Rick.

EASTERN EUROPE

Rick Steves & Cameron Hewitt

Eastern Europe
Overview

e maps on the following pages show more detail.

Baltic Sea

0 km   100   200 km

0 miles   50   100 m

LITHUANIA

KALININGRAD
(RUSSIA)

B
E
L
A
R
U
S

Gdynia • Hel
Sopot • TRI-CITY
Gdańsk

■ Malbork

• Olsztyn

• Białystok

POMERANIA

Toruń   *Wisła*

• Brest

color detail map

★ Berlin

GERMANY

• Poznań

WIELKOPOLSKA

★ Warsaw

MAZOVIA

• Łódź

• Lublin

Elbe

zig

• Dresden

POLAND

MAŁOPOLSKA

• Wrocław

• Częstochowa

SILESIA

Katowice • ★ Kraków

Wisła

• Lviv

TEREZÍN

BOHEMIA   *Labe*

★ Prague

• Kutná Hora

Plzeň •

CZECH

REPUBLIC

Český Krumlov

Vltava

Danube

• Ostrava

• Olomouc

MORAVIA

• Brno

AUSCHWITZ

• Zakopane

HIGH TATRA MTNS.

• Poprad

Spiš • Levoča

• Košice   UKRAINE

SLOVAKIA

★ Bratislava

• Eger

• Tokaj

• Melk

★ Vienna

Győr •

Danube

DANUBE BEND

• Salzburg

AUSTRIA

Sopron •

Szombathely •

Tisza

• Debrecen

★ Budapest

PUSZTA

Lake Balaton

HUNGARY

• Graz

TRANSDANUBIA

★ Szeged

ROMANIA

Klagenfurt •

• Maribor

• Pécs

VOJVODINA

DOLOMITES

JULIAN ALPS

Bled • Bled   Bohinj

Ljubljana ★

• Zagreb ★

SLAVONIA

Novi Sad •

Danube ★

• Osijek

ano •

Kobarid •

Trieste •

SLOVENIA

KARST

Piran •

nice •

• Motovun

ISTRIA

• Rijeka

Plitvice Lakes National Park

• Bihać   • Banja Luka

• Belgrade

SERBIA

• Rovinj

• Pula

CROATIA

BOSNIA - HERZEGOVINA

ITALY

Adriatic Sea

• Zadar

DALMATIAN COAST

★ Sarajevo

rence

• Ancona

Trogir • Split

• Hvar

• Mostar

MONTE-NEGRO

KOSOVO

• Assisi

Korčula •

MEĐUGORJE

Podgorica •

★ Priština

na •

• Dubrovnik

★ Kotor

color detail map

ALBANIA

Skopje • ★

MACEDONIA

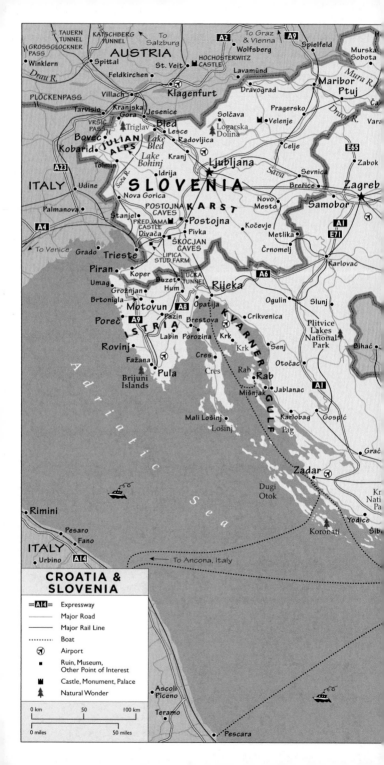

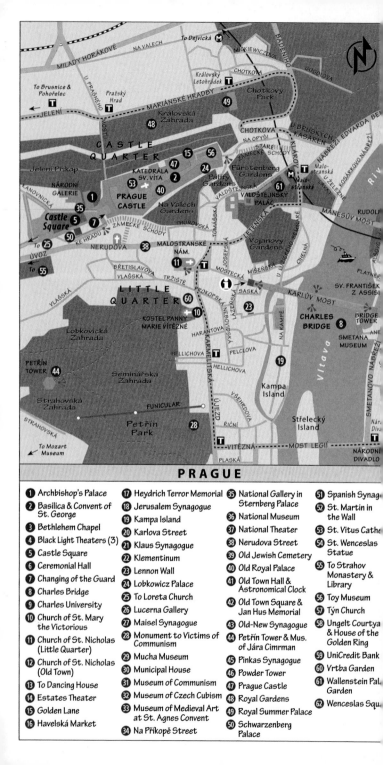

PRAGUE

1. Archbishop's Palace
2. Basilica & Convent of St. George
3. Bethlehem Chapel
4. Black Light Theaters (3)
5. Castle Square
6. Ceremonial Hall
7. Changing of the Guard
8. Charles Bridge
9. Charles University
10. Church of St. Mary the Victorious
11. Church of St. Nicholas (Little Quarter)
12. Church of St. Nicholas (Old Town)
13. To Dancing House
14. Estates Theater
15. Golden Lane
16. Havelská Market
17. Heydrich Terror Memorial
18. Jerusalem Synagogue
19. Kampa Island
20. Karlova Street
21. Klaus Synagogue
22. Klementinum
23. Lennon Wall
24. Lobkowicz Palace
25. To Loreta Church
26. Lucerna Gallery
27. Maisel Synagogue
28. Monument to Victims of Communism
29. Mucha Museum
30. Municipal House
31. Museum of Communism
32. Museum of Czech Cubism
33. Museum of Medieval Art at St. Agnes Convent
34. Na Příkopě Street
35. National Gallery in Sternberg Palace
36. National Museum
37. National Theater
38. Nerudova Street
39. Old Jewish Cemetery
40. Old Royal Palace
41. Old Town Hall & Astronomical Clock
42. Old Town Square & Jan Hus Memorial
43. Old-New Synagogue
44. Petřín Tower & Mus. of Jára Cimrman
45. Pinkas Synagogue
46. Powder Tower
47. Prague Castle
48. Royal Gardens
49. Royal Summer Palace
50. Schwarzenberg Palace
51. Spanish Synag...
52. St. Martin in the Wall
53. St. Vitus Cathe...
54. St. Wenceslas Statue
55. To Strahov Monastery & Library
56. Toy Museum
57. Týn Church
58. Ungelt Courtya... & House of the Golden Ring
59. UniCredit Bank
60. Vrtba Garden
61. Wallenstein Pal... Garden
62. Wenceslas Squa...

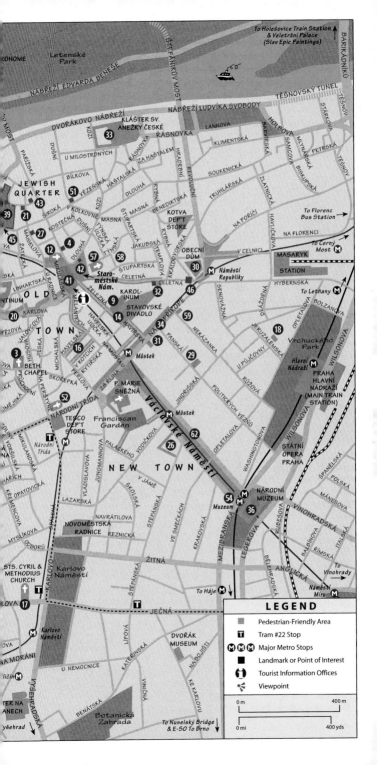

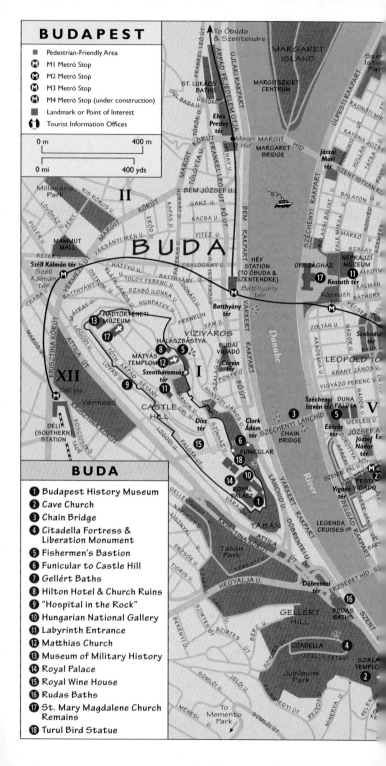

BUDAPEST

- ■ Pedestrian-Friendly Area
- Ⓜ M1 Metró Stop
- Ⓜ M2 Metró Stop
- Ⓜ M3 Metró Stop
- Ⓜ M4 Metró Stop (under construction)
- ■ Landmark or Point of Interest
- ⓘ Tourist Information Offices

0 m   400 m

0 mi   400 yds

BUDA

1. Budapest History Museum
2. Cave Church
3. Chain Bridge
4. Citadella Fortress & Liberation Monument
5. Fishermen's Bastion
6. Funicular to Castle Hill
7. Gellért Baths
8. Hilton Hotel & Church Ruins
9. "Hospital in the Rock"
10. Hungarian National Gallery
11. Labyrinth Entrance
12. Matthias Church
13. Museum of Military History
14. Royal Palace
15. Royal Wine House
16. Rudas Baths
17. St. Mary Magdalene Church Remains
18. Turul Bird Statue

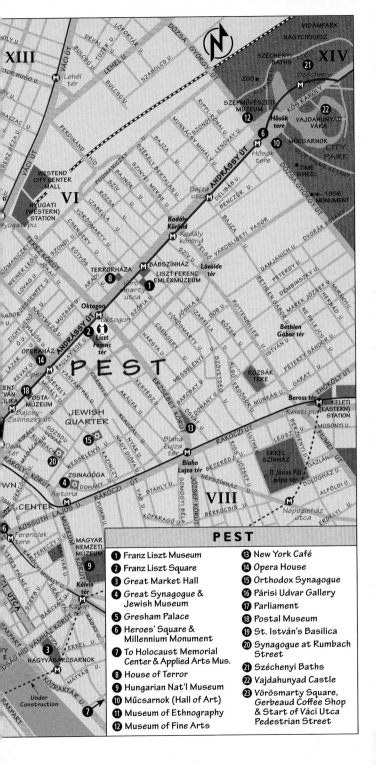

PEST

1. Franz Liszt Museum
2. Franz Liszt Square
3. Great Market Hall
4. Great Synagogue & Jewish Museum
5. Gresham Palace
6. Heroes' Square & Millennium Monument
7. To Holocaust Memorial Center & Applied Arts Mus.
8. House of Terror
9. Hungarian Nat'l Museum
10. Műcsarnok (Hall of Art)
11. Museum of Ethnography
12. Museum of Fine Arts
13. New York Café
14. Opera House
15. Orthodox Synagogue
16. Párisi Udvar Gallery
17. Parliament
18. Postal Museum
19. St. István's Basilica
20. Synagogue at Rumbach Street
21. Széchenyi Baths
22. Vajdahunyad Castle
23. Vörösmarty Square, Gerbeaud Coffee Shop & Start of Váci Utca Pedestrian Street

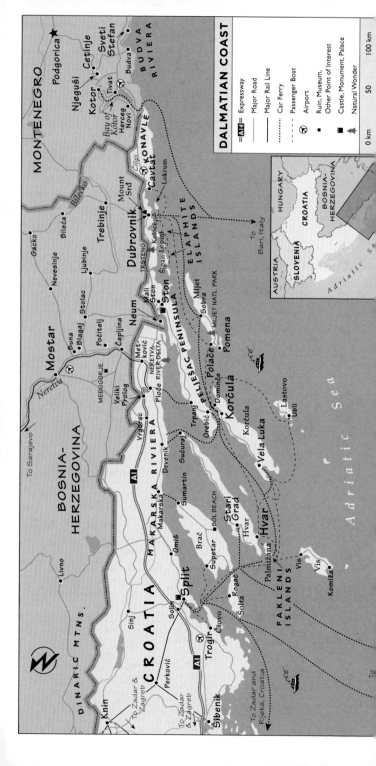

Rick Steves'

EASTERN
EUROPE

AVALON
TRAVEL

CONTENTS

Top Destinations of Eastern Europe

GDAŃSK AND the TRI-CITY

POMERANIA

WARSAW

AUSCHWITZ

KRAKÓW

PRAGUE

NEAR PRAGUE

ČESKÝ KRUMLOV

SPIŠ REGION

BRATISLAVA

EGER

VIENNA

BUDAPEST

PÉCS

LAKE BLED

JULIAN ALPS

LJUBLJANA

ZAGREB

ROVINJ & ISTRIA

PLITVICE LAKES

SPLIT

MOSTAR

KORČULA

DUBROVNIK

DCH

INTRODUCTION

Until 1989, Eastern Europe was a foreboding place—a dark and gloomy corner of the "Evil Empire." But the dismal grays and preachy reds of communism live on only in history books, museums, and kitschy theme restaurants. Today's Eastern Europe is a traveler's delight, with friendly locals, lively squares, breathtaking sights, fascinating history, reasonable prices, and a sense of pioneer excitement.

Wander among Prague's dreamy, fairy-tale spires, bask in the energy of Kraków's Main Market Square, and soak with chess players in a Budapest bath. Ponder Europe's most moving Holocaust memorial at Auschwitz. Enjoy nature as you stroll on boardwalks through the Plitvice Lakes' waterfall wonderland, or glide across Lake Bled to a church-topped island in the shadow of the Julian Alps. Taste a proud Hungarian vintner's wine and say, *"Egészségedre!"* (or stick with "Cheers!").

This book covers Eastern Europe's top big-city, small-town, and back-to-nature destinations—from the Hungarian metropolis of Budapest to the quaint Czech village of Český Krumlov to the rugged High Tatra Mountains of Slovakia. It then gives you all the specifics and opinions necessary to wring the maximum value out of your limited time and money. If you're planning for a month or less in this region, this book is all you need.

Experiencing Europe's culture, people, and natural wonders economically and hassle-free has been my goal for three decades of traveling, tour guiding, and writing. With this book, I pass on to you all of the lessons I've learned.

I've been selective, including only the top destinations and sights. For example, Poland has dozens of medieval castles—but Malbork is a cut above the rest.

The best is, of course, only my opinion. But after spending a

INTRODUCTION

Map Legend

⚲ Viewpoint	✈ Airport	)▬▬(Tunnel	
↑ Entrance	ⓣ Taxi Stand	▬▬▬ Pedestrian Zone	
⊕ Tourist Info	⊤ Tram Stop	▬ ▬ ▬ Railway	
WC Restroom	Ⓜ Métro Stop	⋯⋯⋯ Ferry/Boat Route	
⛫ Castle	⑧ Bus Stop	⊢━┿━┥ Tram	
⛪ Church	Ⓟ Parking	▥▥▥ Stairs	
▦ Synagogue	)(Mtn. Pass	▪ ▪ ▪ Walk/Tour Route	
▪ Statue/Point of Interest	▦ Park	▬ ▬ ▬ Trail	
		⊶▦▦▦⊷ Funicular	

Use this legend to help you navigate the maps in this book.

third of my adult life exploring and researching Europe, I've developed a sixth sense for what travelers enjoy. Just thinking about the places featured in this book makes me want to polka.

About This Book

Rick Steves' Eastern Europe is a personal tour guide in your pocket. Better yet, it's actually two tour guides in your pocket: The co-author of this book is Cameron Hewitt. Cameron writes and edits guidebooks for my travel company, Rick Steves' Europe Through the Back Door. Inspired by his Polish roots and by the enduring charm of the Eastern European people, Cameron has spent the last decade closely tracking the exciting changes in this part of the world. Together, Cameron and I keep this book up-to-date and accurate (though for simplicity we've shed our respective egos to become "I" in this book).

This book is organized by destinations. Each destination is a mini-vacation on its own, filled with exciting sights, strollable neighborhoods, affordable places to stay, and memorable places to eat. In the following chapters, you'll find these sections:

Planning Your Time suggests a schedule for how to best use your limited time.

Orientation includes specifics on public transportation, helpful hints, local tour options, easy-to-read maps, and tourist information.

Sights describes the top attractions and includes their cost and hours.

Self-Guided Walks take you through interesting neighborhoods, with a personal tour guide in hand.

Sleeping describes my favorite hotels, from good-value deals to cushy splurges.

Eating serves up a range of options, from inexpensive eateries

Key to This Book

Updates

This book is updated regularly, but things change. For the latest, visit www.ricksteves.com/update. For a valuable list of reports and experiences—good and bad—from fellow travelers, check www.ricksteves.com/feedback.

Abbreviations and Times

I use the following symbols and abbreviations in this book:
Sights are rated:

▲▲▲	**Don't miss**
▲▲	**Try hard to see**
▲	**Worthwhile if you can make it**
No rating	**Worth knowing about**

Tourist information offices are abbreviated as **TI,** and bathrooms are **WCs.** To categorize accommodations, I use a **Sleep Code** (described on page 27).

Like Europe, this book uses the **24-hour clock.** It's the same through 12:00 noon, then keep going: 13:00, 14:00, and so on. For anything over 12, subtract 12 and add p.m. (14:00 is 2:00 p.m.).

When giving **opening times,** I include both peak season and off-season hours if they differ. So, if a museum is listed as "May-Oct daily 9:00-16:00," it should be open from 9:00 a.m. until 4:00 p.m. from the first day of May until the last day of October (but expect exceptions).

For **transit** or **tour departures,** I first list the frequency, then the duration. So, a train connection listed as "2/hour, 1.5 hours" departs twice each hour, and the journey lasts an hour and a half.

to fancy restaurants.

Connections outlines your options for traveling to destinations by train, bus, and boat. In car-friendly regions, I've included route tips for drivers, with recommended roadside attractions along the way.

Country Introductions give you an overview of each country's culture, customs, money, history, current events, cuisine, language, and other useful practicalities.

The **Understanding Yugoslavia** chapter sorts out the various countries and conflicts, giving you a good picture of how Yugoslavia was formed, and why it broke apart.

The **appendix** is a traveler's tool kit, with telephone tips, useful phone numbers, transportation basics (on trains, buses, boats, car rentals, driving, and flights), recommended books and films, a festival list, a climate chart, a handy packing checklist, a hotel reservation form, and survival phrases in six languages.

INTRODUCTION

Browse through this book, choose your favorite destinations, and link them up. Then have a great trip! Traveling like a temporary local and taking advantage of the information here, you'll enjoy the absolute most of every mile, minute, and dollar. As you visit places I know and love, I'm happy you'll be meeting some of my favorite Europeans.

Planning

This section will help you get started on planning your trip—with advice on trip costs, when to go, and what you should know before you take off.

Travel Smart

Your trip to Europe is like a complex play—easier to follow and fully appreciate on a second viewing. While no one does the same trip twice to gain that advantage, reading this book before your trip accomplishes much the same thing.

Design an itinerary that enables you to visit sights at the best possible times. Note festivals, holidays, specifics on sights, and days when sights are closed. For example, most museums throughout Eastern Europe close on Mondays. Hotels in resort towns (such as those on the Croatian coast) are most crowded on Fridays and Saturdays, while weekdays are tight in convention cities (for instance, Budapest and Warsaw). Expect seasonal closures, especially in Croatia. Whether you're traveling by public transportation (trains, buses, and boats) or by rental car, read up on my tips in the appendix. A smart trip is a puzzle—a fun, doable, and worthwhile challenge.

Be sure to mix intense and relaxed periods in your itinerary. To maximize rootedness, minimize one-night stands. It's worth a long drive or train/bus ride after dinner to be settled into a town for two nights. Accommodations are more likely to give a better price to someone staying more than one night. Every trip—and every traveler—needs slack time (laundry, picnics, people-watching, and so on). Pace yourself. Assume you will return.

Reread this book as you travel, and visit local TIs. Upon arrival in a new town, lay the groundwork for a smooth departure; get the schedule for the train, bus, or boat you'll take when you depart. Drivers can study the best route to their next destination.

Get online at Internet cafés or your hotel, and buy a phone card or carry a mobile phone: You can find tourist information, learn the latest on sights (special events, English tour schedule, etc.), book tickets and tours, make reservations, reconfirm hotels, research transportation connections, and keep in touch with your loved ones.

What Is "Eastern Europe"?

"Eastern Europe" means different things to different people. To most Americans, Eastern Europe includes any place that was once behind the Iron Curtain, from the former East Germany to Moscow. But people who actually live in many of these countries consider themselves "Central Europeans." In fact, some even get a bit offended by the "Eastern" label. (To them, "Eastern Europe" is *really* eastern: Russia, Ukraine, Belarus, and Romania.)

In this book, I use the term "Eastern Europe" the way most Americans do—to describe the **Czech Republic, Slovakia, Poland, Hungary, Slovenia,** and **Croatia.** I've also thrown in two cities worth a detour: **Vienna** (in Austria) and **Mostar** (in Bosnia-Herzegovina). Vienna is a "gateway city" that feels more Western than Eastern, but it has important historical ties to the region. And Mostar—a mostly Muslim city a short drive or bus trip from Croatia's Dalmatian Coast—provides an opportunity to splice in some diversity.

So what do my six core "Eastern European" countries have in common? All of these destinations fell under communist control during the last half of the 20th century. More importantly, for centuries leading up to World War I, they were all part of the Austrian Habsburg Empire. Before the Habsburgs, the kings and emperors of these countries also frequently governed their neighbors. And all of these countries (except Hungary) are populated by people of Slavic heritage.

I hope that natives, sticklers, and historians will understand the liberties I've taken with the title of this book. After all, would you buy a book called *Rick Steves' Former Habsburg Empire?*

Enjoy the hospitality of the local people. Connect with the culture. Set up your own quest for the best bit of communist kitsch, mug of Czech beer, bowl of borscht, or scenic seafront perch. Slow down and be open to unexpected experiences. Ask questions—most locals are eager to point you toward their idea of the right direction. Keep a notepad in your pocket for confirming prices, noting directions, and organizing your thoughts. Wear your money belt, learn the local currency, and figure out how to estimate prices in dollars. Those who expect to travel smart, do.

Trip Costs

The countries in this book—while just two decades removed from communism—are no longer Europe's bargain basement. Although the global financial crisis has hit their economies along with everyone else's, the cost of living in most of Eastern Europe

Eastern Europe at a Glance

Czech Republic

▲▲▲**Prague** Romantic Czech capital with a remarkably well-preserved Old Town, sprawling hilltop castle, informative Jewish Quarter, and rollicking pubs.

▲**Near Prague** Kutná Hora's offbeat bone church, Terezín's Nazi concentration camp memorial, and three countryside castles.

▲▲**Český Krumlov** Picturesque town hugging a river bend under a castle.

Slovakia

▲**Bratislava** The Slovak capital, with a rejuvenated Old Town and lots of new construction.

The Spiš Region Rugged northern corner of Slovakia, featuring sweeping mountain scenery, few tourists, and the diamond-in-the-rough town of Levoča.

Poland

▲▲▲**Kraków** Poland's cultural, intellectual, and historical capital, with a huge but cozy main square, easy-to-enjoy Old Town, thought-provoking Jewish quarter, and important castle.

▲▲▲**Auschwitz-Birkenau** The largest and most notorious Nazi concentration camp, now a compelling museum and memorial.

▲▲**Warsaw** Poland's modern capital, with an appealing urban tempo, a reconstructed Old Town, and good museums.

▲▲**Gdańsk and the Tri-City** Historic Hanseatic trading city, with a cancan of marvelous facades and the shipyard where the Solidarity trade union challenged the communists in 1980.

▲**Pomerania** The Teutonic Knights' gigantic, Gothic Malbork Castle and the red-brick, gingerbread-scented city of Toruń.

Hungary

▲▲▲**Budapest** Grand Danube-spanning cityscape peppered with opulent late-19th-century buildings, excellent restaurants, layers of epic history, and uniquely exhilarating thermal baths.

▲▲**Eger** Strollable town with a gaggle of gorgeous Baroque buildings and locally produced wines.

▲▲**Pécs** Small city featuring a unique mosque-turned-church on its main square, good museums, and colorfully tiled facades.

Slovenia
▲▲**Ljubljana** Slovenia's vibrant, relaxing capital, with fine architecture and an inviting riverside promenade and market.

▲▲▲**Lake Bled** Photogenic lake resort huddled in mountain foothills, with a church-topped island and cliff-hanging castle.

▲▲**The Julian Alps** Cut-glass peaks easily conquered by a twisty mountain road over the Vršič Pass, ending in the tranquil Soča River Valley, with the fine WWI museum in Kobarid.

Croatia
▲▲▲**Dubrovnik** The "Pearl of the Adriatic" and Croatia's best destination: a giant walled Old Town with a scenic wall walk, tons of crowds, an epic past, and an inspiring recent history.

▲▲**Split** Dalmatian transit hub, with a people-filled seaside promenade next to the remains of a massive Roman palace.

▲**Korčula** Low-key island town with a fjord-like backdrop.

▲▲**Rovinj and Istria** Croatia's most enchanting small coastal town—with a romantic Venetian vibe—plus Roman ruins in the city of Pula and the hill town of Motovun.

▲**Zagreb** Croatia's underrated capital city, with interesting sightseeing and a lively urban bustle.

▲▲▲**Plitvice Lakes National Park** Forested canyon filled with crystal-clear lakes and stunning waterfalls, all laced together by boardwalks and trails.

Other Destinations
▲▲▲**Mostar, Bosnia-Herzegovina** Fascinating town with a striking setting, vital Muslim culture, old Turkish architecture, evocative war damage, and an inspiring, rebuilt Old Bridge.

▲▲▲**Vienna, Austria** Glorious onetime Habsburg capital boasting stately palaces and world-class museums, convivial wine gardens, a rich musical heritage, and a genteel elegance that has long outlived the emperor's reign.

is approaching what it is in the West. But it can still be a good value to travel here. Things that natives buy—such as food and transportation—remain fairly inexpensive. Hotels can be pricey, but if you use my listings to find the best accommodations deals, a trip to these countries can be substantially cheaper than visiting, say, Italy, Germany, or France.

Five components make up your trip costs: airfare, surface transportation, room and board, sightseeing and entertainment, and shopping and miscellany. The prices I've listed below are more or less average for all of the destinations in this book. Prices are generally lower in Poland, Slovakia, and Mostar, and higher in Slovenia, Croatia, and Vienna; the Czech Republic and Hungary are in between. Of course, big cities (such as Prague and Budapest) are much more expensive than smaller towns (like Český Krumlov and Eger).

Airfare: A basic round-trip flight from the US to Prague can cost $700-1,300, depending on where you fly from and when (cheaper in winter). Consider saving time and money in Europe by flying into one city and out of another; for instance, flying into Prague and out of Dubrovnik is almost certainly cheaper than the added expense (and wasted time) of an overland return trip to Prague.

Surface Transportation: For the three-week whirlwind trip described in this chapter, allow $300 per person for public transportation (train, bus, and boat tickets). Train travelers will probably save money by simply buying tickets along the way, rather than purchasing a railpass. Depending on the country, renting a small car costs about $300-450 per week (including tolls, gas, and basic insurance). Car rentals are cheapest if arranged from the US. Exorbitant fees for dropping off in a different country can make car rental prohibitively expensive for a multi-country itinerary. For more on public transportation and car rental, see "Transportation" in the appendix.

Room and Board: You can thrive in Eastern Europe on $100 a day per person for room and board. This allows $15 for lunch, $25 for dinner, and $60 for lodging (based on two people splitting the cost of a comfortable $120 double room that includes breakfast). Students and tightwads can eat and sleep for as little as $50 a day ($30 per hostel bed, $20 for groceries and snacks).

Sightseeing and Entertainment: Sightseeing is cheap here. Figure $3-6 per major sight (with some more expensive sights at around $10), and $10-25 for splurge experiences (e.g., going to concerts, taking an Adriatic cruise, or soaking in a Budapest bath). You can hire your own private guide for four hours for about $100-150—a great value when divided among two or more people. An overall average of $20 a day works for most people. Don't skimp

Not Your Father's Eastern Europe

Americans sometimes approach Eastern Europe expecting grouchy service, crumbling communist infrastructure, and grimy, depressing landscapes. But those who visit are pleasantly surprised at the area's beauty and diversity, as well as how safe and easy it is.

Travel in Eastern Europe today is nearly as smooth as travel in the West. Most natives speak excellent English, and many pride themselves on impressing their guests. Service standards can sometimes be a bit lower than in other parts of Europe, but on the other hand, locals are generally less jaded and more excited to meet you than their counterparts in many big-name Western European destinations. Any rough edges add to the charm and carbonate the experience.

The East-West stuff still fascinates us, but to people here, the Soviet regime is old news, Cold War espionage is the stuff of movies, and oppressive monuments to Stalin are a distant memory (and those under age 25 have no firsthand memories of communism at all). More than two decades after the fall of the Iron Curtain, Eastern Europeans (or, as they prefer to be called, *Central* Europeans) think about communism only when tourists bring it up. Freedom is a generation old, and—for better or for worse—McDonald's, MTV, and mobile phones are every bit as entrenched here as anywhere else in Europe. Most of the countries in this book already belong to the European Union, the others are on track to join soon...and all of them are looking optimistically to the future.

here. After all, this category is the driving force behind your trip—you came to sightsee, enjoy, and experience Eastern Europe.

Shopping and Miscellany: Figure $2 per postcard, coffee, beer, and ice-cream cone. Shopping can vary in cost from nearly nothing to a small fortune, though good budget travelers find that this has little to do with assembling a trip full of lifelong and wonderful memories.

Sightseeing Priorities

Depending on the length of your trip, and taking geographic proximity into account, here are my recommended priorities.

3 days:	Prague
5 days, add:	Budapest
7 days, add:	Kraków and Auschwitz
9 days, add:	Český Krumlov
12 days, add:	Ljubljana and Lake Bled
16 days, add:	Dubrovnik and Split
22 days, add:	Plitvice Lakes, Mostar, Eger, Rovinj

With more time or a special interest, choose among Vienna,

Eastern Europe: Best Three-Week Trip by Public Transportation

Day	Plan	Sleep in
1	Arrive in Prague	Prague
2	Prague	Prague
3	Prague night train to Kraków	Night train
4	Kraków	Kraków
5	Kraków, day trip to Auschwitz	Kraków
6	Kraków, maybe side-trip to Wieliczka Salt Mine, night train to Eger	Night train*
7	Eger	Eger
8	Early to Budapest	Budapest
9	Budapest	Budapest
10	Budapest	Budapest
11	To Ljubljana (catch direct 9.5-hour midday train; no night-train option)	Ljubljana
12	Ljubljana	Ljubljana
13	To Bled	Bled
14	Rent car for day trips around Julian Alps	Bled
15	To Zagreb, sightseeing, then early evening bus to Plitvice Lakes National Park	Plitvice
16	Plitvice hike in morning, then afternoon bus to Split	Split
17	Split	Split
18	Boat to Korčula (for beach fun) or bus to Mostar (for a taste of Bosnia)	Korčula or Mostar
19	Korčula or Mostar	Korčula or Mostar
20	Boat or bus to Dubrovnik	Dubrovnik
21	Dubrovnik	Dubrovnik
22	Side-trip to Mostar or fly home	

The handy Kraków-Eger night train connection runs sporadically (most likely only in summer). If it's not running, you can take the more reliable Kraków-Budapest night train. Once in Budapest, you can either side-trip to Eger, or skip the town entirely.

This ambitious, speedy, far-reaching itinerary works best by public transportation. Most of the time, you'll take the train. There are a few exceptions: Bled and Ljubljana are better connected by bus. To get from Bled to Plitvice, take the bus to Ljubljana, the train to Zagreb, and then the bus to Plitvice. To get from Plitvice to the coast, take the bus to Split. The Dalmatian Coast destinations are best connected to each other by boat or bus (no trains). While night trains can save lots of sightseeing time, the trains themselves don't provide much comfort (see page 1242); consider looking around for affordable flights for the longer trips.

By **car,** this itinerary is exhausting, with lots of long road

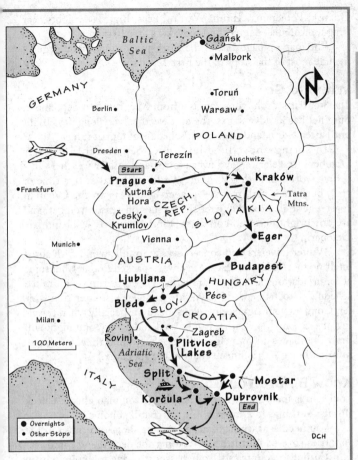

days. Instead, connect long-distance destinations (e.g., Prague to Kraków, Kraków to Eger/Budapest) by night trains or cheap flights, then strategically rent cars for a day or two in areas that merit having wheels (e.g., the Czech or Slovenian countryside). Also consider adding a side-trip to Croatia's Rovinj (and skip Zagreb). But remember that international drop-off fees for rental cars can be astronomical, and plan accordingly (for example, you could drop off your rental car in Slovenia, take the train or bus into Croatia, and then pick up a different rental car for your Croatia visit). This can be a bit of a puzzle to figure out, but it can save you plenty.

Vienna: The Austrian capital is a likely gateway between Western and Eastern Europe, but it's out of the way for the above itinerary. If you really want to see Vienna, give it two days between Budapest and Ljubljana (it also makes sense if you're going directly between Budapest and Prague).

Gdańsk, Pomerania, Toruń, Warsaw, Pécs, Bratislava, sights near Prague, Korčula, Zagreb, and Slovakia's Spiš Region.

The map on page 11 and the three-week itinerary on page 10 include most of the stops in the first 22 days.

When to Go

The "tourist season" runs roughly from May through September. Summer has its advantages: the best weather, very long days (light until after 21:00), and the busiest schedule of tourist fun.

In spring and fall—May, June, September, and early October—travelers enjoy fewer crowds and milder weather. This is my favorite time to travel here. Cities are great at this time of year, but some small towns—especially resorts on the Croatian coast—get quieter and quieter the further off-season you get, and are downright deserted and disappointing in early May and late October.

Winter travelers find concert season in full swing, with absolutely no tourist crowds (except in always-packed Prague), but some accommodations and sights are either closed or run on a limited schedule. Croatian coastal towns are completely shuttered in winter. Confirm your sightseeing plans locally, especially when traveling off-season. The weather can be cold and dreary, and night will draw the shades on your sightseeing before dinnertime. (For more information, see the climate chart in the appendix.)

Know Before You Go

Your trip is more likely to go smoothly if you plan ahead. Check this list of things to arrange while you're still at home.

You need a **passport**—but no visa or shots—to travel in the countries covered in this book. You may be denied entry into certain European countries if your passport is due to expire within three to six months of your ticketed date of return. Get it renewed if you'll be cutting it close. It can take up to six weeks to get or renew a passport (for more on passports, see www.travel.state.gov). Pack a photocopy of your passport in your luggage in case the original is lost or stolen.

Book rooms well in advance if you'll be traveling during **peak season** (July and August in resort towns, September and October in convention cities), or over any major **holidays or festivals** (see list on page 1255).

Call your **debit- and credit-card companies** to let them know the countries you'll be visiting, to ask about fees, and more (see page 17).

Do your homework if you want to buy **travel insurance.** Compare the cost of the insurance to the likelihood of your using it and your potential loss if something goes wrong. Also, check whether your existing insurance (health, homeowners, or renters) covers you and your possessions overseas. For more tips, see www .ricksteves.com/insurance.

If you plan to hire a **local guide,** reserve ahead by email. Popular guides can get booked up. If you're bringing a mobile device, you can download free information from **Rick Steves Audio Europe,** featuring hours of travel interviews and other audio content about Eastern Europe (via www.ricksteves.com /audioeurope, iTunes, or the Rick Steves Audio Europe free smartphone app; for details, see page 1250).

If you're planning on **renting a car** in Eastern Europe, you'll need your driver's license. Many countries require drivers to buy a toll sticker for driving on expressways; for details per country, see page 1243.

Because **airline carry-on restrictions** are always changing, visit the Transportation Security Administration's website (www .tsa.gov/travelers) for an up-to-date list of what you can bring on the plane with you...and what you must check.

Practicalities

Emergency and Medical Help: In all of the countries in this book, dial 112 for medical or other emergencies. For police, dial 112 in Slovakia, Hungary, Poland, or Austria; dial 158 in the Czech Republic; dial 113 in Slovenia; dial 92 in Croatia; and dial 122 in Bosnia-Herzegovina. If you get sick, do as the locals do and go to a pharmacist for advice. Or ask at your hotel for help; they know of the nearest medical and emergency services.

Theft or Loss: To replace a passport, you'll need to go in person to the appropriate embassy or consulate (see page 1237). If your credit and debit cards disappear, cancel and replace them (see "Damage Control for Lost Cards" on page 19). File a police report, either on the spot or within a day or two, and obtain a copy; you'll need it to submit an insurance claim for lost or stolen railpasses or travel gear, and it can help with replacing your passport or credit and debit cards. For more information, see www.ricksteves.com /help. Precautionary measures can minimize the effects of loss: Back up photos and other files frequently, and use passwords to protect any sensitive data on your electronic devices.

Borders: All of the countries in this book, except Croatia and Bosnia-Herzegovina, have officially joined the open-borders Schengen Agreement. That means that there are no border checks between any of these countries, or between them and Western European countries such as Germany, Austria, and Italy. You'll simply zip through the border without stopping.

Croatia and Bosnia-Herzegovina, however, have not yet

joined the Schengen Agreement. (Even after Croatia joins the European Union in 2013, it will likely take until 2015 at the earliest for it to join Schengen—so those borders will remain for a while.) Upon entering or exiting these countries, you'll still have to stop. But whether traveling by car, train, or bus, you'll find that border crossings are generally a non-event—flash your passport, maybe wait a few minutes, and move on. Drivers may be asked to show proof of car insurance ("green card"), so be sure you have it when you pick up your rental car.

When you cross any international border, you must still change phone cards, postage stamps, currencies (in most cases), and underpants.

Time Zones: The countries listed in this book are generally six/nine hours ahead of the East/West Coasts of the US. The exceptions are the beginning and end of Daylight Saving Time: Europe "springs forward" the last Sunday in March (two weeks after most of North America), and "falls back" the last Sunday in October (one week before North America). For a handy online time converter, try www.timeanddate.com/worldclock.

Weekends: Sundays have the same pros and cons as they do for travelers in the US (special events, limited hours, banks and many shops generally closed, limited public-transportation options, no rush hour). Rowdy evenings are rare on Sundays. Saturdays are virtually weekdays, with earlier closing hours and no rush hour (though transportation connections can be less frequent than on weekdays).

Watt's Up? Europe's electrical system is 220 volts, instead of North America's 110 volts. Most newer electronics (such as laptops, battery chargers, and hair dryers) convert automatically, so you won't need a converter, but you will need an adapter plug with two round prongs, sold inexpensively at travel stores in the US. Avoid bringing older appliances that don't automatically convert voltage; instead, buy a cheap replacement in Europe.

Discounts: Discounts are not listed in this book. However, seniors (age 60 and over), youths under 18, and students and teachers with proper identification cards (www.isic.org) can get discounts at many sights. Always ask, though some discounts are available only for local residents or EU citizens.

Smoking: Most Eastern European countries have imposed some restrictions on smoking in public places. Each country handles things differently. The Czech Republic allows each business to decide whether to be smoking, non-smoking, or have a designated non-smoking section. Slovakia and Poland forbid smoking on public transportation and in public indoor spaces (though restaurants and bars may have designated areas for folks to puff away). Hungary's ban on smoking in all public spaces went into effect in January 2012. In Slovenia and Croatia, smoking is banned (to varying degrees) in indoor public spaces, such as restaurants. Since the restrictions are relatively new, it remains to be seen how rigorously they will be enforced; in some places, you'll still get a whiff of the old, nicotine-stained Europe. If you require a completely non-smoking section or hotel room, be very specific in your request, and understand that it may not be granted.

News: Americans keep in touch via the *International Herald Tribune* (published almost daily throughout Europe and online at www.iht.com). Another informative site is www.bbc.co.uk/news. Every Tuesday, the European editions of *Time* and *Newsweek* hit the stands with articles of particular interest to travelers in Europe. Sports addicts can get their daily fix online or from *USA Today*. News in English will be sold only where there's enough demand: in big cities and tourist centers (Prague and Budapest have weekly English-language newspapers). Many hotels have CNN or BBC News television channels available.

Money

This section offers advice on how to pay for purchases on your trip (including getting cash from ATMs and paying with plastic), dealing with lost or stolen cards, VAT (sales tax) refunds, and tipping.

Exchange Rates

Most of the countries in this book still use their traditional currencies...for now. Through the end of 2013, only Slovenia, Slovakia, and Austria officially use the euro currency. But within a few years, the rest are also likely to adopt it.

In countries that don't officially use the euro, many businesses (especially hotels) quote prices in euros anyway. Even if places list prices in euros, they typically prefer payment in the local currency.

Here are the rough exchange rates for each country. Because of currency fluctuations, and to make things easier to convert in your head, these are very loose estimates (for the latest, see www.oanda.com):

1 euro (€) = about $1.40 (used in Slovakia, Slovenia, and Austria). To convert prices in euros to dollars, add 40 percent: €20 = about $28, €50 = about $70, and so on.

18 Czech crowns (*koruna*, Kč) = about $1. To estimate prices in dollars, drop the last digit and divide in half: 150 Kč = about $8.

3 Polish złoty (zł, or PLN) = about $1. To calculate prices in dollars, divide by three: 85 zł = a little under $30.

200 Hungarian forints (Ft, or HUF) = about $1. To figure dollars, divide by two and drop the last two digits: 10,000 Ft = about $50.

5 Croatian kunas (kn, or HRK) = about $1. To estimate dollars, multiply by two and drop the last digit: 70 kn = about $14.

1.40 Bosnian convertible marks (KM, or BAM) = about $1. To convert prices into dollars, subtract 30 percent (or multiply by .7): 60 KM = about $42. Note that most merchants in Mostar will take euros or Croatian kunas.

So, that 20-zł Polish woodcarving is about $7, the 5,000-Ft Hungarian dinner is about $25, and the 2,000-Kč taxi ride through Prague is...uh-oh.

What to Bring

Bring both a credit card and a debit card. You'll use the debit card at cash machines (ATMs) to withdraw local cash for most purchases, and the credit card to pay for larger items. Some travelers carry a third card, in case one gets demagnetized or eaten by a temperamental machine.

For an emergency reserve, bring several hundred dollars in hard cash in easy-to-exchange $20 bills. Avoid using currency exchange booths (lousy rates and/or outrageous fees); if you have foreign currency to exchange, take it to a bank. Don't use traveler's checks—they're not worth the fees or long waits at slow banks.

Cash

Cash is just as desirable in Europe as it is at home. Small businesses (hotels, restaurants, shops, etc.) prefer that you pay your bills with cash. Some vendors will charge you extra for using a credit card,

and many won't take credit cards at all. Cash is the best—and sometimes only—way to pay for bus fare, taxis, and local guides.

Throughout Europe, ATMs are the standard way for travelers to get cash. Most ATMs in Eastern Europe are located outside of a bank. Try to use the ATM when the branch is open; if your card is munched by a machine, you can immediately go inside for help.

To withdraw money from an ATM (known as *Bankomat* in all of these countries), you'll need a debit card (ideally with a Visa or MasterCard logo for maximum usability), plus a PIN code. Know your PIN code in numbers; there are only numbers—no letters—on European keypads. For security, it's best to shield the keypad when entering your PIN at an ATM. Although you can use a credit card for ATM transactions, it's generally more expensive because it's considered a cash advance rather than a withdrawal.

Because most of these countries still use different currencies, you'll likely wind up with leftover cash from the previous country. Coins can't be exchanged once you leave the country, so try to spend them before you cross the border. But bills are easy to convert to the next country's currency. Regular banks have the best rates for changing currency (except in Poland, where *kantors*, or money-changing kiosks, generally offer good rates—check several to find the best). Post offices and train stations usually change money if you can't get to a bank.

When using an ATM, try to withdraw large sums of money to reduce the number of per-transaction bank fees you'll pay. If the machine refuses your request, try again and select a smaller amount (some cash machines limit the amount you can withdraw, especially in Poland and Croatia—don't take it personally). If that doesn't work, try a different machine. It's easier to pay for purchases with smaller bills; if the ATM gives you big bills, try to break them at a major sight or a larger store.

To keep your cash safe, use a money belt—a pouch with a strap that you buckle around your waist like a belt, and wear under your clothes. Pickpockets target tourists. A money belt provides peace of mind, allowing you to safely carry your passport, credit cards, and lots of cash. Don't waste time every few days tracking down a cash machine—withdraw a week's worth of money, stuff it in your money belt, and travel!

Credit and Debit Cards

For purchases, Visa and MasterCard are more commonly accepted than American Express. Just like at home, credit or debit cards work easily at larger hotels, restaurants, and shops. I typically use my debit card to withdraw cash to pay for most purchases. I use my credit card only in a few specific situations: to book hotel reservations by phone, to cover major expenses (such as car rentals, plane tickets, and long hotel stays), and to pay for things near the end of my trip (to avoid another visit to the ATM). While you could use a debit card to make most large purchases, using a credit card offers a greater degree of fraud protection (because debit cards draw funds directly from your account).

Ask Your Credit- or Debit-Card Company: Before your trip, contact the company that issued your debit or credit cards.

• Confirm your card will work overseas, and alert them that you'll be using it in Europe; otherwise, they may deny transactions if they perceive unusual spending patterns.

• Ask for the specifics on transaction **fees.** When you use your credit or debit card—either for purchases or ATM withdrawals—you'll often be charged additional "international transaction" fees

EU Enlargement and the "New Europe"

The Czech Republic, Slovakia, Poland, Hungary, Slovenia, and five other countries joined the European Union in 2004. Two more former communist countries, Bulgaria and Romania, joined in 2007, and Croatia is set to join on July 1, 2013. Though EU membership—and investment—should ultimately benefit everybody, both older and newer members have had their doubts.

For example, Poland survived the communist era without having to collectivize its small family farms. But after it joined the EU, collectivization became mandatory. Traditional Czech cuisine was also in jeopardy. EU hygiene standards dictate that cooked food can't be served more than two hours old. My Czech friend complained, "This makes many of our best dishes illegal." Czech specialties, often simmered, taste better the next day.

A wise Czech grandmother put it best. In her lifetime, she had lived in a country ruled from Vienna (Habsburgs), Berlin (Nazis), and Moscow (communists). She said, "Now that we're finally ruled from Prague, why would we want to turn our power over to Brussels?"

For their part, long-standing EU members have been skeptical about taking on more countries. Wealthy nations have already spent vast fortunes to improve the floundering economies of poorer member countries (such as Portugal, Greece, and Ireland). Most of the new members joined the union expecting a similar financial-aid windfall, especially during these uncertain times. Also on the financial front, Westerners are fretting about an influx of cheap labor from the East (see "The Polish Plumber Syndrome," page 24).

Finally, Western Europeans worry about their political power being diluted. With 12 new nations joining the EU—and more to come—the geographical center of Europe is gradually shifting from Brussels to Prague. In this "New Europe," the old powers of the West have sometimes been startled to find their spunky new Eastern comrades wielding their influence with gusto. The East eagerly embraces the future, intent on distancing itself from its painful recent history, while the West tentatively clings to the past, when its power was at its peak (and French, not English, was the world's language).

As the "New Europe" takes shape, players on both sides will continue to define their roles and seek compromise. So far, the general consensus in the East is that joining the EU was the right move. And Eastern Europeans feel a bit of vindication that it was some of the earliest members—such as Greece, Spain, Portugal, and Italy—that have contributed to the EU's recent economic woes.

of up to 3 percent (1 percent is normal) plus $5 per transaction. If your card's fees are too high, consider getting a card just for your trip: Capital One (credit cards only, www.capitalone.com) and most credit unions have low-to-no international fees.

• If you plan to withdraw cash from ATMs, confirm your daily **withdrawal limit,** and if necessary, ask your bank to adjust it (withdrawal limits are set by your bank, but foreign banks or ATMs often also set maximum withdrawal amounts—usually about $250-400). Some travelers prefer a high limit that allows them to take out more cash at each ATM stop, while others prefer to set a lower limit in case their card is stolen.

• Ask for your credit card's **PIN** in case you encounter Europe's "chip-and-PIN" system; the bank will not reveal your PIN over the phone, so allow time for it to reach you by mail.

Chip and PIN: If your card is declined for a purchase in Europe, it may be because of chip and PIN, which requires cardholders to punch in a PIN instead of signing a receipt. While chip and PIN is not yet common in Eastern European countries, much of Western Europe is adopting it (most often at automated payment machines). If, when you're using your card, you're prompted to enter your PIN but don't know it, ask if the cashier can swipe your card and print a receipt for you to sign instead; if they can't, just pay cash.

Dynamic Currency Conversion: If merchants offer to convert your purchase price into dollars (called dynamic currency conversion, or DCC), refuse this "service." You'll pay even more in fees for the expensive convenience of seeing your charge in dollars.

Damage Control for Lost Cards

If you lose your credit, debit, or ATM card, you can stop people from using it by reporting the loss immediately to the respective global customer-assistance centers. Call these 24-hour US numbers collect: Visa (410/581-9994), MasterCard (636/722-7111), and American Express (623/492-8427).

At a minimum, you'll need to know the name of the financial institution that issued you the card, along with the type of card (classic, platinum, or whatever). Providing the following information will allow for a quicker cancellation of your missing card: full card number, whether you are the primary or secondary cardholder, the cardholder's name exactly as printed on the card, billing address, home phone number, circumstances of the loss or theft, and identification verification (your birth date, your mother's maiden name, or your Social Security number—memorize this, don't carry a copy). If you are the secondary cardholder, you'll also need to provide the primary cardholder's identification-verification details. You can generally receive a temporary card within two or three business days in Europe (see www.ricksteves.com/help for more).

If you promptly report your card lost or stolen, you typically won't be responsible for any unauthorized transactions on your account, although many banks charge a liability fee of $50.

Tipping

A decade ago, tipping was unheard of in Eastern Europe. But then came the tourists. Today, some waiters and taxi drivers have learned to expect Yankee-sized tips when they spot an American—especially in big cities such as Prague and Budapest. Tipping the appropriate amount—not feeling stingy, but also not contributing to the overtipping epidemic—can be nerve-racking to conscientious visitors. Relax! Many locals still don't tip at all, so any tip is appreciated. As in the US, the proper amount depends on your resources, tipping philosophy, and the circumstances, but some general guidelines apply.

Restaurants: Tip only at restaurants that have table service. If you order your food at a counter, don't tip.

At restaurants that have a waitstaff, round up the bill 5-10 percent after a good meal. My rule of thumb is to estimate about 10 percent, then round down slightly to reach a convenient total (for a 370-Kč meal, I pay 400 Kč—a tip of 30 Kč, or about 8 percent). That's plenty. I'm a little more generous in Budapest, where a minimum 10 percent tip is expected (I'll hand over 4,000 Ft for a 3,600-Ft bill—that's a 400-Ft tip, or 11 percent). Anywhere in Eastern Europe, a 15 percent tip is overly generous, verging on extravagant. At some tourist-oriented restaurants, a 10-15 percent "service charge" may be added to your bill, in which case an additional tip is not necessary. (More commonly, menus or bills remind you that the tip is *not* included.) If you're not sure whether your bill includes the tip, just ask.

Taxis: To tip the cabbie, round up about 5 percent (for instance, if the fare is 71 kn, pay 75 kn). If the cabbie hauls your bags and zips you to the airport to help you catch your flight, you might want to toss in a little more. But if you feel like you're being driven in circles or otherwise ripped off, skip the tip.

Special Services: Tour guides at public sites sometimes hold out their hands for tips after they give their spiel. If I've already paid for the tour, I don't tip extra, unless they've really impressed me. At hotels, if you let porters carry your luggage, it's polite to give them the local equivalent of 50 cents for each bag—another reason to pack light. If you like to tip maids, leave a dollar's worth of local cash per overnight at the end of your stay.

In general, if someone in the service industry does a super job for you, a small tip (the equivalent of a dollar or two) is appropriate... but not required.

VAT Rates and Minimum Purchases Required to Qualify for Refunds

Country of Purchase	VAT Standard Rate*	Minimum in Local Currency	Approx. Min. in US Dollars
Austria	20%	€75.01	$105
Croatia	23%	501 kn	$100
Czech Republic	19%	2,001 Kč	$110
Hungary	25%	48,001 Ft	$210
Poland	23%	200 zł	$60
Slovakia	19%	€175.01	$235
Slovenia	20%	€50	$70

* The VAT Standard Rates listed above—while listed as exact amounts—are intended to give you an idea of the rates and minimums involved. But VAT rates fluctuate based on many factors, including what kind of item you are buying. Your refund will also likely be less than the above rate, especially if it's subject to processing fees.

When in doubt, ask: If you're not sure whether (or how much) to tip for a service, ask your hotelier or the TI; they'll fill you in on how it's done on their turf.

Getting a VAT Refund

Wrapped into the purchase price of your souvenirs is a Value-Added Tax (VAT) that varies per country. You're entitled to get most of that tax back if you make a purchase of more than a certain amount at a store that participates in the VAT refund scheme. Typically, you must ring up the minimum at a single retailer—you can't add up your purchases from various shops to reach the required amount.

Getting your refund is usually straightforward and, if you buy a substantial number of souvenirs, well worth the hassle. If you're lucky, the merchant will subtract the tax when you make your purchase. (This is more likely to occur if the store ships the goods to your home.) Otherwise, you'll need to:

Get the paperwork. Have the merchant completely fill out the necessary refund document. You'll have to present your passport. Be sure to retain your original sales receipt.

Get your stamp at the border or airport. Process your VAT document with the customs service at your last stop in the country in which you made your purchase (or, if you bought it in the EU, at your last stop in the EU). If flying, it's best to keep your purchases in your carry-on for viewing. But if they're too large or dangerous to carry on (such as knives), have your purchases easily accessible in the bag you're about to check, ready to show the customs agent. You're not supposed to use your purchased goods before you leave. If you show up at customs wearing your chic Czech shirt, officials might look the other way—or deny you a refund.

Collect your refund. You'll need to return your stamped document to the retailer or its representative. Many merchants work with a service, such as Global Blue (www.global-blue.com) or Premier Tax Free (www.premiertaxfree.com), that has offices at major airports, ports, or border crossings (often after check-in and security, probably strategically located near a duty-free shop). These services, which extract a 4 percent fee, can refund your money immediately in cash or credit your card (within two billing cycles). If the retailer handles VAT refunds directly, it's up to you to contact the merchant for your refund. You can mail the documents from home, or more quickly, from your point of departure (using a stamped, addressed envelope you've prepared or one that's been provided by the merchant). You'll then have to wait—it could take months.

Customs for American Shoppers

You are allowed to take home $800 worth of items per person duty-free, once every 30 days. You can also bring in duty-free a liter of alcohol. As for food, you can take home many processed and packaged foods: vacuum-packed cheeses, dried herbs, jams, chocolate, oil, vinegar, and honey. Fresh fruits and vegetables and most meats are not allowed. Any liquid-containing foods must be packed in checked luggage, a potential recipe for disaster. To check customs rules and duty rates, visit www.cbp.gov.

Sightseeing

Eastern Europe's best attractions are modern museums that chronicle the communist regime and celebrate its demise (such as Budapest's House of Terror and Memento Park, and Gdańsk's "Roads to Freedom" exhibit). But the majority of museums here are dusty, old-fashioned collections of art or historical artifacts. While these don't quite rank with the Louvre or the Prado, many are surprisingly engaging if you take the time to learn more. Generally, you'll follow a confusing, one-way tour route through a maze of rooms with squeaky parquet floors, monitored by grumpy grannies who listlessly point you in the right direction. While some museums label exhibits in English, most don't post full explanations; you'll have to buy a book or borrow laminated translations.

In some cases, neither option is available.

Sightseeing can be hard work. Use these tips to make your visits to Eastern Europe's finest sights meaningful, fun, efficient, and painless.

Plan Ahead

Set up an itinerary that allows you to fit in all your must-see sights. For a one-stop look at opening hours, see the "At a Glance" sidebars for each major city (Prague, Kraków, Warsaw, Budapest, Ljubljana, Dubrovnik, and Vienna). Most sights keep stable hours, but in some areas (especially coastal Croatia), hours tend to fluctuate from season to season. If you have your heart set on visiting particular sights, it's always smart to confirm the latest hours by checking their websites or asking at the local TI.

Don't put off visiting a must-see sight—you never know when a place will close unexpectedly for a holiday, strike, or restoration. On holidays (see list on page 1255), expect reduced hours or closures. In summer, some sights may stay open late. Off-season, many museums have shorter hours.

When possible, visit the major sights in the morning (when your energy is best) and save other activities for the afternoon. At sights, hit the highlights first, then go back to other things if you have the time and stamina.

Going at the right time helps avoid crowds. This book offers tips on specific sights. Try visiting popular sights very early, at lunch, or very late. Evening visits are usually peaceful, with fewer crowds.

Study up. To get the most out of the sight descriptions in this book, read them before you visit. Note: To avoid redundancy, many cultural or historical details are explained for one sight in this book and not repeated for another; to get the full picture, read the entire chapter for each destination you'll visit.

At Sights

Here's what you can typically expect:

Some important sights have metal detectors or conduct bag searches that will slow your entry, while others require you to check daypacks and coats. They'll be kept safely. If you have something you can't bear to part with, stash it in a pocket or purse. To avoid checking a small backpack, carry it under your arm like a purse as you enter. From a guard's point of view, a backpack is generally a problem, while a purse is not.

Flash photography is often banned, but taking photos without a flash is usually allowed. Look for signs or ask. Flashes damage oil paintings and distract others in the room. Even without a flash, a handheld camera will take a decent picture (or buy postcards or

The Polish Plumber Syndrome

You'll likely enjoy a taste of Eastern European culture on your next trip...to London or Dublin. When several Eastern European countries joined the European Union in 2004, three EU members immediately welcomed their new comrades to work without a visa: Great Britain, the Republic of Ireland, and Sweden. This sparked a wave of immigration into these wealthy countries, as Eastern Europeans flocked to the land of plenty to find work. Many ended up in the hospitality industry.

The result has been mixed in each region. The transplants enjoyed more money and an irreplaceable cross-cultural experience. But Eastern Europe went through a somewhat alarming "brain drain," as many of its youngest and most westward-thinking residents rushed away. In Britain and Ireland, tourists began to encounter desk clerks who didn't quite speak fluent English. More recently, the global financial crisis has tightened up the job market—making the arrangement less appealing both to the expat workers, and to the native job-seekers in the countries that are hosting them. Quite a few of these transplants have lost their jobs and returned home to the East.

Other Western European countries have contemplated opening their borders, but it's controversial. One popular  symbol—invented by a right-wing French politician—was an invading "Polish plumber" who'd put French plumbers out of a job. The Polish tourist board countered by putting up clever ads in France featuring an alluring Polish hunk stroking a pipe wrench, saying, "I'm staying in Poland...come visit me!"

This is just one more step in the Europe-wide process of integration. Europeans in their twenties have been dubbed the "Erasmus Generation"—after the Erasmus Student Network, an EU organization that fosters study-abroad opportunities within Europe. As European twentysomethings have grown up accustomed to attending universities in other countries, it seems natural for them to identify as "Europeans" rather than as Spaniards, Slovenes, or Swedes. Multilingualism, international résumés, and cross-cultural marriages are the norm.

posters at the museum bookstore). If photos are permitted, video cameras generally are OK, too.

Museums may have special exhibits in addition to their permanent collection. Some exhibits are included in the entry price, while others come at an extra cost (which you may have to pay even if you don't want to see the exhibit).

Expect changes—items can be on tour, on loan, out sick, or shifted at the whim of the curator. To adapt, pick up any available free floor plans as you enter, and ask museum staff if you can't find a particular item.

Some sights rent audioguides, which offer recorded descriptions in English, but they're usually dull and rarely worth the cost (about $6-8). If you bring along your own pair of headphones and a Y-jack, you can sometimes share one audioguide with your travel partner and save money. As an alternative, several museums now offer smartphone audio tours (often free, sometimes for a fee). Use your smartphone to log on to the museum's Wi-Fi network and access a room-by-room tour (bring earbuds). While this sounds complicated, it generally works great.

Some sights also run short films featuring their highlights and history. These are generally well worth your time. I make it standard operating procedure to ask when I arrive at a sight if there is a film in English.

A few sights have on-site cafés or cafeterias (usually good places to rest and have a snack or light meal). The WCs at sights are free and generally clean (it's smart to carry tissues in case a WC runs out of TP).

Many sights sell postcards that highlight their attractions. Before you leave a sight, scan the postcards and thumb through the biggest guidebook (or skim its index) to be sure you haven't overlooked something that you'd like to see.

Most sights stop admitting people 30-60 minutes before closing time, and some rooms close early (often about 45 minutes before the actual closing time). Guards usher people out, so don't save the best for last.

Every sight or museum offers more than what is covered in this book. Use the information in this book as an introduction—not the final word.

Sleeping

I favor hotels and restaurants that are handy to your sightseeing activities. Rather than list hotels scattered throughout a city, I describe two or three favorite neighborhoods and recommend the best accommodations values in each, from dorm beds to fancy doubles with all the comforts.

A major feature of this book is its extensive listing of good-value rooms. I like places that are clean, central, relatively quiet at night, reasonably priced, friendly, English-speaking, professional-feeling but small enough to have a hands-on owner and stable staff, run with a respect for local traditions, and not listed in other guidebooks. I'm more impressed by a convenient location and a fun-loving philosophy than flat-screen TVs and shoe-shine machines. My favorites are small, family-run hotels (which aren't as prevalent in Eastern Europe as in the West), and friendly local people who rent hotelesque private rooms without a reception desk. I've also thrown in a few hostels and other cheap options for budget travelers.

Book your accommodations well in advance if you'll be traveling during busy times. See page 1255 for a list of major holidays and festivals in Eastern Europe; for tips on making reservations, see page 30.

Travel Review Websites: TripAdvisor (www.tripadvisor.com) and similar review websites are popular tools for finding hotels, but have drawbacks. To write a review, people need only an email address—making it easy to hide their true identity. If a hotel is well reviewed in a guidebook or two, and also gets good ratings on TripAdvisor, it's probably a safe bet—but I wouldn't stay at a hotel based solely on a TripAdvisor recommendation.

Rates and Deals

Accommodations in Eastern Europe cost about as much as comparable beds in the West. While most accommodations listed in this book cluster at about $80-120 per double, they range from $15 bunks to $500-plus splurges (maximum plumbing and more).

I've described my recommended accommodations using a Sleep Code (see the sidebar). Prices listed are for one-night stays in peak season and assume you're booking directly (not through a TI or online hotel-booking engine). Using an online booking service costs the hotel 15-20 percent and logically closes the door on special deals. Book direct.

Some accommodations quote their rates in euros, while others use the local currency. Occasionally I've converted a few prices to make it easier for you to compare hotel rates—so you might notice a little variation between the rates listed here and those quoted by hotels.

As you look over the listings, you'll notice that a few accommodations promise special prices to my readers who book direct (without using a room-finding service or hotel-booking website, which take a commission). To get these rates, you must mention this book when you reserve, and then show the book upon arrival. Some readers with ebooks have reported difficulty getting a Rick

Sleep Code

To help you easily sort through these listings, I've divided the accommodations into three categories based on the price for a double room with bath during high season:

$$$	**Higher Priced**
$$	**Moderately Priced**
$	**Lower Priced**

I always rate hostels as $, whether or not they have double rooms, because they have the cheapest beds in town. Prices can change without notice; verify the hotel's current rates online or by email. For other updates, see www.rick steves.com/update.

Abbreviations

To pack maximum information into minimum space, I use the following code to describe accommodations in this book. Prices listed are per room, not per person. When a price range is given for a type of room (such as double rooms listing for €80-100), it means the price fluctuates with the season, size of room, or length of stay; expect to pay the upper end for peak-season stays. In Croatia, where accommodation prices vary dramatically by season, I've separated high-, mid-, and low-season rates with slashes (explained in each destination's "Sleep Code.")

S = Single room (or price for one person in a double).

D = Double or twin room. "Double beds" can be two twins sheeted together and are usually big enough for non-romantic couples.

T = Triple (often a double bed with a single).

Q = Quad (usually two double beds; adding an extra child's bed to a T is usually cheaper).

b = Private bathroom with toilet and shower or tub.

s = Private shower or tub only (the toilet is down the hall).

According to this code, a couple staying at a "Db-2,700 Kč" place in Prague would pay a total of 2,700 Czech crowns (about $150) for a double room with a private bathroom. At hotels, unless otherwise noted, staff speak basic English, breakfast is included, and credit cards are accepted (though private accommodations rarely provide breakfast or accept credit cards).

If I mention "Internet access" in a listing, there's a public terminal in the lobby for guests to use. If I specify "Wi-Fi," you can generally access it in public areas and often (though not always) in your room, but only if you have your own laptop or other wireless device. If you see "cable Internet," it means you can get online in your room with your laptop, provided you have (or borrow) an Ethernet cable to plug in.

Steves discount. If this happens to you, please show this to the hotelier: Rick Steves discounts apply to readers with ebooks as well as printed books.

Given the economic downturn, many larger hotels are willing and eager to make a deal. Try to avoid paying the inflated, official "rack rates." I'd suggest emailing several hotels to ask for their best price—you'll find some eager to discount and others more passive. This can save you big bucks—with prices potentially far below those listed in this guidebook. Comparison-shop and make your choice.

Three or four people can save money by requesting one big room. Traveling alone can be expensive: A single room is often only 20 percent cheaper than a double. In general, prices can soften if you do any of the following: offer to pay cash, stay at least three nights, or mention this book. You can also try asking for a cheaper room or a discount, or offer to skip breakfast. Before accepting a room, confirm your understanding of the complete price (including, for example, surcharges for short stays).

Helpful Hints

If asked whether they have non-smoking rooms, most hoteliers in Eastern Europe will say yes. When pressed, they'll sheepishly admit, "Well, *all* of our rooms are non-smoking"...meaning they air them out after a smoker has stayed there. I've described accommodations as "non-smoking" only if they have specially designated rooms for this purpose. Be specific and assertive if you need a strictly non-smoking room.

For environmental reasons, towels are often replaced in hotels only when you leave them on the floor. In private accommodations and some cheap hotels, they aren't replaced at all, so hang them up to dry and reuse. The cord that dangles over the tub or shower in big resort hotels is not a clothesline—you pull it if you've fallen and can't get up.

If you're arriving early in the morning, your room probably won't be ready. You should be able to safely check your bag at the place you're staying and dive right into sightseeing.

If you suspect night noise will be a problem (if, for instance, your room is over a nightclub), ask for a quiet room in the back or on an upper floor. To guard against theft in your room, keep valuables out of sight. Fancier rooms come with a safe, and other hotels have safes at the front desk. Use them if you're concerned.

Your host can be a great help and source of advice. Most know their city well, and can assist you with everything from public transit and airport connections to finding a good restaurant, the nearest launderette, or an Internet café. But even at the best places, mechanical breakdowns occur: Air-conditioning malfunctions, sinks leak, hot water turns cold, and toilets gurgle and smell. Report your concerns clearly and calmly. For more complicated problems, don't expect instant results. Above all, don't expect things to be the same as back home. Keep a positive attitude. Remember, you're on vacation. If your accommodations are a disappointment, spend more time out enjoying the places you came to see.

Pay your bill the evening before you leave to avoid the time-wasting crowd at the reception desk in the morning, especially if you need to rush off to catch a boat or train. This also gives you time to discuss and address any points of contention. The only tip my recommended accommodations would like is a friendly, easygoing guest. And, as always, I appreciate feedback on your experiences.

Types of Accommodations
Hotels
In Eastern Europe, you can choose from a delightful variety of stylish and charming hotels and guest houses. A few dreary old  communist-era hotels remain, but most Eastern European hotels are relatively new (built since the end of communism). This means that hotel prices can be higher than you might expect. You can find a central, basic, comfortable double for $100 just about anywhere. Plan on spending $90-130 per double in big cities, and $60-90 in smaller towns. You can uncover some bargains, but I think it's worth paying a little more for comfort and a good location.

When you check in, the receptionist will normally ask for your passport and keep it for a couple of hours. Don't worry. Hotels are legally required to register each guest with the local police. Americans are notorious for making this chore more difficult than it needs to be.

Breakfast, almost always served buffet style, usually includes rolls, cold cuts, cheese, cereal, yogurt, fruit, coffee, milk, and juice; some places also provide eggs.

Most hotel rooms have a TV and telephone, and Internet access (either wireless or with a cable) is increasingly becoming standard. Pricier hotels also have air-conditioning and a minibar.

Private Rooms
Private accommodations—which are particularly prevalent in Croatia—offer travelers a characteristic and money-saving alternative for a fraction of the price of a hotel. Rooms in private homes

Making Reservations

Given the erratic accommodations values in Eastern Europe—and the quality of the places I've found for this book—I recommend that you reserve your rooms in advance, particularly if you'll be traveling during peak season. Book several weeks ahead, or as soon as you've pinned down your travel dates. Note that some holidays jam things up and merit your making reservations far in advance (see "Holidays and Festivals" on page 1255).

Phoning: To make international calls to line up hotel reservations, you'll need to know the country codes. For detailed instructions on telephoning, see page 1230 in the appendix.

Requesting a Reservation: To make a reservation, contact hotels directly by email, phone, or fax. Email is the clearest and most economical way to make a reservation. Or you can go straight to the hotel website; many have secure online reservation forms and can instantly inform you of availability and any special deals. But be sure you use the hotel's official site and not a booking agency's site—otherwise you may pay higher rates than you should. Most recommended accommodations are accustomed to guests who speak only English.

Your hotelier or host wants to know these key pieces of information (also included in the sample request form in the appendix):

- number and type of rooms
- number of nights
- date of arrival
- date of departure
- any special needs (e.g., bathroom in the room or down the hall, twin beds vs. double bed, air-conditioning, quiet, view, ground floor, etc.)

When you request a room, use the European style for writing dates: day/month/year. For example, for a two-night stay in July 2013, I would request: "1 double room for 2 nights, arrive 16/07/13, depart 18/07/13." Consider in advance how long you'll stay; don't just assume you can tack on extra days once you arrive. Make sure you mention any discounts—for Rick Steves readers or otherwise—when you make the reservation.

Confirming a Reservation: If the hotel's response includes its room availability and rates, it's not a confirmation. You

are called *sobe* in Slovenia and Croatia; the German word *Zimmer* works there, too, and throughout Eastern Europe. These places are inexpensive, at least as comfortable as a cheap hotel, and a good way to get some local insight. The boss changes the sheets, so people staying several nights are most desirable—and those who stay less than three nights are often charged a lot more (typically 20-50 percent; this surcharge is often waived outside of peak season). For more on Croatian *sobe*, see page 823.

must tell them that you want that room at the given rate. Many hoteliers will request your credit-card number for a one-night deposit to hold the room. While you can email your credit-card information (I do), it's safer to share that confidential info via phone call, fax, split between two successive emails, or via a secure online reservation form (if the hotel has one on its website).

Canceling a Reservation: If you must cancel your reservation, it's courteous to do so with as much advance notice as possible. Simply make a quick phone call or send an email. Family-run hotels and smaller places lose money if they turn away customers while holding a room for someone who doesn't show up. Understandably, many hoteliers bill no-shows for one night.

Cancellation policies can be strict: For example, you might lose a deposit if you cancel within two weeks of your reserved stay, or you might be billed for the entire visit if you leave early. Internet deals may require prepayment, with no refunds for cancellations. Ask about cancellation policies before you book.

If canceling via email, request confirmation that your cancellation was received to avoid being accidentally billed.

Reconfirming a Reservation: Always call to reconfirm your room reservation a few days in advance. Smaller places appreciate knowing your estimated time of arrival. If you'll be arriving late (after 17:00), let them know. On the small chance that a hotel loses track of your reservation, it's good to have a hard copy of their emailed or faxed confirmation.

Reserving Rooms as You Travel: You can make reservations as you travel, calling places a few days to a week before your arrival. If everything's full, don't despair. Call a day or two in advance and fill in a cancellation. If you'd rather travel without any reservations at all, you'll have greater success snaring rooms if you arrive at your destination early in the day. When you anticipate crowds (weekends are worst), call hotels at about 9:00 or 10:00 on the day you plan to arrive, when the hotel clerk knows who'll be checking out and just which rooms will be available. If you encounter a language barrier, ask the fluent receptionist at your current hotel to call for you.

Hostels

For $20-30 a night, travelers of any age can stay at a youth hostel. While Hostelling International (IYHF) hostels admit nonmembers for an extra fee, it can be easier to join the club's US affiliate before you go (US tel. 301/495-1240 or order online at www.hiusa .org). To increase your options, consider the many independent hostels that don't require a membership card.

If you're used to hosteling elsewhere in Europe, you may be

unpleasantly surprised by some Eastern European hostels. In general, official IYHF hostels are inconveniently located and particularly institutional, while independent hostels are more loosely run and grungier than the European norm. In each town, I've tried to list the best-established, most reputable hostel options, both independent and official—sometimes with lots of caveats. But this scene is evolving so fast that avid hostelers will do better getting tips from fellow travelers and searching on sites such as www.hostels.com, www.hostelworld.com, www.hostelz.com, and www.hostelseurope.com.

At hostels, cheap meals are sometimes available, and kitchen facilities are usually provided for do-it-yourselfers. Most offer Internet access and Wi-Fi, and some have a self-service laundry. Bring a sleeping sheet or rent one as you go. While many hostels have a few doubles or family rooms available upon request for a little extra money, plan on dorms with 4 to 20 beds per room. At official hostels, dorms are generally gender-segregated; at independent hostels, it's more likely mixed. In summer, expect crowds, snoring, and lots of noisy backpacker bonding in the common room while you're trying to sleep. Hosteling is ideal for those traveling single: Prices are per bed, not per room, and you'll have an instant circle of friends. At most hostels, you can reserve online or by phoning ahead (usually with a credit card).

Eating

Eastern Europe offers good food for relatively little money—especially if you steer clear of the easy-to-avoid tourist trap restaurants. This is affordable sightseeing for your palate.

Slavic cuisine has a reputation for being heavy and hearty, with lots of pork, potatoes and cabbage...which is true. But the food here is also delicious, and there's a lot more diversity from country to country than you might expect. Tune in to the regional and national specialties and customs (see each country's introduction in this book for details).

If you need a break from Slavic fare, seek out vegetarian, Italian, Indian, Chinese, and similar places, which are especially good in big cities such as Prague, Budapest, or Kraków (I've listed a few tasty options). Hungarian cuisine is rich and spicy (think paprika), while Slovenia and Croatia have good seafood and lots of Italian-style dishes (pastas and pizzas).

How Was Your Trip?

Were your travels fun, smooth, and meaningful? If you'd like to share your tips, concerns, and discoveries, please fill out the survey at www.ricksteves.com/feedback. I value your feedback. Thanks in advance—it helps a lot.

When restaurant-hunting, choose a spot filled with locals, not the place with the big neon signs boasting, "We Speak English and Accept Credit Cards." Venturing even a block or two off the main drag leads to higher-quality food for less than half the price of the tourist-oriented places. Most restaurants tack a menu onto their door for browsers and have an English menu inside. If the place isn't full, you can usually just seat yourself (get a waiter's attention to be sure your preferred table is OK)—the American-style "hostess," with a carefully managed waiting list, isn't common here. Once seated, feel free to take your time. In fact, it might be difficult to dine in a hurry. Only a rude waiter will rush you. Good service is relaxed (slow to an American).

When you're in the mood for something halfway between a restaurant and a picnic meal, look for take-out food stands, bakeries (with sandwiches and savory pastries to go), shops selling pizza by the slice, or simple little eateries offering fast and easy sit-down restaurant food. In Poland, don't miss the deliriously cheap "milk bar" cafeterias (see page 269). Many grocery stores sell pre-made sandwiches, and others might be willing to make one for you from what's in the deli case.

The Czech Republic is beer country, with Europe's best and cheapest brew. Poland also has fine beer, but the national drink is *wódka*. Hungary, Slovenia, and Croatia are known for their wines. Each country has its own distinctive liqueur, most of them a variation on *slivovice* (SLEE-voh-veet-seh)—a plum brandy so highly valued that it's the de facto currency of the Carpathian Mountains (often used for bartering with farmers and other mountain folk). Menus list drink size by the tenth of a liter, or deciliter (dl). Non-drinkers will find all the standard types of Coke and Pepsi, along with some fun-to-sample local alternatives (such as Slovenia's Cockta, described on page 709).

Traveling as a Temporary Local

We travel all the way to Europe to enjoy differences—to become temporary locals. You'll experience frustrations. Certain truths that we find "God-given" or "self-evident," such as cold beer, ice in drinks, bottomless cups of coffee, hot showers, and bigger being better, are suddenly not so true. One of the benefits of travel is the eye-opening realization that there are logical, civil, and even better alternatives. A willingness to go local ensures that you'll enjoy a full dose of hospitality.

Fortunately for you, hospitality is a local forte. The friendliness of the Eastern Europeans seems to have only been enhanced during the communist era: Tangible resources were in short supply, so an open door and a genial conversation were all that people had to offer. For many Eastern Europeans, the chance to chat with an American is still a delightful novelty. Even so, some people—hardened by decades of being spied on by neighbors and standing in long lines to buy food for their family—seem brusque at first. In my experience, all it takes is a smile and a little effort to befriend these residents of the former "Evil Empire."

Europeans generally like Americans. But if there is a negative aspect to their image of Americans, it's that we are big, loud, aggressive, impolite, rich, superficially friendly, and a bit naive.

While Europeans look bemusedly at some of our Yankee excesses—and worriedly at others—they nearly always afford us individual travelers all the warmth we deserve.

Judging from all the happy feedback I receive from travelers who have used this book, it's safe to assume you'll enjoy a great, affordable vacation—with the finesse of an independent, experienced traveler.

Thanks, and happy travels!

Back Door Travel Philosophy
From *Rick Steves' Europe Through the Back Door*

Travel is intensified living—maximum thrills per minute and one of the last great sources of legal adventure. Travel is freedom. It's recess, and we need it.

Experiencing the real Europe requires catching it by surprise, going casual..."Through the Back Door."

Affording travel is a matter of priorities. (Make do with the old car.) You can eat and sleep—simply, safely, and enjoyably—anywhere in Europe for $120 a day plus transportation costs (allow more for bigger cities). In many ways, spending more money only builds a thicker wall between you and what you traveled so far to see. Europe is a cultural carnival, and time after time, you'll find that its best acts are free and the best seats are the cheap ones.

A tight budget forces you to travel close to the ground, meeting and communicating with the people. Never sacrifice sleep, nutrition, safety, or cleanliness to save money. Simply enjoy the local-style alternatives to expensive hotels and restaurants.

Connecting with people carbonates your experience. Extroverts have more fun. If your trip is low on magic moments, kick yourself and make things happen. If you don't enjoy a place, maybe you don't know enough about it. Seek the truth. Recognize tourist traps. Give a culture the benefit of your open mind. See things as different, but not better or worse. Any culture has plenty to share.

Of course, travel, like the world, is a series of hills and valleys. Be fanatically positive and militantly optimistic. If something's not to your liking, change your liking.

Travel can make you a happier American, as well as a citizen of the world. Our Earth is home to seven billion equally precious people. It's humbling to travel and find that other people don't have the "American Dream"—they have their own dreams. Europeans like us, but with all due respect, they wouldn't trade passports.

Thoughtful travel engages us with the world. In tough economic times, it reminds us what is truly important. By broadening perspectives, travel teaches new ways to measure quality of life.

Globetrotting destroys ethnocentricity, helping us understand and appreciate other cultures. Rather than fear the diversity on this planet, celebrate it. Among your most prized souvenirs will be the strands of different cultures you choose to knit into your own character. The world is a cultural yarn shop, and Back Door travelers are weaving the ultimate tapestry. Join in!

CZECH REPUBLIC
Česká Republika

CZECH REPUBLIC

 Despite their difficult 20th-century experience, the Czechs have managed to preserve their history. In Czech towns and villages, you'll find a simple joy of life—a holdover from the days of the Renaissance. The deep spirituality of the Baroque era still shapes the national character. The magic of Prague, the beauty of Český Krumlov, and the lyrical quality of the countryside relieve the heaviness caused by the turmoil that passed through here. Get beyond Prague and explore the country's medieval towns. These rugged woods and hilltop castles will make you feel as if you're walking through the garden of your childhood dreams.

Of the Czech Republic's three main regions—Bohemia, Moravia, and small Silesia—the best-known is Bohemia. It has nothing to do with beatnik bohemians, but with the Celtic tribe of Bohemia that inhabited the land before the coming of the Slavs. A longtime home of the Czechs, Bohemia, with Prague as its capital, is circled by a naturally fortifying ring of mountains and cut down the middle by the Vltava River. The winegrowing region of Moravia (to the east) is more Slavic and colorful, and more about the land.

Tourists often conjure up images of Bohemia when they think of the Czech Republic. But the country consists of more than rollicking beer halls and gently rolling landscapes. It's also about dreamy wine cellars and fertile Moravian plains, with the rugged Carpathian Mountains on the horizon. Politically and geologically, Bohemia and Moravia are two distinct regions. The soils and climates in which the hops and wine grapes grow are very different...and so are the two regions' mentalities. The boisterousness of the Czech polka contrasts with the melancholy of the Moravian ballad; the political viewpoint of the Prague power broker is at odds with the spirituality of the Moravian bard.

Only a tiny bit of Silesia—around the town of Opava—is part of the Czech Republic today; the rest of the region is in Poland and Germany. (The Habsburgs lost traditionally Czech Silesia to Prussia in the 1740s, and 200 years later, Germany in turn ceded most of it to Poland.) People in Silesia speak a wide variety of dia-

lects that mix Czech, German, and Polish. Perhaps due to their diverse genes and cultural heritage, women from Silesia are famous for being intelligent and beautiful.

Since 1989, the year that the Czechs won their independence from Soviet control, people have been working harder—but the average monthly wage is still only about $1,500. Roads have been patched up, facades have gotten facelifts, and supermarkets have been pushed out by hypermarkets.

In communist times, it was routine to be married and start a family by age 22. Once a Czech finished training school and (for men) the compulsory two-year military service, there was little else to aspire to. Everyone was assigned essentially the same mediocre job ("They pretended to pay us, we pretended to work"), with little hope of career progress—unless you were willing to cut ties with your friends by entering the Communist Party or working for the secret police. Children (and summer homes) were the only way for people to project their dreams. Parenting was subsidized. In the countryside, young families were guaranteed housing, and in cities, flats were allocated according to long waiting lists that gave priority to married couples with children.

But after the fall of communism in 1989, many more options became available to young people who, as children or teenagers, had not even dreamed of such possibilities. Young Czechs embraced the new freedoms: Everyone wanted to travel—to the West to study law, or to the East to meditate in a cave. And everyone wanted to work—for big bucks at a multinational investment bank, or for pennies at a nonprofit organization in Afghanistan. Marriage was no longer the expected "next step." And shacking up was no longer a problem; you needed money, rather than a marriage certificate, to get a place to live. More and more young adults

Czech Republic Almanac

Official Name: It's the Česká Republika, born on January 1, 1993, along with Slovakia, when the nation of Czechoslovakia—formed after World War I and dominated by the USSR after World War II—split into two countries.

Population: 10.2 million people. About 90 percent are ethnic Czechs, who speak Czech. Unlike some of their neighbors (including the very Catholic Poles and Slovaks), Czechs are inclined to be agnostic: One in four is Roman Catholic, but the majority (60 percent) list their religion as unaffiliated.

Latitude and Longitude: 50°N and 15°E (similar latitude to Vancouver, British Columbia).

Area: 31,000 square miles (similar to South Carolina or Maine).

Geography: The Czech Republic comprises three regions—Bohemia (Čechy), Moravia (Morava), and a small slice of Silesia (Slezsko). The climate is generally cool and partly cloudy.

Biggest Cities: Prague (the capital, 1.2 million), Brno (380,000), Ostrava (336,000), and Plzeň (165,000).

Economy: The gross domestic product equals about $254 billion (similar to that of Indiana). The GDP per capita is approximately $25,000 (just over half that of the average American). Some major moneymakers for the country are machine parts, cars and trucks (VW subsidiary Škoda has become a highly respected automaker), and beer (including Pilsner Urquell and the original Budweiser—called "Czechvar" in the US). The recent economic crisis caused a major decline in machine parts, cars, and trucks—

waited until after 30 to get married, and those already married reconsidered their choices in the light of new circumstances. Fewer Czechs had children, and many got divorced.

By 2004, the falling birthrate and shrinking size of the Czech nation was a regular topic in newspaper columns. To stimulate production, the socialist government began paying new parents a baby bonus—one month's wages—in addition to the standard three years of paid maternity leave already promised to one parent.

Ironically—as if to prove that Czechs will never listen to what the government tells them to do—as soon as the newly elected conservatives revoked the monthly baby bonus in 2006, everyone between the ages of 25 and 35 suddenly decided to have children. The biggest baby boom in a generation is still on: Maternity wards are overflowing, signs regulating stroller traffic are popping up in public parks, and politicians are blaming each other for imprudently closing down many state-run nurseries.

Yet, even though they're faced with a bright and baby-filled future, some Czechs maintain a healthy dose of pessimism and

but not in beer consumption, which dropped minimally (the vast majority of Czech beer is consumed domestically). More than a third of trade is with next-door-neighbor Germany; therefore, Germany's economic health one year will generally predict the Czech Republic's fortunes the next. Privatization of formerly government-run industries goes on. Next to be sold are the airlines and the energy company.

Currency: 18 Czech crowns (koruna, Kč) = about $1.

Government: From 1948 to 1989, Czechoslovakia was a communist state under Soviet control. Today, the Czech Republic is a member of the European Union (since 2004) and a vibrant democracy, with about a 60 percent turnout for elections. Its parliament is made up of 200 representatives elected every four years and 81 senators elected for six years. No single political party dominates. Although the left-of-center Social Democrats technically won the 2010 election with a little over one-fifth of the vote, a coalition government was formed by three right-of-center parties united in their emphasis on fiscal responsibility. The fifth party in the parliament, the Communists, joined the Social Democrats in opposition. The president (currently Václav Klaus, a conservative) is selected every five years by the legislators.

Flag: The Czech flag is red (bottom), white (top), and blue (a triangle along the hoist side).

The Average Czech: The average Czech has 1.2 kids (slowly rising after the sharp decline that followed the end of communism), will live 76 years, and has one television in the house.

seem reluctant to dive headlong into the Western rat race. Life still goes a little slower here, and people find pleasure in simple things.

Czech children, adults, and grandparents delight in telling stories. In Czech fairy tales, there are no dwarfs and monsters. To experience the full absurdity and hilarity of Czech culture, you need a child's imagination and the understanding that the best fun comes from being able to laugh at yourself. Czech writers invented the robot, the pistol, and Black Light Theater (an absurd show of illusion, puppetry, mime, and modern dance—see page 135).

Literature and film are the most transparent windows into the Czech soul. The most famous Czech literary figure is the title character of Jaroslav Hašek's *Good Soldier Švejk*, who frustrates the World War I Austro-Hungarian army he serves by cleverly playing dumb. Other well-known Czech writers include Václav Havel (playwright who went on to become Czechoslovakia's first post-communist president—he authored many essays and plays, including *The Garden Party*); Milan Kundera (author of *The Unbearable Lightness of Being*, set during the "Prague Spring" uprising); and

Karel Čapek (novelist and playwright who created the robot in the play *R.U.R.*). But the most famous Czech writer of all is the existentialist great, Franz Kafka, a Prague Jew who wrote in German about a person turning into a giant cockroach *(The Metamorphosis)* and an urbanite being pursued and persecuted for crimes he knows nothing about *(The Trial)*.

Ninety percent of the tourists who visit the Czech Republic see only Prague. But if you venture outside the capital, you'll enjoy traditional towns and villages, great prices, a friendly and gentle countryside dotted by nettles and wild poppies, and almost no Western tourists. Since the time of the Habsburgs, fruit trees have lined the country roads for everyone to share. Take your pick.

Helpful Hints

Telephone: Dial 112 for medical or other emergencies and 158 for police. If a number starting with 0800 doesn't work, replace the 0800 with 822. For more details on dialing, see page 1231.

Toll Sticker: To drive on Czech expressways, you are required to display a toll sticker (*dálniční známka*, 200 Kč/15 days, 300 Kč/2 months). Check to see if your rental car already has one; if not, buy one at a gas station when you enter the country.

Railpasses: The Czech Republic is covered by a Czech Republic railpass, a Germany-Czech or an Austria-Czech railpass, the five-country European East pass, the Eurail Global pass, and the Eurail Selectpass. If your train travel will be limited to a handful of rides and/or short distances (e.g., within the Czech Republic), you're probably better off without a pass—Czech tickets are cheap to buy as you go. But if you're combining Prague with international destinations, a railpass could save you money. For all the details, check out my free Guide to Eurail Passes at www.ricksteves.com/rail.

Czech History

The Czechs have always been at a crossroads of Europe—between the Slavic and Germanic worlds, between Catholicism and Protestantism, and between Cold War East and West. As if having foreseen all of this, the mythical founder of Prague—the beautiful princess Libuše—named her city "Praha" (meaning "threshold" in Czech). Despite these strong external influences, the Czechs have retained their distinct culture...and a dark, ironic sense of humor to keep them laughing through it all.

Charles IV and the Middle Ages

Prague's castle put Bohemia on the map in the ninth century. About a century later, the region was incorporated into the German Holy Roman Empire. Within two hundred years, Prague was one of Europe's largest and most highly cultured cities.

The 14th century was Prague's Golden Age, when Holy Roman Emperor Charles IV (1316-1378) ruled. Born to a Luxemburger nobleman and a Czech princess, Charles IV was a dynamic man on the cusp of the Renaissance. He spoke five languages, counted Petrarch as a friend, imported French architects to make Prague a grand capital, founded the first university north of the Alps, and invigorated the Czech national spirit. (He popularized the legend of the good king Wenceslas to give his people a near-mythical, King Arthur-type cultural standard-bearer.) Much of Prague's history and architecture (including the famous Charles Bridge, Charles University, and St. Vitus Cathedral) can be traced to this man's rule. Under Charles IV, the Czech people gained esteem among Europeans.

Jan Hus and Religious Wars

Jan Hus (c. 1370-1415) was a local preacher and professor who got in trouble with the Vatican a hundred years before Martin Luther. Like Luther, Hus preached in the people's language rather than Latin. To add insult to injury, he complained about Church corruption. Tried for heresy and burned in 1415, Hus became both a religious and a national hero. While each age has defined Hus to its liking, the way he challenged authority while staying true to his beliefs has long inspired and rallied the Czech people. (For more on Hus, see page 77.)

Inspired by the reformist ideas of Hus, the Czechs rebelled against both the Roman Catholic Church and German political control. This burst of independent thought led to a period of religious wars and, ultimately, the loss of autonomy to Vienna. Ruled by the Habsburgs of Austria, Prague stagnated—except during the rule of King Rudolf II (1552-1612), a Holy Roman Emperor. With Rudolf living in Prague, the city again emerged as a cultural and intellectual center. Astronomers Johannes Kepler and Tycho Brahe flourished, as did other scientists, and much of the inspiration for Prague's great art can be attributed to the king's patronage.

Not long after this period, Prague entered one of its darker

Notable Czechs

These prominent historical figures are listed in chronological order.

St. Wenceslas (907-935): Bohemian duke who allied the Czechs with the Holy Roman Empire. He went on to become the Czech Republic's patron saint, and it is he who is memorialized as a "good king" in the Christmas carol. For more on Wenceslas, see page 97.

Jan Hus (c. 1370-1415): Proto-Protestant Reformer who was burned at the stake (see page 77).

John Amos Comenius (Jan Amos Komenský in Czech, 1592-1670): "Teacher of Nations" and Protestant exile, whose ideas paved the way for modern education.

Antonín Dvořák (1841-1904): Inspired by a trip to America, he composed his *New World Symphony*.

Tomáš Garrigue Masaryk (1850-1937): Sociology professor, writer, politician, and spiritual reformer. He was idolized during his lifetime as the "dearest father" of the Czechoslovak democracy (see page 122).

Jára Cimrman (c. 1853-1914): Illustrious but fictional inventor, explorer, philosopher, and all-around genius. Despite being overwhelmingly voted the "Greatest Czech of All Time" in a nationwide poll, he was not awarded the title (see page 116).

Alfons Mucha (1860-1939): You might recognize his turn-of-the-century Art Nouveau posters of pretty girls entwined in vines. Visit his museum in Prague, marvel at his stained-glass window in St. Vitus Cathedral, and bask in his magnum opus, the *Slav Epic* (on display in Prague; see page 102).

Franz Kafka (1883-1924): While working for a Prague insurance firm, he wrote (in German) *The Metamorphosis* (man awakes as a cockroach), *The Trial, The Castle,* and other psychologically haunting stories and novels.

Milan Kundera (1929-): Wrote the novel *The Unbearable Lightness of Being* (which became a film), among others.

Václav Havel (1936-2011): The country's first post-Soviet president, also well-known as a playwright and philosopher.

Madeleine Albright (1937-): Born in Prague as Marie Jana Korbelová, Albright was the first woman to serve as US Secretary of State, from 1997-2001, under Bill Clinton.

Martina Navrátilová (1956-): Tennis star of the 1980s.

spells. The Thirty Years' War (1618-1648) began in Prague when Czech Protestant nobles, wanting religious and political autonomy, tossed two Catholic Habsburg officials out of the window of the castle. (This was one of Prague's many defenestrations—a uniquely Czech solution to political discord, in which offending politicians are literally thrown out the window.) The Czech Estates Uprising lasted for two years, ending in a crushing defeat of the Czech army in the Battle of White Mountain (1620), which marked the end of Czech freedom. Twenty-seven leaders of the uprising were executed (today commemorated by crosses on Prague's Old Town Square), most of the old Czech nobility was dispossessed, and Protestants had to convert to Catholicism or leave the country. Often called "the first world war" because it engulfed so many nations, the Thirty Years' War was particularly tough on Prague. During this period, its population dropped from 60,000 to 25,000. The result of this war was 300 years of Habsburg rule from afar, as Prague became a German-speaking backwater of Vienna.

Czech Nationalist Revival

The end of Prague as a "German" city came gradually. As the Industrial Revolution attracted Czech farmers and peasants to the cities, the demographics of the Czech population centers began to shift. Between 1800 and 1900, though it remained part of the Habsburg Empire, Prague went from being an essentially German town to a predominantly Czech one. As in the rest of Europe, the 19th century was a time of great nationalism, when the age of divine kings and ruling families came to a fitful end. The Czech spirit was stirred by the completion of Prague's St. Vitus Cathedral, the symphonies of Antonín Dvořák, and the operas of Bedřich Smetana, which were performed in the new National Theater.

After the Habsburgs' Austro-Hungarian Empire suffered defeat in World War I, their vast holdings broke apart and became independent countries. Among these was a union of Bohemia, Moravia, and Slovakia, the brainchild of a clever politician named Tomáš Garrigue Masaryk. The new nation, Czechoslovakia, was proclaimed in 1918, with Prague as its capital.

Troubled 20th Century

Independence lasted only 20 years. In the notorious Munich Agreement of September 1938—much to the dismay of the Czechs and Slovaks—Great Britain and France peacefully ceded to Hitler the so-called Sudetenland (a fringe around the edge of Bohemia, populated mainly by people of German descent). It wasn't long before Hitler seized the rest of Czechoslovakia...and the Holocaust began.

Czech Sports

Prague's top sports are soccer (that's "football" here) and hockey. Surprisingly, the Czechs have often been a world power in both.

The Czech national **soccer** team reached the finals of the 1996 Euro Cup and the semifinals of the 2004 Euro Cup, but failed to qualify for the 2010 World Cup. The team's mounting losses highlight the degree to which the Czech Republic lacks—in professional sports as much as in other sectors of the economy—the financial muscle to challenge the European biggies. However, the Czechs did qualify for the 2012 Euro Cup, in neighboring Poland.

Within the Czech Republic, the two oldest and most successful soccer clubs are the bitter Prague rivals, AC Sparta and AC Slavia. Sparta's 1970s-era stadium is at Letná (behind the giant Metronome ticking above the river in Letenské Park). Slavia's stadium is in Vršovice (12 stops from the National Theater on tram #22). Other teams in the country occasionally challenge the supremacy of the two S's, as was the case in 2011, when FC Viktoria Plzeň (Pilsen) won the Czech Cup and qualified for the highly lucrative, 32-club European Champions League—becoming only the third Czech team to do so.

Between 1996 and 2005, the Czech national **hockey** team won five of the annual world championships. In 1998, they won the gold medal at the Olympic Games in Nagano, Japan. However, the golden generation is retiring—and younger players have been slow to fill the gap. Following a disappointing performance at the 2010 Vancouver Olympics, it seemed the Czech

For centuries, Prague's cultural makeup had consisted of a rich mix of Czech, German, and Jewish people—historically, they were almost evenly divided. But only 5 percent of the Jewish population survived the Holocaust. And after World War II ended, the three million people of Germanic descent who lived in Czechoslovakia were pushed into Germany. Their forced resettlement—which led to the deaths of untold numbers of Germans—was the idea, among others, of Czechoslovak President Edvard Beneš, who had ruled from exile in London throughout the war (see page 194). As a result of both events (the Holocaust and the expulsion of Germans), today's Czech Republic is largely homogenous—about 95 percent Czechs.

Although Prague escaped the bombs of World War II, it went directly from the Nazi frying pan into the communist fire. A local uprising freed the city from the Nazis on May 8, 1945, but the Soviets "liberated" them on May 9.

The early communist era (1948-1968) was a mixture of misguided zeal, Stalinist repressions, and attempts to wed social-

CZECH REPUBLIC

team, with no big-name players, had hit rock bottom. But it managed to pull off a major upset by beating the fired-up Russians to win the 2010 world championship. Currently, more than 40 Czech players take the ice in America's NHL; think of Jaromír Jágr, one of the NHL's all-time leading scorers (who made a surprise return to NHL with the Philadelphia Flyers for the 2011-2012 season), and Dominik "The Dominator" Hašek, a top goaltender (now retired from US hockey). Sparta and Slavia, the traditional Czech soccer powers, also have hockey teams, but their rivalry is less intense, as the teams from smaller towns are more than their equals. Slavia plays in the state-of-the-art Sazka Arena, which was built for the 2004 World Hockey Championships (right at the Českomoravská Metro stop).

Back in the old days, ice hockey was the only battleground on which Czechoslovaks could seek revenge on their Russian oppressors. The hockey rink is still where Czechs are proudest about their nationality. If you are in town in May during the hockey championships, join locals cheering their team in front of a giant screen on the Old Town Square, as well as on other main squares around the country.

Ice hockey is also the most popular sport in Slovakia. To understand the friendly relationship between Czechs and Slovaks after their Velvet Divorce, just walk into any Czech or Slovak pub during the hockey championships. Unless the two teams are playing each other, all Czechs passionately support the Slovak team, and vice versa.

ism with democracy. The "Prague Spring" period—initiated by a young generation of reform-minded communists in 1968—came to an abrupt halt under the treads of Soviet tanks.

The uprising's charismatic leader, Alexander Dubček, was exiled (and made a backwoods forest ranger), and the years following the unsuccessful revolt were particularly disheartening. In the late 1980s, the communists began constructing Prague's huge Žižkov TV tower (now the city's tallest structure)—not only to broadcast Czech TV transmissions, but also to jam Western signals. The Metro, built at about the same time, was intended for mass transit, but was also designed to be a giant fallout shelter for protection against capitalist bombs.

But the Soviet empire crumbled. Czechoslovakia regained its freedom in the student- and artist-powered 1989 "Velvet Revolution" (so-called because there were no casualties...or even broken windows; see the sidebar on page 107). Václav Havel, a writer who had been imprisoned by the communist regime, became Czechoslovakia's first post-communist president. In 1993, the Czech and Slovak Republics agreed on the "Velvet Divorce" and became two separate countries (see the sidebar on page 216). In recent times, the Czech Republic's most significant turning points occurred on May 1, 2004, when the country joined the European Union; and January 1, 2008, when it entered the Schengen Agreement, effectively erasing its borders for the purposes of travel.

The Czech Republic Today

Václav Havel left office in 2003, and died in 2011. While he's fondly remembered by Czechs for having been a great thinker, writer, and fearless leader of the opposition movement during the communist days, many consider him to have been less successful as a president. Some believe that the split of Czechoslovakia was partly caused by Havel's initial insensitivity to Slovak demands.

The current president, Václav Klaus, was the pragmatic author of the economic reforms in the 1990s. Klaus' surprising win in the 2003 election symbolized a change from revolutionary times, when philosophers became kings, to modern humdrum politics, when offices are gained by bargaining with the opposition (Communist votes in the Parliament were the decisive factor in Klaus' election).

In 2008, Klaus was narrowly re-elected by the Parliament for a second five-year term, despite revelations that his economic reforms had resulted in widespread corruption in the privatizing business sector. The scandal became the defining issue of the election, with Klaus and his conservative party denying responsibility for (and even the existence of) the abuses. The Greens and the Social Democrats had chosen as their candidate University of Michigan economic professor Jan Švejnar, the most outspoken critic of Klaus' reforms in the 1990s. And though public support was evenly divided between the two candidates, behind-the-scenes deals in the Parliament allowed the ruling conservatives to maintain their majority and keep Klaus in power.

In the first half of 2009, the Czech Republic held the rotating presidency of the EU, during which time they focused on ending Europe's energy dependence on Russia and on more workforce mobility. Halfway through the presidency, Czech minority parties, along with two defectors from the conservatives, pushed a vote of no confidence through the Parliament, leaving the country and the EU without a prime minister—and effectively confirming the widespread European suspicion that the Czechs were unreliable. Ironically, one of the defectors' objections was the government's willingness to allow the US to build a part of its anti-missile defense system on Czech territory, a plan that was shelved by the Obama administration in September 2009.

The main task of the current, conservative administration,

elected in 2010, has been to introduce fiscal austerity measures to reduce the country's growing debt and to preserve its relative fiscal stability and trustworthiness in the global marketplace.

Today, while not without its problems, the Czech Republic is still enjoying a growing economy and a strong democracy, and Prague is one of the most popular tourist destinations in Europe.

Czech Food

The Czechs have one of Europe's most stick-to-your-ribs cuisines. Heavy on meat, potatoes, and cabbage, it's hearty and tasty—designed to keep peasants fueled through a day of hard work. Some people could eat this stuff forever, while others seek a break in the form of ethnic restaurants (bigger towns such as Prague, Český Krumlov, and Kutná Hora have several options).

A Czech restaurant is a social place where people come to relax. Tables are not private. You can ask to join someone, and you will most likely make some new friends. After a sip of beer, ask for the *jídelní lístek* (menu).

Polévka (soup) is the most essential part of a meal. The saying goes: "The soup fills you up, the dish plugs it up." Some of the thick soups for a cold day are *zelná* or *zelňačka* (cabbage), *čočková* (lentil), *fazolová* (bean), and *dršťková* (tripe—delicious if fresh, chewy as gum if not). The lighter soups are *hovězí* or *slepičí vývar s nudlemi* (beef or chicken broth with noodles), *pórková* (leek), and *květáková* (cauliflower). *Pečivo* (bread) is either delivered with the soup or you need to ask for it; it's always charged separately depending on how many *rohlíky* (rolls) or slices of *chleba* (yeast bread) you eat.

Main dishes can either be *hotová jídla* (quick, ready-to-serve standard dishes, in some places available only during lunch hours, 11:30-14:30) or the more specialized *jídla na objednávku* or *minuy* (plates prepared when you order). Even the supposedly quick *hotová jídla* will take longer than the fast food you're used to back home.

Hotová jídla come with set garnishes. The standard menu across the country includes *smažený řízek s bramborem* (fried pork fillet with potatoes), *svíčková na smetaně s knedlíkem* (beef tenderloin in cream sauce with dumplings), *vepřová s knedlíkem a se zelím* (pork with dumplings and cabbage), *pečená kachna s knedlíkem a se zelím* (roasted duck with dumplings and cabbage), *maďarský guláš s knedlíkem* (the Czech version of Hungarian goulash), and *pečené kuře s bramborem* (roasted chicken with potatoes).

In this landlocked country, fish options are typically limited to *kapr* (carp) and *pstruh* (trout), prepared in a variety of ways and served with potatoes or fries—although recently, Czech perch and Norwegian salmon have cropped up on many local menus. Vegetarians can go for the delicious *smažený sýr s bramborem* (fried

CZECH REPUBLIC

Czech Beer

Czechs are among the world's most enthusiastic beer *(pivo)* drinkers—adults drink an average of 80 gallons a year. The

pub is a place to have fun, complain, discuss art and politics, talk hockey, and chat with locals and visitors alike. The *pivo* that was drunk in the country before the Industrial Revolution was much thicker, providing the main source of nourishment for the peasant folk. Even today, it doesn't matter whether you're in a *restaurace* (restaurant), *hostinec* (pub), or *hospoda* (bar)—a beer will land on your table upon the slightest hint to the waiter, and a new pint will automatically appear when the old glass is almost empty. (You must tell the waiter *not* to bring more.) Order beer

from the tap (*točené* means "draft," *sudové pivo* means "keg beer"). A *pivo* is large (0.5 liter—17 oz); a *malé pivo* is small (0.3 liter—10 oz). Men invariably order the large size. *Pivo* for lunch has me sightseeing for the rest of the day on Czech knees.

The Czechs invented Pilsner-style lager in nearby Plzeň ("Pilsen" in German), and the result, Pilsner Urquell, is on tap in many local pubs. But be sure to venture beyond this famous beer. The Czechs produce plenty of other good beers, including Krušovice, Gambrinus, Staropramen, and Kozel. Budvar, from the town of Budějovice ("Budweis" in German), is popular with Anheuser-Busch's attorneys. (The Czech and

the American breweries for years disputed the "Budweiser" brand name. The solution: The Czech Budweiser is sold under its own name in Europe, China, and Africa, while in America it is marketed as Czechvar.)

The big degree symbol on bottles does not indicate the percentage of alcohol content. Instead, it is a measurement used by brewers to track the density of certain ingredients. As a rough guide, 10 degrees is about 3.5 percent alcohol, 12 degrees is about 4.2 percent alcohol, and 11 and 15 degrees are dark beers. The most popular Czech beers are about as potent as German beers and only slightly stronger than typical American beers.

Each establishment has only one kind of beer on tap; to try a particular brand, look for its sign outside. A typical pub serves only one brand of 10-degree beer, one brand of 12-degree beer, and one brand of dark beer. Czechs do not mix beer with anything, and they do not hop from pub to pub (in one night, it is said, you must stay loyal to one woman and to one beer). *Na zdraví* means "to your health" in Czech.

cheese with potatoes) or default to *čočka s vejci* (lentils with fried egg). If you are spending the night out with friends, have a beer and feast on the huge *vepřové koleno s hořčicí a křenem* (pork knuckle with mustard and horseradish sauce) with *chleba* (yeast bread).

The range of the *jídla na objednávku* (meals prepared to order) depends on the chef. You choose your starches and garnishes, which are charged separately.

Czech dumplings *(knedlíky)* resemble steamed white bread. They come in plain or potato *(bramborové)* varieties; are meant to be drowned in gravy (dumplings never accompany sauceless dishes); and are eaten with a knife and fork.

Šopský salát, like a Greek salad, is usually the best salad option (a mix of tomatoes, cucumbers, peppers, onion, and feta cheese with vinegar and olive oil). The waiter will bring it with the main dish, unless you specify that you want it before.

For *moučník* (dessert), there are *palačinka* (crêpes served with fruit or jam), *lívance* (small pancakes with jam and curd), or *zmrzlinový pohár* (ice-cream sundae). Sweet dumplings are a tempting option during summer, when they are loaded with fresh strawberries, blueberries, apricots, or plums, and garnished with custard and melted butter. Beware, though, that many restaurants cheat by filling the sticky dough with a smattering of jam or fruit preserve; before ordering, ask the waiter for details, or discreetly inspect that plate at your neighbor's table. Dumplings with frozen fruit lose some of the flavor, but are still good to try. Many restaurants will offer different sorts of *koláče* (pastries) and *štrůdl* (apple strudel), but it's much better to get these directly from a bakery.

No Czech meal is complete without a cup of strong *turecká káva* (Turkish coffee—finely ground coffee that only partly dissolves, leaving "mud" on the bottom, highly caffeinated and drunk without milk). Although espressos and instant coffees have made headway in the past few years, some Czechs regard them as a threat to tradition.

Czech mineral waters *(minerálka)* have a high mineral content. They're naturally carbonated because they come from the springs in the many Czech spas (Mattoni, the most common brand, is from Carlsbad). If you want still water, ask for *voda bez bublinek* (water without bubbles). Tap water is generally not served. Water comes bottled and generally costs more than beer.

Bohemia is beer country, with Europe's best and cheapest brew (for all the details, see the sidebar). Moravians prefer wine and *slivovice* (SLEE-voh-veet-seh)—a plum brandy so highly valued that it's the de facto currency of the Carpathian Mountains (often used for bartering with farmers and other mountain folk). *Medovina* ("honey wine") is mead.

In bars and restaurants, you can go wild with memorable

liqueurs. Experiment. *Fernet,* a bitter drink made from many herbs, is the leading Czech aperitif. Absinthe, made from wormwood and herbs, is a watered-down version of the hallucinogenic drink that's illegal in much of Europe. It's famous as the muse of many artists (including Henri de Toulouse-Lautrec in Paris more than a century ago). *Becherovka,* made of 13 herbs and 38 percent alcohol, was used to settle upset aristocratic tummies and as an aphrodisiac. This velvety drink remains popular today. *Becherovka* and tonic mixed together is nicknamed *beton* ("concrete"). If you drink three, you'll find out why.

You can stay in a pub as long as you want—no one will bring you the *účet* (bill) until you ask for it: *"Pane vrchní, zaplatím!"* (PAH-neh VURCH-nee zah-plah-TEEM; "Mr. Waiter, now I pay!").

Czech Language

Czech is a Slavic language closely related to its Polish and Slovak neighbors. These days, English is commonly spoken, and you'll find the language barrier minimal. Among older people, German is a common second language.

Czech pronunciation can be tricky. The language has a dizzying array of diacritical marks (little doo-hickeys over some letters that affect pronunciation). Most notably, some letters can be topped with a *háček* (*č, š, ž, ň, ě*). Here are some clues for Czech pronunciation:

- **j** sounds like "y" as in "yarn"
- **c** sounds like "ts" as in "cats"
- **č** sounds like "ch" as in "chicken"
- **š** sounds like "sh" as in "shrimp"
- **ž** sounds like "zh" as in "leisure"
- **ň** sounds like "ny" as in "canyon"
- **ě** sounds like "yeh" as in "yet"
- **ď** sounds like the "dj" sound in "ledge"

Czech has one sound that occurs in no other language: ř (as in "Dvořák"), which sounds like a cross between a rolled "r" and "zh." It takes a lot of practice, but if you can master this sound, you'll impress the Czechs.

An acute accent (*á, é, í, ó, ú, ý*) means you linger on that vowel; it does not indicate stress, which invariably falls on the first syllable. For example, the word for "please" is *prosím,* with the emphasis on the first syllable but a long "i" sound at the end: PROH-zeeeem.

Prague is flooded with tourists, most of whom don't bother to learn a single word of the local language. To ingratiate yourself to your hosts—not to mention be a sensitive traveler—take some time to learn the Czech essentials. You'll find a selection of Czech survival phrases on page 1263.

When navigating town, these words might be helpful: *město* (MYEHS-toh, town), *náměstí* (NAH-myehs-tee, square), *ulica* (OO-leet-sah, street), *nábřeži* (NAH-bzheh-zhee, embankment road), and *most* (mohst, bridge).

PRAGUE

Praha

For many travelers, Prague is their first stop in Eastern Europe. And for good reason. Few places can match Prague's over-the-top romance, evocative Old World charm...and tourist crowds. Whether you use it as a tentative first foray into the East or a springboard for a lengthy Slavic adventure, Prague (whose name means "threshold" in Czech) has always been a natural entry point to Eastern Europe.

With its privileged position on a major river in the very center of bowl-shaped Bohemia, Prague has long been the beating heart and soul of the Czech people. From the Czechs' humble beginnings under a duke named Wenceslas, to the flourishing of culture under Holy Roman Emperor Charles IV, to the devastating Catholics-versus-Protestants warfare of the 17th century, Prague has seen more than its share of history rumble through its cobbled streets. In the 19th century—back when most of its residents were elite German-speakers proud to be subjects of the Habsburg monarchs—Prague was a low-rent mini-Vienna (and played host to the likes of Mozart). But by century's end, the city had become a hotbed for the Czech national revival, as people across Eastern Europe looked to Prague as the region's cultural capital and standard-bearer for shunning imposed Germanic ways and embracing their own deep Slavic roots.

While the 20th century (and its four decades of communism) was hard on Prague, at least the city escaped the bombs of the world wars—making it uniquely well-preserved among Central European capitals. Now that the shroud of communism has lifted, and the facades have been dutifully scrubbed, visitors can fully enjoy the streets and lanes of today's Prague—a veritable textbook of architectural styles. I love bringing first-time visitors to Prague's Old Town Square at twilight. After gaping their way around the square, invariably they nudge me and whisper, "This is better than Disneyland!"

In addition to its glorious buildings, Prague intoxicates visitors with its almost mystically beautiful cityscape, entertains us with an endless array of cheap classical concerts, tickles our inner artist with slinky Art Nouveau works by Alfons Mucha, educates us with its historic sites and sobering Jewish Quarter, bends our minds with the uniquely Czech phenomenon of Black Light Theater, and keeps us lubricated with Europe's best beer. Hike up to the world's biggest castle for a lesson in Czech history and sweeping views across the city's spires and domes. Cross the famous Charles Bridge, and commune with with vendors, artists, tourists, and a stoic lineup of Czech saints in stone. Escape the crowds into the back lanes and pretend you're strolling through the 18th century. Join the local gang over a *pivo* at a rollicking beer hall and learn some Czech soccer songs. Delve into one of Europe's top stops.

PRAGUE

Planning Your Time

Prague demands a minimum of two full days (with three nights, or two nights and a night train). You can easily fill more time in the city or with side-trips to nearby sights (such as Kutná Hora, Terezín Concentration Camp Memorial, or a variety of countryside castles—described in the next chapter). From Budapest, Warsaw, or Kraków, you can reach Prague on a handy overnight train. From Munich, Berlin, and Vienna, Prague is a four- to six-hour train ride by day (you also have the option of night trains from Vienna, Amsterdam, and Zürich).

With two days in Prague, I'd spend one morning seeing the castle and another morning in the Jewish Quarter. Use your afternoons for loitering around the Old Town, Charles Bridge, and the Little Quarter, and split your nights between beer halls and live music. Keep in mind that Jewish Quarter sights close on Saturday and Jewish holidays. Some museums, mainly in the Old Town, are closed on Monday.

Orientation to Prague

Residents call their town "Praha" (PRAH-hah). It's big, with 1.2 million people, but during a quick visit, you'll focus on its relatively compact old center. As you wander, take advantage of brown street signs directing you to tourist landmarks. Self-deprecating Czechs note that while the signs are designed to help tourists (locals never use them), they're only printed in Czech. Still, thanks to the

little icons, the signs can help smart visitors who are sightseeing on foot.

The Vltava River divides the west side (Castle Quarter and Little Quarter) from the east side (New Town, Old Town, Jewish Quarter, Main Train Station, and most of the recommended hotels).

Prague addresses come with references to a general zone: Praha 1 is in the old center on either side of the river; Praha 2 is in the New Town, southeast of Wenceslas Square; Praha 3 (and higher) indicates a location farther from the center. Virtually everything I list is in Praha 1.

Tourist Information

TIs are at several key locations, including on the **Old Town Square** (in the Old Town Hall, just to the left of the Astronomical Clock; Easter-Oct Mon-Fri 9:00-19:00, Sat-Sun 9:00-18:00; Nov-Easter

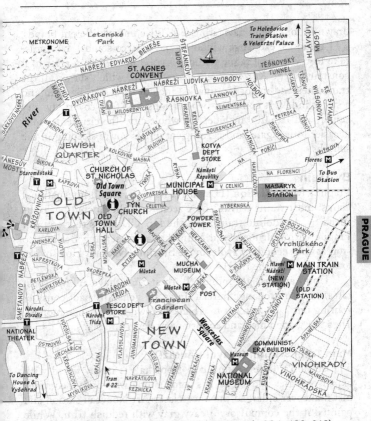

Mon-Fri 9:00-18:00, Sat-Sun 9:00-17:00; tel. 224-482-018); on
the castle side of **Charles Bridge** (Easter-Oct daily 10:00-18:00,
closed Nov-Easter); and in the Old Town, around the corner from
Havelská Market (at Rytířská 31, April-Oct Mon-Sat 9:00-19:00,
closed Nov-March). For general tourist information in English,
dial 12444 (Mon-Fri 8:00-19:00) or check the useful TI website:
www.praguewelcome.cz.

The TIs offer maps, a helpful transit guide, and information
on guided walks and bus tours. They can book local guides, concerts, and hotel rooms.

Monthly event guides—all of them packed with ads—include
the *Prague Guide* (29 Kč), *Prague This Month* (free), and *Heart of
Europe* (free, summer only). The English-language weekly *Prague
Post* newspaper is handy for entertainment listings and current
events (60 Kč at newsstands).

Arrival in Prague

No matter how you arrive, your first priority is buying a city map,
with trams and Metro lines marked and tiny sketches of the sights

drawn in for ease in navigating (30-70 Kč, many different brands; sold at kiosks, exchange windows, and tobacco stands). It's a mistake to try doing Prague without a good map—you'll refer to it constantly. The *Kartografie Praha* city map, which shows all the tram lines and major landmarks, includes a castle diagram and a street index. It comes in two versions: 1:15,000 covers the city center, and 1:25,000 includes the whole city. The city center map is easier to navigate, and is sufficient unless you're sleeping in the suburbs.

By Train

Prague's **Main Station** (Hlavní Nádraží) serves all international trains; most trains within the Czech Republic, including high-speed SC Pendolino trains; and the DB-ČD buses that connect Prague with Nürnberg and Munich. Trains serving Berlin also stop at the secondary **Holešovice Station** (Nádraží Holešovice, located north of the river).

Upon arrival, get money. Both stations have ATMs (best rates) and an exchange bureau (rates are generally bad; consider waiting until you can get to a bank in town to exchange money). Then buy a good map and confirm your departure plans.

Main Train Station (Hlavní Nádraží)

The station's underground two-floor hall is newly filled with expensive cafés and shops. It's come a long way since a communist makeover enlarged the once-classy Art Nouveau station and painted it the compulsory dreary gray with reddish trim. While the underground hall now looks great, the deteriorated above-ground complex remains untouched under scaffolding.

First named for Emperor Franz Josef, the station was later renamed for President Woodrow Wilson (see the commemorative plaque in the main exit hall leading away from the tracks), because his promotion of self-determination led to the creation of the free state of Czechoslovakia in 1918. Under the communists (who weren't big fans of Wilson), it was bluntly renamed Hlavní Nádraží—"Main Station."

Upon arrival, take any of the three parallel tunnels that connect the tracks to the arrival hall. The first area you reach (with low ceilings) has an **exchange office** with **Internet** booths, and signs pointing to the "official" taxi stand to the right (avoid these rip-off cabbies—explained later). If you turn around and go up another floor, you'll find the **Fantova Kavárna,** a decrepit café beneath an Art Nouveau cupola. Outside is the stop for the **AE bus** to the airport (buy 50-Kč ticket from driver, runs every half-hour daily 6:35-22:05, 40 minutes) and the **DB-ČD bus** to Nürnberg and Munich (6/day).

Prague Essentials

English	Czech	Pronounced
Main Train Station	*Hlavní Nádraží*	hlav-NEE NAH-drah-zhee
Old Town	*Staré Město*	STAH-reh MYEHS-toh
Old Town Square	*Staroměstské Náměstí*	STAR-roh-myehst-skeh NAH-myehs-tee
New Town	*Nové Město*	NOH-vay myehs-toh
Little Quarter	*Malá Strana*	MAH-lah strah-nah
Jewish Quarter	*Josefov*	YOO-zehf-fohf
Castle Quarter	*Hradčany*	HRAD-chah-nee
Charles Bridge	*Karlův Most*	KAR-loov most
Wenceslas Square	*Václavské Náměstí*	VAHT-slahf-skeh NAH-myehs-tee
Vltava River	*Vltava*	VUL-tah-vah

Straight down from the low-ceilinged area is the main hall, where you'll find four Metro entrances in the center (two for each direction). One **ATM** is along the right wall, while two more are in front of the ticketing area under the central stairs. The **Billa supermarket**, which stocks food perfect for a picnic, is in the corner under the left stairs. You can get Czech mobile-phone SIM cards at the **Vodafone** store in the main hall.

The **Czech Railways (České Dráhy) ticket office** is in the middle of the main hall under the stairs. Its tiny **ČD Travel center,** on the left as you enter the main office, sells both domestic and international tickets, and is your best bet for information in English (Mon-Fri 9:00-18:00, Sat 9:00-14:00, closed Sun, shorter hours in winter, tel. 972-241-861, www.cd.cz/en). The regular ticket desks are faster if you already know your schedule and destination, but not all attendants speak good English.

The **RegioJet travel office** (with desks at both sides of the main ticket office) sells international train tickets from the DB (German railways) system and offers various DB deals and discounts. RegioJet also runs its own trains to Olomouc at lower prices than Czech Railways. The office, a branch of the **Student Agency bus company**, sells a variety of domestic (e.g., to Český Krumlov) and international (Vienna) bus tickets without a commission (Mon-Sat 8:30-12:30 & 13:00-18:30, closed Sun, tel. 539-000-511, www.regiojet.cz, jizdenky@regiojet.cz). Despite its name, RegioJet does not sell plane tickets.

Touristpoint (with your back to the tracks, it's on your right under the stairs) arranges last-minute rooms in hotels and pensions,

Rip-Offs in Prague

There's no particular risk of violent crime in Prague, but green, rich tourists do get taken by con artists. Simply be on guard, particularly when traveling on trains (thieves thrive on overnight trains), changing money (tellers with bad arithmetic and inexplicable pauses while counting back your change), dealing with taxis (see "Getting Around Prague—By Taxi," on page 67), paying in restaurants (see "Eating in Prague," on page 149), and wandering through seedy neighborhoods.

Anytime you pay for something, make a careful mental note of how much it costs, how much you're handing over, and how much you expect back. Count your change. Someone selling you a phone card marked 190 Kč might first tell you it's 790 Kč, hoping to pocket the difference. If you call his bluff, he'll pretend that it never happened.

Plainclothes policemen "looking for counterfeit money" are con artists. Don't show them any cash or your wallet. If you're threatened with an inexplicable fine by a "policeman," conductor, or other official, you can walk away, scare him away by saying you'll need a receipt (which real officials are legally required to provide), or ask a passerby if the fine is legit. On the other hand, do not ignore the plainclothes inspectors on the Metro and trams who show you their badges.

Pickpockets target Western tourists, and they can be little children or adults dressed like professionals—sometimes even as tourists. Many thieves drape jackets over their arms to disguise

as well as car rentals, sightseeing tours, and adrenaline experiences. They accept any currency and credit cards, and also sell maps and international phone cards. A phone is available for calling a **taxi,** and the driver will come to the desk to get you (daily 8:00-22:00, tel. 224-946-010, www.touristpoint.cz, info@touristpoint.cz).

Getting to Your Hotel: Even though the main train station is basically downtown, it can be a little tricky to get to your hotel. The biggest challenge is that the **taxi** drivers at the train station's run-down "official" stand are a gang of no-neck mafia thugs just waiting for the chance to charge an arriving tourist five times the regular rate. To get an **honest cabbie,** exit the station's main hall through the big glass doors, then cross 50 yards through a park to Opletalova street (a few taxis are usually waiting in front of the Hotel Chopin, on the corner of Jeruzalémská street). You can also call a taxi from the Touristpoint office, described earlier (AAA Taxi—tel. 14-014; City Taxi—tel. 257-257-257). Before getting into a taxi, always confirm the maximum price to your destination, and make sure the driver turns on the meter—it should cost no more than 300 Kč to get to your hotel.

busy fingers. Thieves work the crowded and touristy places in teams. They use mobile phones to coordinate their bumps and grinds. Be careful if anyone creates a commotion at the door of a Metro or tram car (especially around the Národní Třída and Vodičkova tram stops, or on the made-for-tourists tram #22)—it's a smokescreen for theft.

Car theft is also a big problem in Prague (many Western European car-rental companies don't allow their rentals to cross the Czech border). Never leave anything valuable in your car—not even in broad daylight on a busy street.

The sex clubs on Skořepka and Melantrichova streets, just south and north of Havelská Market, routinely rip off naive tour-

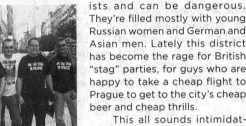

ists and can be dangerous. They're filled mostly with young Russian women and German and Asian men. Lately this district has become the rage for British "stag" parties, for guys who are happy to take a cheap flight to Prague to get to the city's cheap beer and cheap thrills.

This all sounds intimidating. But Prague is safe. It has its share of petty thieves and con artists, but very little violent crime. Don't be scared—just be alert.

Better yet, take the **Metro**. It's dirt cheap and easy, with frequent departures. Once you're on the Metro, you'll wonder why you would ever bother with a taxi (inside the station's main hall, look for the red *M* with two directions: Háje or Letňany). To purchase tickets from the automated machine by the Metro entrance, you'll need Czech coins (get change at the change machine in the corner near the luggage lockers, or break a bill at a newsstand or grocery). Validate your ticket in the yellow machines *before* you go down the stairs to the tracks. To get to hotels in the Old Town, catch a Háje-bound train to the Muzeum stop, then transfer to the green line (direction: Dejvická) and get off at either Můstek or Staroměstská; these stops straddle the Old Town.

Most hotels I list in the Old Town are within a 20-minute **walk** of the train station. Exit the station into a small park, walk through the park, and then cross the street on the other side. Head down Jeruzalémská street to the Jindřišská Tower and tram stop, walk under a small arch, then continue slightly to the right down Senovážná street. At the end of the street, you'll see the Powder Gate—the grand entry into the Old Town—to the left.

Alternatively, Wenceslas Square in the New Town is a 10-minute walk—exit the station, cross the park, and walk to the left along Opletalova street.

The nearest **tram** stop is to the right as you exit the station (about 200 yards away). Tram #9 (headed away from railway tracks) takes you to the neighborhood near the National Theater and the Little Quarter, but isn't useful for most Old Town hotels.

For more information on Prague's taxis and public transportation, see "Getting Around Prague," later.

Holešovice Train Station (Nádraží Holešovice)

This station, slightly farther from the center, is suburban mellow. The main hall has all the services of the main train station in a more compact area. On the left are international and local ticket windows (open 24 hours), and an information office. On the right is an uncrowded café with Internet access (1 Kč/minute, daily 8:00–19:30). Two ATMs are just outside the first glass doors, and the Metro is 50 yards to the right (follow signs toward *Vstup*, which means "entrance"; it's three stops to Hlavní Nádraží—the Main Station—or four stops to the city-center Muzeum stop). Taxis and trams are outside to the right (allow 300 Kč for a cab to the center).

By Bus

Prague's main bus station is at Florenc, east of the Old Town (Metro: Florenc). But some connections use other stations, including Roztyly (Metro: Roztyly), Na Knížecí (Metro: Anděl), the Nádraží Holešovice train station (Metro: Nádraží Holešovice), Hradčanská (Metro: Hradčanská), or the main train station (Metro: Hlavní Nádraží). Be sure to confirm which station your bus uses.

By Plane

Prague's modern, tidy, low-key **Ruzyně Airport,** located 12 miles (about 30 minutes) west of the city center, is as user-friendly as any airport in Western Europe or the US. The new Terminal 2 serves destinations within the EU except for Great Britain (no passport controls); Terminal 1 serves Great Britain and everywhere else. The airport has ATMs (avoid the change desks), desks promoting their transportation services (such as city transit and shuttle buses), kiosks selling city maps and phone cards, and a tourist service with few printed materials. Airport info: tel. 220-113-314, operator tel. 220-111-111, www.prg.aero/en.

Getting between the airport and downtown is easy. Leaving either airport terminal, you have four options, listed below from cheapest to priciest:

Dirt Cheap: Take bus #119 to the Dejvická Metro station, or #100 to the Zličín Metro station (20 minutes), then take the Metro into the center (32 Kč, buy tickets at info desk in airport arrival hall).

Budget: Take the airport express (AE) bus to the main train station, or to the Masarykovo Nádraží station near Náměstí Republiky—Republic Square (50 Kč, runs every half-hour daily 5:46-21:16, 40 minutes, look for the *AE* sign in front of the terminal and pay the driver, www.cd.cz). From either station, you can take the Metro, hire a taxi, or walk to your hotel. The Masarykovo Nádraží stop is slightly closer to downtown.

Moderate: Take the Čedaz minibus shuttle (from exit F at Terminal 1 or exit E at Terminal 2) to the Náměstí Republiky station, at the entrance to the Old Town. The shuttle stop is on V Celnici street, across the street from Hotel Marriott and near the recommended Brasserie La Gare (pay 120 Kč directly to driver, daily 7:30-19:00, 2/hour, info desk in arrival hall).

Expensive: Catch a taxi. Cabbies wait at the curb directly in front of the arrival hall. Or book a yellow AAA taxi through their office in the airport hall—you'll get a 50 percent discount coupon for the trip back (book your return trip by calling 221-111-111). AAA taxis wait in front of exit D at Terminal 1 and exit E at Terminal 2 (metered rate, generally 500-600 Kč to downtown).

Helpful Hints

Medical Help: A 24-hour **pharmacy** is at Palackého 5 (a block from Wenceslas Square, tel. 224-946-982). For standard assistance, there are two state hospitals in the center: the **General Hospital** (open daily 24 hours, moderate wait time, right above Karlovo Náměstí at U Nemocnice 2, Praha 2, use entry G, tel. 224-962-564) and the **Na Františku Hospital** (on the embankment next to Hotel InterContinental, Na Františku 1, go to the main entrance, for English assistance call Mr. Juřina between 7:30-16:30 on weekdays, tel. 222-801-278—serious problems only). The reception staff may not speak English, but the doctors do.

For above-standard assistance in English (including dental service), consider the top-quality **Hospital Na Homolce** (less than 1,000 Kč for an appointment, from 8:00 to 16:00 call 252-922-146, for after-hours emergencies call 257-211-111; bus #167 from Anděl Metro station, Roentgenova 2, Praha 5). The **Canadian Medical Care Center** is a small, private clinic with an English-speaking Czech staff at Veleslavínská 1 in Praha 6 (3,000 Kč for an appointment, 4,500 Kč for a house call, halfway between the city and the airport, tel. 235-360-133, after-hours emergency tel. 724-300-301).

PRAGUE

Internet Access: Internet cafés are well-advertised and scattered through the Old and New Towns. Consider **Bohemia Bagel** near the Jewish Quarter at Masná 2. **Káva Káva Káva Coffee,** on the boundary between the Old and New Towns, is in the Platýz courtyard off Národní 37.

Bookstores: Shakespeare and Sons is a friendly English-language bookstore with a wide selection of translations from Czech, the latest publications, and a reading space downstairs overlooking a river channel (daily 11:00-19:00, one block from Charles Bridge on Little Quarter side at U Lužického Semináře 10, tel. 257-531-894, www.shakes.cz). The tiny **Big Ben Bookshop** is more central, near the Old Town Square (Mon-Sat 9:00-20:00, Sun 11:00-18:00, across the street from the Church of St. James at Malá Štupartská 5, tel. 224-826-565, www.bigbenbookshop.com).

Laundry: A **full-service laundry** near most of the recommended hotels is at Karolíny Světlé 11 (200 Kč/8-pound load, wash and dry in 3 hours, Mon-Fri 7:30-19:00, closed Sat-Sun, 200 yards from Charles Bridge on Old Town side, mobile 721-030-446); another laundry is at Rybná 27 (290 Kč/8-pound load, same-day pickup, Mon-Fri 8:00-18:00, Mon and Wed from 7:00, closed Sat-Sun, tel. 224-812-641). Or surf the Internet while your undies tumble-dry at the **self-service launderette** at Korunní 14 (160 Kč/load wash and dry, Internet access-2 Kč/minute, daily 8:00-20:00, near Náměstí Míru Metro stop, Praha 2).

Local Help: Magic Praha is a tiny travel service run by Lída Jánská. A Jill-of-all-trades, she can help with accommodations and transfers throughout the Czech Republic, as well as private tours and side-trips to historic towns (mobile 604-207-225, www.magicpraha.cz, magicpraha@magicpraha.cz).

Bike Rental: Prague recently improved its network of bike paths, making bicycles a feasible option for exploring the center of the town and beyond (see http://doprava.praha-mesto.cz for a map). Two bike-rental shops located near the Old Town Square are **Praha Bike** (daily 9:00-22:00, Dlouhá 24, mobile 732-388-880, www.prahabike.cz) and **City Bike** (daily 9:00-19:00, Králodvorská 5, mobile 776-180-284, www.citybike -prague.com). They rent bikes for about 300 Kč for two hours or 500 Kč per day (with a 1,500-Kč deposit), and also organize guided bike tours. Or try an **electric bike** (590 Kč/half-day, 890 Kč/day, April-Oct daily 9:00-19:00, tours available, just above American Embassy in Little Quarter at Vlašská 15, mobile 604-474-546, www.ilikeebike.com).

Car Rental: All the biggies have offices in Prague (check each company's website, or ask at the TI). For a locally operated alternative, consider **Prima Rent** (Mon-Fri 8:00-16:30, closed Sat-Sun, Kolbenova 40, Metro: Kolbenova, mobile 602-608-494, www.car-rental-czech.com, info@primarent.cz). The cheaper models are a great value (900 Kč/day with basic insurance and limited mileage, plus 250 Kč/day for full theft and damage insurance; 350 Kč for hotel or airport delivery).

Best Views: Enjoy the "Golden City of a Hundred Spires" during the early evening, when the light is warm and the colors are rich. Good viewpoints—from highest to lowest—include the Strahov Monastery's garden terrace (above the castle), the many balconies and spires at Prague Castle, the Villa Richter restaurants overlooking the city (just below the castle past the Golden Lane), the top of either tower on Charles Bridge, the Old Town Square clock tower (has an elevator), the Restaurant u Prince Terrace overlooking the Old Town Square (also with an elevator), and the steps of the National Museum overlooking Wenceslas Square.

Getting Around Prague

You can walk nearly everywhere. But after you figure out the public transportation system, the Metro is slick, the trams fun, and the taxis quick and easy. Prague's tram system is especially wonderful—trams rumble by every 5-10 minutes and take you just about anywhere. Be bold and you'll swing through Prague like Tarzan with a transit pass. For details, pick up the transit guide at the TI. City maps show the Metro, tram, and bus lines.

By Metro, Tram, and Bus

Excellent, affordable public transit is perhaps the best legacy of the communist era (locals ride all month for 550 Kč). The three-line Metro system is handy and simple, but doesn't always get you right to the tourist sights (landmarks such as the Old Town Square and Prague Castle are several blocks from the nearest Metro stops).

Tickets: The Metro, trams, and buses all use the same tickets:
- 30-minute short-trip ticket *(krátkodobá)*—24 Kč; transfers allowed.
- 90-minute standard ticket *(základní)*—32 Kč; transfers allowed.
- 24-hour pass *(jízdenka na 24 hodin)*—110 Kč.
- 3-day pass *(jízdenka na 3 dny)*—310 Kč.

Buy tickets from your hotel, at Metro stops, newsstand kiosks, or from automated machines (select ticket price, then insert coins). For convenience, buy all the tickets that you think you'll need—but estimate conservatively. Remember, Prague is a great walking town, so unless you're commuting from a hotel far outside the center, you'll likely find that individual tickets work best. Be sure

PRAGUE

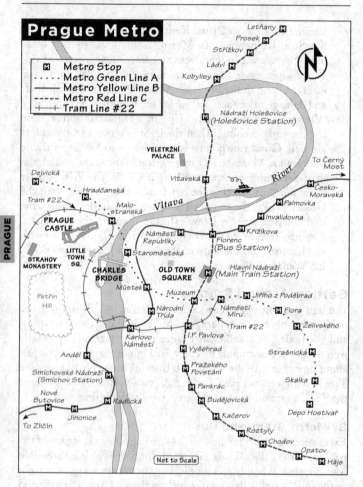

to validate your ticket as you board the tram or bus, or in the Metro station, by sticking it in the machine (which stamps a time on it; watch locals and imitate). Inspectors routinely ambush ticketless riders (including tourists) and fine them 700 Kč on the spot. You can also get fined for using counterfeit tickets, even if you thought they were authentic when you bought them.

Tips: Navigate by signs that list the end stations. When you come to your stop, push the yellow button if the doors don't automatically open. Although it seems that all Metro doors lead to the neighborhood of Výstup, that's simply the Czech word for "exit." Tram stops are not always clearly marked, so carefully follow along with a map to be sure you get off at the right place. Further confusing matters, when a tram pulls up to a stop, two different names are announced: the name of the stop you're currently at, followed

by the name of the stop that's coming up next. Confused tourists, thinking they've heard their stop, are notorious for rushing off the tram one stop too soon.

Schedules and Frequency: Trams run every 5-10 minutes in the daytime (a schedule is posted at each stop). The Metro closes at midnight, and the nighttime tram routes (identified with white numbers on blue backgrounds at tram stops) run all night at 30-minute intervals. You can find more information and a complete route planner in English at www.dpp.cz/en.

Handy Tram: Tram #22 is practically made for sightseeing, connecting the New Town with the Castle Quarter (find the line marked on the color map at the beginning of this book). The tram uses some of the same stops as the Metro (making it easy to get to—or travel on from—the tram route). Of the many stops this tram makes, the most convenient are two in the New Town (Národní Třída Metro stop, between the bottom of Wenceslas Square and the river; and Národní Divadlo, at the National Theater), two in the Little Quarter (Malostranské Náměstí and Malostranská Metro stop), and three above Prague Castle (Královský Letohrádek, Pražský Hrad, and Pohořelec; for details, see "Getting to Prague Castle—By Tram" on page 119).

By Taxi

Prague's taxis—notorious for hyperactive meters—are being tamed. New legislation is in place to curb crooked cabbies, and police will always take your side in an argument. Still, many cabbies are crooks who consider it a good day's work to take one sucker for a ride. You'll make things difficult for a dishonest cabbie by challenging an unfair fare.

While most hotel receptionists and guidebooks advise that you avoid taxis, I find Prague to be a great taxi town and use them routinely. With the local rate, they're cheap (read the rates on the door: drop charge starts at 36 Kč; per-kilometer charge—29 Kč;

Prague's Four Towns

Until about 1800, Prague was actually four distinct towns with four town squares, all separated by fortified walls. Each town had a unique character, which came from the personality of the people who initially settled it. Today, much of Prague's charm survives in the distinct spirit of each of its towns.

Castle Quarter (Hradčany): Since the ninth century, when the first castle was built on the promontory overlooking a ford across the Vltava River, Castle Hill has been occupied by the ruling class. When Christianity arrived in the Czech lands, this hilltop—oriented along an east-west axis—proved a perfect spot for a church and, later, the cathedral (which, according to custom, had to be built with the altar pointing east). Finally, the nobles built their representative palaces in proximity to the castle to compete with the Church for influence on the king. Even today, you feel like clip-clopping through this neighborhood in a fancy carriage. The Castle Quarter—which hosts the offices of the president and the foreign minister—has high art and grand buildings, little commerce, and few pubs.

Little Quarter (Malá Strana): This Baroque town of fine palaces and gardens rose from the ashes of a merchant settlement that burned down in the 1540s. The Czech and European nobility who settled here took pride in the grand design of their gardens. In the 1990s, after decades of decay, the gardens were carefully restored. While some are open only to the successors of the former nobility—including the Czech Parliament and the American, German, and Polish Embassies—many are open to visitors.

Old Town (Staré Město): The Charles Bridge connects the Little Quarter with the Old Town. A boomtown since the 10th century, this area has long been the busy commercial quarter—filled with merchants, guilds, and supporters of the Church reformer Jan Hus (who wanted a Czech-style Catholicism). Trace the walls of this town in the modern road plan (the Powder Tower is a remnant of a wall system that completed a fortified ring, the other half of which was formed by the river). The marshy area closest to the bend—least habitable and therefore allotted to the Jewish community—became the ghetto (today's Josefov, or Jewish Quarter).

New Town (Nové Město): The New Town rings the Old Town—cutting a swath from riverbank to riverbank—and is forti-

---

waiting time per minute—5 Kč). The key is to be sure the cabbie turns on the meter at the #1 tariff (look for the word *sazba*, meaning "tariff," on the meter). Avoid cabs waiting at tourist attractions and train stations. To improve your odds of getting a fair meter rate—which starts only when you take off—call for a cab (or have your hotel or restaurant call one for you). **AAA Taxi** (tel. 14-014) and **City Taxi** (tel. 257-257-257) are the most likely to have

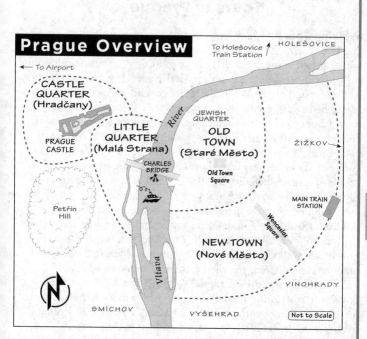

Prague Overview

To Holešovice Train Station

← To Airport

HOLEŠOVICE

CASTLE QUARTER (Hradčany)

PRAGUE CASTLE

River

JEWISH QUARTER

LITTLE QUARTER (Malá Strana)

OLD TOWN (Staré Město)

CHARLES BRIDGE

ŽIŽKOV

Old Town Square

Petřín Hill

MAIN TRAIN STATION

Wenceslas Square

Vltava

NEW TOWN (Nové Město)

VINOHRADY

SMÍCHOV

VYŠEHRAD

Not to Scale

PRAGUE

fied with Prague's outer wall. In the 14th century, the king created this town, tripling the size of what would become Prague. Wenceslas Square was once the horse market of this busy working-class district. Even today, the New Town is separated from the Old Town by a "moat" (the literal meaning of the street called Na Příkopě). As you cross bustling Na Příkopě, you leave the glass and souvenir shops behind, and enter a town of malls and fancy shops that cater to locals and visitors alike.

The Royal Way: Cutting through the four towns—from St. Vitus Cathedral down to the Charles Bridge, and then from the bridge to the Powder Tower—is the Royal Way (Královská Cesta), the ancient path of coronation processions. Today, this city spine is marred by tacky trinket shops and jammed by tour groups. Use it for orientation only; try to avoid it if you want to see the real Prague.

English-speaking staff and honest cabbies. I also find that hailing a passing taxi usually gets me a decent price, although at a slightly higher rate than when reserving by phone. If a cabbie surprises you at the end with an astronomical fare, simply pay 300 Kč, which should cover you for a long ride anywhere in the center. Then go into your hotel. On the miniscule chance that he follows you, the receptionist will back you up.

Tours in Prague

Walking Tours—Many small companies offer walking tours of the Old Town, the castle, and more (for the latest, pick up the walking tour fliers at the TI). Since guiding is a routine side-job for university students, you'll generally get hardworking young guides at good prices. While I'd rather go with my own local guide (described next), public walking tours are cheaper (about 450 Kč for a 4-hour tour), cover themes you might not otherwise consider, connect you with other English-speaking travelers, and allow for spontaneity. The quality depends on the guide rather than the company. Your best bet is to show up at the Astronomical Clock a couple of minutes before 8:00, 10:00, or 11:00, then chat with a few of the umbrella-holding guides there. Choose the one you click with. Guides also have fliers advertising additional walks.

▲▲Local Guides—Guides meet you wherever you like and tailor the tour to your interests. Visit their websites in advance for details on various walks, airport transfers, countryside excursions, and other services offered, and then make arrangements by email.

Small Companies: PragueWalker is run by Katka Svobodová, a hardworking historian-guide who knows her stuff and manages a team of enthusiastic and friendly guides (600 Kč/hour for individuals, families, and small groups; mobile 603-181-300, www.praguewalker.com, katerina@praguewalker.com). **Personal Prague Guide Service**'s Šárka Kačabová uses her teaching background to help you understand Czech culture, and has picked a team of personable and knowledgeable guides for her company (600 Kč/hour for 2-3 people, 800 Kč/hour for 4-8 people, fifth hour free, mobile 777-225-205, www.prague-guide.info, sarka @me.com). **Athos Travel**'s licensed guides can lead you on a general sightseeing tour or fit the walk to your interests: music, Art Nouveau, architecture, and more (600-700 Kč/hour for 1-5 people, tel. 277-004-677, www.a-prague.com/tours, info@a-prague.com).

Individual Guides: These guides typically charge about 2,000-2,500 Kč for a half-day tour. **Jana Hronková** has a natural style—a welcome change from the more strict professionalism of some of the busier guides—and a penchant for the Jewish Quarter (mobile 732-185-180, www.experience-prague.info, janahronkova @hotmail.com). **Zuzana Tlášková** speaks English as well as Hebrew (mobile 774-131-335, tlaskovaz@seznam.cz). **Martin Bělohradský,** who guides on the side when not doing his organic chemistry work, is particularly enthusiastic about fine arts and architecture (mobile 723-414-565, martinb@uochb.cas.cz). **Kamil and Petra Vondrouš** design tours to fit individual interests; they also guide/drive beyond Prague, as far as Vienna or Dresden (mobile 605-701-861, www.prague-extra.com, info@prague-extra

.com). My readers also recommend **Renata Blažková,** who has a special interest in the history of Prague's Jewish Quarter (tel. 222-716-870, mobile 602-353-186, blazer@volny.cz); **Václav Štorek,** who specializes in history (mobile 603-743-523, www.storek.guide-prague.cz, vaclavstorek@post.cz); and **Petr Zídek** (mobile 721-286-869, www.bohemiantours.cz, petr@bohemiantours.cz). For a list of more guides, see www.guide-prague.cz.

Jewish-Themed Tours: Jewish guides (of varying quality) meet small groups twice daily in season for three-hour tours of the Jewish Quarter in English. **Wittman Tours** charges an 880-Kč fee that includes entry to the Old-New Synagogue and the six other major Jewish Quarter sights (which cost 480 Kč total), so the tour actually costs only 400 Kč (May-Oct Sun-Fri at 10:30 and 14:00, Nov-Dec and mid-March-April Sun-Fri at 10:30 only, no tours Sat and Jan-mid-March, minimum 3 people). Tours meet in the little park (just beyond the café), directly in front of Hotel InterContinental at the end of Pařížská street (tel. 603-168-427 or 603-426-564, www.wittmann-tours.com).

Weekend Tours for Students: Andy Steves (Rick's son) runs Weekend Student Adventures, offering experiential three-day weekend tours for €199, designed for American students studying abroad (www.wsaeurope.com for details on tours of Prague and other great cities).

Outside Prague: To get beyond the sights listed in most guidebooks, call Tom and Marie Zahn from **P.A.T.H. Finders International.** Tom is American, Marie is Czech, and together they organize and lead family-friendly day excursions (in Prague and throughout the country). Their tours are creative and affordable, and they teach travelers how to find off-the-beaten-track destinations on their own. Their specialty is Personal Ancestral Tours & History (P.A.T.H.)—with sufficient notice, they can help Czech descendants find their ancestral homes, perhaps even a long-lost relative. Tom and Marie can also help with other parts of your Eastern European travel by linking you with associates in other countries, especially Germany, Hungary, Poland, Romania, Slovakia, and Ukraine (US tel. 360-450-5959, Czech tel. 257-940-113, www.pathfinders.cz, info@pathfinders.cz).

Reverend Jan Dus, an enthusiastic pastor who lived in the US for several years, now serves a small congregation about 100 miles east of Prague. Jan can design itineraries and likes to help travelers connect with locals in little towns, particularly in northeastern Bohemia and Moravia. He also has an outstanding track record in providing genealogical services (toll-free US tel. 800-807-1562, www.revjan.com, rev.jan.services@gmail.com).

Bus Tours—Although I generally recommend cheap big-bus orientation tours for an efficient, once-over-lightly look at great cities,

Prague at a Glance

Rather than a checklist of museums, Prague is a fine place to wander around and just take in the fun atmosphere. Plan some worthwhile outdoor activities—hire a local guide (page 70), enjoy a concert (page 136), or go for a scenic paddle on the river (page 74).

In the Old Town

▲▲▲Old Town Square Magical main square of Old World Prague, with dozens of colorful facades, the dramatic Jan Hus Memorial, looming Týn Church, and fanciful Astronomical Clock. **Hours:** Týn Church—generally open to sightseers Tue-Sat 10:00-13:00 & 15:00-17:00; clock strikes on the hour daily 8:00-21:00, until 20:00 in winter; clock tower open Tue-Sun 9:00-17:30, Mon 11:00-17:30. See page 76.

▲▲▲Charles Bridge An atmospheric, statue-lined bridge that connects the Old Town to the Little Quarter and Prague Castle. **Hours:** Always open and crossable. See page 85.

▲▲▲Jewish Quarter The best collection of Jewish sights in Europe, featuring various synagogues and an evocative cemetery. **Hours:** The quarter can be visited any time; sights open April-Oct Sun-Fri 9:00-18:00, Nov-March Sun-Fri 9:00-16:30, always closed Sat and on Jewish holidays. See page 88.

▲▲Museum of Medieval Art The best Gothic art in the land, at St. Agnes Convent. **Hours:** Tue-Sun 10:00-18:00, closed Mon, may close sporadically due to budget cuts. See page 82.

▲Havelská Market Colorful open-air market that sells crafts and produce. **Hours:** Daily 9:00-18:00. See page 83.

▲Klementinum National Library's lavish Baroque Hall and Observatory Tower (with views), open by 45-minute tour only. **Hours:** Mon-Fri 14:00-19:00, Sat-Sun 10:00-19:00, shorter hours off-season. See page 84.

In the New Town

▲▲Wenceslas Square Lively boulevard at the heart of modern Prague. **Hours:** Always open. See page 95.

▲▲Mucha Museum Easy-to-appreciate collection of Art Nouveau works by Czech artist Alfons Mucha. **Hours:** Daily 10:00-18:00. See page 101.

▲▲Municipal House Pure Art Nouveau architecture, including Prague's largest concert hall and several eateries. **Hours:** Daily 10:00-18:00. See page 104.

▲▲**Museum of Communism** The rise and fall of the regime, from start to Velvet finish. **Hours:** Daily 9:00-21:00. See page 106.

▲**National Memorial to the Heroes of the Heydrich Terror** Tribute to the resistance, which assassinated a Nazi war criminal. **Hours:** Tue-Sun 9:00-17:00, closed Mon. See page 110.

In the Little Quarter
▲**Petřín Hill** Little Quarter hill with public art, a funicular, a replica of the Eiffel Tower, and the quirky museum of a nonexistent Czech hero. **Hours:** Funicular—daily 8:00-22:00; tower and museum—daily 10:00-22:00. See page 116.

Church of St. Nicholas Jesuit centerpiece of Little Quarter Square, with ultimate High Baroque decor and a climbable bell tower. **Hours:** Church—daily 9:00-17:00; tower—April-Oct daily 10:00-18:00, closed Nov-March. See page 112.

Wallenstein Palace Garden Largest and beautiful Renaissance palace garden. **Hours:** April-Oct daily 10:00-18:00, closed Nov-March. See page 114.

In the Castle Quarter
▲▲▲**St. Vitus Cathedral** The Czech Republic's most important church, featuring a climbable tower and a striking stained-glass window by Art Nouveau artist Alfons Mucha. **Hours:** Daily April-Oct 9:00-18:00, Nov-March 9:00-16:00, closed Sunday mornings year-round for Mass. See page 125.

▲▲**Prague Castle** Traditional seat of Czech rulers, with St. Vitus Cathedral (see above), Old Royal Palace, Basilica of St. George, shop-lined Golden Lane, and lots of crowds. **Hours:** Castle sights—daily April-Oct 9:00-18:00, Nov-March 9:00-16:00; castle grounds—daily 5:00-24:00. See page 119.

▲▲**Lobkowicz Palace** The most entertaining palace in town. **Hours:** Daily 10:00-18:00. See page 130.

▲**Strahov Monastery and Library** Baroque center of learning, with ornate reading rooms and old-fashioned science exhibits. **Hours:** Daily 9:00-11:45 & 13:00-17:00. See page 132.

Beyond the Center
▲▲▲**Alfons Mucha's *Slav Epic*** Twenty enormous canvases at Veletržní Palace depicting momentous events of Slavic history. **Hours:** Tue-Sun 10:00-18:00, closed Mon. See page 102.

Prague's sightseeing core (Castle Quarter, Charles Bridge, and the Old Town) is not accessible by bus. In fact, most bus tours of the city are basically walking tours that use buses for pickups and transfers. So if you insist on a bus, you're playing basketball with a catcher's mitt.

Bus tours make more sense for day trips out of Prague. Several companies have kiosks on Na Příkopě, where you can comparison-shop. **Premiant City Tours** offers 20 different tours, including one to Karlštejn and Konopiště castles (1,950 Kč, 8.5 hours) and a river cruise. The tours feature live guides and depart from near the bottom of Wenceslas Square at Na Příkopě 23. Get tickets at an AVE travel agency, your hotel, on the bus, or at Na Příkopě 23 (tel. 224-946-922, mobile 606-600-123, www.premiant.cz). **Wittman Tours,** listed earlier, offers an all-day minibus tour to the Terezín Concentration Camp Memorial (www.wittmann-tours.com).

Tour salespeople are notorious for telling you anything to sell a ticket. Some tours, especially those heading into the country-side, can be in as many as four different languages. Hiring a guide, many of whom can drive you around in their car, can be a much better value (described earlier, under "Local Guides").

Cruises—Prague isn't ideal for a boat tour because you might spend half the time waiting to go through the locks. Still, the hour-long Vltava River cruises, which leave from near the castle end of Charles Bridge about hourly, are scenic and relaxing, though not informative (150-200 Kč).

▲Rowboat or Paddleboat Cruises—Renting a rowboat or paddleboat on the island by the National Theater is a better way to enjoy the river. You'll float at your own pace among the swans and watch local lovers cruise by in their own boats (40 Kč/hour for rowboats, 60 Kč/hour for paddle-boats, bring photo ID for deposit).

Sights in Prague

I've arranged these sights according to which of Prague's four towns you'll find them in (see "Prague's Four Towns" sidebar on page 68): Old Town, New Town, Little Quarter, or Castle Quarter.

The Old Town (Staré Město)

From Prague's dramatic centerpiece, the Old Town Square, sight-seeing options fan out in all directions. Get oriented on the square before venturing onward. You can learn about Jewish heritage in

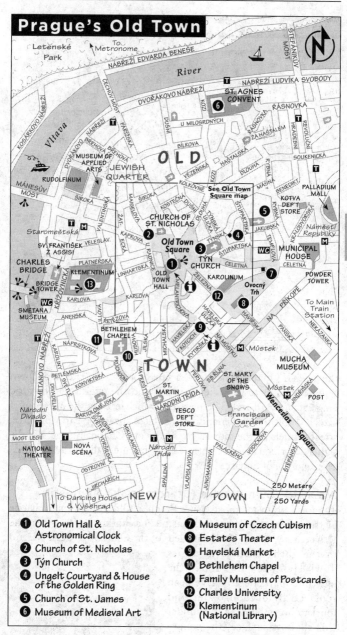

Prague's Old Town

1. Old Town Hall & Astronomical Clock
2. Church of St. Nicholas
3. Týn Church
4. Ungelt Courtyard & House of the Golden Ring
5. Church of St. James
6. Museum of Medieval Art
7. Museum of Czech Cubism
8. Estates Theater
9. Havelská Market
10. Bethlehem Chapel
11. Family Museum of Postcards
12. Charles University
13. Klementinum (National Library)

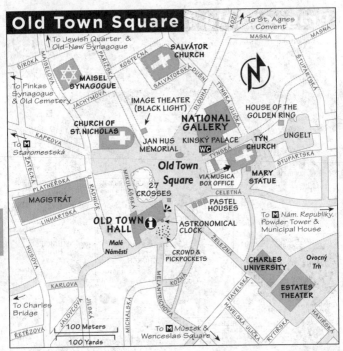

Old Town Square

- To St. Agnes Convent
- To Jewish Quarter & Old-New Synagogue
- SALVÁTOR CHURCH
- MAISEL SYNAGOGUE
- To Pinkas Synagogue & Old Cemetery
- IMAGE THEATER (BLACK LIGHT)
- HOUSE OF THE GOLDEN RING
- CHURCH OF ST. NICHOLAS
- NATIONAL GALLERY
- To M Staroměstská
- JAN HUS MEMORIAL
- KINSKÝ PALACE WC
- TÝN CHURCH
- UNGELT
- Old Town Square
- VIA MUSICA BOX OFFICE
- MARY STATUE
- 27 CROSSES
- PASTEL HOUSES
- MAGISTRÁT
- OLD TOWN HALL
- Malé Náměstí
- ASTRONOMICAL CLOCK
- To M Nám. Republiky, Powder Tower & Municipal House
- CROWD & PICKPOCKETS
- CHARLES UNIVERSITY
- Ovocný Trh
- To Charles Bridge
- ESTATES THEATER
- 100 Meters
- 100 Yards
- To M Můstek & Wenceslas Square

PRAGUE

the Jewish Quarter (Josefov), a few blocks from the Old Town Square. Closer to the square, you'll find the quaint and historic Ungelt courtyard and Celetná street, which leads to the Museum of Czech Cubism and the landmark Estates Theater. Nearby, Karlova street funnels all the tourists to the famous Charles Bridge. All the sights described here are within a five-minute walk of the magnificent Old Town Square.

▲▲▲Old Town Square (Staroměstské Náměstí)

The focal point for most visits, Prague's Old Town Square is one of the city's top sights. This has been a market square since the 11th century. It became the nucleus of the Old Town (Staré Město) in the 13th century, when its Town Hall was built. Today, the old-time market stalls have been replaced by outdoor cafés and touristy horse buggies. But under this shallow surface, the square hides a magic power to evoke the history that has passed through here. The square's centerpiece is a memorial to Jan Hus.

Jan Hus and Martin Luther

The word *catholic* means "universal." The Roman Catholic Church—in many ways the administrative ghost of the Roman Empire—is the only organization to survive from ancient times. For more than a thousand years, it enforced its notion that the Vatican was the sole interpreter of God's word on earth, and the only legitimate way to be a Christian was as a Roman Catholic.

Jan Hus (c. 1369-1415) lived and preached a century before Martin Luther. Both were college professors as well as priests. Both drew huge public crowds as they preached in their university chapels. Both condemned Church corruption and promoted a local religious autonomy. Both helped establish their national languages. (Hus gave the Czech alphabet its unique accent marks so that the letters could fit the sounds.) And both got in big trouble.

Hus was burned at the stake as a heretic, but Luther survived. Thanks to the new printing press, invented by Gutenberg, Luther was able to spread his message cheaply and effectively. Since Luther was high-profile and German, killing him would have caused major political complications. While Hus may have loosened Rome's grip on Christianity, Luther orchestrated the Reformation that finally broke it. Today, both are honored as national heroes as well as religious reformers.

PRAGUE

Jan Hus Memorial—This monument, erected in 1915 (500 years after the Czech reformer's martyrdom by fire), symbolizes the long struggle for Czech freedom. Walk around the memorial. Jan Hus stands tall between two groups of people: victorious Hussite

patriots, and Protestants defeated by the Habsburgs in 1620. One patriot holds a chalice (cup)—in the medieval Church, only priests could drink the wine at Communion. Since the Hussites fought for their right to take both the wine and the bread, the cup is their symbol. Hus looks proudly at Týn Church (described later), which became the headquarters and leading church of his followers. A golden chalice once filled the now-empty niche under the gold bas-relief of the Virgin Mary on the church's facade. After the Habsburg (Catholic) victory over the Czechs in 1620, the Hussite chalice was melted down and made into the image of Mary that shines from that spot high over the square today.

Behind the statue of Jan Hus, the bronze statue of a mother with her children represents the ultimate rebirth of the Czech nation. Because of his bold advocacy for the participation of common people in worship rituals (and his challenges to the state-church hierarchy), Hus was excommunicated and burned in Germany, a century before the age of Martin Luther.

Old Town Square Orientation Spin-Tour—This tour is designed to give you your bearings; most of the important sights are described in greater detail later.

Whirl clockwise to get a look at Prague's diverse architectural styles: Gothic, Renaissance, Baroque, Rococo, and Art Nouveau. Start with the green domes of the Baroque **Church of St. Nicholas.** Originally Catholic, now Hussite, this church is a popular venue for concerts. (There's another green-domed Church of St. Nicholas—also popular for concerts—by the same architect, across the Charles Bridge in the Little Quarter.) The Jewish Quarter (Josefov) is a few blocks behind the church, down the uniquely tree-lined Pařížská—"Paris street."

Pařížská, an eclectic cancan of mostly Art Nouveau facades, leads to a bluff that once sported a 100-foot-tall stone statue of Stalin. Demolished in 1962 after Khrushchev exposed Stalin's crimes, it was replaced in 1991 by a giant ticking **metronome**—partly to commemorate Prague's centennial exhibition (the 1891 exhibition is remembered by the Little Quarter's Eiffel-esque Petřín Tower), and partly to send the message that for every power, there's a time to go.

Spin to the right, past the Hus Memorial and the fine yellow Art Nouveau building. The large Rococo palace on the right (with a public WC in the courtyard) is part of the **National Gallery** and houses an exhibit of Asian art (Tue-Sun 10:00-18:00, closed Mon, may close sporadically due to budget cuts—ask at TI).

To the right, you can't miss the towering Gothic **Týn Church** (pronounced "teen"), with its fanciful spires flanking the gold bas-relief of Mary. For 200 years after Hus' death, this was Prague's leading Hussite church. A narrow lane leading to the church's entrance passes the **Via Musica,** the most convenient ticket office in town (stop by here to consider all of your concert options). Behind Týn Church is a gorgeously restored medieval courtyard called **Ungelt.** The row of pastel houses in front of Týn Church has a mixture of Gothic, Renaissance, and Baroque facades. To the right of these buildings,

shop-lined **Celetná street** leads to a square called Ovocný Trh (with the Estates Theater and Museum of Czech Cubism) and, beyond that, to the Municipal House and Powder Tower in the New Town.

Continue spinning right, taking in more gloriously colorful architecture, until you reach the pointed 250-foot-tall spire mark-

ing the 14th-century **Old Town Hall** (with the famous Astronomical Clock and the only elevator-accessible tower in town). The chunk of pink building attached to the tower of the Neo-Gothic City Hall is the town's "memorial" to sore losers. The building once stretched all the way to the Church of St. Nicholas. Then, in the last days of World War II (May 1945), German tanks knocked off this landmark—to the joy of many Prague citizens who considered it an ugly, oversized 19th-century stain on the medieval square. Across the square from the Old Town Hall (opposite the Astronomical Clock), touristy **Melantrichova street** leads directly to the New Town's Wenceslas Square, passing the craft-packed Havelská Market along the way.

PRAGUE

Twenty-seven Crosses—Embedded in the pavement at the base of the Old Town Hall tower (near the snack stand), you'll see white inlaid crosses marking the spot where 27 Protestant nobles, merchants, and intellectuals were beheaded in 1621 after rebelling against the Catholic Habsburgs. The execution ended Czech independence for 300 years and is still one of the grimmest chapters in the country's history.

▲▲Astronomical Clock—Join the gang for the striking of the hour on the Town Hall clock (daily 8:00-21:00, until 20:00 in winter). As you wait, see if you can figure out how the clock works.

With revolving discs, celestial symbols, and sweeping hands, this clock keeps several versions of time. Two outer rings show the hour: Bohemian time (gold Gothic numbers on black background, counts from sunset—find the zero, between 23 and 1...supposedly the time of tonight's sunset) and modern time (24 Roman numerals, XII at the top being noon, XII at the bottom being midnight). Five hundred years ago, everything revolved around the earth (the fixed middle background—with Prague marking the center, of course).

To indicate the times of sunrise and sunset, arcing lines and moving spheres combine with the big hand (a sweeping golden sun) and the little hand (a moon that spins to show various stages). Look for the orbits of the sun and moon as they rise through day (the blue zone) and night (the black zone).

If this seems complex to us, it must have been a marvel in the early 1400s, when the clock was installed here. The clock was heavily damaged during World War II, and much of what you see today is a reconstruction. The circle below (added in the 19th century) shows the signs of the zodiac, scenes from the seasons of a rural peasant's life, and a ring of saints' names—one for each day of the year, with a marker showing today's special saint (at top).

Four statues flanking the clock represent the 15th-century outlook on time and prejudices. A Turk with a mandolin symbolizes hedonism, a Jewish moneylender is greed, and the figure staring into a mirror stands for vanity. All these worldly goals are vain in the face of Death, whose hourglass reminds us that our time is unavoidably running out.

At the top of the hour (don't blink—the show is pretty quick): First, Death tips his hourglass and pulls the cord, ringing the bell; the windows open and the 12 apostles parade by, acknowledging the gang of onlookers; the rooster crows; and, finally, the hour is rung. The hour is often off because of Daylight Saving Time (completely senseless to 15th-century clockmakers). At the top of the next hour, stand under the tower—protected by a line of banner-wielding concert salespeople in powdered wigs—and watch the tourists.

Clock Tour and Tower Climb: The main TI, to the left of the Astronomical Clock, sells tickets at its information desk. You have two options: zipping up the Old Town Hall tower by elevator (60 Kč, Tue-Sun 9:00-17:30, Mon 11:00-17:30, good views); or taking a 45-minute tour of the Old Town Hall, which includes a Gothic chapel and a close-up look at the inner guts of the Astronomical Clock, plus its statues of the 12 apostles (50 Kč, 2/hour). The most straightforward entry to the tower is to the right of the Astronomical Clock.

▲**Týn Church**—Though this church has a long history, it's most notable for its 200-year stint as the leading church of the Hussite movement. It was Catholic before the Hussites, and was returned to Catholicism after the Hussites were defeated. As if to insult the Hussite doctrine of simplicity, the church's once elegant and pure

Gothic columns are now encrusted with noisy Baroque altars. The church interior is uncharacteristically bright for a Gothic building because of its clear Baroque windowpanes and whitewash. Read the Catholic spin on the church's history—told with barely a mention of Hus (rear-left side, in English). The fine 16th-century, carved John the Baptist altar (right aisle) is worth a look. As you enjoy this church, try to ignore its unwelcoming signs telling you what not to do.

Outside, on the side of the church facing Celetná street, find a statue of the Virgin Mary resting on a temporary column in an ignored niche. Catholics are still waiting for a chance to re-install Mary in the middle of the Old Town Square, where she stood for about 250 years until being torn down in 1918 by a mob of anti-Habsburg (and therefore anti-Catholic) demonstrators.

Cost and Hours: Free but 20 Kč donation suggested, generally open to sightseers Tue-Sat 10:00-13:00 & 15:00-17:00, Sun 10:30-12:00, closed Mon.

Behind Týn Church

▲**Ungelt Courtyard (Týnský Dvůr)**—This fortified courtyard was the commercial nucleus of medieval Prague. Step through its stout gate (immediately behind Týn Church). The Ungelt courtyard once served as a hostel for foreign merchants, much like a Turkish caravanserai. Here the merchants (usually German) would store their goods and pay taxes before setting up stalls on the Old Town Square (where two old trade routes crossed). Notice that, for the purpose of guaranteeing the safety of goods and merchants, there are only two entrances to the complex. After decades of disuse, the courtyard had fallen into such disrepair by the 1980s that authorities considered demolishing it. But now, marvelously restored, the Ungelt courtyard is the most pleasant area in the Old Town for dining outdoors (such as at the recommended Indian Jewel). It's a fine place for elegant shopping, too: Sort through wooden crafts, and page through English-language books. Although Prague has undoubtedly lost some of its dreamy character to the booming tourist industry, places such as Ungelt stand as testimony to the miracles that money can work. Had the communists stayed in power for a few more years, Ungelt would have been a black hole by now. Ungelt also reminds us that Prague, for most of its history, has been a cosmopolitan center.

Church of St. James (Kostel Sv. Jakuba)—Perhaps the most beautiful church in the Old Town, the Church of St. James is just behind the Ungelt courtyard. The Minorite Order has occupied this church and the adjacent monastery almost as long as merchants have occupied Ungelt. A medieval city was a complex phenomenon: Commerce, prostitution, and a life of contemplation existed side by side. (I guess it's not that much different from today.) Artistically, St. James (along with the Church of the Ascension of St. Mary at Strahov Monastery) is a stunning example of how simple Gothic spaces could be transformed into sumptuous feasts of Baroque decoration. The blue light in the altar highlights one of Prague's most venerated treasures—the bejeweled *Madonna Pietatis*. Above the *pietà*, as if held aloft by hummingbird-like angels, is a painting of the martyrdom of St. James

As you leave, find the black shriveled-up arm with clenched fingers (15 feet above and to the left of the door). According to legend, a thief attempted to rob the *Madonna Pietatis* from the altar, but his hand was frozen the moment he touched the statue. The monks had to cut off his arm to get the hand to let go. The desiccated arm now hangs here as a warning—and the entire delightful story is posted nearby in English.

Cost and Hours: Free, daily 9:30-12:00 & 14:00-16:00.

North of the Old Town Square, near the River

▲▲Museum of Medieval Art (Středověké umění v Čechách a Střední Evropě)—The St. Agnes Convent houses the Museum of Medieval Art in Bohemia and Central Europe (1200-1550). The 14th century was Prague's Golden Age, and the religious art displayed in this Gothic space is a testament to the rich cultural life of the period. Each exquisite piece is well-lit and thoughtfully described in English. Follow the arrows for a chronological sweep through Gothic art history. The various Madonnas and saints were gathered here from churches all over Central Europe.

Cost and Hours: 100 Kč, Tue-Sun 10:00-18:00, closed Mon, may close sporadically due to budget cuts—ask at TI, two blocks northeast of the Spanish Synagogue, along the river at Anežská 12, tel. 224-810-628, www.ngprague.cz/en.

On Celetná Street, Toward the New Town

Celetná, a pedestrian-only street, is a convenient and relatively untouristy way to get from the Old Town Square to the New Town (specifically the Municipal House and Powder Tower, described on pages 104 and 105). Along the way, at the square called Ovocný Trh, you'll find these sights.

Museum of Czech Cubism (Muzeum Českého Kubismu)—Cubism was a potent force in Prague in the early 20th century. The fascinating Museum of Czech Cubism in the House of the Black Madonna (Dům u Černé Matky Boží) offers the complete Cubist experience: Cubist architecture (stand back and see how masterfully it makes its statement while mixing with its neighbors...then get up close and study the details), a great café (one flight up), a ground-floor shop, and, of course, a museum. Take the elevator

to the top floor and work your way down. On three floors you'll see paintings, furniture, graphics, and architectural drafts by Czech Cubists. Cubists recognized that preservation without growth was stagnation. A city needs growth—but in harmony with its environment. This building is an example of what has long been considered the greatest virtue of Prague's architects: the ability to adapt grandiose plans to the existing cityscape. Even if you're not interested in touring the museum, consider a drink upstairs in the similarly decorated Grand Café Orient (described on page 157).

Cost and Hours: 100 Kč, Tue-Sun 10:00-18:00, closed Mon, corner of Celetná and Ovocný Trh at Ovocný Trh 19, tel. 224-301-003, www.ngprague.cz/en.

Estates Theater (Stavovské Divadlo)—Built by a nobleman in the 1770s, this Classicist building—gently opening its greenish walls onto Ovocný Trh—was the prime opera venue in Prague at a time when an Austrian prodigy was changing the course of music. Wolfgang Amadeus Mozart premiered Don Giovanni in this building; he directed many of his works here. Prague's theatergoers would whistle arias from Mozart's works on the streets the morning after they premiered. Today, the Estates Theater (part of the National Theater group) continues to produce *The Marriage of Figaro*, *Don Giovanni*, and occasionally *The Magic Flute*. For a more intimate encounter with Mozart, go to Villa Bertramka (see "Entertainment in Prague," later).

On Melantrichova Street

Skinny, tourist-clogged Melantrichova street leads directly from the Old Town Square's Astronomical Clock to the bottom of Wenceslas Square. But even along this most crowded of streets, a genuine bit of Prague remains.

▲Havelská Market—This open-air market, offering crafts and produce, was first set up in the 13th century for the German trading community. Though heavy on souvenirs these days, the market still feeds hungry locals and vagabonds cheaply. It's ideal for a healthy snack— merchants are happy to sell a single vegetable or piece of fruit—and you'll find a washing fountain and plenty of inviting

benches midway down the street. The market is also a fun place to browse for crafts. It's a homegrown, homemade kind of place; you'll often be dealing with the actual artist or farmer. The many cafés and little eateries circling the market offer a relaxing vantage point from which to view the action.

Hours: Market open daily 9:00-18:00, produce best on weekdays; more souvenirs, puppets, and toys on weekends.

From Old Town Square to the Charles Bridge

Karlova Street—This street winds through medieval Prague from the Old Town Square to the Charles Bridge (it zigzags—just follow the crowds). The touristy feeding-frenzy of Prague is at its ugliest along this commercial gauntlet. Street signs keep you on track, and *Karlův most* signs point to the bridge. Obviously, you'll find few good values on this drag. Two favorite places providing a quick break from the crowds are just a few steps off Karlova on Husova street: **Cream and Dream Ice Cream** (Husova 12) and the recommended **U Zlatého Tygra,** a colorful pub that serves great, cheap beer in a classic and untouristy setting (Husova 17).

▲Klementinum—The Czech Republic's massive National Library borders touristy Karlova street. The contrast could not be starker: Step out of the most souvenir-packed stretch of Eastern Europe, and enter the meditative silence of Eastern Europe's biggest library. Jesuits built the Klementinum in the 1600s to house a new college; they had been invited to Prague by the Catholic Habsburgs to offset the influence of the predominantly Protestant Charles University nearby. The building was transformed into a library in the early 1700s, when the Jesuits took firm control of the university. Their books, together with the collections of several noble families (written in all possible languages...except Czech), form the nucleus of the National and University Library, which is now six million volumes strong. (Note that the Klementinum's Chapel of Mirrors is a popular venue for evening concerts.)

Library Tour and Tower Climb: While much of the Klementinum building is simply a vast library, its magnificent original Baroque Hall and Observatory Tower are open to the public by tour only (45 minutes, in English). You'll belly up to a banister at the end of the ornate library with its many centuries-old books, fancy ceilings with Jesuit leaders and saints overseeing the pursuit of knowledge, and Josef II—the enlightened Habsburg emperor—looking on from the far end. Then you'll climb the Observatory Tower, learning how early astronomers charted the skies over Prague. The tour finishes with a grand Prague view from the top.

Cost and Hours: 220 Kč, departs on the hour Mon-Fri 14:00-19:00, Sat-Sun 10:00-19:00, shorter hours off-season, tel. 221-663-

165, mobile 603-231-241, www.klementinum.com; strolling down Karlova, turn at the intersection with Liliová through an archway into the Klementinum's courtyard.

▲▲▲Charles Bridge (Karlův Most)

Among Prague's defining landmarks, this much-loved bridge offers one of the most pleasant and entertaining 500-yard strolls in Europe. Enjoy the bridge at different times of day. It's most memorable early—before the crowds—and late, during that photographers' "magic hour" when the sun is low in the sky.

At the Old Town end of the bridge, in a little square, is a statue of the bridge's namesake, **Charles IV** (Karlo Quatro—the guy on the 100-Kč bill), the Holy Roman Emperor

who ruled his vast empire from Prague in the 14th century. This statue was erected in 1848 to celebrate the 500th anniversary of Prague's university. Charles is holding a contract establishing the university, the first in Northern Europe. The women around the pedestal symbolize the school's four subjects: the arts, medicine, law, and theology. (From the corner by the busy street, many think the emperor's silhouette makes it appear as if he's peeing on the tourists. Which reminds me, public WCs are in the passageway opposite the statue.)

The magically aligned spot on the Old Town side (see sidebar) is occupied by the **bridge tower,** considered one of the finest Gothic gates anywhere. Contemplate the fine sculpture on the Old Town side of the tower, showing the 14th-century hierarchy of kings, bishops, and angels. Climbing the tower rewards you with wonderful views over the bridge (40 Kč, daily 10:00-19:00, as late as 22:00 in summer).

In the 17th century, there were no statues on the bridge—only a **cross,** which you can still see as part of the third sculpture on the

Charles Bridge: Past and Present

Bridges had previously been built at this location, as the tower from the earlier Judith Bridge attests (it's the smaller of the two bridge towers at the far end), but all were washed away by floods. After a major flood in 1342, Emperor Charles IV decided against repairing the old bridge and instead commissioned an entirely new structure. Initially called the Stone Bridge, it was Prague's only bridge across the Vltava River for more than 400 years.

The bridge has long fueled a local love of legends—including one tied to numbers. According to medieval records, the bridge's foundation was laid in 1357. In the late 1800s, an amateur astronomer noticed a curious combination of numbers, leading to a popular theory about Charles IV. Charles is known to have been interested in numerology and astrology, and was likely aware of the significance of this date: the ninth of July at 5:31 in the morning. Written out in digits—as the year, month, day, hour, and minute—it's a numerical palindrome: 135797531. It's said that Charles must have chosen that precise moment (which also coincides with a favorable positioning of the earth and Saturn) to lay the foundation stone of the bridge. Further "corroboration" of this remarkable hypothesis was provided by the discovery that the end of the bridge on the Old Town side aligns perfectly with

right. The gilded Hebrew inscription from the Book of Isaiah celebrates Christ ("Holy, holy, holy is the Lord of hosts"). The inscription was paid for by a fine imposed on a Prague Jew—the result of a rivalry within the Jewish community (fellow Jews turned him in for mocking the cross).

In the space between the third and fourth statues after the cross, look for a small **brass relief** depicting a floating figure with a semicircle of stars above him. This marks the spot where St. John of Nepomuk, the national saint of the Czech people, was tossed off the bridge into the river (I'll tell you that story a bit later). The relief is a replica of a Baroque original that was badly damaged by a flood in 1890, marred by protesters in the 1920s, and finally removed by the communists. In May 2009, this replacement was installed by Prague's archbishop to help revive traditional celebrations of the saint. Devout pilgrims believe that touching the relief of St. John will make a wish come true. But you get only one chance in life to make this wish, so think carefully before you touch the saint.

the tomb of St. Vitus (in the cathedral across the river) and the setting sun at summer solstice. In the absence of accurate 14th-century records, this intriguing proposition has delighted the modern Czech imagination. The number "135797531" is bound to remain celebrated as the adopted birthday of Prague's most beloved structure.

But even the most auspicious numbers could not protect the bridge from periodic damage caused by floods, ice, and inept repairs. Scheduled to last for more than a decade, a long-overdue reconstruction project began in the summer of 2007, days after the city celebrated the bridge's 650-year anniversary.

Aware of the blow that closing the entire bridge would deal to the tourist industry, the city chose a more costly and tech-nologically challenging "chessboard" strategy. With this plan, only a small section is closed at any one time, allowing people to continue using the bridge (but leading to midday crowds in the resulting bottleneck). To give everyone the opportunity to peek inside the centuries-old structure, and thus turn the bridge reno-vation into Prague's new attraction, the mayor requested (to the dismay of many archaeologists) that the construction site be at all times surrounded only by light, transparent fences.

The reconstruction is being carried out in two stages. During the first major stage—preceded by archaeological excavations and completed in 2010—historic gas lighting was returned to the bridge, and the sewage system, insulation, and pavement were installed. In the next stage, deteriorated sandstone blocks will be replaced by new ones. To minimize the impact on nearby areas, most of the building materials are being transported by river.

The relief is the ideal location from which to survey your sur-roundings. Looking **downstream** from right to left, you'll see the modern Four Seasons Hotel (doing a pretty good job of fit-ting in). Farther down, the large Neo-Renaissance facade hides the concert hall of the Czech Philharmonic. Across the river and up the hill, the red needle of a metronome ticks at the spot where a 50-foot-tall granite Joseph Stalin—flanked by eight equally tall deputies—stood from 1955 to 1962. To the right of Stalin's former perch (hiding under the trees and worth the climb on a hot sum-mer day) is Prague's most popular beer garden. Visible between the trees to the left of the metronome is the small but attractive Art Nouveau Havana pavilion, now a fancy restaurant. To the left of it is a red-brick villa, the residence of the Czech prime minister. Finally, the green roof in the shape of an upturned ship along the tree-lined horizon belongs to the Royal Summer Palace, an exqui-site Renaissance structure built by Emperor Ferdinand I.

Looking **upstream,** notice the icebreakers protecting the

abutments upon which the bridge sits (ice flow has historically threatened the very survival of the bridge). Look farther upstream for the tiny locks on either side of the weir. While today's river traffic is limited to tourist boats, in earlier times timber was floated down the river lashed like rafts. The building with the gilded awning on the left by the next upstream bridge is the National Theater. On the other side of the river, a large sculpture of a chair stands in front of the white Kampa Museum, a private art collection situated in a pleasant public park on Kampa Island.

Pause for a moment to enjoy the musicians, artisans, and parade of people on the bridge itself—my favorite strolling bridge in all of Europe.

Continuing across the bridge, you'll reach the bronze Baroque statue depicting **St. John of Nepomuk** (look for the guy with the

five golden stars around his head, near the Little Quarter end of the bridge on the right). This statue always draws a crowd. John was a 14th-century priest to whom the queen confessed all her sins. According to a 17th-century legend, the king wanted to know his wife's secrets, but Father John dutifully refused to tell. He was tortured and eventually killed by being thrown off the bridge. When he hit the water, five stars appeared. The shiny plaque at the base of the statue depicts the heave-ho. Notice the date on the inscription: This oldest

statue on the bridge was unveiled in 1683, on the supposed 300th anniversary of the martyr's death.

Most of the other Charles Bridge statues date from the late 1600s and early 1700s. Today, half of them are replicas—the originals are in city museums, out of the polluted air. At the far end of the Charles Bridge, you reach the **Little Quarter** (described later).

▲▲▲Jewish Quarter (Josefov)

Prague's Jewish Quarter neighborhood and its well-presented, profoundly moving museum tell the story of this region's Jews. For me, this is the most interesting collection of Jewish sights in Europe, and well worth seeing. The Jewish Quarter is an easy walk from Old Town Square, up delightful Pařížská street (next to the green-domed Church of St. Nicholas).

As the Nazis decimated Jewish communities in the region, Prague's Jews were allowed to collect and archive their treasures here. Although the archivists were ultimately killed in concentration camps, their work survives. Seven sights scattered over a

Prague's Jewish Quarter

INTERCONTINENTAL HOTEL (MEETING POINT FOR WITTMANN TOURS)

DINITZ KOSHER RESTAURANT

SPANISH SYNAGOGUE

KOLKOVNA RESTAURANT

CEREMONIAL HALL

OLD-NEW SYNAGOGUE

JEWISH TOWN HALL & HIGH SYNAGOGUE

KLAUS SYNAGOGUE

RUDOLFINUM

MUSEUM OF APPLIED ARTS

Old Cemetery

PINKAS SYNAGOGUE

FRANZ KAFKA CAFÉ

MAISEL SYNAGOGUE

CHURCH OF ST. NICHOLAS

Nam. Jana Palacha

Staroměstská

RESTAURANT U KNIHOVNY

To Charles Bridge

Old Town Square

100 Meters / 100 Yards

Vltava River

PRAGUE

three-block area make up the tourists' Jewish Quarter. Six of the sights—all except the Old-New Synagogue—are part of the Jewish Museum in Prague (Židovské Muzeum v Praze) and are covered by one admission ticket. Your ticket comes with a map that locates the sights and lists admission appointments—the times you'll be let in if it's very busy. (Ignore the times unless it's really crowded.) You'll notice plenty of security.

Going from sight to sight in the Jewish Quarter, you'll walk through perhaps Europe's finest Art Nouveau neighborhood. Make a point to enjoy the circa-1900 buildings with their marvelous trimmings and oh-wow entryways. While today's modern grid plan has replaced the higgledy-piggledy medieval streets of old, Široká ("Wide Street") was and remains the main street of the ghetto.

Cost and Hours: A discount ticket covering all seven Jewish Quarter sights is 480 Kč (ticket available at any of the sights; separately, you'd pay 300 Kč for the six sights that make up the Jewish Museum, and 200 Kč for the Old-New Synagogue). The **museum** sights are open April-Oct Sun-Fri 9:00-18:00; Nov-March Sun-Fri 9:00-16:30; closed year-round on Sat—the Jewish Sabbath—and on Jewish holidays; check the website for a complete list of holiday closures, especially if you are visiting in the fall (tel. 222-317-191, www.jewishmuseum.cz). The **Old-New Synagogue** is open Sun-Thu 9:30-18:00, Fri 9:30-17:00 or until sunset, closed

Prague's Jewish Heritage

The Jewish people from the Holy Land (today's Israel) were dispersed by the Romans 2,000 years ago. Over the centuries, their culture survived in enclaves throughout the world: "The Torah was their sanctuary which no army could destroy." Jews first came to Prague in the 10th century. The Jewish Quarter's main intersection (Maiselova and Široká streets) was the meeting point of two medieval trade routes.

During the Crusades in the 12th century, the pope declared that Jews and Christians should not live together. Jews had to wear yellow badges, and their quarter was walled in and became a ghetto. In the 16th and 17th centuries, Prague had one of the biggest ghettos in Europe, with 11,000 inhabitants. Within its six gates, Prague's Jewish Quarter was a gaggle of 200 wooden buildings. It was said that "Jews nested rather than dwelled."

These "outcasts" of Christianity relied mainly on profits from money-lending (forbidden to Christians) and community solidarity to survive. While their money bought them protection (the kings taxed Jewish communities heavily), it was often also a curse. Throughout Europe, when times got tough and Christian

Sat and on Jewish holidays (tel. 222-317-191, www.synagogue.cz). Admission includes a worthwhile 10-minute tour and entry to the Art Nouveau Jerusalem Synagogue in the New Town (see page 106).

Free View of Cemetery: The Old Jewish Cemetery—with its tightly packed, topsy-turvy tombstones—is, for many, the most evocative part of the experience. Unfortunately, there's no ticket just to see the cemetery, and most of the free viewpoints have been closed off. If the museum ticket is too steep and you just want a free glimpse of the famous cemetery, climb the steps to the covered porch of the Ceremonial Hall (but don't rest your chin on the treacherous railing).

Photos: While *No Photo* signs are posted everywhere, photos without flash (except during actual prayer times at the Old-New Synagogue) seem to be allowed.

Tours: Because the exhibitions of the Jewish Museum are scattered throughout the neighborhood, many tourists think they need a guide, but for most, a private guided tour is unnecessary. Besides what's covered in this guidebook, rely on the helpful com-

debts to the Jewish community mounted, entire Jewish communities were evicted or killed.

In the 1780s, Emperor Josef II, motivated more by economic concerns than by religious freedom, eased much of the discrimination against Jews. In 1848, the Jewish Quarter's walls were torn down, and the neighborhood—named Josefov in honor of the emperor who provided this small measure of tolerance—was incorporated as a district of the Old Town.

In 1897, ramshackle Josefov was razed and replaced by a new modern town—the original 31 streets and 220 buildings became 10 streets and 83 buildings. This is what you'll see today: an attractive neighborhood of pretty, mostly Art Nouveau buildings, with a few surviving historic Jewish structures. By the 1930s, Prague's Jewish community was hugely successful, thanks largely to their ability to appreciate talent—a rare quality in small Central European countries whose citizens, as the great Austrian novelist Robert Musil put it, "were equal in their unwillingness to let one another get ahead."

Of the 120,000 Jews living in the area in 1939, just 10,000 survived the Holocaust to see liberation in 1945. Today there are only 3,000 "registered" Jews in the Czech Republic, and of these, only 1,700 are in Prague. (There are probably more Jewish people here, but after their experiences with the Nazis and communists, you can understand why many choose not to register.) Today, in spite of their tiny numbers, the legacy of Prague's Jewish community lives on.

mentary thoughtfully posted in English throughout the quarter. Group tours flow like chain gangs through the congested and emotional museum sights. The 250-Kč audioguide is slow-moving and not worth the time or expense (rent and return at Pinkas Synagogue, ID required).

Touring on Your Own: A do-it-yourself visit is really quite simple: Buy your ticket at Pinkas Synagogue, and tour the synagogue and the adjacent Old Jewish Cemetery, which leads you to the Ceremonial Hall and Klaus Synagogue (at the far side of the cemetery). After visiting those buildings, walk a block to the Old-New Synagogue. Take a coffee break (the recommended Franz Kafka Café is nearby) before finishing up at the museum-like Maisel Synagogue and the Spanish Synagogue. (Note that Prague's fine Museum of Medieval Art, described earlier, is only a few blocks from the Spanish Synagogue.)

Pinkas Synagogue (Pinkasova Synagóga)—A site of Jewish worship for 400 years, this synagogue (built in 1535) is a poignant memorial to the victims of the Nazis. The walls are covered with the handwritten names of 77,297 Czech Jews who were sent from here to the gas chambers at Auschwitz and other camps. (As you ponder this sad sight, you'll hear the somber reading of the names alternating with a cantor singing the Psalms.) The names are carefully organized by hometown (in gold, listed alphabetically). Family names are in red, followed in black by the individual's first name, birthday, and last date known to be alive. Notice that families generally perished together. Extermination camps are listed on the east wall. Climb eight steps into the women's gallery. When the communists moved in, they closed the synagogue and erased virtually everything. With freedom, in 1989, the Pinkas Synagogue was reopened and the names were rewritten. (The names in poor condition near the ceiling are original.) Note that large tour groups may disturb this small memorial's compelling atmosphere between 10:00 and 12:00.

Upstairs is the **Terezín Children's Art Exhibit** (very well-described in English), displaying art drawn by Jewish children who were imprisoned at the Terezín concentration camp and later perished. Terezín makes an emotionally moving day trip from Prague (see next chapter).

Old Jewish Cemetery (Starý Židovský Hřbitov)—From the Pinkas Synagogue, you enter one of the most wistful scenes in Europe—Prague's Old Jewish Cemetery. As you wander among 12,000 evocative tombstones, remember that from 1439 until 1787, this was the only burial ground allowed for the Jews of Prague. Guides claim the tombs are layered seven or eight deep, and say there are close to 100,000 tombs here. The tombs were  piled atop each other because of limited space, the sheer number of graves, and the Jewish belief that the body should not be moved once buried. With its many layers, the cemetery became a small plateau. And as things settled over time, the tombstones got crooked. The Hebrew word for cemetery means "House of Life." Many Jews believe that death is the gateway into the next world. Pebbles on the tombstones are "flowers of the desert," reminiscent of the old days when rocks were placed upon a sandy gravesite to keep the body covered. Wedged under some of the pebbles are scraps of paper that contain prayers.

Ceremonial Hall (Obřadní Síň)—Leaving the cemetery, you'll find a Neo-Romanesque mortuary house (on the left) built in 1911 for the purification of the dead. It's filled with a worthwhile exhibition, described in English, on Jewish medicine, death, and burial traditions. A series of crude but instructive paintings (hanging on walls throughout the house) show how the "burial brotherhood" took care of the ill and buried the dead. As all are equal before God, the rich and poor alike were buried in embroidered linen shrouds similar to the one you'll see on display.

Klaus Synagogue (Klauzová Synagóga)—This 17th-century synagogue (also near the cemetery exit) is the final wing of a museum devoted to Jewish religious practices. Exhibits on the ground floor explain the Jewish calendar of festivals. The central case displays a Torah (the first five books of the Bible) and the solid silver pointers used when reading it—necessary since the Torah is not to be touched. Upstairs is an exhibit on the rituals of Jewish life (circumcisions, bar and bat mitzvahs, weddings, kosher eating, and so on).

Old-New Synagogue (Staronová Synagóga)—For more than 700 years, this has been the most important synagogue and the cen-

tral building in Josefov. Standing like a bomb-hardened bunker, it feels as though it has survived plenty of hard times. Stairs take you down to the street level of the 13th century and into the Gothic interior. Built in 1270, it's the oldest synagogue in Eastern Europe. Snare an attendant, who is likely to love showing visitors around.

The separate, steep, 200-Kč admission keeps many away, but even if you decide not to pay, you can see the exterior and a bit of the interior. (Go ahead...pop in and crane your cheapskate neck.)

The lobby (down the stairs, where you show your ticket) has two fortified old lockers—in which the most heavily taxed community in medieval Prague stored its money in anticipation of the taxman's arrival. As 13th-century Jews were not allowed to build, the synagogue was erected by Christians (who also built the St. Agnes Convent nearby). The builders were good at four-ribbed vaulting, but since that resulted in a cross, it wouldn't work for a synagogue. Instead, they made the ceiling using clumsy five-ribbed vaulting.

The interior is pure 1300s. The Shrine of the Ark in front is the focus of worship. The holiest place in the synagogue, it holds the sacred scrolls of the Torah. The old rabbi's chair to the right remains empty (notice the thin black chain) out of respect. The red banner is a copy of the one that the Jewish community carried through town during medieval parades. On the banner, within the Star of David, is pictured the yellow-pointed hat that the pope ordered all Jewish men to wear in 1215. Twelve is a popular number (e.g., windows), because it symbolizes the 12 tribes of Israel. The horizontal slit-like windows are an 18th-century addition, allowing women to view the male-only services. While Nazis routinely destroyed synagogues, this most historic synagogue in the country survived because the Nazis intended it to be part of their "Museum of the Extinct Jewish Race."

Maisel Synagogue (Maiselova Synagóga)—This synagogue was built as a private place of worship for the Maisel family during the 16th-century Golden Age of Prague's Jews. Maisel, the wealthy financier of the Habsburg king, lavished his riches on the synagogue's Neo-Gothic interior. In World War II, it served as a warehouse for the accumulated treasures of decimated Jewish communities, a collection that Hitler planned to use for his

Jewish museum (see earlier). Before entering, notice the facade featuring—as is standard in synagogues—the Ten Commandments top and center. Below that is the symbol for Prague's Jewish community: the Star of David, with the pointed hat local Jews wore here through medieval times. The one-room exhibit shows a thousand years of Jewish history in Bohemia and Moravia. Well-explained in English, topics include the origin of the Star of David, Jewish mysticism, the history of discrimination, and the creation of Prague's ghetto. Notice the eastern wall, with the Holy Ark containing the scroll of the Torah. The central case shows the silver ornamental Torah crowns that capped the scroll.

Spanish Synagogue (Španělská Synagóga)—Displays of Jewish history through the 18th, 19th, and tumultuous 20th centuries continue in this ornate, Moorish-style synagogue built in the 1800s. The upstairs is particularly intriguing, with circa-1900 photos of Josefov, an exhibit on the fascinating story of this museum and its relationship with the Nazi regime, and life in Terezín. The Winter Synagogue (also upstairs) shows a trove of silver—Kiddush cups, Hanukkah lamps, Sabbath candlesticks, Torah ornaments—gathered from countryside Jewish neighborhoods that were depopulated in the early 1940s, giving you a glimpse of the treasures the Nazis stole and stockpiled.

The New Town (Nové Město)

Enough of pretty, medieval Prague—let's leap into the modern era. The New Town, with Wenceslas Square as its focal point, is today's urban Prague. This part of the city offers bustling boulevards and interesting neighborhoods. The New Town is one of the best places to view Prague's remarkable Art Nouveau art and architecture, and to learn more about its recent communist past.

▲▲Wenceslas Square (Václavské Náměstí)

More a broad boulevard than a square (until recently, trams rattled up and down its park-like median strip), this city landmark is named for King Wenceslas—featured both on the 20-Kč coin and the equestrian statue that stands at the top of the boulevard. Wenceslas Square functions as a stage for modern Czech history: The creation of the Czechoslovak state was celebrated here in 1918; in 1968, the Soviets suppressed huge popular demonstrations at the square; and, in 1989, more than 300,000 Czechs and Slovaks converged here to claim their freedom.

⊘ Self-Guided Walk: Let's take a stroll down Prague's urban centerpiece.

• *Starting near the Wenceslas statue (Metro: Muzeum), look to the building crowning the head of the square.*

National Museum (Národní Muzeum): This museum—closed for renovation through 2014—stands grandly at the top

of Wenceslas Square. While its collection is dull (a skippable assemblage of Czech fossils and animals), the interior is richly decorated in the Czech Revival Neo-Renaissance style that heralded the 19th-century rebirth of the Czech nation. A grand purpose-built national museum made perfect sense in 19th-century Europe. As different political powers wrangled over territory, some groups would end up with countries and others would become "nations without states." During this tumultuous time, people did their best to prove their distinctive identities and affirm their right to exist. The light-colored patches in the museum's columns fill holes where Soviet bullets hit during the crackdown against the 1968 Prague Spring uprising. Masons—defying their communist bosses, who wanted the damage to be forgotten—showed their Czech spirit by intentionally mismatching their patches.

The nearby Metro stop (Muzeum) is the crossing point of two Metro lines built with Russian know-how in the 1970s.

• *To the left of the National Museum (as you face it) is a...*

PRAGUE

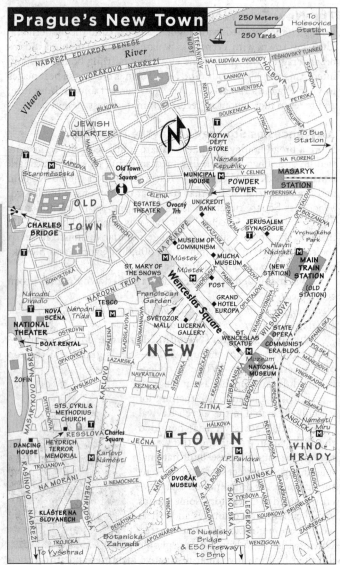

Prague's New Town

250 Meters
250 Yards

To Holesovice Station

Communist-Era Building: This structure housed the rubber-stamp Czechoslovak Parliament back when it voted with Moscow. A Socialist Realist statue showing triumphant workers still stands at its base. Between 1994 and 2008, this building was home to Radio Free Europe. After communism fell, RFE lost some of its funding and could no longer afford its Munich headquarters. In gratitude for its broadcasts—which had kept the people of

Eastern Europe in touch with real news—the Czech government offered this building to RFE for 1 Kč a year. But as RFE energetically beamed its American message deep into the Muslim world from here, it drew attention—and threats—from Al-Qaeda. So in 2009, RFE moved to a new fortress-like headquarters at an easier-to-defend locale farther from the center.

Today, this building is run by the National Museum and hosts special exhibits. However, the real draw here is to see and get the feel of a typical fancy government building from the days of Brezhnev—visitors are welcome just to stroll its halls. It costs 80 Kč to enter, but you're welcome to pop in and enjoy the Prager café for free—sitting in the same big leather chairs that communist big shots did a generation ago.

• *In front of the National Museum is the equestrian...*

St. Wenceslas Statue: Wenceslas (Václav) is the "good king" of Christmas-carol fame. He was the wise and benevolent 10th-

century Duke of Bohemia. A rare example of a well-educated and literate ruler, King Wenceslas I was credited by his people for Christianizing his nation and lifting the culture. He astutely allied the Czechs with Saxony, rather than Bavaria, giving the Czechs a vote when the Holy Roman Emperor was selected (and therefore more political clout).

After his murder in 929, Wenceslas was canonized as a saint. He became a symbol of Czech nationalism and statehood, and remains an icon of Czech unity whenever the nation has to rally. Legend has it that when the Czechs face their darkest hour, Wenceslas will come riding out of Blaník Mountain (east of Prague) with an army of knights to rescue the nation. In 1620, when Austria stripped the Czechs of their independence, many people went to Blaník Mountain to see whether it had opened up. They've done the same at other critical points in their history (in 1938, 1948, and 1968), but Wenceslas never emerged. Although the Czech Republic is now safely part of NATO and the European Union, Czechs remain realistic: If Wenceslas hasn't come out yet, the worst times must still lie ahead...

Study the statue. Wenceslas, on the horse, is surrounded by the four other Czech patron saints. Notice the focus on books. A small nation without great military power, the Czech Republic chose national heroes who enriched the culture by thinking, rather than fighting. This statue is a popular meeting point. Locals say, "I'll see you under the tail."

Take a moment at this spot to survey the square. You'll see businesspeople, families, dumpster divers, security guards, the Pepsi generation, and students. The vision for the square is a matter of controversy among locals. The city plans to turn it into a long, tree-lined pedestrian mall, with trams running up and down the middle (as they once did), and to hide the busy freeway underground (currently it separates the museum from the square).

This freeway originated as part of a 1970s plan by communists to connect the city with inner and outer freeway rings, while running the busiest thoroughfare into the heart of the city—but they only completed a small portion of the grandiose plan. After 1989, the project moved forward, thanks to the aid of EU funds and a boost in local car production, as manufacturers hoped to realize the dream of a car for every person. (This project is a good illustration of how decision makers have continued the trends and policies started under the communists rather than break from them.)

Prague's tunnel-to-tunnel inner circle (the city's "Big Dig") is scheduled to be completed by 2014, at an astronomical price. In keeping with the current era of austerity, parts of the tunnel not already begun have been eliminated from the plan, meaning that automobiles will continue to spit their fumes on the museum's facade (the most polluted spot in the city) for decades to come. Few Czechs enjoy strolling in this part of Prague—notice that locals here are decidedly on the run.

• *Begin walking down the square. Thirty yards below the big horse is a small garden with a low-key...*

Memorial: This commemorates victims of communism such

as Jan Palach. In 1969, a group of patriots decided that an act of self-immolation would stoke the fires of independence. Palach, a philosophy student who loved life—but wanted to live in freedom—set himself on fire on the steps of the National Museum for the cause of Czech independence. He died a few days later in a hospital ward. Czechs are keen on anniversaries, and huge demonstrations swept the city on the 20th anniversary of Palach's death. These protests led, 10 months later, to the overthrow of the Czech communist government in 1989.

This grand square is a gallery of modern architectural styles. As you wander downhill, notice the fun mix, all post-1850: Romantic Neo-Gothic, Neo-Renaissance, and Neo-Baroque from the 19th century; Art Nouveau from about 1900; ugly Functionalism from the mid-20th century (the "form follows function" and "ornamentation is a crime" answer to Art Nouveau); Stalin Gothic from the 1950s "communist epoch" (a good example is the Hotel Jalta building, halfway downhill on the right); and the glass-and-steel buildings of the 1970s.

• *Walk a couple of blocks downhill through the real people of Prague (not tourists) to Grand Hotel Evropa, with its dazzling yellow Art Nouveau exterior and plush café interior full of tourists. Stop for a moment to consider the events of...*

November of 1989: This huge square was filled every evening with more than 300,000 ecstatic Czechs and Slovaks who believed freedom was at hand. Assembled on the balcony of the building opposite Grand Hotel Evropa (look for the *Marks & Spencer* sign) were a priest, a rock star (famous for his unconventional style, which constantly unnerved the regime), Alexander Dubček (hero of the 1968 revolt), and Václav Havel (the charismatic playwright, newly released from prison, who was every freedom-loving Czech's Nelson Mandela). Through a sound system provided by the rock star, Havel's voice boomed over the gathered masses, announcing the resignation of the Politburo and the imminent freedom of the Republic of Czechoslovakia. Picture that cold November evening, with thousands of Czechs jingling their key chains in solidarity, chanting at the government, "It's time to go now!" (To quell this revolt, government tanks could have given it the Tiananmen Square treatment, which had spilled protesters' blood in China just six months earlier. Locals believe that the Soviet head of state, Mikhail Gorbachev, must have made a phone call recommending a nonviolent response.) For more on the events leading up to this climactic rally, see "The Velvet Revolution of 1989" sidebar, later.

• *Immediately opposite Grand Hotel Evropa is the Lucerna Gallery (use the entry marked* Pasáž Rokoko *and walk straight in).*

Lucerna Gallery: This grand mall retains some of its Art Deco glamour from the 1930s, with shops, theaters, a ballroom in the basement, and the fine Lucerna Café upstairs. You'll see a sculpture—called *Wenceslas Riding an Upside-Down Horse*—hanging like a swing from a glass dome. David Černý, who created the statue in 1999, is one of the Czech Republic's most original contemporary artists. Always aspiring to provoke controversy, Černý has painted a menacing Russian tank pink, attached crawling babies to the rocket-like Žižkov TV tower, defecated inside the

National Gallery to protest the policies of its director, and sunk a shark-like Saddam Hussein inside an aquarium. His art hoax *Entropa* was created to commemorate the Czech presidency of the European Union in 2009. But when it was unveiled in Brussels, it insulted many EU nations with its satirical symbolism (Bulgaria was represented by squat toilets, Germany consisted of twisted autobahns hinting at a swastika, and so on).

Inside the gallery, you'll find a **Ticketpro box office** (with a line on concerts and events, daily 9:30-18:00, 30 Kč fee), a lavish 1930s Prague cinema (under the upside-down horse, shows films in original language with Czech subtitles, 115 Kč), and the popular **Lucerna Music Bar** in the basement ('80s and '90s video parties, 100 Kč, from 21:00 on Fri and Sat, concerts on other nights).

Leave the mall from the side of the gallery, then cross busy Vodičkova street (with a handy tram stop) and enter **Světozor mall.** The 1930s glass window advertising Tesla, a defunct Czech radio manufacturer, lends a retro brightness to the place. Find the **World of Fruit Bar Světozor,** every local's favorite ice-cream joint. They also sell cakes, milkshakes, and "little breads"—delightful Czech-style open-face sandwiches. Ask at the counter for an English menu.

• *Walk under the Tesla sign to exit the mall, and head left into the peaceful...*

Franciscan Garden (Františkánská Zahrada): Its white benches and spreading rosebushes are a universe away from the fast beat of the city, which throbs behind the buildings that surround the garden. Its peacefulness reflects the purpose of its Franciscan origin. (If you need a WC, there's one just out the far side of the garden, and another in the tiny wine bar coming up on this walk.)

Back on Wenceslas Square, if you're in the mood for a mellow hippie teahouse, consider a break at the recommended **Dobrá Čajovna** ("Good Teahouse") near the bottom of the square (#14).

The bottom of Wenceslas Square is called **Můstek,** which means "Bridge"; a bridge used to cross a moat here, allowing entrance into the Old Town (you can still see the original Old Town entrance down in the Metro station).

• *Your Wenceslas Square walk ends here, but there's more to see. From the bottom of the square, you can either head right, to Prague's top Art Nouveau sights (described next); or left, toward the river and the National Theater (described later).*

Na Příkopě: Art Nouveau Prague

At the bottom of Wenceslas Square, the street running to the right is called Na Příkopě. Meaning "On the Moat," this busy boulevard follows the line of the Old Town wall, leading to one of the wall's former gates, the Powder Tower (the black tower spire in the

Art Nouveau

Prague is the best Art Nouveau town in Europe, with fun facades gracing streets all over the city. Art Nouveau, born  in Paris, is "nouveau" because it wasn't inspired by Rome. It's neo-nothing...a fresh answer to all the revival styles of the later 19th century and an organic response to the Eiffel Tower art of the Industrial Age. The style liberated the artist in each architect. Notice the unique curves and motifs expressing originality on each Art Nouveau facade. Artists such as Alfons Mucha believed that the style should apply to all facets of daily life. They designed everything from buildings and furniture to typefaces and cigarette packs.

Prague's three top Art Nouveau architects are Jan Koula, Josef Fanta, and Osvald Polivka (whose last name sounds like the Czech word for "soup"). Think "Cola, Fanta, and Soup"— easy to remember and a good way to impress your local friends.

Prague's Art Nouveau highlights include the facades lining the streets of the Jewish Quarter, the Jerusalem Synagogue, the Mucha window in St. Vitus Cathedral, and the Grand Hotel Evropa on Wenceslas Square. The top two sights for Art Nouveau fans are the Mucha Museum and the Municipal House.

distance). Along the way, it passes the Museum of Communism and two of Prague's best Art Nouveau sights: the Mucha Museum (featuring the work of my favorite Art Nouveau artist) and the Municipal House (with my favorite Art Nouveau interior anywhere). Seeing the interior of the UniCredit Bank building, also on Na Příkopě, will help you understand how the Art Nouveau movement came about.

City tour buses (see "Tours in Prague—Bus Tours," earlier) leave from along this street, which offers plenty of shopping temptations (such as these malls: Slovanský Dům at Na Příkopě 22 and Černá Růže at Na Příkopě 12, next door to Mosers, which has a crystal showroom upstairs).

• *Start strolling up Na Příkopě. Turn right at Panská to reach the...*

▲▲**Mucha Museum (Muchovo Museum)**—This is one of Europe's most enjoyable little museums. I find the art of Alfons Mucha (MOO-kah, 1860-1939) insistently likeable. See the crucifixion scene he painted as an eight-year-old boy. Read how this popular Czech artist's posters, filled with Czech symbols and

Mucha's *Slav Epic*

Alfons Mucha (1860-1939), born in the small Moravian town of Ivančice, made a hugely successful commercial career for himself in Paris and in the US as *the* Art Nouveau poster artist and illustrator. In Paris, Mucha conceived the idea of dedicating the second half of his life to a work that would edify his nation. Throughout history, bards in every culture have composed poems eulogizing the best moments of their tradition. Mucha would do the same for the Czechs and the Slavs, on a grand, epic scale...and on canvas.

Mucha convinced the Chicago industrialist Charles Crane to sponsor his project. Both men believed that the purpose of a truly patriotic work was to inspire human beings to understand one another better, thereby bringing humanity closer together. By 1912 Mucha finished the first of three paintings (each 25 by 20 feet) in the series. It was another 16 years before he completed the cycle of 20 enormous canvases known as the *Slav Epic*. The response of his fellow artists was lukewarm—in the experimental age of Picasso, Mucha's representational style and overt nationalism were out of fashion.

During World War II, the patriotic work was damaged while being hidden from the Nazis. After years of restoration, in 1963 the paintings were put on display in a castle in the town of Moravský Krumlov, near Mucha's birthplace.

Mucha had originally dedicated the *Slav Epic* to Prague, but the gift came with strings: Prague was to build a suitable structure in which to display the paintings. But rather than finding a good location and raising the necessary funds, Prague officials simply waited until—60 years after Mucha's death—the copyright on his work expired. Then they cited the dilapidated condition of the Krumlov castle as legal grounds to "temporarily relocate" the canvases to Prague's National Gallery. Following a series of highly publicized standoffs and court battles, in November of 2011 the *Slav Epic* was stripped from the walls of Moravský Krumlov's castle, rolled up, and taken to Prague's Veletržní Palace, where it will be exhibited in 2012 and 2013.

Cost and Hours: 250 Kč, Tue-Sun 10:00-18:00, closed Mon, tel. 224-301-122, www.ngprague.cz.

Getting There: Veletržní Palace (which houses the National Gallery's modern art collection) is located near Holešovice Station at Dukelských Hrdinů 47. Any of three trams will get you to Veletržní: You can take tram #17 from the Staroměstská Metro stop for four stops; or tram #12 from Malostranská for three stops; or tram #14 from Náměstí Republiky for three stops.

Viewing the Paintings: Allow two hours to appreciate the work.

Although Mucha's magnum opus continues to be scorned by many Czech intellectuals because of its overtly nationalistic theme, the *Slav Epic* rises above the typically shallow products of the politicized 19th century. A brilliant craftsman and designer, Mucha captures the viewer's attention with his strong composition and sense of color. Like any true artistic masterpiece, Mucha's work goes beyond the style of the time, beyond Art Nouveau, and beyond Slavic nationalism.

PRAGUE

Consider contemplating Mucha's canvases on three lev-

els. First, use the captions (or handouts, if available) to understand what the paintings are depicting. The great feast is the celebration of the Slavic pagan god; the zealous preacher is Jan Hus (the revolutionary Czech priest); and the subdued old man contemplating the dark horizon is the first Czech exile and great educator, John Amos Comenius. Red is the color of war, white is the color of peace, blue is the past, and orange is the future.

When you get tired of being told what's what, step back and figure out Mucha's intention. His technique will help you. The grand-scale background, which shows the historic events, is executed in egg-based tempera. Against that low-resolution foggy base, the figures painted in oil come sharply into focus: the terrified couple, the mother and child, the bearded sage with the young man, the face of the lady-in-waiting. The lucid detail tells the experience of these single, often-anonymous individuals, suggesting that the *Slav Epic* is not about the monumental depiction of a particular event, but about the fate of the individual against the backdrop of history. The entire weight of events is condensed into the expressions on their faces. In the scene of a print shop, the young man in the foreground is Mucha's self-portrait.

Finally, step even farther back and contemplate the painting as a work of an Impressionist or an abstract artist. The fusion of colors stands far beyond any particular meaning. Like the tones of a 19th-century symphony, Mucha's visual concert has the power to stir the deepest emotions.

expressing his people's ideals and aspirations, were patriotic banners that aroused the national spirit. And check out the photographs of his models (to get the most from his sessions with models, he photographed them from all angles). With the help of an abundant supply of sultry models, Mucha became a founding father of the Art Nouveau movement. Partly overseen by Mucha's grandson, the museum is two blocks off Wenceslas Square, and its collection is wonderfully displayed on one comfortable floor.

The included 30-minute video is definitely worthwhile (in English, generally at :15 and :45 past the hour—check the starting time); it describes the main project of Mucha's life—the *Slav Epic* (see sidebar).

Cost and Hours: 160 Kč, daily 10:00-18:00, good English descriptions, Panská 7. Tel. 224-233-355, www.mucha.cz.

• *Backtrack to Na Příkopě and turn right. At the corner of Na Příkopě and Nekázanka is the...*

▲**UniCredit Bank (Pre-Art Nouveau)**—Pop into this bank building to understand the origins of Art Nouveau. Climb up the stairs and sit in the main hall. The Neo-Renaissance UniCredit Bank building (formerly Živnostenská Banka, Prague's oldest banking institution) was, until the early 1990s, the only place in town to get hard currency or traveler's checks. Any Czech who traveled would sit here dreaming of upcoming adventures.

But let's go back not 20 years, but 100 years—to when cool air (created by ice that filled the vaults below) flowed out of the circa 1880s air-conditioning vents that flank the top of the staircase. You're surrounded by textbook Historicism. In the 19th century, Prague existed in the Viennese cultural realm, and this was it: a Neo-Renaissance celebration of the professions (identify the statues), with the coats of arms of cities in the Czech realm. Imagine a young Alfons Mucha or Gustav Klimt sitting in a lobby similar to this one—talented young artists surrounded by all this, with their deep-seated need to escape this conformity on steroids...to secede. In simple terms, that was what the Secessionist movement (born in Vienna, circa 1897, and kicking off the Art Nouveau era) was all about.

• *Continue one more block up Na Příkopě to the...*

▲▲**Municipal House (Obecní Dům)**—The Municipal House, which celebrated its centennial birthday in 2011, is the "pearl of Czech Art Nouveau." Stand in front and study the Homage to Prague mosaic on the building's striking facade. Featuring a goddess-like Praha presiding over a land of peace and high culture, the image stoked cultural pride and nationalist sentiment.

The building (1905-1911) is Neo-Baroque with a dusting of Art Nouveau. The cultural and artistic leaders who financed it wanted a ceremonial palace to reinforce self-awareness of the Czech nation.

Built under Catholic Habsburg rule, it was drenched in patriotic Czech themes to emphasize how the Protestant Czechs were a distinct culture. In 1918, Czechoslovakia's independence was declared from the building's balcony.

While the exterior is impressive, the highlight is inside—arguably Europe's finest Art Nouveau interior. The Municipal House features Prague's largest concert hall, a recommended Art Nouveau café (Kavárna Obecní Dům), and two other restaurants. While you can poke around its entrance halls (daily 10:00-18:00) or wander around the lobby of the concert hall, to really appreciate the building you must attend a concert or take a tour.

PRAGUE

Tours: Daily one-hour tours give you a guided look at all the sumptuous halls and banquet rooms (English-only, 280 Kč, usually 3/day, leaving between 11:00 and 17:00). Buy your ticket (and pay 55 Kč extra to take photos) from the ground-floor shop where tours depart. Tel. 222-002-101, www.obecnidum.cz.

Concerts: Performances are held regularly in the lavish Smetana Hall (see the schedule at www.obecnidum.cz/web/en/programme). Note that many concerts brag they are held in the Municipal House, but are performed in a smaller, less impressive hall in the same building.

Powder Tower—Next to the Municipal House, the big, black Powder Tower (not worth touring inside) was the Gothic gate of the town wall, built to house the city's gunpowder. The decoration on the tower is the best 15th-century sculpture in town. This is the only surviving bit of wall that was built to defend the city in the 1400s. Look at your city map and conceptualize medieval Prague's smart design. The city was encircled by the river and its wall (now a main street), which arced from a bend in the river. The only river crossing back then was the fortified Charles Bridge. The road from Vienna arrived at the foot of the Powder Tower—it was the city's formal front door. When Empress Maria Theresa was crowned the Queen of Bohemia here, she came down that road and through this gate. Go back 500 years and look up at the impressive welcoming committee, reminding all of the hierarchy of our mortal

existence: from artisans flanking Prague's coat of arms, up to a pair of Czech kings with seals of alliance of neighboring regions, and finally to angels heralding the heavenly zone with Saints Peter and Paul flanking Jesus.

• *OK, got it...let's go in. Pass through the tower to reach commercial and touristy Celetná Street, which leads directly to the Old Town Square (see page 76). Or consider a side-trip to visit another of Prague's Art Nouveau buildings, the...*

Jerusalem Synagogue (Jeruzalémské Synagóga)—This colorful synagogue, also known as the Jubilee Synagogue, is a fascinating combination of Moorish Renaissance and Viennese Art Nouveau styles. It was built from 1905 to 1906 in commemoration of the first 50 years of Franz Josef's liberal, relatively Jewish-friendly rule. Recently restored, still serving the Prague Jewish community, and sparsely visited, this is the most contemplative as well as visually stunning of Prague's synagogues.

Cost and Hours: 80 Kč, 200-Kč combo-ticket includes entry to Old-New Synagogue in the Jewish Quarter—see page 93, April-Oct Sun-Fri 13:00-17:00, closed Sat, closed in winter and on Jewish holidays, between Powder Tower and Main Train Station at Jeruzalémská 7, tel. 222-319-002, www.synagogue.cz/Jerusalem.

Národní Třída: Communist Prague

From Můstek at the bottom of Wenceslas Square, you can head west on Národní Třída (in the opposite direction from Na Příkopě and the Art Nouveau sights) for an interesting stroll through urban Prague to the National Theater and the Vltava River. But first, consider dropping into the Museum of Communism, a few steps down Na Příkopě (on the right).

▲▲Museum of Communism (Muzeum Komunismu)—This museum traces the story of communism in Prague: the origin, dream, reality, and nightmare; the cult of personality; and, finally, the Velvet Revolution—all thoughtfully described in English. Along the way, it gives a fascinating review of the Czech Republic's 40-year stint with Soviet economics, "in all its dreariness and puffed-up glory." You'll find propaganda posters, busts of communist All-Stars (Marx, Lenin, Stalin), and a photograph of the massive stone Stalin that overlooked Prague until 1962.

Slices of communist life are re-created here, from a bland store counter to a typical classroom (with textbooks using Russia's Cyrillic alphabet—no longer studied—and a poem on the chalkboard that extols the virtues of the tractor). Don't miss the Jan Palach exhibit and the 20-minute video (plays continuously, English subtitles) that shows how the Czech people chafed under the big Red yoke from 1969 through 1989.

Cost and Hours: 180 Kč, daily 9:00-21:00, Na Příkopě 10,

The Velvet Revolution of 1989

On the afternoon of November 17, 1989, 30,000 students gathered in Prague's New Town to commemorate the 50th anniversary of the suppression of student protests by the Nazis, which had led to the closing of Czech universities through the end of World War II. The 1989 demonstration—initially planned by the Communist Youth as a celebration of the communist victory over fascism—spontaneously turned into a protest *against* the communist regime. "You are just like the Nazis!" shouted the students. The demonstration was supposed to end in the National Cemetery at Vyšehrad (the hill just south of the New Town). But when the planned events concluded in Vyšehrad, the students, making history, decided to march on toward Wenceslas Square.

As they worked their way north along the Vltava River toward the New Town's main square, the students were careful to keep their demonstration peaceful. Any hint of violence, the demonstrators knew, would incite brutal police retaliation. Instead, as the evening went on, the absence of police became conspicuous. (In the 1980s, the police never missed a chance to participate in any demonstration...preferably outnumbering the demonstrators.) At about 20:00, as the students marched down this very stretch of street toward Wenceslas Square, three rows of policemen suddenly blocked the demonstration at the corner of Národní and Spálená streets. A few minutes later, military vehicles with fences on their bumpers (having crossed the bridge by the National Theater) appeared behind the marching students. This new set of cops compressed the demonstrators into the stretch of Národní Třída between Voršilská and Spálená. The end of Mikulandská street was also blocked, and policemen were hiding inside every house entry. The students were trapped.

At 21:30, the "Red Hats" (a special anti-riot commando force known for its brutality) arrived. The Red Hats lined up on both sides of this corridor. To get out, the trapped students had to run through the passageway as they were beaten from the left and right. Police trucks ferried captured students around the corner to the police headquarters (on Bartolomějská) for interrogation.

The next day, university students throughout Czechoslovakia decided to strike. Actors from theaters in Prague and Bratislava joined the student protest. Two days later, the students' parents—shocked by the attacks on their children—marched into Wenceslas Square. Sparked by the events of November 17, 1989, the wave of peaceful demonstrations ended later that year on December 29, with the election of Václav Havel as the president of a free Czechoslovakia.

above a McDonald's and next to a casino—Lenin is turning over in his Red Square mausoleum. Tel. 224-212-966, www.muzeum komunismu.cz.

Národní Třída and the Velvet Revolution—Národní Třída (National Street) is where you feel the pulse of the modern city. The

street, which connects Wenceslas Square with the National Theater and the river, is a busy thoroughfare running through the heart of urban Prague. In 1989, this unassuming boulevard played host to the first salvo of a Velvet Revolution that would topple the communist regime.

Make your way down Národní Třída until you hit the tram tracks (just beyond the Tesco department store). On the left, look for the photo of Bill Clinton playing saxophone, with Václav Havel on the side (this is the entrance to **Reduta,** Prague's best jazz club; next door are two recommended eateries, **Café Louvre** and **Le Patio**). Just beyond that, you'll come to a short corridor with white arches. Inside this arcade is a simple **memorial** to the hundreds of students injured here by the police in the Velvet Revolution, which took place on November 17, 1989. For the fascinating story, see the sidebar on previous page.

Along the Vltava River

I've listed these sights from north to south, beginning at the grand, Neo-Renaissance National Theater, which is five blocks south of the Charles Bridge and stands along the riverbank at the end of Národní Třída.

National Theater (Národní Divadlo)—Opened in 1883 with Smetana's opera *Libuše,* this theater was the first truly Czech venue in Prague. From the very start, it was nicknamed the "Cradle of Czech Culture." The build-

ing is a key symbol of the Czech national revival that began in the late 18th century. In 1800, "Prag" was predominantly German. The Industrial Revolution brought Czechs from the countryside into the city, their new urban identity defined by patriotic teachers and priests. By 1883, most of the city spoke Czech, and the opening of this theater represented the birth of the modern Czech nation. It remains an important national icon: The state annually pours more subsidies into this theater than into all of Czech film production. It's the most beautiful venue in town for opera and ballet, often with world-class singers (for more details on performances, see "Entertainment in Prague," later).

Next door (just inland, on Národní Třída) is the boxy, glassy facade of the **Nová Scéna.** This "New National Theater" building, dating from 1983 (the 100th anniversary of the original National Theater building), reflects the bold and stark communist aesthetic.

Across the street from the National Theater is the former haunt of Prague's intelligentsia, the recommended **Kavárna Slavia,** a Viennese-style coffeehouse that is fine for a meal or drink with a view of the river.

• Just south of the National Theater, in the Vltava you'll find...

Prague's Islands—From the National Theater, the Bridge of Legions (Most Legií) leads across the island called **Střelecký Ostrov.** Covered with chestnut trees, this island boasts Prague's best beach (on the sandy tip that points north to Charles Bridge). You might see a fisherman pulling out trout from a river that's now much cleaner than it used to be. Bring a swimsuit and take a dip just a stone's throw from Europe's most beloved bridge. In summer, the island hosts open-air movies (most in English or with English subtitles, nightly mid-July-early Sept at about 21:00, www.strelak.cz).

In the mood for boating instead of swimming? On the next island up, **Slovanský Ostrov,** you can rent a boat (40 Kč/hour for rowboats, 60 Kč/hour for paddleboats, bring a picture ID as deposit). A lazy hour paddling around Střelecký Ostrov—or just floating sleepily in the middle of the river surrounded by this great city's architectural splendor—is a delightful experience on a sunny day. It's cheap, easy fun (and it's good for you).

• A 10-minute walk (or one stop on tram #17) south from the National Theater, beyond the islands, is Jirásek Bridge (Jiráskův Most), where you'll find the...

Dancing House (Tančící Dům)—If ever a building could get your toes tapping, it would be this one, nicknamed "Fred and Ginger" by American architecture buffs. This metallic samba is the work of Frank Gehry (who designed the equally striking Guggenheim Museum in Bilbao, Spain, and Seattle's Experience Music Project). Eight-legged Ginger's wispy

dress and Fred's metal mesh head are easy to spot. Some Czechs prefer to think that the two "figures" represent the nation's greatest 20th-century heroes, Jozef Gabčík and Jan Kubiš (explained next).

The building's top-floor restaurant, **Céleste,** is a fine place for a fancy French meal. Whether you go up for lunch (reasonable, 12:00-14:30), a drink (16:00-18:00), or an expensive dinner, you'll be a louse in the Gehry haircut (tel. 221-984-160).

• *Two blocks up Resslova street is the Sts. Cyril and Methodius Church, which contains in its crypt the...*

▲National Memorial to the Heroes of the Heydrich Terror (Národní Památník Hrdinů Heydrichiády)—In 1942, WWII

paratroopers Jozef Gabčík and Jan Kubiš assassinated the SS second-in-command Reinhard Heydrich, who controlled the Nazi-occupied Czech lands and was one of the main architects of the Holocaust. In the weeks following his assassination, the two paratroopers hid, along with other freedom fighters, in the crypt of the Greek Orthodox Sts. Cyril and Methodius Church on Resslova street. Today, a modest exhibition in  the church's crypt retells their story, along with the history of the Czech resistance movement. Outside, notice the small memorial, including bullet holes, plaque, and flowers on the street. Around the corner is the entry into the museum and the crypt.

Cost and Hours: 75 Kč, Tue-Sun 9:00-17:00, closed Mon, 2 blocks up from the Dancing House at Resslova 9A, tel. 224-916-100, full history explained in small 25-Kč booklet.

• *Farther up Resslova street is...*

Charles Square (Karlovo Náměstí)—Prague's largest square is covered by lawns, trees, and statues of Czech writers. It's a quiet antidote to the bustling Wenceslas and Old Town squares. The Gothic New Town Hall at the top-left corner of the square has excellent views and labeled panoramic photographs that help you orient yourself. The little parlor across the street has some of the best gelato in town.

The Little Quarter (Malá Strana)

This charming neighborhood, huddled under the castle on the west bank of the river, is low on blockbuster sights but high on ambience. The most enjoyable approach from the Old Town is across the Charles Bridge. From the end of the bridge (TI in tower), Mostecká street leads two blocks up to the Little Quarter Square (Malostranské Náměstí) and the huge Church of St. Nicholas. But before you head up there, consider a detour to Kampa Island.

Between Charles Bridge and Little Quarter Square

Kampa Island—About one hundred yards before the tower at the castle end of the Charles Bridge, easy-to-miss stairs on the

left (watch for the small gap in the balustrade) lead down to the island, depositing you at the start of the island's long, skinny, tree-lined main square. The island (mostly created from the rubble of the Little Quarter, which was destroyed in a 1540 fire) features relaxing pubs, a breezy park, hippies, lovers, a fine contemporary art gallery, and river access. From the main square, Hroznová lane (on the right) leads to a bridge. The high-water mark at the end of the bridge dates from 1890. The **old water wheel** is the last survivor of many mills that once lined the canal here. Each mill had its own protective water spirit *(vodník)*. The padlocks adorning the bridge are the scourge of romantic spots throughout Europe these days, popular with not-very-creative Romeos who think that clinching a lock onto something (mill, bridge, whatever) proves their enduring love.

• *Fifty yards beyond the bridge (on the right, under the trees) is the...*

Lennon Wall (Lennonova Zeď)—While Lenin's ideas hung like a water-soaked trench coat upon the Czech people, rock

singer John Lennon's ideas gave many locals hope and a vision. When Lennon was killed in 1980, a large wall was spontaneously covered with memorial graffiti. Night after night, the police would paint over the "All You Need Is Love" and "Imagine" graffiti. And day after day, it would reappear. Until independence came in 1989, travelers, freedom lovers, and local hippies gathered here. Silly as it might seem, this wall is remembered as a place that gave hope to locals craving freedom. Even today, while the tension and danger associated with this wall are gone, people come here to imagine. *"John žije"* is Czech for "John lives."

• *From here, continue up to the Little Quarter Square.*

On or near Little Quarter Square

The focal point of this neighborhood, the Little Quarter Square (Malostranské Náměstí) is dominated by the huge Church of St.

PRAGUE

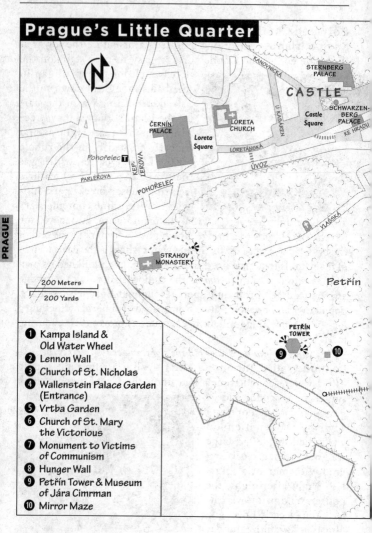

Prague's Little Quarter

1 Kampa Island & Old Water Wheel
2 Lennon Wall
3 Church of St. Nicholas
4 Wallenstein Palace Garden (Entrance)
5 Vrtba Garden
6 Church of St. Mary the Victorious
7 Monument to Victims of Communism
8 Hunger Wall
9 Petřín Tower & Museum of Jára Cimrman
10 Mirror Maze

Nicholas. Note that there's a handy Via Musica ticket office across from the church.

Church of St. Nicholas (Kostel Sv. Mikuláše)—When the Jesuits came to Prague, they found the perfect piece of real estate for their church and its associated school—right on Little Quarter Square. The church (built 1703-1760) is the best example of High Baroque in town. It's giddy with curves and illusions. The altar features a lavish gold-plated Nicholas, flanked by the two top Jesuits: the founder, St. Ignatius Loyola, and his missionary follower, St. Francis Xavier.

Climb up the **gallery** through the staircase in the left tran-

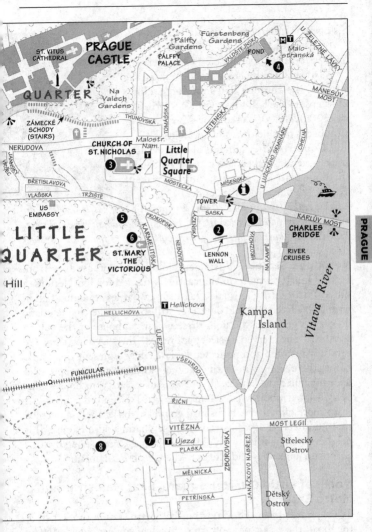

sept for a close-up look at a collection of large canvases and illu-
sionary frescoes by Karel Škréta, who is considered the greatest
Czech Baroque painter. Notice that at first glance the canvases
are utterly dark, but as sunbeams shine through the window,
various parts of the painting brighten up. Like a looking-glass,
the image reflects the light, creating a play of light and dark. This
painting technique represents a central Baroque belief: The world
is full of darkness, and the only hope that makes it come alive
emanates from God. The church walls seem to nearly fuse with
the sky, suggesting that happenings on earth are closely connected to heaven. In the center of the ceiling, find St. Nick with

his bishop's miter, on his way to heaven.

Cost and Hours: 60 Kč, church open daily 9:00-17:00, opens at 8:30 for prayer.

Tower Climb: For a good look at the city and the church's 250-foot dome, climb 215 steps up the bell tower (50 Kč, April-Oct daily 10:00-18:00, closed Nov-March, tower entrance is outside the right transept).

Concerts: The church is also an evening concert venue; tickets are usually on sale at the door (450 Kč, generally nightly except Tue, at 18:00, www.psalterium.cz).

• *From here, you can hike 10 minutes uphill to the castle (and 5 more minutes to the Strahov Monastery). For information on these sights, see "The Castle Quarter," later. If you're walking up to the castle, consider going via...*

Nerudova Street—This steep, cobbled street, leading from Little Quarter Square to the castle, is named for Jan Neruda, a gifted 19th-century journalist (and somewhat less-talented fiction writer). It's lined with old buildings still sporting the characteristic doorway signs (e.g., the lion, three violinists, house of the golden suns) that once served as street addresses. The surviving signs are carefully restored and protected by law. They represent the family name, the occupation, or the various passions of the people who once inhabited the houses. (If you were to replace your house number with a symbol, what would it be?) In 1777, in order to collect taxes more effectively, Habsburg empress Maria Theresa decreed that numbers be used instead of these quaint house names. This neighborhood is filled with old noble palaces, now generally used as foreign embassies and offices of the Czech Parliament.

North of Little Quarter Square, near Malostranská Metro Station

Twenty yards from the Malostranská Metro station (go left from the top of the escalator and turn right when you get outside), a few blocks north of Little Quarter Square, is a lovely palace and garden. If you want to reach Little Quarter Square from here, follow Valdštejnská street.

Wallenstein Palace Garden (Valdštejnská Palac Zahrada)—Of the neighborhood's many impressive palace gardens, this is by far the largest and most beautiful. The complex—consisting of a palace (generally closed) and the surrounding garden (generally open)—was commissioned during the Thirty Years' War by the Habsburg general and Czech nobleman Albrecht z Valdštejna (or, in German, Albrecht von Wallenstein). The inconspicuous entry to the palace's Wallenstein Garden is by

the Malostranská Metro station. The garden, renovated in the late 1990s, features a large pool surrounded by peacocks. The statues that line the central walkway (inspired by Greek mythology) were created by the Danish artist Adriaen de Vries—arguably the best Renaissance sculptor outside of Italy. Notice the elegant classical shapes, a sharp contrast to the chubbiness of the Baroque figures on the Charles Bridge and elsewhere in the city. The original statues were stolen by invading Swedish armies in 1648 and are still in Sweden; the present replicas were cast in the early 1900s.

Cost and Hours: Free, April-Oct daily 10:00-18:00, closed Nov-March.

South of Little Quarter Square

The following sights lie along Karmelitská street, which leads south (along the tram tracks) from Little Quarter Square.

Vrtba Garden (Vrtbovská Zahrada)—This terraced Baroque garden makes for an interesting comparison to the Renaissance garden at Wallenstein Palace Garden, described earlier.

Cost and Hours: 100 Kč, daily 10:00-18:00, just south of Little Quarter Square at Karmelitská 25, www.vrtbovska.cz.

• *Continue past the gardens to the...*

Church of St. Mary the Victorious (Kostel Panny Marie Vítězné)—This otherwise ordinary Carmelite church displays Prague's most worshipped treasure, the Infant of Prague (Pražské Jezulátko). Kneel at the banister in front of the tiny lost-in-gilded-Baroque altar, and find the prayer in your language (of the 13 in the folder). Brought to Czech lands during the Habsburg era by a Spanish noblewoman who came to marry a Czech nobleman, the Infant has become a focus of worship and miracle tales in Prague and Spanish-speaking countries. South Americans come on pilgrimage to Prague just to see this one statue. An exhibit upstairs shows tiny embroidered robes given to the Infant, including ones from Habsburg Empress Maria Theresa of Austria (1754) and the country of Vietnam (1958), as well as a video showing a nun lovingly dressing the doll-like sculpture.

Cost and Hours: Free, Mon-Sat 9:30-17:30, Sun 13:00-17:00, English-language Mass Sun at 12:00, Karmelitská 9, www.pragjesu.info.

• *Continue a few more blocks down Karmelitská to the south end of the Little Quarter (roughly where the street, now called Újezd, intersects with Vitézna). Here you find yourself at the base of...*

Jára Cimrman: Czech Genius

"I am such a complete atheist that I am afraid God will punish me." Such is the pithy wisdom of Jára Cimrman, the man overwhelmingly voted the "Greatest Czech of All Time" in a 2005 national poll. Who is Jára Cimrman? A philosopher? An explorer? An inventor? He is all these things, yes, and much more.

Born in the mid-19th century to a Czech tailor of Jewish descent and an Austrian actress, Cimrman (TSIM-mehr-mahn) studied in Vienna before starting off on his journeys around the world. He traversed the Atlantic in a steamboat he designed himself, taught drama to peasants in Peru, and drifted across the Arctic Sea on an iceberg. Other astounding feats soon followed. Cimrman was the first to come within 20 feet of the North Pole. He was the first to invent the lightbulb (unfortunately, Edison beat him to the patent office by five minutes). It was he who suggested to the Americans the idea for a Panama Canal, though, as usual, he was never credited. Indeed, Cimrman surreptitiously advised many of the world's greats: Eiffel on his tower, Einstein on his theories of relativity, Chekhov on his plays. ("You can't just have *two* sisters," Cimrman told the playwright. "How about three?") In 1886, long before the world knew of Sartre or Camus, Cimrman was writing tracts such as *The Essence of the Existence*, which would become the foundation for his philosophy of "Cimrmanism," also known as "nonexistentialism." (Its central premise: "Existence cannot not exist.")

This man of unmatched genius would have won the honor of "Greatest Czech of All Time" if not for the bureaucratic narrowmindedness of the poll's sponsors, who had a single objection to Cimrman's candidacy: He's not real. Jára Cimrman is the brainchild of two Czech humorists—Zdeněk Svěrák and Jiří Šebánek—who brought their patriotic Renaissance Man to life in 1967 in a satirical radio play. So, even though Cimrman handily won the initial balloting in January 2005, Czech TV officials—blatantly biased against his nonexistentialism—refused to let him into the final rounds of the competition.

How should we interpret the fact that the Czechs would rather choose a fictional character as their greatest countryman

▲Petřín Hill (Petřínské Sady)

This hill, topped by a replica of the Eiffel Tower, features several unusual sights.

Monument to Victims of Communism (Pomník Obětem Komunismu)—The sculptural figures of this moving memorial, representing victims of the totalitarian regime, gradually atrophy as they range up the hillside steps. They do not die but slowly disappear, one limb at a time. The statistics inscribed on the steps say it all: From 1948 until 1989, in Czechoslovakia alone, 205,486 people were imprisoned, 248 were executed, 4,500 died in prison, 327 were

over any of their flesh-and-blood national heroes—say, Charles IV (the 14th-century Holy Roman Emperor who established Prague as the cultural and intellectual capital of Europe), Jan Hus (the 15th-century religious reformer who challenged the legitimacy of the Catholic Church), Comenius (the 17th-century educator and writer, considered one of the fathers of modern education), or Martina Navrátilová (someone who plays a sport with bright green balls)? The more cynically inclined—many Czechs among them—might point out that the Czech people have largely stayed behind their mountains for the past millennia, with little interest in, or influence on, happenings elsewhere in the world. Perhaps Cimrman is so beloved because he embodies that most prickly of ironies: a Czech who was greater than all the world's greats, but who for some hiccup of chance has never been recognized for his achievements.

I like to think that the vote for Cimrman says something about the country's rousing enthusiasm for blowing raspberries in the face of authority. Throughout its history—from the times of the Czech kings who used crafty diplomacy to keep the German menace at bay, to the days of Jan Hus and his questioning of the very legitimacy of any ruler's power, to the flashes of anti-communist revolt that at last sparked the Velvet Revolution in 1989—the Czechs have maintained a healthy disrespect for those who would tell them what is best or how to live their lives. Other countries soberly choose their "Greatest" from musty tomes of history, but the Czechs won't play this silly game. Their vote for a fictional personage, says Cimrman's co-creator Svěrák, shows two things about the Czech nation: "That it is skeptical about those who are major figures and those who are supposedly the 'Greatest.' And that the only certainty that has saved the nation many times throughout history is its humor."

Cimrman would agree. A man of greatness, he was always a bit skeptical of those who saw themselves as great, or who marched forward under the banner of greatness. As Cimrman liked to say, "There are moments when optimists should be shot."

shot attempting to cross the border, and 170,938 left the country.
• *To the left of the monument is the...*
Hunger Wall (Hladová Zed')—This medieval defense wall was Charles IV's 14th-century equivalent of FDR's work-for-food projects.

• *On the right (50 yards away) is the base of a handy **funicular**—hop on to reach Petřín Tower (uses tram/Metro ticket, runs daily every 10-15 minutes from 8:00–22:00).*
Summit and Tower—The summit of Petřín Hill is considered the best place in Prague to take your date for a romantic city view. Built

for an exhibition in 1891, the 200-foot-tall **Petřín Tower** is one-fifth the height of its Parisian big brother, which was built two years earlier. But, thanks to this hill, the top of the tower sits at the same elevation as the real Eiffel Tower. Climbing the 400 steps rewards you with amazing views of the city. Czech wives drag their men to Petřín Hill each May Day to reaffirm their love with a kiss under a blooming sour-cherry tree.

• *In the tower's basement is the...*

Museum of Jára Cimrman (Muzeum Járy Cimrmana)—The museum, the funniest sight in Prague, traces the life of the fictional Jára Cimrman, the famously popular Czech antihero. Pictures and English descriptions of the thinker's overlooked inventions are featured. For more on the enigmatic Cimrman, see the sidebar on the previous page (my thanks to Victor Chen for writing this "biography").

Cost and Hours: 100 Kč includes tower and Cimrman museum, daily 10:00-22:00; the mirror maze next door is nothing special, but fun to wander through quickly since you're already here—50 Kč, daily 10:00-22:00.

The Castle Quarter (Hradčany)

Looming above Prague, dominating its skyline, is the Castle Quarter. Prague Castle and its surrounding sights are packed with Czech history, as well as with tourists. In addition to the castle, I enjoy visiting the nearby Strahov Monastery—which has a fascinating old library and beautiful views over all of Prague.

Castle Square (Hradčanské Náměstí)—right in front of the castle gates—is at the center of this neighborhood. Stretching along the promontory away from the castle is a regal neighborhood that ends at the Strahov Monastery. Above the castle are the Royal Gardens, and below the castle are more gardens and lanes leading down to the Little Quarter.

Visit the castle early or late to minimize crowds. If you plan to see both the castle and the monastery, start with the castle if you can get there early. For an afternoon visit, begin at the monastery, then hike down to the castle.

Getting to Prague Castle

If you're not up for a hike, the tram offers a sweat-free ride up to the castle. Taxis are expensive, as they have to go the long way round (200 Kč).

By Foot: Begin in the Little Quarter, just across Charles

Bridge from the Old Town. Hikers can follow the main cobbled road (Mostecká) from Charles Bridge to Little Quarter Square, marked by the huge, green-domed Church of St. Nicholas. (The nearest Metro stop is Malostranská, from which Valdštejnská street leads down to Little Quarter Square.) From Little Quarter Square, hike uphill along Nerudova street (described earlier). After about 10 minutes, a steep lane on the right leads to the castle. (If you continue straight, Nerudova becomes Úvoz and climbs to the Strahov Monastery.)

By Tram: Tram #22 takes you up to the castle. While you can catch the tram in various places, these three stops are particularly convenient: the Národní Třída Metro stop (between Wenceslas Square and the National Theater in the New Town); in front of the National Theater (Národní Divadlo, on the riverbank in the New Town); and at Malostranská (the Metro stop in the Little Quarter).

Which Tram Stop for the Castle? After rattling up the hill, the tram makes three stops near the castle.

The first stop, **Královský Letohrádek,** allows a scenic but slow approach through the Royal Gardens.

For the quickest commute to the castle, stay on the tram one more stop to get off at **Pražský Hrad,** then simply walk along U Prašného Mostu over the bridge into the castle.

If you'd like to start with the Strahov Monastery, stay on the tram for two more stops—passing the Brusnice stop—to the **Pohořelec** stop. Tour the monastery, then hike down to the castle.

▲▲Prague Castle (Pražský Hrad)

For more than a thousand years, Czech leaders have ruled from

Prague Castle. Today, Prague's Castle is, by some measures, the biggest on earth.

Cost: Admission to the grounds is free, but you need a ticket to enter the sights. Choose the short-tour ticket (250 Kč), which covers the highlights: St. Vitus Cathedral (entry to the vestibule is free, but to go farther requires a ticket), the Old Royal Palace, the Basilica of St. George, and the Golden Lane. Buy tickets in the palace or at the ticket offices on the two castle courtyards; look for the green *i*. Hang on to your ticket; you must present it at each sight. The comprehensive long-tour ticket (350 Kč) includes a few additional sights that aren't worth visiting.

Hours: Castle sights are open daily April-Oct 9:00-18:00, Nov-March 9:00-16:00, last entry 15 minutes before closing;

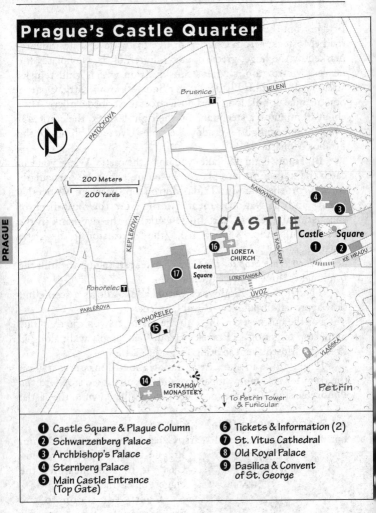

Prague's Castle Quarter

1 Castle Square & Plague Column
2 Schwarzenberg Palace
3 Archbishop's Palace
4 Sternberg Palace
5 Main Castle Entrance (Top Gate)
6 Tickets & Information (2)
7 St. Vitus Cathedral
8 Old Royal Palace
9 Basilica & Convent of St. George

grounds are open daily 5:00-24:00. St. Vitus Cathedral is closed Sunday mornings for Mass. Be warned that the cathedral can be closed unexpectedly due to special services—consider calling ahead to confirm (tel. 224-373-368 or 224-372-434).

Tours: Hour-long tours in English depart from the main ticket office near the cathedral entrance about three times a day, but they cover only the cathedral and Old Royal Palace (100 Kč plus entry ticket, tel. 224-373-368). You can rent an **audioguide** at the main desk. It's perfectly shareable if you have a cheek-to-cheek partner and not much money. The audioguide also entitles you to priority entrance at the cathedral—when the line in front of the entrance is long, walk to the exit door on the right and show the

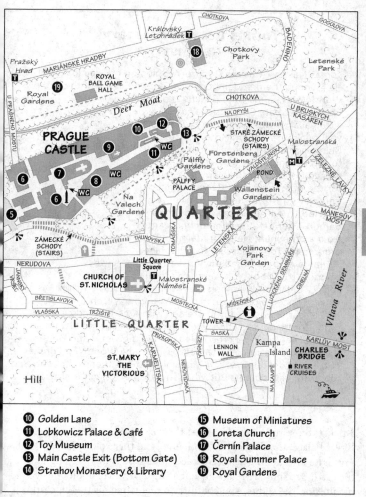

10 Golden Lane
11 Lobkowicz Palace & Café
12 Toy Museum
13 Main Castle Exit (Bottom Gate)
14 Strahov Monastery & Library

15 Museum of Miniatures
16 Loreta Church
17 Černín Palace
18 Royal Summer Palace
19 Royal Gardens

audioguide to the guard to be let in.

Crowd-Beating Tips: Huge throngs of tourists turn the grounds into a sea of people during peak times (9:30-12:30). The small, free entrance area in St. Vitus Cathedral is the most crowded part of the castle complex. If you're visiting in the morning, be at the cathedral entrance promptly at 9:00, when the doors open. For 10 minutes you'll have the sacred space to yourself (after about 9:15, tour guides cram unwieldy groups into the free entrance area, forming a noisy human traffic jam). I'd avoid the castle entirely in mid-morning.

Even if you do hit crowds, keep in mind that most groups stick to the free areas. For fewer crowds, head for the sights that require

PRAGUE

Tomáš Garrigue Masaryk
(1850-1937)

Tomáš Masaryk was the George Washington of Czechoslovakia. He founded the first democracy in Eastern Europe at the end of World War I, uniting the Czechs and the Slovaks to create Czechoslovakia.

Masaryk was born into a poor servant family in southern Moravia. After finishing high school, the village boy set off to attend university in Vienna. Masaryk earned his Ph.D. in sociology just in time for the opening of the Czech-language university in Prague. By then, he was married to an American music student named Charlotta Garrigue, who came from a prominent New York family. (The progressive Tomáš actually took her family name as part of his own.) Charlotta opened the doors of America's high society to Masaryk. Among the American friends he made was a young Princeton professor named Woodrow Wilson.

Masaryk was greatly impressed with America, and his admiration for its democratic system became the core of his gradually evolving political creed. He traveled the world and went to Vienna to serve in the parliament. By the time World War I broke out, in 1914, Masaryk was 64 years old and—his friends thought—ready for retirement. But while most other Czech politicians

a ticket: St. Vitus Cathedral (past the free entrance area), the Old Royal Palace, the Basilica of St. George, and the Golden Lane.

Late afternoon is least crowded; tour groups are napping and the castle grounds are relatively uncrowded. If you're not interested in entering the sights, you could try a nighttime visit—the castle grounds are free, safe, peaceful, floodlit, and open late (see www.hrad.cz for more information).

Eateries: The castle complex has several forgettable cafés scattered within it, but good eateries are nearby: between the castle and Strahov Monastery, and also near the castle-complex exit (see map on page 160, with listings on page 162). I like the scenic, creative café at Lobkowicz Palace (see page 131).

Sightseeing Plan: Begin at Castle Square, then tour St. Vitus Cathedral, the Old Royal Palace, the Basilica of St. George, the Golden Lane, and Lobkowicz Palace (a non-castle sight, requiring a separate admission fee, at the bottom of the castle complex). Note that if you're interested in Strahov Monastery and Loreto Church, which sit above the castle, the most efficient plan is to

stayed in Prague and supported the Habsburg Empire, Masaryk went abroad in protest and formed a highly original plan: to create an independent, democratic republic of Czechs and Slovaks. Masaryk and his supporters recruited an army of 100,000 Czech and Slovak soldiers who were willing to fight with the Allies against the Habsburgs, establishing a strong case to put on his friend Woodrow Wilson's Oval Office desk.

On the morning of October 28, 1918, news of the unofficial capitulation of the Habsburgs reached Prague. Local supporters of Masaryk's idea quickly took control of the city and proclaimed the free republic. As the people of Prague tore down double-headed eagles (a symbol of the Habsburgs), the country of Czechoslovakia was born.

On November 11, 1918, four years after he had left the country as a political unknown, Masaryk arrived in Prague as the greatest Czech hero since the revolutionary priest Jan Hus. The dignified old man rode through the masses of cheering Czechs on a white horse. He told the jubilant crowd, "Now go home—the work has only started." Throughout the 1920s and 1930s, Masaryk was Europe's most vocal defender of democratic ideals against the rising tide of totalitarian ideologies.

In 2001, the US government honored Masaryk's dedication to democracy by erecting a monument to him in Washington, DC. He is one of only three foreign leaders (along with Gandhi and Churchill) to have a statue in the American capital.

begin at the monastery (Pohořelec tram stop) and work your way downhill through the castle sights. However, if you're rushing to reach the castle by 9:00 (to avoid crowds), it may be worth backtracking uphill to Strahov and Loreto later.

Castle Square (Hradčanské Náměstí)

This is the central square of the Castle Quarter. Enjoy the awesome city view and the two entertaining bands that play regularly

at the gate. (If the Prague Castle Orchestra is playing, say hello to friendly, mustachioed Josef, and consider getting the group's terrific CD.) The recommended **Espresso Kajetánka** café, with dramatic city views, hides a few steps down (immediately to the right as you face the castle). From the café, stairs lead down to the

Little Quarter.

Castle Square was the focal point of medieval power—the king, the most powerful noblemen, and the archbishop lived here. Look uphill from the gate. The Renaissance **Schwarzenberg Palace** (Svancenberský Palác, on the left, with the big, envelope-like rectangles scratched on the wall) was where the noble Rožmberk family "humbly" stayed when they were in town visiting from their Český Krumlov estates. The Schwarzenberg family inherited the Krumlov estates and aristocratic prominence in Bohemia, and stayed in the palace until the 20th century. The palace now houses the National Gallery's collection of Czech Baroque paintings, displayed in recently restored rooms that have great views of the city (150 Kč, Tue-Sun 10:00-18:00, cheaper after 16:00, closed Mon, www.ngprague.cz/en).

The archbishop still lives in the yellow Rococo **palace** across the square (with the three white goose necks in the red field—the coat of arms of Prague's archbishops).

Through the portal on the left-hand side of the palace, a lane leads to the **Sternberg Palace** (Šternberský Palác), filled with the National Gallery's collection of European paintings—including minor works by Albrecht Dürer, Peter Paul Rubens, Rembrandt, and El Greco (150 Kč, Tue-Sun 10:00-18:00, closed Mon, www .ngprague.cz/en).

The black Baroque sculpture in the middle of the square is a **plague column.** Erected as a token of gratitude to the saints who saved the population from the epidemic, these columns are an integral part of the main square of many Habsburg towns.

The statue marked *TGM* honors **Tomáš Garrigue Masaryk** (1850-1937), a university prof and a pal of Woodrow Wilson. At the end of World War I, Masaryk united the Czechs and the Slovaks into one nation and became its first president (see sidebar).

Castle Gate and Courtyards

Standing in the square, survey the castle—the tip of a 1,500-foot-long series of courtyards, churches, and palaces. The guard changes on the hour from 5:00-23:00 at every gate: top, bottom, and side. The most ceremony and music occurs at noon at the top gate.

Walk under the fighting giants, under an arch, through the passageway, and into the courtyard. The modern green awning with the golden-winged cat (just to the right of the fountain) marks the offices of the Czech president, who is elected by the

parliament rather than by popular vote and serves more as a figurehead than a power broker. The current president is Václav Klaus. His consistent politics have brought him popularity from like-minded Czechs, but bitter resentment from those who see him as incapable of considering points of view other than his own. Outside the Czech Republic, Klaus is known for his unconstructive criticism of the European Union and denunciation of the campaign against global warming (the reality of which he denies).

• As you walk through another passageway, you'll find yourself facing...

▲▲▲St. Vitus Cathedral (Katedrála Sv. Víta)

The Roman Catholic cathedral symbolizes the Czech spirit—it contains the tombs and relics of the most important local saints and kings, including the first three Habsburg kings.

❷ Self-Guided Tour: Before entering, check out the facade. What's up with the guys in suits carved beneath the big, round window? They're the architects and builders who finished the church. Started in 1344, construction was stalled by wars and plagues. But, fueled by the 19th-century rise of Czech nationalism, Prague's top church was finished in 1929 for the 1,000th anniversary of the death of St. Wenceslas. While it looks all Gothic, it's actually two distinct halves: the original 14th-century Gothic area around the high altar and the modern Neo-Gothic nave. For 400 years, a temporary wall sealed off the functional, yet unfinished, cathedral.

• Enter the cathedral through the door on the left, make your way through the crowds in the vestibule, show your ticket (at the left of the roped-off area), and find the third window just beyond the ticket check.

Mucha Stained-Glass Window: This masterful 1931 Art Nouveau window was designed by Czech artist Alfons Mucha and executed by a stained-glass craftsman (if you like this, you'll love the Mucha Museum in the New Town and Mucha's masterpiece, the *Slav Epic*—described on pages 101 and 102).

Notice Mucha's stirring nationalism: Methodius and Cyril, widely considered the fathers of Slavic-style Christianity, are top and center. Cyril—the monk in black holding the Bible—brought the word of God to the Slavs. They had no written language in the ninth century, so he designed the necessary alphabet (Glagolitic, which later developed into Cyrillic). Methodius, the bishop, is shown baptizing a mythic, lanky, long-haired Czech man—a reminder of how he brought Christianity to the Czech people. Scenes from the lives of Cyril (on the left) and Methodius (on the right) bookend the stirring and epic Slavic story. In the center are a kneeling boy and a prophesying elder—

that's young St. Wenceslas and his grandmother, St. Ludmila. In addition to being specific historical figures, these characters are also symbolic: The old woman, with closed eyes, stands for the past and memory; the young boy, with a penetrating stare, represents the hope and future of a nation. Notice how master designer Mucha draws your attention to these two figures through the use of colors—the dark blue on the outside gradually turns into green, then yellow, and finally the gold of the woman and the crimson of the boy in the center. In Mucha's color language, blue stands for the past, gold for the mythic, and red for the future. Besides all the meaning, Mucha's art is simply a joy to behold. (And on the bottom, the tasteful little ad for *Banka Slavie*, which paid for the work, is hardly noticeable.)

Royal Mausoleum: Continue circulating around the church. A slight incline near the middle takes you into the older, 14th-century section (you will need to show your ticket here). The big royal tomb (within the black iron fence) contains the remains of the first Habsburgs to rule Bohemia, including Ferdinand I, his wife Anne, and Maximilian II. The tomb dates from 1590, when Prague was a major Habsburg city.

Relief of Prague: As you walk around the high altar (Neo-Gothic, circa 1900), study the fascinating carved-wood relief of Prague. It depicts the action after the Battle of White Mountain, when the Protestant King Frederic escaped over the Charles Bridge (before it had any statues). Carved in 1630, 10 years after the famous event occurred, the relief gives you a peek at Prague in 1620, stretching from the Týn Church to the cathedral (half-built at that time, up to where you are now). Notice that back then, the Týn Church was Hussite, so the centerpiece of its facade is not the Virgin Mary, but a chalice, a symbol of Jan Hus' ideals. The old city walls—now replaced by the main streets of the city—stand strong. The Jewish Quarter (the slummy, muddy zone along the riverside below the bridge on the left) fills land no one else wanted.

Apse: Circling around the high altar, you pass graves of bishops, including the tomb of St. Vitus (with a rooster at his feet). The stone sarcophagi contain kings from the Přemysl dynasty (12th-14th centuries). Locals claim the gigantic, shiny tomb of St. John of Nepomuk has more than a ton of silver (for more on St. John of Nepomuk, see page 88). About three yards after the tomb (above on the right) is a finely carved wood relief, circa 1630. It gives a Counter-Reformation spin on the Wars of Religion, showing the "barbaric" Protestant nobles destroying the Catholic icons in the cathedral after their short-lived victory.

Ahead on the left, look up at the royal oratory, a box supported by busy late-Gothic vine-like ribs. This is where the king would go to attend Mass in his jammies (an elevated corridor connected his private apartment with his own altar-side box pew).

• *From here, walk 25 paces and look left through the crowds and door to see the richly decorated chapel containing the tomb of St. Wenceslas. The best views are around the corner, ahead and to the left.*

Wenceslas Chapel: A fancy roped-off chapel (right transept) houses the tomb of St. Wenceslas, surrounded by walls encrusted with precious and semiprecious stones. (Lead us not into temptation.) The scene evokes heavenly Jerusalem to anyone entering with a 14th-century mindset. Above are circa-1590 frescoes showing scenes of the saint's life (for more on Wenceslas, see page 97) and a locked door leading to the crown jewels. Get as close as you can. Notice the Tupperware-toned stained-glass windows from the 1950s. The Czech kings used to be crowned right here in front of the coffin, draped in red. You can view the chapel from either door (if the door facing the nave is crowded, duck around to the left to find a door that is most likely open).

Back Outside the Cathedral: Leaving the cathedral, turn left (past the clean and free public WC). The **obelisk** was erected in 1928—a single piece of granite celebrating the 10th anniversary of the establishment of Czechoslovakia and commemorating the soldiers who fought for its independence. It was originally much taller, but broke in transit—an inauspicious start for a nation destined to last only 70 years. Up in the fat, green tower of the cathedral is the Czech Republic's biggest bell, nicknamed "Zikmund." In June 2002, it cracked, and two months later, the worst flood in recorded history hit the city—the locals saw this as a sign. As a nation sandwiched between great powers, Czechs are deeply superstitious when

PRAGUE

it comes to the tides of history. Often feeling unable to influence their own destiny, they helplessly look at events as we might look at the weather and other natural phenomena—trying to figure out what fate has in store for them next. You can view the bell as you climb up the 287 steps of the **tower** to the observation deck at the top (150 Kč, daily 10:00-18:30, until 16:30 in winter, enter near sculpture of St. George).

Find the 14th-century **mosaic** of the Last Judgment outside on the right transept (above the church's "golden gate"). It was commissioned in the Italian style by King Charles IV, who, in 1370 was modern, cosmopolitan, and ahead of his time. Jesus oversees the action, as some go to heaven and some go to hell. The Czech king and queen kneel directly beneath Jesus and six patron saints. On coronation day, they would walk under this arch, a reminder to them (and their subjects) that even those holding great power are not above God's judgment. The royal crown and national jewels are kept in a chamber (see the grilled windows) above this entryway, which was the cathedral's main entry for centuries while the church remained uncompleted.

• *Across the square and 20 yards to the right, a door leads into the Old Royal Palace (in the lobby, there's a WC with a window shared by the men's and women's sections—meet your partner to enjoy the view).*

Old Royal Palace (Starý Královský Palác)

Starting in the 12th century, this was the seat of the Bohemian princes. While extensively rebuilt, the **large hall** is late Gothic, designed as a multipurpose hall for the old nobility. It was big enough for jousts—even the staircase (which you'll use as you exit) was designed to let a mounted soldier gallop in. It was filled with market stalls, giving nobles a chance to shop without going into town. In the 1400s, the nobility met here to elect their king. The tradition  survived until modern times, as the parliament crowded into this room into the late 1990s to elect the president of Czechoslovakia, and later, the Czech Republic (more recently, elections have happened in another, far more lavish hall in the castle). Look up at the flower-shaped, vaulted ceiling.

On your immediate right, enter the two small Renaissance rooms known as the **"Czech Office."** From these rooms (empty today except for their 17th-century porcelain heaters), two governors used to oversee the Czech lands for the Habsburgs in Vienna. In 1618, angry Czech Protestant nobles poured into these rooms and threw the two Catholic governors out the window. An old law actually permits this act—called defenestration—which usually targets bad politicians. Old prints on the wall show the second of Prague's many defenestrations. The two governors landed—fittingly—in a pile of horse manure. Even though they suffered only broken arms and bruised egos, this event kicked off the huge and lengthy Thirty Years' War.

Look down on the chapel from the end, and go out on the balcony for a sweeping view of Prague. Is that Paris' Eiffel Tower in the distance? No, it's Petřín Tower (described earlier), a fine place for a relaxing day at the park, offering sweeping views over Prague.

As you reenter the main hall, head for the door immediately opposite. It opens into a room with a fine Gothic ceiling, a crimson throne, and benches for the nobility who once served as the high court. Notice the balcony on the left where scribes recorded the proceedings (without needing to mix with the aristocrats). The portraits on the walls depict Habsburg rulers (including Maria Theresa), and the display case on the right contains replicas of the Czech crown jewels. The originals are locked up inside the cathedral.

Return to the main hall; the next door to your right is the exit. As you leave, pause at the door to consider the subtle yet racy little Renaissance knocker. Go ahead—play with it for a little sex in the palace (be gentle).

• *Across from the palace exit is the...*

Basilica and Convent of St. George (Bazilika Sv. Jiří)

Step into the beautiful-in-its-simplicity Basilica of St. George to see Prague's best-preserved Romanesque church and the burial

place of Czech royalty. Notice the characteristic double windows on the gallery, as well as the walls made of limestone (the bedrock underlying Prague). In those early years, building techniques were not yet advanced, and the ceiling is made of wood, rather than arched with stone. St. Wenceslas' grandmother, St. Ludmila, who established this first Bohemian convent, was reburied

here in 973. Her stone tomb is in the space just to the right of the altar. Look for the restored Gothic fresco (from the 12th century) depicting this cultured woman (under the arch, to the right of the altar space). The St. John of Nepomuk chapel (through which you exit the church) comes with scary-looking bones under the altar.

(These are replicas—neither St. John's nor real.)
• *Continue walking downhill through the castle grounds. The next street on the left leads to the popular ...*

Golden Lane (Zlatá Ulička)

The tiny old buildings of this picturesque street originally housed castle servants, and perhaps goldsmiths. Well-written English texts explain the history of the lane and its cannon towers, which served as prisons. The houses themselves were occupied until World War II—Franz Kafka lived briefly at #22. These days, the dwellings are filled with a mix of shops and reconstructions portraying medieval life in the lane, including a pub and a goldsmith's workshop. There's a deli/bistro at the top end. The street is jammed during the day with tourists, but in the morning (before 9:00) and at night (after 18:00 in summer, 16:00 in winter), the tiny street is empty and romantic. Exit the lane through a corridor at the last house (#12).

More Castle-Area Sights

Extend your visit by dropping by a nobleman's palace and a toy museum with an entire floor devoted to the Barbie doll. Each sight requires a separate admission ticket; they're not included in any castle tickets.

▲▲**Lobkowicz Palace (Lobkowiczký Palác)**—This palace, at the bottom of the castle complex, displays the private collection of a prominent Czech noble family, including paintings, ceramics, and musical scores. The Lobkowiczes' property was confiscated twice in the 20th century: first by the Nazis at the beginning of World War II, and then by the communists in 1948. In 1990, William Lobkowicz, then a Boston investment banker, returned to Czechoslovakia to fight a legal battle to reclaim his family's property and, eventually, to restore the castles and palaces to their former state.

A conscientious host, William himself narrates the delightful, included audioguide. As you pass by the portraits of his ancestors, listen to their stories, including that of Polyxena, whose determination saved the two Catholic governors defenestrated next door (according to family legend, she hid the bruised officials under the folds of her skirt). The museum's highlights are Pieter Bruegel the Elder's magnificently preserved *Haymaking*, from 1565, one of the earliest entirely secular landscape paintings in Europe (showing an idyllic and almost heroic connection between peasants and nature), along with the manuscript of Beethoven's *Heroica* (dedicated to his sponsor, Prince Lobkowicz), displayed near Mozart's reorchestration of Handel's *Messiah*. While the National Gallery may seem a more logical choice for the art enthusiast, the obvious care that went into creating this museum, the collection's variety, and the personal insight that it opens into the past and present of Czech nobility make the Lobkowicz worth an hour of your time.

Cost and Hours: 275 Kč, includes audioguide, daily 10:00-18:00, last entry one hour before closing, tel. 233-312-925, www.lobkowicz.cz.

Eating: The Lobkowicz Palace Café by the exit has a creative cosmopolitan menu and stunning panoramic views of the city (daily 10:00-18:00). If a charming young man is selling ice cream out front, it may be William's son, Will.

Toy Museum (Muzeum Hraček)—Across the street from Lobkowicz Palace, a courtyard and a long wooden staircase lead to two entertaining floors of old toys and dolls, thoughtfully described in English. You'll see a century of teddy bears, some 19th-century model train sets, old Christmas decor, and an incredible Barbie collection (the entire top floor). Find the buxom 1959 first edition, and you'll understand why these capitalistic sirens of material discontent weren't allowed here until 1989.

Cost and Hours: 70 Kč, 120 Kč family ticket, daily 9:30-17:30, WC next to entrance.

Leaving the Castle Complex

Tourists squirt slowly through a fortified door at the bottom end of the castle. From there, you can head to the nearest Metro/tram station, the Strahov Monastery, the Little Quarter, or Castle Square.

To the Malostranská Metro/Tram Station: You can follow the steep lane directly back to the riverbank...or turn right about halfway down the steps to visit the Fürstenberg Gardens, with 3,500 flowering plants and 2,200 rose bushes (80 Kč, April-Oct daily from 10:00 until one hour before sunset). For a gentler descent, start heading down the steep lane. About 40 yards below the castle exit, a gate on the left leads you through a scenic vineyard and past the recommended Villa Richter restaurants to the station.

To the Strahov Monastery: As the monastery sits above the castle complex, you could backtrack uphill through the grounds to reach it. For an easier (but more time-consuming) approach, you can follow directions to the Malostranská Metro/tram station (above), then catch the tram back up to the Pohořelec stop.

To the Little Quarter or Castle Square (and Monastery): As you leave the castle gate, take a hard right and stroll through the long, delightful park. Along the way, notice the Modernist layout of the Na Valech Gardens, designed by the 1920s court architect, Jože Plečnik of Slovenia (for more on this great Slovene, see page 742). Halfway through the long park is a viewpoint overlooking the terraced Pálffy Gardens (80 Kč, April-Oct daily 10:00-18:00, closed Nov-March). You can zigzag down through these gardens into the Little Quarter. Or, if you want to walk to Castle Square, continue uphill along the castle wall and through the garden to the square. You can hike up to the monastery from here.

Strahov Monastery and Nearby

Twin Baroque domes high above the castle mark the Strahov Monastery. It's best reached from the Pohořelec stop on tram #22 (from the stop, follow the tram tracks uphill for 50 yards, enter the fancy gate on the left near the tall red-brick wall, and you'll see the twin spires of the monastery; the library entrance is in front of the church on the right). If you're coming on foot from the Little Quarter, allow 15 minutes for the uphill hike. After seeing the monastery, hike down to the castle (a 10-minute walk), or detour into the tiny Museum of Miniatures.

▲**Strahov Monastery and Library (Strahovský Klášter a Knihovna)**—As you enter the grounds, consider that medieval monasteries were a mix of industry, agriculture, and education, as well as worship and theology.

Cost and Hours: Grounds—free and always open; Library—80 Kč, daily 9:00-11:45 & 13:00-17:00, www.strahovsky klaster.cz.

Touring the Complex: In its heyday, the **monastery** had a booming economy of its own, with vineyards, a brewery, and a sizeable beer hall—all open once again. Its main church, dedicated to the Assumption of St. Mary, is an originally Romanesque structure decorated by the monks in textbook Baroque (usually closed, but look through the window inside the front door to see its interior).

The adjacent **library** offers a peek at how enlightened thinkers in the 18th century influenced learning. Cases in the library

gift shop show off illuminated manuscripts, described in English. Some are in old Czech, but because the Enlightenment promoted the universality of knowledge (and Latin was the universal language of Europe's educated elite), there was little place for regional dialects— therefore, few books here are in the Czech language.

Two rooms (seen only from the door) are filled with 10th- to 17th-century books, shelved under elaborately painted ceilings. The theme of the first and bigger hall is philosophy, with the history of man's pursuit of knowledge painted on the ceiling. The other hall focuses on theology. As the Age of Enlightenment began to take hold in Europe at the end of the 18th century, monasteries still controlled the books. Notice the gilded, locked case containing the *libri prohibiti* (prohibited books) at the end of the room. Only the abbot had the key, and you had to have his blessing to read these books—by writers such as Nicolas Copernicus and Jan Hus, and even including the French encyclopedia. The hallway connecting the two library rooms was filled with cases illustrating the new practical approach to natural sciences. Find the dried-up elephant trunks, baby dodo bird (which became extinct in the 17th century), and one of the earliest models of an electricity generator.

Nearby Views: Just downhill from the monastery, past the venerable linden trees (a symbol of the Czech people) and through the gate, the views from the **monastery garden** are among the finest in Prague. The Bellavista Restaurant, with perhaps the city's best view tables, serves basic food at high prices. From the public perch beneath the tables, you can see St. Vitus Cathedral (the heart of the castle complex), the green dome of the Church of St. Nicholas (marking the center of the Little Quarter), the two dark towers fortifying both ends of Charles Bridge, and the fanciful black spires of the Týn Church (marking the Old Town Square). On the horizon is the modern Žižkov TV and radio tower (conveniently marking the liveliest nightlife zone in town). Begun in the 1980s, the tower was partly meant to jam Radio Free Europe's broadcast from Munich. By the time it was finished, communism was dead, and Radio Free Europe's headquarters had moved to Prague.

Getting from the Monastery to the Castle: From the monastery, take Loretánská (the upper road, passing Loreta Square, with Loreta Church—described later) to the castle; this is a more interesting route than the lower road, Úvoz, which takes you down a steep hill, below Castle Square.

• *Or, for one more little sight, consider visiting the Museum of Miniatures. From the monastery garden viewpoint, backtrack through the gate to the big linden trees and leave through a passage on your right. At the door is the miniscule...*

Museum of Miniatures (Muzeum Miniatur)—You'll see 40 teensy exhibits, each under a microscope, crafted by an artist from St. Petersburg. Yes, you could fit the entire museum in a carry-on-size suitcase, but good things sometimes come in very, very small packages—it's fascinating to examine minutiae such as a padlock on the leg of an ant. An English loaner flier explains it all. Notice how the Russian staff has a certain gentility.

Cost and Hours: 70 Kč, kids-50 Kč, daily 9:00-17:00, tel. 233-352-371, www.muzeumminiatur.com.

Loreta Square, Between the Monastery and the Castle

From the monastery, take Loretánská street to Loreta Square (Loretánské Náměstí).

Loreta Church—This church has been a hit with pilgrims for centuries, thanks to its dazzling bell tower, peaceful yet plush cloister, sparkling treasury, and much-venerated Holy House.

Cost and Hours: 110 Kč, audioguide-150 Kč, Tue-Sun 9:00-12:15 & 13:00-16:30, closed Mon, tel. 220-516-740, www.loreta.cz.

Touring the Church: Once inside, follow the one-way clockwise route. While you stroll along the cloister, notice that the ceiling is painted with the many places Mary has miraculously appeared to the faithful in Europe.

In the garden-like center of the cloister stands the ornate **Santa Casa (Holy House)**, considered by some pilgrims to be part of Mary's home in Nazareth. Because many pilgrims returning from the Holy Land docked at the Italian port of Loreto, it's called the Loreta Shrine. The Santa Casa is the "little Bethlehem" of Prague. It is the traditional departure point for Czech pilgrims setting out on the long, arduous journey to Europe's most important pilgrimage site, Santiago de Compostela, in northwest Spain. Inside, on the left wall, hangs what some consider to be an original beam from the house of Mary. It's overseen by a much-venerated statue of the Black Virgin. The Santa Casa itself might seem like a bit of a letdown, but generations of believers have considered this to be the holiest spot in the country.

The small **Baroque church** behind the Santa Casa is one of the most beautiful in Prague. The decor looks rich—but the marble and gold are all fake (tap the columns). From the window in the back, you can see a stucco relief on the Santa Casa that shows angels rescuing the house from a pagan attack in Nazareth and making a special delivery to Loreto in Italy.

Continue around the cloister. In the last corner is **"St. Bearded Woman"** (Svatá Starosta). This patron saint of unhappy marriages is a woman whose family arranged for her to marry a pagan man. She prayed for an escape, sprouted a beard...and the guy said, "No way." While she managed to avoid the marriage, it angered her father, who crucified her. The many candles here are from people suffering through unhappy marriages.

Take a left just before the exit and head upstairs, following signs to the **treasury**—a room full of jeweled worship aids (well-described in English). The highlight here is a monstrance

(Communion wafer holder) from 1699, with more than 6,000 diamonds.

Enjoy the short **carillon concert** at the top of the hour; from the lawn in front of the main entrance, you can see the racks of bells being clanged. (At the exit, you'll find a schedule of English-language Masses and upcoming *pouť*—pilgrimages—departing from here.)

Entertainment in Prague

Prague booms with live and inexpensive theater, classical music, jazz, and pop entertainment. Everything is listed in several

monthly cultural events programs (free at TIs) and in the *Prague Post* newspaper (60 Kč at newsstands).

Tickets: You'll be tempted to gather fliers as you wander through town. Don't bother. To really understand all your options (the street Mozarts are pushing only their concerts), drop by a **Via Musica** box office. There are two:

One is next to Týn Church on the Old Town Square (daily 10:30-19:30, tel. 224-826-969), and the other is in the Little Quarter across from the Church of St. Nicholas (daily 10:30-18:00, tel. 257-535-568). The event schedule posted on the wall clearly shows everything that's playing today and tomorrow, including tourist concerts, Black Light Theater, and marionette shows, with photos of each venue and a map locating everything (www.viamusica.cz).

Ticketpro sells tickets for the serious concert venues and most music clubs (English-language reservations tel. 296-329-999, www.ticketpro.cz). Ticketpro has several outlets: at Rytířská 31 (daily 8:00-12:00 & 12:30-16:30, between Havelská Market and Estates Theater); in the Lucerna Gallery (daily 9:30-18:00, on Wenceslas Square, opposite Grand Hotel Evropa); and in the privately run Tourist Center at Rytířská 12 (Mon-Fri 11:00-19:00, closed Sat-Sun). As with most ticket box offices, you'll pay about 30 Kč extra per ticket.

Dress Code: Locals dress up for the more "serious" concerts, opera, and ballet, but many tourists wear casual clothes—as long as you don't show up in shorts, sneakers, or flip-flops, you'll be fine.

Black Light Theater

A kind of mime/modern dance variety show, Black Light Theater has no language barrier and is, for some, more entertaining than a classical concert. Unique to Prague, Black Light Theater originated in the 1960s as a playful and mystifying theater of the absurd. These days, aficionados and critical visitors lament that it's becoming a cheesy variety show, while others are uncomfortable with the sexual flavor of some acts. Still, it's an unusual theater experience that many enjoy. Shows last about an hour and a half. Avoid the first four rows, which get you so close that it ruins the illusion. Each theater has its own spin on what Black Light is supposed to be:

Ta Fantastika is traditional and poetic, with puppets and a little artistic nudity (*Aspects of Alice* nightly at 21:30, 650 Kč, reserved seating, near east end of Charles Bridge at Karlova 8, tel. 222-221-366, www.tafantastika.cz).

Image Theater has more mime and elements of the absurd, with shows including *Black Box, Cabinet,* and *The Best of Image:* "It's precisely the fact that we are all so different that unites us" (shows nightly at 18:00 and 20:00, 480 Kč, open seating—arrive early to grab a good spot, just off Old Town Square at Pařížská 4, tel. 222-314-448, www.imagetheatre.cz).

Laterna Magica, in the big, glassy building next to the National Theater, mixes Black Light techniques with film projection into a multimedia performance that draws Czech audiences (*Wonderful Circus, Legends of Magic, Graffiti,* shows Mon-Sat at 20:00, no shows on Sun, 680 Kč, tel. 224-931-482, www .laterna.cz).

The other Black Light theaters advertised around town aren't as good.

Classical Concerts

Each day, six to eight classical concerts designed for tourists fill delightful Old World halls and churches with music of the crowd-pleasing sort: Vivaldi, Best of Mozart, Most Famous Arias, and works by the famous Czech composer Antonín Dvořák. Concerts typically cost 400-1,000 Kč, start anywhere from 13:00 to 21:00, and last about an hour. Typical venues include two buildings on the Little Quarter Square (the Church of St. Nicholas and the Prague Academy of Music in Liechtenstein Palace), the Klementinum's Chapel of Mirrors, the Old Town Square (in a different Church of St. Nicholas), and the stunning Smetana Hall in the Municipal House (see page 104). Musicians vary from excellent to amateurish.

To ensure a memorable venue and top-notch musicians, choose a concert in one of three places (Municipal House's Smetana Hall, Rudolfinum, or National Theater) featuring Prague's finest ensembles (such as the Prague Symphony Orchestra or Czech Philharmonic).

The **Prague Symphony Orchestra** plays in the gorgeous Art

Nouveau Municipal House. Their ticket office is on the right side of the building, on U Obecního Domu street opposite Hotel Paris (Mon-Fri 10:00-18:00, tel. 222-002-336, www.fok.cz, pokladna @fok.cz). A smaller selection of tickets is sold in the information office inside the Municipal House.

The **Czech Philharmonic** performs in the classical Neo-Renaissance Rudolfinum in the Jewish Quarter. Their ticket office is on the right side of the Rudolfinum, under the stairs (250-1,000 Kč, open Mon-Fri 10:00-18:00, and until just before the show starts on concert days, on Palachovo Náměstí on the Old Town side of Mánes Bridge, tel. 227-059-352, www.ceskafilharmonie.cz, info@cfmail.cz).

Both orchestras perform in their home venues about five nights a month from September through June. Most other nights these spaces are rented to agencies that organize tourist concerts of varying quality for double the price (as described earlier). Check first whether your visit coincides with either ensemble's performance.

Mozart's Villa: During his frequent visits to Prague, Wolfgang Amadeus Mozart (1756-1791) stayed with his friends in the beautiful, small, Neoclassical **Villa Bertramka,** now the Mozart Museum. The Salzburg prodigy felt more appreciated in Prague than in Austria, and the villa, surrounded by a peaceful garden, preserves artifacts from his time there. Intimate concerts are held some afternoons and evenings, either in the garden or in the small concert hall (museum entry—110 Kč, daily April-Oct 9:30-18:00, Nov-March 9:30-17:00, Mozartova 169, Praha 5; from Metro: Anděl, it's a 10-minute walk—head to Hotel Mövenpick and then go up alley behind hotel; tel. 257-317-465, www.bertramka.cz).

Jam Session: A good bet is the session held every Monday at 17:00 at **St. Martin in the Wall,** where some of Prague's best musicians gather to tune in and chat with one another (400 Kč, Martinská 8, just north of the Tesco department store in the Old Town).

Buskers: The **Prague Castle Orchestra,** one of Prague's most entertaining acts, performs regularly on Castle Square. This trio—Josef on flute, Radek on accordion, and Zdeněk on bass—plays a lively Czech mélange of Smetana, swing, old folk tunes, and 1920s cabaret songs. Look for them if you're visiting the castle, and consider picking up their fun CD. They're also available for private functions (mobile 603-552-448, josekocurek@volny.cz).

Opera and Ballet

The **National Theater** (Národní Divadlo), on the New Town side of Legií Bridge, is best for opera and ballet. Enjoy its Neo-Renaissance interior (shows from 19:00, 300-1,000 Kč, tel. 224-912-673, www.nationaltheatre.cz).

The **Estates Theater** (Stavovské Divadlo) is where Mozart premiered and personally directed many of his most beloved works (see page 83). *Don Giovanni, The Marriage of Figaro,* and *The Magic Flute* are on the program a couple of times each month (shows from 20:00, 800-1,400 Kč, between the Old Town Square and the New Town on a square called Ovocný Trh, tel. 224-214-339, www.estatestheatre.cz). A handy ticket office for both of these theaters is in the little square (Ovocný Trh) behind the Estates Theater, next to a pizzeria.

The **State Opera** (Státní Opera) operates on a smaller budget and is also not as architecturally rewarding as the National Theater (shows at 19:00 or 20:00, 400-1,200 Kč, buy tickets at the theater, 101 Wilsonova, on the busy street between the main train station and Wenceslas Square, see map on page 96, tel. 224-227-693, www.opera.cz).

Festivals

World-class musicians are in town during these musical festivals: **Prague Spring** (May 12-June 4 in 2012, www.festival.cz), **Prague Proms** (late June-late July, www.pragueproms.cz), and the newer **Dvořák's Prague** (Sept, www.dvorakovapraha.cz).

Shopping in Prague

Prague's entire Old Town seems designed to bring out the shopper in visitors. Puppets, glass, and ceramics are traditional. Shop your way from the Old Town Square up Celetná street to the Powder Tower, then along Na Příkopě to the bottom of Wenceslas Square. The city center is tourist-oriented—most locals do their serious shopping in the suburbs.

Celetná is lined with big stores selling all the traditional Czech goodies. Tourists wander endlessly here, mesmerized by the window displays. Celetná Crystal, about midway down the street, offers the largest selection of affordable crystal. You can have the glass safely shipped home directly from the shop.

Náměstí Republiky (Republic Square) boasts Prague's newest and biggest mall, Palladium (Sun-Wed 9:00-21:00, Thu-Sat 9:00-22:00). It's hidden behind a pink Neo-Romanesque facade and the brown steel-and-glass 1980s department store Kotva ("Anchor"), an obsolete beast on the verge of extinction (Mon-Fri 9:00-20:00, Sat-Sun 10:00-18:00).

Na Příkopě has a couple of good modern malls. The best is Slovanský Dům (daily 10:00-20:00, Na Příkopě 22), where you'll wander deep past a 10-screen multiplex into a world of classy restaurants and designer shops surrounding a peaceful, park-like inner courtyard. Another modern mall is Černá Růže (daily 10:00-

20:00, Na Příkopě 12), with a great Japanese restaurant around a small garden. Next door is Moser, which has a museum-like crystal showroom upstairs. The Galerie Myslbek, directly across the street, has fancy stores in a space built to Prague's scale.

Národní Třída (National Street) is less touristy and lined with some inviting stores. The big Tesco department store in the middle sells anything you might need, from a pin for a broken watchband to a swimsuit (generally daily 9:00-21:00, Národní Třída 26).

Crystal: Along with shops on Celetná and Na Příkopě, a small square just off the Old Town Square, Malé Náměstí, is ringed by three major crystal retailers (generally open daily 10:00-20:00): Moser, Rott Crystal, and Crystalex (which claims to have "factory-direct" prices, at #6 on the square).

"Bohemian Garnets": These fiery red, gemstone-quality garnets, with unique refractive—some claim even curative—properties, were mined from a mountainous area of Bohemia. This region was the major source of garnet gems from the Renaissance through the Victorian Age, and is now largely mined out. Traditional hand-crafted designs pack many small garnets together, and much of the authentic jewelry you'll see today is Victorian-era. Of the many garnet shops in Prague's shopping districts, Turnov Granát Co-op has the largest selection (with shops at Dlouhá 28 and Panská 1, www.granat.eu). If you buy garnet jewelry, shop around, use a reputable dealer, and ask for a certificate of authenticity to avoid buying a glass imitation.

Sleeping in Prague

Peak months for hotels in Prague are May, June, and September. Easter and New Year's are the most crowded times, when prices are jacked up a bit. I've listed peak-time prices—if you're traveling in July or August, you'll find rates generally 15 percent lower, and from November through March, about 30 percent lower. It's often possible to negotiate a discount off the official rack rate (a hotel's highest, published rate). Most rack rates are pitched in euros, so the listed prices in crowns may differ somewhat due to currency fluctuations.

Room-Booking Services

Prague is awash with fancy rooms on the push list; private, small-time operators with rooms to rent in their apartments; and roving agents eager to book you a bed and earn a commission. You can

PRAGUE

Sleep Code

(18 Kč = about $1, country code: 420)
S = Single, **D** = Double/Twin, **T** = Triple, **Q** = Quad, **b** = bathroom,
s = shower only. Unless otherwise noted, credit cards are
accepted, and breakfast and tax are included. Everyone listed
here speaks English.

To help you easily sort through these listings, I've divided
the accommodations into three categories based on the price
for a double room with bath during high season:

$$$ Higher Priced—Most rooms 3,500 Kč or more.
  $$ Moderately Priced—Most rooms between 2,500-3,500 Kč.
    $ Lower Priced—Most rooms 2,500 Kč or less.

Prices can change without notice; verify the hotel's
current rates online or by email. For other updates, see www
.ricksteves.com/update.

save about 30 percent by showing up without a reservation and
finding accommodations upon arrival. However, it can be a hassle,
and you won't necessarily get your ideal choice. If you're coming in
by train or car, you'll encounter booking agencies. They can almost
always find you a reasonable room, and, if it's in a private guest
house, your host can even come and lead you to the place.

Athos Travel has a line on 200 properties (ranging from hostels to five-star hotels), 90 percent of which are in the Old Town.
To book a room, call them or use their handy website, which allows
you to search for a room based on various criteria (best to arrange
in advance during peak season, can also help with last-minute
booking off-season, tel. 241-440-571, fax 241-441-697, www.a
-prague.com, info@a-prague.com). Readers report that Athos is
aggressive with its business policies—although there's no fee if you
cancel well in advance, they strictly enforce penalties on cancellations within 48 hours.

Touristpoint, at the main train station (Hlavní Nádraží),
is another booking service (daily 8:00-22:00). They have a slew
of hotels and small pensions available (2,000-Kč pension doubles
in the Old Town, 1,500-Kč doubles a Metro ride away). You can
reserve by email, using your credit card as a deposit (tel. 224-946-
010, www.touristpoint.cz, info@touristpoint.cz), or just show up at
the office and request a room. Be clear on the location before you
make your choice.

Lída Jánská's **Magic Praha** can help with accommodations (mobile 604-207-225, www.magicpraha.cz, magicpraha
@magicpraha.cz; see page 64). Lída rents a well-located apartment

with a river view near the Jewish Quarter.

Web-booking services, such as Priceline.com and Bidding fortravel.com, enable budget travelers to snare fancy rooms for half the rack rate. It's not unusual to find a room in a four-star hotel for 1,300 Kč—but keep in mind that many of these international business-class hotels are far from the city center.

Old Town Hotels and Pensions
You'll pay higher prices to stay in the Old Town, but for many travelers, the convenience is worth the expense. These places are all within a 10-minute walk of the Old Town Square.

$$$ Hotel Metamorphis is a splurge, with solidly renovated rooms in Prague's former caravanserai (hostel for foreign merchants). Its breakfast room is in a spacious medieval cellar with modern artwork. Some of the street-facing rooms, located above two popular bars, are noisy at night (Db-3,800 Kč, manager David promises a 20 percent discount to my readers, also check website for last-minute discounts, Internet access, Malá Štupartská 5, tel. 221-771-011, fax 221-771-099, www.metamorphis.cz, hotel@metamorphis.cz).

$$ Hotel Maximilian is a sleek, mod, 70-room place with Art Deco black design; big, plush living rooms; and all the business services and comforts you'd expect in a four-star hotel. It faces a church on a perfect little square just a short walk from the action (Db-3,300 Kč, extra bed-1,200 Kč; online deal sometimes offered: stay 3 days and pay for 2; Internet access, Haštalská 14, tel. 225-303-111, fax 225-303-110, www.maximilianhotel.com, reservation@maximilianhotel.com).

$$ Pension u Medvídků ("By the Bear Cubs") has 31 comfortably renovated rooms in a big, rustic, medieval shell with dark wood furniture. Upstairs, you'll find lots of beams—or, if you're not careful, they'll find you (Sb-2,000 Kč, Db-3,000 Kč, Tb-4,000 Kč, extra bed-500 Kč, "historical" rooms-10 percent more, apartment-20 percent more, manager Vladimír promises my readers a 10 percent discount with cash if you book direct, Internet access, Na Perštýně 7, tel. 224-211-916, fax 224-220-930, www.umedvidku .cz, info@umedvidku.cz). The pension is above a brewpub and a popular, recommended beer-hall restaurant that features live music most Fridays and Saturdays until 23:00—request an inside room for maximum peace.

$$ Design Hotel Jewel Prague (U Klenotníka), with 11 modern, comfortable rooms in a plain building, is three blocks off the Old Town Square (Sb-2,250 Kč, small double-bed Db-3,000 Kč, bigger double or twin-bed Db-3,400 Kč, Tb-3,750 Kč, 10 percent off when you book direct and mention this book, Wi-Fi, Rytířská 3, tel. 224-211-699, fax 224-221-025, www.jewelhotel prague.cz, info@jewelhotel.cz).

Hotels in Prague's Old Town

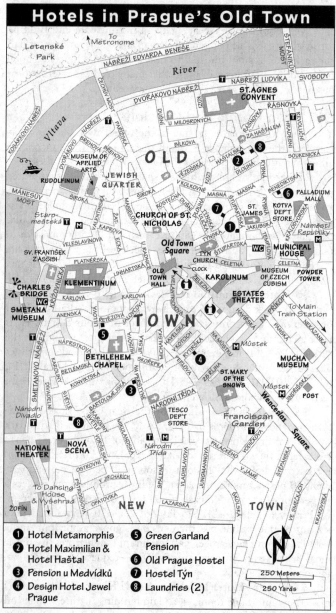

1. Hotel Metamorphis
2. Hotel Maximilian & Hotel Haštal
3. Pension u Medvídků
4. Design Hotel Jewel Prague
5. Green Garland Pension
6. Old Prague Hostel
7. Hostel Týn
8. Laundries (2)

$ Green Garland Pension (U Zeleného Věnce), on a central but delightfully quiet cobbled lane, has a warm and personal feel rare for the Old Town. Located in a thick 14th-century building with open beams, it has a blond-hardwood charm decorated with a woman's touch. Its nine rooms are clean and simply furnished (big Sb-1,700 Kč, Db-2,200 Kč, bigger Db-2,500 Kč, Tb-2,800 Kč, family suite, Wi-Fi, Řetězová 10, tel. 222-220-178, fax 224-248-791, www.uzv.cz, pension@uzv.cz).

$ Hotel Haštal is next to Hotel Maximilian (listed earlier) on the same quiet, hidden square in the Old Town. A popular hotel back in the 1920s, it has been renovated to complement the neighborhood's vibrant circa-1900 architecture. Its 24 rooms are comfortable, and its thin walls have recently been insulated against noise (Sb-1,500 Kč, Db-2,000 Kč, extra bed-550 Kč; manager Patrick promises my readers a 20 percent discount off their lowest online price, book via email to get the discount and avoid their online booking fee; air-con, Wi-Fi, Haštalská 16, tel. 222-314-335, www.hastal.com, info@hastal.com).

Under the Castle, in the Little Quarter

The first and third listings below are buried on quiet lanes deep in the Little Quarter, among cobbles, quaint restaurants, rummaging tourists, and embassy flags. Hotel Julián is a 10-minute walk up the river on a quiet and stately street, with none of the intense medieval cityscape of the others.

$$$ Vintage Design Hotel Sax's 22 rooms are decorated in a retro, meet-the-Jetsons fashion. With a fruity atrium and a distinctly modern, stark feel, this is a stylish, no-nonsense place (Sb-3,800-4,300 Kč, Db-3,800-4,500 Kč, Db suite-5,000 Kč, extra bed-750 Kč, 10 percent off with this book, elevator, Internet access, Jánský Vršek 3, tel. 257-531-268, fax 257-534-101, www.sax.cz, hotel@sax.cz).

$$$ Hotel Julián is an oasis of professional, predictable decency in an untouristy neighborhood. Its 32 spacious, fresh, well-furnished rooms and big, homey public spaces hide behind a noble Neoclassical facade. The staff is friendly and helpful. Their official "rack rates" are ridiculous, but with the Rick Steves discount, you can generally get a double here for around 2,200 Kč (Sb-3,725 Kč, Db-3,975 Kč, suites and bigger rooms available, check website for discounts, 15 percent discount off best website price when you book direct and mention this book, air-con, Wi-Fi, elevator, plush and inviting lobby, summer roof terrace, parking lot; Metro: Anděl, then an 8-minute walk, or take tram #6, #9, #12, or #20 for two stops; Elišky Peškové 11, Praha 5, reservation tel. 257-311-150, reception tel. 257-311-145, fax 257-311-149, www.julian.cz, info@julian.cz). Free lockers and a shower

PRAGUE

are available for those needing a place to stay after checkout (for example, while waiting for an overnight train).

$$ Dům u Velké Boty ("House at the Big Boot"), on a quiet square in front of the German Embassy, is the rare quintessential family hotel in Prague: homey, comfy, and extremely friendly. Charlotta, Jan, and their two sons treat every guest as a (thirsty) friend, and the wellspring of their stories never runs dry. Each of their 12 rooms is uniquely decorated, most in a tasteful, 19th-century Biedermeier style. There's no hotel sign on the house—look for the splendid geraniums that Jan nurtures in the windows (tiny Sb-2,100 Kč, two D rooms that share a bathroom-2,250 Kč each, Db-2,900-3,600 Kč, extra bed-725 Kč, 10 percent off with advance reservation and this book, prices can be soft when slow, cash only, children up to age 10 sleep free—toys provided, free Internet access and Wi-Fi, Vlašská 30, tel. 257-532-088, www.bigboot.cz, info@bigboot.cz).

Away from the Center

Moving just outside central Prague saves you money—and gets you away from the tourists and into some more workaday residential neighborhoods. The following listings are great values compared with the downtown hotels listed previously, and are all within a 5- to 15-minute tram or Metro ride from the center. For locations, see the map on the next page.

Beyond Wenceslas Square

These hotels are in urban neighborhoods on the outer fringe of the New Town, beyond Wenceslas Square. But they're still within several minutes' walk of the sightseeing zone and are well-served by trams.

$$ Louren Hotel, with 20 rooms, is a quality four-star business-class hotel in an upscale, circa-1900 residential neighborhood (Vinohrady) that has recently become popular with Prague's expat community. They do a good job of being homey and welcoming (Sb-2,900 Kč, Db-3,200 Kč, extra bed-1,600 Kč, fourth night free, 20 percent discount when you book direct and mention this book, 30 percent discount for last-minute reservations, air-con, elevator, Internet access, 3-minute walk to Metro: Jiřího z Poděbrad, or tram #11, Slezská 55, Praha 3, tel. 224-250-025, fax 224-250-027, www.louren.cz, reservations@louren.cz).

$$ Hotel 16 is a sleek and modern business-class place with an intriguing Art Nouveau facade, polished cherry-wood elegance, high ceilings, and 14 fine rooms (Sb-2,300 Kč, Db-2,900 Kč, Tb-3,500 Kč, 10 percent discount when you book direct and mention this book, check website for last-minute discounts, triple-paned windows, complimentary tea, back rooms facing the garden are quieter, air-con, elevator, free Internet access, limited free

Hotels & Restaurants in the New Town & Beyond

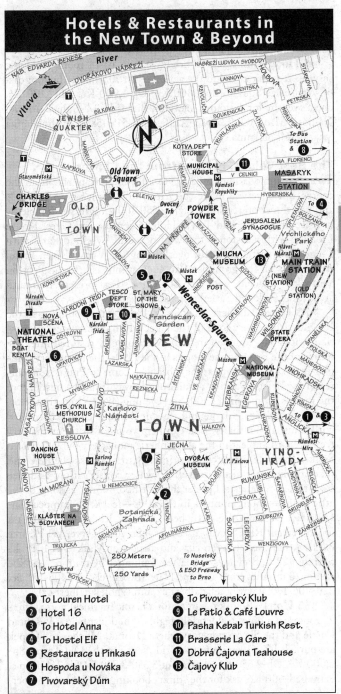

1. To Louren Hotel
2. Hotel 16
3. To Hotel Anna
4. To Hostel Elf
5. Restaurace u Pinkasů
6. Hospoda u Nováka
7. Pivovarský Dům
8. To Pivovarský Klub
9. Le Patio & Café Louvre
10. Pasha Kebab Turkish Rest.
11. Brasserie La Gare
12. Dobrá Čajovna Teahouse
13. Čajový Klub

parking, 10-minute walk south of Wenceslas Square, Metro: I.P. Pavlova, Kateřinská 16, Praha 2, tel. 224-920-636, fax 224-920-626, www.hotel16.cz, hotel16@hotel16.cz).

$ Hotel Anna offers 24 bright, simple, pastel rooms and basic service. It's a bit closer to the action—just 10 minutes by foot east of Wenceslas Square (Sb-1,600 Kč, Db-1,900 Kč, Tb-2,100 Kč, check website for discounts, elevator, Budečská 17, Praha 2, Metro: Náměstí Míru, tel. 222-513-111, fax 222-515-158, www.hotelanna.cz, sales@hotelanna.cz).

The Best Values, Farther from the Center

These accommodations are a 10- to 20-minute tram ride from the center, but once you make the trip, you'll see it's no problem—and you'll feel pretty smug saving $50-100 a night per double by not sleeping in the Old Town. Hotel u Šemíka and Guest House Lída are within a stone's throw of peaceful Vyšehrad Park, with a legendary castle on a cliff overlooking the Vltava River. Hotel Adalbert is on the grounds of an ancient monastery, and Pension Větrník is adjacent, with two of Prague's best-preserved natural areas (Star Park and Šárka) just a short walk away.

$$ Hotel Adalbert occupies an 18th-century building in the Břevnov Monastery (one of the Czech Republic's oldest monastic institutions, founded in 993). Meticulously restored after the return of the Benedictine monks in the 1990s, the monastery complex is the ultimate retreat for those who come to Prague for soul-searching or just wanting a quiet place away from the bustle. Join the monks for morning (7:00) and evening (18:00) Mass in the St. Margaret Basilica, a large and elegant Baroque church decorated with unusual simplicity. You can help yourself in the monastery fruit orchard and eat in the atmospheric monastery pub (Klášterní Šenk). The hotel itself caters primarily to business clientele and takes ecology seriously: recycling, water conservation, and free tram tickets for guests. I prefer the first-floor rooms, as some of the attic rooms—room numbers in the 200s—feel a bit cramped (Sb-1,800 Kč, Db-2,600 Kč, extra bed-1,000 Kč, less on weekends, ask for 15 percent Rick Steves discount when you reserve, Wi-Fi, free parking, halfway between city and airport at Markétská 1, Praha 6, tram #22 to Břevnovský Klášter; 5 minutes by tram beyond the castle, 20 minutes from Old and New Towns; tel. 220-406-170, fax 220-406-190, www.hoteladalbert.cz, info@hoteladalbert.cz).

$$ Hotel u Šemíka, named for a heroic mythical horse, offers 25 rooms in a quiet residential neighborhood just below Vyšehrad Castle and the Slavín cemetery where Dvořák, Mucha, and Čapek are buried. It's a 10-minute tram ride south of the Old Town (Sb-2,000 Kč, Db-2,650 Kč, apartment-3,350-3,700 Kč for 2-4 people, extra bed-600 Kč, ask for the "direct booking" Rick Steves 10 percent discount when you reserve, Internet access; from the center, take tram #3, #17, or #21 to Výtoň, go under rail bridge, and walk 3 blocks uphill to Vratislavova 36; Praha 2, tel. 224-920-736, fax 224-911-602, www.usemika.cz, usemika@usemika.cz).

$ Pension Větrník fills an attractive white-and-orange former 18th-century windmill in one of Prague's most popular residential areas, right next to the Břevnov Monastery and midway between the airport and the city. The talkative owner, Miloš Opatrný, is a retired prizewinning Czech chef whose culinary work took him as far as Japan. On request, he will gladly prepare a meal you won't forget. The six rooms here are the pride of the Opatrný family, who live on the upper floors. The garden has a red-clay tennis court—rackets and balls are provided (Db-1,800 Kč, suite-2,300 Kč, extra bed-500 Kč, Internet access, U Větrníku 1, Praha 6; airport bus #179 stops near the house, tram #18 goes straight to Charles Bridge, both take 20 minutes; tel. 220-513-390, www.vetrnik1722 .cz, pension@vetrnik1722.cz).

$ Guest House Lída, with 12 homey and spacious rooms, fills a big house in a quiet residential area farther inland, a 15-minute tram ride from the center. Jan, Jitka, Jiří, and Jana Prouzas—who run the place—are a wealth of information and know how to make people feel at home (Sb-1,380 Kč, small Db-1,440 Kč, Db-1,760 Kč, Tb-2,110 Kč, Qb-2,530 Kč, cash only, family rooms, top-floor family suite with kitchenette, Internet access, parking garage-200 Kč/day, Metro: Pražského Povstání; exit Metro and turn left on Lomnického between the Metro station and big blue-glass ČSOB building, follow Lomnického for 500 yards, then turn left on Lopatecká, go uphill and ring bell at Lopatecká #26; Praha 4, tel. & fax 261-214-766, www.lidabb.eu, lidabb@seznam.cz). The Prouzas brothers also rent two **apartments** across the river, an equal distance from the center (Db-1,400 Kč, Tb-1,700 Kč, Qb-2,000 Kč).

Hostels in the Center

It's tough to find a double for less than 2,500 Kč in the old center. But Prague has an abundance of fine hostels—each with a distinct personality, and each excellent in its own way for anyone wanting a 300-500-Kč dorm bed or an extremely simple twin-bedded room for about 1,300 Kč. With travelers seeking cheaper options these days, it's good to keep in mind that hostels are no longer the exclusive domain of backpackers. The first two hostels are centrally located, but lack in care and character; the last two are found in workaday neighborhoods and have atmospheric interiors.

$ Old Prague Hostel is a small place with 70 beds on the second and third floors of an apartment building on a back alley near the Powder Tower. The spacious rooms were once apartment bedrooms, so it feels less institutional than most hostels. You can hang out in the comfy TV lounge/breakfast room (D-1,400 Kč, bunk in 4- to 8-person room-400-500 Kč; includes breakfast, sheets, towels, lockers, and free Internet access; in summer reserve 2 weeks ahead for doubles, a few days ahead for bunks; Benediktská 2, see map on page 142 for location, tel. 224-829-058, www.oldpraguehostel.com, info@oldpraguehostel.com).

$ Hostel Týn is a quiet, mature, and sterile place hidden in a silent courtyard two blocks from the Old Town Square. The management is very aware of its valuable location, so they don't have to bother being friendly (D-1,240 Kč, T-1,410 Kč, bunk in 4- to 5-bed co-ed room-420 Kč, lockers, Internet access, kitchen, no breakfast, reserve one week ahead, Týnská 19, see map on page 142 for location, tel. 224-828-519, mobile 776-122-057, www.hosteltyn.com, roomservice@seznam.cz).

$ Sir Toby's is in a 1930s working-class neighborhood—a newly popular residential and dining-out area that's a 12-minute tram ride from the center. The owners have taken great pains to stamp the place with character: restored hardwood floors, a back garden with tables made out of sewing machines, and rooms filled with vintage 1930s furniture and photographs. Amenities include self- and full-service laundry, an on-site pub, and a friendly staff (120 beds, Sb-1,400 Kč, D-1,300 Kč, Db-1,700 Kč, Tb-1,840 Kč, bunk in 4- to 6-bed co-ed room-450 Kč, bunk in 8- to 10-bed co-ed room-350 Kč, take tram #5 from the main train station or tram #3 from the middle of Wenceslas Square to Dělnická, at Dělnická 24, Praha 7, tel. 246-032-610, www.sirtobys.com, info@sirtobys.com). The owners also run two contemporary-design hostels in Vinohrady.

$ Hostel Elf, a 10-minute walk from the main train station or one bus stop from the Florenc Metro station, is fun-loving; ramshackle; covered with noisy, self-inflicted graffiti; and the wildest of these hostels. They offer cheap, basic beds, a helpful staff, and lots of creative services—kitchen, free luggage room, free Internet access, laundry, no lockout, free tea, cheap beer, a terrace, and lockers (120 beds, D-1,100 Kč, bunk in 6- to 11-person room-320 Kč, includes sheets and breakfast, cash only, reserve four days ahead, Husitská 11, Praha 3, take bus #133 or #207 from Florenc Metro station for one stop to U Památníku, tel. 222-540-963, www.hostelelf.com, info@hostelelf.com).

Eating in Prague

A big part of Prague's charm is found in wandering aimlessly through the city's winding old quarters, marveling at the architecture, watching the people, and sniffing out fun restaurants. You can eat well here for very little money. What you'd pay for a basic meal in Vienna or Munich will get you a feast in Prague. In addition to meat-and-potatoes Czech cuisine (see "Czech Food" on page 49), you'll find trendy, student-oriented bars and lots of fine ethnic eateries. For ambience, the options include traditional, dark Czech beer halls; elegant Art Nouveau dining rooms; and hip, modern cafés.

Watch out for scams. Many restaurants put more care into ripping off green tourists (and even locals) than into their cooking. Tourists are routinely served cheaper meals than what they ordered, given a menu with a "personalized" price list, charged extra for things they didn't get, or shortchanged. Speak Czech. Even saying "Hello" in Czech (*Dobrý den;* see also "Czech Survival Phrases" on page 1263) will get you better service. Avoid any menu without clear and explicit prices. Be careful of waiters padding the tab. Closely examine your itemized bill and understand each line (a 10 percent service charge is sometimes added—in that case, there's no need to tip extra). Tax is always included in the price, so it shouldn't be tacked on later.

Make it a habit to pay for your meals with cash that you've withdrawn from an ATM. Part with very large bills only if necessary, and deliberately count your change. If you pay with a credit card, never let it out of your sight.

Remember, there are two parallel worlds in Prague: the tourist town and the real city. Generally, if you walk two minutes away from the tourist flow, you'll find better value, atmosphere, and service. (For more on scams, see "Rip-Offs in Prague" on page 60.)

I've listed these eating and drinking establishments by neighborhood. The most options—and highest prices—are in the Old Town. For a light meal, consider one of Prague's many cafés (see the "Cafés in the Old and New Towns" section). Many of the places listed here are handy for an efficient lunch, but may not offer fine evening dining. Others make less sense for lunch, but are great for a slow, drawn-out dinner. Read the descriptions to judge which is which.

Fun, Touristy Neighborhoods: Several areas are pretty and well-situated for sightseeing, but lined only with touristy restaurants. While these places are not necessarily bad values, I've listed only a few of your many options—just survey the scene in these spots and choose whatever looks best: **Kampa Square,** just off the Charles Bridge, feels like a small-town square. **Havelská Market**

is surrounded by colorful little eateries, any of which offer a nice perch for viewing the market scene while you munch. The massive **Old Town Square** is the place to nurse a drink or enjoy a meal while watching the tide of people, both tourists and locals, sweep back and forth. There's often some event on this main square, and its many restaurants provide tasty and relaxing vantage points.

Dining with a View: For great views, consider these options: **Hotel u Prince's terrace** (rooftop dining above a fancy hotel, completely touristy but with awesome views, described on page 156); **Villa Richter** (next to Prague Castle, above Malostranská Metro stop, described on page 162); **Bellavista Restaurant** at the Strahov Monastery; **Petřínské Terasy** and **Nebozízek** next to the funicular stop halfway up Petřín Hill; and **Čertovka** in the Little Quarter (superb views of the Charles Bridge; described on page 85). For the best cheap riverside dinner, have a picnic on a paddleboat (see page 74). There's nothing like drifting down the middle of the Vltava River as the sun sets, while munching on a picnic meal and sipping a beer with your favorite travel partner.

Cheap-and-Cheery Sandwich Shops: All around town you'll find modern little sandwich shops (like the Panería chain) offering inexpensive fresh-made sandwiches (grilled if you like), pastries, salads, and drinks. You can get the food to go, or eat inside at simple tables.

In the Old and New Towns
Characteristically Czech Places

With the inevitable closing of cheap student pubs (replaced by shops and hotels that make more money), it's getting difficult to find a truly Czech pub in the historic city center. Most Czechs no longer go to "traditional" eateries, preferring the cosmopolitan taste of the world to the mundane taste of sauerkraut. As a result, ancient institutions with "authentic" Czech ambience have become touristy—but they're still great fun, a good value, and respected by locals. Expect wonderfully rustic spaces, smoke, surly service, and reasonably good, inexpensive food. Understand every line on your bill. For locations, see the maps on pages 145 and 151.

Restaurace u Pinkasů, founded in 1843, is known among locals as the first place to serve Pilsner beer. You can sit in its traditional interior, in front to watch the street action, or out back in a garden shaded by the Gothic buttresses of the St. Mary of the Snows Church. While the prices are straightforward, some of the waiters could win the rudest-service award (daily 9:00-24:00, 90-Kč lunch menu, near the bottom of Wenceslas Square, between Old and New Towns, Jungmannovo Náměstí 16, tel. 221-111-150).

Restaurants in the Old Town

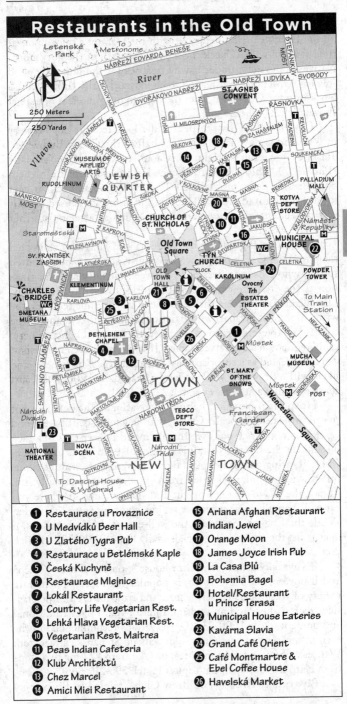

1. Restaurace u Provaznice
2. U Medvídků Beer Hall
3. U Zlatého Tygra Pub
4. Restaurace u Betlémské Kaple
5. Česká Kuchyně
6. Restaurace Mlejnice
7. Lokál Restaurant
8. Country Life Vegetarian Rest.
9. Lehká Hlava Vegetarian Rest.
10. Vegetarian Rest. Maitrea
11. Beas Indian Cafeteria
12. Klub Architektů
13. Chez Marcel
14. Amici Miei Restaurant
15. Ariana Afghan Restaurant
16. Indian Jewel
17. Orange Moon
18. James Joyce Irish Pub
19. La Casa Blú
20. Bohemia Bagel
21. Hotel/Restaurant u Prince Terasa
22. Municipal House Eateries
23. Kavárna Slavia
24. Grand Café Orient
25. Café Montmartre & Ebel Coffee House
26. Havelská Market

Restaurace u Provaznice ("By the Ropemaker's Wife") has all the Czech classics, peppered with the story of a once-upon-a-time-faithful wife. (Check the menu for details of the gory story.) Natives congregate under bawdy frescoes for the famously good "pig leg" with horseradish and Czech mustard (daily 11:00–24:00, a block into the Old Town from the bottom of Wenceslas Square at Provaznická 3, tel. 224-232-528).

U Medvídků ("By the Bear Cubs") started out as a brewery in 1466 and is now a flagship beer hall of the Czech Budweiser. The one large room is bright, noisy, touristy, and a bit smoky (daily 11:30–23:00, a block toward Wenceslas Square from Bethlehem Square at Na Perštýnì 7, tel. 224-211-916). The small beer bar next to the restaurant (daily 16:00–3:00 in the morning) is used by university students during emergencies—such as after most other pubs have closed.

U Zlatého Tygra ("By the Golden Tiger") has long embodied the proverbial Czech pub, where beer turns strangers into kindred spirits, who cross the fuzzy line between memory and imagination as they tell their hilarious life stories to each other. Today, "The Tiger" is a buzzing shrine to one of its longtime regulars, the writer Bohumil Hrabal, whose fictions immortalize many of the colorful characters that once warmed the wooden benches here. Only regulars have reserved tables. If you find a rare empty spot, you'll be treated as a surprise guest rather than as a customer—and likely will wait quite a while to land a beer (daily 15:00–23:00, just south of Karlova at Husova 17, tel. 222-221-111).

Hospoda u Nováka, behind the National Theater (i.e., not so central), is emphatically Czech, with few tourists. It takes good care of its regulars (you'll see the old monthly beer tabs in a rack just inside the door). Nostalgic communist-era signs are everywhere. During that time, pubs like this were close-knit communities where regulars escaped from the depression of daily life. Today, the U Nováka is a bright and smoky hangout where you can still happily curse whatever regime you happen to live under. While the English menu lists the well-executed Czech classics, it doesn't list the cheap daily specials (daily 10:00–23:00, V Jirchářích 2, tel. 224-930-639).

Pivovarský Dům ("The Brewhouse"), on the corner of Ječná and Lípová in the New Town, is popular with locals for its rare variety of fresh beers (yeast, wheat, and fruit-flavored), fine classic Czech dishes, and an inviting interior that mixes traditional and modern (daily 11:00–23:00, reservations recommended in the evenings, variety of beer mugs sold; walk up Štěpánská street from Wenceslas Square for 10 minutes, or take tram #22 for two stops from Národní to Štěpánská; Lípová 15, tel. 296-216-666).

Pivovarský Klub ("The Brew Club," related to Pivovarský

Dům, above) serves the widest selection of Czech microbrews in town in a modern, blond-wood restaurant near the Florenc Metro station. Every week different beers are featured on tap on the ground floor, while small breweries hold regular presentations in the basement (daily 11:30-23:30, evening reservations recommended; about 50 yards on the left along Křižíkova from Florenc Metro station, Křižíkova 17, tel. 222-315-7770).

Restaurace u Betlémské Kaple, behind Bethlehem Chapel, is not "ye olde" Czech. It has light wooden decor, cheap lunch deals, and fish specialties that attract natives and visitors in search of a good Czech bite for good Czech prices (daily 11:00-23:00, Betlémské Náměstí 2, tel. 222-221-639).

Česká Kuchyně ("Czech Kitchen") is a blue-collar cafeteria serving steamy old Czech cuisine. It's fast, practical, cheap, and traditional as can be. Pick up your tally sheet as you enter, grab a tray, point to whatever you'd like, and keep the paper to pay as you exit. It's extremely cheap...unless you lose your paper. As you enter, you'll come across serving stations in this order: salads, fruit dumplings and sweets, soups, main dishes, and finally, drinks (daily 9:00-20:00, very central, across from Havelská Market at Havelská 23, tel. 224-235-574).

Restaurace Mlejnice ("The Mill") is a fun little pub strewn with farm implements and happy eaters, located just out of the tourist crush two blocks from the Old Town Square. They serve hardy traditional and modern Czech plates for 150-180 Kč. Reservations are smart in the evening (daily 11:00-24:00, between Melantrichova and Železná at Kožná 14, tel. 224-228-635).

Lokál ("The Dump") is a new hit with residents for its good-quality Czech classics at low prices. Filling a long, arched space, the restaurant plays on customers' nostalgia: the stark interior is a deliberate 1980s retro design, and the waiters have been instructed to be curt (but not impolite)—just as if they were serving in one of Prague's notorious train station "dumps" (daily 11:00-1:00 in morning, ask for English menu at the front by the tap, Dlouhá 33, tel. 222-316-265). The same group has a smaller branch, **Lokál u Bílé Kuželky,** in the Little Quarter (see listing later).

Hip Restaurants

Country Life Vegetarian Restaurant is a bright, easy, non-smoking cafeteria with a well-displayed buffet of salads and hot veggie dishes. It's midway between the Old Town Square and the bottom of Wenceslas Square. They're serious about their vegetarianism, serving only plant-based, unprocessed, and unrefined food. Its quiet dining area is elegant for a cafeteria, with a few tables outside in the courtyard (Sun-Thu 9:00-20:30, Fri 9:00-17:00, closed Sat, through courtyard at Melantrichova 15/Michalská 18, tel. 224-213-366).

Lehká Hlava Vegetarian Restaurant ("Clear Head"), tucked away on a cul-de-sac, has a mission to provide a "clear atmosphere for enjoying food." Sitting in an enchanted-forest setting, diners enjoy dishes from around the world. Reserve in advance for evenings (100-150-Kč plates, two-course 90-Kč daily special, no eggs, no smoke, lots of vegan dishes, daily 11:30-23:30, between Bethlehem Chapel and the river at Boršov 2, tel. 222-220-665).

Vegetarian Restaurant Maitrea, just off the Old Town Square alongside the Týn Church, serves imaginative dishes in a swoopy modern interior where every inch is curved to ensure the "unobstructed flow of energy." Its organic woody basement is even more seductive than the ground floor. The 105-Kč lunch special is a great value (Mon-Fri 11:30-23:30, Sat-Sun 12:00-23:30, Týnská ulička 6, tel. 221-711-631).

Beas Indian Cafeteria is a spartan little vegetarian restaurant ruled by a Punjabi chef. Diners grab a steel tray and point to whatever looks good. The food is sold by weight—you'll likely spend 140 Kč for lunch. Tucked away in a courtyard behind the Týn Church, this place is popular with university students (Mon-Sat 11:00-20:00, Sun 12:00-18:00, Týnská 19, mobile 608-035-727).

Klub Architektů, next to Bethlehem Chapel, is a modern hangout in a medieval cellar with a fun menu offering excellent original dishes, hearty salads, Moravian wines, and Slovak beer (daily 11:30-24:00, Betlémské Náměstí 169, tel. 224-401-214).

Le Patio, on the big and busy Národní Třída, has a hip, continental feel. But for a place that also sells furniture (head straight back and down the stairs), it definitely needs comfier dining chairs. Hanging lanterns and live music (Fri-Sat) contribute to the pleasant atmosphere. Dishes are from India, France, and points in between, and there's always a serious vegetarian option (200-350-Kč plates, daily 8:00-23:00, Národní 22—see map on page 145, tel. 224-934-375).

Pasha Kebab Turkish Restaurant, near the bottom of Wenceslas Square, has American fast-food chain ambience, good ingredients, and wonderful, authentic ready-to-eat Turkish dishes (120-Kč meals, daily 10:00-22:00, a block from Můstek Metro stop, just beyond Franciscan garden at Jungmannova 27, tel. 224-948-481).

Brasserie La Gare, just off Náměstí Republiky, opened with the mission to prove to Czechs that French food can be simple and inexpensive. The menu includes such classics as escargots de Bourgogne and coq au vin. The red-hued, modern interior also contains a French bakery and a deli (250-Kč main dishes, 89-Kč lunch specials, daily 11:00-24:00, V Celnici 3, tel. 222-313-712).

Ethnic Eateries and Bars near Dlouhá Street

Dlouhá, the wide street leading away from the Old Town Square behind the Jan Hus Memorial, is lined with ethnic restaurants catering mostly to cosmopolitan locals. Within a couple of blocks, you can eat your way around the world. From Dlouhá, wander the Rámová/Haštalská/Vězeňská area to survey a United Nations of eateries: You'll find French (**Chez Marcel** at Haštalská 12); Italian (the expensive **Amici Miei** at Vězeňská 5 prides itself on fresh *pesci* and *frutti di mare*); and Afghan (**Ariana** at Rámová 6). These five deserve special consideration:

Indian: **Indian Jewel,** in the Ungelt courtyard behind the Týn Church, is the best place in Prague to find a full Indian menu that actually tastes Indian. Located in a pleasant, artfully restored courtyard, this is my choice for outdoor dining, with seriously executed sub-Continental classics and good-value lunch specials (daily 11:00-23:00, Týn 6, tel. 222-310-156).

Thai: **Orange Moon** specializes in Thai curries, but you'll also find dishes from Myanmar (Burma) and India, served in a space delightfully decorated with artwork from Southeast Asia. This restaurant attracts a mixture of locals, expats, and tourists (daily 11:30-23:30, reservations recommended, Rámová 5, tel. 222-325-119).

Irish: **James Joyce Irish Pub** may seem like a strange recommendation in Prague—home of some of the world's best beer—but it has the kind of ambience that locals (and few tourists) seek out. Expats have favored this pub (formerly known as Molly Malone's) for Guinness ever since the Velvet Revolution enabled the Celts to return to one of their homelands. Worn wooden floors, dingy walls, and the Irish manager transport you right into the heart of blue-collar Dublin, which was, after all, a popular place for young Czechs to seek jobs in the high-tech industry—before the recent recession hit (daily 11:00-1:00, U Obecního Dvora 4, tel. 224-818-851).

Latin American: **La Casa Blů,** with cheap lunch specials, Mexican plates, Staropramen beer, and greenish mojitos, is your own little pueblo in Prague. It's one of the last student bastions in the Old Town. Painted in warm oranges and reds, energized by upbeat music, and guarded by creatures from Mayan mythology, La Casa Blů attracts a fiesta of happy eaters and drinkers (Mon-Sat 11:00-23:00, Sun 14:00-23:00, non-smoking, on the corner of Kozí and Bílkova, tel. 224-818-270).

North American: **Bohemia Bagel** is hardly authentic—exasperated Czechs insist that bagels have nothing to do with Bohemia. Owned by an American, this practical café caters mostly to youthful tourists, with good sandwiches (100-125 Kč), a little garden out back, and Internet access. If homesick, you'll love the menu, with everything from Philly cheesesteaks to bacon and eggs (daily 7:00-24:00, Masná 2, tel. 224-812-560). Outside of meal times, it's a quiet and comfy hangout.

In the Jewish Quarter

These eateries are well-located to break up a demanding tour of the Jewish Quarter—all within two blocks of each other on or near Široká (see map on page 89). Also consider the nearby ethnic eateries listed above.

Kolkovna, the flagship restaurant of a chain allied with Pilsner Urquell, is big and woody yet modern, serving a fun mix of Czech and international cuisine—ribs, salads, cheese plates, and beer. It feels a tad formulaic...but in a good way (a bit overpriced but good energy, daily 11:00-24:00, across from Spanish Synagogue at V Kolkovně 8, tel. 224-819-701).

Franz Kafka Café, with a cool, dark interior strewn with historic photos of the ghetto and a few good sidewalk tables, is great for a relaxing salad, sandwich, snack, or drink (150-Kč salads, daily 10:00-21:00, one block from the cemetery at Široká 12).

Restaurace u Knihovny ("By the Library"), situated steps away from the City and National Libraries as well as the Pinkas Synagogue, is a favorite lunch spot for locals who work nearby. The cheap daily lunch specials consist of seven imaginative variations on traditional Czech themes. The service is friendly, and the stylish red-brick interior is warm (daily 11:00-23:00, smoke-free at lunch, on the corner of Veleslavínova and Valentinská, mobile 732-835-876).

Dinitz Kosher Restaurant, around the corner from the Spanish Synagogue, is the most low-key and reasonably priced of the kosher restaurants in the Jewish Quarter (Sun-Thu 11:30-22:30, Fri 11:30-14:30, 800-Kč Shabbat meals by prepaid reservation only, Bílkova 12, tel. 222-244-000). For Shabbat meals, the fancier **King Solomon Restaurant** is a better value (Široká 8, tel. 224-818-752).

Dining with an Old Town Square View

The **Hotel u Prince Terasa,** atop the five-star hotel facing the Astronomical Clock, is designed for foreign tourists. A sleek elevator takes you to the rooftop terrace, where every possible inch is used to serve good food (international with plenty of fish) from their open-air grill. The view is arguably the best in town—especially at sunset. The menu is a fun but overpriced mix, with photos that make ordering easy. Being in such a touristy spot, waiters are experts at nicking you with confusing menu charges; don't be afraid to confirm exact prices before ordering. This place is also great for a drink at sunset or late at night (fine salads, 240-300-Kč plates, daily until 24:00, brusque staff, outdoor heaters when necessary, Staroměstské Náměstí 29, tel. 224-213-807, no reservations possible).

Art Nouveau Splendor in the Municipal House

The **Municipal House** (Obecní Dům), the sumptuous Art Nouveau concert hall, has three restaurants: a café, a French res-

taurant, and a beer cellar (all at Náměstí Republiky 5). The dressy café, **Kavárna Obecní Dům,** is drenched in chandeliered, Art Nouveau elegance and offers the best value and experience here. Light, pricey meals and drinks come with great atmosphere and bad service (280-Kč three-course

special daily for lunch or dinner, open daily 7:30-23:00, live piano or jazz trio 16:00-20:00, tel. 222-002-763). The fine and formal French restaurant in the next wing oozes Mucha elegance (700-1,000-Kč meals, daily 12:00-16:00 & 18:00-23:00, tel. 222-002-777). The beer cellar is overpriced and touristy (daily 11:30-23:00).

Cafés in the Old and New Towns

Dripping with history, these places are as much about the ambience as they are about the coffee. Most cafés also serve sweets and light meals.

Kavárna Slavia, across from the National Theater (facing the Legií Bridge on Národní street), is a fixture in Prague, famous as a hangout for its literary elite. Today, it's tired and clearly past its prime, with an Art Deco interior, lousy piano entertainment, and celebrity photos on the wall. But its iconic status makes it a fun stop for a coffee—skip the food (daily 8:00-23:00, sit as near the river as possible, Smetanovo Nábřeží 2, tel. 224-218-493). Notice the *Drinker of Absinthe* painting on the wall (and on the menu for 55 Kč)—with the iconic Czech writer struggling with reality.

Café Louvre is a longtime elegant favorite (opened in 1902) that still draws an energetic young crowd. From the big and busy Národní street, you walk upstairs into a venerable world of newspapers on sticks (including English) and waiters in vests and aprons. The back room has long been the place for billiard tables (100 Kč/hour). An English flier tells its history (200-Kč plates, 120-Kč two-course lunch offered 11:00-15:00, open daily 8:00-23:30, Národní 22—see map on page 145, tel. 224-930-949).

Grand Café Orient is just one flight up off busy Celetná street, yet a world away from the crush of tourism below. Located in the House of the Black Madonna, the café is upstairs, above the entrance to the Museum of Czech Cubism and fittingly decorated with a Cubist flair. With its stylish, circa-1910 decor toned to dark green, this space is full of air and light—and a good value as well. The café takes its Cubism seriously: Traditionally round desserts are served square (salads, sandwiches, great balcony seating, Mon-Fri 9:00-22:00, Sat-Sun 10:00-22:00, Ovocný Trh 19, at the corner of Celetná near the Powder Tower, tel. 224-224-240).

Café Montmartre, on a small street parallel to Karlova, combines Parisian ambience with unbeatable Czech prices for coffee (no food served). Dreamy Czech minds found their quiet asylum here after Kavárna Slavia (listed earlier) and other longtime favorites either closed down or became stuck in their past. The main room is perfect for discussing art and politics; the intimate room behind the courtyard is where you recite poetry to your partner (Mon-Fri 9:00-23:00, Sat-Sun 12:00-23:00, Řetězová 7, tel. 222-221-244).

Ebel Coffee House, next door to Café Montmartre, prides itself on its wide assortment of fresh brews from every coffee-bean-growing country in the world, inviting cakes, and a colorful setting that delights the mind as much as the caffeine (daily 9:00-22:00, Řetězová 3, tel. 224-895-788).

Teahouses

Many Czech people are bohemian philosophers at heart and prefer the mellow, smoke-free environs of a teahouse to the smoky, traditional beer hall. Young Czechs are much more interested in traveling to exotic destinations like Southeast Asia, Africa, or Peru than to Western Europe, so the Oriental teahouses set their minds in vacation mode.

While there are teahouses all over town, a fine example in a handy locale is Prague's original one, established in 1991—just after freedom. **Dobrá Čajovna** ("Good Teahouse"), only a few steps off the bustle of Wenceslas Square, takes you into a very peaceful world that elevates tea to an almost religious ritual. You'll be given an English menu—which lovingly describes each tea—and a bell. The menu lists a world of tea (very fresh, prices by the small pot), "accompaniments" (such as Exotic Miscellany), and light meals "for hungry tea drinkers." When you're ready to order, ring your bell to beckon a tea monk—likely a member of the Lovers of Tea Society (Mon-Sat 10:00-21:30, Sun 14:00-21:30, near the base of Wenceslas Square, opposite McDonald's at Václavské Náměstí 14, see map on page 145, tel. 224-231-480).

For an actual taste of tea from Prague's newly emerging Chinese middle class (rather than from some Czech's dreams of the Orient), head to **Čajový Klub** ("Tea Club"), just opposite the Jerusalem Synagogue. Creatively run by a cultured man from Beijing, here you'll find red cherry-wood decor, expertly served tea, and the freshest green leaves in town (Mon-Sat 10:00-21:00, closed Sun, Jeruzalémská 10, see map on page 145, tel. 222-721-072).

In the Little Quarter

These characteristic eateries are handy for a bite before or after your Prague Castle visit. For locations, see the map on page 160.

Malostranská Beseda, in the impeccably restored former Town Hall, weaves together an imaginative menu of traditional Czech dishes (both classic and little known), vegetarian fare, and fresh fish. It feels a bit sterile and formulaic, but that follows a local trend. You can choose among three settings: the non-smoking ground-floor restaurant on the left; the café on the right (serves meals but it's OK to just have coffee or cake); or the packed beer hall downstairs, where Pilsner Urquell is served well (daily 11:00-23:00, Malostranské Náměstí 21, tel. 257-409-112). The restaurant has a recommended music club upstairs.

U Zavěšenýho Kafe ("By the Hanging Coffee"), up 20 yards on the right after Nerudova turns into Úvoz, is a creative little pub/restaurant that has attracted a cult following among Prague's cognoscenti. You can "hang" a coffee here for a local vagabond by paying for an extra coffee on your way out (daily 11:00-24:00, Úvoz 6, look for the only house covered by vines, mobile 605-294-595).

U Hrocha ("By the Hippo"), a small authentic pub with tar dripping from its walls, is packed with beer drinkers. Expect simple, traditional meals—basically meat starters with bread. Just below the castle near Little Quarter Square (Malostranské Náměstí), it's actually the haunt of many members of Parliament, which is located around the corner (daily 12:00-23:00, chalkboard lists daily meals in English, Thunovská 10, tel. 257-533-389).

Lokál u Bílé Kuželky ("By the White Bowling Pin"), a branch of the Old Town's recommended Lokál restaurant, is the best bet for quick, cheap, well-executed Czech classics on this side of the river (Mon-Fri 11:30-24:00, Sat-Sun 12:00-22:00, non-smoking section, Míšeňská 12; from the Charles Bridge, turn right around the U Tří Pštrosů Hotel just before the Little Quarter gate; tel. 257-212-014).

Čertovka, down an alley so narrow that it requires a signal to regulate foot traffic, offers outdoor seating on two small terraces right on the water, with some of the best views of the Charles Bridge. Given the location, the prices are reasonable (400-Kč meals, daily 11:30-23:30, off the little square at U Lužického Semináře 24, no reservations taken, arrive early to claim a spot, tel. 257-534-524).

PRAGUE

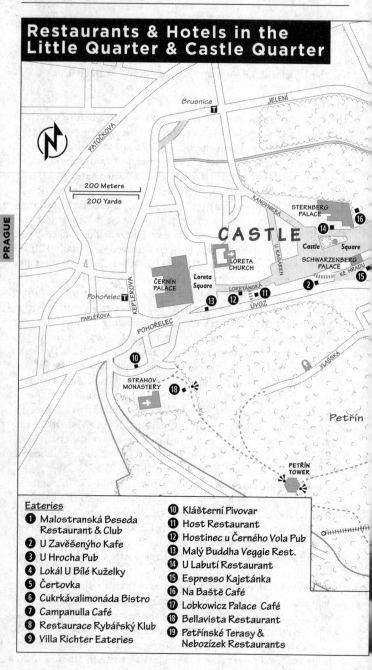

Restaurants & Hotels in the Little Quarter & Castle Quarter

Eateries

1. Malostranská Beseda Restaurant & Club
2. U Zavěšenýho Kafe
3. U Hrocha Pub
4. Lokál U Bílé Kuželky
5. Čertovka
6. Cukrkávalimonáda Bistro
7. Campanulla Café
8. Restaurace Rybářský Klub
9. Villa Richter Eateries
10. Klášterní Pivovar
11. Host Restaurant
12. Hostinec u Černého Vola Pub
13. Malý Buddha Veggie Rest.
14. U Labutí Restaurant
15. Espresso Kajetánka
16. Na Baště Café
17. Lobkowicz Palace Café
18. Bellavista Restaurant
19. Petřínské Terasy & Nebozízek Restaurants

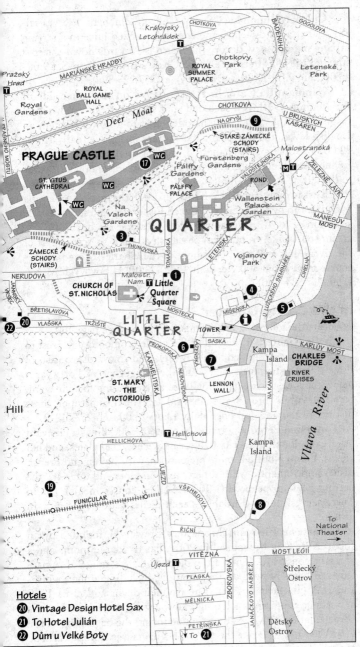

Prague map showing Prague Castle, Little Quarter, Charles Bridge, and the Vltava River.

Hotels
20 Vintage Design Hotel Sax
21 To Hotel Julián
22 Dům u Velké Boty

Cukrkávalimonáda ("Sugar, Coffee, Lemonade") serves salads, ciabatta sandwiches, and freshly squeezed juice in a setting mixing old and new decor. The bistro is 50 yards down the first street to the left after you exit the Charles Bridge (Mon-Sat 9:00-23:00, Sun 9:00-19:00, Lázeňská 7, tel. 257-225-396).

Campanulla Café, in the courtyard on the other side of the Lennon Wall, is a secluded spot serving fresh sandwiches, raspberry drinks, and Italian coffee next to a flower garden, an English lawn, and one of the oldest trees in Prague (daily 11:00-22:00, Velkopřevorské Náměstí 4, look for small gate at left end of Lennon Wall, entrance to indoor seating area is another 20 yards to the left, tel. 257-217-736).

Restaurace Rybářský Klub, just off the park on Kampa Island, is run by the Society of Czech Fishermen and serves a wide selection of local freshwater fish. Dine along the dock on fish-cream soup, pike, trout, carp, or catfish at a not-so-scenic part of the river—but still with a glimpse of the Charles Bridge (three-course meal about 500 Kč, daily 12:00-23:00, U Sovových Mlýnů 1, tel. 257-534-200).

In the Castle Quarter

To locate the following restaurants, see the map on page 160.

Villa Richter, at the end of the castle promontory (closest to the river) and surrounded by newly replanted vineyards, consists of three classy restaurants, each with killer Prague views. Forty yards below the lower castle gate, you'll see a gate leading to a vineyard. Stroll downhill through the vineyard and you'll come upon three distinct restaurants (all open daily 10:00-23:00, tel. 257-219-079). At **Panorama Pergola,** a string of outdoor tables lines a vineyard terrace overlooking the city (wine, sandwiches, cold plates, and hot views). **Piano Nobile** is more pretentious, with Italian and French dishes and romantic white-linen tables indoors and out—it's the perfect place to propose (1,000-Kč three-course meals). **Piano Terra** serves more affordable Czech dishes (200-300-Kč main dishes).

Klášterní Pivovar ("Monastery Brewery"), founded by an abbot in 1628 and reopened in 2004, has two large rooms and a pleasant courtyard. This is the place to taste a range of unpasteurized beers brewed on the premises, including amber, wheat, and IPA (India Pale Ale). The wooden decor and circa-1900 newspaper clippings (including Habsburg Emperor Franz Josef's "Proclamation to My Nations," announcing the beginning of the First World War) evoke the era when Vienna was Europe's artistic capital, Prague was building its faux Eiffel Tower, and life moved much slower. To accompany the beer, try the strong beer-flavored cheese served on toasted black-yeast bread (daily 10:00-22:00, Strahovské Nádvoří 301, tel. 233-353-155). It's directly across from the entrance to the Strahov Library (don't confuse it with the enormous, tour group-oriented Klášterní Restaurace next door, to the right).

Host Restaurant is hidden in the middle of a staircase that connects Loretánská and Úvoz streets. This spot, which boasts super views of the Little Quarter and Petřín Hill, has a modern black-and-white design and an imaginative menu. Most main dishes are priced around 350 Kč, but try asking for the "business lunch" menu (two courses for 145 Kč) advertised only in Czech (daily 11:30-22:00, as you go up Loretánská, watch for stairs leading down to the left at #15—just before the arcaded passageway, mobile 728-695-793).

Hostinec u Černého Vola ("By the Black Ox") is a smoky, dingy old-time pub—its survival in the midst of all the castle splendor and tourism is a marvel. It feels like a kegger on the banks of the river Styx, with classic bartenders serving up Kozel beer (traditional "Goat" brand with excellent darks) and beer-friendly gut-bomb snacks (fried cheese, local hot dogs). The pub is located on Loretánská (50 yards from Loreta Church, no sign outside, sniff for cigarette smoke and look for the only house on the block without an arcade, daily 10:00-22:00, English menu on request, tel. 220-513-481).

Malý Buddha ("Little Buddha") serves delightful food— especially vegetarian—and takes its theme seriously. You'll step into a mellow, low-lit escape of bamboo and peace, where you'll be served by people with perfect complexions and almost no pulse to the no-rhythm of meditative music. Eating in their little back room is like being in a temple (100-200-Kč meals, Tue-Sun 12:00-22:30, closed Mon, non-smoking, between the castle and Strahov Monastery at Úvoz 46, tel. 220-513-894).

U Labutí ("By the Swans") offers reasonably priced, classic Czech food in a quiet courtyard, just across from the Plague Column on Castle Square (daily 10:00-22:00, Hradčanské Náměstí 11, tel. 220-511-191).

Espresso Kajetánka, just off Castle Square, has magnificent city views. It's a handy, though overpriced, place for a coffee in a plastic cup or a snack as you start or end your castle visit (daily 10:00-20:00, Ke Hradu, tel. 257-533-735).

Na Baště, serene but not as scenic, is in a garden through the gate to the left of the main castle entry. The outdoor seating, among Jože Plečnik's ramparts and obelisks, is the castle at its most quiet (100-Kč sandwiches, 250-Kč salads, daily 10:00-18:00, tel. 281-933-010).

Prague Connections

Centrally located Prague is a logical gateway between Western and Eastern Europe. From here, convenient, direct night trains head eastward to Budapest, Kraków, and Warsaw, and westward to Amsterdam, Vienna, Frankfurt, and Zurich; several trains also leave daily for Munich, Berlin, and Vienna. You'll find handy Czech train and bus schedules at www.idos.cz; for trains, you can also check out Germany's all-Europe timetable at www.bahn.com. Remember that for all train connections, it's important to confirm which of Prague's stations to use.

From Prague's Main Station by Train to: Konopiště Castle (train to **Benešov**, 2/hour, 1 hour, then 30-minute walk to castle), **Karlštejn** (2/hour, 40 minutes, then a 20-minute walk to castle), **Křivoklát** (hourly, 1.5 hours total, transfer in Beroun), **Kutná Hora** (11/day, 1 hour, more with change in Kolín), **Terezín** (train to Bohušovice station, nearly hourly, 1-1.5 hours, then 5-minute taxi or bus ride—bus is better), **Český Krumlov** (8/day, 1/day direct, 4 hours—bus is faster, cheaper, and easier), **Budapest** (3/day, 7 hours; more with 2-3 changes, 8.5 hours; 1 night train, 7.5 hours), **Kraków** (1/day direct, 7.5 hours; 4/day with 1-2 changes, 8.25 hours; 1 night train, 9.5 hours), **Warsaw** (1/day direct, 8.75 hours; 3/day with 1-2 changes, 8.5-10 hours; 1 night train, 10 hours), **Vienna** (that's *Vídeň* in Czech, 5/day direct, 4-4.5 hours, more with 1 change, 5-6 hours; 1 night train, 7.5 hours), **Berlin** (6/day, 4.5-5 hours), **Dresden** (about hourly, 2-2.5 hours), **Munich** (2/day direct, 6.25 hours; also 6/day via ExpressBus, 4.75-6 hours, operated by German Railways and covered by any railpass that includes the Czech Republic and Germany, more bus connections possible with change to a train in Nürnberg; no night train), **Frankfurt** (6/day via ExpressBus to Nürnberg then train to Frankfurt, 6.5 hours total; 1 night train, 9.5 hours), **Amsterdam** (1 night train, 15 hours), **Zürich** (1 night train, 15 hours), **Paris** (5/day, 12.5-13.5 hours; 1 night train possible via Mannheim or Berlin).

From Prague by Bus to: Terezín (hourly, 50 minutes, 10 more minutes to **Litoměřice**, departs from Nádraží Holešovice train station), **Český Krumlov** (7/day, 3.5 hours, some leave from Florenc station, others leave from Na Knížecí station or Roztyly station). The handy ExpressBus to Munich or Nürnberg (mentioned above) departs from in front of the main train station.

By Car with a Driver: Mike's Chauffeur Service is a reliable, family-run company with fair and fixed rates around town and beyond. Friendly Mike's motto is, "We go the extra mile for you" (round-trip fares, with waiting time included, guaranteed through 2012 with this book: Český Krumlov-3,800 Kč, Terezín-1,900 Kč, Karlštejn-1,700 Kč, 4 percent surcharge for credit-card payment;

these prices for up to 4 people, minibus for up to 7 also available; tel. 241-768-231, mobile 602-224-893, www.mike-chauffeur.cz, mike.chauffeur@cmail.cz). On the way to Český Krumlov, Mike will stop at no extra charge at Hluboká Castle or České Budějovice, where the original Bud beer is made. For day trips from Prague, Mike can bring bicycles along and will pedal with you.

Mike also offers "Panoramic Transfers" to **Vienna** (7,000 Kč, depart Prague at 8:00, arrive Český Krumlov at 10:00, stay up to 6 hours, 1-hour scenic Czech riverside-and-village drive, then a 2-hour autobahn ride to your Vienna hotel, maximum 4 people); **Budapest** (8,900 Kč, 6 hours, Bratislava or Český Krumlov options); and **Kraków** (8,900 Kč, Auschwitz stop). Check Mike's website for special deals on last-minute transfers (see his "Hot News" sidebar), including super-cheap "deadhead" rides when you travel in the opposite direction of a full-fare client.

By Plane: For information on Prague's airport, see page 62.

PRAGUE

NEAR PRAGUE

Kutná Hora • Terezín Concentration Camp Memorial •
Konopiště Castle • Karlštejn Castle • Křivoklát Castle

Prague has plenty to keep a traveler busy, but don't overlook the interesting day trips in the nearby Bohemian countryside. Within an hour of Prague (in different directions), you'll find a rich medieval town, a sobering concentration camp, and three grand castles.

Down-to-earth Kutná Hora was once home to the world's largest silver mine; it's now known for its opulent cathedral, built with riches from the mining bonanza. Terezín, a walled town, served as an internment camp for Jews during World War II. Two of the country's most popular castles—Konopiště (better interior) and Karlštejn (better exterior)—give you a good look at the Czech version of this European medieval architectural form. And Křivoklát Castle is one of the purest Gothic structures in the country, and a less touristy alternative to the other two castles.

Kutná Hora

Kutná Hora (KOOT-nah HO-rah) is a refreshingly authentic town of 20,000, on top of what was once Europe's largest silver mine. In its heyday, the mine was so productive that Kutná Hora was Bohemia's "second city" after Prague. Much of Europe's standard coinage was minted here. By about 1700, the mining and minting petered out, and the city slumbered. Once rich, then ignored, Kutná Hora is now appreciated by tourists looking for a handy side-trip from Prague. Visitors are charmed by this wonderfully preserved town and its interesting sights: the fine St.

Day Trips

GERMANY

POLAND

To Berlin

Dresden

Bautzen

Görlitz

Zgorzelec

Elbe

E 40

E 40

Bad Schandau

170

Zinnwald

Děčín

Cínovec

E 55

8

Ústí nad Labem

Teplice

Litoměřice

Terezín

CONCENTRATION CAMP MEMORIAL

50 Kilometers

50 Miles

C Z E C H   R E P U B L I C

Mělník

Křivoklát Park

Slaný

E 55

9

To Karlovy Vary

E 6

Lidice

RUZYNĚ AIRPORT

Labe   River

To Hradec Králové

Rakovník

Lány

E 67

Prague

Křivoklát Castle

Nižbor

12

Beroun

Karlštejn Castle

603

Kolín

2

Berounka   River

Revnice

Kutná Hora

E 50

Vltava River

4

Konopiště Castle

Beneşov

To Brno

To Plzeň

E 50

To Brno

To Tábor & Český Krumlov

NEAR PRAGUE

Barbara's Cathedral, the fascinating silver mine, and the eerie Sedlec Bone Church.

Kutná Hora, unlike dolled-up Český Krumlov, is a typical Czech town. The shops on the main square cater to locals, and the factory between the Sedlec Bone Church and the train station—since the 1930s, the biggest tobacco processor in the country—is now Philip Morris' headquarters for Central Europe. After touristy Prague, Kutná Hora is about as close to quintessential Czech life as you can get.

Getting to Kutná Hora

The town is 40 miles east of Prague. Direct trains from Prague's Main Station stop at Kutná Hora's Main Station, two miles from the town center (11/day, 1 hour; other trains are slower and require transfer in Kolín). From there, a local train shuttles visitors to Sedlec Station (near the Sedlec Bone Church), then to the central Město Station (near the rest of the sights). For train schedules, see www.jizdnirady.idnes.cz.

In Prague, make sure to buy a ticket to the Kutná Hora Město Station rather than its Main Station—the price is nearly the same, and this gives you the flexibility to get off and on at any of the three Kutná Hora stations.

Planning Your Time

For the most efficient visit, visit the Sedlec Bone Church first, then St. Barbara's Cathedral, and end with the Museum of Silver.

Here are the specifics: At Kutná Hora's Main Station, transfer to the local train. Get off at its first stop (Kutná Hora-Sedlec), and walk one block down the street perpendicular to the tracks, passing a large church on your right. Cross the main street and find the small Bone Church in the middle of the cemetery directly ahead. After your visit, ride the Bone Church's tourist minivan to St. Barbara's Cathedral in the town center. From the cathedral, walk to the Museum of Silver and reserve your spot on the next English-language tour (it's also possible to call the museum ahead to reserve). At the end of the day, walk to the Kutná Hora Město Station to catch the train back to Prague.

Orientation to Kutná Hora

Tourist Information

The main TI is on **Palackého Náměstí,** housed in the same building as the Alchemy Museum (April-Sept daily 9:00-18:00; Oct-March Mon-Fri 9:00-17:00, Sat-Sun 9:00-16:00; tel. 327-512-378, www.kutnahora.cz). It offers Internet access and also rents bicycles (220 Kč/day, mobile 605-802-874).

A small TI kiosk, with handy WCs, is in front of the **cathedral;** you can also hire a local guide here. Reserve ahead if you can (500 Kč/hour Tue-Sun, no tours Mon, tel. 327-516-710, mobile 736-485-408, infocentrum@kh.cz).

Sights in Kutná Hora

St. Barbara's Cathedral (Chrám Sv. Barbory)—The cathedral was founded in 1388 by miners, who dedicated it to their patron. The dazzling interior celebrates the town's sources of wealth, with frescoes featuring mining and minting. Even the Renaissance vault—a stunning feat of architecture by the two Gothic geniuses of Prague, Matyáš Rejsek and Benedict Ried—is decorated with miners' coats of arms. The artistic highlight is the Smíšek Chapel to the right of the altar. The late-Gothic frescoes—*The Arrival of the Queen of Sheba, The Trial of Trajan,* and especially the fresco under the chapel's window depicting two men with candles—are the only remaining works of a Dutch-trained master in Gothic Bohemia.

Cost and Hours: 50 Kč, daily 9:00-18:00 in summer, shorter hours off-season.

Art Gallery of the Central Bohemian Region (GASK)—The former Baroque Jesuit college (on your left as you exit the cathedral) was recently converted into an art museum. It boasts the second-biggest exhibition space in the country (after the National Gallery in Prague), filled with ever-changing temporary exhibits of 20th- and 21st-century art.

The statues of saints on the artificial terrace in front of the gallery are a reminder of the building's Jesuit past. The Jesuits arrived here in 1626 with a mission: to make the Protestant population Catholic again. These chubby sandstone figures, just like those on the Charles Bridge in Prague, were initially commissioned as Counter-Reformation propaganda pieces.

Cost and Hours: Combo-ticket for all exhibits-120 Kč, single exhibit-60 Kč, Tue-Sun 10:00-18:00, closed Mon, Barborská 51-53, www.gask.cz.

Hrádek Castle and the Czech Museum of Silver (České Muzeum Stříbra)—This museum, located in Kutná Hora's 15th-century Hrádek castle, features an exhibit on mining and an intriguing horse-powered winch that once hoisted 2,000 pounds of rock at a time out of the mine. Don a miner's coat and helmet, and climb deep into the mine for a wet, dark, and claustrophobic 45-minute tour of the medieval shafts that honeycomb the rock beneath the town. Try to time your visit to join an English-language tour (ask for the charming Mr. Matuška, a retired miner). You can try calling ahead (the day before or the morning of your visit) to ask when English tours are scheduled—wait through the Czech recording, ask to speak with an English-speaker, and reserve a slot. Otherwise, drop by the museum soon after you arrive in Kutná Hora to find out the schedule and reserve.

Cost and Hours: 110 Kč, April-Oct Tue-Sun 10:00-18:00, closed Mon and Nov-March, tours generally every half-hour, tel. 327-512-159, www.cms-kh.cz.

Stone Fountain (Kamenná Kašna)—Because of intensive mining under the town, Kutná Hora has always struggled with obtaining clean drinking water. Water was brought to town by

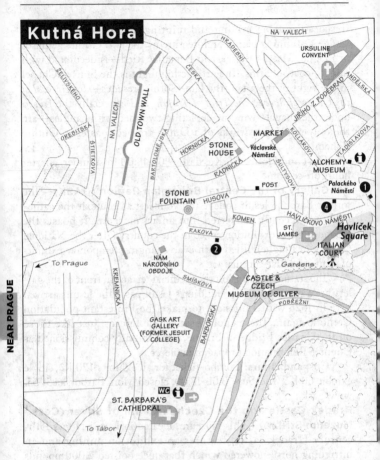

Kutná Hora

a sophisticated system of water pipes and then stored in large tanks. At the end of the 15th century, the architect Rejsek built a 12-sided, richly decorated Gothic structure over one of these tanks. Although no longer functioning, the fountain survives unchanged—the only structure like it in Bohemia (on the square called Rejskovo Náměstí).

Stone House (Kamenný Dům)—Notice the meticulous detail in the grape leaves, branches, and animals on this house's facade and up in its gable. Talented Polish craftsmen delicately carved the brittle stone into what was considered a marvel of its time. Skip the boring museum of local arts and crafts inside.

Cost and Hours: 40 Kč, daily 10:00-17:00, Radnická 183, www.cms-kh.cz.

Alchemy Museum (Muzeum Alchymie)—The only one of its kind in the Czech Republic, situated in the surprisingly deep medieval cellars of this otherwise unassuming house, this museum

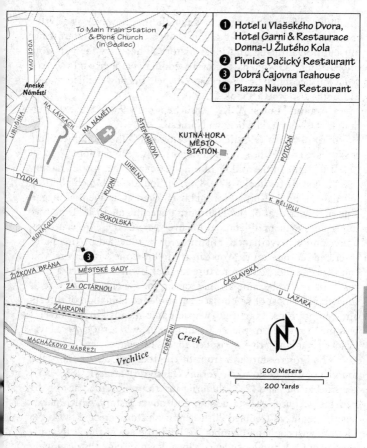

Map Legend:
1. Hotel u Vlašského Dvora, Hotel Garni & Restaurace Donna-U Žlutého Kola
2. Pivnice Dačický Restaurant
3. Dobrá Čajovna Teahouse
4. Piazza Navona Restaurant

features a laboratory dedicated to the pursuit of *prima materia* (primal matter). The English descriptions do a good job explaining the goals and methods of alchemy and the fate of its failed practitioners. The rare Gothic tower in the rear of the house is set up as an alchemist's study (complete with ancient books), looking much as it did when a prince used this vaulted space in his quest to purify matter and spirit.

Cost and Hours: 60 Kč, daily April-Sept 9:00-18:00, Oct-March 9:00-17:00, on the main square in the same building as the TI, tel. 327-512-378.

Nearby: Upstairs from the TI (in the same building) is another quirky museum, featuring a collection of baby strollers from the Victorian era to the present.

Italian Court (Vlašský Dvůr)—This palace, located on the site where Czech currency was once made, became Europe's most important mint and the main residence of Czech kings in the 1400s. Most of the present-day building, however, is a 19th-century reconstruction. Today, it hosts a moderately interesting museum on minting and local history. The entry fee gets you into the main Gothic hall (now a wedding chamber) and the Art Nouveau-decorated St. Wenceslas Chapel. The flower-filled square in front is also worth a look.

Cost and Hours: 70 Kč, April-Sept daily 9:00-18:00, shorter hours Oct-March, Havlíčkovo Náměstí.

Havlíček Square (Havlíčkovo Náměstí)—The monuments on this square are a Who's Who of important Czech patriots.

The statue in the middle of the square (and the square's namesake) is **Karel Havlíček** (1821-1856), the founder of Czech political journalism. From Kutná Hora, Havlíček ran an influential magazine highly critical of the Habsburg government. In 1851, he was forced into exile and detained for five years in the Tirolean Alps under police surveillance. His integrity is reflected by the quote inscribed on the statue: "You can try to bribe me with favors, you can threaten me, you can torture me, yet I will never turn a traitor." His motto became an inspiration for generations of Czech intellectuals, most of whom faced a similar combination of threats and temptations. Havlíček (whose name means "little Havel") was much revered in the 1970s and 1980s, when the *other* Havel (Václav) was similarly imprisoned for his dissent.

The bronze statue in front of the Italian Court honors the founder of Czechoslovakia, **Tomáš Garrigue Masaryk** (1850-1937; see sidebar on page 122). The brief inscription on the back of the pedestal recounts the statue's up-and-down history, which parallels the country's troubled 20th-century history: erected by Kutná Hora townspeople on October 27, 1938 (the eve of the 20th anniversary of Czech independence); torn down in 1942 (by occupying Nazis, who disliked Masaryk as a symbol of Czech independence); erected again on October 27, 1948 (by freedom-loving locals, a few months after the communist coup); torn down again in 1957 (by the communists, who considered Masaryk an enemy of the working class); and erected once again on October 27, 1991. Notice that the Czechs, ever practical, have left a blank space below the last entry....

On the wall to the left of the gate, you'll find a small bronze tablet covered with barbed wire. This is an unassuming little **memorial** to the victims of the communist regime's misrule and torture.

Walk down the steps into a little park, and then turn right to reach a great viewpoint. It overlooks the tent-shaped roof of the cathedral and the scenic valley below. You might want to take a rest on nearby benches under some linden trees—and think about those whom the memorial commemorates.

Market (Tržiště)—This double row of stalls selling fake Nike shoes and cheap jeans is as much a part of Czech urban life today as farmers markets were in the past. The stalls are often run by Vietnamese immigrants, the Czech Republic's third-largest minority (after Slovaks and Poles). Many came here in the 1970s as part of a communist solidarity program that sent Vietnamese workers to Czech textile factories. They learned the language, adapted to the environment, and, after 1989, set off on a road to entrepreneurial success that allowed them to bring over friends and relatives (Mon-Fri 7:30-16:45, shorter hours Sat, closed Sun, near Stone House).

Near Kutná Hora

Sedlec Bone Church (Kostnice u Sedlci)—Located a mile away from the center of town, in Sedlec, this little church looks

normal on the outside. But inside, the bones of 40,000 people decorate the walls and ceilings. The 14th-century plagues and 15th-century wars provided all the raw material necessary for the creepily creative monks who made these designs. Those who first placed these bones 400 years ago wanted viewers to remember that the earthly church is a community of both the living and the dead, a countless multitude that will one day stand before God. Later bone-stackers were more interested in design than theology...as evidenced by the chandelier that includes every bone in the human body.

Cost and Hours: 60 Kč, daily April-Sept 8:00-18:00, March and Oct 9:00-17:00, Nov-Feb 9:00-16:00, tel. 327-561-143, www.kostnice.cz.

Shuttle: The Bone Church runs a tourist minivan that can shuttle you from the church to sights in town (35 Kč/person, requires 3 passengers or else pay the 105-Kč minimum fee, April-Sept 9:00-18:00, Oct-March 9:00-17:00, inquire at the desk, mobile 731-402-307).

Sleeping in Kutná Hora

Although one day is enough for Kutná Hora, staying overnight saves you money (hotels are much cheaper here than in Prague) and allows you to better savor the atmosphere of a small Czech town.

$$ Hotel u Vlašského Dvora and **Hotel Garni** are two renovated townhouses run by the same management. Furnished in a

NEAR PRAGUE

Sleep Code

(18 Kč = about $1, country code: 420)
S = Single, **D** = Double/Twin, **T** = Triple, **Q** = Quad, **b** = bathroom,
s = shower only. Unless otherwise noted, English is spoken,
credit cards are accepted, and breakfast is included.

To help you easily sort through these listings, I've divided
the accommodations into three categories based on the price
for a double room with bath during high season:

$$$ Higher Priced—Most rooms 1,500 Kč or more.
$$ Moderately Priced—Most rooms between 1,000-1,500 Kč.
$ Lower Priced—Most rooms 1,000 Kč or less.

Prices can change without notice; verify the hotel's
current rates online or by email. For other updates, see www
.ricksteves.com/update.

mix of 1930s and modern style, the hotels come with access to a
fitness center and sauna. Hotel Garni is slightly nicer (Db-1,200
Kč, a few steps off main square at Havlíčkovo Náměstí 513, tel.
327-515-773, www.vlasskydvur.cz).

Eating in Kutná Hora

Pivnice Dačický has made a theme of its namesake, a popular
17th-century author who once lived in the house. Solid wooden
tables rest under perky illustrations of medieval town life, and a
once-local brew, also named after Dačický, flows from the tap.
They serve standard Czech fare, as well as excellent game and fish.
While its regulars still come here for the cheap lunch specials,
during tourist season the crowd is mostly international. Service
can be slow when a group arrives (daily 11:00-23:00, Rakova 8, tel.
327-512-248, mobile 603-434-367).

Dobrá Čajovna Teahouse also offers the chance to escape—
not to medieval times, but to a Thai paradise. Filled with tea cases,
water pipes, and character, this place is an ideal spot to dawdle
away the time that this ageless town has reclaimed for you (daily
14:00-22:00, Jungmannovo Náměstí 16, mobile 777-028-481).

Restaurace Donna-U Žlutého Kola serves the fastest, tasti-
est Czech dishes in town, attracting a local crowd. There's a long
menu in English, but the lunch specials are only listed on a separate sheet in Czech. When the weather's nice, sit in the shady
courtyard behind the restaurant (open daily, lunch specials until
15:00, on Havlíčkovo Náměstí, right above Hotel Garni).

Piazza Navona features irritating English-language advertising ("the only true Italian restaurant in town"), but it still draws loyal customers thanks to its decent food and superb location on the main square (open daily).

Terezín Concentration Camp Memorial

Terezín (TEH-reh-zeen), an hour by bus from Prague, was originally a fortified town named after Habsburg Empress Maria Theresa (it's called "Theresienstadt" in German). It was built in the 1780s with state-of-the-art, star-shaped walls designed to keep out the Prussians. In 1941, the Nazis removed the town's 7,000 inhabitants and brought in 60,000 Jews, creating a concentration camp. Ironically, the town's medieval walls, originally meant to keep Germans out, were later used by Germans to keep the Jews in.

This was the Nazis' model "Jewish town," a concentration camp dolled up for propaganda purposes. Here, in this "self-governed Jewish resettlement area," Jewish culture seemed to

thrive, as "citizens" put on plays and concerts, published a magazine, and raised their families. But it was all a carefully planned deception, intended to convince Red Cross inspectors that the Jews were being treated well. Virtually all of Terezín's Jews (155,000 over the course of the war) ultimately ended up dying either here (35,000) or in extermination camps farther east.

One of the notable individuals held at Terezín was Viennese artist Friedl Dicker-Brandeis. This daring woman, a leader in the Bauhaus art movement, found her life's calling in teaching children freedom of expression. She taught the kids in the camp to distinguish between the central things—trees, flowers, lines—and peripheral things, such as the conditions of the camp. In 1944, Dicker-Brandeis volunteered to be sent to Auschwitz after her husband was transported there; she was killed a month later.

Of the 15,000 children who passed through Terezín from 1942 to 1944, fewer than 100 survived. The artwork they created at Terezín is a striking testimony to the cruel horror of the Holocaust. In 1994, Hana Volavková, a Terezín survivor and the director of the Jewish Museum in Prague, collected the children's artwork

Petr Ginz, Young Artist and Writer

Born in 1928 to a Jewish father and non-Jewish mother, Prague teenager Petr Ginz excelled at art and was a talented writer who penned numerous articles, short stories, and even a science-fiction novel. Petr was sent to the concentration camp at Terezín in 1942, where he edited the secret boys' publication *Vedem (We Are Ahead)*, writing poetry and drawing illustrations, and paying contributors with food rations he received from home.

Some of Petr's artwork and writings were preserved by Terezín survivors and archived by the Jewish Museum in Prague. In 2003, Ilan Ramon, the first Israeli astronaut and the son of a Holocaust survivor, took one of Petr's drawings—titled *Moon Country*—into space aboard the final, doomed mission of the space shuttle Columbia.

The publicity over the Columbia's explosion and Petr's drawing spurred a Prague resident to come forward with a diary he'd found in his attic. It was Petr's diary from 1941 to 1942, hidden decades earlier by Petr's parents and chronicling the year before the teen's deportation to Terezín. *The Diary of Petr Ginz* has since been published in more than 10 languages.

In the diary, Petr matter-of-factly documented the increasing restrictions on Jewish life in occupied Prague, interspersing the terse account with dry humor. In the entry for September 19, 1941, Petr wrote, "They just introduced a special sign for Jews" alongside a drawing of the Star of David. He continued, "On the way to school I counted 69 'sheriffs,'" referring to people wearing the star.

Petr spent two years at Terezín before being sent to Auschwitz, where he died in a gas chamber. He was 16.

and poems in the book *I Never Saw Another Butterfly*. Selections of the Terezín drawings are also displayed and well-described in English in Prague's Pinkas Synagogue (described on page 91).

The most well-known of the cultural activities that took place at Terezín was the children's opera *Brundibár*. Written just before the war, the anti-Fascist opera premiered secretly in Prague at a time when Jewish activities were no longer permitted. From 1943 to 1944, the play, performed in Czech, ran 55 times in the camp. After the war it was staged internationally, and was recently rewritten as a children's book in the US by Tony Kushner and Maurice Sendak (whose version later appeared on Broadway).

Today, Terezín is an unforgettable day trip from Prague for those interested in touring a concentration camp memorial and museum. Allow three to six hours to see the entire camp.

Getting to Terezín

The camp is about 40 miles northwest of Prague. It's most convenient to visit Terezín by **bus** (described next) or **tour bus** (see page 71).

Buses to Terezín leave hourly from Prague's Holešovice train station (Nádraží Holešovice, on Metro line C). When you get off the Metro (coming from the city center), head toward the front of the train, go upstairs, turn right, and walk to the end of the corridor. You'll see bus stands directly ahead, outside the station. The Terezín bus departs from platform 7 (direction: Litoměřice, buy ticket from driver). You'll arrive in Terezín 50 minutes later at the public bus stop on the main square, around the corner from the Museum of the Ghetto. Some buses also stop earlier, by the Small Fortress. The driver and fellow passengers may tell you to get off there, but my self-guided tour works best if you begin at the stop in town (after the bus passes a field of crosses on your right and travels across the river).

For bus schedules, see www.idos.cz—you want "Terezín LT" (be sure to check the return schedule, too; for details on getting back to Prague, see "Terezín Connections," later).

Orientation to Terezín

Cost and Hours: The 200-Kč combo-ticket includes all parts of the camp. Most sights, including the Museum of the Ghetto, Magdeburg Barracks, and Hidden Synagogue, are open daily April-Oct 9:00-18:00, Nov-March 9:00-17:30. The columbarium and crematorium are closed Sat. The crematorium opens at 10:00 year-round and closes at 16:00 Nov-March, and the Small Fortress opens at 8:00 year-round and closes at 16:30 Nov-March.

Tours: Guided tours in English are offered if enough people request them; call ahead to get the schedule and reserve a spot (included in entry).

Information: Tel. 416-782-225, mobile 606-632-914, www .pamatnik-terezin.cz.

Eating: In Terezín town, the **Parkhotel Restaurant** is the most elegant place for lunch (daily 10:00-22:00, around the block from Museum of the Ghetto at Máchova 163, tel. 416-782-260, cell 775-068-734).

The Small Fortress has a **cafeteria.** But avoid the stale sandwiches in the Museum of the Ghetto's dingy basement cafeteria, where most tour guides inexplicably bring their clients.

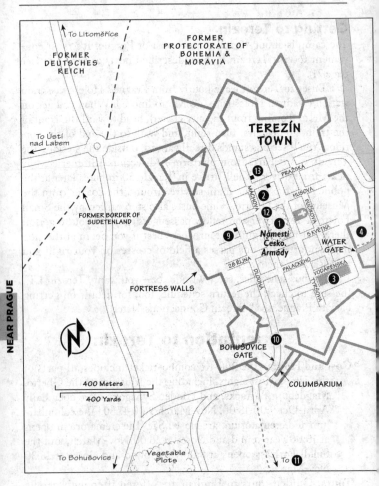

Self-Guided Tour

On this visit, you'll see Terezín town and the Small Fortress, which is a long half-mile walk to the east across the river.

• *The bus from Prague drops you off at Terezín town's spacious...*

Main Square (Náměstí Československé Armády): Picture the giant circus tent and barbed-wire fence that stood on this square for two years during the war. Inside, Jewish workers boxed special motors for German vehicles being used on the frigid Soviet front. As part of year-long preparations for the famous Red Cross visit (which lasted all of six hours on June 23, 1944), the tent and fence were replaced by flower beds (which you still see on the square today) and a pavilion for outdoor music performances.

• *Walk around the corner to the...*

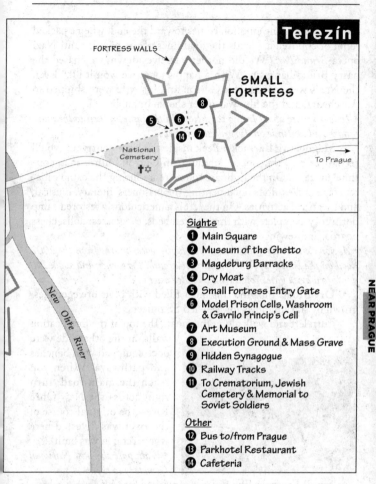

Terezín

FORTRESS WALLS

SMALL FORTRESS

National Cemetery

To Prague

New Ohře River

Sights
1. Main Square
2. Museum of the Ghetto
3. Magdeburg Barracks
4. Dry Moat
5. Small Fortress Entry Gate
6. Model Prison Cells, Washroom & Gavrilo Princip's Cell
7. Art Museum
8. Execution Ground & Mass Grave
9. Hidden Synagogue
10. Railway Tracks
11. To Crematorium, Jewish Cemetery & Memorial to Soviet Soldiers

Other
12. Bus to/from Prague
13. Parkhotel Restaurant
14. Cafeteria

Museum of the Ghetto: You can buy the Terezín combo-ticket here (note film show-times posted near ticket desk). You'll find two floors of exhibits about the development of the Nazis' "Final Solution" and a theater showing four excellent films. One film documents the history of the ghetto, and two focus on children's art in the camp. The fourth is made up of clips from *Der Führer schenkt den Juden eine Stadt (The Führer Gives a City to the Jews)* by Kurt Gerron. Gerron, a Berlin Jew, was a 1920s movie star who appeared with Marlene Dietrich in *Blue Angel*. Deported to Terezín, Gerron in 1944 was asked by the Nazis to produce a propaganda film. The resulting film depicts healthy (i.e., recently arrived) "Jewish settlers" in Terezín happily viewing concerts, playing soccer, and sewing in their rooms—yet an unmistakable, deadly desperation radiates from their pallid faces. The only moment of genuine emotion comes toward the end, when a packed room of children applauds the final lines of the popular anti-Nazi opera *Brundibár:* "We did not let ourselves down, we chased the nasty Brundibár away. With a happy song, we won it all." Even the Nazis were not fooled: Gerron and his wife were shipped to Auschwitz, and the film was never shown in public.

• *To learn more about living conditions in the camp, return to the main square and continue on Tyršova street to the...*

Magdeburg Barracks: Peek inside the large courtyard (you'll recognize it as the "soccer stadium" in Gerron's film), then continue upstairs. On the right are rooms reproducing the camp cabaret stage and exhibits documenting the prisoners' literary, musical, and theatrical activities. On the left is a meticulously restored camp dormitory, complete with three-tiered beds, eyeglasses, dolls, chess boards, and sewing kits.

• *As you exit the barracks (notice the high-water marks from the 2002 flood on the house opposite), turn right around the corner and walk 100 yards to a brick gate. You'll cross a bridge over a...*

Dry Moat: Imagine this moat filled with plots of vegetables, grown by starving Jews for well-fed SS officers.

Turn left and walk along the moat. The top of the fortification

walls on the other side were once equipped with benches and pathways. When you reach the main road, turn right across the New Ohře River (the original course of the river was diverted here when Terezín was built).

• *Walk past the vast National Cemetery to the...*

Small Fortress: The fortress is marked by a black-and-white-striped gate. From 1940 to 1945, this fortress functioned as a Gestapo prison, through which 32,000 inmates passed (nearly 10 percent died here)—chiefly members of the Czech resistance and communists. The 1,500 Jews interned here were treated with particular severity.

• *Inside the gate, turn left toward the notorious* Arbeit Macht Frei *sign (a postwar replica), painted above an arched gate. In the courtyard behind, you will first find...*

Model Prison Cells: The washroom in the left corner was built solely for the purpose of fooling Red Cross inspectors. Go ahead, turn the faucets: No pipes were ever installed to bring in water. The **shower room** farther to the left, on the other hand, was used to fool the Jews. Here they got used to the idea of communal bathing, so they wouldn't be suspicious when they were later taken

to similar-looking installations at Auschwitz. (There were no gas chambers at Terezín—most of the deaths here were caused by malnutrition, disease, and, to a lesser extent, execution.)

Before the Nazis, the Small Fortress was used as a prison by the Austrian monarchy. The little courtyard preserves the cell of the most famous prisoner from that time, Bosnian Serb **Gavrilo Princip,** whose assassination of Archduke Franz Ferdinand and his wife Žofie in 1914 sparked World War I (see sidebar on page 184). Princip died here in 1918 of tuberculosis.

• *Return through the* Arbeit Macht Frei *gate, then turn left into a large courtyard. On your right is an...*

Art Museum: This features two floors of paintings by prominent Czech artists, with themes of camp life and the Spanish Civil War.

• *Farther to the left is a path leading to the...*

Execution Ground and Mass Grave: Many of Terezín's victims were buried in mass graves along the fortress ramparts. The National Cemetery, outside the fortress, was created after World War II to hold remains exhumed from the mass graves (it now holds the last remains of 10,000 people).

• *At this point you could head to the handy cafeteria by the entry gate to the Small Fortress and take a break. The wood-and-metal chandeliers inside were produced by Jewish workers for the SS officers who once dined in these two rooms.*

With more time, consider continuing your tour in Terezín town with the less-frequented sights that lie along or just off a main road called Dlouhá. At Dlouhá 17, look for the unique...

Hidden Synagogue: This is the only one of the camp's eight synagogues that survived. Although entry is included with your combo-ticket, you may need to ring the bell for the guard to open the door. Inside you'll find a courtyard; the bakery that used to be here hid the synagogue behind it. The atmospheric space is still inscribed with two Hebrew captions, which are translated as "May my eyes behold, how You in compassion return to Sinai," and "If I forget Jerusalem, may my tongue rot and my right arm fall off." These words indicate that the prayer room belonged to a congregation of Zionists (advocates of a Jewish state), who, one would expect, were specifically targeted by the Nazis.

• *Continue down Dlouhá toward the Bohušovice gate. On the ground, look for the remnants of...*

Railway Tracks: In the early years of the camp, Jews arrived

at the train station in the nearby
town of Bohušovice and then had
to walk the remaining two miles
to Terezín. This was too public a
display for the Nazis, who didn't
want townspeople to observe the
transports and become suspicious,
so the Jewish prisoners at Terezín
were forced to construct a railway
line that led right to Terezín...and
back out again to Auschwitz.

As you exit the walled-in area, on the right you will find
Jewish and Christian ceremonial halls and the main morgue; on
the left is a **columbarium,** where the Nazis deposited cardboard
boxes containing the ashes of dead prisoners. The Germans originally promised that the remains would be properly buried after the
war, but in 1945, to erase evidence, the ashes of Terezín victims
were dumped into the New Ohře River.

• *Continue along the road, then turn left past bucolic vegetable plots and
fruit gardens to reach the...*

Crematorium, Jewish Cemetery, and a **Memorial to Soviet
Soldiers:** Days before Terezín was liberated (on May 8, 1945), an
epidemic of typhus spread through the camp. In the weeks after
the war ended, scores of Soviet soldiers and medical workers who
tried to contain the epidemic died, along with hundreds of former
prisoners.

• *Our tour ends here. As you ponder Terezín, remember the message of
all such memorials: Never again.*

Terezín Connections

The bus for **Prague** leaves from Terezín's main square (hourly, 50
minutes). If the return bus doesn't fit your schedule, consider taking a taxi from Terezín to the Bohušovice station (5 minutes from
Terezín, trains to Prague depart nearly hourly, 1-1.5 hours). There
is no taxi service from Bohušovice to Terezín, making the train a
good option only for the return journey. If you're continuing from
Terezín to **Dresden,** Germany, take the train from Bohušovice to
Ústí, then switch to the international express train. For bus and
train schedules, see www.idos.cz.

Konopiště Castle

Konopiště (KOH-noh-peesh-tyeh), the huge, Neo-Gothic residence of the Archduke Franz Ferdinand d'Este, is 30 miles south of Prague.

Construction of the castle began in the 14th century, but today's exterior and furnishings date from about 1900, when the

heir to the Habsburg throne, Archduke Franz Ferdinand, renovated his new home. As one of the first castles in Europe to have an elevator, a WC, and running water, Konopiště shows "modern" living at the turn of the 20th century. Touring the castle gives you a good sense of who this powerful Habsburg was, as well as a glimpse at one of the best medieval arms collections in the world (and lots of hunting trophies).

While the stretch between the parking lot and the castle entrance is overrun by tour groups, the **gardens** and the **park** are surprisingly empty. In the summer, the flowers and goldfish in the rose garden are a big hit with visitors. The peaceful 30-minute walk through the woods around the lake (wooden bridge at the far end) offers gorgeous castle views.

Tucked away in the bushes behind the pond is a pavilion coated with tree bark, a perfect picnic spot. This simple structure, nicknamed the **Kaiser's Pavilion,** was the site of a fateful meeting between the German Kaiser Wilhelm and the Archduke Franz Ferdinand (explained in the sidebar).

Cost and Tours: Entrance to the castle is by one-hour guided tour only. Choose from three different routes: Route I (210 Kč, includes public and guest rooms, hunting hall, and shooting range), Route II (210 Kč, includes the oldest part of the castle, armory, elevator, and chapel), and Route III (310 Kč, includes private top-floor rooms of Franz Ferdinand and his family). While Route II gives you the most comprehensive look into the castle, its history, and celebrated collections, Route III—reopened after the rooms were meticulously restored to match 1907 photographs—launches you right into a turn-of-the-20th-century time capsule. Space on Route III is limited to 8 people per hour: It's best to reserve a spot in advance by calling one day ahead or on the morning of your visit. All tickets are 30 percent cheaper if you join a Czech-speaking tour (you'll be given an English audioguide).

Hours: May-Aug Tue-Sun 9:00-12:30 & 13:00-17:00; April and Oct Tue-Fri 9:00-15:00, Sat-Sun 9:00-16:00; Sept Tue-Fri

Archduke Franz Ferdinand
(1863-1914)

Archduke Franz Ferdinand was the nephew of the Habsburg Emperor Franz Josef, who ruled from 1848 to 1916 (longer than Queen Victoria; for more on Franz Josef, see page 1142). Ferdinand was the impatient successor to the Austro-Hungarian throne. Local legends (whose veracity historians categorically deny) say that Franz Ferdinand even built a chapel at Konopiště for the sole purpose of praying that his old, hated uncle might soon die...but the emperor went on to outlive the young archduke.

Franz Ferdinand fell out of his uncle's favor when he married a beautiful but low-ranking Czech countess, Žofie Chotková (often known by her German name, Sophie). Žofie was "only" aristocratic, not royal. To get out of his relatives' sight, Franz Ferdinand bought Konopiště and moved here.

Obsessed with hunting, Franz Ferdinand traveled around the world twice, shooting at anything in sight: deer, bears, tigers, elephants, and crocodiles. He killed about 300,000 animals in all, many of whom stare morbidly at you as hunting trophies covering the walls at Konopiště.

In the Kaiser's Pavilion on the grounds of Konopiště, Franz Ferdinand met with German Kaiser Wilhelm and tried to talk him out of plotting a war against Russia. Wilhelm argued that a war would work to the mutual benefit of Germany and Austria: Germans wanted colonies, and Austria—crippled by the aspirations of its many nationalities—could use a war to divert attention from its domestic problems. But Franz Ferdinand foresaw that war would be suicidal for Austria's overstretched monarchy.

Soon after, Franz Ferdinand and Žofie went to Sarajevo, in the Habsburg-annexed territories of Bosnia and Herzegovina. On that trip, young Gavrilo Princip, a Bosnian Serb, shot the Habsburg archduke who so loved shooting. (Žofie was also killed.) Franz Ferdinand's assassination ironically gave the Germans (and their pro-war allies in the Austro-Hungarian administration) the pretext for starting the war against Serbia and its ally, Russia. World War I soon broke out. The event Franz Ferdinand had tried to prevent was, in fact, sparked by his death.

9:00-16:00, Sat-Sun 9:00-17:00; closed Nov-March and Mon year-round.

Information: Tel. 317-721-366, www.zamek-konopiste.cz.

Getting to Konopiště Castle: Trains from Prague's Main Station drop you in Benešov (2/hour, one hour, www.idos.cz); a well-marked trail goes from the station to the castle (1.5 miles). To walk to the castle, as you exit the Benešov train station, turn left and walk along the street parallel to the railroad tracks. Turn left at the first bridge you see crossing over the tracks. Along the way you'll see trail markers on trees, walls, and lampposts—one yellow stripe between two white stripes. Follow these markers. As you leave town, watch for a marker with an arrow pointing to a path in the woods. Take this path to bypass the castle's enormous parking lot, which is clogged with souvenir shops and bus fumes.

Eating at Konopiště Castle

Three touristy restaurants sit under the castle, but I'd bring picnic supplies from Prague (or buy them at the grocery store by the Benešov train station). While the crowds wait to pay too much for lousy food in the restaurants, you'll enjoy the peace and thought-provoking ambience of a **picnic** in the shaded Kaiser's Pavilion. Or eat cheaply on Benešov's main square (try **U Zlaté Hvězdy**—"The Golden Star").

Karlštejn Castle

One of the Czech Republic's top attractions, Karlštejn Castle (KARL-shtayn) was built by Charles IV in about 1350 to house the crown jewels of the Holy Roman Empire. While it looks like a striking, fairy-tale castle from a distance, it's not much inside. The highlight of the castle's interior—the much venerated and sumptuous Chapel of the Holy Cross (built to house the crown jewels)—can be seen only with an advance reservation.

Cost and Tours: The Chapel of the Holy Cross—basically the only thing inside Karlštejn worth seeing—is part of tour Route II, which requires a reservation (300 Kč, hourly, 15 people maximum). To reserve a spot, send an email (rezervace@stc.npu.cz) with the date you'd like to visit. They'll reply with an available time slot and instructions for how to pay the 30-Kč/person reservation fee by credit card. Your reservation will be confirmed upon payment. Route I is nowhere near as interesting (270 Kč, no reservation required, bigger groups, shorter tour).

Hours: July-Aug daily 9:00-12:00 & 12:30-18:00; May-June and Sept Tue-Sun 9:00-12:00 & 12:30-18:00, closed Mon; March-April and Oct Tue-Sun 9:00-12:00 & 13:00-17:00, closed Mon; Nov-Feb Sat-Sun 10:00-12:00 & 13:00-15:00, closed Mon-Fri.

Information: Tel. 274-008-154 or 274-008-155, www.hrad karlstejn.cz.

Getting to Karlštejn Castle: The castle, 20 miles southwest of Prague, is accessible by train (2/hour, 40 minutes, then a 20-minute walk; depart from Prague's Main Station in the direction of Beroun, www.idos.cz).

When you leave the Karlštejn station, turn right, walk to the next road, turn left, and cross the bridge over the river. From here, follow the pedestrian-only street up to the castle. Warning: This half-mile stretch has a concentration of crystal and souvenir shops as intense as Karlova street in Prague.

Hike to Srbsko: From Karlštejn Castle, an easy one-hour hike along a well-marked trail (look for markers with one red stripe between two white stripes) leads you away from the tourists through a quiet forest to Srbsko. There you'll find two good Czech restaurants and a train station (the Karlštejn-Prague train stops in Srbsko).

Křivoklát Castle

Křivoklát (KREE-vohk-laht), an original 14th-century castle, is beautiful for its simplicity and setting, amid the hills and deep woods near the lovely Berounka River valley. Originally a hunting residence of Czech kings, it was later transformed into a royal prison that "entertained" a number of distinguished guests, among them the most notorious alchemist of the 1500s, Englishman Edward Kelly.

In summer, Křivoklát comes alive with craftspeople—woodcarvers, blacksmiths, and basket-weavers—who work as if it were the 15th century. The absence of tacky souvenir shops, the plain Gothic appearance, and the background noise of hammers and wood chisels give Křivoklát an engaging character.

The tour of the interior lasts a sensible half-hour. The highlight is the king's audience hall, with its delicately arched ceiling.

Cost and Tours: 240 Kč with an English-speaking guide; 190 Kč if you go with a Czech group (pick up an explanation sheet in English, and you'll be fine with the Czechs).

Hours: Open May-Sept Tue-Sun 9:00-12:00 & 13:00-17:00, closed Mon; April and Oct Tue-Sun 10:00-16:00, closed Mon; Nov-Dec Sat-Sun 10:00-15:00, closed Mon-Fri; Jan-March Mon-Sat 10:00-15:00, closed Sun.

Information: Tel. 313-558-440, www.krivoklat.cz.

Getting to Křivoklát Castle: Trains leave Prague's Main Station for Beroun (hourly, 40 minutes), running through the delightful valley of the dreamy Berounka River. In Beroun, transfer to the cute little motor train to Křivoklát (dubbed by Czech hikers the "Berounka Pacific"; every 2 hours, allow 1.5 hours total for trip from Prague). From Křivoklát's train station, it's a 10-minute walk uphill to the castle. At the train station, confirm the schedule back—one train leaves just before noon, and three others depart in the afternoon. For train schedules, see www.idos.cz.

ČESKÝ KRUMLOV

Lassoed by its river and dominated by its castle, this enchanting town feels lost in a time warp. While Český Krumlov is the Czech Republic's answer to Germany's Rothenburg, it has yet to be turned into a medieval theme park. When you see its awe-inspiring castle, delightful Old Town of shops and cobbled lanes, characteristic little restaurants, and easy canoeing options, you'll understand why having fun is a slam-dunk here.

Český Krumlov (CHESS-key KROOM-loff) means, roughly, "Czech Bend in the River." Calling it "Český" for short sounds silly to Czech-speakers (since dozens of Czech town names begin with "Český"). However, "Krumlov" for short is OK.

The sharp bend in the Vltava provides a natural moat, so it's no wonder Český Krumlov has been a choice spot for eons. Celtic tribes first settled here a century before Christ. Then came German tribes. The Slavic tribes arrived in the ninth century. The Rožmberks—Bohemia's top noble family—ran the city from 1302 to 1602. You'll see their rose symbol all over town.

In many ways, the 16th century was the town's Golden Age, when Český Krumlov hosted artists, scientists, and alchemists from all over Europe. In 1588, the town became home to an important Jesuit college. The Habsburgs bought the region in 1602, ushering in a more Germanic period. After that, as many as 75 percent of the town's people were German—until 1945, when most Germans were expelled.

Český Krumlov's rich mix of Gothic, Renaissance, and Baroque buildings is easy to miss. As you wander, look up...notice the surviving details in the stonework. Step into shops. Snoop into back lanes and tiny squares. Gothic buildings curve with the winding streets. Many precious Gothic and Renaissance frescoes were whitewashed in Baroque times (when the colorful trimmings of earlier periods were way out of style). Today, these frescoes are being rediscovered and restored.

With the town's rich German heritage, it was easy for Hitler to claim that this region—the Sudetenland—was rightfully part of Germany, and in 1938, the infamous Munich Agreement made it his. Americans liberated the town in 1945. Due to Potsdam Treaty-approved ethnic cleansing, three million Germans in Czech lands were sent west to Germany. Emptied of its German citizenry, Český Krumlov turned into a ghost town, partially inhabited by Roma (Gypsies—see page 248).

In the post-WWII world drawn up by Stalin, Churchill, and FDR at Yalta, the border of the Soviet and American spheres of influence fell about here. Although the communist government established order, the period from 1945 to 1989 was a smelly interlude, as the town was infamously polluted. Its now-pristine river was foamy with effluent from the paper mill just upstream, while the hills around town were marred with prefab-concrete apartment blocks. The people who moved in never fully identified with the town—in Europe, a place without ancestors is a place without life. But the bleak years of communism paradoxically provided a cocoon to preserve the town. There was no money, so little changed, apart from a buildup of grime.

In the early 1990s, tourists discovered Český Krumlov, and the influx of money saved the buildings from ruin. Color returned to the facades, waiters again dressed in coarse linen shirts, and the main drag was flooded with souvenir shops.

With its new prosperity, the center of today's Český Krumlov looks like a fairy-tale town. In fact, movie producers consider it ideal for films. *The Adventures of Pinocchio* was filmed here in 1995, as was the opening sequence for the 2006 film *The Illusionist*.

After Prague, Český Krumlov is the Czech Republic's second-biggest tourist magnet (1.5 million visits annually), with enough tourism to make things colorful and easy—but not so much that it tramples the place's charm. This town of 15,000 attracts a young, bohemian crowd, drawn here for its simple beauty, cheap living, and fanciful bars.

Planning Your Time

Because you can visit the castle and theater only with a guide (and English-language tours are offered just a few times a day), serious sightseers should reserve both tours first thing in the morning in person at the castle and theater (or call the castle), and then build your day around your tour times. Those who hate planning ahead on vacation can join a Czech tour anytime

(English information sheets provided).

A paddle down the river to Zlatá Koruna Abbey is a high-light (three hours), and a 20-minute walk up to the Křížový Vrch (Hill of the Cross) rewards you with a fine view of the town and its unforgettable riverside setting. Other sights are quick visits and worthwhile only if you have a particular interest (Viennese artist Egon Schiele, puppets, torture, and so on).

The town itself is the major attraction. Evenings are for atmospheric dining and drinking. Sights are generally open 10:00-17:00 and closed on Monday.

Orientation to Český Krumlov

Český Krumlov is extremely easy to navigate. The twisty Vltava River, which makes a perfect S through the town, ropes the Old Town into a tight peninsula. Above the Old Town is the Castle Town. Český Krumlov's one main street starts at the isthmus and heads through the peninsula. It winds through town and continues across a bridge before snaking through the Castle Town, the castle complex (a long series of courtyards), and the castle gardens high above. The main square, Náměstí Svornosti—with the TI, ATMs, and taxis—dominates the Old Town and marks the center of the peninsula. All recommended restaurants and hotels are within a few minutes' walk of this square. No sight in town is more than a five-minute stroll away.

Tourist Information

The helpful TI is on the **main square** (daily 9:00-19:00, July-Aug until 20:00, shorter hours in winter, tel. 380-704-622, www .ckrumlov.info). Pick up the free city map. The 129-Kč *City Guide* book explains everything in Český Krumlov and includes a fine town and castle map in the back. The TI has a baggage-storage desk and can check train, bus, and flight schedules. Ask about concerts, city walking tours in English, and canoe trips on the river. A second, less-crowded TI—actually a private business—is just below the **castle** (daily 9:00-19:00, tel. 380-725-110).

Arrival in Český Krumlov

By Train: The train station is a 20-minute walk from town (turn right out of the station, then walk downhill onto a steep cobbled path leading to an overpass into the town center). Taxis are standing by to zip you to your hotel (about 100 Kč), or call 602-113-113 to summon one.

By Bus: The bus station is just three blocks away from the Old Town. To walk from the bus-station lot to the town center, drop down to the main road and turn left, then turn right at the grocery store (*potraviny*). Figure on 60 Kč for a taxi from the station to your hotel.

Helpful Hints

Festivals: Locals drink oceans of beer and celebrate their medieval roots at big events such as the Celebration of the Rose (Slavnosti Růže), where blacksmiths mint ancient coins, jugglers swallow fire, mead flows generously, and pigs are roasted on open fires (June 22-24 in 2012). The summer also brings a top-notch international jazz and alternative music festival to town, performed in pubs, cafés, and the castle gardens (Aug 20-25 in 2012, www.festivalkrumlov.cz). During the St. Wenceslas celebrations, the square becomes a medieval market and the streets come alive with theater and music (Sept 28-30 in 2012). Reserve a hotel well in advance if you'll be in town for these events.

Internet Access: Fine Internet cafés are all over town, and many of my recommended accommodations offer Wi-Fi or Internet access. The TI on the main square has several fast, cheap, stand-up stations. Perhaps the best cybercafé is behind the TI by the castle (tel. 380-725-117).

Bookstore: Shakespeare and Sons is a good little English-language bookstore (daily 11:00-19:00, a block below the main square at Soukenická 44, tel. 380-711-203, www.shakes.cz).

Laundry: Pension Lobo runs a self-service launderette near the castle. Since there are only a few machines, you may have to wait (200 Kč to wash and dry, includes soap, daily 9:00-20:00, Latrán 73).

Bike Rental: You can rent bikes at the **train station** (150 Kč/day with train ticket, prices slightly higher otherwise, tel. 380-715-000), **Vltava Sport Service** (see listing under "Canoeing and Rafting the Vltava" on page 200), and the recommended **Hostel 99**.

Tours in Český Krumlov

Walking Tours—Since the town itself, rather than its sights, is what it's all about here, taking a guided walk is the key to a meaningful visit. The TI sells tickets for two different guided walks. They are affordable, in English, and well worth your time. Both meet in front of the TI on the main square. No reservations are necessary—just drop in and pay the guide. The **Old Town Tour** offers the best general town introduction and is most likely to run (250 Kč, daily May-Oct at 10:30 and 15:00, Nov-April at 11:00, weekends only in Feb, 1.5 hours). The **Brewing History Tour,** the most intimate of the many brewery tours in this land that so loves its beer, takes you through the Eggenberg Brewery (200 Kč, daily May-Oct at 12:30, Nov-April at 13:00, weekends only in Feb, 1 hour). For a self-guided town walk, consider renting an **audioguide** from the TI (100 Kč/one hour).

Local Guides—**Oldřiška Baloušková** is a hardworking young guide who offers a wonderful tour around her hometown (400 Kč/hour, mobile 737-920-901, oldriskab@gmail.com). **Jiří (George) Václavíček,** a gentle and caring man who perfectly fits mellow Český Krumlov, is a joy to share this town with (450 Kč/hour, mobile 603-927-995, www.krumlovguide.cz, jiri.vaclavicek@gmail .com). **Karolína Kortušová** is an enthusiastic woman with great organizational skills. Her company, Krumlov Tours, can set you up with a good local tour guide, palace and theater admissions, river trips, and more (guides-400 Kč/hour, mobile 723-069-561, www.krumlovtours.com, info@krumlovtours.com).

Self-Guided Walk

▲▲▲Welcome to Český Krumlov

The town's best sight is its cobbled cityscape, surrounded by a babbling river and capped by a dramatic castle. All of Český Krumlov's

modest sights are laced together in this charming walk from the top of the Old Town, down its spine, across the river, and up to the castle.

• *Start at the bridge over the isthmus, which was once the fortified grand entry gate to the town.*

Horní Bridge: From this "Upper Bridge," note the natural fortification provided by the tight bend in the river. The last building in town (just over the river) is the Eggenberg Brewery (with daily tours—see "Tours in Český Krumlov," earlier). Behind that, on the horizon, is a pile of white apartment high-rises—built in the last decade of the communist era and considered the worst places in town to call home. Left of the brewery stands a huge monastery (not generally open to the public). Behind that, on Kleť Mountain, the highest hilltop, stands a TV tower that locals say was built to jam Voice of America broadcasts. Facing the town, on your left, rafters take you to the river for the sloppy half-hour float around town to the takeout spot just on your right.

• *A block downhill on Horní (Upper) street is the...*

Museum of Regional History: This small museum gives you a quick look at regional costumes, tools, and traditions. When you pay, pick up the English translation of the displays (it also includes

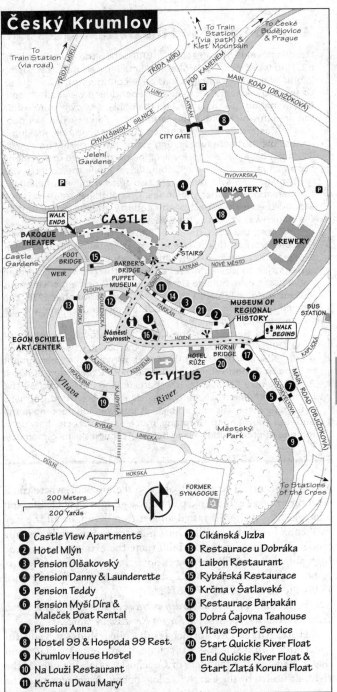

Český Krumlov

1. Castle View Apartments
2. Hotel Mlýn
3. Pension Olšakovský
4. Pension Danny & Launderette
5. Pension Teddy
6. Pension Myší Díra & Maleček Boat Rental
7. Pension Anna
8. Hostel 99 & Hospoda 99 Rest.
9. Krumlov House Hostel
10. Na Louži Restaurant
11. Krčma u Dwau Maryí
12. Cikánská Jizba
13. Restaurace u Dobráka
14. Laibon Restaurant
15. Rybářská Restaurace
16. Krčma v Šatlavské
17. Restaurace Barbakán
18. Dobrá Čajovna Teahouse
19. Vltava Sport Service
20. Start Quickie River Float
21. End Quickie River Float & Start Zlatá Koruna Float

ČESKÝ KRUMLOV

Edvard Beneš and the German Question

Czechoslovakia was created in 1918, when the vast, multiethnic Habsburg Empire broke into smaller nations after losing World War I. The principle that gave countries such as Poland, Czechoslovakia, and Romania independence was called "self-determination": Each nation had the right to its own state within the area in which its people formed the majority. But the peoples of Eastern Europe had mixed over the centuries, making it impossible to create functioning states based purely on ethnicity. In the case of Czechoslovakia, the borders were drawn along historical rather than ethnic boundaries. While the country was predominantly Slavic, there were also areas with overwhelmingly German and Hungarian majorities. One of these areas—a fringe around the western part of the country, mostly populated by Germans—was known as the Sudetenland.

At first, the coexistence of Slavs and Germans in the new republic worked fine. German parties were important power brokers and participated in almost every coalition government. Hitler's rise to power, however, led to the growth of German nationalism, even outside Germany. Soon 70 percent of Germans in Czechoslovakia voted for the Nazis. In September 1938, the Munich Agreement ceded the Sudetenland to Germany, and the Czech minority had to leave.

Edvard Beneš was the first Czechoslovak secretary of state (1918-1934) and later became the country's second president (1934-1948), leading the Czechoslovak exile government in London during World War II. Like most Czechs and Slovaks, Beneš believed that after the hard feelings produced by the Munich Agreement, peaceful coexistence of Slavs and Germans in a single state was impossible. His postwar solution: move the Sudeten Germans to Germany, much as the Czechs had been forced out of the Sudetenland before. Through skillful diplomacy,

a lengthy history of Krumlov). Start on the top floor, where you'll see a Bronze Age exhibit, old paintings, a glimpse of noble life, and a look at how the locals rafted lumber from Krumlov all the way to Vienna (partly by canal). Don't miss the fun-to-study ceramic model of Český Krumlov in 1800 (note the extravagant gardens high above the town). The lower floor comes with fine folk costumes and domestic art (50 Kč, daily 10:00-17:00, July-Aug until 18:00, Horní 152, tel. 380-711-674).

• *Below the museum, a little garden overlook affords a fine castle view. Immediately across the street, notice the Renaissance facade of...*

Hotel Růže: This former Jesuit college hides a beautiful courtyard. Pop inside to see a couple of bronze busts that stand like a shrine to the founders of Czechoslovakia. The one on the right, dedicated by the Czech freedom fighters, commemorates the

Beneš got the Allies to sign on to this idea.

Shortly after the end of World War II, three million people of German ancestry were forced to leave their homes in Czechoslovakia. Millions of Germanic people in Poland, Romania, Ukraine, and elsewhere met with a similar fate. Many of these families had been living in these areas for centuries. The methods employed to expel them included murder, rape, and plunder. (Today, we'd call it "ethnic cleansing.")

In 1945, Český Krumlov lost 75 percent of its population, and Czechs moved into the vacated German homes. Having easily acquired the property, the new residents didn't take care of the houses. Within a few years, the once-prosperous Sudetenland was reduced to shabby towns and uncultivated fields—a decaying, godforsaken region. After 1989, displaced Sudeten Germans—the majority of whom now live in Bavaria—demanded that the Czechoslovak government apologize for the violent way in which the expulsion was carried out. Some challenged the legality of the decrees, and for a time the issue threatened otherwise good Czech-German relations.

Although no longer such a hot-button diplomatic issue, the so-called Beneš Decrees remain divisive in Czech politics. While liberals consider the laws unjust, many others—especially the older generations—see them as fair revenge for the behavior of the Sudeten Germans prior to and during the war. In the former Sudetenland, where Czech landowners worry that the Germans will try to reclaim their property, Beneš is a hugely popular figure. His bust in Český Krumlov's Hotel Růže is one of the first memorials to him in the country. The bridge behind the Old Town has been named for Beneš since the 1990s. The main square—the center of a thriving German community 70 years ago—is now, ironically, called "Square of Concord."

first Czechoslovak president, Tomáš Garrigue Masaryk (in office 1918-1934; see sidebar on page 122). The bust on the left recalls Masaryk's successor, Edvard Beneš (in office 1934-1948; see sidebar, above).

• *Walk another block down the main drag, until you reach steps on the left leading to the...*

Church of St. Vitus: Český Krumlov's main church was built as a bastion of Catholicism in the 15th century, when the Roman Catholic Church was fighting the Hussites. The 17th-century Baroque high altar shows a totem of religious figures: the Virgin Mary (crowned in heaven); St. Vitus (above Mary); and, way up on top, St. Wenceslas, the patron saint of the Czech people—long considered their ambassador in heaven. The canopy in the back, though empty today, once supported a grand statue of a Rožmberk atop a horse. The statue originally stood at the high altar. (Too egotistical for Jesuits, it was later moved to the rear of the nave, and then lost for good.) As you listen to the river, notice the empty organ case. While the main organ is out for restoration, the cute little circa-1716 Baroque beauty is getting plenty of use (see photos of the restoration work on the far wall, church open daily 10:00–19:00, Sunday Mass at 9:30, tel. 380-711-336).

• *Continuing on Horní street, you'll come to the…*

Main Square (Náměstí Svornosti): Lined with a mix of Renaissance and Baroque homes of burghers (all built on 12th-century Gothic foundations), the main square has a grand charm. There's continuity here. Lékárna, with the fine red Baroque facade on the lower corner of the square, is still a pharmacy, as it has been since 1620. McDonald's tried three times to get a spot here but was turned away each time. The Town Hall flies both the Czech flag and the town flag, which shows the rose symbol of the Rožmberk family, who ruled the town for 300 years.

Imagine the history that this square has seen: In the 1620s, the rising tide of Lutheran Protestantism threatened Catholic Europe. Krumlov was a seat of Jesuit power and learning, and the intellectuals of the Roman church allegedly burned books on this square. Later, when there was a bad harvest, locals blamed witches—and burned them, too. Every so often, terrible plagues rolled through the countryside. In a nearby village, all but two residents were killed by a plague.

But the plague stopped before devastating the people of Český Krumlov, and in 1715—as thanks to God—they built the plague monument that stands on the square today. Much later, in 1938, Hitler stood right here before a backdrop of long Nazi banners to celebrate the annexation of the Sudetenland. And in 1968, Russian tanks spun their angry treads on these same cobblestones to intimidate locals who were demanding freedom. Today, thankfully, this square is part of an unprecedented time of peace and prosperity for the Czech people.

• *The following three museums are grouped around the main square.*

Puppet Museum: In three small rooms, you'll see fascinating displays of more than 200 movable creations (overwhelmingly of Czech origin, but also some from Burma and Rajasthan). At the model stage, children of any age can try their hand at pulling the strings on their favorite fairy tale (80 Kč, daily 10:00-18:00, longer hours in July-Aug, Dlouhá 29, tel. 380-713-422, www .krumlovskainspirace.cz).

Torture Museum: This is just a lame haunted house: dark, with sound effects, cheap modern models, and prints showing off the cruel and unusual punishments of medieval times (100 Kč, daily 9:00-20:00, shorter hours off-season, English descriptions, Náměstí Svornosti 1, tel. 380-766-343).

Egon Schiele Art Center: This classy contemporary art gallery has temporary exhibits, generally featuring 20th-century Czech artists. The top-floor permanent collection celebrates the Viennese artist Egon Schiele (pronounced "Sheila"), who once spent a few weeks here during a secret love affair. A friend of Gustav Klimt and an important figure in the Secession movement in Vienna, Schiele lived a short life, from 1890 to 1918. His cutting-edge lifestyle and harsh art of graphic nudes didn't always fit the conservative, small-town style of Český Krumlov, but townsfolk are happy today to charge you to see this relatively paltry collection of his work (120 Kč, daily 10:00-18:00 except closed Mon in Jan, café, Široká 71, tel. 380-704-011, www.schieleartcentrum .cz). The Schiele collection in Vienna's Belvedere Palace is far better (see page 1160).

• *From the main square, walk up Radniční street and cross the...*

Barber's Bridge (Lazebnicky Most): This wooden bridge, decorated with two 19th-century statues, connects the Old Town and the Castle Town. In the center stands a statue of St. John of Nepomuk, who's also depicted by a prominent statue on Prague's Charles Bridge (see page 88). Among other responsibilities, he's the protector against floods. In the great floods of August 2002, the angry river submerged the bridge (but removable banisters minimized the damage). Stains just above the windows of the adjacent building show you how high the water rose.

• *After crossing the bridge, hike up the hill. Your next stop is Krumlov Castle.*

Sights in Český Krumlov

▲▲Krumlov Castle (Krumlovský Zámek)

No Czech town is complete without a castle—and now that the nobles are gone, their mansions are open to us common folk. The Krumlov Castle complex includes bear pits, a rare Baroque theater, groomed gardens—and the castle itself (www.castle.ckrumlov.cz).

Round Tower (Zâmecká Věž)—The strikingly colorful round tower marks the location of the first castle, built here to guard the medieval river crossing. With its 16th-century Renaissance paint job colorfully restored, it looks exotic, featuring fancy astrological decor, terra-cotta symbols of the zodiac, and a fine arcade. Climb its 162 steps for a great view.

Cost and Hours: 50 Kč, daily 9:00-18:00, last entry 17:30.

Bear Pits (Medvědí Příkop)—At the site of the castle drawbridge, the bear pits hold a family of European brown bears, as they have since the Rožmberks added bears to their coat of arms in the 16th century to demonstrate their (fake) blood relation to the distinguished Italian family of Orsini (the name means "bear-like"). Featured on countless coats of arms, bears have long been totemic animals for Europeans. Pronouncing the animal's real name was taboo in many cultures, and Czechs still refer to bears only indirectly. For example, in most Germanic languages the word "bear" is derived from "brown," while the Slavic medvěd literally means "honey-eater."

Castle (Zámek)—The immense castle is a series of courtyards with shops, contemporary art galleries, and tourist services. The

interior is accessible only by tour, which gives you a glimpse of the places where the Rožmberks, Eggenbergs, and Schwarzenbergs dined, studied, worked, prayed, entertained, and slept. (By European standards, the castle's not much, and the tours move slowly.) Imagine being an aristocratic guest here, riding the dukes' assembly line of fine living: You'd promenade through a long series of elegant spaces and dine in the sumptuous dining hall before enjoying a concert in the Hall of Mirrors, which leads directly to the Baroque Theater (described next). After the play, you'd go out into the château garden for a fireworks finale.

Cost and Hours: To see the interior, you must take a one-hour escorted tour: Tour I (Gothic and Renaissance rooms, of the most general interest) or Tour II (19th-century castle life). Tours run June-Aug Tue-Sun 9:00-12:00 & 13:00-18:00, spring and fall until 17:00, closed Mon and Nov-March. Tours in Czech cost 150 Kč plus a 10-Kč reservation fee, leave regularly, and include an adequate flier in English that contains about half the information imparted by the guide (generally a student who's simply memorized the basic script). English tours are preferable, but cost more

(200 Kč plus a 10-Kč reservation fee), run less frequently, and are often booked solid. Make your reservation when you arrive in town—just walk up to the castle office—or you can call 380-704-721, though the number is often busy. You'll be issued a ticket with your tour time printed on it. Be in the correct courtyard at that time, or you'll be locked out.

▲▲**Baroque Theater (Zámecké Divadlo)**—Europe once had several hundred Baroque theaters. Using candles for light and fireworks for special effects, most burned down. Today, only two survive in good shape and are open to tourists: one at Stockholm's Drottningholm Palace; and one here, at Krumlov Castle. During the 40-minute tour, you'll sit on benches in the theater and then go under the stage to see the wood-and-rope contraptions that enabled scenes to be scooted in and out within seconds (while fireworks and smoke blinded the audience). Due to the theater's fragility, the number of visitors is strictly regulated. There are only five English tours a day, limited to 20 people per group, and generally sold out in advance. While it's a lovely little theater with an impressive 3-D effect that makes the stage look deeper than it really is, I wouldn't bother with the tour unless you can snare a spot on an English one. The theater is used only once a year for an actual performance, with attendance limited to Baroque theater enthusiasts. You can call 380-704-721 to get English-language tour times and reserve a space; but as with the castle tour, you will likely do best visiting the ticket office in person.

Cost and Hours: 300 Kč plus a 10-Kč reservation fee for English tour, 250 Kč plus a 10-Kč reservation fee for Czech tour, tours Tue-Sun May-Oct, no tours Mon and Nov-April; English departures at 10:00, 11:00, 13:00, 14:00, and 15:00; buy theater tour tickets at castle ticket office.

Castle Museum (Hradní Muzeum)—A newly opened exhibit assembled from the castle's archives focuses on key moments in the lives of the town's various ruling families. While generally skippable, on summer Mondays it provides the only chance to peek inside the castle.

Cost and Hours: 100 Kč, April-Aug daily 9:00-17:00, Sept-March Tue-Sun 9:30-16:00, closed Mon.

Castle Gardens (Zámecká Zahrada)—This 2,300-foot-long garden crowns the castle complex. It was laid out in the 17th century, when the noble family would have it lit with 22,000 oil lamps, torches, and candles for special occasions. The lower part is geometrical and symmetrical—French garden-style. The upper is rougher—English garden-style.

Cost and Hours: Free, May-Sept Tue-Sun 8:00-19:00, April and Oct Tue-Sun 8:00-17:00, closed Mon and Nov-March.

Near Český Krumlov

Zlatá Koruna Abbey (Klášter Zlatá Koruna)—Directly above the river at the end of a three-hour float by raft or canoe (see "Activities in Český Krumlov," later), this abbey was founded in the 13th century by the king to counter the growing influence of the Vítek family, the ancestors of the mighty Rožmberks. As you enter the grounds, notice the central linden tree, with its strange, cape-like leaves; it's said to have been used by the anti-Catholic Hussites when they hanged the monks. The short guided abbey tour takes you through the rare two-storied Gothic Chapel of the Guardian Angel, the main church, and the cloister. After the order was dissolved in 1785, the abbey functioned briefly as a village school, before being turned into a factory during the Industrial Revolution. Damage from this period is visible on the cloister's crumbling arches. The abbey was restored in the 1990s and opened to the public only a few years ago.

Cost and Hours: 100 Kč for a tour in Czech—generally runs hourly, 180 Kč for an English tour, Tue-Sun 9:00-15:30, until 16:30 June-Aug, closed Mon and Oct-March, call 380-743-126 to pre-arrange an English tour, access via river float, www.klaster-zlata koruna.eu.

Activities in Český Krumlov

Český Krumlov lies in the middle of a valley popular for canoeing, rafting, hiking, and horseback riding. Boat-rental places are convenient to the Old Town, and several hiking paths start right in town.

▲▲▲Canoeing and Rafting the Vltava

Splash a little river fun into your visit by renting a rubber raft or fiberglass canoe for a quick 30-minute spin around Český Krumlov. Or go for a three-hour float and pad-dle through the Bohemian forests and villages of the nearby country-side. You'll end up at Zlatá Koruna Abbey (described earlier), where the rafting company will shuttle you back to town—or provide you with a bicycle to pedal back on your own along a bike path. This is a great hot-weather activity. Though the river is far from treacherous, be prepared to get wet.

You'll encounter plenty of inviting pubs and cafés for breaks along the way. There's a little whitewater, but the river is so shallow that if you tip, you can simply stand up and climb back in.

(When that happens, pull the canoe up onto the bank to empty it, since you'll never manage to pour the water out while still in the river.)

Choose from a kayak, a canoe (faster, less work, more likely to tip), or an inflatable raft (harder rowing, slower, but very stable). Prices are per boat (2-6 people) and include a map, a waterproof container, and transportation to or from the start and end points. Here are your options:

Quickie Circle-the-Town Float: The easiest half-hour experience is to float around the city's peninsula, starting and ending at opposite sides of the tiny isthmus. Heck, you can do it twice (400 Kč for 1-2 people in a canoe or raft).

Three-Hour Float to Zlatá Koruna Abbey: This is your best basic trip, with pastoral scenery, a riverside pub about two hours down on the left, and a beautiful abbey as your destination (about 9 miles, 700 Kč for 1-2 people). From there you can bike back or catch a shuttle bus home—simply arrange a return plan with the rental company.

Longer and Faster Trips: If you start upriver from Krumlov (direction: Rožmberk), you'll go faster with more whitewater, but the river parallels a road, so it's a little less idyllic. Longer trips in either direction involve lots of paddling, even though you're going downstream. Rafting companies can review the many day-trip options with you.

Rental Companies: Several companies offer this lively activity. Perhaps the handiest are **Půjčovna Lodí Maleček Boat Rental** (open long hours daily April-Oct, closed Nov-March, at recommended Pension Myší Díra, Rooseveltova 28, tel. 380-712-508, www.malecek.cz, lode@malecek.cz) and **Vltava Sport Service** (April-Oct daily 9:00-18:00, closed Nov-March, Hradební 60, tel. 380-711-988, www.ckvltava.cz). Vltava also rents mountain bikes (320 Kč/day) and can bring a bike to the abbey for you to ride back.

Hiking

For an **easy 20-minute hike** to the Křížový Vrch (Hill of the Cross), walk to the end of Rooseveltova street, cross at the traffic light, then head straight for the first (empty) chapel-like Station of the Cross. Turning right, it's easy to navigate along successive Stations of the Cross until you reach the white church on the hill (closed), set in the middle of wild meadows. Looking down into the valley at the medieval city nestled within the S-shaped river, framed by the rising hills, it's hard to imagine any town with a more powerful *genius loci* (spirit of the place). The view is best at sunset.

For **longer hikes,** start at the trailhead by the bear pits below the castle. Red-and-white trail markers guide you on an easy six-mile hike around the neighboring slopes and villages. The green-and-yellow stripes mark a five-mile hiking trail up Kleť Mountain—with an altitude gain of 1,800 feet. At the top, you'll find the Kleť Observatory, the oldest observatory in the country (now a leading center for discovering new planets). On clear days, you can see the Alps (observatory tours-30 Kč, hourly July-Aug Tue-Sun 10:30-15:30, closed Mon, www.hvezdarna.klet.cz).

Horseback Riding

Head about a mile and a half out of town, beyond the Křížový Vrch (Hill of the Cross), for horseback rides and lessons at Slupenec Horseback Riding Club.

Cost and Hours: 300 Kč-1 hour outdoors or in the ring, 2,200 Kč-all-day ride, helmets provided, Tue-Sun 10:00-18:00, closed Mon, Slupenec 1, worth a taxi trip, tel. 380-711-052, www.jk-slupenec.cz, René Srncová.

Sleeping in Český Krumlov

Krumlov is filled with small, good, family-run pensions offering doubles with baths from 1,000 to 1,500 Kč and hostel beds for 300 Kč. Summer weekends and festivals (see page 191) are busiest and most expensive; reserve ahead when possible. Hotels (not a Krumlov forte) have staff that speak some English and accept credit cards; pensions rarely have or do either. While you can find a room upon arrival here, it's better to book at least a few days ahead if you want to stay in the heart of town. Cars are not very safe overnight—locals advise paying for a garage.

In the Old Town

$$$ **Castle View Apartments,** run by local guide Jiří Václavíček, rents seven apartments. These are the plushest and best-equipped rooms I found in town—the bathroom floors are heated, all come with kitchenettes, and everything's done just right. Their website describes each stylish apartment (1,800-4,500 Kč depending on size, view, and season; the big 4,500-Kč apartment sleeps up to six, complex pricing scheme, reserve direct with this book for 10 percent off online prices, non-smoking, breakfast in a nearby hotel, Šatlavská 140, tel. 380-727-015, mobile 731-108-677, www.castleview.cz, info@castleview.cz).

On Parkán Street, Below the Square

Secluded Parkán street, which runs along the river below the square, has a row of pensions with three to five rooms each. These places have a family feel and views of the looming castle above.

Sleep Code

(18 Kč = about $1, country code: 420)
S = Single, **D** = Double/Twin, **T** = Triple, **Q** = Quad, **b** = bathroom,
s = shower only. Unless otherwise noted, English is spoken,
credit cards are accepted, and breakfast is included.

To help you easily sort through these listings, I've divided
the accommodations into three categories based on the price
for a double room with bath during high season:

$$$ Higher Priced—Most rooms 1,500 Kč or more.
$$ Moderately Priced—Most rooms between 1,000-1,500 Kč.
$ Lower Priced—Most rooms 1,000 Kč or less.

Prices can change without notice; verify the hotel's
current rates online or by email. For other updates, see www
.ricksteves.com/update.

$$$ Hotel Mlýn, at the end of Parkán, is a newly opened
and tastefully furnished hotel with more than 30 rooms and all
the amenities (Sb-2,400 Kč, Db-3,000 Kč, elevator, free Wi-Fi,
pay parking, Parkán 120, tel. 380-731-133, fax 380-747-054, www
.hotelmlyn.eu, info@hotelmlyn.eu).

$$ Pension Olšakovský, which has a delightful breakfast
area on a terrace next to the river, treats visitors as family guests
(Db-1,000-1,250 Kč, includes parking, Parkán 114, tel. & fax 380-
714-333, mobile 604-430-181, www.olsakovsky.cz, J.Olsakovsky
@post.cz).

On Latrán Street, at the Base of the Castle

A quiet, cobbled pedestrian street (Latrán) runs below the castle
just over the bridge from the Old Town. It's a 10-minute walk
downhill from the train station. Lined with cute shops, the street
has a couple of fine little family-run, eight-room pensions.

$$ Pension Danny is a little funky place, with homey rooms
and a tangled floor plan above a restaurant (Db-1,050 Kč, apart-
ment Db-1,250 Kč, breakfast in room, Latrán 72, tel. 380-712-710,
www.pensiondanny.cz, recepce@pensiondanny.cz).

On Rooseveltova Street, Between the Bus Station and the Old Town

Rooseveltova street, midway between the bus station and the Old
Town (a four-minute walk from either), is lined with several fine
little places, each with easy free parking. The key here is tranquil-
ity—the noisy bars of the town center are out of earshot.

Little **$$ Pension Teddy** offers three deluxe rooms that share a balcony overlooking the river and have original 18th-century furniture. Or stay in one of four modern-style rooms, some of which also face the river (Db-1,250 Kč, deluxe Db-1,400 Kč, cash only, staff may be unhelpful, free Wi-Fi and Internet access, parking-200 Kč, Rooseveltova 38, tel. 380-711-595, mobile 724-003-981, www.pensionteddy.cz, info@pensionteddy.cz).

$$ Pension Myší Díra ("Mouse Hole") hides eight sleek, spacious, bright, and woody Bohemian contemporary rooms overlooking the Vltava River just outside the Old Town (Db-900-1,400 Kč, bigger deluxe riverview Db-1,900 Kč, prices include transfer to/from bus or train station, Internet access, Rooseveltova 28, tel. 380-712-853, fax 380-711-900, www.malecek.cz). The no-nonsense reception, which closes at 20:00, runs the recommended boat rental company (Půjčovna Lodí Maleček, at the same address), along with three similar pensions with comparable prices: **Pension Wok** down by the river, **Pension Margarita** farther along Rooseveltova, and **Pension u Hada.**

$$ Pension Anna is well-run, with two doubles, five apartments, and a restful little garden. Its apartments are spacious suites, with a living room and stairs leading to the double-bedded loft. The upstairs rooms can get stuffy during the summer (Db-1,250 Kč, Db apartment-1,550 Kč, extra bed-350 Kč, Rooseveltova 41, tel. & fax 380-711-692, www.pensionanna-ck.cz, pension.anna @quick.cz). If you book a standard Db and they bump you up to an apartment, don't pay more than the Db rate.

Hostels

There are several hostels in town. Hostel 99 (closest to the train station) is clearly the high-energy, youthful party hostel. Krumlov House (closer to the bus station) is more mellow. Both are well-managed, and each is a five-minute walk from the main square.

$ Hostel 99's picnic-table terrace looks out on the Old Town. While the gentle sound of the river gurgles outside your window late at night, you're more likely to hear a youthful international crowd having a great time. The hostel caters to its fun-loving young guests, offering a day-long river rafting and pub crawl, with rental bikes and a free keg of beer each Wednesday (65 beds in 4- to 10-bed coed rooms-300 Kč, D-700 Kč, T-990 Kč, Internet access-1 Kč/minute, laundry-200 Kč/load, use the lockers, no curfew or lockout, recommended Hospoda 99 restaurant, 10-minute downhill walk from train station or two bus stops to Spicak, Vezni 99, tel. & fax 380-712-812, www.hostel99.cz, hostel99@hotmail .com).

$ Krumlov House Hostel is take-your-shoes-off-at-the-door, shiny, hardwood-with-throw-rugs mellow. Efficiently run by a Canadian, it has a hip and trusting vibe and feels welcoming to travelers of any age (24 beds, 6 beds in two dorms-300 Kč per bed, Db-800 Kč, 2-person apartment-900 Kč, family room, no breakfast but there is a guests' kitchen, DVD library, Wi-Fi, laundry facilities, Rooseveltova 68, tel. 380-711-935, www.krumlovhostel .com, info@krumlovhostel.com).

Eating in Český Krumlov

Krumlov, with a huge variety of creative little restaurants, is a fun place to eat. In peak times, the good places fill fast, so make reservations or eat early.

Na Louži seems to be everyone's favorite little Czech bistro, with 40 seats in one 1930s-style room decorated with funky old advertisements. They serve inexpensive, tasty local cuisine and hometown Eggenberg beer on tap. If you've always wanted to play the piano for an appreciative Czech crowd in a colorful little tavern...do it here (daily 10:00-23:00, Kájovská 66, tel. 380-711-280).

Krčma u Dwau Maryí ("Tavern of the Two Marys") is a characteristic old place with idyllic riverside picnic tables, serving ye olde Czech cuisine and drinks. The fascinating menu explains the history of the house and makes a good case that the food of the poor medieval Bohemians was tasty and varied. Buck up for buckwheat, millet, greasy meat, or the poor-man's porridge (daily 11:00-23:00, Parkán 104, tel. 380-717-228).

Cikánská Jizba ("Gypsy Pub") is a Roma tavern filling one den-like, barrel-vaulted room. The Roma staff serves Slovak-style food (Slovakia is where most of the Czech Republic's Roma population came from). Krumlov has a long Roma history, and even today 1,000 Roma people live in the town. While this rustic little restaurant—which packs its 10 tables under a mystic-feeling Gothic vault—won't win any cuisine awards, you never know what festive and musical activities will erupt, particularly on Friday nights, when the owner's son's band, Cindži Renta (Wet Rag), performs here (Mon-Sat 15:00-24:00, closed Sun, 2 blocks toward castle from main square at Dlouhá 31, tel. 380-717-585). For more on the Roma of Eastern Europe, see page 248.

Restaurace u Dobráka ("Good Man") is like eating in a medieval garage, with a giant poster of Karl Marx overseeing the action. Lojza, who's been tossing steaks on his open fire for years, makes sure you'll eat well. Locals know it as the best place for grilled steak and fish—expect to pay 350 Kč for a full meal. He charges too much for his beer in order to keep the noisy beer-drinkers away (open daily 17:30-24:00 from Easter until Lojza "has a shoebox full of money," Široká 74, tel. 380-717-776).

Laibon is the modern vegetarian answer to the carnivorous Middle Ages. Settle down inside or head out onto the idyllic river terrace, and lighten up your pork-loaded diet with soy goulash or Mútábúr soup (daily 11:00-23:00, Parkán 105).

Rybářská Restaurace ("Fisherman's Restaurant") doesn't look particularly inviting from the outside, but don't get discouraged. This is *the* place in town to taste freshwater fish you've never heard of (and never will again). Try eel, perch, shad, carp, trout, and more. Choose between indoor tables under fishnets or riverside picnic benches outside (daily 11:00-22:00, on the island by the millwheel, mobile 723-829-089).

Krčma v Šatlavské is an old prison gone cozy, with an open fire, big wooden tables under a rustic old medieval vault, and tables outdoors on the pedestrian lane. It's great for a late drink or roasted game (cooked on an open spit). *Medovina* is the hot honey wine (daily 12:00-24:00, on Šatlavská, follow lane leading to the side from TI on main square, mobile 608-973-797).

Restaurace Barbakán is built into the town fortifications, with a terrace hanging high over the river. It's a good spot for old-fashioned Czech cooking and beer, at the top of town and near the recommended Rooseveltova street accommodations (open long hours daily, reasonable prices, Horní 26, tel. 380-712-679).

Hospoda 99 Restaurace serves good, cheap soups, salads, and meals. It's the choice of hostelers and locals alike for its hamburgers, vegetarian food, Czech dishes, and cheap booze (meals served 10:00-22:00, bar open until 24:00, at Hostel 99, Vezni 99, tel. 380-712-812). This place is booming until late, when everything else is hibernating.

Dobrá Čajovna is a typical example of the quiet, exotic-feeling teahouses that flooded Czech towns in the 1990s as alternatives to smoky, raucous pubs. Though directly across from the castle entrance, it's a world away from the touristic hubbub. As is so often the case, if you want to surround yourself with locals, don't go to a traditional place...go ethnic. With its meditative karma inside and a peaceful terrace facing the monastery out back, it provides a relaxing break (daily 13:00-22:00, Latrán 54, mobile 777-654-744).

Český Krumlov Connections

Almost all trains to and from Český Krumlov require a transfer in the city of České Budějovice, a transit hub just to the north. České Budějovice's bus and train stations are next to each other. All bus and train timetables are online at www.idos.cz.

From Český Krumlov by Train to: Č**eské Bud**ě**jovice** (6/day, 1 hour), **Prague** (8/day, 1/day direct, 4 hours; bus is faster, cheaper, and easier—see below), **Brno** (10/day, 1.25 hours), **Vienna** (6/day, 5-6 hours, 1-2 changes), **Budapest** (6/day with at least one change, 10-15 hours).

From Český Krumlov by Bus to: Prague (7/day, 3.5 hours, 180 Kč; 2 of the daily departures—12:00 and 16:45—can be

reserved and paid for at TI, tickets can be bought from driver if seats are available), Č**eské Bud**ě**jovice** (transit hub for other destinations; about 2/hour, 30-50 minutes, 30 Kč). The Český Krumlov bus station, a five-minute walk out of town, is just a big parking lot with numbered stalls for various buses (bus info tel. 380-711-190). A good place to buy bus tickets online is www.studentagency.cz.

By Shuttle Bus or Private Car to Linz and Beyond: If you can get to Linz, Austria, you'll have your choice of the fast trains running hourly from Linz to Munich, Salzburg, and Vienna.

Two companies with similar pricing run shuttle buses to and from Český Krumlov and **Linz** (3/day, 1.25 hours, 400 Kč), **Vienna** (1/day, 3 hours, 1,090 Kč), and **Salzburg** (1/day, 3 hours, 1,090 Kč). Be sure to book in advance, whether you're going with reliable Sebastian Tours (mobile 607-100-234 or 608-357-581, www .sebastianck-tours.com, sebastiantours@hotmail.com) or Pension Lobo (tel. 380-713-153 or 777-637-374, www.shuttlelobo.cz, lobo @ckrumlov.cz; or reserve in person at Pension Lobo at Latrán 73 or at the main square shuttle office; may cancel with short notice— reconfirm the day before).

SLOVAKIA
Slovensko

SLOVAKIA

Sitting quietly in the very center of Central Europe, wedged between bigger and stronger nations (Hungary, Austria, the Czech Republic, and Poland), Slovakia was brutally disfigured by the communists, then overshadowed by the Czechs. But in recent years, this fledgling republic seems to have finally found its wings. Recent economic reforms are causing two very different Slovakias to emerge: The flatlands of the west, centered in the capital of Bratislava, are modern, industrialized, and affluent; while the mountainous east is traditional, remote, poor, and struggling with high unemployment.

Slovakia is fairly ethnically diverse: In addition to the Slavic Slovaks, it's home to many ethnic Hungarians (about 10 percent of the population, "stranded" here when Hungary lost this land after World War I) and Roma (Gypsies, also about 10 percent). Slovakia has found it challenging to incorporate both of these large and often-mistreated minority groups. Rounding out the cultural cocktail are Czechs, Ruthenians (Carpathian Mountain peasants of Ukrainian origin), and a smattering of Germans.

Though the Slovaks are closely associated with their former countrymen, the Czechs, they actually have more in common culturally with their neighbors to the north, in Poland. Like the Poles, Slovaks tend to be devout Catholics and have a strong agricultural (rather than industrial) heritage.

Why is it hard to think of any great Slovaks? During the period of Czechoslovakia (1919-1993), every time a Slovak excelled in culture or politics or sports, they were considered "Czech" by the rest of the world. (For example, the "Czech" leader of the 1968 Prague Spring uprising against the Soviets, Alexander Dubček, was actually Slovak.) As of 1993, suddenly Slovaks could celebrate their own heroes without the confusion.

Slovakia's biggest city, Bratislava, is also its capital. Situated between Vienna and Budapest on the Danube, up-and-coming Bratislava is becoming a more enticing destination with each passing year, seemingly leaving the rest of the country in its dust. To the north and east, near the Polish border, are the poorest and most beautiful parts of this mountainous nation: the rolling hills of the Spiš Region and the jagged peaks of the High Tatras.

Among travelers, there are two schools of thought about the rural, rough-around-the-edges eastern part of the country. Some people adore the region for its stark natural beauty and cultural authenticity, which provides an exciting detour off the prettified tourist mainstream. Rural Slovakia gives more adventurous travelers the opportunity to feel the pulse of a place that's still struggling to transition into democracy—and yet is stable and safe enough for a comfortable visit. These people enjoy hiking along Slovakia's glorious mountain trails, driving through its humble villages, interacting with its kind people, and pondering the blemishes that communism left on its pastoral landscape.

Other people can't wait to leave rural Slovakia, turned off by its drab industrial skeletons, relative poverty, and dearth of must-see sights compared to the rest of Eastern Europe. Tourists focusing on pretty-as-a-postcard Eastern Europe will want to spend more time elsewhere...and should.

What is clear is that Slovakia is not your standard European country. With lots of pleasant surprises, Slovakia is worth a peek for more adventurous travelers.

For more in-depth information about Slovakia, pick up a copy of *Spectacular Slovakia*, an excellent annual magazine produced by the English-language newspaper in Bratislava (http://travel.spectator.sme.sk). Bratislava-based tour operator Martin Sloboda also publishes a series of well-researched, beautifully photographed

Slovakia Almanac

Official Name: Slovenská Republika, though locals call it Slovensko. The nation is the eastern half of the former Czechoslovakia (split peaceably in 1993).

Population: 5.5 million people. The majority are native Slovaks who are Roman Catholic and speak Slovak. But one in ten has Hungarian roots, and an estimated one in ten is Roma (Gypsy).

Latitude and Longitude: 48°N and 19°E (similar latitude to Paris or Vancouver, BC).

Area: 19,000 square miles (the size of Massachusetts and New Hampshire put together).

Geography: The northeastern half of Slovakia features the beautiful rolling hills and spiky, jagged peaks of the Carpathian Mountains. The southwestern half is quite flat—a continuation of the Great Hungarian Plain. The climate is generally cool and cloudy.

Biggest Cities: Only two cities have more than 100,000 inhabitants: Bratislava in the west (the capital, 430,000) and Košice in the east (235,000).

Economy: The Gross Domestic Product is about $120 billion, and the GDP per capita is about $22,000 (roughly two-thirds that of the average German).

Currency: Slovakia uses the euro currency (€1 = about $1.40). You might occasionally see references to the old currency, the Slovak koruna (30 Sk = about €1).

Government: Slovakia's mostly figurehead president, Ivan Gašparovič (whose second and final term ends in 2014), heads

guidebooks about Slovakia (available locally; for more about Martin, see page 223, or visit www.msagency.sk).

Helpful Hints

Telephone: Dial 112 for medical or other emergencies and 158 for police. Mobile numbers begin with 09. For more details on dialing, see page 1231.

Toll Sticker: Slovakia requires cars on its expressways to display a toll sticker (*úhrada*, €10/10 days, €14/month, www.ndsas .sk). If your car doesn't have one, buy one at a gas station when you cross the border.

Slovak History

The Danube divides Europe's two biggest mountain ranges: the Alps of Western Europe, and the Carpathians of Eastern Europe. Slovakia (and Bratislava in particular) has long been a bridge between East and West. Perhaps for this reason, Slovakia has a government that isn't dominated by any single political party. Slovakia also has a 150-seat National Council (like a parliament), the leader of which is the prime minister (Iveta Radičová, who faces re-election in 2012).

Flag: Horizontal bands of white, blue, and red with a shield bearing a "patriarchal cross" (with two crossbars instead of one) atop three humps. The three humps represent three historic mountain ranges of Slovakia: Mátra (now in northern Hungary, near Eger), Fatra, and Tatra. The double-barred cross represents St. Stephen (István) of Hungary, commemorating the many centuries that Slovakia was part of Hungary.

Slovaks You May Recognize: Andy Warhol (American Pop artist who gained more than his 15 minutes of fame, born to Slovak immigrants), Martina Hingis (Swiss tennis player born in Slovakia), film director Ivan Reitman (*Ghostbusters, Stripes;* born in Slovakia to Jewish Holocaust survivors), actor Paul Newman (whose mother was born in Slovakia), Tomáš Garrigue Masaryk (founder of Czechoslovakia, whose father was Slovak), Alexander Dubček (leader of the 1968 Prague Spring uprising), and Štefan Bani (emigrated to America and invented the parachute).

spent most of its history as someone else's backyard.

For centuries, Slovakia was part of the Hungarian realm and known as "Upper Hungary." When Budapest was taken by the Ottomans in the 1500s, the political and religious elite of Hungary retreated to Bratislava—far from the Ottomans and close to Vienna, but still within greater Hungary, at an easy-to-defend location on the Danube.

In the 1760s, the Ottoman threat was gone, and the strategic military importance of Bratislava was over. Slovakia (and the rest of Hungary) fell under the auspices of the Habsburg Empire, ruled from Vienna. Habsburg Empress Maria Theresa wanted her daughter Christina to stay close, so she built a comfy palace in Bratislava and made her son-in-law Albert the Viceroy of Hungary. This left Bratislava with a fine Habsburg palace and a strong Vienna connection, both of which remain today.

Between 1880 and 1914, a third of the Slovak population emigrated to the US to find new opportunity. There were also lots of Slovak deserters during World War I—those who opted to fight against, rather than with, their Austrian and Hungarian rulers. The Slovak-Hungarian friction continues into the present day; many Hungarians still lament the loss of their old capital, Bratislava, from the post-World War I Treaty of Trianon (see page 511). And it's possible that the historic Hungarian cultural oppression of the Czechs and Slovaks contributed to the creation of modern Czechoslovakia, as those smaller groups sought safety in numbers after World War I.

Czechoslovakia

For most visitors, the most familiar period of Slovak history is the 75-year era—still fresh in the collective memory—in which Slovakia was joined with the Czech Republic as the nation of "Czechoslovakia." That country was formed at the end of World War I, when the Austro-Hungarian Empire was splitting into pieces. During this flurry of new nation-building, a small country of seven million Czechs or two million Slovaks was unlikely to survive. The Czechs were concerned about the huge number of Germans in their territory (in an area called the Sudetenland), while the Slovaks—who had endured relatively oppressive conditions under the Hungarian half of the empire—were unsure of their ability to steer their own nation.

These two Slavic peoples decided that the only way to protect their joint heritage was to combine forces. (It was a delicate balance—there were more Sudeten Germans in Czechoslovakia than there were Slovaks.) The union was logical enough—especially in the eyes of Tomáš Masaryk, Czechoslovakia's first president (and a buddy of Woodrow Wilson's from Princeton). Masaryk was from the border of the two regions and spoke a dialect that mixed elements of Czech and Slovak (for more on Masaryk, see page 122). Czechoslovakia was born.

The United States was a big supporter of Czechoslovakia—which was, between the world wars, the only democracy (and had the strongest economy) in this part of Europe. And yet, the Czechs and the Slovaks were constantly reminded that they were countrymen in name only. In a prelude to World War II, these two peoples were again split along the cultural fault that always divided them: Today's Czech Republic was absorbed into Germany, while much of the Slovak lands went to Nazi-allied Hungary. After the war, the groups were again combined in the communist Czechoslovak Socialist Republic.

During this communist era, the regime converted the Slovak economy from a low-key agricultural model to a base of heavy industry. Since the industry was centrally planned for communist purposes (relying on raw materials imported from elsewhere within the Eastern Bloc), it made sense only as a cog in the communist machine. Many of Slovakia's factories built heavy arms, making the country the biggest producer of tanks in the world. Slovakia became one of the ugliest and most polluted corners of Eastern Europe. The Slovak environment—and economy—are still recovering.

Because of Bratislava's location nearly on the border with Austria (and the West), many bomb shelters were built in the city during the tense times around the Cuban Missile Crisis. (Today these make ideal venues for clubs—right in the heart of town, but amazingly soundproof.)

When the wave of uprisings spread across Eastern Europe in 1989, Czechoslovakia peacefully achieved its own freedom with the Velvet Revolution (see page 107). Then, on January 1, 1993, with the so-called Velvet Divorce, Czechoslovakia amicably split into two nations: the Czech and Slovak Republics (see sidebar, next page). At first, many Slovaks weren't sure this was so wise. More recently, however, it seems that the Czechs and Slovaks are getting along better than ever—by choice, not because they're compelled to. Czechs root for the Slovak hockey team, and Slovaks cheer on the Czech soccer powerhouse...unless, of course, their teams are playing against each other.

After the Divorce: Slovakia Today

Finally on their own after the Velvet Divorce, the Slovaks were initially faced with some challenging times. Communist rule had been particularly unkind to them, and Slovakia's huge armaments industry collapsed—leaving the country in a deep economic hole.

The first president of Slovakia was a former boxer named Vladimír Mečiar, whose authoritarian rule was not much better than the communists' had been. Mečiar was frequently accused of corruption (including pulling issues off the ballot when the polls seemed to be going against him), and he was accused of being involved in the kidnapping, torture, and humiliation of his main political opponent's sons in 1995. He was also notorious for making offensive statements about his country's substantial Hungarian and Roma minorities. Mečiar drew criticism from neighboring Eastern and Western European nations, as well as the US. He was finally defeated at the polls in 2000, but—like a bad penny—he kept turning up, making a strong showing in the elections of 2002 and 2004.

But in recent years—as Mečiar and his voting base have gotten along in years—Slovakia has seen a dramatic political and economic sea change. In the early 2000s, major international corporations began to notice the same thing the communists had: This is a great place to build stuff, thanks to low labor costs and

SLOVAKIA

It's Not You, It's Me: The Velvet Divorce

In the autumn of 1989, hundreds of thousands of Czechs and Slovaks streamed into Prague to demonstrate in Wenceslas Square. Their "Velvet Revolution" succeeded, and Czechoslovakia's communist regime peacefully excused itself. But that was only the first step. In that age of new possibility, the two peoples of Czechoslovakia began to wonder if they belonged together, after all.

Ever since they joined with the Czechs in 1918, the Slovaks felt they were ruled from Prague (unmistakably the political, economic, and cultural center of the country), rather than from their own capital. And the Czechs, for their part, resented the financial burden of carrying their poorer neighbors to the east. In the post-communist world, the Czechs found themselves with a 10 percent unemployment rate...compared to 20 or 30 percent unemployment in the Slovak lands. In this new world of flux and freedom, long-standing tensions came to a head.

The dissolution of Czechoslovakia began over a hyphen, as the Slovaks wanted to rename the country Czecho-Slovakia. Ideally, this symbolic move would come with a redistribution of powers: two capitals and two UN reps, but one national bank and a single currency. The Slovaks were also less enthusiastic about abandoning the communist society altogether, since the Soviet regime had left them with a heavily industrialized economy that depended on a socialist system for survival.

Initially, many Czechs couldn't understand the Slovaks'

a well-trained workforce. Another big factor is Slovakia's central location, with 300 million consumers living within a day's truck drive. It didn't take long for the gap left by armaments to be filled by carmakers. Today Slovakia, with five million people, produces one million cars a year, making the country the world's biggest car producer (per capita) and leading *The New York Times* to dub it "the European Detroit."

The economic turnaround has been partly thanks to some bold political changes. For the last several years, Slovak leadership has been striving to create a pro-business environment with a relatively unregulated employment code (making it easy to hire and fire employees—strikes don't plague the country). One major benchmark was the 2003 implementation of a 19 percent flat tax.

This and other aggressively pro-business policies have not been without their critics—especially in the very impoverished eastern half of the country, where poor people feel they're becoming even poorer. With the rollback of social services and the proverbial cracks widening, many seem to have been left behind by

demands. The first post-communist president of Czechoslovakia, the Czech Václav Havel, inadvertently widened the gap when he took a rare trip to the Slovak half of his country in 1990. In a fit of terrible judgment, Havel boldly promised he'd close the ugly, polluting Soviet factories in Slovakia...seemingly oblivious to the fact that many Slovaks still depended on these factories for survival. Havel left in disgrace and visited the Slovak lands only twice more in the following two and a half years.

In June 1992, the Slovak nationalist candidate Vladimír Mečiar fared surprisingly well in the elections—suggesting that the Slovaks were serious about secession. The politicians plowed ahead, getting serious about the split in September 1992. The transition took only three months from start to finish.

The people of Czechoslovakia never actually voted on the separation; in fact, public opinion polls in both regions were two-thirds *against* the split. This makes Slovakia quite possibly the only country ever to gain independence against the will of its citizens.

The Velvet Divorce became official on January 1, 1993, and each country ended up with its own capital, currency, and head of state. The Slovaks let loose a yelp of excitement, and the Czechs emitted a sigh of relief. For most, the divorce dissolved tensions, and nearly two decades later, Czechs and Slovaks still feel closer to each other than to any other nationality.

Slovakia's dynamic new economy. But there's no doubt it has been a boon for middle-class areas in the west.

If you ignore Slovakia's problem areas—and zoom in on its success story around Bratislava—the evidence is impressive. Slovakia joined the EU (along with nine other nations) in 2004; in 2009, it was just the second of these new additions (after Slovenia)—and the first former Warsaw Pact country—to adopt the euro currency.

Slovakia's leading political and economic class consists mostly of people who were between the ages of 15 and 25 when communism fell in 1989. Because of the Czech domination of Czechoslovak government, between World War I and 1993 the Slovaks effectively had no real political diplomatic class to call their own (Vladimír Mečiar being the exception that proves the rule). But with the Velvet Divorce, many eager, well-educated young Slovak expats returned from the West and quickly took the helm, filling that void.

Today Slovakia's power brokers are about 40 years old, and largely free from the old boys' network (most of whom stayed in the Czech lands). This trend played out in the June 2010 parliamentary elections, where for the first time, no former communist reached the 5 percent threshold needed to gain a seat in parliament. The new "Dream Team," as many Slovaks call the people in power now, is liberal on social issues but realistic—decidedly not populist—on economic issues.

As they set their own course, the Slovaks seem relatively uninterested in the European Union; in EU parliamentary elections, Slovakia routinely has the lowest voter turnout of any of the 27 member nations (usually around 20 percent).

While the rural parts of the country still have dismal unemployment rates, Bratislava has only 2.5 percent unemployment. The measure for standard of living as it relates to local costs puts Bratislava at #10 among European cities. And, while Europe struggles through difficult economic times, much of Slovakia seems poised for its brightest future yet.

Slovak Food

Slovak cuisine shows some Hungarian influence, but in most ways it's closer to Czech cuisine—with lots of starches and gravy, and plenty of pork, cabbage, and potatoes (see "Czech Food," page 49). Slovakia also has a strong tradition of grilling pickled meats. Keep an eye out for the national dish, *bryndzové halušky* (small potato dumplings with sheep's cheese and bits of bacon). Like the Czechs, the Slovaks produce excellent beer (*pivo*, PEE-voh). One of the top brands is Zlatý Bažant ("Golden Pheasant").

Slovak Language

Many people assume Slovak is virtually the same as Czech. To be sure, there are similarities—but they're not identical.

Slovak is handy as a sort of a lingua franca of Slavic tongues. Czechs can understand Poles, but not Slovenes; Poles can understand Croatians, but not Czechs. But Slovak speakers generally find they can understand—and be understood by—speakers of any of these languages.

Slovak's similarity to Czech was exaggerated during the 75 years that these languages shared a country. Soccer games would be broadcast with two commentators—one spoke Czech, and the other spoke Slovak. Anyone growing up in this era grew comfortable using the languages interchangeably. But today's teenagers—who have only spoken exclusively Czech or Slovak—find they have trouble understanding each other across the border.

Slovak uses many of the same diacritical markings as Czech. Many letters are topped with a *mäkčeň* ("softener"), including *č, š, ž,* and *ň*). Here are some guidelines for pronouncing Slovak:

j sounds like "y" as in "yarn"
c sounds like "ts" as in "cats"
č sounds like "ch" as in "chicken"
š sounds like "sh" as in "shrimp"
ž sounds like "zh" as in "leisure"
ň sounds like "ny" as in "canyon"
ä sounds like "eh" as in "get"

An acute accent *(á, é, í, ó, ú, ý)* means you linger on that vowel. What looks like an apostrophe after a consonant—such as *ď, ť,* and *ľ*—indicates that the sound has a palatal pronunciation; this means that you make the sound by tapping the flat part of your tongue to the roof of your mouth (so *ď* sounds not quite like "d," but closer to the "dj" sound in "ledge").

The local "ciao"—used informally for both "hi" and "bye"—is easy to remember: *ahoj* (pronounced "AH-hoy," like a pirate).

When navigating in towns and cities, these words might be helpful: *mesto* (MEHS-toh, town), *námestie* (NAH-mehs-tee, square), *ulica* (OO-leet-sah, road), *nábrežie* (NAH-breh-zhee, embankment road), and *most* (mohst, bridge).

BRATISLAVA

Pozsony/Pressburg

Bratislava (brah-tee-SLAH-vah), long a drab lesson in the failings of the communist system, is turning things around...fast. A decade ago, the city center was grim, deserted, and dangerous—a place where only thieves and fools dared to tread. Today it's downright charming, bursting with colorfully restored facades, lively outdoor cafés, swanky boutiques, in-love-with-life locals, and (on sunny days) an almost Mediterranean ambience.

The rejuvenation doesn't end in the Old Town. The ramshackle quarter to the east is gradually being flattened and redeveloped into a new forest of skyscrapers. Bratislava is working together with its neighbor Vienna to forge a new twin-city relationship for trade and commerce, bridging the former Eastern Europe and the former Western Europe. The hilltop castle is getting a facelift. And even the glum commie suburb of Petržalka is undergoing a Technicolor makeover. Before our eyes, Bratislava is becoming the quintessential post-communist Eastern European city—showing what can happen when government and business leaders make a concerted effort to jump-start a failing city.

You get the feeling that workaday Bratislavans—who strike some visitors as gruff—are being pulled to the cutting edge of the 21st century kicking and screaming. But many Slovaks embrace the changes, and fancy themselves as the yang to Vienna's yin: If Vienna is a staid, elderly aristocrat sipping coffee, then Bratislava is a vivacious young professional jet-setting around Europe. Bratislava at night is a lively place; its very youthful center thrives. While it has tens of thousands of university students, there are no campuses as such—so the Old Town is the place where students go to play.

Bratislava's priceless location—on the Danube (and the tourist circuit) smack-dab between Budapest and Vienna—makes it a very worthwhile "on the way" destination. Frankly, the city used to leave me cold. But all the new changes are positively inspiring.

Planning Your Time

A few hours are enough to get the gist of Bratislava. Head straight to the Old Town and follow my self-guided walk, dropping into your choice of museums and finishing with a walk along the Danube riverbank to the thriving, modern Eurovea development. With more time, ascend to the "UFO" observation deck atop the funky suspension bridge. Or hike up to the castle, which offers great views over the town (if little else). If you spend the evening in Bratislava, you'll find it lively with students, busy cafés, and nightlife.

Note that all museums and galleries are closed on Monday.

Orientation to Bratislava

(area code: 02)
Bratislava, with nearly half a million residents, is Slovakia's capital and biggest city. It has a small, colorful Old Town (Staré Mesto), with the castle on the hill above. This small area is surrounded by a vast construction zone of new buildings and a few colorized communist suburbs (including Petržalka, across the river). The northern and western parts of the city are hilly and cool (these "Little Carpathians" are draped with vineyards), while the southern and eastern areas are flat and warmer.

You've dropped in to visit Bratislava just as the city is undoing the brutally ugly infrastructure inflicted upon it by the communists. Soon, the highway that barrels between the Old Town and the castle will be diverted underground (through a tunnel beneath the Danube); the TGV bullet train from Paris will swoosh to a stop at a slick new train station; and a new six-station subway line will lace the city together. The entire riverfront is being transformed into a people-friendly park (to match the new zone beyond the old iron bridge, in Eurovea).

Tourist Information

The TI is on **Primate's Square** behind the Old Town Hall (Mon-Fri 9:30-18:00, Sat-Sun 9:30-16:30, Klobučnícka 2, tel. 02/16186, www.bkis.sk and www.bratislava.sk). Pick up the free *Bratislava Guide* (with map) and browse their brochures; they can help you find a room in town for a modest fee.

Discount Card: The TI also sells the €10 **Bratislava City Card,** which includes free transit and sightseeing discounts—but it's worthwhile only if you're doing the Old Town walking tour (€14 without the card—see "Tours in Bratislava," later).

Arrival in Bratislava

By Train: Bratislava's **Main Train Station,** called Bratislava Hlavná Stanica, is about a half-mile north of the Old Town. In the next few years, the city plans to tear down most of this station and start from scratch (to accommodate, among other things, a new high-speed rail line connecting Bratislava to Paris). Therefore, these arrival instructions are likely to change; just look for signs.

As you emerge from the tracks, the left-luggage desk is to your right (€1-2, depending on size; look for *ú schovňa batožín;* there are no lockers, and the check desk closes for 30-minute lunch and dinner breaks).

It's an easy 15-minute **walk** to the town center. Leave the station straight ahead, take the overpass across the busy cross street, and continue straight on Štefánikova. This formerly elegant old boulevard is lined with rotting facades from Bratislava's high-on-the-hog Habsburg era. After about 10 minutes, you'll pass the nicely manicured presidential gardens on your left, then the Grassalkovich Palace, Slovakia's "White House." Continue straight through the busy intersection onto Súché Mýto, and head for the green onion-domed steeple (take the narrow street next to the mod, green, white-capped Alizé restaurant). This is St. Michael's Gate, at the start of the Old Town (and the beginning of my self-guided walk, described later).

If you want to shave a few minutes off the trip, go part of the way by **tram** (from train station's main hall, with tracks at your back, look for signs to *električky* on left; take escalator down, buy a €0.50/15-minute ticket from the machine, hop on tram #13, ride it to Poštová, then walk straight down Obchodná street). If the tram is not running (due to reconstruction of the tracks), bus #93 follows a similar route (ride it to the Hodžovo Námestie stop, in front of the Slovak "White House").

If you're coming from Vienna, be aware that about half of the trains from there arrive at Bratislava's other train station (called "ŽST Petržalka"), in the **Petržalka** suburb. From this station, ride bus #80, #93, or #94 to the Zochova stop (near St. Michael's Gate), or bus #91 or #191 to the Nový Most stop (at the Old Town end of the New Bridge). Buses #93 (by day) and #N93 (by night) also connect the two stations.

By Boat or Plane: For information on Bratislava's riverboats and airport, see "Bratislava Connections," at the end of this chapter.

Helpful Hints

Internet Access: You'll see signs advertising Internet cafés around the Old Town. If you have a laptop or other wireless device, you can get online free at the three main squares in the Old Town (Old Town Square, Primate's Square, and Hviezdoslav Square).

Local Guidebook: For in-depth suggestions on Bratislava sightseeing, dining, and more, look for the excellent and eye-pleasing *Bratislava Active* guidebook by Martin Sloboda (see "Tours in Bratislava," next; around €10, sold at every postcard rack).

Tours in Bratislava

Walking Tour—The **TI** offers a one-hour Old Town walking tour in English every day in the summer at 14:00 (€14, free with Bratislava City Card; you must book and pay at least two hours in advance). Those arriving by boat will be accosted by guides selling their own 1.5-hour tours (half on foot and half in a little tourist train, €10, in German and English).

Local Guide—MS Agency, run by **Martin Sloboda** (a can-do entrepreneur and tireless Bratislava booster, and author of the great local guidebook described above), can set you up with a good local

guide (€120/3 hours, €150/4 hours), and can help you track down your Slovak roots. Martin, whose local expertise has made much of this chapter possible, is a fine example of the youthful energy and leadership responsible for Bratislava's success story (tel. 02/5464-1467, www.msagency.sk, info@msagency.sk).

Self-Guided Walk

Bratislava's Old Town

This orientation walk, which passes through the heart of delightfully traffic-free old Bratislava and then down to its new riverside commercial zone, takes about an hour and a half (not including stops). If you're coming from the station, make your way toward the green onion-domed steeple of St. Michael's Gate (explained in "Arrival in Bratislava," earlier). Before going through the passage into the Old Town, peek over the

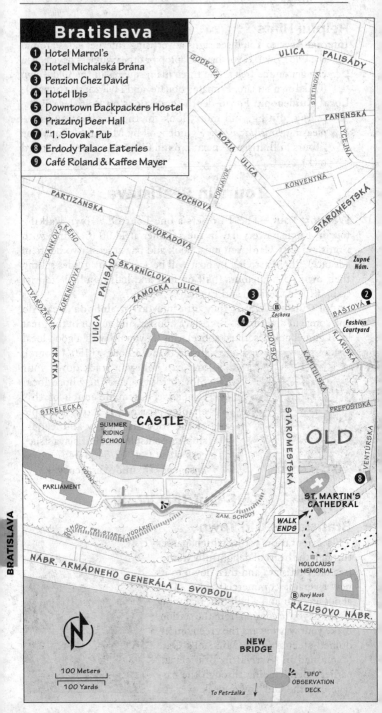

Bratislava

1. Hotel Marrol's
2. Hotel Michalská Brána
3. Penzion Chez David
4. Hotel Ibis
5. Downtown Backpackers Hostel
6. Prazdroj Beer Hall
7. "1. Slovak" Pub
8. Erdody Palace Eateries
9. Café Roland & Kaffee Mayer

BRATISLAVA

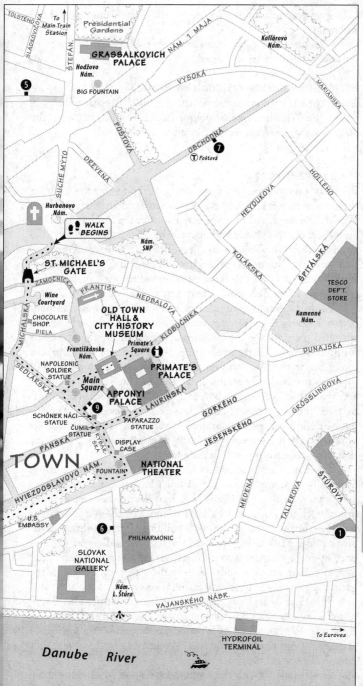

railing on your left to the inviting garden below—once part of the city moat.

• *Step through the first gate, walk along the passageway, and pause as you come through the onion-domed...*

St. Michael's Gate (Michalská Brána)

This is the last surviving tower of the city wall. Just below the gate, notice the "kilometer zero" plaque in the ground, marking the point from which distances in Slovakia are measured.

• *You're at the head of...*

Michalská Street

Pretty as it is now, the Old Town was a decrepit ghost town during the communist era. Bratislava was a damaged husk after World War II. The communist regime cared only for the future—they had no respect for the town's heritage. In the 1950s, they actually sold Bratislava's original medieval cobbles to cute towns in Germany that were rebuilding after the war with elegant Old World character. Locals avoided this desolate corner of the city, preferring to spend time in the Petržalka suburb across the river.

With the fall of communism in 1989, the new government began a nearly decade-long process of restitution—sorting out who had the rights to the buildings, and returning them to their original owners. During this time, little repair or development took place (since there was no point investing in a property until ownership was clearly established). By 1998, most of these property issues had been sorted out, and the Old Town was made traffic-free. The city replaced all of the street cobbles, spruced up the public buildings, and encouraged private owners to restore their buildings. (If you see any remaining decrepit buildings, it's likely that their ownership is still in dispute.)

The cafés and restaurants that line this street are inviting, especially in summer. But if you don't look beyond the facades and outdoor tables, you'll miss much of Bratislava's charm. Poke around. Courtyards and galleries—most of them open to the public—burrow through the city's buildings. For example, a half-block down Michalská street on the left, the gallery at #12 was once home to vintners who lived within the walls for safety; their former cellars are now clubs. Across the street, on the right, the gallery at #7 is home to several fashion designers.

Speaking of fashion...are you noticing a lot of skin? Tight jeans? Low-cut tops? Slovak women are known for their provocative dress. When pressed for a reason for this, one male resident of "Leg-islava" smirked and told me, "Women like to show what they have. Why should they hide it?"

On the left (at #6), the **Čokoládovňa pod Michalom** chocolate shop is highly regarded among locals for its delicious hot chocolate and creamy truffles (Mon-Fri 9:00-21:00, Sat-Sun 10:00-21:00, tel. 02/5443-3945).

Above the shop's entrance, the **cannonball** embedded in the wall commemorates Napoleon's two sieges of Bratislava, which together caused massive devastation—even worse than the city suffered during World War II. Keep an eye out for these cannonballs all over town...somber reminders of one of Bratislava's darkest times.

• *Two blocks down from St. Michael's Gate, the name of this main drag changes to Ventúrska, the street jogs to the right, and the café scene continues. At the jog, detour left (along Sedlárska) and head for the...*

Main Square (Hlavné Námestie)

This is the bustling centerpiece of Old World Bratislava. Cute little kiosks, with old-time cityscape engravings on their roofs,

sell local handicrafts and knick-knacks (Easter through October). Similar stalls fill the square from mid-November until December 23, when the Christmas market here is a big draw (www.vianocne trhy.sk).

Virtually every building around this square dates from a different architectural period, from Gothic (the yellow tower) to Art Nouveau (the fancy facade facing it from across the square). When these buildings were restored a few years ago, great pains were taken to achieve authenticity—each one matches the color most likely used when it was originally built.

Extremely atmospheric cafés line the bottom of the square. You can't go wrong here. Choose the ambience you like best (indoors or out) and nurse a drink with arguably Slovakia's best urban view. **Café Roland** is known for its 1904 Klimt-style mosaics and historic photos of Pozsony/Pressburg. The barista, who stands where a different kind of bean-counter once did, guards a vault that now holds coffee (daily, Hlavné Námestie 5, tel. 02/5443-1372). The classic choice is **Kaffee Mayer,** next door. This venerable café, an institution here, has been selling coffee and cakes to a genteel clientele since 1873. You can enjoy your pick-me-up in the swanky old interior, or out on the square (€2-3 cakes, Mon-Fri 9:30-22:00, Sat-Sun 9:30-23:00, Hlavné Námestie 4, tel. 02/5441-1741).

Peering over one of the benches on the square is a cartoonish statue of a **Napoleonic officer** (notice the French flag marking the embassy right behind him). With bare feet and a hat pulled over his

City of Three Cultures: Pressburg, Pozsony, Bratislava

Historically a Hungarian and Austrian city as much as a Slovak one, Bratislava has always been an Eastern European melting pot. The Hungarians used Pozsony (as they called it) as their capital during the century and a half that Buda and Pest were occupied by Ottoman invaders. Later, the city was a retreat of Habsburg Empress Maria Theresa (who used its German name, Pressburg). Everyone from Hans Christian Andersen to Casanova sang the wonders of this bustling burg on the Danube.

By its late-19th-century glory days, the city was a rich inter-section of cultures. Shop clerks had to be able to greet customers in German, Hungarian, and Slovak. It was said that the mornings belonged to the Slovaks (farmers who came into the city to sell their wares at market), the afternoons to the Hungarians (diplo-mats and office-workers filling the cafés), and the evenings to the Austrians (wine-producers who ran convivial neighborhood wine pubs where all three groups would gather). In those wine pubs, the vintner would listen to which language his customers used, then automatically bring them the correct size glass: 0.3 liters for Hungarians, 0.25 liters for Austrians, and 0.2 liters for Slovaks (a distinction that still exists today). Jews (one-tenth of the popu-lation), Romanians, and Roma (Gypsies) rounded out the city's ethnic brew.

When the new nation of Czechoslovakia was formed from the rubble of World War I, the city shed its German and Hungarian names, proudly taking the new Slavic name Bratislava. The Slovak population—which had been at only about 10 per-cent—was on the rise, but the city remained tri-cultural.

World War II changed all of that. With the dissolution of Czechoslovakia, Slovakia became an "independent" coun-try under the thumb of the Nazis—who all but wiped out the

eyes, it's hardly a flattering portrait—you could call it the Slovaks' revenge for the difficulties they faced at Napoleon's hands.

At the top of the Main Square is the impressive **Old Town Hall** (Stará Radnica), marked by a bold yellow tower. Near the bottom of the tower (to the left of the win-dow), notice the cannonball embedded in the facade—yet another reminder of Napoleon's impact on Bratislava. Over time, the Old Town Hall gradually grew, annexing the buildings next to it and creating a mishmash of architectural styles along this side of the square. (A few steps down the street to the right are the historic apartments and wine

Jewish population. Then, at the end of the war, in retribution for Hitler's misdeeds, a reunited Czechoslovakia expelled people of Germanic descent (including all of those Austrians). And finally, a "mutual exchange of populations" sent the city's ethnic Hungarians back to Hungary.

Bratislava suffered terribly under the communists. It became the textbook example of a historic city whose multilayered charm and delicate cultural fabric were ripped apart, then shrouded in gray by the communist regime. For example, the communists were more proud of their ultramodern New Bridge than of the historic Jewish quarter they razed to make way for it. Now the bridge and its highway slice through the center of the Old Town, and the heavy traffic rattles the stained-glass windows of St. Martin's Cathedral.

But Bratislava's most recent chapter is one of great success. Over the last decade, the city has gone from gloomy victim of communism to thriving economic center and social hub. Its population of 430,000 includes some 70,000 students (at the city's six universities), creating an atmosphere of youthful energy and optimism. Its remarkable position on the Danube, a short commute from Vienna, is prompting its redevelopment as one of Europe's most up-and-coming cities.

Bratislava and Vienna have realized it's in both cities' interest to work together to bring the Slovak capital up to snuff. They're cooperating as a new "twin city" commerce super-zone. In the coming years, foreign investors plan to erect a skyline of 600-foot-tall skyscrapers and a clutch of glittering new megamalls. You'd never have guessed it a few years ago, but today calling Bratislava "the next Berlin on a smaller scale" is only a bit of a stretch.

museum at the **Apponyi House**—described later, under "Sights in Bratislava.")

Step through the passageway into the Old Town Hall's gorgeously restored **courtyard,** with its Renaissance arcades. (The **City History Museum**'s entrance is here—described later.)

Then, to see another fine old square, continue through the other end of the courtyard into **Primate's Square** (Primaciálne Námestie). The pink mansion on the right is the **Primate's Palace,** with a fine interior decorated with six English tapestries (described later). Do you see a lot of people using laptops? In a progressive move befitting its status as an emerging business center of Europe, Bratislava provides free Wi-Fi on three squares in the Old Town. The huge student population (not to mention tourists) happily surfs in this beautiful setting. At the far end of this square is the main

branch of the TI.
• *Backtrack to the Main Square. With your back to the Old Town Hall, go to the end of the square and follow the street to the left (Rybárska Brána). Soon you'll pass a pair of...*

Whimsical Statues

Several playful statues (such as the Napoleonic officer we met earlier) dot Bratislava's Old Town. Most of these date from the late 1990s, when city leaders wanted to entice locals back into the newly prettied-up Old Town.

A half-block down this street (on the left), you'll come to a jovial chap doffing his top hat. This is a statue of **Schöner Náci,**

who lived in Bratislava until the 1960s. This eccentric old man, a poor carpet cleaner, would dress up in his one black suit and top hat, and go strolling through the city, offering gifts to the women he fancied. (He'd often whisper *"schön"*—German for "pretty"—to the women, which is how he got his nickname.) After spending his life cheering up the gloomy streets of communist Bratislava, Schöner Náci now gets to spend eternity greeting visitors outside his favorite café, Kaffee Mayer. As a sad epilogue, the statue's arm was broken off recently by a bunch of drunks. As Prague gets more expensive, Bratislava is becoming the cheaper alternative for weekend "stag parties," popular with Brits lured here by cheap flights

and cheap beer. Locals hope this is a short-lived trend, and that those rowdy louts will move farther east before long.
• *Continue down Rybárska.*

At the end of this block, at the intersection with Panská, watch out on the right

for **Čumil** ("the Peeper"), grinning at passersby from a manhole. This was the first and is still the favorite of Bratislava's statues. There's no story behind this one—the artist simply wanted to create a fun icon and let the townspeople make up their own tales. Čumil has survived being driven over by a truck—twice—and he's still grinning.

For a peek at a third statue—a nosy **Paparazzo**—you can take a side-trip left up

Panská and go one block, watching the corner on the left.
• *Back at Čumil, continue along Rybárska to reach the long, skinny square called...*

Hviezdoslav Square (Hviezdoslavovo Námestie)

This square is yet another part of Bratislava that has undergone a much-needed sprucing-up. The landscaped park in the center is particularly inviting. At this end of the square is the impressive, silver-topped Slovak National Theater (Slovenské Národné Divadlo). Beyond that, the opulent yellow building that seems to be melting is the Philharmonic. The prominence of these two venues is evidence of Bratislava's strong performing arts tradition.

Right in front of the theater (by the McDonald's), look down into the glass **display case** to see the foundation of the one-time Fishermen's Gate into the city. Surrounding the base of the gate is water. This entire square was once a tributary of the Danube, and the Carlton Hotel across the way was a series of inns on different islands. The buildings along the Old Town side of the square mark where the city wall once stood.

Stroll down the long art-and-people-filled park, nicknamed **"The Promenade."** Each summer, as part of an arts festival, the park is ornamented with entertaining modern art. After passing a statue of the square's namesake (Pavol Országh Hviezdoslav, a beloved Slovak poet), you'll come upon an ugly fence and barriers on the left, which mark the fortified US Embassy. The glass pavilion is a popular venue for summer concerts. On the right near the end of the park, a statue of Hans Christian Andersen is a reminder that the Danish storyteller enjoyed his visit to Bratislava, too.
• *Reaching the end of the square (just before the big highway), you come to the...*

Holocaust Memorial

This monument, marking the site of the old synagogue (an image of the building is etched into the marble wall), is a Holocaust memorial. The word "Remember" carved into the base in Hebrew and Slovak commemorates the 90,000 Slovaks who were deported to Nazi death camps. Nearly all were killed. The fact that the town's main synagogue and main church (to the right) were located side by side illustrates the tolerance that characterized Bratislava before Hitler. Ponder the modern statue: The two pages of an open book, faces, hands in the sky, and bullets—all under the Star of David—evoke the fate of 90 percent of the Slovak Jews.

• *Now enter the adjacent church (the door is around on the far side).*

St. Martin's Cathedral (Dóm Sv. Martina)

This historic church isn't looking too sharp these days—and the highway thundering a few feet in front of its door (courtesy of

communist city planners) doesn't help matters. If it were any closer, the off-ramp would go through the nave. Sad as it is now, the cathedral has been party to some pretty important history. While Buda and Pest were occupied by Ottomans for a century and a half, Bratislava was the capital of Hungary. Nineteen Hungarian kings and queens were crowned in this church—more than have been crowned anywhere in Hungary. In fact, the last Hungarian coronation

(not counting the Austrian Franz Josef) was not in Budapest, but in Bratislava. A replica of the Hungarian crown still tops the steeple.

As you leave the church, note that directly in front of the door is a broken bit of the 15th-century town wall. The church was actually built into the wall, which explains its unusual north-side entry. In fact, notice the fortified watchtower (with a WC drop on its left) built into the corner of the church just above you.

Looking toward the river, you can see the **New Bridge** (Nový Most, a.k.a. Most SNP), the communists' pride and joy. As with

most Soviet-era landmarks in former communist countries, locals aren't crazy about this structure—not only for the questionable starship *Enterprise* design, but also because of the oppressive regime it represented. However, the restaurant and observation deck up top—long a stale holdover from

communist times—has been renovated into a posh eatery called (appropriately enough) "UFO." You can visit it for the views, a drink, or a full meal.

• *You could end the walk here. Two sights (both described later, under "Sights in Bratislava") are nearby: You could hike up to the **castle** (take the underpass beneath the highway, go up the stairs on the right marked by the* Hrad/Castle *sign, then turn left up the stepped lane marked*

Zámocké Schody). Or hike over the New Bridge (pedestrian walkway on lower level) to ride the elevator up the "UFO" viewing platform.

*But to really round out your Bratislava visit, head for the river and stroll downstream (left) to a place where you get a dose of modern development in Bratislava—**Eurovea**. Walk about 10 minutes downstream, past the Old Town, boat terminals, and iron bridge, until you come to a big, slick complex with a grassy park leading down to the riverbank.*

Eurovea

Just downstream from the Old Town is the futuristic Eurovea, with four vibrant layers, each a quarter-mile long: a riverside park,

luxury condos, a thriving modern shopping mall, and an office park. Walking out onto the view piers jutting into the Danube and surveying the scene, it looks like a computer-generated urban dreamscape come true. Exploring the Old Town gave you a taste of where this country has been. But wandering this riverside park, enjoying a drink in one of its chic outdoor lounges, and then browsing through the thriving mall, you'll enjoy a glimpse of where Slovakia is heading.

• *Our walk is finished. If you haven't already visited them, consider circling back to some of the sights described below.*

Sights in Bratislava

Most of Bratislava's charm is in its streets, not its museums. But these sights are fine for a rainy day or for "extra credit."

On or near the Old Town's Main Square

City History Museum (Mestské Múzeum)—This museum, in the Old Town Hall, offers an exhibit on town history (including torture equipment, or "feudal justice") and a chance to climb the Old Town Hall tower for a view of the square.

Cost and Hours: €3, Tue-Fri 10:00-17:00, Sat-Sun 11:00-18:00, closed Mon, enter through courtyard of Old Town Hall, Hlavné Námestie 1, tel. 02/5920-5130, www.muzeum.bratislava.sk.

▲Apponyi House (Apponyiho Palác)—This gorgeously restored mansion of a Hungarian aristocrat is meaningless without the included audioguide. This museum has two parts: The cellar holds an interesting exhibit on the vineyards of the nearby "Little Carpathian" hills, with historic presses and barrels, and a replica of an old-time wine-pub table. Upstairs are two floors of urban apartments from old Bratislava: The first floor up shows off the 18th-century Rococo-style rooms of the nobility, while the second floor up (with lower ceilings and simpler wall decorations) illustrates 19th-century bourgeois/middle-class lifestyles, including some fine Empire-style furniture.

Cost and Hours: €6, Tue-Fri 10:00-17:00, Sat-Sun 11:00-18:00, closed Mon, Radničná ulica 1, tel. 02/5920-5135.

▲**Primate's Palace (Primaciálny Palác)**—Bratislava's most interesting museum, this tastefully restored French-Neoclassical mansion (formerly the residence of the archbishop, or "primate") dates from 1781. The religious counterpart of the castle, it filled in for Esztergom when that religious capital of the Hungarians was taken by the Ottomans. Throughout the Ottoman occupation, from 1543 to the late 1800s, this was the winter residence of Hungary's archbishops.

You'll explore one fine floor. The smaller rooms were the archbishop's private quarters, now decorated with Dutch, Flemish, German, and Italian paintings. You'll peer from a bay window down into the archbishop's own private marble chapel. When the archbishop became too ill to walk down to Mass, this window was built for him to take part in the service. The larger rooms were public...designed to impress. Among these is the Mirror Hall, used for concerts, city council meetings, and other important events.

The museum's highlight is its series of six English **tapestries,** illustrating the ancient Greek myth of the tragic love between Hero and Leander. The tapestries—the only complete cycle of royal English tapestries in existence—were woven in England by Flemish weavers for the court of King Charles I (in the 1630s). They were kept in London's Hampton Court Palace until Charles was deposed and beheaded in 1649. Cromwell sold them to France to help fund his civil war, but after 1650, they disappeared. Centuries later, in 1903, restorers broke through a false wall in this mansion and discovered the six tapestries, neatly folded and perfectly preserved. Nobody knows how they got there (perhaps they were squirreled away during the Napoleonic invasion, and whoever hid them didn't survive). The archbishop—who had just sold the palace to the city, but emptied it of furniture before he left—cried foul and tried to get the tapestries back...but the city said, "A deal's a deal."

Cost and Hours: €2, Tue-Fri 10:00-17:00, Sat-Sun 11:00-18:00, closed Mon, Primaciálne Námestie 3, tel. 02/5935-6394.

Bratislava Castle (Bratislavský Hrad)

This imposing fortress, nicknamed the "upside-down table," is the city's most prominent landmark. There surely has been a castle on

this spot for centuries. The oldest surviving chunk is the 13th-century Romanesque watchtower (the one slightly taller than the other three). When Habsburg Empress Maria Theresa took a liking to Bratislava in the 18th century, she transformed the castle from a military fortress to a royal residence suitable for holding court. She added a summer riding school (the U-shaped complex next to the castle), an enclosed winter riding school out back, and lots more. Maria Theresa's favorite daughter, Maria Christina, lived here with her husband Albert when they were newlyweds. Locals nicknamed the place "little Schönbrunn," in reference to the Habsburgs' summer palace on the outskirts of Vienna.

But M.T.'s castle burned to the ground in an 1811 fire, and it was left as a ruin for a century and a half—not reconstructed until 1953. Unfortunately, the communist rebuild was drab and uninviting; the inner courtyard felt like a prison exercise yard.

The good news is that the city is in the midst of a five-year renovation project to rehabilitate the castle from top to bottom (due to wrap up in 2013). They've already reconstructed the summer riding school, and plan to rebuild the winter riding school and terraced French

gardens out back. The bad news is that during the restoration, the castle interior is closed to visitors. But more good news: The interior was never appealing anyway, so the main reason to visit—for up-close views of the castle, over the rooftops of the Old Town, and across the Danube to Petržalka—remains the same (and free).

For details on the best way to hike up to the castle, see page 232.

The "UFO" at New Bridge (Nový Most)

The bizarre, flying-saucer-capped bridge near the Old Town—completed in 1972 in heavy-handed communist style—has been reclaimed by capitalists. It's been spruced up and turned into an overpriced café/restaurant, with an observation deck that allows

BRATISLAVA

visitors sweeping 360-degree views of Bratislava from about 300 feet above the Danube. Think of it as the "Slovak Space Needle."

Cost and Hours: €7, daily 10:00-23:00, elevator free if you have a meal reservation—main courses steeply priced at €25-30, tel. 02/6252-0300, www.u-f-o.sk.

Getting There: Walk across the New Bridge from the Old Town—the elevator entrance is underneath the tower on the Petržalka side.

◑ Self-Guided Tour: The "elevator" that takes you up is actually a funicular—you'll notice you're moving at an angle. At the top, walk up the stairs to the observation deck.

Begin by viewing the **castle** and **Old Town.** Notice the area to the right of the Old Town, between and beyond the skyscrapers—it's a massive construction zone. If you set up a time-lapse camera

here over the next few years, you'd watch skyscrapers pop up like dandelions. International investors are throwing lots of money at Bratislava. (Imagine having so much prime, undeveloped real estate available downtown in the capital of an emerging European economic power...just an hour down the road from Vienna, no less.) Most of the development is taking place along the banks of the Danube. In a decade, this will be a commercial center.

The huge tower capping a forested hill beyond the Old Town is a TV tower. Below and to the left of it, the pointy monument is **Slavín,** where more than 6,800 Soviet soldiers who fought to liberate Bratislava from the Nazis are buried. A nearby church had to take down its steeple so as not to draw attention away from the huge Soviet soldier on top of the monument.

Now turn 180 degrees and cross the platform to face **Petržalka,** a planned communist suburb that sprouted here in the 1970s. The site was once occupied by a village, and the various districts of modern Petržalka still carry

their original names (which now seem ironic): "Meadows" *(Háje),* "Woods" *(Lúky),* and "Courtyards" *(Dvory).* The ambitious communist planners envisioned a city laced with Venetian-style canals to help drain the marshy land, but the plans were abandoned after the harsh crackdown on the 1968 Prague Spring uprising. Today, one in four Bratislavans lives in Petržalka. A few years ago, this was a grim and decaying sea of miserable concrete apartment *panelák* ("panel buildings," so called because they're made of huge prefab panels that were built elsewhere, then brought here to assemble on-site). But things are changing fast. Many of the *panelák* are being retrofitted with new layers of insulation, and the apartments inside are being updated. And, like Dorothy opening the door to Oz, the formerly drab buildings are being splashed with bright new colors. Far from being a slum, Petržalka is a popular neighborhood for Bratislavan yuppies who can't yet afford to build their dream house. Locals read the Czech-language home-improvement magazine *Panel Plus* for ideas on how to give their *panelák* apartments some style (www.panelplus.cz).

Still facing Petržalka, notice that new construction is also happening along this riverbank (such as the supermall down below). But there's still history here. The **park** called Sad Janka Kráľa, a.k.a. "Aupark"—just downriver from the bridge—was technically the first public park in Europe, and is still a popular place for locals to relax and court.

Scanning the **horizon** beyond Petržalka, two things stick out: on the left, the old communist oil refinery (which has been fully updated and is now state-of-the-art); and on the right, a sea of modern windmills. These are just over the border, in Austria...and Bratislava is sure to grow in that direction quickly. Austria is about three miles that way, and Hungary is about six miles farther to the left.

Before you leave, consider nursing a drink at the café (€3 coffee or beer, €5-15 cocktails). If nothing else, be sure to use the memorable WCs (guys can enjoy a classic urinal photo).

Sleeping in Bratislava

A few years ago, there were no sleepable hotels near Bratislava's Old Town. But as new accommodations open every year, the scene is rapidly improving: Search online for the latest options, from hostels to five-star places. I'd still rather sleep in Budapest or Vienna. But if the city entices you to stay longer than a day trip, these options are all inside or within a short walk of the Old Town. Business-oriented places charge more on weekdays (Mon-Thu) than on weekends (Fri-Sun).

Sleep Code

(€1 = about $1.40, country code: 421, area code: 02)
S = Single, **D** = Double/Twin, **T** = Triple, **Q** = Quad, **b** = bathroom.
Unless otherwise noted, credit cards are accepted and breakfast is included. Everyone listed here speaks English.

To help you easily sort through these listings, I've divided the accommodations into three categories, based on the price for a double room with bath during high season:

$$$ Higher Priced—Most rooms €100 or more.
  $$ Moderately Priced—Most rooms between €50-100.
    $ Lower Priced—Most rooms €50 or less.

Prices can change without notice; verify the hotel's current rates online or by email. For other updates, see www.ricksteves.com/update.

$$$ Hotel Marrol's is the town's most enticing splurge. Although it's in a drab urban neighborhood, it's a five-minute walk from the Old Town, and its 54 rooms are luxurious and tastefully appointed Old World country-style. While pricey, the rates drop on weekends (Mon-Thu: Db-€180, Fri-Sun: Db-€125, Sb-€10 less, non-smoking, air-con, computer in room with free cable Internet, Wi-Fi, free minibar, gorgeous lounge, Tobrucká ulica 4, tel. 02/5778-4600, www.hotelmarrols.sk, rec@hotelmarrols.sk).

$$$ Hotel Michalská Brána is a charming boutique hotel hiding down a tight, atmospheric little lane just inside St. Michael's Gate in the Old Town. The 14 rooms are sleek, mod, and classy (Mon-Thu: Db-€105, Fri-Sun: Db-€100, pricier suites also available, non-smoking, air-con, elevator, free cable Internet, Baštová 4, tel. 02/5930-7200, www.michalskabrana.com, michalskabrana @gmail.com).

$$ Penzion Chez David is a spartan, Jewish-themed hotel with 10 budget rooms just outside the Old Town (Mon-Thu: Sb-€59, Db-€76; Fri-Sun: Sb-€49, Db-€66; check website for last-minute specials, air-con, some street noise from busy road and tram—request quieter room, Zámocká 13, tel. 02/5441-3824, www.chezdavid.sk, recepcia@chezdavid.sk).

$$ Hotel Ibis, part of the cookie-cutter chain, offers 120 rooms overlooking a busy tram junction across the street from Penzion Chez David (Mon-Thu: Sb/Db-€85, Fri-Sun: Sb/Db-€69, rates flex with demand, you'll likely save €20 with advance booking on their website, breakfast-€10, Zámocká 38, tel. 02/5929-2000, fax 02/5929-2111, www.ibishotel.com, h3566@accor.com).

$ Downtown Backpackers Hostel is a good hostel option. Funky but well-run, it's near the Grassalkovich (presidential) Palace about a five-minute walk from the Old Town (61 beds in 12 rooms, Db-€70, D-€55, bunk in Qb-€25, bunk in 7-8-bed dorm-€20, bunk in 10-bed dorm-€18, free Wi-Fi, laundry facilities, kitchen, bike rental, Panenská 31, tel. 02/5464-1191, www .backpackers.sk, info@backpackers.sk).

Eating in Bratislava

For a fun drink and snack that locals love, try a Vinea grape soda and a sweet *Pressburger* bagel in any bar or café. Long a wine-pro-

ducing area, the Bratislava region makes the same wines that Vienna is famous for. But, as nearly all is consumed locally, most people don't think of Slovakia as wine country.

Bratislava is packed with inviting new eateries. In addition to the heavy Slovak staples, you'll find trendy new bars and bistros, and a wide range of ethnic offerings. The best plan may be to stroll the Old Town and keep your eyes open for the setting and cuisine that appeals to you most. Or consider one of these options.

Prazdroj ("Urquell") is a Czech-style beer hall with lively ambience and good traditional food. It sprawls through several rooms of a building just off Hviezdoslav Square at the edge of the Old Town (€7-10 main dishes, Mon-Fri 10:00-24:00, Sat-Sun 11:00-24:00, Mostová 8, tel. 02/5441-1108).

1. Slovak Pub (as in "the first") is the Slovak equivalent of Prazdroj, attracting a younger crowd. Enter from a bustling modern shopping street just outside the Old Town, and climb the stairs into a vast warren of rustic, old countryside-style pub rooms. While enjoying the lively, loud, almost chaotic ambience, you'll dine on affordable and truly authentic Slovak fare, made with products from the pub's own farm. This is a good place to try the Slovak specialty, *bryndzové halušky* (€6-9 main dishes, Mon-Sat 10:00-24:00, Sun 12:00-24:00, Obchodná 62, tel. 02/5292-6367).

Erdody Palace, a renovated mansion in the center of the Old Town at Ventúrska 1, is a great place to splurge at one of two eateries with an Andy Warhol theme (after all, Andrej Warhola was Slovak). As the owner is a huge Warhol fan, lots of Warhol art hangs in each restaurant, named for the theme of the works: **Flowers** dishes up Mediterranean fare in a bright, covered court-yard (€7-14 pastas, €15-25 main dishes, daily 11:30-1:00 in the morning, tel. 02/2092-2733). The stuffier **Camouflage** features nouvelle cuisine in a somewhat snooty, white-minimalist setting. While their main menu is pricey (€15-30 main dishes), their local specialty dishes are reasonable and really tasty (Mon-Sat 11:30-24:00, closed Sun, reservations smart, tel. 02/2092-2711). Even if you're not eating here, drop by to see Warhol enjoying the place.

Fast and Cheap: A local chain called **Coffee & Co,** with branches throughout the Old Town and beyond, serves up good €3-4 sandwiches—ideal for a bite on the run (various locations, all open long hours daily).

Bratislava Connections

By Train

Bratislava has two major train stations. The Main Train Station (Hlavná Stanica, abbreviated "Bratislava hl. st." on schedules) is closer to the Old Town, while the Petržalka station (ŽST Petržalka) is in the suburb across the river. When checking schedules (http://bahn.hafas.de/bin/query.exe/en is helpful), pay attention to which station your train uses. Bus #93 connects these two Bratislava stations (5-12/hour, 10 minutes; take bus #N93 at night).

From Bratislava by Train to: Vienna (2/hour, 1 hour, €11 round-trip ticket is cheaper than the €14 one-way fare—you can simply buy it moments before and hop on; departures alternate between the two stations—half from main station, half from Petržalka), **Budapest** (5/day direct, 2.5 hours; more with transfers), **Sopron** (at least hourly, 2.5-3 hours, transfer in Vienna and Weiner Neustadt), **Prague** (3/day direct, 4.25-5.5 hours). For more Hungarian destinations (such as **Eger** or **Pécs**), you'll connect through Budapest.

By Bus

Two different companies, Blaguss and Slovak Lines/Post Bus, run handy buses that connect Bratislava, **Vienna,** and the **airports** in each city. The buses go from Bratislava airport to downtown Bratislava (15 minutes), continue on to Vienna's airport (1 hour), and end in Vienna (Erdberg stop on the U-3 subway line, 1.25 hours). Buses also run in the opposite direction (Blaguss: 10/day each way, €10 from Bratislava airport to Vienna, €6 from downtown Bratislava to Vienna, www.eurolines.at; Slovak Lines/Post Bus: about hourly, similar times and prices, tel. 0810-222-3336, www.slovaklines.sk). It's smart to book in advance.

By Boat

Riverboats connect Bratislava to the nearby capitals of Budapest and Vienna. Conveniently, these boats dock right along the

Danube in front of Bratislava's Old Town. While they are more expensive, less frequent, and slower than the train, some travelers enjoy getting out on the Danube. Passports are not required.

To Budapest: For details on the Mahart boats to and from Budapest, see "Budapest Connections" on page 650.

To Vienna: The **Twin City Liner** offers several daily boat trips between downtown Bratislava and Vienna's Schwedenplatz (where Vienna's town center hits the canal; €28 each way, €17 at less convenient times, €2 more on weekends, 1.25-hour trip; daily April-Oct only, Austrian tel. 01/58880, Slovak tel. 0903-610-716, www.twincityliner.com).

Two competing lines (the Slovak **LOD,** www.lod.sk; and the Hungarian **Mahart,** www.mahartpassnave.hu) connect the cities a little more cheaply, but only once a day. These boats are slower (1.5-1.75 hours), as they use Vienna's Reichsbrücke dock on the main river, and therefore need to go through the locks.

By Plane

Bratislava Airport (Letisko Bratislava, airport code: BTS, www.letiskobratislava.sk) is six miles northeast of downtown. The airport offers budget flights on low-cost carriers Ryanair (www.ryanair.com) and Danube Wings (www.danubewings.eu). Some airlines market it as "Vienna-Bratislava," thanks to its proximity to both capitals. The airport is officially named for Milan Rastislav Štefánik, who worked toward the creation of Czechoslovakia at the end of World War I. It's compact and manageable, with all the usual amenities (including ATMs).

From the Airport to Downtown Bratislava: The airport has easy **public bus** connections to Bratislava's Main Train Station (€0.60, plus €0.30 ticket for each big bag, bus #61, 6/hour in peak times, 3/hour in slow times, trip takes 30 minutes). To reach the bus stop, exit straight out of the arrivals hall, cross the street, buy a ticket at the kiosk, and look for the bus stop on your right. For directions from the train station into the Old Town, see "Arrival in Bratislava," earlier. A **taxi** from the airport into central Bratislava should cost less than €20.

To Budapest: Take the bus or taxi to Bratislava's train station (described above), then hop a train to Budapest.

To Vienna: A slow option is to connect through Bratislava's train station (described above). More direct and still afford-able, you can take a Eurolines bus from Bratislava Airport to the Erdberg stop of Vienna's U-3 subway line (described earlier, under "By Bus"). A taxi from Bratislava Airport directly to Vienna costs €60-90 (depending on whether you use a cheaper Slovak or more expensive Austrian cab).

THE SPIŠ REGION

Levoča • The High Tatras

The most beautiful part of Slovakia is the mountainous north-central region, comprising the jagged High Tatras and the Spiš Region (pronounced "speesh"). The dramatic Carpathian Mountains slice through Eastern Europe here, dividing the Poles and Czechs in the north from the Hungarians and Yugoslavs in the south. With these Carpathian peaks as a backdrop, this region offers fine high-mountain scenery; easy river-rafting trips with fun-loving guides through a breathtaking gorge; a classic Old World walled town with one of Europe's finest Gothic altarpieces; a glimpse at Slovakia's complicated ethnic mix; and treacherous but legendary hiking trails in a place so pretty, they call it "paradise." In many ways, this part of Slovakia is the West Virginia of Europe—poor and relatively undeveloped, but stunningly beautiful in its own rustic way.

Planning Your Time

The Spiš Region is a handy place for drivers to break up the long journey between Kraków and Hungary—on this route, Levoča is worth an overnight to recharge and get a taste of rural Slovakia. But unless you have a special interest, don't go out of your way to reach this area. Train travelers or those on a speedy itinerary should skip it (sleep through Slovakia on the night train).

Getting to the Spiš Region

Seeing the Spiš Region is a real headache without a car. If you're going between Kraków and Hungary (Eger or Budapest), the train line veers around Levoča far to the east, through Košice. From Košice, trains will get you to Prešov or Spišská Nová Ves, and the

Spiš Region

To Nowy Sacz & Kraków

To Kraków

POLAND

Nowy Targ

Dunajec

Dębno

PIENINY

Dunajec Canyon

Lesnica

River

Červený Kláštor

Poronin

Stará L'ubovňa

Plaveč

Zakopane

Łysa Polana

Javorina

SLOVAKIA

Lomnický Štít

Tatranská Kotlina

Spišská Bela

HIGH TATRAS

Tatranská Lomnica

Kežmarok

To Zirina & Bratislava

Starý Smokovec

SPIŠ REGION

To Prešov & Košice

SPIŠ CASTLE

Poprad

Spišský Štvrtok

Levoča

Spiš. Kap.

Hornád River

Spišská Nová Ves

Spiš. Pod.

Žehra

To Banská Bystrica

"SLOVAK PARADISE"

Dedinky

To Košice

10 Kilometers

Dobšiná Ice Caves

10 Miles

To Rožňava (Slovakia), Miskolc & Eger (Hungary)

bus will take you the rest of the way to Levoča. From the west, buses run between Bratislava and Levoča (though it's often faster to take the train to Poprad, then bus to Levoča). For specific schedules, see www.cp.sk.

Levoča

Levoča (LEH-voh-chah) is a diamond in the rough. If you can look past the crumbling facades and potholed roads, you'll see Slovakia's finest small town—with a mostly intact medieval wall, a main square ringed by striking Renaissance facades, and one of the greatest Gothic altarpieces in all of Europe.

Levoča boomed in the Middle Ages, when trade between Hungary and Poland brought abundant merchant traffic through its gates. In the 15th century, the town's centerpiece was built: St. James Church. A local woodcarver named Master Pavol packed the church with one of the most impressive collections of altarpieces in the world—including the pièce de résistance, an exquisite

60-foot-high main altar.

In the 19th century, Levoča vied with Spišská Nová Ves, a town eight miles south, to host a station on an important rail line that was being built. S.N.V. won, and became a transportation hub for the region. While unfortunate for Levoča's economy at the time, this lack of train access has allowed Levoča to remain a wonderfully well-preserved Old World village of 10,000. If all of this makes Levoča feel off the beaten track, so much the better.

Orientation to Levoča

(area code: 053)
Levoča is small—you can walk from one end of the walled burg to the other in 15 minutes—and all roads lead to the town's main square, which is named for the important woodcarver Master Pavol (Námestie Majstra Pavla). The **TI** can answer your questions about the town and put you in touch with a local guide (May-Sept daily 9:00-17:00; Oct-April Mon-Fri 8:30-16:30, closed Sat-Sun; on the main square at #58, tel. 053/451-3763, www.levoca.sk).

Sights in Levoča

▲**Church of St. James (Chrám Sv. Jakuba)**—This huge Gothic church, dominating Levoča's main square, contains 11 ornately decorated altars—including the tallest wooden altarpiece in the world. During your visit, you'll be accompanied by a guide, but you don't have to listen to her spiel (usually Slovak only—but try asking for English). Instead, you can use my self-guided tour or find the talking box in the back of the nave and insert a coin for English.

Cost and Hours: €2, church open July-Aug Mon 11:00-17:00, Tue-Sat 9:00-17:00, Sun 12:00-17:00, tours every 30 minutes; Easter-June and Sept-Oct Mon 11:30-16:00, Tue-Sat 8:30-16:00, Sun 13:00-16:00, tours roughly hourly, though not always at the top of the hour; Nov-Easter Mon 11:30-16:00, Tue-Sat 8:30-16:00, closed Sun, tours roughly hourly; within these timeframes, you can visit only at the specific times posted on the door of the church office, across the street from the church entrance (on the north side of the church, facing the top of the square); tel. 053/451-2347, mobile 0907-521-673, www.chramsvjakuba.sk.

● **Self-Guided Tour:** The church dates from the 14th century. In the late 15th century, neighboring VIPs visited here. The greatest Hungarian king, Mátyás Corvinus, came in 1474 (for more on Corvinus, see sidebar on page 556). Two decades later, representatives of Poland's powerful Jagiellonian dynasty paid a visit. These important guests—both commemorated inside the church—are a

History of the Spiš Region

The Spiš Region is one of the most historic and scenic corners of Slovakia. The area was named Szepes ("beautiful") by the Hungarians, who controlled this area in the Middle Ages. After the Tatars swept through in the 13th century, decimating the local population, the Hungarians invited Saxons (from the region around Dresden in today's Germany) to come and resettle the land. Silver, copper, and iron ore were discovered, and the Spiš became a prosperous mining region, with 24 bustling, richly decorated Saxon towns (including Levoča). The region became a showcase of Gothic and, later, Renaissance architecture.

For centuries, the Spiš was populated by a colorful mix of Saxons, Jews, and Slovaks. But after World War II, Czechoslovakia forced out people of German heritage—including descendants of those Saxon settlers who had arrived here centuries before. The Spiš was abandoned, and many towns were repopulated by Slovaks, while others were settled by Roma (see sidebar on page 248).

Today's Spiš, while still suffering from economic ills, is emerging as a popular tourist destination.

reminder that Slovakia sits at the center of Eastern Europe.

In the early 16th century, the great sculptor Master Pavol left his mark on the church. Master Pavol's unique, almost cartoonish style features figures with too-big heads, strangely weepy eyes, and honest-to-goodness personalities. Pavol's masterpiece is the church's single most impressive sight: the 60-foot-tall **main altar,** carved out of linden wood and bathed in gold paint. The large central figures represent Mary and the Baby Jesus, flanked by St. James (the church's namesake, on left) and St. John the Evangelist (on right). The four panels surrounding these figures depict scenes from James' and John's lives and deaths. Beneath them is a depiction of the Last Supper. Unusual in Gothic art, each apostle has his own individual features (based on the local merchants who financed the work). With this and his other carvings, Master Pavol was knocking on the door of the Renaissance.

The nave is lined with several other altarpieces—some by Master Pavol, some by others. At the front of the right nave (right-hand corner), look for the altar depicting the **Passion of Christ,** carved for the 1474 visit of Hungarian King Mátyás Corvinus. Jesus looks like Mátyás, Mary resembles his Italian wife, and the altar was supposed to bring the couple good luck in having a child.

To the left as you view the main altar, notice the interesting medieval **frescoes** on the wall (splotchy from a bad 19th-century renovation). The frescoes on the left depict the life of St. Dorothy.

On the right are two strips. The upper strip shows a couple performing good deeds (feeding the hungry, visiting prisoners, burying the dead, and so on). In the lower strip, they sit on animals representing the mortal sins.

As you leave, at the back of the left nave, look for another Master Pavol altar with an iconic statue of **Mary.** When the Reformation swept Europe in the 16th century, locals hid statues like Mary (who was tucked away in the Town Hall) to protect them from iconoclasts, Protestants who destroyed religious symbols to simplify their communion with God. Two centuries later, the long-forgotten statues were miraculously discovered and brought back to the church...for you to enjoy.

House of Master Pavol (Dom Majstra Pavla)—The downside of the Church of St. James is that you can see the breathtaking altarpieces only from a distance, so you can't get a sense of what made Pavol the Master. At this museum, replicas of the statues allow you to look Pavol's creations right in their big, weepy eyes.

Cost and Hours: €3.50, Mon-Fri 9:00-17:00, Sat-Sun 13:00-17:00, Námestie Majstra Pavla 20, tel. 053/451-3496, www.spisske muzeum.com.

Levoča Town Hall (Radnica v Levoči)—The huge, Renaissance-style building behind the Church of St. James used to be the Town Hall; now it's a museum devoted to the town and region's history and colorful folk cultures. You'll watch a movie in English before wandering though a grand, wood-carved meeting hall (with a beautifully painted ceiling) and rooms of maps of historic Levoča and the Spiš Region.

Cost and Hours: €3.50, skimpy English information, Mon-Fri 9:00-17:00, Sat-Sun 13:00-17:00, Námestie Majstra Pavla 2, tel. 053/451-2449, www.spisskemuzeum.com.

Mariánska Hora—This humble church, overlooking Levoča from a perch on a nearby hill, has been an important site for pilgrimages for centuries. Every year, on the first weekend of July, hundreds of thousands of Slovaks flock to the hill from the surrounding countryside—many walking as far as 30 miles. In 1995, Pope John Paul II made a pilgrimage here, saying Mass in front of some 650,000 people.

Near Levoča

Spiš Castle (Spišský Hrad)—Just a few miles from Levoča lies one of Europe's largest castles. Spiš Castle watches over the region

from high on a bluff, overlooking a desolate terrain. Though there have been castles on this strategic spot for as long as people have lived here, the current version was built during the 15th century. Since its destruction in 1781, only evocative, photogenic ruins remain. The interior is tourable, though it pales in comparison to the dramatic hilltop setting. However, views of the castle from the surrounding countryside are majestic.

Cost and Hours: €5, includes audioguide, daily May-Sept 9:00-18:00, April and Oct 9:00-16:00, Nov 10:00-16:00, closed Dec-March, last entry one hour before closing, tel. 053/454-1336, www.spisskemuzeum.com or www.spisskyhrad.sk.

Getting There: From Levoča, take the main road (E50) east. After 7.5 miles, you'll see the first turnoff, which takes you scenically past Spišská Kapitula and through Spišské Podhradie (park near town and hike all the way up, or cut through town back to the main road and wind around to the second exit). To get to the castle more directly, stay on E50 past the first exit, and go another two miles, where you'll reach another turnoff to the right leading up to the parking lot behind the castle.

Nearby: Spiš Castle is the centerpiece of a cluster of interesting sights. The town just below the castle is **Spišské Podhradie** ("Under the Spiš Castle"). On a ridge opposite Spiš Castle is **Spišská Kapitula,** the site of the Spiš Region's cathedral, surrounded by a modest village and an imposing 14th-century wall. And tucked behind Spiš Castle is **Žehra,** a village with a simple, onion-domed church that contains some 13th- to 15th-century wall paintings.

Slovak Paradise (Slovenský Raj)—Outdoors enthusiasts from all over Eastern Europe flock to this national park, and for good reason—it features steep river gorges lined with waterfalls and plateaus pocked by caves, offering some of the most enjoyable hikes this side of the Plitvice Lakes. The Slovak Paradise is known for its seemingly treacherous trails—one often-photographed stretch features ladders laid at sharp uphill angles, spanning a gaping gorge. The faint of heart should steer clear of these more challenging hikes, but in other parts of the park, you'll find trails suitable for any hiker (www.slovenskyraj.sk). Spišská Nová Ves is the handiest gateway, on the northeastern fringe of the park (and with a convenient train station).

River Rafting in the Pieniny—A few miles north of Levoča, at the border with Poland, is the Pieniny region (www.pieniny .sk). Here, the Dunajec (DOO-nah-yets) River flows through a

The "Gypsy Question"

Eastern Europe is home to a silent population—mostly in Romania, Bulgaria, Hungary, and Slovakia—of millions of dark-skinned people who speak a unique language and follow their own culture. The once-common term "Gypsy" is now considered both derogatory and inaccurate. It was derived from "Egypt"—the place where these people were once mistakenly thought to have originated. While "Gypsy" is not overtly offensive to most, today's preferred term for these people is "Roma."

The Roma are descended from several low north-Indian castes. (In fact, the language still spoken by about two-thirds of today's European Roma—called Romany—is related to contemporary Indian languages.) A thousand years ago, the Roma began to migrate through Persia and Armenia into the Ottoman Empire, which later stretched across much of southeastern Europe. Known for their itinerant lifestyles, expertise in horse trading, skilled artisanship, and flexibility regarding private property, the Roma were both sought out and suspected in medieval Europe. Similarly, the *gadjos* (non-Roma) and their customs came to be distrusted by the Roma.

The Industrial Revolution removed the Roma's few traditional means of earning a livelihood, making their wandering lifestyle difficult to sustain. Roma became entertainers (fortune telling, music and dancing, horse shows, dancing bears), outlaws, and metalworkers.

Roma were initially not allowed to enter Austrian territory, but as the Habsburgs recaptured lands once controlled by the Ottomans (including Slovakia and Hungary), they permitted the Roma already living there to stay. In the 18th and 19th centuries, as "Gypsy music" funneled into the theaters of Vienna and Budapest, a romantic image of the Roma emerged: a happy-go-lucky nomadic lifestyle; intoxicating music, with dancers swirling around a campfire; and mystical powers over white Europeans.

But white Europe's image of the Roma also had a sinister side. Even today, people might warn their children, "If you don't behave, I'll sell you to the Gypsies!" And when someone is cheated, we say they've been "gypped"—an ethnic slur so deeply ingrained, most don't even realize its origin. This widespread bigotry culminated in the Holocaust—when at least a quarter of a million Roma people were murdered in Nazi death camps.

After World War II, communist governments in the Soviet Bloc implemented a policy of forced assimilation: Roma were required to speak the country's major language, settle in *gadjo* towns, and work in new industrial jobs. But rather than producing well-adjusted citizens, the policy eroded time-honored Roma values and shattered the cohesiveness of their traditional communities. It left the new Roma generation prone to sexual, alcohol, and drug abuse, and filled state-run orphanages with deprived Roma toddlers. When the "obligation and right to work" disappeared with the communist regimes in 1989, rampant unemployment and dependence on welfare joined the list of Roma afflictions.

Today's Roma are Europe's forgotten population—estimates range from 6 to 12 million throughout the continent. As people all over Eastern Europe have found it difficult to adjust to the new economic realities, they've again turned on the Roma as scapegoats, fueling the latent racism that is so characteristic of European history. For example, a small Czech town tried to build a wall between its wealthy neighborhood and the Roma ghetto. Obstetricians in the Czech Republic were accused of sterilizing their female Roma patients without their informed consent.

Those Roma who do their best to integrate with their white neighbors often find themselves shunned both by their fellow Roma, and by the white Europeans they're emulating. Those who make it against the odds and succeed in mainstream society typically do so by turning their backs on their Roma heritage.

Many Roma resist assimilation and live in segregated ghettos, where even the most talented of their children are forced to attend schools for the mentally disabled. For example, in the Spiš Region, some Roma live in small, remote, self-contained villages—a long walk up a dirt road away from the mainstream "civilization." Polygamy is not uncommon, and some girls marry and begin having children at a very early age. Most children start attending school, but a high percentage drop out.

The large Roma population also puts an enormous strain on the already overtaxed social-welfare networks. Unemployment in the Spiš Region among Roma is about 50 percent in the summer (when some seasonal work is available) to 80 percent in the winter. To a white Slovak struggling to succeed, Roma people are often seen as freeloaders. After Romania (with Europe's highest concentration of Roma) joined the EU, various other member nations implemented strict entry requirements for "Romanians"—a thinly veiled measure designed to keep out Roma.

It's easy to criticize these seemingly closed-minded attitudes. But, in the eyes of many white Europeans, the Roma's poor reputation is at least partly deserved. While many Roma are upstanding citizens, others do turn to thievery for survival. The tour-guide refrain, "Watch out for Gypsy thieves!" might seem racist—but it's not necessarily bad advice.

What emerges is a seemingly unsolvable problem—a fundamental cultural misunderstanding, tinged with racist undertones, that separates the people of this region. But many are hopeful that with the EU's increased focus on cooperation and human rights, the Roma will find a place in the new, united Europe.

dramatic gorge in the shadow of sheer limestone cliffs, with Poland on one bank and Slovakia on the other. Floating through this scenery feels like living a scene from *The Lord of the Rings*.

The best way to experience the Pieniny is on a boat cruise. You'll board a *plt'*—a strange, pontoon-type raft made up of five canoe-like skiffs lashed together and bridged with long benches—and ply the waters of the Dunajec River. Your lively conductor is dressed in the traditional costume of the Góral folk who populate this region. The trip is generally smooth—no white water to speak of—and offers a lazy chance to enjoy the scenery.

Rafting trips go roughly from early May through late October, weather permitting (daily 8:30-17:00, until 15:00 Sept-Oct, about €10 per person, float lasts about one hour). The best stretch of river is 5.5-mile-long, U-shaped **Dunajec Canyon,** which begins near the town of **Červený Kláštor** ("Red Cloister"—this old building is near the town itself) and ends at the town of **Lesnica.** Hop on at a raft landing—marked as *prístav plt'í* on signs and maps. When you reach Lesnica, catch the bus back to your starting point...or hike the three miles back to Červený Kláštor.

Sleeping in Levoča

The presidents of all of Central Europe's countries converged on Levoča for a conference in 1998, and you'll see photos of many of them decorating the few proud hotels in town. All of these hotels are right on the main square, Námestie Majstra Pavla.

$$ Hotel u Leva is the town splurge, with 23 nicely decorated rooms (Sb-€39, Db-€68, apartment-€99, breakfast-€6, elevator, cable Internet, Námestie Majstra Pavla 25, tel. 053/450-2311, fax 053/450-2340, www.uleva.sk, hotel@uleva.sk).

$ Hotel Arkada, popular with tours, has 32 nondescript rooms (Sb-€36, Db-€52, suite-€63, 20 percent cheaper mid-Oct-April, extra bed-€13, breakfast-€4, Wi-Fi, Námestie Majstra Pavla 26, tel. 053/451-2372, fax 053/451-2255, www.arkada.sk, hotelarkada @arkada.sk).

$ Hotel Barbakan, near the top of the main square, feels traditional. Though its 15 rooms are darkly furnished, it's a decent option for the price (Sb-€28, Db-€42-48 depending on size, junior suite-€55, 15 percent cheaper mid-Oct-May, extra bed-€15, breakfast-€5, lots of stairs with no elevator, Košická 15, tel. 053/451-4310, fax 053/451-3609, www.barbakan.sk, recepcia@barbakan.sk).

Sleep Code

(€1 = about $1.40, country code: 421, area code: 053)
S = Single, **D** = Double/Twin, **T** = Triple, **Q** = Quad, **b** = bathroom,
s = shower only. At each place, credit cards are accepted and English is spoken. These rates do not include breakfast.

To help you easily sort through these listings, I've divided the accommodations into two categories, based on the price for a double room with bath during high season:

$$ Higher Priced—Most rooms €60 or more.
$ Lower Priced—Most rooms less than €60.

Prices can change without notice; verify the hotel's current rates online or by email. For other updates, see www.ricksteves.com/update.

Eating in Levoča

Hotel Barbakan, listed earlier, has a restaurant. But **Reštaurácia u 3 Apoštolov** ("Three Apostles"), also right on the square, is a cut above, serving tasty Slovak cuisine. The decor is nothing special, but the food is delicious and cheap: pungent garlic soup, excellent trout, and the tasty "Apostle Specialty"—sautéed beef and vegetables in a spicy sauce, wrapped in a potato pancake (€7-10 main dishes, long hours daily, Námestie Majstra Pavla 11, tel. 053/451-2302).

The High Tatras (Vysoké Tatry)

While not technically in the Spiš Region, Slovakia's most breathtaking mountain range is nearby. The High Tatras mountain range is small but mighty—dramatic, nearly 9,000-foot-tall granite peaks spike up from the plains, covering an area of about 100 square miles. The High Tatras are the northernmost and highest part

of the Carpathian Mountains, which stretch across the heart of Eastern Europe all the way to Romania. These cut-glass peaks have quickly become legendary among hardy, in-the-know travelers for their inexpensive, off-the-beaten-track hiking and skiing opportunities.

The High Tatras make up the Polish-Slovak border. Without a car, the most accessible approach is from the Polish resort town of **Zakopane** (an easy 1.5-hour bus or train connection from Kraków). But for more rugged beauty, head to the southern part of the range, in Slovakia.

The mid-sized city of **Poprad**—located on a plain about 10 miles from the mountains—is the most convenient launch pad for venturing into Slovakia's High Tatras. Along the base of the High Tatras are various modest resort towns (including the biggest, Starý Smokovec). There's no shortage of scenic hikes all over the region (good maps and guidebooks available locally). The best no-sweat high-altitude option is to take the **cable car** from the resort village of Tatranská Lomnica up to the viewpoint at Lomnický Štít (8,640 feet; popular and crowded, so visit early).

By car, take road 537 along the base of the High Tatras to connect the various towns. By public transportation, you'll commute by electric trains *(električky)* from Poprad into Starý Smokovec. (There are also direct, one-hour buses from Levoča to Starý Smokovec.) From Starý Smokovec, you can continue by electric train on to Tatranská Lomnica and other villages. Each town has its share of simple resort-type hotels, but serious hikers enjoy staying in the High Tatras' many *chaty* (mountain huts). For more details on the High Tatras, visit www.tanap.sk or www.tatry.net. *Spectacular Slovakia* magazine, mentioned on page 211, also has good coverage of the region (http://travel.spectator.sme.sk).

THE SPIŠ REGION

POLAND
Polska

POLAND

Americans who think of Poland as run-down—full of rusting factories, smoggy cities, and gloomy natives—are speechless when they step into Kraków's vibrant main square, Gdańsk's colorful pedestrian drag, or Warsaw's lively Old Town. While parts of the country are still cleaning up the industrial mess left by the Soviets, Poland also has some breathtaking medieval cities that show off its kind-hearted people, dynamic history, and unique cultural fabric.

The Poles are a proud people—as moved by their spectacular failures as by their successes. Their quiet elegance has been tempered by generations of abuse by foreign powers. The Poles place a lot of importance on honor, and you'll find fewer scams and con artists here than in other Eastern European countries.

In a way, there are two Polands: lively, cosmopolitan urban centers, and countless tiny farm villages in the countryside. City-dwellers often talk about the "simple people" of Poland—those descended from generations of farmers, working the same plots for centuries and living an uncomplicated, agrarian lifestyle. This large contingent of salt-of-the-earth folks—who like things the way they are—is a major reason why Poland was so hesitant to join the European Union, and remains fiercely "Euroskeptic."

Poland is arguably Europe's most devoutly Catholic country. Catholicism has long defined these people, holding them together through times when they had little else. Squeezed between Protestant Germany (originally Prussia) and Eastern Orthodox Russia, Poland wasn't even a country for generations (1795-1918). Its Catholicism helped keep its spirit alive. In the last century, while "under communism" (as that age is referred to), Poles once again found their religion a source of strength as well as rebellion—they could express dissent against the athe-

istic regime by going to church. Some of Poland's best sights are churches, usually filled with locals praying silently. While these church interiors are worth a visit, be especially careful to show the proper respect (maintain silence, keep a low profile, and if you want to snap pictures, do so discreetly).

Visitors are sometimes surprised at how much of Poland's story is a Jewish story. Before World War II, 80 percent of Europe's Jews lived in Poland. Warsaw was the world's second-largest Jewish city (after New York) with 380,000 Jews (out of a total population of 1.2 million). Poland was a magnet for Jews because of its relatively welcoming policies. Still, Jews were forbidden from owning land; that's why they settled mostly in the cities. But the Holocaust (and a later Soviet policy of sending "troublemaking" Jews to Israel) decimated the Jewish population. This tragic chapter, combined with postwar border shifts and population movements, made Poland one of Europe's most ethnically homogeneous countries. Today, virtually everyone in the country is an ethnic Pole, and only a few thousand Polish Jews remain. (For simplicity, in this book I've used the term "Pole" to describe someone who's ethnically Polish as opposed to Jewish—though many Jews were "Polish" in that they were citizens of Poland.)

Poland has long been extremely pro-America. Of course, their big neighbors (Russia and Germany) have been their historic enemies. And when Hitler invaded in 1939, the Poles felt let down by their supposed European friends (France and Britain), who declared war on Germany but provided virtually no military support to the Polish resistance. America, meanwhile, has been regarded as the big ally from across the ocean—and the home of about 10 million Polish Americans. In 1989, when Poland finally

Poland Almanac

Official Name: Rzeczpospolita Polska (Republic of Poland), or Polska for short.

Snapshot History: This thousand-year-old country has been dominated by foreigners for much of the last two centuries, finally achieving true independence (from the Soviet Union) in 1989.

Population: Nearly 38.5 million people, slightly more than California. About 97 percent are ethnic Poles who speak Polish (though English is also widely spoken). Three out of every four Poles are practicing Catholics. The population is younger than most European countries, with an average age of 39 (Germany's is 42).

Latitude and Longitude: 52°N and 20°E (similar latitude to Berlin, London, and Edmonton, Alberta).

Area: 122,000 square miles, the same as New Mexico (or Illinois and Iowa put together).

Geography: Because of its overall flatness, Poland has been a corridor for invading armies since its infancy. The Vistula River (650 miles) runs south-to-north up the middle of the country, passing through Kraków and Warsaw, and emptying into the Baltic Sea at Gdańsk. Poland's climate is generally cool and rainy—40,000 storks love it.

Biggest Cities: Warsaw (the capital, 1.7 million), Kraków (757,000), and Łódź (747,000).

Economy: The Gross Domestic Product is $721 billion, with a GDP per capita of $18,800. The 1990s saw an aggressive and successful transition from state-run socialism to privately owned capitalism. Still, Poland's traditional potato-and-pig-farming society is behind the times, with 16 percent of the country's workers producing less than 3 percent of its GDP. About one in ten Poles is unemployed, and nearly one in five lives in poverty. And yet, perhaps because its economy is so primitive, Poland fared especially well through the recent economic downturn.

Currency: 1 złoty (zł, or PLN) = 100 groszy (gr) = about 30 cents; 3 zł = about $1.

won its freedom, many Poles only half-joked that they should apply to become the 51st state of the US.

Over the last few years, Poland beefed up its infrastructure to prepare for the Euro Cup soccer championship, which it co-hosts with Ukraine in June of 2012. For Europeans, this is just one step down from hosting the Olympics. Cities hosting matches (Warsaw, Gdańsk, Poznań, and Wrocław), as well as the rest of the country, enjoyed a wave of new construction and refurbishment, leaving dingy old quarters refreshed and re-energized. Poland is

Real Estate: A typical one-bedroom apartment in Warsaw (250 square feet) rents for roughly $600 a month.

Government: Poland's mostly figurehead president selects the prime minister and cabinet, with legislators' approval. They govern along with a two-house legislature (Sejm and Senat) of 560 seats. Prime Minister Donald Tusk, leader of the centrist Civic Platform, was re-elected in 2011. President Bronisław Komorowski, also of the Civic Platform, won a five-year term following Lech Kaczyński's tragic death in 2010. (For more on Polish politics, see page 266.)

Flag: The upper half is white, and the lower half is red—the traditional colors of Poland. Poetic Poles claim the white represents honor, and the red represents the enormous amounts of blood spilled by the Poles to honor their nation. The flag sometimes includes a coat of arms with a crowned eagle (representing Polish sovereignty). Under Poland's many oppressors (including the Soviets), the crown was removed from the emblem, and its talons were trimmed. On regaining its independence, Poland coronated its eagle once more.

The Average Pole: In spite of its tragic history, Poland is a relatively upbeat nation: 74 percent of all Poles report they are "quite happy." Half use the Internet, and the average Pole will live to about age 76. The average Polish woman gets married at age 24 and will have 1.3 children.

Not-so-Average Poles: Despite the many "Polack jokes" you've heard (and maybe repeated), you likely know of many famous Polish intellectuals—you just don't realize they're Polish. The "Dumb Polack" Hall of Fame includes Karol Wojtyła (Pope John Paul II), Mikołaj Kopernik (Nicolas Copernicus), composer Fryderyk Chopin, scientist Marie Curie (née Skłodowska), writer Teodor Józef Korzeniowski (better known as Joseph Conrad, author of *Heart of Darkness*), filmmaker Roman Polański (*Chinatown, The Pianist*), politician Lech Wałęsa, Daniel Libeskind (the master architect for redeveloping the 9/11 site in New York City)...and one of this book's co-authors.

using the Euro Cup as an excuse to improve its rail system, creating a network of high-speed trains to more quickly and smoothly link together its major cities.

On my first visit to Poland, I had a poor impression of Poles, who seemed brusque and often elbowed ahead of me in line. I've since learned that all it takes is a smile and a cheerful greeting—preferably in Polish—to break through the thick skin that helped these kind people survive the difficult communist times. With a friendly hello *(Dzień dobry!)*, you'll turn any grouch into an ally. It may help to know that, because of the distinct cadence of Polish, Poles speaking English sometimes sound more impatient, gruff, or irritated than they actually are. Part of the Poles' charm is that they're not as slick and self-assured as many Europeans: They're kind, soft-spoken, and quite shy. On a recent train trip in Poland, I offered my Polish seatmate a snack—and spent the rest of trip enjoying a delightful conversation with a new friend.

Helpful Hints

Restroom Signage: To confuse tourists, the Poles have devised a secret way of marking their WCs. You'll see doors marked with *męska* (men) and *damska* (women)—but even more often, you'll simply see a triangle (for men) or a circle (for women). A sign with a triangle, a circle, and an arrow is directing you to the closest WCs.

Pay to Pee: Many Polish bathrooms charge a small fee. You may even be charged at a restaurant where you're paying to dine. Don't let this minor inconvenience interfere with your enjoyment of your trip. Yes, it's an annoying hassle—but at least it's cheap (usually around 1 zł).

Train Station Lingo: "PKP" is the abbreviation for Polish National Railways ("PKS" is for buses). In larger towns with several train stations, you'll normally use the one called Główny (meaning "Main"—except in Warsaw, where it's Centralna). *Dworzec główny* means "main train station." Underneath most larger stations are mazes of walkways—lined with market stalls—that lead to platforms *(peron)* and exits *(wyjście)*. Most stations have several platforms, each of which has two tracks *(tor)*. Departures are generally listed by the *peron*, so keep your eye on both tracks for your train. Arrivals are *przyjazdy*, and departures are *odjazdy*. Left-luggage counters or lockers are marked *przechowalnia bagażu*. *Kasy* are ticket windows. These can be marked (sometimes only in Polish) for specific needs—domestic tickets, international tickets, and so on; ask fellow travelers to be sure you select the right line. Ticket and "information" windows are more often than not staffed by monolingual grouches. Smile sweetly, write down your destination and time, and hang onto your patience. The line you choose will invariably be the slowest one—leave plenty of time to buy your ticket before your train departs (or, if you're running out of time, buy it on board for 10 zł extra). For longer and/or express journeys, you'll likely be given two separate tickets: one for the trip itself, and the other for your seat assignment. On arriving at a station, to get into town, follow signs for *wyjście do centrum* or *wyjście do miasta*. Ongoing construction to improve Poland's rail lines may make some of your train journeys take much longer than normal, and delays are common.

Top 10 Dates That Changed Poland

A.D. 966—The Polish king, Mieszko I, is baptized a Christian, symbolically uniting the Polish people and founding the nation.

1385—The Polish queen (called a "king" by sexist aristocrats of the time) marries a Lithuanian duke, starting the two-century reign of the Jagiełło family.

1410—Poland defeats the Teutonic Knights at the Battle of Grunwald, part of a Golden Age of territorial expansion and cultural achievement.

1572—The last Jagiellonian king dies, soon replaced by bickering nobles and foreign kings. Poland declines.

1795—In the last of three Partitions, the country is divvied up by its more-powerful neighbors: Russia, Prussia, and Austria.

1918—Following World War I, Poland gets back its land and sovereignty.

1939—The Free City of Gdańsk (then called Danzig) is invaded by Nazi Germany, starting World War II. At war's end, the country is "liberated" (i.e., occupied) by the Soviet Union.

1980—Lech Wałęsa leads a successful strike, demanding more freedom from the communist regime.

1989—Poland gains independence under its first president—Lech Wałęsa. Fifteen years later, Poland joins the European Union.

2010—President Lech Kaczyński and 95 other high-level government officials are killed in a tragic plane crash in Russia.

Museum Tips: Virtually every museum in Poland is closed on Monday. The ticket window for any museum typically closes a half-hour before the museum's closing time, and this last-entry deadline is strictly enforced. Poland's museums are notorious for tweaking their opening times—try to confirm hours locally if you have your heart set on a particular place.

Polish Artists: Though Poland has produced world-renowned scientists, musicians, and writers, the country isn't known for its artists. Polish museums greet foreign visitors with fine artwork by unfamiliar names. If you're planning to visit any museums in Poland, two artists in particular are worth remembering: **Jan Matejko,** a 19th-century positivist who painted grand historical epics (see page 409); and one of his students, **Stanisław Wyspiański,** a painter and playwright who led the charge of the Młoda Polska movement—the Polish answer to Art Nouveau—in the early 1900s (see page 293).

Telephones: Remember these Polish prefixes: 800 is toll-free, and 70 is expensive (like phone sex). Many Poles use mobile phones (which come with the prefix 50, 51, 53, 60, 66, 69, 72, 78, 79, or 88). For details on how to dial, see page 1231.

Polish History

Poland is flat. Take a look at a topographical map of Europe, and you'll immediately appreciate the Poles' historical dilemma: The path of least resistance from northern Europe to Russia leads right through Poland. Over the years, many invaders—from Genghis Khan to Napoleon to Hitler—have taken advantage of Poland's strategic location. The country is nicknamed "God's playground" for the many wars that have rumbled through

its territory. Poland has been invaded by Soviets, Nazis, French, Austrians, Russians, Prussians, Swedes, Teutonic Knights, Tatars, Bohemians, Magyars—and, about 1,300 years ago, Poles.

Medieval Greatness

The first Poles were a tribe called the Polonians ("people of the plains"), a Slavic band that showed up in these parts in the eighth century. In 966, Mieszko I, Duke of the Polonian tribe, adopted Christianity and founded the Piast dynasty (which would last for more than 400 years). Centuries before Germany, Italy, or Spain first united, Poland was born.

Poland struggled against two different invaders in the 13th century: the Tatars (Mongols who ravaged the south) and the Teutonic Knights (Germans who conquered the north—see page 486). But despite these challenges, Poland persevered. The last king of the Piast dynasty was also the greatest: Kazimierz the Great, who famously "found a Poland made of wood and left one made of brick and stone"—bringing Poland (and its capital, Kraków) to international prominence (see page 291). The progressive Kazimierz also invited Europe's much-persecuted Jews to settle here, establishing Poland as a haven for the Jewish people—which it would remain until the Nazis arrived.

Kazimierz the Great died at the end of the 14th century without a male heir. His grand-niece, Princess Jadwiga, became "king" (the Poles weren't ready for a "queen") and married Lithuanian Prince Władysław Jagiełło, uniting their countries against a common enemy, the Teutonic Knights. Their marriage marked the beginning of the Jagiellonian dynasty and set the stage for Poland's Golden Age. During this time, the Polish nobility began to acquire more political might, Italy's Renaissance (and its architectural styles) became popular, and the Toruń-born astronomer Nicholas Copernicus shook up the scientific world with his bold new heliocentric theory. Up on the Baltic coast, the port city of Gdańsk took advantage of its Hanseatic League trading partnership to become one of Europe's most prosperous cities.

Foreign Kings and Partitions

When the Jagiellonians died out in 1572, political power shifted to the nobility. Poland became a republic of nobles governed by its wealthiest 10 percent—the *szlachta*, who elected a series of foreign kings. In the 16th and 17th centuries—with its territory spanning from the Baltic Sea to the Black Sea—the Polish-Lithuanian Commonwealth was the largest state in Europe.

But over time, many of the elected kings made poor diplomatic decisions and squandered the country's resources. To make matters worse, the nobles' parliament (Sejm) introduced the concept of *liberum veto* (literally "I freely forbid"), whereby any measure could be vetoed by a single member of parliament. This policy—which effectively demanded unanimous approval for any law to be passed—paralyzed the Sejm's waning power. Sensing the Commonwealth's weakness, in the mid-17th century forces from Sweden rampaged through Polish and Lithuanian lands—devastating the landscape in the so-called "Swedish Deluge." While Poland eventually reclaimed its territory, a third of its population was dead. The Commonwealth continued to import self-serving foreign kings, including Saxony's Augustus the Strong and his son, who drained Polish wealth to finance vanity projects in their hometown of Dresden.

By the late 18th century, Poland was floundering—and surrounded by three land-hungry empires (Russia, Prussia, and Austria). The Poles were unaware that these neighbors had entered into an agreement now dubbed the "Alliance of the Three Black Eagles" (since all three of those countries, coincidentally, used that bird as their symbol); they began to circle Poland's white eagle like vultures. Stanisław August Poniatowski, elected king with Russian support in 1764, would prove to be Poland's last.

Over the course of less than 25 years, Russia, Prussia, and Austria divided Poland's territory among themselves in a series of three Partitions. In 1772 and again in 1790, Poland was forced into ceding large chunks of its territory to its neighbors. Desperate to reform their government, Poles enacted Europe's first democratic constitution (and the world's second, after the US Constitution) on May 3, 1791—still celebrated as a national holiday. This visionary document protected the peasants, dispensed with both *liberum veto* and the election of the king, and set up something resembling a modern nation. But the constitution alarmed Poland's neighbors, who swept in soon after with the third and final Partition in 1795. "Poland" disappeared from Europe's maps, not to return until 1918.

Even though Poland was gone, the Poles wouldn't go quietly. As the Partitions were taking place, Polish soldier Tadeusz Kościuszko (also a hero of the American Revolution) returned home to lead an unsuccessful military resistance against the Russians in 1794.

Napoleon offered a brief glimmer of hope to the Poles in the early 19th century, when he marched eastward through Europe and set up the semi-independent "Duchy of Warsaw" in Polish lands. But that fleeting taste of freedom lasted only eight years; with Napoleon's defeat, Polish hopes were dashed. The Congress of Vienna, which redistributed Polish territory to Prussia, Russia, and Austria, is sometimes called (by Poles) the "Fourth Partition." In a classic case of "my enemy's enemy is my friend," the Poles still have great affection for Napoleon for how fiercely he fought against their mutual foes.

The Napoleonic connection also established France as a safe haven for refugee Poles. After another failed uprising against Russia in 1830, many of Poland's top artists and writers fled to Paris—including pianist Fryderyk Chopin and Romantic poet Adam Mickiewicz (whose statue adorns Kraków's main square and Warsaw's Royal Way). These Polish artists tried to preserve the nation's spirit with music and words; those who remained in Poland continued to fight with swords and fists. By the end of the 19th century, the image of the Pole as a tireless, idealistic insurgent emerged. During this time, some Romantics—with typically melodramatic flair—dubbed Poland "the Christ of nations" for the way it was misunderstood and persecuted by the world, despite its inherent nobility.

As the map of Europe was redrawn following World War I, Poland emerged as a reborn nation, under the war hero-turned-head of state, Marshal Józef Piłsudski. The newly reformed "Second Polish Republic," which patched together the bits and pieces of territory that had been under foreign rule for decades, enjoyed a diverse ethnic mix—including Germans, Russians, Ukrainians, Lithuanians, and an enormous Jewish minority. A third of Poland spoke no Polish. The historic Baltic port city of Gdańsk—which was bicultural (German and Polish)—had been given a special "free city" status to avoid dealing with the prickly issue of whether to assign it to Germany or Poland. But the peace was not to last.

World War II

On September 1, 1939, Adolf Hitler began World War II by attacking Gdańsk to bring it into the German fold. Before the month was out, Hitler's forces had overrun Poland, and the Soviets had taken over a swath of eastern Poland (today still part of Ukraine, Belarus, and Lithuania).

The Nazis considered the Poles *slawische Untermenschen*, "Slavic sub-humans" who were useful only for manual labor. Remember that Poland was also home to a huge population of another group the Nazis hated, Jews. Nazi Germany annexed Polish regions that it claimed historic ties to, while the rest (including "Warschau" and "Krakau") became a puppet state ruled by the *Generalgouvernement* and Hitler's handpicked governor, Hans Frank. The Nazis considered this area *Lebensraum*—"living space" that wasn't nice enough to actually incorporate into Germany, but served perfectly as extra territory for building things that Germans didn't want in their backyards...such as Auschwitz-Birkenau, the notorious death camp that functioned like a factory for the mass-production of murder.

The Poles anxiously awaited the promised military aid of France and Britain; when help failed to arrive, they took matters into their own hands, forming a ragtag "Polish Home Army" and staging incredibly courageous but lopsided battles against their powerful German overlords (such as the Warsaw Uprising—see page 418). With six million deaths over six years—including both Polish Jews and ethnic Poles—Poland suffered the worst per-capita WWII losses of any nation. By the war's end, one out of every five Polish citizens was dead—and 90 percent of those killed were civilians.

Throughout the spring of 1945, as the Nazis retreated from their failed invasion of the Soviet Union, the Red Army gradually "liberated" Poland from Nazi oppression, guaranteeing it another four decades of oppression under another regime. At the war's end, the victorious Allies shifted Poland's borders significantly westward—folding historically German areas into Polish territory, and appropriating previously Polish areas for the USSR. This prompted a massive movement of populations—which today we'd decry as "ethnic cleansing"—as Germans were forcibly removed from western Poland, and Poles from newly "Soviet" territory were transplanted to Poland proper. Entire cities were repopulated (such as the formerly German metropolis of Breslau, which was suddenly renamed Wrocław and filled with refugee Poles from Lwów—now Lviv, in Ukraine). After millions died in the war, millions more were displaced from their ancestral homes. When the dust settled, Poland was in rubble...but almost exclusively populated by Poles.

Saddle on a Cow: Poland Under Communism

Like other Soviet satellites, Poland suffered under the communists. A postwar intimidation regime was designed to frighten people "on board" and coincided with government seizure of private

POLAND

The Heritage of Communism

While Poland has been free, democratic, and capitalist since 1989, some adults carry lots of psychological baggage from living under communism. Although the young generally embrace the fast new affluence with enthusiasm, many older people tend to be nostalgic about that slower-paced time that came with more security. And even young professionals, with so much energy and hope now, don't condemn everything about that stretch of history. A friend who was 13 in 1989 recalled those days this way:

"My childhood is filled with happy memories. Under communism, life was family-oriented. Careers didn't matter. There was no way to get rich, no reason to rush, so we had time. People always had time.

"But there were also shortages—many things were 'in deficit.' Sometimes my uncle would bring us several toilet paper rolls, held together with a string—absolutely the best gift anyone could give. I remember my mother and father had to 'organize' for special events...somehow find a good sausage and some Coca-Cola.

"Boys in my neighborhood collected pop cans. Since drinks were very limited in Poland, cans from other countries represented a world of opportunities beyond our borders. Parents could buy their children these cans on the black market, and the few families who were allowed to travel returned home with a treasure trove of cans. One boy up the street from me went to Italy, and proudly brought home a Pepsi can. All of the boys in the neighborhood wanted to see it—it was a huge status symbol. But a month later, communism ended, you could buy whatever you wanted, and everyone's can collections were worthless.

"We had real chocolate only for Christmas. The rest of the year, for treats we got something called 'chocolate-like product,' which was sweet, dark, and smelled vaguely of chocolate. And we had oranges from Cuba for Christmas, too. Everybody was excited when the newspapers announced, 'The boat with the oranges from Cuba is just five days from Poland.' We waited with excitement all year for chocolate and those oranges. The smell of Christmas was so special. Now we have that smell every day. Still, my happiest Christmases were under communism."

property, rationing, and food shortages. The country enjoyed a relatively open society under Premier Władysław Gomułka in the 1960s, but the impractical, centrally planned economy began to unravel in the 1970s. Stores were marked by long lines stretching around the block. Poles were issued ration coupons for food staples, and cashiers clipped off a corner when a purchase was made... assuming, of course, the item was in stock. It often wasn't.

The little absurdities of communist life—which today seem almost comical—made every day a struggle. For years, every elderly woman in Poland had hair the same strange magenta color. There was only one color of dye available, so if you had dyed hair, the choice was simple: Let your hair grow out (and look clownishly half red and half white), or line up and go red.

During these difficult times, the Poles often rose up—staging major protests in 1956, 1968, 1970, and 1976. Stalin famously noted that introducing communism to the Poles was like putting a saddle on a cow.

When an anti-communist Polish cardinal named Karol Wojtyła was elected Pope in 1978, then visited his homeland in 1979, it was a sign to his countrymen that change was in the air. (For more on Pope John Paul II, see page 298.) In 1980, Lech Wałęsa, an electrician at the shipyards in Gdańsk, became the leader of the Solidarity movement, the first workers' union in communist Eastern Europe. After an initial 18-day strike at the Gdańsk shipyards, the communist regime gave in, legalizing Solidarity (for more on Solidarity, see page 457).

But the union grew too powerful, and the communists felt their control slipping away. On Sunday, December 13, 1981, Poland's head of state, General Wojciech Jaruzelski, declared martial law in order to "forestall Soviet intervention." (Whether the Soviets actually would have intervened remains a hotly debated issue.) Tanks ominously rolled through the streets of Poland on that snowy December morning, and the Poles were terrified.

Martial law lasted until 1983. Each Pole has his or her own chilling memories of this frightening time. During riots, the people would flock into churches—the only place they could be safe from the ZOMO (riot police). But Solidarity struggled on, going underground and becoming a united movement of all demographics, 10 million members strong (more than a quarter of the population).

In July of 1989, the ruling Communist Party agreed to hold open elections (reserving 65 percent of representatives for themselves). Their goal was to appease Solidarity, but the plan backfired: Communists didn't win a single contested seat. These elections helped spark the chain reaction across Eastern Europe that eventually tore down the Iron Curtain. Lech Wałęsa became Poland's first post-communist president. (For more on Lech Wałęsa, see page 456.)

Poland in the 21st Century

When 10 new countries joined the European Union in May 2004, Poland was the most ambivalent of the bunch. After centuries of being under other empires' authority, the Poles were hardly eager to relinquish some of their hard-fought autonomy to Brussels. Many Poles thought that EU membership would make things worse (higher prices, a loss of traditional lifestyles) before they got better. But most people agreed that their country had to join to survive in today's Europe. Today most Poles begrudgingly acknowledge that the benefits of EU membership have outweighed the drawbacks.

The most obvious initial impact of EU membership was the tremendous migration of young Poles seeking work in other EU countries (mostly Britain, Ireland, and Sweden, which waived visa requirements for Eastern European workers earlier than other EU nations). Many of them found employment at hotels and restaurants. Visitors to London and Dublin are still likely to notice a surprising language barrier at the front desks of hotels, and Polish-language expat newspapers have joined British gossip rags on newsstands. Those who remained in Poland were concerned about the "brain drain" of bright young people flocking out of their country. But with the recent global economic crisis, quite a few Polish expats have returned home. For more on this phenomenon, see "The Polish Plumber Syndrome" sidebar on page 24.

Poland is by far the most populous of the recent EU members, with nearly 39 million people (about the same as Spain, or about half the size of Germany). This makes Poland the sixth-largest of the 27 EU member states—giving it serious political clout, which it has already asserted...sometimes to the dismay of the EU's more established powers.

On the American political spectrum, Poland may be the most "conservative" country in Europe. Like a nation of Newt Gingriches, Poles are phobic when it comes to "big government"—likely because they've been subjugated and manipulated by so many foreign oppressors over the centuries. For most of the 2000s, the country's right wing was represented by a pair of twin brothers, Lech and Jarosław Kaczyński. Their conservative Law and Justice Party is pro-tax cuts, fiercely Euroskeptic (anti-EU), and very Catholic. In the 2005 presidential election, Lech Kaczyński emerged as the victor; several months later, he took the controversial step of appointing his identical twin brother Jarosław as Poland's prime minister. The Kaczyński brothers were child actors who appeared in several popular movies together—their biggest hit was titled *Those Two Who Would Steal the Moon*. As teenagers,

Polish Jokes

Through the dreary communist times, the Poles managed to keep their sense of humor. A popular target of jokes was the riot police, called the ZOMO. Here are just a few of the things Poles said about these unpopular cops:

- It's better to have a sister who's a whore than a brother in the ZOMO.
- ZOMO police are hired based on the 90-90 principle: They have to weigh at least 90 kilograms (200 pounds), and their I.Q. must be less than 90.
- ZOMO are dispatched in teams of three: one who can read, one who can write, and a third to protect those other two smart guys.
- A ZOMO policeman was sitting on the curb, crying. Someone came up to him and asked what was wrong. "I lost my dog!" he said. "No matter," the person replied. "He's a smart police dog. I'm sure he can find his way back to the station." "Yes," the ZOMO said. "But without him, *I* can't!"

The communists gave their people no options at elections: If you voted, you voted for the regime. Poles liked to joke that in some ways, this made communists like God—who created Eve, then said to Adam, "Now choose a wife." It was said that communists could run a pig as a candidate, and it would still win; a popular symbol of dissent became a pig painted with the words, "Vote Red."

There were even jokes about jokes. Under communism, Poles noted that there was a government-sponsored prize for the funniest political joke: 15 years in prison.

they would switch identities and take tests for each other.

The political pendulum swung back toward the center in October of 2007, when the Kaczyński brothers' main political rival, the pro-EU Donald Tusk, led his Civic Platform Party to victory in the parliamentary elections. The name Kaczyński loosely means "duck"—so the Poles quipped that they were led by "Donald and the Ducks."

Tragically, the levity wasn't to last. On April 10, 2010, a plane carrying President Lech Kaczyński crashed in a thick fog near the city of Smolensk, Russia. All 96 people on board—including top government, military, and business officials, high-ranking clergy, and others—were killed, plunging the nation into a period of stunned mourning. Poles wondered why, yet again, an unprecedented tragedy had befallen their nation. (Ironically, the group's trip was intended to put a painful chapter of Poland's history to rest: a commemoration of the Polish officers and enlisted men killed in the Soviet massacre at Katyń.)

The ensuing presidential election pitted the deceased president's brother, Jarosław Kaczyński, against Donald Tusk's Civic Platform compatriot, Bronisław Komorowski. Komorowski's victory—and Donald Tusk's re-election as prime minister in 2011 (the first re-election of a PM since the end of communism)—have given the centrist Civic Platform the reins of Poland for the foreseeable future.

Meanwhile, Poland's economy has just kept chugging along, even as the rest of Europe and much of the world were bogged down by an economic downturn. More than a quarter of Poland's trade is with neighboring Germany—another of Europe's healthiest economies—and Poland was the only European Union country that didn't have a recession in 2009. When I asked some Polish friends about this, they replied—cynically, but not without a hint of truth—"Well, when you have a backwards, agrarian economy, you're pretty resistant to international market fluctuations." Poland is a big, self-sustaining, insular economy. In recent years, Poland's relatively weak currency ("cheaper" than the euro, yet also shielded from euro volatility) and robust economy are luring foreign investment, paradoxically threatening the very autonomy that has buffered it so far. As Europe struggles to deal with its debt crisis and flagging economic might, it will be interesting to see the role that Poland plays.

Polish Food

Polish food is hearty and tasty. Since Poland is north of the Carpathian Mountains, its weather tends to be chilly, which limits the kinds of fruits and vegetables that flourish here. Like other northern European countries (such as Russia or Scandinavia), dominant staples include potatoes, dill, berries, beets, and rye. Much of what you might think of as "Jewish cuisine" turns up on Polish menus (gefilte fish, potato pancakes,  chicken soup, and so forth)—which makes sense, given that Poles and Jews lived in the same area for centuries under the same climatic and culinary influences.

Polish soups are a highlight. The most typical are *żurek* and *barszcz*. *Żurek* (often translated as "sour soup" on menus) is a light-colored soup made from a sourdough base, usually containing a hard-boiled egg and pieces of *kiełbasa* (sausage). *Barszcz,* better known to Americans as borscht, is a savory beet soup that you'll see in several varieties: *Barszcz czerwony* (red borscht) is a broth with a deep red color, sometimes containing dumplings or a

Bar Mleczny (Milk Bar)

When you see a "bar" in Poland, it doesn't mean alcohol—it means cheap grub. Eating at a *bar mleczny* (bar MLECH-neh)

is an essential Polish sightseeing experience. These cafeterias, which you'll see all over the country, are an incredibly cheap way to get a good meal...and, with the right attitude, a fun cultural experience.

In the communist era, the government subsidized the food at milk bars, allowing lowly workers to enjoy a meal out. The tradition continues, and today, Poland still foots the bill for most of your milk-bar meal. Prices are astoundingly low—my bill for a big meal usually comes to about $4-5—and, while communist-era fare was gross, today's milk-bar cuisine is usually quite tasty.

Milk bars usually offer many of the traditional tastes listed in the "Polish Food" section. Common items are soups (like *żurek* and *barszcz*), a variety of cabbage-based salads, *kotlet* (fried pork chops), pierogi (like ravioli, with various fillings), and *naleśniki* (pancakes). You'll see glasses of juice and (of course) milk, but most milk bars also stock bottles of water and Coke.

There are two types of milk bars: updated, modern cafeterias that cater to tourists (English menus), add some modern twists to their traditional fare, and charge about 50 percent more; and time-machine dives that haven't changed for decades. At truly traditional milk bars, the service is aimed at locals—which means no English menu and a confusing ordering system.

Every milk bar is a little different, but here's the general procedure: Head to the counter, wait to be acknowledged, and point to what you want. Handy vocabulary: *to* (sounds like "toe") means "this"; *i* (pronounced "ee") means "and."

If the milk-bar lady asks you any questions, you have three options: nod stupidly until she just gives you something; repeat one of the things she just said (assuming she's asked you to choose between two options, like meat or cheese in your pierogi); or hope that a kindly English-speaking Pole in line will leap to your rescue. If nothing else, ordering at a milk bar is an adventure in gestures. Smiling seems to slightly extend the patience of milk-bar staffers.

Once your tray is all loaded up, pay the cashier, do a double-take when you realize how cheap your bill is, then find a table. After the meal, it's generally polite, if not expected, to bus your own dishes to the little window (watch locals and imitate).

hard-boiled egg. *Barszcz ukraiński* (Ukrainian borscht) is similar, but has vegetables mixed in (usually cabbage, beans, and carrots). In summer, try the "Polish gazpacho"—*chłodnik*, a cream soup with beets, onions, and radishes that's served cold. I never met a Polish soup I didn't like...until I was introduced to *flaki* (sometimes *flaczki*)—tripe soup.

Another familiar Polish dish is pierogi. These ravioli-like dumplings come with various fillings. The most traditional are minced meat, sauerkraut, mushroom, cheese, and blueberry; many restaurants also experiment with more exotic fillings. Pierogi are often served with specks of fatty bacon to add flavor. Pierogi are a budget traveler's dream: Restaurants serving them are everywhere, and they're generally cheap, tasty, and very filling.

Bigos is a rich and delicious sauerkraut stew cooked with meat, mushrooms, and whatever's in the pantry. *Gołąbki* is a dish of cabbage leaves stuffed with minced meat and rice in a tomato or mushroom sauce. *Kotlet schabowy* (fried pork chop)—once painfully scarce in communist Poland—remains a local favorite to this day. *Kaczka* (duck) is popular, as is fish: Look for *pstrąg* (trout), *karp* (carp, beware of bones), and *węgorz* (eel). Poles eat lots of potatoes, which are served with nearly every meal.

For a snack on the go, Poles love *zapiekanki* (singular *zapiekanek*): a toasted baguette with melted cheese, garlic, ketchup, rubbery mushrooms from a can, and sometimes onions or other toppings. It's like the poor cousin of a French-bread pizza, and a favorite late-night snack for bar-hopping young people. The bagel-like rings you'll see sold on the street, *obwarzanki* (singular *obwarzanek*), are also cheap, and usually fresh and tasty.

Poland has good pastries. A *piekarnia* is a bakery specializing in breads. But if you really want something special, look for a *cukiernia* (pastry shop). The classic Polish treat is *pączki*, glazed jelly doughnuts. They can have different fillings, but most typical is a wild-rose jam. *Szarlotka* is apple cake—sometimes made with chunks of apples (especially in season), sometimes with apple filling. *Sernik* is cheesecake, and *makowiec* is poppy-seed cake. *Winebreda* is an especially gooey Danish. *Babeczka* is like a cupcake filled with pudding. You may see *jabłko w cieście*—slices of apple cooked in dough, then glazed. *Napoleonka* is a French-style treat with layers of crispy wafers and custard.

Lody (ice cream) is popular. The tall, skinny cones of soft-serve ice cream are called *świderki*, sometimes translated as "American ice cream." The most beloved traditional candy is *ptasie mleczko* (birds' milk), which is like a semi-sour marshmallow covered with chocolate. E. Wedel is the country's top brand of chocolate, with outlets in all the big cities (see page 428).

Thirsty? *Woda* is water, *woda mineralna* is bottled water

(*gazowana* is with gas/carbonation, *niegazowana* is without), *kawa* is coffee, *herbata* is tea, *sok* is juice, and *mleko* is milk. Żywiec, Okocim, and Lech are the best-known brands of *piwo* (beer).

Wódka (vodka) is a Polish staple—the word means, roughly, "precious little water." Żubrówka, the most famous brand of vodka, comes with a blade of grass from the bison reserves in eastern Poland (look for the bottle with the bison). The bison "flavor" the grass...then the grass flavors the vodka. Poles often mix Żubrówka with apple juice, and call this cocktail *szarlotka* ("apple cake"); it also goes by the name *tatanka* (a Native American word for "bison"). For "Cheers!" say, "*Na zdrowie!*" (nah ZDROH-vyeh).

Unusual drinks to try if you have the chance are *kwas* (a cold, fizzy, Ukrainian-style non-alcoholic beverage made from day-old rye bread) and *kompot* (a hot drink made from stewed berries). Poles are unusually fond of carrot juice (often cut with fruit juice); Kubuś is the most popular brand.

"Bon appétit" *is* "*Smacznego*" (smatch-NEH-goh). To pay, ask for the *rachunek* (rah-KHOO-nehk).

Polish Language

Polish is closely related to its neighboring Slavic languages (Slovak and Czech), with the biggest difference being that Polish has lots of fricatives (hissing sounds—"sh" and "ch"—often in close proximity). Consider the opening line of Poland's most famous tongue-twisting nursery rhyme: *W Szczebrzeszynie chrzaszcz brzmi w trzcinie* ("In Szczebrzeszyn, a beetle is heard in the reeds"—pronounced vuh shih-chehb-zheh-shee-nyeh khzhahshch bzh-mee vuh tzhuh-cheen-yeh...or something like that).

Polish intimidates Americans with long, difficult-to-pronounce words. But if you take your time and sound things out, you'll quickly develop an ear for it. One rule of thumb to help you out: The stress is always on the next-to-last syllable.

Polish has some letters that don't appear in English, and some letters and combinations are pronounced differently than in English:

ć, ci, and **cz** all sound like "ch" as in "church"
ś, si, and **sz** all sound like "sh" as in "short"
ż, ź, zi, and **rz** all sound like "zh" as in "leisure"
dż and **dź** both sound like the "dj" sound in "jeans"
ń and **ni** sound like "ny" as in "canyon"
ę and **ą** are pronounced nasally, as in French: "en" and "an"
c sounds like "ts" as in "cats"
ch sounds like "kh" as in the Scottish "loch"
j sounds like "y" as in "yellow"
w sounds like "v" as in "Victor"
ł sounds like "w" as in "with"

So to Poles, "Lech Wałęsa" isn't pronounced "lehk wah-LEH-sah," as Americans tend to say—but "lehkh vah-WEHN-sah."

The Polish people you meet will be impressed and flattered if you take the time to learn a little of their language. To get started, check out the selection of Polish survival phrases on page 1265.

As you're tracking down addresses, these words will help: *miasto* (mee-AH-stoh, town), *plac* (plahts, square), *rynek* (REE-nehk, big market square), *ulica* (OO-leet-sah, road), *aleja* (ah-LAY-yah, avenue), and *most* (mohst, bridge).

KRAKÓW

Kraków is easily Poland's best destination: a beautiful, old-fashioned city buzzing with history, enjoyable sights, tourists, and college students. Even though the country's capital moved from here to Warsaw 400 years ago, Kraków remains Poland's cultural and intellectual center. Of all of the Eastern European cities laying claim to the boast "the next Prague," Kraków is for real.

Kraków grew wealthy from trade in the late 10th and early 11th centuries. Traders who passed through were required to stop here for a few days and sell their wares at a reduced cost. Local merchants turned around and sold those goods with big price hikes...and Kraków thrived. In 1038, it became Poland's capital.

Tatars invaded in 1241, leaving the city in ruins. Krakovians took this opportunity to rebuild their streets in a near-perfect grid, a striking contrast to the narrow, mazelike lanes of most medieval towns. The destruction also paved the way for the spectacular Main Market Square—still Kraków's best attraction.

King Kazimierz the Great sparked Kraków's Golden Age in the 14th century (see page 291). In 1364, he established the university that still defines the city (and counts Copernicus and Pope John Paul II among its alumni).

But Kraków's power waned as Poland's political center shifted to Warsaw. In 1596, the capital officially moved north. At the end of the 18th century, three neighboring powers—Russia, Prussia, and Austria—partitioned Poland, annexing all of its territory and dividing it among themselves. Warsaw ended up as a satellite of oppressive Moscow, and Kraków became a poor provincial backwater of Vienna. After Napoleon briefly reshuffled the map of

KRAKÓW

Kraków Essentials

English	Polish	Pronounced
Main Train Station	*Kraków Główny*	KROCK-oof GWOHV-nee
Old Town	*Stare Miasto*	STAH-reh mee-AH-stoh
Main Market Square	*Rynek Główny*	REE-nehk GWOHV-nee
Cloth Hall	*Sukiennice*	soo-kyeh-NEET-seh
Floriańska Street	*Ulica Floriańska*	OOH-leet-suh floh-ree-AHN-skah
Park around the Old Town	*Planty*	PLAHN-tee
Castle Hill	*Wawel*	VAH-vehl
Jewish Quarter	*Kazimierz*	kah-ZHEE-mehzh
Vistula River	*Wisła*	VEES-wah
Salt Mine	*Wieliczka*	vee-LEECH-kah
Planned Communist Suburb	*Nowa Huta*	NOH-vah HOO-tah

Europe in the early 19th century, Kraków was granted the status of a semi-independent city-state for about 30 years. The feisty Free City of Kraków, a tiny sliver wedged between three of Europe's mightiest empires, enjoyed an economic boom that saw the creation of the Planty park, the arrival of gas lighting and trams, and the construction of upscale suburbs outside the Old Town. Only after the unsuccessful Kraków Uprising of 1846 was Kraków forcefully brought back into the Austrian fold. But despite Kraków's reduced prominence, Austria's comparatively liberal climate allowed the city to become a haven for intellectuals and progressives (including a young revolutionary thinker from Russia named Vladimir Lenin).

The Nazis overran Poland in September of 1939. In the parts of the country that had no historical ties to Germany (including Kraków), the Nazis installed a ruling body called the *Generalgouvernement*, headed by former attorney Hans Frank. Germany wanted to quickly develop "Krakau" (as they called it) into the German capital of the nation. They renamed the Main Market Square "Adolf-Hitler-Platz," tore down statues of Polish figures (including the Adam Mickiewicz statue that dominates the Main Market Square today), and invested heavily in construction and industrialization (opening the door for Oskar Schindler to come and take over a factory from its Jewish owners). The German overlords imposed a "New Order" that included seizing businesses, rationing, and a strict curfew for Poles and Jews alike. A special set of "Jewish laws" targeted, then decimated, Poland's huge Jewish population (for details, see "Jewish Kraków" on page 328).

Kraków's cityscape—if not its people—emerged from World War II virtually unscathed. But when the communists took over, they decided to give intellectual (and potentially dissident) Kraków an injection of good Soviet values—in the form of heavy industry. They built Nowa Huta, an enormous steelworks and planned town for workers, on Kraków's outskirts—dooming the city to decades of smog. Thankfully, Kraków is now much cleaner than it was 20 years ago.

Pope John Paul II was born (as Karol Wojtyła) in nearby Wadowice, and served as archbishop of Kraków before being called to Rome. Kraków might be the most Catholic town in Europe's most Catholic country; be sure to visit a few of its many churches. University life, small but thought-provoking museums, great restaurants, sprawling parks, and Jewish history round out the city's appeal.

Over the last few years, Kraków has gone through a boom and bust. The early 2000s were kind to the city, but tourist interest peaked around mid-2007; with uncertain economic times, many travelers seem to have retreated to more predictable destinations farther west—leaving local hoteliers scratching their heads and lowering their rates. While the city wasn't selected to host any matches for the Euro Cup 2012 soccer championship, it hopes for a big boost from visitors passing through on their way to the games being held elsewhere in Poland. And someday, this gem of a city will be as swamped with tourists as any big-league destination. Enjoy it now, while it's still relatively quiet.

Planning Your Time

Kraków and its important side-trips deserve at least two full days on the busiest itinerary. Most people can easily fill three days. More than any town in Europe, Kraków is made for aimless strolling.

Ideally, spend two full days in Kraków itself, plus a visit to Auschwitz (either as a side-trip on the third day, or en route to or from Kraków). In a pinch, spend one day sightseeing in Kraków, another at Auschwitz, and two evenings on the Main Market Square.

With only one full day in Kraków, follow this plan: Take my self-guided walk of Kraków's Royal Way to cover the city's core. Have lunch on or near the Main Market Square, and spend the rest of your time visiting any Old Town museums that interest you (such as the Wyspiański Museum, Jagiellonian University Museum, Gallery of 19th-Century Polish Art, or the museums

Kraków's Old Town

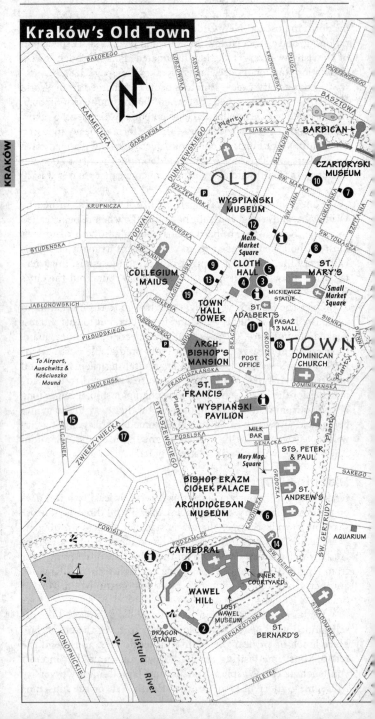

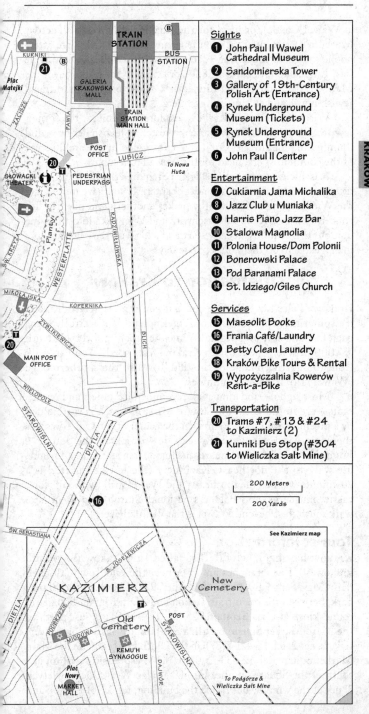

KRAKÓW

Sights
1. John Paul II Wawel Cathedral Museum
2. Sandomierska Tower
3. Gallery of 19th-Century Polish Art (Entrance)
4. Rynek Underground Museum (Tickets)
5. Rynek Underground Museum (Entrance)
6. John Paul II Center

Entertainment
7. Cukiarnia Jama Michalika
8. Jazz Club u Muniaka
9. Harris Piano Jazz Bar
10. Stalowa Magnolia
11. Polonia House/Dom Polonii
12. Bonerowski Palace
13. Pod Baranami Palace
14. St. Idziego/Giles Church

Services
15. Massolit Books
16. Frania Café/Laundry
17. Betty Clean Laundry
18. Kraków Bike Tours & Rental
19. Wypożyczalnia Rowerów Rent-a-Bike

Transportation
20. Trams #7, #13 & #24 to Kazimierz (2)
21. Kurniki Bus Stop (#304 to Wieliczka Salt Mine)

200 Meters

200 Yards

See Kazimierz map

at Wawel Castle), or head for the excellent Schindler's Factory Museum in Kazimierz. If you have any energy left by late afternoon, you could squeeze in a late visit to the Wieliczka Salt Mine (last English tour departs at 18:00, or at 17:00 Oct-May). Savor the Main Market Square over dinner or a drink, or enjoy traditional Jewish music and cuisine in Kazimierz.

With more time in Kraków, explore Kazimierz, the former Jewish quarter—a must for those interested in Jewish heritage, and illuminating for anyone. Or, if you're intrigued by the architecture of the communist era, head for the Nowa Huta suburb.

Auschwitz, an essential side-trip, requires the better part of a day for a round-trip visit (see next chapter). If you have more time, the Wieliczka Salt Mine nearby makes another good day trip. It's conceivably possible to fit Auschwitz and Wieliczka into the same day, but this requires an early start and a local driver—it's far more manageable to do them on separate days.

Orientation to Kraków

Kraków (Poles say KROCK-oof, but you can say KRACK-cow; it's sometimes spelled "Cracow" in English) is mercifully compact, flat, and easy to navigate. While the urban sprawl is big (with 757,000 people), the tourist's Kraków feels small. You can walk from the northern edge of the Old Town to the southern edge (Wawel Hill) in about 15 minutes.

Most sights—and almost all recommended hotels and restaurants—are in the Old Town (Stare Miasto), which is surrounded by a greenbelt called the Planty. In the center of the Old Town lies the Main Market Square (Rynek Główny, a.k.a. "the Square"). From the Main Market Square, the main train station is a 15-minute walk to the northeast; Kazimierz (the Jewish quarter) is a 20-minute walk to the southeast; and Wawel Hill (with a historic castle, museums, and Poland's national church) is a 10-minute walk south. Just beyond Wawel is the Vistula River.

Tourist Information

Kraków has many helpful TIs, called InfoKraków (www.info krakow.pl). Five branches are in or near the Old Town (all open daily May-Sept 9:00-19:00, Oct-April 9:00-17:00): in the **Planty** park, between the main train station and Main Market Square (in round kiosk at ulica Szpitalna 25, tel. 12-432-0110); just north of the Main Market Square on **ulica Św. Jana** (specializes in concert tickets, at #2, tel. 12-421-7787); in the **Cloth Hall** right on the Main Market Square (tel. 12-433-7310); in the **Wyspiański Pavilion** just south of the Square on ulica Grodzka (plac Wszystkich Świętych 3, not at the window but inside the building, tel. 12-616-1886); and just west of **Wawel Hill** (also covers the entire region, Powiśle 11, mobile 513-099-688).

Other TI branches are in **Kazimierz** (daily 9:00-17:00, ulica Józefa 7, tel. 12-422-0471), **Nowa Huta** (Tue-Sat 10:00-14:00, closed Sun-Mon, os. Słoneczne 16, tel. 12-643-0303), and the **airport** (daily 9:00-19:00, tel. 12-285-5341).

At any TI, ask what's new in fast-changing Kraków, browse the brochures, and pick up the free map and the *Kraków Tourist Information Compendium* booklet. The TIs also offer a free room-finding service and sell tickets for bus tours and walking tours (though only for one walking-tour company, See Kraków; for other options, see "Tours in Kraków," later).

Sightseeing Pass: The TI's **Kraków Tourist Card** isn't a good value for most visitors. It covers public transportation, includes admission to several city museums (basically everything except the Wawel Hill sights and Wieliczka Salt Mine), and offers discounts to outlying sights and tours—but Kraków's museums are already cheap, and public transportation is mostly unnecessary (50 zł/2 days, 65 zł/3 days).

Warning: Many private travel agencies, room-booking services, and tour operators masquerade as TIs, with deceptive blue-and-white "i" signs. If I haven't listed them in this section, they're not a real TI.

Arrival in Kraków

By Train: Kraków's main train station (called "Kraków Główny") is just northeast of the Old Town. It shares a broad plaza (plac Dworcowy) with the giant, modern Galeria Krakowska shopping mall.

Taxis from the station are cheap and easy: From the tracks, take the elevator or stairs to the rooftop above you, where you'll find a giant parking lot where taxis wait. Be sure to use a taxi clearly marked with a company name and telephone number. The usual metered rate to downtown is a reasonable 10-15 zł.

Most hotels are within easy **walking** distance of the station. It's about a 15-minute stroll to the Main Market Square—just follow signs to the center (*wyjście do centrum* or *wyjście do miasta*).

Arriving at the Kraków station can be confusing—when you get off the train, it's a bit of a hike to get to the station itself: From the tracks, you'll first walk down some stairs and pass through an underground corridor. When you emerge, turn left up the stairs and walk under the long green canopy to the yellow main terminal building. Exiting on the other side of the main terminal, you'll emerge into the wide-open plaza called plac Dworcowy, fronted by the Galeria Krakowska mall and an old-fashioned post office. Beyond the post office, a broad ramp leads down into a pedestrian underpass beneath the busy ring road; as you emerge from this underpass, bear right (following signs for *Rynek Główny/Main Market*) and head into the Planty park. You'll see the round TI kiosk on your left, and the Main Market Square is a few blocks straight ahead. If you're heading to hotels in Kazimierz, follow the same directions, but when you walk up the ramp into the Planty park, make a sharp right up the stairs to find a tram stop; from here, you can catch tram #7, #13, or #24 to Kazimierz (ride it three stops, to Miodowa—see "Getting to Kazimierz" on page 322).

By Bus: The bus station is right behind the main train station. To get into town, use the passage that takes you under the train tracks (following signs for *PKP*—the train station—and *centrum*). Once at the train station, follow the above directions.

To get *to* the bus station from the Old Town (such as to catch a bus to Auschwitz), first head to the main train station (go through the Planty park and use the underpass). From the train station's main terminal, walk under the long green canopy to the train platforms. Use the pedestrian underpass to go under the tracks (following signs for *dojście do dworca autobusowego*); when you emerge on the other side, the bus station is the blocky, modern building on your left (marked *RDA Dworzec Autobusowy*). Inside are the standard amenities (lockers and toilets), domestic and international ticket windows, and an electronic board showing the next several departures. Some bus departures, marked on the board with a *G*, leave from the upper *(gorna)* stalls, which you can see out the window. Other bus departures, marked with a *D*, leave from the lower *(dolna)* stalls; to find these, go down the easy-to-miss stairs (marked *zejście na dolna płytę*) on the left just beyond the ticket windows. Note that some minibuses, such as those to Auschwitz, also leave from, or near, this station (though the buses and minibuses that go to the Wieliczka Salt Mine leave from elsewhere—see page 337).

By Car: *Centrum* signs lead you into the Old Town—you'll know you're there when you hit the ring road that surrounds the Planty park. Parking garages surround the Old Town. Your hotelier can advise you on directions and parking.

By Plane: The small, modern **John Paul II Kraków-Balice Airport** is about 10 miles west of the center, with separate international and domestic terminals (airport info: tel. 12-295-5800, www.krakowairport.pl). To get to downtown Kraków, you can take a speedy train, a slower public bus, or a taxi.

If you take the **train** downtown, first catch the free, blue shuttle bus from the airport to the nearby train station. The bus serves both the main international terminal (as you exit the terminal, turn right and look for the *PKP* sign for the bus stop) and the domestic terminal (bus stops in front). At the train station, you can buy the 10-zł ticket from the automated machine or from the conductor on the train (2/hour, 18 minutes, arrives at Kraków's main train station, uses platform 1, see train arrival instructions earlier).

To get to Kraków's main bus station downtown by **public bus**, catch bus #208, #292, or (at night) #902 in front of the airport (3.20 zł, 50-minute trip depending on traffic, see bus arrival instructions earlier).

For door-to-door service, hop in a **cab** at the taxi stand in front of the terminal (ask about the fare up front—should be around 70-80 zł, more expensive at night, about 30 minutes). You can also arrange a taxi transfer in advance (such as with recommended driver Andrew Durman, listed later, under "Tours in Kraków").

Note that many budget flights—including those on Wizz Air and Ryanair—use the **International Airport Katowice in Pyrzowice** (Międzynarodowy Port Lotniczy Katowice w Pyrzowicach, www.katowice-airport.com). This airport is about 18 miles from the city of Katowice, which is about 50 miles west of Kraków. Direct buses run sporadically between Katowice Airport and Kraków's main train station (50 zł, trip takes 1.75 hours, generally scheduled to meet incoming flights). You can also take the bus from Katowice Airport to Katowice's train station (hourly, 50 minutes), then take the train to Kraków (hourly, 1.5 hours). Wizz Air's website is useful for figuring out your connection: www.wizz air.com.

Helpful Hints

Sightseeing Schedules: Some sights are closed on Monday (including the Gallery of 19th-Century Polish Art, Wyspiański Museum, and a few museums in Kazimierz), but many sights are open (including the churches and Jagiellonian University Museum, and in Kazimierz, all of the Jewish-themed sights). On Saturday, most of Kazimierz's Jewish-themed sights are closed. Before heading out, check the "Kraków at a Glance" sidebar on page 284.

Internet Access: Virtually every hotel in Kraków has an Internet terminal in its lobby and/or Wi-Fi in its rooms. Otherwise, take your pick of the city's many cheap Internet cafés—it seems there's one on every corner.

Post Office: The main post office (Poczta Główna) is at the intersection of Starowiślna and the Westerplatte ring road, a few blocks east of the Main Market Square (Mon-Fri 7:30-20:30, Sat 8:00-14:00, closed Sun).

Bookstore: For an impressive selection of new and used English books, try **Massolit Books,** just west of the Old Town. They also have a café with drinks and light snacks, and a good children's section (Sun-Thu 10:00-20:00, Fri-Sat 10:00-21:00, ulica Felicjanek 4, tel. 12-432-4150, http://massolit.com).

Laundry: Frania Café is a dream come true for a traveler with dirty laundry. Halfway between the Old Town and Kazimierz, this inviting café/pub has ample washers and driers, relaxing ambience, free Wi-Fi and a loaner laptop, a full bar serving up espresso drinks and laundry-themed hard drinks, very long hours, and a friendly staff. Those in search of a mellow hangout might want to come here even if they don't need to wash clothes (16 zł/load self-service, 26 zł for them to do it for you in 2 hours—consider dropping it off on your way to Kazimierz and picking it up on the way back, likely open daily 10:30-24:00, ulica Starowiślna 26, mobile 783-945-021, www.laundromat.pl).

If you must have something laundered closer to the Old Town, **Betty Clean** is relatively central, but pricey (about 12 zł/shirt, 17 zł/pants, 1 zł/pair of socks or underwear, takes 24 hours, 50 percent more for express 3-hour service, Mon-Fri 7:30-19:30, Sat 8:00-15:30, closed Sun, just outside the Planty park at ulica Zwierzyniecka 6, tel. 12-423-0848).

Getting Around Kraków

Kraków's top sights and best hotels are easily accessible by foot. You'll only need wheels if you're going to the Kazimierz Jewish quarter or the Nowa Huta suburb.

By Public Transit: Trams and buses zip around Kraków's urban sprawl. While most trams are new and modern, a few rickety old trams with big windows (dubbed "aquariums" by locals) also rattle around the city. The same tickets are used for both trams and buses, and can be purchased at most kiosks or at the new automated machines you'll find at most stops. You can buy a ticket from the driver, but they sometimes run out and usually demand exact change, so it's safer to get one before you board. (Better yet, if you know in advance you'll be taking the tram, stock up on tickets ahead of time.) A *bilet jednoprzejazdowy* (basic single ticket, no transfers) costs 2.80 zł; a *bilet godzinny* (one-hour ticket) allows transfers and costs 3.60 zł. For a short ride, such as the one from the Old Town or train station to Kazimierz, buy a 15-minute ticket (2 zł). You can also get longer-term tickets for 24 hours (12 zł), 48 hours (20 zł), and 72 hours (28 zł). These prices are for a "one-zone" ticket, which covers virtually everything of interest in Kraków (including Nowa Huta and the Kościuszko Mound)— unless you're headed for the airport or Wieliczka Salt Mine, which are beyond the city limits and require a slightly more expensive *aglomeracyjny* ticket. Always validate your ticket when you board the bus or tram (24-, 48-, and 72-hour tickets must be validated only the first time you use them).

By Taxi: Just as in other Eastern European cities, only take cabs that are clearly marked with a company logo and telephone number. Kraków taxis start at 7 zł and charge about 3 zł per kilometer. Rides are usually very short and generally run less than 15-20 zł. You're more likely to get the fair metered rate by calling or hailing a cab, rather than taking one waiting at tourist spots. To call a cab, try **Radio Taxi** (tel. 19191).

By Bike: The riverfront bike path is enticing on a nice day; the Planty park, while inviting, can be a bit crowded for biking. **Kraków Bike Tours** rents a wide variety of new, good-quality bikes (10 zł/first hour, cheaper per hour for longer rentals, 50 zł/day, 60 zł/24 hours, daily 10:00-19:00, just off the Square at Grodzka 2; see listing later, under "Tours in Kraków"). Nearby at **Wypożyczalnia Rowerów Rent-a-Bike,** easygoing Michał Bisping rents cheaper bikes (5 zł/hour, 35 zł/day, April-Oct daily 9:00-dusk, less in bad weather, closed Nov-March, ulica Św. Anny 4, mobile 501-745-986).

Tours in Kraków

You have many options for touring Kraków (and beyond): with a local guide or driver, or by foot, bike, bus, buggy, or even golf cart.

Local Guides—Kraków has several affordable guides. I've enjoyed working with two in particular, both of whom can show you the sights in Kraków and also have cars for day-tripping into the countryside: **Marta Chmielowska** (250 zł/half-day, 300 zł with her car; 450 zł/day; mobile 603-668-008, martachm7@gmail.com); or **Anna Gega** (by foot: 250 zł/4 hours, 350 zł/day; by car: 300 zł/4 hours, 500 zł/day—maybe more for long-distance trips; mobile 604-151-293, leadertour@wp.pl).

Either of these guides can also take you to **Auschwitz** for the day for around 600-700 zł. However, only official Auschwitz guides can legally give tours at the concentration camp museum. Therefore, your local guide will probably either do the tour herself (and pay to hire a Polish-speaking guide to tag along and act "official"), or send you with one of the regularly departing English tours. Because of the added expense of hiring the local guide, it's pricey to visit Auschwitz with Marta or Anna. You'll get a better value by going with one of the drivers listed next.

Drivers—Since Kraków is such a useful home base for day trips, it can be handy to splurge on a private driver for door-to-door service. **Andrew (Andrzej) Durman,** a Pole who lived in Chicago and speaks fluent English, is a gregarious driver, translator, miracle worker, and all-around great guy. While not an officially licensed tour guide, Andrew is an eager conversationalist and loves

Kraków at a Glance

▲▲▲**Main Market Square** Stunning heart of Kraków and a people magnet any time of day. **Hours:** Always open. See page 292.

▲▲**Planty** Once a moat, now a scenic park encircling the city. **Hours:** Always open. See page 288.

▲▲**St. Mary's Church** Landmark church with extraordinary wood-carved Gothic altarpiece. **Hours:** Mon-Sat 11:30-18:00, Sun 14:00-18:00. See page 289.

▲▲**Cloth Hall** Fourteenth-century market hall with 21st-century souvenirs. **Hours:** Summer Mon-Fri 9:00-18:00, Sat-Sun 9:00-15:00, sometimes later; winter Mon-Fri 9:00-16:00, Sat-Sun 9:00-15:00. See page 294.

▲▲**St. Francis' Basilica** Lovely Gothic church with some of Poland's best Art Nouveau. **Hours:** Daily 6:00-19:45. See page 296.

▲▲**Wawel Cathedral** Poland's splendid national church, with tons of tombs, a crypt, and a climbable tower. **Hours:** April-Sept Mon-Sat 9:00-17:00, Sun 12:30-17:00; Oct-March Mon-Sat 9:00-16:00, Sun 12:30-16:00. See page 302.

▲▲**Wawel Castle Grounds** Historic hilltop with views, castle, cathedral, courtyard with chakras, and a passel of museums. **Hours:** Grounds open daily 6:00 until dusk, but many of the museums closed Mon. See page 306.

▲▲**Gallery of 19th-Century Polish Art** Worthwhile collection of paintings by should-be-famous artists, upstairs in the Cloth Hall. **Hours:** Tue-Sat 10:00-20:00, Sun 10:00-18:00, closed Mon. See page 311.

▲▲**Wyspiański Museum** Art by the talented leader of the Młoda Polska (Polish Art Nouveau) movement. **Hours:** Wed-Sat 10:00-18:00, Sun 10:00-16:00, closed Mon, Tue only temporary exhibits open. See page 316.

▲▲**Old Cemetery** Poignant Jewish burial site in Kazimierz, with graves from 1552 to 1800. **Hours:** Sun-Fri 9:00-16:00, sometimes until 18:00 May-Aug, closes earlier in winter and at sundown on Fri, closed Sat. See page 323.

▲▲Schindler's Factory Museum Historic building where Oskar Schindler saved more than 1,000 Jewish workers, now filled with engaging exhibit about Kraków's WWII experience. **Hours:** April-Oct Mon 10:00-16:00 (closed first Mon of month), Tue-Sun 10:00-20:00; Nov-March Mon 10:00-14:00 (closed first Mon of month), Tue-Sun 10:00-18:00. See page 331.

▲Czartoryski Museum Varied collection, with European paintings (da Vinci and Rembrandt) and Polish armor, handicrafts, and decorative arts. **Hours:** Likely closed for restoration, otherwise Tue-Sat 10:00-18:00, Sun 10:00-16:00, closed Mon. See page 317.

▲Rynek Underground Museum Super-modern exhibit on medieval Kraków filling excavated cellars beneath the Main Market Square. **Hours:** Mon 10:00-20:00, Tue 10:00-16:00 (closed first Tue of month), Wed-Sun 10:00-22:00. See page 319.

▲Jagiellonian University Museum: Collegium Maius Proud collection of historic university, surrounding a tranquil courtyard where medieval professors lived. **Hours:** Two different tours; 30-minute version—April-Oct departs every 20 minutes Mon-Fri 10:00-15:00, Tue and Thu until 18:00, Sat 10:00-14:00; no tours Sun; Nov-March 14:00-16:00; one-hour version—year-round Mon-Fri at 13:00, no tours Sat-Sun. See page 320.

▲New Cemetery Jewish graveyard with tombs from after 1800, partly restored after Nazi desecration. **Hours**: Sun-Fri 8:00-18:00, until 16:00 in winter, closed Sat. See page 326.

▲Ethnographic Museum Traditional rural Polish life on display. **Hours:** Tue-Sat 11:00-19:00, Thu until 21:00, Sun 11:00-15:00, closed Mon. See page 330.

▲Pharmacy Under the Eagle Small Podgórze exhibit about the Holocaust in Kraków, including three evocative historic films. **Hours:** April-Oct Mon 10:00-14:00, Tue-Sun 9:30-17:00; Nov-March Mon 10:00-14:00, Tue-Thu and Sat 9:00-16:00, Fri 10:00-17:00, closed Sun and the first Tue of each month. See page 331.

▲Museum of Contemporary Art in Kraków Today's thought-provoking art, displayed in renovated old warehouses behind Schindler's Factory Museum. **Hours:** Tue-Sun 11:00-19:00, closed Mon. See page 336.

KRAKÓW

to provide lively commentary while you roll. Although you can hire Andrew for a simple airport transfer or Auschwitz day trip, he also enjoys tackling more ambitious itineraries, from helping you track down your Polish roots to taking you on multiple-day journeys around Poland and beyond (prices are for up to four people if you book direct: 400 zł to Auschwitz—you can meet up with an English tour group there at your own expense or follow my self-guided tour, 200 zł to Wieliczka Salt Mine, 80 zł for transfer from Kraków-Balice Airport, 450 zł for transfer from Katowice Airport, 600 zł for an all-day trip into the countryside—such as into the High Tatras or to track down your Polish roots near Kraków, more to cover gas costs for trips longer than 100 km one-way; long-distance transfers for up to 4 people to Prague, Budapest, or Berlin for 1,600 zł or to Vienna for 1,800 zł; also available for multi-day trips—price negotiable, all prices higher for bigger van, tel. 12-411-5630, mobile 602-243-306, www.tour-service.pl, andrew@tour-service.pl).

Local guide Marta Chmielowska's husband, **Czesław** (a.k.a. Chester), can also drive you to nearby locations (300 zł for all-day trip to Auschwitz for up to 3 people, 380 zł for 4-8 people; to book, see Marta's contact information, above).

Walking Tours—Various companies run city walking tours in English daily in summer. Most do a 2.5-hour tour of the Old Town as well as a 2.5-hour tour of Kazimierz, the Jewish district (40-60 zł per tour, depending on company). Because the scene is continually evolving, it's best to pick up fliers locally (the TI works exclusively with one company, See Kraków, but hotel reception desks generally have more options), then choose the one that fits your interests and schedule. Four people can hire their own great local guide for about the same amount of money.

Crazy Guides—This irreverent company offers tours to the communist suburb of Nowa Huta and other outlying sights. For details, see page 339.

Bike Tours—**Kraków Bike Tours** is a well-established operation that runs 3- to 3.5-hour bike tours in English daily in summer. The tours make 25 stops in the Old Town, Kazimierz, and Podgórze (80 zł, includes loaner bike, April-Oct daily at 13:00, meet tour at their office down the passage at Grodzka 2—right at the bottom of the Square, tel. 12-430-2034, mobile 788-800-231, www.krakowbiketour.com, krakowbiketour@gmail.com).

Bus Tours—As Kraków is so easily seen on foot, taking a bus tour doesn't make much sense here. But they can be handy for reaching outlying sights. Various tour companies run bus-plus-walking itineraries (each of them around 100-130 zł), including Auschwitz (6 hours), Wieliczka Salt Mine (4 hours), and other regional side-trips. Look for fliers around town.

Buggy Tours—Romantic, horse-drawn buggies trot around Kraków from the Main Market Square. The going rate is a hefty 100 zł for a 30-minute tour.

Golf-Cart Tours—Several outfits around town (including on the Square) offer tours on a golf cart with recorded commentary (prices are for up to 4 people: 60 zł for one-way trip up to Wawel Hill, 120 zł for half-hour tour of Old Town or Kazimierz, 200 zł for hour-long tour of both the Old Town and Kazimierz).

Self-Guided Walk

Kraków's Royal Way

Most of Kraków's major sights are conveniently connected by this self-guided walking tour. This route is known as the "Royal Way" because the king used to follow this same path when he returned to Kraków after a journey. After the capital moved to Warsaw, most kings were still crowned and buried in Wawel Cathedral at the far end of town—and they followed this same route for both occasions. You could sprint through this walk in about an hour (less than a mile altogether), but it's much more fun if you take it slow.

• *Begin just outside the main gate at the north end of the Old Town.*

▲Barbican (Barbakan) and City Walls

Tatars invaded Kraków three times in the 13th century. After the first attack destroyed the city in 1241, Krakovians built this wall. The original rampart had 47 watchtowers and eight gates.

The big, round defensive fort standing outside the wall is a barbican. Structures like this provided extra fortification to weak sections. Imagine how it looked in 1500, when this barbican stood outside the town moat with a long bridge leading to the Florian Gate—the city's main entryway. Today you can pay to scramble along the passages and fortifications of the barbican, though there's little to see inside. The same ticket also lets you climb up onto the surviving stretch of Old Town walls flanking the Florian Gate (entry from inside walls).

Cost and Hours: 7 zł, May-Oct daily 10:30-18:00, last entry 30 minutes before closing, closed Nov-April.

• *Before entering the Old Town, look to the left and right of the barbican to see the...*

▲▲Planty

By the 19th century, Kraków's no-longer-necessary city wall had fallen into disrepair. Krakovians decided to tear down what remained, fill in the moat, and plant trees. (The name comes not from the English "plant," but from the Polish *plantovac,* or "flat"—since they flattened out this area

to create it.) Today, the Planty is a beautiful park that stretches 2.5 miles around the entire perimeter of Kraków's Old Town.

• *Now enter the Old Town by walking through the...*

Florian Gate (Brama Floriańska)

Inside the gate, notice the little chapel with a replica of the famous **Black Madonna of Częstochowa,** probably the most

important religious symbol among Polish Catholics. The original, located in Częstochowa (70 miles north of Kraków), is an Eastern Orthodox-style icon of mysterious origin with several mystical legends attached to it. After the icon's believed role in protecting a monastery from Swedish invaders in the mid-17th century, it was named "Queen and Protector of Poland."

• *Once through the gate, you're standing at the head of Kraków's historic (and now touristic) gamut...*

▲Floriańska Street (Ulica Floriańska)

On the inside of the city wall, you'll see a makeshift **art gallery,** where starving students hawk the works they've painted at the Academy of Fine Arts (across the busy street from the barbican). Portraits, still lifes, landscapes, local scenes, nudes...this might just be Kraków's best collection of art. If you were to detour along the gallery (to the right with your back to the gate), in a block you'd arrive at another fine collection—the eclectic Czartoryski Museum. (While it's currently closed for renovation, this museum is normally home to a rare Leonardo da Vinci oil painting.)

Standing at the top of Floriańska street,

you can't miss two restaurant chains: **Coffee Heaven** (the local Starbucks) and **McDonald's.** When renovating the McDonald's building, they discovered a Gothic cellar—so they excavated it and added seating. Today, you can super-size your ambience by dining on a Big Mac and fries under a medieval McVault.

About halfway down the long block, on the left (at #45, round green sign), look for **Cukiarnia Jama Michalika** ("Michael's Cave"). This dark, atmospheric café, popular with locals for its coffee and pastries, began in 1895 as a simple bakery in a claustrophobic back room. A brothel upstairs scared off respectable patrons, so the owner attracted students by creating a cabaret act called "The Green Balloon." To this day, the cabaret—political satire set to music—still runs (in Polish only, Sun at 12:00; you may also see ads for a touristy folk show here). Around the turn of the 20th century, this was a hangout of the Młoda Polska (Young Poland) movement—the Polish answer to Art Nouveau (explained on page 293). The walls are papered with sketches from poor artists who couldn't pay their tabs. Poke around inside, appreciating this unique art gallery. Consider having coffee and dessert here (Sun-Thu 9:00-22:00, Fri-Sat 9:00-23:00), but expect a grouchy greeting and a fee for the obligatory coat-check.

Continue strolling down Floriańska street. Two blocks ahead on the left (at #3, 50 yards before the big church), you'll see **Jazz Club u Muniaka.** In the 1950s, Janusz Muniak was one of the first Polish jazzmen. Now he owns this place, and jams regularly here in a cool cellar surrounded by jazzy art. If you hang around the bar before the show, you might find yourself sitting next to Janusz himself, smoking his pipe...and getting ready to smoke on the saxophone (for details, see "Entertainment in Kraków," later).

• *Continue into the Main Market Square, where you'll run into...*

▲▲St. Mary's Church (Kościół Mariacki)

A church has stood on this spot for 800 years. The original church

was destroyed by the first Tatar invasion in 1241, but all subsequent versions—including the current one—have been built on the same foundation. You can look down the sides to see how the Main Market Square has risen about seven feet over the centuries.

How many church towers does St. Mary's have? Technically, the answer is one. The shorter tower belongs to the church; the taller one is a municipal watchtower, from which you'll hear a bugler playing the hourly *hejnał* song.

According to Kraków's favorite legend, during that first Tatar invasion, a town watchman saw the enemy approaching and sounded the alarm. Before he could finish the tune, an arrow pierced his throat—which is why, even today, the *hejnał* stops suddenly partway through. Today's buglers—12 in all—are firemen first, musicians second. Each one works a 24-hour shift up there, playing the *hejnał* on the hour, every hour (broadcast on national Polish radio at noon).

To see one of the most finely crafted Gothic altarpieces anywhere, it's worth paying admission to enter the church. The front door is open 14 hours a day and is free to those who come to pray, but tourists use the door around the right side (buy your ticket across the little square from this door).

Cost and Hours: 6 zł, audioguide-5 zł, Mon-Sat 11:30-18:00, Sun 14:00-18:00. The famous wooden altarpiece is open between noon and 18:00; try to be here by 11:50 for the ceremonial opening (Mon-Sat) or at 18:00 for the closing (except on Sat, when it's left open for the service on Sun).

Touring the Church: The rusty neck-stock (behind the tourists' left door) was used until the 1700s to publicly humiliate wrongdoers.

Inside, you're drawn to one of the best medieval woodcarvings in existence—the exquisite, three-part **altarpiece** by German Veit Stoss (Wit Stwosz in Polish).
Carved in 12 years and completed in 1489, it's packed with emotion rare in Gothic art. Get as close as you can, and study the remarkable details. Stoss used oak for the structural parts and linden trunks for the figures. When the altar doors are closed, you see scenes from the lives of Mary and Jesus. The open altar depicts the Dormition (death) of the Virgin. The artist catches the apostles around Mary, reacting in the seconds after she collapses. Mary is depicted in three stages: dying, being escorted to heaven by Jesus, and (at the very top) being crowned in heaven (flanked by two Polish saints—Adalbert and Stanisław). The six scenes on the sides are the Annunciation, birth of Jesus, visit by the Three Magi, Jesus' Resurrection, his Ascension, and Mary becoming the mother of the apostles at Pentecost.

There's more to St. Mary's than the altar. While you're admiring this church's art, notice the flowery Neo-Gothic painting covering the choir walls. Stare up into the starry, starry blue ceiling. As you wander around, consider that the church was renovated a century ago by three Polish geniuses from two very different

Kazimierz the Great
(1333-1370)

Out of the many centuries of Polish kings, only one earned the nickname "great," and he's the only one worth remembering: Kazimierz the Great.

K. the G., who ruled Poland from Kraków in the 14th century, was one of those larger-than-life medieval kings who left his mark on all fronts—from war to diplomacy, art patronage to womanizing. His scribes bragged that Kazimierz "found a Poland made of wood, and left one made of brick and stone." He put Kraków on the map as a major European capital. He founded many villages (some of which still bear his name) and replaced wooden structures with stone ones (such as Kraków's Cloth Hall). Kazimierz also established the Kraków Academy (today's Jagiellonian University), the second-oldest university in Central Europe. And to protect all these new building projects, he heavily fortified Poland by building a series of imposing forts and walls around its perimeter.

Most of all, Kazimierz is remembered as a progressive, tolerant king. In the 14th century, other nations were deporting—or even interning—their Jewish subjects, who were commonly scapegoated for anything that went wrong. But the enlightened and kindly Kazimierz actively encouraged Jews to come to Poland by granting them special privileges, often related to banking and trade—establishing the country as a safe haven for Jews in Europe.

Kazimierz the Great was the last of Poland's long-lived Piast dynasty. Although he left no male heir—at least, no legitimate one—Kazimierz's advances set the stage for Poland's Golden Age (14th-16th centuries). After his death, Poland united with Lithuania (against the common threat of the Teutonic Knights), the Jagiellonian dynasty was born, and Poland became one of Europe's mightiest medieval powers.

artistic generations: the venerable positivist Jan Matejko and his Art Nouveau students, Stanisław Wyspiański and Józef Mehoffer (we'll learn more about these two later on our walk). The huge silver bird under the organ loft in back is a crowned eagle, the symbol of Poland.

Tower Climb: Several days a week in the summer, you can actually climb up the 239 stairs to the top of the taller tower to visit the *hejnał* fireman. While it's a huff—with some claustrophobic stone stairs, followed by some steep, acrophobic wooden ones—the view up top is the best you'll find of the Square (5 zł, buy ticket at little tent next to front door; open May-Sept Tue, Thu, and Sat 9:00-11:30 & 13:00-17:30, closed Oct-April).

• *Leaving the church, enjoy the...*

▲▲▲Main Market Square (Rynek Główny), a.k.a. "The Square"

Kraków's marvelous Square, one of Europe's most gasp-worthy public spaces, bustles with street musicians, colorful flower stalls, cotton-candy vendors, loitering teenagers, businesspeople commuting by foot, gawking tourists, and the lusty coos of pigeons. This Square is where Kraków lives. It's often filled with various special events, markets, and festivals. The biggest are the seasonal markets before Easter and Christmas, but you're also likely to stumble on something special going on here anytime between June and August.

The Square was established in the 13th century, when the city had to be rebuilt after being flattened by the Tatars. At the time, it was the biggest square in medieval Europe. It was illegal to sell anything on the street, so everything had to be sold here on the Main Market Square. It was divided into smaller markets, such as the butcher stalls, the ironworkers' tents, and the still-standing Cloth Hall (described later).

Notice the modern **fountain** with the glass pyramid at this end of the Square. If you peer through the water and the glass bottom, you may see people moving around down there. A recent, lengthy excavation of the surrounding area created a museum of Kraków's medieval history that literally sprawls beneath the Square (for more on the **Rynek Underground Museum,** see "Sights in Kraków," later).

The statue in the middle of the Square is of Romantic poet **Adam Mickiewicz** (1789-1855). His epic masterpiece, *Pan Tadeusz,* is still regarded as one of the greatest works in Polish, and Mickiewicz is considered the "Polish Shakespeare." A wistful, nostalgic tale of Polish-Lithuanian nobility, *Pan Tadeusz* stirred patriotism in a Poland that had been dismantled by surrounding empires.

Near the end of the Square, you'll see the tiny, copper-domed **Church of St. Adalbert,** the oldest church in Kraków (10th century). This Romanesque structure predates the Square. Like St. Mary's (described earlier), it seems to be at an angle because it's aligned east-west, as was the custom when it was built. (In other words, the churches aren't crooked—the Square is.)

Drinks are reasonably priced at cafés on the Square (most around 10-15 zł). Find a spot where you like the view and the chairs, then sit and sip. Order a coffee, Polish *piwo* (beer, such

The Młoda Polska (Young Poland) Art Movement

Polish art in the late 19th century was ruled by positivism, a school with a very literal, straightforward focus on Polish history (Jan Matejko led the charge; see page 409). But when the new generation of Kraków's artists came into their own in the early 1900s, they decided that the old school was exactly that. Though moved by the same spirit and goals as the previous generation—evoking Polish patriotism at a time when their country was being occupied—these new artists used very different methods. They were inspired by a renewed appreciation of folklore and peasant life. Rather than being earnest and literal (an 18th-century Polish war hero on horseback), the new art was playful and highly symbolic (the artist frolicking in a magical garden in the idyllic Polish countryside). This movement became known as Młoda Polska (Young Poland)—Art Nouveau with a Polish accent.

Stanisław Wyspiański (vees-PAYN-skee, 1869-1907) was the leader of Młoda Polska. He produced beautiful artwork,

from simple drawings to the stirring stained-glass images in Kraków's St. Francis' Basilica. Wyspiański was an expert at capturing human faces with realistic detail, emotion, and personality. The versatile Wyspiański was also an accomplished stage designer and writer. His patriotic play *The Wedding*—about the nuptials of a big-city artist and a peasant girl—is regarded as one of Poland's finest dramas. The largest collection of Wyspiański's art is in Kraków's Wyspiański Museum, but you'll also see examples in Kraków's St. Francis' Basilica and Warsaw's National Museum.

Józef Mehoffer (may-HOH-fehr), Wyspiański's good friend and rival, was another great Młoda Polska artist. Mehoffer's style is more expressionistic and abstract than Wyspiański's, often creating an otherworldly effect. See Mehoffer's work in Kraków's St. Francis' Basilica and at the artist's former residence (see the Józef Mehoffer House, later); and in Warsaw, at the National Museum.

Other names to look for include **Jacek Malczewski** (mahl-CHEHV-skee), who specialized in self-portraits, and **Olga Boznańska** (bohz-NAHN-skah), the movement's only prominent female artist. Both are featured in Warsaw's National Museum; Malczewski's works also appear in Kraków's Gallery of 19th-Century Polish Art.

as Żywiec, Okocim, or Lech), or a shot of *wódka* (Żubrówka is a good brand; for more on Polish drinks, see page 270). For a higher vantage point, the Cloth Hall's **Café Szał** terrace, overlooking the Square and St. Mary's Church, has one of the nicest views in town (open daily until 24:00, terrace costs 2 zł to enter except free on Sun-Mon and after 20:00, 10-15-zł drinks, some light meals, enter through Gallery of 19th-Century Polish Art entrance).

As the Square buzzes around you, imagine this place before 1989. There were no outdoor cafés, no touristy souvenir stands, and no salesmen hawking cotton candy and quacking or chirping mouthpieces. The communist government shut down all but a handful of the businesses. They didn't want people to congregate here—they should be at home, resting, because "a rested worker is a productive worker." The buildings were covered with soot from the nearby Lenin Steelworks in Nowa Huta. The communists denied the pollution, and when the student "Green Brigades" staged a demonstration in this Square to raise awareness in the 1970s, they were immediately arrested. How things have changed.

· *The huge, yellow building right in the middle of the Square is the...*

▲▲Cloth Hall (Sukiennice)

In the Middle Ages, this was the place where cloth-sellers had their market stalls. Kazimierz the Great turned the Cloth Hall into a permanent structure in the 14th century. In 1555, it burned down, and was replaced by the current building. The letter *S* (at the top of the gable above the entryway) stands for King Sigismund the Old, who commissioned this version of the hall. As Sigismund fancied all things Italian (including women—he

married an Italian princess), this structure is in the Italianate Renaissance style. Sigismund kicked off a nationwide trend, and you'll still see Renaissance-style buildings like this one all over the country—making the style as typically Polish as it is typi-

cally Italian. We'll see more works by Sigismund's imported Italian architects at Wawel Castle.

Recently restored and gleaming, the Cloth Hall is still a functioning market—selling mostly souvenirs, including wood carvings, chess sets, jewelry (especially amber), painted boxes, and trinkets (summer Mon-Fri 9:00-18:00, Sat-Sun 9:00-15:00, sometimes later; winter Mon-Fri 9:00-16:00, Sat-Sun 9:00-15:00). Cloth Hall prices are slightly inflated, but still cheap by American standards. You're paying a little extra for the convenience and the atmosphere, but you'll see locals buying gifts here, too.

WCs and telephones are at each end of the Cloth Hall. The upstairs of the Cloth Hall is home to the excellent **Gallery of 19th-Century Polish Art** (described later, under "Sights in Kraków").

• *Browse through the Cloth Hall passageway. As you emerge into the other half of the Square, the big tower on your left is the...*

Town Hall Tower

This is all that remains of a town hall building from the 14th century—when Kraków was the powerful capital of Poland. (The model to the right of the stairs shows the complete, original structure.) After the 18th-century partitions of Poland, Kraków's prominence took a nosedive. By the 19th century, Kraków was Nowheresville. As the town's importance crumbled, so did its town hall. It was cheaper to tear down the building than to repair it, and all that was left standing was this nearly 200-foot-tall tower. In summer, you can climb the tower, stopping along the way to poke around an exhibit on Kraków history—but the views from up top are disappointing.

Cost and Hours: 6 zł, April-Oct daily 10:30-18:00, last entry 30 minutes before closing, closed Nov-March.

Nearby: The **gigantic head** at the base of the Town Hall Tower (the opposite end from the Cloth Hall) is a sculpture by

 contemporary artist Igor Mitoraj, who studied here in Kraków. Typical of Mitoraj's works, the head is an empty shell that appears to be wrapped in cloth. It was originally intended to be placed near the train station. But because of construction delays at the station, it found a home here on the Square. While some locals enjoy having a work by their fellow Krakovian in such a prominent place, others disapprove of its sharp contrast with the Square's genteel Old World ambience. Tourists enjoy playing peek-a-boo with the head's eyes.

• *When you're finished on the Square, we'll head toward Wawel Hill. But we'll take a one-block detour from the Royal Way to introduce you to one of Kraków's best churches. Leave on the street called ulica Bracka, in the middle of the bottom of the Square (next to the Deutsche Bank, straight ahead from the end of the Cloth Hall). Follow this one long*

KRAKÓW

block (and across the busy Franciszkańska street) directly to the side door of a big red-brick church. Go ye.

▲▲St. Francis' Basilica (Bazylika Św. Franciszka)

This beautiful Gothic church, which was Pope John Paul II's home church while he was archbishop of Kraków, features some of Poland's best Art Nouveau in situ (in the setting for which it was intended). After an 1850 fire, it was redecorated by the two leading members of the Młoda Polska (Young Poland) movement: Stanisław Wyspiański and Józef Mehoffer. These two talented and fiercely competitive Krakovians were friends who apprenticed together under Poland's greatest painter, Jan Matejko. The glorious decorations of this church are the result of their great rivalry run amok. (For more Wyspiański or Mehoffer, visit their museums—described later, under "Sights in Kraków.")

Cost and Hours: Free, daily 6:00-19:45—but frequent services, so be discreet.

⊙ Self-Guided Tour: To the right of the side door, notice the board displaying death announcements for community mem-

bers. Entering through this door, turn left into the altar area to enjoy the paintings and stained-glass windows by **Stanisław Wyspiański.** The windows flanking the high altar represent the Blessed Salomea (left, the church's founder, buried in a side chapel) and St. Francis (right, the church's namesake). Salomea was a medieval Polish woman who became queen of Hungary, but later returned to Poland and entered a convent after her husband's death. Notice she's dropping a crown—repudiating the earthly world and giving herself over to the simple, stop-and-smell-God's-roses lifestyle of St. Francis.

As you face the back of the church, look at the window in the rear of the nave: *God the Father Let It Be,* Wyspiański's finest masterpiece. The colors beneath the Creator change from yellows and oranges (fire) to soothing blues (water), depending on the light. Wyspiański was supposedly inspired by

Michelangelo's vision of God in the Sistine Chapel, though he used a street beggar to model God's specific features. Wyspiański also painted the delightful floral designs decorating the walls of the nave—fitting for a church dedicated to a saint so famous for his spiritual connection to nature. (For more on Wyspiański, see page 293.)

The chapel on the right side of the nave (as you face the back of

the church) contains some evocative Stations of the Cross. This is **Józef Mehoffer**'s response to Wyspiański's work. The centerpiece of the room is a replica of the Shroud of Turin—which, since it touched the original shroud, is also considered a holy relic.

Back out in the nave, the modern painting (with an orange-and-blue background, midway up the nave on the left as you face the back of the church) depicts **St. Maksymilian Kolbe,** the Catholic priest who sacrificed his own life to save a fellow inmate at Auschwitz (see his story on page 371). Kolbe is particularly beloved here, as he actually served at this church.

Just before going out the back door (below Wyspiański's stained-glass window), find the **silver plate** labeled "Jan Paweł II" on the second pew from the last (on right); this was Pope John Paul II's favorite place to pray when he lived in the Archbishop's Palace across the street.

• *Stepping outside (through the back door), look to the right. The light-yellow building across the street is the...*

Archbishop's Palace

This building (specifically, the window over the stone entryway) was Pope John Paul II's residence when he was the archbishop of Kraków. When he became Pope, it

remained his home-away-from-Rome for visits to his hometown. After a long day of saying formal Mass during his visits to Kraków, he'd wind up here. Weary as he was, before going to bed he'd stand in the window for hours, chatting casually with the people assembled below—about religion, but also about sports, current events, and whatever was on their minds. In 2005, when the Pope's health deteriorated, this street filled with his

Karol Wojtyła (1920-2005): The Life and Death of the Greatest Pole

Karol Wojtyła was born to a humble family in the town of Wadowice near Kraków on May 18, 1920. Karol's mother died when he was a young boy. When he was older, he moved with his father to Kraków to study philosophy and drama at Jagiellonian University. Young Karol was gregarious and athletic—an avid skier, hiker, swimmer, and soccer goalie. During the Nazi occupation in World War II, he was forced to work in a quarry. In defiance of the Nazis, he secretly studied theology and appeared in illegal underground theatrical productions. When the war ended, he resumed his studies, now at the theology faculty.

After graduating in 1947, Wojtyła swiftly rose through the ranks of the Catholic Church hierarchy. By 1964, he was archbishop of Kraków, and just three years later, he became the youngest cardinal ever in the Roman Catholic Church. Throughout the 1960s, he fought an ongoing battle with the regime when they refused to allow the construction of a church in the Kraków suburb of Nowa Huta. After years of saying Mass for huge crowds in open fields, Wojtyła finally convinced the communists to allow the construction of the Lord's Ark Church in 1977. A year later, just as Poland was facing its darkest hour, Karol Wojtyła was called to the papacy—the first non-Italian pope in more than four centuries. In 1979, he paid a visit to his native Poland. In a series of cautiously provocative speeches, he demonstrated to his countrymen the potential for mass opposition to communism.

Imagine you're Polish in the 1970s. Your country was devastated by World War II, and has struggled under an oppressive regime ever since. Food shortages are epidemic. Lines stretch around the block even to buy a measly scrap of bread. Life is bleak, oppressive, and hopeless. Then someone who speaks your language—someone you've admired your entire life, and one of the only people you've seen successfully stand up to the regime—becomes one of the world's most influential people. A Pole like you is the leader of a billion Catholics. He makes you believe that the impossible can happen. He says to you again and again: *"Nie lękajcie się"*—"Have no fear." And you begin to believe it.

In addition to encouraging his countrymen, the Pope had a knack for challenging the communists. He'd push at them strongly enough to get his point across, but never went so far

supporters, even though the Pope was in Rome. For days, somber locals focused their vigil on this same window, their eyes fixed on a black crucifix that had been placed here. At 21:37 on the night of April 2, 2005, the Pope passed away in Rome. Ten thousand Krakovians were in this street, under this window, listening to a Mass broadcast on loudspeakers from the church. When the priest announced the Pope's death, every single person simultaneously

as to jeopardize the stature of the Church in Poland. Gentle but pointed wordplay was his specialty. The inspirational role he played in the lives of Lech Wałęsa and the other leaders of Solidarity gave them the courage to stand up to the communists (for more on Solidarity, see page 457). Many people (including Mikhail Gorbachew) credit Pope John Paul II for the collapse of Eastern European communism.

Even as John Paul II's easy charisma attracted new worshippers to the Church (especially young people), his conservatism on issues such as birth control, homosexuality, and female priests pushed away many Catholics. Under his watch, the Church struggled with embarrassing pedophilia scandals in the US, Ireland, and elsewhere. Many still fault him for turning a blind eye and not putting a stop to these abuses much earlier. By the end of his papacy, John Paul II's failing health and old-fashioned politics had caused him to lose stature in worldwide public opinion. And yet, approval of the Pope never waned in Poland. His countrymen—even the relatively few atheists and agnostics—saw John Paul II both as the greatest hero of their people...and as a member of the family, like a kindly grandfather.

When Pope John Paul II died on April 2, 2005, the mourning in Poland was particularly deep and sustained. Though the Pope's passing was hardly unexpected, it created an overwhelming wave of grief that flooded the country for weeks. Musical performances of all kinds were canceled for a week after his death, and the irreverent MTV-style music channel simply went off the air out of respect.

Since John Paul II's death, Kraków has improvised some modest collections that celebrate his legacy. While there's still no definitive museum about the man, you'll find items relating to his life at the Archdiocesan Museum and John Paul II Center (both on Kanonicza street below the castle), and at the John Paul II Wawel Cathedral Museum (facing the cathedral); all of these are described in this chapter.

A speedy six years after his death, Karol Wojtyła was beatified in May of 2011; sainthood is all but certain to follow. Out of 265 popes, only two have been given the title "great." There's already talk in Rome of increasing that number to three. Someday soon we may speak of this man as "John Paul the Great." His countrymen already do.

fell to their knees in silence. For the next several days, thousands of the faithful continued to stand in this street, staring intently at the window where they last saw the man they considered to be the greatest Pole.

• *Now turn right, walk along the side of the church, pass a few monuments and a tram stop, and turn right again down busy...*

KRAKÓW

Grodzka Street

Now you're back on the Royal Way proper. At the corner of Grodzka street stands the modern, copper-colored **Wyspiański Pavilion.** In addition to housing a handy TI (inside—not the ticket window out front) and a conference center, this building features three new stained-glass windows based on designs Wyspiański once submitted for a contest to redecorate Wawel Cathedral. While these designs were rejected back then, they were finally realized on the hundredth anniversary of his death (in 2007). Visible from inside the building during the day (step inside to see them), and gloriously illuminated to be seen outside the building at night, they represent three Polish historical figures: The gaunt St. Stanisław (Poland's first saint), the skeletal Kazimierz the Great (in the middle), and the swooning King Henry the Pious.

Now continue down Grodzka street. This lively thoroughfare, connecting the Square with Wawel, is teeming with shops— and some of Kraków's best restaurants (see "Eating in Kraków," later). Survey your options now, and choose (and maybe reserve) your favorite for dinner tonight. This street is also characterized by its fine arcades over the sidewalks. While this might seem like a charming Renaissance feature, the arcades were actually added by the Nazis after they invaded in 1939; they wanted to convert Kraków into a city befitting its status as the capital of their Polish puppet state.

This is also a good street to find some of Kraków's **milk bars** (three are listed on page 357). The most traditional one is about two blocks down, on the right (at #45), with a simple *Bar Mleczny* sign. These government-subsidized cafeterias are the locals' choice for a quick, cheap, filling, lowbrow lunch. Prices are deliriously cheap (soup costs less than a dollar), and the food isn't bad. For more on milk bars, see page 269. Or, for an even quicker bite, buy an *obwarzanek* (ring-shaped roll, typically fresh) from a street vendor.
• *One more block ahead, the small square on your right is...*

Mary Magdalene Square (Plac Św. Marii Magdaleny)

Back when Kraków was just a village, this was its main square. Today it offers a great visual example of Kraków's deeply religious character. In the Middle Ages, Kraków was known as "Small Rome" for its many churches. Today, there are 142 churches and monasteries within the city limits (32 in the Old Town alone)— more per square mile than anywhere outside Rome. You can see several of them from this spot: The nearest, with the picturesque white façade and red dome, is the **Church of Saints Peter and Paul** (Kraków's first Baroque church, and a popular tourist concert venue). The statues lining this church's façade are the 11 apostles (minus Judas), plus Mary Magdalene, the square's namesake. The next church to the right, with the twin towers, is the Romanesque **St. Andrew's** (now with a Baroque interior). According to legend, a spring inside this church provided water to citizens who holed up here during Tatar invasions in the 13th century. If you look farther down the street, you can see three more churches. And the square next to you used to be a church, too—it burned in 1855, and only its footprint survives.

• *Go through the square (admiring the sculpture on the column that won Kraków's distinguished "ugliest statue" award in 2002), and turn left down...*

Kanonicza Street (Ulica Kanonicza)

With so many churches around here, the clergy had to live somewhere. Many lived on this well-preserved street—supposedly the oldest street in Kraków. As you walk, look for the cardinal hats over three different doorways. The Hotel Copernicus, on the left, is named for a famous guest who stayed here five centuries ago. On the right at #17, the **Bishop Erazm Ciołek Palace** hosts a good exhibit of medieval art and Orthodox icons. Next door, the yellow house on the right (#19) is where Karol Wojtyła lived for 10 years after World War II—long before he became Pope John Paul II. Today this building houses the **Archdiocesan Museum,** which features a few sparse exhibits about Kraków's favorite son. Across the street is the **John Paul II Center,** which has another modest exhibit about the late pontiff, and also provides information about a major complex being built in his honor. These two exhibits are worth visiting if you want to know more about the man. All three of these sights are described later, under "Sights in Kraków."

• *At the end of Kanonicza street, our self-guided walk is finished. But there's still much more to see. Across the busy street, a ramp leads up to the most important piece of ground in all of Poland: Wawel.*

Sights in Kraków

Wawel Hill

Wawel (VAH-vehl), a symbol of Polish royalty and independence, is sacred territory to every Polish person. A castle has stood here since the beginning of Poland's recorded history. Today, Wawel—awash in tourists—is the most visited sight in the country. Crowds and an overly complex admissions system for the hill's many

historic sights can be exasperating. Thankfully, a stroll through the cathedral and around the castle grounds requires no tickets, and—with the help of the following commentary—is enough. I've described these sights in the order of a handy self-guided walk. The many museums on Wawel (all described in this section) are mildly interesting, but can be skipped (grounds open daily from 6:00 until dusk, inner courtyard closes 30 minutes earlier).

• *From Kanonicza street—where my self-guided walk ends—head up the long ramp to the castle entry.*

Entry Ramp

Huffing up this ramp, it's easy to imagine how this location—rising above the otherwise flat plains around Kraków—was both strategic and easy to defend. When Kraków was part of the Habsburg Empire in the 19th century, the Austrians turned this castle complex into a fortress, destroying much of its delicate beauty. When Poland regained its independence after World War I, the castle was returned to its former glory. The bricks you see on your left as you climb the ramp bear the names of Poles from around the world who donated to the cause.

The jaunty equestrian statue ahead is **Tadeusz Kościuszko** (1746-1817)—a familiar name to many Americans. Kościuszko was a hero of the American Revolution and helped design West Point. When he returned to Poland, he fought bravely but unsuccessfully against the Russians (during the Partitions that would divide Poland's territory among three neighboring powers). Kościuszko also gave his name to several American towns, a county in Indiana, a type of mustard from Illinois, and the tallest mountain in Australia.

• *Hiking through the Heraldic Gate next to Kościuszko, you pass the ticket office (if you'll be going into the museums, use the other ticket office, with shorter lines, on top of the hill—see "Tickets and Reservations," later). As you crest the hill, on your left is...*

▲▲Wawel Cathedral

Poland's national church is its Westminster Abbey. While the history buried here is pretty murky to most Americans, to Poles, this church is *the* national mausoleum. It holds the tombs of nearly all of Poland's most important rulers and greatest historical figures.

Cost and Hours: It's usually free to walk around the main part of the church. You must buy a 12-zł ticket to climb up the tall-

est tower, visit the crypt and the royal tombs, and tour the John Paul II Wawel Cathedral Museum. Buy this ticket at the house across from the cathedral entry, where you can also rent an audio-guide (7 zł). The cathedral is open April-Sept Mon-Sat 9:00-17:00, Sun 12:30-17:00; Oct-March Mon-Sat 9:00-16:00, Sun 12:30-16:00; last entry 15 minutes before closing (tel. 12-429-9516, www .katedra-wawelska.pl). Note that the cathedral's museum (described later) is closed on Sunday.

Cathedral Exterior—Go around to the far side of the cathedral to take in its profile. This uniquely eclectic church is the product of centuries of haphazard additions...yet somehow, it works. It began as a simple, stripped-down Romanesque church in the 12th century. (The white base of the nearest tower is original. In fact, anything at Wawel that's made of white limestone like this was probably part of the earliest Romanesque structures.) Kazimierz the Great and his predecessors gradually surrounded the cathedral with some 20 chapels, which were further modified over the centuries—making this beautiful church a happy hodgepodge of styles. To give you a sense of the historical sweep, scan the chapels from left to right: 14th-century Gothic, 12th-century Romanesque (the base of the tower), 17th-century Baroque (the inside is Baroque, though the exterior is a copy of its Renaissance neighbor), 16th-century Renaissance, and 18th- and 19th-century Neoclassical. (This variety in styles is even more evident in the chapels' interiors, which we'll see soon.)

Pay attention to the two particularly interesting domed chapels to the right of the tall tower. The gold one is the Sigismund Chapel, housing memorials to the Jagiellonian kings—including Sigismund the Old, who was responsible for Kraków's Renaissance renovation in the 16th century. Poles consider this chapel, made with 80 pounds of gold, to be the finest Renaissance chapel north of the Alps. The copper-domed chapel next to it, home to the Swedish Waza dynasty, resembles its neighbor (but it's a copy built 150 years later, and without all that gold). The tallest tower, called the Sigismund Tower, has a clock with only an hour hand.

Go back around and face the front entry for more architectonic silliness. You see Gothic chapels (with pointy windows) flanking the door, a Renaissance ceiling, lavish Baroque decoration over the door, and some big bones (thought to have come from extinct animals). Years ago, these were taken for the bones of giants and put here as an oddity to be viewed by the public. (Back then, there were no museums, so notable items like these were used to lure people to the church.) It's said that as long as the bones hang here, the cathedral will stand. The door is the original from the 14th century, with fine wrought-iron work. The *K* with the crown stands for Kazimierz the Great. The black marble frame is made of Kraków stone from nearby quarries.

Cathedral Interior—The cathedral interior is slathered in Baroque memorials and tombs, decorated with tapestries, and soaked in Polish history.

❷ Self-Guided Tour: After you step inside, you'll follow the one-way, clockwise route that leads you through the choir, then

around the back of the apse, then back to the entry.

At the entry, look straight ahead to see the silver tomb under a **canopy,** inspired by the one in St. Peter's Basilica at the Vatican. It contains the remains of the first Polish saint, Stanisław (from the 11th century).

Go behind this canopy into the ornately carved **choir** area. For 200 years, the colorful chair to the right of the high altar has been the seat of Kraków's archbishops, including Karol Wojtyła, who served here for 14 years before becoming pope.

Now you'll continue into the left aisle. From here, if you have a ticket, you can enter two of the optional attractions: Seventy claustrophobic wooden stairs lead up to the 11-ton **Sigismund Bell** and pleasant views of the steeples and spires of Kraków. Then, closer to the front of the church, descend into the little **crypt** (with a rare purely Romanesque interior), which houses the remains of Adam Mickiewicz—the Romantic poet whose statue dominates the Main Market Square.

Now continue around the apse (behind the main altar). After curving around to the right, look for the red-marble tomb (on the right) of The Great One—**Kazimierz,** of course. (Look for *Kazimierz Wielki*—at his feet is what appears to be a beaver.) A few more steps toward the entrance, on the left, is the **Chapel of the Blessed John Paul II.** While Karol Wojtyła's remains are in St. Peter's Basilica in Rome, this chapel was recently converted to honor him—with a plaque in the floor and an altar with his picture. Someday, Poles hope, he may be moved here (but, the Vatican says, don't hold your breath).

On the right is the white sarcophagus of **St. Jadwiga** (with a dog at her feet). This 14th-century "King" of Poland helped Christianize Lithuania, fought the Teutonic Knights, kicked off

the grand Jagiellonian dynasty, and was sainted by Pope John Paul II in 1997. (The sexist bigwigs of the time begrudgingly allowed her to take the throne, but refused to call her "Queen.") All the flowers here prove she remains popular with Poles today. Across from Jadwiga, peek into the gorgeous 16th-century **Sigismund Chapel,** with its silver altar (this is the gold-roofed chapel you just saw from outside). Then, look into the **Waza Chapel**: Remember that its exterior matches the restrained, Renaissance style of the Sigismund Chapel, but the interior is clearly Baroque, slathered with gold and silver.

Just beyond is a door leading back outside. If you don't have a ticket, your tour is finished—head out here. But those with a ticket can keep circling around.

To the left of the main door, take a look at the Gothic **Holy Cross Chapel,** with its seemingly Orthodox-style 14th-century frescoes.

In the back corner of the church is the entrance to the **royal tombs** (you'll exit outside the church, so be sure you're done in here first). The first big room houses Poland's greatest war heroes: Kościuszko (of American Revolution fame), Jan III Sobieski (who successfully defended Vienna from the Ottomans; he's in the simple black coffin with the gold inscription *J III S*), Sikorski, Poniatowski, and so on. Then you'll wander through several rooms of second-tier Polish kings, queens, and their kids. Marshal Józef Piłsudski, the WWI hero who seized power and ruled Poland from 1926 to 1935, has the last grave (in the room on the right, just before you exit). His tomb was moved here so the rowdy soldiers who came to pay their respects wouldn't disturb the others. You may notice that there's one VIP (Very Important Pole) who's missing...Karol Wojtyła, a.k.a. John Paul II. The late pontiff left no specific requests for his body, and the Vatican controversially (to Poles, at least) chose to entomb him in Vatican City, instead of sending him back home to Wawel.

• *Nearby (and covered by the same ticket as the tower and crypt) is the cathedral's museum.*

John Paul II Wawel Cathedral Museum—This small museum, up the little staircase across from the cathedral entry, was recently spiffed up and re-dedicated to Kraków's favorite archbishop. It fills four rooms with artifacts relating to both the cathedral and John Paul II.

Downstairs is the Royal Room, with vestments, swords, regalia, holy robes, and items that were once buried with the kings,

KRAKÓW

as well as early treasury items (from the 11th through 16th centuries). Upstairs are a later treasury collection (17th through 20th centuries) and a "Papal Room" with items from John Paul II's life: his armchair, vestments, and miter (pointy pope hat—notice how the golden decorations on this one incorporate the Black Madonna of Częstochowa), plus souvenirs from his travels.

As admission to this museum is included with your ticket to the cathedral's special options (Sigismund Bell tower, plus crypt and royal tombs), this collection is worth a quick look if you have the time—especially if you're interested in John Paul II (covered by 12-zł cathedral ticket; April-Sept Mon-Sat 9:00-17:00, closed Sun; Oct-March Mon-Sat 9:00-16:00, closed Sun; pick up free brochure at entrance, tel. 12-429-3321).

• *When you're finished with the cathedral sights, stroll around the...*

▲▲Wawel Castle Grounds

In the rest of the castle, you'll uncover more fragments of Kraków's history, and have the opportunity to visit several museums. While I consider the museums skippable, if you want to visit them, buy tickets before you enter the inner courtyard. Read the descriptions on page 309 to decide which museums appeal to you.

◑ Self-Guided Walk: This tour, which doesn't enter any of the attractions, is plenty for most visitors.

• *Behind the cathedral, a grand green-and-pink entryway leads into the palace's dramatically Renaissance-style...*

Inner Courtyard: If this space seems to have echoes of Florence, that's because it was designed and built by young Florentines after Kazimierz's original castle burned down. Notice the three distinct levels: The ground floor housed the private apartments of the higher nobility (governors and castle administrators); the middle level held the private apartments of the king; and the top floor—much taller, to allow more light to fill its large spaces—were the public state rooms of the king. The ivy-covered wing to the right of where you entered served as the headquarters of the notorious Nazi governor of German-occupied Poland, Hans

Frank. (He was tried and executed in Nürnberg after the war.) At the far end of the courtyard is a false wall, designed to create a pleasant Renaissance symmetry, and also to give the illusion that the castle is bigger than it is. Looking through the windows, notice that there's nothing but air on the other side. When foreign dignitaries visited, these windows could be covered to complete the illusion. The entrances to most Wawel museums are around this courtyard, and some believe that you'll find something even more special: chakra.

Adherents to the Hindu concept of **chakra** believe that a powerful energy field connects all living things. Some believe that, mirroring the seven chakra points on the body (from head to groin), there are seven points on the surface of the earth where this energy is most concentrated: Delhi, Delphi, Jerusalem, Mecca, Rome, Velehrad...and Wawel Hill—specifically over there in the corner (immediately to your left as you enter the courtyard). Look for peaceful people (here or elsewhere on the castle grounds) with their eyes closed. One thing's for sure: They're not thinking of Kazimierz the Great. The smudge marks on the wall are from people pressing up against this corner, trying to absorb some good vibes from this chakra spot.

The Wawel administration seems creeped out by all this. They've done what they can to discourage this ritual (such as putting up information boards right where the power is supposedly most focused), but believers still gravitate from far and wide to hug the wall. Give it a try...and let the Force be with you. (Just for fun, ask a Wawel tour guide about the chakra, and watch her squirm—they're forbidden to talk about it.)

• If you want to visit some of the **castle museums** (you can enter four of the five from this courtyard), you'll first need to buy tickets elsewhere. Stick with me for a little longer to finish up our tour of the grounds, and we'll wind up near a ticket office.

Head back out to the side of the cathedral to survey the...

Field of History: This hilltop has seen lots of changes over the years. Kazimierz the Great turned a small fortress into a mighty Gothic castle in the 14th century. Today, you'll see the cathedral and a castle complex, but little remains of Kazimierz's grand fortress, which burned to the ground in 1499. In the grassy field across from the cathedral, you'll see the **foundations** of two Gothic churches that were destroyed when the Austrians took over Wawel in the 19th century and needed a parade ground for their troops. (They built the red-brick hospital building beyond the field, now used by the Wawel administration.)

• *Head across to the gap in the buildings beyond the field, to the...*

Viewpoint over the Vistula: Belly up to the wall and enjoy the panorama over the Vistula River and Kraków's outskirts. From here, you can see some unusual landmarks, including the odd wavy-roofed building just across the river (which houses the Manggha Japanese art gallery). The symmetrical little bulge that tops the highest hill on the horizon is the **Kościuszko Mound** (see page 341).

Now look directly below you, along the riverbank, to find a fire-belching monument to the **dragon** that was instrumental in the founding of Kraków. Once upon a time, a prince named Krak founded a town on Wawel Hill. It was the perfect location—except for the fire-breathing dragon who lived in the caves under the hill and terrorized the town. Prince Krak had to feed the dragon all of the town's livestock to keep the monster from going after the townspeople. But Krak, with the help of a clever shoemaker, came up with a plan. They stuffed a sheep's skin with sulfur and left it outside the dragon's cave. The dragon swallowed it, and before long, developed a terrible case of heartburn. To put the fire out, the dragon started drinking water from the Vistula. He kept drinking and drinking until he finally exploded. The town was saved, and Kraków thrived.

If you want to head down to see the Vistula and the dragon close up, take a shortcut through the nearby **Dragon's Den** (Smocza Jama, enter at the little copper-roofed brick building). It's just a 135-step spiral staircase and a few underground caverns—worthwhile only as a quick way to get from the top of Wawel down to the banks of the Vistula (3 zł, pay at machine—coins only, April-Oct daily 10:00-17:00, July-Aug until 18:00, closed Nov-March).

If you'd like a higher viewpoint on the riverfront, you can pay 4 zł to climb 137 stairs to the top of the **Sandomierska Tower** (at the far end of the hill, past the visitors center, no elevator). But I'd skip it—disappointingly, the view from up top is only through small windows (May-Sept daily 10:00-18:00, June-Aug until 19:00, Oct Sat-Sun only 10:00-17:00, closed Nov-April).

• *Our Wawel tour is finished. If you'd like to explore some of the museums, you can buy your tickets in the nearby visitors center (head back into the main Wawel complex—with the empty field—and turn right); here you'll also find WCs,*

*a café, a gift shop, and other amenities. Or go down to the riverfront
park: Walk downhill (through the Dragon's Den, or use the main ramp
and simply circle around the base of the hill) to reach the park—one of
the most delightful places in Kraków to simply relax, with beautiful
views back on the castle complex.*

Wawel Castle Museums

There are five museums and exhibits in Wawel Castle (not including the cathedral and Cathedral Museum, the Dragon's Den, or
the Sandomierska Tower—all described above). Each has its own
admission and slightly different hours (tel. 12-422-5155, ext. 219,
www.wawel.krakow.pl). The castle sights don't have an audioguide, but English descriptions are posted. If you're visiting all of
the sights, start with the Royal State Rooms and/or Royal Private
Apartments (which share an entrance), then see the Oriental Art
exhibit (on your way back down from the Royal State Rooms), and
finally the Crown Treasury and Armory (back near where you
entered). Then head back out into the outer courtyard for the Lost
Wawel exhibit.

Tickets and Reservations: Each sight has individual ticket
prices (listed below). A 62-zł combo-ticket includes the Royal
State Rooms, Royal Private Apartments, and Crown Treasury and
Armory; for another 17 zł, you can add any other sight.

Wawel has two ticket windows. Most people line up at the
top of the entry ramp, but it's faster to buy tickets at the visitors
center at the far corner of the castle grounds (across the field from
the cathedral, near the café). You can buy tickets directly at the
door for two of the exhibits: Oriental Art and Lost Wawel.

A limited number of tickets are sold for the Royal State
Rooms, Royal Private Apartments (entry by guided, included tour
only), and Crown Treasury and Armory. Boards show how many
tickets for each of these are still available on the day you're there.
Tickets come with an assigned entry time (though you can usually
sneak in before your scheduled appointment). In the summer, ticket
lines can be long, and sights can sell out by midday. You can make
a free reservation for the tour of the Royal Private Apartments,
but if you book the Royal State Rooms and the Crown Armory
and Treasury in advance, you'll pay a 16-zł reservation fee for up to
nine people (tel. 12-422-1697). Frankly, the sights aren't worth all
the fuss—if they're sold out, you're not missing much.

Hours: Unless otherwise noted, the museums are open April-
Oct Tue-Fri 9:30-17:00, Sat-Sun 11:00-17:00, closed Mon; Nov-
March Tue-Sat 9:30-16:00, closed Sun-Mon; last entry one hour
before closing.

In summer (April-Oct), visiting on Mondays has its advantages: Although three of the museums are closed, the Lost Wawel

and the Crown Treasury and Armory are free and open 9:30-13:00. Off-season (Nov-March), everything is closed on Monday, but similar caveats apply to Sundays (when the Crown Treasury and Armory is closed, but Lost Wawel and the Royal State Rooms remain open).

▲Royal State Rooms (Komnaty Królewskie)—While precious to Poles, these rooms are mediocre by European standards.

Still, this is the best of the Wawel museums. First, climb up to the top floor and wander through some ho-hum halls with paintings and antique furniture. Along the way, you'll walk along the outdoor gallery (enjoying views down into the courtyard). Finally, you'll reach the Throne Room, with 30 carved heads in the ceiling. According to legend, one of these heads got mouthy when the king was trying to pass judgment—so its mouth has been covered to keep it quiet. Continue into some of the palace's finest rooms, with 16th-century Brussels tapestries (140 of the original series of 300 survive), remarkably decorated wooden ceilings, and gorgeous leather-tooled walls. Wandering these halls (with their period furnishings), you get a feeling for the 16th- and 17th-century glory days of Poland, when it was a leading power in Eastern Europe. The Senate Room, with its throne and elaborate tapestries, is the climax.

Cost and Hours: 18 zł, see hours above, plus Nov-March also open—and free—Sun 10:00-16:00, enter through courtyard.

Royal Private Apartments (Prywatne Apartamenty Królewskie)—The rooms, which look similar to the State Rooms, can only be visited with a guided (and included) tour.

Cost and Hours: 25 zł, request English tour when buying your ticket—they depart 3/hour, see hours listed above, enter through courtyard.

Oriental Art (Sztuka Wschodu)—While small, this exhibit displays swords, carpets, banners, vases, and remarkable Turkish tents used by the Ottomans during the 1683 Battle of Vienna. These are trophies of Jan III Sobieski, the Polish king who led a pan-European army to victory in that battle.

Cost and Hours: 8 zł, tickets sold at the door, see hours listed earlier, enter through courtyard; don't miss entry on your way back downstairs from Royal State Rooms.

Crown Treasury and Armory (Skarbiec i Zbrojownia)—This is a decent collection of swords, saddles, and shields; ornately decorated muskets, crossbows, and axes; and cannons in the base-

ment. Off in a smaller side room are some of the most precious
items. Look for the regalia given to Jan III Sobieski as thanks for
his defeat of the Ottoman invaders in the Battle of Vienna: giant
swords consecrated by the pope and the mantle (robe) of the Order
of the Holy Ghost from France's King Louis XIV. Nearby is the
13th-century coronation sword of the Polish kings, and some gorgeously inlaid rifles.

Cost and Hours: 18 zł, see hours listed earlier, plus April-Oct
also open—and free—Mon 9:30-13:00, enter through courtyard.

▲**Lost Wawel (Wawel Zaginiony)**—This exhibit traces the
history of the hill and its various churches and castles. Begin by
viewing the model of the entire castle complex in the 18th century
(pre-Austrian razing). From here, the one-way route leads through
scarcely explained excavations of a 10th-century church. The collection includes models of the cathedral at various historical stages
(originally Romanesque—much simpler, before all the colorful,
bulbous domes, chapels, and towers were added—then Gothic,
and so on). Circling back to the entrance, find the display of fascinating decorative tiles from 16th-century stoves that once heated
the place.

Cost and Hours: 8 zł, tickets sold at the door, see hours listed
earlier, plus April-Oct also open—and free—Mon 9:30-13:00;
Nov-March also open—and free—Sun 9:30-13:00; enter near
snack bar across from side of cathedral.

National Museum Branches

Kraków's National Museum (Muzeum Narodowe) is made up
of a series of small but interesting collections scattered throughout the city (www.muzeum.krakow.pl). I've listed the best of the
National Museum's branches below. All of these are free to enter
on Sunday.

▲▲**Gallery of 19th-Century Polish Art (Galeria Sztuki
Polskiej XIX Wieku)**—This surprisingly enjoyable collection of
works by obscure Polish artists fills the recently renovated upper
level of the Cloth Hall. While you probably won't recognize any
of the Polish names in here—and this collection isn't quite as fine
as Warsaw's National Gallery—some of these paintings are just
plain good. It's worth a visit to see some Polish canvases in their
native land, and to enjoy views over the Square from the hall's
upper terraces.

Cost and Hours: 12 zł, free on Sun, dry audioguide-5 zł,
comprehensive guidebook-40 zł, Tue-Sat 10:00-20:00, Sun 10:00-
18:00, closed Mon, last entry 30 minutes before closing, entrance
on side of Cloth Hall facing Adam Mickiewicz statue, tel. 12-424-
4600.

Background: Keep in mind that during the 19th century—

when every piece of art in this museum was created—there was no "Poland." The country had been split up among its powerful neighbors in a series of three Partitions, and would not appear again on the map of Europe until after World War I. Meanwhile, the 19th century was a period of national revival throughout Europe, when various until-then-marginalized ethnic groups began to take pride in what made them different from their neighbors. So the artists you see represented here were grappling with trying to forge a national identity at a time when they didn't even have a nation. You'll sense a pessimism that comes from a country that feels abused by foreign powers, mingled with a resolute spirit of national pride.

◊ Self-Guided Tour: The small collection fills just four rooms. On a quick visit, skip the museum's audioguide and guidebook and just enjoy the canvases, focusing on the highlights I mention here.

Entering the Cloth Hall, buy your ticket and head up the stairs—pausing to peek out onto the inviting café terrace for a fine view of the Square and St. Mary's. Then continue up to the main exhibit.

The first two small rooms don't feature much of interest. You enter **Room I** (Bacciarelli Room), with works from the Enlightenment; straight ahead is **Room II** (Michałowski Room), featuring Romantic works from 1822 to 1863.

The two larger rooms merit a linger. From Room I, turn right into **Room III** (Siemiradzki Room). This hall features art of the Academy, which was "conformist" art embraced by the art critics of the day. Entering the room, turn right and survey the canvases counterclockwise. The space is dominated by the works of Jan Matejko, a remarkably productive painter who specialized in epic historical scenes that he presented in such a way as to comment on his own era (for more on Matejko, see page 409). The first big canvas is his depiction of Wenyhora, a (possibly fictional) late-18th-century Ukrainian soothsayer who, according to legend, foretold Poland's hardships—the three Partitions, Poland's pact with Napoleon, and its difficulties regaining nationhood. Like many Poles of the era, Matejko was preoccupied with Poland's tragic fate, imbuing this scene with an air of inevitable tragedy. A similar gloominess is reflected in the *Death of Ellenai*, by Jacek Malczewski, although this artist comes from a younger generation. The main characters in a Polish Romantic poem, Ellenai and Anhelli, have been exiled to a remote cabin in Siberia (in Russia—

one of the great powers occupying Poland). Just when they think things can't get worse, Ellenai dies. Anhelli sits immobilized by grief.

Farther down is a gigantic canvas by Matejko: Tadeusz Kościuszko—a hero of the American Revolution, now back in

his native Poland fighting the Russians—doffs his hat after his unlikely victory at the battle at Racławice. In this battle (which ultimately had little bearing on Russia's drive to overtake Poland), a ragtag army of

Polish peasants defeated the Russian forces. Kościuszko is clad in an American uniform, symbolizing Matjeko's respect for the American ideals of democracy and self-determination.

To the left, a smaller Matejko painting shows the last Grand Master of the fearsome Teutonic Knights swearing allegiance to the Polish king in 1525. This historic ceremony took place in the Main Market Square in Kraków, the capital at the time. Notice the Cloth Hall and the spires of St. Mary's Church in the background. Matejko has painted his own face on one of his favorite historical figures, the jester Stańczyk (at the foot of the throne; for more on Stańczyk, see page 409).

Dominating the far wall is *Nero's Torches,* by Henryk Siemiradzki. On the left, Roman citizens eagerly gather to watch Christians being burned

at the stake (on the right). The symbolism is clear: The meek and downtrodden (whether Christians in the time of Rome, or Poles in the heyday of Russia

and Austria) may be persecuted now, but we have faith that their noble ideals will ultimately prevail.

On the next wall, Pantaleon Szyndler's *Bathing Girl* evokes the orientalism popular in 19th-century Europe, when romanticized European notions of the Orient (such as harem slave girls) were popular artistic themes. Already voyeuristic, the painting was originally downright lewd until Szyndler painted over a man leering at the woman from the left side of the canvas.

The predominantly pessimistic theme continues with Matejko's *Rejtan: The Fall of Europe,* in which a prince, who has just been poisoned, clutches his chest and breathes his last. On a lighter note, Tadeusz Ajdukiewicz's portrait of Helena Modrzejewska depicts a popular actress of the time attending a party in this very building.

Finally, backtrack through Room I and continue into **Room IV** (Chełmoński Room). Featuring works of the late 19th century, this section includes Realism and the first inklings of Symbolism and Impressionism. Just as elsewhere in Europe (including Paris, where many of these artists trained), artists were beginning to throw off the conventions of the Academy and embrace their own muse.

As you proceed counterclockwise through the room, the next stretch of canvases features landscapes and genre paintings. Tune into a couple of appealing nature scenes: Józef Chełmoński's small and misty *Cranes*, and Władyslaw Malecki's *A Gathering of Storks*, in which the majestic birds stand under big willows in front of the setting sun. Even seemingly innocent wildlife paintings have a political message: Storks are particularly numerous in Poland, making them a subtle patriotic symbol.

Linger over Józef Brandt's excellent battle scenes (often involving a foe from the East). The Jewish artist Samuel Hirszenberg's *School of Talmudists* features young Jewish students poring over the Talmud (including one, deeply lost in thought, who may be pondering more than ancient Jewish law).

Dominating the end of the room is Józef Chełmoński's energy-charged *Four-in-Hand*, depicting a Ukrainian horseman giving a lift to a pipe-smoking nobleman.

Heading back toward the entrance, on the right wall, watch for Witold Pruszkowski's *Water Nymphs*. Based on Slavic legends (and wearing traditional Ukrainian costumes), these mischievous ladies have just taken one victim (see his hand in the foreground) and are about to descend on another (seen faintly in the upper-right corner). Beyond this painting are

some travel pictures from Italy and France (including some that are very Impressionistic, suggesting a Parisian influence).

Flanking the door are two of this room's best works. First, on the right, is Władysław Podkowiński's gripping *Frenzy* (whose title, tellingly, has variously been translated as *Ecstasy* or *Insanity*). A pale, sensuous woman—possibly based on a socialite for whom the artist fostered a desperate but unrequited love—clutches an all-fired-up black stallion. This sexually charged painting caused a frenzy indeed at its 1894 unveiling—leading the unbalanced artist to attack his own creation with a knife (you can still see the slash marks in the canvas).

On the other side of the door is Jacek Malczewski's poignant *Introduction*, showing a young painter's apprentice on a bench contemplating his future. Surrounded by nature and with his painter's tools beside him, it's easy to imagine this as a self-portrait of the artist as a young man...wondering if he's choosing the correct path.

More Art Treasures Possibly on Display at the Gallery: While the Czartoryski Museum (described later) is closed for restoration, its two finest pieces may be temporarily displayed in this museum. When you visit, ask about the following works—although they're neither 19th century nor Polish, they're a thrill even for non-art-lovers:

Lady with an Ermine **(1489 or 1490), by Leonardo da Vinci:** This small (21" x 16"), simple portrait of a teenage girl is one of the most influential paintings in art history, and a rare surviving work by one of history's greatest minds. The girl is likely Cecilia Gallerani, the young mistress of the Duke of Milan, Leonardo's employer. The ermine (white during winter) suggests several overlapping meanings, including a symbol of chastity (thus praising Cecilia's questioned virtue) and a naughty reference to the Duke's nickname, "Ermellino"—notice that his mistress is sensually, um, "stroking the ermine."

Painted before the *Mona Lisa*, the portrait was immediately recognized as revolutionary. Cecilia turns to look off-camera at someone. Leonardo catches her in an unguarded moment, giving the viewer a behind-the-scenes look unheard-of in the days of the posed, front-facing formal portrait. Her simple gestures and faraway gaze speak volumes about her inner thoughts and personality. Leonardo tweaks the generic Renaissance "pyramid" composition by turning it to three-quarters angle and softening it with curved lines—from her eyes, down her cheek and sloping shoulders, then doubling back across her folded arms. The background—once gray and blue—was painted black in the 19th century.

Lady with an Ermine is one of only three surviving oil paintings by Leonardo. It's better preserved than her famous cousin in Paris *(Mona Lisa)*, and—many think—simply more beautiful. Can we be sure it's really by the enigmatic Leonardo? Yep—the master's fingerprints were literally found pressed into the paint (he was known to work areas of his paintings directly with his fingertips).

Landscape with the Good Samaritan **(1638), by Rembrandt van Rijn:** This small, remarkably detailed painting depicts the popular parable. On the right, the barely visible Samaritan helps the wounded, half-naked man onto his horse (as a little boy and girl look on). To the left, much farther down the road (just beyond the waterfall and bridge), find the two tiny figures walking: the priest and the Levite who had passed the injured man by. The churning sky—with bright sunlight clashing against black clouds—seems to reflect the inner conflict that comes with doing the right thing...or not. Instead of using a strict interpretation of the parable's Holy Land setting, Rembrandt chooses to combine disparate elements—such as the juxtaposition of classic Dutch windmills with the domed city of Jericho in the distance—to make the parable feel even more universal and immediate.

▲▲**Wyspiański Museum (Muzeum Wyspiańskiego)**—If you enjoyed Stanisław Wyspiański's stained glass and wall paintings in St. Francis' Basilica, visit the museum that collects his work. Housed in a renovated mansion, this museum traces the personal history and artistic development of the Młoda Polska poster boy. For more on Wyspiański, see page 293.

Cost and Hours: 8 zł, free on Sun, dry audioguide-5 zł, good English descriptions posted in most rooms, Wed-Sat 10:00-18:00, Sun 10:00-16:00, closed Mon, Tue only temporary exhibits open, last entry 30 minutes before closing, 1 block northwest of the Square at ulica Szczepańska 11, tel. 12-292-8183.

◒ Self-Guided Tour: Buy your ticket and climb the stairs. Turn left at the top of the first flight of stairs, and begin circling this floor clockwise. To the left, find the room devoted to Wyspiański's youth, including some of his precocious childhood sketchbooks. In the next room are works (including designs for beautiful stained-glass windows) from Wyspiański's youthful col-

laboration with his teacher Jan Matejko and his friend Józef Mehoffer; together they renovated St. Mary's Church. The "applied art" section shows off furniture Wyspiański designed, and a fine pastel drawing of St. Mary's spires.

In the next room, hiding behind a curtain (to protect it from damaging sunlight—ask an attendant to raise it for you) is his design for the dramatic stained-glass *Apollo*, which hangs in the House of the Medical Society (which, unfortunately, is closed to the public).

A room of portraits by various artists includes a self-portrait by Wyspiański himself. The next section demonstrates that Wyspiański was also a playwright—you'll see costumes and sets that he designed for his own plays, and copies of his printed works (which he also designed himself). Finally are more portraits, including some by other artists (such as Wyspiański's talented Młoda Polska compatriot, Jacek Malczewski).

In the stairwell up to the third floor are more stained-glass designs, this time for Wyspiański's masterpiece, *God the Father Let It Be*, from St. Francis' Basilica.

On the top floor, go left and circle the collection clockwise. After seeing various furniture and lesser works by other artists,

you'll reach the model of the elaborate acropolis Wyspiański planned for the top of Wawel Hill, with a domed palace, an amphitheater, and a circus maximus. In the same room is a haunting painting of the Planty park in winter, with Wawel Castle hovering in the background.

The next few rooms contain more stained-glass designs, and designs for the painted floral decorations of St. Francis' Basilica. Then, filling another room, are portraits of Wyspiański's family—including his daughter Helenka just waking up, and his wife breastfeeding their son Staś. Helenka circles around to get good views of both of them, appearing twice in the painting. Yet another Helenka portrait shows her curiously fingering a vase of flowers. Rounding out the collection is a room filled with countryside scenes.

Bishop Erazm Ciołek Palace (Pałac Biskupa Erazma Ciołka)—This branch of the National Museum features two separate art collections. Upstairs, the extensive "Art of Old Poland" section shows off works from the 12th through the 18th centuries, with room after room of altarpieces, sculptures, paintings, and more. The "Orthodox Art of the Old Polish Republic" section on the ground floor offers a taste of the remote Eastern reaches of Poland, with icons and other ecclesiastical art from the Orthodox faith. You'll see a sizeable section of the iconostasis (wall of icons) from the town of Lipovec. Both collections are covered by the same ticket and are very well-presented in a modern facility; while items are labeled in English, there's not much description.

Cost and Hours: 12 zł, free on Sun, audioguide-5 zł, Tue-Sat 10:00-18:00, Sun 10:00-16:00, closed Mon, Kanonicza 17, tel. 12-424-9371.

▲Czartoryski Museum (Muzeum Czartoryskich)—This eclectic collection, displaying armor, handicrafts, decorative arts, and paintings, is one of Kraków's best-known (and most over-rated) museums. It's closed for several years for a major restora-

tion, during which most of its collection is scheduled to be temporarily exhibited at a castle outside of town (not worth the trip). However, its top two paintings—Leonardo da Vinci's *Lady with an Ermine* and Rembrandt's *Landscape with the Good Samaritan* (both described earlier)—may be displayed at Kraków's Gallery of 19th-Century Polish Art in the Cloth Hall, unless they're on loan to another city (they were recently shown in London) or simply in storage. Ask around.

The collection was due in part to Poland's 1791 constitution (Europe's first), which inspired Princess Izabela Czartoryska to begin gathering bits of Polish history and culture. She fled with the collection to Paris after the 1830 insurrection, and 45 years later, her grandson returned it to its present Kraków location. When he ran out of space, he bought part of the monastery across the street, joining the buildings with a fancy passageway. The Nazis took the collection to Germany, and although most of it has been returned, some pieces are still missing.

If the museum is open, you'll wander through rooms of ornate armor (including a ceremonial Turkish tent from the 1683 siege of Vienna, plus feathered Hussar armor), tapestries, treasury items, majolica pottery, and Meissen porcelain figures. Rounding out the exhibits are painting galleries (including Italian, French, and Dutch High Renaissance and Baroque, as well as Czartoryski family portraits) and ancient art (mostly sculptures and vases).

Cost and Hours: If museum is open—around 12 zł, free on Sun, audioguide-15 zł, Tue-Sat 10:00-18:00, Sun 10:00-16:00, closed Mon, last entry 30 minutes before closing, 2 blocks north of the Main Market Square at ulica Św. Jana 19, tel. 12-422-5566, www.czartoryski.org.

More National Museum Branches—While less interesting than the branches listed above, the National Museum's **Main Branch** (Gmach Główny) is worth a visit for museum completists. It features 20th-century Polish art and temporary exhibits (10 zł, west of the Main Market Square at aleja 3 Maja 1). You can also check out the museum of Wyspiański's friend and rival, the **Józef Mehoffer House** (Dom Józefa Mehoffera, 6 zł, ulica Krupnicza 26, tel. 12-421-1143), and the former residence of their mentor, the **Jan Matejko House** (Dom Jana Matejki, 8 zł, ulica Floriańska 41, tel. 12-422-5926).

Other Attractions

The following sights are worth considering if you're looking to fill out your Kraków sightseeing experience.

▲**Rynek Underground Museum (Podziemia Rynku)**—Recent work to renovate the Square's pavement unearthed a wealth of remains from previous structures. Now you can do some urban spelunking with a visit to this high-tech medieval-history museum, which is literally underground— beneath all the photo-snapping tourists on the Square above.

Cost and Hours: 17 zł, Mon 10:00-20:00, Tue 10:00-16:00 (but closed first Tue of each month), Wed-Sun 10:00-22:00, last entry 1.25 hours before closing, enter at north end of Cloth Hall near the fountain, Rynek Główny 1, tel. 12-426-5060, www.podziemiarynku.com.

Reservations: Advance reservations are recommended, as the museum allows 30 people to enter every 15 minutes. You can reserve online or by phone (see contact information above), or drop by the information office a few hours (or ideally up to a day) before your visit. (This office faces the Town Hall Tower, on the opposite side of the Cloth Hall.) If you already have a reservation, report to the museum entrance.

Touring the Museum: You'll enter through a door near the north end of the Cloth Hall (close to the fountain, facing St. Mary's). Climb down a flight of stairs, buy your ticket, then follow the numbered panels through the exhibit (all in English except a few unimportant video clips). Cutting-edge museum technology illuminates life and times in medieval Kraków: Touchscreens let you delve into topics that intrigue you, 3-D virtual holograms resurrect old buildings, lots of surround-sound effects convincingly immerse you in a medieval burg, and video clips illustrate everyday life on unexpected surfaces (such as a curtain of fog).

All of this is wrapped around large chunks of early structures that still survive beneath the Square; several "witness columns" of rock and dirt are accompanied by diagrams helping you trace the layers of history. Interactive maps emphasize Kraków's Europe-wide importance as an intersection of major trade routes, and several models, maps, and digital reconstructions give you a good look at Kraków during the Middle Ages—when the Old Town looked barely different from today. You'll see a replica of a blacksmith's shop, and learn how "vampire prevention burials" were used to ensure that the suspected undead wouldn't return from the grave.

In the middle of the complex, look up through the glass of the Square's fountain to see the towers of St. Mary's above.

Deeper in the exhibit, explore the long corridors of ruined buildings that once ran alongside the length of the Cloth Hall. In this area, you'll find a series of five rooms, each showing a brief, excellent film outlining a different period of Kraków's history. These "Kraków Chronicles" provide a big-picture context to what otherwise seems like a loose collection of cool museum gizmos, and also help you better appreciate what you'll see outside the museum's doors.

▲Jagiellonian University Museum: Collegium Maius— Kraków had the second university in Central Europe (founded

in 1364, after Prague's), boasting such illustrious grads over the centuries as Copernicus and Pope John Paul II. With around 150,000 students (including 500 Norwegian med students), this city is still very much a university town, and Jagiellonian University proudly offers tours of its historic oldest building, the 15th-century Collegium Maius (one block west of the Main Market Square at ulica Jagiellońska 15). In the Middle Ages, professors were completely devoted to their scholarly pursuits. They

were unmarried and lived, ate, and slept here in an almost monastic environment. They taught downstairs and lived upstairs. In many ways, this building feels more like a monastery than a university.

Tours: Student guides lead visitors through the musty and mildly interesting interior of the complex. You'll choose between two different guided tours: 30 minutes (very popular) or one hour. It's smart to call ahead to find out when the shorter tour is scheduled in English, and to reserve for either tour (tel. 12-663-1307 or 12-663-1521, www.maius.uj.edu.pl).

The **30-minute tour** books up long in advance—especially on Tuesday afternoons, when it's free. Its "main exhibition" route includes the library, refectory (with a gorgeously carved Baroque staircase), treasury (including Polish filmmaker Andrzej Wajda's honorary Oscar), assembly hall, and some old scientific instruments (12 zł, a few tours per day in English, 20 people maximum, leaves every 20 minutes Mon-Fri 10:00-15:00, Tue and Thu until 18:00 in April-Oct, Sat 10:00-14:00, last tour departs 40 minutes before closing, no tours Sun). On Tuesday afternoons, entrance is free (April-Oct 15:00-18:00, last tour departs 17:20; Nov-March 14:00-16:00, last tour departs at 15:20).

The **one-hour tour** adds some more interiors, room after

room of more old scientific instruments, medieval art (mostly church sculptures), a Rubens, a small landscape from the shop of Rembrandt, and Chopin's piano (16 zł, usually in English year-round Mon-Fri at 13:00, no tours Sat-Sun).

Aside from the courtyard, the only part of the Collegium Maius you can see without a tour is an interactive exhibit that allows you to tinker with replicas of old scientific tools (7 zł, open Mon-Sat 9:00-13:30, closed Sun).

Before you leave, enjoy a cup of hot chocolate at the chocolate shop (down the stairs near the entrance)—widely regarded as the best in town.

Archdiocesan Museum (Muzeum Archidiecezjalne)—This museum, in a building where John Paul II lived both as a priest and as a bishop, does its best to capture some of his story. The museum consists of several parts: the underwhelming ground-floor collection of sacral art (with altars, paintings, and vestments); various temporary exhibits; and the top-floor museum devoted to John Paul II. Wandering past the scores of paintings and photographs, the late pontiff's cult of personality is almost palpable. Unfortunately, since the collection mostly consists of elaborate gifts received by the Holy Father from around the world, it offers little intimacy or insight into the man himself. Still, admirers of John Paul II will appreciate it.

Cost and Hours: 5 zł, Tue-Fri 10:00-16:00, Sat-Sun 10:00-15:00, closed Mon, Kanonicza 19-21, tel. 12-421-8963, www.muzeumkra.diecezja.pl.

John Paul II Center (Centrum Jan Pawła II)—This modest exhibition space, across the street from the Archdiocesan Museum, is also the headquarters for the construction of a sprawling John Paul II Center on the outskirts of Kraków. The new complex will include a church, museum, meeting spaces, retreat center with accommodations, and other facilities for John Paul II pilgrims (possibly open in late 2012, more likely in 2013 or later). In the meantime, in this small center, you can see exhibits (with photographs, artifacts, and English descriptions), watch films (subtitled in English) about the late pontiff, and get construction updates.

Cost and Hours: Free, daily 10:00-16:00, Kanonicza 18, tel. 12-429-6471, www.janpawel2.pl.

Kraków Aquarium—Landlocked Kraków and marine life don't quite seem to go together. But this facility—the brainchild of an armchair ichthyologist and expat American—is surprisingly modern and engaging, and one of the only truly kid-friendly attractions in town. With 130 different species of fish, reptiles, snakes, and even tamarinds (cute little monkeys) thoughtfully displayed on two floors, it offers a refreshing break from historic old Kraków. High-tech touchscreen displays give you more detail on each of the animals, and everything's kid-oriented and well-described in English. Rounding out the collection are items from the former Natural History Museum that once filled this building, including the skeleton of a 30,000-year-old woolly rhinoceros and two mammoth skulls.

Cost and Hours: Adults-20 zł, kids under 16-14 zł, family ticket for 2 adults and 2 kids-59 zł, Mon-Fri 9:00-19:00, Sat 9:00-20:00, Sun 10:00-12:00, near Wawel Hill just outside the Planty park at ulica Św. Sebastiana 9, tel. 12-429-1049, www.aquarium krakow.com.

Kazimierz (Jewish Quarter)

The neighborhood of Kazimierz (kah-ZHEE-mezh), 20 minutes by foot southeast of Kraków's Old Town, is the historic heart of Kraków's once-thriving Jewish community. After years of neglect, the district has been rediscovered by Krakovians and tourists alike. Visitors expecting a polished, touristy scene like Prague's Jewish Quarter will be surprised...and maybe disappointed. This is basically a local-feeling, slightly run-down neighborhood with a handful of Jewish cemeteries, synagogues, and restaurants, and often a few pensive Israeli tour groups wandering the streets. But for many, this is where you'll find the true soul of the European Jewish experience.

Try to visit any day except Saturday, when most Jewish-themed sights are closed (except the Old Synagogue, High Synagogue, and Galicia Jewish Museum). Monday comes with a few closures: the Ethnographic Museum, Museum of Contemporary Art in Kraków, and Museum of Municipal Engineering (along with Schindler's Factory Museum, but only on the first Monday of the month).

Note that it's respectful for men to cover their heads while visiting a Jewish cemetery or synagogue. While some of these sights offer loaner yarmulkes, it's easiest to just bring your own hat.

Getting to Kazimierz: From the Old Town, it's about a 20-minute **walk,** which gets you out of the fairy-tale tourist zone and into the real, soot-stained, workaday Kraków (that's a good thing). From the Main Market Square, walk down ulica Sienna (near St. Mary's Church). At the fork, bear right through the Planty park. At the intersection with the busy Westerplatte ring road, you'll continue straight ahead (bear right at fork, then continue straight across the busy ring road) down Starowiślna for 15 more minutes. To hop the **tram,** go to the stop on the left-hand side of ulica Sienna (at the intersection with Westerplatte, across the street from the Poczta Główna, or main post office). Catch tram #7, #13, or #24 and go two stops to Miodowa. Walking or by tram, at the intersection of Starowiślna and Miodowa, you'll see a small park across the street and to the right. To reach the heart of Kazimierz—ulica Szeroka—cut through this park. You can also take this tram from near the train station (see "Arrival in Kraków," earlier). To return to the Old Town, catch tram #7, #13, or #24 from the intersection of Starowiślna and Miodowa (kitty-corner from where you got off the tram), and go two stops back to the Poczta Główna stop.

Orientation: Start your visit to Kazimierz on **ulica Szeroka** (which is more of a long, parking-lot square than a street), surrounded by Jewish-themed restaurants, hotels, and synagogues.

Check in at the **Jarden Bookshop** at the top of the square (Mon-Fri 9:00-18:00, Sat-Sun 10:00-18:00, ulica Szeroka 2, tel. 12-429-1374, www.jarden.pl, jarden@jarden.pl). While there are many new bookstores in Kazimierz (mostly inside the various museums and synagogues), this is the original. It serves as a sort of TI for the neighborhood, and sells a wide variety of fairly priced books on Kazimierz and Jewish culture in the region (including a good 4-zł Kraków map of Jewish monuments and the well-illustrated 18-zł *Jewish Kraków* guidebook). They also run several tours (prices based on the number of people; I've listed the price per person for 2 people): Jewish Kazimierz overview (70 zł, 2 hours, walking tour), Kazimierz and the WWII ghetto (90 zł, 3 hours, walking, the best overview), *Schindler's List* sights (120 zł, 2 hours, by car), and Auschwitz-Birkenau (180 zł, 6-7 hours, by car). Call to reserve ahead, as tours are by appointment only. Pairs or singles may be able to join an already scheduled tour (which lowers the price for everybody).

There's also an official **TI** just a few blocks off the bottom of ulica Szeroka, at ulica Józefa 7 (daily 9:00-17:00, tel. 12-422-0471).

Several Kazimierz restaurants offer live traditional Jewish **klezmer music** nightly in summer, and the district is home to many of the city's best bars, cafés, nightspots, and hangouts. For more suggestions in Kazimierz, see page 343 of "Entertainment in Kraków," page 353 of "Sleeping in Kraków," and page 358 of "Eating in Kraków."

Central Kazimierz

Ulica Szeroka is the core of Kazimierz; within a few blocks of here, you'll find two cemeteries (quite different and both worth a visit), six synagogues, and three museums, as well as the lively market square called plac Nowy.

▲▲**Old Cemetery (Stary Cmentarz)**—This small cemetery was used to bury members of the Jewish community from 1552 to 1800. It has been renovated—so in a way, it actually feels "newer" than the New Cemetery. After the New Cemetery (described next) was opened in 1800, this one gradually fell into disrepair. What

KRAKOW

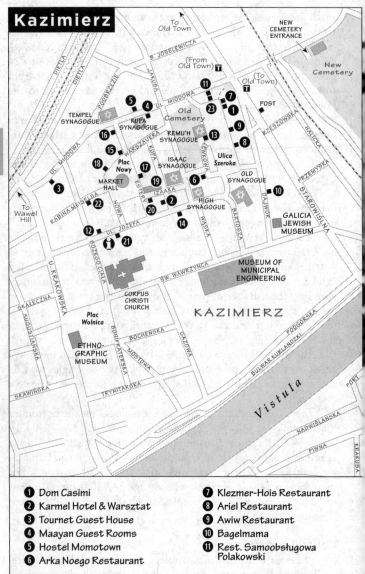

Kazimierz

1 Dom Casimi
2 Karmel Hotel & Warsztat
3 Tournet Guest House
4 Maayan Guest Rooms
5 Hostel Momotown
6 Arka Noego Restaurant
7 Klezmer-Hois Restaurant
8 Ariel Restaurant
9 Awiw Restaurant
10 Bagelmama
11 Rest. Samoobsługowa Polakowski

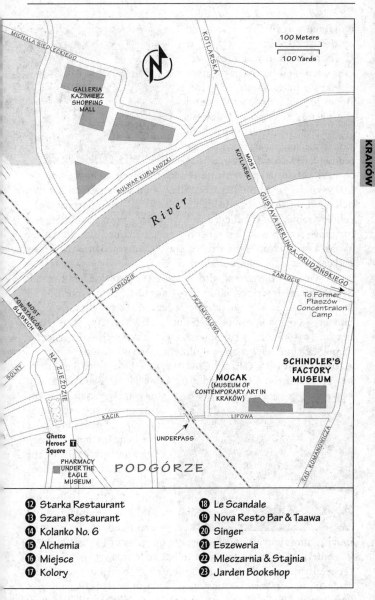

12 Starka Restaurant
13 Szara Restaurant
14 Kolanko No. 6
15 Alchemia
16 Miejsce
17 Kolory

18 Le Scandale
19 Nova Resto Bar & Taawa
20 Singer
21 Eszeweria
22 Mleczarnia & Stajnia
23 Jarden Bookshop

remained was further desecrated by the Nazis during World War II. In the 1950s, it was discovered, excavated, and put back together as you see here. Shattered gravestones form a mosaic wall around the perimeter. As in all Jewish cemeteries, you'll see many small stones stacked on the graves (originally placed over desert graves to cover the body and prevent animals from disturbing it). Behind the little synagogue to the left, the tallest tombstone next to the tree belonged to Moses Isserles (a.k.a. Remu'h), an important 16th-century rabbi. He is believed to have been a miracle worker, and his grave was one of the only ones that remained standing after World War II. Notice the written prayers crammed into the cracks and crevices of the tombstone.

Cost and Hours: 5 zł, also includes entry to attached Remu'h Synagogue—described later; very sporadic hours according to demand—especially outside peak season—but generally open Sun-Fri 9:00-16:00, can be open until 18:00 May-Aug, closes earlier off-season and by sundown on Fri, always closed Sat, enter through Remu'h Synagogue at ulica Szeroka 40.

▲**New Cemetery (Nowy Cmentarz)**—This much larger site has graves of those who died after 1800. Nazis also vandalized

this cemetery, selling many of its gravestones to stonecutters, and using others as pavement in their concentration camps. Many of the gravestones have since been returned to their original positions. Other headstones could not be replaced, and were used to create the moving mosaic wall and Holocaust monument (on the right as you enter). Most gravestones are in one of four languages: Hebrew (generally the oldest, especially if there's no other language, though some are newer "retro" tombstones); Yiddish (sounds like a mix of German and Hebrew, and uses the Hebrew alphabet); Polish (Jews who assimilated into the Polish community); and German (Jews who assimilated into the German community). The earliest graves are simple stones, while later ones imitate graves in Polish Catholic cemeteries—larger, more elaborate, and with a long stone jutting out to cover the body. Notice that some new-looking graves have old dates. These were most likely put here well after the Holocaust (or even after the communist era) by relatives of the dead.

Cost and Hours: Free, Sun-Fri 8:00-18:00, until 16:00 in winter, closed Sat. It's tricky to find: Go under the railway bridge at the east end of ulica Miodowa, and jog left as you emerge. The cemetery is to your right (enter through gate with small *cmentarz żydowski* sign).

Synagogues—Six different synagogues in Kazimierz welcome visitors. Each of the interiors is a variation on the same theme: a large central prayer hall, often with an altar-like ark (facing east, toward Jerusalem) where the Torah is kept. The elevated platform in the center, sometimes surrounded by a cage-like structure, is the equivalent of a pulpit in a Christian church. You may see segregated areas (often a balcony or an arcade) where women would worship separately from men. Some synagogues have been converted into museums, while others are still used for services. The first two synagogues listed below are on Kazimierz's main square, ulica Szeroka; the next four are all within three blocks to the west (all are shown on the map on page 324).

Remu'h Synagogue, which is tight, cozy, and dates from 1553, has been carefully renovated and is fully active (included in 5-zł entry fee for Old Cemetery, same unpredictable hours as Old Cemetery, ulica Szeroka 40).

The **Old Synagogue** (Stara Synagoga), the oldest surviving Jewish building in Poland, is now a good three-room museum on local Jewish culture, with informative English descriptions. Most of the exhibits are displayed in the impressive main prayer hall (8 zł, free on Mon, good 50-stop audioguide-10 zł; April-Oct Mon 10:00-14:00, Tue-Sun 10:00-17:00; Nov-March Mon 10:00-14:00, Wed-Thu and Sat-Sun 9:00-16:00, Fri 10:00-17:00, closed Tue; ulica Szeroka 24, tel. 12-422-0962).

The recently renovated **High Synagogue**—so called because its prayer room is upstairs—displays changing exhibits, most of which focus on the people who lived here before and after the Holocaust (9 zł, daily 10:00-19:00, shorter hours in winter, just around the corner from the Old Synagogue at ulica Józefa 38, tel. 12-430-6889).

Isaac Synagogue (Synagoga Izaaka), one of Kraków's biggest, was built in the 17th century. On the walls in the prayer hall are giant wall paintings of prayers for worshippers who couldn't afford to buy books (with translations posted below). It also serves as the local center for the Hasidic Jewish group Chabad, with a

Jewish Kraków

After King Kazimierz the Great encouraged Jews to come to Poland in the 14th century, a large Jewish community settled in and around Kraków. According to legend, Kazimierz (the king) established Kazimierz (the village) for his favorite girlfriend— a Jewish woman named Ester—just southeast of the city walls. (If you have a 50-zł note, take a look at it: That's Kazimierz the Great on the front, and on the back are his capital, Cracovia, and the most important town he founded, Casmirus.)

It's a cute legend, but the village of Kazimierz didn't really become a Jewish enclave until much later. By the end of the 15th century, there were large Jewish populations in both Kazimierz and in Kraków. Kraków's Jewish community and the university students clashed, and when a destructive fire broke out in 1495, the Jews were blamed. The king at the time forced all of Kraków's Jews to move to Kazimierz.

Kazimierz was an autonomous community, with its own Town Hall, market square, and city walls (though many Jews still commuted into Kraków's Main Market Square to do business). Within Kazimierz, the Christian (west) and Jewish (east) neighborhoods were also separated by a wall. But by 1800, the walls came down, Kazimierz became part of Kraków, and the Jewish community flourished.

By the start of World War II, 65,000 Jews lived in Kraków

kosher restaurant and a library (5 zł; Sun-Thu 9:00-18:00, open later in summer depending on sunset—until 20:00 in July-Aug, Fri 9:00-15:00, closed Sat, a block west of ulica Szeroka at ulica Kupa 18, tel. 12-430-2222). In addition to its Sabbath services, this is Kraków's only synagogue that has daily prayers (at 8:30).

Tempel Synagogue (Synagoga Templu) has the grandest interior—big and dark, with elaborately decorated, gilded ceilings and balconies—and the most lived-in feel of the bunch (5 zł, Sun-Fri 10:00-16:00, sometimes until 18:00, closed Sat, corner of ulica Miodowa and ulica Podbrzezie).

The smaller **Kupa Synagogue** (Synagoga Kupa), clean and brightly decorated, sometimes hosts temporary exhibits (Miodowa 27).

▲**Galicia Jewish Museum (Galicja Muzeum)**—This museum focuses on the present rather than the past. With a series of photographs displayed around a restored Jewish furniture factory, the permanent "Traces of Memory" exhibit shows today's remnants of

KRAKÓW

(mostly in Kazimierz)—making up more than a quarter of the city's population. When the Nazis arrived, they immediately sent most of Kraków's Jews to the ghetto in the eastern Polish city of Lublin. Soon after, they forced Kraków's remaining 15,000 Jews into a walled ghetto at Podgórze, across the river. The Jews' cemeteries were defiled, and their buildings ransacked and destroyed. In 1942, the Nazis began transporting Kraków's Jews to death camps (including Płaszów—just on Kraków's outskirts—and Auschwitz). Many others were worked to death in the Podgórze ghetto. Only a few thousand Kraków Jews survived the war. During World War II, Poland was the only Nazi-controlled country where residents could be executed for helping Jews—making even more remarkable the number of Poles who risked their lives to help escapees.

Today's Kraków has only about 200 Jewish residents. During the communist era, this waning population was ignored or mistreated. But in recent years, Kazimierz has enjoyed a renaissance of Jewish culture—thanks largely to the popularity of *Schindler's List* (which was partly filmed here). Look for handwritten letters from Steven Spielberg and the cast in local restaurants (such as Ariel) and hotels. While few Jews live here now, the spirit of the Jewish tradition lives on in the many synagogues, as well as in the soulful cemeteries.

yesterday's Judaism in the area around Kraków (a region known as "Galicia"). From forgotten synagogues to old Jewish gravestones flipped over and used as doorsteps, these giant postcards of Jewish artifacts (with good English descriptions) ensure that an important part of this region's heritage won't be forgotten. Complementing this permanent collection are good temporary exhibits.

Cost and Hours: 15 zł, daily 10:00-18:00, 1 block east of ulica Szeroka at ulica Dajwór 18, tel. 12-421-6842, www.galiciajewish museum.org. The museum also serves as a sort of cultural center, with a good bookstore, café, and programming that caters to both locals and visitors (pick up the monthly program).

Kazimierz Market Square (Plac Nowy)—The natives shop at plac Nowy's market stalls. This is a gritty, factory-workers-on-lunch-break contrast to Kraków's touristy Main Market Square (stalls open Tue-Sun 6:00-14:00, a few also open later, closed Mon). Consider dropping by here for some shopping, people-watching, or a quick, cheap, and local lunch (see page 360). For dessert, buy some fruit from a vendor. There's a fun antiques shop at #3. This square also has the highest concentration of nightlife in town, and several fun and funky spots are open during the day as stay-awhile cafés (see "Entertainment in Kraków," later).

▲**Ethnographic Museum (Muzeum Etnograficzne)**—This clever and refreshingly good museum hides a few blocks west of the Jewish area of Kazimierz, in the former town hall. It sits on plac Wolnica, which was Kazimierz's primary market square and was once almost as big as Kraków's. On the ground floor, you'll find models of traditional rural Polish homes, as well as musty replicas of the interiors (like an open-air folk museum moved inside). The exhibit continues upstairs, where each in a long lineup of traditional Polish folk costumes is identified by specific region. You'll see exhibits on village lifestyles, rustic tools, and musical instruments (including a Polish bagpipe). A highlight is the explanation of traditional holiday celebrations—from elaborate crèche scenes at Christmas, to a wall of remarkably painted Easter eggs. Some items are labeled in English, but it's mostly in Polish. The top floor features temporary exhibits.

Cost and Hours: 9 zł, free on Sun, open Tue-Sat 11:00-19:00, Thu until 21:00, Sun 11:00-15:00, closed Mon, ulica Krakowska 46, tel. 12-430-6023, www.etnomuzeum.eu.

Museum of Municipal Engineering (Muzeum Inżynierii Miejskiej)—This pleasant museum fills the immaculately restored red-brick buildings of an old tram depot in a quiet part of Kazimierz. Exhibits include a history of the town's public-transit system (including several antique trams); old Polish-made cars and motorcycles (among them the tiny commie-era Polski Fiat); typography and historical printing presses; and a hands-on area for kids called "Around the Circle."

Cost and Hours: 8 zł, family ticket-24 zł, Tue-Sun 10:00-16:00, until 18:00 on Tue and Thu June-Sept, closed Mon, Św. Wawrzyńca 15, tel. 12-421-1242.

Near Kazimierz: Podgórze

The neighborhood called Podgórze (POD-goo-zheh), directly across the Vistula from Kazimierz, has one of Kraków's most famous sights: Schindler's Factory Museum.

Background: This is the neighborhood where the Nazis forced Kraków's Jews into a ghetto in early 1941. (*Schindler's List* and the films in the Pharmacy Under the Eagle museum depict the sad scene of the Jews loading their belongings onto carts and trudging over the bridge into Podgórze.) Non-Jews who had lived here were displaced to make way for the new arrivals. The ghetto was surrounded by a wall with a fringe along the top that resembled Jewish gravestones—a chilling premonition of what was to come.

A short section of this wall still stands along Lwowska street. The tram continued to run through the middle of Podgórze, without stopping—giving Krakovians a chilling glimpse at the horrifying conditions inside the ghetto.

Getting There: To get to Ghetto Heroes' Square, continue through Kazimierz on tram #7, #13, or #24 (described earlier, under "Getting to Kazimierz") to the stop called plac Bohaterow Getta. You can also simply continue walking along Starowiślna, about 10 minutes past the other Kazimierz sights—it's just across the bridge.

Ghetto Heroes' Square (plac Bohaterow Getta)—This unassuming square is the focal point of the visitor's Podgórze. Today the

square is filled with a recent monument consisting of several empty metal chairs. This is intended to remind viewers that the Jews of Kazimierz were forced to carry all of their belongings—including furniture—to the ghetto on this side of the river. It was also here that many Jews waited to be sent to extermination camps. The small, gray building at the river end of Ghetto Heroes' Square feels like a train car inside, evocative of the wagons that carried people from here to certain death.

▲**Pharmacy Under the Eagle (Apteka pod Orłem)**—This modest museum, on Ghetto Heroes' Square, tells the story of Tadeusz Pankiewicz, a Polish Catholic pharmacist who chose to remain in Podgórze when it became a Jewish ghetto. During this time, the pharmacy was an important meeting point for the ghetto residents, and Pankiewicz and his staff heroically aided and hid Jewish victims of the Nazis. (Pankiewicz survived the war and was later acknowledged by Israel as one of the "Righteous Among the Nations"—non-Jews who risked their lives to help the Nazis' victims during World War II.) Today the pharmacy hosts an exhibit about the Jewish ghetto. Three small video screens display footage from that era: One shows Kazimierz before the Nazis arrived; another documents the forced transition to the Podgórze ghetto; and a third is secret surveillance footage of Płaszów Concentration Camp, on Kraków's outskirts.

Cost and Hours: 6 zł, free on Mon, some English descriptions, good 45-minute audioguide-10 zł; April-Oct Mon 10:00-14:00, Tue-Sun 9:30-17:00; Nov-March Mon 10:00-14:00, Tue-Thu and Sat 9:00-16:00, Fri 10:00-17:00, closed Sun and the first Tue of each month in winter; plac Bohaterow Getta 18, tel. 12-656-5625.

▲▲**Schindler's Factory Museum (Fabryka Emalia Oskara Schindlera)**—One of Europe's best museums about the Nazi

Oskar Schindler (1908-1974) and His List

Steven Spielberg's instant-classic, Oscar-winning 1993 film, *Schindler's List,* brought the world's attention to the inspiring story of Oskar Schindler, the compassionate German business-man who did his creative best to save the lives of the Jewish workers at his factory in Kraków. Spielberg chose to film the story right here in Kazimierz, where the historical events actually unfolded. Today the Schindler's Factory Museum gives visitors the chance to learn not just about the man and his workers, but about the historical context of their story: the Nazi occupation of Poland.

Oskar Schindler was born in 1908 in the Sudetenland (currently Moravia in the Czech Republic, then predominantly German). Early on, he displayed an idiosyncratic interpretation of ethics that earned him both wealth and enemies. As Nazi aggres-sions escalated, Schindler (who was very much a Nazi) carried out espionage against Poland; when Germany invaded the coun-try in 1939, Schindler smelled a business opportunity. Early in the Nazi occupation of Poland, Schindler came to Kraków and lived in an apartment at ulica Straszewskiego 7 (a block from Wawel Castle, but unmarked and not available for tours). He took over the formerly Jewish-owned Emalia factory at ulica Lipowa 4, which produced metal pots and pans that were dipped into protective enamel (later the factory also began producing arma-ments for the Nazi war effort). The factory was staffed by about 1,000 Jews from the nearby Płaszów Concentration Camp, which was managed by the ruthless SS officer Amon Göth (depicted in *Schindler's List*—based on real events—shooting at camp inmates for sport from his balcony).

At a certain point, Schindler began to sympathize with his Jewish workers, and gradually did what he could to protect them and offer them better lives. Schindler fed them far better than most concentration-camp inmates, and allowed them to sell some of the pots and pans they made on the black market to

occupation fills the actual factory building (named "Emalia") where Oskar Schindler and his Jewish employees worked. It's worth ▲▲▲ to those interested in World War II history gener-ally, or in Schindler specifically, but it's fascinating to anyone. While the museum tells the story of Schindler and his work-ers, it broadens its perspective to take in the full experience of all of Kraków during the pain-ful era of Nazi rule—making it the single best WWII museum

make money. After he saw many of his employees and friends murdered during an SS raid in 1943, he ramped up these efforts even further. He would come up with bogus paperwork to classify those threatened with deportation as "essential" to the workings of the factory—even if they were unskilled. He sought and was granted permission to build a "concentration camp" barracks for his workers on the factory grounds, where they lived in far better conditions than those at Płaszów. These lucky few became known as *Schindlerjuden*—"Schindler's Jews."

As the Soviet army encroached on Kraków in October of 1944, word came that the factory would need to be relocated west, farther from the front line. While Schindler could easily have simply turned his workers over to the concentration-camp system and certain death—as most other industrialists did—he decided to bring them with him to his new factory at Brünnlitz (Brněnec, in today's Czech Republic). He assembled a list of 700 men and 300 women who worked with him, along with 200 other Jewish inmates, and at great personal expense, moved them to Brünnlitz. At the new factory, Schindler and the 1,200 people he had saved produced grenades and rocket parts—virtually all of them, the workers later claimed, mysteriously defective.

After the war, Schindler—who had spent much of his fortune protecting his Jewish workers—hopped around Germany and Argentina, repeatedly attempting but failing to break back into business (often with funding from Jewish donors). He died in poverty in 1974. In accordance with his final wishes, he was buried in Jerusalem, and today, his grave is piled high with small stones left there by appreciative Jewish visitors. He has since been named one of the "Righteous Among the Nations" for his efforts to save Jews from the Holocaust. Thomas Keneally's 1982 book *Schindler's Ark* brought the industrialist's tale to a wide audience that included Steven Spielberg, who vaulted Schindler to the ranks of a pop-culture icon.

in this country that was so profoundly affected by that war. It's loaded with in-depth information (all in English), and touch-screens throughout invite you to learn more and watch eyewitness interviews. Scattered randomly between the exhibits are replicas of everyday places from the age—a photographer's shop, a tram car, a hairdresser's salon—designed to give you a taste of 1940s Kraków. Throughout the museum are calendar pages outlining wartime events, which you can stamp with seals and symbols from each era, then take along with you.

Cost and Hours: 15 zł, limited free entry on Mon (first-come, first-served, so consider reserving ahead on their website); open April-Oct Mon 10:00-16:00 (except closed first Mon of month),

Tue-Sun 10:00-20:00; Nov-March Mon 10:00-14:00 (except closed first Mon of month), Tue-Sun 10:00-18:00; last entry 1.5 hours before closing, tel. 12-257-1017, www.mhk.pl.

Getting There: It's in a depressed industrial area a five-minute walk from Ghetto Heroes' Square (plac Bohaterow Getta): Head up Kącik street (use the pedestrian underpass, then head to the left of the big, glass skyscraper), go under the railroad underpass marked *Kraków-Zabłocie*, and continue two blocks, past MOCAK (the Museum of Contemporary Art in Kraków, described later) to the second big building on the left (ulica Lipowa 4). Look for signs to *Emalia*.

➋ Self-Guided Tour: You'll begin on the ground floor, where you'll buy your ticket and have the chance to tour the special exhibits. There's also a "film café" with refreshments. Then head upstairs to the first floor.

First Floor: The 35-minute **film**, called *Lipowa 4* (this building's address), sets the stage with interviews of both Jews and non-Jews describing their wartime experience (subtitled in English, runs continuously 10:15-15:50). From here, the one-way route winds through the permanent exhibit, called **Kraków Under Nazi Occupation 1939-1945**. "Stereoscopic" (primitive 3-D) photos of prewar Kraków capture an idyllic age when culture flourished and the city's Jews (more than one-quarter of the population)

blended more or less smoothly with their Catholic-Pole neighbors. A video explains the Nazi invasion of Poland in early September of 1939: It took them only a few weeks to overrun the country (which desperately awaited the promised-for help of their British and French allies, who never arrived). Watch the film clip of SS soldiers marching through the Main Market Square—renamed "Adolf-Hitler-Platz"—and read stories about how the Nazis' *Generalgouvernement* attempted to reshape the life of its new capital, "Krakau." You'll see the story of a newly German-owned shop selling Nazi propaganda, and learn how professors at Kraków's Jagiellonian University were arrested to prevent them from fomenting rebellion among their students. During this time, Polish secondary schools were closed—effectively prohibiting learning among Poles, whom the Nazis considered inferior. But Polish students continued to meet clandestinely with their teachers. The exhibit also details how early Nazi policies targeted Jews, with roundups, torture, and execution. (Down the staircase is an eerie simulation of a cellar prison.) As the Nazis ratcheted up their genocidal activities, troops swept through Kraków on March

3, 1941, forcing all the remaining Jews in town to squeeze into the newly created Podgórze ghetto.

Second Floor: Climb upstairs using the long **staircase**, which was immortalized in a powerful scene in *Schindler's List*. At the top of the stairs on the right is a small room that served as "Schindler's office" for the film; more recently, they've determined that his actual office was elsewhere (we'll see it soon).

You'll walk through a corridor lined by a replica of the wall that enclosed the **Podgórze ghetto,** and see exhibits about the horrific conditions there (including a replica of the cramped living quarters). The Nazis claimed that Jews had to be segregated here, away from the general population, because they "carried diseases."

KRAKÓW

Continue into the office of Schindler's secretary, with exhibits about Schindler's life and video touchscreens that play testimonial footage of Schindler's grateful employees. Then proceed into the actual **Schindler's office.** The big map (with German names for cities) was uncovered only in recent years when the factory was being restored. Because Schindler's short tenure here was the only time in the factory's history that these

Polish place names would appear in German, it's believed that this map was hung over his desk. Nearby is a giant monument of enamel pots and pans, like those that were made in this factory, and walls lined with names from The List.

Continuing through the exhibit, you'll learn more about everyday life, including the Polish resistance (see the Home

Army's underground print shop). More eyewitness accounts relate the terrifying days of March 13 and 14, 1943, when the Podgórze ghetto was liquidated, sending survivors to the nearby Płaszów Concentration Camp. The replica of the Płaszów quarry, where inmates were forced to work in unimaginably difficult conditions, provides a poignant memorial for those who weren't fortunate enough to be on Schindler's list.

Now head all the way back down to the ground floor.

Ground Floor: Exhibits here capture the uncertain days near the end of the war in the summer of 1944, when Nazis arrested between 6,000 and 8,000 suspected saboteurs after the Warsaw Uprising, and sent them to Płaszów (see the replica of a basement hideout for 10 Jews who had escaped the ghetto); and later, when many Nazis had fled Kraków, leaving residents to await the Soviet Union's Red Army (see the replica air-raid shelters). The Red Army arrived here on January 18, 1945—at long last, the five years, four months, and twelve days of Nazi rule were over. The Soviets caused their own share of damage to the city before beginning a whole new occupation that would last for generations...but that's a different museum.

Finally, walk along the squishy floor into the Hall of Choices, where six rotating pillars tell the stories of people who chose to act—or not to act—when they witnessed atrocities. Think about the ramifications of the choices they made...and what you would have done in their shoes. The final room holds two books: a white book listing those who tried to help, and a black book listing Nazi collaborators.

Before heading back to downtown Kraków, consider paying a visit to the excellent—and very different—museum that fills the buildings on the factory grounds, behind this main building.

▲**Museum of Contemporary Art in Kraków (Muzeum Sztuki Współczesnej w Krakowie)**—Called "MOCAK" for short, this

museum exhibits a changing array of innovative and thought-provoking works by contemporary artists, often with heavy themes tied to the surrounding sites. With the slogan *Kunst macht frei* ("Art will set you free"—a pointed spin on the Nazis' *Arbeit macht frei* concentration-camp motto), the museum occupies warehouse buildings once filled by Schindler's workers. Now converted to wide-open, bright-white halls, the buildings house many temporary exhibits as well as two permanent ones (the MOCAK Collection in the basement, and the library in the smaller side building). Pick up the floor plan as you enter. It's all well-described in English, and engaging even for non-art-lovers.

Cost and Hours: 10 zł, free on Tue, open Tue-Sun 11:00-19:00, closed Mon, Lipowa 4, tel. 12/263-4001, www.mocak.pl.

Outside of Central Kraków

Each of these three sights—an impressive salt mine, a purpose-built communist town, and an unusual earthwork—requires a bus or tram ride to reach.

▲▲Wieliczka Salt Mine (Kopalnia Soli Wieliczka)

Wieliczka (veel-EECH-kah), a salt mine 10 miles southeast of Kraków, is beloved by Poles. Deep beneath the ground, the mine is filled with sculptures that miners have lovingly carved out of the salt. You'll explore this unique gallery—learning both about the art and about medieval mining techniques—on a required tour. Though the sight is a bit overrated, it's unique and practically obligatory if you're in Kraków for at least two days.

Cost and Hours: Visits cost 68 zł and are by guided tour only. English tours are offered daily year-round (June-Sept every half-hour 8:30-18:00, Oct-May every hour 9:00-17:00), with the exception of a few holidays when the mine is closed. If you miss the English-language tour (or decide to just show up and take whatever's going next), you can rent an audioguide for an extra 10 zł. The mine is in the town of Wieliczka at ulica Daniłowicza 10 (tel. 12-278-7302, www.kopalnia.pl).

You'll pay an extra 10 zł for permission to use your camera—but be warned that flash photos often don't turn out, thanks to the irregular reflection of the salt crystals. Dress warmly—the mine is a constant 57 degrees Fahrenheit.

Your ticket includes a dull **mine museum** at the end of the tour. It adds an hour to the mine tour and is discouraged by locals ("1.5 miles more walking, colder, more of the same"). Make it clear when you buy your ticket that you're not interested in the museum.

Getting There: The salt mine, 10 miles from Kraków, is best reached by **bus #304** (3.20-zł *aglomeracyjny* ticket, 3/hour, 40-minute trip, catch bus at Kurniki stop across from church near Galeria Krakowska mall, get off at stop called Wieliczka Kopalnia Soli). You can also get there by **minibus** (2.50 zł, 4/hour or with demand, *Wieliczka Soli* sign in window, 30-40 minutes), but the departure point for the minibuses is constantly changing—ask the TI where you can find them now (likely near the main post office). These options are better than taking the train, which deposits you in the town of Wieliczka, far from the mine.

Background: Wieliczka Salt Mine has been producing salt since at least the 11th century. Under Kazimierz the Great, one-third of Poland's income came from these precious deposits. Wieliczka miners spent much of their lives underground, leaving for work before daybreak and returning after sundown, rarely emerging into daylight. To pass the time, and to immortalize their national pride and religiosity in art, 19th-century miners began to carve figures, chandeliers, and eventually even an elaborate chapel out of the salt. Until a few years ago, the mine still produced salt. Today's miners—about 400 of them—primarily work on maintaining the 200 miles of chambers. This entire network is supported by wooden beams (because metal would rust).

Touring the Mine: From the lobby, your guide leads you 380 steps down a winding staircase. From this spot you begin a 1.5-mile stroll, generally downhill (more than 800 steps down altogether), past 20 of the mine's 2,000 chambers (with signs explaining when they were dug), finishing 443 feet below the surface. When you're done, an elevator beams you back up.

The tour shows how the miners lived and worked, using horses who spent their whole adult lives without ever seeing the light of day. It takes you through vast underground caverns, past subterranean lakes, and introduces you to some of the mine's many sculptures (including one of Copernicus—who actually visited here in the 15th century—as well as an army of salt elves, and this region's favorite son, Pope John Paul II). Your jaw will drop as you enter the enormous  **Chapel of St. Kinga,** carved over three decades in the early 20th century. Look for the salt-relief carving of the Last Supper (its 3-D details are astonishing, considering it's just six inches deep).

While advertised as two hours, your tour finishes in a deep-down shopping zone 1.5 hours after you started (they hope you'll hang out and shop). Note when the next elevator departs (just 3/ hour), and you can be outta there on the next lift. Zip through the shopping zone in two minutes, or step over the rope and be immediately in line for the great escape (you'll be escorted 300 yards to the skinny industrial elevator, into which you'll be packed like mine workers).

▲Nowa Huta

Nowa Huta (NOH-vah HOO-tah, "New Steel Works"), an enormous planned workers' town, offers a glimpse into the stark, grand-scale aesthetics of the communists. Since it's five miles east of central Kraków and a little tricky to see on your own, skip it unless you're determined. But architects and communist sympathizers may want to make a pilgrimage here.

Getting There: Trams #4 and #15 go from near Kraków's Old Town (catch the tram on the ring road near Kraków's main train station, at the Basztowa stop) along Pope John Paul II Avenue (aleja Jana Pawła II) to Nowa Huta's main square, plac Centralny (about 30 minutes total). From there, tram #4 (but not #15) continues a few minutes farther to the main gate of the Tadeusz Sendzimir Steelworks, and then it returns to Kraków.

Tours: True to its name, Mike Ostrowski's **Crazy Guides** is a loosely run operation that takes tourists to Nowa Huta in genuine communist-era vehicles (mostly Trabants and Polski Fiats). While the content is good, Mike and his comrades are laid-back, very informal, and sometimes crude. If you're offended by a foulmouthed guide who reminds you of a scruffy college student, or if you don't like the idea of careening down the streets of Kraków in a car that feels like a cardboard box with a lawnmower engine, skip this tour. For the rest of us, it's a fun and convenient way to experience Nowa Huta (129 zł/person for 2.5-hour Nowa Huta tour; 169 zł/person for 4-hour Communism Deluxe tour that also includes their makeshift "museum"—a communist-era apartment that's decorated to give you a taste of the way things were; 159 zł/person for 4-hour Real Kraków tour that covers the basic Nowa Huta trip plus outlying sights; other crazy experiences also available, cash only, reserve ahead and they'll pick you up at your hotel, mobile 500-091-200, www.crazyguides.com, info@crazyguides.com).

Background: Nowa Huta was the communists' idea of paradise. It's one of only three towns outside the Soviet Union that

were custom-built to showcase socialist ideals. (The others are Dunaújváros—once called Sztálinváros—south of Budapest, Hungary; and Eisenhüttenstadt—once called Stalinstadt—near Brandenburg, Germany.) Completed in just 10 years (1949-1959), Nowa Huta was built primarily because the Soviets felt that smart and sassy Kraków needed a taste of heavy industry. Farmers and villagers were imported to live and work in Nowa Huta. Many of the new residents, who weren't accustomed to city living, brought along their livestock (which grazed in the fields around unfinished buildings). For commies, it was downright idyllic: Dad would cheerily ride the tram into the steel factory, mom would dutifully keep house, and the kids could splash around at the man-made beach and learn how to cut perfect red stars out of construction paper. But Krakovians had the last laugh: Nowa Huta, along with Lech Wałęsa's shipyard in Gdańsk, was one of the home bases of the Solidarity strikes that eventually brought down the regime. Now, with the communists long gone, Nowa Huta remains a sooty suburb of Poland's cultural capital, with a whopping 200,000 residents.

Touring Nowa Huta: Nowa Huta's focal point used to be known simply as **Central Square** (plac Centralny), but in a fit of poetic justice, it was recently renamed for the anti-communist Ronald Reagan. This square is the heart of the planned town. A map of Nowa Huta looks like a clamshell: a semi-circular design radiating from Central/Reagan Square. Numbered streets fan out like spokes on a wheel, and trolleys zip workers directly to the immense factory.

Believe it or not, the inspiration for Nowa Huta was the Renaissance (which, thanks to the textbook Renaissance design of the Cloth Hall and other landmarks, Soviet architects considered typically Polish). Notice the elegantly predictable arches and galleries that would make Michelangelo proud. The settlement was loosely planned on the gardens of Versailles (comparing aerial views of those two very different sites—both with axes radiating from a central hub—this becomes clear). When first built (before it was layered with grime), Nowa Huta was delightfully orderly, primly painted, impeccably maintained, and downright beautiful... if a little boring. It was practical, too: Each of the huge apartment blocks is a self-contained unit, with its own grassy inner courtyard, school, and shops. Driveways (which appear to dead-end at underground garage doors) lead to vast fallout shelters.

Today's Nowa Huta is a far cry from its glory days. Wander around. Poke into the courtyards. Reflect on what it would be like to live here. It may not be as bad as you imagine. Ugly as they seem from the outside, these buildings are packed with happy little apartments filled with color, light, and warmth.

The wide boulevard running northeast of Central/Reagan Square, now called Solidarity Avenue (aleja Solidarności, lined with tracks for tram #4), leads to the **Tadeusz Sendzimir Steelworks.** Originally named for Lenin, this factory was supposedly built using plans stolen from a Pittsburgh plant. It was designed to be a cog in the communist machine—reliant on iron ore from Ukraine, and therefore worthless unless Poland remained in the Soviet Bloc. Down from as many as 40,000 workers at its peak, the steelworks now employs only about 10,000. Today there's little to see other than the big sign, stern administration buildings, and smokestacks in the distance. Examine the twin offices flanking the sign—topped with turrets and a decorative frieze inspired by Italian palazzos, these continue the Renaissance theme of the housing districts.

Another worthwhile sight in Nowa Huta is the **Lord's Ark**

Church (Arka Pana, several blocks northwest of Central/Reagan Square on ulica Obrońców Krzyża). Back when he was archbishop

of Kraków, Karol Wojtyła fought for years to build a church in this most communist of communist towns. When the regime refused, he insisted on conducting open-air Masses before crowds in fields—until the communists finally capitulated. Consecrated on May 15, 1977, the Lord's Ark Church has a Le Corbusier–esque design that looks like a fat, exhausted Noah's Ark resting on Mount Ararat—encouraging Poles to persevere through the floods of communism. While architecturally interesting, the church is mostly significant as a symbol of an early victory of Catholicism over communism.

▲Kościuszko Mound (Kopiec Kościuszki)

On a sunny day, the parklands west of the Old Town are a fine place to get out of the city and commune with Krakovians at play. On the outskirts of town is the Kościuszko Mound, a nearly perfectly conical hill erected in 1823 to honor the Polish and American military hero, Tadeusz Kościuszko. The mound incorporates soil that was brought here from battlefields where the famous general fought, both in Poland and in the American Revolution. Later, under Habsburg rule, a citadel with a chapel was built around the mound, which provided a fine lookout over this otherwise flat terrain. And more recently, the hill was reinforced with steel and cement to prevent it from eroding away. You'll pay to enter the walls and walk to the top—up a curlicue path that makes the mound resemble a giant soft-serve cone—and inside you'll find a modest Kościuszko museum. While not too exciting, this is a pleasant place for an excursion on a nice day.

Cost and Hours: 10 zł, includes museum, mound open daily 9:00-dusk, museum open daily 9:30-16:30, café, tel. 12-425-1116, www.kopieckosciuszki.pl.

Getting There: Ride tram #1 (from in front of the Wyspiański Pavilion or the main post office) to the end of the line, called Salvator, then follow the well-marked path uphill for 20 minutes.

Shopping in Kraków

Two of the most popular Polish souvenirs—amber and pottery—come from areas far from Kraków. Amber *(bursztyn)* is found on northern Baltic shores (see page 449). "Polish pottery," with distinctive blue-and-white designs, is made in the region of Silesia, west of Kraków (mostly in the town of Bolesławiec). Because neither of these items actually comes from Kraków, you won't find any great bargains. Somewhat more local are the many wood carvings you'll see.

The **Cloth Hall,** smack-dab in the center of the Main Market Square, is the most convenient place to pick up any Polish souvenirs. It has a great selection, respectable prices, and the city's highest concentration of pickpockets (summer Mon-Fri 9:00-18:00, Sat-Sun 9:00-15:00, sometimes later; winter Mon-Fri 9:00-16:00, Sat-Sun 9:00-15:00).

A small but swanky mall called **Pasaż 13** is a few steps off the southeast corner of the Main Market Square, where Grodzka street enters the Square. Enter the mall under the balcony marked *Pasaż 13* (Mon-Sat 9:00-21:00, Sun 11:00-17:00).

Two new, enormous shopping malls lie just beyond the tourist zone. The gigantic **Galeria Krakowska,** with 270 shops, shares a square with the train station (Mon-Sat 9:00-22:00, Sun 10:00-21:00, can't miss it right next to the main train station). Note that nearby landmarks are signposted inside this massive, labyrinthine mall (*PKP/PKS* leads to the train and bus stations; *Stare Miasto* goes to the Old Town). Only slightly smaller is the **Galeria Kazimierz** (Mon-Sat 10:00-22:00, Sun 10:00-20:00, just a few blocks east of the Kazimierz sights, along the river at Podgórska 24).

Entertainment in Kraków

As a town full of both students and tourists, Kraków has plenty of fun options, especially at night.

In the Old Town

Main Market Square—Intoxicating as the Square is by day, it's even better at night...pure enchantment. Have a meal or nurse a drink at an outdoor café, or just grab a bench and enjoy the scene. There's often live, al fresco music coming from somewhere (either at restaurants, at a temporary stage set up near the Town Hall Tower, or from talented buskers). You could spend hours doing slow laps around the Square after dark, and never run out of diversions.

Concerts—You'll find a wide range of musical events, from tourist-oriented "Chopin's greatest hits" in quaint old ballrooms, to folk-dancing shows, to serious philharmonic performances. Popular venues include churches (such as the churches of Sts. Peter and Paul on ulica Grodzka, St. Adalbert on the Square, or St. Idziego/Giles at the foot of Wawel Hill), various gardens around town (July-Aug only), and fancy mansions on the Main Market Square (including the Polonia House/Dom Polonii at #14, near ulica Grodzka; the Bonerowski Palace near the top of the Square at ulica Św. Jana 1; and the Pod Baranami Palace, at #27). Because Kraków's live-music scene is continually evolving, it's best to inquire locally about what's on during your visit. Hotel lobbies are stocked with fliers for upcoming concerts. But to get all of your options, visit any TI. The TI on ulica Św. Jana, which specializes in cultural events, can book tickets for most concerts (no extra fee) and tell you how to get tickets for the others. The free, monthly *Karnet* cultural-events book lists everything (half in Polish and half in English, also online at www.karnet.krakow.pl).

Jazz—For something a little more edgy, delve into Kraków's thriving jazz scene. Several popular clubs hide on the streets surrounding the Main Market Square (open nightly, most shows start around 21:30). The most famous and best for all-around jazz in a sophisticated cellar environment is **Jazz Club u Muniaka** (10-20-zł cover, open nightly 19:00-1:00 in the morning, live music nightly from 21:30, best music when the owner Janusz plays on Thu-Sat, ulica Floriańska 3, tel. 12-423-1205; described earlier on my self-guided walk). **Harris Piano Jazz Bar,** right on the Square (at #28), is more casual and offers a mix of traditional and updated "fusion" jazz, plus blues (free most nights, 10-zł cover for more serious shows on Sat, music nightly from 21:30, tel. 12-421-5741, www.harris.krakow.pl). **Stalowa Magnolia** is a bit more youthful, clubby-feeling, and snooty, with jazz about two nights a week and rock or pop the other nights (no cover on weeknights, on weekends 15-zł cover for men and free for women, music nightly from 22:00, ulica Św. Jana 15, tel. 12-422-8472, www.stalowemagnolie.com).

Nightlife in the Old Town—The entire Old Town is crammed with nightclubs and discos pumping loud music on weekends. On a Saturday, the pedestrian streets can be more crowded at midnight than at noon. However, with the exception of the jazz clubs mentioned earlier, most of the nightspots in the Old Town are garden-variety dance clubs, completely lacking the personality and creativity of the Kazimierz nightspots described next. Worse, to save money, local young people stand out in front of nightclubs to drink their own booze (BYOB), rather than pay high prices for the drinks inside—making the streets that much more crowded and noisy. For low-key hanging out, people choose a café on the Square; otherwise, they head for Kazimierz.

In Kazimierz

Aside from the Old Town's gorgeous Square, Kraków's best area to hang out after dark is Kazimierz, the former Jewish quarter.

Klezmer Music—Several restaurants offer traditional Jewish klezmer music most evenings for a steep 25-zł cover charge (plus the cost of food); for details, see page 358. On most summer evenings, a klezmer concert or two can be found at theater venues (generally 50 zł; look for posters and fliers around town). The music is lively and evocative, but this is a fairly sedate scene—most of the people around you will be going to bed right after the show. If you'd like to stay up a bit later, there's no better way to spend your time than exploring the bars of Kazimierz (described next).

Bars and Clubs—Squeezed between centuries-old synagogues and cemeteries are wonderful hangouts running the full gamut from sober and tasteful to wild and clubby. The classic recipe for a Kazimierz bar: Find a dilapidated old storefront, fill the interior with ramshackle furniture, turn the lights down low, and pipe in old-timey jazz music from the 1920s. Sprinkle with alcohol. Serves one to two dozen hipsters. After a few clubs of this type caught on, a more diverse cross-section of nightspots began to move in, including some loud dance clubs. The whole area is bursting with life—it's the kind of place where people just spontaneously start dancing—and locals still outnumber tourists. I've listed websites for places that feature periodic live music and other events.

On and near Plac Nowy: The highest concentration of bars ring the plac Nowy market square. While most of these are nondescript, a few stand out. **Alchemia**, one of the first—and still one of the best—bars in Kazimierz, is candlelit, cluttered, and claustrophobic, with cave-like rooms crowded with rickety old furniture, plus a cellar used for live performances (Estery 5, www.alchemia .com.pl). Hiding just a half-block down the street is **Miejsce** ("The Place"), which is brighter and more minimalist than the norm, with stripped-down walls and carefully chosen Scan-design old furniture—it's run by the owners of a design firm specializing in decor from the 50s, 60s, and 70s (Estery 1). Fronting the square, **Kolory** has a pleasant Parisian brasserie ambience (Estery 10), while **Le Scandale** is all black leather and serves Italian food (plac Nowy 9). Late at night, the little windows in the plac Nowy **market hall** do a big business selling *zapiekanki* (baguette with toppings) to hungry bar-hoppers.

On Rabina Meiselsa street, just a half-block off plac Nowy, two places share a long courtyard: **Mleczarnia**, a top-notch beer garden with rickety tables squeezed under the trees and its cozy old-fashioned pub across the street (at #20); and **Stajnia**, at the far end of the courtyard, where scenes from *Schindler's List* were filmed. Its interior feels like a Polish village drenched in red light and turned into a dance hall.

Near Isaac Synagogue: A block east of plac Nowy, a few more places cluster on the wide street in front of Isaac Synagogue. The huge **Nova Resto Bar** dominates the scene with a long covered terrace, a vast interior, and seating in their courtyard—all with a cool-color-scheme Las Vegas polka-dot style. This feels upscale and a bit pretentious compared to many of the others, but it's *the* place to be seen (25-40-zł meals, Estery 18). Upstairs is the similarly trendy music club **Taawa** (www.taawa.pl). Facing this double-decker wall of style are some smaller, more accessible options: **Singer** is classy and mellow, with most of its tables made of old namesake sewing machines (Estery 20), while **Warsztat** has an exploding-instruments-factory ambience (Izaaka 3; also recommended later, under "Eating in Kraków").

On Józefa Street: More good bars are just a short block south. Along Józefa, you'll find a pair of classic Kazimierz joints: **Eszeweria**, which wins the "best atmosphere" award, feels like a Polish speakeasy that's been in mothballs for the last 90 years—a low-key, unpretentious, and inviting hangout (Józefa 9). Their less enticing but still enjoyable sister bar, Esze, is across the street. A block up, look for **Kolanko No. 6,** with a cozy bar up front, a pleasant beer garden in the inner courtyard, and a fun events hall in back (Józefa 17, www.kolanko.net; also recommended later, under "Eating in Kraków").

In Podgórze: If you run out of diversions in the heart of Kazimierz, head south. With the construction of a new pedestrian bridge over the river just south of this area, Kazimierz's nightlife scene is spreading to **Podgórze,** just across the river. Here in this fast-evolving zone, prices are a bit lower.

Sleeping in Kraków

Healthy competition—with new, cleverly run places cropping up all the time—keeps Kraków's accommodation prices reasonable and makes choosing a hotel fun rather than frustrating. Rates are soft; hoteliers don't need much of an excuse to offer you 10 to 20 percent off, especially on weekends or off-season. I've focused my accommodations in two areas: in and near the Old Town; and in Kazimierz, a local-style, more affordable neighborhood that is home to both the old Jewish quarter and a thriving dining and nightlife zone.

While the Old Town used to be sleepy, it's now jam-packed with discos that thump loud music on weekend nights to attract roving gangs of rowdy students, backpackers, and obnoxious "stag parties" of drunken louts from the UK in town for a weekend of carousing. The "quiet after 22:00" law is flagrantly ignored. Kazimierz is also home to various hip dance clubs. Because of all these clubs, virtually all of my accommodations come with some risk of noise; to help your odds, ask for a quiet room when you reserve, and bring earplugs.

Sleep Code

(3 zł = about $1, country code: 48)

S = Single, **D** = Double/Twin, **T** = Triple, **Q** = Quad, **b** = bathroom, **s** = shower only. Unless otherwise noted, credit cards are accepted, and breakfast is included. Everyone listed here speaks English.

To help you easily sort through these listings, I've divided the accommodations into three categories based on the price for a double room with bath during high season:

\$\$\$ Higher Priced—Most rooms 400 zł or more.

\$\$ Moderately Priced—Most rooms between 300-400 zł.

\$ Lower Priced—Most rooms 300 zł or less.

Prices can change without notice; verify the hotel's current rates online or by email. For other updates, see www .ricksteves.com/update.

In the Old Town

While you could stay away from the center, accommodations values here are so good that there's little sense in sleeping beyond the Planty park. Most of my listings are inside (or within a block or two of) the former city walls.

The Old Town has four basic types of accommodations: small, well-run guest houses (my favorite); big hotels (comfortable but overpriced); apartments (cheap, but you're on your own); and funky youth hostels. I've listed the best of each type.

Guest Houses

These good-value pensions almost invariably come with lots of stairs (no elevators), and are run by smart, can-do, entrepreneurial owners. They're all located in the heart of the Old Town along busy pedestrian streets, and most don't have air-conditioning—so they can be noisy with the windows open in the summer, especially on weekends. (Light sleepers should request quiet rooms.) These places book up fast, especially in summer—reserve as far ahead as possible. Don't expect a 24-hour reception desk; it's always smart to tell them your arrival time, especially if it's late in the day.

\$\$ Tango House, run by tango dance instructor Marcin Miszczak, is in a well-located building with an ancient-feeling stairwell decorated with faded Art Nouveau paintings. Its eight long, skinny, stylish rooms have parquet floors (tiny Sb-220 zł, standard Sb-300 zł, Db-340 zł, big Db-380 zł, prices can be soft in slow times, about 100 zł cheaper Nov-March, free Wi-Fi, ask for quieter courtyard room to avoid rowdy street noise on weekends, ulica Szpitalna 4, tel. 12-429-3114, www.tangohouse.pl, info @tangohouse.pl).

$ Golden Lion Guest House has 12 smallish rooms with modern flair on a bustling pedestrian street a block off the Main Market Square (Sb-180 zł, Db-300 zł, 10 percent cheaper Nov-Feb, ask for quieter room in back, air-con in some rooms, free Internet access and Wi-Fi, guest kitchen, no parking, ulica Szewska 19, tel. 12-422-9323, fax 12-421-9775, www.goldenlion.pl, reservation @goldenlion.pl, Łodziński family and Tyson, a smelly boxer dog).

$ Globtroter Guest House offers 18 rustic-feeling rooms with high ceilings and big beams around a serene garden courtyard. Jacek (Jack), who really understands and respects travelers, conscientiously focuses on value—keeping prices as low as possible by not offering needless extras (June-Aug: Sb-190 zł, Db-310 zł; April-May and Sept-Oct: Sb-170 zł, Db-290 zł; Nov-March: Sb-120 zł, Db-180 zł; ask for 10 percent discount with this book, 2 people can cram into a single to save money—a little more than the Sb price, larger suites for up to five also available, no breakfast at hotel but you can buy 14-zł breakfast from nearby restaurant, free Internet access and Wi-Fi, fun 700-year-old brick cellar lounge down below, go down passageway at #7 at the square called plac Szczepański, tel. 12-422-4123, fax 12-422-4233, www.globtroter -krakow.com, globtroter@globtroter-krakow.com).

$ La Fontaine B&B, run by a French-Polish family, offers eight rooms and five apartments just off the Main Market Square. Tastefully decorated with French flair, it's cute as a poodle. Each room has a little lounge with a microwave and fridge (most on the hall, some inside the room). If you don't mind lots and lots of stairs (it's on the fifth floor), this is a decent value (Sb-249 zł, Db-269 zł, extra bed-60 zł, apartment for up to four-460 zł, apartment for up to six-659 zł, gigantic apartment-727 zł, cheaper Oct-Easter, aircon, low slanted ceilings in some rooms, free Wi-Fi, guest kitchen, free self-service laundry machine—or pay them 25 zł to wash clothes for you, ulica Sławkowska 1, tel. 12-422-6564, fax 12-431-0955, www.bblafontaine.com, biuro@bblafontaine.com). They also have six newer rooms and two apartments in another, equally convenient Old Town location, just south of the Square; you'll check in at the main hotel, then walk five minutes to your room (similar prices and stairs as main hotel).

Hotels

For this section, I've listed the official, published "rack rates"—which are very soft. Most hotels discount their rates substantially, especially in slow times. Consider asking several hotels for their lowest price during your visit, and take the best deal.

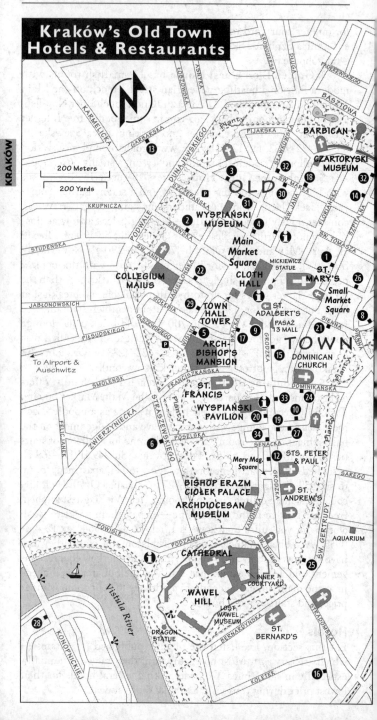

Kraków's Old Town Hotels & Restaurants

KRAKÓW

1. Tango House
2. Golden Lion Guest House
3. Globtroter Guest House
4. La Fontaine B&B #1
5. La Fontaine B&B #2
6. Hotel Maltański
7. Hotel Pugetów
8. Hotel Gródek
9. Wentzl Hotel, Wierzynek Rest. & Słodki Wentzl
10. Hotel Wawel
11. Hotel Classic
12. Hotel Senacki & Bar Grodzki
13. Hotel Amber
14. Kraków City Apts.
15. Grodzka Apt. House
16. Nathan's Villa Hostel
17. Mama's Hostel
18. Restauracja Farina
19. Miód Malina Restaurant
20. Restauracja pod Aniołami
21. Aperitif Restaurant
22. Chimera Cafeteria
23. Restauracja Jarema
24. Ancora Restaurant
25. Pod Wawelem Beer Hall
26. Cyklop Pizza
27. Pizzeria Trzy Papryczki
28. Pizza Garden
29. Aqua e Vino
30. Indus Tandoor
31. Polskie Smaki
32. U Babci Maliny (2)
33. Kwandras Lunch Bar
34. Bar Mleczny

$$$ Donimirski Boutique Hotels, with three different locations in or near Kraków's Old Town, set the bar for splurge hotels in Kraków (website for all: www.donimirski.com). All Donimirski hotels offer my readers a 15 percent discount. You can expect any of these hotels to have some of the friendliest staff in Kraków and all of the classy little extras that add up to a memorable hotel experience. **Hotel Maltański**—my home away from home in Kraków— has 16 rooms in the beautifully renovated former royal stables, just outside the Planty park and only two blocks from Wawel Castle (Sb-430 zł, Db-510 zł, 80 zł more for "deluxe" room with air-con, cheaper Nov-March, no elevator but only 2 floors, free Wi-Fi, parking-50 zł/day, ulica Straszewskiego 14, tel. 12-431-0010, fax 12-431-0615, maltanski@donimirski.com). **Hotel Pugetów,** with seven small but plush and cozy rooms and a fun breakfast cellar, is on the other side of town, in a slightly dingy but convenient neighborhood between the Main Market Square and Kazimierz (Sb-280 zł, Db-490 zł, Db suite-640 zł, cheaper Nov-March, air-con, free cable Internet, parking-50 zł/day, ulica Starowiślna 13-15, tel. 12-432-4950, pugetow@donimirski.com). **Hotel Gródek**—by far the fanciest and most central of the bunch—offers 23 rooms a three-minute walk behind St. Mary's Church on a quiet dead-end street overlooking the Planty park. This place is easily the best splurge in town, with a handy location, gorgeously decorated rooms, and a top-notch breakfast served in a room surrounded by a mini-museum of artifacts discovered during the recent renovation (Sb-470 zł, bigger "deluxe" Sb-630 zł, Db-610 zł, bigger "deluxe" Db-690 zł, suite-920 zł, cheaper Nov-March, free Internet access, free cable Internet, good cellar restaurant serves Polish cuisine, parking-50 zł/day, Na Gródku 4, tel. 12-431-9030, grodek @donimirski.com). If you have a car, ask about rooms at their countryside castle, Zamek Korzkiew. Their fifth property, Hotel Kościuszko, has five stars and reasonable prices, but is located far from the center.

$$$ Wentzl Hotel is your splurge-right-on-the-Square option, with 18 rooms. The decor is over-the-top-classy Old World with modern touches, like state-of-the-art TVs and bathrooms. When reserving, request a room with a view on the Square— which can be noisy, especially on weekends—or one of the three quieter back rooms (Sb-665 zł, Db-700 zł, bigger "deluxe" rooms cost 50 zł more, air-con, elevator, free Wi-Fi, Rynek Główny 19, tel. 12-430-2664, fax 12-430-2665, www.wentzl.pl, hotel @wentzl.pl).

$$$ Hotel Wawel has 39 rooms on a well-located street that's quieter than the Old Town norm. It feels plush for the price, though its colorful decor verges on gaudy; above the swanky marble lobby are hallways creatively painted with the history of the building and images from around Kraków (Sb-340 zł, Db-480 zł, extra bed-100 zł/adult or 50 zł/child, rates are soft so ask for best price, 20 percent less Nov-March, non-smoking, air-con, elevator—but doesn't go to top floor, free Internet access and Wi-Fi, ulica Poselska 22, tel. 12-424-1300, fax 12-424-1333, www.hotel wawel.pl, hotel@hotelwawel.pl).

$$$ Hotel Classic, a modern home in old Kraków (on a nondescript street just inside the Planty park), has 30 Scan-designed rooms, a sleek marble lobby, professional staff, decent prices, and little character (April-Oct: Sb-495 zł, Db-540 zł, suite-740 zł, cheaper Nov-March, Rick Steves readers get a 20 percent discount on weekdays and 25 percent discount Fri-Sun with a 2-night minimum stay, non-smoking floor, air-con, elevator, free Wi-Fi and cable Internet, request one of the few quiet back rooms to avoid weekend disco noise from across the street, ulica Św. Tomasza 32, tel. 12-424-0303, fax 12-429-3680, www.hotel-classic.pl, hotel @hotel-classic.pl).

$$$ Hotel Senacki is a business-class place renting 20 aging rooms with parquet floors between Wawel Castle and the Main Market Square. Nine of the rooms have air-conditioning for no extra charge—if you'll be here in summer, request this when you reserve. Top-floor "attic" rooms have low beams, skylight windows, and a flight of stairs after the elevator (prices change constantly with demand, but generally Sb-400 zł, Db-500 zł, deluxe Db-550 zł, extra bed-90 zł, cheaper Nov-March, non-smoking rooms, elevator—but doesn't go to "attic" rooms, free Wi-Fi, parking-50 zł/day, ulica Grodzka 51, tel. 12-422-7686, fax 12-422-7934, www.osti-hotele.pl, senacki@osti-hotele.pl).

$$ Hotel Amber sits on a grimy but safe and quiet street just outside the Planty park, less than a 10-minute walk from the Square. With 18 rooms, attentive service, and modern style, it's a good-value alternative to the places inside the Old Town (Sb-350 zł, standard Db-438 zł, bigger "superior" Db-479 zł, "deluxe" Db with fancier touches-499 zł, cheaper Nov-March, air-con, elevator, free Wi-Fi, Garbarska 10, tel. 12-421-0606, www.hotel-amber.pl, office@hotel-amber.pl).

Apartments

You can save money by staying in your own apartment rather than a hotel. Apartments come with great locations, simple kitchens, and relatively low prices, but no reception desk or big-hotel services (such as having your room cleaned daily)...you're on your own. Apartments aren't just for long stays—these places welcome even one-nighters. While the apartments themselves are neat and modern, most are in old buildings with dreary entryways and stairways. Be sure to clearly communicate your arrival time.

$ Kraków City Apartments, conscientiously run by Andzej and Katarzyna, is 10 clean, modern apartments tucked away in a quiet courtyard at the corner of the Old Town (small Db-200 zł, standard Db-260 zł, bigger apartment-350 zł, 20 percent cheaper Oct-April, non-smoking, elevator in one building, free Wi-Fi, ulica Szpitalna 34, tel. 12-431-0041, mobile 504-235-925, www.krakowapartments.info, info@krakowapartments.info).

$ Grodzka Apartment House offers 11 new-feeling, stylishly decorated apartments around a courtyard along one of Kraków's most happening streets, just a few steps off the Main Market Square. The studio apartments are as nice as a hotel room and a good value (studio-250 zł, 1-bedroom-330 zł, 2-bedroom-450 zł, prices soft, cheaper Nov-March, no breakfast but can buy 25-zł breakfast at nearby café, reception open daily 11:00-21:00, some apartments have street noise—light sleepers ask for quiet room, lots of stairs with no elevator, free Wi-Fi, go down the passage at Grodzka 4, tel. 12-421-4835, mobile 660-541-085, www.grodzka.net.pl, info@grodzka.net.pl, Mikołaj). They also have more apartments (though not quite as nice) in two other Old Town buildings.

Hostels

New hostels are born—and go extinct—every other day in Kraków. But these three are well-established.

$ Nathan's Villa Hostel, in an up-and-coming neighborhood between Wawel Hill and Kazimierz, is well-run by an energetic young Bostonian and his wife. It's loose, easygoing, and fun, with 120 beds in 21 cleverly painted rooms, a bar, a beer garden, an art gallery, a cheap BBQ every night in summer, and plenty of backpacker bonding. Their advertising promises advice on how to "get hammered," and the bar has regular drinking contests...if that's not your scene, sleep elsewhere (bunk in 4-bed room-65 zł, in 6-bed room-60 zł, in 8-bed room-55 zł, in 10-bed room-45 zł, D-160 zł, Db-180 zł, apartment with kitchenette for up to four-280 zł, rates are 5 zł/person less Nov-Feb; includes breakfast, sheets, laundry facilities, and lockers; free Internet access and Wi-Fi, non-smoking, no curfew or lockout time, ulica Św. Agnieszki 1, tel. 12-422-3545, www.nathansvilla.com, krakow@nathansvilla.com).

$ Mama's Hostel is ideally located (just steps off the Main Market Square) and more dignified than most hostels—like an old apartment taken over by vagabonds with good manners, but who still know how to have a good time. With 54 beds in 7 rooms and mellow public spaces, it's a winner (60 zł/person in a 6-bed room, 55 zł in a 10-bed room, 50 zł in a 12-bed room, D-180 zł; includes sheets, breakfast, and lockers; non-smoking, no curfew, lots of stairs with no elevator, free Internet access and Wi-Fi, kitchen,

pay laundry, ulica Bracka 4, tel. & fax 12-429-5940, www.mamas
hostel.com.pl, hostel@mamashostel.com.pl).

$ Hostel Momotown, in Kazimierz (described next), is a
smidge more institutional and less party-oriented than the above
options, but still loose and friendly. Run by Paweł Momot, it has 52
dorm beds and a fun garden for hanging out (bunk in 4-bed dorm-
60 zł, in 6-bed dorm-55 zł, in 8-bed dorm-55 zł, in 10-bed dorm-
45 zł, includes breakfast and sheets, towels-2.50 zł, free Internet
access and Wi-Fi, kitchen, laundry, lockers, ulica Miodowa 28,
tel. 12-429-6929, www.momotownhostel.com, info@momotown
hostel.com). Two blocks away, they also rent 14 basic but cheap
private rooms that share a kitchenette, overlooking Kazimierz's
main square, ulica Szeroka (Sb-140 zł, Db-180 zł).

In Kazimierz

Sleep in Kazimierz to be close to Kraków's Jewish heart—or simply to experience a cheaper, less touristy, more local-feeling neighborhood outside the Old Town. With the highest concentration
of pubs and nightclubs in town, Kazimierz rivals the Old Town
for nightlife—which means that all of these places can be subject
to some noise, especially on weekends. Keep in mind that these
accommodations put you a 20-minute walk or a 5-minute tram
ride from the medieval ambience of Kraków's old center (for details
on getting to Kazimierz from the Old Town, see page 323). Some
of the klezmer music restaurants listed under "Eating in Kraków"
also rent rooms, but they're generally an afterthought to the food
and music, and not a good value. Note that Hostel Momotown—
listed above—is also in Kazimierz. For locations, see the map on
page 324.

$$ Dom Casimi is nicely located, with 12 rooms at the top
of ulica Szeroka in the heart of Jewish Kazimierz (Sb-155-260 zł,
Db-220-370 zł, Tb-240-430 zł, price depends on size, season, and
style of room—pricier rooms have antique furniture, rates are soft
so ask for best price, stairs with no elevator, free Wi-Fi and cable
Internet, free loaner bikes for guests, ulica Szeroka 7/8, tel. 12-426-
1193, fax 12-426-1194, www.casimi.pl, casimi@casimi.pl).

$$ Karmel Hotel, with 11 rooms on a pleasant side street
near the heart of Kazimierz, offers elegance at a reasonable price
(Sb-260 zł, tight twin Db-298 zł, more spacious "komfort plus"
Db with one big bed and air-con-398 zł, pricier suites also available, extra bed-70 zł, about 15-20 percent less Nov-March, upstairs
with no elevator, free Internet access and Wi-Fi, some night noise
on weekends, ulica Kupa 15, tel. 12-430-6697, fax 12-430-6726,
www.karmel.com.pl, hotel@karmel.com.pl).

$ Tournet Guest House, well-run by friendly Piotr and
Sylwia Działowy, is a great budget option offering 19 clean, colorful

rooms near the edge of Kazimierz toward Wawel Hill. The "basic" rooms don't include breakfast (7.50 zł extra) or TV sets (basic Sb-110 zł, standard Sb-150 zł, basic Db-140 zł, standard Db-200 zł, Tb-250 zł, extra bed-50 zł, 10 zł/person less Nov-March, lots of stairs with no elevator, free Wi-Fi, reception open 7:00-22:00, ulica Miodowa 7, tel. 12-292-0088, fax 12-292-0089, www.nocleg .krakow.pl, tournet@accommodation.krakow.pl).

$ **Maayan Guest Rooms** offers 11 simple, cozy, cheap rooms surrounding the 17th-century Kupa Synagogue. You can walk through the balconies overlooking the synagogue's prayer hall (S-70 zł, Sb-120 zł, D-100 zł, Db-180 zł, T-160 zł, Tb-210 zł, cash only, no breakfast, non-smoking, free Internet access and Wi-Fi, café, bike rental, some nightclub noise on weekends—ask for quiet room, ulica Miodowa 27, tel. 12-431-0170, maayanhotel@gmail.com).

Eating in Kraków

Kraków has a wide array of great restaurants—for every one I've listed, there are two or three nearly as good. (The downside is a lack of variation; little distinguishes one place from another.) Polish food is rivaled by Italian in popularity. As the restaurant scene changes constantly, I've chosen places that are well-established and have a proven track record for reliably good food.

In the Old Town

Kraków's Old Town is loaded with dining options. Prices are reasonable even on the Main Market Square. And a half-block away, they get even better. All of these eateries (except the milk bars) are likely to be booked up on weekends—always reserve ahead.

Restauracja Farina, with a fish-and-bottles theme, features a welcoming atmosphere and Polish and Mediterranean cuisine with an emphasis on fresh fish (30-35-zł pastas, 30-60-zł main dishes). They serve some special seafood dishes (60-100 zł) only on the days that they get their fresh delivery (about twice weekly; open daily 12:00-23:00, 2 blocks north of the Square at ulica Św. Marka 16, at intersection with ulica Św. Jana, tel. 12-422-1680).

Miód Malina ("Honey Raspberry") is a delightful Polish-Italian fusion restaurant filled with the comforting aroma of its wood-fired oven. The menu is half Polish and half Italian—yet, remarkably, they do both cuisines equally well. For example, you can start with borscht and follow it with lasagna Bolognese. Sit in the cozy, warmly painted interior, or out in the courtyard (19-zł pierogi, 25-zł pastas, 40-70-zł main dishes, reservations smart, daily 12:00-23:00, ulica Grodzka 40, tel. 12-430-0411).

Restauracja pod Aniołami ("Under Angels") offers a dressy, candlelit atmosphere on a wonderful covered patio, or in a deep, steep, romantic cellar with rough wood and medieval vaults. Peruse the elaborately described menu of medieval noblemen's dishes. The cuisine is traditional Polish, with an emphasis on grilled meats and trout (on a wood-fired grill). Every meal begins with *smalec* (spread made with lard, fried onion, bacon, and apple). Don't go here if you're in a hurry—only if you want to really slow down and enjoy your dinner. Reservations are smart (15-30-zł starters, 40-70-zł main dishes, daily 13:00-24:00, ulica Grodzka 35, tel. 12-421-3999).

Aperitif is a stylish bistro serving tasty international cuisine with Mediterranean flair on the appealing Small Market Square (Mały Rynek) behind St. Mary's Church. It's classy but casual, with a cozy interior and a pleasant garden in back. Their 19- or 25-zł lunch specials, served on weekdays, are a great deal (22-26-zł pastas, 35-50-zł main dishes, daily 10:00-23:00, ulica Sienna 9, tel. 12-432-3333).

Chimera, just off the Main Market Square, is a cafeteria that serves fast traditional meals to a steady stream of students. You'll order at the counter, then eat outside on their quiet courtyard (good salad buffet: small plate-12 zł, big plate-16 zł; 12-19-zł main dishes, good for vegetarians, daily 9:00-22:00, near university at ulica Św. Anny 3). I'd skip their expensive full-service restaurant (in the basement), which shares an entryway.

Restauracja Jarema (yah-RAY-mah) offers a tasty reminder that Kraków used to rule a large swath of Ukraine and Lithuania. They serve eastern Polish/Ukrainian cuisine (with well-described specialties) amid 19th-century aristocratic elegance—you'll feel like you're dining in an old mansion. It's very sedate and feels a bit tired, but the food satisfies (30-55-zł main dishes, several good vegetarian options, daily 12:00-22:00, usually live music from 19:00, reservations wise, across the street from barbican at plac Matejki 5, tel. 12-429-3669).

Fine Dining: **Ancora** attempts to bring a touch of modern class and creativity to Kraków's otherwise staid and predictable culinary landscape. Chef Adam Chrząstowski, who worked under world-famous chef Thomas Keller, offers modern international food with a Polish accent. It's not cheap—you're basically paying Square-view prices for a sleek minimalist dining room tucked alongside the Dominican Church—but the food is a notch above (30-40-zł starters, 55-70-zł main dishes; fixed-price meals: 155 zł/5 courses, 190 kn/7 courses; daily 11:00-22:30, Dominikańska 3, tel. 12-357-3355).

Beer Hall: **Pod Wawelem** ("Under Wawel") is a rollicking Austrian-style beer hall right on the Planty park near Wawel Castle. It's packed with locals seeking big, sloppy, greasy portions of meaty fare, with giant mugs of various beers on tap (including Polish and Bavarian). Choose between the bustling interior, or the outdoor terrace right on the Planty (20-30-zł main dishes, different specials every day—such as giant schnitzel, pork ribs, or roasted chicken; daily 12:00-24:00, ulica Św. Gertrudy 26-29, tel. 12-421-2336).

Pizza: Two well-established places in the Old Town are reliable choices. **Cyklop,** with 10 tables wrapped around the cook and his busy oven, has good wood-fired pizzas (14-23-zł one-person pizzas, 15-26-zł two-person pizzas, daily 11:00-23:00, near St. Mary's Church at Mikołajska 16, tel. 12-421-6603). **Pizzeria Trzy Papryczki** ("Three Peppers"), whose wood-fired pizzas aren't quite as good as Cyklop's, has better ambience, either inside or out in the welcoming garden (17-25-zł one-person pizzas, 20-29-zł two-person pizzas, daily 11:00-23:00, ulica Poselska 17, tel. 12-292-5532). But the best pizza in town is at **Pizza Garden,** run by Stanisław, who worked at a respected New York City pizzeria for a decade and has brought the art of brick-oven pizza back home. The catch is that his place is well outside the Old Town, about a 10-minute walk across the river from Wawel Hill (the walk is mostly along the pretty riverside parkland and across Dębnicki Bridge, with great views back on the castle). This makes it a good post-Wawel lunch or dinner spot (16-30-zł one-person pizzas, 20-25-zł two-person pizzas, Mon-Wed 13:00-22:00, Thu-Sun 13:00-23:00; cross Dębnicki Bridge, then look right to find M. Konopnickiej 11/1; tel. 12-266-7309).

Serious Italian: The Italian-owned **Aqua e Vino** offers good food in a mellow, mod, black-and-white cellar decorated with giant stills from old movies. Probably the most authentic Italian eatery in town, it has a loyal following among the Italian expat community (20-40-zł pastas, 45-65-zł main dishes, daily 12:00-24:00, ulica Wiślna 5/10, tel. 12-421-2567).

Indian: **Indus Tandoor** is Kraków's oldest Indian restaurant, and the best I've tried in town. If you're ready for a break from Polish fare, this is the place (20-35-zł dishes, daily 12:00-22:00, Fri-Sat until 24:00, Sławkowska 13-15, tel. 12-423-2282).

Milk Bars

Kraków is a good place to try the cheap cafeterias called "milk bars." For pointers on eating at a milk bar, review the sidebar on page 269. I've listed them by neighborhoods: north or south of the Main Market Square.

North of the Main Market Square

These two options, easy to squeeze into a busy day of sightseeing, are my favorites in Kraków.

Polskie Smaki ("Polish Flavors") is a homey little self-service cafeteria with a surprisingly elegant interior. They serve fast, inexpensive, and tasty traditional meals a block off the Square, with good borscht and *gołąbki* (stuffed cabbage rolls) at a fraction of what you'd pay elsewhere (9-13-zł main dishes, daily 10:00-22:00, ulica Św. Tomasza 5, tel. 12-422-4822).

U Babci Maliny, with a grinning Granny on the sign, is another well-established and popular upmarket milk bar (6-18-zł main dishes). One location is across the street from the National Theater building at Szpitalna 38 (daily 11:00-23:00), while another—frequented almost entirely by Krakovians—is designed for university students and staff and is tucked into an inner court-yard of the Science Academy (find the door at Sławkowska 17, Mon-Fri 11:00-21:00, Sat-Sun 12:00-21:00).

On Grodzka Street, South of the Main Market Square

Ulica Grodzka, the busy street that cuts south from the Main Market Square, has a convenient little pocket of three milk bars within a few steps of each other (all are open daily for lunch and dinner, but only until 19:00 or 20:00, sometimes later in summer). Survey all three options before you dive in. If they look full, just wait—there's a lot of turnover, so a table should free up soon.

Approaching from the Square, the first one you'll come to (just after the modern copper-colored Wyspiański Pavilion, on the left) is the most modern and trendy of the three, more popular with students than with their grandparents: **Kwandras Lunch Bar** ("Quarter"—as in, you can eat here in a quarter-hour; pierogi and other dishes for 9-12 zł, full dinner for 13 zł, ulica Grodzka 32, tel. 12-294-2222).

Two blocks down the street and on the right (at the corner with Senacka) is the most basic and traditional milk bar, with a sign reading simply **Bar Mleczny** ("Milk Bar"; low-profile sign over the door reads *Restauracja "pod Temidą"*). The next best thing to a time machine to the communist era, this place has grumpy monolingual service, a mostly local clientele, and cheap but good food (8-15-zł main dishes).

A few more steps down, also on the right (just before the two churches), is **Bar Grodzki,** a single tight little room with shared tables. In addition to the standard milk-bar fare, Bar Grodzki special-izes in tasty potato pancake dishes *(placki ziemniaczane)*. Order high on the menu and

try the rich and hearty "Hunter's Delight"—potato pancake with sausage, beef, melted cheese, and spicy sauce for 20 zł. The English menu posted by the counter makes ordering easy. Order, sit, and wait to be called to fetch your food (most main dishes 9-20 zł).

Splurging on the Main Market Square

You'll find plenty of relatively expensive, tourist-oriented restaurants on the Square. While all of these places have rich interiors, there's not much point in paying a premium to dine here unless you're sitting outside on the Square (one exception is Pod Krzyżkiem at #39, with a surrealistic interior that boldly attempts to one-up Eastern Europe's top square). While tourists go for ye olde places, natives hang out at pizza joints (like Sphinx, part of a wildly popular Poland-wide chain). Poles generally afford this zone on their meager incomes by just having a drink on the Square after eating at home. If any place on the Square is a cut above, it's probably **Wierzynek**—the most famous restaurant on the Square (and maybe in all of Poland)—with a heritage dating back to 1364 and a guest list of notables ranging from heads of state to movie stars. It lives up to its big reputation with good food at not-too-outrageous prices in two dining zones (both with seating either indoors, or out on the Square—if dining outside, be clear on which area you want). The fancier restaurant serves sophisticated Polish fare (22-35-zł starters, 60-85-zł main dishes, daily 13:00-23:00), while the simpler café is a good budget alternative, with salads for under 30 zł and 20-40-zł Polish traditional classics (daily 10:00-23:00; both at #15, tel. 12-424-9600).

And for Dessert: **Słodki Wentzl** ("Sweets") is a local favorite for enjoying dessert on the Square. Consider dining more cheaply elsewhere, then finishing up with coffee, ice cream, or cake here (12-25-zł desserts, daily 11:00-23:00, at #19).

In Kazimierz

The entire district is bursting with lively cafés and bars—it's a happening night scene. Jewish food is the specialty here, but in general the neighborhood offers more diversity than the Old Town. The non-Jewish places I've listed are fast, cheap, and convenient. For locations, see the map on page 324.

Klezmer Concerts and Jewish Food

Kazimierz is a hub of Jewish restaurants, featuring cuisine and music that honors the neighborhood's Jewish heritage (and caters to its Jewish visitors). On a balmy summer night, the air is filled with the sound of klezmer music—traditional Jewish music from 19th-century Poland, generally with violin, string bass, clarinet, and accordion. Skilled klezmer musicians can make their instruments weep or laugh like human voices. Several places on ulica Szeroka (Kazimierz's main square) offer klezmer concerts around 20:00. All of these have several rooms, which the musicians move between as the evening goes on. While most places claim to do concerts nightly year-round, in reality they can be canceled anytime it's slow (especially off-season). For this reason—and because these places fill up—it's important to reserve ahead. (If you're in Kazimierz for some daytime sightseeing, visit several places, pick your favorite, and reserve dinner.) Each restaurant has a similar menu, with main dishes for 20-55 zł. Sometimes you'll need to order sides and starches separately. You'll pay an additional cover charge just for the music (about 25 zł/person). Don't expect great cuisine—you're here for the music.

Arka Noego ("Noah's Ark") has a good reputation for its music and its food (slightly cheaper food than the others, daily 10:00-2:00 in the morning, Izaaka 7, tel. 12-429-1528, mobile 669-635-106).

At **Klezmer-Hois,** which fills a venerable former Jewish ritual bathhouse, you'll feel like you're dining in a rich grandparent's home (daily 8:00-22:00, at #6, tel. 12-411-1245).

Ariel is popular but has gone downhill in recent years, and receives mixed reviews for its food (daily 10:00-24:00, music in up to six different rooms, best upstairs in the larger dining hall, at #18, tel. 12-421-7920).

Awiw is the poor man's option for live klezmer music. Each evening from 18:00 to 23:00, they have live music outside on their patio on ulica Szeroka with no cover charge. (You can also hear it just fine sitting at other restaurants and bars facing the square.) They also serve a menu of affordable Jewish and Polish food (30-50-zł main dishes, daily 10:00-23:00, Szeroka 13, tel. 12-341-4279).

Fast and Cheap

Bagelmama, run by an American named Nava (who has worked as a private chef for US tennis star John McEnroe), is a casual bagel shop that's understandably popular with expats. Nava and his staff serve up a wide range of sandwiches, soups, salads, burritos, desserts, and good espresso drinks. The bagels come dressed with a wide variety of spreads, from simple cream cheese or peanut butter to lox, tuna, or curried chicken. You can eat in or get it to go (most items 10-17 zł, 16-21-zł salads, selection of "bagel tapas" with various toppings for 18.50 zł/person for 2 people, daily 9:00-18:00, possibly later in summer, ulica Dajwór 10, tel. 12-346-1646).

Restauracja Samoobsługowa Polakowski is a glorified milk bar with country-kitchen decor, and cheap and tasty Polish fare. Curt service...cute hats (9-12-zł main dishes, borrow the English menu and/or point to what you want, daily 9:00-22:00, just behind the top of ulica Szeroka at ulica Miodowa 39).

The **plac Nowy market** offers a fully authentic, very cheap, blue-collar Polish experience—join the workers on their lunch break at the little food windows on Kazimierz's market square. This area is particularly known for its *zapiekanki*—the uniquely Polish fast food of a toasted baguette with cheese, ketchup, and other toppings (Bar Endzior is well-regarded). More recently, a wide range of trendy restaurants and bars has sprung up around the square. Survey your options and choose your favorite.

Dining in Kazimierz

For a good-quality sit-down meal, consider these options.

Starka has romantic, dark-red decor and walls hung with sketches from a circa 1910 Berlin cartoonist. In addition to good Polish cuisine, they have 16 types of their own homemade flavored vodkas (12-18-zł starters, 30-45-zł main dishes, daily 12:00-23:00, Józefa 14, tel. 12-430-6538).

Szara is a well-respected Kraków institution (with another location near the Main Market Square). This popular spot—a bit more upscale and dressy than the tired klezmer joints—provides refined food at reasonable prices (20-30-zł starters, 35-60-zł main dishes, 40-zł lunch special includes soup and a main dish, open daily, Szeroka 39, tel. 12-429-1219).

Kazimierz Bars with Food

Two of my favorite atmospheric Kazimierz bars also serve food. It's not high cuisine—the food is an afterthought to the busy bar.

Kolanko No. 6 has a classic Kazimierz atmosphere. The bar up front is filled with old secondhand furniture. Walking toward the back, you discover an inviting garden with tables, and beyond that, a hall where they host events. They serve light meals, specializing in crêpes, toasted sandwiches, and salads (13-17 zł, daily 10:00-24:00, Józefa 17, tel. 12-292-0320).

Warsztat ("Workshop") is littered with musical instruments: The bar is a piano, and the tight interior is crammed with other instruments and rakishly crooked lampshades. The menu is an odd hybrid of Italian, Middle Eastern, and Polish cuisine (15-25-zł salads, pizzas, and pastas, 30-45-zł meat dishes, daily 9:00-24:00, Izaaka 3, tel. 12-430-1451).

Kraków Connections

For getting between Kraków and **Auschwitz,** see page 377 in the next chapter.

From Kraków by Train to: Warsaw (hourly, 2.75-3.25 hours, requires seat reservation, see below), **Gdańsk** (4/day direct, 2 more with change in Warsaw, 8.5 hours—shorter after new rail line completed; plus 2 night trains, 10.5-11.5 hours), **Toruń** (3/day direct, 7.75-9 hours; better to transfer at Warsaw's Zachodnia station: 10/day, 6-6.75 hours), **Prague** (1 early-morning direct train/day, 7.5 hours; 4/day with 1-2 changes, 8.25 hours; 1 night train, 9.5 hours), **Berlin** (1/day direct, 10 hours; otherwise transfer in Warsaw, 8.25-8.5 hours; plus 2 night trains, 10.5-11.5 hours), **Budapest** (3/day, 9.5-11 hours, transfer in Katowice, Poland, and Břeclav, Czech Republic; plus 1 night train/day, 10.75 hours), and **Vienna** (1/night direct, 8.5 hours; 3 decent daytime options, 7.75-8.75 hours with 1-3 changes).

The express train to **Warsaw**—which requires a reservation, even if you have a railpass—is particularly pleasant: A speedy 2.75 to 3.25 hours without stopping, from city center to city center. You'll be offered a free drink and snack to nibble on as you enjoy the pastoral scenery.

Night Trains to Hungary: If your next stop is Hungary, it can be convenient to sleep your way there on a night train. A night train from Kraków to **Budapest** runs nightly year-round (10.75 hours). If you'd rather head for **Eger,** in the summer (late June-late Aug) it may be possible to take a night train to Füzesabony, Hungary, where you can change to an Eger-bound train. However, this service has been in flux in recent years. If it's not running, ride the night train from Kraków to Budapest, then connect to Eger (either right away, or as a side-trip later). To research the latest schedules, see www.bahn.com.

AUSCHWITZ-BIRKENAU

The unassuming regional capital of Oświęcim (ohsh-VEENCH-im) was the site of one of humanity's most unspeakably horrifying tragedies: the systematic murder of at least 1.1 million innocent people. From 1941 until 1945, Oświęcim was the home of Auschwitz, the biggest, most notorious concentration camp in the Nazi system. Today, Auschwitz is the most poignant memorial anywhere to the victims of the Holocaust.

A visit here is obligatory for Polish 14-year-olds; students usually come again during their last year of school, as well. You'll often see Israeli high school groups walking through the grounds waving their Star of David flags. Many visitors, including Germans, leave flowers and messages. One of the messages reads, "Nations who forget their own history are sentenced to live it again."

Orientation to Auschwitz

"Auschwitz" (OWSH-vits) actually refers to a series of several camps in Poland—most importantly Auschwitz I, in the village of Oświęcim (50 miles, or a 1.25-hour drive, west of Kraków), and Auschwitz II, a.k.a. Birkenau (about 2 miles west of Oświęcim). Those visiting Auschwitz generally see both parts. **Auschwitz I,** where public transportation from Kraków arrives, has the main museum building, the *Arbeit Macht Frei* gate, and indoor museum exhibits in former prison buildings. Then a brief shuttle-bus ride takes visitors to **Birkenau** (BEER-keh-now)—on a much bigger scale and mostly outdoors, with the famous guard tower (and another bookshop and more WCs), a vast field with ruins of barracks, a few tourable rough barracks, the notorious "dividing

Greater Auschwitz

1 Kilometer
1 Mile

To Katowice
To Kraków

Vistula R.

933

KONOPNICKIEJ

TRAIN STATION

Brzezinka (Town)

AUSCHWITZ II - BIRKENAU

MĘCZEŃSTWA NARODNÓW

Oświęcim (Town)

WYZWOLENIA

LEGIONÓW

P

JUDENRAMPE MEMORIAL

AUSCHWITZ I

To Bielsko-Biała & Cieszyn

933   Soła R.   948

950

platform," a giant monument flanked by remains of destroyed crematoria, and a prisoner processing facility called "the Sauna."

Begin at Auschwitz I. The museum's main building has ticket booths (to pay for a tour or to make a donation), bookshops (consider the good *Guide-Book* brochure or the bigger laminated map), exchange offices, WCs, and basic eateries. You'll also find maps of the camp (posted on the walls) and a theater that shows a powerful film. A helpful **information desk**—where you can ask questions, buy tickets for the tour (see "Tours at Auschwitz," later), and find out about bus schedules for the return trip to Kraków—is halfway down the main entrance hall on the right, in the back corner behind the little tables.

Cost and Hours: Entrance to the camp is free, but donations are gladly accepted. During busy times (May-Oct 10:00-15:00), you'll pay 40 zł to join a required organized tour (private guides also available; see "Tours at Auschwitz," later). The museum opens every day at 8:00, and closes June-Aug at 19:00, May and Sept at 18:00, April and Oct at 17:00, March and Nov at 16:00, and Dec-Feb at 15:00. Information: Tel. 33-844-8100, www.auschwitz.org.

Getting There: For details on getting between Kraków and Auschwitz, see "Auschwitz Connections," at the end of this chapter.

Getting from Auschwitz I to Birkenau: Buses shuttle visitors two miles between the camps (free, about 4/hour in peak season, less off-season, times posted at the bus stop outside the main building of each site, timed to correspond with tours). Taxis are also standing by (about 15 zł). Many visitors, rather than wait for the next bus, decide to walk the 20 minutes between the camps—

Why Visit Auschwitz?

Why visit a notorious concentration camp on your vacation? Auschwitz-Birkenau is one of the most moving sights in Europe, and certainly the most important of all the Holocaust memorials. Seeing the camp can be difficult: Many visitors are overwhelmed by a combination of sadness and anger over the tragedy, as well as inspiration at the remarkable stories of survival. Auschwitz survivors and victims' families want tourists to come here and experience  the scale and the monstrosity of the place. In their minds, a steady flow of visitors will ensure that the Holocaust is always remembered—so nothing like it will ever happen again.

Auschwitz isn't for everyone. But I've never met anyone who toured Auschwitz and regretted it. For many, it's a profoundly life-altering experience—and at the very least, it will forever affect the way you think about the Holocaust.

offering a much-needed chance for reflection. Along the way, you'll pass the Judenrampe, an old train car like the ones used to transport prisoners, explained by an informational sign.

Film: The 17-minute movie (too graphic for children) was shot by Ukrainian troops days after the Red Army liberated the camp (3.50 zł, buy ticket on arrival; always in English at 10:00, 11:00, 13:00, and 15:00, sometimes more—ask when you arrive).

Photography: Because the philosophy of the camp is to spread the story of Auschwitz, taking photographs of anything outdoors is encouraged. However, to ease the movement of visitors, photography is not allowed inside certain museum buildings.

Eating: There's a café and decent cafeteria (Bar Smak) at the main Auschwitz building. More options are in the commercial complex across the street.

Etiquette: The camp encourages visitors to remember that Auschwitz is the place where more than a million people lost their lives; behave here as you would at a cemetery.

Tours at Auschwitz

Visiting Auschwitz on your own works well, given the abundance of English descriptions (and this chapter's self-guided tour). However, due to crowd-control issues, from May to October individual visitors are not allowed to enter the Auschwitz I part of

Auschwitz Renovation

The International Auschwitz Council is planning to renovate the site over the next several years. The museum at Auschwitz I, widely considered the oldest Holocaust exhibit in the world, has remained largely unchanged in the more than 50 years since it opened. Now the museum displays will be modernized and better organized to accommodate the growing number of visitors. The key elements described in this chapter (such as the displays of human hair, eyeglasses, and suitcases) will still be part of the exhibit, but will likely be spread into more buildings (mostly on the ground floor, to avoid congestion on stairways). At Birkenau, restorers will build retaining walls to prevent the remains of the huge crematoria—key evidence of Nazi crimes—from slowly sinking into the ground.

Because of the renovation, be aware that the information in this chapter (especially the locations of exhibits on the self-guided tour) is subject to change. Ask about recent developments when you arrive at the camp.

the complex on their own between the peak times of 10:00 and 15:00. Instead, you're required to either join one of the museum's organized tours, or reserve your own private museum guide (both options are explained below). Note that even during these busy times, individuals may enter the Auschwitz II/Birkenau part of the complex without a guide.

Organized Museum Tours—The Auschwitz Museum's network of excellent guides are serious and frank, and feel a strong sense of responsibility about sharing the story of the camp. Appropriately, these well-trained guides are more historians than entertainers. The regularly scheduled 3.5-hour English tour covers Auschwitz, Birkenau, and the film (40 zł, buy ticket halfway down the main entry hall, on the right, in the back corner behind the tables). Most of the year, there are generally at least four English tours scheduled each day. You'll watch the film first, and the actual tour begins 30 minutes later (film at 10:00, 11:00, 13:00, and 15:00; possibly more with demand—as soon as 10 English-speakers gather, ask for a tour; in winter generally at 10:00, 11:00, 12:00, and 13:00). Try to arrive at least 20-30 minutes ahead, because if the tour's full, you might have to wait until the next one.

Private Official Museum Guides—If you have a special interest, a small group, or just want a more personalized visit, it's affordable and worthwhile to hire one of the museum's guides for a private tour. Choose between the basic 3.5-hour tour of the camp (250 zł), or a longer "study tour" (320 zł/4 hours, 400 zł/6 hours, 500 zł/8 hours spread over 2 days). Because English-speaking guides are limited, it's essential to reserve as far ahead as possible—at least two weeks in advance (fill out the online form at www.auschwitz .org, or call 33-844-8099 or 33-844-8100). At busy times, individuals might not be able to reserve a private guide between 10:00 and 14:00, when they're needed for bigger groups.

Tours from Kraków—Various Kraków-based companies sell round-trip tours from Kraków to Auschwitz (generally around 130 zł; see "Tours in Kraków," page 283). While these take care of transportation for you and include a guided tour, you'll pay triple and have to adhere to a strict schedule, and the tours tend to be impersonal.

Local Guides and Drivers from Kraków—For hassle-free transportation to the camp, you can hire a Kraków-based local guide or driver to bring you to Auschwitz; I've listed my favorites on page 283. However, since these people are not officially registered museum guides, they technically aren't allowed to show you around the site. Instead, they will most likely arrange a private museum guide to join you, or time your visit so you can join an organized English tour (both options described earlier). While it's pricey, some travelers consider hiring a driver/guide to be a worthwhile splurge, since you'll have door-to-door service to the camp and three hours in the car with a local expert.

Self-Guided Tour

Auschwitz I

Before World War II, this camp was a base for the Polish army. When Hitler occupied Poland, he took over these barracks and turned it into a concentration camp for his Polish political enemies. The location was ideal, with a nearby rail junction and rivers providing natural protective boundaries. In 1942, Auschwitz became a death camp for the extermination of European Jews and others whom Hitler considered "undesirable." By the time  the camp was liberated in 1945, at least 1.1 million people had been murdered here—approximately 960,000 of them Jewish.

As you exit the entry building's back door and go toward the camp, you see the notorious **gate** with the cruel message, *Arbeit Macht Frei* ("Work Sets You Free"). Note that the "B" was welded on upside down by belligerent inmates. On their arrival, new prisoners were told the truth: The only way out of the camp was through the crematorium chimneys. This gate was in the news

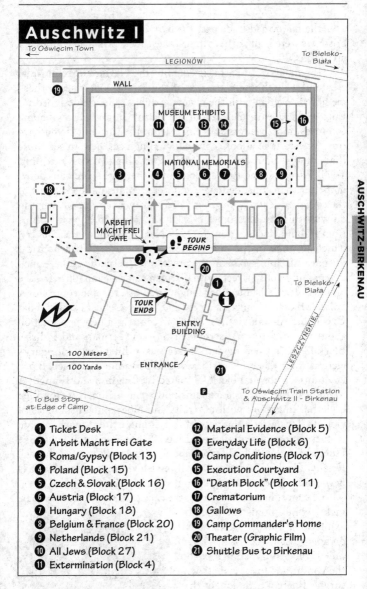

Auschwitz I

To Oświęcim Town ←

LEGIONÓW

To Bielsko-Biała →

WALL

MUSEUM EXHIBITS

NATIONAL MEMORIALS

ARBEIT MACHT FREI GATE

TOUR BEGINS

TOUR ENDS

ENTRY BUILDING

ENTRANCE

100 Meters
100 Yards

To Bus Stop at Edge of Camp

To Bielsko-Biała

To Oświęcim Train Station & Auschwitz II - Birkenau

LESZCZYŃSKIEJ

AUSCHWITZ-BIRKENAU

1 Ticket Desk
2 Arbeit Macht Frei Gate
3 Roma/Gypsy (Block 13)
4 Poland (Block 15)
5 Czech & Slovak (Block 16)
6 Austria (Block 17)
7 Hungary (Block 18)
8 Belgium & France (Block 20)
9 Netherlands (Block 21)
10 All Jews (Block 27)
11 Extermination (Block 4)
12 Material Evidence (Block 5)
13 Everyday Life (Block 6)
14 Camp Conditions (Block 7)
15 Execution Courtyard
16 "Death Block" (Block 11)
17 Crematorium
18 Gallows
19 Camp Commander's Home
20 Theater (Graphic Film)
21 Shuttle Bus to Birkenau

in December of 2009, when the original sign that still hung here was stolen one night, then recovered cut into three pieces two days later. While the original is now safely in the museum's possession, the sign you see here is a replica.

Just inside the gate and to the right, the camp orchestra (made up of prisoners) used to play marches; having the prisoners march made them easier to count.

The main road leads past the barracks. An average of 14,000 prisoners were kept at this camp at one time. (Birkenau could hold up to 100,000.)

The first row of barracks contains the **National Memorials,** created by the home countries of the camps' victims. As these memorials overlap with the general exhibits, and are designed for Europeans to learn more about the victims from their own home countries, most visitors skip this part of the site. But if you have time later to take a look, consider circling back here to see those that interest you. Block 13 houses the **Roma (Gypsy)** exhibit. You'll learn that the Roma, along with the Jews, were considered no better than "rats, bedbugs, and fleas," and explore elements of the so-called *Zigeunerfrage*—the "Gypsy question" about what to do with this "troublesome" population. Block 15 honors victims from **Poland,** focusing on the 1939 Nazi invasion of the country, which resulted in the immediate internment of Polish political prisoners. Exhibits explain the process of "Germanization"—such as renaming Polish streets with German names—and (upstairs) the underground resistance that fought to re-assert some control over Poland. Block 16 contains a new and well-presented exhibit about **Czech and Slovak** victims. Block 17 contains a new presentation about victims from **Austria** (but only in German and Polish). Block 18 holds a very modern, conceptual exhibit about **Hungary**'s victims, with an eerie heartbeat sound pervading the space. Block 20, a former hospital block, is shared by **Belgium** and **France.** A room near the entrance explains how some prisoners were killed by lethal injection, with portraits and biographical sketches of victims. Upstairs is the powerful Belgium exhibit, with a room featuring portraits of victims. Block 21 honors **Dutch Jews;** like Hungary's, the exhibit is experiential, with a walk-through tunnel. Finally, Block 27 is devoted to all **Jewish victims** of Auschwitz (a new exhibit is scheduled to open here in 2012).

The most interesting part of the camp is the second row of barracks, which holds the museum exhibitions. Blocks 4 and 5 focus on how Auschwitz prisoners were killed. Blocks 6, 7, and 11 explore the conditions for prisoners who survived here a little longer than most.

Block 4 features exhibits on **extermination.** In the first room is a map showing the countries from which Auschwitz prisoners were brought—as far away as Norway and Greece. You'll also find an urn filled with ashes, a symbolic memorial to all of the camp's victims. In Room 2, a map shows how the victims were

Chilling Statistics: The Holocaust in Poland

The majority of people murdered by the Nazis during the Holocaust were killed right here in Poland. For centuries, Poland was known for its relative tolerance of Jews, and right up until the beginning of World War II, Poland had Europe's largest concentration of Jews: 3,500,000. Throughout the Holocaust, the Nazis murdered 4,500,000 Jews in Poland (many of them brought in from other countries) at camps, including Auschwitz, and in ghettos such as Warsaw's.

By the end of the war, only 300,000 Polish Jews had survived—less than 10 percent of the original population. Many of these survivors were granted "one-way passports" (read: deported) to Israel by the communist government in 1968 (following a big student demonstration with a strong Jewish presence). Today, only about 10,000 Jews live in all of Poland.

transported here from all over Europe. To prevent a riot, the Nazis claimed at first that this was only a transition camp for resettlement in Eastern Europe. Room 3 displays some of the only photos that exist of victims inside the camp—taken by arrogant SS men.

Upstairs in Room 4 is a chilling model of a Birkenau crematorium. People entered on the left, then got undressed in the underground rooms (hanging their belongings on numbered hooks and encouraged to remember their numbers to retrieve their clothes later). They then moved into the "showers" and were killed by Zyklon-B gas (hydrogen cyanide), a German-produced cleaning agent that is lethal in high doses. This efficient factory of murder took about 20 minutes to kill 20,000 people in four gas chambers. Elevators brought the bodies up to the crematorium. Members of the *Sonderkommand*—Jewish inmates who were kept isolated and forced by the Nazis to work here—removed the corpses' gold teeth and shaved off their hair (to be sold) before putting the bodies in the ovens. It wasn't unusual for a *Sonderkommand* worker to discover a wife, child, or parent among the dead. A few of these workers committed suicide by throwing themselves at electric fences; those who didn't were systematically executed by the Nazis after a two-month shift. Across from the model of the crematorium are canisters of Zyklon-B. Across the hall in Room 5 is a wall of victims' hair—4,400 pounds of it. Also displayed is cloth made of the hair, used to make Nazi uniforms.

Back downstairs in Room 6 is an exhibit on the plunder of victims' personal belongings. People being transported here were encouraged to bring luggage—and some victims had even paid in advance for houses in their new homeland. After they were killed, everything of value was sorted and stored in warehouses that prisoners named "Canada" (after a country they associated with great wealth). Although the Canada warehouses were destroyed, you can see a few of these items in the next building.

Block 5 focuses on **material evidence** of the crimes that took place here. It consists mostly of piles of the victims' goods, a tiny fraction of everything the Nazis stole. As you wander through the rooms, you'll see eyeglasses; fine Jewish prayer shawls; crutches and prosthetic limbs (the first people the Nazis exterminated were mentally and physically ill German citizens); a seemingly endless mountain of shoes; and suitcases with names of victims—many marked *Kind,* or "child." Visitors often wonder if the suitcase with the name "Frank" belonged to Anne, one of the Holocaust's most famous victims. After being discovered in Amsterdam by the Nazis, the Frank family was transported here to Auschwitz, where they were split up. Still, it's unlikely this suitcase was theirs. Anne Frank and her sister Margot were sent to the Bergen-Belsen camp in northern Germany, where they died of typhus shortly before the war ended. Their father, Otto Frank, survived Auschwitz and was found barely alive by the Russians, who liberated the camp in January of 1945.

Although the purpose of Auschwitz was to murder its inmates, not all of them were killed immediately. After an initial evaluation, some prisoners were registered and forced to work. (This did not mean they were chosen to live—just to die later.) In Block 6, you see elements of the **everyday life** of prisoners. The halls are lined with photographs of victims. The dates of arrival *(przybył)* and death *(zmarł)* show that those registered survived here an average of two to three months. (Flowers are poignant reminders that these victims are survived by loved ones.) Room 1 displays drawings of the arrival process—sketched by survivors of the camp. After the initial selection, those chosen to work were showered, shaved, and photographed.

19472
DĄBROWSKI JAN
ur. 8.2.1929 r., robotnik
przybył: 30.7.1941, zginął: wrzesień 1942.

After a while, photographing each prisoner got to be too expensive, so prisoners were tattooed instead (see photographs): on the chest, on the arm, or—for children—on the leg. A display shows the symbols that prisoners had to wear to show their reason for internment—Jew, Roma (Gypsy), homosexual, political prisoner, and so on.

Room 4 shows the starvation that took place here. The 7,500 survivors that the Red Army found when the camp was liber-

St. Maksymilian Kolbe
(1894-1941)

Among the many inspirational stories of Auschwitz is that of a Polish priest named Maksymilian Kolbe. Before the war, Kolbe traveled as a missionary to Japan, then worked in Poland for a Catholic newspaper. While he was highly regarded for his devotion to the Church, some of his writings had an unsettling anti-Semitic sentiment. But during the Nazi occupation, Kolbe briefly ran an institution that cared for refugees—including Jews.

In 1941, Kolbe was arrested and interned at Auschwitz. When a prisoner from Kolbe's block escaped in July of that year, the Nazis punished the remaining inmates by selecting 10 of them to put in the Starvation Cell until they died—based on the Nazi "doctrine of collective responsibility." After the selection had been made, Kolbe offered to replace a man who expressed concern about who would care for his family. The Nazis agreed. (The man Kolbe saved is said to have survived the Holocaust.)

All 10 of the men—including Kolbe—were put into Starvation Cell 18. Two weeks later, when the door was opened, only Kolbe had survived. The story spread throughout the camp, and Kolbe became an inspiration to the inmates. To squelch the hope he had given the others, Kolbe was executed by lethal injection.

In 1982, Kolbe was canonized by the Catholic Church. Some critics—mindful of his earlier anti-Semitic rhetoric—still consider Kolbe's sainthood controversial. But most Poles feel he redeemed himself for his earlier missteps through this noble act at the end of his life.

ated were essentially living skeletons (the "healthier" inmates had been forced to march to Germany). Of those liberated, 20 percent died soon after of disease and starvation. Look for a display of the prisoners' daily ration (in the glass case): a pan of tea or coffee in the morning; thin vegetable soup in the afternoon; and a piece of bread (often made with sawdust or chestnuts) for dinner. This makes it clear that Auschwitz was never intended to be a "work camp," where people were kept alive, healthy, and efficient to do work. Rather, people were meant to die here—if not in the gas chambers, then through malnutrition and overwork.

You can see scenes from the prisoner's workday (sketched by survivors after liberation) in Room 5. Prisoners worked as long as the sun shone—eight hours in winter, up to twelve hours in summer—mostly on farms or in factories. Room 6 is about Auschwitz's child inmates, 20 percent of the camp's victims. Blond, blue-eyed children—like the girl in the bottom row on the right—were either "Germanized" in special schools or, if younger, adopted by German families. Dr. Josef Mengele conducted gruesome experiments here on children, especially twins and triplets, ostensibly to find ways to increase fertility for German mothers.

Block 7 shows **living and sanitary conditions** at the camp—which you'll see in more detail later at Birkenau. Blocks 8-10 are vacant (medical experiments were carried out in Block 10).

Step into the **courtyard** between Blocks 10 and 11. The wall at the far end is where the Nazis shot several thousand political prisoners, leaders of camp resistance, and religious leaders. Notice that the windows are covered, so that nobody could witness the executions. Also take a close look at the memorial—the back of it is made of a material designed by Nazis to catch the bullets without a ricochet. Inmates were shot at short range—about three feet. The pebbles represent prayers from Jewish visitors.

The most feared place among prisoners was the **"Death Block"** (#11), from which nobody ever left alive. In Room 5, you can see how prisoners lived in these barracks—three-level bunks, with three prisoners sleeping in each bed (they had to sleep on their sides so they could fit). Death here required a trial (the room in which sham trials were held—lasting about two minutes each—is on display). In Room 6, people undressed before they were executed. In the basement, you'll see several different types of cells. The Starvation Cell (#18) held prisoners selected to starve to death when a fellow prisoner escaped; Maksymilian Kolbe spent two weeks here to save another man's life (see sidebar). In the Dark Cell (#20), which held up to 30, people had only a small window for ventilation—and if it became covered with snow, the prisoners suffocated. At the end of the hall in Cell 21, you can see where a prisoner scratched a crucifix (left) and image of Jesus (right) on the wall. In the Standing Cells (#22), four people would be forced to stand together for hours at a time (the bricks went all the way to the ceiling then). Upstairs is an exhibit on resistance within the camp.

Before you leave Auschwitz, visit the **crematorium** (from Block 11, exit straight ahead and go past the first row of barracks, then turn right and go straight on the road between the two rows of barracks; pass through the gap in the fence and look for the chimney on your left). People undressed outside, or just inside the door. Up to 700 people at a time could be gassed here. Inside the door, go into the big room on the right. Look for the vents in the ceiling—this is where the SS men dropped the Zyklon-B. Through the door is a replica of the furnace. This facility could burn 340 bodies a day—so it took two days to burn all of the bodies from one round of executions. (The Nazis didn't like this inefficiency, so they built four more huge crematoria at Birkenau.)

Shortly after the war, camp commander Rudolf Höss was tried, convicted, and sentenced to death. Survivors requested that he be executed at Auschwitz, and in 1947, he was hanged here. The **gallows** are preserved behind the crematorium (about a hundred yards from his home where his wife—who loved her years here—read stories to their children, very likely by the light of a human-skin lampshade).

Take your time with Auschwitz I. When you're ready, con-tinue to the second stage of the camp—Birkenau (see "Getting from Auschwitz I to Birkenau" on page 363).

Auschwitz II—Birkenau

In 1941, realizing that the original Auschwitz camp was too small to meet their needs, the Nazis began a second camp in some nearby

farm fields. The original plan was for a camp that could hold 200,000 people, but at its peak, Birkenau (Brzezinka) held only about 100,000. They were still adding onto it when the camp was liberated in 1945.

Train tracks lead past the main building and into the camp.

The first sight that greeted prisoners was the **guard tower** (familiar to many visitors from the stirring scenes in *Schindler's List*). Climb to the top of the entry building (also houses WCs and bookstore) for an overview of the massive camp. As you look over the camp, you'll see a vast field of chimneys and a few intact wooden and brick barracks. The train tracks lead straight back to the dividing

platform, and then dead-end at the ruins of the crematorium and camp monument at the far side.

Some of the barracks were destroyed by Germans. Most were dismantled to be used for fuel and building materials shortly after the war. But the first row has been recon-structed (using components from the original structures). Visit the barracks on the right.

The first of these barrack build-ings was the **latrine**: The front half

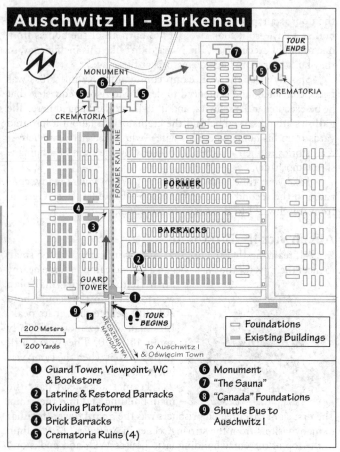

Auschwitz II – Birkenau

MONUMENT

TOUR ENDS

CREMATORIA

FORMER RAIL LINE

CREMATORIA

FORMER

BARRACKS

GUARD TOWER

TOUR BEGINS

MIESIĘŃSKIEGO NARODÓW

To Auschwitz I & Oświęcim Town

200 Meters

200 Yards

☐ Foundations
▬ Existing Buildings

1 Guard Tower, Viewpoint, WC & Bookstore
2 Latrine & Restored Barracks
3 Dividing Platform
4 Brick Barracks
5 Crematoria Ruins (4)
6 Monument
7 "The Sauna"
8 "Canada" Foundations
9 Shuttle Bus to Auschwitz I

AUSCHWITZ-BIRKENAU

of the building contained washrooms, and the back was a row of toilets. There was no running water, and prisoners were in charge of keeping the latrine clean. Because of the resulting unsanitary conditions and risk of disease, the Nazis were afraid to come in here—so the latrine became the heart of the black market and the inmates' resistance movement.

The fourth **barrack** was a bunk building. Each inmate had a personal number, a barrack number, and a bed number. Inside, you can see the beds (angled so that more could fit). An average of 400 prisoners—but up to 1,000—would be housed in each of these buildings. These wooden

structures, designed as stables by a German company (look for the horse-tying rings on the wall), came in prefab pieces that made them cheap and convenient. Two chimneys connected by a brick duct provided a little heat. The bricks were smoothed by inmates who sat here to catch a bit of warmth.

Follow the train tracks toward the monument about a half-mile away, at the back end of Birkenau. At the intersection of these tracks and the perpendicular gravel road (halfway to the monument) was the gravel **dividing platform.** A Nazi doctor would stand facing the guard tower and evaluate each prisoner. If he pointed to the right, the prisoner was sentenced to death, and trudged—unknowingly—to the gas chamber. If he pointed to the left, the person would be registered and live a little longer. It was here that families from all over Europe were torn apart forever.

On the left-hand side of the tracks are some **brick barracks.** Go inside one of them. The supervisors lived in the two smaller rooms near the door. Farther in, most barracks still have the wooden bunks that held about 700 people per building. Four or five people slept on each bunk, including the floor—reserved for new arrivals. There were chamber pots at either end of the building. After a Nazi doctor died of typhus, sanitation improved, and these barracks got running water.

As you walk along the camp's only road, which leads along the tracks to the crematorium, imagine the horror of this place—no grass, only mud, and all the barracks packed with people, with smoke blowing in from the busy crematoria. This was an even worse place to die than Auschwitz I.

The train tracks lead to the camp memorial and crematorium. At the end of the tracks, go 50 yards to the left and climb the three concrete steps to view the ruin of the **crematorium.** This is one of four crematoria here at Birkenau, each with a capacity to cremate more than 4,400 people per day. At the far-right end of the ruins, see the stairs where people entered the rooms to undress. They were given numbered lockers, conning them into thinking they were coming back. (The Nazis didn't want a panic.) Then they piled into the "shower room"—the underground passage branching away from the memorial—and were killed. Their bodies were burned in the crematorium (on the left), giving off a scent of sweet almonds (from the Zyklon-B). Beyond the remains of the crematorium is a hole—once a gray lake where tons of ashes were dumped. This efficient factory of death was destroyed by the Nazis as the Red Army approached, leaving the haunting ruins you see today.

When the Soviets arrived on January 27, 1945, the nightmare of Auschwitz-Birkenau was over. The Polish parliament voted to turn these grounds into a museum, so that the world would

On the Way to Auschwitz: The Polish Countryside

You'll spend about an hour gazing out the window as you drive or ride to Auschwitz. This may be your only real look at the Polish countryside. Ponder these thoughts about what you're passing...

The small houses you see are traditionally inhabited by three generations at the same time. Nineteenth-century houses (the few that survive) often sport blue stripes. Back then, parents announced that their daughters were now eligible by getting out the blue paint. Once they saw these blue lines, local boys were welcome to come a-courtin'.

Big churches mark small villages. Like in the US, tiny roadside memorials and crosses indicate places where fatal accidents have occurred.

Polish farmers traditionally had small lots that were notorious for not being very productive. These farmers somewhat miraculously survived the communist era without having to merge their farms. For years, they were Poland's sacred cows: producing little, paying almost no tax, and draining government resources. But since Poland joined the European Union in 2004, they're being forced to get up to snuff...and, in many cases, collectivize their farms after all.

Since most people don't own cars, bikes are common and public transit is excellent. There are lots of bus stops, as well as minibuses that you can flag down anywhere for a 2-zł ride. The bad roads are a legacy of communist construction, exacerbated by heavy truck use and brutal winters.

Poland has more than 2,000 counties, or districts, each with its own coat of arms; you'll pass several along the way. The forests are state-owned, and locals enjoy the right to pick berries in the summer and mushrooms in the autumn (you may see people—often young kids—selling their day's harvest by the side of the road). The mushrooms are dried and then boiled to make tasty soups in the winter.

understand, and never forget, the horror of what happened here. The **monument** at the back of the camp, built in 1967 (by the communist government in its heavy "Socialist Realism" style), represents gravestones and the chimney of a crematorium. The plaques, written in each of the languages spoken by camp victims (including English, far right), explain that the memorial is "a cry of despair and a warning to humanity."

With more time, you could continue deeper into the camp—to the reception and disinfection building that prisoners called **"the Sauna"** (the long building with four tall chimneys). It was

here that prisoners would be forced to strip and be de-loused; their belongings were seized and taken to the "Canada" warehouses (described earlier) to be sorted. Walking through here (on glass floors designed to protect the original structure below), you'll see artifacts of the queasy efficiency with which prisoners were "processed"—their heads were shaved, they were tattooed with a serial number, and they were assigned uniforms and wooden clogs to wear. Portraits at the end of the building humanize those who passed through here. Look for the cart, which was used to dispose of ashes. In front of the Sauna is a field of foundations of the **"Canada" warehouses.** Nearby are the other two destroyed **crematoria.**

Auschwitz Connections

The Auschwitz Museum is in the town of Oświęcim, about 50 miles west of Kraków. By bus, minibus, or train, the journey takes around an hour and 45 minutes each way; driving shaves off about 10-20 minutes.

From Kraków to Auschwitz

The easiest way to reach Auschwitz is with a **package tour** (figure around 130 zł per person) or **private guide or driver** (300-500 zł for the carload); both of these options are described on page 283. While the package tours are more convenient than going on your own, three people can hire their own driver for less and have a more intimate experience.

If you're using public transportation, here are your choices:

The most comfortable public-transit option is to take one of the frequent **buses,** mostly run by PKS Oświęcim (10 zł, at least hourly, 1.75 hours, get the most recent schedule at any Kraków TI, buses depart from Kraków's main bus station behind the train station). Buy a one-way ticket from the bus-station ticket office or from the driver to leave your options open for getting home. Look for buses to "Oświęcim" (not necessarily "Auschwitz"). Note that these buses can be full, and since most come from other towns, there's no way to reserve a seat—so line up early (generally about 15 minutes ahead). If you don't get on a bus, you'll have to wait for the next one (or, if there's a minibus leaving sooner, you can take one of those—described next). Once in the town of Oświęcim, buses from Kraków stop first at the train station, then continue on to one of two stops near the museum: About half of the buses go directly into the parking lot at the museum itself, while the rest use a low-profile bus stop on the edge of the Auschwitz camp grounds (you'll see a small *Muzeum Auschwitz* sign on the right just before the stop, and a blue *Oświęcim Muzeum PKS* sign at the stop itself). From this bus stop, follow the sign down the road and into the parking lot; the main museum building is across the lot on your left. Note that since some buses don't actually go into the museum's parking lot, the Auschwitz stop can be easy to miss—don't be shy about letting your driver know where you want to go: "*Muzeum?*"

Several **minibuses** from Kraków head for Auschwitz (10 zł, sporadic departures—generally 1-2/hour, 1.75 hours). Like the buses, some go directly to the museum, while others use the bus stop at the edge of camp (see above). These generally depart from the lower platform of the main bus station (but confirm the departure point at the TI). Some of my readers report that the minibuses are a bit more cramped than the buses and, while intended for local commuters, can be crammed with tourists. But they work fine in a pinch.

You could ride the **train** to Oświęcim, but it's less convenient than the bus because it leaves you at the train station, farther from the museum (15/day, less Sat-Sun, 1.5 hours, 14 zł). If you do wind up at the Oświęcim train station, it's about a 20-minute walk to the camp (turn right out of station, go straight, then turn left at roundabout, camp is several blocks ahead on left). Or you can take a taxi (around 15 zł).

Returning from Auschwitz to Kraków

Upon arrival at Auschwitz I, plan your departure by visiting the information window inside the main building (halfway down the main entry hall, on the right, in the back corner behind the tables). They can give you a schedule of departures and explain where the bus or minibus leaves from. (If you'll be staying late into the afternoon, make a point of figuring out the last possible bus or train back to Kraków, and plan accordingly.) Remember to allow enough time to make it from Birkenau back to Auschwitz I to catch your bus.

Although most minibuses and a few buses back to Kraków leave from the camp parking lot itself, if you're taking the bus, you'll most likely catch it from the stop on the edge of the Auschwitz I grounds. To reach this bus stop, leave the Auschwitz I building through the main entry and walk straight along the parking lot, then turn right on the road near the end of the lot. At the T-intersection, cross the street to the little bus stop with the blue

Oświęcim Muzeum PKS sign. Don't be distracted by the ads for a nearby travel agency—you can buy tickets on board. Again, be aware that there's no public transportation back to Kraków from Birkenau, where most people end their tours; you'll have to take the shuttle bus back to Auschwitz I first.

WARSAW

Warszawa

Warsaw (Warszawa, vah-SHAH-vah in Polish) is Poland's capital and biggest city. It's huge, famous, and important...but not particularly romantic. If you're looking for Old World quaintness, head for Kraków. If you're tickled by spires and domes, get to Prague. But if you want to experience a truly 21st-century city, Warsaw's your place.

Stroll down revitalized boulevards that evoke the city's glory days, pausing at an outdoor café to sip coffee and nibble at a *pączek* (the classic Polish jelly doughnut). Commune with the soul of Poland through its artists (at the National Museum), its favorite composer (at the Chopin Museum), its dramatic history (at the Warsaw Historical Museum and Warsaw Uprising Museum), its dedication to the sciences (at the Copernicus Science Center), and its Jewish story (in the former Jewish Ghetto and—beginning in 2013—the brand-new Museum of the History of Polish

Jews). And ponder the wide range of Warsaw's postwar urban architecture, from dreary communist monstrosities to innovative skyscrapers designed by *the* top names in global architecture.

Warsaw is modernizing—fast. Mindful of its history, yet optimistic about its future, Warsaw has happily emerged from a long hibernation. Varsovians are embracing their role as the capital city of an influential nation in the "New Europe." The European Union has two universities aimed at educating future political leaders (or "Eurocrats"). One is in Bruges, Belgium, just down the road from the EU capital of Brussels. The other one is right here. You can almost feel Warsaw peeling back the layers of communist grime as it replaces pot-holed highways with pedestrian-friendly parks. Today's Warsaw has gleaming new office towers and street signs, stylishly dressed locals, cutting-edge shopping malls, swarms of international businesspeople, and a gourmet coffee shop on every corner. More recently, the city built a futuristic new stadium and an even more spiffed-up infrastructure to host key matches for the Euro Cup 2012 soccer championship.

Warsaw has good reason to be a city of the future: The past hasn't been very kind. Since becoming Poland's capital in 1596, Warsaw has seen wave after wave of foreign rulers and invasions—especially during the last hundred years. But in this horrific cru-cible, the enduring spirit of the Polish people was forged. As one proud Varsovian told me, "Warsaw is ugly because its history is so beautiful."

The city's darkest days came during the Nazi occupation of World War II. First, its Jewish residents were forced into a tiny ghetto. They rose up...and were slaughtered. Then, its Polish resi-dents rose up...and were slaughtered. Hitler sent word to system-atically demolish this troublesome city. At the war's end, Warsaw was devastated. An estimated 800,000 residents were dead—nearly two out of every three Varsovians.

The Poles almost gave up on what was then a pile of rubble to build a brand-new capital city elsewhere. But ultimately they decided to rebuild, creating a city of contrasts: painstakingly restored medieval lanes, crumbling communist apartment blocks (*bloki* in Polish), and sleek skyscrapers. Between the buildings, you'll find fragments of a complex, sometimes tragic, and often inspiring history.

A product of its complicated past, sprinkled with the big-city style and sophistication of its present, Warsaw remains quintessen-tially Polish. It is a place worth grappling with to understand the Poland of today...and the Europe of tomorrow.

Planning Your Time

Warsaw can easily fill two or three days, but if you're pressed for time, one full day is enough for most visitors. Get your bearings by taking a stroll through Polish history on the Royal Way, using my self-guided walk. Then enjoy the Old Town area. Visit other sights according to your interests: Polish artists, Holocaust history, the Warsaw Uprising, royalty, hands-on science gizmos, or Chopin. To slow down and take a break from the city, relax in Łazienki Park.

Orientation to Warsaw

Warsaw sprawls with 1.7 million residents. Everything is on a big scale—it seems to take forever to walk just a few "short" blocks. Get comfortable with public transportation and plan your sightseeing wisely to avoid backtracking.

Virtually everything of interest to travelers is on a mild hill on the west bank of the Vistula River. The city's central train station (Warszawa Centralna) is in the shadow of its biggest landmark: the can't-miss-it, skyscraping Palace of Culture and Science. From here, the avenue called aleja Jerozolimskie runs east toward the river, past the National Museum. It crosses the "Royal Way" boulevard, which connects the sights in the north (Old Town and New Town) with those in the south (Łazienki Park, and at the outskirts of town, Wilanów Palace). Most major sights and recommended hotels and restaurants are along or near these two thoroughfares (aleja Jerozolimskie and the Royal Way).

Another tip: You'll hear about two distinct uprisings against the Nazis during World War II. They're easy to confuse, but try to keep them straight: the **Ghetto Uprising** was staged by Warsaw's dwindling Jewish population in the spring of 1943 (see page 415); the **Warsaw Uprising,** a year later, was led by the (mostly non-Jewish) Polish Home Army (see page 418).

Tourist Information

Warsaw's helpful, youthful TI has five offices: on the **Royal Way** (in the Kordegarda building directly across the street from Radziwiłł Palace, daily May-Aug 11:00-21:00, Sept-April 11:00-19:00), on the **Old Town Market Square** (daily May-Aug 9:00-21:00, March-April and Sept-Oct 9:00-19:00, Nov-Feb 9:00-18:00), at the **central train station** (daily 8:00-20:00), at the **Palace of Culture and Science** (daily 8:00-20:00), and at the **airport** (daily May-Aug 8:00-20:00, March-April and Sept-Oct 8:00-19:00, Nov-Feb 8:00-18:00). The general information number for all TIs is 19431 from inside Warsaw, or 22-19431 from outside Warsaw. All branches offer several free, useful materials: a city map (with key phone numbers on the back), a well-produced booklet called *Warsaw: In Short,* and a series of brochures on sights and activities ("city breaks," Jewish heritage, Chopin, mermaids, and so on, as well as info for kids, active types, and travelers with limited mobility); everything is also available

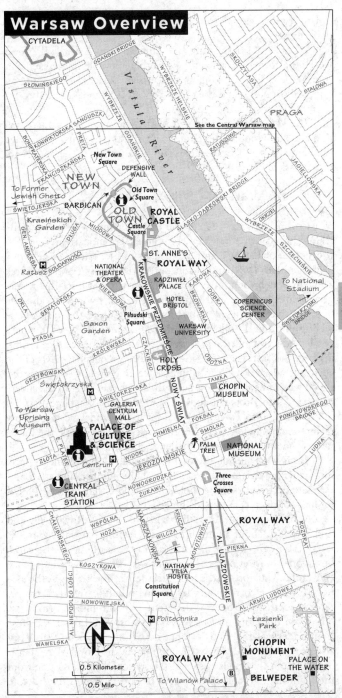

online (www.warsawtour.pl). The TI also has a free room-booking service.

Warsaw has a thriving live-music scene. Ask the TI for a weekly performance schedule. For light, enjoyable music events in summer, consider the Chopin concerts in Łazienki Park (only on Sun, see page 413) and the organ concerts in the Cathedral of St. John the Baptist (daily except Sun, see page 403).

The **Warsaw Tourist Card,** which covers public transportation and admission or discounts to nearly 30 museums, might save you some money if you're sightseeing like crazy (as the details are in flux, ask about it at the TI).

Arrival in Warsaw
By Train

Most trains arrive at the **central train station** (Warszawa Centralna), a recently renovated communist-era monstrosity next to the Palace of Culture and Science. It can be tricky to get your bearings here: Two parallel concourses run across the tracks, creating an underground maze where it's easy to get lost. The underground area includes well-signed lockers, ticket windows, and lots of shops and eateries. I'd start by heading up to the vast, open-feeling **main hall** (follow signs for *main hall/hala główna*), where you'll find a row of ticket windows, a rail customer service center, a TI (in the "Service Point" kiosk), and (from outside) views of the adjacent Palace of Culture and Science and Złota 44 skyscrapers. If you have time to kill, you can walk across the street to the super-modern **Złote Tarasy Shopping Mall** (described on page 407).

Getting into Town: To reach the tourist zone and most of my recommended hotels, taxis are the easiest choice, while the bus is more economical (but more challenging to find).

Taxis wait outside the main hall (many are dishonest—look for one with a company logo and telephone number, and ask for an estimate up front; the fare should be no more than about 20-30 zł for most of my recommended hotels).

From the station, **bus #175** takes you to the Royal Way and Old Town in about 10 minutes (see "Getting Around Warsaw," later). You can catch this bus—and others going in the same direction—in front of the skyscraper with the LOT airlines office and Hotel Marriott across busy aleja Jerozolimskie from the station. From the corridors under the main hall, carefully track *Al. Jerozolimskie* signs. Several different exits are marked this way, but if you hone in on *Hotel Marriott* signs, you'll reach a pedestrian underpass that pops you out next to the bus stop. **Bus #160** also goes to the Old Town (though not via the Royal Way), but it departs from the opposite side of the station: To find its stop from the main hall, go out the side door toward *ul. Emilii Plater*. Note

Warsaw Essentials

English	Polish	Pronounced
Warsaw	*Warszawa*	vah-SHAH-vah
Central Train Station	*Warszawa Centralna*	vah-SHAH-vah tsehn-TRAHL-nah
Palace of Culture and Science	*Pałac Kultury i Nauki (or simply "Pałac")*	PAH-wahts nah-OO-kee
New Town	*Nowe Miasto*	NOH-vay mee-AH-stoh
Old Town	*Stare Miasto*	STAH-reh mee-AH-stoh
Old Town Market Square	*Rynek Starego Miasta*	REE-nehk stah-RAY-goh mee-AH-stah
Royal Way	*Szlak Królewski*	shwock kroh-LEHV-skee
Popular restaurant street on Royal Way	*Nowy Świat*	NOH-vee SHVEE-aht
Attraction-lined street on Royal Way	*Krakowskie Przedmieście*	krah-KOHV-skyeh pzhehd-MYESH-cheh
Royal Castle	*Zamek Królewski*	ZAH-mehk kroh-LEHV-skee
Castle Square	*Plac Zamkowy*	plahts zahm-KOH-vee
Piłsudski Square	*Plac Marszałka Józefa Piłsudskiego*	plahts mar-SHAW-kah yoh-ZEH-fah pew-sood-SKYAY-goh
Łazienki Park	*Park Łazienkowski*	park wah-zhehn KOV-skee
Vistula River	*Wisła*	VEES-wah

that it's easiest to buy your bus ticket in the underground zone (at any kiosk marked *RUCH*) before you surface.

Buying Train Tickets: Lining one wall of the main arrival hall *(hala główna)* are 16 **ticket windows;** the two farthest to the right are designated for international tickets. A much more user-friendly **customer service center** is in the corner (daily 9:00-20:00). While it can be slower to buy tickets or make reservations here (take a number as you enter), staff members speak English and are generally more patient in helping explain your options. If you're in a hurry and the lines at the ticket windows in the main hall are way too long, you can find more ticket windows in the maze of corridors under the station. Allow yourself plenty of time to wait in line to buy tickets. Some locals bypass these lines altogether and

Warsaw at a Glance

▲▲**Royal Castle** Warsaw's best palace, rebuilt after World War II, but retaining its former opulence and many original furnishings. **Hours:** May-Sept Mon-Sat 10:00-18:00, Sun 11:00-18:00; Oct-April Tue-Sat 10:00-16:00, Sun 11:00-16:00, closed Mon. See page 399.

▲▲**Old Town Market Square** Re-creation of Warsaw's glory days, with lots of colorful architecture. **Hours:** Always open. See page 404.

▲▲**National Museum** Collection of mostly Polish art, with unknown but worth-discovering works by Jan Matejko and the Młoda Polska (Art Nouveau) crew. **Hours:** Tue 10:00-17:00, Wed-Thu 10:00-16:00, Fri 12:00-21:00, Sat-Sun 12:00-18:00, closed Mon. See page 408.

▲▲**Warsaw Uprising Museum** High-tech exhibit tracing the history of the Uprising and celebrating its heroes. **Hours:** Mon, Wed, and Fri 8:00-18:00; Thu 8:00-20:00; Sat-Sun 10:00-18:00; closed Tue. See page 419.

▲▲**Copernicus Science Center** Spiffy new science museum with well-explained, hands-on exhibits in English; Warsaw's best family activity. **Hours:** Tue-Fri 9:00-18:00, Sat-Sun 10:00-19:00, closed Mon. See page 412.

▲**Castle Square** Colorful spot with whiffs of old Warsaw—Royal Castle, monuments, and a chunk of the city wall—and cafés just

buy their tickets on the train for an extra charge (10 zł extra; find the conductor before he finds you).

Note that even if you have a railpass, a reservation is still required on certain trains (including express trains to Kraków)—if you're not sure, it's worth asking at the rail service center.

To get to your train, first find your way to the right platform (*peron*, as noted on schedules), then keep an eye on both tracks *(tor)* for your train. Train info: Tel. 19436 (22-19436 from outside Warsaw), www.rozklad-pkp.pl.

By Plane

Warsaw's **Fryderyk Chopin International Airport** (Port Lotniczy im. Fryderyk Chopina) is about six miles southwest of the center. The airport terminal has two zones: the old southern hall (areas A and B) and the newer northern hall (areas C, D, E). At the airport, you'll find a TI, ATMs, and exchange offices *(kantor)*.

off the square. **Hours:** Always open. See page 398.

▲**Łazienki Park** Lovely, sprawling green space with Chopin statue, peacocks, and Neoclassical buildings. **Hours:** Always open. See page 413.

Chopin Museum Elegant old mansion features slick exhibits but not much substance about Chopin; occasional piano concerts worthwhile. **Hours:** Tue-Sun 12:00-20:00, closed Mon. See page 410.

Warsaw Historical Museum Glimpse of the city before and after World War II, with excellent movie in English. **Hours:** Museum—Tue and Thu 11:00-18:00, Wed and Fri 10:00-15:30, until 18:00 mid-July-Sept, Sat-Sun 10:30-16:30, closed Mon; Movie—Tue-Sun at noon. See page 404.

Palace of Culture and Science Huge "Stalin Gothic" sky-scraper with a more impressive exterior than interior, housing theaters, multiplex cinema, observation deck, and more. **Hours:** Observation deck—daily June-Aug 9:00-20:00, until 24:00 Fri-Sat; Sept-May 9:00-18:00. See page 406.

Jewish Ghetto: Path of Remembrance Pilgrimage from Ghetto Heroes Square to the infamous Nazi "transfer spot" where Jews were sent to death camps. **Hours:** Always open. See page 416.

From either hall (AB or CDE), **bus #175** runs into the city center (central train station, the Royal Way, and Old Town; 3.60 zł, buy ticket at kiosk or from driver—though sometimes drivers can't make change and require the exact amount, 4-6/hour, 30-45 minutes). Only certain **taxi** companies are authorized to pick up arriving travelers at the airport; go to the official taxi stand, and avoid random hucksters offering you a ride out front (these creeps are notorious for overcharging). The 30-minute taxi ride to the center shouldn't cost you more than 50 zł. The trip into town can take much longer during rush hour. Airport info: tel. 22-650-4220, www.lotnisko-chopina.pl/en.

Modlin Airport, an abandoned military facility about 21 miles northwest of the city center, was recently refurbished to serve primarily low-cost airlines (likely open by mid-2012). A 30-minute train connection to downtown is planned; in the meantime, there is a bus connection (for updates, see www.modlinairport.pl).

By Car

Warsaw is a stressful city to drive and park in. Arrange parking with your hotel, and get around by foot or public transit.

Getting Around Warsaw

By Public Transit: In this big city, it's essential to get a handle on public transportation. The Metro will remain mostly useless to tourists until the new line opens in late 2013, but the buses and trams are great. All three systems use the same tickets. A single ticket costs 3.60 zł (called *bilet jednorazowy,* good for one trip, no transfers); a 24-hour ticket costs 12 zł *(bilet dobowy)*; and a three-day ticket is 24 zł *(bilet trzydniowy)*. For shorter trips, you can also buy time-limited tickets, such as the 2.60-zł "20-minute city travelcard" (*bilet 20-minutowy;* also available in 40- and 60-minute versions). Buy your ticket at any kiosk with a *RUCH* sign. Be sure to validate your ticket as you board by inserting it in the little yellow box (24-hour and three-day tickets need only be validated the first time you ride). Some, but not all, buses have automated machines for buying tickets on board (coins only—no bills or credit cards), but it's safer to buy them in advance from a kiosk. Transit info: www.ztm.waw.pl.

Most of the city's major attractions line up on a single axis, the Royal Way, which is served by several different buses (but no trams). **Bus #175,** particularly useful on arrival, links the airport, the central train station, the Royal Way, and Old Town. Once in town, the designed-for-tourists **bus #180** conveniently connects virtually all of the significant sights and neighborhoods: the former Jewish Ghetto, Castle Square/Old Town, the Royal Way, Łazienki Park, and Wilanów Palace (south of the center). This particularly user-friendly bus lists sights in English on the posted schedule inside (other buses don't). Those two buses, as well as buses **#116, #195,** and **#222,** go along the most interesting stretch of the Royal Way (between aleja Jerozolimskie and Castle Square in the Old Town). **Bus #178** conveniently connects Castle Square to the Warsaw Uprising Museum. Bus routes beginning with "E" (and marked in red on schedules) are express, so they go long distances without stopping.

Note that on Saturdays and Sundays in summer (June-Sept), the Nowy Świat section of the Royal Way is closed to traffic, so the above routes take a detour along a parallel street.

While Warsaw's original **Metro** line is largely unhelpful to visitors (it runs roughly parallel to the Royal Way, several blocks to the west), a new Metro line is under construction that could prove very useful. Due to begin running in late 2013, this line cuts through the city from west to east, effortlessly connecting two otherwise hard-to-reach sights (Warsaw Uprising Museum and

Copernicus Science Center), and also stopping at Nowy Świat (near the Copernicus Monument) and the National Stadium.

By Taxi: As in most big Eastern European cities, it's wise to use only cabs that are clearly marked with a company logo and telephone number (or call your own: Locals like MPT Radio Taxi, tel. 19191; or Ele taxi, tel. 22-811-1111). All official taxis have similar rates: 6 zł to start, then 3 zł per kilometer (4.50 zł after 22:00 or in the suburbs). The drop fee may be higher if you catch the cab in front of a fancy hotel.

Tours in Warsaw

For a big and important city, Warsaw suffers from a lack of good tour options. Each year, new companies crop up offering **walking tours** in Warsaw; as none is well-established, get the latest advice from the TI.

Various companies offer **bus tours** (which include some walking; 140 zł, 3 hours, get information at TI or your hotel). The same companies offer private, guided minivan tours to various destinations.

Two different companies offer **hop-on, hop-off bus tours.** While City Sightseeing runs more frequently, it's still meager (1/hour); Warsaw City Tour runs even less often (every 2 hours), but has a farther-reaching route that includes more sights (such as the Jewish Quarter, not covered by City Sightseeing).

A **tourist train** does a 30-minute circuit, leaving from in front of the Royal Castle (22 zł, daily May-Oct, doesn't run Mon Nov-April).

Self-Guided Walk

Warsaw's Royal Way

The Royal Way (Szlak Królewski) is the six-mile route that the kings of Poland used to take from their main residence (at Castle Square in the Old Town) to their summer home (Wilanów Palace, south of the center and not worth visiting). In the heart of the city, the Royal Way is a busy boulevard with two different names: At the south end, hip and vibrant **Nowy Świat** offers lots of shops and restaurants, and a good glimpse of urban Warsaw; to the north, and ending at the Old Town, **Krakowskie Przedmieście** is lined with historic landmarks and better for sightseeing.

Since this spine connects most hotels, restaurants, and sights, you'll almost certainly use it—on foot or by bus—sometime during your trip (key buses are noted earlier, under "Getting Around Warsaw"). This self-guided walk should make your commute more interesting. Not counting sightseeing stops, figure about

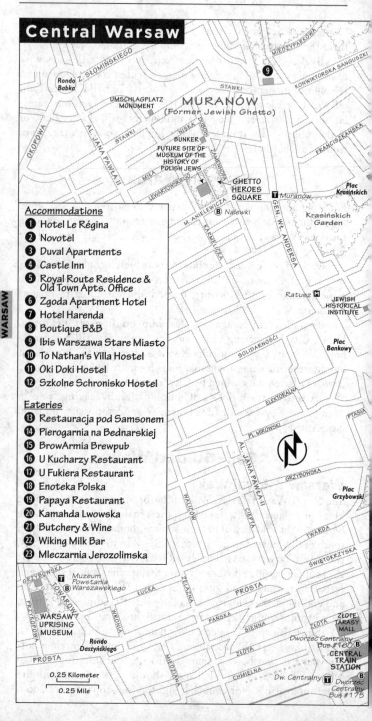

Central Warsaw

WARSAW

Accommodations

1. Hotel Le Régina
2. Novotel
3. Duval Apartments
4. Castle Inn
5. Royal Route Residence & Old Town Apts. Office
6. Zgoda Apartment Hotel
7. Hotel Harenda
8. Boutique B&B
9. Ibis Warszawa Stare Miasto
10. To Nathan's Villa Hostel
11. Oki Doki Hostel
12. Szkolne Schronisko Hostel

Eateries

13. Restauracja pod Samsonem
14. Pierogarnia na Bednarskiej
15. BrowArmia Brewpub
16. U Kucharzy Restaurant
17. U Fukiera Restaurant
18. Enoteka Polska
19. Papaya Restaurant
20. Kamahda Lwowska
21. Butchery & Wine
22. Wiking Milk Bar
23. Mleczarnia Jerozolimska

0.25 Kilometer

0.25 Mile

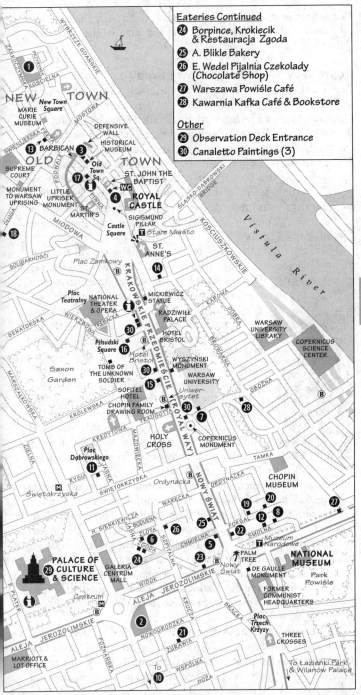

Eateries Continued
24 Borpince, Krokiecik & Restauracja Zgoda
25 A. Blikle Bakery
26 E. Wedel Pijalnia Czekolady (Chocolate Shop)
27 Warszawa Powiśle Café
28 Kawarnia Kafka Café & Bookstore

Other
29 Observation Deck Entrance
30 Canaletto Paintings (3)

WARSAW

15 minutes to walk along Nowy Świat ("Part 1"), then another 30 minutes along Krakowskie Przedmieście to the Old Town ("Part 2").

Royal Way Walk Part 1: Nowy Świat

Begin at the head of the boulevard called Nowy Świat, at the intersection with busy **aleja Jerozolimskie** ("Jerusalem Avenue"). This street once led to a Jewish settlement called New Jerusalem. Like so much else in Warsaw, it's changed names many times. Between the World Wars, it became "May 3rd Avenue," celebrating Poland's 1791 constitution (Europe's first). But this was too nationalistic for the occupying Nazis, who called it simply Bahnhofstrasse ("Train Station Street"). Then the communists switched it back to "Jerusalem"—strangely disregarding the religious connotations of that name. (Come on, guys—what about a good, old-fashioned "Stalin Avenue"?)

WARSAW

You can't miss the giant, out-of-place **palm tree** in the middle of aleja Jerozolimskie. When a local artist went to the real Jerusalem, she was struck at how many palm trees she saw there. She decided it was only appropriate that one should grace Warsaw's own little stretch of "Jerusalem." This artificial palm tree—with a trunk from France and leaves from California, where theme parks abound with such fake trees—went up years ago as a temporary installation. It was highly controversial, dividing the neighborhood. One snowy winter day, the pro-palm tree faction—who appreciated the way the tree spiced up this otherwise predictable metropolis—camped out here in bikinis and beachwear to show their support. They prevailed, and the tree still stands.

Look to the corner across the street from the palm tree, where a statue of **Charles de Gaulle** strides confidently up the street. A gift from the government of France, this celebrates the military tactician who came to Warsaw's rescue when the Red Army invaded from the USSR after World War I. The giant roundabout surrounding the palm tree is also named for de Gaulle.

As you face the palm tree, look across the street and up the block to the left to see the **National Museum**—a good place for a Polish art lesson (more interesting than it sounds—described later, under "Sights in Warsaw").

To the right of the National Museum, directly across from Nowy Świat stands a big, blocky building marked *RICOH* that used to be the **headquarters of the Communist Party**. The translation for Nowy Świat is "New World." A popular communist-era joke: What do you see when you turn your back on the Communist Party? A "New World."

Today's Poland is confidently striding into a new world...and so should we. Get marching.

Nowy Świat is a charming shopping boulevard lined with boutiques, cafés, and restaurants—the most upscale, elegant-

feeling part of the city. Before World War II, Nowy Świat was Warsaw's most popular neighborhood. And today, once again, rents are higher here than anywhere else in town. While most tourists flock into the Old Town, Varsovians and visiting business-people prefer this zone. The city has worked hard to revitalize this strip with new, broader, pedestrian-friendly sidewalks, flower boxes, and old-time lampposts.

Ulica Chmielna, the first street to the left, is an appealing pedestrian boutique street leading to Emil Wedel's chocolate heaven (a five-minute walk away; described later, under "Eating in Warsaw"). Between here and the Palace of Culture and Science stretches one of Warsaw's trendiest shopping neighborhoods (culminating at the Galleria Centrum mall, just across from the Palace).

Across the street from Chmielna (on the right) is the street called **Foksal,** one of Warsaw's most pleasant and trendy dining zones. On a balmy summer evening, this street is filled with chatty al fresco diners, sipping drinks and nibbling at plates of cutting-edge international cuisine.

A few steps down Nowy Świat, on the left, don't miss the recommended **A. Blikle** pastry shop and café—*the* place in Poland to buy sweets, especially *pączki* (rose-flavored jelly doughnuts; see page 270). Or, if you're homesick for Starbucks, drop into one of the many gourmet coffee shops that line this stretch of Nowy Świat—with American-style lattes "to go."

A half-block down the street (on the left) is a rare surviving bit of pre-glitz Nowy Świat: Bar Mleczny Familijny, a classic **milk bar**—a government-subsidized cafeteria filled with locals seeking a cheap meal (an interesting cultural artifact, but not recommended for a meal; for more about milk bars, see page 269). Don't be surprised if it's gone by the time you visit; in this high-rent district, it's unlikely that these few remaining holdovers from the old days will survive for much longer.

The next two blocks are more of the same. Eat and shop your way up Nowy Świat, until you reach the big Copernicus statue.

WARSAW

Royal Way Walk Part 2: Krakowskie Przedmieście

The street name changes to Krakowskie Przedmieście at the big statue of **Copernicus** (by the great Danish sculptor Bertel Thorvaldsen), in front of the Polish Academy of Science. Mikołaj Kopernik (1473-1543) was born in Toruń and went to college in Kraków. The Nazis stole

this statue and took it to Germany (which, like Poland, claims Copernicus as its own). Now it's back where it belongs. Nearby,

in the glass case, find a replica of a Canaletto painting of this same street scene in 1778, and compare it to today's reality. (Paintings like this were used to rebuild the city after World War II.) You may see other Canalettos like this one scattered around the city.

We'll pass many churches along this route, but the **Church of the Holy Cross** is unique (Kościół Św. Krzyża, across from Copernicus, free entry). Composer Fryderyk Chopin's heart is inside one of the pillars of the nave (first big pillar on the left, look for the marker). After two decades of exile in France, Chopin's final wish was to have his heart brought back to his native Poland after his death. During World War II, the heart was hidden away in the countryside for safety. Check out the bright gold chapel, located on the left as you face the altar, near the front of the church. It's dedicated to a saint whom Polish Catholics believe helps them with "desperate and hopeless causes." People praying here are likely dealing with some tough issues. The beads draped from the altarpieces help power their prayers, and the many little brass plaques are messages of thanks for prayers answered. In the back-right corner (as you face the altar), behind the giant barbed wire, is a memorial to the 22,000 Polish POWs—mostly officers and prominent civilians—massacred by Soviet soldiers in 1940 near Katyń, a village in today's Russia.

Leave the church and cross the street (appreciating how pedestrian-friendly it's become in recent years). A long block up the street on the right, you'll see the gates (marked *Uniwersytet*) to the main campus of **Warsaw University,** founded in 1816. This area is a lively student district with plenty of bookstores and cafés.

The 18th century was a time of great political decline for Poland, as a series of incompetent foreign kings mishandled crises and squandered funds. But ironically, it was also Warsaw's biggest economic boom time. Along this boulevard, aristocratic families of the period built **mansions**—most of them destroyed during World War II and rebuilt since. Some have curious flourishes (just past the university on the right, look for the doorway supported by four bearded brutes admiring their overly defined abs). Over time, many of these families donated their mansions to the university. (Across the street on the corner, look for the recommended BrowArmia brewpub, with some of the best people-watching al fresco tables on the Royal Way.)

The bright-yellow church a block up from the university is the Church of the Nuns of the Visitation (Kościół Sióstr Wizytek). The monument in front commemorates **Cardinal Stefan Wyszyński,** who was the Polish primate (the head of the Polish Catholic Church) from 1948 to 1981. He took this post soon after the arrival of the communists, who opposed the Church, but also realized it would be risky for them to shut down the churches in such an ardently religious country. The Communist Party and the Catholic Church coexisted tensely in Poland, and when Wyszyński protested a Stalinist crackdown in 1953, he was arrested and imprisoned. Three years later, in a major victory for the Church, Wyszyński was released. He continued to fight the communists, becoming a great hero of the Polish people in their struggle against the regime. Across the street is another then-and-now Canaletto illustration.

Farther up (on the right) is the elegant, venerable Hotel Bristol. Leave the Royal Way briefly here to reach Piłsudski Square (a block away on the left, up the street opposite Hotel Bristol).

The vast, empty-feeling **Piłsudski Square** (Plac Marszałka Józefa Piłsudskiego) has been important Warsaw real estate for centuries, constantly changing with the times. In the 1890s, the Russians who controlled this part of Poland began construction of a huge and magnificent Orthodox cathedral on this spot. But soon after it was completed, Poland regained its independence, and anti-Russian sentiments ran hot. So in the 1920s, just over a decade after the cathedral went up, it was torn down again. During the Nazi occupation, this square took the name "Adolf-Hitler-Platz." Under the communists, it was Zwycięstwa, meaning "Victory" (of the Soviets over Hitler's fascism). When the regime imposed martial law in 1981, the people of Warsaw silently protested by filling the square with a giant cross made of flowers. The huge plaque in the ground near the road commemorates two monumental communist-era Catholic events on this square: John Paul II's first visit as pope to his homeland on June 2, 1979; and the May 31, 1981 funeral of Cardinal Stefan Wyszyński, whom we met across the street. The cross nearby also honors the 1979 papal visit, with one of his most famous and inspiring quotes to his countrymen: "Let thy spirit descend, let thy spirit descend, and renew the face of the earth—*this* earth" (meaning Poland, in a just-barely-subtle-enough dig against the communist regime that was tolerating his visit). More recently, on April 17, 2010, more than 100,000 Poles convened on this square for a more solemn occasion: a memorial service for President Lech Kaczyński, who had died in a tragic plane crash in Russia.

Stand near the giant plaque, with the Royal Way at your back, for this quick spin-tour orientation: Ahead are the Tomb of the Unknown Soldier and Saxon Garden (explained later); 90 degrees to the right is the old National Theater, eclipsed by a modern business center/parking garage; another 90 degrees to the right is a statue of Piłsudski (which you passed to get here—described later); and 90 more degrees to the right is the Sofitel—formerly the Victoria Hotel, the ultimate plush, top-of-the-top hotel where all communist-era VIPs stayed. To the right of the hotel, on the horizon, you can see Warsaw's newly emerging skyline. The imposing Palace of Culture and Science, which once stood alone over the city, is now joined by a cluster of brand-new skyscrapers, giving Warsaw a Berlin-esque vibe befitting its important role as a business center of the "New Europe."

Walk to the fragment of colonnade by the park that marks the **Tomb of the Unknown Soldier** (Grób Nieznanego Żołnierza). The colonnade was once part of a much larger palace built by the Saxon prince electors (Dresden's Augustus the Strong and his son), who became kings of Poland in the 18th century. After the palace was destroyed in World War II, this fragment was kept to memorialize Polish soldiers. The names of key battles are etched into the columns, the urns contain dirt from major Polish battlefields, and the two soldiers are pretty stiff.

Just behind the Tomb is the stately **Saxon Garden** (Ogród Saski), inhabited by genteel statues and a spurting fountain. This park was also built by the Saxon kings of Poland. Like most foreign kings, Augustus the Strong and his son cared little for their Polish territory, building gardens like these for themselves instead of investing in more pressing needs. Poles say that foreign kings such as Augustus did nothing but  "eat, drink, and loosen their belts" (it rhymes in Polish). According to Poles, these selfish absentee kings were the culprits in Poland's eventual decline.

Walk back out toward the Royal Way, stopping at the statue you passed earlier. In 1995, the square was again renamed—this

time for **Józef Piłsudski** (1867-1935), the guy with the big walrus moustache. With the help of a French captain named Charles de Gaulle (whom we met earlier), Piłsudski forced the Russian Bolsheviks out of Poland in 1920 in the so-called Miracle on the Vistula. Piłsudski is credited with creating a once-again-independent Poland after more than a century of foreign oppression, and he essentially ran Poland as a virtual dictator after World War I. Of course, under the communists, Piłsudski was swept under the rug. But since 1989, he has enjoyed a renaissance as many Poles' favorite prototype anti-communist hero (his name adorns streets, squares, and bushy-mustachioed monuments all over the country).

Return to Hotel Bristol, turn left, and continue your Royal Way walk. Next door to the hotel, you'll see the huge **Radziwiłł Palace.** The Warsaw Pact was signed here in 1955, officially uniting the Soviet satellite states in a military alliance against NATO. This building has also, from time to time, served as the Polish "White House." A **TI** is in the old guardhouse (Kordegarda) across the street.

Beyond Radziwiłł Palace, you'll reach a statue (on a pillar) of **Adam Mickiewicz,** Poland's national poet. Polish high school students have a big formal ball (like a prom) 100 days before graduation. After the ball, if students come here and hop around the statue on one leg, it's supposed to bring them good luck on their finals. Mickiewicz, for his part, looks like he's suffering from a heart attack—perhaps in response to the impressively ugly National Theater and Opera a block in front of him.

Continue to the end of the Royal Way, marked by the big pink

palace. For a scenic finale to your Royal Way stroll, climb the 150 steps of the view tower by **St. Anne's Church** (5 zł, sporadic hours but generally open daily 10:00-18:00, in summer until 21:00 or 22:00 depending on weather, closed in bad winter weather, on the right just before Castle

Square). You'll be rewarded with a great view of the Old Town, river, and Warsaw's skyline.

From St. Anne's Church, it's just another block—past inviting art galleries and restaurants—to Castle Square, the TI, and the start of the Old Town.

Sights in Warsaw

The Old Town

In 1945, not a building remained standing in Warsaw's "Old" Town (Stare Miasto). Everything you see is rebuilt, mostly finished by 1956. Some think the Old Town feels artificial and phony, in a Disney World kind of way. For others, the painstaking postwar reconstruction feels just right, with Old World squares and lanes charming enough to give Kraków a run for its money. Before 1989, stifled by communist repression and choking on smog, the Old Town was an empty husk of its historic self. But now, the outdoor restaurants and market stalls have returned, and Varsovians and tourists are out strolling.

These sights are listed in order from south to north, beginning at Castle Square and ending at the entrance to the New Town. For the best route from the central train station to the Old Town, see the "Royal Way" self-guided walk, earlier.

▲Castle Square (Plac Zamkowy)—This lively square is dominated by the big, pink Royal Castle that is the historic heart of Warsaw's political power.

After the second great Polish dynasty—the Jagiellonians—died off in 1572, it was replaced by the Republic of Nobles (about

10 percent of the population), which elected various foreign kings to their throne. The guy on the 72-foot-tall **pillar** is Sigismund III, the first Polish king from the Swedish Waza family. In 1596, he relocated the capital from Kraków to Warsaw. This move made sense, since Warsaw was closer to the center of 16th-century Poland (which had expanded to the east), and because the city had gained political importance over the past 30 years as the meeting point of the Sejm, or parliament of nobles. Along the right side of the castle, notice the two previous versions of this pillar lying on a lawn. The first one, from 1644, was falling apart and had to be replaced in 1887 by a new one made of granite. In 1944, a Nazi tank broke this second pillar—a symbolic piece of Polish heritage—into the four pieces (still pockmarked with bullet holes) that you see here today. As Poland

rebuilt, its citizens put Sigismund III back on his pillar. Past the pillars are great views of Warsaw's brand-new, red-and-white National Stadium across the river.

Across the square from the castle, you'll see the partially reconstructed **defensive wall**. This rampart once enclosed the entire Old Town. Warsaw—like all of Poland—has seen invasion from all sides.

Explore the café-lined lanes that branch off Castle Square. Street signs indicate the year that each lane was originally built.

The first street leading off the square is **ulica Piwna** ("Beer Street"), where you'll find **St. Martin's Church** (Kościół Św. Martina, on the left). Run by Franciscan nuns, this church has a simple, modern interior. Walk up the aisle and find the second pillar on the right. Notice the partly destroyed crucifix—it's the only church artifact that survived World War II. Across the street and closer to Castle Square, admire the carefully carved doorway of the house called *pod Gołębiami* ("Under Doves")—dedicated to the memory of an old woman who fed birds amidst the Old Town rubble after World War II.

Back on Castle Square, find the white **plaque** in the middle of the second block (by plac Zamkowy 15/19). It explains that 50 Poles were executed by Nazis on this spot on September 2, 1944. You'll see plaques like this all over the Old Town, each one commemorating victims or opponents of the Nazis. The brick planter under the plaque is often filled with fresh flowers to honor the victims.

▲▲**Royal Castle (Zamek Królewski)**—A castle has stood here since the Mazovian dukes built a wooden version in the 14th cen-

tury. It has shifted shape with the tenor of the times, being rebuilt and remodeled by many different kings. When Warsaw became the capital in 1596, this massive building served a dual purpose: It was both the king's residence and the meeting place of the parliament (Sejm). It reached its peak under Stanisław August Poniatowski— the final Polish king—who imported artists and architects to spiff up the interior, leaving his mark all over the place. After Luftwaffe bombs destroyed it in World War II (only one wall remained standing), rebuilding began again in the 1950s. It was not completed until the 1970s.

Warsaw's Royal Castle has a gorgeous interior—the most opulent I've seen in Poland. Many of the furnishings are original (hidden away when it became clear the city would be demolished in

World War II). A visit to the castle is like perusing a great Polish history textbook. In fact, you'll likely see grade-school classes sitting cross-legged on the floors. Watching the teachers quizzing eager young history buffs, you can imagine what it's like to be a young Pole, with such a tumultuous history.

Cost and Hours: 22 zł, free on Sun, audioguide-17 zł; open May-Sept Mon-Sat 10:00-18:00, Sun 11:00-18:00; Oct-April Tue-Sat 10:00-16:00, Sun 11:00-16:00, closed Mon; last entry one hour before closing; Plac Zamkowy 4, tel. 22-355-5170, www.zamek-krolewski.pl. A public WC is on the courtyard just around the corner of the castle.

❸ Self-Guided Tour: The castle has good posted English information and a well-produced audioguide (worth the extra cost if you want the full story). For the basics, use this commentary to follow the one-way route through the castle. Because the castle visit procedure is always changing, it's possible you won't see these rooms in this exact order; if that happens, match the labels in each room to the corresponding text below.

Entering the courtyard, go to the left to buy tickets, then cross to the opposite side to tour the interior. (If you want an audioguide, go downstairs to rent it first.) Head up the stairs and follow *Castle Route* signs.

Start in the Oval Gallery, then head into the **Council Chamber,** where a "Permanent Council" consisting of the king, 18 senators, and 18 representatives met to chart Poland's course. Next is the **Great Assembly Hall,** heavy with marble and chandeliers. The statues of Apollo and Minerva flanking the main door are modeled after King Stanisław August Poniatowski and Catherine the Great of Russia, respectively. (The king enjoyed a youthful romantic dalliance with Catherine on a trip to Russia, and never quite seemed to get over her...much to his wife's consternation, I'm sure.)

The **Knights' Hall** features the Polish Hall of Fame, with paintings of great events and busts and portraits of VIPs—Very Important Poles. The statue of Chronos—god of time, with the globe on his shoulders—is actually a functioning clock, though now it's stopped at 11:15 to commemorate the exact time in 1944 when the Nazis bombed this palace to bits. Just off this hall is the **Marble Room,** with more portraits of Polish greats ringing the top of the room. Above the fireplace is a portrait of Stanisław August Poniatowski.

Continuing back through the Knights' Hall, you'll wind up in the remarkable **Throne Room.** Notice the crowned eagle, the symbol of Poland, decorating the banner behind the throne. The Soviets didn't allow anything royal or aristocratic, so postwar restorations came with crown-less eagles. Only after 1989 were the crowned eagles reinstated (one of the original eagles from this banner somehow turned up in the United States, and was used as a model for the ones you see here). Peek into the **Conference Rooms,** with portraits of other major European monarchs—Russia's Catherine the Great, England's George III, and France's Louis XVI—in whose esteemed company Stanisław August Poniatowski liked to consider himself.

After four more grand rooms (including the King's Bedroom, with a gorgeous silk canopy over the bed), you'll enter the **Canaletto Room,** filled with canvases of late-18th-century Warsaw painted in exquisite detail by this talented artist. (This Canaletto, also known for his panoramas of Dresden, was the nephew of another artist with the same nickname, famous for painting Venice's canals.) Paintings like these helped post-WWII restorers resurrect the city from its rubble. To the left, on the lower wall, the big canvas features the view of Warsaw from the Praga district across the river; pick out the few landmarks that are still standing (or, more precisely, have been resurrected). Notice the artist's self-portrait in the lower-left. On the right side of the room is Canaletto's depiction of the election of Stanisław August Poniatowski as king, in a field outside Warsaw (notice the empty throne in the middle of the group). Among the assembled crowd, each flag represents a different Polish province. From here, head into the **side chapel,** reserved for the king. In the box to the left of the altar is the heart of Tadeusz Kościuszko, a hero of both the American Revolution and the Polish struggle against the Partitions (for more about the Partitions, see page 261).

As you cross over to the other part of the castle, you'll pass through the **Four Seasons Gallery** (with some fine but faded Gobelin tapestries) before entering a few rooms occupied by the houses of parliament—a reminder that this "castle" wasn't just the king's house, but also the meeting place of the legislature. In the **Parliamentary Chambers,** notice the maps showing Poland's constantly in-flux borders—a handy visual aid for the many school groups who visit here.

After several rooms, you'll reach the grand **Senators' Chamber,** with the king's throne, surrounded by different coats of arms. Each one represents a region that was part of Poland during its Golden Age, back when it was united with Lithuania and its territory stretched from the Baltic to the Black Sea (see the map on the wall). In this room, Poland adopted its 1791 constitution (notice

the replica in the display case to the left of the throne). It was the first in Europe, written soon after America's and just months before France's. And, like the Constitution of the United States, it was very progressive, based on the ideals of the Enlightenment. But when the final Partitions followed in 1793 and 1795, Poland was divided between neighboring powers and ceased to exist as a country until 1918—so the constitution was never fully put into action.

Next, the **Crown Princes Room** features paintings by Jan Matejko that capture the excitement surrounding the adoption of this ill-fated constitution (for more on Matejko, see page 409). The next room has another Matejko painting: King Stefan Batory negotiating with Ivan the Terrible's envoys to break their siege of a Russian town. Notice the hussars—fearsome Polish soldiers wearing winged armor. Finally, you'll wind through more rooms with yet more paintings of great historical events and portraits of famous Poles.

Other Castle Sights: Consider a detour to the **Kubicki Arcades** (Arkady Kubiciego), the impressively excavated arcades

deep beneath the castle. From the entrance lobby, head downstairs to the area with the cloakroom, bathrooms, and bookshop, then find the long escalator that takes you down to the arcades. It's free to wander the long, cavernous, and newly clean and gleaming space, made elegant by grand drapes. To visit the exhibit branching off the arcade, which explains the excavation and refurbishment, you'll have to buy an 8-zł ticket (free on Sun, purchase from main ticket desk). I'd skip the exhibit and just enjoy the space.

The castle has a vast collection, which it organizes into various exhibitions—some permanent (well, as permanent as anything around here) and some temporary. The extensive **oriental carpet collection** in the "tin-roofed castle" (Pałac pod Blachą) is sparsely described and skippable for most; the same building also features seven unimpressive apartments of Prince Józef Poniatowski, the king's brother (14 zł for both, free on Sun, same hours as castle, around the right side of the castle as you face it—past the two

WARSAW

fallen columns, buy ticket at main ticket desk). When you're buying your castle ticket, keep an eye out for **temporary exhibits** of interest.

• *After you finish touring the castle and are ready to resume exploring the Old Town, turn left at the end of the square onto...*

St. John's Street (Świętojańska)—On the plaque under the street name sign, you can guess what the dates mean, even if you don't know Polish: This building was constructed from 1433 to 1478, destroyed in 1944, and rebuilt from 1950 to 1953.

• *Partway down the street on the right, you'll come to the big brick...*

Cathedral of St. John the Baptist (Katedra Św. Jana Chrzciciela)—This cathedral-basilica is the oldest (1339) and most important church in Warsaw.

Superficially unimpressive, the church's own archbishop admitted that it was "modest and poor"—but "the historical events that took place here make it magnificent." Poland's constitution was consecrated here on May 3, 1791. Much later, this church became the final battleground of the 1944 Warsaw Uprising—when a Nazi "tracked mine" (a huge bomb on tank tracks—this one appropriately named *Goliath*) drove into the church and exploded, massacring the rebels. You can still see part of that tank's tread hanging on the outside wall of the church (through the passage on the right side, near the end of the church).

Head inside. Typical of brick churches, it has a "hall church" design, with three naves of equal height. Look for the crucifix ornamented with real human hair (chapel left of high altar). The high altar holds a copy of the Black Madonna—proclaimed "everlasting queen of Poland" after a victory over the Swedes in the 17th century. The original Black Madonna is in Częstochowa (125 miles south of Warsaw)—a mecca for Slavic Catholics, who visit in droves in hopes of a miracle. In the back-left corner, find the chapel with the tomb of Cardinal Stefan Wyszyński. The crypt (2 zł) holds graves of several important Poles, including Stanisław August Poniatowski (the last Polish king) and Nobel Prize-winning author Henryk Sienkiewicz.

Cost and Hours: Free, crypt-2 zł, good guidebook-5 zł, open to tourists daily 10:00-13:00 & 15:00-17:30, closed during services and organ concerts. The cathedral hosts organ concerts in summer—9 zł, May-late Sept Mon-Sat at 12:00, 25 minutes, no concerts Sun or late Sept-April.

• *Continue up the street and enter Warsaw's grand...*

▲▲Old Town Market Square (Rynek Starego Miasta)—
Seventy-five years ago, this was one of the most happening spots
in Central Europe. Sixty-five years ago, it was rubble. And today,
like a phoenix from the ashes, it's risen to remind residents and
tourists alike of the prewar glory of the Polish capital.

Go to the **mermaid fountain** in the middle of the square.
The mermaid is an important symbol in Warsaw—you'll see her

everywhere. Legend has it that a
mermaid *(syrenka)* lived in the Vistula
River and protected the townspeople.
While this siren supposedly serenaded
the town, Varsovians like her more
for her strength (hence the sword).
In fact, the woman who modeled for
this sculpture, Krystyna Krahelska
(code name: "Danuta"), served as a
paramedic for the Polish Home Army
during the Warsaw Uprising. On the
second day of the fighting, she was
shot in the chest and died, becoming
a martyr for the Polish people. But life goes on in Warsaw, as it
always has. I've often seen children frolicking here, oblivious to
the turmoil their forebears withstood. When the fountain gurgles,
the kids giggle.

Each of the square's four sides is named for a prominent 18th-
century Varsovian: Kołłątaj, Dekert, Barss, and Zakrzewski. These
men served as "Presidents" of Warsaw (mayors, more or less), and
Kołłątaj was also a framer of Poland's 1791 constitution. Take some
time to explore the square. Enjoy the colorful architecture. Notice
that many of the buildings were intentionally built to lean out into
the square—to simulate the higgledy-piggledy wear and tear of the
original buildings.

• *On the Dekert (north) side of the square is the...*

**Warsaw Historical Museum (Muzeum Historyczne
Warszawy)**—This labyrinthine museum rambles through several
reconstructed buildings fronting the Old Town Market Square.
They recently excavated a series of cellars that run beneath the
square, which now also house museum exhibits. The English
descriptions are limited, making it a bit difficult to appreciate. As
you twist your way through room after room of historical bric-
a-brac, keep an eye out for the model of 18th-century Warsaw,
which is worth a close look. The final third of the collection, which
focuses on the tumultuous 20th century, is the most updated—and
the most interesting.

Cost and Hours: 8 zł, free on Sun, open Tue and Thu 11:00-

18:00, Wed and Fri 10:00-15:30—until 18:00 mid-July-Sept, Sat-Sun 10:30-16:30, closed Mon, last entry 45 minutes before closing, Rynek Starego Miasta 28/42, tel. 22-635-1625, www.mhw.pl.

Film: Unless you're fascinated by Warsaw's history, I'd skip the museum collection and just buy the separate 6-zł ticket to watch the excellent 20-minute film in English, worth ▲▲; unfortunately, it runs only at 12:00 (Tue-Sun). With somber narration and black-and-white scenes from before, during, and after the wartime devastation, this film is best appreciated after you've had a chance to see some of today's Warsaw (especially along the Royal Way). The movie ends with, "They say that there are no miracles. Then what is this city on the Vistula?" Emotionally drained, you can only respond, "Amen."

• *Leave the square on Nowomiejska (at the mermaid's 2 o'clock, by the*

second-story niche sculpture of St. Anne). After a block, you'll reach the...

Barbican (Barbakan)—This defensive gate of the Old Town, similar to Kraków's, protected the medieval city from invaders.

• *Once you've crossed through the barbican, you're officially in Warsaw's...*

New Town (Nowe Miasto)—This 15th-century neighborhood is "new" in name only: It was the first part of Warsaw to spring up outside of the city walls (and therefore slightly newer than the Old Town). The New Town is a fun place to wander: Only a little less charming than the Old Town, but with a more real-life feel—people live and work here. Its centerpiece is the **New Town Square** (Rynek Nowego Miasta), watched over by the distinctive green dome of St. Kazimierz Church.

Marie Skłodowska-Curie Museum—Scientists might want to pay homage at the museum (and birthplace) of Warsaw native Marie Skłodowska-Curie, a.k.a. Madame Curie (1867-1934), just off the square. This Nobel Prize winner was the world's first radiologist—discovering both radium and polonium (named for her native land) with her husband, Pierre Curie. Since she lived at a time when Warsaw was controlled by oppressive Russia, she conducted her studies in France. The museum—with photos, furniture, artifacts, and a paucity of English information—is a bit of a snoozer, best left to true fans.

Cost and Hours: Overpriced at 11 zł, Tue 8:30-16:00, Wed-Fri 9:30-16:00, Sat 10:00-16:00, Sun 10:00-15:00, closed Mon, ulica Freta 16, tel. 22/831-8092, http://muzeum-msc.pl.

From the New Town to Castle Square—You can backtrack the way you came, or, to get a look at Warsaw's back streets, consider this route from the big, round barbican gate (where the New Town meets the Old): Go back through the barbican and over the little bridge, turn right, and walk along the houses that line the inside of the wall. You'll pass a leafy garden courtyard on the left—a reminder that people actually live in the tourist zone within the Old Town walls. Just beyond the garden on the right, look for the carpet-beating rack, used to clean rugs (these are common fixtures in people's backyards). Go left into the square called Szeroki Dunaj ("Wide Danube") and look for another mermaid (over the Thai restaurant). Continue through the square and turn right at Wąski Dunaj ("Narrow Danube"). After about 100 yards, you'll pass the city wall. Just to the right (outside the wall), you'll see the monument to the **Little Upriser** of 1944, a child wearing a grown-up's helmet and too-big boots, and carrying a machine gun. Children—and especially Scouts (Harcerze)—played a key role in the resistance against the Nazis. Their job was mainly carrying messages and propaganda.

Now continue around the wall (the upper, inner part is more pleasant). Admire more public art as you head back to Castle Square.

Near the Central Train Station

These sights are near Nowy Świat, within a few blocks of the central train station.

Palace of Culture and Science (Pałac Kultury i Nauki, or PKiN)—This massive skyscraper, dating from the early 1950s, is the tallest building between Frankfurt and Moscow (760 feet with the spire—though several new buildings are threatening to eclipse that peak). It was a "gift" from Stalin that the people of Warsaw couldn't refuse. Varsovians call it "Stalin's Penis"...using cruder terminology than that. (There were seven such "Stalin Gothic" erec-

tions in Moscow.) Because it was to be "Soviet in substance, Polish in style," Soviet architects toured Poland to absorb local culture before starting the project. Notice the frilly decorative friezes that top each level—evocative of Poland's many Renaissance buildings (such as Kraków's Cloth Hall). The clock was added in 1999 as

WARSAW

part of the millennium celebrations. Since the end of communism, the younger generation doesn't mind the structure so much—and some even admit to liking it for the way it enlivens the new, predictable, glass-and-steel skyline springing up around it.

Everything about the Pałac is big. It's designed to show off the strong, grand-scale Soviet aesthetic and architectural skill. The Pałac contains various theaters (the Culture), museums of evolution and technology (the Science), a congress hall, a multiplex (showing current movies), an observation deck, and lots of office space. With all of this culture and science under one roof, it's a shame that none of it makes for worthwhile sightseeing. While the interior is highly skippable, viewing the building from the outside is a quintessential Warsaw experience, worth ▲▲.

If you're killing time between trains, you could zip up to the observation deck in 20 seconds on the retrofitted Soviet elevators. Better yet, snap a photo from down below and save your money—it's overpriced and the view's a letdown. While you'll get a nice overview of Warsaw's forest of new skyscrapers, you can hardly see the Old Town, and Warsaw's most prominent big building—the Pałac itself—is missing.

Cost and Hours: Free entry, observation deck—20 zł, includes Polish-oriented special exhibitions; deck open daily June-Aug 9:00-20:00, until 24:00 Fri-Sat; Sept-May 9:00-18:00, enter through main door on east side of Pałac—opposite from central train station, tel. 22-656-7600, www.pkin.pl.

Złote Tarasy Shopping Mall—Tucked behind the central train station, "Golden Terraces" is a super-modern shopping mall with a funky, undulating glass-and-steel roof. Even though you didn't come all the way to Poland to visit a shopping mall, it's worth detouring here to get a taste of Poland's race into the future. In many ways, this—and not humble farmers munching pierogi—is the face of today's Poland.

Hours: Mon-Sat 10:00-22:00, Sun 10:00-20:00, lots of designer shops, good food court on top level, www.zlotetarasy.pl.

Złota 44—This dramatic skyscraper, rising high from the Złote Tarasy shopping mall, was designed by world-renowned architect Daniel Libeskind (who is also redeveloping the 9/11 site in New York City). Born in Poland, at a very young age Libeskind emigrated with his family to the US, returning only recently to embark on this project. Its shape evokes an eagle (a common symbol for Poland) just beginning to take flight. Of all the shiny new towers popping up in Warsaw's skyline, this is the most architecturally interesting—and offers a striking counterpoint to the Stalinist Palace of Culture and Science nearby. (For more on the building, visit www.zlota44tower.com.)

Between Nowy Świat and the River

▲▲**National Museum (Muzeum Narodowe)**—While short on big-name pieces, this museum interests art-lovers and offers a good, accessible introduction to some talented Polish artists who are largely unknown outside their home country.

Cost and Hours: 12 zł, more for temporary exhibits, permanent collection free on Sat; open Tue 10:00-17:00, Wed-Thu 10:00-16:00, Fri 12:00-21:00, Sat-Sun 12:00-18:00, closed Mon, last entry 45 minutes before closing; one block east of Nowy Świat at aleja Jerozolimskie 3, tel. 22-629-3093, www.mnw.art.pl.

◐ Self-Guided Tour: As this collection was recently renovated, some of the items listed below may have moved.

On the ground floor are exhibits of ancient art (from Egyptian and Greek pieces to works by early Polish tribes), as well as room upon room of medieval altarpieces and crucifixes (including some of the most graphic ones I've seen). The upper floors have temporary exhibits and collections of Polish and European decorative arts and European paintings. But the reason we're here is the Gallery of Polish Painting, one floor up. Focus on the two most important eras, at opposite ends of the building.

First, find the **Jan Matejko** room. From the lobby, take the left staircase up one level, then walk along the railing and go in the door on the left. Bear right through this door, then walk to the very back of this wing, where Matejko hides (if you can't find him, ask the guards, "mah-TAY-koh?"). On the way, you'll pass through a whole room of Napoleon portraits. The Poles loved Napoleon, who bravely marched on Russia in an era when this part of Poland was occupied and oppressed by the Russians...sadly, not for the last time.

The Matejko room is dominated by the enormous *Battle of Grunwald*. This epic painting commemorates one of Poland's high-water marks—the dramatic victory of a Polish-Lithuanian army over the Teutonic Knights, who had been terrorizing northern Poland for decades (for more on the Teutonic Knights, see page 486). On July 15, 1410, some 40,000 Poles and Lithuanians (led by the sword-waving Lithuanian in red, Grand Duke Vytautas) faced off against 27,000 Teutonic Knights (under their Grand Master, in white) in one of the medieval world's bloodiest battles. Matejko plops us right in the thick of the battle's chaos, painting life-size figures and framing off a 32-foot-long slice of the actual two-mile battle line.

In the center of the painting, the Teutonic Grand Master is about to become a shish kebab. Duke Vytautas, in red, leads the final charge. And waaaay up on a hill (in the upper right-hand corner, on horseback, wearing a silver knight's suit) is Władysław Jagiełło, the first king of the Jagiellonian dynasty...ensuring his

Jan Matejko
(1838-1893)

Jan Matejko (yawn mah-TAY-koh) is Poland's most important painter, period. In the mid- to late-19th century, the nation of Poland had been dissolved by foreign powers, and Polish artists struggled to make sense of their people's place in the world. Rabble-rousing Romanticism seemed to have failed (inspiring many brutally suppressed uprisings), so Polish artists and writers turned their attention to educating the people about their history, with the goal of keeping their traditions alive.

Matejko was at the forefront of this so-called "positivist" movement. Matejko saw what the tides of history had done to Poland, and was determined to make sure his countrymen learned from it. He painted two types of works: huge, grand-scale epics depicting monumental events in Polish history; and small, intimate portraits of prominent Poles. Polish schoolchildren study history from books with paintings of virtually every single Polish king—all painted by the incredibly prolific Matejko.

Matejko is admired not for his technical mastery (he's an unexceptional painter) or for the literal truth of his works—he was notorious for fudging historical details in order to give his canvases a bit more propagandistic punch. But he is revered for the emotion behind—and inspired by—his works. His paintings are utilitarian, straightforward, and dramatic enough to stir the patriot in any Pole. The intense focus on history by Matejko and other positivists is one big reason why today's Poles are still so in touch with their heritage.

You'll see Matejko's works in Warsaw's National Museum and Royal Castle, as well as in Kraków's Gallery of 19th-Century Polish Art (above the Cloth Hall). You can also visit his former residence in Kraków.

bloodline will survive another 150 years.

Matejko spent three years covering this 450-square-foot canvas in paint. The canvas was specially made in a single seamless piece. This was such a popular work that almost as many fans turned out for its unveiling as there are figures in the painting.

From Poland's high point in the *Battle of Grunwald*, turn to the canvas immediately to the left, *Stańczyk After the Loss of Smolensk*, to see how Poland's fortunes shifted drastically a century later. This smaller, more intimate portrait by Matejko depicts a popular Polish figure: the court jester Stańczyk, who's smarter than the king, but not allowed to say so. This complex character, representing the national conscience, is a favorite symbol of Matejko's. Stańczyk slumps in gloom. He's just read the news (on the table beside him) that the city of Smolensk has fallen to the Russians after a three-year siege (1512-1514). The jester had tried to warn the king to send more troops, but the king was too busy partying (behind the curtain). The painter Matejko—who may have used his own features for Stańczyk's face—also blamed the nobles of his own day for fiddling while Poland was partitioned.

Other Matejko paintings include one depicting the tragic couple of the last Jagiellonian king, Stanisław August Poniatowski (here identified as Sigismund Augustus), and his wife, Barbara—whom the king loved deeply, even though she couldn't bear him an heir. (In the next room, see the painful end to their sad tale: Barbara on her deathbed.)

Next, take a look at the **Młoda Polska** ("Young Poland") collection, featuring paintings from Poland's version of Art Nouveau (see page 293). It's in the same position as the Matejko room, only on the opposite side of the building: From the lobby, take the right staircase up, then go in the right-hand door, bear left, and work around all the way to the back. In addition to a room of works by movement headliner Stanisław Wyspiański, you'll see the hypnotic *Strange Garden* by Wyspiański's friend and rival, Józef Mehoffer. In the next room are several paintings by Jacek Malczewski, many of them depicting the goateed, close-cropped artist in a semi-surrealistic, Polish countryside context. There's also a room of canvases by the only prominent female Polish painter, Olga Boznańska (past the Wyspiański room)—with a softer and more impressionistic touch than her male Młoda Polska counterparts.

Chopin Museum (Muzeum Fryderyka Chopina)—The reconstructed Ostrogski Castle houses this museum honoring Poland's most famous composer.

The museum was recently overhauled for the "Year of Chopin" in 2010, when all of Poland celebrated the composer's 200th birthday. Unfortunately, what could have been a fantastic opportunity to introduce people to Chopin instead was squandered on slick, high-tech presentations that are all style and no substance. The museum features actual Chopin artifacts (manuscripts, letters, and original handwritten compositions), video screens that delve into specific facets of his life, and listening stations for hearing his music, but completely lacks an overarching narrative of his life and any sense of who he was as a person. While Chopin devotees may find it riveting, those with only a passing familiarity with the composer leave feeling like they knew less about him than when they entered.

Cost and Hours: 22 zł, free on Tue, open Tue-Sun 12:00-20:00, closed Mon, 3 blocks east of Nowy Świat at ulica Okólnik 1, tel. 22-441-6251, www.chopin.museum.

Getting Tickets: Only 70 people can enter each hour, and because the museum is very popular, tickets can quickly sell out. While it's possible to reserve online, the system is challenging to figure out for non-Polish-speakers; instead, if your heart's set on seeing the museum, call ahead to ask what time you should arrive to ensure getting in.

Touring the Museum: Buy your ticket at the small, adjacent building, then go up the stairs and enter the mansion that houses the exhibit. You'll be given an electronic card to wear around your neck; tap it against glowing red dots to access additional information. You'll proceed more or less chronologically through the composer's life, with various opportunities to hear his compositions. In the cellars is a virtual "Guest Book," where you can record your thoughts about Chopin to be added to the montage. Then head up into the mansion interior, with a replica of Chopin's drawing room in Paris, and his last piano, which he used for composing during the final two years of his life (1848-1849). Exhibits here trace themes of the composer's life, such as the women he knew (including his older sister Ludwika, his mother, and George Sand—the French author who took a male pseudonym in order to be published, and who was romantically linked with Chopin). The exhibit ends with Chopin's bronze death mask, featuring his distinctively Polish nose, shaped like an eagle's beak.

Concerts: In the cellar under the palace is a new **concert hall,** open for special concerts. If you're in town for one, go. There's nothing like hearing Chopin's music passionately played by a teary-eyed Pole who really feels the music (call museum to ask for concert schedule).

Other Chopin Sights: The **Chopin Family Drawing Room** is the Royal Way apartment where Chopin lived with his family, and where he wrote and premiered many of his earliest compositions (3 zł, free on Wed, open Mon-Fri 10:00-18:00, closed Sat-Sun, upstairs in the Krasiński Palace—now the Academy of Fine Arts—at Krakowskie Przedmieście 5, tel. 22-320-0275). Chopin's tourable **birth house** is in a park in Żelazowa Wola, 34 miles from Warsaw. While interesting to Chopin devotees, it's not worth the trek for most. On summer weekends, the Chopin Museum sometimes runs a handy bus to the house—ask at the museum (departs from Marszałkowska street, 30 minutes each way; 7 zł for the bus, 7 zł for the park, 23 zł for the park and birth house, 39 zł also includes museum in Warsaw; birth house open Tue-Sun 9:00-19:00, Oct-March until 17:00, closed Mon year-round, tel. 46-863-3300).

▲▲Copernicus Science Center (Centrum Nauki Kopernik)—
This brand-new facility, a wonderland of completely hands-on scientific doodads that thrill kids
and adults alike, is a futuristic
romper room. Filling two floors
of an industrial-mod, purpose-
built space, this is Warsaw's
best family activity. Exhibits are
grouped more or less thematically
and described in both Polish and
English.

Cost and Hours: 22 zł, 13 zł for kids 19 and under, 57-zł
family ticket for up to four people; open Tue-Fri 9:00-18:00, Sat-
Sun 10:00-19:00, closed Mon, last entry one hour before closing;
Wybrzeże Kościuszkowskie 20, tel. 22-596-4100, www.kopernik
.org.pl.

Crowd-Beating Tips: As a relatively new attraction, the center can get crowded—especially on weekends and school holidays,
when the line can be hours long. On weekdays, it's generally no
problem to walk right in.

Getting There: It's an easy downhill walk from Warsaw's
Royal Way, but the hike back up is fairly steep. The nearest bus
stop, called Pomnik Syreny, is on a nearby corner, next to the modern bridge; from here, bus #102 goes to Nowy Świat, then up the
Royal Way (Uniwersytet and Zachęta stops) before heading south
to the central train station (4/hour). When the new Metro line
opens (likely in late 2013), it will connect this center to the Royal
Way and Warsaw Uprising Museum.

Touring the Center: Your ticket is actually a plastic "log-in
card" that you can insert into certain interactive exhibits. On the
ground floor, the **Roots of Civilization** features working models of various tools and machines, demonstrating how humanity
has mastered the mechanics of physics. By playing with a model
piston, I grasped for the first time how that technology works.
Other exhibits let you play archaeologist in a sandbox, listen to
Ode to Joy while tuning into different instruments (depending on
where you sit), and see a small "fire tornado" (every bit as cool as
it sounds). A playroom for toddlers, called **Buzzz!**, has a nature
theme. Meanwhile, **RE: generation** targets teens and adults with
computer touchscreens that investigate the biological underpin-
nings of emotion—from what makes you laugh to what grosses
you out—and examines how cultures around the world are both
similar and different.

The **planetarium** requires a separate ticket (18 zł, 11 zł for
kids 19 and under, in Polish with English headset, show starts at
the top of each hour, ask for schedule at ticket desk).

The fun continues upstairs, where **Humans and the Environment** illuminates the human body (find out just how long your intestines are, identify and place the organs, and see how various joints work like hinges). One area focuses on exercise, including the engaging arena, where you can compete with various virtual animals (can you jump as high as a kangaroo or hang like a chimp?). The **LightZone** illustrates how light travels in waves, lets you try out an old-fashioned but still impressive camera obscura, and use prisms and lenses to play a game of "light billiards." **On the Move** features fascinating hands-on physics demos, including an earthquake simulator, an air cannon, and a tube that lets you harness sound waves to make water vibrate.

Nearby: The **Discovery Park** surrounding the museum was created when the busy riverfront highway was rerouted into an underground tunnel, creating this delightful people zone. From here, you have fine views of the modern Holy Cross Bridge (Most Świętokrzyski, from 2000) and the brand-new National Stadium, built to host matches for the 2012 Euro Cup and proudly wrapped in the patriotic red and white of the Polish flag.

Two short blocks inland from the science center is the architecturally innovative **Warsaw University Library** (Biblioteka Uniwersytecka w Warszawie, or BUW), with its distinctive oxidized-copper-colored facade decorated with open books from various cultures. The facade is fun to ogle, and the rooftop holds a huge and inviting garden.

South of the Center

▲**Łazienki Park (Park Łazienkowski)**—This huge, idyllic park is where Varsovians go to play. The park is sprinkled with fun Neoclassical buildings, strutting peacocks, and young Poles in love. It was built by Poland's very last king (before the final Partition), Stanisław August Poniatowski, to serve as his summer residence and provide a place for his citizens to relax.

On the edge of the park (along Belwederska) is a **monument to Fryderyk Chopin.** The monument, in a rose garden, is flanked by platforms, where free summer piano **concerts** of Chopin's music are given weekly (mid-May-late Sept only, generally Sun at 12:00 and

16:00—confirm at TI). The statue shows Chopin sitting under a wind-blown willow tree. While he spent his last 20 years and wrote most of his best-known music in France, his inspiration came from wind blowing through the willow trees of his native land, Poland. The Nazis melted the original statue (from 1926) down for its metal. Today's copy was recast after World War II. Savor this spot; it's great in summer, with roses wildly in bloom, and in autumn, when the trees provide a golden backdrop for the black, romantic statue.

Venture to the center of the park, where (after a 10-minute hike) you'll find King Poniatowski's striking **Palace on the Water** (Pałac na Wodzie)—literally built in the middle of a river. Nearby, you'll spot a clever amphitheater with seating on the riverbank and the stage on an island. The king was a real man of the Enlightenment, hosting weekly dinners here for artists and intellectuals. But Poland's kings are long gone, and proud peacocks now rule this roost.

Getting There: The park is just south of the city center on the Royal Way. Buses #116, #180, and #195 run from Castle Square in the Old Town along the Royal Way directly to the park (get off at the stop called Łazienki Królewskie, by Belweder Palace—you'll see Chopin squinting through the trees on your left). Maps at park entrances locate the Chopin monument, Palace on the Water, and other park attractions.

Jewish Warsaw

After centuries of living peacefully in Poland, Warsaw's Jews suffered terribly at the hands of the Nazis. Several sights in Warsaw commemorate those who were murdered, and those who fought back. Because the Nazis leveled the ghetto, there is literally nothing left except the street plan, some monuments, and the heroic spirit of its former residents. However, a brand-new museum promises to rejuvenate the area, making it even more of a magnet for those interested in this chapter of Polish history.

Museum of the History of Polish Jews (Muzeum Historii Żydów Polskich)—Designed by Finnish architect Rainer Mahlamäki, the blocky museum building is pierced with a dramatically asymmetrical passage (visible from the outside). The permanent exhibition, likely to open sometime in 2013, will trace the nearly millennium-long story of Jews in Poland—high-tech, interactive exhibits will mingle with actual artifacts to bring history to life. Its first section, **First Encounters,** sends visitors through a simulated forest, evocative of legends about the Jews' arrival in Poland. **Paradisus Judaeorum** explains the ways Jewish culture flourished in medieval Poland. **Into the Country** traces the spread of Jews throughout the Eastern European countryside, where they

Warsaw's Jews and the Ghetto Uprising

From the Middle Ages until World War II, Poland was a relatively safe haven for Europe's Jews. While other kings were imprisoning and deporting Jews in the 14th century, the progressive king Kazimierz the Great welcomed Jews into Poland, even granting them special privileges (see page 291).

By the 1930s, there were more than 380,000 Jews in Warsaw—nearly a third of the population (and the largest concentration of Jews in any European city). The Nazis arrived in 1939. Within a year, they had pushed all of Warsaw's Jews into one neighborhood and surrounded it with a wall, creating a miserably overcrowded ghetto (crammed full of half a million people, including many from nearby towns). Over the next year, the Nazis brought in more Jews from throughout Poland, and the number grew by a million.

By the summer of 1942, more than a quarter of Warsaw's Jews had either died of disease, committed suicide, or been murdered. The Nazis started moving Warsaw's Jews (at the rate of 5,000 a day) into what they claimed were "resettlement camps." Most of these people were actually murdered at Treblinka or Auschwitz. After hundreds of thousands of Jews had been taken away, the waning population—now about 60,000—began to get word from concentration camp escapees about what was actually going on there. Spurred by this knowledge, Warsaw's surviving Jews staged a dramatic uprising.

On April 19, 1943, the Jews attacked Nazi strongholds and had some initial success. But within a month, the Nazis crushed the Ghetto Uprising. The ghetto's residents and structures were "liquidated." About 300 of Warsaw's Jews survived, thanks in part to a sort of "underground railroad" of courageous Varsovians.

Warsaw's Jewish sights are emotionally moving, but even more so if you know some of their stories. You may have heard of **Władysław Szpilman,** a Jewish concert pianist who survived the war with the help of Jews, Poles, and even a Nazi officer. Szpilman's life story was turned into the highly acclaimed, Oscar-winning 2002 film *The Pianist,* which powerfully depicts events in Warsaw during World War II.

Less familiar to non-Poles—but equally affecting—is the story of Henryk Goldszmit, better known by his pen name, **Janusz Korczak.** Korczak wrote imaginative children's books that are still enormously popular among Poles. He worked at an orphanage in the Warsaw ghetto. When his orphans were sent off to concentration camps, the Nazis offered the famous author a chance at freedom. Korczak turned them down, choosing to die at Treblinka with his children.

forged a unique type of settlement called a *shtetl*. **Encounters with Modernity** examines how, after the Partitions (when Polish territory was divided among neighboring powers), the Jews struggled to integrate with the respective societies of their new overlords. **The Street** re-creates an early 20th-century shopping street from a Jewish community, demonstrating how Jewish culture thrived in the vibrant urban life of Poland. The **Holocaust** section explains the horrific events that claimed the lives of some 9 out of every 10 Polish Jews. Finally, **The Postwar Years** follows Holocaust survivors as they navigate an unfriendly, anti-Semitic communist regime—and embrace a world of new possibility with the fall of communism. Temporary exhibits and a cultural center will fill the rest of the museum's space. (For the latest news, see www.jewish museum.org.pl.)

Ghetto Walking Tour—For a quick walking tour of the former ghetto site, begin at **Ghetto Heroes Square** (plac Bohaterow Getta). To get here from the Old Town you can hop a taxi (10 zł), take a bus (to the Nalewki stop—though this stop may be renamed when the museum opens; bus #180 is particularly useful), or walk (go through barbican gate two blocks into New Town, turn left on Świętojerska, and walk straight 10 minutes—passing the new green-glass Supreme Court building—until you reach a grassy park on Zamenhofa Street). The square is in the heart of what was the Jewish ghetto—now surrounded by bland Soviet-style apartment blocks. After the uprising, the entire ghetto was reduced to dust by the Nazis, leaving the communists to rebuild to their own specifications. The district is called Muranów ("Rebuilt") today.

The **monument** in the middle of the square commemorates those who fought and died, "for the dignity and freedom of the Jewish Nation, for a free Poland, and for the liberation of humankind." Across the street is the brand-new **Museum of the History of Polish Jews** (described earlier).

Facing the monument, head left (with the park on your left) up Zamenhofa—which, like many streets in this neighborhood, is named for a hero of the Ghetto Uprising. From the monument, you'll follow a series of three-foot-tall black stone monuments to uprising heroes—the **Path of Remembrance.** Like Stations of the Cross, each recounts an event of the uprising. Every April 19th (the day the uprising began), huge crowds follow this path. In a block, at the corner of Miła (partly obscured by some bushes), you'll find a **bunker** where organizers of the uprising hid (and where they committed suicide when the Nazis discovered them on May 8, 1943).

Continue following the black stone monuments up Zamenhofa (which becomes Dubois), then turn left at the corner (onto Stawki) and, later on that same block, cross busy Stawki street. A long block up Stawki and on the right, you'll see the **Umschlagplatz** monument—shaped like a cattle car. That's German for "transfer place," and it marks the spot where the Nazis brought Jewish families to prepare them to be loaded onto trains bound for Treblinka or Auschwitz (a harrowing scene vividly depicted in *The Pianist*). In the walls of the monument are inscribed the first names of some of the victims.

Jewish Historical Institute of Poland (Żydowski Instytut Historyczny)—For more in-depth information about Warsaw's Jewish community, including the Ghetto Uprising, visit this museum housed in the former Jewish Library building. The main floor displays well-described old photos. The 37-minute movie about life and death in the ghetto—played in English upon request—is graphic and powerful. Upstairs, you'll find more on Jewish art and culture, along with temporary exhibits.

Cost and Hours: 10 zł, Mon-Wed and Fri 9:00-16:00, Thu 11:00-18:00, Sun 10:00-18:00, closed Sat, last entry 30 minutes before closing, just north of Saxon Garden at ulica Tłomackie 3/5, tel. 22-827-9221, www.jhi.pl.

Nearby: The Peugeot building next door—appropriately dubbed "the blue tower" by locals—was built on the former site of Warsaw's biggest synagogue, destroyed by the Nazis as a victorious final kick.

Warsaw Uprising Sights

While the 1944 Warsaw Uprising is a recurring theme in virtually all Warsaw sightseeing, two sights in particular—one a monument, the other a museum—are worth a visit for anyone with a special interest. Neither is right on the main tourist trail; the monument is closer to the sightseeing action, while the museum is a tram or taxi ride away.

Warsaw Uprising Monument—The most central sight relat-

ing to the Warsaw Uprising is the monument at plac Krasińskich (intersection of ulica Długa and Miodowa, one long block and about a five-minute walk northwest of the New Town). Larger-than-life soldiers and civilians race for the sewers in a desperate attempt to flee the Nazis. Just

The Warsaw Uprising

By the summer of 1944, it was becoming clear that the Nazis' days in Warsaw were numbered. The Red Army drew near, and by late July, Soviet tanks were within 25 miles of downtown Warsaw.

The Varsovians could have simply waited for the Soviets to cross the river and force the Nazis out. But they knew that Soviet "liberation" would also mean an end to Polish independence. The Polish Home Army numbered 400,000—30,000 of them in Warsaw alone—and was the biggest underground army in military history. The uprisers wanted Poland to control its own fate, and they took matters into their own hands. The resistance's symbol was an anchor made up of a *P* atop a *W* (which stands for *Polska Walcząca,* or "Poland Fighting"— you'll see this icon all around town). Over time, the Home Army had established an extensive network of underground tunnels and sewers, which allowed them to deliver messages and move around the city without drawing the Nazis' attention. These tunnels gave the Home Army the element of surprise.

On August 1, 30,000 Polish resistance fighters launched an attack on their Nazi oppressors. They poured out of the sewers and caught the Nazis off guard. The ferocity of the Polish fighters stunned the Nazis, who thought they'd put down the uprising within hours. But the Nazis regrouped, and within a few days, they had retaken several areas of the city— murdering tens of thousands of innocent civilians as they went. In one notorious incident, some 5,500 Polish soldiers and 6,000 civilians who were surrounded by Nazis in the Old Town were forced to flee through the sewers; many drowned or were shot. (This scene is depicted in the Warsaw Uprising Monument on plac Krasińskich.)

Just two months after it had started, the Warsaw Uprising was over. The Home Army called a cease-fire. About 18,000 Polish uprisers had been killed, along with nearly 200,000 innocent civilians. An infuriated Hitler ordered that the city be destroyed—which it was, systematically, block by block, until virtually nothing remained.

Through all of this, the Soviets stood still, watched, and waited. When the smoke cleared and the Nazis left, the Red Army marched in and claimed the wasteland that was once called Warsaw. After the war, General Dwight D. Eisenhower said that the scale of destruction here was the worst he'd ever seen. The communists later tracked down the surviving Home Army leaders, killing or imprisoning them.

Depending on whom you talk to, the desperate uprising of Warsaw was incredibly brave, stupid, or both. As for the Poles, they remain fiercely proud of their struggle for freedom. The city of Warsaw has recently commemorated this act of bravery with the new Warsaw Uprising Museum.

behind the monument is the oxidized-copper facade of Poland's Supreme Court.

▲▲**Warsaw Uprising Museum (Muzeum Powstania Warszawskiego)**—This museum opened on August 1, 2004— the 60th anniversary of the Warsaw Uprising. Thorough, modern, and packed with Polish field-trip groups, the museum celebrates the heroes of the uprising. It's a bit cramped, and finding your way through the exhibits can be confusing, but it thoughtfully illuminates this complicated chapter of Warsaw's history. The location is inconvenient (a 10-minute tram or bus ride west of central train station) and, because it eats up about a half-day to come here, may not be worth the trek for those with a casual interest. But for history buffs, it's Warsaw's single best museum.

Cost and Hours: 14 zł; Mon, Wed, and Fri 8:00-18:00; Thu 8:00-20:00; Sat-Sun 10:00-18:00; closed Tue; last entry 30 minutes before closing, tel. 22-539-7947, www.1944.pl.

Audioguide: The informative, two-hour audioguide is ideal if you really want to delve into the whole story (10 zł, rent it in the gift shop). A well-illustrated, 20-zł guidebook is also sold in the shop. For a quick overview, take my self-guided tour.

Getting There: It's on the western edge of downtown at ulica Przyokopowa 28; the nearest tram and bus stop is called Muzeum Powstania Warszawskiego. While it looks close on the map, it's actually a long hike through Warsaw's dullest quarter. Instead, take tram #22 or #24 from near the central train station (from the underground passageways, follow signs for *Ochota* to find the tram tracks), or across the street from the National Museum (near the start of Nowy Świat). You can also get to the museum by taking bus #109 (departs in front of the central train station—from the main hall, go out the door with the bus icon). From Castle Square in the Old Town, bus #178 goes to the museum. On the Royal Way, catch bus #105 from the Uniwersytet stop (next to the university building) or the Nowy Świat stop. All of these trams and buses take you to the Muzeum Powstania Warszawskiego stop. From this stop, cross the tracks and the busy street, walk straight one short block up Grzybowska, and take a left on Przyokopowa. The museum is the big, red-brick building on the left.

When the new Metro line opens (likely in late 2013), it will connect this museum (Rondo Daszyńskiego Station) to the Royal Way and Copernicus Science Center.

◑ **Self-Guided Tour:** The museum has several parts. The beautifully restored 1905 red-brick building, once an electrical plant, houses the permanent exhibition. The more recent gray addition behind it displays temporary exhibitions. And the park stretching around the back of the complex also has some evocative sights. Buy your ticket at the little house on the left (marked *kasa*), then head into the main hall.

The high-tech **main exhibit** sprawls across three floors. It chronologically tells the story of the uprising, with a keen focus on military history. While it's easy to get turned around, look for directional signs and don't be afraid to explore. Everything is well-described in English; also look for the printed pages of English information.

The ground floor focuses on Germany's invasion and occupation of Poland. The children's area (to the right as you enter) reminds visitors that Varsovian kids played a role in the Warsaw Uprising, too. Then you'll take the elevator to the top floor (signed 2), which features exhibits on the uprising itself. You'll meet some of the uprising's heroes, and learn about their weapons and methods. Inside the big tent is an exhibit about the Wola Massacre, during which 40,000 people were killed after the Nazis issued a take-no-prisoners decree in retribution for the uprising. Another exhibit looks at its impact on civilians and hospitals. The "Kino Palladium" movie screen shows subtitled Home Army newsreel footage from the period. To the right of the screen, you'll walk through a simulated sewer, reminiscent of the one that many Home Army soldiers and civilians used to evade the Germans. Imagine terrified troops quietly traversing a more than mile-long sewer line like this one (but with lower ceilings)—and doing it while knee-deep in liquid sewage.

The exhibit continues downstairs. If you need a break, straight ahead from the stairs are WCs and a café (past the exhibit on the USSR's role in the Warsaw Uprising, and in "liberating" and terrorizing postwar Poland). The café is oddly pleasant, serving drinks and light snacks amidst genteel ambience from prewar Warsaw.

Back in the main exhibit, one room honors the Field Postal Service, which, at great personal risk, continued mail delivery of both military communiqués and civilian correspondences. Many of these brave "mailmen" were actually Scouts who were too young to fight. The later days of the uprising are outlined, battle by battle. A chilling section describes how Warsaw became a "city of graves," with burial mounds and makeshift crosses scattered everywhere.

As you learn about the uprising's aftermath, consider that the Nazis destroyed Warsaw four separate times during World War II (at the outbreak of war, to put down the Ghetto Uprising, to put down the Warsaw Uprising, and finally just to be mean).

Occupying the center of the main hall are two large-scale

exhibits: a replica of an RAF Liberator B-24 J, used for airborne surveillance of wartime Warsaw; and a giant movie screen showing more fascinating newsreels assembled by the Home Army's own propaganda unit during the uprising. Under the screen, behind the black curtains, is yet another exhibit, this one about life in Nazi-occupied Warsaw, along with another, more claustrophobic walk-through sewer.

The newest feature is the five-minute 3-D film *City of Ruins,* with aerial footage of the postwar devastation.

The **park** features several thought-provoking sights. Around the right side are several monuments, with photographs along the side wall showing the history of the museum building. Along the back is the Wall of Memory, a Vietnam War Memorial-type monument to soldiers of the Polish Home Army who were killed in action. You'll see their rank and name, followed by their code name, in quotes. The Home Army observed a strict policy of anonymity, forbidding members from calling each other by anything but their code names. The bell in the middle is dedicated to the commander of the uprising, Antoni Chruściel (code name "Monter").

Sleeping in Warsaw

Most accommodations in central Warsaw are either overpriced business-class hotels (whose rates can drop dramatically when demand is low—especially on weekends and in summer), or gloomy, impersonal communist-holdover hotels. Thankfully, there are a few happy exceptions—such as Boutique B&B and Duval Apartments, easily the best options in Warsaw. Expect hotel rates to go through the roof during June of 2012, when Warsaw hosts Euro Cup soccer matches. For locations, see the map on page 390.

$$$ Hotel Le Régina is a tempting splurge buried in the quiet and charming New Town (just beyond the Old Town). From its elegant public spaces to its 61 top-notch rooms, everything here is done with class. Choose between plenty nice "standard" and "classic" rooms, or pay an extra 200 zł for bigger "superior" rooms, with hand-painted frescoes over each bed. While the official rates are ridiculously high (standard Db-1,140 zł, superior Db-1,290 zł), you'll often find amazingly lower promotional prices on their website (for a standard room in summer figure Db-550 zł on weekdays, as low as 350 zł on weekends, prices change constantly—check online for latest deals, more expensive during winter convention season, prices don't include the 90-zł breakfast—skip this very overpriced option, pricier suites, elevator, non-smoking floor, free Internet access and Wi-Fi, exercise room, pool, Kościelna 12, tel. 22-531-6000, www.leregina.com, reception.leregina@mamaison.com).

WARSAW

Sleep Code

(3 zł = about $1, country code: 48)
S = Single, **D** = Double/Twin, **T** = Triple, **Q** = Quad, **b** = bathroom, **s** = shower only. Unless otherwise noted, credit cards are accepted, and breakfast is included. Everyone listed here speaks English.

To help you easily sort through these listings, I've divided the accommodations into three categories, based on the price for a double room with bath during high season:

$$$ Higher Priced—Most rooms 400 zł or more.
$$ Moderately Priced—Most rooms between 300-400 zł.
$ Lower Priced—Most rooms 300 zł or less.

Prices can change without notice; verify the hotel's current rates online or by email. For other updates, see www.ricksteves.com/update.

$$$ Novotel, a chain hotel with 733 uninspired cookie-cutter rooms across the street from the Palace of Culture and Science, overlooks Poland's busiest intersection. Recently renovated inside and out, this is a good option for a big, business-class, downtown hotel that's handy to the central train station (official rate is Sb/Db-785 zł and possibly much higher on busy weekdays, but in slow times—especially weekends—you might pay 250-450 zł, best deals are online, optional breakfast-65 zł, non-smoking rooms, elevator; free Internet access, cable Internet, and Wi-Fi; Marszałkowska 94/98, tel. 22-596-0000, fax 22-625-0476, www.novotel.com, h3383@accor.com).

$$ Duval Apartments, named for a French woman who supposedly had an affair with the Polish king in this building, offers four beautifully appointed rooms above a restaurant (called Same Fusy) a few steps off the square in the Old Town. Each room has a different theme: traditional Polish, Japanese, glass, or retro (Sb-280 zł, Db-320 zł, Tb-400 zł, includes breakfast, lots of stairs with no elevator, some restaurant noise—light sleepers should request a quiet room, free Wi-Fi, Nowomiejska 10, mobile 608-679-346, tel. & fax 22-831-9104, www.duval.net.pl, duval@duval.net.pl). There's no reception, and the rooms aren't officially affiliated with the restaurant, so arrange a meeting time with Agnieszka (or, if she's busy, Marcin) when you reserve. On arrival, go up the stairs and ring doorbell #5; the restaurant closes at 23:00.

$$ Castle Inn, sitting right on Castle Square at the entrance to the Old Town, is the next rung up the ladder for youth hostelers who've outgrown the grungy backpacker scene. Run by the owners of Oki Doki Hostel (described later), it has 22 creative and colorful rooms, each with completely different but equally artsy decor. Youthful and funky, it provides a welcome jolt of new energy on Warsaw's hotel scene (very slushy rates depending on demand, generally Sb-255-303 zł, Db-270-360 zł, "delux" Db-350-440 zł, "delux" Tb-355-492 zł, 35 zł extra for continental breakfast—have it delivered to your room for the same price, lots of stairs and no elevator, free Internet access and Wi-Fi, Świętojańska 2, tel. 22-425-0100, www.castleinn.pl, castleinn@castleinn.pl).

$$ Old Town Apartments offers 25 studio, one-bedroom, and two-bedroom apartments inside Warsaw's Old Town. The prices are good and the location is excellent, but you're pretty much on your own (no real reception, no breakfast but all have kitchens). View the apartments on their website, pick the one that looks best, and set up a meeting to get the keys at their Nowy Świat office (prices flex with demand, but figure studio-300 zł, 1-bedroom-350 zł, 2-bedroom-450 zł, some more expensive "featured" apartments on the square also available, slightly cheaper Oct-April and last-minute, tel. 22-887-9800, fax 22-831-4956, www.apartmentsapart .com, warsaw@bookaa.net). They also rent 15 pricey apartments on Nowy Świat, called **Royal Route Residence** (studio-400 zł, 1-bedroom-500 zł, 2-bedroom-600 zł, breakfast-25 zł, corner of Nowy Świat and Chmielna). For either place, you'll check in at the office at #3 Nowy Świat 29 (Mon-Fri 10:00-20:00, Sat-Sun 9:00-17:00, at other times arrange a meeting to get the keys). After checking in here, they'll send you in a taxi to your Old Town apartment.

$$ Zgoda Apartment Hotel is conveniently located on an urban street between the Palace of Culture and Science and the Royal Way. With 51 classy-feeling apartments designed for business travelers, it's a comfortable home base in the city center (small Sb/Db-368 zł, studio Sb-395 zł, bigger "comfort" Sb/Db-435, twin-bedded "comfort plus" Sb/Db-455 zł, fancier rooms also available, rates are soft—especially for longer stays, extra bed-90 zł, breakfast-30 zł or use the kitchenette, air-con, elevator, free Internet access and Wi-Fi, Zgoda 6, tel. 22-553-6200, www .apartamenty-zgoda.pl, apartamenty@dipservice.pl).

$$ Hotel Harenda, a reliable old standby, has 43 rooms with leather-bound doors on the second and third floors of an office building right in the middle of the Royal Way, by the Copernicus monument. The tired, communist-era rooms are crying out for a renovation, but the location is ideal, and the ground-floor pub is a popular hangout (May-June and Sept-Oct: Sb-340 zł, Db-380 zł; July-Aug and Nov-April: Sb-310 zł, Db-340 zł; breakfast-25 zł, second night is free Fri-Sun, some rowdy street noise—especially on weekends—so request a quiet room, lots of stairs with no elevator, free Internet access and Wi-Fi, Krakowskie Przedmieście 4/6, tel.

WARSAW

& fax 22-826-0071, www.hotelharenda.com.pl, rezerwacja@hotel
harenda.com.pl).

$ Boutique B&B offers more comfort and class than a hotel
twice its price, in a beautifully renovated and well-located old
building near the National Museum.
Jarek Chołodecki, who lived near
Chicago for many years, returned to
Warsaw and converted apartments
into this wonderful bed-and-break-
fast with 16 rooms. It's a friendly,
casual, stylish place, creatively decorated and impeccably maintained.
You'll feel like you're staying with

your Warsaw sophisticate cousin—quirky, charismatic Jarek loves
to chat with his guests, many of whom return and become his
good friends. Each morning, lively conversation percolates at the
big, family-style breakfast table over a morning meal made mostly
from organic and locally sourced foods. A small drawing room
plays host to occasional piano concerts and other convivial activities. When Jarek is out of town, his right-hand-man Paweł capably
holds down the fort. Let them know what time you'll be arriving
(Sb-270 zł, standard Db-300 zł, junior suite-320 zł, big suite-420
zł, these special rates are for Rick Steves readers, elevator, free
Internet access and Wi-Fi, ulica Smolna 14/6, tel. 22-829-4801, fax
22-829-4802, www.bedandbreakfast.pl, office@bedandbreakfast
.pl). To make things easier, Jarek can arrange for a no-stress ride in
from the airport for the same price as a taxi (45 zł, more at night,
request when you reserve your room).

$ Ibis Warszawa Stare Miasto, with 333 cookie-cutter
rooms, is the place for predictable comfort with zero personality. This hotel, part of the popular European chain, overlooks a
WWII memorial in a nondescript, businessy-feeling neighborhood a 10-minute walk north of the Old Town (Sb/Db-289 zł,
or 219 zł Fri-Sun, can be higher during conventions, sometimes
better deals online, breakfast-33 zł, air-con, non-smoking rooms,
elevator, Muranowska 2, tel. 22-310-1000, fax 22-310-1010, www
.ibishotel.com, h3714@accor.com).

Hostels

$ Nathan's Villa Hostel is the most appealing hostel option in
Warsaw. Run by a sharp Bostonian entrepreneur with hostels all
over Poland, Nathan's has 13 dorm rooms (with 95 beds) and 6
private rooms overlooking a cozy courtyard, and plenty of opportunities for backpacker bonding. The catch: It's less conveniently
located than my other listings, requiring a 15-minute walk or easy
bus ride south of the central train station area (dorm bed in 4-bed

room-72 zł, in 6-bed room-60 zł, in 12-bed room-50 zł, D-184 zł, Db-194 zł, Db with kitchen-204 zł, Tb/Qb-234 zł, all rates about 10 zł/person less on off-season weeknights, includes basic breakfast and sheets, lockers, free Internet access and Wi-Fi, laundry service-15 zł, guest kitchen, hiding behind a modern glass office building at ulica Piękna 24/26—the nearby square called plac Konstytucji has easy bus connections, for location see map on page 390, tel. & fax 22-622-2946, www.nathansvilla.com).

$ Oki Doki Hostel, on a pleasant square a few blocks in front of the Palace of Culture and Science, is colorful, creative, and easygoing. Each of its 37 rooms was designed by a different artist with a special theme—such as Van Gogh, Celtic spirals, heads of state, or Lenin. It's run by Ernest—a Pole whose parents loved Hemingway—and his wife Łucja, with help from their sometimes-jaded staff (complicated pricing structure flexes with demand: dorm bed in 4-bed room-50-67 zł, in 5- to 6-bed room-40-58 zł, in 8-bed room-40-53 zł; S-120-160 zł, D-150-180 zł, Db-192-219 zł, T-180-219 zł; prices include breakfast except for dorm-dwellers—who pay 15 zł, free Internet access and Wi-Fi, laundry service-15 zł, kitchen, lots of stairs with no elevator, plac Dąbrowskiego 3, tel. 22-826-5112, fax 22-828-0122, www.okidoki.pl, okidoki@okidoki.pl).

$ The IYHF **Szkolne Schronisko** hostel, with 110 beds and lots of school groups, is institutional, well-run, bright, and clean. The downside: It's five floors up, with no elevator (nonmembers welcome, all prices per person: dorm beds-40 zł, S-70 zł, twin D-65 zł, T-60 zł, Q-50 zł, sheets-6 zł, towel-3 zł, no breakfast but members' kitchen, 10 percent cheaper for hostel members, closed 10:00-16:00, curfew at 24:00; email or fax ahead to reserve limited S, D, and T rooms; good location across the street from National Museum at ulica Smolna 30, tel. & fax 22-827-8952, www.hostelsmolna30.pl, info@hostelsmolna30.pl).

Eating in Warsaw

While the Old Town has a tourist-friendly atmosphere and traditional Polish food, Varsovians know that these days, the Nowy Świat area is where it's at—with trendy international restaurants and an enticing al fresco scene on balmy summer evenings. This is especially enticing, since Warsaw offers your best break from traditional Polish food. (Though if you do want traditional Polish, just wander along the Royal Way or the Old Town and

take your pick of the many interchangeable, ye olde options.) Most restaurants are open until the "last guest," which usually means about 23:00 (sometimes later in summer).

In or near the Old Town

Rather than spending too much to eat on the Old Town Market Square, I prefer to venture a few blocks to find a place with good food and much lower prices. For locations, see the map on page 390.

At **Restauracja pod Samsonem** ("Under Samson"), dine on affordable Jewish and Polish comfort food with well-dressed locals. The ambience is pleasant, the service is playfully opinionated, and the low prices make up for the fact that you have to pay to check your coat and use the bathroom (10-20-zł starters, most main dishes 20-35 zł, enjoyable outdoor seating in summer, daily 10:00-23:00, ulica Freta 3/5, tel. 22-831-1788).

Pierogarnia na Bednarskiej brags, "only our grandmothers make better pierogi." In addition to the classic Polish dumplings, the menu includes soups and a fun variety of drinks (from unusual fruit juices to *kvas*, the non-alcoholic, rye-flavored dark beer). Order at the counter and take a seat—they'll call you when your food's ready. With mellow country decor, wooden menus, and a loyal local crowd, this is a handy spot for a quick, cheap meal along the Royal Way (13-16-zł plates of pierogi, 18-zł combo-plate includes soup and salad, daily 12:00-20:00, hiding down a quiet street behind the statue of Adam Mickiewicz at ulica Bednarska 28/30, tel. 22-828-0392).

BrowArmia is a hit with beer-lovers. This sprawling brewpub makes four different types of beer (plus special seasonal beers) and serves decent pub grub. The dark, mod, long interior fills two levels (including a fun cellar), but in good weather I'd stake out a spot on the terrace—ideal for people-watching along the Royal Way (18-32-zł starters, 30-65-zł main dishes, daily 12:00-24:00, live music or DJ in cellar on weekends, right on Krakowskie Przedmieście near Piłsudski Square at ulica Królewska 1, tel. 22-826-5455).

U Kucharzy ("By the Cooks") is the most innovative of Warsaw celebrity chef-turned-restaurateur Magda Gessler's growing empire. The kitchen of this former hotel restaurant (tucked behind the Hotel Europejski building, facing Piłsudski Square) has been converted into a dining room, with tables scattered throughout the white-tiled cooking and prep areas—so you'll get the behind-the-scenes experience of watching the chefs prepare the food. The menu is upmarket Polish classics, the ambience is dressy, and the service can be less than snappy, but it's a memorable and good-quality dining experience. Reservations are smart (25-40-zł starters, 50-70-zł main dishes, daily 12:00-24:00, live piano music in the evenings, Ossolińskich 7, tel. 22-826-7936).

On the Old Town Market Square: You'll pay triple to eat right on the square, but some visitors figure it's worth the splurge. Compare menus and views to find the spot you like best. If you want to go for the venerable old favorite—and money's no object— check out **U Fukiera**. This place offers traditional Polish and pan-European meals in a sophisticated setting with carefully designed prewar atmosphere. In summer, sit at their tables out on the square, or find your way to the cozy courtyard garden in back (30-90-zł starters, 45-105-zł main dishes, daily 12:00-24:00, at #27, tel. 22-831-1013).

Italian: **Enoteka Polska** is a dressy wine cellar serving Italian food at rustic tables squeezed between crates of wine bottles. Although the location is in the middle of nowhere (about a 10-minute walk through drab sprawl from the Old Town), the decor is nicely modern, and there's a pleasant garden in the summer. Reservations are smart (20-30-zł starters, 30-45-zł pastas, 35-50-zł main dishes, daily 12:00-23:00, Sun 13:00-21:00, Długa 23/25, tel. 22-831-3443).

On or near Nowy Świat

While most Old Town eateries are traditional and cater to tourists, locals flock to the Nowy Świat neighborhood (near the National Museum and central train station) for a fun night on the town.

Fancy Eateries on Foksal Street: Foksal—the first cross street as you go down Nowy Świat from aleja Jerozolimskie—has a thriving assortment of about a half-dozen cafés and restaurants: Mexican, Italian, Asian, international, and more. Most have inviting outdoor seating that's ideal on a balmy summer evening. The clientele is young and sophisticated, and there's not a pierogi in sight. Find the place with the cuisine and ambience you like best. **Papaya** has tasty pan-Asian fare and a trendy, minimalist, black-and-white interior (30-60-zł main dishes plus pricier splurges, daily 12:00-24:00, at #16, tel. 22-826-1199). A block beyond this area is a far more traditional option, **Kamahda Lwowska,** named for the former Polish city that's now in Ukraine. It has a few outdoor seats and a charming, cluttered old cellar (20-25-zł starters, 30-45-zł main dishes, daily 10:00-24:00, Foksal 10, tel. 22-828-1031).

Classy Steakhouse: **Butchery & Wine,** in an unassuming location on a drab urban street, is a pocket of chic international cuisine in the heart of Warsaw. While a bit farther from the heart of Nowy Świat than the others listed here, it's worth the walk. The waiters, smartly dressed in pinstripe aprons, serve upscale comfort food (specializing in steaks) to a small, lively room of business travelers. The wine list is extensive, and reservations are smart (15-60-zł starters, 50-85-zł steaks, Mon-Sat 12:00-22:00, closed Sun,

WARSAW

across aleja Jerozolimskie from Nowy Świat at Żurawia 22, tel. 22-502-3118).

Cheap Milk Bars: Wiking Bar, a colorful milk bar, serves up Polish grub right on Nowy Świat (10-15-zł main dishes, Mon-Fri 7:30-21:30, Sat 10:00-21:30, Sun 10:00-20:30, Nowy Świat 28). **Mleczarnia Jerozolimska,** just around the corner on busy aleja Jerozolimskie, is a more classic milk-bar experience (4-8-zł soups, 9-12-zł main dishes, Mon-Fri 10:00-20:00, Sat 12:00-17:00, Sun 12:00-18:00, aleja Jerozolimskie 32). For more on milk bars, see page 269.

Hungarian and Polish Cuisine on Zgoda Street: Borpince ("Wine Cellar") is a cozy cellar serving up very authentic Hungarian fare a long block off of Nowy Świat (toward the Palace of Culture and Science). As you dive into spicy goulash and *paprikás,* you'll see just how different the cuisine can be on the other side of the Carpathians. If you won't be visiting Hungary on your trip, this is the next best way to sample Hungarian favorites. The restaurant also has a long list of Hungarian wines (15-25-zł soups including goulash, 35-60-zł main dishes, daily 12:00-23:00, closes earlier when it's slow, ulica Zgoda 1, tel. 22-828-2244). For Magyar flavors at lower prices, try **Krokiecik** ("Croquette"), the simpler self-service restaurant located next door, at street level. Choose from Polish or Hungarian food, order at the counter, then take a seat (7-12-zł soups, 12-25-zł main dishes, daily 9:00-21:00, ulica Zgoda 1, tel. 22-827-3037). **Restauracja Zgoda,** across the street and owned by the same people, has affordable, reliable Polish cuisine in an Old World setting; it's popular among traditionalists dining out (8-12-zł soups, 17-zł salads, 25-40-zł fish and meat dishes, Mon-Sat 9:00-23:00, Sun 12:00-23:00, Zgoda 4, tel. 22-827-9934).

Uniquely Polish Treats

These two places are on or close to the busy Nowy Świat boulevard.

A. Blikle, Poland's most famous pastry shop, serves a wide variety of delicious treats. This is where locals shop for cakes when they're having someone special over for coffee. The specialty: *pączki* (PONCH-kee), the quintessential Polish doughnut, filled with rose-flavored jam. You can get your goodies "to go" in the shop (2.60-zł *pączki,* Mon-Sat 9:00-19:00, Sun 10:00-18:00), or pay more to enjoy them with coffee in the swanky, classic café with indoor or outdoor seating (6-zł *pączki,* Mon-Sat 9:00-22:00, Sun 10:00-22:00; both at Nowy Świat 35, tel. 22-828-6601). While they also have a sit-down restaurant (30-50-zł main dishes), I come here only for the *pączki.*

E. Wedel Pijalnia Czekolady thrills chocoholics. Emil Wedel made Poland's favorite chocolate, and today, his former residence houses this chocolate shop and genteel café. This is the spot for delicious pastries and a *real* hot chocolate—*czekolada do picia* ("drinking chocolate"), a cup of actual melted chocolate, not just hot chocolate milk (12 zł). The menu describes it as, "True Wedel ecstasy for your mouth that will take you to a world of dreams and desires." Or, if you fancy chocolate mousse, try *pokusa* ("Wedel Temptation"). Wedel's was *the* Christmas treat for locals under communism. Cadbury bought the company when Poland privatized, but they kept the E. Wedel name, which is close to all Poles' hearts...and taste buds (Mon-Fri 8:00-22:00, Sat 10:00-22:00, Sun 10:00-21:00, between Palace of Culture and Science and Nowy Świat at ulica Szpitalna 8, tel. 22-827-2916).

Hangout Cafés near the River

If you just want to grab a drink (and possibly a light meal) and watch the world go by, Warsaw has two inviting cafés downhill, near the river, that are worth the short trip from the main tourist zone. The first one serves mostly drinks and is a hip hangout by day and by night; the second has a wider menu of food and is open only during the day.

Warszawa Powiśle occupies the old, communist-style ticket office for the suburban train station of the same name. Now it's

been taken over by hipsters and converted into one of the most happening hangouts in town. Tucked picturesquely along a bike lane beneath the towering legs of a bridge, its sidewalk is jammed with cool Varsovians and in-the-know visitors living well. The building itself has some indoor seating, but it's quite small—making this a better good-weather option (light sandwiches, daily 10:00 until late, Kruczkowskiego 3B, tel. 22-474-4084). The most direct way to get here from the palm tree at the head of Nowy Świat is to walk down aleja Jerozolimskie toward the bridge, enter the rail station, go down the stairs, walk all the way along *peron* (platform) 1 to the end, then go down the stairs at the far end: You'll pop out right at the bar. Alternatively, you can walk partway across the bridge at aleja Jerozolimskie, then go down the stairs at the first tower.

Kawarnia Kafka combines a used bookstore (with books sold by weight) with a hip and creative café. You'll find comfy chairs, stay-awhile tables, and checkerboard tiles inside, while outside on the lawn across from the café, guests lounge in slingback chairs (10-12-zł sandwiches and crêpes, 20-zł pastas and salads, free

Wi-Fi, Mon-Fri 9:00-22:00, Sat-Sun 10:00-22:00, Oboźna 3, tel. 22-826-0822).

Warsaw Connections

Virtually all trains into and out of Warsaw go through the hulking central train station (described earlier, under "Arrival in Warsaw"; pay special attention to the "Buying Train Tickets" section). If you're heading to Gdańsk, note that the red-brick Gothic city of Toruń and the impressive Malbork Castle are on the way (though on separate train lines, so you can't do both en route; see Gdańsk and Pomerania chapters). Also be aware that express trains to many destinations—including Kraków—require seat reservations (free), even if you have a railpass.

Through 2012, the duration of any train journey in Poland may be in flux, as the country builds a network of new high-speed rail lines. Confirm specific times online (www.rozklad-pkp.pl) or at the central train station. If there is construction along your route, you'll likely experience additional delays even beyond what's scheduled.

From Warsaw's Central Station by Train to: Kraków (hourly, 2.75-3.25 hours, requires seat reservation), **Gdańsk** (9/day, 5.5-6.5 hours—but will drop to 3 hours when new line is finished), **Toruń** (9/day, 2.75 hours direct, longer with a transfer in Kutno), **Malbork** (6/day direct, 4.5 hours—but will drop to 2.5 hours when new line is finished), **Prague** (2/day direct, including 1 night train, more with changes, 8.5-10 hours), **Berlin** (4/day direct, 5.5-6 hours), **Budapest** (2/day direct, including 1 night train, 10.5-11.5 hours; plus 1 each per day with transfer in Győr, Hungary, or Břeclav, Czech Republic, 10 hours), **Vienna** (2/day direct, 8-8.5 hours; plus 1 night train, 9.5 hours). An overnight train leaves nightly at 20:36, splitting to reach both **Prague** (arriving at 7:45) and **Budapest** (arriving at 8:35).

GDAŃSK & THE TRI-CITY

Gdańsk (guh-DAYNSK) is a true find on the Baltic Coast of Poland. You may associate Gdańsk with dreary images of striking dockworkers from the nightly news in the 1980s—but there's so much more to this city than shipyards, Solidarity, and smog. It's surprisingly easy to look past the urban sprawl to find one of northern Europe's most historic and picturesque cities.

Gdańsk is second only to Kraków as Poland's most appealing destination. The gem of a Main Town boasts block after block of red-brick churches and narrow, colorful, ornately decorated Hanseatic burghers' mansions. Its history is also fascinating—from its medieval Golden Age to the headlines of our own generation, big things happen here. You might even see old Lech Wałęsa still wandering the streets.

And yet, Gdańsk is also looking to its future, finally repairing some of its WWII damage after a long communist hibernation. Things have picked up even more in recent years, as the city prepared to host matches for the Euro Cup 2012 soccer championship tournament. The recent flurry of construction has included a futuristic new stadium, shaped like a translucent glob of amber, and high-speed train lines, which will more efficiently link the city to the rest of Poland. Newly spiffed up and excited to host hordes of European visitors, Gdańsk is poised to reclaim its former greatness as a top European city.

Gdańsk and two nearby towns (Sopot and Gdynia) together form an area known as the "Tri-City," offering several day-trip opportunities north along the coast. The once-faded, now-revitalized elegance of the seaside resort of Sopot beckons to tourists, while the modern burg of Gdynia sets the pace for today's

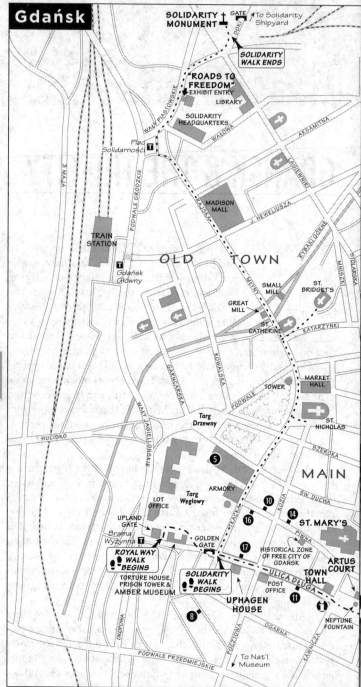

Gdańsk

SOLIDARITY MONUMENT †
GATE → To Solidarity Shipyard

SOLIDARITY WALK ENDS

"ROADS TO FREEDOM"
EXHIBIT ENTRY
LIBRARY

SOLIDARITY HEADQUARTERS

WAŁY PIASTOWSKIE

WAŁOWA

AKSAMITNA

Plac Solidarności

ŁAGIEWNIKI

PODWALE GRODZKIE

MADISON MALL

J. HEWELIUSZA

3 MAJA

TRAIN STATION

KYDAŃ GÓRNE

STOLARSKA

MINISZKI

OLD   TOWN

Gdańsk Główny

MŁYNY

SMALL MILL

ST. BRIDGET'S

GREAT MILL

ST. CATHERINE

KATARZYNKI

GARNCARSKA

KOWALSKA

PODWALE

TOWER

MARKET HALL

ST. NICHOLAS

HUCISKO

WAŁY JAGIELLOŃSKIE

Targ Drzewny

SZEROKA

5

MAIN

ARMORY

Targ Węglowy

10

KOŁA

ŚW. DUCHA

LOT OFFICE

16

14

ST. MARY'S

UPLAND GATE

TKACKA

PIWNA

Brama Wyżynna

GOLDEN GATE

17

HISTORICAL ZONE OF FREE CITY OF GDAŃSK

ARTUS COURT

ROYAL WAY WALK BEGINS

ULICA DŁUGA

TOWN HALL

TORTURE HOUSE, PRISON TOWER & AMBER MUSEUM

SOLIDARITY WALK BEGINS

POST OFFICE

11

8

UPHAGEN HOUSE

NEPTUNE FOUNTAIN

OKOPOWA

POCZTOWA

OGARNA

ŁAWNICZA

PODWALE PRZEDMIEJSKIE

→ To Nat'l Museum

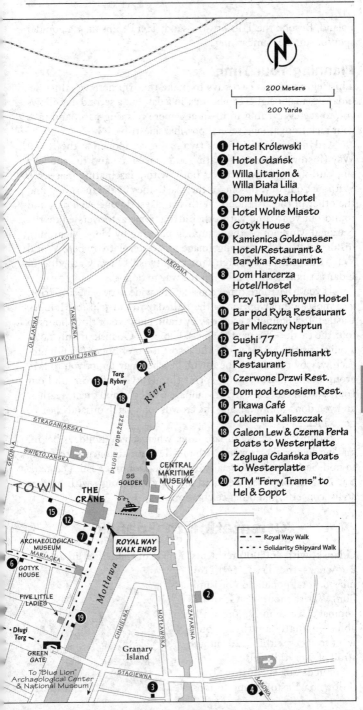

200 Meters
200 Yards

1. Hotel Królewski
2. Hotel Gdańsk
3. Willa Litarion & Willa Biała Lilia
4. Dom Muzyka Hotel
5. Hotel Wolne Miasto
6. Gotyk House
7. Kamienica Goldwasser Hotel/Restaurant & Baryłka Restaurant
8. Dom Harcerza Hotel/Hostel
9. Przy Targu Rybnym Hostel
10. Bar pod Rybą Restaurant
11. Bar Mleczny Neptun
12. Sushi 77
13. Targ Rybny/Fishmarkt Restaurant
14. Czerwone Drzwi Rest.
15. Dom pod Łososiem Rest.
16. Pikawa Café
17. Cukiernia Kaliszczak
18. Galeon Lew & Czerna Perła Boats to Westerplatte
19. Żegluga Gdańska Boats to Westerplatte
20. ZTM "Ferry Trams" to Hel & Sopot

- · - · - · Royal Way Walk
- - - - - Solidarity Shipyard Walk

GDAŃSK & THE TRI-CITY

Poland. Beyond the Tri-City, the sandy Hel Peninsula is a popular spot for summer sunbathing.

Planning Your Time

This region merits two days to make the trip here worthwhile. Gdańsk's major sights can be seen in a day, but a second day allows you to see everything in town at a more relaxing pace, and take your pick from among several possible side-trips.

Gdańsk sightseeing has two major components: the Royal Way (historic main drag with good museums) and the modern shipyard where Solidarity was born (with a fascinating museum). With just one day, do one of these activities in the morning, and the other in the afternoon. With two days, do one each day, and round out your time with other attractions: art-lovers enjoy the National Museum (with a stunning painting by Hans Memling), history buffs make the pilgrimage to Westerplatte (where World War II began), and church fans might visit Oliwa Cathedral in Gdańsk's northern suburbs (on the way to Sopot).

If you have more time, consider the wide variety of side-trips. The most popular option is the half-day round-trip to Malbork Castle (40-50 minutes each way by train, plus two or three hours to tour the castle—see next chapter). Closer to Gdańsk, it only takes a quick visit to get a feel for the resort town of Sopot (25 minutes each way by train), but the town's beaches may tempt you to laze around longer. Consider a sprint through Gdynia to round out your take on the Tri-City. If you have a full day and great weather, and you don't mind fighting the crowds for a patch of sandy beach, go to Hel.

Gdańsk gets busy in late June, when school holidays begin, and it's downright crowded with mostly German tourists from July to mid-September—especially during St. Dominic's Fair (Jarmark Św. Dominika, three weeks in late July-mid-Aug), with market stalls, concerts, and other celebrations.

Orientation to Gdańsk

Gdańsk, with 460,000 residents, is part of the larger urban area known as the Tri-City (Trój-miasto, total population of 1 million). But the tourist's Gdańsk is compact, welcoming, and walk-able—virtually anything you'll want to see is within a 20-minute stroll of everything else.

Focus on the Main Town (Główne Miasto), home to most

GDAŃSK & THE TRI-CITY

of the sights described, including the spectacular Royal Way main drag, ulica Długa. The Old Town (Stare Miasto) has a handful of old brick buildings and faded, tall, skinny houses—but the area is mostly drab and residential, and not worth much time. Just beyond the northern end of the Old Town (about a 20-minute walk from the heart of the Main Town) is the entrance to the Gdańsk Shipyard, with the excellent Solidarity museum. From here, shipyards sprawl for miles.

The second language in this part of Poland is German, not English. As this was a predominantly German city until the end of World War II, German tourists flock here in droves. But you'll win no Polish friends if you call the city by its more familiar German name, Danzig.

Tourist Information

Gdańsk's official TI—the only one I've seen with a tip jar—is in a red, high-gabled building across **ulica Długa** from the Town Hall. Pick up the free map and brochure, and browse through the other brochures and guidebooks (May-Sept Mon-Fri 9:00-18:00, Sat-Sun 10:00-18:00, until 20:00 during busy times; Oct-April Mon-Fri 9:00-18:00, Sat-Sun 9:00-16:30; ulica Długa 45, tel. 58-301-9151, www.gdansk4u.pl or www.pttk-gdansk.pl). There are also small TIs at the **main train station** (Mon-Sat 9:00-17:00, Sun 9:00-16:00, tel. 58-721-3277) and the **airport** (same hours as train station TI, tel. 58-348-1368).

Sightseeing Card: Busy sightseers should consider the **Tourist Card,** which includes entry to 24 sights in Gdańsk, Gdynia, and Sopot, and discounts at others (such as 20 percent off admission to Malbork Castle). Check the list of what's covered (most of the biggies in town are free with the card, while the Solidarity museum is 50 percent off), and do the arithmetic. If you'll be seeing several included museums, this card could save you some money ("standard" card: 22 zł/24 hours, 35 zł/72 hours; "max" card also includes local public transit: 45 zł/24 hours, 75 zł/72 hours; sold at TIs).

Arrival in Gdańsk

By Train: Gdańsk's main train station (Gdańsk Główny) is a pretty brick palace on the western edge of the old center. (To save money, architects in Colmar, France, copied this exact design to build their city's station.) Trains to other parts of Poland (marked *PKP*) use tracks 1-3; regional trains with connections to the Tri-City (marked *SKM*) use the shorter

GDAŃSK & THE TRI-CITY

tracks 3-5 (for instructions on riding these regional SKM trains, see page 476).

Inside the terminal building, you'll find lockers, ATMs, ticket windows, and a helpful TI (look for *it* sign). Outside, the pedestrian underpass by the McDonald's takes you beneath the busy road (go down the stairs and turn right; first set of exits: tram stop; end of corridor: Old Town). To reach the heart of the Main Town, you can ride the **tram** (buy tickets—*bilety*—at the *RUCH* kiosk by track 4 or at any window marked *Bilety ZKM* in pedestrian underpass; access tram stop via underpass, then board tram #2, #3, #6, #8, or #11 going to the right with your back to the station; go just one stop to Brama Wyżynna, in front of the LOT airlines office). But by the time you buy your ticket and wait for the tram, you might as well **walk** the 15 minutes to the same place (go through underpass, exit to the right and follow the busy road until you reach LOT airlines office, then head left toward all the brick towers). Or even easier, take a **taxi** (which shouldn't cost more than 15 zł to any of my recommended hotels).

By Plane: Gdańsk's small airport, named for Lech Wałęsa, is about five miles west of the city center (tel. 58-348-1163, www .airport.gdansk.pl). The airport has a TI desk and ATMs. Public **bus** #210 connects the airport with downtown, stopping near the main train station and at Brama Wyżynna, near the heart of the Main Town (2.80 zł if bought from TI desk, more if purchased on board, 2/hour on weekdays, 1/hour on weekends, 40 minutes, exit terminal and turn right to find bus stop). The **Airportbus shuttle** zips you directly to various points downtown, though the schedule is sporadic and it must be booked in advance (9-12 zł depending on where you go, 11/day, reserve at www.mpapoland.pl). The 25-minute **taxi** ride into town will cost you about 50 zł.

Helpful Hints

Blue Monday: In the off-season, most of Gdańsk's museums are closed Monday. In the busy summertime, the Gdańsk Historical Museum branches are open—and free—for limited hours on Monday. If museums are closed, Monday is a good day to visit churches or take a side-trip to Sopot (but not to Malbork Castle, which is also closed Mon).

Internet Access: You'll find several free Wi-Fi hotspots in major tourist zones around central Gdańsk.

Getting Around Gdańsk

If you're staying at one of my recommended hotels, everything is within easy walking distance. Public transportation is generally unnecessary for sightseers (except for reaching outlying sights such as Oliwa Cathedral, Westerplatte, Sopot, Gdynia, and

Hel—transportation options for these places are described in their listings).

By Public Transportation: Gdańsk's trams and buses work on the same tickets: Choose between a single-ride ticket (2.80 zł), one-hour ticket (3.40 zł), and 24-hour ticket (11 zł). Buy tickets *(bilety)* at kiosks marked *RUCH* or *Bilety ZKM*, or on board (1-hour and 24-hour tickets only sold on board). In the city center, the stops worth knowing about are Plac Solidarnośći (near the shipyards), Gdańsk Główny (in front of the main train station), and Brama Wyżynna (near the heart of the tourist zone, in front of LOT airlines office). When buying tickets, don't confuse *ZKM* (the company that runs Gdańsk city transit) with *SKM* (the company that runs regional trains to outlying destinations).

By Taxi: Taxis cost about 7 zł to start, then 2 zł per kilometer (or 3 zł at night). Find a taxi stand, or call a cab (try Super Hallo Taxi, tel. 191-91).

Tours in Gdańsk

Walking Tours—In peak season, the TI sometimes offers a pricey 2.5-hour English walking tour (80 zł/person, offered with demand in July-Aug only, no set schedule—ask at TI).

Private Guide—Hiring your own local guide is an exceptional value. **Agnieszka Syroka** is bubbly and personable, and also does tours of Malbork Castle (400 zł for up to 4 hours, more for all day, mobile 502-554-584, www.tourguidegdansk.com, asyroka@interia.pl or syroka.agnieszka@gmail.com).

Self-Guided Walks

▲▲▲Gdańsk's Royal Way

In the 16th and 17th centuries, Gdańsk was Poland's wealthiest city, with gorgeous architecture (much of it in the Flemish

Mannerist style) rivaling that in the two historic capitals, Kraków and Warsaw. During this Golden Age, Polish kings would visit this city of well-to-do Hanseatic League merchants, and gawk along the same route trod by tourists today. The following walk introduces you to the best of historic Gdańsk. It only takes about 30 minutes, not counting multiple worthwhile sightseeing stops. This stroll turns tourists into poets. On my last visit, a traveler gasped to me, "It's like stepping into a Fabergé egg."

Begin at the west end of the Main Town, between the white gate and the big brick gate (near the LOT airlines office, the busy road, and the Brama Wyżynna tram stop).

City Gates: Medieval Gdańsk had an elaborate network of protection for the city, including several moats and gates—among them the white **Upland Gate** (Brama Wyżynna); the red-brick **Torture House** (Wieża Więzienna); and the taller, attached red-brick **Prison Tower** (Katownia). The three gates were all connected back then, and visitors had to pass through all of them to enter the city. The Torture House/Prison Tower complex, with walls up to 15 feet thick, now holds the fine **Amber Museum** (described later, under "Sights in Gdańsk").

Now walk around the left side of the Torture House and Prison Tower. Look to your left to see a long brick building with four gables (next to the modern theater building). This is the 16th-century **Armory** (Zbrojownia), one of the best examples of Dutch Renaissance architecture in Europe. Though this part of the building looks like four separate house facades, it's a kind of urban camouflage to hide its real purpose from potential attackers. But there's at least one clue to what it's for: Notice the exploding cannonballs at the tops of the turrets. The round, pointy-topped tower next door is the **Straw Tower** (Baszta Słomiana). Gunpowder was stored here, and the roof was straw—so if it exploded, it would blow its top without destroying the walls.

· *Continue around the brick buildings until you're face-to-face with the...*

Golden Gate (Złota Brama): The other gates were defensive, but this one's purely ornamental. The four women up top represent virtues that the people of Gdańsk should exhibit toward outsiders: Peace, Freedom, Prosperity, and Fame. The inscription, a psalm in medieval German, compares Gdańsk to Jerusalem: famous and important. In the middle is one of the coats of arms of Gdańsk—two white crosses under a crown on a red shield. We'll see this symbol many times today.

· *Now go through the gate, entering the "Long Street"...*

Ulica Długa: Look back at the gate you just came through. The women on top of this side represent virtues the people of Gdańsk should cultivate in themselves: Wisdom, Piety, Justice, and Concord (if an arrow's broken, let's take it out of the quiver and fix it).

Wander this intoxicating promenade. Gdańsk was cosmopolitan and exceptionally tolerant in the Middle Ages, attracting a wide range of people, including many who were persecuted elsewhere: Jews, Scots, Dutch, Flemish, Italians, Germans, and more. Members of each group brought with them strands of their culture, which they wove into the tapestry of this city—demonstrated by the eclectic homes along this street.

This lovely street wasn't always so lively and carefree. At the end of World War II, ulica Długa was in ruins. The city was badly damaged when the Nazis first invaded, but the worst devastation came when the Soviets arrived. This was the first traditionally German city that the Red Army reached on their march toward Berlin—and the soldiers were set loose to level the place in retaliation for all the pain the Nazis had caused. (Soviets didn't destroy nearby Gdynia—which they considered Polish, not German.) Soviet officers turned a blind eye as their soldiers raped and brutalized residents. An entire order of horrified nuns committed suicide by throwing themselves into the river. Upwards of 80 percent of this area was destroyed. It was only thanks to detailed drawings and photographs that these buildings could be so carefully reconstructed, mostly using the original brick.

During Gdańsk's Golden Age, these houses were taxed based on frontage (like the homes lining Amsterdam's canals)—so they were built skinny and deep. The widest houses belonged to the super-elite. Different as they are from the outside, every house had the same general plan inside. Each had three parts, starting with the front and moving back: First was a fancy drawing room, to show off for visitors. Then came a narrow corridor to the back rooms—often along the side of an inner courtyard. Because the houses had only a few windows facing the outer street, this courtyard provided much-needed sunlight to the rest of the house. The residential quarters were in the back, where the family actually lived: bedroom, kitchen, office. To see the interior of one of these homes, pay a visit to the very interesting **Uphagen House** (#12, on the right, a block and a half in front of the Golden Gate; described later, under "Sights in Gdańsk").

Across the street and a little farther down are some of the most striking **facades** along ulica Długa. The blue-and-white house with

the three giant heads is from the 19th century, when the hot style was eclecticism—borrowing bits and pieces from various architectural eras. This was one of the few houses on the street that survived World War II.

At the next corner on the right is the huge, blocky, red **post office,** which doesn't quite fit with

Gdańsk History

Visitors to Gdańsk are surprised at how "un-Polish" the city's history is. In this cultural melting pot of German, Dutch, and Flemish merchants (with a smattering of Italians and Scots), Poles were only a small part of the picture until the city became exclusively Polish after World War II. However, in Gdańsk, cultural backgrounds traditionally took a back seat to the bottom line. Wealthy Gdańsk was always known for its economic pragmatism—no matter who was in charge, merchants here made money.

Gdańsk is Poland's gateway to the waters of Europe—where its main river (the Vistula) meets the Baltic Sea. The town was first mentioned in the 10th century, and was seized in 1308 by the Teutonic Knights (who called it "Danzig"; for more on the Teutonic Knights, see page 486). The Knights encouraged other Germans to settle on the Baltic coast, and gradually turned Gdańsk into a wealthy city. In 1361, Gdańsk joined the Hanseatic League, a trade federation of mostly Germanic merchant towns that provided mutual security. By the 15th century, Gdańsk was a leading member of this mighty network, which virtually dominated trade in northern Europe (and also included Toruń, Kraków, Lübeck, Hamburg, Bremen, Bruges, Bergen, Tallinn, Novgorod, and nearly a hundred other cities).

In 1454, the people of Gdańsk rose up against the Teutonic Knights, burning down their castle and forcing them out of the city. Three years later, the Polish king borrowed money from wealthy Gdańsk families to hire Czech mercenaries to take the Teutonic Knights' main castle, Malbork (described in the next chapter). In exchange, the Gdańsk merchants were granted special privileges, including exclusive export rights. Gdańsk now acted as a middleman for much of the trade passing through Polish lands, but paid only a modest annual tribute to the Polish king.

The 16th and 17th centuries were Gdańsk's Golden Age. Now a part of the Polish kingdom, the city had access to an enormous hinterland of natural resources to export—yet it maintained a privileged, semi-independent status. Like Amsterdam, Gdańsk became a tolerant, progressive, and booming merchant

the skinny facades lining the rest of the street. But step inside. With doves fluttering under an airy glass atrium, the interior's a class act. (To mail postcards, take a number—category C—from the machine on the left.)

Across the street and a few doors down from the post office, notice the colorful **scenes** just overhead on the facade of the cocktail bar. These are slices of life from 17th-century Gdańsk: drinking, talking, buying, fighting, playing music. The ship is a *koga*, a typical symbol of Gdańsk.

A couple of doors down from the cocktail bar is **Neptun**

city. Its mostly Germanic and Dutch burghers imported Dutch, Flemish, and Italian architects to give their homes an appropriately Hanseatic flourish. At a time of religious upheaval in the rest of Europe, Gdańsk became known for its tolerance—a place that opened its doors to all visitors (many Mennonites and Scottish religious refugees emigrated here). It was also a haven for great thinkers, including philosopher Arthur Schopenhauer and scientist Daniel Fahrenheit (who invented the mercury thermometer).

Gdańsk declined, along with the rest of Poland, in the late 18th century, and became a part of Prussia (today's northern Germany) during the Partitions. But the people of Gdańsk—even those of German heritage—had taken pride in their independence, and weren't enthusiastic about being ruled from Berlin. After World War I, in a unique compromise to appease its complex ethnic makeup, Gdańsk did not fall under German or Polish control, but once again became an independent city-state: the Free City of Danzig (populated by 400,000 ethnic Germans and only 15,000 Poles). The city, along with the so-called Polish Corridor connecting it to Polish lands, effectively cut off Germany from its northeastern territory. On September 1, 1939, Adolf Hitler started World War II when he invaded Gdańsk in order to bring it back into the German fold. Nearly 80 percent of the city was destroyed in the war.

After World War II, Gdańsk officially became part of Poland, and was painstakingly reconstructed (mostly replicating the buildings of its Golden Age). In 1970, and again in 1980, the shipyard of Gdańsk witnessed strikes and demonstrations that would lead to the fall of European communism. Poland's great anti-communist hero and first post-communist president—Lech Wałęsa—is Gdańsk's most famous resident, and still lives here.

A city with a recent past that's both tragic and uplifting, Gdańsk celebrated its 1,000th birthday in 1997. This occasion, and preparations for the Euro Cup 2012 soccer matches, kicked off a wave of renovation and refurbishment that has the gables of the atmospheric Hanseatic quarter gleaming once again.

Cinema (marked *KINO*). In the 1980s, this was the only movie theater in the city, and locals lined up all the way down the street to get in. Adults remember coming here with their grandparents to see a full day of cartoons. Now, as with traditional main-street cinemas in the US, this one is threatened by the rising popularity of multiplexes outside the town center.

Across the street from the theater are three houses belonging to the very influential medieval **Ferber family,** which produced many burghers, mayors, and even a bishop. On the house with the little dog over the door (#29), look for the heads in the circles. These are Caesars of Rome. At the top of the building is Mr. Ferber's answer to the constant question, "Why build such an elaborate house?"—*PRO INVIDIA*, "For the sake of envy."

A few doors down, notice the outdoor tables for Gdańsk's most popular milk bar, the recommended **Bar Mleczny Neptun**. Now you're just a few steps from the **Main Town Hall** (Ratusz Głównego Miasta). Consider climbing its observation tower and visiting its superb interior, which features ornately decorated meeting rooms for the city council (described later, under "Sights in Gdańsk"). The **TI** is across the street, on the right.

• *Just beyond the Main Town Hall, ulica Długa widens and becomes...*

Długi Targ (Long Square): The centerpiece of this square is one of Gdańsk's most important landmarks, the statue of **Neptune**—god of the sea. He's a fitting symbol for a city that dominates the maritime life of Poland. Behind him is another fine museum, the **Artus Court** (described later, under "Sights in Gdańsk"). This meeting hall for various Gdańsk brotherhoods is home to the most impressive stove you've ever seen.

As you continue down Długi targ, notice the **balconies** extending out into the square, with access to cellars underneath. These were a common feature on ulica Długa in Gdańsk's Golden Age, but were removed in the 19th century to make way for a new tram system. You can find more balconies like these on Mariacka street, which runs parallel to this one (2 blocks to the left).

• *At the end of Długi targ is the...*

Green Gate (Zielona Brama): This huge gate was actually built as a residence for visiting kings...who usually preferred to stay back by Neptune instead (maybe because the river, just on the other side of this gate, stank). It might not have been good enough for kings and queens, but it's plenty fine for a former president—Lech Wałęsa's office is upstairs (see the plaque, *Biuro Lecha Wałęsy*). Other parts of the building are used for temporary exhibitions.

Notice that these bricks are much smaller than the ones we've seen earlier on this walk, which were locally made. These, however, are Dutch: Boats from Holland would come here empty of cargo but with a load of bricks for ballast. Traders filled their ships with goods for the return trip, leaving the bricks behind to be turned into this gate.

• *Now go through the gate, and turn left along the...*

Riverfront Embankment: The Motława River—actually a side channel of the mighty Vistula—was the source of Gdańsk's phenomenal Golden Age wealth. This embankment was jam-packed in its heyday, the 14th and 15th centuries. It was so crowded with boats that you would hardly have been able see the water, and boats had to pay a time-based tax for tying up to a post. Instead of an actual embankment (which was built later), a series of wooden piers connected the boats directly to the gates of the city. Now it's a popular place to stroll and to buy amber. Keep an eye out for old-fashioned **galleons** plying the waters here—these boats depart hourly for a fun cruise to Westerplatte and back. While kitschy, the galleons are a fun way to get out on the water (details on page 474).

Across the river is **Granary Island** (Spichrze), where grain was stored until it could be taken away by ships. Before World War II, there were some 400 granaries here; today the island is still in ruins. Three granaries that have been reconstructed on the next island up house exhibits for the Central Maritime Museum (described later, under "Sights in Gdańsk"); two others are now recommended hotels (Hotel Gdańsk and Hotel Królewski). A big international company has bought this island, and plans to develop the prime real estate into a new city-center zone of shops, restaurants, houses, and hotels.

Continue along the embankment until you see the five big, round stones on your left. These are the **five little ladies**—mysterious ancient sculptures. If you look closely, you can make out their features, especially the chubby one on the end.

In the next block, the huge red-brick fort houses the **Archaeological Museum** and a tower you can climb for a good view (described later, under "Sights in Gdańsk"). The gate in the middle of the building leads to **Mariacka street,** a calm, atmospheric drag lined with old balconies, amber shops, and imaginative gargoyles (which locals call "pukers" when it rains).

Consider taking a few minutes to window-shop your way up Mariacka street, comparison-pricing amber souvenirs. At the end of the street on the left (at #1), the recommended **Gotyk House** hotel has a characteristic little shop in the cellar that sells heavenly gingerbread from the town of Toruń. If you're not headed to Toruń (described in the next chapter), this is a good opportunity to buy some of its tasty treats. As that city was the hometown of Nicholas Copernicus—and Copernicus' former lover supposedly once lived in this very house—the shop also has a fondly presented mini-museum dedicated to the couple. Just after Gotyk House and the gingerbread shop, you're face-to-face with **St. Mary's Church** (enter around the far side; described later, under "Sights in Gdańsk").

• Back on the embankment, head past a few tempting eateries (including the recommended Kamienica Goldwasser and Sushi 77)—consider *scouting a table here for dinner later tonight—before running right into Gdańsk's number-one symbol, and our last stop...*

The Crane (Żuraw): This monstrous 15th-century crane was once used for loading ships, picking up small crafts for repairs, and uprighting masts...beginning a shipbuilding tradition that continued to the days of Lech Wałęsa. The crane mechanism was operated by several hardworking sailors scrambling around in giant hamster wheels up top (you can see the wheels if you look up). The Crane belongs to the Central Maritime Museum. Just beyond the Crane, they're rebuilding several structures that will house museum exhibits. And along here, you might see a stand selling smoked fish.

• *Our orientation tour is over. Now get out there and enjoy Gdańsk... do it for Lech!*

From the Main Town to the Solidarity Shipyard

This lightly guided walk links Gdańsk's two most important sight-seeing areas. Along the way, we'll see some historic landmarks, tour two of Gdańsk's more interesting red-brick churches, and wander through the city's best shopping district. The stroll takes about 20 minutes, not counting stops for sightseeing and shopping.

Begin at the top of ulica Długa, with your back to the Golden Gate. Head a few steps down the street and take a left on Tkacka. After one long block, on the left, you can see the back of the **Armory** building (described earlier). This pearl of Renaissance architecture recently had a striking facelift—examine the exquisite decorations.

After three short blocks, detour to the right down Świętojańska and use the side door to enter the brick **St. Nicholas Church** (Kościół Św. Mikołaja, with the ornate towers on the ends). Archaeologists have found the bodies of 3,000 Napoleonic soldiers buried here. Near the end of World War II, when the Soviet army reached Gdańsk on its march westward, they were given the order to burn all the churches. Only this one—dedicated to Russia's patron saint—was spared. As the best-preserved church in town, it has a more impressive interior than the others, with lavish black-and-gold Baroque altars.

Backtrack out to the main street and continue north. Immediately after the church (on the right) is Gdańsk's renovated **Market Hall.** Look for the coat of arms of Gdańsk over each of its four doors (two white crosses on a red shield). Inside you'll find mostly local shoppers—browsing through produce, other foods, and clothing—as well as the graves of medieval Dominican monks, which were discovered in the basement when the building was refurbished. Look up to appreciate the delicate steel-and-glass canopy.

Across the street from the Market Hall is a round, red-brick **tower,** once part of the city's protective wall. This marks the end of the Main Town and the beginning of the Old Town.

Another long block up the street is the huge **St. Catherine's Church** (Kościół Św. Katarzyny, on the right). "Katy," as locals call it, is the oldest church in Gdańsk. In May of 2006, a carelessly discarded cigarette caused the church roof to burst into flames. Local people ran into the church and pulled everything outside, so nothing valuable was damaged; even the carillon bells were saved. However, the roof and wooden frame were totally destroyed. The people of Gdańsk were determined to rebuild this important symbol of the city. Within days of the fire, fund-raising concerts were held to scrape together most of the money needed to raise the roof once more.

The church hiding behind Katy—named for Catherine's daughter Bridget—has important ties to Solidarity, and is worth a quick detour. To get there, walk up ulica Katarzynki, along the side of St. Catherine's Church, and past the monument to Pope John Paul II.

St. Bridget's Church (Kościół Św. Brygidy) was the home church of Lech Wałęsa during the tense days of the 1980s. This church and its priest, Henryk Jankowski, were particularly aggressive in supporting the ideals of Solidarity. Jankowski became a mouthpiece for the movement, and Wałęsa named his youngest daughter Brygida in gratitude for the church's support. In the back corner, under the wall of wooden crosses, find the memorial to Solidarity martyr Jerzy Popiełuszko, a famously outspoken Warsaw priest who in 1984 was kidnapped, beaten, and murdered by the communist secret police. Notice that the figure's hands and feet are tied. At the front of the church, check out the enormous, unfinished altar made entirely of amber, featuring the Black Madonna of Częstochowa and a royal Polish eagle. If and when it's finished, it'll be 36 feet high, 20 feet wide, and 10 feet deep. But some locals criticize this ambitious project as an example of Father Jankowski's missteps. Despite his fame and contributions to Solidarity, Jankowski's public standing took a nosedive near the end of his life—thanks to ego-driven projects like this, as well as accusations of anti-Semitism and implications of pedophilia and corruption. Forced to retire in 2007, Jankowski died in 2010.

Backtrack out past St. Catherine's Church to the main street. Just across from the church is a red-brick building with a lot of

Gdańsk at a Gdlance

▲▲▲**Ulica Długa** Gdańsk's colorful showpiece main drag, cutting a picturesque swath through the heart of the wealthy burghers' neighborhood. **Hours:** Always open. See page 438.

▲▲▲**Solidarity Sights and Gdańsk Shipyard** Home to the beginning of the end of European communism, housing a towering monument and an excellent museum. **Hours:** Memorial and shipyard gate—always open. "Roads to Freedom" exhibit—May-Sept Tue-Sun 10:00-18:00, Oct-April Tue-Sun 10:00-17:00, closed Mon year-round. See page 457.

▲▲**Main Town Hall** Ornately decorated meeting rooms, exhibits of town artifacts, and climbable tower with sweeping views. **Hours:** Mid-June-late Sept Mon 10:00-15:00, Tue-Sat 10:00-18:00, Sun 11:00-18:00; late Sept-mid-June Tue 10:00-15:00, Wed-Sat 10:00-16:00, Sun 11:00-16:00, closed Mon. See page 450.

▲▲**Artus Court** Grand meeting hall for guilds of Golden Age Gdańsk, boasting an over-the-top tiled stove. **Hours:** Mid-June-late Sept Mon 10:00-15:00, Tue-Sat 10:00-18:00, Sun 11:00-18:00; late Sept-mid-June Tue 10:00-15:00, Wed-Sat 10:00-16:00, Sun 11:00-16:00, closed Mon. See page 451.

▲▲**St. Mary's Church** Giant red-brick church crammed full of Gdańsk history. **Hours:** June-Sept Mon-Sat 9:00-18:30, Sun 13:00-18:30; closes progressively earlier off-season. See page 452.

▲**Amber Museum** High-tech new exhibit of valuable golden globs of petrified tree sap. **Hours:** Mid-June-late Sept Mon 10:00-15:00, Tue-Sat 10:00-18:00, Sun 11:00-18:00; late Sept-mid-June Tue 10:00-15:00, Wed-Sat 10:00-16:00, Sun 11:00-16:00, closed Mon. See page 448.

▲**Uphagen House** Tourable 18th-century interior, typical of the pretty houses that line ulica Długa. **Hours:** Mid-June-late Sept

little windows in the roof. This is the **Great Mill** (Wielki Młyn), which has been converted into a shopping mall (daily 10:00-19:00). As you continue north and cross the stream, you'll also see the picturesque **Small Mill** (Mały Młyn) straddling the stream on your right.

After another block, on your right, is the modern **Madison shopping mall** (Mon-Sat 9:00-21:00, Sun 10:00-20:00). Two blocks to your left (up Heweliusza) are more shopping malls and the main train station.

Mon 10:00-15:00, Tue-Sat 10:00-18:00, Sun 11:00-18:00; late Sept-mid-June Tue 10:00-15:00, Wed-Sat 10:00-16:00, Sun 11:00-16:00, closed Mon. See page 450.

▲Central Maritime Museum Sprawling exhibit on all aspects of the nautical life, housed in several venues (including the land-mark medieval Crane and a permanently moored steamship) connected by a ferry boat. **Hours:** July-Aug daily 10:00-18:00; Sept-Oct and March-June Tue-Sun 10:00-16:00, closed Mon; Nov-Feb Tue-Sun 10:00-15:00, closed Mon. See page 455.

Historical Zone of the Free City of Gdańsk Tiny museum examining Gdańsk's unique status as a "Free City" between the World Wars. **Hours:** May-Nov Tue-Sun 11:00-18:00, Dec-April Tue-Sun 13:00-17:00, closed Mon year-round. See page 454.

Archaeological Museum Decent collection of artifacts from this region's past. **Hours:** July-Aug Tue-Fri 9:00-17:00, Sat-Sun 10:00-17:00, closed Mon; Sept-June Tue and Thu-Fri 8:00-16:00, Wed 9:00-17:00, Sat-Sun 10:00-16:00, closed Mon. See page 454.

National Museum in Gdańsk Ho-hum art collection with a single blockbuster highlight: Hans Memling's remarkable *Last Judgment* altarpiece. **Hours:** Tue-Wed and Fri-Sat 10:00-18:00, Thu and Sun 12:00-19:00, closed Mon. See page 464.

"Blue Lion" Archaeological Education Center New, kid-friendly exhibit about medieval Gdańsk. **Hours:** May-Aug Tue-Sun 10:00-18:00, Sept-April Tue-Sun 9:00-17:00, closed Mon year-round. See page 465.

Oliwa Cathedral Suburban church with long, skinny nave and playful organ. **Hours:** Church open long hours daily; frequent organ concerts in summer. See page 466.

But to get to the **shipyard,** keep heading straight up Rajska. After another long block, jog right (between the big, green-glass skyscraper and today's Solidarity headquarters) and head for the three tall crosses.

On the way, you'll see signs leading to the **"Roads to Freedom" exhibit** (the entrance to this underground museum is actually a freestanding kiosk by the side of the road).

But before you visit this museum, head to the shipyard to begin my self-guided tour there (see page 457). Near the entrance to the museum are two artifacts from communist times. First, parked in front of the museum is an **armored personnel carrier,** just like the ones used by the ZOMO (riot police) to terrorize Polish citizens after martial law was declared in 1981. Nearby, watch for the two big chunks of **wall:** on the left, a piece of the Berlin Wall; and on the right, a chunk of the shipyard wall Lech Wałęsa scaled to get inside and lead the strike. The message: What happened behind one wall eventually led to the fall of the other Wall.

For the whole story, continue to the monument with the three tall crosses, and turn to page 457.

Sights in Gdańsk

Main Town (Główne Miasto)
The following sights are all in the Main Town, listed roughly in the order you'll see them on the self-guided walk of the Royal Way.

Gdańsk Historical Museum
The Gdańsk Historical Museum has four excellent branches: the Amber Museum, Uphagen House, Main Town Hall, and Artus Court. All have the same cost and hours, but you must buy a separate ticket for each.

Cost and Hours: 10 zł apiece, free Mon in summer and Tue off-season; open mid-June-late Sept Mon 10:00-15:00, Tue-Sat 10:00-18:00, Sun 11:00-18:00; late Sept-mid-June Tue 10:00-15:00, Wed-Sat 10:00-16:00, Sun 11:00-16:00, closed Mon; last entry 30 minutes before closing.

Information: The museums share a phone number and website (central tel. 58-767-9100, www.mhmg.gda.pl).

▲**Amber Museum (Muzeum Bursztynu)**—Housed in a pair of connected brick towers just outside the Main Town's Golden Gate, this museum has two oddly contradictory parts. One shows off Gdańsk's favorite local resource, amber, while the other focuses on implements of torture (cost and hours above, overpriced 1.5-hour audioguide—25 zł, enter at end facing Golden Gate).

Partially explained in English, the Amber Museum offers a good introduction to the globby yellow stuff, but you'll have to walk up several flights of stairs to see it all. For a primer before you go, check out the "All About Amber" sidebar.

Climb up one flight of stairs, buy your ticket, then head up to the second floor for a scientific look at amber. View inclu-

All About Amber

Poland's Baltic seaside is known as the Amber Coast. You can see amber *(bursztyn)* in Gdańsk's Amber Museum, in the collection at Malbork Castle (see next chapter)—and in shop windows everywhere. This fossilized tree resin originated here on the north coast of Poland 40 million years ago. It comes in as many different colors as Eskimos have words for snow: 300 distinct shades, from yellowish white to yellowish black, from opaque to transparent. (I didn't believe it either, until I toured Gdańsk's museum.) Darker-colored amber is generally mixed with ash and sand—making it more fragile, and generally less desirable. Lighter amber is mixed with gasses and air bubbles.

Amber has been popular since long before there were souvenir stands. Archaeologists have found Roman citizens (and their coins) buried with crosses made of amber. Almost 75 percent of the world's amber is mined in northern Poland, and it often simply washes up on the beaches after a winter storm. Some of the elaborate amber sculptures displayed at the museum are joined with "amber glue"—melted-down amber mixed with an adhesive agent. More recently, amber craftsmen are combining amber with silver to create artwork—a method dubbed the "Polish School."

In addition to being good for the economy, some Poles believe amber is good for their health. A traditional cure for arthritis pain is to pour strong vodka over amber, let it set, and then rub it on sore joints. Other remedies call for mixing amber dust with honey or rose oil. It sounds superstitious, but users claim that it works.

sions (items trapped in the resin) through a magnifying glass and microscope, and see dozens of samples showing the full rainbow of amber shades. Interactive video screens explain the creation of amber. The third-floor exhibit explains the "Amber Route" (the ancient Celtic trade road connecting Gdańsk to Italy), outlines medicinal uses of the stuff, and displays a wide range of functional items made from amber—clocks, pipe stems, candlesticks, chandeliers, jewelry boxes, and much more. The fourth floor shows off more artistic items made of amber—sculptures, candelabras, beer steins, chessboards, and a model ship with delicate sails made of amber. At the top floor, you'll find a modern gallery showing more recent amber craftsmanship, and displays about amber's role in fashion today.

On your way back down, detour along the upper level of the courtyard to find the museum's dark side (the Torture Museum). First is a brief exhibit about the building's history, including its chapter as a prison tower. The rest of the exhibit—with sound effects, scant artifacts, and mannequins helpfully demonstrating the grisly equipment—tries hard to make medieval torture and imprisonment interesting.

▲**Uphagen House (Dom Uphagena)**—This interesting place at ulica Długa 12 is your chance to glimpse what's behind the colorful facades lining this street (see cost and hours above). Check out the cutaway model just inside the entry to see the three parts you'll visit: dolled-up visitors' rooms in front, a corridor along the courtyard, and private rooms in the back. As you enter, the costumed staffers will likely usher you to the top floor, which houses temporary exhibits. Back down on the middle floor, ogle the finely decorated salon, which was used to show off for guests. Most of this furniture is original (saved from WWII bombs by locals who hid it in the countryside). Passing into the dining room, note the knee-high paintings of hunting and celebrations. Along the passage to the back, each room has a theme: butterflies in the smoking room, then flowers in the next room, then birds in the music room. In the private rooms at the back, notice how much simpler the decor is. Downstairs, you'll pass through the kitchen, the pantry, and a room with photos of the house before the war, which were used to reconstruct what you see today.

▲▲**Main Town Hall (Ratusz Głównego Miasta)**—This landmark building contains remarkable decorations from Gdańsk's Golden Age (see cost and hours on page 446). You can also climb to the top of the **tower** for commanding views (5 zł extra, mid-June–mid-Sept only).

Touring the Main Town Hall: Buy your ticket down below (good gift shop), then head up the stairs and inside.

In the entry room, examine the photo showing this building at the end of World War II (you'll see more upstairs). The ornately carved wooden **door,** which we'll pass through in a minute, also deserves a close look. Above the door are two crosses under a crown. This seal of Gdańsk is being held—as it's often depicted—by a pair of lions. The felines are stubborn and independent, just like the citizens of Gdańsk. Close the door partway to look at the carvings of crops. Around the frame of the door are mermen, reminding us that this agricultural bounty, like so many of Poland's resources, is transported on the Vistula and out through Gdańsk.

Go through the door into the **Red Hall,** where the Gdańsk city council met in the summertime. (The lavish fireplace—with another pair of lions holding the coat of arms of Gdańsk—was just for show.) City council members would sit in the seats around the room, debating city policy. The shin-level paintings depict the earth; the exquisitely detailed inlaid wood just over the seats are animals; the paintings on the wall above represent the seven virtues the burghers meeting in this room should have; and the ceiling is all about theology. Examine that ceiling. It has 25 paintings in total, with both Christian and pagan themes—meant to inspire the decision-makers in this room to make good choices. The smaller ones around the edges are scenes from mythology and the Bible. The one in the middle (from 1607) shows God's relationship to Gdańsk. In the foreground, the citizens of Gdańsk go about their daily lives. Above them, high atop the arch, God's hand reaches down (from within clouds of Hebrew characters) and grasps the city's steeple. The rainbow arching above also symbolizes God's connection to Gdańsk. Mirroring that is the Vistula River, which begins in the mountains of southern Poland (on the right), runs through the country, and exits at the sea in Gdańsk (on the left, where the rainbow ends).

Continue into the not-so-impressive Winter Hall, with another fireplace and coat of arms held by lions. Keep going through the next room, into a room with before-and-after photos of **WWII damage.** At the foot of the destroyed crucifix is a book with a bullet hole in it. The twist of wood is all that's left of the main support for the spiral staircase (today reconstructed in the room where you entered). Ponder the inspiring ability of a city to be reborn after the tragedy of war.

Upstairs are some temporary exhibits and several examples of **Gdańsk-style furniture.** These pieces are characterized by three big, round feet along the front, lots of ornamentation, and usually a virtually impossible-to-find lock (sometimes hidden behind a movable decoration). You can also see a coin collection, from the days when Gdańsk had the elite privilege of minting its own currency.

▲▲**Artus Court (Dwór Artusa)**—In the Middle Ages, Gdańsk was home to many brotherhoods and guilds (like businessmen's clubs). For their meetings, the city provided this elaborately decorated hall, named for King Arthur—a medieval symbol for pres-

tige and power. Just as in King Arthur's Court, this was a place where powerful and important people came together. Such halls were once common in Baltic Europe, but this is the only original one that survives (cost and hours on page 446, dry and too-thorough audioguide-5 zł; in tall, white, triple-arched building behind Neptune statue at Długi targ 43-44).

In the grand hall, various **cupboards** line the walls. Each organization that met here had a place to keep its important documents and office supplies. Suspended from the ceiling are seven giant **model ships** that depict Baltic vessels, symbolic of the city's connection to the sea.

In the far-back corner is the museum's highlight: a gigantic **stove** decorated with 520 colorful tiles featuring the faces of kings, queens, nobles, mayors, and burghers. Half of these people were Protestant, and half were Catholic, mixed together in no particular order—a reminder of Gdańsk's religious tolerance. Virtually all the tiles are original, having survived WWII bombs. But not all of the original tiles are here: Three of them were recently discovered by a bargain-hunter wandering through a flea market in the southern part of the country, who returned them to their rightful home.

Notice the huge **paintings** on the walls above, with 3-D animals emerging from flat frames. Hunting is a popular theme in local artwork. Like minting coins, hunting was a privilege usually reserved for royalty, but extended in special circumstances to the burghers of special towns...like Gdańsk. If you look closely, it's obvious that these "paintings" are new, digitally generated reproductions of the originals, which were damaged in World War II.

The next room—actually in the next-door building—is a typical front room of the burghers' homes lining ulica Długa. Ogle the gorgeously carved wooden staircase. Upstairs (through the door to the right of the stairs) is a hall of knights—once again evoking Arthurian legend. If you've rented an audioguide, take it back up front to return it; otherwise, exit through the back, just down the street from St. Mary's Church; to get back to the main drag, go back around the block, to the left.

Other Museums and Churches in the Main Town

▲▲St. Mary's Church (Kościół Mariacki)—
Gdańsk has so many striking red-brick churches, it's hard to keep track of them. But if you visit only one, make it St. Mary's. This is the biggest brick church in the world, accommodating up to 25,000 people. Built over 159 years in the 14th and 15th centuries, the church is an important symbol of Gdańsk.

Cost and Hours: 3 zł; June-Sept Mon-Sat 9:00-18:30, Sun 13:00-18:30; closes progressively earlier off-season, tel. 58-301-3982, www.bazylikamariacka.pl.

Touring the Church: As you enter the

church, notice all the white, empty space—unusual in a Catholic country, where frilly Baroque churches are the norm. In the Middle Ages, Gdańsk's tolerance attracted people who were suffering religious persecution. As the Protestant population grew, they needed a place to worship. St. Mary's, like most other Gdańsk churches, eventually became Protestant—leaving these churches with the blank walls you see now. Today you'll find only one Baroque church in central Gdańsk (the domed pink-and-green chapel behind St. Mary's).

Most Gothic stone churches are built in the basilica style—with a high nave in the middle, shorter aisles on the side, and flying buttresses to support the weight. (Think of Paris' Notre-Dame.) But that design doesn't work with brick. So, like all Gdańsk churches, St. Mary's is a "hall church"—with three naves the same height, and no exterior buttresses.

Also like other Gdańsk churches, St. Mary's gave refuge to the Polish people after the communist government declared martial law in 1981. When a riot broke out and violence seemed imminent, people would flood into churches for protection. The ZOMO riot police wouldn't follow them inside.

Most of the church decorations are original. A few days before World War II broke out in Gdańsk, locals hid precious items in the countryside. Take some time now to see a few of the highlights.

Head up the right nave and find the opulent family marker to the right of the main altar, high on the pillar. Look for the falling baby (under the crown). This is Constantine Ferber. As a precocious child, Constantine leaned out his window on ulica Długa to see the king's processional come through town. He slipped and fell, but landed in a salesman's barrel of fish. Constantine grew up to become the mayor of Gdańsk.

Look on the side of the same pillar for a coat of arms with three pigs' heads. It relates to another member of the illustrious Ferber clan. An enemy army that was laying siege to the town tried to starve its people out. A clever Ferber decided to load the cannons with pigs' heads to show the enemy that they had plenty of food—it worked, and the enemy left.

Circle around, past the front of the beautifully carved main altar. Behind it is the biggest stained-glass window in Poland. Below the window (behind the main altar) is a huge, empty glass case. The case was designed to hold Hans Memling's *Final Judgment* painting, which used to be on display here, but is currently being held hostage by the National Museum. To counter the museum's claim that the church wasn't a good environment for such a precious work, the priest had this display case built—but that still wasn't enough to convince the museum to give the painting back. You can see a smaller replica up by the main door of the church (in the little chapel on the right just before you exit), but true art fans will want to venture to the National Museum (described later) to see the much larger and masterful original.

Before you head back out to the mini-Memling (and the exit), venture to the far side of the altar and check out the elaborate **astronomical clock**—supposedly the biggest wooden clock in the world. Below is the circular calendar showing the saint's day, and above are zodiac signs and the time (only one hand).

Tower Climb: If you've got the energy, climb the 408 steps up the church's 270-foot-tall tower. You'll be rewarded with sweeping views of the entire city (tower climb-5 zł; July-Aug Mon-Sat 9:00-18:00, Sun 13:00-18:00; April-June and Sept-Oct Mon-Sat 9:00-17:00, Sun 13:00-17:00; closed Nov-March; entrance in back corner).

Historical Zone of the Free City of Gdańsk (Strefa Historyczna Wolne Miasto Gdańsk)—In a city so obsessed with its Golden Age and Solidarity history, this charming little collection illuminates a unique but often-overlooked chapter in the story of Gdańsk: The years between World Wars I and II, when—in an effort to find a workable compromise in this ethnically mixed city—Gdańsk was not part of Germany nor of Poland, but a self-governing "free city" *(wolne miasto)*. Like a holdover from medieval fiefdoms in modern times, the city-state of Gdańsk even issued its own currency and stamps. This modest museum earnestly shows off artifacts from the time—photos, stamps, maps, flags, promotional tourist leaflets, and other items from the free city, all marked with the Gdańsk symbol of two white crosses under a crown on a red shield. The brochure explains that four out of five people living in the free city identified themselves not as German or Poles, but as "Danzigers." While some might find the subject obscure, this endearing collection is a treat for WWII history buffs.

Cost and Hours: 5 zł, May-Nov Tue-Sun 11:00-18:00, Dec-April Tue-Sun 13:00-17:00, closed Mon year-round, a few steps in front of St. Mary's at ulica Piwna 19-21, tel. 58-320-2828, www.tpg.info.pl.

Archaeological Museum (Muzeum Archeologiczne)—This modest museum is worth a quick peek for those interested in archaeology. The ground floor has exhibits on excavated finds from Sudan, where the museum has a branch program. Upstairs, look for the distinctive urns with cute faces, which date from the Hallstatt Period and were discovered in slate graves around Gdańsk. Also upstairs are some Bronze and Iron Age tools; before-and-after photos of WWII Gdańsk; and a reconstructed 12th-century Viking-like Slavonic longboat. You can also climb the building's tower, with good views up Mariacka street toward St. Mary's Church.

Cost and Hours: Museum-8 zł, tower-3 zł; July-Aug Tue-Fri 9:00-17:00, Sat-Sun 10:00-17:00, closed Mon; Sept-June Tue and Thu-Fri 8:00-16:00, Wed 9:00-17:00, Sat-Sun 10:00-16:00, closed Mon; ulica Mariacka 25-26, tel. 58-322-2100, www.archeologia.pl.

▲**Central Maritime Museum (Centralne Muzeum Morskie)**—Gdańsk's history and livelihood are tied to the sea. This collection, spread among several buildings on either side of the river, examines all aspects of this connection. While nautical types may get a thrill out of the creaky, sprawling museum, most visitors find it little more than a convenient way to pass some time and enjoy a cruise across the river. The museum's lack of English information is frustrating; fortunately, some exhibits have descriptions you can borrow.

Cost and Hours: Individually, each of the three parts of the museum costs 8 zł, but an 18-zł ticket gets you in everywhere and also covers the ferry across the river. It's open July-Aug daily 10:00-18:00; Sept-Oct and March-June Tue-Sun 10:00-16:00, closed Mon; Nov-Feb Tue-Sun 10:00-15:00, closed Mon; ulica Ołowianka 9-13, tel. 58-301-8611, www.cmm.pl.

Touring the Museum: The exhibit has three parts, with a fourth on the way. The first is on the Main Town side of the river: The landmark medieval **Crane** (Żuraw)—Gdańsk's most important symbol—houses an exhibit on living in the city during its Golden Age (16th-17th centuries). You can see models of Baltic buildings (including the Crane you're inside), plus traditional tools and costumes. For more on the Crane itself, see page 444. The brand-new **Maritime Cultural Center** is due to open in 2012.

The rest of the museum is across the river on Ołowianka Island, which you can reach via the little **ferry** (*prom*, 1 zł one-way, included in 18-zł museum ticket). The ferry runs about every 15 minutes in peak season (during museum hours only), but frequency declines sharply in the off-season (and it doesn't run if the river freezes). This also gives fine views back on the Crane.

Once on the island, visit the three rebuilt **Old Granaries** (Spichlerze). These make up the heart of the exhibit, tracing the history of Gdańsk—particularly as it relates to the sea—from prehistoric days to the present. Models of the town and region help

put things into perspective. Other exhibits cover underwater exploration, navigational aids, artifacts of the Polish seafaring tradition, peek-a-boo cross-sections of multilevel ships, and models of the modern-day

Lech Wałęsa

In 1980, the world was turned on its ear by a walrus-mustachioed shipyard electrician. Within three years, this seemingly run-of-the-mill Pole had precipitated the collapse of communism, led a massive 10-million-member trade union with enormous political impact, was named *Time* magazine's Man of the Year, and won a Nobel Peace Prize.

Lech Wałęsa was born in Popowo, Poland, in 1943. After working as a car mechanic and serving two years in the army, he became an electrician at the Gdańsk Shipyard in 1967. Like many Poles, Wałęsa felt stifled by the communist government, and was infuriated that a system that was supposed to be for the workers clearly wasn't serving them.

When the shipyard massacre took place in December of 1970 (see description on page 458), Wałęsa was at the forefront of the protests. He was marked as a dissident, and in 1976, he was fired. Wałęsa hopped from job to job and was occasionally unemployed—under communism, a rock-bottom status reserved for only the most despicable derelicts. But he soldiered on, fighting for the creation of a trade union and building up quite a file with the secret police.

In August of 1980, Wałęsa heard news of the beginnings of the Gdańsk strike and raced to the shipyard. In an act that has since become the stuff of legend, Wałęsa scaled the shipyard wall to get inside.

Before long, Wałęsa's dynamic personality won him the unofficial role of the workers' leader and spokesman. He negotiated with the regime to hash out the August Agreements, becoming a rock star-type hero during the so-called 16 Months of Hope...until martial law came crashing down in December of 1981. Wałęsa was arrested and interned for 11 months in a coun-

shipyard where Solidarity was born. This place is home to more miniature ships than you ever thought you'd see, and the Nautical Gallery upstairs features endless rooms with paintings of boats.

Finally, crawl through the holds and scramble across the deck of a decommissioned steamship docked permanently across from the Crane, called the *Sołdek* (ship generally closed in winter). This was the first postwar vessel built at the Gdańsk shipyard. Below decks, you can see where they shoveled the coal; wander through a maze of pipes, gears, valves, gauges, and ladders; and visit the rooms where the sailors lived, slept, and ate. You can even play captain in the bridge.

try house. After being released, he continued to struggle underground, becoming a symbol of anti-communist sentiment.

Finally, the dedication of Wałęsa and Solidarity paid off, and Polish communism dissolved—with Wałęsa rising from the ashes as the country's first post-communist president. But the skills that made Wałęsa a rousing success at leading an uprising didn't translate to the president's office. Wałęsa proved to be a stubborn, headstrong politician, frequently clashing with the parliament. He squabbled with his own party, declaring a "war at the top" of Solidarity and rotating higher-ups to prevent corruption and keep the party fresh. He also didn't choose his advisors well, enlisting several staffers who wound up immersed in scandal. His overconfidence was his Achilles' heel, and his governing style verged on authoritarian.

Unrefined and none too interested in scripted speeches, Wałęsa was a simple man who preferred playing Ping-Pong with his buddies to attending formal state functions. Though lacking a formal education, Wałęsa had unsurpassed drive and charisma... but that's not enough to lead a country—especially during an impossibly complicated, fast-changing time, when even the savviest politician would certainly have stumbled.

Wałęsa was defeated at the polls, by the Poles, in 1995, and when he ran again in 2000, he received a humiliating 1 percent of the vote. Since leaving office, Wałęsa has kept a lower profile, but still delivers speeches worldwide. Many poor Poles grumble that Lech, who started life simple like them, has forgotten the little people. But his fans point out that he gives much of his income to charity. And on his lapel, he still always wears a pin featuring the Black Madonna of Częstochowa—the symbol of Polish Catholicism.

Poles say there are at least two Lech Wałęsas: the young, working-class idealist Lech, at the forefront of the Solidarity strikes, who will always have a special place in their hearts; and the failed President Wałęsa, who got in over his head and tarnished his legacy.

▲▲▲Solidarity (Solidarność) and the Gdańsk Shipyard (Stocznia Gdańska)

Gdańsk's single best experience is exploring the shipyard that witnessed the beginning of the end of communism's stranglehold on Eastern Europe. Here in the former industrial wasteland that Lech Wałęsa called the "cradle of freedom," this evocative site tells the story of the brave Polish shipyard workers who took on—and ultimately defeated—an Evil Empire.

A visit to the Solidarity sights has two main parts: the memorial and gate out in front of the shipyard, and the excellent "Roads to Freedom" exhibit nearby. Begin at the towering monument—

with three anchor-adorned crosses—near the entrance gate to the shipyard, and allow two hours for the whole visit.

Getting to the Shipyard: The Solidarity monument and shipyard are at the north end of the Old Town, about a 20-minute walk from ulica Długa. For the most interesting approach, follow my self-guided "From the Main Town to the Solidarity Shipyard" walk on page 444.

Background: After the communists took over Eastern Europe at the end of World War II, oppressed peoples throughout the Soviet Bloc rose up in different ways. The most dramatic uprisings—Hungary's 1956 Uprising (see page 570) and Czechoslovakia's 1968 "Prague Spring" (see page 47)—were brutally crushed under the treads of Soviet tanks. The formula for freedom that finally succeeded was a patient, decade-long series of strikes spearheaded by Lech Wałęsa and his trade union, called Solidarność— "Solidarity." (The movement also benefited from good timing, as it coincided with the *perestroika* and *glasnost* policies of the Soviet premier Mikhail Gorbachev.) While some American politicians might like to take credit for defeating communism, Wałęsa and his fellow workers were the ones fighting on the front lines, armed with nothing more than guts.

Monument of the Fallen Shipyard Workers

The seeds of August 1980 were sown a decade before. Since becoming part of the Soviet Bloc, the Poles staged frequent strikes,

protests, and uprisings to secure their rights, all of which were put down by the regime. But the bloodiest of these took place in December of 1970—a tragic event memorialized by this monument.

The 1970 strike was prompted by price hikes. The communist government set the prices for all products. As Poland endured drastic food shortages in the 1960s and 1970s, the regime frequently announced what it called "regulation of prices." Invariably, this meant an increase in the cost of essential foodstuffs. (To be able to claim "regulation" rather than "increase," the regime would symbolically lower prices for a few select items—but these were always nonessential luxuries, such as elevators and TV sets, which nobody could afford anyway.) The regime was usually smart enough to raise prices on January 1—when the people were fat and happy after Christmas, and too hung-over to complain. But on December 12, 1970, bolstered by an ego-stoking visit by West German Chancellor Willy Brandt, Polish premier

Władysław Gomułka increased prices. The people of Poland—
who cared more about the price of Christmas dinner than relations
with Germany—struck back.

A wave of strikes and sit-ins spread along the heavily industrialized north coast of Poland, most notably in Gdańsk, Gdynia,
and Szczecin. Thousands of angry demonstrators poured through
the gate of this shipyard, marched into town, and set fire to the
Communist Party Committee building. In an attempt to quell the
riots, the government-run radio implored the people to go back
to work. On the morning of December 17, workers showed up at
shipyard gates across northern Poland—and were greeted by the
army and police. Without provocation, the Polish army opened
fire on the workers. While the official death toll for the massacre stands at 44, others say the true number is much higher. This
monument, with a trio of 140-foot-tall crosses, honors those lost to
the regime that December.

Go to the middle of the wall behind the crosses, to the
monument of the worker wearing a flimsy plastic work helmet,
attempting to shield himself from bullets. Behind him is a list—
pockmarked with symbolic bullet holes—of workers murdered
on that day. *Lat* means "years old"—many teenagers were among
the dead. The quote at the top of the wall is from Pope John Paul
II, who was elected eight years after this tragedy. The Pope was
known for his clever way with words, and this very carefully
phrased quote—which served as an inspiration to the Poles during
their darkest hours—skewers the regime in a way subtle enough to
still be tolerated: "Let thy spirit descend, and renew the face of the
earth—*this* earth" (that is, Poland). Below that is the dedication:
"They gave their lives so you can live decently."

Stretching to the left of this center wall are plaques representing labor unions from around Poland—and around the world
(look for the Chinese characters)—expressing solidarity with these
workers. To the right is an enormous Bible verse: "May the Lord
give strength to his people. May the Lord bless his people with the
gift of peace" (Psalms 29:11).

More than a decade after the massacre, this monument was
finally constructed. It marked the first time a communist regime
ever allowed a monument to be built to honor its own victims.
Wałęsa called it a harpoon in the heart of the communists. Inspired
by the brave sacrifice of their true comrades, the shipyard workers
rose up here in August of 1980, formulating the "21 Points" of a
new union called Solidarity. The demands included the right to
strike and form unions, the freeing of political prisoners, and an
increase in wages. These 21 Points are listed in Polish on the panel
at the far end of the right wall, marked *21 X TAK Solidarność* ("21
times yes Solidarity").

• *Now continue to the gate and peer through into the birthplace of Eastern European freedom.*

Gdańsk Shipyard (Stocznia Gdańska) Gate #2

When a Pole named Karol Wojtyła was elected Pope in 1978—and visited his homeland in 1979—he inspired his 40 million countrymen to believe that impossible dreams can come true. Prices continued to go up, and the workers continued to rise up. By the summer of 1980, it was clear that the dam was about to break.

In August, Anna Walentynowicz—a Gdańsk crane operator and known dissident—was fired unceremoniously just short of her retirement. This sparked a strike in the Gdańsk Shipyard (then called the Lenin Shipyard) on August 14, 1980. An electrician named Lech Wałęsa had been fired as an agitator years before and wasn't allowed into the yard. But on hearing news of the strike, Wałęsa went to the shipyard and climbed over the wall to get inside. The strike now had a leader.

Imagine being one of the 16,000 workers who stayed here for 18 days during the strike—hungry, cold, sleeping on sheets of Styrofoam, inspired by the new Polish pope, excited about finally standing up to the regime...and terrified that at any moment you might be gunned down, like your friends had been a decade before. Workers, afraid to leave the shipyard, communicated with the outside world through this gate—wives and brothers showed up here and asked for a loved one, and those inside spread the word until the striker came forward. Occasionally, a truck pulled up inside the gate, with Lech Wałęsa standing atop its cab with a megaphone. Facing the thousands of people assembled outside the gate, Wałęsa gave progress reports on the negotiations and pleaded for supplies. The people of Gdańsk responded, bringing armfuls of bread and other food to keep the workers going. This truly was Solidarity.

During the strike, two items hung on the fence. One of them (which still hangs there today) was a picture of Pope John Paul II—a reminder to believe in your dreams and have faith in God (for more on the pope and his role in Solidarity, see page 298). The other item was a makeshift list of the strikers' 21 Points—demands scrawled in red paint and black pencil on pieces of plywood.
• *You'll likely see construction in the area beyond the gate.*

Today's Shipyard

This part of the shipyard, long abandoned, is gradually being redeveloped into a **"Young City"** (Młode Miasto)—envisioned as a new city center for Gdańsk, with shopping, restaurants, and homes. Rusting shipbuilding equipment will be torn down, and old brick buildings will be converted into gentrified flats. Just behind the monument will be the new European Center of Solidarity (still an active union in some countries). The shipyard gate, monument, and other important sites from the Solidarity strikes will stay put. Work will likely wrap up in 2013.

• *Walk to the right and go through the gate.*

The path leading into the shipyard passes through two huge **symbolic gateways.** The first resembles the rusted hull of a ship, representing the protest of the shipbuilders. The next gateway—a futuristic, colorful tower—is a small-scale contemporary reinterpretation of a 1,000-foot-tall monument planned in 1919 by the prominent Russian constructivist artist Vladimir Tatlin. Tatlin's unrealized design represented the optimism of the communist "utopia" before it was fatally perverted by totalitarianism.

The path leads to a low-profile, red-brick building—the **BHP Conference Hall,** where the communists sat down across the table from Lech Wałęsa and worked out a compromise. Today it houses an interesting exhibition about that page of history.

• *The museum where we'll learn the rest of the story is about 100 yards back toward the Main Town. With the main shipyard gate to your back, walk straight ahead, passing the green-and-yellow building on your right. Cross the street and walk toward the green skyscraper. After about a block, note the stairs leading underground, into the...*

"Roads to Freedom" Exhibit

This small but outstanding museum captures (better than any other sight in the country) the Polish reality under communism, and traces the step-by-step evolution of the Solidarity movement.

Cost and Hours: 6 zł, 2 zł on Wed; open May-Sept Tue-Sun 10:00-18:00, Oct-April Tue-Sun 10:00-17:00, closed Mon year-round; Wały Piastowskie 24, tel. 58-308-4428, museum: www.ecs .gda.pl, organization: www.fcs.org.pl.

◐ Self-Guided Tour: Walk downstairs—startled by angry shouts from the ZOMO—and buy your ticket, which is designed to look like the communist ration coupons that all Poles had to carry and present before they could buy certain goods. Cashiers would stand with scissors at the ready, prepared to snip off a corner of your coupon after making the sale. Consider picking up a Solidarity book or other souvenir at the excellent gift shop here before moving on.

To the right of the ticket desk are some depressing reminders of the communist days. The phone booth is marked *Automat Nieczynny*—"Out of Order"—as virtually all phone booths were back then. In the humble, authentic commie WC, notice that instead of toilet paper, there's a wad of old newspapers. Actual toilet paper was cause for celebration. Notice the mannequin with several rolls on a string around her neck—time to party!

Across from the ticket desk is a typical **Polish shop** (marked *spożyw*, a truncated version of *spożywczy*, "grocery store") from the 1970s, at the worst of the food shortages. Great selection, eh? Often the only things in stock were vinegar and mustard. Milk and bread were generally available, but they were low quality—it wasn't unusual to find a cigarette butt in your loaf. The few blocks of cheese and other items in the case weren't real—they were props, placed there so the shop wouldn't look completely empty. Sometimes they'd hang a few pitiful, phony salamis from the hooks—otherwise, people might think it was a tile shop. The only real meat in here were the flies on the flypaper. Despite the meager supplies, shoppers (mostly women) would sometimes have to wait in line literally all day long just to pick over these scant choices. People didn't necessarily buy what they needed; instead, they'd buy anything that could be bartered on the black market. On the counter, notice the little jar holding clipped-off ration coupons.

Continue into the exhibit. The first room explains the **roots** of the shipyard strikes, including the famous uprisings in Hungary and Czechoslovakia, and the December 1970 riots in Poland. (Interactive computer screens tell you more about these events.) The prison cell is a reminder of Stalin's strong-arm tactics for getting the people of Eastern Europe to sign on to his new system.

Then head into the heart of the exhibit, **August 1980.** Near the plaster statue of Lenin are several tables. These were the actual tables used (in the red-brick building back in the shipyard) when the communist authorities finally agreed to negotiate after 18 days of protests. On the afternoon of August 31, 1980, the Governmental Commission and the Inter-Factory Strike Committee (MKS) came together and signed the August Agreements, which legalized Solidarity—the first time any communist government permitted a workers' union. Photos and a video show the giddy day, as the Polish Bob Dylan laments the evils of the regime. Lech Wałęsa— sitting at the big table, with his characteristic walrus moustache— signed the agreement with a big, red, souvenir-type pen adorned with a picture of Pope John Paul II (displayed across the room). Other union reps, sitting at smaller tables, tape-recorded the proceedings, and played them later at their own factories to prove that the unthinkable had happened. Near the end of this room are replicas of the plywood boards featuring the 21 Points, which hung on the front gate we just saw.

While the government didn't take the agreements very seriously, the Poles did...and before long, 10 million of them—one out of every four—joined Solidarity. So began the **16 Months**

of Hope—the theme of the next room. Newly legal, Solidarity continued to stage strikes and make its opposition known. Slick Solidarity posters and children's art convey the childlike enthusiasm with which the Poles seized their hard-won kernels of freedom. The poster with a baby in a Solidarity T-shirt—one year old, just like the union itself—captures the sense of hope. The communist authorities' hold on the Polish people began to slip. The rest of the Soviet Bloc looked on nervously, and the Warsaw Pact army assembled at the Polish border and glared at the uprisers. The threat of invasion hung heavy in the air.

Turn the corner to see Solidarity's progress come crashing down. On Sunday morning, December 13, 1981, the Polish head of state, General Wojciech Jaruzelski, appeared on national TV and announced the introduction of **martial law.** Solidarity was outlawed, and its leaders were arrested. Frightened Poles heard the announcement and looked out their windows to see Polish Army tanks rumbling through the snowy streets. Jaruzelski claimed that he imposed martial law to prevent the Soviets from invading. Today, many historians question whether martial law was really necessary—though Jaruzelski remains unremorseful. Martial law was a tragic, terrifying, and bleak time for the Polish people. It didn't, however, kill the Solidarity movement, which continued its fight after going underground. Notice that the movement's martial-law-era propaganda was produced with far more primitive printing equipment than their earlier posters.

In the next room, you see a clandestine print shop like those used to create that illegal propaganda. Surrounding the room are sobering displays of **ZOMO riot gear.** A film reveals the ugliness of martial law. Watch the footage of General Jaruzelski—wearing his trademark dark glasses—reading the announcement of martial law. Chilling scenes show riots, demonstrations, and crackdowns by the ZOMO police—including one in which a demonstrator is run over by a truck. An old woman is stampeded by a pack of fleeing demonstrators.

The next room shows a film tracing the whole history of **communism in Poland** (with a copy of Lech Wałęsa's Nobel Peace Prize).

For a happy ending, head into the final room, with an uplifting film about the **fall of the Iron Curtain** across Eastern Europe—right up through the 2004 "Orange Revolution" in Ukraine.

Here's how it happened in Poland: By the time the Pope visited his homeland again in 1983, martial law had finally been lifted, and Solidarity—still technically illegal—was gaining momentum, gradually pecking away at the communists. With the moral support of the Pope and the entire Western world, the brave Poles were the first European country to throw off the shackles of communism when, in the spring of 1989, the "Round Table Talks" led to the opening up of elections. The government arrogantly called for parliamentary elections, reserving 65 percent of seats for themselves. The plan backfired, as virtually every open seat went to Solidarity. This success inspired people all over Eastern Europe, and by that winter, the Berlin Wall had crumbled and the Czechs and Slovaks had staged their Velvet Revolution. Lech Wałęsa—the shipyard electrician who started it all by jumping over a wall—became the first president of post-communist Poland. And a year later, in Poland's first true elections since World War II, 29 different parties won seats in the parliament. This celebration of democracy was brought to the Polish people by the workers of Gdańsk.

South of the Main Town

A 10- to 15-minute walk south of the Main Town, these two sights are probably not worth the trek on a short visit.

National Museum in Gdańsk (Muzeum Narodowe w Gdańsku)—This art collection, housed in what was a 15th-century Franciscan monastery, is worth ▲▲ to art-lovers for one reason: Hans Memling's glorious *Last Judgment* triptych altarpiece, one of the two most important pieces of art to be seen in Poland (the other is da Vinci's *Lady with an Ermine*, usually in Kraków's Czartoryski Museum). If you're not a purist, you can settle for seeing the much smaller replica in St. Mary's Church. But if medieval art is your bag, make the 10-minute walk here from the Main Town.

Cost and Hours: 15 zł, Tue-Wed and Fri-Sat 10:00-18:00, Thu and Sun 12:00-19:00, closed Mon, last entry 45 minutes before closing; walk 10 minutes due south from ulica Długa's Golden Gate, take pedestrian underpass beneath the big cross-street, then continue down the busy street until you see signs for the museum; ulica Toruńska 1, tel. 58-301-7061, www.muzeum.narodowe.gda.pl.

Touring the Museum: From the entry, the altarpiece by Hans Memling (c. 1440-1494) is at the top of the stairs and to the right. The history of the painting is as interesting as the work itself. It was commissioned in the mid-15th century by the Medicis' banker in Florence, Angelo di Jacopo Tani. The ship delivering the painting from Belgium to Florence was hijacked by a Gdańsk pirate, who brought the altarpiece to his hometown to be displayed in St. Mary's Church. For centuries, kings, emperors, and czars admired it from afar, until Napoleon seized it in the early 19th century and took it to Paris to hang in the Louvre. Gdańsk finally got the painting back, only to have it exiled again—this time into St. Petersburg's Hermitage Museum—after World War II. On its return to Gdańsk in 1956, this museum claimed it—though St. Mary's wants it back.

Have a close look at Memling's well-traveled work. It's the end of the world, and Christ rides in on a rainbow to judge humankind. Angels blow reveille, waking the dead, who rise from their graves. The winged archangel Michael—dressed for battle and wielding the cross like a weapon—weighs the grace in each person, sending them either to the fires of hell (right panel) or up the sparkling-crystal stairway to heaven (left).

It takes all 70 square feet of paneling to contain this awesome scene. Jam-packed with dozens of bodies, a Bible's worth of symbolism, and executed with astonishing detail, the painting can keep even a non-art-lover occupied. Notice the serene, happy expressions of the righteous, as they're greeted by St. Peter (with his giant key) and clothed by angels. And pity the condemned, their faces filled with terror and sorrow as they're tortured by grotesque devils more horrifying than anything Hollywood could devise.

Tune into the exquisite details: the angels' robes, the devils' genetic-mutant features, the portrait of the man in the scale (a Medici banker), Michael's peacock wings. Get as close as you can to the globe at Christ's feet and Michael's shining breastplate: You can just make out the whole scene in mirror reflection. Then back up and take it all in—three panels connected by a necklace of bodies that curves downward through hell, crosses the earth, then rises up to the towers of the New Jerusalem. On the back side of the triptych are reverent portraits of the painting's patron, Angelo Tani, and his new bride, Catarina.

Beyond the Memling, the remainder of the collection isn't too thrilling. The rest of the upstairs has more Flemish and Dutch art, as well as paintings from Gdańsk's Golden Age and various works by Polish artists. The ground floor features a cavernous, all-white cloister filled with Gothic altarpiece sculptures, gold and silver wares, majolica and Delft porcelain, and characteristic Gdańsk-style furniture.

"Blue Lion" Archaeological Education Center (Centrum Edukacji Archeologicznej "Błękitny Lew")—Hiding far from the Main Town on Granary Island, this kid-friendly exhibit re-creates the atmosphere of medieval Gdańsk. Occupying a rebuilt granary called the "Blue Lion," its highlight is a full-scale replica of an atmospheric medieval street, populated by mannequins whose features are based on actual human remains. Also telling the tale are artifacts from the period, a selection of films (subtitled in English), and touchscreens that provide some background. While information is a bit sparse (especially along the medieval street), the collection tries hard not to be just another fuddy-duddy, dusty old museum, making it popular with kids on field trips.

Cost and Hours: 10 zł, May-Aug Tue-Sun 10:00-18:00, Sept-April Tue-Sun 9:00-17:00, closed Mon year-round, ulica Chmielna 53, tel. 58-320-3188, www.archeologia.pl.

Outer Gdańsk

These two sights—worthwhile only to those with a special interest—are each within the city limits of Gdańsk, but they take some serious time to see round-trip.

Oliwa Cathedral (Katedra Oliwska)—The suburb of Oliwa, at the northern edge of Gdańsk, is home to this visually striking church. The quirky, elongated facade hides a surprisingly long and skinny nave. The ornately decorated 18th-century organ over the main entrance features angels and stars that move around when the organ is played. While locals are proud of this place, it's hard to justify the effort it takes to get out here. Skip it unless you just love Polish churches or you're going to a concert.

Concerts: The animated organ performs its 20-minute show frequently, especially in summer (concerts at the top of each hour: July-Aug Mon-Fri 10:00-13:00 & 15:00-17:00, Sat 10:00-15:00, Sun 15:00-17:00; June Mon-Sat 10:00-13:00 & 15:00-16:00, Sun 15:00-17:00; May and Sept Mon-Sat 10:00-13:00, Sun at 15:00 and 16:00; 1-2/day off-season, www.archikatedraoliwa.pl). Confirm the schedule at the TI before making the trip. Note that on Sundays and holidays, there are no concerts before 15:00.

Getting There: Oliwa is about six miles northwest of central Gdańsk, on the way to Sopot and Gdynia. To get to Oliwa, you have two options: Take **tram** #6 or #12 from Gdańsk's main train station. These trams let you off right at the entrance to Oliwski Park. Go straight through to the back of the park; near the end, you can see the copper roof and two skinny, pointy spires of the cathedral on your right. Exit through the back of the park, bear right, and go one block to find the entrance to the church. Your other option is to take a **commuter SKM train** from Gdańsk's main train station 15 minutes to the "Gdańsk Oliwa" stop (see "Getting Around the Tri-City," page 476). From the Oliwa train station, it's a 15-minute walk or 10-zł taxi ride to the cathedral. Walk straight ahead out of the station and turn right when you get to the busy road. Cross the road at the light and enter the tree-filled Park Oliwski at the corner, then follow the directions above.

Westerplatte—World War II began on September 1, 1939, when Adolf Hitler sent the warship *Schleswig-Holstein* to attack this Polish munitions depot, which was guarding Gdańsk's harbor. Though it may interest serious WWII history buffs, most visitors will find little to see here aside from a modest museum, a towering monument, and some old bunkers. As it's surrounded by shipyard sprawl, it's not a particularly scenic trip, either.

Getting There: The most enjoyable approach is on a cruise—either on a modern boat, or on the fun old-fashioned galleons (45-50 minutes each way; see page 474). You can also take **bus #106** from Brama Wyżynna (just outside the Main Town) to the end (about 30 minutes).

Shopping in Gdańsk

The big story in Gdańsk is amber *(bursztyn),* a fossil resin available in all shades, shapes, and sizes (see the "All About Amber" sidebar, earlier). While you'll see amber sold all over town, the best place to browse and buy is along the atmospheric ulica Mariacka (between the Motława River and St. Mary's Church). This pretty street, with old-fashioned balconies and dozens of display cases, is fun to wander even if you're not a shopper. Other good places to buy amber are along the riverfront embankment and on ulica Długa. To avoid rip-offs—such as amber that's been melted and reshaped—always buy it from a shop, not from someone standing on the street. (But note that most shops also have a display case and salesperson out front, which are perfectly legit.) Prices everywhere are about the same, so rather than seeking out a specific place, just window-shop until you see what you want. Styles range from gaudy necklaces with huge globs of amber, to tasteful smaller pendants in silver settings, to cheap trinkets. All shades of amber—from near-white to dark brown—cost about the same, but you'll pay more for inclusions (bugs or other objects stuck in the amber).

Gdańsk also has several modern shopping malls, most of them in the Old Town or near the main train station. The walk between the Main Town and the Solidarity shipyard goes past some of the best malls (see page 446).

Sleeping in Gdańsk

Gdańsk's accommodations scene is booming. New hotels open every year, forcing dreary old ones to up their standards and/or lower their rates. Even with all those new rooms, many hotels are booked up (mostly with German tourists) in peak season (mid-June-mid-Sept), when prices increase—book ahead.

Across the River

These hotels are across the river from the Main Town. While that puts you a bit farther from the sightseeing action, it's a relatively short walk (no more than 10 minutes from any of these), and the rooms are a better value.

Sleep Code

(3 zł = about $1, country code: 48)

S = Single, **D** = Double/Twin, **T** = Triple, **Q** = Quad, **b** = bathroom, **s** = shower only. Unless otherwise noted, English is spoken, credit cards are accepted, and breakfast is included.

To help you easily sort through these listings, I've divided the accommodations into three categories, based on the price for a double room with bath during high season:

$$$ Higher Priced—Most rooms 400 zł or more.
$$ Moderately Priced—Most rooms between 300-400 zł.
$ Lower Priced—Most rooms 300 zł or less.

Prices can change without notice; verify the hotel's current rates online or by email. For other updates, see www.ricksteves.com/update.

$$$ Hotel Królewski, a classy hotel in a beautifully renovated red-brick granary, offers 30 stylish rooms, good rates, and a friendly staff. It's just beyond the three granaries of the Central Maritime Museum, across the river from the Crane (Sb-380 zł, Db-470 zł, fancier suite-like Db "plus"-520 zł, pricier apartments, lower rates mid-Oct-April, 50 zł to reserve a view room—or try asking for one when you check in for no extra charge, non-smoking rooms, elevator, free Wi-Fi, good restaurant, ulica Ołowianka 1, tel. 58-326-1111, fax 58-326-1110, www.hotelkrolewski.pl, office @hotelkrolewski.pl). You can commute to your sightseeing by ferry (take the 1-zł boat trip across the river offered by the Maritime Museum). But the ferry runs only during the museum's opening hours, and is sporadic off-season. If the ferry isn't running, it's a scenic 10-minute walk along the river and over the bridge into the Main Town.

$$$ Hotel Gdańsk is a splurge hotel over a brewpub. Also in a rehabbed granary across the river from the embankment, it's a bit closer to the Main Town than the Królewski. The 90 elegant rooms are divided between the old granary (with tiny windows and big beams) and a modern annex (Mon-Thu: Sb-490 zł, Db-590 zł, bigger "premium" Db-630 zł; Fri-Sun: Sb-460 zł, Db-560 zł, premium Db-590 zł; cheaper Nov-March, elevator, free Internet access and Wi-Fi, sauna and spa, ulica Szafarina 9, tel. 58-300-1717, www.hotelgdansk.pl, rezerwacja@hotelgdansk.pl).

On Ulica Spichrzowa: Several small, similar, relatively new hotels are on the back side of a charmingly restored row of colorful houses on the island just across the river from the main drag.

While they overlook a dreary vacant lot, these places (and others on the same street) offer a good value in a convenient location. As these buildings are tall and skinny, expect plenty of stairs and no elevator. **$$ Willa Litarion** is run by the eager Owsikowski family. Each of the 13 small rooms has a totally different design, but all are artsy and mod (Sb-255 zł, Db-330 zł, bigger "deluxe" Db-360 zł, 20-25 percent cheaper Oct-April, extra bed-60 zł, free cable Internet, parking garage-30 zł, ulica Spichrzowa 18, tel. 58-320-2553, fax 58-320-2563, www.litarion.pl, recepcja@litarion.pl). **$$ Willa Biała Lilia** ("Villa of the White Lily"), next door, has 14 uninspired but modern and comfortable rooms (Sb-260 zł, Db-340 zł, extra bed-70 zł, slightly cheaper Oct-April, free Wi-Fi, reserve ahead for parking garage-30 zł, ulica Spichrzowa 16, tel. 58-301-7074, fax 58-320-1473, www.bialalilia.pl, bialalilia@bialalilia.pl).

$$ Dom Muzyka rents 87 simple, tidy rooms in a nondescript residential neighborhood. The catch: It's very difficult to find, hiding in the back of the big Academy of Music building (Akademia Muzyczna). But the prices are worth the hunt, and once you're set up, it's an easy 10-minute walk to the sights. Their "deluxe" rooms, mostly twins, are bigger and overlook the quiet courtyard; most of the standard rooms face a busy street but have good windows and air-conditioning (Sb-250 zł, standard Db-340 zł, deluxe Db-360 zł, apartment-500 zł, extra bed-100 zł, cheaper Oct-April, elevator, free Internet access and Wi-Fi, popular with tour groups, good restaurant, ulica Łąkowa 1-2, tel. 58-326-0600, fax 58-326-0601, www.dommuzyka.pl, biuro@dommuzyka.pl). From the Main Town's Green Gate, cross the two bridges, then walk a long block along the modern commercial building and turn right just before the park (on Łąkowa, across from the big brick church). Walk to the end of this block; before the busy road, go through the gate just before the big yellow-brick building on the right. Once inside the gate checkpoint, the hotel is around the back of the yellow building, the farthest door down. If you get lost, just ask people, "Hotel?"

In the Main Town

You'll pay a premium to sleep in the Main Town itself, but many find it worth the extra expense.

$$ Hotel Wolne Miasto ("Free City") offers rich, wood-carved public spaces with photos of old Gdańsk and 67 elegant, well-priced rooms on the edge of the Main Town, just two blocks from the main drag. Since it's above a popular disco that gets noisy on weekends (Thu-Sat nights), request a quieter room when you reserve (Sb-350 zł, Db-400 zł, bigger "deluxe" Db-500 zł, cheaper Oct-March, air-con in some rooms, elevator, free Internet access and Wi-Fi, ulica Świętego Ducha 2, tel. 58-322-2442, fax 58-322-2447, www.hotelwm.pl, rezerwacja@hotelwm.pl).

$$ Gotyk House, a good value, is run with warmth and pride by the Rybicki family. Owner Andrzej is an energetic armchair historian who works hard to make his little hotel comfortable while still respecting the sanctity of what's supposedly Gdańsk's oldest house. The chimes from St. Mary's Church, next door, provide a pleasant soundtrack. The cellar houses a gingerbread museum and small shrine to Copernicus (whose longtime lover may have lived here). The seven straightforward rooms share a tiny breakfast room, so you'll have to tell them what time you'd like to eat (Sb-280 zł, Db-310 zł, cheaper Oct-April, free Wi-Fi in most rooms, tight public spaces, ulica Mariacka 1, tel. 58-301-8567, mobile 516-141-133, www.gotykhouse.eu, reservation@gotykhouse.eu).

$$ Kamienica Goldwasser, renting seven rooms over a recommended restaurant, is perfectly located, right on the river embankment next door to the Crane. Each room is different, but all are thoughtfully decorated, with windows facing both the river and the back. Three smaller rooms—similar to the bigger rooms, but with tight bathrooms, are an especially good value (small Sb-240 zł, big Sb-340 zł, small Db-340 zł, big Db-440 zł, extra bed-100 zł, lots of stairs and no elevator, free Wi-Fi, Długie Pobrzeże 22, tel. 58-301-8878, fax 58-301-1244, www.goldwasser.pl, kamienica@goldwasser.pl).

$ Dom Harcerza is a Polish-style budget hotel/hostel with 21 old, musty, but well-maintained rooms on the second floor of a dreary office building. This institutional-feeling place won't win any prizes for personality, and communication can be difficult, but it's cheap and nicely located in a corner of the Main Town just two blocks south of the Golden Gate (S-60 zł, D-120 zł, Db-200 zł, T-150 zł, Tb-252 zł, Q-160 zł, 25 percent cheaper Oct-April, includes sheets, breakfast-9 zł, cash only, all twin beds, ground-floor café, ulica Za Murami 2-10, tel. 58-301-3621, fax 58-301-2472, www.domharcerza.pl, rezerwacje@domharcerza.pl).

$ Przy Targu Rybnym, a three-minute walk from the Crane at the north end of the embankment, is Gdańsk's most central hostel. Waldemar runs this easygoing, low-key, slightly grungy place with a spirit of fun that permeates the chummy common room. Aside from dorm beds, it offers private rooms for two to four people, most with shared bathrooms down the hall (bunk in dorm or crowded basement slumbermill-55 zł, D-200 zł, Db-250 zł, T-240 zł, Q-280 zł, cheaper Sept-April, prices include sheets and breakfast, free Internet access, 20-zł laundry service, ulica Grodzka 21, tel. 58-301-5627, www.gdanskhostel.com.pl, gdansk hostel@hotmail.com).

Eating in Gdańsk

In addition to traditional Polish fare, Gdańsk has some fine Baltic seafood. Herring *(śledź)* is popular here, as is cod *(dorsz)*. Natives brag that their salmon *(łosoś)* is better than Norway's. For a stiff drink, sample *Goldwasser* (similar to Goldschlager). This sweet and strong liqueur, flecked with gold, was supposedly invented here in Gdańsk. The following options are all in the Main Town, within three blocks of ulica Długa.

Budget Restaurants in the City Center

These two places are remarkably cheap, tasty, quick, and wonderfully convenient—on or very near ulica Długa. They're worth considering even if you're not on a tight budget.

Bar pod Rybą ("Under the Fish") is nirvana for fans of baked potatoes *(pieczony ziemniak)*. They offer more than 20 varieties, piled high with a wide variety of toppings and sauces, from Mexican beef to herring to Polish cheeses. They also serve fish dishes with salad and potatoes, making this a cheap place to sample local seafood. The tasteful decor—walls lined with old bottles, antique wooden hangers, and paintings by the owner—is squeezed into a single cozy room packed with happy eaters. In the summer, order inside, and they'll bring your food to you at an outdoor table (potatoes and fish dishes are each about 15-25 zł, daily 10:00-22:00, ulica Piwna 61/63, tel. 58-305-1307).

Bar Mleczny Neptun is your best milk-bar option in the Main Town. A hearty meal, including a drink, runs about 15-20 zł. This popular place has more charm than your typical institutional milk bar, including outdoor seating along the most scenic stretch of the main drag, and an upstairs dining room overlooking it all. Most of the items on the counter are for display—rather than take what's there, point to what you want and they'll dish it up fresh (Mon-Fri 7:30-18:00, until 20:00 in summer, Sat-Sun 10:00-17:00, free Wi-Fi, ulica Długa 33-34, tel. 58-301-4988). For more on milk bars, see page 269.

On the Riverfront Embankment

Perhaps the most appealing dining zone in Gdańsk stretches along the riverfront embankment near the Crane. On a balmy summer evening, the outdoor tables here are enticing. As it's a popular area, consider scouting a table during your sightseeing, and reserve your choice for dinner later that night. While you have several good options along here, the following are particularly well-regarded.

Kamienica Goldwasser, which also rents rooms (see listing on page 470), offers good Polish and international cuisine at fair prices. Choose between cozy, romantic indoor seating on several levels, or scenic outdoor seating (most main dishes 40-60 zł, daily 10:00-24:00, occasional live music, Długie Pobrzeże 22, tel. 58-301-8878).

Baryłka ("Barrel"), next door to Goldwasser, has a similar menu and outdoor seating. The elegant upstairs dining room, with windows overlooking the river, is appealing (40-65-zł main dishes, daily 9:00-24:00, Długie Pobrzeże 24, tel. 58-301-4938).

Sushi 77, serving up a wide selection of surprisingly good sushi right next to the Crane, is a refreshing break from ye olde Polish food. Choose between the outdoor tables bathed in red light, or the mod interior (30-50-zł sushi sets, daily 12:00-23:00, Długie Pobrzeże 30, tel. 58-682-1823).

Targ Rybny/Fishmarkt ("The Fish Market")—run by the Goldwasser people (see listing, page 470)—is farther up the embankment, overlooking a park and parking lot. The outdoor seating isn't too scenic, but the warm, mellow-yellow nautical ambience inside is pleasant, making this a good bad-weather option. It features classy but not stuffy service, and an emphasis on fish (most main dishes 30-50 zł, plus pricier seafood splurges, daily 10:00-23:00, ulica Targ Rybny 6C, tel. 58-320-9011).

Other Restaurants in Central Gdańsk

Czerwone Drzwi ("The Red Door") serves up tasty Polish and international cuisine in a single-room, six-table restaurant. The decor is artsy, and there's live piano music nightly at 19:00; at other times, recorded jazz sets the mood (22-28-zł pierogi, big 20-25-zł salads, 30-45-zł main dishes, daily 10:00-22:00, ulica Piwna 52/53, tel. 58-301-5764).

Dom pod Łososiem ("House Under the Salmon") is a venerable old standby with over-the-top formality. This place will make you feel like a rich burgher's family invited you over for dinner (right down to the greeting by a stiff, bow-tied maître d'). This elegant splurge restaurant has been serving guests for more than 400 years, racking up an impressive guest list (some pictured in the lobby)—and, somewhere in there, inventing *Goldwasser*. Reservations are smart for dinner (most main dishes 50-80 zł, emphasis on fish, small portions, daily 12:00-23:00, ulica Szeroka 52-54, tel. 58-301-7652).

Coffee and Sweets

Gdańsk's Main Town is full of hip cafés that lure in young people with long menus of exotic coffee drinks and tasty cakes. Here are two good options—one new, one old.

Pikawa (as in "3.14 Coffee," pronounced "pee-kah-vah") is a trendy, atmospheric café with a wide variety of coffee drinks and herbal teas, best accompanied by the delicious *szarlotka* (Polish apple cake). The decor is cozy Old World, the outdoor seating is pleasant, and the café is packed with socializing locals (8-16-zł cakes, daily 10:00-22:00, until 24:00 in summer, ulica Piwna 5-6, tel. 58-309-1444).

Cukiernia Kaliszczak, a bakery right on ulica Długa, is a no-frills throwback to the communist days. It's cheap but not cheery, with delicious 3-zł cakes and ice cream and no-nonsense service—just line up and place your order, comrade. If you want ice cream, order first at the register rather than at the display case (daily 9:00-22:00, ulica Długa 74, tel. 58-301-0895).

Gdańsk Connections

By Train

Gdańsk is well-connected to the Tri-City via the commuter SKM trains (explained later, under "Getting Around the Tri-City"). It also has frequent connections to Warsaw and handy night trains to Berlin and Kraków. You'll likely encounter some disruptions, however, as new high-speed rail lines are built between Gdańsk and points south (aiming to be complete in 2012).

From Gdańsk by Train to: Hel (town on Hel Peninsula, 3/day direct July-Aug only, 2.25-3.25 hours; otherwise about hourly with transfer in Gdynia), **Malbork** (about 2/hour, 40-50 minutes), **Toruń** (6/day direct, 3.25-3.75 hours; at least hourly with a transfer in Bydgoszcz, 3-4 hours), **Warsaw** (9/day, 5.5-6.5 hours—but will drop to 3 hours when new line is finished), **Kraków** (4/day direct, 2 more with change in Warsaw, 8.5 hours—shorter when new rail line is complete; plus 2 night trains, 10.5-11.5 hours), **Berlin** (4/day, 7-7.5 hours, transfer in Szczecin or Poznań).

By Boat

Various boats depart from Gdańsk's embankment to nearby destinations, including **Westerplatte** (the monument marking where World War II started) and **Hel** (the beachy peninsula, described below). While boats also run sporadically to Sopot and Gdynia, the train is better for those trips (described under "Getting Around the Tri-City," later). As these boat schedules tend to change from year to year, confirm your plans carefully at the TI. All boat trips are weather permitting, especially the faster hydrofoils. In shoulder season (April-June and Sept-Oct), even though most boats stop running from Gdańsk, several routes still run between Sopot, Gdynia, and Hel. Boats generally don't run in winter (Nov-March).

To Westerplatte: To travel by boat to the monument at Westerplatte, you have two options. It's more enjoyable to ride the replica **17th-century galleons,** either the *Galeon Lew* ("Lion Galleon") or the *Czerna Perła*
("Black Pearl"). These over-the-top, touristy boats depart hourly from near the Crane for a lazy 1.5-hour round-trip cruise to Westerplatte and back. (You can choose to get off at Westerplatte after 45 minutes and take a later boat back.) The *Czerna Perła* has English commentary; both boats

often have live nautical music on the return trip (if you've ever wanted to hear "What Shall We Do with a Drunken Sailor?" in Polish, here's your chance). It's not exactly pretty—you'll see more industry than scenery—but it's a fun excuse to set sail, even if you don't care about Westerplatte (40 zł round-trip, 27 zł one-way, the two boats take turns departing at the top of each hour 10:00-19:00 in July-Aug, fewer departures May-June and Sept, from the embankment near the Crane, mobile 501-571-383, www.rejsy turystyczne.pl). The duller alternative is to take a modern **Żegluga Gdańska** boat (45 zł round-trip, 30 zł one-way, 50 minutes each way, daily April-Oct, 3-6/day in each direction, www.zegluga.pl).

To Hel: Various boats—mostly the ZTM "ferry trams" *(tramwaj wodny)*—zip out to Hel in two hours three times a day from June through August, with a stop in Sopot (sometimes also runs on weekends in shoulder season; 20 zł each way, carefully confirm departure point, which can change but will likely be at the north end of the embankment, past the Crane).

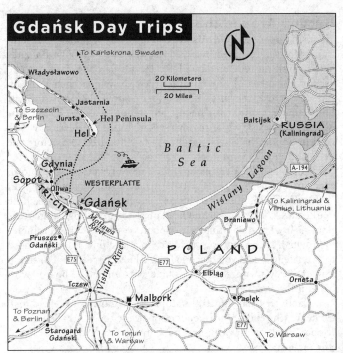

Near Gdańsk: The Tri-City (Trójmiasto)

Gdańsk is the anchor of the three cities that make up the metropolitan region known as the Tri-City (Trójmiasto). The other two parts are as different as night and day: a once-swanky resort town (Sopot) and a practical, nose-to-the-grindstone business center (Gdynia). The Tri-City as a whole is home to bustling industry and a sprawling university, with several campuses and plenty of well-dressed, English-speaking students. Beyond the Tri-City, the long, skinny Hel Peninsula—a sparsely populated strip of fishing villages and fun-loving beaches—arches dramatically into the Baltic Sea.

Sopot—boasting sandy beaches, tons of tourists, and a certain elegance—is clearly the most appealing day-trip option. Gdynia offers a glimpse into workaday Poland, but leaves most visitors cold. Hel, which requires the better part of a day to visit, is worthwhile only if you've got perfect summer weather and a desire to lie on the beach.

Getting Around the Tri-City

Gdańsk, Sopot, and Gdynia are connected by regional commuter trains (*kolejka*, operated by SKM) as well as by trains of Poland's national railway (operated by PKP). Tickets for one system can't be used on the other. While trains for the two systems chug along on the same tracks, they use different (but nearby) platforms/stations. For example, at Gdańsk's main train station, national PKP trains use platforms 1-3, while regional SKM trains use platforms 3-5. And in Sopot, the SKM station is a few hundred feet before the PKP station.

Regional SKM trains are much more frequent—they go in each direction about every 10-15 minutes (less frequently after 19:30). In Gdańsk, buy tickets at the automated ticket machine marked *SKM Bilety* (near the head of platform 4, English instructions, 3.40 zł and 25 minutes to Sopot, or 4.40 zł and 40 minutes to Gdynia). If you buy your ticket from a machine, there's no need to validate it. But if you buy one from a kiosk, you'll need to stamp it in the easy-to-miss yellow or blue slots under the boards with SKM information.

Each city has multiple stops. In Gdańsk, use "Gdańsk Główny" (the end of the line); for Sopot, use the stop called simply "Sopot" (only one word); and for Gdynia, it's "Gdynia Główna" (the main station).

The bigger PKP trains are faster, but less frequent—unless you notice one that happens to be leaving at a convenient time, I'd skip them and stick with the easy SKM trains. But note that trains to Hel are always operated by PKP.

For a more romantic—and much slower—approach, consider the boat (see "Gdańsk Connections," earlier).

Sopot

Sopot (SOH-poht), dubbed the "Nice of the North," was a celebrated haunt of beautiful people during the 1920s and 1930s, and remains a popular beach getaway to this day.

Sopot was created in the late 19th century by Napoleon's doctor, Jean Georges Haffner, who believed Baltic Sea water to be therapeutic. By the 1890s, it had become a fashionable seaside resort. This gambling center boasted enough high-roller casinos to garner comparisons to Monte Carlo.

The casinos are gone, but the health resorts remain, and you'll

still see more well-dressed people here per capita than just about anywhere in the country. While it's not quite Cannes, Sopot feels relatively high class, which is unusual in otherwise unpretentious Poland. But even so, a childlike spirit of summer-vacation fun pervades this St-Tropez-on-the-Baltic, making it an all-around enjoyable place.

Planning Your Time

You can get the gist of Sopot in just a couple of hours. Zip in on the train, follow the main drag to the sea, wander the pier, get your feet wet at the beach, then head back to Gdańsk. Why not come here in the late afternoon, enjoy those last few rays of sunshine, stay for dinner, then take a twilight stroll on the pier?

Orientation to Sopot

The main pedestrian drag, Monte Cassino Heroes street (ulica Bohaterów Monte Cassino), leads to the Molo, the longest pleasure pier in Europe. From the Molo, a broad, sandy beach stretches in each direction. Running parallel to the surf is a tree-lined, people-filled path made for strolling.

Tourist Information

Sopot's helpful TI is directly in front of the PKP train station (look for blue *it* sign). Pick up the free map, info booklet, and events schedule. They also offer a free room-booking service (daily June-mid-Sept 9:00-20:00, mid-Sept-May 10:00-18:00, ulica Dworcowa 4, tel. 58-550-3783, www.sopot.pl).

Arrival in Sopot

From the SKM station, exit to the left and walk down the street. After a block, you'll see the PKP train station on your left—detour here to find the TI (described above). Then continue on to the can't-miss-it main drag, ulica Bohaterów Monte Cassino (marked by the big red-brick church steeple). Follow it to the right, down to the seaside.

Sights in Sopot

▲Monte Cassino Heroes Street (Ulica Bohaterów Monte Cassino)—Nicknamed "Monciak" (MOHN-chak) by locals, this in-love-with-life promenade may well be Poland's most manicured street. Especially after all the suburban and industrial dreck you passed through to get here, it's easy to be charmed by this pretty drag. The street is lined with happy tourists, trendy cafés, al fresco restaurants, movie theaters, and late-19th-century facades (known for their wooden balconies).

The most popular building along here (on the left, about half-way down) is the so-called **Crooked House** (Krzywy Domek), a trippy, Gaudí-inspired building that looks like it's melting. Hard-partying Poles prefer to call it the "Drunken House," and say that when it looks straight, it's time to stop drinking.

At the bottom of the boulevard, just before the Molo, pay 4 zł to climb to the top of the Art Nouveau lighthouse for a waterfront panorama.

Molo (Pier)—At more than 1,600 feet long, this is Europe's longest wooden entertainment pier. While you won't find any amusement-park rides, you will be surrounded by vendors, artists, and Poles having the time of their lives. Buy a *gofry* (Belgian waffle topped with whipped cream and fruit) or an oversized cloud of *wata cukrowa* (cotton candy), grab your partner's hand, and stroll with gusto (5 zł, free Oct-April, open long hours daily).

Scan the horizon for sailboats and tankers. Any pirate ships? For a jarring reality check, look over to Gdańsk. Barely visible from the Molo are two of the most important sites in 20th-century history: the towering monument at Westerplatte, where World War II started, and the cranes rising up from the Gdańsk Shipyard, where Solidarity was born and European communism began its long goodbye.

In spring and fall, the Molo is a favorite venue for pole vaulting—or is that Pole vaulting?

The Beach—Yes, Poland has beaches. Nice ones. When I heard Sopot compared to places like Nice, I'll admit that I scoffed. But when I saw those stretches of inviting sand as far as the eye can see, I wished I'd packed my swim trunks. (You could walk from Gdańsk to Gdynia on beaches like this.) The sand is finer than anything I've seen in Croatia...though the water's not exactly crystal-clear. Most of the beach is public, except for a small private stretch in front of the Grand Hotel Sopot. Year-round, it's crammed with locals. At these northern latitudes, the season for bathing is brief and crowded.

Overlooking the beach next to the Molo is the **Grand Hotel Sopot.** It was renovated to top-class status just recently, but its history goes way back. They could charge admission for room #226, a multiroom suite that has hosted the likes of Adolf Hitler, Marlene Dietrich, and Fidel Castro (but not all at the same time). With all the trappings of Sopot's belle époque—dark wood, plush upholstery, antique furniture—this room had me imagining Hitler sitting at the desk, looking out to sea, and plotting the course of World War II.

Gdynia

Compared to its flashier sister cities, straightforward Gdynia (guh-DIN-yah) has retained a more working-class vibe, still in touch with its salty, fishing-village roots. Gdynia is less historic than Gdańsk or Sopot, as it was mostly built in the 1920s to be Poland's main harbor after Gdańsk became a free city. Although nowhere as attractive as Gdańsk or Sopot, Gdynia has an authentic feel and a fine waterfront promenade (www.gdynia.pl).

Gdynia is a major business center, and—thanks to its youthful, progressive city government—has edged ahead of the rest of Poland in transitioning from communism. It enjoys one of the highest income levels in the country. Many of the crumbling downtown buildings have been renovated, and Gdynia is becoming known for its top-tier shopping—all the big designers have boutiques here. If a local woman has been shopping on Świętojańska street in Gdynia, it means that she's got some serious złoty.

Because Gdańsk's port is relatively shallow, the biggest cruise ships must put in at Gdynia...leaving confused tourists to poke around town looking for some medieval quaintness, before coming to their senses and heading for Gdańsk. Gdynia is also home to a major military harbor and an important NATO base.

To get a taste of Gdynia, take the SKM train to the "Gdynia Główna" station, follow signs to *wyjście do miasta*, cross the busy street, and walk 15 minutes down Starowiejska. When you come to the intersection with the broad Świętojańska street, turn right (in the direction the big statue is looking) and walk two blocks to the tree-lined park on the left. Head through the park to the Southern Pier (Molo Południowe). This concrete slab—nowhere near as charming as Sopot's wooden-boardwalk version—features a modern shopping mall and a smattering of sights, including an aquarium and a pair of permanently moored museum boats.

Hel Peninsula (Mierzeja Helska)

Out on the edge of things, this slender peninsula juts 20 miles into the ocean, providing a sunny retreat from the big cities—even as it shelters them from Baltic winds. Trees line the peninsula, and the northern edge is one long, sandy, ever-shifting beach.

On hot summer days, Hel is a great place to frolic in the sun with Poles. Sunbathing and windsurfing are practically religions here. Small resort villages line Hel Peninsula: Władysławowo (at the base), Chałupy, Kuźnica, Jastarnia, Jurata, and—at the tip—a town also called Hel. Beaches right near the towns can be crowded in peak season, but you're never more than a short walk away from your own stretch of sand. There are few permanent residents, and the waterfront is shared by budget campgrounds, hotels hosting middle-class families, and mansions of Poland's rich and famous (former president Aleksander Kwaśniewski has a summer home here).

The easiest way to go to Hel—aside from coveting thy neighbor's wife—is by boat (see "Gdańsk Connections," earlier). Trains from Gdańsk also reach Hel (summer only), and from Gdynia, you can take a train, bus, or minibus. But overland transit is crowded and slow—especially in summer, when Hel is notorious for its hellish traffic jams.

POMERANIA

Malbork Castle • Toruń

The northwestern part of Poland—known as Pomerania (Pomorze)—has nothing to do with excitable little dogs, but it does offer plenty of attractions. Two in particular are worth singling out, both conveniently located between Gdańsk and Warsaw. Malbork, the biggest Gothic castle in Europe, is one of the most interesting castles in Eastern Europe. Farther south, the Gothic town of Toruń—the birthplace of Copernicus, and a favorite spot of every proud Pole—holds hundreds of red-brick buildings (and, it seems, even more varieties of tasty gingerbread).

Planning Your Time

Malbork works well as a side-trip from Gdańsk (frequent trains, 40-50 minutes each way), and it's also on the main train line from

Gdańsk to Warsaw. While Toruń doesn't merit a long detour, it's worth a stroll or an overnight if you want to sample a smaller Polish city. Unfortunately, Toruń is on a different train line than Malbork—if you visit both in one day, it'll be a very long one. Ideally, if traveling round-trip from Warsaw, see one of these destinations coming to Gdańsk, and visit the other on the way back. (Note: Due to renovations at Malbork's train station, there may be no luggage storage; instead, you might have to take your bags with you to the castle to check them there.) Or do Malbork as a side-trip from Gdańsk, then visit Toruń on the way to Warsaw.

Malbork Castle

Malbork Castle is soaked in history. The biggest brick castle in the world, the largest castle of the Gothic period, and one of Europe's most imposing fortresses, it sits smugly on a marshy plain at the edge of the town of Malbork, 35 miles southeast of Gdańsk. This was the headquarters of the notorious Teutonic Knights, a Germanic band of ex-Crusaders who dominated northern Poland in the Middle Ages.

When the Teutonic Knights were invited to Polish lands to convert neighboring pagans in the 13th century, they found the perfect site for their new capital here, on the bank of the Nogat River. Construction began in 1274. After the Teutonic Knights conquered Gdańsk in 1308, the order moved its official headquarters from Venice to Malbork, where they remained for nearly 150 years. They called the castle Marienburg, the "Castle of Mary," in honor of the order's patron saint.

At its peak in the early 1400s, Malbork was both the imposing home of a seemingly unstoppable army and Europe's final bastion of chivalric ideals. Surrounded by swamplands, with only one gate in need of defense, it was a tough nut to crack. Malbork Castle was never taken by force in the Middle Ages, though it had to withstand various sieges by the Poles during the Thirteen Years' War (1454-1466)—including a campaign that lasted over three years. Finally, in 1457, the Polish king gained control of Malbork by buying off Czech mercenaries guarding the castle. Malbork became a Polish royal residence for 300 years. But when Poland was partitioned in the late 18th century, this region went back into German hands. The castle became a barracks, windows were sealed up, delicate vaulting was damaged, bricks were quarried for new buildings, and Malbork deteriorated.

In the late 19th century, Romantic German artists and poets rediscovered the place. An architect named Konrad Steinbrecht devoted 40 years of his life to Malbork, painstakingly restoring the palace to its medieval splendor. A half-century later, the Nazis used the castle to house POWs, and about half of it was destroyed by the Soviet army, who saw it as a symbol of long-standing German domination. But it was restored once again, and today Malbork has been returned to its Teutonic glory.

Getting There

Malbork is on the train line between Gdańsk and Warsaw. Coming by train from Gdańsk, you'll enjoy views of the castle on your right as you cross the Nogat River.

Unfortunately, due to ongoing renovation, there may be **no**

luggage storage at the Malbork train station. If you can't find anywhere to leave your bags at the station, you'll have to carry them
with you to the castle, then check them at the guardhouse (the
small wooden house near the castle exit, along the river).

To get from the station to the castle, consider taking a **taxi**
(shouldn't cost more than 10 zł, though many corrupt cabbies
charge twice that—keep asking until someone agrees to 10 zł).
Or you can **walk** 15 minutes to the castle: Leave the station to
the right, walk straight, and go through the pedestrian underpass
beneath the busy road (by the red staircase). When you emerge on
the other side, follow the busy road (noticing peek-a-boo views on
your right of the castle's main tower) and take your first right turn
(onto Kościuszki, the main shopping street). On Kościuszki, you'll
pass the fancy pink building housing the TI on the right. Near
the bottom of Kościuszki, at the fountain and the McDonald's,
jog right, then bear left over two moats. Turn right and follow the
castle wall to the end, where you'll find the ticket office (marked
kasa).

Orientation to Malbork Castle

Cost and Hours: Mid-April–mid-Sept—39 zł, castle exhibits
open Tue-Sun 9:00-19:00, grounds until 20:00; mid-Sept–
mid-April—29 zł, castle exhibits open Tue-Sun 10:00-15:00,
grounds until 16:00. Ask about slightly discounted family
tickets (it's also cheaper to visit within 1.25 hours of closing).
On Mondays year-round, most of the castle is closed, with
only a few sparse exhibits remaining open (8 zł to enter), but
there's little point in making the trip on a Monday. The ticket
office opens 30 minutes before the castle. For details, see
www.zamek.malbork.pl.

Tours: You are technically required to enter the castle with a
three-hour tour or audioguide (Polish version included in
your ticket), but most non-Polish speakers simply split off
from their guide and tour the place on their own—just enter
with any tour, wander off, and explore the castle using my
self-guided tour (see next page). You can also rent an English
audioguide for 6 zł.

In July and August, **English tours** run three times a day
(likely at 11:00, 13:30, and 15:30; 8 zł extra). Otherwise, year-
round, you can pay 210 zł for a private English tour (English
guides are easy to arrange in summer—even on short notice—
but more difficult in winter). Ideally, contact the castle a few
days ahead to reserve a guide (tel. 55-647-0978, fax 55-647-
0976, kasa@zamek.malbork.pl), or hire your own guide in
Gdańsk (such as Agnieszka Syroka—see page 437).

POMERANIA

Alternatively, if you show up and there's no scheduled English tour, ask if an English-speaking guide is available. Then take the initiative, play "tour organizer," and get together a group of frustrated English-speakers by the cashier. On my last trip, it took me only a few minutes to gather a dozen strangers eager for some English information—bringing the per-person cost of the private tour down to less than 20 zł.

Expect Changes: Future plans may revamp the tour system and create several shorter tour routes. Restoration of the moat area may cause the relocation of the castle entrance (possibly in 2013).

Best Views: The views of massive Malbork are stunning—especially at sunset, when its red brick glows. Be sure to walk out across the bridge over the Nogat River. The most scenic part of the castle is probably the twin-turreted, riverside Bridge Gate, which used to be connected by a bridge to the opposite bank.

Sound-and-Light Show: Every night from mid-April through mid-September, there's a sound-and-light show in the castle courtyard. Though the commentary is in Polish, the show gives you a different perspective on the mighty fortress (20 zł, buy tickets at castle drawbridge, begins after dark—which can be as late as 22:00 at these northern latitudes). Don't make a special trip (or stay late) just for this show—it really only makes sense if you're spending the night (see "Sleeping at Malbork Castle," later).

Self-Guided Tour

The official tour of Malbork lasts about three hours. And, while there's plenty to see, this self-guided tour allows you to see the highlights at your own pace. (Remember, you can split off from your group at any time.) This tour also works if you're tagging along with a Polish group, since it corresponds more or less to the route most Malbork guides take. Still, every guide is a little different, exhibits tend to move around, and entrances can close unexpectedly. Use the map on the opposite page to navigate and jump around as needed. The castle complex is a bit of a maze, with various entrances and exits for each room, often behind closed (but unlocked) doors. Don't be shy about grabbing a medieval door-knob and letting yourself in.

POMERANIA

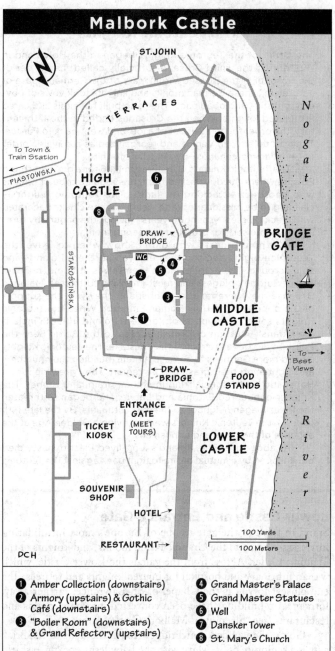

Malbork Castle

ST. JOHN

TERRACES

To Town & Train Station

PIASTOWSKA

HIGH CASTLE

STAROŚCIŃSKA

N o g a t

BRIDGE GATE

DRAW-BRIDGE

WC

MIDDLE CASTLE

DRAW-BRIDGE

FOOD STANDS

To Best Views

ENTRANCE GATE (MEET TOURS)

LOWER CASTLE

R i v e r

TICKET KIOSK

SOUVENIR SHOP

HOTEL→

RESTAURANT→

DCH

100 Yards

100 Meters

POMERANIA

❶ Amber Collection (downstairs)
❷ Armory (upstairs) & Gothic Café (downstairs)
❸ "Boiler Room" (downstairs) & Grand Refectory (upstairs)
❹ Grand Master's Palace
❺ Grand Master Statues
❻ Well
❼ Dansker Tower
❽ St. Mary's Church

The Teutonic Knights

The Order of the Teutonic Knights began in the Holy Land in 1191, during the Third Crusade. Officially called the "Order of the Hospital of the Blessed Virgin Mary of the German House of Jerusalem," these German monks and knights took vows of poverty, chastity, and obedience. They also built hospitals and cared for injured knights. When the Crusades ended in the 12th century, the order found itself out of a job, and went back to Europe. They set up shop in Venice and reorganized as a chivalric order of Christian mercenaries—pagan-killers for hire.

The Teutonic Knights were hired in 1226 for a gig in northern Poland, where the duke asked them to subdue a tribe of pagans who had been attacking his lands. The Teutonic Knights—claiming to be missionaries (and wearing white cloaks decorated with black crosses)—spent 60 years "saving" the pagans by turning them into serfs or brutally massacring them.

Like houseguests who didn't know when to leave, the Teutonic Knights decided they enjoyed northern Poland—and stuck around. The Knights made themselves at home, building one of Europe's biggest and most imposing fortresses: Malbork. Because they were fanatical Christians, they won the support of the pope and the Holy Roman Emperor. When the Teutonic Knights seized large parts of northern Poland in 1308, including Gdańsk—cutting off Polish access to the Baltic Sea—the Polish royals began to realize their mistake. The Teutonic Knights invited more Germans to come join them, building their numbers and tightening their grasp on the region. They grew rich from Hanseatic trade, specializing in amber, grain, and timber. The Knights conquered Estonia and Latvia, and began to threaten the Poles' pagan neighbor to the east, Lithuania. By the late 14th century, the Teutonic Knights were enjoying a Golden Age at the expense of the Poles and Lithuanians.

At about this time, Poland's long-lived Piast dynasty died out. Inspired by a mutual desire to fight back against the Teutonic

Lower Castle and Entrance Gate

Stand in front of the gate to one of Europe's most intimidating fortresses—home to the Grand Master, monks, and knights of the Teutonic Order. Across from the gate is the Lower Castle, which was an infirmary and hospital for injured knights and retirees. The end closest to you is the Chapel of St. Lawrence; farther away, former farm buildings have been converted into hotel rooms and restaurants (see "Sleeping at Malbork Castle," later).

Go up the wooden drawbridge. Above the door to the brick gate is a sculpture of St. Mary with the Baby Jesus...next to a shield and helmet. The two messages to visitors: This castle is protected by Mary, and the Teutonic Knights are here to convert pagans—by

Knights, the Poles and the Lithuanians decided to join their two kingdoms. In 1386, Polish Princess Jadwiga married Lithuanian Prince Władysław Jagiełło (who converted to Christianity for the occasion), uniting Poland and Lithuania and kick-starting a grand new dynasty, the Jagiellonians.

Just as every American knows the date July 4, 1776, every Pole knows the date July 15, 1410—the Battle of Grunwald. King Władysław Jagiełło and Grand Duke Vytautas the Great led a ragtag army of some 40,000 soldiers—Lithuanians, Poles, other Slavs, and even speedy Tatar horsemen—against 27,000 Teutonic Knights. At the end of the day, some 18,000 Poles and Lithuanians were dead—but so were half of the Teutonic Knights (and the other half had been captured). Poland and Lithuania were victorious. Though the Teutonic Knights remained in Poland—extending their Germanic cultural influence on the region well into the 20th century—their political power waned, they pulled out of Lithuania, and they once again allowed free trade on the Vistula. A generation later, the Thirteen Years' War (1454-1466) finally put an end to the Teutonic Knights' domination of northern Poland. The order officially dissolved in 1575, when they converted to Protestantism (though some conspiracy theorists claim the Teutonic Knights are still very much active).

The Knights' influence on Poland persists today—even beyond the striking red-brick churches and castles scattered around the northern part of the country. The Polish novelist Henryk Sienkiewicz's *The Teutonic Knights* is a cultural benchmark and a favorite work of many Poles. The 19th-century Romantics who fanned the flames of Polish patriotism turned the Teutonic Knights into a symbol of Germanic oppression. Even today, Poles—and all Slavs—think of the Teutonic Knights as murderous invaders...while the Germans see them as a mere footnote in their history.

force, if necessary (or, as it turned out, even if not necessary).

Pass through this gate, into the entry area. Imagine the gate behind you closing. Look up to see wooden chutes where archers are preparing to rain arrows down on you. Your last thought: Maybe we should have left the Teutonic Knights alone, after all.

Before you're pierced by arrows, read the castle's history in its walls: The foundation is made of huge stones, which are rare in these marshy lands—they were brought from Sweden. But most of the castle, like so many other buildings in northern Poland, was built with handmade red brick. Throughout the castle, the darker-colored, rougher brick is original, and the lighter-colored, smoother brick was used during later restorations (in the 19th century, and again after World War II).

Venture through two more enclosed spaces, watching for the holes in the wall (for more guards and soldiers). The Teutonic Knights connected nearby lakes to create a system of canals, forming a moat around the castle that could be crossed only by this drawbridge. Ponder the fact that you have to go through five separate, well-defended gates to reach the...

Middle Castle (Zamek Średni)

This part of Malbork, built at an uphill incline to make it even more imposing, was designed to impress. Knights and monks lived here.

Let's get oriented: To your left is the east wing, where guests would sleep. Today this houses the Amber Collection (ground floor) and the armory (upstairs). To the right (west) as you enter the main courtyard is the Grand Refectory (closer to the entrance) and the Grand Master's Palace (the taller, squarer building at the far end).

• *Before we move on, this is a good time to read up on the history of the Teutonic Knights (see sidebar). When you're ready to continue, enter the ground floor of the building on the left (remember, don't be shy about opening closed doors), and visit the...*

Amber Collection

This exhibit will make jewelry shoppers salivate. (Even as someone with zero interest in amber, I enjoyed it.) For a primer, read the "All About Amber" sidebar on page 449. Begin at the huge chunks of raw amber and the illuminated display of inclusions (bugs stuck in the amber, à la *Jurassic Park*). Some of the ancient amber artifacts displayed here are up to 3,000 years old. These were found in graves, put there by people who thought amber would help the deceased enter a better world. Wandering the hall, you'll see all manner of amber creations: boxes, brooches, necklaces, chess sets, pipes, miniature ships, wine glasses, and belts for skinny-waisted, fashion-conscious women. Look for two truly exquisite pieces: a small casket and an altar. Many of the finely decorated jewelry boxes and chests have ivory, silver, or shell inlays—better for contrast than gold. The portable religious shrines and altars allowed travelers to remain reverent on the road and still pack light. Find the amber crucifix. This is a small replica of a six-foot-tall amber and silver cross presented to Pope John Paul II by the people of Gdańsk. Another exhibit case contains necklaces displaying the full range of amber colors, from opaque white at the top, to transparent yellow in the middle, to virtually black at the bottom.

• *Go back outside and turn left, to the wooden staircase above the Gothic Café (worth considering for a meal, and described later, under "Eating at Malbork Castle"). Go up that staircase, and several more inside, to the top-floor...*

Armory

Browse your way through the impressive array of swords, armor, and other armaments (English descriptions). Look for the 600-year-old "hand-and-a-half" swords—too big to be held in one hand. At the end, in the display of cannons, pikes, and spears, find the giant shield. These shields could be lined up to form a portable "wall" to protect the knights.

Head downstairs to the second room of the armory, displaying suits of armor (including one for horses). On the wall behind the first suit of armor, look for some five-foot-long "two-hand swords" even bigger than the ones upstairs. Halfway down the hall on the left, find the suit of armor from the Hussars—Polish horseback knights who had wings on their armor, which created a terrifying sound when galloping.

• *Head back outside (noticing the handy WC straight ahead) and cross the main courtyard, entering the smaller courtyard through the passage next to the dark-wood-topped tower. Find the steep steps down into the...*

"Boiler Room"

The Teutonic Knights had a surprisingly sophisticated method for heating this huge complex. You see a furnace down below, and a sort of holding area for super-heated rocks above. The radiant heat given off by the rocks spread through the vents without also filling them with smoke. This is one of 11 such "boiler rooms" in the castle complex. As you tour the rest of the castle, keep an eye out for little saucer-sized vents in the floor where the heat came through.

• *Head back out into the main courtyard and turn right, going uphill about 30 yards. At the upper part of this castle are two doors; take the one on the right, then climb up the stairs into the...*

Grand Master's Palace

This was one of the grandest royal residences in medieval Europe, used in later times by Polish kings and German kaisers. (Today it's sometimes used for special exhibitions.)

• *From the top of the stairs, head down the hall to the right. Notice the troughs in the ground—anyone wanting an audience with the Grand Master had to wash both his hands and his feet.*

At the end of the hall, on the left, enter the elegant...

POMERANIA

Summer Refectory: This was where the G.M. dined. With big stained-glass windows, and all the delicate vaulting supported by a single pillar in the middle, this room was clearly not designed with defense in mind. In fact, medieval Polish armies focused their attacks on this room. On one legendary occasion, the attackers—tipped off by a spy—knew that an important meeting was going on here, and fired a cannonball into the room. It just missed the pillar. (You can see where the cannonball hit the wall, just above the fireplace.) The ceiling eventually did collapse during World War II.

As you continue into the **Winter Refectory,** notice that it has fewer windows (better insulation) and little manhole-like openings in the floor where the "central heating" entered the room.

• *Keep going, and you'll circle back around to where you came in. Go through the door just to the left of the stairs, into the...*

Private Rooms of the Grand Master: Though the Teutonic Order dictated that the monks sleep in dormitories, the Grand Master made an exception for himself. Near the entrance, you'll see his private bedroom (with rough original frescoes of four female martyrs). Exploring the rest of the Top Knight's residence, appreciate the show-off decor (including some 15th-century original frescoes of wine leaves and grapes). The Grand Master even had his own chapel, dedicated to St. Catherine.

• *You'll enter a small hall at the very end of these rooms. If it's open, go through the little door at the right end of this hall, and walk down to the...*

Grand Refectory: This enormous dining hall, damaged in World War II, recently re-opened after a decade-long restoration project. With remarkable palm vaulting and grand frescoes, the Grand Refectory hosted feasts for up to 400 people to celebrate a military victory or to impress visiting dignitaries.

• *Head outside. You're back by the boiler room. Go back out into the main courtyard and walk to the top. Look for the four...*

Grand Master Statues

These four statues came from a 19th-century Prussian monument that was mostly destroyed when the Soviets took Malbork at the end of World War II. Though this was a religious order, these powerful guys look more like kings than monks. From right to left, shake hands with Hermann von Salza (who was Grand Master when the Teutonic Knights came to Poland); Siegfried von Feuchtwangen (who actually moved the T.K. capital from Venice to Malbork, and who conquered Gdańsk for the Knights—oops, can't shake his hand, which was supposedly chopped off by Soviet troops); Winrich von Kniprode (who oversaw Malbork's Golden Age, and turned it into a castle fit for a king); and Markgraf Albrecht von Hohenzollern (the last Grand Master before the order dissolved and converted to Protestantism).

• *To the right of the statues, continue over the...*

Drawbridge

As you cross, notice the extensive system of fortifications and moats protecting the innermost part of the castle. Check out the cracks in the walls—an increasing threat to this ever-settling castle set on marshy, unstable terrain. The passage is lined with holes (for surveillance), with chutes up above (to pour scalding water or pitch on unwanted visitors). It's not quite straight—so a cannon fired here would hit the side wall of the passage, rather than entering the High Castle. Which is what you're about to do now.

High Castle (Zamek Wysoki)

This is the beating heart of the castle, and its oldest section. As much a monastery as a fortress, the High Castle was off-limits to all but 60 monks of the Teutonic Order and their servants. (The knights stayed in the Middle Castle.) Here you'll find the monks' dormitories, chapels, church, and refectory. As this was the nerve center of the Teutonic Knights—the T.K. HQ—it was also their last line of defense. They stored enormous amounts of food here in case of a siege.

In the middle of the High Castle courtyard is a **well**—an essential part of any inner castle, especially one as prone to sieges as Malbork. At the top is a sculpture of a pelican. Because this noble bird was believed to kill itself to feed its young (notice that it's piercing its own chest with its beak), it was often used in the Middle Ages as a symbol for the self-sacrifice of Jesus.

• *Take some time to explore the...*

Ground Floor

Work clockwise around the courtyard from where you entered. A door leads to the prison and torture chamber (with small "solitary confinement" cells near the entrance), behind which you'll find a long hall with a single tiny window. Along the back of the cloister is a post-WWII photo of Malbork. Beyond that, hiding in the far corner, is an exhibit on medieval stained-glass windows. Somewhere around here, you should see a demonstration of how medieval money was made. The Teutonic Knights minted their own coins—and you can buy your very own freshly minted replica today.

• *Continuing around the courtyard (to the right from where you entered), you'll find the most interesting exhibit on this floor, the...*

Kitchen: This exhibit really gives you a feel for medieval monastery life. The monks who lived here ate three meals a day, along with lots of beer (made here) and wine (imported from France, Italy, and Hungary). A cellar under the kitchen was used as a primitive refrigerator—big chunks of ice were cut from the frozen river in winter, stored in the basement, and used to keep food cool in summer. Behind the long table, see the big dumbwaiter (with shelves), which connects this kitchen with the refectory upstairs. Step into the giant stove and look up the biggest chimney in the castle.

• *Now go back out into the courtyard, and climb up the stairs near where you first entered.*

Middle Floor

• *From the top of the stairs, the first door on the left (with the colorfully painted arch) leads to the most important room of the High Castle, the...*

Chapter Room: Monks gathered here after Mass, and it was also the site for meetings of Teutonic Knights from around the countryside. If a Grand Master was killed in battle, the new one would be elected right here. Each monk had his own seal and a name over his seat. The big chair belonged to the Grand Master. Above his chair, notice the little windows, connecting this room to St. Mary's Church next door (described later). Church music would filter in through these windows...imagine the voices of 60 monks bouncing around with these acoustics.

While monks are usually thought to pursue simple lives, the elegant vaulting in this room is anything but plain. The 14th-century frescoes (restored in the 19th century) depict Grand Masters. In the floor are more vents for the central heating.

• *Leave the Chapter House and walk straight ahead, imagining the monk-filled corridors of Teutonic times. The first door on the right is the...*

Treasury: As you explore the rooms of the tax collector and the house administrator, notice the wide variety of safes and other lock boxes. Near the end, look for the small bed—fit for a small medieval person.

• *Continue around the cloister. At the end of the corridor, spot the little devil at the bottom of the vaulting (on the right, about eye level). He's pulling his beard and crossing his legs—pointing you down the long corridor to the...*

Dansker Tower: From the devil's grimace, you might have guessed that this tower houses the latrine. For obvious sanitary (and olfactory) reasons, it's set apart from the main part of the castle. The toilets dropped straight down into the moat. The bins above them are filled with cabbage leaves, used by the T. K. as TP. This tower could also serve as a final measure of defense—it's easier to defend than the entire castle. Food was stored above, just in case.

• *Head back toward the main part of the High Castle. On the right-hand side of the long passage, a door leads into the...*

Church Exhibition: Once dormitories for the monks, these rooms today display a wide range of relics from the church (with English descriptions). The first room features various statues, including an evocative, hands-less 15th-century Christ praying in the Garden of Gethsemane. The next room displays pictures of Malbork Castle through the years, as well as some fragments of statues rescued from the destroyed St. Mary's Church. The huge, mangled crucifix dates from the mid-14th century. At the end of this exhibition is a replica of a Gothic altarpiece, with graphic paintings of the murder and dismemberment of Poland's patron saint, Adalbert.

• *Go back out into the main cloister, turn right, and continue down to the end, arriving at the...*

Golden Gate: This elaborate doorway—covered in protective glass—marks the entrance to St. Mary's Church. Ringed with

detailed carvings from the Old Testament, and symbolic messages about how monks of the Teutonic Order should live their lives, it's a marvelous example of late-13th-century art. At the bottom left end of the arch, find the five wise virgins who, having filled their lamps with oil and conserved it wisely, are headed to heaven. On the right, the five foolish virgins who overslept and used up all their oil are damned, much to their dismay.

• *Go through this door into...*

St. Mary's Church: This holy site was destroyed in World War II and sat for decades with no roof. After so much neglect, it's finally being renovated...slowly. Pictures of the original church with English descriptions explain some of the fragments.

• *Go through the narrow door next to the one where you entered the church, and hike up the tight spiral staircase to the final set of exhibits.*

Top Floor

Walk through the long hallway of temporary exhibits. At the end, go down the stairs into the monks' common room (on the left). Over the fireplace is a relief depicting the Teutonic Knights fighting the pagans. To the left of that (see the stone windows) is a balcony where musicians entertained the monks after a meal. The next, very long room, with seven pillars, is the refectory, where the monks ate in silence.

Along the right-hand wall are confessional-like, lockable storage boxes. At the end of this room, just beyond another decorated fireplace, notice the grated hole in the wall. This is where the dumbwaiter comes up from the kitchen (which we saw below). Beyond this room is an exhibit about the architectural renovation of the castle. On your way back out, you'll have the opportunity to pay 8 zł to climb the very tight and steep steps to the top of the tower for a view over the castle complex.

• *Your Malbork tour ends here. When finished, you can head back the way you came. En route, you can walk around terraces lining the inner moat, between the castle walls (stairs lead down off of the drawbridge). It's hardly a must-see, but it's pleasant enough, with the Grand Master's garden, a cemetery for monks, and the remains of the small St. Anne's Chapel (with Grand Master tombs).*

Sleeping at Malbork Castle

Malbork is so well-connected by rail to Gdańsk and Warsaw that there's little sense in sleeping here. If you do stay, consider the nighttime sound-and-light show in the castle courtyard.

$$ Hotel Zamek is housed in Malbork's Lower Castle, a red-brick building that was once a hospital, just across from the main part of the fortress. The 42 rooms are overpriced, dark, musty, old-feeling, and a little creepy...but, hey—you're next door to one of Europe's grandest Gothic castles (Sb-210 zł, Db-310 zł, Tb-390 zł, cheaper off-season, elevator, ulica Starościńska 14, tel. 055-272-8400, www.hotelprodus.pl, hotelprodus@hotelprodus.pl).

Eating at Malbork Castle

Several cheap food stands cluster outside the castle (by the river). For a meal inside the castle complex, your best bet is the **Gothic Café,** under the stairs to the armory in the Middle Castle. Serving traditional Polish food in a nondescript cellar setting, it's handy for its 29-zł lunch deal that includes a main dish and soup (25-40-zł main dishes, Tue-Sun 9:00-17:00 or 18:00 depending on demand, tel. 50-620-8560).

Sleep Code

(3 zł = about $1, country code: 48)
S = Single, **D** = Double/Twin, **T** = Triple, **Q** = Quad, **b** = bathroom,
s = shower only. At each place, credit cards are accepted,
breakfast is included, and English is spoken.

　　To help you easily sort through these listings, I've divided
the accommodations into two categories, based on the price
for a double room with bath during high season:

　　$$　Higher Priced—Most rooms 200 zł or more.
　　$　Lower Priced—Most rooms less than 200 zł.

　　Prices can change without notice; verify the hotel's
current rates online or by email. For other updates, see www
.ricksteves.com/update.

Malbork Connections

From Malbork by Train to: Gdańsk (about 2/hour, 40-50 minutes), **Toruń** (about every 2 hours, 3 hours, transfer in Tczew), **Warsaw** (6/day direct, 4.5 hours—but will drop to 2.5 hours when new line is finished).

Toruń

Toruń (TOH-roon) is a pretty, lazy Gothic town conveniently located about halfway between Warsaw and Gdańsk. It's worth a

couple of hours to stroll the lively streets, ogle the huge red-brick buildings, and savor the flavor of Poland's most livable city.

　　With about 210,000 residents and 30,000 students (at Copernicus University), Toruń is a thriving burg. Locals brag that their city is a "mini-Kraków." But that sells both cities short.

Toruń lacks Kraków's over-the-top romanticism, and its sights are quickly exhausted. On the other hand, Toruń may well be Poland's most user-friendly city: tidy streets with a sensible grid plan (and English signposts to keep you on track), wide pedestrian boulevards crammed with locals who greet each other like they're long-lost friends, and an easygoing ambience that seems to say, "Hey—relax." And, while it has its share of tourists, Toruń feels more off-the-beaten-path than the other Polish destinations in this book.

Toruń clings fiercely to its two claims to fame: It's the proud birthplace of the astronomer Copernicus (Mikołaj Kopernik), and home to a dizzying variety of gingerbread treats (*piernika;* pyer-NEE-kah).

Orientation to Toruń

Everything in Toruń worth seeing is in the walled Old Town, climbing up a gentle hill from the Vistula River. The broad, traffic-free main drag, ulica Szeroka (called Różana at the entrance of town) bisects the Old Town, running parallel to the river.

Arrival in Toruń

Toruń's main train station (called Toruń Główny) is about a mile away—and across the river—from the Old Town. The main hall has ticket windows, an ATM, and lockers.

To reach the Old Town, you have two options: If you go out the door from the main hall, you'll spot **taxis** waiting to take you into town (the trip costs around 15-20 zł). To take the **bus,** buy a 2.50-zł ticket from the *RUCH* kiosk overlooking the tracks near the main hall. Then follow the pedestrian underpass beneath track 4 (entrance to underpass marked with low-profile *wyjście do miasta* sign and bus icon, outside main hall and to the left). When you emerge on the other side, the bus stop for bus #22, #25, or #27 into the center is ahead and on your right. Take the bus to Plac Rapackiego, the first stop after the long bridge. To return to the station, catch bus #22, #25, or #27 across the busy road from where you got off.

Tourist Information

The TI is on the main square, behind the Old Town Hall. Pick up the free map, and get information about hotels in town and city tours (Tue-Fri 9:00-18:00, Mon and Sat 9:00-16:00; closed Sun except May-Sept, when it's open 11:00-15:00; Rynek Staromiejski 25, tel. 56-621-0931, www.it.torun.pl).

Self-Guided Walk

Welcome to Toruń

This very lightly guided introductory stroll takes you through the heart of Toruń. With no stops, you could do it in 15 minutes.

From the Plac Rapackiego bus stop, head into the town through the passageways under the colorful buildings. Within a block, you're at the bustling **Old Town Market Square** (Rynek

Staromiejski), surrounded by huge brick buildings and outdoor restaurants buzzing with lively locals. The big building in the center is the **Old Town Hall** (Ratusz Staromiejski), with a boring museum and a climbable tower. The building with the pointy spires on the right (across from the Old Town Hall) is the **Artus Court,** where the medieval town council and merchants' guilds met (sadly, unlike the similar court in Gdańsk, it's not open to the public).

The guy playing his violin in front of the Old Town Hall is a **rafter** *(retman)*—one of the medieval lumberjacks who lashed tree trunks together and floated them down the Vistula to Gdańsk. This particular rafter came to Toruń when the town was infested with frogs. He wooed them with his violin and marched them out of town. (Hmm...sounds like a certain piper in another medieval Hanseatic city, Bremen....)

The bigger statue, at the other end of the Old Town Hall, depicts **Mikołaj Kopernik,** better known as Nicholas Copernicus (1473-1543). This Toruń-born son of aristocrats turned the world on its ear when he suggested that the sun, not the earth, is the center of the universe (an idea called the "heliocentric theory"). Toruń is serious about this local boy done good—he's the town mascot, as well as the namesake of the local university. Among its fields of study, Copernicus U. has a healthy astronomy program. There's a planetarium in the Old Town (just past the far corner of the square) and a giant radio telescope on the town outskirts. Despite all the local fuss over Copernicus, there's some dispute about his ethnicity; he was born in Toruń, all right, but at a time when it was a predominantly German town. So is he Polish or German? (For more on Copernicus, visit his birth house—now a modest museum on the astronomer—just two blocks away, and described later, under "Sights in Toruń").

What's that sweet smell in the air? For Poles, Toruń is synonymous with **gingerbread** *(piernika)*. This Toruń treat can be topped with different kinds of jams or glazes, and/or dipped in chocolate. You'll see gingerbread shops all over town, mostly selling the same stuff. The shop in the Artus Court building on the Old Town Market Square is handy and atmospheric; more are around the corner on ulica Żeglarska (toward the river; the shop on the right near the end of the block has a handy bulk system—point to what looks good and get exactly the amount and types you want).

Having satisfied your ginger tooth, head back to the square and join the human stream down the appropriately named **ulica Szeroka** ("Wide Street"), an enjoyable pedestrian promenade through the heart of town. Just before the road forks at the white Empik building, look down Przedzamcze to the right to see fragments of the town wall. This marks the border between the Old Town and the New Town (chartered only about 30 years later—both in the 13th century). While these areas are both collectively known today as the unified "Old Town," they were quite different in the Middle Ages—each with its own market square, and separated by a wall. (If you're curious to see the New Town Square and Town Hall, continue up ulica Szeroka and bear left at the fork.)

To end our walk, follow the wall to the right, down Przedzamcze, to reach the **ruins** of a castle built by the Teutonic Knights who were so influential in northern Poland in the Middle Ages (see page 486). The castle was destroyed in the 15th century by the locals—who, aside from a heap of bricks, left only the tower that housed the Teutonic toilets.

Beyond the castle ruins is the **Vistula** riverbank. The road that runs along the river here is called Bulwar Filadelfijski—for Toruń's sister city in Pennsylvania.

Sights in Toruń

Toruń is more about strolling than it is about sightseeing—the town's museums are underwhelming. Aside from its half-dozen red-brick churches (any of which are worth dropping into), the following attractions are worth considering on a rainy day.

Gingerbread Museum (Muzeum Piernika)—This fun attraction—by far Toruń's liveliest—is an actual, working gingerbread bakery of yore. Barefoot, costumed medieval bakers walk you through the traditional process of rolling, cutting out, baking, and tasting your own batch of gingerbread cookies (30-40 minutes, start to finish). After aging for 12 weeks to achieve the proper consistency, the dough bakes only 12 minutes—or, according to the medieval bakers, about 50 Hail Marys.

Cost and Hours: 11 zł, may have to wait a few minutes for an English guide to help you, daily 9:00-18:00, 2 blocks toward the river from Old Town Market Square at Rabiańska 9, tel. 56-663-6617, www.muzeumpiernika.pl.

Copernicus House (Dom Kopernika)—Filling a pair of beautiful, gabled brick buildings, this dull, overpriced little museum celebrates the hero of Toruń. As much about medieval Toruń as about the famous astronomer, and sprawling over several floors in the two buildings, the exhibits loosely explain Nicolaus Copernicus' life and achievements. While the displays—mostly copies of important documents and paintings, models of his instruments, and English descriptions—are pretty flat, it's mildly interesting to walk around the creaky interiors. The second part of the exhibit is an 18-minute "sound-and-light show" (slideshow with recorded commentary) about medieval Toruń, with a model of the city that lights up dramatically at appropriate moments (ask for English show when you enter). Finally, there's a "World of Toruń's Gingerbread" exhibit, about the city's favorite product.

Cost and Hours: Museum only-10 zł, gingerbread exhibit only-10 zł, model/slideshow only-12 zł; combo-ticket for any two-18 zł; May-Sept Tue-Sun 10:00-18:00, Oct-April Tue-Sun 10:00-16:00, closed Mon year-round; Kopernika 15/17, tel. 56-662-7038, www.muzeum.torun.pl. To get to the museum from the Old Town Market Square, head down Żeglarska and take the first right—on Kopernika, of course.

Ethnographic Park (Park Etnograficzny)—This open-air folk museum, while not ranking with Europe's best, is at least your most convenient opportunity to stroll through some traditional buildings from the region. It's in the middle of a pleasant park just outside the Old Town. Even if you're not interested in the museum, the park is a fine place to pass some time.

Cost and Hours: 14 zł; mid-April-June Tue and Thu 9:00-17:00, Wed and Fri 9:00-16:00, Sat-Sun 10:00-18:00; July-Sept Tue, Thu, and Sat-Sun 10:00-18:00, Wed and Fri 9:00-16:00; Oct-mid-April Tue-Fri 9:00-16:00, Sat-Sun 10:00-16:00; closed Mon year-round; Wały Gen. Sikorskiego 19, www.etnomuzeum.pl. To get there from the Old Town Market Square, walk up Chełmińska with the river at your back and the Old Town Hall on your left. Cross the busy road, and you're in the park.

Sleeping in Toruń

Toruń's Old Town has more than its share of good-value hotels (Db-200-300 zł). The TI has a brochure listing the options, and can help you find a room for no extra charge.

$$ Hotel Karczma "Spichrz" ("Granary") is a fresh, atmospheric hotel in a renovated old granary. Its 23 rooms and public spaces are a fun blend of old and new—with huge wooden beams around every corner, and the scent of the restaurant's wood-fired grill wafting through the halls. It's comfortable, central, well-priced, and a little kitschy (Sb-230 zł, Db-290 zł, 10-20 percent cheaper on weekends, tall people may not appreciate low ceilings and beams, elevator, a block off the main drag toward the river at ulica Mostowa 1, tel. 56-657-1140, fax 56-657-1144, www.spichrz .pl, hotel@spichrz.pl). The restaurant is also good (30-55-zł grilled meat dishes, daily 12:00-23:00).

$ Hotel Retman ("Rafter") has 29 older but nicely appointed rooms over a restaurant just down the street from the Gingerbread Museum (Sb-190 zł, Db-250 zł; Fri-Sun prices drop to Sb-160 zł, Db-200 zł; ulica Rabiańska 15, tel. 56-657-4460, fax 56-657-4461, www.hotelretman.pl, recepcja@hotelretman.pl).

Toruń Connections

Toruń is a handy stopover on the way between Warsaw and Gdańsk. It's on a different train line than Malbork—so visiting both Toruń and the mighty Teutonic castle in the same day is surprisingly time-consuming.

From Toruń by Train to: Warsaw (9/day, 2.75 hours direct, longer with a transfer in Kutno), **Gdańsk** (6/day direct, 3.25-3.75 hours; at least hourly with a transfer in Bydgoszcz, 3-4 hours), **Kraków** (2/day direct, 6.5-8 hours; better to transfer at Warsaw's Zachodnia station: 10/day, 6-6.75 hours), **Berlin** (4/day, 5.75-6 hours, transfer in Poznań).

HUNGARY
Magyarország

HUNGARY

Hungary is an island of Asian-descended Magyars in a sea of Slavs. Even though the Hungarians have thoroughly integrated with their Slavic and German neighbors in the millennium-plus since they arrived, there's still something about the place that's distinctly Magyar (MUD-jar). Here in quirky, idiosyncratic Hungary, everything's a little different from the rest of Europe—in terms of history, language, culture, customs, and cuisine—but it's hard to put your finger on exactly how.

Just a century ago, this country controlled half of one of Europe's grandest realms: the Austro-Hungarian Empire. Today, perhaps clinging to their former greatness, many Hungarians remain old-fashioned and nostalgic. With their dusty museums and bushy moustaches, they love to remember the good old days. Buildings all over the country are marked with plaques boasting *MŰEMLÉK* ("historical monument").

Thanks to this focus on tradition, the Hungarians you'll encounter are generally polite, formal, and professional. Hungarians have class. Everything here is done with a proud flourish. People in the service industry seem to wear their uniforms as a badge of honor rather than a burden. When a waiter comes to your table in a restaurant, he'll say, *"Tessék parancsolni"*—literally, "Please command, sir." The standard greeting, *"Jó napot kívánok,"* means "I wish you a good day." Women sometimes hear the even more formal greeting, *"Kezét csókolom"*—"I kiss your hand." And when your train or bus makes a stop, you won't be alerted by a mindless, blaring beep—but instead, peppy music. (You'll be humming these contagious little ditties all day.)

Hungarians are also orderly and tidy...in their own sometimes unexpected ways. Yes, Hungary has its share of litter, graffiti, and crumbling buildings—but you'll find great reason within the chaos. My favorite town name in Hungary: Hatvan. This means "Sixty" in Hungarian...it's exactly 60 kilometers from Budapest. You can't argue with that kind of logic.

This tradition of left-brained thinking hasn't produced many great Hungarian painters or poets who are known outside their

homeland. But the Hungarians, who are renowned for their ingenuity, have made tremendous contributions to science, technology, business, and industry. Hungarians of note include Edward Teller (instrumental in creating the A-bomb), John von Neumann (a pioneer of computer science), Andy Grove (who, as András Gróf, immigrated to the US and founded Intel), and George Soros (the billionaire investor famous—or notorious—for supporting left-wing causes). A popular local joke claims that Hungarians are so clever that they can enter a revolving door behind you and exit in front of you.

Perhaps the most famous Hungarian "scientist" invented something you probably have in a box in your basement: Ernő Rubik, creator of the famous cube. Hungarians' enjoyment of a good mind-bending puzzle is also evident in their fascination with chess, which you'll see played in cafés, parks, and baths.

Like their Viennese neighbors, Hungarians know how to enjoy the good life. Favorite activities include splashing and soaking in their many thermal baths (see page 606). "Taking the waters," Hungarian-style, deserves to be your top priority while you're here. Though public baths can sound intimidating, they're a delight. In this book I recommend my three favorite baths in Budapest, a fine bath in Eger, and another just outside of Eger. For each one, I've included careful instructions to help you enjoy the warm-water fun like a pro. (To allay your first fear: Yes, you can wear your swimsuit the entire time.)

Hungarians are also reviving an elegant, Vienna-style café culture that was dismantled by the communists. Whiling away

Hungary Almanac

Official Name: Simply Magyarország (Hungary).

Snapshot History: Settled by the Central Asian Magyars in A.D. 896, Hungary became Catholic in the year 1000, and went on to become Christian Europe's front line in fighting against the Ottomans (Muslims from today's Turkey) in the 16th-17th centuries. After serving as co-capital of the vast Austro-Hungarian Empire and losing World Wars I and II, Hungary became a Soviet satellite until achieving independence in 1989.

Population: Hungary's 10 million people (similar to Michigan) are 92 percent ethnic Hungarians who speak Hungarian. One in 50 is Roma (Gypsy). Half the populace is Catholic, with 20 percent Protestant and 25 percent listed as "other" or unaffiliated. Of the world's approximately 12 million ethnic Hungarians, one in six lives outside Hungary (mostly in areas of Romania, Slovakia, Serbia, and Croatia that were once part of Hungary).

Latitude and Longitude: 47°N and 20°E; similar latitude to Seattle, Paris, and Vienna.

Area: 36,000 square miles, similar to Indiana or Maine.

Geography: Hungary is situated in the Carpathian Basin, bound on the north by the Carpathian Mountains and on the south by the Dinaric Mountains. Though it's surrounded by mountains, Hungary itself is relatively flat, with some gently rolling hills. The Great Hungarian Plain—which begins on the east bank of the Danube in Budapest—stretches all the way to Asia. Hungary's two main rivers—the Danube and Tisza—run north-south through the country, neatly dividing it into three regions.

Biggest Cities: Budapest (the capital on the Danube, 1.7 million), Debrecen (in the east, 205,000), and Miskolc (in the north, 170,000).

the afternoon at a genteel coffeehouse, as you nurse a drink or a delicate dessert, is a favorite pastime. (For the best options in Budapest, see "Budapest's Café Culture" on page 647.)

Classical music is revered in Hungary, perhaps as nowhere else outside Austria. Aside from scientists and businessmen, the best-known Hungarians are composers: Béla Bartók, Zoltán Kodály, and Franz Liszt.

While one in five Hungarians lives in Budapest, the countryside plays an important role in Hungary's economy—this has always been a highly agricultural region. You'll pass through fields of wheat and corn, but the grains are secondary to Hungarians' (and tourists') true love: wine. Hungarian winemaking standards plummeted under the communists, but many vintner families are now reclaiming their lands, returning to their precise traditional

HUNGARY

Economy: The Gross Domestic Product is $188 billion (less than a third of Poland's), but the GDP per capita is $18,800 (equal to Poland's). Thanks to its progressive "goulash communism," Hungary had a head start on many other former Soviet Bloc countries and is now thriving, privatized...and largely foreign-owned. In the 1990s, many communist-era workers (especially women) lost their jobs. Today, the workforce is small (only 57 percent of eligible workers) but highly skilled. Grains, metals, machinery, and automobiles are major exports, and about one quarter of trade is with Germany.

Currency: 200 forints (Ft, or HUF) = about $1.

Government: The single-house National Assembly (200 seats) is the only ruling branch directly elected by popular vote. The legislators in turn select the figurehead president (currently Pál Schmitt, a onetime Olympic gold medalist in fencing) and the ruling prime minister (Viktor Orbán); both belong to the right-of-center Fidesz party.

Flag: Three horizontal bands, top to bottom: red (representing strength), white (faithfulness), and green (hope). It's identical to the Italian flag, but flipped 90 degrees counterclockwise. It often includes the Hungarian coat of arms: horizontal red-and-white stripes (on the left); the patriarchal, or double-barred, cross (on the right); and the Hungarian crown (on top).

The Average János: The typical Hungarian eats a pound of lard a week (they cook with it). The average family has three members, and they spend almost three-fourths of their income on (costly) housing. According to a recent condom-company survey, the average Hungarian has sex 131 times a year (behind only France and Greece), making them Europe's third-greatest liars.

methods, and making wines worth being proud of once more. (For details, see the "Hungarian Wines" sidebar, later.)

Somehow Hungary, at the crossroads of Europe, has managed to become cosmopolitan while remaining perfectly Hungarian. In the countryside, where less mixing has occurred, traditional Magyar culture is more evident. But in the cities, Hungarians—like the country itself—are a cross-section of Central and Eastern European cultures: Magyars, Germans, Czechs, Slovaks, Poles, Serbs, Jews, Ottomans, Romanians, Roma (Gypsies), and many others. Still, no matter how many generations removed they are from Magyar stock, there's something different about Hungarians—and not just the language. Look a Hungarian in the eye, and you'll see a glimmer of the marauding Magyar, stomping in from the Central Asian plains a thousand years ago.

HUNGARY

Helpful Hints

First Name Last: Hungarians list a person's family name first, and the given name is last—just as in many other Eastern cultures (think of Kim Jong Il). So the composer known as "Franz Liszt" in German is "Liszt Ferenc" in his homeland. (To help reduce confusion, many Hungarian business cards list the surname in capital letters.)

Hello Goodbye: Hungarians have a charming habit of using the English word "hello" for both "hi" and "bye," just like the Italians use "ciao." You might overhear a Hungarian end a telephone conversation with a cheery "Hello!"

Telephones: Like many things in Hungary, the telephone system is uniquely confusing. You must dial different codes whether you're calling locally, long distance within the country, or internationally to Hungary.

Dialing Fixed Lines: To dial a number in the same city, simply dial direct, with no area code.

To dial long-distance within Hungary, you have to add the prefix 06, followed by the area code (e.g., Budapest's area code is 1, so you dial 06-1, then the rest of the number).

To make an international call to Hungary, start with the international access code (00 if calling from Europe, 011 from the United States or Canada), then Hungary's country code (36), then the area code (but not the 06) and number.

To make an international call from Hungary, dial 00, the country code of the country you're calling (see chart in appendix), the area code if applicable (may need to drop initial zero), and the local number.

Dialing Mobile Phones and Other Unusual Numbers: Certain Hungarian phone numbers are particularly tricky to dial. Numbers beginning with 0620, 0630, or 0670 are mobile phones; those beginning with 0680 are toll-free; and 0690 and 0691 are expensive toll lines.

To call these numbers from within Hungary, simply dial the number direct, as it appears in this book.

To dial these numbers from outside Hungary, you need to replace the initial 06 with 011-36 (from the US) or 00-36 (from Europe). So, to call my favorite Budapest guide from a fixed line inside Hungary, you'd dial 0620-926-0557; from North America, you'd dial 011-36-20-926-0557; and from another European country, you'd dial 00-36-20-926-0557.

Toll Sticker: Driving on Hungarian expressways requires a toll sticker (*autópálya matrica*, 1,650 Ft/4 days, 2,750 Ft/week, 4,500 Ft/month, www.motorway.hu). Your rental car likely has one (if you're picking it up on Hungary); if not, buy one at a gas station when you cross the border.

Hungarian History

The Hungarian story—essentially the tale of a people finding their home—is as epic as any in Europe. Over the course of a millennium, a troublesome nomadic tribe that was the scourge of Europe gradually assimilated with its neighbors and—through a combination of tenacity and diplomacy—found itself controlling a vast swath of Central and Eastern Europe. Locals toss around the names of great historical figures such as István, Kossuth, and Nagy as if they're talking about old friends. Take this crash course so you can keep up.

The story begins long, long ago and far, far away....

Welcome to Europe

The land we call Hungary today has long been considered the place—culturally, if not geographically—where the West (Europe) meets the East (Asia). The Roman province of Pannonia extended to the final foothills of the Alps that constitute the Buda Hills, on the west side of the Danube. Across the river, Rome's empire ended and the barbarian wilds began. From here, the Great Hungarian Plain stretches in a long, flat expanse all the way to Asia—hemmed in to the north by the Carpathian Mountains. (Geologists consider this prairie-like plain to be the westernmost steppe in Europe—resembling the terrain that covers much of Central Asia.) After Rome collapsed and Europe fell into the Dark Ages, Hungary became the territory of Celts, Vandals, Huns, and Avars...until some out-of-towners moved into the neighborhood.

The seven Magyar tribes, led by the mighty Árpád (and, according to legend, guided by the mythical Turul bird), thundered

into the Carpathian Basin in A.D. 896. They were a rough-and-tumble nomadic people from Central Asia who didn't like to settle down in one place. And yet, after their long and winding westward odyssey, the Great Hungarian Plain felt comfortingly like home to the Magyars—reminiscent of the Asian steppes of their ancestors.

The Magyars would camp out in today's Hungary in the winters, and in the summers, they'd go on raids throughout Europe. They were notorious as incredibly swift horsemen, whose use of stirrups (an eastern innovation largely unknown in Europe at the time) allowed them to easily outmaneuver foes and victims. Italy, France, Germany's Rhine, the Spanish Pyrenees, all the way to Constantinople (modern-day Istanbul)—the Magyars had the run of the Continent.

Now planted in the center of Europe, the Hungarians effectively drove a wedge in the middle of the sprawling Slavic populations of the Great Moravian Kingdom (basically today's "Eastern Europe"). The Slavs were split into two splinter groups, north and south—a division that persists today: Czechs, Slovaks, and Poles to the north; and Croats, Slovenes, Serbs, and Bosniaks to the south. (You can still hear the division caused by the Magyars in the language: While Czechs and Russians call a castle *hrad,* Croats and Serbs call it *grad.*)

For half a century, the Magyars ranked with the Vikings as the most feared people in Europe. But they were finally defeated by a German and Czech army at the Battle of Augsburg in 955. The Magyars' King Géza—realizing that if they were to survive, his people had to put down roots and get along with their neighbors—made the fateful decisions that would forever shape Hungary's

future: He adopted Christianity; baptized his son, Vajk; and married him to a Bavarian princess at a young age.

On Christmas Day in the year 1000, Vajk changed his name to István (Stephen) and was symbolically crowned by the pope (for more on István, see page 561). The domestication of the nomadic Magyars was difficult, thanks largely to the resistance of István's uncles, but was ultimately successful. Hungary became a legitimate Christian kingdom, welcomed by its neighbors.

The Tatars, the Ottomans, and Other Outsiders (A.D. 1000-1686)

One of Hungary's earliest challenges came at the hands of fellow invaders from Central Asia. Through the first half of the 13th century, the Tatars swept into Eastern Europe from Mongolia. They sacked and plundered Hungarian towns, laying waste to the kingdom. When they left, the Hungarian king at the time, Béla IV, was left to rebuild his ruined kingdom from the rubble—constructing many of the stout hilltop castles that still line the Danube.

Each of Béla's successors left his own mark on Hungary, as the Magyar kingdom flourished. They barely skipped a beat when the original Árpád dynasty died out in 1301, as they imported French kings (from the Naples-based Anjou, or Angevin, dynasty) to continue building their young realm.

For more than 150 years, Hungary did not have a Hungarian-blooded king. This changed in the late 15th century, when a shortage of foreign kings led to the ascension to the throne of the

enlightened King Mátyás (Matthias) Corvinus. The son of popular military hero János Hunyadi, King Matthias fostered the arts, sparked a mini-Renaissance, and successfully balanced foreign threats to Hungarian sovereignty (the Habsburgs to the north and west, and the Ottomans to the south and east). Under Matthias, Hungarian culture and political power reached a peak. (For more on this great Hungarian king, see page 556.)

But even before the reign of "good king Matthias," the Ottomans (from today's Turkey) had already begun slicing their way through the Balkan Peninsula toward Eastern Europe. In 1526, the Ottomans entered Hungary when Sultan Süleyman the Magnificent killed Hungary's King Lajos II at the Battle of Mohács. By 1541, they took Buda. The Ottomans would dominate Hungarian life (and history) until the 1680s—nearly a century and a half.

The Ottoman invasion divided Hungary into thirds: Ottoman-occupied "Lower Hungary" (more or less today's Hungary); rump "Upper Hungary" (basically today's Slovakia), with its capital at Bratislava (which they called "Pozsony"); and the loosely independent territories of Transylvania (in today's Romania), ruled by Hungarian dukes. During this era, the Ottomans built many of the thermal baths that you'll still find throughout Hungary.

Ottoman-occupied Hungary became severely depopulated, and many of its towns and cities fell into ruins. While it was advantageous for a Hungarian subject to adopt Islam (for lower taxes and other privileges), the Ottomans rarely resorted to forced conversion—unlike the arguably more oppressive Catholics who controlled other parts of Europe at the time (such as the monarchs of Spain, who expelled the Jews and conducted the Spanish Inquisition). Ottoman rule meant that Hungary took a different course than other parts of Europe during this time. The nation fully enjoyed the Renaissance, but missed out on other major European historical events—both good (the Age of Discovery and Age of Reason) and bad (the devastating Catholic-versus-Protestant wars that plagued much of the rest of Europe).

Crippled by the Ottomans and lacking power and options, Hungarian nobles desperately offered their crown to the Austrian Habsburg Empire, in exchange for salvation from the invasion. The Habsburgs instead used Hungary as a kind of "buffer zone" between the Ottoman advance and Vienna. And that was only the beginning of a very troubled relationship between the Hungarians and the Austrians.

Habsburg Rule, Hungarian National Revival, and Revolution (1686-1867)

In the late 17th century, the Habsburg army, starting from Vienna, began a sustained campaign to push the Ottomans out of Hungary in about 15 years. They finally wrested Buda and Pest from the Ottomans in 1686. The Habsburgs repopulated Buda and Pest with Germans, while Magyars reclaimed the countryside.

The Habsburgs governed Hungary as an outpost of Austria. The Hungarians—who'd had enough of foreign rule—fought them tooth and nail. Countless streets, squares, and buildings throughout the country are named for the "big three" Hungarian patriots who resisted the Habsburgs during this time: Ferenc Rákóczi (who led the unsuccessful War of Independence in 1703-1711), István Széchenyi (a wealthy count who funded grand structures to give his Magyar countrymen something to take pride in), and Lajos Kossuth (who led the Revolution of 1848; pictured).

The early 19th century saw a thawing of Habsburg oppression. Here as throughout Europe, "backward" country traditions began to trickle into the cities, gaining more respect and prominence. It was during this time of reforms that Hungarian (rather than German) became the official language. It also coincided with a Romantic Age of poets and writers (such as Mihály Vörösmarty and Sándor Petőfi) who began to use the Hungarian tongue to create literature for the first time. By around 1825, the Hungarian National Revival was under way, as the people began to embrace the culture and traditions of their Magyar ancestors. Like people across Europe—from Ireland to Italy, and from Prague to Scandinavia—the Hungarians were beginning to celebrate what made them a unique people.

In March of 1848, a wave of Enlightenment-fueled nationalism that began in Paris spread like wildfire across Europe, igniting a revolutionary spirit in cities such as Budapest. On March 15, the Revolution of 1848 began on the steps of the National Museum in Pest. In the spring of 1849, the Hungarians mounted a bloody but successful offensive to take over a wide swath of territory, including Buda and Pest. But in June, some 200,000 Russian reinforcements flooded into Hungary, crushing the revolution. After the final battle, the Habsburgs executed 13 Hungarian generals, then celebrated by clinking mugs of beer. To this very day, clinking beer mugs is, for many traditional Hungarians, just bad style.

For a while, the Habsburgs cracked down on their unruly

Hungarian subjects. But after an important military loss to Bismarck's Prussia in 1866, Austria began to realize that it couldn't control its rebellious Slavic holdings all by itself. And so, just 18 years after crushing the Hungarians in a war, the Habsburgs handed them the reins. With the Compromise *(Ausgleich)* of 1867, Austria granted Budapest the authority over the eastern half of their lands, creating the so-called Dual Monarchy of the Austro-Hungarian Empire. Hungary was granted their much-prized "home rule," where most matters (except finance, foreign policy, and the military) were administered from Budapest rather than Vienna. The Habsburg emperor, Franz Josef, agreed to a unique "king and emperor" *(König und Kaiser)* arrangement, where he was emperor of Austria, but only king of Hungary. In 1867, he was crowned as Hungarian king in both Buda (at Matthias Church) and Pest (on today's Roosevelt tér). The insignia "K+K" (*König und Kaiser*, king and emperor)—which you'll still see everywhere—evokes these grand days.

Budapest's Golden Age (1867-1918)

The *Ausgleich* marked a dramatic turning point for the Hungarians, who once again governed their traditional holdings: large parts of today's Slovakia, Serbia, and Transylvania (northwest Romania), and smaller parts of today's Croatia, Slovenia, Ukraine, and Austria. To better govern their sprawling realm, in 1873, the cities of Buda, Pest, and Óbuda merged into one mega-metropolis: Budapest.

Serendipitously, Budapest's new prominence coincided with the 1,000th anniversary of the Hungarians' ancestors, the Magyars, arriving in Europe...one more excuse to dress things up. Budapest's long-standing rivalry with Vienna only spurred them to build bigger and better. The year 1896 saw an over-the-top millennial celebration, for which many of today's greatest structures were created (see page 539).

It was clearly Budapest's Golden Age. No European city grew faster in the second half of the 19th century than Budapest; in the last quarter of the 19th century alone, Budapest doubled in size. By 1900, the city was larger than Rome, Madrid, or Amsterdam. But before long, the Hungarians began to make the same mistakes the Habsburgs had—disrespecting the rights of their minorities, and enforcing a policy of "Magyarization" that compelled subjects from all ethnic backgrounds to adopt the Hungarian language and culture. Soon the Golden Age came crashing to an end, and Hungary plunged into its darkest period.

The Crisis of Trianon (1918-1939)

World War I marked the end of the age of divine monarchs, as

Pre-Trianon Hungary

- Pre-Trianon Hungary (1920)
- Current Hungarian Border

200 Miles
100 Km

POLAND
UKRAINE
CZECH. REP.
SLOVAKIA
MOLDOVA
Danube R.
Vienna
Budapest
AUSTRIA
TRANSYLVANIA
SLOVENIA
ROMANIA
ITALY
CROATIA
VOJVODINA
BOSNIA-HERZ.
Danube R.
Black Sea
Adriatic Sea
SERBIA
BULGARIA

the Romanovs of Russia, the Ottomans of Asia Minor, and, yes, the Habsburgs of Austria-Hungary saw their empires break apart. Hungary, which had been riding the Habsburgs' coattails to power and prominence for the past half-century, now paid the price. As retribution for their role on the losing side of World War I, the 1920 Treaty of Trianon reassigned two-thirds of Hungary's former territory and half of its population to Romania, Ukraine, Czechoslovakia, and Yugoslavia (Slovenia, Croatia, and Serbia).

It is impossible to overstate the impact of the Treaty of Trianon on the Hungarian psyche—and on Hungarian history. Not unlike the overnight construction of the Berlin Wall, towns along the new Hungarian borders were suddenly divided down the middle. Many Hungarians found themselves unable to visit relatives or commute to jobs that were in the same country the day before. This sent hundreds of thousands of Hungarian refugees— now "foreigners" in their own towns—into Budapest, sparking an enormous but bittersweet boom in the capital.

To this day, the Treaty of Trianon is regarded as one of the greatest tragedies of Hungarian history. Like the Basques and the Serbs, the Hungarians feel separated from each other by circumstances outside their control. Today, more than two million ethnic Hungarians live outside Hungary (mostly in Romania)— and many Hungarians claim that these lands still belong to the Magyars. You'll see maps, posters, and bumper stickers with the distinctive shape of a much larger, pre-WWI Hungary...patriotically displayed by Magyars who feel as strongly about Trianon as if it happened yesterday.

After Trianon, the newly shrunken Kingdom of Hungary had to reinvent itself. The Hungarian crown sat unworn in the

Royal Palace, as if waiting for someone worthy to claim it. The WWI hero Admiral Miklós Horthy had won many battles with the Austro-Hungarian navy. Though the new Hungary had no sea and no navy, Horthy retained his rank and ruled the country as a regent. A popular joke points out that during this time, Hungary was a "kingdom without a king" and a landlocked country ruled by a sea admiral. This sense of compounded deficiency pretty much sums up the morose attitude Hungarians have about those gloomy post-Trianon days.

A mounting financial crisis, and lingering resentment about the strict post-WWI reparations, made Hungary fertile ground for some bold new fascist ideas.

World War II and the Arrow Cross (1939-1945)

As Adolf Hitler rose to power, some countries that had felt unfairly treated in the aftermath of World War I—including Hungary—saw Nazi Germany as a vehicle to greater independence. Admiral Horthy joined forces with the Nazis with the hope that they might help Hungary regain the crippling territorial losses of Trianon. In June 1941, Hungary (reluctantly) declared war on the Soviet Union—and against the US and Britain in December.

Being an ally to the Nazis, rather than an occupied state, also allowed Hungary a certain degree of self-determination through the war—temporarily saving its sizeable Jewish population from immediate deportation. Winning back chunks of Slovakia, Transylvania, and Croatia in the early days of World War II also bolstered the Nazis' acceptance in Hungary.

As Nazism took hold in Germany, the Hungarian fascist movement—spearheaded by the Arrow Cross Party (Nyilaskeresztes Párt)—gained popularity within Hungary. As Germany increased its demands for Hungarian soldiers and food, Admiral Horthy resisted...until Hitler's patience wore thin. In March of 1944, the Nazis invaded and installed the Arrow Cross in power. The Arrow Cross made up for lost time, immediately beginning a savage campaign of executing Hungary's Jews—not only sending them to death camps, but butchering them in the streets. As the end of the war neared, Hungarian Nazi collaborators resorted to more desperate measures, such as lining up Jews along the Danube and shooting them into the river. To save bullets, they'd sometimes tie several victims together, shoot one of them, and throw him into the freezing Danube—dragging the others in with him. Hungary lost nearly 600,000 Jews to the Holocaust. The Soviet Army eventually "liberated" Hungary, but at the expense of Budapest: A months-long siege, from Christmas of 1944 to mid-February of 1945, reduced the proud city to rubble. One in 10 Hungarian citizens perished in the war.

HUNGARY

Communism...with a Pinch of Paprika (1945-1989)

After World War II, Hungary was gradually compelled to adopt Moscow's system of government. The Soviet-puppet hardliner Mátyás Rákosi ruled Hungary with an iron fist. Everyday people were terrorized by the KGB-style secret police, called the ÁVO and ÁVH, to accept the new regime. Non-Hungarians were deported, potential and actual dissidents disappeared into the horrifying gulag system of Siberia, food shortages were epidemic, people were compelled to spy on their friends and families, and countless lives were ruined.

Beginning on October 23, 1956, the Hungarians courageously staged a monumental uprising, led by Communist Party reformer Imre Nagy. Initially, it appeared that one of the cells of the Soviet Bloc might win itself the right to semi-autonomy. But Moscow couldn't let that happen. In a Tiananmen Square-style crackdown, the Soviets sent in tanks to brutally put down the uprising and occupy the city. When the dust settled, 2,500 Hungarians were dead, and 200,000 fled to the West. (If you know any Hungarians in the US, their families more than likely fled there in 1956.) Nagy was arrested, given a sham trial, and executed in 1958. For more on these events, see the "1956" sidebar on page 570.

After the uprising, the USSR installed János Kádár—a colleague of Nagy's who was also loyal to Moscow—to lead Hungary. For a few years, things were bleak, as the secret police ratcheted up their efforts against potential dissidents. But in the 1960s, Kádár's reformist tendencies began to cautiously emerge. While still mostly cooperating with Moscow, Kádár gradually allowed the people of Hungary more freedom than citizens of neighboring countries had—a system dubbed "goulash communism." The "New Economic Mechanism" of 1968 partly opened Hungary to foreign trade. People from other Warsaw Pact countries—Czechs, Slovaks, and Poles—flocked to Budapest's Váci utca to experience "Western evils" unavailable to them back home, such as Adidas sneakers and Big Macs. People half-joked that Hungary was the happiest barrack in the communist camp.

In the late 1980s, the Eastern Bloc began to thaw. And Hungary—which was always skeptical of the Soviets (or any foreign rule)—was one of the first satellite states that implemented real change. In February of 1989, the Hungarian communist parliament, with little fanfare, essentially voted to put an expiration date on their own regime. There were three benchmarks in that fateful year: May 2, when Hungary was the first Soviet Bloc country to effectively open its borders to the West (by removing its border fence with Austria); June 16, when communist reformer Imre Nagy and his comrades were given a proper, ceremonial reburial on Heroes' Square in Budapest; and August 19, when, in the first tentative steps toward the reunification of Europe, Hungarians and Austrians came together in a field near the town of Sopron for the so-called "Pan-European Picnic." (Some 900 East Germans seized this opportunity to make a run for the border...and slipped into the West while Hungarian border guards refused their orders to shoot defectors.) On October 23—the anniversary of the 1956 Uprising—the truly democratic Republic of Hungary triumphantly replaced the People's Republic of Hungary.

Hungary Today (1989-Present)

The transition from communism to capitalism has been rocky in Hungary. While many Hungarians were eager for the freedom to travel and pursue the interests that democracy allowed them, many others struggled to cope with the sudden reduction of government-provided services. In 2004, Hungary took the monumental step of joining the European Union. But the EU hasn't solved all of the country's problems. Hungary's leaders continue to struggle with how to afford the generous social-welfare network its people have come to expect. The Hungarian Socialist Party, which took control of parliament in 2002, stubbornly maintained and even extended some social programs, prompting experts to worry that the mounting public debt would bankrupt the country.

Hungary made international headlines in 2006, when Prime Minister Ferenc Gyurcsány gave a secret speech to the party's lead-

ers after his Hungarian Socialist Party won re-election in April. The intent of his shockingly frank remarks was to give his colleagues a wake-up call. But Gyurcsány's method—ranting on and on about how badly they'd fouled things up (and using very colorful language)—was ill-advised. Someone in the meeting recorded the whole thing, waited a few months, then turned the audiotape over to the press. On September 17, 2006, Hungarians turned on their TVs to hear their prime minister detailing the ways he and his party had driven their country to the brink of ruin: "We have screwed up. Not a little but a lot. No country in Europe has screwed up as much as we have...We did not actually do anything for four years. Nothing...We lied morning, noon, and night." The following night, demonstrators showed up at two strategic squares in downtown Budapest, demanding Gyurcsány's resignation. Gyurcsány refused, and held on to power for another three years. He finally resigned in early 2009, acknowledging that he was getting in the way of Hungary's economic recovery.

HUNGARY

Viktor Orbán, of the right-of-center Fidesz Party, became prime minister in May of 2010. Fidesz took its huge two-thirds majority as a mandate to completely remake Hungary. Even before Orbán formally took office, Fidesz passed a law extending Hungarian citizenship to people of Hungarian descent living in neighboring countries (stoking age-old Hungarian resentment about the post-WWI Treaty of Trianon territorial losses). This strained the always-tense relations with Slovakia; Slovak government officials retaliated by saying that anyone choosing to accept Hungarian citizenship would lose their Slovak citizenship. In early 2011, Orbán's party created a new FCC-like media authority with broad latitude for suppressing material that it considers inappropriate. Attacked by both Hungarian and international critics for its potential to infringe on the free press, this new media law has been submitted to EU authorities for review. Fidesz has also pursued reforming the government in ways that, both the US and European governments have stated, may place alarming limits on Hungary's democracy.

Fortunately, tourists visiting today's Hungary are scarcely aware of its economic and political woes. The Hungarian people—relieved to be free of oppression, and allowed to pursue their lovably quirky customs with a renewed vigor—enthusiastically welcome and charm visitors. It's been a long road for the Hungarians from those distant, windblown steppes of Central Asia...but today they seem to be doing better than ever.

Hungarian Food

Hungarian cuisine is the undisputed best in Central Europe. It delicately blends Magyar peasant cooking (with rich spices), refined by the elegance of French preparation, with a delightful smattering of flavors from the vast, multiethnic Austro-Hungarian Empire (including Germanic, Balkan, Jewish, and Carpathian). Everything is heavily seasoned: with paprika, tomatoes, and peppers of every shape, color, size, and flavor.

An *étterem* ("eatery") is a nice sit-down restaurant, while a *vendéglő* is usually more casual (similar to a tavern or an inn). A *söröző* ("beer place") is a pub that sells beer and food, ranging from a small selection of snacks to a full menu. A *kávéház* ("coffeehouse"), or café, is where Budapesters gather to meet friends, get a caffeine fix...and sometimes to have a great meal. Other cafés serve only light food, or sometimes only desserts. But if you want a wide choice of cakes, look for a *cukrászda* (pastry shop—*cukr* means "sugar").

When foreigners think of Hungarian cuisine, what comes to mind is goulash. But tourists are often disappointed when "real Hungarian goulash" isn't the thick stew that they were expect-

ing. The word "goulash" comes from the Hungarian *gulyás leves,* or "shepherd's soup"—a tasty, rustic, nourishing dish originally eaten by cowboys and shepherds on the Great Hungarian Plain. Here in its homeland, it's a clear, spicy broth with chunks of meat, potatoes, and other vegetables. Elsewhere (such as in Hungary's Germanic and Slavic neighbors), the word "goulash" does describe a thick stew.

Aside from the obligatory *gulyás,* make a point of trying another unusual Hungarian specialty: cold fruit soup *(hideg gyümölcs leves).* This sweet, cream-based treat—generally eaten before the meal, even though it tastes more like a dessert—is usually made with *meggy* (sour cherries), but you'll also see versions with *alma* (apples) or *körte* (pears). Other Hungarian soups *(levesek)* include *bableves* (bean soup), *zöldségleves* (vegetable soup), *gombaleves* (mushroom soup), *halászlé* (fish broth with paprika), *húsleves* (meat or chicken soup), and *pörkölt* (a simmered-meat soup similar to goulash but without the potatoes). The ultimate staple of traditional Hungarian home-cooking, but rarely served in restaurants, is *főzelék*—a simple but tasty wheat flour–thickened stew that can be supplemented with various vegetables and meats (served at cheap restaurants around Budapest—see the Főzelékfaló Ételbár listing on page 646).

Hungarians adore all kinds of meat *(hús). Csirke* is chicken, *borjú* is veal, *kacsa* is duck, *liba* is goose, *sertés* is pork, *sonka* is ham, *kolbász* is sausage, *szelet* is schnitzel (*Bécsi szelet* means Wiener schnitzel)—and the list goes on. *Libamáj* is goose liver, which shows up everywhere (for example, anything prepared "Budapest style" is topped with goose liver). Lard is used extensively in cooking, making Hungarian cuisine very rich and filling.

Meat is often covered with delicious sauces or garnishes, from rich cream sauces to spicy pastes to fruit jam. For classic Hungarian flavors, you can't beat chicken or veal *paprikás* (described later in the "Paprika Primer" sidebar).

Vegetarians have a tricky time in traditional Hungarian restaurants, many of which offer only a plate of deep-fried vegetables. They haven't quite figured out how to do a good, healthy,

Paprika Primer

The quintessential ingredient in Hungarian cuisine is paprika. In Hungarian, the word *paprika* can mean both peppers (red or green) and the spice that's made from them. Peppers can be stewed, stuffed, sautéed, baked, grilled, or pickled. For seasoning, red shakers of dried paprika join the salt and pepper on tables.

Locals say paprika is best from the sunny south of Hungary. There are more than 40 varieties of paprika spice, with two main types: hot (*csípős* or *erős*) and sweet (*édesnemes* or simply *édes,* often comes in a white can; sometimes also called *csemege*—"delicate"). Hungarians typically cook with sweet paprika to add flavor and color. Then, at the table, they put out hot paprika so each diner can adjust the heat to his or her preferred taste. A can or bag of paprika is a handy and tasty souvenir of your trip (see the "Shopping in Budapest" section).

On menus, anything cooked *paprikás* (PAW-pree-kash) comes smothered in a spicy, creamy red stew. Most often you'll see this option with *csirke* (chicken) or *borjú* (veal), and it's generally served with dumpling-like boiled egg noodles called *nokedli* (similar to German *Spätzle*). This dish is *the* Hungarian staple—if you sample just one dish in Hungary, make it chicken or veal *paprikás*.

To add even more kick to your food, ask for a jar of the bright-red paste called *Erős Pista* (EH-rewsh PEESH-taw). Literally "Spicy Steve," this Hungarian answer to Tabasco is best used sparingly. Or try *Édes Anna* (AY-desh AW-naw, "Sweet Anna"), a newer variation that's more sweet than spicy.

---

leafy salad; a traditional restaurant will generally offer only marinated cucumbers (listed on menus as "cucumber salad"), a plate of sliced-up pickles ("pickled cucumbers"), marinated spicy peppers, or something with cabbage—using lettuce only as a garnish. Fortunately, the more modern, trendy eateries in the capital often offer excellent vegetarian options.

Starches *(köretek)*—which you'll sometimes order separate from the meat course—can include *nokedli* (small potato dumplings, a.k.a. *Spätzle*), *galuska* (noodles), *burgonya* (potatoes), *krumpli* (French fries), *krokett* (croquettes), or *rizs* (rice). *Kenyér* (bread) often comes with the meal.

Sometimes your main dish will come with steamed, grilled, or deep-fried vegetables. A common side dish is *káposzta* (cabbage, often prepared like sauerkraut). You may also see *töltött káposzta* (cabbage stuffed with meat) or *töltött paprika* (stuffed peppers). Look for the traditional (and increasingly in-vogue) dish called *lecsó* (LEH-chew). Basically the Hungarian answer to ratatouille, this is a mix of tomatoes, peppers, and other vegetables.

Thin, crêpe-like pancakes *(palacsinta)* are sometimes served as a main dish. A delicious traditional Hungarian dish is *Hortobágyi palacsinta* (Hortobágy pancakes, named for the Hungarian Great Plain where the dish originates). This is a savory crêpe wrapped around a tasty meat filling and drenched with creamy paprika sauce.

Pancakes also appear as desserts, stuffed and/or covered with fruit, jam, chocolate sauce, walnuts, poppy seeds, or whipped cream. Most famous is the *Gundel palacsinta*, named for *the* top-of-the-line Budapest restaurant—stuffed with walnuts and raisins in a rum sauce, topped with chocolate sauce, and flambéed.

Pastries are a big deal in Hungary. In the late 19th century, pastry-making caught on here in an attempt to keep up with the

renowned desserts of rival Vienna. Today Hungary's streets are still lined with *cukrászda* (pastry shops), where you can simply point to whichever treat you'd like. Try the *Dobos torta* (a many-layered chocolate-and-caramel cream cake), *somlói galuska* (a dumpling with vanilla, nuts, and chocolate), anything with *gesztenye* (chestnuts), and *rétes* (strudel with various fillings, including *túrós*, curds). And many *cukrászda* also serve *fagylalt* (ice cream, *fagyi* for short), sold by the *gomboc* (ball).

When the server comes to take your order, he or she might say *"Tessék"* (TEHSH-shayk), or maybe the more formal *"Tessék parancsolni"* (TEHSH-shayk PAW-rawn-chohl-nee)—"Please command, sir." When they bring the food, they will probably say, *"Jó étvágyat!"* (yoh AYT-vah-yawt)—"Bon appétit." When you're ready for the bill, you can simply say, *"Fizetek"* (FEE-zeh-tehk)—"I'll pay."

Drinks

Kávé (KAH-vay) and *tea* (TEH-aw) are coffee and tea. As for water *(víz*, veez) it comes as *szódavíz* (soda water, sometimes just carbonated tap water) or *ásványvíz* (spring water, more expensive).

Hungarian Wines

Wine *(bor)* is an essential part of Hungarian cuisine. Whites *(fehér)* can be sweet *(édes)*, half-dry *(félszáraz)*, or dry *(száraz)*. Whites include the standards (Riesling, Chardonnay), as well as some wines made from more typically Hungarian grapes: **Leányka** ("Little Girl"), a half-dry, fairly heavy, white table  wine; **Cserszegi Fűszeres,** a spicy, light white that can be fruity; the half-dry, full-bodied **Hárslevélű** ("Linden Leaf"); and the dry **Furmint** and **Kéknyelű** ("Blue Stalk").

Reds *(vörös)* include the familiar varieties (Cabernet Sauvignon, Cabernet Franc, Merlot, Pinot Noir), and some that are less familiar. **Kekporto** is better known as Blauer Portugieser in German-speaking countries. In Eger, don't miss **Bull's Blood,** a.k.a. Egri Bikavér, a distinctive blend of reds that comes with a fun local legend (described on page 669). The spicy, medium-body **Kékfrankos** ("Blue Frankish") supposedly got its name because when Napoleonic soldiers were here, they could pay either with valuable blue-colored bank notes, or unstable white ones...and local vintners wanted the blue francs. (Like most wine origin legends, this story is untrue—Kékfránkos wasn't cultivated here until after Napoleon's time.)

Probably the most famous Hungarian wine is **Tokaji Aszú,**

Hungary is first and foremost a wine country. For the complete rundown on Hungarian wines, see the sidebar.

Hungary isn't particularly well-known for its beer *(sör,* pronounced "shewr"), but Dreher and Borsodi are two of the better brands. *Villagos* is lager; if you prefer something darker, look for *barna* (brown).

Hungary is almost as proud of its spirits as its wines. Unicum is a unique and beloved Hungarian bitter liquor made of 40 different herbs and aged in oak casks. The flavor is powerfully unforgettable—like Jägermeister, but harsher. A swig of Unicum is often gulped before the meal, but it's also used as a cure for an upset stomach (especially if you've eaten too much rich food—not an uncommon problem in Hungary). Unicum has a history as complicated as its flavor. Invented by a Doctor Zwack in the late 18th century, the drink impressed Habsburg Emperor Josef II, who supposedly declared: *"Das ist ein Unikum!"* ("This is a specialty!") A newer version, called Unicum Next, has a softer cherry flavor; its ads target the new generation of Hungarian drinkers. To get your

a sweet, late-harvest, honey-colored dessert wine made primarily from Furmint grapes. Known as the "wine of kings, and the king of wines," Tokaji Aszú is a D.O.C. product, meaning that to have that name, it must be grown in a particular region. Tokaj is a town in northeastern Hungary (not far from Eger), while Aszú is a "noble rot" grape. The wine's unique, concentrated flavor is made possible by a fungus *(Botrytis cinerea)* that thrives on the grapes

in the late fall. The grapes are left on the vine, where they burst and wither like raisins before they are harvested in late October and November. This sucks the water out of the grape, leaving behind a very high sugar content and a deep golden color. Tokaji Aszú wines are numbered, from three to six, indicating how many eight-gallon tubs *(puttony)* of these "noble rot" grapes were added to the base wine—the higher the number, the sweeter the wine. Other variations on Tokaji can be less sweet. (The similarly named French Tokay wine—which derives from the same word—is a different story altogether.)

Finally, note that, except for Bull's Blood and Tokaji Aszú, Hungarian wines are not widely available in the US. Packing home a bottle or two (in your checked luggage) is a unique souvenir.

own taste of this family saga, look for the round bottle with the red cross on the label (www.zwack.hu).

For a more straightforward spirit, try the local firewater, *pálinka*, a powerful schnapps made from various fruits (most often plum, *szilva;* or apricots, *barack*). Also look for the pear-flavored Vilmos brandy.

If you're drinking with some new Magyar friends, impress them with the standard toast: *Egészségedre* (EH-gehs-shay-geh-dreh; "to your health").

Hungarian Language

Even though Hungary is surrounded by Slavs, Hungarian is not at all related to Slavic languages (such as Polish, Czech, or Croatian). In fact, Hungarian isn't related to *any* European language, except for very distant relatives Finnish and Estonian. It isn't even an Indo-European language. English is more closely related to Hindi, Russian, and French than it is to Hungarian.

Hungarian is agglutinative, which means that you start with a simple root word and then start tacking on suffixes to create mean-ing—sometimes resulting in a pileup of extra sounds at the end of a very long word. The emphasis always goes on the first syllable, and the following syllables are droned in a kind of a monotone—giving the language a distinctive cadence that Hungary's neigh-bors love to tease about.

While the language is overwhelming for tourists, one easy word is *"Szia"* (SEE-yaw), which means both hello and goodbye (like "ciao" or "aloha"). Confusingly, sometimes Hungarians sim-ply say the English word "hello" to mean either "hi" or "bye."

Hungarian pronunciation is straightforward, once you remember a few key rules. The trickiest: *s* alone is pronounced "sh," while *sz* is pronounced "s." This explains why you'll hear in-the-know travelers pronouncing Budapest as "BOO-daw-pesht." You might catch the *busz* up to Castle Hill—pronounced "boose." And "Franz Liszt" is easier to pronounce than it looks: It sounds just like "list." To review:

s sounds like "sh" as in "shirt"

sz sounds like "s" as in "saint"

Hungarian has a set of unusual palatal sounds that don't quite have a counterpart in English. To make these sounds, gently press the thick part of your tongue to the roof or your mouth (instead of using the tip of your tongue behind your teeth, as we do in English):

gy sounds like "dg" as in "hedge"

ny sounds like "ny" as in "canyon" (not "nee")

ty sounds like "tch" as in "itch"

cs sounds like "ch" as in "church"

As for vowels: The letter *a* almost sounds like o (aw, as in "hot"); but with an accent *(á)*, it brightens up to the more standard "ah." Likewise, while *e* sounds like "eh," *é* sounds like "ay." An accent *(á, é, í, ó, ú)* indicates that you linger on that vowel, but not necessarily that you stress that syllable. Like German, Hungarian has umlauts *(ö, ü)*, meaning you purse your lips when you say that vowel: roughly, *ö* sounds like "ur" and *ü* sounds like "ew." A long umlaut *(ő, ű)* is the same sound, but you hold it a little longer. Words ending in *k* are often plural.

Here are a few other letters that sound different in Hungarian than in English:

c and **cz** both sound like "ts" as in "cats"

zs sounds like "zh" as in "leisure"

j and **ly** both sound like "y" as in "yellow"

OK, maybe it's not *so* simple. But you'll get the hang of it...and Hungarians will appreciate your efforts. For a list of Hungarian survival phrases, see page 1267 in the appendix.

As you navigate, remember these key Hungarian terms: *tér*

(pronounced "tehr," square), *utca* (OOT-zaw, street), *út* (oot, boulevard), *körút* (KUR-root, ring road), *híd* (heed, bridge), and *város* (VAH-rohsh, town). To better match what you'll see locally, in the following chapters I've mostly used these Hungarian terms (instead of the English equivalents).

BUDAPEST

Budapest (locals say "BOO-daw-pesht") is, in so many ways, the capital of Eastern Europe. Europe's most underrated big city, Budapest is a unique metropolis at the heart of a unique nation. Feel your stress ebb away as you soak in hundred-degree water, surrounded by opulent Baroque domes...and by Speedo- and bikini-clad Hungarians. Ogle some of Europe's most richly decorated interiors, which faintly echo a proud little nation's bygone glory days. Open your ears to a first-rate performance at one of the world's top opera houses—at bargain prices. Ponder the region's bleak communist era as you stroll amidst giant Soviet-style statues designed to evoke fear and obedience. Try to wrap your head around Hungary's colorful history...and your tongue around some of its notoriously difficult words. Dive into a bowl of goulash, the famous paprika-flavored peasant soup with a kick. Go for an after-dinner stroll along the Danube, immersed in a grand city that's bathed in floodlights.

Budapest is as challenging as it is enchanting. The Hungarian capital on the banks of the Danube excites good travelers...and exasperates bad ones. It's a city of nuance and paradox—cosmopolitan, complicated, and tricky for the first-timer to get a handle on. Like a full-bodied Hungarian wine, Budapest can overwhelm visitors, even as it intoxicates them with delights. But if you equip yourself with the information in this chapter, delving into the city can be an exhilarating experience.

Planning Your Time

Budapest is quite decentralized, making efficient sightseeing tricky. You'll have to zig and zag, refer to your map constantly, rely on public transit, and strategize to maximize your sightseeing time. Visitors attempting to "do" Budapest in just one day leave dazed, exhausted...and yearning for more. Two days are the bare minimum, and force you to tackle the city at a breakneck pace (and you still won't see everything). Three or four days are ideal.

I've left your **evenings** open for your choice of activities: enjoying good restaurants, taking in an opera or concert, snuggling on a romantic floodlit river cruise, exploring the city's unique "ruin pubs," or simply strolling the Danube embankments and bridges. (Your options are outlined under "Entertainment in Budapest" on page 616.)

Budapest in Two Days

Spend **Day 1** in Pest. Begin at the Parliament and stroll through Leopold Town, then walk through Pest Town Center to the Great Market Hall. From there, circle around the Small Boulevard to Deák tér and consider strolling up Andrássy út to Heroes' Square and City Park. Or, if you're exhausted already, just take the M1/yellow Metró line to Hősök tere, ogle the Heroes' Square statues and Vajdahunyad Castle, and reward yourself with a soak at Széchenyi Baths. (Note that this leaves virtually no time for entering any museums—though you might be able to fit in one or two big sights, such as the Parliament, Opera House, Great Synagogue, or House of Terror.)

On the morning of **Day 2,** tackle any Pest sights you didn't have time for yesterday (or take the bus out to Memento Park). After lunch, ride bus #16 from Deák tér to Castle Hill. Head back to Pest for some final sightseeing and dinner.

Budapest in Three or Four Days

Use the above plan as a starting point, but spread the Pest sights over two (or three) days. This much time allows you to actually enter many of the sights you'd otherwise only have time to sprint past. Consider devoting one Pest day to Leopold Town, the Town Center, and the Small Boulevard sights; another day to Andrássy út and Heroes' Square/City Park; and—if you have it—yet another day to visit Memento Park, slow down, and enter even more sights.

Orientation to Budapest

Budapest is huge, with nearly two million people. Like Vienna, the city was built as the head of a much larger empire than it currently governs—which can make it feel a bit too grandiose for the capital of a small country. But Budapest is surprisingly easy to manage once you get the lay of the land and learn the excellent

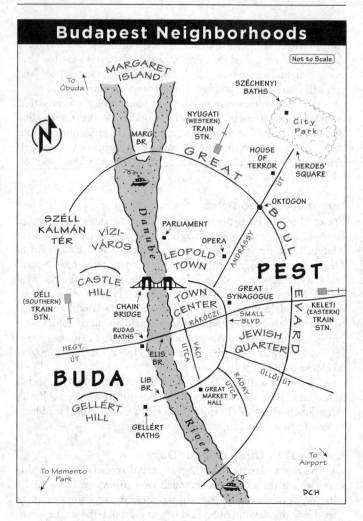

Budapest Neighborhoods

Not to Scale

public transportation network. Those who are comfortable with the Metró, trams, and buses have the city by the tail (see "Getting Around Budapest," later).

The city is split down the center by the Danube River. On the west side of the Danube is hilly **Buda,** and on the east is flat **Pest** (pronounced "pesht"). A third part of the city, **Óbuda,** sits to the north of Buda.

Buda: Buda is dominated by **Castle Hill** (packed with tourists by day, dead at night). The pleasant **Víziváros** ("Water Town"; VEE-zee-vah-rohsh) neighborhood is between the castle and the river; nearby is the square called Batthyány tér (a handy hub for the Metró—M2/red line—plus tram lines and the HÉV suburban

railway). To the south is the taller, wooded **Gellért Hill,** capped by the Liberation Monument, with a pair of thermal baths at its base (Gellért and Rudas).

Pest: Just across the river from Castle Hill, **"Downtown" Pest** is divided into two sections: The more genteel northern half, called **Leopold Town** (Lipótváros), surrounds the giant Parliament building. This is the governmental, business, and banking district (sleepy after hours). The southern half, the grittier and more urban-feeling **Town Center** (Belváros, literally "Inner Town"), is a thriving shopping, dining, nightlife, and residential zone that bustles day and night. Major landmarks here include the famous (and overrated) Váci utca shopping street and the vast Great Market Hall.

Roads: The Town Center is hemmed in by the first of Pest's four concentric **ring roads** *(körút)*. The innermost ring is called the Kiskörút, or "Small Boulevard." The next ring, several blocks farther out, is called the Nagykörút, or "Great Boulevard." These ring roads change names every few blocks, but they are always called *körút*. Arterial **boulevards,** called *út*, stretch from central Pest into the suburbs like spokes on a wheel. One of these boulevards, **Andrássy út,** begins near Deák tér in central Pest and heads out to Heroes' Square and City Park; along the way it passes some of the city's best eateries, hotels, and sights (Opera House, House of Terror).

Bridges: Buda and Pest are connected by a series of characteristic bridges. From north to south, there's the low-profile **Margaret Bridge** (Margit híd, crosses Margaret Island), the famous **Chain Bridge** (Széchenyi lánchíd), the white and modern **Elisabeth Bridge** (Erzsébet híd), and the green **Liberty Bridge** (Szabadság híd). These bridges are fun to cross by foot, but it's faster to go under the river (on the M2/red Metró line), or to cross over it by tram or bus. (Four more bridges lie beyond the tourist zone: the Petőfi and Rákóczi Bridges to the south, and Árpád and Megyeri Bridges to the north.)

Districts: Budapest uses a district system (like Paris and Vienna). There are 23 districts *(kerület)*, identified by Roman numerals. For example, Castle Hill is in district I and City Park

BUDAPEST

Snapshot History of Budapest

When describing the story of this grand metropolis, it's tempting to fall back on the trusty onion metaphor: Budapest, which has been adored and destroyed by many different groups across the centuries, is layered with a rich history...sometimes stinky, sometimes sweet. You could spend days, years, or an entire lifetime peeling back those layers. But here's the quick version:

Budapest is hot—literally. The city sits on a thin layer of earth above thermal springs, which power its many baths. Even the word "Pest" comes from a Slavic word for "oven." Two thousand years ago, the Romans had a settlement (called Aquincum) on the northern edge of today's Budapest. Several centuries later, in A.D. 896, a mysterious nomadic group called the Magyars arrived from the steppes of Central Asia and took over the Carpathian Basin (roughly today's Hungary). After running roughshod over Europe for a time, the Magyars—the ancestors of today's Hungarians—settled down, adopted Christianity, and became fully European. The twin towns of Buda and Pest emerged as the leading cities of Hungary.

In the 16th century, the Ottomans invaded and occupied the region for nearly a century and a half. The Habsburgs (monarchs of neighboring Austria) finally forced them out, but Buda and Pest were in ruins. The cities were rebuilt in a more Austrian style.

After many decades of Hungarian uprisings, the Compromise of 1867 granted Hungary an equal stake in the Austro-Hungarian Empire. Six years later, the cities of Buda, Pest, and Óbuda united to form the capital city of Budapest, which governed a huge chunk of Eastern Europe. For the next few decades, Budapest boomed, and Hungarian culture enjoyed a Golden Age. The

is in district XIV. Notice that the district number does not necessarily indicate how central a location is: Districts II and III are to the north of Buda, where few tourists go, while the heart of Pest is district V. Addresses often start with the district number (as a Roman numeral).

Tourist Information

Budapest has several TIs (www.budapestinfo.hu, tel. 1/438-8080). The main branch is a few steps from the M2 and M3 Metró station at **Deák tér** (daily 8:00-20:00, Sütő utca 2, near the McDonald's, district V). Other locations include **Franz Liszt Square,** a block south of the Oktogon on Andrássy út (March-Oct daily 12:00-20:00; Nov-Feb Mon-Fri 10:00-18:00, closed Sat-Sun; Liszt Ferenc tér 11, district VII, M1: Oktogon, tel. 1/322-4098) and in both terminals at the **airport** (TIs at Terminals 1 and 2A open daily 8:00-22:00; at Terminal 2B open daily 10:00-20:00). The helpfulness

expansion reached its peak with a flurry of construction surrounding the year 1896—Hungary's 1,000th birthday.

But with Hungary's defeat in World War I, the city's fortunes reversed. World War II left Budapest in ruins...and in the hands of the Soviets. A bold uprising in 1956 was brutally dealt with, but before long a milder "goulash communism" emerged in Hungary. Budapest, though still oppressed, was a place where other Eastern Europeans could come to experiment with "Western evils"...from Big Macs to Nikes.

Since communism's graceful exit in 1989, Budapest has once again been forced to reinvent itself. During this time of transition, the city has struggled with whether to cling to its past glory days, or to leave all that behind and create something new. The architectural tendency here has been to renovate stately old buildings exactly as they were (rather than incorporating modern elements, as is the trend in much of the world). Budapest is one of Europe's most nostalgic places—although to many locals, the city sometimes feels trapped by its own sentimentality. Investors and city planners are increasingly attempting to jolt Budapest into the future with some modern flourishes. It will be fascinating to see which of these influences wins out in the end, as this dynamic, living city continues to grow.

Through it all, Budapest—atmospherically shot through with the crumbling elegance of former greatness—remains the heart and soul of Eastern Europe. It's a rich cultural stew made up of Hungarians, Germans, Slavs, and Jews, with a dash of Turkish paprika—simmered for centuries in a thermal bath. Each group has left its mark, but through it all, something has remained that is distinctly...Budapest.

of Budapest's TIs can vary, but they do produce some free, useful publications, including a good city map, the *Budapest Panorama* events guide, and the information-packed *Budapest Guide* booklet. At all of the TIs, you can also collect a pile of other free brochures (for sights, bus tours, and more) and buy a Budapest Card.

Sightseeing Passes: The **Budapest Card** includes free use of all public transportation, free walking tours of Buda and Pest, a few free museum admissions (Budapest History Museum, Museum of Fine Arts, Museum of Ethnography, Hungarian National Gallery), and 10 to 50 percent discounts on many other major museums and attractions (5,500 Ft/24 hours, 6,900 Ft/48 hours, 8,300 Ft/72 hours, includes handy 100-page booklet with maps, updated hours, and brief museum descriptions; www .budapest-card.com). If you take advantage of the included walking tours, this could be a good value for a very busy sightseer—do the arithmetic.

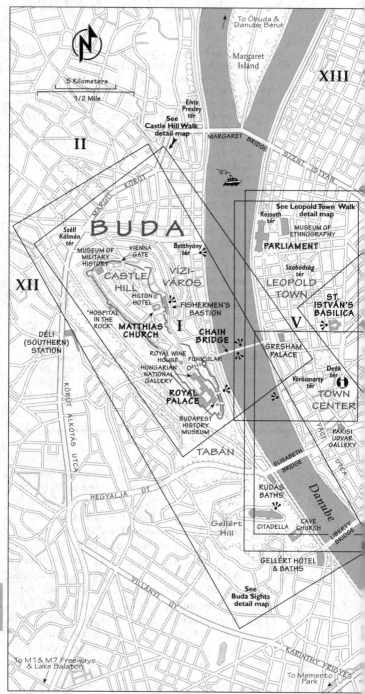

Budapest Overview

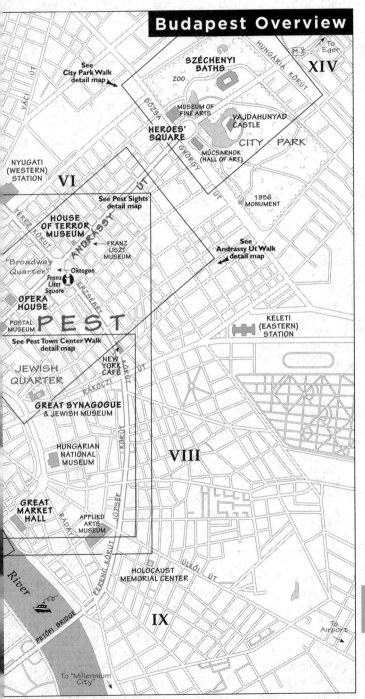

To Eger
M-3

SZÉCHENYI BATHS

HUNGÁRIA KÖRÚT

ZOO

XIV

See City Park Walk detail map

VÁCI ÚT

DÓZSA GYÖRGY ÚT

MUSEUM OF FINE ARTS

HEROES' SQUARE

VAJDAHUNYAD CASTLE

CITY PARK

MŰCSARNOK (HALL OF ART)

NYUGATI (WESTERN) STATION

TERÉZ KÖRÚT

VI

See Pest Sights detail map

ANDRÁSSY ÚT

1956 MONUMENT

HOUSE OF TERROR MUSEUM

FRANZ LISZT MUSEUM

"Broadway Quarter"

Oktogon

ERZSÉBET KÖRÚT

Franz Liszt Square

See Andrassy Ut Walk detail map

OPERA HOUSE

P E S T

POSTAL MUSEUM

GYÖRGY ÚT

KELETI (EASTERN) STATION

See Pest Town Center Walk detail map

JEWISH QUARTER

NEW YORK CAFÉ

ERZSÉBET KÖRÚT

RÁKÓCZI ÚT

GREAT SYNAGOGUE & JEWISH MUSEUM

HUNGARIAN NATIONAL MUSEUM

JÓZSEF KÖRÚT

VIII

GREAT MARKET HALL

RÁDAY

APPLIED ARTS MUSEUM

FERENC KÖRÚT

River

ÜLLŐI ÚT

HOLOCAUST MEMORIAL CENTER

PETŐFI BRIDGE

IX

To Airport

To "Millennium City"

Budapest Essentials

English	Hungarian	Pronounced
Pest Town Center	Belváros	BEHL-vah-rohsh
Pest's Leopold Town	Lipótváros	LEE-poht-vah-rohsh
Pest Town Center's Main Pedestrian Street	Váci utca	VAHT-see OOT-zaw
Pest Town Center's Main Square	Vörösmarty tér	VEW-rewsh-mar-tee tehr
Pest's Grand Boulevard	Andrássy út	AWN-drah-shee oot
Heroes' Square	Hősök Tere	HEW-shewk TEH-reh
City Park	Városliget	VAH-rohsh-lee-geht
(Buda) Castle	(Budai) Vár	BOO-die vahr
Castle Hill	Várhegy	VAHR-hayj
Buda's "Water Town"	Víziváros	VEE-zee-vah-rohsh
Chain Bridge	Széchenyi Lánchíd	SAY-chehn-yee LAHNTS-heed
Liberty Bridge (green, a.k.a. Franz Josef Bridge)	Szabadság híd	SAW-bawd-shahg heed
Elisabeth Bridge (white, modern)	Erzsébet híd	EHR-zay-beht heed
Margaret Bridge (crosses Margaret Island)	Margit híd	MAWR-geet heed
Danube River	Duna	DOO-naw
Eastern Train Station	Keleti pályaudvar	KEH-leh-tee PAH-yuh-uhd-vawr
Western Train Station	Nyugati pályaudvar	NYOO-gaw-tee PAH-yuh-uhd-vawr
Southern Train Station	Déli pályaudvar	DAY-lee PAH-yuh-uhd-vawr
Suburban Train System	HÉV	hayv

Discover Budapest: Ben Frieday, an American in love with Budapest (and one of its women), runs this agency, which specializes in answering questions Americans (especially backpackers) have about Budapest and Hungary. It's conveniently located near Andrássy út, behind the Opera House at Lázár utca 16 (district VI, M1: Opera). At their office, you can use the Internet (200 Ft/15 minutes) or rent a bike (May-Oct daily 9:00-20:00, shorter hours off-season, tel. 1/269-3843, www.discoverbudapest.com).

This location also houses the Tree Hugger Dan secondhand bookstore (described later, under "Helpful Hints") and is the meeting point for Ben's various tours: Yellow Zebra bike tours, Absolute Walking Tours, and City Segway Tours (all described later, under "Tours in Budapest").

Arrival in Budapest

By Train

Budapest has three major train stations (*pályaudvar,* abbreviated *pu.*): Keleti ("Eastern") Station, Nyugati ("Western") Station, and Déli ("Southern") Station. A century ago, the name of the station indicated which part of Europe it served. But these days, there's no correlation: Trains going to the east might leave from the Western Station, and vice versa. Even more confusing, the station used by a particular train can change from year to year. Before departing from Budapest, it's essential to carefully confirm which station your train leaves from.

Keleti/Eastern Station and Nyugati/Western Station are both cavernous, slightly run-down, late-19th-century Erector-set masterpieces in Pest. Déli/Southern Station, behind Castle Hill in Buda, mingles its dinginess with modern flair. At all stations, access to the tracks is monitored—you might have to show your ticket to reach the platforms (though this is very loosely enforced). A few key words: *pénztár* is ticket window, *vágány* is track, *induló vonatok* is departures, and *érkező vonatok* is arrivals.

The taxi stands in front of each train station are notorious for ripping off tourists; it's better to call for a taxi. For tips on this—and on using the Metró system to connect into downtown Budapest—see "Getting Around Budapest," later.

Here's the rundown, station by station:

Keleti/Eastern Station

Keleti train station (Keleti pu.) is just south of City Park, east of central Pest. The area in front of the

station has been undergoing renovation (as they build the new M4/green Metró line), so things might be chaotic for your visit. Here's what you'll likely find: On arrival, go to the front of long tracks 6-9 to reach the exits and services. Several travel agencies masquerading as TIs cluster near the head of the tracks. There is no official TI at the station, but the railroad runs an information office with train advice and basic city info (near the front of track 9). Along track 6, you'll find a left-luggage

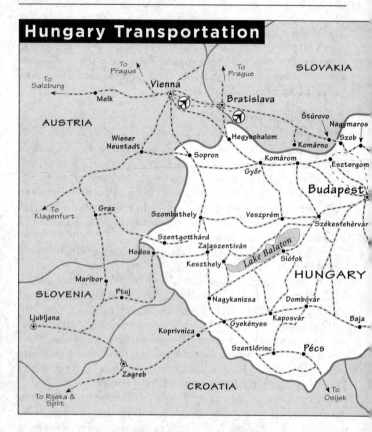

Hungary Transportation

desk, money-exchange booths (avoid Interchange, which has bad rates), and a narrow passage marked *Exit*. Following this passage leads you to a broad, beautifully renovated hallway leading (to the left) to pay WCs, and (to the right) to an Internet café and international information and ticket windows (look for *nemzetközi pénztár*, and take a number). Back in the main hall, domestic ticket windows are across the tracks, near track 9. The big staircase at the head of the tracks leads down to more domestic ticket windows, WCs, telephones, and lockers.

Frustratingly, as of this writing (late 2011), there was no **ATM** inside the train station. If you arrive from another country and need forints, you have two options: Change a small amount of cash at one of the bad-rates exchange offices near the head of the tracks, to hold you over until you can get to an ATM; or walk five minutes to the nearest bank with a 24-hour ATM. To get to the bank, go out the front door and look straight ahead and a bit to the right, to find the yellow *Raffeisen Bank* sign. Find your way along surface streets (through possible construction) to the bank; it's just up the street

from the Burger King, the route to which is generally well-signed.

To get **into the center,** the easiest option is to take the Metró (M2/red line). To find the Metró entrance, exit straight out the front door of the train station and turn left; at the corner of the building, you'll see stairs leading down to the Metró. (Once construction is completed, you'll probably be able to walk from inside the station straight down the main staircase to the Metró.) In front of the train station (or nearby), you'll also stumble across a cluster of suspicious-looking, unmarked taxis. You can try to negotiate with these goons—the fair rate to downtown is about 1,500 Ft—but it's far more reliable and less of a hassle to phone for a taxi (buy phone card at newsstand, go to the phone bank downstairs, call 211-1111 or 266-6666, tell the English-speaking dispatcher where you are, and go out front to meet your taxi).

Nyugati/Western Station

Nyugati train station (Nyugati pu.) is the most central of Budapest's stations, on the northeast edge of downtown Pest. Most international arrivals use tracks 1-9, which are set back from the main entrance. From the head of these tracks, exit straight ahead into a parking lot with taxis and buses, or use the stairs or escalator just inside the doors to reach an underpass and the Metró (M3/blue line). Note that the taxi

drivers here are often crooked—it's far better to call for your own cab (see instructions and phone numbers above).

Ticket windows are through an easy-to-miss door across the tracks by platform 13 (marked *cassa* and *információ;* once you enter the ticket hall, international windows are in a second room at the far end—look for *nemzetközi,* daily 7:30-19:00). Lockers are down the hall next to the international ticket office, and on the left (400-600 Ft).

From the head of tracks 10-13, exit straight ahead and you'll be on Teréz körút, the very busy Great Boulevard. (Váci utca, at the center of Pest, is dead ahead, about 20 minutes away by foot.) In front of the building is the stop for the handy trams #4 and #6 (which zip around Pest's Great Boulevard ring road); to the right you'll find stairs leading to an underpass (use the underpass to avoid crossing this busy intersection, or to reach the Metró's M3 line); and to the left you'll see the classiest Art Nouveau McDonald's on the planet. (Seriously. Take a look inside.)

Déli/Southern Station

In the late 19th century, local newlyweds caught the train at Déli train station (Déli pu.) for their honeymoon in Venice. Renovated by the heavy-handed communists, today the station—tucked behind Castle Hill on the Buda side—is dreary, dark-stone, smaller, and more modern-feeling than the other train stations. From the tracks, go straight ahead into the vast, empty-feeling main hall, with well-marked domestic and international ticket windows at opposite ends. A left-luggage desk is outside, beyond track 1. Downstairs, you'll find several shops and eateries, and access to the very convenient M2/red Metró line, which takes you to several key points in town: Batthyány tér (on the Buda embankment, at the north end of the Víziváros neighborhood), Deák tér (the heart of Pest, with connections to other Metró lines), and Keleti train station.

By Plane at Budapest Liszt Ferenc Airport

Budapest's airport is 10 miles southeast of the center (airport code: BUD, tel. 1/296-7000, www.bud.hu). Many Hungarians still call the airport by its former name, "Ferihegy." The airport has two passenger terminals, which are about three miles from each other. Terminal 1 is used by the low-cost airlines. Terminal 2 has two adjacent parts: 2A is for flights from EU/Schengen countries (no passport control required), while 2B is for flights from other countries. (If you're flying out of Budapest, confirm which terminal your flight leaves from.) Both terminals have similar services, including ATMs and TI desks (TIs at Terminals 1 and 2A open daily 8:00-22:00; at Terminal 2B open daily 10:00-20:00). There is no free bus between terminals. **Public bus #200E** frequently connects Terminals 1, 2A, and 2B (covered by 320-Ft transit ticket at an automated machine, 400 Ft if purchased from driver), or you can connect them by using the airport shuttle minibus (700 Ft, described below).

From the Airport to Budapest: If you're using **Terminal 1,** consider taking the handy **train** that heads straight to Nyugati/Western train station near downtown Pest (365 Ft, plus 520 Ft supplement for InterCity trains, 3-7/hour depending on the day and time, 25 minutes). Buy your ticket from the TI desk inside Terminal 1 before leaving the airport. Then, as you exit Terminal 1, bear left and follow signs to the train tracks (use colorful pedestrian overpass to reach the platform).

If you're using **Terminal 2A or 2B,** it's a hassle to get to Terminal 1 to catch the train (bus #200E to "Liszt Ferenc Airport 1" stop, go inside terminal to buy ticket from TI desk, then go back out to catch train). Instead, I'd consider one of these options (which also work from Terminal 1):

The fastest door-to-door option is to take a **taxi.** Zóna Taxi has a monopoly at the taxi stand out front, with a fixed off-meter price depending on where you're going (about 5,200-5,400 Ft to downtown, 1,000 Ft less from downtown to the airport, about 30 minutes, 1,700 Ft between terminals, tel. 1/365-5555, www.zonataxi.eu). Note that you can also call any other taxi company to take you to or from the airport (see "Getting Around Budapest—By Taxi" on page 547).

The **airport shuttle** minibus is cheaper for a solo traveler, but two people will pay only a few dollars more for a taxi (3,000 Ft/1 person, 4,500 Ft/2 people for minibus ride to any hotel in the city center, about 30-45 minutes depending on hotel location; they can also take you between terminals for 700 Ft; tel. 1/296-8555, www.airportshuttle.hu; if arranging a minibus transfer *to* the airport, call at least 24 hours in advance). Because they prefer to take several people at once, you may have to wait awhile for a quorum to show up (about 20 minutes in busy times, up to an hour when it's slow—they can give you an estimate).

Finally, the cheapest option is to take **public bus #200E** from any of the terminals to the Kőbánya-Kispest station on the M3/ blue Metró line, and then take the Metró all the way into town (covered by basic 320-Ft transit ticket, allow about an hour total for the trip to the center).

By Car

Avoid driving in Budapest if you can. Especially during rush hour (7:00-9:00 and 16:00-18:00), congestion is maddening, and ongoing roadwork only complicates matters. Do not drive down roads marked with a red circle, or in lanes marked for buses; these can be monitored by automatic traffic cameras, and you could get a ticket in the mail.

While in Budapest, park the car at your hotel and take public transportation. Public parking costs 150-600 Ft per hour (pay in advance at machine and put ticket on dashboard—watch locals and imitate; free parking Mon-Fri 18:00-8:00 and all day Sat-Sun—but you'll have to pay all the time in tourist zones). Be careful to park within the lines—otherwise, your car is likely to get "booted" (I've seen more than one confused tourist puzzling over the giant red brace on his or her wheel). A guarded parking lot is safer, but more expensive (figure 3,000-4,000 Ft/day, ask your hotel or look for the blue *P*s on maps). As rental-car theft can be a problem, ask at your hotel for advice. For driving info in Budapest, visit www.fovinform.hu.

Helpful Hints

Construction Alert: Budapest is a city in transition. The good news: They're improving the city by pedestrianizing formerly traffic-clogged streets and building a new Metró line. The bad news: Construction can wreak havoc on walking routes and public transportation. Be prepared to run into some hassles during your visit; stay patient and ask locals for advice on getting around the obstacles.

Rip-Offs: Budapest feels—and is—safe, especially for a city of its size. While there's little risk of violent crime, and I've rarely had someone try to rip me off here, you might run into a petty crook or two (such as con artists or pickpockets). As in any big city, it's especially important to secure your valuables and wear a money belt in crowded and touristy places, particularly on the Metró and in trams. Keep your wits about you and refuse to be bullied or distracted. Any deal that seems too good to be true...probably is.

Restaurants on the Váci utca shopping street are notorious for overcharging tourists. Here or anywhere in Budapest, don't eat at a restaurant that doesn't list prices on the menu, and always check your bill carefully. Increasingly, restaurants

Tonight We're Gonna Party Like It's 1896

Visitors to Budapest need only remember one date: 1896. For the millennial celebration of their ancestors' arrival in Europe, Hungarians threw a huge blowout party. In the thousand years between 896 and 1896, the Magyars had gone from being

a nomadic Central Asian tribe that terrorized the Continent to sharing the throne of one of the most successful empires Europe had ever seen.

Much as the year 2000 saw a fit of new construction worldwide, Budapest used its millennial celebration as an excuse to build monuments and buildings appropriate for the co-capital of a huge empire, including:

- **Heroes' Square** and the **Millennium Monument**
- **Vajdahunyad Castle** (in City Park)
- The riverside **Parliament** building (96 meters tall, with 96 steps at the main entry)
- **St. István's Basilica** (also 96 meters tall)
- The M1/yellow Metró line, a.k.a. *Földalatti* ("Underground")—the first subway on the Continent
- The **Great Market Hall** (and four other market halls)
- **Andrássy út** and most of the fine buildings lining it
- The **Opera House**
- A complete rebuilding of **Matthias Church** (on Castle Hill)
- The **Fishermen's Bastion** decorative terrace (by Matthias Church)
- The green **Liberty Bridge** (then called Franz Josef Bridge, in honor of the ruling Habsburg emperor)

Ninety-six is the key number in Hungary—even the national anthem (when sung in the proper tempo) takes 96 seconds. But after all this fuss, it's too bad that the date was wrong: A commission—convened to establish the exact year of the Magyars' debut—determined it happened in 895. But city leaders knew they'd never make an 1895 deadline, and requested the finding be changed to 896.

are adding a (legitimate) service charge of 10 to 15 percent to your bill; if you don't notice this, you might accidentally double-tip (for more on tipping, see page 20).

If you're a male in a touristy area and a gorgeous local girl takes a liking to you, avoid her. She's a *konzumlány* ("consumption girl"), and the foreplay going on here will climax in your grand rip-off. You'll wind up at her "favorite bar," with astronomical prices enforced by a burly bouncer.

Budapest's biggest crooks? Unscrupulous cabbies. For tips on outsmarting them, see page 547. Bottom line: Locals *always* call for a cab, rather than hail one on the street or at a taxi stand. If you're not comfortable making the call yourself, ask your hotel or restaurant to call for you.

Medical Help: Near Buda's Széll Kálmán tér, **FirstMed Centers** is a private, pricey, English-speaking clinic (by appointment or urgent care, call first, Hattyú utca 14, 5th floor, district I, M2: Széll Kálmán tér, tel. 1/224-9090, www.firstmed centers.com).

Pharmacies: The helpful **Dorottya Gyógyszertár** pharmacy is dead-center in Pest, between Vörösmarty and Széchenyi squares. Because they cater to clientele from nearby international hotels, they have a useful directory that lists the Hungarian equivalent of US prescription medicines (Mon-Fri 8:00-20:00, closed Sat-Sun, Dorottya utca 13, district V, M1: Vörösmarty tér, for location see map on page 628, tel. 1/317-2374). Each district has one pharmacy that stays open 24 hours (these should be noted outside the entrance to any pharmacy).

Calling Mobile Numbers: In Hungary, mobile numbers (generally beginning with 0620, 0630, or 0670) are dialed differently, depending on where you're calling from. I've listed them as you'd dial them from a fixed line within Hungary. From another country, or from a mobile phone in Hungary, omit the initial 06, and replace it with the international access code (011 from the US, 00 from Europe, or + on a mobile phone), then 36, then the number. For more tips on calling, see page 1231.

Monday Closures: Most of Budapest's museums are closed on Mondays. But you can still take advantage of these sights and activities: all three major baths, Memento Park, Great Synagogue and Jewish Quarter, Matthias Church on Castle Hill, St. István's Basilica, Parliament tour, Great Market Hall, Opera House tour, City Park (and Zoo), Danube cruises, concerts, and bus, walking, and bike tours.

Train Tickets: Ticket-buying lines can be long at train stations, particularly for long-distance international trains. If you want to buy your ticket in advance, **MÁV** (Hungarian Railways) has a very convenient ticket office right in the heart of downtown Pest. They generally speak English and sell tickets for no additional fee (Mon-Fri 9:00-18:00, closed Sat-Sun, just up from the Chain Bridge and across from Erzsébet tér at József Attila utca 16, district V, M1: Vörösmarty tér, for location see map on page 566).

Internet Access: Most hotels have Wi-Fi or cable Internet in the rooms (usually free, sometimes for a fee). Internet cafés are everywhere—just look for signs or ask your hotel. In Pest, I like **Discover Budapest,** with fast access and good prices (free Wi-Fi, Internet terminals-200 Ft/15 minutes; for location, hours, and contact information, see "Discover Budapest" listing on page 532).

Post Offices: These are marked with a smart green *posta* logo (usually open Mon-Fri 8:00-18:00, Sat 8:00-12:00, closed Sun).

Laundry: Budapest doesn't have a handy coin-op, self-serve launderette. But two places in Pest can do your laundry for a reasonable price. Your best option is **Laundromat-Mosómata,** just behind the Opera House (2,100 Ft to wash and dry a big load, generally takes 3-5 hours, Mon-Fri 10:00-18:00, Sat 10:00-16:00, closed Sun; walk straight behind the Opera House and turn right on Ó utca, then look left for signs at #24-26, district VI, M1: Opera, for location see map on page 625; mobile 0670-340-0478). Another option—closer to the Town Center, but with more difficult communication—is **Patyolat Gyorstisztító.** They say it's "self-service," but usually you can just drop off your clothes with the monolingual laundry ladies in the morning and pick them up in the afternoon (borrow the English information sheet, allow 2,500 Ft to wash and dry a small load, Mon-Fri 7:00-19:00, Sat 7:00-13:00, closed Sun, just up from Váci utca at the corner of Vármegye utca and Városház utca, district V, M3: Ferenciek tere, for location see map on page 628).

English Bookstores: The **Central European University Bookshop** offers the best selection anywhere of scholarly books about this region (and beyond). They also sell guidebooks, literary fiction, and some popular American magazines—all in English (Mon-Fri 10:00-19:00, Sat 10:00-14:00, closed Sun, just down the street in front of St. István's Basilica at Zrínyi utca 12, district V, for location see map on page 566, tel. 1/327-3096). **Tree Hugger Dan,** which bills itself as a "local bookstore with a global conscience," is crammed with a wide variety of English books (in the Discover Budapest office just behind the Opera House—see hours on page 532). **Red Bus Bookstore** has a great selection of used books in English (also buys used books, Mon-Fri 11:00-18:00, Sat 10:00-14:00, closed Sun, Semmelweis utca 14, district V, M2: Astoria, for location see map on page 628, tel. 1/337-7453).

Bike Rental: You can rent a bike at **Yellow Zebra,** part of Discover Budapest (2,000-3,000 Ft/all day, 3,000-4,500 Ft/24 hours, price depends on type of bike; for location, hours, and contact information, see "Discover Budapest" listing on page 532).

Drivers: Friendly, English-speaking **Gábor Balázs** can drive you around the city or into the surrounding countryside (3,600 Ft/hour, 3-hour minimum in city, 4-hour minimum in countryside—good for a Danube Bend excursion, mobile 0620-936-4317, bgabor.e@gmail.com). **József Király** runs a 10-car company, Artoli (20,000 Ft/4 hours within town, 40,000 Ft/8 hours to Danube Bend, these prices for up to 4 people—more for bigger groups, tel. 1/240-4050, mobile 0620-369-8890, www.artolibus.com, artoli@t-online.hu). Note that these are drivers, not tour guides. For tour guides who can drive you to outlying sights, see "Tours in Budapest," later.

Best Views: Budapest is a city of marvelous vistas. Some of the best are from the Citadella fortress (high on Gellért Hill), the promenade in front of the Royal Palace and the Fishermen's Bastion on top of Castle Hill, and the embankments or many bridges spanning the Danube (especially the Chain Bridge). Don't forget the view from the tour boats on the Danube—lovely at night.

Getting Around Budapest

Budapest sprawls. Connecting your sightseeing by foot is tedious and unnecessary. It's crucial to get comfortable with the public transportation system—a well-coordinated network of Metró lines, trams, and buses that can take you virtually anywhere you want to go.

The same tickets work for the entire system. Buy them at kiosks, Metró ticket windows, or machines. The new machines are slick and easy (with English instructions). The old orange ones are tricky: Put in the appropriate amount of money, then wait for your ticket or press the button. As it can be frustrating to find a ticket machine (especially when you see your tram or bus approaching), I generally invest in a multi-day ticket to have the freedom of hopping on at will.

Your options are as follows:

• **Single ticket** (*vonaljegy*, for a ride of up to an hour on any means of transit; transfers are allowed only within the Metró system)—320 Ft (or 400 Ft if bought from the driver)

• **Short single Metró ride** (*Metrószakaszjegy*, 3 stops or fewer on the Metró)—260 Ft

• **Transfer ticket** (*átszállójegy*—allowing up to 90 minutes, including one transfer)—490 Ft

• **Pack of 10 single tickets** (*10 darabos gyűjtőjegy*), which can

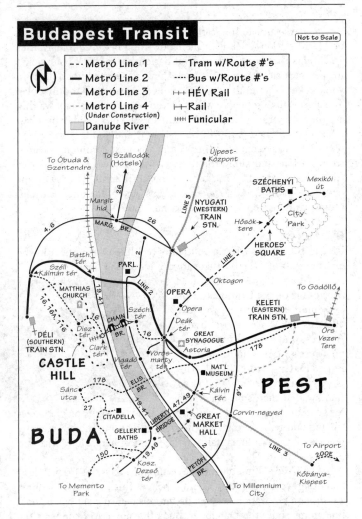

be shared—2,800 Ft (that's 280 Ft per ticket, saving you 40 Ft per ticket; note that these must stay together as a single pack—they can't be sold separately)

• Unlimited multi-day tickets for Metró, bus, and tram, including a **one-day ticket** (*napijegy*, 1,550 Ft/24 hours), **three-day ticket** (*turistajegy*, 3,850 Ft/72 hours), and **weekly ticket** (*hetijegy*, 4,600 Ft/7 days)

• A **family ticket,** which covers one or two adults and up to seven kids aged 14 and under (2,200 Ft/48 hours)

• The **Budapest Card,** which combines a multi-day ticket with sightseeing discounts (but it's generally a bad value—see page 529).

Always validate single-ride tickets as you enter the bus, tram, or Metró station (stick it in the elbow-high box). On older buses and trams that have little red validation boxes, stick your ticket in the black slot, then pull the slot toward you to punch holes in your ticket. The multi-day tickets need be validated only once. The stern-looking people with blue-and-green armbands waiting as you enter or exit the Metró want to see your validated ticket. Cheaters are fined 6,000 Ft on the spot, and you'll be surprised how often you're checked (inspectors are most commonly seen at train stations and along the touristy M1/yellow line). All public transit runs from 4:30 in the morning until 23:10. *Megálló* means "stop" or "station," and *Végállomás* means "end of the line." A useful route-planning website is www.bkv.hu.

By Metró

Riding Budapest's Metró, you really feel like you're down in the efficient guts of the city. There are three working lines:

• **M1/yellow**—The oldest Metró line on the Continent, this extremely handy line runs just 20 steps below street level under Andrássy út from Vörösmarty tér (Pest's main square) to City Park. Dating from 1896, "the Underground" *(Földalatti)* is so shallow that there's no underpass for switching platforms—you must follow the signs on the street (listing end points) to gauge the right direction. Though recently renovated, the M1 line retains its 1896 atmosphere, along with fun black-and-white photos of the age.

• **M2/red**—Built during the communist days, it's 115 feet deep and designed to double as a bomb shelter. This line has undergone a thorough renovation, leaving its stations new and shiny. The only line going under the Danube to Buda (for now), M2 connects the Déli/Southern train station, Széll Kálmán tér (where you catch bus #16, #16A, or #116 to the top of Castle Hill), Batthyány tér (Víziváros and the HÉV suburban railway), Kossuth tér (behind the Parliament), Astoria (near the Great Synagogue on the Small Boulevard), and the Keleti/Eastern train station.

• **M3/blue**—This line makes a broad, boomerang-shaped swoop north to south on the Pest side. It hasn't been renovated and is noticeably older, but its number will come up soon. Key stops include the Nyugati/Western train station, Ferenciek tere (in the heart of Pest's Town Center), and Kálvin tér (near the Great Market Hall and many recommended hotels).

• **M4/green; likely not yet running**—Under construction

for the last few years, this brand-new line is nearing completion (though you still might run into construction for its stations). The line will run from southern Buda to the Gellért Baths, under the Danube to the Great Market Hall and Kálvin tér (where it will cross the M3/blue line), then up to Keleti/Eastern train station (where it will cross the M2/red line). The city-center portion of this line may open in 2014 or 2015; as stations farther out are finished, the line will get longer and longer. To check progress, see www.metro4.hu.

The three original lines—M1, M2, and M3—cross only once: at the **Deák tér** stop (often signed as *Deák Ferenc tér*) in the heart of Pest, near where Andrássy út begins.

Aside from the historic M1 line, most Metró stations are at intersections of ring roads and other major thoroughfares. You'll usually exit the Metró into a confusing underpass packed with kiosks, fast-food stands, and makeshift markets. Directional signs (listing which streets, addresses, and tram or bus stops are near each exit) help you find the right exit. Or do the prairie-dog routine: Surface to get your bearings, then head back underground to find the correct stairs up to your destination.

Metró stops themselves are usually very well-marked, with a list of upcoming stops on the wall behind the tracks. Digital clocks either count down to the next train's arrival, or count up from the previous train's departure; either way, you'll rarely wait more than five minutes.

HÉV: Budapest's suburban rail system, or HÉV (pronounced "hayv"), branches off to the outskirts and beyond. The HÉV line that begins at Batthyány tér in Buda's Víziváros neighborhood (at the M2/red line stop of the same name) heads through Óbuda to the charming Danube Bend town of Szentendre; from Örs vezér tere, a different line runs east to the royal palace at Gödöllő. The HÉV is covered by standard transit tickets and passes for rides within the city of Budapest (such as to Óbuda). But if going beyond—such as to Szentendre or Gödöllő—you'll have to pay more (tell the ticket-seller where you're going). However, on a short visit, it's unlikely that you'll need to use the HÉV.

By Tram

Budapest's trams are handy and frequent, taking you virtually anywhere the Metró doesn't. Here are some trams you might use (note that all of these run in both directions):

Tram #2: Follows Pest's Danube embankment, parallel to Váci utca. From north to south, it begins at the Great Boulevard (near Margaret Bridge) and passes the Parliament, Széchenyi István tér and the Chain Bridge, Vigadó tér, and the Great Market Hall. (Note that a similar route might also be operated by tram #2A.)

Trams #19 and #41: Run along Buda's Danube embankment from Batthyány tér (with an M2/red Metró station, and HÉV trains to Óbuda and Szentendre). From Batthyány tér, these trams run (north to south) through Víziváros to Clark Ádám tér (the bottom of the Castle Hill funicular, near the stop for bus #16 up to Castle Hill), then under Elisabeth Bridge (get off at Döbrentei stop for the Rudas Baths) and around the base of Gellért Hill to the Gellért Hotel and Baths (Gellért tér stop).

Trams #4 and #6: Zip around Pest's Great Boulevard ring road (Nagykörút), connecting Nyugati/Western train station and the Oktogon with the southern tip of Margaret Island and Buda's Széll Kálmán tér (with M2/red Metró station).

Trams #47 and #49: Connect the Gellért Baths in Buda with Pest's Small Boulevard ring road (Kiskörút), with stops at the Great Market Hall, the National Museum, the Great Synagogue (Astoria stop), and Deák tér (end of the line).

Note: For the last several years, construction on the new Metró line has caused several tram lines to be ripped up. When this happens, the trams are replaced by buses that follow similar routes. Look for a bus with the same number, ending in *V* (for *villamospótló*, "tram substitute"; for example, #47-49V to replace trams #47 and #49).

By Bus

I use the Metró and trams for most of my Budapest commuting. But some buses are useful for shortcuts within the city, or for reaching outlying sights. Note that the transit company draws a distinction between gas-powered "buses" and electric "trolley buses" (which are powered by overhead cables). Unless otherwise noted, you can assume the following are standard buses:

Buses #16, #16A, and #116: All head up to the top of Castle Hill (get off at Dísz tér, near the Royal Palace). You can catch any of these three at Széll Kálmán tér (on M2/red Metró line). When coming from the other direction, bus #16 makes several handy stops in Pest (Deák tér, Széchenyi István tér), then crosses the Chain Bridge for more stops in Buda (including Clark Ádám tér, at Buda end of Chain Bridge).

Trolley buses #70 and #78: Zip from near the Opera House (intersection of Andrássy út and Nagymező utca) to the Parliament (Kossuth tér).

Bus #178: Goes from Keleti/Eastern train station to central Pest (Astoria and Ferenciek tere Metró stops), then over the Elisabeth Bridge to Buda.

Bus #26: Begins at Nyugati/Western train station and heads around the Great Boulevard to Margaret Island, making several stops along the island.

Bus #27: Runs from either side of Gellért Hill to just below the Citadella fortress at the hill's peak (Búsuló Juhász stop).

Bus #150: Goes from Kosztolányi Dezső tér (several blocks beyond Gellért Hotel and Baths, in Buda) to Memento Park.

Bus #200E: Connects both terminals at Liszt Ferenc Airport to the Kőbánya-Kispest M3/blue Metró station.

By Taxi

Budapest's public transportation is good enough that you probably won't need to take many taxis. But if you do, you're likely to run into a dishonest driver. Arm yourself with knowledge: Cabbies are not allowed to charge more than a drop rate of 300 Ft, and then 240 Ft/kilometer. (The prices go up at night, between 22:00 and 6:00 in the morning: 420 Ft drop, 350 Ft/kilometer.) The big companies charge even less than these rates. Prices are per ride, not per passenger. A 10 percent tip is expected. A typical ride within central Budapest shouldn't run more than 2,000 Ft. Despite what some slimy cabbies may tell you, there's no legitimate extra charge for crossing the river.

Instead of hailing a taxi on the street, do as the locals do and call a cab from a reputable company—it's cheaper and you're more likely to get an honest driver. Try **City Taxi** (tel. 1/211-1111), **Taxi 6x6** (tel. 1/266-6666), or **Főtaxi** (1/222-2222). Most dispatchers speak English, but if you're uncomfortable calling, you can ask your hotel or restaurant to call for you. (Request that they call a "City Taxi"—otherwise, they might call a pricier company to get a bigger kickback.)

Many cabs you'd hail on the streets are there only to prey on rich, green tourists. Avoid unmarked taxis and cabs waiting at tourist spots and train stations. If you do wave down a cab on the street, choose one that's marked with an official company logo and telephone number, and has a yellow license plate (if the plate's not yellow, it's not official). Ask for a rough estimate before you get in—if it doesn't sound reasonable, walk away. If you wind up being dramatically overcharged for a ride, simply pay what you think is fair and go inside. If the driver follows you (unlikely), your hotel receptionist will defend you.

Tours in Budapest

By Foot

▲▲**Local Guides**—Budapest has an abundance of enthusiastic, hardworking, young guides who speak perfect English and enjoy showing off their city. Given the reasonable fees and efficient use of your time, hiring your own personal expert is an excellent value. While they might be available last-minute, it's better to reserve in advance by email. I have two favorites, either of whom can do half-day or full-day tours, and can also drive you into the coun-

tryside: **Péter Pölczman** is an exceptional guide who really puts you in touch with the Budapest you came to see (€90/4 hours, €150/8 hours, mobile 0620-926-0557, www.budapestyourself.com, polczman@freestart.hu or peter@budapestyourself.com). **Andrea Makkay** is also great, with professional polish (€80/4 hours, €140/8 hours, mobile 0620-962-9363, www.privateguidebudapest .com, amakkay@t-online.hu—arrange details by email; if Andrea is busy, she can arrange to send you with another guide).

Elemér Boreczky, a semi-retired university professor, leads walking tours with a soft-spoken, scholarly approach, emphasizing Budapest's rich tapestry of architecture as "frozen music." Elemér is ideal if you want a walking graduate-level seminar about the easy-to-miss nuances of this grand metropolis (€25/hour, tel. 1/386-0885, mobile 0620-340-3598, www.culturaltours.mlap.hu, boreczky.elemer@gmail.com).

Péter, Andrea, and Elemér were all indispensable help to me in writing this book.

Walking Tours—Budapest has several backpacker-oriented walking-tour companies. The self-guided walks and tours in this book, and the availability of the excellent local guides listed above, make these tours less appealing. But they can be worth considering.

Budapest's best-established outfit is **Absolute Walking Tours,** run by Oregonian Ben Frieday, offering tours that are informal but informative. Travelers with this book pay half-price for the Absolute Walk and Hammer & Sickle Tour, and get a 500-Ft discount on any specialty tour. The Absolute Walk gives you a good overview of Budapest (8,000 Ft—or 4,000 Ft for Rick Steves readers, daily at 10:00, 3.5 hours). The Hammer & Sickle Tour includes a walk through the Jewish Quarter (with an emphasis on WWII history), sites related to the 1956 Uprising, and a visit to a mini-museum of communist artifacts (7,000 Ft—or 3,500 Ft for Rick Steves readers, 2-3/week, 3.5 hours). The Hungro Gastro Food and Wine Tasting Tour gives you information on traditional recipes and ingredients, and a chance to taste several specialties at a local restaurant (8,000 Ft, 4/week, 1/week in winter, 2.5 hours, reservations required). In the evening, consider the Night Stroll, which includes a one-hour cruise on the Danube (7,500 Ft, 4/week March-Oct, 2/week Nov-Feb, 3 hours); or the rowdier Pub Crawl, which sometimes continues late into the night (4,500 Ft, departs 20:30, 4/week April-Oct, 2/week Nov-March, at least 3 hours). They also offer a fashion and shopping tour, a Christmas Market tour (December only), and an "Alternative Budapest" tour that visits artsy, edgy, off-the-beaten path parts of town (for details on any of their tours, see www.absolutetours.com or contact the Discover Budapest office, tel. 1/269-3843). All tours (except the pub crawl) depart from the Discover Budapest office behind the Opera House (see page 532); the pub crawl departs from the blocky, green-domed Lutheran church at Deák tér, near the Metró station. If you pre-book online, you're still eligible for the Rick Steves discount (enter the coupon code RICK), and you'll have the option of booking a 1,000-Ft transfer from your hotel to your walk's starting point.

You'll also see various companies advertising **"free" walking tours.** While there is no set fee to take these tours, guides are paid only if you tip (they're hoping for 2,000 Ft per person). There's a basic 2.5-hour introduction to the city, as well as itineraries focusing on the communist era and the Jewish Quarter. Because they're working for tips, the generally good-quality, certified guides are highly motivated to impress their customers. But because the "free" tag attracts very large groups, these tours tend to be less intimate than paid tours, and (especially the introductory tours) take a once-over-lightly "infotainment" approach. Still, these "free" tours get rave reviews from travelers and offer an inexpensive introduction to the city. As this scene is continually evolving, look for local fliers to learn about the options and meeting points.

By Boat

▲▲**Danube Boat Tours**—Cruising the Danube, while touristy, is fun and convenient. The most established company, **Legenda,** is a class act that runs new, glassed-in panoramic boats day and night. All cruises include a free drink and headphone commentary. By night, TV monitors show the interiors of the great buildings as you float by.

I've negotiated a special discount with Legenda for my readers (but you must book direct in person and ask for the Rick Steves price). By **day,** the one-hour cruise costs 2,700 Ft for Rick Steves readers, or pay 3,200 Ft to also include a one-hour walking tour around Margaret Island (8/day May-Aug, 7/day April and

Budapest at a Glance

In Buda

▲▲**Matthias Church** Landmark Neo-Gothic church with gilded history-book interior and revered 16th-century statue of Mary and Jesus. **Hours:** Mon-Sat 9:00-17:00, Sun 13:00-17:00, sometimes closed Sat after 13:00 for weddings. See page 559.

▲▲**Gellért Baths** Touristy baths in historic Buda hotel. **Hours:** Daily 6:00-20:00. See page 564.

▲▲**Rudas Baths** Half-millennium-old Turkish dome over a series of hot-water pools. **Hours:** Daily 6:00-20:00. See page 564.

▲▲**Memento Park** Larger-than-life communist statues collected in one park, on the outskirts of town. **Hours:** Daily 10:00-sunset. See page 598.

▲**Hungarian National Gallery** Top works by Hungarian artists, housed in the Royal Palace. **Hours:** Tue-Sun 10:00-18:00, closed Mon. See page 556.

▲**"Hospital in the Rock"** Fascinating underground network of hospital and bomb-shelter corridors from WWII and the Cold War. **Hours:** Tue-Sun 10:00-20:00, closed Mon. See page 562.

In Pest

▲▲▲**Széchenyi Baths** Budapest's steamy soaking scene in City Park—the city's single best attraction. **Hours:** Swimming pool—daily 6:00-22:00, thermal bath—daily 6:00-19:00. See page 596.

▲▲**Hungarian Parliament** Vast riverside government center with remarkable interior. **Hours:** English tours usually daily at 10:00, 12:00, and 14:00. See page 564.

▲▲**Great Market Hall** Colorful Old World mall with produce, eateries, souvenirs, and great people-watching. **Hours:** Mon 6:00-17:00, Tue-Fri 6:00-18:00, Sat 6:00-15:00, closed Sun. See page 579.

▲▲**Great Synagogue** The world's second-largest, with fancy interior, good museum, and memorial garden. **Hours:** April-Oct Sun-Thu 10:00-17:30, Fri 10:00-15:30; Nov-March Sun-Thu 10:00-

15:30, Fri 10:00-14:30; always closed Sat and Jewish holidays. See page 582.

▲▲**Hungarian State Opera House** Neo-Renaissance splendor and affordable opera. **Hours:** Lobby/box office open Mon-Sat from 11:00 until show time—generally 19:00; Sun open 3 hours before performance—generally 16:00-19:00, or 10:00-13:00 if there's a matinee; English tours nearly daily at 15:00 and 16:00. See page 586.

▲▲**House of Terror** Harrowing remembrance of Nazis and communist secret police in former headquarters/torture site. **Hours:** Tue-Sun 10:00-18:00, closed Mon. See page 588.

▲▲**Heroes' Square** Mammoth tribute to Hungary's historic figures, fronted by art museums. **Hours:** Square always open. See page 593.

▲▲**City Park** Budapest's backyard, with Art Nouveau zoo, Transylvanian Vajdahunyad Castle replica, amusement park, and Széchenyi Baths. **Hours:** Park always open. See page 595.

▲▲**Holocaust Memorial Center** Excellent memorial and museum honoring Hungarian victims of the Holocaust. **Hours:** Tue-Sun 10:00-18:00, closed Mon. See page 597.

▲**St. István's Basilica** Budapest's largest church, with a saint's withered fist and great city views. **Hours:** Daily 9:00-19:00 except closed for weddings (often Sat afternoon) and other services (various times on Sun); observation deck has shorter hours. See page 572.

▲**Hungarian National Museum** Expansive collection of fragments from Hungary's history. **Hours:** Tue-Sun 10:00-18:00, closed Mon. See page 581.

▲**Postal Museum** Funky, charming tribute to old postal service objects in venerable, old Andrássy út mansion. **Hours:** Tue-Sun 10:00-18:00, closed Mon. See page 586.

▲**Margaret Island** Budapest's traffic-free urban playground, with spas, ruins, gardens, a game farm, and fountains, set in the middle of the Danube. **Hours:** Park always open. See page 576.

Sept, 4/day March and Oct, 1/day Nov-Feb). By **night,** the one-hour cruise (with no Margaret Island visit) costs 4,100 Ft for Rick Steves readers (4/day March-Oct, 1/day Nov-Feb). They also offer a dinner cruise (also discounted for my readers).

The Legenda dock is in front of the Marriott on the Pest embankment (find pedestrian access under tram tracks just downriver from Vigadó tér, district V, M1: Vörösmarty tér, tel. 1/317-2203, www.legenda.hu). Competing river-cruise companies are nearby, but given the discount, Legenda offers the best value.

On Wheels

Bike Tours—Various companies offer bike tours around the city; as the most interesting part of town (Pest) is quite flat and spread out, this is a good way to see the place. The best-established option is **Yellow Zebra,** a sister company of Absolute Walking Tours (5,500 Ft, 500-Ft discount for Rick Steves readers, 3.5 hours; July-Aug daily at 11:00 and 17:00; April-June and Sept-Oct daily at 11:00; Nov and March Fri-Sun at 11:00—cancelled in below-freezing temperatures; no tours Dec-Feb; meet at Discover Budapest office behind the Opera House—see page 532, tel. 1/269-3843, www.yellowzebrabikes.com; if booking online, enter coupon code "RICK").

City Segway Tours—Discover Budapest also offers tours of the city by Segway (stand-up electric scooter). Although expensive, it's a unique way to see Budapest while trying out a Segway. Each tour begins with a 30- to 45- minute training; my readers get a 10 percent discount. Options include a full-length tour (16,500 Ft/2.5-3 hours, daily at 10:00, also April-Sept daily at 14:30) or a mini-tour (14,000 Ft/1.5 hours, April-Sept daily at 14:30; 15,500 Ft/2 hours, April-Sept daily at 18:00). Reserve and prepay online (www.citysegwaytours.com, enter coupon code RICK) or call the office when in Budapest (tel. 1/269-3843).

Bus Tours—Several different companies run essentially the same bus tours that glide past all the big sights (figure around 3,500 Ft for a 2-hour tour). Various companies run hop-on, hop-off bus tours, which make 12 to 16 stops as they cruise around town on a two-hour loop with headphone commentary (4,500 Ft for a 24-hour ticket). Most companies also offer a wide variety of other tours, including dinner boat cruises and trips to the Danube Bend. Pick up fliers about all these tours at the TI or in your hotel lobby.

Sights in Budapest

A real highlight of visiting Budapest is touring the opulent interiors of its late-19th-century Golden Age buildings—an experience worth ▲▲▲. The best interiors belong to the Opera House and

BUDAPEST

Parliament, and "honorable mentions" go to St. István's Basilica, the Great Synagogue, New York Café, and both the Széchenyi and the Gellért Baths.

In Buda

Nearly all of Buda's top sights are concentrated on or near its two riverside hills: Castle Hill and Gellért Hill.

Castle Hill (Várhegy)

Once the seat of Hungarian royalty, and now the city's highest-profile tourist zone, Castle Hill is a historic spit of land looming above the Buda bank of the Danube. Scenic from afar, but (frankly) a bit soulless from up close, it's best seen quickly. The major landmarks are the huge, green-domed Royal Palace at the south end of the hill (housing a pair of museums) and the frilly-spired Matthias Church near the north end (with the hill's best interior). In between are tourist-filled pedestrian streets and dull but historic buildings. Perhaps best of all are the bird's-eye views from up here across the Danube to Pest. I've listed the sights in order from south to north, and linked them together on a self-guided walk.

When to Visit: Castle Hill is packed with tour groups in the morning, but it's much less crowded in the afternoon. Castle Hill is an ideal after-lunch activity. Restaurants up here are mediocre, but if you're having lunch here, see page 644.

Getting to Castle Hill: The Metró and trams won't take you to the top of Castle Hill. Instead, you can hike, taxi, catch a bus, or ride the funicular.

For most visitors, the easiest bet is to hop on **bus #16,** with handy stops in both Pest (at the Deák tér Metró hub—near the old bus building in Erzsébet tér; and at Széchenyi István tér at the Pest end of the Chain Bridge) and Buda (at Clark Ádám tér at the Buda end of the Chain Bridge—across the street from the lower funicular station, and much cheaper than the funicular). Or you can go via Széll Kálmán tér (on the M2/red Metró line); from here, bus **#16,** as well as buses **#16A** and **#116,** head up the hill (at Széll Kálmán tér, catch the bus just uphill from the Metró station—in front of the red-brick, castle-looking building). All buses stop at Dísz tér, at the crest of the hill, about halfway along its length (most people on the bus will be getting off there, too). From Dísz tér, go past the war-damaged building (the old Ministry of War), walk five minutes along the row of flagpoles, then bear left to find the big Turul bird statue.

The pricey **funicular** (*sikló,* SHEE-kloh), lifts visitors from the Chain Bridge to the top of Castle Hill (840 Ft one-way, 1,450 Ft round-trip, not covered by transit pass, daily 7:30-22:00, departs

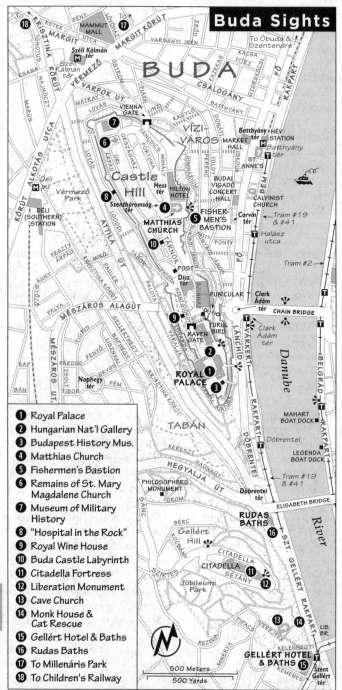

Buda Sights

1. Royal Palace
2. Hungarian Nat'l Gallery
3. Budapest History Mus.
4. Matthias Church
5. Fishermen's Bastion
6. Remains of St. Mary Magdalene Church
7. Museum of Military History
8. "Hospital in the Rock"
9. Royal Wine House
10. Buda Castle Labyrinth
11. Citadella Fortress
12. Liberation Monument
13. Cave Church
14. Monk House & Cat Rescue
15. Gellért Hotel & Baths
16. Rudas Baths
17. To Millenáris Park
18. To Children's Railway

BUDAPEST

every 5 minutes, closed for maintenance every other Mon). It leaves you right at the Turul bird statue.

• *Orient yourself from the top of the funicular, enjoying the views over the Danube. At the top of the nearby staircase, notice the giant bird that looks like a vulture. This is the...*

Turul Bird—This mythical bird of Magyar folktales suppos- edly led the Hungarian migrations from the steppes of Central Asia in the ninth century. He dropped his sword in the Carpathian Basin, indicating that this was to be the permanent home of the Magyar people. While the Hungarians have long since integrated into Europe, the Turul remains a symbol of Magyar pride. During a surge of nationalism in the 1920s, a movement named after this bird helped revive traditional Hungarian culture. And today, the bird is invoked by right-wing nationalist politicians.

• *We'll circle back this way later. But for now, climb down the stairs by the Turul and walk along the broad terrace in front of the...*

Royal Palace (Királyi Palota)—The imposing palace on Castle Hill barely hints at the colorful story of this hill since the day that the legendary Turul dropped his sword. In the early 15th century,

the Renaissance King Mátyás (Matthias) Corvinus—whom we'll learn more about soon— converted a humble medieval palace on this site into one of Europe's most extravagant residences, putting Buda and Hungary on the map. Just

a few decades later, the invading Ottomans occupied Buda and turned the palace into a military garrison. When the Habsburgs laid siege to the hill for 77 days in 1686, gunpowder stored in the cellar exploded, destroying the palace. The Habsburgs took the hill, but Buda was deserted and in ruins. The palace was rebuilt, then damaged again during the 1848 Revolution, then repaired again. As World War II drew to a close, Budapest became the front line between the Nazis and the approaching Soviets. The Red Army laid siege to the hill for 100 days. They eventually succeeded in taking Budapest...but the city—and the hill—were devastated.

While impressive from afar, the current version of the pal- ace—a historically inaccurate, post-WWII reconstruction—is a loose rebuilding of previous versions, lacking the style and sense of history that this important site deserves. Fortunately, the palace

Mátyás (Matthias) Corvinus: The Last Hungarian King

The Árpád dynasty—descendants of the original Magyar tribes—died out in 1301. For more than 600 years, Hungary would be ruled by foreigners...with one exception.

In the middle of the 15th century, Hungary had bad luck hanging on to its foreign kings: Two of them died unexpectedly within seven years. Meanwhile, homegrown military general János Hunyadi was enjoying great success on the battlefield against the Ottomans. When five-year-old László V was elected king, Hunyadi was appointed regent and essentially ruled the country.

Hunyadi defeated the Ottomans in the crucial 1456 Battle of Belgrade, which kept them out of Hungary (at least for another 70 years) and made him an even greater hero to the Hungarian people. But soon afterward, Hunyadi died from the plague, which he had contracted during that fateful battle. When the young king also died (at the tender age of 16), the nobles looked for a new leader. At first their sights settled on Hunyadi's eldest son, László. But the Habsburgs—who were trying to project their influence from afar—felt threatened by the Hunyadi family, and László was killed.

At this dark moment, the Hungarians turned to the younger Hunyadi son, Mátyás (or Matthias in English). At the time, Matthias (whose first wife was a Czech princess) was at court in Prague. According to legend, Matthias' mother sent for him with a raven with a ring in its beak. The raven supposedly flew nonstop from

does house some worthwhile museums (described later), and boasts the fine terrace you're strolling on, with some of Budapest's best views.

• *Behind the big equestrian statue is the main entrance to the...*

▲**Hungarian National Gallery (Magyar Nemzeti Galéria)**— The best place in Hungary to appreciate the works of homegrown artists, this art museum offers a peek into the often-morose Hungarian worldview. The collection includes a remarkable group of 15th-century, wood-carved altars from Slovakia (then "Upper Hungary"); piles of gloomy canvases dating from the dark days after the failed 1848 Revolution; and several works by two great Hungarian Realist painters, Mihály Munkácsy and László Paál. Don't miss the three works by Tivadar Csontváry Kosztka, the "Hungarian Van Gogh" (for more on Csontváry, see page 684). At the second-floor landing, you'll see a few of this well-trav-

Transylvania to Prague. The raven-with-ring motif became part of the family crest, as well as the family name: Corvinus (Latin for "raven").

Matthias Corvinus returned to Buda, becoming the first Hungarian-descended king in more than 150 years. Progressive and well-educated in the Humanist tradition, Matthias Corvinus (r. 1458-1490) was the quintessential Renaissance king. A lover of the Italian Renaissance, he patronized the arts and built palaces legendary for their beauty. Also a benefactor of the poor, he dressed up as a commoner and ventured into the streets to see firsthand how the nobles of his realm treated his people.

Matthias was a strong, savvy leader. He created Central Europe's first standing army—30,000 mercenaries known as the Black Army. No longer reliant on the nobility for military support, Good King Matthias was able to drain power from the nobles and make taxation of his subjects more equitable—earning him the nickname the "people's king."

King Matthias was also a shrewd military tactician. Realizing that quarreling with the Ottomans would squander his resources, he made peace with the Ottoman sultan to stabilize Hungary's southern border. Then he swept north, invading Moravia, Bohemia, and even Austria. By 1485, Matthias moved into his new palace in Vienna, and Hungary was enjoying a Golden Age.

Five years later, Matthias died mysteriously at the age of 47, and his empire disintegrated. It is said that when Matthias died, justice died with him. To this day, Hungarians consider him the greatest of all kings, and they sing of his siege of Vienna in their national anthem. They're proud that for a few decades in the middle of half a millennium of foreign oppression, they had a truly Hungarian king—and a great one at that.

eled painter's destinations: the giant canvas in the center depicts the theater at Taormina, Sicily; on the left are the waterfalls of Schaffhausen, Germany; and on the right is a cedar tree in Lebanon. Typical of Csontváry's style, these are colorful, allegorical, and expressionistic.

Cost and Hours: 1,200 Ft, may be more for special exhibitions, 1,500 Ft extra to take photos, Tue-Sun 10:00-18:00, closed Mon, required bag check for large bags, café, in the Royal Palace—enter from terrace by Eugene of Savoy statue, district I, mobile 0620-439-7325, www.mng.hu.

• *Head back outside and face the palace. Go through the passage to the right of the National Gallery entrance (next to the café). You'll emerge into a courtyard decorated with a gorgeous* **fountain** *dedicated to King Matthias Corvinus (see sidebar). Go around the right side of the fountain and through the passage, into the palace courtyard. At the far end of* *this too-big space is the entrance to the...*

Budapest History Museum (Budapesti Történeti Múzeum)

—This earnest but dusty collection strains to bring the history of this city to life. The dimly lit fragments of 14th-century sculptures, which depict early Magyars, allow you to see how Asian those original Hungarians truly looked. The "Budapest in the Modern Times" exhibit deliberately but effectively traces the union between Buda and Pest. Rounding out the collection are exhibits on prehistoric residents and a sprawling cellar that unveils fragments from the oh-so-many buildings that have perched on this hill over the centuries.

Cost and Hours: 1,400 Ft, audioguide-850 Ft, some good English descriptions posted; March-Oct Tue-Sun 10:00-18:00, closed Mon; Nov-Feb Tue-Sun 10:00-16:00, closed Mon; last entry 30 minutes before closing, district I, tel. 1/487-8800, www.btm.hu.

Walk to Matthias Church

—Leaving the palace courtyard, walk straight up the slight incline, passing under a gate with a raven holding a ring in its mouth (a symbol of King Matthias).

As you walk along the line of flagpoles, you'll pass a big field on your right. Look closely to spot the remains of a medieval monastery and church. Along the left side (past the flagpoles) is the ongoing excavation of the medieval Jewish quarter—more reminders that most of what you see on today's Castle Hill has been destroyed and rebuilt many times over.

Beethoven once performed in the yellow **National Dance Theater** (on the right). The hulking, war-damaged building beyond that (at the end of the lawn, partially covered by the huge banner) used to house the **Ministry of War.** Most of the bullet holes are from World War II, while others were left by the Soviets who occupied this hill in response to the 1956 Uprising. The building is a political hot potato—prime real

estate, but nobody can decide what to do with it.

Just after the Ministry of War, at the cross street, you reach **Dísz tér** ("Parade Square"), which has a convenient bus stop for connecting to other parts of Budapest (bus #16, #16A, or #116 to Széll Kálmán tér; or bus #16 to the Pest side of the Chain Bridge).

If you walk a few steps down the street to the left, on the left-hand side you'll find an entrance to the rampart garden between the castle walls. A short walk through this area takes you to the **Royal Wine House and Wine Cellar Museum,** where you can tour a network of old wine cellars burrowed under Castle Hill...and taste some Hungarian wines, if you choose (990 Ft for museum entry, tastings cost 2,000-6,000 Ft depending on number and quality, sparkling wine and schnapps tastings also available, daily 12:00-20:00, maybe shorter hours and closed Mon off-season, Budavár kerület, district I, tel. 1/267-1100, www.kiralyiborok.com).

Cross the street in front of the Ministry of War, noticing the handy post office on your left. On the right, behind the yellow wall, is a courtyard with an open-air Hungarian **crafts market.** While it's fun to browse, prices here are high (haggle away). The Great Market Hall has a better selection, and its prices are generally lower (see page 579).

Continue straight uphill on **Tárnok utca.** This area often disappoints visitors. After being destroyed by Ottomans, it was rebuilt in sensible Baroque, lacking the romantic time-capsule charm of a medieval old town. But if you poke your head into some courtyards, you'll almost always see some original Gothic arches and other medieval features.

• *Continue on Tárnok utca up to the little park (on your right). The green, circular building in the park, marked as if it's a TI, is actually a private **travel agency**—but they do answer questions and dispense a free, handy* Castle Walks *map.*

*Across the street from the park (on the left), the **CBA grocery store** sells reasonably priced cold drinks, and has a coffee shop upstairs (Mon-Fri 7:00-20:00, Sat 8:00-20:00, Sun 9:00-18:00). Just beyond it, the same store runs a "Szendwics" shop selling cheap and basic sandwiches and sides (to go, or sit at the tables out front). Down the street next to the grocery store, in a little courtyard, is a good spot for dessert: **Rétesbár**, selling* rétes *(strudel) of various flavors for 250 Ft (daily 8:00-19:00).*

*Just beyond the park, a warty plague column from 1713 marks **Szentháromság tér** ("Holy Trinity Square"), the main square of old Buda.*

Dominating the square is the...

▲▲**Matthias Church (Mátyás-Templom)**—Budapest's best church has been destroyed and rebuilt several times in the 800 years since it was founded by King Béla IV. Today's version—renovated at great expense in the late 19th century and restored after World War II—is an ornately decorated lesson in Hungarian history. While it's officially named the "Church of Our Lady," everyone calls it the Matthias Church, for the popular Renaissance king who got married here—twice.

Cost and Hours: 990 Ft, includes Museum of Ecclesiastical Art, 12-stop audioguide-500 Ft, Mon-Sat 9:00-17:00, Sun 13:00-17:00, may close Sat after 13:00 for weddings, Szentháromság tér 2, district I, tel. 1/488-7716, www.matyas-templom.hu.

◑ Self-Guided Tour: Examine the **exterior.** While the nucleus of the church is Gothic, most of what you see outside—including the frilly, flamboyant steeple—was added in 1896, for the celebrations surrounding the 1,000th anniversary of the Magyars' arrival in Europe (see sidebar on page 539). At the top of the spire facing the river, notice the raven—the ever-present symbol of King Matthias Corvinus.

Buy your **ticket** (and rent a 500-Ft audioguide, if you want) across the square, at the ticket windows embedded in the wall. (The same windows sell tickets for the Fishermen's Bastion, described later.) Then enter the church.

The sumptuous **interior** is wallpapered with gilded pages from a Hungarian history textbook. Different eras are represented by symbolic motifs. For example, the wall immediately to the left of the entry represents the Renaissance, with a giant coat of arms of the beloved King Matthias Corvinus. (The tough guys in armor on either side are members of his mercenary Black Army, the source of his power.) Notice another raven, with a ring in its beak. Meanwhile, the wall across from the entry—with Oriental motifs—commemorates the Ottoman reign of Buda.

Work your way clockwise around the church from the entry. The first chapel (in the back corner, by the closed main doors)—the **Loreto Chapel**—holds the church's prize possession. Peer through the black iron grill to see the 1515 statue of Mary and Jesus. Anticipating Ottoman plundering, locals walled over this precious statue. The occupying Ottomans used the church as their primary mosque—oblivious to the statue plastered over in the niche. Then, a century and a half later, during the siege of Buda in 1686, gunpowder stored in the castle up the street detonated, and the wall crumbled. Mary's triumphant face showed through, terrifying the Ottomans. Supposedly this was the only part of town taken from the Ottomans without a fight.

As you look down the **nave,** notice the banners. They've hung here since the Mass that celebrated Habsburg monarch Franz Josef's coronation at this church on June 8, 1867. In a sly political compromise to curry favor in the Hungarian part of his territory, Franz Josef was "emperor" *(Kaiser)* of Austria, but only "king" *(König)* of Hungary. (If you see the old German phrase "K+K"—still used today as a boast of royal quality—it refers to this *"König und Kaiser"* arrangement.) So, after F. J. was crowned emperor in Vienna, he came down the Danube and said to the Hungarians, "King me."

Along the left aisle is the entrance to the upstairs gallery, which holds the **Museum of Ecclesiastical Art** (Egyházművészeti Gyűjteménye, same ticket and hours as church). The original Hungarian crown is under the Parliament's dome—but a replica is up here, and worth a peek.

The church also hosts **concerts** (Oct-Feb only, maybe a few in shoulder season, none in summer; ask at ticket windows or church entry, or look for posted schedules).

• *Back outside, at the end of the square next to the Matthias Church, is the...*

Fishermen's Bastion (Halászbástya)—This Neo-Romanesque fantasy rampart offers beautiful views over the Danube to Pest.

In the Middle Ages, the fish market was just below here (in today's Víziváros, or "Water Town"), so this part of the rampart actually was guarded by fishermen. The current structure, however, is completely artificial—yet another example of Budapest sprucing itself up for 1896. Its seven pointy towers represent the seven Magyar tribes. The cone-headed arcades are reminiscent of tents the nomadic Magyars called home before they moved west to Europe. While some suckers pay for the views from here, parts of the rampart are free and always open—just poke around to find your own, free view. Note that the grand staircase leading down from the bastion offers a handy shortcut to the Víziváros neighborhood.

Cost and Hours: 500 Ft, buy ticket at ticket office along the park wall across the square from Matthias Church, daily mid-March-mid-Oct 9:00-21:00; after closing time and off-season, no tickets are sold, but bastion is open and free to enter; Szentháromság tér 5, district I.

• *Between the bastion and the church stands a statue of...*

St. István—Hungary's first Christian king, István (c. 967-1038) tamed the nomadic, pagan Magyars and established strict laws and the concept of private property. In the late 900s, King Géza of Hungary lost a major battle against the forces of Christian Europe—and realized that he must raise his son Vajk as a Catholic and convert his people, or they would be forcefully driven out of Europe. Vajk took the Christian name István (EESHT-vahn, "Stephen") and was baptized in the year 1000. The reliefs on this statue show the commissioners of the pope crowning

St. István, bringing Hungary into the fold of
Christendom. This put Hungary on the map as a
fully European kingdom, forging alliances that
would endure for centuries. Without this pivotal event, Hungarians believe that the Magyar
nation would have been lost.

• *Directly across from Matthias Church is a charming little street called...*

Szentháromság Utca—Halfway down this
street on the right, look for the venerable, recommended **Ruszwurm** café—the oldest in
Budapest (see page 650). Then continue out to
the terrace and appreciate views of the Buda
Hills—the "Beverly Hills" of Budapest, draped with orchards,
vineyards, and the homes of the wealthiest Budapesters.

• *If you go down the stairs here, then turn right up the street, you'll reach
the entrance of the...*

**▲"Hospital in the Rock" Secret Military Hospital and
Nuclear Bunker (Sziklakórház és Atombunker)**—Sprawling
beneath Castle Hill is a 25,000-square-foot labyrinthine network
of hospital and fallout-shelter corridors built during the mid-20th
century. And now, after decades in mothballs, it's been opened
to tourists. While pricey, this visit is a must for doctors, nurses,
and World War II buffs. First you'll watch an eight-minute movie
(with English subtitles) about the history of the place. Then, on
the required tour, your guide will lead you through the tunnels
to see room after room of perfectly preserved WWII and 1960s-
era medical supplies and equipment, most still in working order.
More than a hundred wax figures engagingly bring the various
hospital rooms to life: giant sick ward, operating room, and so on.
On your way to the fallout shelter, you'll pass the decontamina-
tion showers, and see primitive radiation detectors and communist
propaganda directing comrades how to save themselves in case of
capitalist bombs or gas attacks. In the bunker, you'll also tour the
various mechanical rooms that ventilated and provided water to
this sprawling underground city.

Cost and Hours: 3,000 Ft for required one-hour tour, 30
percent discount with Memento Park ticket, Tue-Sun 10:00-
20:00, English tours at the top of each hour, last tour departs at
19:00—couples get a "lovers' discount" rate of 4,000 Ft for two
people on this tour only, closed Mon, gift shop like an army-sur-
plus store, Lovas utca 4C, district I, mobile 0670-701-0101, www
.hospitalintherock.com.

• *Our Castle Hill walk is finished. If you're ready to head back down to
the river (and the Víziváros neighborhood), you can make a graceful exit
down the big staircase below the Fishermen's Bastion.*

If you'd like to spend more time exploring Castle Hill, poke around the northern part of the hill. In this area, you'll find several interesting sights. Next door to the Matthias Church, the modern **Hilton Hotel** is built around the fragments of a 13th-century Dominican church (to see them, go inside, find the lounge, and look out the window toward Pest). A few blocks farther north stand the remains of **St. Mary Magdalene Church**, which was destroyed during the Ottoman occupation but whose bell tower has been rebuilt. Around the corner is the dusty **Museum of Military History**. And along the tree-shaded terrace at the northern tip of the hilltop, look for the **Turkish grave** of a pasha (Ottoman ruler).

From the northern end of the hill, you can head out through the Vienna Gate and follow the road downhill to bustling Széll Kálmán tér and its handy Metró stop (M2/red line).

Gellért Hill (Gellérthegy) and Nearby

The hill rising from the Danube just downriver from the castle is Gellért Hill. When King István converted Hungary to Christianity

in the year 1000, he brought in Bishop Gellért, a monk from Venice, to tutor his son. But some rebellious Magyars had other ideas. They put the bishop in a barrel, drove long nails in from the outside, and rolled him down this hill...tenderizing him to death. Gellért became the patron saint of Budapest and gave his name to the hill that killed him. Today the hill is a fine place to commune with nature on a hike or jog, followed by a restorative splash in its namesake baths.

Citadella—This strategic, hill-capping fortress was built by the Habsburgs after the 1848 Revolution to keep an eye on their Hungarian subjects. There's not much to do up here (no museum or exhibits), but it's a good destination for an uphill hike, and provides the best panoramic view over all of Budapest. The hill is crowned by the **Liberation Monument,** featuring a woman holding aloft a palm branch. Locals call it "the lady with the big fish" or "the great bottle opener." A heroic Soviet soldier, who once inspired the workers with a huge red star from the base of the monument, is now in Memento Park (see page 598).

Getting There: It's a steep hike up from the river to the Citadella. Bus #27 cuts some time off the trip, taking you up to the Búsuló Juhász stop (from which it's still an uphill hike to the fortress). You can catch bus #27 from either side of Gellért Hill. From the southern edge of the hill, catch this bus at the Móricz Zsigmond körtér stop (easy to reach: ride trams #19 or #41 south from anywhere along Buda's Danube embankment, or trams #47 or #49 from Pest's Small Boulevard ring road; you can also catch any of these trams at Gellért tér, in front of the Gellért Hotel).

▲▲Gellért Baths—Located at the famous and once-exclusive Gellért Hotel, right at the Buda end of the Liberty Bridge, this elegant bath complex has long been the city's top choice for a swanky, hedonistic soak. For details, see "Experiences in Budapest," later.

Cave Church (Sziklatemplom)—Hidden in the hillside on the south end of the hill (across the street from Gellért Hotel) is Budapest's atmospheric cave church—literally burrowed into the rock face. The communists bricked up this church when they came to power, but now it's open for visitors once again (500 Ft, unpredictable hours, closed to sightseers during frequent services).

▲▲Rudas Baths—Along the Danube toward Castle Hill from Gellért Baths, Rudas (ROO-dawsh) offers Budapest's most old-fashioned, Turkish-style bathing experience. In fact, the main pools sit under a 500-year-old Ottoman dome. On weekdays, it's a nude, gender-segregated experience, as bathers move from pool to pool to tweak their body temperature. It becomes more accessible (and mixed) on weekends, when men and women put on swimsuits and mingle beneath that historic dome. For details, see "Experiences in Budapest," later.

In Pest

Most of Pest's top sights cluster in four neighborhoods: **Leopold Town** and the **Town Center** (together forming the city's "downtown," along the Danube); along **Andrássy út;** and at **Heroes' Square and City Park.** Several other sights are along the **Small Boulevard** (Kiskörút); along the **Great Boulevard** (Nagykörút); and along the boulevard called Üllői út.

Leopold Town (Lipótváros)

The Parliament building, which dominates Pest's skyline, is the centerpiece of a banking and business district. Called Lipótváros ("Leopold Town"), this area is one of Budapest's most genteel quarters, and features some of the best of Budapest's many monuments. I've linked up the best sights in Leopold Town as a self-guided walk, starting at the grandiose Parliament building.

▲▲Hungarian Parliament (Országház)—The Parliament was built from 1885 to 1902 to celebrate the Hungarian millennium year of 1896 (see sidebar on page 539). Its elegant, frilly spires and riverside location were inspired by its counterpart in London (where the

architect studied). When completed, the Parliament was a striking and cutting-edge example of the mix-and-match Historicist style of the day—just as Frank Gehry's undulating buildings are examples of today's bold new aesthetic. Like the Hungarian people, this building is at once grandly ambitious and a somewhat motley hodgepodge of various influences—a Neo-Gothic palace topped with a Neo-Renaissance dome, which once had a huge, red communist star on top of the tallest spire. Fittingly, it's the city's top icon. The best views of the Parliament are from across the Danube—especially in the late-afternoon sunlight.

Touring the building offers the chance to stroll through one of Budapest's best interiors. On the 45-minute **tour,** you'll first pass through a security checkpoint, then climb up a 96-step staircase. Stops include the monumental entryway, the Hungarian crown (under the ornate gilded dome), and the legislative chamber of the now-disbanded House of Lords. Your guide will explain the history and symbolism of the building's intricate decorations and offer a lesson in the Hungarian parliamentary system. You'll find out why a really good speech was nicknamed a "Havana" by cigar-aficionado parliamentarians.

Cost and Hours: 3,400 Ft, free for EU citizens if you show your passport; English tours usually daily at 10:00, 12:00, and 14:00—but there can be more tours with demand, and fewer tours (for no apparent reason), so confirm in advance; on Mondays when parliament is in session—generally Sept-May—the only English tour is generally at 10:00; Kossuth tér 1-3, district V, M2: Kossuth tér, tel. 1/441-4904, www.parlament.hu.

Getting Tickets: There are two lines behind the security barrier: one to buy tickets and get your appointed time, the other to meet your tour guide and begin your tour. The ticket office opens each day at 8:00 (tickets sold for same-day tours only). On busy days, ticket-buyers line up, and tours can sell out (especially if a tour group has reserved a large block of tickets, which individuals can't do). If your heart is set on getting in, buy your tickets early (for morning tours, I'd try to arrive by 9:00; the ticket-buying line is longest around 10:30). Behind the Parliament, follow signs to the entry marked "X" (slightly right of center as you face the back of the giant building), and find the line at the fence marked *For Buying Tickets*. Wait for the guard to let you enter door X, pay the cashier to get your English tour ticket and time, and return to the mob to wait for your tour.

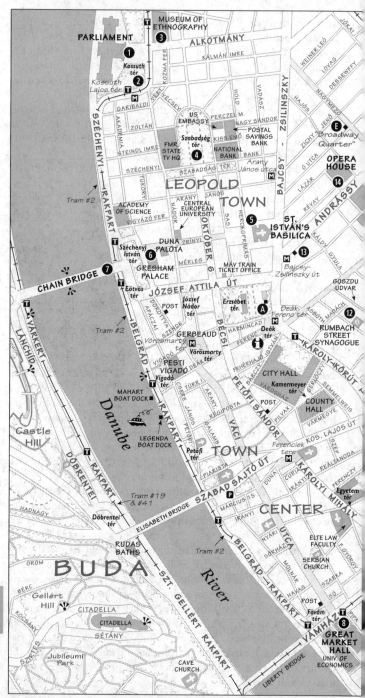

BUDAPEST

Pest Sights

1. Hungarian Parliament
2. Kossuth (Lajos) Tér
3. Museum of Ethnography
4. Szabadság Tér
5. St. István's Basilica
6. Gresham Palace
7. Chain Bridge
8. Great Market Hall
9. Hungarian National Museum
10. Great Synagogue
11. Orthodox Synagogue
12. Synagogue at Rumbach Street
13. Postal Museum
14. Hungarian State Opera House
15. House of Terror
16. Franz Liszt Museum
17. New York Café
18. To Holocaust Memorial Center
19. Applied Arts Museum

Nightlife
A. Gödör Klub
B. Szimpla Kert
C. Szimpla Kávézó
D. Mumus
E. Instant
F. Szóda
G. Corvintető

To Heroes' Square & City Park

Vörösmarty utca

PUPPET THEATER

Tram #4 & #6

HOUSE OF TERROR

FMR. ACADEMY OF MUSIC

Hunyadi tér

EÖTVÖS

TERÉZ KÖRÚT

MOZSÁR

Jókai tér

Oktogon

POST

SZOFIA

KIRÁLY

CSENGERY

HARSFA

KERTÉSZ

ERZSÉBET KÖRÚT

Lizst Ferenc tér

ACADEMY OF MUSIC

Opera

DRESCHLER PALACE

NEW THEATER

PAULAY EDE

HEGEDÜ

KIRÁLY

CSÁNYI

AKÁCFA

KLAUZÁL

KIS DIÓFA

KÁZINCZY

VASVÁRI

KÜRT

JEWISH QUARTER
(& "Ruin Pub" District)

ORTHODOX SYNAGOGUE

CARL LUTZ MEM.

TREE OF LIFE

GREAT SYNAGOGUE AND JEWISH MUSEUM

DOHÁNY

DOB

WESSELÉNYI

NAGY DIÓFA

NYÁR

AKÁCFA

Blaha Lujza tér

NEW YORK CAFÉ

KÖRÚT

LUTHER

ERKEL SZÍNHÁZ

KÉNYÉR

Astoria

RÁKÓCZI

Tram #47 & #49

MÚZEUM KÖRÚT

ELTE CAMPUS

Károlyi Park

HUNGARIAN NATIONAL MUSEUM

MÚZEUM

Kálvin tér

ÚT

STÁHLY

MAGYAR

TREFORT

PUSKIN

BRÓDY SÁNDOR

POLLACK MIHÁLY

SZENTKIRÁLYI

ÖT

SZABÓ REV.

PEST

MOGYI BÉLA

KŐFARAGÓ

BÉKÉSI

MÁRIA

RÖKK SZILÁRD

KRÚDY LŐRINC

Blaha Lujza tér

Rákóczi tér

BERKÖSCSI

VÁSÁR

JÓZSEF

BACSÓ

NÉMET

SALÉTROM

RIGÓ

Tram #4 & #6

LOVASSY LÁSZLÓ

SZSZ

BAROSS UTCA

Kálvin tér

BAROSS UTCA

KIS STÁCIÓ

HOCK

KÖRÚT

ÜLLŐI ÚT

RÁDAY

GÖNCZY PÁL

ERKEL

MÁTYÁS

CZUCZOR

LÓNYAY

IMRE

KINIZSI

KÖZTELEK

CSEPREGHY

PÁL

KISFALUDY

NAP

PRÁTER

APPLIED ARTS MUSEUM

HŐGYÉS ENDRE

Corvin-negyed

N

500 Meters

500 Yards

To 18

BUDAPEST

• *Behind the Parliament is...*

Kossuth (Lajos) Tér—This square is sprinkled with interesting monuments and packed with Hungarian history—including an **eternal flame** honoring the victims of the 1956 Uprising (near the ticket-buying line for Parliament visits); and, at the far end of the nearby park, a statue of the square's namesake, **Lajos Kossuth,** who led the 1848 Revolution against the Habsburgs. The street that leaves this square behind Kossuth is Falk Miksa utca, Budapest's **"antique row"**—a great place to browse for nostalgic souvenirs.

• *Walk halfway across the big, empty asphalt lot behind the Parliament. Look back and across the street to see the...*

Museum of Ethnography (Néprajzi Múzeum)—This museum, housed in one of Budapest's majestic venues, feels deserted. Its fine collection of Hungarian folk artifacts (mostly from the late 19th century) takes up only a small corner of the cavernous building. The permanent exhibit, with surprisingly good English explanations, shows off costumes, tools, wagons, boats, beehives, furniture, and ceramics of the many peoples who lived in pre-WWI Hungary, which also included much of today's Slovakia and Romania (1,000 Ft, may be more for special exhibitions, Tue-Sun 10:00-18:00, closed Mon, Kossuth tér 12, district V, M2: Kossuth tér, tel. 1/473-2200, www.neprajz.hu).

• *Now continue through the lot to the opposite end. At the edge of the grassy park, find the Hungarian flag with a hole cut out of the center.*

1956 Uprising Monument—This flag commemorates the 1956 Uprising, when protesters removed the communist seal the Soviets had added to their flag. Two days into that revolt, on October 25, the ÁVH (communist police) and Soviet troops on the rooftop above opened fire on demonstrators gathered in this square—massacring many and leaving no doubt that Moscow would not tolerate dissent. For more on this tragic chapter of Hungarian history, see the "1956" sidebar.

In the field behind this flag, you'll see a monument to yet another rebel: **Ferenc Rákóczi,** who valiantly (but unsuccessfully) led the Hungarians in their War of Independence (1703-1711) against the Habsburgs.

More Monuments—Three powerful monuments are near this square. First, walk along the path between the Parliament and the park toward the river. When you reach the tram tracks, turn right and continue past the little guardhouse toward the Danube. You'll see (with his back to you) a statue of **Attila József** (1905-1937). This beloved modern poet lived a tumultuous, productive, and short life before he killed himself by jumping in front of a train at age 32. József's poems of life, love, and death—mostly written in the 1920s and 1930s—are considered the high point of Hungarian literature. Here József re-enacts a scene from one of his best-loved poems, "At the Danube."

To find the next monument, continue straight down toward the Danube and stand at the top of the big staircase over the busy road. If you visually trace the Pest riverbank to the left, just before the tree-filled, riverfront park, you can just barely see several low-profile dots lining the embankment. This is a **Holocaust Monument** consisting of 50 pairs of bronze shoes. This monument commemorates the Jews who were killed when the Nazis' puppet government, the Arrow Cross, came to power in Hungary in 1944. While many Jews were sent to concentration camps, the Arrow Cross massacred

some of them right here, shooting them and letting their bodies fall into the Danube.

Backtrack past Attila József, cross the tram tracks, and walk along the ugly building (with an entrance to the Métró) up to the

back corner of Kossuth tér. Across the street in a little park (at Vértanúk tere), you'll see a monument to **Imre Nagy** (EEM-ray nodge, 1896-1958). When the 1956 Uprising broke out on October 23, Imre Nagy was drafted (reluctantly, some say) to become the head of the movement to soften the severity of the communist regime. Because he was a communist insider, it briefly seemed that Nagy might hold the key to finding a middle path (represented by the bridge he's standing on) between the suffocating totalitarian model of Moscow and the freedom of the West. But the optimism was short-lived. The

Soviets violently put down the uprising, arrested and sham-tried Nagy, executed him, and buried him face-down in an unmarked grave. The regime forced Hungary to forget about Nagy. But the Hungarians didn't oblige—and today, thanks to this monument, Nagy keeps a watchful eye on today's lawmakers in the Parliament across the way.

• *Go up the short, diagonal street behind Nagy, called Vécsey utca. After just one block, you emerge into...*

▲**Szabadság Tér ("Liberty Square")**—One of Budapest's most genteel squares is dominated by a stout obelisk, a **Soviet War Memorial** commemorating "Liberation Day": April 4, 1945, when the Soviets officially forced the Nazis out of Hungary. As a very rare reminder of the Soviet days—you almost never see

BUDAPEST

1956

The year 1956 is etched into the Hungarian psyche. In that year, the people of Budapest staged the first major uprising against the communist regime. It also marked the first time in the Eastern Bloc that the Soviets implicitly acknowledged, in brutally putting down the uprising, that the people of Eastern Europe were not "communist by choice."

The seeds of revolution were sown with the death of a tyrant: Josef Stalin passed away on March 5, 1953. Suddenly the choke-hold that Moscow had held on its satellite states loosened. During this time of "de-Stalinization," Hungarian premier Imre Nagy presided over two years of mild reform, before his political opponents (and Moscow) became nervous and demoted him.

In 1955, Austria declared its neutrality in the Cold War. This thrust Hungary to the front line of the Iron Curtain, and raised the stakes both for Hungarians who wanted freedom and for Soviets who wanted to preserve their buffer zone. When Stalin's successor, Nikita Khrushchev, condemned Stalin's crimes in a "secret speech" to communist leaders in February of 1956, it emboldened the Soviet Bloc's dissidents. A workers' strike in Poznań, Poland, in October inspired Hungarians to follow their example.

On October 23, 1956, the Hungarian uprising began. A student union group gathered in Budapest at 15:00 to articulate a list of 16 demands against the communist regime. Then they marched toward Parliament, their numbers gradually swelling. One protester defiantly cut the Soviet-style insignia out of the center of the Hungarian flag, which would become the uprising's symbol.

By nightfall, some 200,000 protesters filled Kossuth tér behind Parliament, calling for Imre Nagy, the one communist leader they believed could bring change. Nagy finally appeared around 21:00. Ever the pragmatic politician, he implored patience. Following the speech, a large band of protesters took matters into their own hands, marched to City Park, and tore down the hated Stalin statue that stood there (see page 594).

Another group went to the National Radio building to read their demands on the air. The ÁVH (communist police) refused to let them do it, and eventually opened fire on the protesters. The peaceful protests evolved into an armed insurrection, as frightened civilians gathered weapons and supplies.

Overnight, Moscow decided to intervene. Budapesters awoke on October 24 to find Red Army troops occupying their city. That morning, Imre Nagy—who had just been promoted again to prime minister—promised reforms and tried to keep a lid on the simmering discontent.

The next day, October 25, a huge crowd gathered on Kossuth tér behind the Parliament to hear from Nagy. In the hubbub, shots rang out as Hungarian and Soviet soldiers opened fire on the (mostly unarmed) crowd. At least 70 protesters were killed and more than 100 injured.

The Hungarians fought back with an improvised guerilla resistance. They made use of any guns they could get their hands on, as well as Molotov cocktails, to strike against the Soviet occupiers. Many adolescents (the celebrated "Pest Youth") participated. The fighting tore apart the city, and some of the fallen were buried in impromptu graves in city parks.

Political infighting in Moscow paralyzed the Soviet response, and an uneasy cease-fire fell over Budapest. For 10 tense days, it appeared that the Soviets might allow Nagy to push through some reforms. Nagy, a firmly entrenched communist, had always envisioned a less repressive regime...but within limits. While he was at first reluctant to take on the mantle of the uprising's leadership, he gradually began to echo what he was hearing on the streets. He called for free elections, the abolishment of the ÁVH, the withdrawal of Soviet troops, and Hungary's secession from the Warsaw Pact.

But when the uprisers attacked and killed ÁVH officers and communist leaders in Budapest, it bolstered the case of the Moscow hardliners. On November 4, the Red Army launched a brutal counterattack in Budapest that left the rebels reeling. At 5:20 that morning, Imre Nagy's voice came over the radio to beg the world for assistance. Later that morning, he sought asylum at the Yugoslav Embassy across the street from City Park. He was never seen alive in public again.

János Kádár—an ally of Nagy's who was palatable to the uprisers, yet firmly loyal to Moscow—was installed as prime minister. The fighting dragged on for about another week, but the uprising was eventually crushed. By the end, 2,500 Hungarians and more than 700 Soviets were dead, and 20,000 Hungarians were injured. Communist authorities arrested more than 15,000 people, of whom at least 200 were executed (including Imre Nagy). Anyone who had participated in the uprising was blacklisted; fearing this and other forms of retribution, some 200,000 Hungarians fled to the West.

Though the 1956 Uprising met a tragic end, within a few years Kádár did succeed in softening the regime, and the milder, so-called "goulash communism" emerged. And today, even though the communists are long gone, the legacy of 1956 pervades the Hungarian consciousness. Some Budapest buildings are still pockmarked with bullet holes from '56, and many Hungarians who fled the country in that year still have not returned. October 23 remains a major Hungarian holiday.

hammers-and-sickles in the streets of Hungary anymore—it has often been defaced, which is why a fence surrounds it. Nearby, look for a new statue honoring **Ronald Reagan,** erected in 2011 by right-wing Hungarian politicians.

• *Walk around the memorial and stand in the middle of Szabadság tér. Turn with your back to the obelisk, and look down to the far end of the square.*

The genteel open-air **café** in the middle of the park is an inviting place for a coffee break. Across the square (on the left), the yellow corner building is the **US Embassy.** This is where Cardinal József Mindszenty famously holed up for 15 years during the Cold War to evade arrest by the communist authorities.

• *Next we're headed for Perczel Mór utca, the street next to the US Embassy—but you'll have to detour a bit to the left (and tiptoe around some barricades) to get there. After one block on Perczel Mór utca, turn right onto Hold utca. You'll pass a **market hall** (on the left), then— on the right—Ödön Lechner's elaborate **Postal Savings Bank** (notice the beehive motif along the roofline—bees store honey like people store money), and after that, the **National Bank of Hungary.** Continue two blocks straight ahead up Hercegprímás utca. You'll emerge into a broad plaza in front of Budapest's biggest church...*

▲St. István's Basilica (Szent István Bazilika)—The church is only about 100 years old—like most Budapest landmarks, it was

built around the millennial celebrations of 1896. Designed by three architects over more than 50 years, St. István's is particularly eclectic. Each architect had a favorite style: Neoclassical, Neo-Renaissance, Neo-Baroque. Construction was delayed for a while when the giant dome collapsed midway through. Step inside. While it's dimly lit and a bit gloomy, it has been recently renovated and shows off a gorgeous interior. You'll see not Jesus, but St. István (Stephen), Hungary's first Christian king, glowing above the high altar.

The church's main claim to fame is the **"holy right hand" of St. István.** The sacred fist—a somewhat grotesque, 1,000-year-old withered stump—is in a jeweled box in the chapel to the left of the main altar (follow signs for *Szent Jobb Kápolna,* chapel often closed).

Pop in a 200-Ft coin for two minutes of light, and ask the guard for tips on taking the best photo. Posted information describes the hand's unlikely journey to this spot (chapel open April-Sept Mon-Sat 9:00-16:30, Sun 13:00-16:30; Oct-March Mon-Sat 10:00-16:00, Sun 13:00-16:30).

The church also has a panoramic **observation deck.** While the views over Budapest's rooftops are pretty distant (and disappointing without a good zoom lens), it offers a good sense of the sprawl of the city. You have various options: You can walk up the entire way (302 steps); or you can take an elevator to midlevel (with WCs), where you can follow signs to another elevator (plus 42 steps) or climb 137 steps to the top.

The church also hosts regular **organ concerts** (advertised near the entry).

Cost and Hours: Interior—free but 200-Ft donation strongly requested, daily 9:00-19:00 except closed for weddings (often Sat afternoon) and other services (various times on Sun); Observation deck—500 Ft, daily July-Aug 10:00-21:00, Sept 10:00-19:00, June and Oct 10:00-18:00, Nov-May 10:00-17:00; Szent István tér, district V, M1: Bajcsy-Zsilinszky út or M3: Arany János utca.

• *From here, you're very close to the boulevard called **Andrássy út**, which leads to various interesting sights, including the Opera House, House of Terror, and City Park (all described starting on page 586). To get there, walk around the right side of the basilica, and turn right on busy Bajcsy-Zsilinszky út; Andrássy út begins across the street, on your left.*

*But for now, consider heading to the Danube for a good look at the mighty Chain Bridge. Walk straight ahead from St. István's main staircase down **Zrínyi Utca**. This recently pedestrianized people zone passes (on the right) **Central European University**, a graduate school largely funded by Hungarian-American George Soros, and its good CEU Bookshop. Later, after crossing Nádor utca, on the left you'll find **Duna Palota**, a venue and ticket office for Hungária Koncert's popular tourist shows (described on page 618).*

Zrínyi utca dead-ends at the big traffic circle called Széchenyi István tér. Turn left and walk a half-block to the entrance (on the left) of the...

▲**Gresham Palace**—This was Budapest's first building in the popular Historicist style, and also incorporates elements of Art Nouveau. Budapest boomed at a time when architectural eclecticism—mashing together bits and pieces of different styles—was in vogue. But because much of the city's construction was compressed

Old Places, New Names

Since taking power both in Budapest and in the national parliament in 2010, the right-wing Fidesz party has introduced big changes in Hungary. One of Mayor István Tarlós' bold, controversial initiatives has been to rename many of the capital's streets and public spaces, including some of its most prominent squares. If you're using a map of Budapest that's even just a year or two old, you may still see the old names for some key landmarks. (The old street signs—crossed by a red slash—will remain up through 2013, and it may take locals even longer to start using the new names.) Of the two dozen or so new names, here's a decoder for the ones you're most likely to encounter:

Old Name	New Name
Roosevelt tér	**Széchenyi István tér**
Moszkva tér	**Széll Kálmán tér**
Köztársaság tér	**II. János Pál pápa tér ("John Paul II Square")**
Lágymányosi híd (bridge)	**Rákóczi híd**
Ferenc körút (Metró stop)	**Corvin-negyed**
Ferihegy Airport	**Liszt Ferenc (Franz Liszt) Airport**

The Fidesz party also christened a previously unnamed park (at the Buda end of Margaret Bridge) **Elvis Presley tér**. They wanted to honor The King for using his appearance on the *Ed Sullivan Show*—soon after the 1956 Uprising—to speak out in sup-

into a short window of time, even these disparate styles enjoy an unusual harmony. Damaged in World War II, the building was an eyesore for decades. In 1999, the Gresham Palace was meticulously restored to its former glory. Even if you can't afford

to stay here, saunter into the lobby and absorb the gorgeous details. For example, not only did they have to re-create the unique decorative tiles—they had to rebuild the original machines that made the tiles.

• *Grandly spanning the Danube from this spot is Budapest's best bridge...*

▲**Chain Bridge (Lánchíd)**—One of the world's great bridges connects Pest's Széchenyi István tér and Buda's Clark Ádám tér. This historic, iconic bridge, guarded by lions (symbolizing power),

port of the Hungarians and sing "Peace in the Valley" as a fundraiser for the country. Fidesz also honored another American, President Ronald Reagan, by erecting a larger-than-life statue of him—in charismatic stride—on one of Budapest's most important squares (Szabadság tér). But don't mistake this as a sign of widespread Hungarian support for the great American conservative; Fidesz simply considers the anti-communist crusader Reagan a handy stand-in for their own struggle against Hungary's Socialist Party.

Unsurprisingly, many of Fidesz's new names are politically motivated. Their decision to finally rename "Moscow Square" (Moszkva tér) has obvious anti-socialist overtones. Renaming a major square in honor of Pope John Paul II is both a nod to their Catholicism (Fidesz controversially inserted a reference to Hungary's Christian origins into the constitution) and a way to honor another anti-communist crusader. Other names are even more provocative—such as Wass Albert tér, for the Transylvanian writer who is embraced by the nationalistic Hungarian minority in Romania. Even the country got a new name. Formerly the "Republic of Hungary," on January 1, 2012, it was renamed simply "Hungary." Said one Fidesz politician, dismissively, "Far as I know, Hungary has always been called Hungary."

Mapmakers and everyday Hungarians alike have been frustrated by all of this fiddling around, and hope that this renaming trend doesn't stick. In the meantime, you may need to attack your Budapest map with a red pen to avoid getting lost.

is Budapest's most enjoyable and convenient bridge to cross on foot.

Until the mid-19th century, only pontoon barges spanned the Danube between Buda and Pest. In the winter, the pontoons had to be pulled in, leaving locals to rely on ferries (in good weather) or the river freezing over. People often walked across the frozen Danube, only to get stuck on the other side during a thaw, with nothing to do but wait for another cold snap.

Count István Széchenyi was stranded for a week trying to get to his father's funeral. After missing it, Széchenyi commissioned Budapest's first permanent bridge—which was also a major symbolic step toward another of Széchenyi's pet causes, the unification of Buda and Pest.

The Chain Bridge was built by Scotsman Adam Clark between 1842 and 1849, and it immediately became an important symbol of Budapest. Széchenyi—a man of the Enlightenment—charged both commoners and nobles a toll for crossing his bridge, making it an emblem of equality in those tense times. Like all of the city's bridges, the Chain Bridge was destroyed by the Nazis at the end of World War II, but was quickly rebuilt.

· *As you look out to the Danube from here, to the right you can see the tip of...*

▲**Margaret Island (Margitsziget)**—In the Middle Ages, this island in the Danube (just north of the Parliament) was known as the "Isle of Hares." In the 13th century, a desperate King Béla IV swore that if God were to deliver Hungary from the invading Tatars, he would dedicate his youngest daughter Margaret to the Church. Hungary was spared...and Margaret was shipped to a nunnery here. But, the story goes, Margaret embraced her new life as a castaway nun, and later refused her father's efforts to force her into a politically expedient marriage with a Bohemian king. She became St. Margaret of Hungary, and this island was named for her.

Today, Margaret Island remains Budapest's playground. Budapesters come to relax in this huge, leafy park...in the midst of the busy city, yet so far away (no cars are allowed on the island—just public buses). The island rivals City Park as the best spot in town for strolling, jogging, biking (you can rent a bike at Bringóhintó, with branches at both ends of the island), and people-watching. Rounding out the island's attractions are an iconic old water tower, the remains of Margaret's convent, a rose garden, a game farm, and a "musical fountain" that performs to the strains of Hungarian folk tunes.

Getting There: Bus #26 begins at Nyugati/Western train station, crosses the Margaret Bridge, then drives up through the middle of the island—allowing visitors to easily get from one end to the other (3-6/hour). **Trams** #4 and #6, which circulate around the Great Boulevard, cross the Margaret Bridge and stop at the southern tip of the island, a short walk from some of the attractions.

· *If you'd like to head for the heart of Pest, Vörösmarty tér (and the sights listed next), it's just two long blocks away: Turn left out of the Gresham Palace, and walk straight on Dorottya utca.*

Pest Town Center (Belváros)

Pest's Belváros ("Inner Town") is its gritty urban heart—simultaneously its most beautiful and ugliest district. Here you'll see fancy facades, some of Pest's best views from the Danube embankment, genteel old coffee houses that offer a whiff of the city's Golden Age, inviting oasis-like parks tucked between densely populated streets, and a cavernous, colorful market hall filled with Hungarian goodies. But you'll also experience crowds, grime, and pungent smells like nowhere else in Budapest. Remember: This is a city in transition. Within a decade, all of those rough edges will be sanded off... and tourists like you will be nostalgic for the "authentic" old days.

▲**Vörösmarty Tér**—The central square of the Town Center, dominated by a giant statue of the revered Romantic poet Mihály

Vörösmarty, is the hub of Pest sightseeing.

At the north end of the square is the landmark **Gerbeaud** café and pastry shop. Between the World Wars, the well-to-do ladies of Budapest would meet here after shopping their way up Váci utca. Today it's still *the* meeting point in Budapest (for tourists, at least). Consider stepping inside to appreciate the elegant old decor, or for a cup of coffee and a slice of cake. (Better yet, read "Budapest's Café Culture" for some other, more authentic café options near here—see page 647.) The yellow **M1 Metró stop** between the Vörösmarty statue and Gerbeaud is the entrance to the shallow *Földalatti*, or "underground"—the first subway on the Continent (built for the Hungarian millennial celebration in 1896). Today, it still carries passengers to Andrássy út sights, running under that street all the way to City Park.

• *Extending straight ahead from Vörösmarty tér is a broad, bustling, pedestrianized shopping street called...*

Váci Utca—Dating from 1810-1850, Váci utca (VAHT-see OOT-zah) is one of the oldest streets of Pest. This has long been the street where the elite of Pest would go shopping, then strut their stuff for their neighbors on an evening promenade. Today, the tourists do the strutting here—and the Hungarians go to American-style shopping malls.

This boulevard—Budapest's tourism artery—was a dreamland for Eastern Bloc residents back in the 1980s. It was here that they fantasized about what it might be like to be free, while drooling over Nikes, Adidas, and Big Macs before any of these "Western evils" were introduced elsewhere in the Warsaw Pact region. In fact, partway down the street (on the right, at Régi Posta utca) is the **first McDonald's behind the Iron Curtain,** where people from all over the Eastern Bloc flocked to dine. Since you had to wait in a long line—stretching around the block—to get a burger, it wasn't "fast food"...but at least it was "West food."

Ironically, this street—once prized by Hungarians and other Eastern Europeans because it felt so Western—is what many

Western tourists today mistakenly think is the "real Budapest." Visitors mesmerized by this people-friendly stretch of souvenir stands, Internet cafés, and upscale boutiques are likely to miss some more interesting and authentic areas just a block or two away. Don't fall for this trap. You could have a fun and fulfilling trip to this city without setting foot on Váci utca.

• *For a more appealing people zone than Váci utca, detour from Vörösmarty tér a block toward the river, to the inviting...*

Danube Promenade (Dunakorzó)—Some of the best views in Budapest are from this walkway facing Castle Hill—especially this stretch, between the white Elisabeth Bridge (left) and the iconic Chain Bridge (right). This is a favorite place to promenade *(korzó),* strolling aimlessly and greeting friends.

Dominating this part of the promenade is the Neo-Romantic–style **Pesti Vigadó**—built in the 1880s, and today undergoing a thorough renovation. Charmingly, the word *vigadó*—used to describe a concert hall—literally means "joyous place." In front is a playful statue of **a girl with her dog,** which captures the fun-loving spirit along this drag. At the gap in the railing, notice the platform to catch **tram #2,** which goes frequently in each direction along the promenade—a handy and scenic way to connect river-side sights in Pest. (You can ride it to the right, to the Parliament; or to the left, to the Great Market Hall.)

About 20 yards to the right, find the little statue wearing a jester's hat. She's playing on the railing with the castle behind her. The *Little Princess* is one of Budapest's cherished symbols and a favorite photo-op for tourists. While many of the city's monuments have interesting back-stories, more recent statues (like this one) are simply whimsical and fun.

Look to the riverfront below. Lining the **embankment** are several long boats: Some are excursion boats for sightseeing trips up and down the Danube, while others are overpriced (but scenic) restaurants. If you're interested in taking a cruise—which is especially pleasant at night—you could cross the road here (using the tram underpass 20 yards to the left), then walk 100 yards downriver (farther left) to the Danube Legenda boat dock. For details on the cruises, see page 549.

• *From here, both the promenade and Váci utca cut south through the Town Center. At the end of this zone is one of Budapest's top attractions, the Great Market Hall. Between here and there are the next two sights. While Váci utca is the most direct route, use your map to navigate the side streets in this area, and to locate these two potentially hard-to-find escapes.*

Párisi Udvar Gallery—This "Parisian Courtyard" is the grandest of Pest's many hidden galleries. Once used for elegant shopping, it's now dark, faded, and largely unused. The building is owned by the city and protected as a historic landmark: It can't be renovated in modern style, but it's too expensive to restore it to its original condition. And, as in many towns and cities in the US, many locals would rather shop at suburban malls than at inner-city alternatives like this one...gorgeous though they might be. For now, it's all yours to explore. Enjoy the delicate woodwork, the fine mosaics that glitter evocatively in the

low light, and the breathtaking stained-glass dome. While many of the storefronts inside are abandoned, a few are still alive and kicking (including the local answer to Starbucks, Coffee Heaven). This place is a reminder that if you only experience what's on the main streets in Budapest, you'll miss a big part of the story.

Getting There: A bit tricky to find, it's on the big square called Ferenciek tere, about halfway between Vörösmarty tér and the Great Market Hall. You can enter either at Kossuth Lajos út 11, or around the corner at Petőfi Sándor utca 2.

Károlyi Park (Károlyi Kert)—This delightful, flower-filled oasis offers the perfect break from loud and gritty urban Pest. Once

the private garden of the aristocratic Károlyi family from eastern Hungary (whose mansion it's behind), it's now a public park beloved by people who live, work, and go to school in this neighborhood. The park is filled with tulips in the spring, potted palm trees in the summer, and rich colors in the fall. On a sunny summer day, locals escape here to read books, gossip with neighbors, or simply lie in the sun. Many schools are nearby. Teenagers hang out here after school, while younger kids enjoy the playground. You'll find the park two blocks southeast of Ferenciek tere and the gallery described above; it's a block off Károlyi Mihály utca, to the left up Ferenczy István utca.

▲▲Great Market Hall (Nagyvásárcsarnok)—"Great" indeed is this gigantic marketplace. The Great Market Hall has somehow succeeded in keeping local shoppers happy, even as it's evolved

into one of the city's top tourist attractions. Goose liver,
embroidered tablecloths, golden
Tokaji Aszú wine, pickled peppers, communist-kitsch T-shirts,
patriotic green-white-and-red
flags, kid-pleasing local candy
bars, and paprika of every level
of spiciness...if it's Hungarian,
you'll find it here.

This market hall (along with four others) was built—like so
much of Budapest—around the millennial celebration year of
1896. Appreciate the colorful Zsolnay tiles lining the roof—frost-
proof and harder than stone, these were an integral part of the
Hungarian national style that emerged in the late 19th century.

Step inside the market
and get your bearings: The
cavernous interior features
three levels. The ground
floor has produce stands,
bakeries, butcher stalls,
heaps of paprika, goose
liver, and salamis. Upstairs
are stand-up eateries and
souvenirs. And in the basement are a supermarket, a fish market,
and piles of pickles.

Stroll down the "main drag," enjoying a combination of produce stands and vendors selling authentic Hungarian products.

About halfway down, detour
to the left to find the **Csárdi és
Csárdi** stall (near the outer wall),
where you can sample both types
of paprika: sweet (*édes*, used for
flavor) and hot (*csípős*, used sparingly to add some kick). Note the
difference, choose your favorite,
and buy some to take home (for

more information, see "Paprika Primer" on page 518).

After you've worked your way to the far end of the hall, take
the escalator to the **upper level.** You're immersed in a world of
Hungarian **souvenirs** (for tips, see "Shopping in Budapest," page
621). The left wall (as you face the front) is lined with fun, cheap,
stand-up, Hungarian-style fast-food joints and six-stool pubs.
About two-thirds of the way along the hall (after the second
bridge), the **Lángos** stand is the best eatery in the market, serving
up the deep-fried snack called *lángos*—similar to elephant ears, but

savory rather than sweet. The most typical version is *sajtos tejfölös*—with sour cream and cheese. You can also add garlic *(fokhagyma)*. The **Fakanál Étterem** cafeteria above the main entrance is handy but pricey.

For a less glamorous look at the market, head down the escalators to the **basement.** In addition to the handy supermarket down here, the basement is pungent with tanks of still-swimming carp, catfish, and perch, and piles of pickles (along the left side). Stop at one of the pickle stands and take a look. Hungarians pickle just about anything: peppers and cukes, of course, but also cauliflower, cabbage, beets, tomatoes, garlic, and so on. Vendors are usually happy to give you a sample; consider picking up a colorful jar of mixed pickled veggies for your picnic.

Hours and Location: Mon 6:00-17:00, Tue-Fri 6:00-18:00, Sat 6:00-15:00, closed Sun, Fővám körút 1-3, district IX, M3: Kálvin tér.

Along the Small Boulevard (Kiskörút)

These two sights are along the Small Boulevard, between the Liberty Bridge/Great Market Hall and Deák tér.

▲**Hungarian National Museum (Magyar Nemzeti Múzeum)**—One of Budapest's biggest museums features all

manner of Hungarian historic bric-a-brac, from the Paleolithic age to a more recent infestation of dinosaurs (the communists). Artifacts are explained by good, if dry, English descriptions. Upstairs, 20 rooms provide a historic overview from the arrival of the Magyars in 896 up to the 1989 revolution. The museum adds substance to your understanding of Hungary's story—but it helps to have a pretty firm foundation first (read "Hungarian History" on page 507). The most engaging part is room 20, with an exhibit on the communist era, featuring both pro- and anti-Party propaganda. The exhibit ends with video footage of the 1989 end of communism—demonstrations, monumental parliament votes, and a final farewell to the last Soviet troops leaving Hungarian soil. Another uprising—the 1848 Revolution against Habsburg rule—was declared from the steps of this impressive Neoclassical building.

Cost and Hours: 1,100 Ft, audioguide-750 Ft/hour, Tue-Sun 10:00-18:00, closed Mon, last entry 30 minutes before closing, near Great Market Hall at Múzeum körút 14-16, district VIII, M3: Kálvin tér, tel. 1/327-7773, www.hnm.hu.

▲▲**Great Synagogue (Zsinagóga)**—Also called the "Dohány Street Synagogue," Budapest's gorgeous synagogue is the biggest in Europe and the second biggest in the world (after the Temple Emanu-El of New York). With its ornately decorated interior, attached museum offering a concise lesson in the Jewish faith, and evocative memorial garden (with its weeping-willow *Tree of Life* sculpture), it's well worth a visit.

Cost and Hours: 2,650 Ft for Great Synagogue and Jewish Museum, *Tree of Life* and memorial garden are always free; April-Oct Sun-Thu 10:00-17:30, Fri 10:00-15:30; Nov-March Sun-Thu 10:00-15:30, Fri 10:00-14:30; always closed Sat and Jewish holidays, last entry 30 minutes before closing. Dohány utca 2, district VII, near M2: Astoria or the Astoria stop on trams #47 and #49. Tel. 1/344-5131, www.aviv.hu.

Tours: Aviv Travel, with a well-marked kiosk just outside the synagogue entrance, leads tours of the synagogue, museum, and related sights. You have four options: A quick 45-minute tour combines the Great Synagogue and the *Tree of Life* (2,400 Ft). A longer 80-minute tour covers the above, plus a guided visit to the Jewish Museum (2,750 Ft). The 90-minute version includes the Great Synagogue, *Tree of Life*, and the nearby synagogue on Rumbach Street, but not the museum (3,150 Ft). And the 110-minute version covers the whole shebang: both synagogues, museum, and *Tree of Life* (3,400 Ft). Tours leave every 30 minutes during the Great Synagogue's opening hours (last tour departs one hour before closing).

❍ Self-Guided Tour: While the tours described above are worthwhile, the following commentary covers the basics.

First, go through the security checkpoint at the entrance. You can buy tickets for the synagogue interior and the museum at the end of the courtyard on the right. Then visit the sights in the following order. (Note that you can visit the *Tree of Life* and memorial garden even if you don't buy a ticket for the synagogue. Or, if the synagogue is closed, go around left side to view the monument through a fence.)

1. Great Synagogue: Before going inside, check out the synagogue's striking **facade,** and consider the rich history of the building and the people it represents: The synagogue was built in 1859 just outside what was then the city limits (where the Small Boulevard ring road is today). Although Budapest's Jews held fast to their own faith, they also wished to prove their worth, and to demonstrate how well-integrated they were with the greater community. The two tall towers (designed to

evoke the Temple of Solomon in Jerusalem) and the rosette (rose window) helped the synagogue resemble Christian churches of the time. (In fact, when it was built, the synagogue was cynically dubbed by one onlooker as "the most beautiful Catholic synagogue in the world.")

Now step **inside.** (Men will need to cover their heads, and women their shoulders; loaner yarmulkes and scarves are available

at the door.) Notice that it really feels like a church with the symbols switched—with a basilica floor plan, three naves, two pulpits, and even a pipe organ. The Moorish-flavored decor—which looks almost Oriental—is a sign of the Historicist style of the time, which borrowed eclectic elements from past styles. Specifically, it evokes how Jewish culture flourished among the Sephardic Jews of Iberia (the origin of many Hungarian Jews). In the ark, behind the burgundy curtain, 25 original Torah scrolls are kept. Catholic priests hid these scrolls during World War II (burying them temporarily in a cemetery). The two-tiered balconies on the sides were originally for women, who worshipped separately from the men.

Ponder this building's recent history: While it survived World War II, the Great Synagogue sat neglected for 40 years. But since the thawing of communism, Hungarian Jews have taken a renewed interest in their heritage. In 1990, this synagogue was painstakingly restored. As you tour this place, think of all of the famous and important people of Hungarian-Jewish descent: Harry Houdini (born Erich Weisz), Elie Wiesel, Theodor Hertzl, Joseph Pulitzer, Estée Lauder, Goldie Hawn, Peter Lorre, Eva and Zsa Zsa Gabor, and Tony and Jamie Lee Curtis.

• When you're finished inside, exit through the main doors, turn right, and go to the opposite end of the front courtyard. Here you'll find the entrance to the...

2. Jewish Museum (Zsidó Múzeum): This small but informative museum illuminates the Jewish faith, with artifacts and succinct but engaging English explanations. You'll find descriptions of rituals and holidays, from Rosh Hashanah and Yom Kippur to Passover and Chanukah. The exhibit also explains ancient symbols (prayer shawls, the mezuzah, etc.) and traces Jewish family life, from birth to marriage to death. The final room holds a small exhibit about the Holocaust, including some actual items from concentration camps—such as drums that the Nazis fashioned out of Torah scrolls, and a menorah made by a resourceful inmate out of scraps of bread. (For more information about this tragic chapter of the Hungarian Jewish experience, don't miss the outstanding Holocaust Memorial Center, described on page 597.)

• *Exiting back into the front courtyard, go down the passageway between the synagogue and the museum (across from the security checkpoint, past the gift shop).*

3. *Tree of Life* and Memorial Garden: Dominating the garden behind the synagogue is the ***Tree of Life***, sculpted by renowned artist Imre Varga. The willow makes an upside-down menorah, and each of the 4,000 metal leaves is etched with the name of a Holocaust victim. In the center of the courtyard is a symbolic **grave of Raoul Wallenberg.** He was a

humanitarian and diplomat who came here from Sweden to do what he could to rescue Hungary's Jews from the Nazis.

Other Synagogues—If you have time and interest, two nearby, smaller synagogues are also worth a visit. The **Orthodox Synagogue** is located on a nondescript urban street two blocks from the Great Synagogue. Built in the Vienna-inspired Secession style in 1912, damaged and deserted for decades after World War II, and now undergoing a long-overdue renovation, this temple invites visitors to see its colorful, sumptuously decorated interior (800 Ft, Sun-Thu 10:00-16:00, Fri 10:00-13:00, closed Sat, two blocks behind the Great Synagogue at Kazinczy utca 27, enter down little alley, district VII, M2: Astoria). Still rough around the edges, the **Synagogue at Rumbach Street** awaits a more thorough restoration. In the meantime, it's open for visitors to walk around the Moorish-style interior, designed by Otto Wagner (500 Ft, Sun-Thu 10:00-17:30, Fri 10:00-14:30, closed Sat, from the *Tree of Life* it's two blocks down Rumbach utca toward Andrássy út, district VII, M2: Astoria).

Andrássy Út

Connecting downtown Pest to City Park, Andrássy út is Budapest's main boulevard, lined with plane trees, shops, theaters, cafés, and locals living well. Budapesters like to think of Andrássy út as the Champs-Elysées and Broadway rolled into one. While that's a stretch, it is a good place to stroll, get a feel for today's urban Pest, and visit a few top attractions (most notably the Opera House and the House of Terror).

I've arranged these sights in the order you'll reach them if you walk up the boulevard from where it begins, near Deák tér. The handy M1/yellow Metró line runs every couple of minutes just under the street, making it easy to skip several blocks ahead, or to

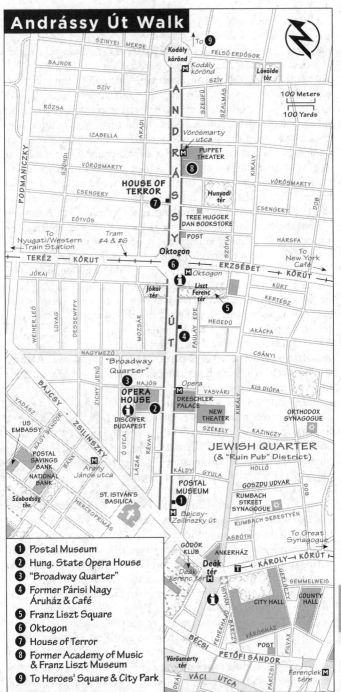

Andrássy Út Walk

1. Postal Museum
2. Hung. State Opera House
3. "Broadway Quarter"
4. Former Párisi Nagy Áruház & Café
5. Franz Liszt Square
6. Oktogon
7. House of Terror
8. Former Academy of Music & Franz Liszt Museum
9. To Heroes' Square & City Park

BUDAPEST

backtrack (stops marked by yellow signs).

• *Near the Bajcsy–Zsilinszky Métró stop at the beginning of Andrássy út, on the right side of the street, look for the red mailboxes flanking the entrance (at #3, dial 10 to get inside) to the...*

▲**Postal Museum (Postamúzeum)**—This quirky and unexpectedly enjoyable museum, in a fine old apartment from Budapest's Golden Age, features a collection of postal artifacts. You'll see post office coats of arms, 100-year-old postal furniture, antique telephone boxes, historic mailman uniforms, and all manner of postal paraphernalia that was cutting-edge a century ago. The exhibits are displayed in an elegant old merchant's mansion with big Murano crystal chandeliers, all the original ornate woodwork, and creaky parquet floors. The apartment—decorated as it was when built in the 1880s—is at least as interesting as the museum's collection. If it's not too busy, one of the nostalgic women staff members (who seem to be of a similar vintage as the apartment) might show you around and lovingly demonstrate the still-working equipment.

Cost and Hours: 500 Ft, Tue-Sun 10:00-18:00, closed Mon, loaner English information in each room, just up the street from St. István's Basilica at Andrássy út 3, look for easy-to-miss sign and dial 10 to get upstairs, district VI, M1: Bajcsy-Zsilinszky út, tel. 1/269-6838, www.postamuzeum.hu.

• *Three blocks up Andrássy út on the left is the...*

▲▲**Hungarian State Opera House (Magyar Állami Operaház)**—The Neo-Renaissance home of the Hungarian State Opera features performances (almost daily except during outdoor music season, late June-early Sept) and delightful tours. The building dates from the 1890s, not long after Budapest had become co-capital of the Habsburg Empire. Designed by Miklós Ybl, it was built using almost entirely Hungarian materials. After being damaged in World War II, it was painstakingly restored in the early 1980s. Today, with lavish marble-and-gold-leaf decor, a gorgeous gilded interior slathered with paintings of Greek myths, and high-quality performances at bargain prices, this is one of Europe's finest opera houses.

You can drop in whenever the box office is open to ogle the ostentatious **lobby** (Mon-Sat from 11:00 until show time—generally 19:00; Sun open 3 hours before the performance—generally 16:00-19:00, or 10:00-13:00 if there's a matinee; Andrássy út 22, district VI, M1: Opera).

The 45-minute **tours** of the Opera House are a must for music-lovers, and enjoyable to anyone. With an English-speaking guide (who spouts plenty of fun, if silly, legends), you'll see the main entryway, the snooty lounge area, some of the cozy but plush boxes, and the lavish auditorium. You'll find out why secret lovers would meet in the cigar lounge, how the Opera House is designed to keep the big spenders away from the rabble in the nosebleed seats, and how to tell the difference between real marble and fake marble (2,900 Ft, 500 Ft to take photos, 500 Ft extra for 5-minute mini-concert of two arias after the tour, tours nearly daily at 15:00 and 16:00, tickets are easy to get—just show up right before the tour, buy ticket in opera shop—enter the main lobby and go left, shop open Mon-Fri 10:30-12:45 & 13:30-17:00, Sat-Sun 13:30-17:00, open later during performances, tel. 1/332-8197).

To experience the Opera House in action, take in an excellent and refreshingly affordable **performance** (see "Entertainment in Budapest," page 616).

• *The Opera House marks the beginning of an emerging dining-and-nightlife zone dubbed the...*

"Broadway Quarter"—The traffic-free street just behind the Opera House, **Hajós utca,** is a budding outdoor-dining zone with a smattering of trendy restaurants. The next major cross-street, **Nagymező utca,** features a chic cluster of restaurants, bars, and theaters. This is an enjoyable place to stroll on a summer evening. Many of my recommended restaurants described under "Eating in Budapest," later, are in this neighborhood.

A half-block down on the right (at #39) is a grand old early-20th-century building marked **Párisi Nagy Áruház** (Paris

Department Store), with a fine café inside. One of the city's first department stores, this was a popular shopping stop for years. But as was common in Budapest, the store closed down and sat deserted and glum for years until investors came along to rescue it. The new owners, the Alexandra bookstore chain, turned the main area into a great bookshop, created office space above, and—inside, up the escalator at the back—fully restored the sumptuous Lotz Hall to create an excellent café with tinkling-piano ambience and reasonable prices. Dip inside to check it out (daily 10:00-22:00; for more details, see page 649).

• *One more block up the boulevard is Budapest's outdoor-dining mecca...*

Franz Liszt Square (Liszt Ferenc Tér)—This leafy square is surrounded by hip, expensive cafés and restaurants. (The best is the kitschy communist-themed restaurant Menza, described later, under "Eating in Budapest.") This is *the* scene for Budapest's yuppies. The square is named for **Franz Liszt** (pronounced "list," 1811-1886; look for his statue playing an imaginary piano in the middle of the park). This master composer, conductor, pedagogue, and (above all) pianist was prodigiously talented and traveled far and wide to share his skill ("Liszt played here" signs are plastered on buildings all over Hungary). Although Liszt was raised speaking German, he had a Hungarian surname and ancestry, and loved what he considered his homeland of Hungary. (We'll see a museum dedicated to Liszt farther along Andrássy út.)

• *One block up from Franz Liszt Square is the gigantic crossroads known as the...*

Oktogon—This vast intersection with its corners snipped off—where Andrássy út meets the Great Boulevard ring road (Nagykörút)—was called Mussolini tér during World War II, then November 7 tér in honor of the Bolshevik Revolution. Today kids have nicknamed it American tér for the fast-food joints littering the square and streets nearby. Standing (carefully) in the center of Andrássy út, you can already see the column of Heroes' Square at the end of the boulevard.

From here, if you have time to delve into workaday Budapest, consider a trip on tram #4 or #6, which trundle in both directions around the ring road. Or take a short detour to the most opulent coffee break of your life, at **New York Café** (described on page 647): Just hop on a tram to the right (tram #6 toward Móricz Zsigmond körtér, or tram #4 toward Fehérvári út), and get off at the Wesselényi utca stop.

• *There's one more major sight between here and Heroes' Square. You can either walk two more blocks up Andrássy út, or hop on the Metró and take it one stop to Vörösmarty utca, to reach the...*

▲▲House of Terror (Terror Háza)—The building at Andrássy út 60 was home to the vilest parts of two destructive regimes: first the Arrow Cross (the Gestapo-like enforcers of Nazi-occupied Hungary), then the ÁVO and ÁVH secret police (the insidious KGB-type wing of the Soviet satellite government). Now re-envisioned as the "House of Terror," this building uses high-tech, highly conceptual, bombastic exhibits to document (if not proselytize about) the ugliest moments in Hungary's difficult 20th century. Enlightening and well-presented, it rivals Memento Park as Budapest's best attraction about the communist age.

Cost and Hours: 2,000 Ft, possibly more for special exhibitions, audioguide-1,300 Ft, Tue-Sun 10:00-18:00, closed Mon, last entry 30 minutes before closing, Andrássy út 60, district VI, M1: Vörösmarty utca—*not* the Vörösmarty tér stop, tel. 1/374-2600, www.terrorhaza.hu.

Audioguide: The 1,300-Ft English audioguide is good but almost too thorough, and can be difficult to hear over the din of Hungarian soundtracks in each room. As an alternative, my self-guided tour (next page) covers the key points.

Background: In the lead-up to World War II, Hungary initially allied with Hitler—both to retain a degree of self-determination and to try to regain its huge territorial losses after World War I's devastating Treaty of Trianon (see page 511). But in March of 1944, the country was taken over by the Nazi-affiliated Arrow Cross. The Arrow Cross immediately set to work exterminating Budapest's Jews (most of whom had survived until then). The Nazi surrogates deported nearly 440,000 Jewish people to Auschwitz, murdered thousands more on the streets of Budapest, and executed hundreds in the basement of this building. When the communists moved into Hungary, they took over the same building as headquarters for their secret police (the ÁVO, later renamed ÁVH). To keep dissent to a minimum, the secret police terrorized, tried, deported, or executed anyone suspected of being an enemy of the state.

○ Self-Guided Tour: Buy your ticket (and rent an audioguide, if you wish) and head into the museum. The **atrium** features

a Soviet tank and a huge wall covered with portraits of 3,200 of this building's victims.

The one-way exhibit begins two floors up, then spirals down to the cellar. To begin, you can either take the elevator (to floor 2), or walk up the red stairwell nearby, decorated with old sculptures from the communist days.

Once on the second floor, enter the exhibition. In the **Double Occupation** room, the video sets the stage for Hungary's 20th century: its territorial losses after World War I; its alliance with, then invasion by, the Nazis; and its "liberation," then occupation, by the USSR.

After passing through a room displaying uniforms and other gear belonging to Hungarian Nazis, you'll reach a room devoted to the **Gulag.** The word "gulag" refers to a network of secret Soviet prison camps, mostly in Siberia. These were hard-labor camps where potential and actual dissidents were sent to be punished, to remove their dangerous influence from society, and to make an example of those who would dare to defy the regime. On the

carpet, a giant map of the USSR
shows the locations of some of
these camps, where an estimated
600,000-700,000 Hungarian
civilians and prisoners of war
were sent...about half of whom
never returned.

The **Changing Clothes**
room—with rotating figures dressed alternately in Arrow Cross
and communist uniforms—satirizes the readiness of many
Hungarians to align with whoever was in power.

The room about **The Fifties** examines the gradual insinuation
of the communist regime into the fabric of Hungary. Their meth-

ods ranged from pre-marked
ballots to glossy propaganda—
such as the paintings celebrating the peasants of the "people's
revolution" and romanticized
depictions of communist leaders (look for Lenin as the brave
sailor). Behind the distorted
stage is the dark underbelly of
the regime: the constant surveillance that bred paranoia among the people.

The **Resistance** room features three very different kitchen
tables, symbolizing the way that resistance to the regime emerged
in every walk of life. The exhibit continues downstairs, where
the **Resettlement and Deportation** section considers the ethnic
cleansing (or, in the more pleasant parlance of the time, "mutual
population exchange") that took place throughout Central and
Eastern Europe in the years following World War II. In Hungary,
230,000 Germans were uprooted and deported. Meanwhile, hundreds of thousands of Hungarians who had become ethnically
"stranded" in other nations after the Treaty of Trianon were sent to
Hungary.

In **Surrender of Property and Land,** we learn that under the
communists, the Hungarian people had to survive on increasingly
sparse rations. Enter the labyrinth of pork-fat bricks, which remind
old-timers of the harsh conditions of the 1950s (lard on bread for
dinner). Look for the ration coupons, which people had to present
before being allowed to buy even these measly staples.

The next room examines the **ÁVO,** the communist secret
police who intimidated the common people of Hungary—
equivalent to the KGB in the Soviet Union. Before they were finished, the ÁVO imprisoned, abused, or murdered one person from
every third Hungarian family. Their power came from enlisting

untold numbers of civilians as informants.

After passing through Gábor Péter's Office (he was the first director of the ÁVO), you'll reach the **"Justice"** exhibit, which explores the concept of "show trials"—high-profile, loudly publicized, and completely choreographed trials of people who had supposedly subverted the regime. The burden of proof was on the accused, not on the accuser, and coerced confessions were fair game. From 1945 until the 1956 Uprising, more than 71,000 Hungarians were accused of political crimes, and 485 were executed.

Next you'll pass through another, more upbeat method for

controlling the people: bright, cheery communist **Propaganda.** The poster about the *Amerikai Bogár* warns of the threat of the "American Beetle" (from *Kolorádó*), which threatened Hungarian crops. When the communists collectivized traditional family farm plots, they removed the trees and hedgerows that separated them—in the process removing the birds that had kept pest populations in check. When a potato beetle epidemic hit, rather than acknowledging their own fault, the communists blamed an American conspiracy.

Rounding out this floor are sections on **"The Hungarian Silver"** (actually aluminum—lampooning the lowbrow aesthetic of the communist era) and **Religion** (those who openly practiced their faith risked being blacklisted or worse by the atheistic regime). Then you'll board an **elevator** that gradually lowers down into the cellar, while you watch a three-minute video of a guard explaining the grotesque execution process.

When the door opens, you're in the **Prison Cellar.** You'll wander through former cells used for different purposes. In the large room after the cells, you'll see a stool with a lamp; nearby are the primitive torture devices: hot pads and electrical appliances. The bucket and hose were used to revive torture victims who had blacked out. After the torture room, in a small room on the right, you'll see a gallows that was used for executions, as you just heard described in the elevator. The **Internment** exhibit explains

that, while the most notorious gulag network was in Siberia, a similar system of prison camps also emerged in the Soviet satellites—including Hungary.

The room commemorating the **1956 Uprising** features a symbol of the

BUDAPEST

uprising—a Hungarian flag with a hole cut out of the middle—and the slogan *Ruszkik Haza!* ("Russkies go home!"). For more on '56, see page 570.

After a sobering room displaying gallows, the **Emigration** room features a wall of postcards. More than 200,000 Hungarians simply fled the country after the uprising.

The **Hall of Tears** memorial commemorates all of the victims of the communists from 1945 to 1967 (when the final prisoners were released from this building). The **Room of Farewell** shows several color video clips that provide a (relatively) happy ending: the festive and exhilarating days in 1991 when the Soviets departed, making way for freedom; the reburial of the Hungarian hero, Imre Nagy; and the dedication of this museum.

The chilling finale: walls of photographs of the **Victimizers**—members and supporters of the Arrow Cross and ÁVO, many of whom are still living and who were never brought to justice. The Hungarians have a long way to go to reconcile everything they lived through in the 20th century. For many of them, this museum is an important first step.

• *Across the street and a few steps up Andrássy út is the...*

Franz Liszt Museum—In this surprisingly modest apartment where the composer once resided, you'll find a humble but appealing collection of artifacts. A pilgrimage site for Liszt fans, it's housed in the former Academy of Music, which also hosts Saturday-morning concerts (museum entry-800 Ft, dry English audioguide with a few snippets of music-600 Ft, otherwise scarce English information—borrow the information sheet as you enter, Mon-Fri 10:00-18:00, Sat 9:00-17:00, closed Sun, 35 Vörösmarty utca, district VI, M1: Vörösmarty utca—*not* Vörösmarty tér stop, tel. 1/322-9804, www.lisztmuseum.hu).

• *While you can walk from here to Heroes' Square (visible in the distance, about a 15-minute walk), there's less to see along the rest of Andrássy út. If you prefer, hop on the Metró here and ride it three stops to Hősök tere.*

Heroes' Square and City Park

The grand finale of Andrássy út, at the edge of the city center, is also one of Budapest's most entertaining quarters. Here you'll find the grand Heroes' Square, dripping with history; the vast tree-filled expanse of City Park, dressed up with fanciful buildings; and, tucked in the middle of it all, Budapest's finest thermal spa and single best experience: the Széchenyi Baths. If the sight-

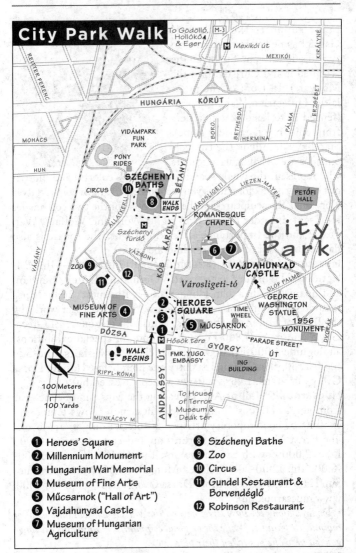

City Park Walk

To Gödöllő, Hollókő & Eger   M-3

Mexikói út

MEXIKÓI

KIRÁLYNÉ

HUNGÁRIA KÖRÚT

VIDÁMPARK FUN PARK

PONY RIDES

SZÉCHENYI BATHS

CIRCUS ⑩ ⑧ **WALK ENDS**

Széchenyi fürdő

ROMANESQUE CHAPEL

PETŐFI HALL

City Park

⑥ ⑦ **VAJDAHUNYAD CASTLE**

ZOO ⑨

⑫

⑪

Városligeti-tó

GEORGE WASHINGTON STATUE

1956 MONUMENT

MUSEUM OF FINE ARTS ④

② **HEROES' SQUARE**

③

⑤ MŰCSARNOK

TIME WHEEL

DÓZSA

①

WALK BEGINS

Hősök tere

"PARADE STREET"

FMR. YUGO. EMBASSY

GYÖRGY ÚT

ING BUILDING

100 Meters
100 Yards

RIPPL-RÓNAI

To House of Terror Museum & Deák tér

MUNKÁCSY M.

ANDRÁSSY ÚT

① Heroes' Square
② Millennium Monument
③ Hungarian War Memorial
④ Museum of Fine Arts
⑤ Műcsarnok ("Hall of Art")
⑥ Vajdahunyad Castle
⑦ Museum of Hungarian Agriculture

⑧ Széchenyi Baths
⑨ Zoo
⑩ Circus
⑪ Gundel Restaurant & Borvendéglő
⑫ Robinson Restaurant

seeing grind gets you down, take a mini-vacation from your busy vacation like the Budapesters do...and escape to City Park. To reach this area directly, take the M1/yellow Metró line to Hősök tere (district XIV).

▲▲**Heroes' Square (Hősök Tere)**—Built in 1896 to celebrate the 1,000th anniversary of the Magyars' arrival in Hungary, this vast square culminates at a bold **Millennium Monument**. The granddaddy of all Magyars, Árpád, stands proudly at the bottom of the pillar, peering down Andrássy út. The 118-foot-tall pillar supports the archangel Gabriel as he offers the crown to Árpád's descendant, St. István (he accepted it and Christianized the Magyars). In front of the pillar is the Hungarian War Memorial (fenced in to keep skateboarders from enjoying its perfect slope). Standing stoically in the two colonnades are 14 Hungarian leaders  who represent the whole span of this nation's colorful and illustrious history. Look for names you recognize: István, Béla IV, Mátyás Corvinus. The sculptures on the top corners of the two colonnades represent, in order from left to right: Work and Welfare, War, Peace, and the Importance of Packing Light. The square is also flanked by a pair of museums (described next).

Museum of Fine Arts (Szépművészeti Múzeum)—This collection of Habsburg art—mostly Germanic, Dutch, Belgian, and Spanish, rather than Hungarian—is Budapest's best chance to appreciate some European masters. You'll see lesser works by the likes of Dürer, the Bruegels, Murillo, Velázquez, El Greco, Goya, and more (1,800 Ft, may be more for special exhibitions, audioguide-1,000 Ft, WC and coat check downstairs, Tue-Sun 10:00-17:30, closed Mon, last entry one hour before closing, Dózsa György út 41, tel. 1/469-7100, www.szepmuveszeti.hu).

Műcsarnok ("Hall of Art")—Facing the Museum of Fine Arts from across Heroes' Square, the Műcsarnok shows temporary exhibits by contemporary artists—of interest only to art-lovers. The Ernst Museum wing features up-and-coming artists (1,900 Ft, or 2,000 Ft with Ernst Museum; Tue-Wed and Fri-Sun 10:00-18:00, Thu 12:00-20:00, closed Mon; Ernst Museum open Tue-Sun 11:00-19:00, closed Mon; Dózsa György út 37, tel. 1/460-7000, www.mucsarnok.hu).

• *The area along the busy street beyond the Műcsarnok was once used for communist parades. While the original communist monuments are long-gone, a new one has taken their place...*

1956 Monument—This monument, which sits just beyond the parking lot behind the Műcsarnok, celebrates the historic uprising against the communists (see page 570). During the early days of the Soviet regime, this was the site of a giant monument to Josef Stalin that towered 80 feet high (Stalin himself was more than 25 feet tall). While dignitaries stood on a platform at Stalin's feet, military parades would march past. From the inauguration of the monument in 1951, the Hungarians saw it as a hated symbol of an unwanted regime. When the 1956 Uprising broke out, the removal of the monument was high on the protestors' list of 16 demands.

The night the uprising began, October 23, some rebels came here to cut off Stalin just below the knees, and toppled him from his platform. (Memento Park has a reconstruction of the monument's base, including Stalin's boots.) In 2006, to commemorate the 50th anniversary of the uprising, this new monument was erected. Symbolizing the way Hungarians came together to attempt the impossible, it begins with scattered individuals at the back (rusty and humble), gradually coming together and gaining strength and unity near the front—culminating in a silver ship's prow boldly plying the ground.

▲▲**City Park (Városliget)**—Budapest's not-so-central "Central Park," which sprawls beyond Heroes' Square, was the site of the

overblown 1896 Millennium Exhibition, celebrating Hungary's 1,000th birthday. Explore the fantasy castle of Vajdahunyad (described next). Visit the animals and ogle the playful Art Nouveau buildings inside the city's zoo, ride a rollercoaster at the amusement park, or enjoy a circus under the big top. Go for a stroll, rent a rowboat, eat some cotton candy, or challenge a local Bobby Fischer to a game of chess. Or (best of all) take a dip in Budapest's ultimate thermal spa, the Széchenyi Baths. This is a fine place to just be on vacation.

▲▲**Vajdahunyad Castle (Vajdahunyad Vára)**—Many of the buildings for Hungary's Millennial National Exhibition were

erected with temporary materials, to be torn down at the end of the festival—as was the case for most world fairs at the time. But locals so loved Vajdahunyad Castle that they insisted it stay, so it was rebuilt in brick and stone. The complex actually has four parts, each representing a high point in Hungarian architectural style: Romanesque chapel, Gothic gate, Renaissance castle, and Baroque palace (free and always open to walk around the grounds).

From this direction, the **Renaissance castle** dominates the view. It's a replica of a famous castle in Transylvania that once belonged to the Hunyadi family (János and Mátyás Corvinus—described on page 556).

Cross over the bridge and through the **Gothic gateway.** Once inside the complex, on the left is a replica of a 13th-century Romanesque **Benedictine chapel.** Consecrated as an actual church, this is Budapest's most popular spot for weddings on summer weekends. Farther ahead on the right is a big Baroque mansion housing the **Museum of Hungarian Agriculture** (Magyar Mezőgazdasági Múzeum). The museum brags that it's Europe's biggest agriculture museum, but most visitors will find the lavish interior more interesting than the exhibits (800 Ft; April-Oct Tue-Sun 10:00-17:00, closed Mon; Nov-March Tue-Fri 10:00-16:00, Sat-Sun 10:00-17:00, closed Mon; last entry 30 minutes before closing, tel. 1/363-2711).

Facing the museum entry is a monument to **Anonymous**—specifically, the Anonymous from the court of King Béla IV who penned the first Hungarian history in the Middle Ages.

▲▲▲**Széchenyi Baths (Széchenyi Fürdő)**—My favorite activity in Budapest, the Széchenyi Baths are an ideal way to

reward yourself for the hard work of sightseeing and call it a culturally enlightening experience. You'll soak in hundred-degree water, surrounded by portly Hungarians squeezed into tiny swimsuits, while jets and cascades pound away your tension. Go for a vigorous swim in the lap pool, giggle and bump your way around the whirlpool, submerge yourself to the nostrils in water green with minerals, feel the bubbles from an underwater jet gradually caress their way up your leg, or challenge the locals to a game of Speedo-clad chess. And it's all surrounded by an opulent yellow palace with shiny copper domes. The bright blue-and-white of the sky, the yellow of the buildings, the pale pink of the skin, the turquoise of the water...Budapest simply doesn't get any better. It's in City Park, just beyond Vajdahunyad Castle; for all the details, see "Experiences in Budapest," later.

Museums near Üllői Út

These two museums are near the city center, on the boulevard called Üllői út. You could stroll there in about 10 minutes from the Small Boulevard ring road (walking the length of the Ráday utca café street gets you very close), or hop on the M3/blue Metró line to Corvin-negyed (just one stop beyond Kálvin tér).

▲▲Holocaust Memorial Center (Holokauszt Emlék-központ)—This sight honors the nearly 600,000 Hungarian victims of the Nazis...one out of every ten Holocaust victims. The impressive modern complex (with a beautifully restored 1920s synagogue as its centerpiece) is a museum of the Hungarian Holocaust, a monument to its victims, a space for temporary exhibits, and a research and documentation center of Nazi atrocities. Interesting to anybody, but essential to those interested in the Holocaust, this is Budapest's (and one of Europe's) best sights about that dark time. You'll pass through a security checkpoint to reach

the courtyard. Once inside, a black marble wall is etched with the names of victims. Head downstairs to buy your ticket. The excellent permanent exhibit, called "From Deprivation of Rights to Genocide," traces in English the gradual process of marginalization, exploitation, and dehumanization that befell Hungary's Jews as World War II wore on. The finale is the interior of the synagogue, now a touching memorial filled with glass seats, each one etched with the image of a Jewish worshipper who once filled it.

Cost and Hours: 1,400 Ft, 850-Ft English audioguide repeats posted English information, Tue-Sun 10:00-18:00, closed Mon, Páva utca 39, district IX, M3: Ferenc körút, tel. 1/455-3333, www.hdke.hu.

Getting There: From the Corvin-negyed Metró stop, use the exit marked *Holokauszt Emlékközpont* and take the left fork at the exit. Walk straight ahead two long blocks, then turn right down Páva utca.

Applied Arts Museum (Iparművészeti Múzeum)—This remarkable late-19th-century building, a fanciful green-roofed castle that seems out of place in an otherwise dreary urban area, was designed by Ödön Lechner. The interior is equally striking: Because historians of the day were speculating about possible ties between the Magyars and India, Lechner decorated it with Mogul motifs (from the Indian dynasty best known for the Taj Mahal). Strolling through the forest of dripping-with-white-stucco arches and columns, you might just forget to pay attention to the exhibits. The small permanent collection displays furniture, clothes, ceramics, and other everyday items, with an emphasis on curvy Art Nouveau (all described in English). This and various temporary exhibits are displayed around a light and airy atrium. If you're visiting the nearby Holocaust Memorial Center, consider dropping by here for a look at the building.

Cost and Hours: 2,000-Ft ticket includes permanent and several temporary exhibits, audioguide-1,000 Ft, Tue-Sun 10:00-18:00, closed Mon, Üllői út 33-37, district IX, M3: Corvin-negyed, tel. 1/456-5100, www.imm.hu.

Getting There: From the Corvin-negyed Métró stop, follow signs to *Iparművészeti Múzeum* and bear right up the stairs.

▲▲Memento Park (a.k.a. Statue Park)

When regimes fall, so do their monuments. Just think of all those statues of Stalin and Lenin—or Saddam Hussein—crashing to the ground. Throughout
Eastern Europe, peo-
ple couldn't wait to get
rid of these remind-
ers of their oppres-
sors. But some clever
entrepreneur hoarded
Budapest's, collect-
ing them in a park in

the countryside just southwest of the city—where tourists flock to get a taste of the communist era. Though it can be time-consuming to visit, this collection is worth ▲▲▲ for those fascinated by Hungary's commie past. You'll see the great figures of the Soviet Bloc, both international (Lenin, Marx, and Engels) and Hungarian (local bigwig Béla Kun). And you'll see gigantic, stoic figures representing Soviet ideals.

Cost and Hours: 1,500 Ft, 30 percent discount with "Hospital in the Rock" ticket (see page 562), daily 10:00-sunset, tel. 1/424-7500, www.mementopark.hu.

Getting There: It's six miles southwest of the city center, at the corner of Balatoni út and Szabadka út (district XXII). The park runs a convenient **direct bus** from Deák tér in downtown Budapest (where all three Métró lines converge; bus stop is at corner of busy Bajcsy-Zsilinszky út and Harmincad utca). The trip takes 2.5 hours total, including a 1.5-hour visit to the park (4,500-Ft fee includes round-trip and park entry, runs year-round daily at 11:00, July-Aug also at 15:00). The **public transit** option is more frequent and less expensive, but also less convenient: First take tram #19 (from along Buda's Danube embankment) or #49 (from Pest's Small Boulevard ring road) to Kosztolányi Dezső tér. From there, catch bus #150 in the direction of Campona and ask for "Memento Park" (stop can be easy to miss—ask fellow passengers for help; 3/hour Mon-Fri, 2/hour Sat-Sun, 30-minute trip, covered by one transit ticket or multi-day pass). Other connections are possible, but they're too complicated.

Background: Under the communists, creativity was dis-

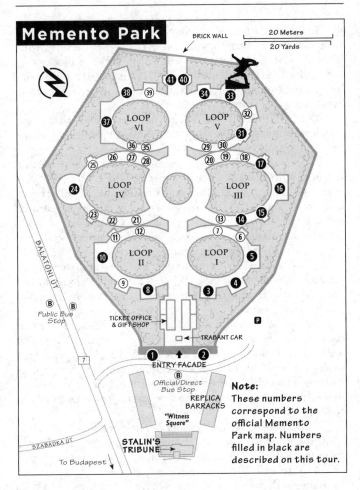

Memento Park

BRICK WALL

20 Meters
20 Yards

LOOP VI
LOOP V
LOOP IV
LOOP III
LOOP II
LOOP I

BALATONI ÚT

Public Bus Stop

7

TICKET OFFICE & GIFT SHOP

TRABANT CAR

P

ENTRY FACADE

Official/Direct Bus Stop

REPLICA BARRACKS

"Witness Square"

STALIN'S TRIBUNE

SZABADKA ÚT

To Budapest ↓

Note:
These numbers correspond to the official Memento Park map. Numbers filled in black are described on this tour.

couraged. The primary purpose of art was to further the goals of the state, with creative expression only as an afterthought. This **Socialist Realistic** art served two purposes: It was Realistic, breaking with the "decadent" bourgeois art that came before it (Impressionism, Post-Impressionism, and other modern -isms); and Socialistic, encouraging complicity with the brave new world the communists were forging. From 1949 until 1956, Socialist Realism was legally enforced as the sole artistic style of the Soviet Bloc.

As propaganda was an essential weapon in the Soviet arsenal, the regime made ample use of Socialist Realistic art. Aside from a few important figureheads, individuals didn't matter. Everyone was a cog in the machine—strong, stoic, doing their job well and proudly for the good of the people. Individual characteristics and distinguishing features were unimportant; people were represented as automatons serving their nation. Artistic merit was virtually ignored. Most figures are trapped in stiff, unnatural poses that ignore the 3,000 years of artistic evolution since the Egyptians. Sculptures and buildings alike from this era were designed to evoke feelings of power and permanence.

⊙ **Self-Guided Tour:** The numbers in the following tour match the statue labels in the park, the official park map, and the map on the previous page.

As you approach the park, you're greeted by an imposing red-brick **entry facade** featuring three of the Communist All-Stars—❶ **Lenin** and ❷ **Marx** and **Engels.** (They couldn't save the biggest "star" of all, Stalin—all statues of him were destroyed in the 1956 Uprising.) Like the rest of the park, this gate is highly conceptual in its design: It looks impressive and monumental...but, like the rotted-out pomp of communism, there's nothing behind it. It's a glossy stage-set with no substance. If you try to go through the main, central part of the gate, you'll run into an always-locked door. Instead, as with the communist system, you have to find another way around (in this case, the smaller gate to the left).

Once inside and past the ticket-window building, notice that the main road takes you confidently toward...a dead end (the brick wall). Once again, as with life under the communists, you'll have to deviate from this main axis to actually accomplish anything. Even so, notice that the six cul-de-sacs branching off the main road all bring you right back to where you started—the futility of communism.

Work your way counterclockwise around the park.

Liberation Monuments (Loop I): Dominating this loop is a ❸ **giant soldier** holding the Soviet flag. This statue once stood at the base of the Liberation Monument that still overlooks the Danube from Gellért Hill. Typical of Socialist Realistic art, the soldier has a clenched fist (symbolizing strength) and a face that is inspired by his egalitarian ideology. To the left of this soldier, see the ❹ **two comrades**  stiffly shaking hands: the Hungarian worker thrilled to meet the Soviet soldier—protector of the proletariat. Beyond them is a ❺ **long wall,** with a triumphant worker breaking through the left end—too busy doing his job to be very excited. Just another brick in the wall.

• *Cross "main street" to a group of statues commemorating the key communist holiday of...*

April 4, 1945 (Loop II): On this date, the Soviets forced the final Nazi soldier out of Hungary. The tall panel nearest the entrance shows a Hungarian woman and a Soviet woman setting free the ❽ **doves of peace.** According to the inscription, "Our freedom and peace is founded upon the enduring Hungarian-Soviet friendship." (With friends like these....) At the back of the loop, the ❿ **Hungarian worker and Soviet soldier** (who appear to be doing calisthenics) are absurdly rigid even though they're trying to be dynamic. (Even the statues couldn't muster genuine enthusiasm for communist ideals.)

• *Cross over and head up to the next loop, to pay homage to...*

Heroes of the Workers' Movement (Loop III): This loop has a ⓮ bust and a ⓯ statue of the Bulgarian communist leader **Georgi Dimitrov** (ruled 1946-1949)—one of communist Hungary's many Soviet Bloc comrades. At the back of this loop are ⓰ three blocky portraits. The middle figure is the granddaddy of Hungarian communism, **Béla Kun** (1886-1938). To the left is one of the park's best-loved, most-photographed, and most artistic statues: ⓱ **Vladimir Lenin,** in his famous "hailing a cab" pose.

• *Cross over—passing the giant red star made of flowers—to meet...*

More Communist Heroes (Loop IV): This group is dominated by a ㉔ dramatic, unusually emotive sculpture by a genuine artist, Imre Varga. Designed to commemorate the 100th anniversary of Béla Kun's birth, this clever statue accomplishes seemingly contradictory feats. On the one hand, it reinforces the communist message: Under the able leadership of Béla Kun

(safely overlooking the fray from above), the crusty, bourgeois old regime of the Habsburg Empire (on the left, with the umbrellas and fancy clothes) was converted into the workers' fighting force of the Red Army (on the right, with the bayonets). And yet, those silvery civilians in back seem more appealing than the lunging soldiers in front. And notice the lamppost next to Kun: In Hungarian literature, a lamppost is a metaphor for the gallows. This reminds viewers that Kun—in spite of his groundbreaking and heroic work for the communist movement in Hungary—was ultimately executed by the communists during Stalin's purges of the late 1930s.

• Zig and head up again, for a lesson in...

Communist Concepts (Loop V): Look for a rusty pair of ③① **workers' hands** holding a sphere (which was once adorned with

a red star). The sphere represents the hard-won ideals of communism, carefully protected by the hands—but also held out for others to appreciate. Dominating this group is a ③③ **communist worker** charging into the future, clutching the Soviet flag. Budapesters of the time had a different interpretation: a thermal bath attendant running after a customer who'd forgotten his towel. To the left is a monument to the communist version of the Boy Scouts: the elementary school-age ③④ **Little Drummers,** and the older Pioneers. While these organizations existed before the communists, they were slowly infiltrated and turned into propaganda machines by the regime. These kids—with their jaunty red and blue neckerchiefs—were sent to camp to be properly raised as good little communists; today, many of them have forgotten the brainwashing, but still have fond memories of the socializing.

• Now zag once more to learn about...

More Communist Concepts (Loop VI): The ③⑦ long, white **wall** at the back of this section tells quite a story (from left to

right): The bullet holes lead up to a jumbled, frightful clutter (reminiscent of Pablo Picasso's Guernica) representing World War II. Then comes the bright light of the Soviet system, and by the end everyone's properly regimented and looking boldly to the future (and enjoying a bountiful crop, to boot). Next is a ③⑧ **fallen hero** with arm outstretched, about to collapse to the ground—mortally wounded, yet victorious. This monument to "the Martyrs of the Counter-Revolution" commemorates those who died attempting to put down the 1956 Uprising.

• Now continue down the main drag to, um, a....

Dead End: Where the main path dead-ends at the wall (symbolizing life's frustrations under communism), it's flanked by statues of two Soviet officers who negotiated with the Nazis to end the WWII siege of Budapest. ④⓪ **Captain Miklós Steinmetz** (on the right) was killed by a Nazi land mine, while ④① **Ilja Ostapenko** (on the left) was shot under mysterious circumstances as he returned

from a successful summit. Both became heroes for the communist cause. Were they killed by wayward Nazi soldiers, as the Soviets explained—or by their own Red Army, to create a pair of convenient martyrs?

Heading back out to the entry gate, peruse the fun parade of communist kitsch at the **gift shop.** The stirring music may just move you to pick up the CD of *Communism's Greatest Hits,* and maybe a model of a Trabant (the classic two-stroke commiemobile). A real **Trabant** is often parked just inside the gate.

• *Across the parking lot, you'll find a replica of...*

Stalin's Tribune: This re-creates the giant grandstand from which Hungarian and Soviet leaders would survey ceremonial processions (described on page 594). Notice the giant boots—the only part of a giant Stalin statue that survived the 1956 Uprising. Flanking the tribune are replica **barracks,** reminiscent of the ones where political prisoners lived in communist-era work camps. These hold special exhibits. Sit down for the short and creepy film, *The Life of an Agent,* which was actually used to train spies on secret-police methods and policies.

• *Our tour is over. Now, inspired by the bold propaganda of your Hungarian comrades, march proudly into the dawn of a new day.*

Near Budapest

On a visit of a few days, Budapest will keep even the most avid sightseer busy. And after Budapest, Eger and Pécs—each covered in a chapter of its own—are the best Hungarian towns. But for a longer stay, a few outlying sights are worth knowing about.

Óbuda—"Old Buda," just north of Buda, is the oldest part of Budapest, with roots going back to Celtic and Roman times. It has various sights that cluster around the Árpád híd stop of the HÉV suburban train line (catch the HÉV from the Batthyány tér Metró stop in Buda). The most interesting museum displays works by Hungarian sculptor **Imre Varga,** who worked from the 1950s through the 1990s, and created many popular sculptures in Budapest and throughout Hungary. You'll also find a museum filled with eye-popping, colorful paintings by **Victor Vasarely,** the founder of Op Art. If you ride the HÉV farther north to the Aquincum stop, you'll reach a museum at the remains of the 2,000-year-old Roman town of **Aquincum** and its amphitheater. All of these sights are closed on Mondays.

Gödöllő Royal Palace—Holding court in an unassuming town on the outskirts of Budapest, this pink Baroque palace was once the residence of Habsburg Emperor Franz Josef and his wife, Empress Elisabeth—better known to her beloved Hungarian subjects as Sisi (see pages 1140 and 1141). While the Habsburg sights in Vienna and near Prague are better, this is the best place in Hungary to learn about its former monarchs (open daily April-Oct, closed Mon Nov-March, www.kiralyikastely.hu; take the M2/red Metró line to Örs vezér tere, then catch the HÉV suburban train from to Gödöllő—figure about one hour each way from downtown Budapest).

The Danube Bend—This string of three river towns north of Budapest offers a convenient day-trip getaway for urbanites who want to commune with nature. While I find "the Bend" less than thrilling, it's undeniably convenient to reach from the capital by train or boat; these destinations make for handy stopovers if you're driving between Budapest and Bratislava or Vienna.

Szentendre is a colorful, Balkan-feeling artist colony. With a tidy main square, a few engaging art galleries, and several Orthodox churches built by the Serbs and Greeks who settled the town, it offers a relaxing escape from the city. This is the easiest pleasant small town to reach from Budapest—which means it's also deluged by tourists. To reach Szentendre, hop on the HÉV suburban train at Budapest's Batthyány tér Metró (the same one that goes to Óbuda, described above).

Visegrád offers a small riverside museum at the scant remains of a Renaissance palace built by King Matthias Corvinus, and a dramatic hilltop castle with fine views over the Bend. While you can get here by boat or by train (to the Nagymaros-Visegrád station, then boat across the river), it's not worth the trip unless you're driving.

Esztergom Basilica is Hungary's biggest and most important church, built on the site where István, Hungary's first Christian king, was crowned in A.D. 1000. Packed with history, it looms grandly above the Danube (free, daily April-mid-Oct 8:00-19:00, mid-Oct-March 8:00-16:00). The easiest way to reach it is by bus from Budapest's Újpest-Városkapu bus station (at the Metró stop of the same name); trains and other buses from Budapest take you to the far end of town, an inconvenient 45-minute walk to the basilica.

Sopron—This little Baroque town, jam-packed with historic buildings and dusty museums, is conveniently located between Budapest and Bratislava, tucked between alpine foothills. Its square—watched over by the town's symbol, the Fire Tower—might be Hungary's most romantic. While fun to explore, Sopron is small and sleepy enough that its sightseeing options are quickly exhausted.

Experiences in Budapest

Thermal Baths (Fürdő)

Splashing and relaxing in Budapest's thermal baths is the city's top attraction. Though it might sound daunting, bathing with

the Magyars is far more accessible than you'd think. The first two thermal baths I've described below (Széchenyi and Gellért) are basically like your home-town swimming pool—except the water is 100 degrees, there are plenty of jets and bubbles to massage away your stress, and you're surrounded by scantily clad Hungarians. Overcome your jitters, follow my instructions, and dive in...or miss out on *the* quintessential Budapest experience.

The three baths listed here are the best-known, most representative, and most convenient for first-timers: The Széchenyi Baths are more casual and popular with locals; the Gellért Baths are touristy, famous, and genteel; and the Rudas Baths are old-school Turkish, with more nudity and less "fun" (unless you find public nudity fun...but that's a whole other book). To me, Széchenyi is second to none, but some travelers prefer the Gellért or Rudas experience. As they're all quite different, doing more than one is an excellent idea. For more information on all of Budapest's baths, see www.budapestgyogyfurdoi.hu or www.spasbudapest.com.

▲▲▲Széchenyi Baths (Széchenyi Fürdő)

To soak with the locals, head for this bath complex—the big, yellow, copper-domed building in the middle of City Park. Széchenyi

(SAY-chehn-yee) is the best of Budapest's many bath experiences. Relax and enjoy some Hungarian good living. Magyars of all shapes and sizes stuff themselves into tiny swimsuits and strut their stuff. Housewives float blissfully in the warm water. Intellectuals and elder statesmen stand in chest-high water around chessboards and ponder their next moves. This is Budapest at its best.

Cost: 3,100 Ft for locker (in gender-segregated locker room), 400 Ft more for personal changing cabin, 150 Ft more on weekends, cheaper if you arrive before 8:00 or after 19:00. The price

Taking the Waters

American tourists often feel squeamish at the thought of bathing with Speedo-clad, pot-bellied Hungarians. Relax! It's less intimidating than it sounds—and the fun you'll have far outweighs the jitters. I was nervous on my first visit, too. But now I feel like a trip to Hungary just isn't complete without a splish-splash in the bath.

While Budapest has several mostly nude, gender-segregated Turkish baths (such as Rudas), my favorites—Széchenyi and Gellért—are less intimidating: Men and women are usually together, and you can keep your swimsuit on the entire time. (Even at mixed baths, there generally are a few clothing-optional, gender-segregated areas, where locals are likely to be nude—or wearing a *kötény,* a loose-fitting loincloth.)

Bring along these items, if you have them: a swimsuit, towel, flip-flops, soap and shampoo for a shower afterward, a comb or brush, and maybe sunscreen and leisure reading. Hotels typically frown on guests taking their room towels to the baths. Try asking nicely if they have some loaner towels just for this purpose (they'll probably tell you to rent one there...but what they don't know won't hurt them). At Budapest's baths, you can usually rent a towel or swimsuit (for men, Speedos are always available, trunks sometimes).

Each bath complex has multiple pools, used for different purposes. Big pools with cooler water are for serious swimming, while the smaller, hotter thermal baths (*gyógyfürdő,* or simply *gőz*) are for relaxing, enjoying the jets and current pools, and playing chess. The water bubbles up from hot springs at 77° Celsius (170° Fahrenheit), then is mixed with cooler water to achieve the desired temperatures. Most pools are marked with the water temperature in Celsius (cooler pools are about 30°C/86°F; warmer pools are closer to 36°C/97°F or 38°C/100°F, about like the hot tub back home; and the hottest are 42°C/108°F... yowtch!). Locals hit the cooler pools first, then work their way up to the top temps. While the lap pools are chlorinated, most of the thermal baths are only lightly chlorinated, or not at all. Unlike swimming pools in the US—where the water is recycled back into the pool—water here is slowly drained out and replaced with fresh water from the hot springs. Locals figure this makes chemicals unnecessary.

You'll also usually find a dry sauna, a wet steam room, a cold plunge pool (for a pleasurable jolt when you're feeling overheated), and sunbathing areas (which may be segregated and clothing-optional). Some baths have fun flourishes: bubbles, whirlpools, massage jets, wave pools, and so on.

The most difficult part of visiting a Hungarian bath is the inevitably complicated entrance procedure. This is one of today's best time-travel experiences to communist Eastern Europe. Expect monolingual staff, a complex payment scheme, and lengthy menus of massages and other treatments. I've carefully outlined the specifics for each bath, but be forewarned that they can change from year to year, or even from day to day. Keep track of any receipt or slip of paper you're given, as you may be asked to show it later (for example, to get your deposit back). Hang in there, go where people direct you, and enjoy this unique cultural experience. Remember, they're used to tourists—so don't be afraid to act like one. If you can make it through those first few confusing minutes, you'll soon be relaxing like a pro.

Budapest's baths recently upgraded to a system that uses a plastic, watch-like wristband as your ticket. When you enter, touch the wristband to the entry turnstile, then again to be assigned a changing cabin or locker, then again each time you want to unlock your cabin or locker. When you're done, drop the wristband into a slot as you exit the turnstile. This wristband system frees you up to enjoy and explore the baths, since you don't have to rely on a grumpy attendant to lock and unlock your cabin.

While enjoying the baths, you can leave your clothing and other belongings in your locked cabin or locker. Although I've found these to be safe, and bath employees assure me that thefts are rare (a cabin is safer than a locker), it's at your own risk. Another option is to leave valuables in a safe (generally costs 500 Ft, ask when you buy ticket). On rare occasions, people have been known to steal rental towels from around the pools to collect the deposit—keep an eye on your towels and any other belongings you bring poolside. Many locals bring plastic shopping bags to hold their essentials: towels, leisure reading, and sunscreen.

Be aware that the jets, bubbles, waves, waterfalls, and whirlpools sometimes take turns running. For example, a current pool runs for 10 minutes, then a series of jets starts up and the current pool stops for 10 minutes, then the current pool starts up again, and so on. If a particularly fun feature of the pool doesn't seem to be working, just give it a few minutes.

Here are some useful phrases:

English	Hungarian	Pronounced
Bath	*Fürdő*	FEWR-dur
Men	*Férfi*	FAYR-fee
Women	*Női*	NUR-ee
Changing Cabin	*Kabin*	KAH-been
Locker	*Szekrény*	SEHK-rayn
Ticket Office	*Pénztár*	PAYNZ-tar
Thermal Bath	*Gyógyfürdő, Gőz*	JODGE-fewr-dur, gorz

Please trust me, and take the plunge. My readers almost unanimously report that the thermal baths were their top Hungarian experience. If you go into it with an easygoing attitude and a sense of humor, I promise you'll have a blast.

includes the outdoor swimming pool area and the indoor thermal bath and sauna (but note that the indoor sections close earlier—see below). Couples can share a changing cabin: One person pays the cabin rate, the other pays the locker rate, but both use the same cabin.

Hours: Swimming pool (the best part, outdoors) open daily 6:00-22:00, indoor thermal bath and sauna open daily 6:00-19:00, last entry one hour before closing.

Location and Entrances: In City Park at Állatkerti körút 11, district XIV, M1: Széchenyi fürdő. The huge bath complex has three entrances. The busiest one—technically the **"thermal bath entrance"**—is the grand main entry, facing south (roughly toward Vajdahunyad Castle). I avoid this entrance—there's often a line during peak times, and it's a bit more confusing to find your way once inside. Instead, I prefer the **"swimming pool entrance,"** facing the zoo on the other side of the complex—it's faster and more user-friendly, has shorter lines, and is open later. A third, smaller **"medical entrance,"** to the right as you face the zoo entry (near the Metró station), provides access to either the thermal bath changing rooms or the swimming pool changing rooms, but can also have long lines.

Massage: A wide array of massages and other special treatments is offered—find the English menu in the lobby. If you're interested in this, set up an appointment and pay at the office near the towel-rental desk (3,000-9,000 Ft, expect 15-30-minute wait for your appointment when it's busy). For something more hedonistic than medicinal, you can get a Thai massage at the upper level of the complex (above the swimming pool entrance)—just follow the signs (11,000 Ft/1 hour).

Night Bathing: The baths are a joy in the evening, when both the price and the crowds are reduced. In cool weather, or even rain or snow, the pools maintain their hot temperatures—making this a delightful after-hours activity. Busy sightseers can be extremely efficient by closing down the museums, then heading to the baths. The only caveat: The indoor (and less appealing) thermal bath sections close after 19:00.

Entry Procedure: While the following details might seem intimidating, it's easier than it sounds. Take your time and you'll eventually find your way. These instructions assume that you're using the swimming pool entrance (from this entrance, there are parallel facilities in each direction).

First, in the grand lobby, pay

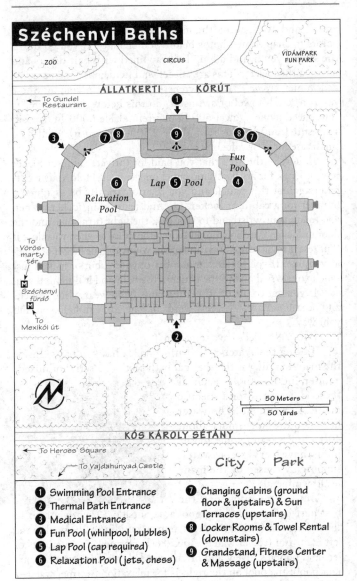

Széchenyi Baths

ZOO CIRCUS VIDÁMPARK FUN PARK

ÁLLATKERTI KÖRÚT

← To Gundel Restaurant

❶

❸ ❼ ❽ ❾ ❽ ❼

Fun Pool

❻ *Lap* ❺ *Pool* ❹

Relaxation Pool

To Vörös-marty tér

Ⓜ Széchenyi fürdő

Ⓜ Mexikói út

❷

50 Meters
50 Yards

KÓS KÁROLY SÉTÁNY

← To Heroes' Square

↙ To Vajdahunyad Castle

City Park

❶ Swimming Pool Entrance	❼ Changing Cabins (ground floor & upstairs) & Sun Terraces (upstairs)
❷ Thermal Bath Entrance	
❸ Medical Entrance	
❹ Fun Pool (whirlpool, bubbles)	❽ Locker Rooms & Towel Rental (downstairs)
❺ Lap Pool (cap required)	
❻ Relaxation Pool (jets, chess)	❾ Grandstand, Fitness Center & Massage (upstairs)

the cashier. You'll be given a waterproof, watch-like wristband with an electronic chip inside. Touch your wristband to the panel on the turnstile to enter the complex. Just after the turnstile, pause to get oriented: Straight ahead is a row of private changing cabins. At the start of this row is a stairwell. If you go **up the stairs,** you'll find another floor of changing cabins (as well as the Thai massage area, gender-segregated "solarium" sun terraces, and a fun grandstand overlooking the main pool—these are ideal vantage points to snap some photos before you change). If you go **down the stairs,** you'll find a long hallway lined with hair dryers and mirrors; the locker rooms are at each end (remember, men are *férfi* and women are *nöi*). Also down here, you'll find the counter where you can rent a towel or swimsuit (do this before you change, as you'll need money: towel-600 Ft plus refundable 1,000-Ft deposit; swimsuit-1,000 Ft plus refundable 2,500-Ft deposit). Renting a small safe for your valuables costs 500 Ft.

Report to the area that you paid for (private cabin or locker room). Look for an electronic panel on the wall. Hold your wrist-band against this panel, and you'll automatically be assigned a number for a **cabin** or **locker.** Go find your cabin/locker. When you touch your wristband to the lock, the light turns blue and the door unlocks. The door should lock automatically when you close it (but test it to be sure). You can reopen your cabin or locker as often as you like. If you forget the number of your cabin or locker, just touch your wristband to the panel in the hall, and it'll remind you.

If you get confused, the attendants (who wear white smocks and occasionally speak a few words of English) can help you find your way.

Phew. Now let's have some fun.

Taking the Waters: The bath complex has two parts. Inside the main building is the thermal bath section, a series of mixed-gender indoor pools; each of these is designed for a specific medical treatment. The water here is quite hot—most about 40°C/104°F—and some of the pools have very green water, supposedly caused by the many healthy minerals.

But for most visitors, the best part is the swimming pool area outside. Orient yourself to the three pools (facing the main, domed building): The pool to the left is for fun (cooler water—30°C/86°F, warmer in winter, lots of jets and bubbles, lively and often crowded, includes circular cur-rent pool); the pool on the right is for relaxation (warmer water—38°C/100°F, mellow atmosphere, a few massage jets, chess); and the main pool in the center is all business (coolest water, people doing laps, swimming cap required). Stairs to saunas are below the doors to the inside pools. You get extra credit for joining the gang in a chess match.

There's a basic **snack bar** right in the middle of the com-plex, but you're allowed to bring in your own food if you munch discreetly.

For good **views**—or to use the well-equipped **fitness center**—climb up the stairs near the front of the changing-cabin hallways. There you'll find the grandstand area overlooking the main pool, with the fitness center just above it.

If you're feeling waterlogged and need a break from the baths, it's fun just to explore the sprawling complex. It's a bit of a maze, but don't be afraid to poke around (but keep in mind that several areas—such as the solarium sun terraces up top—are gender-segregated; again, men are *férfi* and women are *nõi*). Go for a photo safari, and don't miss the grandstand.

Exit Procedure: If you rented a towel or swimsuit, return it to the desk where you got it, and present your receipt to get your deposit back. Then, as you exit the complex, insert your wristband into the little slot at the turnstile to exit. Then continue your sightseeing...soggy, but relaxed.

If you're heading to the **Metró,** the station is very close, but easy to miss: It's basically a pair of nondescript stairwells in the middle of the park, roughly toward Heroes' Square from the thermal bath entrance (look for the low-profile, yellow *Földalatti* sign; to head for downtown, take the stairwell marked *a Vörösmarty tér felé*).

▲▲Gellért Baths (Gellért Fürdő)

Using the baths at Gellért (GEH-layrt) Hotel costs a bit more than the Széchenyi Baths, and you won't run into nearly as many locals; this is definitely a more upscale, touristy, spa-like scene. Because most of the warmest pools are in gender-segregated areas (except on Sundays), it's not ideal for opposite-sex couples or families who want to spend time together. But if you want a soothing, luxurious bath experience in an elegant setting, this is the place. And if it's fun you're looking for, the Gellért Baths have something that Széchenyi doesn't: a

huge, deliriously enjoyable wave pool that'll toss you around like a queasy surfer (summer only).

Cost: 3,600 Ft for a locker, 300 Ft more for a personal changing cabin, 150 Ft more on weekends, cheaper if you arrive after 17:00.

Hours: Daily 6:00-20:00, last entry one hour before closing. Note that on Sundays, the thermal bath areas are mixed; on other days, they're gender-segregated.

Location: It's on the Buda side of the green Liberty Bridge (trams #47 and #49 from Deák tér in Pest, or trams #19 and #41 along the Buda embankment from Víziváros below the castle, Gellért tér stop). The entrance to the baths is under the white dome opposite the bridge (Kelenhegyi út 4-6, district XI, tel. 1/466-6166, ext. 165).

Entry Procedure: The grand entry hall is fully open to visitors, so feel free to poke around to get the lay of the land before

buying your ticket (good views from the walkways up above). The entrance doors are flanked by ticket windows, and on the left is a window where you can deposit valuables in the safe (500 Ft). Halfway down the hall on the right is an information booth that usually has English-speaking staff.

In the summer, they sell two different tickets based on which changing area you'll use (same price for either ticket). With a **thermal bath ticket,** you'll change in a large, gender-segregated area that connects directly to the also-segregated thermal baths (so some people walk nude directly from their cabins to the bath); opposite-sex couples can't share a changing cabin here. With a **swimming pool ticket,** you'll go to a mixed area where opposite-sex couples can share a cabin (this area also has gender-segregated locker rooms). Both tickets allow you to move freely between the thermal baths and swimming pool areas once you're inside.

A dizzying array of **massages** and other treatment options are also sold at the ticket windows. Most are available only with a doctor's note, but some massages are for anyone (generally 2,900 Ft/20 minutes, 3,900 Ft/30 minutes, 4,800 Ft/40 minutes; book when you buy your ticket). Upstairs, you can also book a Thai massage.

Buy your ticket (and, if you like, arrange for a massage), and you'll be issued a plastic wristband that acts as your ticket. Then

glide through the swanky lobby. The indoor swimming pool is on your right, about halfway down the main hall. Looking through the window to the pool, visualize the perfectly symmetrical bath complex: The men's thermal bath, changing cabins, and lockers are on the left, while the identical women's facilities are on the right. The two sections meet at this shared pool in the center.

If you bought a swimming pool ticket, you'll touch your wristband to the turnstile and enter here: Men/*férfi* go down the stairs on the left, and women/*női* on the right (either way, you'll head down a long hallway, then up several flights of stairs and through a maze to the changing areas; for couples sharing a cabin, go to the section corresponding to the partner who bought the cabin ticket). If you have a thermal bath ticket, the entrances are a bit farther away: women to the right, closer to the entrance; and men to the left, at the end of the hall.

Once inside the changing area, hold your wristband against the electronic panel to be assigned a changing cabin or locker number. Once you track it down, touch your wristband to the cabin or locker to open it. The door locks automatically behind you (but test it just to be sure).

If you want to rent a towel (600 Ft) or swimsuit (1,000 Ft; both with a 4,000-Ft deposit, cash only), you'll find them offered along the way.

Taking the Waters: Once you've changed, you can spend your time either indoors or out. Inside, the central, mixed-gender, genteel-feeling hall is home to a cool-water swimming pool (swimming cap required—free loaners available) and a crowded hot-water pool. Back toward the window and main hall are doors to the gender-segregated, clothing-optional massage rooms and thermal baths, with nude or loincloth-wearing bathers stewing in pools at 36°C (97°F) and 38°C (100°F). Notice that these temperatures perfectly flank the normal temperature of the human body, allowing you to toggle your temp at will. You'll also find a sauna (near the showers), steam rooms (at the far end of the bath), and a cold plunge pool. If you paid for a massage, report to the massage room in this section when you're ready (no appointments—first-come, first-served; you might wait 30 minutes or more).

To get outside, head upstairs (which also has a fine view over the main indoor pool). Out here, you'll find several sunbathing areas and a warm thermal pool (up the stairs at the end). But the main attraction is the big, unheated wave pool in the center (generally closed Oct-April, weather-dependent). Not for the squeamish, this pool thrashes fun-loving swimmers around like driftwood. The swells in the deeper area are fun and easy to float on, but the crashing waves at the shallow end are vigorous, if not dangerous. If there are no waves, just wait around awhile (you'll hear a garbled message on the loudspeaker five minutes before the tide comes in).

Exit Procedure: When you're finished, return your towel and swimsuit to reclaim your deposit, then insert your wristband into the slot at the exit turnstile.

▲▲Rudas Baths (Rudas Fürdő)

To get to the Turkish roots of Budapest's obsession with thermal baths, head for Rudas (ROO-dawsh). The most historic,

local, and potentially intimidating of the three baths I list, Rudas feels more like the classic Turkish baths of yore: On most days, it's men-only, and those men wander around nude or in flimsy loincloths under a 500-year-old dome first built by the Ottoman Turks. These baths are not about splashy fun—there are no jets, bubbles, or whirlpools. Instead, Rudas is about history, and about serious temperature modulation—stepping your body temperature up and down between very hot and very cold. While not for the skittish, Rudas offers adventurous travelers and bath connoisseurs another facet of the Budapest baths experience. Be aware that all of Budapest's single-sex, nude baths are (to varying degrees) a popular meeting point for the local gay community—though Rudas is less so than some others (such as Király Baths). Rudas becomes far more widely accessible to all visitors on weekends (Sat-Sun), when men and women mingle together in swimsuits under the fine old dome; then, at nighttime (Fri-Sat only), this old chamber becomes a modern nightclub until the wee hours.

Cost: The thermal bath costs 2,800 Ft, 100 Ft more on weekends, cheaper weekdays after 17:00; the swimming pool has a separate ticket for 1,900 Ft, but there's no point coming here for the swimming pool (boring and modern; the ones at Széchenyi and Gellért are better).

Hours: The thermal baths (the part you're interested in) are open daily 6:00-20:00, last entry one hour before closing. The baths are open only to men Mon and Wed-Fri; only to women Tue; and to both men and women Sat-Sun.

Night Bathing: In addition to normal opening hours, the baths are open—to both men and women, in swimsuits—with a dance hall ambience Fri-Sat 22:00-4:00 in the morning (3,300 Ft; once a month, it hosts a wild "sparty" called Cinetrip for 8,000 Ft—see www.cinetrip.hu).

Location: It's in a grungy-looking, low-profile building at the foot of Gellért Hill, next to the white Elisabeth Bridge (Döbrentei tér 9, district I, tel. 1/375-8373). From the Döbrentei stop on trams #19 and #41 (along the Buda riverfront, between the Gellért Baths and Batthyány tér), walk under the off-ramps for the big white bridge, pass the statue of Elisabeth, and go through the tunnel. The baths are straight ahead.

Entry Procedure: Buy your ticket, and if you want, rent a towel (600 Ft for a towel or 300 Ft for a "bath sheet," plus 1,000-Ft refundable deposit) or a swimsuit (1,000 Ft plus 4,000-Ft deposit), or book a massage (basic types are soapy/wet or traditional; 2,900 Ft/20 minutes, 3,900 Ft/30 minutes, 4,800 Ft/40 minutes).

You'll be issued a plastic wristband, which you'll use to go through the turnstile into the changing area (two floors of private cabins—there are no lockers in the thermal bath section). If you paid to rent a towel or swimsuit, give your receipt to the attendant to claim it now. Hold your wristband against the electronic panel on the wall for a few seconds to be assigned a cabin number, then find that cabin and touch your wristband to the lock in order to open it. After you change and are ready to explore the complex, the cabin should lock automatically.

If you're here on a mixed day (Sat-Sun), the dress code is swimsuits. On other days, bathers can go nude, and many of the men wear a flimsy loincloth called a *kötény* (issued as you enter). If you're a self-conscious, gawky tourist (it happens to the best of us), you can wear your swimsuit...although you might get some funny looks.

Taking the Waters: This historic complex was thoroughly renovated a few years ago, making the outer section feel almost institutional. But the innermost section transports you half a millennium back.

Rudas is all about modulating your body temperature—pushing your body to its limit with heat, then dousing off quickly with a bucket of cold water, then heating up again, and so on. The different temperatures are designed to let you do this as gradually or quickly as you like.

The central chamber, under an original 35-foot-high Turkish dome supported by eight pillars, is the historic core of the baths. The main, octagonal pool in the center is surrounded by four smaller pools, each in its own corner. Working clockwise from the right as you enter, the four corner pools get progressively hotter: 28°C (82°F), 30°C (86°F), 33°C (91°F), and 42°C (108°F). While the hottest pool feels almost scalding at first, you can ease your way into it, the same way you would into cold water. Conveniently, the largest, central pool—at 36°C (97°F)—is not too hot, not too cold...juuuust right.

Along one wall are entrances to the wet sauna (*nedves gőzkamra*, to the left), with 50°C (122°F) scented steam; and the dry sauna (*hőlégkamra*, to the right), with three progressively hotter rooms ranging from 45°C (113°F) to 72°C (161°F). Near the entrance to each one is a shower or—if you don't want to beat around the bush—a bucket of frigid water (pull the rope for immediate relief if you're feeling overheated).

Surrounding this central chamber are hallways with other areas: resting rooms, tanning beds (*szolarium*, costs extra), massage rooms, a cold plunge pool, and a scale to see how much sweat you've lost.

Float on your back for a while in the main octagonal pool, pondering the faintly glittering translucent tiles embedded in the old Turkish dome. You'll notice that the voices echoing around that dome are mostly Hungarian—there are very few tourists here. You might see people stretching, moving from pool to pool very purposefully, or even doing chin-ups from the metal supports; some are athletes, training for their next event.

Exit Procedure: After changing, return your rental towel and swimsuit to the attendant and get your receipt; present this at the front desk (along with your original towel receipt) to get your deposit back. Then drop your wristband through the little slot at the turnstile, head out the door, and stumble along the Danube... as relaxed as you'll ever be.

Aaaaahhh.

Entertainment in Budapest

Budapest is endlessly entertaining. Whether it's opera, folk music and dancing, a twilight stroll or boat trip, or holing up in one of the city's uniquely ramshackle "ruin pubs," Budapest offers something for everybody.

For **event schedules,** pick up the free, monthly *Budapest Panorama*, which makes things easy—listing performances with dates, venues, performers, and contact information for getting tickets (get it at the TI, or visit www.budapestpanorama.com). Other helpful websites include www.wherebudapest.hu (general), www.budapestsun.hu (the local English-language newspaper), www.muzsikalendarium.hu (classical), and www.funzine.hu (nightlife). Hungarian-only websites include www.pestiest.hu (nightlife) and www.pestimusor.hu (cutting-edge arts).

To buy **tickets,** I've given strategies for the top options (Opera House and Hungária Koncert). Resources such as *Budapest Panorama* usually explain how you can get tickets for specific performances. There are ticket offices around town, but they usually sell for only some (not all) performances. You can search for information about—and buy tickets for—many Budapest events at www.kulturinfo.hu and www.jegymester.hu.

What's on can vary by **season.** For example, the Hungarian State Opera and other indoor cultural events tend to take a summer break from late June into early September (though that's prime time for outdoor music and Hungária Koncert's touristy shows).

Budapest's Music Scene

Budapest is a great place to catch a good—and inexpensive—musical performance. In fact, music-lovers from Vienna often make the three-hour trip here just to take in a fine opera in a luxurious setting at a bargain price. Options range from a performance at one of the world's great opera houses to light, touristy Hungarian folk concerts. The tourist concerts are the simplest option—you'll see the fliers everywhere—but you owe it to yourself to do a little homework and find something that really appeals to you. See the resources listed earlier, including the good classical music schedules at www.muzsikalendarium.hu. Locals dress up for the more "serious" concerts and opera, but many tourists wear casual clothes—as long as you don't show up in shorts, sneakers, or flip-flops, you'll be fine.

A Night at the Opera—Consider taking in an opera by one of the best companies in Europe, in one of Europe's loveliest opera

houses, for bargain prices. The Hungarian State Opera performs almost nightly, both at the main Opera House (Andrássy út 22, district VI, M1: Opera, see page 586) and in the Erkel Színház theater (not nearly as impressive). Be careful to get a performance in the Opera House—not the Erkel Színház. Note that there are generally no performances from late June into early September. Most performances are in the original language with Hungarian supertitles.

Ticket prices range from 1,000 to 17,000 Ft, but the best music deal in Europe may be the 500-Ft, obstructed-view tickets (easy to get, as they rarely run out—even when other tickets are sold out). If you buy one of these $2.50 opera tickets, you'll get a seat in one of two places: If you're sitting at the back of one of the boxes along the side of the theater, you can either sit comfortably, and see nothing; or stand and crane your neck to see about half the stage. If you sit on the top of the side balcony, you can stand near the door for a view of the stage. If the seats in front of you don't fill up, scooting up to an empty seat when the show starts is less than a capital offense. Either way, you'll hear every note along with the big spenders. If a full evening of opera is too much for you, you can leave early or come late (but buy your ticket ahead of time, since the box office closes when the performance starts).

To get tickets, book online (www.opera.hu or www.jegy mester.hu), print your e-ticket, and waltz right in. Or you can book by phone with a credit card (tel. 1/332-7914, phone answered Mon-Fri 10:00-17:00), then pick up your ticket at the Opera House before the performance. Maybe best of all, just drop by in person and see what's available during your visit. There are often a few tickets for sale at the door, even if it's supposedly "sold out" (box office open Mon-Sat from 11:00 until show time—generally 19:00; Sun open 3 hours before the performance—generally 16:00-19:00, or 10:00-13:00 if there's a matinee; second ticket office around the left side as you face the main entrance, open Mon-Fri 10:00-17:00, closed Sat-Sun).

Tourist Concerts by Hungária Koncert—Hungária Koncert offers a wide range of made-for-tourists performances of tradi-

tional music. These take place in one of two historic venues: the Budai Vigadó ("Buda Concert Hall," on Corvin tér in Víziváros, between Castle Hill and the Danube, district I, M2: Batthyány tér—for location, see the map on page 634); or in the former Budapest Ritz, now called the Duna Palota ("Danube Palace," 3 long blocks north of Vörösmarty tér in Pest, behind Széchenyi István tér and the Gresham Palace at Zrínyi utca 5, district V, M1: Vörösmarty tér).

While highbrow classical music buffs will want a more serious concert, these shows are crowd-pleasers. The most popular options are Hungarian folk music-and-dance shows by various inter-changeable troupes (3,600-6,200 Ft, June-Oct Sun-Fri at 20:00, can be at either theater) and classical "greatest hits" by the Danube Symphony Orchestra (with some traditional Hungarian instruments as well; 6,400-8,900 Ft, June-Oct Sat at 20:00, always at Duna Palota). Or you can take in an organ concert (usually mixing Bach and Mozart with Liszt or Bartók) in the impressive St. István's Basilica (4,500-7,800 Ft, May-Sept Sat at 20:00).

If you book direct, you'll get a 10 percent Rick Steves discount on anything they offer (must book in person, by phone, or by email—discount not valid if you buy your tickets on their website or through your hotel). The main office is in the Duna Palota at Zrínyi utca 5 (daily April-Dec 8:00-21:00, Jan-March 8:00-18:00, open later during concerts, tel. 1/317-2754 or 1/317-1377, www.ticket.info.hu, hunkonc@ticket.info.hu). Hungária Koncert also offers dinner cruises on the Danube and in-depth tours of the Jewish Quarter.

Nightlife in Budapest

Budapest is a youthful and lively city, with no shortage of after-hours fun. I've listed these roughly in increasing order of edginess, from "asleep by 10:00 (p.m.)" to "asleep by 10:00 (a.m.)."

Low-Impact Nightlife—This beautiful city is gorgeously lit after dark. Strolling along either the Buda or the Pest **promenade** along the Danube rewards you with wonderful views.

For a different angle on Budapest, consider joining a fun, romantic, crowd-pleasing **boat trip** on the Danube. Danube Legenda's cruises include two drinks and evocative commentary about the floodlit buildings you pass (for details, see page 549).

If you need some rejuvenation after a busy day of sightseeing, soak and splash at **Széchenyi Baths.** The indoor thermal baths close down at 19:00, but the outdoor pools—which are the best part anyway—stay open until 22:00 (last entry at 21:00). Better yet, the mysterious, Turkish-style **Rudas Baths** become a nightclub on Friday and Saturday nights until the wee hours (22:00-4:00 in the morning, wear your bathing suit). For details, see page 614.

Yuppie Drinking Zones—Young locals meet up for happy hour after work at the many trendy bars in two areas: on **Franz Liszt Square** (Liszt Ferenc tér, on page 587) and along **Ráday utca** (described on page 639). Many of these places also serve food. For something a bit more genteel—evocative of this city's late-19th-century Golden Age—locals pass their evenings sipping wine or nibbling dessert at a **café** (see "Budapest's Café Culture" on page 647).

In the "National Ditch"—**Gödör Klub** ("Ditch Club") fills the foundation for the never-completed new National Theater, in the very center of Pest at Erzsébet tér (next to Deák tér, where the three Metró lines converge). It's a café by day and a music club by night, when the sprawling subterranean art-gallery space (which is faintly visible below the surface of the park's shallow pond) hosts an eclectic range of concerts. In the summer, people fill the tables on the terraces that lead down into the club, and hang out on the lawn nearby—creating a fun and engaging local scene. Contemporary dance classes accompanied by live music happen almost every night. If you want to learn how to pop-and-lock with the Magyars, anyone can join in (1,000 Ft for a one-hour class, sometimes bigger concerts and events as well; events begin around 20:00 or 21:00, Erzsébet tér, district V, M1/M2/M3: Deák tér, mobile 0620-201-3868, www.godorklub.hu or www.vilagveleje.hu).

"Ruin Pub" Crawl—If you're looking for memorable, lively, smoke-filled, trendy pubs crammed with twentysomething Budapesters and backpackers, explore the dingy streets of the

Jewish Quarter, behind the Great Synagogue. (This area is between the Small and Great Boulevards, south of Király utca and north of Rákóczi út.) Here you'll find a funky new breed of bars, dubbed "ruin pubs" *(romkocsma)*. The low-profile entryways look abandoned, but once you walk back through a maze of hallways, you'll emerge into large halls and open-air courtyards filled with people huddled around ramshackle tables...rickety-chic. Note that most of these places have vast outdoor zones, but small interiors—so they're better in good weather. (Instant is the exception, with a sprawling labyrinth of indoor rooms.)

Szimpla Kert ("Simple Garden") was the first and remains the best of Budapest's "ruin pubs." This place sprawls through an old building that ought to be condemned, and spills out into an equally shoddy courtyard. It oozes nostalgia for young Budapesters who have fond memories of their communist-era childhoods. Even the snacks are communist kitsch, and along with a full range of alcohol, they serve the old commie soft drinks (such as grape-flavored Traubisoda and sour cherry Meggymárka). Although it's on the route of the tourist pub-crawls, Szimpla is still mostly frequented by locals (daily 12:00-4:00 in the morning, Kazinczy utca 14, district VII, M2: Astoria, tel. 1/352-4198, www.szimpla.hu). They have a second, smaller, far less impressive café, **Szimpla Kávézó,** a few blocks away (Kertész utca 48).

Mumus is another place expertly combining cool and ramshackle. It has a few indoor rooms, but most of the action happens in the cool graffitied garden, which has mismatched furniture strewn under scaffolding. They usually have live jazz on Wednesdays and Sundays (open Mon-Sat 15:00-late, Sun 16:00-late, at the corner of Sip and Dob streets, Dob utca 18).

Instant—a few blocks away, closer to the Opera House and the "Little Broadway" quarter—fills three floors and a warren of dozens of rooms and alcoves in a historic-feeling (but appropriately run-down) building. Each room is decorated differently, but always creatively (I like the upside-down room, with furniture on the ceiling). Find your own little private room, and just chill (daily 16:00 until late, Nagymező utca 38, www.instant.co.hu).

Wesselényi utca, the street that stretches

up past the Great Synagogue, is lined with other appealing bars and cafés; while not strictly "ruin pubs," they have the same spirit. One of the best is **Szóda** (named for the seltzer bottles that line the wall). It's lively and maintains a healthy reverence for the Red old days, with secondhand communist furniture and a sprawling open-air courtyard in good weather (nightly until late, dance floor in cellar, Wesselényi utca 18, district VII, M2: Astoria, tel. 1/461-0007, www.szoda.com).

Corvintető ("Corvin Roof")—also not exactly a ruin pub—has a less enjoyable atmosphere and isn't quite as widely accessible as the ones listed above. However, it's got a memorable location at the top floor of an old department store. You'll hike up several flights of stairs to a maze of bars and dance halls, eventually emerging onto an outdoor terrace looking out over the rooftops of Pest (good weather only; nightly 20:00-5:00 in the morning; a bit farther away from the others, on top of the Corvin department store, across from New York Café at Blaha Lujza tér 1-2, enter on Somogyi Béla utca, district VII, M2: Blaha Lujza tér; www.corvinteto.hu).

Shopping in Budapest

While it's not quite a shopper's mecca, Budapest does offer some enjoyable opportunities to hunt for that perfect Hungarian souvenir.

For a look at local life and a chance to buy some mementos, Budapest's single best shopping venue is the **Great Market Hall** (described in detail on page 579). In addition to all the colorful produce downstairs, the upstairs gallery is full of fiercely competitive souvenir vendors. There's also a **folk-art market on Castle Hill** (near the bus stop at Dísz tér), but it's generally more touristy and a little more expensive. And, while **Váci utca** has been Budapest's main shopping thoroughfare for generations, today it features the city's highest prices and worst values. At touristy markets (but not established shops), haggling is common for pricier items (more than about 4,000 Ft)—but you'll likely only get the merchant to come down about 10 percent (maybe down to 20 percent for multiple items). If you pay with a credit card, you're less likely to snare a discount.

To see how Hungarian urbanites renovate their crumbling concrete flats, don't miss the home-improvement shops that line **Király utca,** which runs parallel to Andrássy út (two short blocks south). For a taste of the good old days—which somehow just feels right, here in nostalgic Budapest—wander up the city's **"antique row,"** Falk Miksa utca, just north of the Parliament. Budapest also has several excellent **English bookstores.** For details, see page 541.

BUDAPEST

Budapesters do most of their shopping in big, American-style **shopping malls** (most shops generally open Mon-Sat 10:00-21:00, Sun 10:00-18:00). The biggest and most convenient options include **WestEnd City Center,** next door to Nyugati/Western train station (Váci út 1-3, district VI, M3: Nyugati pu., tel. 1/374-6573, www.westend.hu); **Mammut** ("Mammoth"), two separate malls a few steps from Buda's Széll Kálmán tér (Lövőház utca 2-6, district II, M2: Széll Kálmán tér, tel. 1/345-8020, www.mammut.hu); and **Arena Plaza,** near Keleti/Eastern train station (Kerepesi út 9, district XIV, M2: Keleti pu., tel. 1/880-7000, www.arenaplaza.hu).

Souvenir Ideas

The most popular souvenir is that quintessential Hungarian spice, **paprika.** Sold in metal cans, linen bags, or porcelain vases—and often accompanied by a tiny wooden scoop—it's a nice way to spice up your cooking with memories of your trip. (But remember that only sealed containers will make it through customs on your way back home.) For more, see "Paprika Primer" on page 518.

Special drinks are a fun souvenir, though they're tricky to bring home (you'll have to wrap them very carefully and put them in your checked luggage—not permitted in carry-on; for customs regulations, see page 22). Consider the unique Hungarian spirit **Unicum,** or a bottle of Hungarian **wine** (both described on page 520).

Hungary has two major **porcelain** manufacturers—Herend and Zsolnay. While very pricey, their works might interest collectors (each one has shops around the city—see www.herend.com and www.zsolnay.hu).

Another popular local item is a hand-embroidered **linen tablecloth.** The colors are often red and green—the national colors of Hungary, of course—but white-on-white designs are also available (and classy). If the thread is thick and the stitching is very even, it was probably done by machine, and obviously is less valuable.

Other handicrafts to look for include **chess sets** (most from Transylvania) and **nesting dolls.** While these dolls have more to do with Russia than with Hungary, you'll see just about every modern combination available: from classic girl dolls, to *South Park* characters, to Russian heads of state, to infamous terrorists, to American presidents. Tacky...but fun.

Fans of **communist kitsch** can look for ironic T-shirts that poke fun at that bygone era. But remember that the best selection is at the Memento Park gift shop, which also sells communist memorabilia and CDs of commie anthems (see page 598).

Music-lovers can shop for a CD of **Hungarian music** at the Opera House gift shop (see page 586).

Sleeping in Budapest

September is extremely tight (because of conventions), with October close behind; book as far ahead as possible for these times. The Formula 1 races (one weekend in late July or early Aug) send rates through the roof. Most rates drop 10-25 percent in the off-season (generally Nov-March). Budapest's hoteliers have been struggling with the weak economy; in desperation, most hotels in town have reduced their rates by about 10-25 percent. I've listed the prevailing rates at the time of this writing (early 2011), but if the economy rebounds, expect rates to increase. In general, the prices I list here are very unreliable; check each hotel's website (or email to ask them) for the latest rates and deals. Since my €100 listings are substantially nicer than my €85 listings, I'd spring for the extra expense to have a comfortable home base.

A flurry of new hotel construction over the last few years has flooded the market with top-end rooms. Outside of busy convention times (Sept-Oct), many of these places offer prices that are only a little more than a mid-range hotel (these deals are often listed on the hotel's website; I've noted specifics in the listings).

If you're on a tight budget, don't overlook the good-value Bellevue B&B (page 635) and Mária and István's place (page 631).

The majority of hotels don't include the 3 percent tourist tax in their rates. Be warned that some big chains also don't include the whopping 21 percent sales tax, which can make your hotel cost nearly a quarter more than you expected. (Independent hotel rates typically do include sales tax.)

Sleep Code

(€1 = $1.40, 200 Ft = about $1, country code: 36, area code: 1)
S = Single, **D** = Double/Twin, **T** = Triple, **Q** = Quad, **b** = bathroom. Unless otherwise noted, credit cards are accepted, and breakfast is included. Everyone listed here speaks English.

To help you easily sort through these listings, I've divided the accommodations into three categories based on the price for a double room with bath during high season (or for a bunk at a hostel):

$$$ Higher Priced—Most rooms €100 or more.
$$ Moderately Priced—Most rooms between €70-100.
$ Lower Priced—Most rooms €70 or less.

Prices can change without notice; verify the hotel's current rates online or by email. For other updates, see www.ricksteves.com/update.

Most hotels listed here include a buffet breakfast. Some smaller budget places serve no breakfast at all, while larger chain hotels charge (too much) extra for it; in these cases, I've noted it in the listing. Consider having breakfast instead at one of three good cafés I've recommended under "Eating in Budapest": Gerlóczy Café, Centrál Kávéház, or Callas.

In Pest

Most travelers find staying in Pest more convenient than sleeping in Buda. Most sights worth seeing are in Pest, which also has a much higher concentration of Metró and tram stops, making it a snap to get around. Pest feels more lively and local than stodgy, touristy Buda, but it's also much more urban (if you don't enjoy big cities, sleep in Buda instead). I've arranged my listings by neighborhood, clustered around the most important sightseeing sectors.

Near Andrássy Út

Andrássy Boulevard is handy, local-feeling, and fun. With its ample restaurants, upscale-residential vibe, and easy connection to downtown (via the M1/yellow line), it's the neighborhood where I prefer to sleep. Most of the hotels listed here (except Cotton House) are within a two-block walk of this main artery. The Queen Mary and Cotton House, which are often mysteriously empty, are likely to have rooms when other hotels are full. For specific locations, see the map on the next page.

$$$ K+K Hotel Opera is wonderfully situated beside the Opera House in the fun "Broadway Quarter"—my favorite home-base location in Budapest. It's a regal splurge, with 206 classy rooms and helpful, professional service. The published rates are sky-high (Sb-€213, Db-€265), but most of the time you can score a better deal (often Sb-€120-140 and Db-€120-160 in summer, Sb/Db-€100-120 in winter, €25 more for bigger and fancier "executive" rooms, non-smoking floors, air-con, elevator, free Internet access and cable Internet in rooms, parking garage-€15/day, Révay utca 24, district VI, M1: Opera, tel. 1/269-0222, fax 1/269-0230, www.kkhotels.com, kk.hotel.opera@kkhotels.hu).

$$$ Kapital Inn is an upscale, gay-friendly boutique B&B tucked behind the House of Terror. Its four rooms are pricey but perfectly stylish—there's not a pillow out of place. Albert, who lived in Boston, gives his B&B a sense of real hospitality (D-€79-89—a good value if you don't mind sharing a bathroom, Db-€99-125, lower rates are for Nov-March, air-con, free Internet access and Wi-Fi, pleasant breakfast terrace, free communal minibar, up several flights of stairs with no elevator, Aradi utca 30, district VI, M1: Vörösmarty utca, mobile 0630-931-1023, www.kapitalinn.com, kapitalinn@kapitalinn.com).

BUDAPEST

Andrássy Út Hotels & Restaurants

- 1 K+K Hotel Opera
- 2 Kapital Inn
- 3 Hotel Pest
- 4 Cotton House
- 5 Hotel Queen Mary
- 6 Hotel Medosz
- 7 easyHotel
- 8 To Aventura Hostel
- 9 Home Made Hostel
- 10 Menza Rest.
- 11 Klassz Bistro
- 12 Bock Bisztró
- 13 Két Szerecsen
- 14 Millennium da Pippo
- 15 Shalimar Rest.
- 16 Duran Szendvics
- 17 Főzelékfaló Ételbár
- 18 Hummus Bar
- 19 Alexandra Café
- 20 Callas Café
- 21 Művész Kávéház
- 22 Laundry
- 23 Discover Budapest & Tree Hugger Dan Bookstore

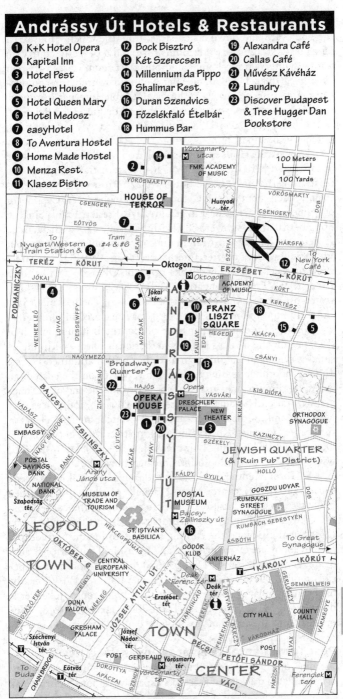

$$ Hotel Pest is nicely located a block off Andrássy út (across the boulevard and down a side-street from the Opera House). Its 25 newish, straightforward rooms surround a peaceful courtyard with a winter-garden lounge and breakfast room (rates vary, but usually Sb-€86, Db-€96, cheaper Nov-mid-March, air-con, elevator, free Internet access in lobby and cable Internet in rooms, request a quieter courtyard room, Paulay Ede utca 31, district VI, M1: Opera, tel. 1/343-1198, fax 1/351-9164, www.hotelpest.hu, hotelpest@hotelpest.hu).

$$ Cotton House, a bit farther from Andrássy út than the others listed here (near the Nyugati/Western train station), is a blast-from-the-past theme hotel. Its 22 retro rooms have 1930s themes; each room is devoted to a different mobster (Al Capone) or old-time performer (Ella Fitzgerald, Elvis Presley, Frank Sinatra; Sb/Db-€70 with shower, €80 with bathtub, €90 with Jacuzzi, 15 percent cheaper Jan-March, air-con, non-smoking rooms but smoky lobby, elevator, free Internet access and Wi-Fi, some street noise on weekends, a few blocks from the Oktogon at Jókai utca 26, district VI, M3: Nyugati pu., tel. 1/354-2600, fax 1/354-1341, www.cottonhouse.hu, info@cottonhouse.hu). The basement jazz club is fun to explore (closes at 24:00, may be closed in summer).

$ Hotel Queen Mary (named not for the British monarch or ship, but for the owner's wife) is mysteriously cheap, with impersonal service and 26 unimaginative but well-maintained rooms. The neighborhood is dingy and gloomy, but it's on the cusp of an emerging dining zone, just two blocks beyond the end of the happening Franz Liszt Square (Sb-€40, Db-€46, Tb-€56, prices vary with demand, 20 percent cheaper Nov-March, air-con, elevator, free cable Internet, Kertész utca 34, district VII, between M1: Oktogon and M2: Blaha Lujza tér, tel. 1/413-3510, fax 1/413-3511, www.hotelqueenmary.hu, info@hotelqueenmary.hu).

$ Hotel Medosz is cheap and dumpy, overlooking a seedy square. But the prices are low, it's gradually getting a much-needed makeover, and the location is enticing—around the corner from the Oktogon and across busy Andrássy út from the trendy Franz Liszt Square. Beyond the chilling concrete communist facade and gloomy lobby are 69 rooms—old and uninspired but perfectly adequate, comrade (Sb-€49, Db-€59, €20 more for renovated "superior" rooms, €10 cheaper Nov-March, elevator, free Wi-Fi, nearby bars can be noisy—ask for a quieter courtyard room, Jókai tér 9, district VI, M1: Oktogon, tel. 1/374-3000, fax 1/332-4316, www.medoszhotel.hu, info@medoszhotel.hu).

Pest Town Center (Belváros), near Váci Utca

Sleeping on the very central and convenient Váci utca comes with overly inflated prices. But these less expensive options—just a block or two off Váci utca—offer some of the best values in Budapest.

$$$ Gerlóczy Café & Rooms, which also serves good meals (see page 638), is the best spot in central Budapest for affordable elegance. The 15 rooms, set around a classy old spiral-staircase atrium with a stained-glass ceiling, are thoughtfully and stylishly appointed. This gem is an exceptional value (Sb-€95, Db-€105, includes great breakfast, some restaurant noise on lower floors until 23:00, air-con, elevator, free Wi-Fi, 2 blocks from Váci utca, just off Városház utca at Gerlóczy utca 1, district V, M3: Ferenciek tere, tel. 1/501-4000, www.gerloczy.hu, info@gerloczy.hu).

$$$ Peregrinus Hotel, just a block off Váci utca, has 25 high-ceilinged, spacious, institutional-feeling rooms (most of which lack air-conditioning—in summer, request a room with air-con for the same price). Because it's owned by the big ELTE university, many of its guests are visiting professors and lecturers (Sb-€70, Db-€100, Tb-€125, 20 percent cheaper Nov-March, rates very soft—email to ask about deals, elevator, free Internet access and Wi-Fi, free loaner bikes, Szerb utca 3, district V; 5-minute walk to M3: Kálvin tér, or tram #47 or #49 to Fövám tér; tel. 1/266-4911, fax 1/266-4913, www.peregrinushotel.hu, peregrinushotel@elte.hu).

$$ Kálvin-Ház, a long block up from the Great Market Hall, offers 38 big rooms with old-fashioned furnishings and squeaky parquet floors. The newer top-floor rooms have a bit less classic character, but are air-conditioned and tidier than the older rooms (all rooms cost the same: Sb-€49-70, Db-€59-95, apartment-€79-120, price depends on demand, extra bed-€20, elevator, free Internet access and Wi-Fi, Gönczy Pál utca 6, district IX, M3: Kálvin tér, tel. 1/216-4365, fax 1/216-4161, www.kalvinhouse.hu, info@kalvinhouse.hu).

$$ Leo Panzió (a.k.a. Leo Hotel) is a peaceful oasis with 14 modern but worn rooms hiding upstairs in a giant, hulking building that's seen better days. The location is central, if you can get past the dingy neighborhood. Once inside, the antique elevator is enjoyably rickety, and the double-paned windows keep out most of the noise from the busy street below. Rooms #1 and #7 overlook a quieter courtyard (Sb-€63, Db-€80, extra bed-€27, includes tax, 5 percent discount if you mention Rick Steves when booking, 25 percent cheaper Nov-March, all rooms have a strange but well-marked little step down in the middle of the room, entirely non-smoking, air-con, free Wi-Fi, tiny and tight breakfast room, Kossuth Lajos utca 2A—dial 58 at the door to call reception, district V, M3: Ferenciek tere, tel. 1/266-9041, www.leopanzio.hu, leo@leopanzio.hu).

$$ Ibis Hotel Budapest Centrum, with 126 rooms, is part of the no-frills chain that's sweeping Europe, with cookie-cutter

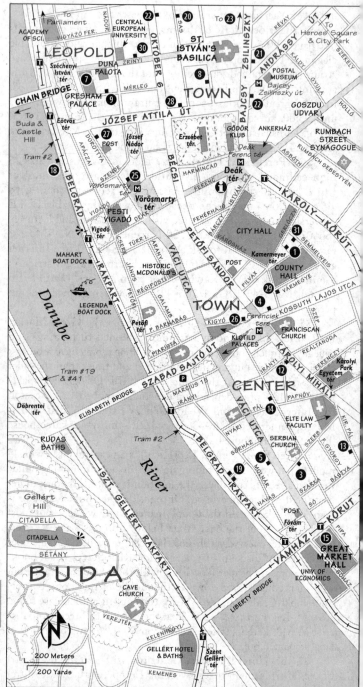

BUDAPEST

To Parliament
ACADEMY OF SCI.
VIGYÁZÓ FER.
NÁDOR
CENTRAL EUROPEAN UNIVERSITY 22
SAS 20
To 23
REVAY
ÚT
To Heroes' Square & City Park
KÁLDY GYULA
SZÉKELY
LEOPOLD
OKTÓBER 6
ST. ISTVÁN'S BASILICA
8
21
ANDRÁSSY
Széchenyi István tér
DUNA PALOTA
ZRINYI
30
7
MÉRLEG
POSTAL MUSEUM Bajcsy-Zsilinszky út 22
GOSZDU UDVAR
HOLLÓ
CHAIN BRIDGE
GRESHAM PALACE
9
TOWN
RUMBACH STREET SYNAGOGUE
To Buda & Castle Hill
Eötvös tér
28
JÓZSEF ATTILA ÚT
ANKERHÁZ
RUMBACH SEBESTYÉN
Tram #2
18
POST
27
DOROTTYA
APÁCZAI
SZENDE
József Nádor tér
BÉCSI
Erzsébet tér
GÖDÖR KLUB
Deák Ferenc tér
ASBÓTH
KÁROLY
BELGRÁD
25
Vörösmarty tér
DEÁK
HARMINCAD
FERENC
Deák tér
T
KÖRÚT
GERLÓCZY
Vörösmarty tér
FEHÉRHAJÓ ISTVÁN
SEMMELWEIS
PESTI VIGADÓ
VIGADÓ
ARANY
RÉGIPOSTI U.
DEÁK
CITY HALL
31
Vigadó tér
TÜRR I.
CSERE
PETŐFI SÁNDOR
VÁROSHÁZ
Kamermeyer tér
1
MAHART BOAT DOCK
HISTORIC McDONALD'S
JÁNOS
PETŐFI
GALAMB
POST
PILVAX
COUNTY HALL
VÁRMEGYE
Danube
LEGENDA BOAT DOCK
Petőfi tér
P. BARNABÁS
TOWN
4
29
KOSSUTH LAJOS UTCA
SZÉP
RÉALTANODA
PIARISTA
KIGYÓ
26
Ferenciek tere
FRANCISCAN CHURCH
FERENCZY
Károlyi Park
KLOTILD PALACES
KÁROLY MIHÁLY
Egyetem tér
Tram #19 & #41
SZABAD SAJTÓ ÚT
IRÁNYI
12
CENTER
PAPNÖV.
Károlyi tér
Döbrentei tér
ELISABETH BRIDGE
MÁRCIUS 15
IRÁNYI
14
VÁCI UTCA
PÁL
ELTE LAW FACULTY
AIR. PÁL
ELTE LAW FACULTY
RUDAS BATHS
Tram #2
BELGRÁD RAKPART
NYÁRI
SÖRHÁZ
SERBIAN CHURCH
SZERB
F. GYÖRGY
13
River
5
19
MOLNÁR
3
SZARKA
SÓ
BÁLYA
KÖRÚT
Gellért Hill
CITADELLA
CITADELLA
POST
Fővám tér
PIPA
VÁMHÁZ
SÉTÁNY
B U D A
15
GREAT MARKET HALL
SZT. GELLÉRT RAKPART
CAVE CHURCH
UNIV. OF ECONOMICS
VEREJTÉK
N
200 Meters
200 Yards
KELENHEGYI
LIBERTY BRIDGE
GELLÉRT HOTEL & BATHS
Szent Gellért tér
KEMENES

Pest Town Center Hotels & Restaurants

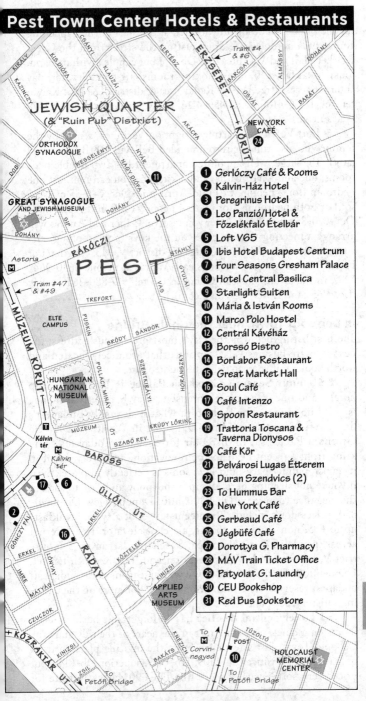

1. Gerlóczy Café & Rooms
2. Kálvin-Ház Hotel
3. Peregrinus Hotel
4. Leo Panzió/Hotel & Főzelékfaló Ételbár
5. Loft V65
6. Ibis Hotel Budapest Centrum
7. Four Seasons Gresham Palace
8. Hotel Central Basilica
9. Starlight Suiten
10. Mária & István Rooms
11. Marco Polo Hostel
12. Centrál Kávéház
13. Borssó Bistro
14. BorLabor Restaurant
15. Great Market Hall
16. Soul Café
17. Café Intenzo
18. Spoon Restaurant
19. Trattoria Toscana & Taverna Dionysos
20. Café Kör
21. Belvárosi Lugas Étterem
22. Duran Szendvics (2)
23. To Hummus Bar
24. New York Café
25. Gerbeaud Café
26. Jégbüfé Café
27. Dorottya G. Pharmacy
28. MÁV Train Ticket Office
29. Patyolat G. Laundry
30. CEU Bookshop
31. Red Bus Bookstore

BUDAPEST

predictability and utterly no charm. But it's cheap, well-equipped for the price, and beautifully located at the start of the happening Ráday utca outdoor café drag, just up the street from the Great Market Hall and Váci utca (Sb/Db-€71 but can flex with demand, lousy breakfast-€10, non-smoking rooms, air-con, elevator, pay Internet access, free Wi-Fi, Ráday utca 6, district IX, M3: Kálvin tér, tel. 1/456-4100, fax 1/456-4116, www.ibis-centrum.hu, h2078 @accor.com).

$ **Loft V65** is an apartment right on Váci utca, rented by the family who also run the recommended Bellevue B&B (described later). The large, well-appointed apartment has two double bedrooms, one and a half baths, and a kitchen. You can rent just one bedroom (for 2 people, €70 mid-April-mid-Oct, €40-55 off-season) or both bedrooms (for up to 4 people, €100 mid-April-mid-Oct, €70-85 off-season). After you reserve, Gábor and András will arrange a meeting time to give you the keys (non-smoking, air-con, elevator, free Wi-Fi, Váci utca 65, district V, M3: Kálvin tér or Ferenciek tere, in the mornings call András at mobile 0630-964-7287, in the afternoons call Gábor at US tel. 917-880-3656, www.LoftV65.com, LoftV65@gmail.com).

In Leopold Town, near the Chain Bridge

The first listing below is the city's most prestigious address; the next two are business-class options that are nicely located and worth booking if you can get a discounted rate.

$$$ **Four Seasons Gresham Palace** is Budapest's top hotel—and one of its most expensive. Stay here only if money is truly no object. You'll sleep in what is arguably Budapest's finest Art Nouveau building. Damaged in World War II, the Gresham Palace sat in disrepair for decades. Today it's sparkling from a recent head-to-toe renovation, and every detail in its lavish public spaces and 179 rooms is perfectly in place. Even if you're not sleeping here, dip into the lobby and café to soak in the elegance (non-view Db-€300-400, Danube-view Db-€490-830, prices don't include 21 percent tax—not a typo, breakfast-up to €35, non-smoking rooms, air-con, elevator, free Internet access, pay Wi-Fi, top-floor spa, Széchenyi István tér 5-6, district V, between M1: Vörösmarty tér and M2: Kossuth tér, tel. 1/268-6000, fax 1/268-5000, www.fourseasons.com/budapest, budapest.reservations@fourseasons.com). For more on the building's history, see page 573.

$$ **Hotel Central Basilica** has 48 forgettable business-class rooms on a quiet, pleasant street in the heart of the tidy and sane Leopold Town, just a few steps from the inviting plaza in front of St. István's Basilica (Sb-€109, Db-€119, superior Db-€149, but prices very soft—usually more like Db-€90; check website for

deals, or find best price on a booking site and try to cut a deal directly with the hotel; even cheaper Nov-March, air-con, elevator, free Wi-Fi in lobby and cable Internet in rooms, Hercegprímás utca 8, district V, M1: Bajcsy-Zsilinszky út, tel. 1/328-5010, www .hotelcentral-basilica.hu, info@hotelcentral-basilica.hu).

$$ Starlight Suiten has 54 big suites—with living room, bedroom, and kitchenette—directly behind the Gresham Palace (listed above). While rates can range widely (€80-130), you can often get a suite for €90—making this place a great deal (includes continental breakfast, air-con, elevator, pay Internet access and Wi-Fi, free fitness room, Mérleg utca 6, district V, M1: Vörösmarty tér, tel. 1/484-3700, www.starlighthotels.com, manager.merleg @starlighthotels.com).

"Hostel Alternative" Budget Beds

Although Budapest's hostels (listed in the next section) welcome travelers of any age, those over 30 might not enjoy bunking with the backpacker set. Below you'll find several good-value alternatives to the youth-hostel scene. (Don't miss the excellent **Bellevue B&B,** across the river in Buda, and listed on page 635.)

$ Mária and István, your chatty Hungarian aunt and uncle, are saving a room for you in their Old World apartment. For warmth and hospitality at youth-hostel prices, consider bunking in one of their two simple, old-fashioned rooms, which share a bathroom. The smaller room is cheaper and quieter; the bigger room gets  some street noise on weekends (S-€20-24, D-€30-36, T-€42-48, price depends on size of room and length of stay—longer is cheaper, no breakfast but guests' kitchen, cash only, elevator plus a few stairs, Ferenc körút 39, district IX, M3: Corvin-negyed, tel. & fax 1/216-0768, www.mariaistvan.hu, mariaistvan@upcmail.hu). From the Corvin-negyed Metró stop, follow signs for the *Ferenc körút 41-45* exit, bear right up the stairs, and walk straight about a block and a half, looking for #39 (on the left, after the post office; dial 19 at the door). Mária and István also rent two apartments that are two Metró stops farther from the center (Db-€50-56, Tb-€60-66, Qb-€68-80, family apartment, both near M3: Nagyvarad tér).

$ Budapesting, run by friendly Marton Andrássy, his family, and his business partner Peter, rents eight apartments scattered around central neighborhoods in Pest (mostly districts V, VI, and VII). Generally located in nondescript residential buildings, each apartment comes equipped with a kitchen, free Wi-Fi, a washing machine, and mostly modern but some mix-and-match furnishings. You can rent the whole apartment (2-3 bedrooms, €50-90; rates cheaper Oct-May), or just a room in an apartment (D-€25-40), in which case you'll share the bathroom and kitchen with another traveler. Marton, Peter, and the gang have a youthful enthusiasm and pride themselves on offering a warm welcome (arrange a time to meet them at the apartment, or they can pick you up at the airport or train station for the same price as a taxi) and getting to know their guests—they'll happily get you oriented to the city (check out options at www.budapesting.com, mobile 0670-275-5690).

The **$ easyHotel** chain follows a similar model to its parent company, the no-frills easyJet airline: They charge you very little up front, then nickel-and-dime you with optional extras—so you pay only for what you want (pick up the list at entry: TV access-€7.50/24 hours; cable Internet access-€2/hour, €10/24 hours; hair dryer-€1/24 hours; laundry-€10/load; room-cleaning during your stay-€10; and so on). With 59 rooms just a block off the busy Great Boulevard and around the corner from the Oktogon, the location is handy and the hotel is well-run by Zoltán. The rooms feel popped out of a plastic mold, with a nauseating orange color scheme, sterile quasi-linoleum floors, and tiny prefab ship's-head bathrooms. But the price is right...if you can resist the extras (Sb/Db-€19-43 depending on demand, average rate is €33 for a small room and €37 for a standard room, no breakfast, 24-hour reception, non-smoking, air-con, elevator, two wheelchair-accessible rooms, Eötvös utca 25A, district VI, M1: Oktogon, tel. 1/411-1982, www.easyhotel.com, info@budapestoktogon.easyhotel.com).

Hostels

"Official" IYHF hostels are rare in Hungary, but independent hostels prevail. Budapest has seemingly dozens of apartments that have been taken over by young entrepreneurs, offering basic, rough-around-the-edges hostel charm. You'll buzz in at the door and climb up a creaky, dank, and smelly staircase to a funky little enclave of fellow backpackers. Most of these places have just three rooms (one double and two small dorms) and feel more like communes than some of the finely tuned, high-capacity youth-hostel machines in many other cities. As each of these fills a niche (party, artsy, communist-themed, etc.), it's hard to recommend just one—read reviews on a hostel site (such as www.hostels.com) and find one that suits your hosteling philosophy. Amenities also vary, but you'll generally have access to kitchen facilities, Internet terminals and/or Wi-Fi, and laundry. Of the places I've seen, I particularly liked Aventura and Home Made; Marco Polo has less personality but more beds.

$ Aventura Hostel is a colorful and stylish option in a dreary urban neighborhood near the Nyugati/Western train station. Well-run by Agnes, this homey place is tastefully mod, friendly, clean, and low-key, with imaginatively decorated rooms (3 rooms, bunk in 5- to 8-bed dorm-€11-19, D-€40-50, price depends on season, breakfast-450 Ft, includes sheets, towel rental-450 Ft, free Internet access and Wi-Fi, kitchen, laundry service, massage available, across the busy Great Boulevard ring road and a very long block from Nyugati train station at 12 Visegrádi utca—dial 5 at door, district XIII, M3: Nyugati pu., tel. 1/239-0782, www.aventura hostel.com, reservation@aventurahostel.com). They also rent two apartments near Andrássy út (Db-€50-70).

$ Home Made Hostel is a fun-and-funky slumbermill artfully littered with secondhand furniture. It's run and decorated with a sense of humor. With 20 beds in four rooms located near the Oktogon, it's another good option (bunk in 4- to 8-bed dorm-€12-15, D-€37, apartment Db-€41, includes sheets and towels, no breakfast, free Internet access and Wi-Fi, kitchen, laundry service, Teréz körút 22, district VI, M1: Oktogon, tel. 1/302-2103, www .homemadehostel.com, info@homemadehostel.com).

$ Marco Polo Hostel has six 4- to 12-bed dorms and 36 twin rooms (with bathrooms). Although it's very institutional and the location is a bit less handy, the private rooms attract a slightly older crowd (dorm bed-€12, Db-€39, 20 percent cheaper Nov-Feb, cash only, includes sheets, towel rental-500 Ft, breakfast-€4, pay Internet access, pay laundry, Nyár utca 6, district VII, M2: Blaha Lujza tér, tel. 1/413-2555, fax 1/413-6058, www.marcopolohostel .com, sales@marcopolohostel.com).

In Buda
Víziváros

The Víziváros neighborhood—or "Water Town"—is the lively part of Buda squeezed between Castle Hill and the Danube, where fishermen and tanners used to live. Víziváros is the most pleasant central area to stay on the Buda side of the Danube. Located across the river from the Parliament building, it comes with fine views. It's expensive and a little less convenient than Pest, but this area also feels less urban.

The following hotels (except Hotel Papillon) are in district I, between the Chain Bridge and Buda's busy Margit körút ring road. Trams #19 and #41 zip along the embankment in either direction. Batthyány tér, a few minutes' walk away, is a handy center with lots of restaurants (see "Eating in Budapest," later), a Metró stop (M2/red line), and the HÉV train to Óbuda and Szentendre. All of these places come with professional, helpful staff.

Buda Hotels & Restaurants

1. Hotel Victoria
2. art'otel
3. Carlton Hotel
4. Bellevue B&B
5. To Hotel Papillon
6. Hilton Budapest
7. Hotel Castle Garden
8. Burg Hotel
9. 21 Magyar Vendéglő
10. Tabáni Terasz Rest.
11. Matróz Kocsma Rest.
12. Pater Marcus Beer Hall
13. Batthyány tér Eateries
14. Ruszwurm Café
15. To Szent Jupát Rest.

$$$ Hotel Victoria, with 27 business-class rooms—each with a grand river view—is a winner. This tall, narrow place (three rooms on each of nine floors) is run with pride and attention to detail by on-the-ball manager Zoltán and his friendly staff (Sb-€102, Db-€107, extra bed-€30, 30 percent cheaper Nov-March, air-con, elevator, free Internet access and Wi-Fi, free sauna, reserve ahead for €13/day parking garage or park free on street, Bem rak-part 11, tel. 1/457-8080, fax 1/457-8088, www.victoria.hu, victoria @victoria.hu). The painstakingly restored 19th-century Hubay Palace behind the hotel (entrance next to reception) is used for con-certs and other events. It feels like a museum, with inlaid floors, stained-glass windows, and stuccoed walls and ceilings—even if you're not staying at Hotel Victoria, drop in and ask to see it.

$$$ art'otel impresses even New York City sophisticates. Every detail—from the breakfast dishes to the carpets to the good-luck blackbird perched in each room—was designed by American artist Donald Sultan. This stylish, fun hotel has 165 rooms spread between two attached buildings: The new section fronting the Danube, and a restored older house just behind it (high rack rates, but usually Sb/Db-€99-165 depending on season, figure Sb/Db-€129 in summer, Danube view-€20 more, bigger "executive" rooms-€30 more, deluxe "art suites"-€60 more, breakfast-€14, non-smoking rooms, air-con, elevator, free Internet access in busi-ness lounge, free Wi-Fi, free sauna and mini-exercise room, Bem rakpart 16-19, tel. 1/487-9487, fax 1/487-9488, www.artotel.hu, budapest@artotel.hu).

$$$ Carlton Hotel, with 95 smallish, somewhat long-in-the-tooth rooms, is all business and no personality. But the location—where the Castle Hill funicular meets the Chain Bridge—is handy for getting to both Castle Hill and Pest (official rates: Sb-€95, Db-€110—but very soft so ask for best price, suites available, extra bed-€25, 20 percent cheaper Nov-March, non-smoking rooms, elevator, free Internet access and Wi-Fi, parking garage-€12/day, Apor Péter utca 3, tel. 1/224-0999, fax 1/224-0990, www.carlton hotel.hu, carltonhotel@t-online.hu).

$ Bellevue B&B is Budapest's best deal. It hides in a quiet residential area on the Víziváros hillside just below the Fishermen's Bastion staircase. This gem is run by retired economists Judit and Lajos Szuhay, who lived in Canada for four years and speak flaw-less English. The breakfast room and some of the six straightfor-ward, comfortable rooms have views across the Danube to the Parliament and Pest. Judit (YOO-deet) and Lajos (LIE-yosh) love to chat, and pride themselves on offering genuine hospitality and a warm welcome (let them know what time you're arriving). As this B&B is understandably popular, book ahead (Sb-€55-62, Db-€65-72, price depends on room size and view, 20-30 percent cheaper mid-Oct-mid-April, cash only, non-smoking, air-con, free Internet access and Wi-Fi; M2: Batthyány tér plus a 10-minute uphill walk, or bus #16 from Deák, Széchenyi, or Adam Clark squares to Dónati utca plus a 2-minute walk uphill, then downhill—they'll email you detailed directions; Szabó Ilonka utca 15/B, mobile 0630-370-8678 or 0630-951-5494, www.bellevuebudapest.com, judit@bellevue budapest.com). The same family rents the Loft V65 in central Pest (described on page 630).

$ **Hotel Papillon** is farther north, in a forgettable residential area a 10-minute uphill walk past Széll Kálmán tér. It's a cheery little place with 30 homey, pastel rooms, a garden with a tiny swimming pool, and affordable prices (Sb-€44, older Db-€54, newer "superior" Db with air-con and balcony-€64 and worth the extra money, 25 percent cheaper Nov-March, elevator, pay Internet access, free Wi-Fi in some parts of hotel, restaurant, tram #4 or #6 from Széll Kálmán tér to Mechwart liget stop then an uphill walk, Rózsahegy utca 3, district II, tel. 1/212-4750, fax 1/212-4003, www.hotelpapillon.hu, papillon2@t-online.hu).

Castle Hill

Romantics often like calling Castle Hill home (district I). The Hilton and Burg hotels share Holy Trinity Square (Szentháromság tér) with Matthias Church. They couldn't be closer to the Castle Hill sights, but they're in a tourist zone—dead at night, and less convenient to Pest than other listings.

$$$ **Hilton Budapest** is a 322-room landmark—the first big Western hotel in town, opened back in the gloomy days of communism. Today, while a bit faded, it still offers a complete escape from Hungary and a chance to be surrounded by rich tourists mostly from Japan, Germany, and the United States (very flexible rates, but usually about Db-€130 in slower times—a great deal, check for better prices online, best rates are for 3-week advance booking with nonrefundable prepayment in full, €30 more for Danube-view rooms, prices do not include 21 percent tax, breakfast-€28/ person, non-smoking floors, elevator, pay Wi-Fi, Hess András tér 1-3 on Castle Hill next to Matthias Church, tel. 1/889-6600, fax 1/889-6644, www.budapest.hilton.com, reservations.budapest @hilton.com).

$$ **Hotel Castle Garden,** huddled in a tranquil, park-like neighborhood just outside the castle's Vienna Gate (north end), has 39 modern, business-class rooms in a contemporary building. As it's roughly on the way between the castle and Széll Kálmán tér, it's relatively handy, though still less convenient than the Víziváros listings (Sb-€105, Db-€120, but usually more like Db-€79—a great deal at this price, "superior" room with terrace for €20-30 more, air-con, elevator, free Internet access and cable Internet, Lovas út

41, M2: Széll Kálmán tér; exit the castle through the Vienna Gate and turn left along the wall, or hike up from Széll Kálmán tér and turn right along the castle wall; tel. 1/224-7420, fax 1/224-7421, www.castlegarden.hu, hotel@castlegarden.hu).

$$ Burg Hotel, with 26 overpriced rooms, is simply efficient: concrete, spacious, and comfy, with a professional staff. You'll find more conveniently located hotels for less money elsewhere, but if you simply *must* stay in a modern hotel across the street from Matthias Church, this is it (official rates: Sb-€105, Db-€115, Db apartment-€134, but rates very soft—usually more like €85-99, extra bed-€39, 10 percent discount on their official online rate if you book direct and mention this book—unless they're very busy, cheaper for 3-night stays, 20 percent cheaper Nov-March, request view room for no extra charge, entirely non-smoking, no elevator, top-floor rooms are extremely long, family rooms, free Internet access and Wi-Fi, Szentháromság tér 7-8, tel. 1/212-0269, fax 1/212-3970, www.burghotelbudapest.com, info@burghotel budapest.com, Lajos).

Eating in Budapest

Thanks to Budapest's ever-evolving culinary scene, there's no shortage of places to dine. A few years ago, I had to scrape the bottom of the barrel to recommend eateries here. Now, I can barely keep track of what's new—and scouting new restaurants is the highlight of my research chores. The broad range of options and healthy sense of one-upmanship among local chefs keeps prices reasonable and quality high. This also means that the foodie scene here is boom-and-bust: A place quickly acquires a huge and enthusiastic following, but soon falls from grace as an even more enticing competitor opens up shop.

While you'll find the standard Hungarian fare, most big-city restaurants like to dabble in international cuisine. Most of my listings feature an international menu with some Hungarian flourishes. (If you want truly traditional Hungarian fare, you'll actually do a bit better in smaller towns.) The good news: Most Hungarian chefs are so skilled that any cuisine is well-executed here.

Most Hungarians dine between 19:00 and 21:00, peaking around 20:00; trendy zones such as Franz Liszt Square and Ráday utca, which attract an after-work crowd, are lively earlier in the evening.

While most Hungarian restaurateurs are honest, rip-off joints abound in downtown Budapest's tourist zone—especially along the main walking street, Váci utca. (Frankly, I'd never eat on Váci utca, which practically guarantees bad food and service for high prices.) Avoid any place with a menu that doesn't list prices, and tune in to the fine print. For example, many restaurants automatically add a 10-15 percent service charge to the bill. The extra charge should be noted on the menu (if it's not, complain), and appears as a line item after the subtotal on the bill (look for "service," "tip," *felszolgálási díj*, or *szervízdíj*). In these cases, an additional tip is not necessary. For more on tipping, see page 20.

In Pest

I've listed these options by neighborhood, for easy reference with your sightseeing.

In Pest's Town Center (Belváros), near Váci Utca

When you ask natives about good places to eat on Váci utca, they just roll their eyes. But wander a few blocks off the tourist route, and you'll discover alternatives with fair prices and better food. For locations, see the map on page 628.

Gerlóczy Café is tucked on a peaceful little square next to the giant City Hall. This classy café features international cuisine with

several seating options (out on the square, in the coffee-house interior, or upstairs in the non-smoking section). There's a good permanent menu along with weekly specials. The clientele is a mix of tourists and upscale-urban Budapesters, includ-

ing local politicians and actors from several nearby theaters. With a take-your-time ambience that's arguably more Parisian than Hungarian—and with live harp music most evenings inside—this is a particularly inviting spot (1,700-4,000-Ft main dishes; weekday lunch specials: 1,400 Ft/two courses, 1,800 Ft/three courses; good breakfasts, excellent fresh-baked pastries and bread, daily 7:00-23:00, 2 blocks from Váci utca, just off Városház utca at Gerlóczy utca 1, district V, M3: Ferenciek tere, tel. 1/501-4000). They rent good rooms, too (see page 627).

Centrál Kávéház, while famous as a grand, old-fashioned

café, is also one of Budapest's best spots for a central, characteristic meal, and offers some good home-style Hungarian dishes you don't often find in restaurants. Live music (most evenings) adds to the elegant, early-1900s ambience (1,400-2,000-Ft starters, 2,500-4,500-Ft main dishes;

lunch special: 1,200 Ft/two courses, 1,600 Ft/three courses; open daily 8:00-23:00, Károlyi Mihály utca 9, district V, M3: Ferenciek tere, tel. 1/266-2110).

Borssó Bistro, in the newly spiffed-up area near University Square (Egyetem tér), is the latest rising star on the Budapest restaurant scene. Featuring deconstructed Hungarian cuisine with French flair, they offer up reasonably sized portions of delicately assembled fare in a cozy two-story interior. The ambience, like the cuisine, is an elegant yet accessible blend of old and new. They offer outdoor tables and occasional live music. Reservations are smart at this pricey, popular place (2,500-5,000-Ft main dishes, daily 12:00-23:00, Király Pál utca 14, district V, M3: Kálvin tér, tel. 1/789-0975).

BorLabor ("Wine Lab") features traditional, regional, updated Hungarian specialties at reasonable prices in a mod, romantic wine-cellar atmosphere (2,000-3,000-Ft main dishes, daily 12:00-24:00, a block north of Váci utca at Veres Pálné utca 7, district V, M3: Ferenciek tere, tel. 1/328-0382).

Great Market Hall: At the far south end of Váci utca, you can eat a quick lunch on the upper floor of the Great Market Hall (Nagyvásárcsarnok). **Fakanál Étterem**—the glassed-in, sit-down cafeteria above the main entrance—is overpriced and touristy, but offers good seating (2,000-2,700-Ft main dishes). The sloppy, stand-up stalls along the right side of the building are cheaper, but quality can vary (grab a bar stool or you'll stand while you munch). Locals love the **Lángos** stand, for deep-fried bread slathered with sour cream and cheese (add garlic for some kick).

Or you can assemble a **picnic**—produce and butcher stands line the main floor, and there's a big, modern, easy-to-miss grocery store in the basement (the end nearest Váci utca; Mon 6:00-17:00, Tue-Fri 6:00-18:00, Sat 6:00-15:00, closed Sun, Fővám körút 1-3, district IX, M3: Kálvin tér).

Ráday Utca

While tourists blow their budgets a few blocks away on Váci utca, Budapesters hang out at Ráday utca's trendy, inventive eateries and pubs. As this is a prime pre-dinner drink spot, many places serve no food, only drinks. The outdoor seating along here is inviting on a balmy evening. Just take the M3/blue Metró line to Kálvin tér—a three-minute walk from the Great Market Hall—and stroll south (district IX). If you can't decide among the many options, consider these:

Soul Café is one of the best-regarded eateries along this drag, with a spacious yet romantic interior, lively sidewalk tables, and international fare with a few Hungarian options. Portions are big enough to split (1,000-Ft sandwiches before 18:00, 1,600-3,400-Ft main dishes anytime, salad options, open daily 12:00-24:00, Ráday utca 11-13, tel. 1/217-6986).

Café Intenzo hides around the corner from the start of Ráday utca, where it meets the busy ring road. Low-key and with a loyal local following, they serve Hungarian and international cuisine, either in a nondescript interior or out in a pleasant courtyard garden (1,100-Ft sandwiches, 1,200-1,900-Ft pastas, 1,900-3,300-Ft main dishes, daily 11:00-24:00, closed Sat-Sun if construction is still going on outside, Kálvin tér 9, tel. 1/219-5243).

Danube Promenade

The riverbank facing the castle is lined with hotel restaurants and permanently moored restaurant boats. You'll find bad service, mediocre food, mostly tourists, and sky-high prices...but the atmosphere and people-watching are marvelous.

Among the ships moored here, the hip, upscale **Spoon** (in front of the InterContinental Hotel next to the Chain Bridge) is the most appealing option—with pricey, elaborately prepared international cuisine with an emphasis on seafood, plus some Hungarian standards (3,500-6,000-Ft main dishes, daily 12:00-24:00, often booked for special events—call ahead to be sure it's open and to reserve a riverside table, Vigadó tér, dock #3, district V, M1: Vörösmarty tér, tel. 1/411-0933).

For a more affordable and more local experience, head a bit farther south, near the green Liberty Bridge. Along the embankment road called Belgrád Rakpart, you'll find a cluster of fun and lively ethnic restaurants (including good Italian at **Trattoria Toscana**, #13, and a mini-Santorini with Greek fare at **Taverna Dionysos**, #16).

Various companies run **dinner cruises** along the Danube (including Danube Legenda and Hungária Koncert, both of which offer a discount to Rick Steves readers—see pages 549 and 618). While these can be romantic, Budapest's real restaurants are too tempting to pass up. Instead, dine at your choice of eateries, then take the Danube Legenda nighttime cruise (see page 549).

Near St. István's Basilica

For the locations of these restaurants, see the map on page 628.

On Sas Utca, in Front of St. István's Basilica: The street called Sas utca, running along the bottom of the grand plaza in front of

St. István's, is lined with a handful of trendy, pricey, well-regarded, and somewhat snobby restaurants (such as Mokka and Dío). For something top-notch but a bit less expensive, head for **Café Kör** ("Circle"). This stylish but unsnooty eatery serves up mostly Hungarian and some Mediterranean fare in a tasteful, tight, one-room interior and at a few sidewalk tables. It prides itself on being friendly and providing a good value. Because it's beloved by local foodies, reservations are smart anytime—and essential on weekends (2,000-4,000-Ft main dishes, small portions for 30 percent less, good salads, daily specials, cash only, Mon-Sat 10:00-22:00, closed Sun, Sas utca 17, district V, between M3: Arany János utca and M1: Bajcsy-Zsilinszky út, tel. 1/311-0053).

Behind St. István's Basilica: **Belvárosi Lugas Étterem** is your cheap-and-charming, no-frills option. *Lugas* is a Hungarian word for a welcoming garden strewn with grapevines, and the cozy dining room—with a dozen tables of happy eaters under overhanging vines—captures that spirit. Or sit at one of their sidewalk tables outside on busy Bajcsy-Zsilinszky Boulevard. The food is simply good Hungarian (1,300-2,800-Ft main dishes, order starches separately, daily 12:00-23:30, directly behind and across the street from St. István's Basilica at Bajcsy-Zsilinszky út 15, district VI, M1: Bajcsy-Zsilinszky út, tel. 1/302-5393).

Near Andrássy Út and the Oktogon

Some of Budapest's best eateries are in this area, which is a hotbed for capable chefs and restaurateurs. For the locations of these eateries, see the map on page 625.

Franz Liszt Square (Liszt Ferenc Tér): Franz Liszt Square, a leafy park on the most interesting stretch of Andrássy út, boasts a stylish cluster of pricey, pretentious yuppie restaurants, many with outdoor seating (lively on a summer evening). This is the place for Budapesters (who can afford it) to see and be seen (main dishes 2,500-4,000 Ft). My favorite Liszt Square eatery, **Menza**

(the old communist word for "School Cafeteria"), wins the "Best Design" award. Recycling 1970s furniture and an orange-and-brown color scheme, it's a postmodern parody of an old communist café—half kitschy-retro, half brand-new feeling. When locals come in here, they can only chuckle and say, "Yep. This is how it was." With tasty and well-priced updated Hungarian cuisine, embroidered leather-bound menus, brisk but efficient service, breezy jazz on the soundtrack, and indoor or outdoor seating, it's a memorable spot (1,900-2,800-Ft main dishes, daily 10:00-24:00, halfway up Andrássy út at Liszt Ferenc tér 2, district VII, tel. 1/413-1482, www.menza.co.hu). If you like the Franz Liszt Square scene, you'll find more on Kertész utca beyond the end of the square, and in the "Broadway Quarter" near the Opera House (on Hajós utca and Nagymező utca).

Right on Andrássy út: **Klassz** is a trendy bistro with a similarly postmodern "eclectic-mod" aesthetic, both in its decor and its food (though the service can be standoffish). Serving up surprisingly affordable international/nouvelle cuisine with Hungarian flair, it's a favorite among Budapest's value-seeking foodies (1,700-3,500-Ft main dishes, Mon-Sat 11:30-23:00, Sun 11:30-18:00, Andrássy út 41, district VI, between M1: Opera and M1: Oktogon, no reservations possible—try to arrive by 19:00).

On the Great Boulevard: **Bock Bisztró,** run by a prominent Hungarian vintner from Villány, serves up traditional Hungarian staples with some modern flourishes in a casual-feeling wine bar with cork-filled tables. Pricey but unpretentious and well-regarded, with 250 different wines on the menu (including 60 by the glass), it's a good opportunity to sample food and wine from around the country (3,000-4,700-Ft main dishes, Mon-Sat 12:00-24:00, closed Sun, in the Corinthia Grand Royal Hotel, a couple of blocks west of the Oktogon on the Great Boulevard, Erzsébet körút 43-49, district VII, M1: Oktogon, right by Király utca stop on trams #4 and #6, tel. 1/321-0340).

On Nagymező utca: **Két Szerecsen** ("Two Saracens"), named for a historic coffee shop at this location a century ago that a trader filled with exotic goods, features eclectic and well-executed international cuisine—including Mediterranean and Asian. With good indoor and outdoor seating, reasonable prices, and relatively small portions, it's a reliable choice (800-1,400-Ft tapas, 1,600-1,900-Ft pastas, 1,400-2,400-Ft salads, 1,900-3,000-Ft main dishes, daily 9:00-24:00, a block off Andrássy út at Nagymező utca 14, district VI, M1: Opera, tel. 1/343-1984).

Italian: **Millennium da Pippo,** run by a Sicilian who speaks only Italian, greets you with a robust *"Buona sera!"* A neighborhood favorite for pasta and pizza, it's a handy choice near the House of Terror (1,900-2,600-Ft pizza and pastas, 2,800-4,700-Ft meat dishes, daily 12:00-24:00, Andrássy út 76, district VI, M1: Vörösmarty utca, tel. 1/374-0880).

Indian: Hungarians seem to have an affinity for Indian cooking, as both cuisines blend powerful spices. **Shalimar** hides in a stuffy cellar in a dreary neighborhood two blocks beyond the end of Franz Liszt Square. Everything about this place is unexceptional...except the food, which is my favorite for a break from pork and kraut. I can never resist the *murg makhani*...and I'm never disappointed. If the non-smoking section is filled with too-loud Americans, I sit with the young locals in the smoking section (1,800-2,600-Ft main dishes, half-portions for 40 percent less, daily 12:00-16:00 & 18:00-24:00, reservations smart on weekends, Dob utca 50, district VII, between M1: Oktogon and M2: Blaha Lujza tér, tel. 1/352-0297).

In City Park

These three touristy eateries cluster around the end of the lake behind the Millennium Monument in City Park (district XIV, M1: Hősök tere). All are open for both lunch and dinner. The first one is Budapest's best-known, fanciest splurge; the other two are more reasonable and casual, but still pretty pricey. For locations, see the map on page 593.

Gundel Restaurant has been *the* dining spot for VIPs and celebrities since 1894. The pricey place is an institution—President Bill Clinton ate here. Pope John Paul II didn't, but when his people phoned out for dinner, they called Gundel. The elegant main room is decorated with fine 19th-century Hungarian paintings and an Art Deco flair, while the more casual garden terrace is leafy and delightful (same menu for both). The Hungarian cuisine flirts with sophisticated international influences (4,000-10,000-Ft main courses, 24,000-40,000-Ft fixed-price meals). At lunch, choose from the same pricey à la carte items, or opt for a more affordable fixed-price meal (4,000-5,000 Ft). Sunday brunch, with a different theme each week, is popular (6,400 Ft, served 11:30-15:00). Reserve ahead for dinner, and ask to sit either near or far from the live "Gypsy" music (daily 12:00-15:00 & 18:30-24:00, music nightly, Állatkerti út 2, tel. 1/468-4040, www.gundel.hu). The dress code is formal: Jackets are required for men having dinner in the dining room, but not for lunch, for Sunday brunch, or if you sit outside. (You can borrow a free jacket at the door if you travel like me. Ties and dresses are not required.)

Gundel's **Borvendéglő** ("Wine Cellar") offers similar food in a more casual atmosphere at half the price. With an even more extensive wine list than the main restaurant upstairs, this option is ideal for wine-lovers. In addition to full dinners, including some "home-style" dishes (2,000-6,000 Ft, pricier 10,500-13,500-Ft tasting *menus* with wine pairings), they offer wine-and-cheese tastings (5,000-8,000 Ft; Mon-Sat 18:00-23:00, closed Sun, downstairs from Gundel at Állatkerti út 2, tel. 1/468-4041).

Robinson, stranded on an island in City Park's lake, is a hip, playful, mellow theme restaurant. With island-castaway ambience and more outdoor seating than indoor, it's made to order for lazing away a sunny afternoon at the park. The terrace and elegant, glassed-in dining room feature pricey international and Hungarian cuisine—or you can just sip a coffee or have a slice of cake on the terrace (3,000-6,000-Ft main dishes, 1,100-Ft desserts, daily 11:00-16:00 & 18:00-23:00, reserve ahead and ask for lakefront seating, Városligeti tó, tel. 1/422-0222).

In Buda

Eateries on Castle Hill are generally overpriced and touristy—as with Váci utca, locals never eat here. The Víziváros ("Water Town") neighborhood, between the castle and the river, is a bit better. Even if sleeping in Buda, try to dine in Pest—that's where you'll find the city's best restaurants. All of the restaurants listed below (except Szent Jupát) are in district I.

Castle Hill

If you must eat atop Castle Hill, and just want a quick bite, visit the handy, affordable **CBA** grocery store and its sandwich shop (see page 559). For coffee and cakes, try the historic **Ruszwurm** (described later, under "Budapest's Café Culture"). If you'd rather have a meal—and don't want to head down to Víziváros—try the following choice:

21 Magyar Vendéglő ("21 Hungarian Kitchen") features traditional Hungarian fare in a mod environment, with seating indoors or outside on pretty Fortuna utca (near the north end of the hill). While touristy and overpriced—as you'd expect in this location—it's well-regarded (2,000-2,900-Ft light meals, 3,500-5,000-Ft bigger meals, chalkboard specials, daily 11:00-24:00, Fortuna utca 21, tel. 1/202-2113).

Víziváros

My first listing is just beyond the southern tip of Castle Hill, near the Elisabeth Bridge. The others are in the heart of Víziváros, right between Castle Hill and the river. For locations, see the map on page 634.

Tabáni Terasz, between the castle and the white Elisabeth Bridge, is the best restaurant on this side of the river. They serve tasty Hungarian and international food to a mix of locals and tourists. The historic 250-year-old building has several seating options: in a cozy, classy drawing-room interior; on a terrace out front; in the inner courtyard; or in a wine cellar (2,500-4,000-Ft main dishes, daily 12:00-24:00, by the single-spired yellow church at Apród utca 10, Döbrentei stop on trams #19 and #41, tel. 1/201-1086).

Matróz Kocsma ("Sailor Inn") features specialties from up and down the Danube—mostly Hungarian, but also German, Transylvanian, Serbian, and more. Each dish's place of origin is noted in the menu. Very convenient to most of my recommended

Víziváros hotels, this eatery has jaunty nautical decor inside and out (2,200-4,300-Ft main dishes, daily 10:00-24:00, Halász utca 1, tel. 1/212-3817).

Pater Marcus is a well-established beer hall, serving up more than a hundred types of Belgian beers with Hungarian and international cuisine near the Chain Bridge. The outdoor alley seating is nothing special, but the cellar restaurant will transport you to Brussels (2,300-2,700-Ft main dishes, daily 12:00-24:00, Apor Péter utca 1, tel. 1/212-1612).

Batthyány Tér

This bustling square—the transportation hub for Víziváros—is overlooked by a recently renovated, late-19th-century market hall (today housing a supermarket and various shops). Several worthwhile, affordable eateries cluster around this square. Survey your options before settling in.

Nagyi Palacsintázója ("Granny's Pancakes")—just to the right of the market hall entrance—serves up cheap and tasty crêpes *(palacsinta)* to a local crowd (300-600-Ft sweet or savory crêpes, convenient 800-1,000-Ft combo-meals, communication can be challenging—ask for English menu, open 24 hours daily, Batthyány tér 5).

As you face the market hall, go up the street that runs along its left side (Markovits Iván utca) to reach more good eateries: At the end of the block on the right is **Éden Vegetarian Restaurant,** a self-service, point-and-shoot place (main dishes for less than 1,000 Ft, Mon-Thu 8:00-21:00, Fri 8:00-18:00, Sun 11:00-21:00, closed Sat, tel. 1/375-7575). And around the back side of the market hall is **Bratwursthäusle/Kolbászda,** a fun little beer hall/beer garden with specialties and blue-and-white checkerboard decor from Bavaria. Sit outside, or in the woody interior (1,000-Ft sausages, daily 11:00-23:00, Gyorskocsi utca 6, tel. 1/225-3674).

Near Széll Kálmán Tér

Szent Jupát is a reliable choice for large portions of basic, stick-to-your-ribs, traditional Hungarian cuisine (a relative rarity in Budapest). Vegetarians and weight-watchers need not apply. Just a couple of blocks off Széll Kálmán tér (the terminus for buses from the castle), near the corner of the giant Mammut shopping mall, it's a good place to head for an extremely filling meal after a busy day of Castle Hill sightseeing. Choose between the woody interior or the covered terrace beer garden out back (1,500-2,800 splittable main dishes, daily from 12:00 until very late, corner of Retek utca and Dékán utca, district II, M2: Széll Kálmán tér, tel. 1/212-2923).

Snacks and Light Meals

A popular snack is *lángos*—a savory deep-fried doughnut (similar to an elephant ear or Native American fry bread). Sold at stands on the street, the most typical versions are spread with cheese and sour cream, and sometimes topped with garlic. Some restaurants serve a fancier version (often with meat) as an entrée. The Lángos stand upstairs in the Great Market Hall is a local favorite (see page 639).

All around town, you'll see cheery **open-face sandwich shops,** each displaying a dozen or so tempting little treats in its front window—thin slices of bread piled with egg salad, veggies, cold cuts, cream spreads, cheese, salmon, affordable caviar, or other toppings for 160-280 Ft apiece. There's no English menu—just point at what looks good. Two sandwiches and a drink make a quick and healthy meal for less than $5 (they'll also box things to go for a classy picnic). There are various chains, but **Duran Szendvics** is the dominant operation (convenient location near the start of Andrássy út at Bajcsy-Zsilinszky út 7, district VII, M1: Bajcsy-Zsilinszky út, tel. 1/267-9624; also in Leopold Town at Október 6 utca 15, district V, M3: Arany János utca). These shops are generally open for lunch or an early dinner (Mon-Fri 8:00-18:00, Sat 8:00-14:00, Sun 8:00-12:00).

For quick, inexpensive, and very local grub, head for the chain called **Főzelékfaló Ételbár** (roughly, "Soup Slurper Eating Bar"). This self-service cafeteria dishes up simple fare to businesspeople on their lunch breaks. *Főzelék,* a simple soup that's thickened with roux (wheat flour mixed into lard or butter) and can be supplemented with various vegetables, is a staple of Hungarian home cooking. Go to the counter, choose your *főzelék* soup (various flavors, 300-400 Ft), then choose from a variety of basic meat dishes (chicken, pork, meatballs, and more for 500-1,000 Ft apiece; some English spoken, but pointing also works). A filling meal here typically runs 1,000-2,000 Ft. Because of the limited seating, most people get their grub to go (though the location near Andrássy út has fine outdoor tables). There are two locations in central Pest: One is just off Andrássy út in the "Broadway Quarter" (Mon-Fri 9:00-22:00, Sat 10:00-21:00, Sun 11:00-18:00, Nagymező utca 22, a block north of the Opera House, district VI, M1: Opera); the other is in a big building along the busy highway at Ferenciek tere (Mon-Fri 10:00-21:30, Sat 12:00-20:00, closed Sun, same building as the recommended Leo Panzió/Hotel, Kossuth Lajos utca 2A, district V, M3: Ferenciek tere). You'll also find them in the WestEnd City Center and Arena Plaza shopping malls.

Hummus Bar, while not authentically Hungarian, is a popular expat-run local chain that offers cheap Middle Eastern vegetarian meals to grateful backpackers and young locals. Their falafel is tasty (600 Ft for a pita-wrapped sandwich, combination plates for 800-1,500 Ft). I'd get it to go and enjoy it on a park bench to avoid the cramped interior (one location just beyond the end of Franz Liszt Square at Kertesz utca 39, district VII, M1: Oktogon, open daily 12:00-24:00; another in Leopold Town at Alkotmány utca 20, district V, M2: Kossuth tér, open daily 10:00-22:00; additional locations near Szabadság tér on Oktober 6 utca and at the Nyugati/Western train station).

For a fast snack, you'll see **Fornetti** stands everywhere (on street corners and Metró underpasses). This Hungary-based chain, which is becoming wildly popular across Central and Eastern Europe, sells small, tasty, freshly baked phyllo dough–based pastries by weight. They have both sweet and savory varieties. For a bite on the go, just point to what you want and hold your fingers up for how many you'd like of each type (150 Ft/100 grams). If you smell something heavenly in the Metró passages...it's probably a Fornetti.

Budapest's Café Culture

In the late 19th century, a vibrant café culture boomed here in Budapest, just as it did in Vienna and Paris. The *kávéház* ("coffeehouse") was a local institution. By 1900, Budapest had more than 600 cafés. In this crowded and fast-growing cityscape, a neighborhood café allowed urbanites to escape their tiny flats (or get a jolt of caffeine to power them through a 12-hour workday). Local people (many who'd moved to the city from the countryside) didn't want to pay to heat their homes during the day. So instead, for the price of a cup of coffee, they could come to a café to enjoy warmth, companionship, and loaner newspapers. Realizing that these neighborhood living rooms were breeding grounds for dissidents, the communists closed the cafés or converted them into *eszpresszós* (with uncomfortable stools instead of easy chairs) or *bisztrós* (stand-up fast-food joints with no chairs at all). Today, nostalgia is bringing back the *kávéház* culture—both as a place to get coffee and food, and as a social institution. While some serve only coffee and cakes, most serve light meals, and some serve full meals (as noted below).

On the Great Boulevard: **New York Café** makes the others listed here look like Starbucks. Originally built in 1894 as part of the "New York Palace" (and it really is palatial), this fanciful, over-the-top explosion of Neo-Baroque and Neo-Renaissance epitomizes the "mix and match, but plenty of everything" Historicist style of the day. In the early 20th century, artists, writers, and musicians came here to sip overpriced coffee and bask in opulence. After decades of neglect, Italian investors completely restored it in 2006, and now it once again welcomes guests. Tourists and gawkers

are not encouraged—you'll be stopped at the door and asked if you want a table. If you're up for a coffee break, this place might actually be worth an $8 cup of coffee or an overpriced meal. Read the fun history on the place-mat. While it's a few blocks beyond the tourist zone, it's worth the trip out here for the ultimate in turn-of-the-20th-century Budapest elegance (900-1,400-Ft coffee and hot chocolate drinks, 1,100-2,000-Ft desserts, 2,700-3,500-Ft pastas and light dishes, 4,000-6,000-Ft main dishes, 4,000-5,000-Ft breakfasts and 1,200-1,700-Ft à la carte items served 9:00-12:00, open daily 9:00-24:00, Erzsébet körút 9-11, district VII, tel. 1/886-6167). Take the M2/red Metró line to Blaha Lujza tér, and exit toward *Erzsébet körút pártalan oldal/6É Margit híd*. Bear left up the stairs, then turn right and walk a block. You can also take tram #4 or #6 from the Oktogon (at Andrássy út) around the Great Boulevard to the Wesselényi utca stop.

Two blocks up from Váci utca: **Centrál Kávéház** and **Gerlóczy Café,** both listed as restaurants on page 638, nicely recapture Budapest's early-1900s ambience, with elegant cakes and coffees, loaner newspapers on racks, and a management that encourages loitering. After the New York Café, these are Budapest's top two cafés.

On Vörösmarty tér: **Gerbeaud** (zhehr-BOH) isn't just a café—it's a 150-year-old landmark, the most famous gathering place in

Budapest. While it feels faded and dull compared to the others listed here, it's a local institution, and handy for people-watching (best on a sunny day from its out-door tables). I'd avoid the bad-value meals here, and just sip a coffee and nibble a cake (700-900-Ft coffee drinks, 850-Ft cakes, 1,700-3,100-Ft salads and sandwiches, daily 9:00-21:00, on Vörösmarty tér, district V, M1: Vörösmarty tér, tel. 1/429-9000). They also have a cellar pub downstairs and a separate Onyx restaurant around the side.

Near Ferenciek tere: **Jégbüfé** is where Pest urbanites get their quick, cheap, stand-at-a-counter fix of coffee and cakes. And for those feeling nostalgic for the communist days, little has changed at this typical *bisztró*. First, choose what you want at the counter.

Then try to explain it to the cashier across the aisle. Finally, take your receipt back to the appropriate part of the counter (figure out the four different zones: coffee, soft drinks, ice cream, cakes), trade your receipt for your goodie, go to the bar, and enjoy it standing up (cakes for under 300 Ft, Mon-Sat 7:00-21:30, Wed until 20:30, Sun 8:00-21:30, Ferenciek tere 10, district V, M3: Ferenciek tere). If you're not sure what to get, consider these traditional Hungarian favorites: *krémes* (KRAY-mesh) is custard sandwiched between delicate wafers. *Rákóczi turós* (RAH-koh-tsee TOO-rohsh) is a cake of sweet cottage cheese (a Hungarian dessert staple) with jam on top. *Dobos torta* (DOH-bohsh TOR-taw) has alternating layers of chocolate and vanilla cake topped with caramelized sugar. *Somlói galuska* (SHOM-lowee GAW-losh-kaw) is made of pieces of moist sponge cake soaked in rum and drizzled with chocolate. And *flódni* (FLOHD-nee)—in the pie section (in this area, you can pay directly at the counter)—has layers of nut paste and poppy seeds...another Hungarian dessert staple.

On Andrássy út, near the Opera House: Three fine and very different cafés are within a block of the Opera. The **Alexandra**

bookstore—in the Lotz Hall of the newly refurbished Párisi Nagy Áruház (Paris Department Store)—hides a spectacular gilded café that immerses you in turn-of-the-century splendor (walk straight in and go up the escalator). Because this prominent local chain encourages loitering, the service here is no-pressure, and the drinks and desserts are bargain-priced (300-500-Ft coffee drinks and cakes). Rounding out this café's appeal are the occasional live piano music, periodic evening concerts, and mirrors at either end that make the hall seem to go on forever (daily 10:00-22:00, Andrássy út 39, district VI, M1: Opera, tel. 1/461-5835). **Callas** features ideal outdoor seating facing the Opera House, and one of the finest Art Nouveau interiors in town, with gorgeous *Jugendstil* chandeliers. While their full meals are pricey (2,500-5,000 Ft), this is a wonderful spot on Andrássy út for a coffee break, a tasty dessert, or breakfast (ham and eggs plus coffee for 1,800 Ft, 400-800-Ft pastries, daily 10:00-24:00, Andrássy út 20, district VI, M1: Opera, tel. 1/354-0954). Across the street and a block toward the Oktogon, **Művész Kávéház** ("Artists Coffee House") is a classic café with 19th-century elegance, a hoity-toity high-ceilinged interior, snobby staff, and fine outdoor seating on Andrássy út. True to its name, this institution in the "Broadway Quarter" is a favorite after-rehearsal haunt of famous-to-Hungarians actors and musicians (700-900-Ft cakes, 1,100-2,000-Ft sandwiches, 2,000-3,000-Ft main dishes, 900-1,900-Ft breakfasts, daily 9:00-23:45, Andrássy út 29, district VI, M1: Opera, tel. 1/333-2116).

In Buda, atop Castle Hill: **Ruszwurm** lays claim to being Budapest's oldest café (since 1827). Tiny but classy, with old-style Biedermeier furnishings, it carries on its venerable reputation with pride. Its dead-central location—a block in front of St. Matthias' Church in the heart of the castle district—means that it has become a popular tourist spot (though it remains dear to locals' hearts). Look for gussied-up locals chatting here after the 10:00 Sunday-morning Mass at the church (600-Ft coffees, 400-600-Ft desserts, daily 10:00-19:00, Szentháromság utca 7, district I, tel. 1/375-5284).

Budapest Connections

By Train

Remember that Budapest has three stations: Keleti/Eastern, Nyugati/Western, and Déli/Southern (for all the details, see page 533). There's no telling which station each train will use, especially since it can change from year to year—always confirm carefully which station your train leaves from. For specific schedules, check http://bahn.hafas.de/bin/query.exe/en or http://elvira.mav-start .hu. You can also check Hungary's own timetable website, at http://elvira.mav-start.hu. For general rail information in Hungary, call 1/461-5400; for information about international trains, call 1/461-5500.

It's best to buy your ticket in advance at the MÁV ticket office in downtown Pest (see page 540). Be aware that ticket lines can be very long at the train stations; if you're buying a ticket there, it's smart to arrive with plenty of time to spare.

From Budapest by Train to: Eger (5/day direct, 2.5 hours, more with transfer in Füzesabony, usually from Budapest's Keleti/Eastern Station), **Pécs** (8/day direct, 3 hours; a few more connections possible with transfer at the suburban Budapest-Kelenföld station), **Sopron** (5/day direct, 3 hours, more with a transfer in Győr), **Visegrád** (trains arrive at Nagymaros-Visegrád station, across the river—take shuttle boat to Visegrád; hourly, 40-50 minutes, usually from Budapest's Nyugati/Western Station), **Esztergom** (hourly, 1.5 hours, usually from Budapest's Nyugati/Western Station), **Bratislava** (that's **Pozsony** in Hungarian, 5/day direct, 2.5 hours; more with transfers), **Vienna** (that's **Bécs** in Hungarian, every 2 hours direct, 3 hours; more with transfers), **Prague** (5/day direct, 7-7.5 hours, more with transfers in Győr and Vienna; plus 1 night train/day, 7.5 hours), **Kraków** (1/day direct, 9.25 hours; plus 1 direct night train/day, 10.5 hours; otherwise transfer in Břeclav,

Czech Republic), **Zagreb** (3/day direct, 6-7.5 hours), **Ljubljana** (1/day direct, plus 2/day with a transfer in Zagreb, 9.5 hours; also possible in 8.5 hours with changes at Vienna/Wien Meidling and Maribor; no convenient night train), **Munich** (1/day direct, 7.5 hours; plus 1 direct night train/day, 10 hours; otherwise transfer in Vienna and Salzburg), **Berlin** (1/day direct, 11.75 hours), and **Venice** (1 direct night train/day, 14.25 hours).

By Bus

Buses can be relatively inexpensive, but are typically slower and less convenient than trains. The only bus you're likely to take is the one to **Eger** (2/hour, 2 hours), which leaves from the Stadionok bus station (at the M2/red line stop of the same name). You can search bus schedules at the (Hungarian-only) website www.menetrendek.hu (click on "VOLÁN Menetrend").

Orange Ways Buses: For long-distance international journeys, consider Orange Ways buses, which offer affordable express connections from Budapest to **Bratislava** (1-4/day, 2.5 hours), **Vienna** (3-4/day, 3 hours), **Kraków** (5/week, 6.5 hours), **Prague** (1-4/day, 6.5-7.5 hours; this same bus sometimes continues to **Dresden** and **Berlin**), and more (www.orangeways.com).

By Boat

In the summer, Mahart runs daily high-speed hydrofoils up the Danube to **Vienna**. It's not particularly scenic, and it's slower than the train, but it's a fun alternative for nautical types. The boat leaves Budapest at 9:00 and arrives in Vienna at 15:30 (daily in Aug; May-July and Sept-early Oct Tue, Thu, and Sat only). On the return trip, a boat leaves from Vienna at 9:00 and reaches Budapest at 14:30 (daily in Aug; May-July and Sept-early Oct Wed, Fri, and Sun only). The trip costs €89 one-way between Budapest and Vienna; you can also ride between Budapest and the Slovak capital, **Bratislava** (€79 one-way). To confirm times and prices, and to buy tickets, contact Mahart in Budapest (tel. 1/484-4010, www.mahart passnave.hu) or DDSG Blue Danube in Vienna (tel. 01/58880, www.ddsg-blue-danube.at).

By Plane

For information about Budapest's Liszt Ferenc Airport, see "Arrival in Budapest—By Plane" on page 536.

Route Tips for Drivers

For pointers on driving into (and parking in) Budapest, see "Arrival in Budapest—By Car" on page 538. Remember, to use Hungary's expressways, you'll need to buy a toll sticker (see page 506). To get out of town, here are some pointers.

BUDAPEST

To Eger and Other Points East: Head out of the city center on Andrássy út, circling behind Heroes' Square to access Kós Károly sétány through the middle of City Park. You'll pass Széchenyi Baths on the left, then (exiting the park) go over the Hungária körút ring road, before getting on M3. This expressway zips you conveniently to Eger (exit #114 for Füzesabony; go north on road 33, then follow 3, then 25 into Eger).

To Bratislava, Vienna, and Other Points West: From central Pest, head over the Danube on the white, modern Elisabeth Bridge (Erzsébet híd). Once in Buda, the road becomes Hegyalja út; simply follow *Wien* signs to get on M1.

EGER

Eger (EH-gehr) is a county-seat town in northern Hungary, with about 60,000 people and a thriving teacher-training college. While many travelers have never heard of Eger, among Hungarians, the town has various claims to fame. It's a bishopric whose powerful bishops have graced it with gorgeous churches. It has some of the best and most beloved spas in this hot-water-crazy country (including the excellent Salt Hill Thermal Spa in the nearby countryside). And, perhaps most of all, Eger makes Hungarians proud as the town that, against all odds, successfully held off the Ottoman advance into Europe in 1552. This stirring history makes Eger the mecca of Hungarian school field trips. If the town is known internationally for anything, it's for the surrounding wine region (its best-known red wine is Bull's Blood, or Egri Bikavér).

And yet, refreshingly, enchanting Eger remains mostly off the

tourist trail. Egerites go about their daily routines amidst lovely Baroque buildings, watched over by one of Hungary's most important castles. Everything in Eger is painted with vibrant colors, and even the communist apartment blocks seem quaint. The sights are few but fun, the ambience is great, and strolling is a must. It all comes together to make Eger an ideal introduction to small-town Hungary.

Planning Your Time

Mellow Eger is a fine side-trip from Budapest. It's doable round-trip in a single day (2.5 hours by train or 2 hours by bus each way), but it's much more satisfying and relaxing to spend the night.

A perfect day in Eger begins with a browse through the very local-feeling market and a low-key ramble on the castle ramparts. Then head to the college building called the Lyceum to visit the library and astronomy museum, and climb up to the thrillingly low-tech camera obscura. Take in the mid-day organ concert in the cathedral across the street from the Lyceum (mid-May–mid-Oct only). In the afternoon, unwind on the square or, better yet, at a thermal bath (in Eger, or at the Salt Hill Thermal Spa in nearby Egerszalók). If you need more to do, consider a drive into the countryside (including visits to local vintners—get details at TI). Round out your day with dinner on Little Dobó Square, or a visit to Eger's touristy wine caves in the Sirens' Valley.

Orientation to Eger

(area code: 36)

Eger Castle sits at the top of the town, hovering over Dobó Square (Dobó István tér). This main square is divided in half by Eger Creek, which bisects the town. Two blocks west of Dobó Square is the main pedestrian drag, Széchenyi utca, where you'll find the Lyceum and the cathedral. A few blocks due south from the castle (along Eger Creek) are Eger's various spas and baths.

Tourist Information

Eger's TI (TourInform) offers a free brochure and town map, as well as piles of other brochures about the city and region. They can't book rooms, but they can help you find one—or anything else you're looking for (mid-June–mid-Sept Mon-Fri 9:00-18:00, Sat-Sun 9:00-13:00 & 15:00-19:00; mid-Sept–mid-June Mon-Fri 9:00-17:00, Sat 9:00-13:00, closed Sun; Bajcsy-Zsilinszky utca 9, tel. 36/517-715, www.eger.hu or www.egerpanorama.hu). You can also get online here (200 Ft/30 minutes).

Arrival in Eger

By Train: Eger's tiny train station is a 20-minute walk south of the center. The baggage-deposit desk is by track 1, between the WCs (500 Ft/day, daily 7:00-19:00, attendant often waits in the adjacent *büfé*). For those in need of Hungarian cash, the closest ATM is at the Spar grocery store just up the street (turn left out of station, walk about 100 yards, and look for red-and-white supermarket on your right; ATM is around front).

Taxis generally wait out front to take new arrivals into town

EGER

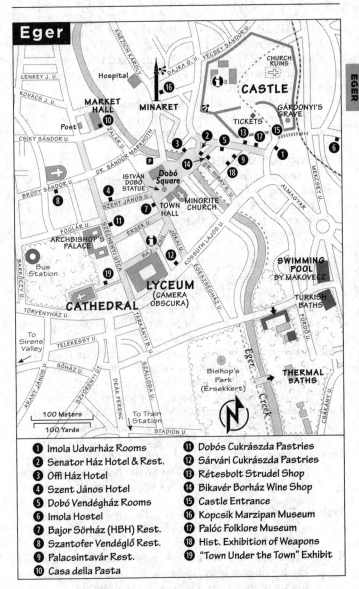

Eger

1. Imola Udvarház Rooms
2. Senator Ház Hotel & Rest.
3. Offi Ház Hotel
4. Szent János Hotel
5. Dobó Vendégház Rooms
6. Imola Hostel
7. Bajor Sörház (HBH) Rest.
8. Szantofer Vendéglő Rest.
9. Palacsintavár Rest.
10. Casa della Pasta
11. Dobós Cukrászda Pastries
12. Sárvári Cukrászda Pastries
13. Rétesbolt Strudel Shop
14. Bikavér Borház Wine Shop
15. Castle Entrance
16. Kopcsik Marzipan Museum
17. Palóc Folklore Museum
18. Hist. Exhibition of Weapons
19. "Town Under the Town" Exhibit

(1,000-1,400 Ft). Even in little Eger, it's always best to take a taxi with a company name and number posted.

To catch the **bus** toward the center, go a block straight out of the station. Buses #11 and #12 cut about 10 minutes off the walk into town (220 Ft, buy ticket from driver; or 150 Ft if you buy it at the train station newsstand facing track 1—ask for *helyijárat buszj-egy*). Get off the bus when you reach the big yellow cathedral.

To **walk** all the way, leave the station straight ahead, turn right with the road, and then continue straight (on busy Deák Ferenc utca) until you run into the cathedral. With your back to the cathedral entry, the main square is two blocks ahead of you, then a block to the left.

By Car: In this small town, most hotels will provide parking or help you find a lot. For a short visit, the most central lot is behind the department store on Dobó Square.

Getting Around Eger

Everything of interest in Eger is within walking distance. But a taxi can be helpful to reach outlying sights, including the Sirens' Valley wine caves and the Salt Hill Thermal Spa in Egerszalók (taxi meter starts at 250 Ft, then around 250 Ft/km; try City Taxi, tel. 36/555-555).

Helpful Hints

Phoning: Confusingly, Hungary's country code is the same as Eger's city code (36). This means that if you're calling from another country, you'll have to dial 36 twice. For example, to call my favorite Eger hotel from the US, I'd dial 011-36-36-411-711.

Blue Monday: Note that the castle museums and the Lyceum are closed on Mondays. But you can still visit the cathedral (and enjoy its organ concert), swim in the thermal bath, explore the market, see the castle grounds, and enjoy the local wine.

Organ Concert: Daily from mid-May to mid-October, Hungary's second-biggest organ booms out a glorious 30-minute concert in the cathedral (700 Ft, Mon-Sat at 11:30, Sun at 12:45).

Internet Access: The TI has one terminal (200 Ft/30 minutes; see "Tourist Information," earlier). The town's many Internet cafés come and go—ask the TI or your hotelier for current options.

Walking Tours: The TI offers an affordable town walking tour in English once weekly in summer (300 Ft, likely Sat at 10:00, early June-Sept only).

Tourist Train: A hokey little tourist train leaves the main square at the top of each hour. It does a circuit around town, then heads out to the Sirens' Valley wine caves (600 Ft, 50-minute trip).

Sights in Eger

▲▲Dobó Square (Dobó István Tér)

Dobó Square is the heart of Eger. In most towns this striking, the main square is packed with postcard stalls and other tourist traps.

Refreshingly, Eger's square seems mostly packed with Egerites. Ringed by pretty Baroque buildings, decorated with vivid sculptures depicting the city's noble past, and watched over by Eger's historic castle, this square is one of the most pleasant spots in Hungary.

The statue in the middle is **István Dobó** (EESHT-vahn DOH-boh), the square's namesake and Eger's greatest hero, who defended the city—and all of Hungary—from an Ottoman invasion in 1552 (see his story in the sidebar). Next to Dobó is his co-commander, István Mekcsey. And right at their side is one of the brave women of Eger—depicted here throwing a pot down onto the attackers.

Dominating the square is the exquisitely photogenic pink

Minorite Church—often said to be the most beautiful Baroque church in Hungary. The shabby interior (free entry) is less interesting, but has some appealing details. Notice that each of the hand-carved wooden pews has a different motif. Pay close attention to the side altars that flank the nave: The first set (left and right) are 3-D illustrations, painted to replicate the wood altars that burned in a fire; the next set are real. And looking up at the faded ceiling frescoes, you'll see (in the second one from the entrance) the church's patron: St. Anthony of Padua, who's preaching God's word to the fishes after the townspeople refused to hear him.

Next to the Minorite Church is the Town Hall, then an old-fashioned pharmacy. The **monument** in front of the Town Hall also commemorates the 1552 defense of Eger: one Egerite against two Ottoman soldiers, reminding us of the townspeople's bravery despite the odds.

Use the square to orient yourself to the town. Behind the statue of Dobó is a bridge over the stream that bisects the city. Just before you reach that bridge, look to the left and you'll see the northernmost Ottoman **minaret** in Europe—once part of a mosque, it's now a tourist attraction. Across the bridge is the charming **Little Dobó Square** (Kis-Dobó tér), home to the town's best hotels, its outdoor dining zone, and a handy and atmospheric opportunity to sample local wines at the Bikavér Borház wine shop (see page 669). Hovering above Little Dobó Square is Eger Castle;

EGER

István Dobó and the Siege of Eger

In the 16th century, Ottoman invaders swept into Hungary. They easily defeated a Hungarian army—in just two hours—

at the Battle of Mohács in 1526. When Buda and Pest fell to the Ottomans in 1541, all of Europe looked to Eger as the last line of defense. István Dobó and his second-in-command, István Mekcsey, were put in charge of Eger's forces. They prepared the castle (which still overlooks the square) for a siege and waited.

On September 11, 1552—after a summer spent conquering more than 30 other Hungarian fortresses on their march northward—40,000 Ottomans arrived in Eger. Only about 2,000 Egerites (soldiers, their wives, and their children) remained to protect their town. The Ottomans expected an easy victory, but the siege dragged on for 39 days. Eger's soldiers fought valiantly, and the women of Eger also joined the fray, pouring hot tar down on the Ottomans...everyone pitched in. A Hungarian officer named Gergely Bornemissza, sent to reinforce the people of Eger, startled the Ottomans with all manner of clever and deadly explosives. One of his brilliant inventions was a "fire wheel"—a barrel of gunpowder studded with smaller jars of explosives, which they'd light and send rolling downhill to wreak havoc until the final, deadly explosion. Ultimately, the Ottomans left in shame, Eger was saved, and Dobó was a national hero.

The unfortunate epilogue: The Ottomans came back in 1596 and, this time, succeeded in conquering an Eger Castle guarded by unmotivated mercenaries. The Ottomans sacked the town and then controlled the region for close to a century.

In 1897, a castle archaeologist named Géza Gárdonyi moved from Budapest to Eger, where tales of the siege captured his imagination. Gárdonyi wrote a book about István Dobó and the 1552 Siege of Eger called *Egri Csillagok* ("Stars of Eger," translated into English as *Eclipse of the Crescent Moon,* available at local bookstores and souvenir stands). The book—a favorite of many Hungarians—is taught in schools, keeping the legend of Eger's heroes alive today.

to get there, hang a right at the Senator Ház Hotel and go up Dobó utca. (All of these places are described later in more detail.)

Now face in the opposite direction, with the castle at your back. On your right is a handy department store (with an ATM by the door). At the bottom end of this square, various pedestrian shopping lanes lead straight ahead two short blocks to Eger's main "walking street," Széchenyi utca (with the cathedral and the Lyceum at its left end). To reach the TI, jog left at the end of this square, then right onto Bajcsy-Zsilinszky utca (TI one block ahead on right). The market hall is in the opposite direction: Leave Dobó Square to the right (on Zalár József utca, with department store on your right-hand side; you'll see the market hall on the left).

▲Dobó Utca

This street, which leads to the entrance of the castle (up the street to the right of Senator Ház Hotel), is lined with colorful shops and attractions. You'll encounter these sights in the following order as you head from the main square toward the castle:

The **Rétesbolt** strudel shop (#10) offers a delightful chance to watch them make mouthwatering strudel...and then eat one (360 Ft, daily 10:00-17:00).

The **Historical Exhibition of Weapons** (#9, actually just down Fazola Henrik utca) features centuries of Eger armaments: clubs, rifles, and everything in between (400 Ft, Tue-Sun 10:00-18:00 except in winter 12:00-17:00, closed Mon, 450-Ft booklet labels weapons in English, 1,600-Ft English book gives a full weapon-by-weapon tour).

The **Palóc Folklore Museum** (#12) displays a handful of traditional tools, textiles, ceramics, costumes, and pieces of furniture (200 Ft, no English information, May-Sept Tue-Sun 9:15-17:15, closed Mon and Oct-April).

The **wine-tasting courtyard** (#18) features a different local winery each week from May through October. Pop into the brightly lit vaulted tasting room in the back to try a glass (cheap and good).

The **antique shop** (at #24) is worth a peek. If musty old things from the communist era—a painting of Lenin or a classic old radio—are cluttering your attic, you can sell them here.

▲Eger Castle (Egri Vár)

This castle is Hungary's Alamo, where István Dobó defended Eger from the Ottomans in 1552—as depicted in the relief just outside the entry gate. These days, it's usually crawling with schoolchildren on field trips from all over the country. Every Hungarian sixth grader reads and enjoys the thrilling *Eclipse of the Crescent Moon*, which explains the heroic siege of Eger.

The great St. István—Hungary's first Christian king—founded a church on this hill a thousand years ago. The church was destroyed by Tatars in the 13th century, and this fortress was built to repel another attack.

The castle grounds feature two small museums. The **history museum** (in the top floor of the main building of the garrison) is the best of its kind in town, with lots of artifacts and good English descriptions. The **picture gallery** (top floor of building to the left as you enter the castle) is worth a few minutes, with paintings giving you a look at traditional life in Hungary.

On the **grounds,** you'll see the remains of a once-grand cathedral and a smaller rotunda dating from the days of St. István (10th or 11th century). The underground **casements** (tunnels through the castle walls, which include the Heroes' Hall with the symbolic grave of István Dobó) are accessible only by guided tour.

For those of us who didn't grow up hearing the legend of István Dobó, the complex is hard to appreciate, and English information is sparse. Most visitors find that the most rewarding plan is to stroll up, wander around the grounds, and enjoy the view overlooking the town (find the minaret and other landmarks).

Cost: While a 700-Ft "walking ticket" gets you into the castle grounds only (free Nov-March), the 1,400-Ft ticket includes the big castle sights (history museum, art gallery, casements tour—see next).

Tours: The underground casements and Heroes' Hall are only accessible by a one-hour Hungarian tour, with some posted information in English (included in ticket price, tours depart frequently in summer, sporadically off-season).

Hours: Castle grounds—April-Aug daily 8:00-20:00, Sept until 19:00, March and Oct until 18:00, Nov-Feb until 17:00; castle museums—Tue-Sun 9:00-17:00, closed Mon. General castle info: tel. 36/312-744, www.div.iif.hu.

Other Castle Sights: The castle hosts a few privately run exhibits (with sporadic hours and prices).

The **waxworks,** or "Panoptikum" (500 Ft, daily April-Oct 9:00-18:00, Nov-March 9:00-16:00), while kind of silly, is fun for kids or those who never really grew up. Think of it as a very low-tech, walk-through *Ottomans of the Caribbean.* You'll see a handful of eerily realistic heroes and villains from the siege of Eger (including István Dobó himself and the leader of the Ottomans sitting in his colorful tent). Notice the exaggerated Central Asian features

N

of the Egerites—a reminder that the Magyars were more Asian than European. A visit to the waxworks lets you scramble through a segment of the tunnels that run inside the castle walls (a plus since it's not really worth it to wait around through the similar, Hungarian-language casements tour).

Additional sights include an **archery** exhibit (look for archers just inside inner gate in summer, and pay them for the chance to shoot old-fashioned bows and crossbows—1 arrow/100 Ft, 5 arrows/400 Ft, 10 arrows/700 Ft); the **mint,** with a display of former currencies and a chance to make your own souvenir (entry-500 Ft, souvenirs extra, in cellar of Gothic palace); and **temporary exhibits** in the pink round tower.

Getting There: To reach the castle from Dobó Square, cross the bridge toward Senator Ház Hotel, then jog right around the hotel, turning right onto Dobó utca (with its own set of attractions, described earlier). Take this street a few blocks until it swings down to the right; the ramp up to the castle is across the little park to your left.

On Széchenyi Utca

▲▲**Lyceum (Líceum)**—In the mid-18th century, Bishop Károly Eszterházy wanted a university in Eger, but Habsburg Emperor

Josef II refused to allow it. So instead, Eszterházy built the most impressive teacher-training college on the planet, and stocked it with the best books and astronomical equipment that money could buy. The Lyceum still trains local teachers (enrollment: about 2,000). The halls of the Lyceum are also roamed by tourists who have come to visit its classic old library, and its astronomy museum, with a fascinating camera obscura. The library and museum are tucked away in the big, confusing building; a flier that comes with your ticket helps you find your way.

Cost and Hours: Library—800 Ft, museum—850 Ft; both open April-Sept daily 9:30-15:30; Oct-March Tue-Sun 9:30-15:30, closed Mon; Eszterházy tér 1, at south end of Széchenyi utca at intersection with Kossuth utca, enter through main door across from cathedral and buy tickets just inside and to the left.

Ⓞ Self-Guided Tour: First, visit the old-fashioned **library** one floor up (from the main entry hall, cut through the middle of the courtyard, go up the stairs, and look for room 223, marked *Bibliothek*). This library houses 60,000 books (here and in the two adjoining rooms, with several stacked two deep). Dr. Imre Surányi and his staff have spent the last decade cataloging these books. This is no easy task, since they're in over 30 languages—from Thai to Tagalog—and are shelved according to size, rather than topic. You'll likely meet the resident tour guide, Katalin Bódi, who's happy to show you the collection's most prized pieces, and explain how only one percent of the books

are in Hungarian—but half of them are in Latin. The shelves are adorned with golden seals depicting great minds of science, philosophy, and religion. Marvel at the gorgeous ceiling fresco, dating from 1778. To thank the patron of this museum, say *köszönöm* to the guy in the second row up, to the right of the podium (above the entry door, second from left, not wearing a hat)—that's Bishop Károly Eszterházy.

Turn right as you leave the library to find the staircase that leads up the Astronomical Tower (follow signs several flights up) to the **Astronomical Museum.** Some dusty old stargazing instruments occupy one room, as well as a meridian line in the floor (a dot of sunlight dances along this line each day around noon). Across the hall is a fun, interactive **magic room,** where you can try out scientific experiments—such as using air pressure to make a ball levitate or sending a mini "hot-air balloon" up to the ceiling.

A few more flights up is the Lyceum's treasured **camera obscura**—one of just two originals surviving in Europe (the other is in Edinburgh). You'll enter a dark room around a big, bowl-like canvas, and the guide will fly you around the streets of Eger (presentations about 2/hour, maybe more when busy). Fun as it is today, this camera must have astonished viewers when it was built in 1776—well before anyone had seen "moving pictures." It's a bit of a huff to get up here (nine flights of stairs, 302 steps)—but the camera obscura, and the actual view of Eger from the outdoor terrace just outside, are worth it.

▲▲Eger Cathedral—Eger's 19th-century bishops peppered the city with beautiful buildings, including the second-biggest church in Hungary (after Esztergom's—see page 604). With a quirky, sumptuous, Baroque-feeling interior, Eger's cathedral is well worth a visit.

Cost and Hours: Free entry, open long hours daily. The cathedral is the big, can't-miss-it yellow building at Pyrker János tér 1, just off Széchenyi utca.

⊘ Self-Guided Tour: Eger Cathedral was built in the 1830s

by an Austrian archbishop who had previously served in Venice, and who thought Eger could use a little more class. The colonnaded Neoclassical **facade,** painted a pretty Habsburg yellow, boasts some fine Italian sculpture. As you walk up the main stairs, you'll pass saints István and László—Hungary's first two Christian kings—and then the apostles Peter and Paul.

Enter the cathedral and walk to the first collection box, partway down the nave. Then, turning back to face the door, look up

at the ornate **ceiling fresco:** On the left, it shows Hungarians in traditional dress; and on the right, the country's most important historical figures. At the bottom, you see this cathedral, celestially connected with St. Peter's in Rome (opposite). This symbol of devotion to the Vatican was a brave state-

ment when it was painted in 1950. The communists were closing churches in other small Hungarian towns, but the Eger archbishop had enough clout to keep this one open.

Continue to the transept, stopping directly underneath the main dome. The **stained-glass windows** decorating the north and south transepts were donated to the cathedral by a rich Austrian couple to commemorate the 1,000th anniversary of Hungary's conversion to Christianity—notice the dates 1000 (when St. István converted the Magyars to Christianity) and 2000.

As you leave, notice the enormous **organ**—Hungary's second-largest—above the door. In the summer, try to catch one of the cathedral's daily half-hour organ concerts (700 Ft, mid-May-mid-Oct Mon-Sat at 11:30, Sun at 12:45, no concerts off-season).

Nearby: If you walk up Széchenyi utca from here, you'll see the fancy Archbishop's Palace on your left—still home to Eger's archbishop.

Just to the right of the steps leading up to the cathedral is the entrance to the...

EGER

Town Under the Town (Város a Város Alatt)—Here you can take a 45-minute guided tour of the archbishop's former wine-cellar network, which honeycombs the land behind the Archbishop's Palace (1,000 Ft, departs at the top of each hour, 5-person minimum, you'll get a little English sprinkled in with the Hungarian, daily April-Sept 10:00-20:00, Oct-March 10:00-17:00, last tour departs one hour before closing, www.varosavarosalatt.hu).

North of Dobó Square

▲**Market Hall (Piaccsarnok)**—Wandering Eger's big indoor

market will give you a taste of local life—and maybe some samples of local food, too. It's packed with Egerites choosing the very best of the fresh produce. Tomatoes and peppers of all colors and sizes are abundant—magic ingredients that give Hungarian food its kick (opens daily at 6:00; while open most afternoons, it's best in the mornings).

Minaret—Once part of a mosque, this slender, 130-foot-tall min-

aret represents the century of Ottoman rule that left its mark on Eger and all of Hungary. The little cross at the top symbolizes the eventual Christian victory over Hungary's Ottoman invaders. You can climb the minaret's 97 steps for fine views of Eger, but it's not for those scared of heights or enclosed spaces. Because the staircase was designed for one man to climb to call the community to prayer, it's very tight. To avoid human traffic jams, they allow groups of visitors in about twice an hour.

Cost and Hours: 200 Ft, April-Oct daily 10:00-18:00, closed Nov-March; if it's locked, ask around for the key.

▲**Kopcsik Marzipan Museum (Kopcsik Marcipánia)**—Lajos

Kopcsik is a master sculptor who's found his medium: marzipan. Kopcsik can make this delicate mixture of sugar, ground almonds, egg whites, and edible paints take virtually any form. Pass through the entryway, filled with awards, to enter this surprisingly engaging little museum. You'll see several remarkable, colorful examples of Kopcsik's skill: sword, minaret, gigantic wine bottle, suitcase, Russian stacking dolls, old-timey phonograph, grandfather clock, giant bell...and paintings galore (including Van Gogh's sunflowers and Picasso's musicians). The list literally goes on for four pages. Who'd have thought you could do so much with candy? Don't miss the European map celebrating May 1, 2004, when much of Eastern Europe joined the EU; and the "Baroque room"—furnished and decorated entirely in marzipan.

Cost and Hours: 800 Ft, ask for printed English information; daily 10:00-18:00, Harangöntő utca 4, tel. 36/412-626.

Experiences in Eger

Aqua Eger

Swimming and water sports are as important to Egerites as good wine. They're proud that many of Hungary's Olympic medalists in aquatic events have come from this county. The men's water polo team took the gold for Hungary at each of the last three Olympics, and swimmer László Cseh might have been a multiple gold medalwinner at Beijing in 2008 if he hadn't been swimming next to Michael Phelps. The town's Bitskey Aladár swimming pool—arguably the most striking building in this part of Hungary—is practically a temple to water sports.

Eger also has two of the most appealing thermal bath complexes outside of Budapest: one right in town, and the other a few miles away (near the village of Egerszalók). Budapest offers classier bath experiences, but the Eger options are more modern and a bit more accessible, and allow you to save your Budapest time for big-city sights. Before you go, be sure to read "Taking the Waters" on page 606.

In Eger

Note that you can't rent a swimsuit or a towel at either of these places; bring both with you, along with shower sandals for the locker room (if you've got them).

Bitskey Aladár Pool—This striking swimming pool was

designed by Imre Makovecz, the father of Hungary's Organic architectural style. Some Eger taxpayers resented the pool's big price tag, but it left the city with a truly distinctive building befitting its love of water sports. You don't need to be an architecture student to know that the pool is special. It's worth the five-minute

Hungary's Organic Architecture

In recent years, a unique, eye-catching style of architecture has caught on in Hungary: Organic. The Hungarian brand of Organic was developed and championed by Imre Makovecz (1935-2011). After being blacklisted by the communists for his nationalistic politics, Makovecz was denied access to building materials, so he taught himself to make impressive structures with nothing more than sticks and rocks. Makovecz was inspired by Transylvanian village architecture: whitewashed walls with large, overhanging mansard roofs to maximize attic space (resembling a big mushroom).

After the fall of the regime, Makovecz became Hungary's premier architect—but he still kept things simple. He believed that a building should be a product of its environment, rather than a cookie-cutter copy. Organic buildings use indigenous materials (especially wood) and take on unusual forms—often inspired by animals or plants—that blend in with the landscape. Organic buildings look like they're rising up out of the ground, rather than plopped down on top of it. You generally won't find this back-to-nature style in big cities like Budapest; Makovecz preferred to work in small communities such as Eger (see photo on previous page) instead of working for corporations. For more on Makovecz, visit www.makovecz.hu.

Organic architecture has become *the* post-communist style in Hungary. Even big supermarket chains are now imitating Makovecz—a sure sign of architectural success.

walk from Dobó Square just to take a look. Oh, and you can swim in it, too.

Cost and Hours: 970 Ft, Mon-Fri 6:00-21:30, Sat-Sun 7:30-18:00, follow Eger Creek south from Dobó Square to Frank Tivadar utca, tel. 36/511-810, www.egertermal.hu.

▲**Eger Thermal Bath (Eger Thermálfürdő)**—For a refreshing break from the sightseeing grind, consider a splash at the spa. This is a fine opportunity to try a Hungarian bath: relatively accessible (men and women are clothed and together most of the time), but frequented mostly by locals.

Cost and Hours: 1,700 Ft; July-Aug Sun-Wed 8:30-18:30, Thu-Sat 8:30-23:00; May-June and Sept Sun-Wed 8:30-18:30, Thu-Sat 8:30-21:00; Oct-April Sun-Wed 9:00-18:30, Thu-Sat 9:00-21:00; Petőfi tér 2, tel. 36/510-558, www.egertermal.hu.

Getting There: It's easy to reach and

within a 10-minute walk of most hotels. From Dobó Square, follow the stream four blocks south (look for signs for *Strand*). You'll come first to the main entrance (on the left after crossing busy street, roughly facing the fancy swimming-pool building on Petőfi tér). However, as this entrance is a bit more confusing and farther from the best pools, I'd use the side entrance instead: Continue following the stream as it runs along the side of a park (to the right of the main entrance building). Soon you'll see the side entrance to the bath on your left over a bridge.

Entry Procedure: You'll enter and be given a little barcode bracelet, which acts as your ticket (keep it on until you leave). If you use the main entrance, you'll change in the blocky white buildings just inside the entry (get a hanger from the desk, change in one of the free little cabins, then bring your clothes-laden hanger back for them to store it, 400 Ft extra to use safe-deposit box). At the better side entrance, you'll show your bracelet to get a key to a locker (1,000-Ft deposit per key, which will be refunded; private changing cabins available in the locker room for no extra charge). After you change and stow your stuff, put the key around your wrist, then join the fun.

Taking the Waters: There's a sprawling array of different pools, each one thoughtfully described in English and labeled with its depth and temperature. From the main entrance, you'll see them in this order: big and small warm pools, a very hot sulfur pool (where Egerites sit peacefully, ignore the slight stink, and supposedly feel their arthritis ebb away), the adventure bath, a kids' pool with splashy slide fun, and a lap pool (some of these are closed off-season). The best part is the green-domed, indoor-outdoor adventure bath, right at the side entrance. Its cascades, jets, bubbles, geysers, and powerful current pool will make you feel like a kid again.

Near Eger, in Egerszálok

▲▲**Salt Hill Thermal Spa**—This spa complex, in the hills about four miles outside of Eger, is the most modern and accessible thermal bath I've visited in Hungary. While it lacks the old-fashioned class of the Budapest options, it trumps them in user-friendliness and overall soggy fun.

For decades, Egerites would come to this "salt hill" (a natural terraced formation caused by mineral-rich spring water running down the hillside) in the middle of nowhere and cram together to baste in pools of hot water. Then the developers arrived. Today, those same simple pools are still used by local purists, but a giant new hotel and spa complex has been built nearby. With 12 indoor pools and five outdoor ones—many cleverly overlapping one another on several levels—these cutting-edge baths are worth the trip outside of Eger.

Ideal for kids but fun for anyone, the complex has pools with mineral water as well as plain old swimming-pool water.

Cost and Hours: 2,500 Ft for up to 2.5 hours, additional 600 Ft per half-hour after that, daily maximum payment of 4,300 Ft. Entry is discounted to 1,350 Ft after 17:00 on Mon-Fri. You'll pay 1,500 Ft extra to access "sauna world," with five different saunas. Towel rental is 1,000 Ft; massages and other treatments also available. Open June-Aug daily 10:00-20:00, likely less off-season—call ahead to check. Tel. 36/688-500, www.egerszalokfurdo.hu.

Getting There: It's about a mile outside the village of Egerszalók, which is itself about three miles from Eger. You can take a public **bus** from Eger's bus station to the baths (take bus going toward Demjén, you want the *Egerszalók Gyógyfürdő* stop—tell the bus driver "EH-gehr-sah-lohk FEWR-dur"—just after leaving the town of Egerszalók, 9/day Mon-Fri, 2/day Sat, 1/day Sun, 17-minute trip, 200 Ft). Check the return bus information carefully (especially on weekends, when frequency plummets). Or you can take a **taxi** from Eger (about 2,500 Ft; tel. 36/555-555 for a return taxi from Egerszalók). Here's a fun and very hedonistic afternoon plan: Take the bus or taxi to the spa, taxi back to Eger's Sirens' Valley for some wine-cave hopping, then taxi back to your Eger hotel.

Note: The humble little baths beside the parking lot are a whole other story—fun but very traditional (just sitting in hot water). Don't mistake these for the new complex. To find the big one, continue walking about five minutes beyond the parking lot to the hotel.

Entry Procedure: You pay and are given a watch-like wristband, which serves as your ticket, locker key, and credit card. Press it against a nearby computer screen to find out which locker you've been assigned. Find that locker in the common locker room (you can change in one of the private cabins), stow your stuff there, and have fun. Take some time to explore the sprawling complex. Everything is labeled in English, and each pool is clearly marked with the depth and temperature (in Celsius). You can buy food or drinks with the wristband, too—it's keeping tabs so you can be charged when you leave.

Eger Wine

Eger is at the heart of one of Hungary's best-known wine regions, internationally famous for its **Bull's Blood** (Egri Bikavér). You'll likely hear various stories as to how Bull's Blood got its name during the Ottoman siege of Eger. My favorite version: The Ottomans were amazed at the ferocity displayed by the Egerites, and wondered what they were drinking that boiled their blood and stained their beards so red...it must be potent stuff. Local merchants, knowing that the Ottomans were Muslim and couldn't drink alcohol, told them it was bull's blood. The merchants made a buck, and the name stuck.

Creative as these stories are, they're all bunk—the term dates only from 1851. Egri Bikavér is a blend (everyone has their own recipe), so you generally won't find it at small producers. Cabernet Sauvignon, Merlot, Kékfrankos, and Kékoportó are the most commonly used grapes.

Of course, there's so much more to Hungarian wines than Bull's Blood—and the Eger region produces many fine options. For all the details, see "Hungarian Wines" on page 520.

While it would be enjoyable to drive around the Hungarian countryside visiting wineries, the most accessible way to get a quick taste of local wine is at a wine shop in town. I like the Kenyeres family's **Bikavér Borház,** right on Little Dobó Square (across from Offi Ház Hotel). In addition to a well-stocked (if slightly overpriced) wine shop, they have a wine bar with indoor and outdoor seating (six tastings and two cheeses for less than 2,000 Ft, or wine by the glass, some English spoken, menu lists basic English description for each wine, daily 10:00-22:00, Kis-Dobó tér 10, tel. 36/413-262).

Sirens' Valley (Szépasszony-völgy)—When the Ottoman invaders first occupied Eger, residents moved into the valley next door, living in caves dug into the hillside. Eventually the Ottomans were driven out, the Egerites moved back to town, and the caves became wine cellars. (Most Eger families who can afford it have at least a modest vineyard in the countryside.) There are more than 300 such caves in the valley to the southwest of Eger, several of which are open for visitors.

The best selection of these caves (about 50) is in the Sirens' Valley (sometimes also translated as "Valley of the Beautiful Women"—or, on local directional signs, the less poetic "Nice Woman Valley"). While the valley can feel vacant and dead (even sometimes in the summer), if you visit when it's busy it can be a fun scene—locals showing off their latest vintage, with picnic tables and tipsy tourists spilling out into the street. At some places, you'll be offered free samples; others have a menu for tastes or glasses of wine. While you're not expected to buy a bottle, it's a nice gesture to buy one if you've spent a while at one cave (and it's usually very cheap). Most caves offer something light to eat with the wine, and you'll also see lots of non-cave, full-service restaurants. Some of the caves are fancy and finished, staffed by multilingual waiters in period costume. Others feel like a dank basement, with grandpa leaning on his moped out front and a monolingual granny pouring the wine inside. (The really local places—where the decor is cement, bottles don't have labels, and food consists of potato chips and buttered Wonder Bread—can be the most fun.)

This experience is a strange mix of touristy and local, but not entirely accessible to non-Hungarian-speakers—it works best with a bunch of friends and an easygoing, social attitude. Hopping from cave to musky cave can make for an enjoyable evening, but be sure to wander around a bit to see the options before you dive in (cellars generally open 10:00-21:00 in summer, best June-Aug after 19:00 and good-weather weekends in the shoulder season; it's sleepy and not worth a visit off-season, when only a handful of cellars remain open for shorter hours).

Getting to the Sirens' Valley: The valley is on the southwest outskirts of Eger. Figure no more than 1,000 Ft for a **taxi** between your hotel and the caves. During the summer, you can take the 500-Ft **tourist train** from Eger's main square to the caves (see "Helpful Hints" on page 656), then catch a later one back.

You can **walk** there in about 25 minutes: Leave the pedestrian zone on the street next to the cathedral (Törvényház utca), with the cathedral on your right-hand side. Take the first left just after the back end of the cathedral (onto Trinitárius utca), go one long block, then take the first right (onto Király utca). At the fork, bear to the left. You'll stay straight on this road—crossing busy Koháry István utca—for several blocks, passing through some nondescript residential areas (on Szépasszony-völgy utca). When you crest the hill and emerge from the houses, you'll see the caves (and tour buses) below you on the left—go left (downhill) at the fork to get there. First you'll come to a stretch of touristy non-cave restaurants; keep going past these, and eventually you'll see a big loop of caves on your left.

Nightlife in Eger

Things quiet down pretty early in this sedate town. Youthful student bars and hangouts cluster along the main "walking street," Széchenyi utca. Older travelers feel more at home on Little Dobó Square, with schmaltzy live music until 21:00 or 22:00 in summer.

Sleeping in Eger

Eger is a good overnight stop, and a couple of quaint, well-located hotels in particular—Senator Ház and Offi Ház—are well worth booking in advance. The TI can help you find a room; if you're stumped, the area behind the castle has a sprinkling of cheap guesthouses *(vendégház)*. Elevators are rare—expect to climb one or two flights of stairs to reach your room. A tax of 360 Ft per person will be added to your bill (not included in the prices listed here). Parking is generally free and easy.

$$$ Imola Udvarház rents six spacious apartments—with kitchen, living room, bedroom, and bathroom—all decorated in modern IKEA style. They're pricey, but roomy and well-maintained, with a great location near the castle entrance (Sb-18,000 Ft, Db-20,000 Ft, 2,000 Ft more July-Aug, 4,000 Ft less in winter, extra person-2,000 Ft, air-con, free Wi-Fi, enter through restaurant courtyard at Dózsa György tér 4, tel. & fax 36/516-180, www.imolaudvarhaz.hu, udvarhaz@imolanet.hu).

$$ Senator Ház Hotel is one of my favorite small, family-run hotels in Eastern Europe. Though the 11 rooms are a bit worn, this place is cozy and well-run by András Cseh and his right-hand man, Viktor. With oodles of character, all the right quirks, and a picture-perfect location just under the castle on Little Dobó Square, it's a winner (Sb-13,200 Ft, Db-18,000 Ft, extra bed-6,000 Ft, 1,000

Ft more in July-Aug, less in winter, András offers 10 percent cash discount for Rick Steves readers who book direct and mention this book, air-con, free Internet access and Wi-Fi, Dobó István tér 11, tel. & fax 36/411-711, www.senatorhaz.hu, senator@enternet.hu). The Cseh family also runs **Pátria Vendégház**—two doubles (same prices as main hotel) and four luxurious apartments (Db-20,000 Ft, Tb-27,000 Ft).

$$ Offi Ház Hotel shares Little Dobó Square with Senator Ház. Its five rooms are classy and romantic, but a bit tight, with slanted ceilings (Sb-13,500 Ft, Db-17,500 Ft, Db suite-19,500 Ft, Tb suite-23,000 Ft, extra bed-4,500 Ft, 15 percent cheaper Nov-March, non-smoking, air-con, free cable Internet, Dobó István tér 5, tel. & fax 36/518-210, www.offihaz.hu, offihaz@t-online.hu, Offenbächer family).

$$ Szent János Hotel, less charming and more business-like than the Senator Ház and Offi Ház, offers a good but less

Sleep Code

(200 Ft = about $1, country code: 36, area code: 36)
S = Single, **D** = Double/Twin, **T** = Triple, **Q** = Quad, **b** = bathroom.
Unless otherwise noted, English is spoken, credit cards are
accepted, and breakfast is included.

To help you easily sort through these listings, I've divided
the accommodations into three categories, based on the price
for a double room with bath during high season:

$$$ Higher Priced—Most rooms 20,000 Ft or more.
$$ Moderately Priced—Most rooms between
15,000-20,000 Ft.
$ Lower Priced—Most rooms 15,000 Ft or less.

Prices can change without notice; verify the hotel's
current rates online or by email. For other updates, see www
.ricksteves.com/update.

Phone Tip: Remember, if calling or faxing Eger internationally, you'll have to dial 36 twice (once for the country
code, again for the area code).

atmospheric location, 11 straitlaced rooms, and a pleasant winter
garden to relax in (Sb-13,000 Ft, Db-16,500 Ft, extra bed-5,000
Ft, 15 percent cheaper Nov-April, non-smoking rooms, air-con,
free cable Internet, street noise on weekends can be a problem—
request a quiet back room, a long block off Dobó Square at Szent
János utca 3, tel. 36/510-350, fax 36/517-101, www.hotelszentjanos
.hu, hotelszentjanos@hotelszentjanos.hu).

$ Dobó Vendégház, run by warm Mariann Kleszo, has seven
basic but colorful rooms just off Dobó Square. Mariann speaks
nothing but Hungarian, but gets simple reservation emails and
faxes translated by a friend (Sb-9,500 Ft, Db-13,500 Ft, Tb-19,000
Ft, Qb-22,000 Ft, cash only, no air-con, Wi-Fi, Dobó utca 19, tel.
36/421-407, fax 36/515-715, www.dobovendeghaz.hu, info@dobo
vendeghaz.hu).

$ Imola Hostel, a big, modern, and comfy hostel, is basi-
cally a college dormitory that welcomes travelers of any age into its
dorm rooms in summer (July-Aug only). As there are several hundred beds, finding a place should be easy (bunk in 2-3-bed room-
3,500 Ft, includes sheets but no breakfast; a short hike up behind
the castle or a 5-minute walk from the Old Town at Leányka utca
2; tel. 36/520-430, www.imolanet.hu/imolahostel, hostel@imola
net.hu).

Eating in Eger

Bajor Sörház (known to locals as "HBH" for the brand of beer on tap) is favored by tourists and locals alike for its excellent Hungarian cuisine. Everything's good here. You could make a meal of the giant 700-Ft bowl of their spicy *gulyás leves* soup (that's *real* Hungarian goulash, described on page 516)—but it's fun to supplement it with some other well-prepared Hungarian dishes. This is a good place for two or more people to split several dishes. They also feature some Bavarian specialties...but with a Hungarian accent (most main dishes 1,200-1,500 Ft, daily 11:30-22:00, outdoor tables in summer, right at the bottom of Dobó Square at Bajcsy-Zsilinszky utca 19, tel. 36/515-516). Say hello to animated István "Call Me Steve Miller" Molnár, one of my favorite Hungarians.

Restaurant Senator Ház, at the top end of Dobó Square, offers the best setting for al fresco dining in town, with good Hungarian and international food (main dishes 1,500-2,500 Ft). Sure, you pay extra for the setting—but it's worth it. With its post-card-perfect outdoor seating from which to survey the Little Dobó Square action, and cheesy live music pouring from their gazebo on summer evenings, this place might just tempt you to savor an after-dinner glass of wine (open long hours daily). Neighboring restaurants (such as Offi Ház) offer the same ambience.

Szantofer Vendéglő serves traditional Hungarian food at local prices to both Egerites and tourists. The good, unpretentious, fill-the-tank grub is designed for the neighborhood gang (most main dishes 1,400-2,100 Ft, daily 11:30-22:00, Bródy Sándor utca 3, tel. 36/517-298).

Palacsintavár ("Pancake Castle"), near the ramp leading up to the castle, isn't your hometown IHOP. This cellar bar serves up inventive, artfully presented crêpe-wrapped main courses to a mostly student clientele. It's decorated with old cigarette boxes, and cutting-edge rock music plays on the soundtrack (most main dishes 1,300-1,500 Ft, daily 12:00-22:00, Dobó utca 9).

Casa della Pasta, above the market hall, has a pleasant tree-house ambience. As it's outside of the cute zone, it attracts more locals than tourists. Sit indoors or enjoy covered terrace seating that's delightful in warm weather. The menu is mostly Italian, with pasta and pizzas (1,000-1,400 Ft) and main dishes (1,600-2,000 Ft), and a few Hungarian standbys thrown in (1,600-2,000 Ft; daily 12:00-23:00, Katona István tér 2, tel. 36/412-452).

Dessert: *Cukrászda* (pastry shops) line the streets of Eger. For deluxe, super-decadent pastries of every kind imaginable—most for less than 450 Ft—drop by **Dobós Cukrászda** (daily 9:30-21:00, point to what you want inside and they'll bring it out to your table,

Széchenyi utca 6, tel. 36/413-335). For a more local scene, find the tiny **Sárvári Cukrászda,** a block behind the Lyceum. Their pastries are good, but Egerites line up here for homemade gelato (170 Ft/scoop, Mon-Fri 7:00-19:00, Sat-Sun 10:00-19:00, Kossuth utca 1, between Jókai utca and Fellner utca).

Eger Connections

By Train

The only major destination you'll get to directly from Eger's train station is **Budapest** (5/day direct to Budapest's Keleti/Eastern Station, 2.5 hours; more frequent and faster with a change in Füzesabony—see next). For other destinations, you'll connect through Füzesabony or Budapest.

Eger is connected to the nearby junction town of **Füzesabony** (FOO-zesh-ah-boyn) by frequent trains (13/day, 17 minutes). The very rustic Füzesabony station does not have lockers or an ATM, but—oddly enough—does have a modest museum of local artifacts. To find an ATM, exit straight from the station, walk about two blocks, and you'll find one on your right.

In Füzesabony, you can transfer to Budapest (including some speedy InterCity trains—with a 900-Ft supplement—that get you to Budapest in 2 hours total).

Night Train to Kraków: If you're connecting to Poland, it may be possible to use a night train between Budapest and Kraków that stops at Füzesabony. If you want to start (or end) your Hungarian trip in Eger, this allows you to sleep into (or out of) Eger with a handy change at Füzesabony, rather than backtracking to Budapest. However, recently this train has run sporadically (summer only, or maybe not at all); sometimes the Budapest-Kraków night train is routed through the Czech Republic instead. If this option intrigues you, investigate your options carefully at http://bahn.hafas.de/bin/query.exe/en.

By Bus

Eger's bus station (unlike its train station) is right in town, a five-minute uphill walk behind Eger's cathedral and the Archbishop's Palace: Go behind the cathedral and through the park, and look for the modern, green, circular building. Blue electronic boards in the center of the station show upcoming departures.

From Eger to Budapest: The direct Eger-Budapest bus service is cheaper and slightly faster than the train (2,500 Ft, 2/hour, 2 hours, departs at about :15 and :45 past the hour, tickets always available just before departure, regular and express buses nearly the same speed). While Eger's bus station is closer to the town center than its train station, this bus takes you to a somewhat less central point in Budapest (near Budapest's Stadionok bus station, on the M2/red Metró line).

To Salt Hill Thermal Spa: Buses from the same station also connect Eger to the Salt Hill Thermal Spa near Egerszalók (see "Getting There" on page 668). However, buses marked for *Egerszalók* do not actually go to the spa; instead, you need a bus going *beyond* Egerszalók, marked for *Demjén*.

PÉCS

An established settlement for nearly 2,000 years, Pécs (pronounced "paych") is a historic, museum-packed, and oh-so-pretty town near Hungary's southern frontier. Cheerful, inviting Pécs, with colorful buildings dripping with lavish Zsolnay porcelain decoration, feels unusually proud and prosperous. Of course, it's a relative backwater, and compared to Budapest, its charms are modest and humble...but they're also delightfully accessible. And you'll hardly see another tourist, as this place is rarely visited by Americans.

Owing to its illustrious history, Pécs offers surprisingly engaging sightseeing for a city of its size; museum-going is fun and enlightening here. You'll gradually peel back the many layers of Pécs' past: Walk in the footsteps of Romans through ancient crypts, stroll the medieval trade-town street plan, explore some rare surviving artifacts of the Ottoman occupation, ogle colorful Baroque and Art Nouveau buildings...and enjoy the energetic bustle of one of Hungary's leading cities. The city's symbol—a mosque-turned-church—says it all.

The Mecsek Hills gently cradle the city, blocking out the colder weather from the north to give Pécs a mild Mediterranean climate closer to Croatia's than to Budapest's. It's no surprise that this bright and invigorating city has earned a reputation as a leading art colony. Its streets are lined with museums devoted to local artists both obscure and well-known (including Vasarely and Csontváry, considered the two great figures of Hungarian art). Students love it, too. Hungary's first university was founded here in 1367, and today's U. of Pécs rivals Budapest's ELTE as the country's biggest university. More than 30,000 students give Pécs a youthful buzz.

Planning Your Time

One full day is plenty to get your fill of Pécs. Like Eger, it's a long day trip from Budapest (three hours each way by train), so it's worth spending the night. With the better part of a day in Pécs, go for a walk through town following my self-guided commentary, dipping into the museums that appeal to you. Everything is within a few minutes' walk of the main square.

Orientation to Pécs

(area code: 72)

With about 170,000 people, Pécs is Hungary's fifth-largest city. But it feels like a small town, right down to the convivial strolling atmosphere that combusts along its pedestrian zone. The Belváros, or Inner Town, is hemmed in by a ring road (the site of the former town wall, some of which still stands). You can walk from one end of this central tourist zone to the other in about 15 minutes. All roads lead to the main square, Széchenyi tér, marked by the palatial yellow Town Hall and giant mosque/church. Because Pécs is nestled up against a gentle hillside, you'll go gradually uphill as you head north.

Tourist Information

The Pécs TI is right on the main square, Széchenyi tér, in the ornately decorated County Hall building (April-Sept Mon-Fri 9:00-18:00, Sat-Sun 9:00-14:00; Oct-March Mon-Fri 9:00-16:00, closed Sat-Sun; Széchenyi tér 9, tel. 72/213-315, www.pecs.hu).

Arrival in Pécs

By Train: The Pécs train station is three-quarters of a mile due south of the city center's Széchenyi tér. Inside, the station is long but straightforward (with ATM, lockers, and all the usual amenities).

A **taxi** to any of my recommended hotels should cost no more than 1,000 Ft.

You can **walk** from the train station to the town center in about 15 minutes: Exit straight ahead from the station and walk up the tree-lined, slightly angled Jókai út, which funnels you directly to Széchenyi tér.

Various **bus** lines (#38, #38A, #39, #40, and #43) shave a few minutes off the walk downtown, taking you to the Árkád shopping center just south of the pedestrianized old center. As you exit

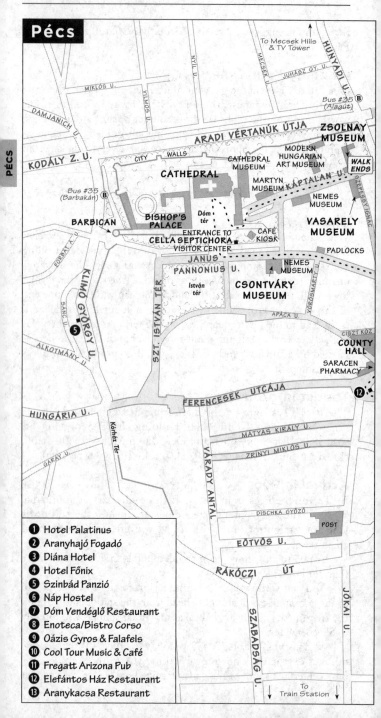

Pécs

PÉCS

Key locations on map:
- To Mecsek Hills & TV Tower
- HUNYADI U.
- NYÍL U.
- MECSEK U.
- JUHÁSZ GY. U.
- MIKLÓS U.
- DAMJANICH U.
- Bus #35 (Alagút)
- ARADI VÉRTANÚK ÚTJA
- ZSOLNAY MUSEUM
- KODÁLY Z. U.
- CITY WALLS
- CATHEDRAL MUSEUM
- MODERN HUNGARIAN ART MUSEUM
- WALK ENDS
- CATHEDRAL
- MARTYN MUSEUM
- KÁPTALAN U.
- Bus #35 (Barbakán)
- NEMES MUSEUM
- BARBICAN
- BISHOP'S PALACE
- Dóm tér
- CELLA SEPTICHORA
- ENTRANCE TO VISITOR CENTER
- CAFÉ KIOSK
- VASARELY MUSEUM
- SZÉCHENYI IGNÁC
- FORBÁT A. U.
- KLIMÓ GYÖRGY U.
- JANUS PANNONIUS U.
- NEMES MUSEUM
- PADLOCKS
- SÁNC U.
- István tér
- CSONTVÁRY MUSEUM
- VÖRÖSMARTY U.
- ALKOTMÁNY U.
- SZT. ISTVÁN TÉR
- APÁCA U.
- CISZT KÖZ
- COUNTY HALL
- SARACEN PHARMACY
- HUNGÁRIA U.
- Kórház Tér
- FERENCESEK UTCÁJA
- GARAY U.
- MÁTYÁS KIRÁLY U.
- ZRINYI MIKLÓS U.
- VÁRADY ANTAL
- DISCHKA GYŐZŐ
- POST
- EÖTVÖS U.
- RÁKÓCZI ÚT
- SZABADSÁG U.
- JÓKAI U.
- To Train Station

1. Hotel Palatinus
2. Aranyhajó Fogadó
3. Diána Hotel
4. Hotel Főnix
5. Szinbád Panzió
6. Náp Hostel
7. Dóm Vendéglő Restaurant
8. Enoteca/Bistro Corso
9. Oázis Gyros & Falafels
10. Cool Tour Music & Café
11. Fregatt Arizona Pub
12. Elefántos Ház Restaurant
13. Aranykacsa Restaurant

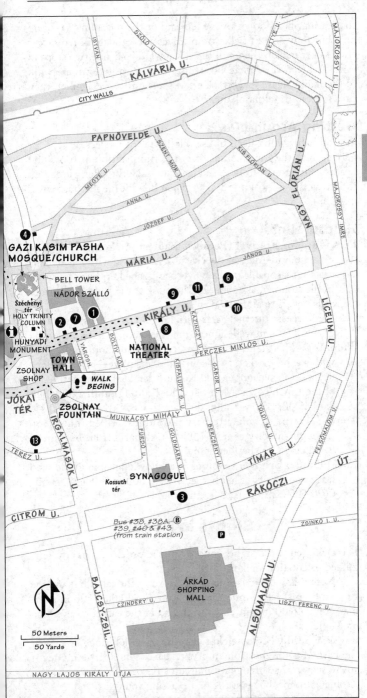

KÁLVÁRIA U.

ISTVÁN U.

SZALÓ U.

CITY WALLS

PAPNÖVELDE U.

MECSE U.

SZENT MÓR U.

ANNA U.

KIS FLÓRIÁN U.

NAGY FLÓRIÁN U.

MAJOROSSY I. U.

MAJOROSSY MRE

PÉCS

JÓZSEF U.

MÁRIA U.

JÁNOS U.

4

GAZI KASIM PASHA MOSQUE/CHURCH

← BELL TOWER

NÁDOR SZÁLLÓ

9 **11**

6

Széchenyi tér
HOLY TRINITY COLUMN

2 **7** **1**

KIRÁLY U.

8

10

KAZINCZY U.

LICEUM U.

HUNYADI MONUMENT

VÁROSH. KÖZ.

BÓLTY KÖZ.

NATIONAL THEATER

PERCZEL MIKLÓS U.

TOWN HALL

ZSOLNAY SHOP

KISFALUDY S. U.

GÁBOR U.

WALK BEGINS

JÓKAI TÉR

ZSOLNAY FOUNTAIN

MUNKÁCSY MIHÁLY U.

FÜRDŐ U.

GOLDMARK U.

BERCSÉNYI U.

TOLDI M. U.

IRGALMASOK U.

TÍMÁR U.

FELSŐMALOM U.

13

TERÉZ U.

Kossuth tér

SYNAGOGUE

RÁKÓCZI

ÚT

CITROM U.

3

ZSINKÓ I. U.

Bus #38, #38A, #39, #40 & #43 (from train station)

B

P

BAJCSY-ZSIL. U.

CZINDERY U.

ÁRKÁD SHOPPING MALL

ALSÓMALOM U.

LISZT FERENC U.

N

50 Meters
50 Yards

NAGY LAJOS KIRÁLY ÚTJA

the station, head down to the left end of the bus stops, and hop on a bus (buy 360-Ft ticket from driver and validate in red box— stick ticket in slot, then pull the slot toward you; ride two stops to Árkád). From the Árkád bus stop, it's about a five-minute walk to the main square (backtrack a few steps up Rákóczi street, then turn right up Irgalmasok utcája).

Getting Around Pécs

You probably won't need to use public transit in Pécs, except for getting into the town center from the train station or (possibly) heading up into the hills. A single ticket is 280 Ft when purchased in advance at a kiosk, or 360 Ft when bought on the bus (www .pkrt.hu).

Helpful Hints

Pécs Outdoor Festival (Pécsi Szabadtéri Játékok): Each June through mid-August, the city hosts a festival with lots of concerts at reasonable prices (www.pecsiszabadteri.hu). If visiting in the summer, ask about it. The kiosk at the National Theater sells tickets to all festival events.

Internet Access: Internet cafés with long hours and fair prices are easy to find and well-signed from the main walking zone.

Shopping: The giant, American-style **Árkád** shopping mall— with a supermarket, food court, and lots more—is just a block beyond the synagogue and Kossuth tér, at the southern edge of the Inner Town (Mon-Sat 7:00-21:00, Fri until 22:00, Sun 8:00-19:00, Bajcsy-Zsilinszky utca 11, www.arkadpecs.hu).

Tourist Train: A hokey tourist train does a 40-minute loop through the city center (1,000 Ft, departs from bottom of Széchenyi tér, May-Sept only).

Local Guide: Brigitta Gombos is a knowledgeable guide who leads good tours of her hometown (12,000 Ft/3 hours, mobile 0670-505-3531, gerluc@freemail.hu).

Sights in Pécs

I've arranged these sights roughly in the order of a handy self-guided orientation walk through town.

Note that most museums in Pécs (except the cathedral and the Roman crypts) have similar **hours:** Tue-Sun 10:00-18:00 in summer, 10:00-16:00 in winter. Everything but the cathedral is closed on Monday.

The 3,000-Ft **day ticket** *(napijegy),* which does not cover the cathedral or the Roman crypts, saves you a little money if you're seeing the three main museums (Csontváry, Vasarely, and Zsolnay). Simply buy it at the first museum you visit.

• *Begin in front of the little church next to the Town Hall, at the...*

▲Zsolnay Fountain (Zsolnay-kút)

This fountain, an icon of Pécs, was a gift from the beloved local Zsolnay (ZHOL-nay) family. The family created an innovative type of ceramics called pyrogranite that allowed colorful, delicate-seeming porcelain to be made frost-proof and hard as steel—ideal for external building decoration. The ox heads—modeled after an ancient drinking vessel found in Pécs—are specially glazed with another Zsolnay invention, eosin. Notice how eosin glaze glimmers with a unique range of colors. (Since this glaze compromises the pyrogranite, the fountain must be covered in winter.) Above the oxen heads are traditional symbols of

Pécs. One is the shield with five tall churches, dating from the Middle Ages. (Germans still call the town Fünfkirchen.) This seal was appropriated by the Zsolnay family as a symbol of their porcelain. The other seal is Pécs' coat of arms: a walled city under vineyard-strewn hills.

This is the first of many gorgeous Zsolnay decorations we'll see all over town. But Pécs is just the beginning. In the late 19th and early 20th centuries, Budapest and cities all over Europe covered their finest buildings with decorations from this city's Zsolnay Porcelain Manufacture. (For all the details, see the "Zsolnay Porcelain" sidebar on page 694.)

• *Across the wide street and 20 yards uphill is the entrance to an enjoyable pedestrian zone called...*

Jókai Tér

As you enter the traffic-free area, notice the **game boards** on top of the little pillars. When this street was renovated in 2000—with funky benches and other playful elements—the designers wanted to remind locals to take time to relax.

On the right (at #2), notice the **Zsolnay porcelain shop.** Although the company was reduced to an industrial supplier under the communists, today Zsolnay is proudly reclaiming its role as a maker of fine art. Dipping into the shop, notice that some of the decorative items use the same distinctive eosin glaze as the fountain's oxen heads...and are priced accordingly.

Continuing to the corner, you enter a fine little square with a kid-pleasing fountain. Look down the newly pedestrianized street called **Ferencesek utcája.** When Pécs was a walled market town,

this street—and Király utca to the east, also now pedestrianized—
made up the main east-west road. At the house on the uphill corner, notice the elephant. This used to be a grocery store, which
likely imported exotic Eastern goods, symbolized by the then-
mysterious pachyderm.

Hang a right around the elephant house, noticing the former
tram tracks preserved in the street. The yellow bricks were pretty
standard in 20th-century Hungary. Imagine how unappealing this
drag was when it was choked with tram and car traffic. At the corner (on the left), look for the old-time **Saracen Pharmacy** (marked
with the words *Sipöcz István* and an African prince over the door).
Its interior features gorgeous woodwork, little porcelain medicine
pots, and a Zsolnay fountain.

• *Continuing up the street, you'll emerge into the main square...*

▲▲Széchenyi Tér

In the Middle Ages, Pécs was a major trading crossroads, located
at the intersection of two Byzantine trade routes. Széchenyi tér
was a natural meeting point and
market zone. Today the market is
gone, but this square remains the
bustling city center, where both
political demonstrations and the
annual New Year's Eve festivities
percolate.

Let's get oriented. Stand
at the base of the square (across
from the McDonald's). Face the green-domed **Gazi Kasim Pasha
Mosque** at the top of the square (described in detail later). On
the right (housing the McDonald's), the giant yellow-and-white
building with the tower is the **Town Hall** (Városház, 1908),
strategically located here since the olden days to watch over the
market activities. The Town Hall's tower plays laid-back organ
ditties throughout the day. Across the square (housing the TI) is
the gorgeous, red-roofed **County Hall** (Megyháza, 1898), frosted

like a wedding cake with
sumptuous Zsolnay decora-
tions. Because the building
was originally a bank, it's
adorned with beehives (one
at the very peak of the building, and two more between
the top-floor windows).
Industrious bees, who carefully collect and store away their golden
deposits, are a common symbol for banking. Farther up the square
on the right is the pink **Nádor Szálló.** In the early 20th century,

this hotel was a popular gathering place for artists and intellectuals (but now it's awaiting a massive renovation).

The square has two monuments. On the right is an equestrian statue of **János Hunyadi,** the war hero who fended off the Ottoman invaders at the 1456 Battle of Belgrade. Later those Ottomans took Pécs and built the mosque at the top of the square. But Hunyadi gets the last laugh: If you position yourself just right, it appears that Hunyadi's club is smashing the crescent at the top of the mosque. (Try it.) This statue is a popular meeting point: Locals say, "I'll meet you under the horse's...tail." With perhaps unintended irony, Hunyadi—who died of the plague soon after that battle—shares the square with the **Holy Trinity Plague Column,** which townspeople built to give thanks to God after surviving a nasty bout of the plague in the late 17th century. Around its base are three saints known for protecting against disease or injury: Sebastian, who was killed by arrows (on left); Rocco, with his trusty dog and trademark leg wound (on right); and Anthony of Padua, who offers help recovering that which is lost—including health (behind the pillar).

• *We'll visit the mosque/church soon. But first, head down the street branching off to the right, next to the Town Hall....*

▲The Walking Street: Király Utca

This vibrant Technicolor people zone—combined with Jókai tér and Ferencesek utcája, across the

square—bisects the city center. Király utca ("Royal Street") is a delight to stroll. Walk its entire length, simply enjoying street musicians and people-watching, and noting its personality-filled architecture.

There are several recommended restaurants along this street (see "Eating in Pécs," later). Also keep an eye out for the gorgeous, horseshoe-shaped Hotel Palatinus (on the left at #5; step into its lobby for a taste of genteel Secession architecture) and a bike-rental place (VeloSophie, at #9).

A few steps farther, you'll reach the square in front of the **National Theater,** built (along with most of the other houses on this square) for the Hungarian millennial celebrations of 1896

Tivadar Csontváry Kosztka
(1853-1919)

Adored by Hungarians, but virtually unknown outside his home-land, Tivadar Csontváry Kosztka had a life as fascinating as his paintings. Because of the time in which he lived and his struggles with mental illness (schizophrenia)— if not for his talent—Csontváry (CHONT-vah-ree) is often com-pared to Van Gogh. While that's a bit of a stretch, viewing Csontváry's works gives you a glimpse into the Hungarian psyche, and into his own fractured mind.

Tivadar Kosztka was born to an upper-class family, seemingly bound for a humdrum lot in life. He didn't pick up a paintbrush until his 27th year. Then one day, while idly sketching sleeping oxen, he had a revelation (or, perhaps, a psychotic episode): A voice told him that he was destined to become "the world's greatest *plein air* painter, greater even than Raphael."

He adopted the pseudonym "Csontváry" and became driven by an almost pathological compulsion to prepare him-self for what he believed to be his destiny. He figured it would take him 20 years, working as a pharmacist to finance his quest. By age 41, he had saved enough to attend art school (in Munich and in Paris). Seeking the ideal subjects for his outdoor style, he traveled extensively around Europe and the Middle East:

(see page 539). The decorations on the theater—including the stone-like statues—are all made of Zsolnay pyrogranite. This is a popular venue in this city of culture, and hosts the local philhar-monic (their season runs Sept-May). Duck into the box office here any time of year to see what's on, either here or elsewhere in town.

Farther along, you'll find a good ice-cream parlor; a very cool "ruin pub" (the recommended **Cool Tour**—a play on words from the formal "Kultur" label for local cultural centers, with an inviting garden out back); and, finally, a contemporary Hungarian painting gallery (at #31).

While this part of Pécs appears wealthy and manicured, the region is struggling. In the early 1950s, Pécs had only about 50,000 residents. Coal and uranium mines kick-started the econ-omy, causing the population to more than triple over the last 50 years. However, both mines are now closed, and while Pécs' uni-versity and business center continue to thrive, outlying commu-

Italy, Croatia, Bosnia-Herzegovina, Greece, Egypt, Lebanon, Jerusalem, and the Tatra Mountains of his own homeland. By the time he began painting in earnest, he had only six productive years (1903-1909).

Csontváry's rough, autodidactic (self-taught) style reveals his untrained origins, but contains a depth of meaning and of composition that exceeded his technical skill. While classified as a Post-Impressionist, Csontváry forged a style all his own. Like his contemporary Marc Chagall, he worked in almost childlike bright colors and often reverted to big, bold themes. His most common subjects are the destinations he traveled to that inspired him.

After exhibitions in 1909 and 1910 failed to win him the praise he so desperately sought, he became consumed by his schizophrenia and created only bizarre, surrealistic works. He died in obscurity in 1919.

After Csontváry's death, his family planned to sell his works to wagon-makers, who wanted the valuable canvas to stretch over their wagons. Fortunately, a Budapest art collector bought them instead, preserving the legacy of this important figure in Hungarian art history.

Csontváry remained largely unappreciated until the 1960s, when art-lovers began to take notice. But one discerning eye for talent knew greatness when he saw it, before many others did: Pablo Picasso reportedly discovered Csontváry's canvases at a 1949 exhibition, and proceeded to lock himself in the room with them for an hour. Finally emerging, he told his friend Marc Chagall that Chagall could never produce a work half as good as Csontváry's.

nities are grappling with 30 percent unemployment.

• *Head back to Széchenyi tér to visit the...*

▲Gazi Kasim Pasha Mosque (Gázi Kászim Pasa Dzsámija)/Inner Town Parish Church

It's rare to find such a well-preserved Ottoman structure in Hungary. The Ottomans—who began their 150-year stay in Pécs in 1543—lived here in the Inner Town, while the dwindling Hungarian population moved to the outskirts. The Ottomans tore down the church that stood on this spot and used the stones to build the structure you see today. After the Ottomans were forced out, the Catholic Church reclaimed this building and turned it into a church—which is why it's still intact today. Despite renovations over the years, it remains an offbeat hybrid of the Islamic and Christian faiths.

Cost and Hours: Free but donations are requested—consider buying a postcard or booklet; mid-April-mid-Oct Mon-Sat 10:00-16:00, Sun 11:30-16:00; mid-Oct-mid-April Mon-Sat 10:00-12:00, Sun 11:30-14:00.

❍ Self-Guided Tour: From the **outside,** notice the crescent moon of Islam capping the dome—but it's topped by the victorious Christian cross. The only decorations on the austere facade are the striped ogee arches over the windows. Before entering, notice the fig trees; locals are proud that their mild climate can support these heat-seekers.

Go **inside** and let your eyes adjust to the low light. Are you in a church, or a mosque...or both? The striped arches over the windows are also visible inside. Notice the colorful Islamic-style stalactite decorations at the tops of the corners. The painting on the underside of the dome seems to combine Christian figures with the geometric designs of Islam. To the right of the main altar is a verse from the Quran trans-

lated into Hungarian and used for Christian worship (a reminder that Islam and Christianity are founded on many of the same principles). Look for gray patches with faint Arabic script peeking through—most were whitewashed over during the church-ification.

Looking back to where you entered, you'll see a large **prayer niche** (mihrab) next to the door. This niche, which faces Mecca

(southeast from here), indicated to Muslim worshippers where they had to face to pray. The holy water basin in the niche and the crucifix suspended above it make it clear who's in charge now.

Mentally erase these and other Christian elements, and imagine worshipping here during the Ottoman period. There were no pews, and carpets covered the floor. Worshippers—men in front, women segregated in back—stood and knelt as they prayed toward the mihrab. A step-stair pulpit, called a mimber, likely stood off to one side of the mihrab.

When the Christians reclaimed this building, they flipped it around, creating an entrance near the mihrab, and an altar at the former entrance. Much later, in 1939, they added the giant **apse** (semi-circular area behind the altar). Explore this area, with its striking 1930s-style murals. In the corners you'll see small stone basins. These once stood outside the building, where the Ottoman worshippers performed their ablution, or ritual washing before prayer. The modern paintings depict Bible scenes and events in Hungary's Christian history. And the giant organ is an Angster (made by a local Hungarian organ-maker).

Exiting the building, head around back to find the latest addition to this constantly evolving structure: the modern **bell tower** and a concrete footprint that recalls the original church that preceded the mosque. The statue is St. Bartholomew, the patron of this church. Depicted (as he always is) with his skin peeling away, he steps on a serpent, representing victory over evil (Islam?). Every day at 12:00 and 19:00, the bell tower mechanically rises 40 feet into the air to play a tune.

• *While interesting, this is not Pécs' main church. To see that (and a lot more), go down the street at the upper-left corner of the square...*

Janus Pannonius Utca

About a block down this street, watch (on the right) for a railing that's completely covered in **padlocks**. Nobody knows for sure

how this local tradition began, back in the 1980s. Some say it was a clever way for graduating students to get rid of the padlocks from their lockers. These days, the padlocks mostly belong to lovers who want to pledge themselves to each other. You can see that many of the locks are marked (or even engraved) with couples' names. Farther down the same block, the tradition continues at the padlock-covered gate. (Not missing a sales opportunity, guess what the nearby shop sells.)

• *Continue along the street until you emerge into the little square. In the pretty off-white building on the left (with the gray roof), you'll find Pécs' best art museum...*

▲▲Csontváry Museum (Csontváry Múzeum)

This small but delightful collection showcases the works of beloved Hungarian painter Tivadar Csontváry Kosztka. Csontváry produced only 100 paintings and 20 drawings, and about half are collected here. For a crash course in this enigmatic painter, read the sidebar above before visiting.

The museum is divided into five rooms. In Room 1, see Csontváry's art-school sketches that capture people at unguarded moments and show the work of a budding genius. Room 2 shows mostly scenes from around Hungary. *Storm on the Great Hortobágy* is a dynamic snapshot of life on the Great Hungarian Plain, where cowherds tend longhorn cattle. A storm brews on the horizon as a horseman races across the bridge. Notice the balance between movement and stillness, and between the yellow sky and the blue clouds. In Room 3, Csontváry's most acclaimed work, *The Lonely Cedar,* depicts a windblown tree on a ridge above the sea. The tree seems boldly independent even as it longs for companionship. Rooms 3 and 4 are filled with other "postcards" of Csontváry's far-flung travels, where he found inspiration in the Middle East (Baalbek, Jerusalem, Nazareth) and Europe (France, Sicily, Croatia, Bosnia-Herzegovina, Greece). The last room (5) displays Csontváry's final major painting, *Riders on the Seashore.* This haunting valedictory canvas, with an equestrian party pausing by an eerily deep-blue cove, hints at the troubled depths of Csontváry's own psyche. Other works in this room date from Csontváry's final days, when—in his worsening mental state—he sketched large-scale, absurdist scenes.

Cost and Hours: 1,200 Ft, covered by 3,000-Ft day ticket, borrow the English information sheet, May-Oct Tue-Sun 10:00-18:00, Nov-April Tue-Sun 10:00-16:00, closed Mon year-round, Janus Pannonius utca 11, tel. 72/224-255.

• *Leaving the museum, cross the street and continue left down the tree-lined, pedestrian-only path. Soon you'll see a beautiful yellow kiosk (on the right)—an inviting place for a coffee break. A few steps beyond that, look for the modern entrance to the...*

▲Cella Septichora Visitor Center (Roman Crypts)

This unique, modern, well-presented museum allows visitors to take a peek inside some remarkably preserved Roman crypts. (Note: If you skip this museum, sneak a free look at some of the ruins through the glass behind the yellow kiosk.)

Cost and Hours: 1,200 Ft; April-Oct Tue-Thu 10:00-18:00, Fri-Sun 10:00-20:00, closed Mon; Nov-March Tue-Sun 10:00-16:00, closed Mon; Dóm tér, tel. 72/224-755.

Tours: For an extra fee, you can join a 45-minute English tour (for details, call 72/224-755). For a brief visit, my self-guided tour (below)—and the good posted English descriptions—will guide you through the basics.

Background: There was a Roman settlement in today's Pécs

from the year A.D. 30, and by the second century it was a provincial capital called Sopinae. During that time, this part of town was a vast cemetery, which included the graves of early Christian martyrs. Later, after Christianity became the state religion in the early fourth century, these tombs attracted pilgrims from afar.

Wealthy Christian families were now free to build a double-decker structure to hold the remains of their relatives: a sealed crypt below ground (painted with Bible scenes and floral motifs), with a chapel directly above for remembering and praying for the dead. About a century later, Rome fell. Nomadic invaders lived in the chapels and raided the crypts (then carefully re-covered them). Today the remains of some of these crypt-chapels have been discovered, excavated, and opened to visitors.

⊙ Self-Guided Tour: Buy your ticket and head into the first area (under the glass roof), the foundation of a **giant chapel with seven apses.** (The exhibit is named for this—Cella Septichora means "seven-apsed chapel.") Experts believe that the crypt of a different martyr would have been placed in each apse, and pilgrims would come here to worship. However, the structure was never finished.

From here, follow signs to the highlights, and then exit as you climb through the subterranean exhibit. Unlike Rome's famous catacombs, these crypts were not originally connected underground; modern archaeologists built the tunnels you'll pass through to allow visitors easier access to all the tombs.

Find the **Wine Pitcher Burial Chamber.** The model shows the two-tiered structure. Peer through the window to see the paintings that decorate the crypt. Its nickname comes from the wine jug and glass painted in the niche above the body. Romans used wine to toast to the memory of the departed (the Roman version of "pour one out for the homies who ain't here"). Climb up the stairs to what was ground level, where you can view the foundation of the chapel and look down into the crypt. From here, you'll see other paintings (representing paradise), as well as the drain at the bottom of the sarcophagus. The Romans, ever the clever engineers, provided drainage so that accumulating

groundwater would not defile the body.

Retrace your steps, then follow signs to the Peter and Paul crypt. Along the way, you'll pass through an area with several **smaller crypts.** Notice that these didn't have large chapels up top; rather, worshippers would kneel and look inside a small decorative chapel. In one, a hole in the floor of the chapel indicates where tomb raiders broke in to search for valuables. Turn right into the **octagonal chapel,** which—like the seven-apsed chapel—was likely designed to be a pilgrim church. Finally you'll pass another small crypt that's more intact, showing the barrel vaulting that once covered all of these.

Take the spiral stairs down to the bottom to enter the **Peter and Paul Burial Chamber.** Standing under the painted tomb, you'll see faded Sts. Peter and Paul flanking the Christogram (an ancient Christian symbol). The side walls are painted with biblical scenes, while the ceiling features another Christogram, four portraits (possibly the Four Evangelists), and more nature motifs—plants and birds. (An artist's rendering of the original version is nearby.) Notice the little window above the body. Experts believe that a ribbon tied to the sarcophagus led through this window up into the chapel, so the faithful could have a tangible connection to the dead.

Retracing your steps on your way out, you'll pass through even more crypts (they've unearthed more than 20), as well as some simple brick sarcophagi used by poorer families to bury their dead.

• *Exiting the exhibit, turn right and continue down Janus Pannonius utca, which deposits you at...*

István Tér and Dóm Tér

These two squares—the lower István Square, which belonged to the people, and the upper Cathedral Square, which was the bishop's—used to be separated by a wall and moat. But later, the enlightened

Bishop Szepesy turned them into one big park. In the statue that dominates the square, the bishop is stepping down from the pulpit clutching a Bible—a reminder that he's believed to have been the first priest to use Hungarian.

Walk up the stairs and into Cathedral Square. The brown, Neo-Renaissance building on the left is the Bishop's Palace. At the corner of this building, notice the engaging statue of **Franz Liszt** by popular 20th-century sculptor Imre Varga. Liszt was a friend of the bishop, and Liszt's visit here in 1846 is still the stuff of legend.

• *Now turn your attention to the massive, four-towered....*

▲▲Cathedral

With an imposing exterior and an elaborately decorated interior, Pécs' cathedral merits a close look. St. István established a bish-

opric in Pécs in the year 1009, and this church building grew in fits and starts from then on. By the 14th century, it had roughly the same floor plan as today, and gradually morphed with the styles of the day: Romanesque, Gothic, Renaissance. The Ottomans preserved the building, using it first as a mosque and later as a stable,

a grain store, and a library. Later, when it became the cathedral again, it got a Baroque makeover. Finally, in the 1880s, a bishop (likely hoping to be remembered as a visionary) grew tired of the architectural hodgepodge, gutted the place, and turned it into the Neo-Romanesque fortress of God you see today. The 12 apostles stand along the roofline, and the four distinctive corner towers anchor and fortify the massive structure.

Cost and Hours: 1,000 Ft, 300 Ft more to also visit cathedral museum and bishop's wine cellar for a tasting; April-mid-Oct Mon-Sat 9:00-17:00, Sun 13:00-17:00; mid-Oct-March Mon-Sat 10:00-16:00, Sun 13:00-16:00; can be closed for weddings Sat afternoons—especially in summer, tel. 72/513-030.

❷ **Self-Guided Tour:** Study the symbolic **bronze gate** from 2000. The vines, grapes, and branches are all connected, symbolizing our connection to God. If you look closely, you'll find animals representing good (birds) and evil (snake, scorpion, frog). On the left, St. István gives Pécs to the first bishop; on the right, Jesus offers his hand to St. Peter.

Stepping inside, you're struck by the rich Neo-Romanesque, 19th-century decor. It's clear that the renovating bishop did not subscribe to the "less is more" school of church decoration. Like the Matthias Church in Budapest (see page 559)—renovated at about the same time—every square inch is covered by a thick and colorful layer of paint. Along the **nave** are paintings depicting the lives of the church's patrons, Sts. Peter and Paul. Above the arches are biblical scenes. The coffered ceiling of the nave depicts the 12 apostles and (near the organ) John the Baptist.

The **altar,** with its highly decorated canopy, is a replica of the 13th-century original. The mosaic on the apse dome (behind the

altar, not entirely visible from here) features Jesus flanked by Peter and Paul (on the right) and, on the left, István and Mary (the patron saint of Hungary).

To the right of the organ is the **bishop's treasury,** in the Chapel of Mary. (This is the only one of the cathedral's four such chapels open to tourists.) Pop in to see vestments, goblets, and monstrances, all surrounded by paintings of events from the Christian history of Hungary. At the far end of the chapel is a remarkably detailed 16th-century alabaster sculpture, done by a Dutch sculptor for an Italian family who decided they didn't want it after all (so the Pécs bishop bought it instead).

Back in the main church, to the right of the altar are the stairs down to the **crypt.** This 11th-century forest of columns (redecorated like the rest of the church) is part of the original church building on this site. The bust at the back depicts the bishop who decided to renovate the church.

• *From in front of the cathedral, if you want to take a look at part of the old* **city wall,** *you can go down the stairs and turn right at the wide path, which will take you to a barbican (round tower) that helped fortify the walls. (For more on these walls, see next page.)*

Otherwise, exiting the cathedral, turn left, pass through the archway, walk over the glassed-in Roman ruins, and walk down...

Káptalan Utca: Pécs' "Museum Row"

A cluster of museums line tranquil Káptalan Street ("Chapterhouse Street," where priests once lived). A few of the smaller museums are skippable, but the Zsolnay and Vasarely museums are worthwhile (www.jpm.hu). Remember, all of these have the same hours and are covered by the same 3,000-Ft day ticket (explained on page 680).

▲**Viktor Vasarely Museum (Vasarely Múzeum)**—You might not know Viktor Vasarely (1908-1997), but you know his work. Think optical illusions, and the dizzying Op Art that inspired the psychedelic 1960s. Here in his hometown, you can see a museum of Vasarely's eye-popping creations. Inspired by nature, Vasarely discovered that the repetition and slight variation of lines and forms can play with the viewer's brain to create illusions of depth

and movement. In other words, black-and-white lines undulating across a canvas are trippy, baby. It's easy to get lost in Vasarely's mind-bending designs—such as, in the first room, a pair of carpets with zebras—which make you go cross-eyed before you stumble up the stairs to see him add more color to the mix.

PÉCS

Cost and Hours: 1,200 Ft, covered by 3,000-Ft day ticket, borrow the English information, Káptalan utca 3, tel. 72/514-040.

▲**Zsolnay Porcelain Museum (Zsolnay Múzeum)**—This museum, situated in the former mansion of the Zsolnay family, is as much a shrine to the family as a showcase of their work. (For more on the family and their legacy, see the "Zsolnay Porcelain" sidebar, next page.) The collection is divided into two parts: architectural elements and decorative ware. Each room is well-described in English. In the architectural elements section, you'll see impressively detailed and colorful decorations for the many buildings the Zsolnays were involved in renovating (including Budapest's Matthias Church and Parliament). You'll also see a playful duck fountain with its colorful eosin glaze, and some beautiful pieces of the destroyed István Stove that once warmed Budapest's Royal Palace. The decorative-ware collection displays vases, sculptures, and other objects that demonstrate the evolution of porcelain style. Notice how trends came and went over time. A spinning table allows you to easily inspect each place setting of Zsolnay dinnerware.

Cost and Hours: 1,200 Ft, covered by 3,000-Ft day ticket, Káptalan utca 4, tel. 72/514-040, www.zsolnay.hu.

Other Museums—Nearby are museums that showcase the work of yet two more local artists, Ferenc Martyn and Endre Nemes, and the Modern Hungarian Art Museum.

• *From Káptalan utca, you're just a block above the main square and our starting point. If you have more time, consider some of these sights....*

Elsewhere in Pécs

City Walls—Several segments of the city walls around the northern part of Pécs are still standing (most notably around the cathedral area). Built after the Tatar invasions of the 13th century, and beefed

PÉCS

Zsolnay Porcelain

Because of the pioneering Zsolnay (ZHOL-nay) family of Pécs, buildings all over Hungary are slathered with gorgeously colorful porcelain.

Miklós Zsolnay (1800-1880) opened a porcelain factory in Pécs in 1853. But the real breakthrough came at the hands of his innovative son, Vilmos Zsolnay (1828-1900), who experimented with glazes and additives, and revolutionized the use of porcelain in building materials. He invented a type of ceramic called pyrogranite to create porcelain decorative elements that were as resilient as steel and weatherproof, but could still be delicately sculpted and painted any color of the rainbow. Zsolnay pyrogranite  made a splash at the 1873 World Exhibition in Vienna, winning an avalanche of orders from all over Europe. The twists and curves that Zsolnay porcelain allowed for were a perfect fit for the slinky, organic Art Nouveau style of the day. Exhibits at further world fairs added to the Zsolnay family's renown and wealth.

In 1893, Vilmos Zsolnay unveiled his latest innovation: eosin, a shimmering—almost metallic—iridescent glaze. Named for the Greek word for "dawn," it has an otherworldly way of making porcelain resemble light striking a precious gemstone or the glistening surface of a soap bubble. This eosin technique is exemplified by Pécs' Zsolnay Fountain (described on page 681).

Boom time for the Zsolnays also coincided with the 1896 millennial celebrations in Budapest (see page 539). The city's

up in the 15th century, the walls were no match for the Ottoman invaders who took the town in 1543. Still standing just west of the cathedral area is the round, stout barbican defensive gate, which you can actually climb.

Synagogue (Zsinagóga)—Just south of the old center, overlooking Kossuth tér, is Pécs' colorful synagogue. Dating from the 1860s, but recently restored, this building is a powerful reminder of Pécs' Jewish heritage. The  city had a thriving population of 4,000 Jews; only a few hundred survived the Holocaust (500 Ft, May-Sept Sun-Fri 10:00-17:00, closed Sat and Oct-April, Kossuth tér, tel. 72/315-881).

architects, who had ample resources and imagination, were striving to create a unique Hungarian national style. Many of them adopted colorful pyrogranite tiles and other decorations as an integral part of that style. In Budapest alone, the Great Market Hall, Matthias Church and National Archives on Castle Hill, and Ödön Lechner's Postal Savings Bank and Museum of Applied Arts are roofed with Zsolnay pyrogranite tiles. Zsolnay decorative elements also adorn the Hungarian Parliament, Gellért Baths, and many other buildings. To this day, Zsolnay tiles are synonymous with Budapest (and Hungarian) architecture.

All of that porcelain generated a lot of work for the Pécs factory. By the time World War I broke out, the Zsolnay family business was actually the Austro-Hungarian Empire's biggest company (unlikely but true). But the stripped-down modern styles that emerged in the 20th century had little use for the fanciful Zsolnay decorations. The factory was nationalized by the communists, the Zsolnay name was abandoned, and quality plummeted.

In the 1990s, private investors took over and have made great strides toward rehabilitating the Zsolnay name. All over Hungary, you'll see shops selling beautiful Zsolnay tableware, some with designs as innovative as ever. But to keep up with our modern economy, Zsolnay also creates everyday items. In fact, they recently signed a big deal to make dishes for IKEA.

Mecsek Hills—Pécs is picturesquely nestled in the Mecsek (MEH-chek) Hills, a popular place to go for a hike. To get an aerial view of Pécs, ride bus #35 about 30 minutes up to the TV tower overlooking the city and surrounding region (catch this bus at the train station, or at the northern entrance to city center). Ascend the 580-foot-tall TV tower for views over the town and region (650 Ft, daily 9:00-20:00).

Sleeping in Pécs

Most of Pécs' city-center accommodations are affordable pensions with simple but sleepable rooms. Elevators are rare.

$$$ Hotel Palatinus is your impersonal big-hotel option, perfectly located right on the main walking street. You'll rarely find a more impressive facade, lobby, and breakfast room; the showpiece

Sleep Code

(200 Ft = about $1, country code: 36, area code: 72)
S = Single, **D** = Double/Twin, **T** = Triple, **Q** = Quad, **b** = bathroom.
Unless otherwise noted, English is spoken, credit cards are accepted, and breakfast is included—but the modest tourist tax (350 Ft per person, per night) is not.

To help you easily sort through these listings, I've divided the accommodations into three categories, based on the price for a double room with bath during high season:

$$$ Higher Priced—Most rooms 16,000 Ft or more.
$$ Moderately Priced—Most rooms between 10,000-16,000 Ft.
$ Lower Priced—Most rooms 10,000 Ft or less.

Prices can change without notice; verify the hotel's current rates online or by email. For other updates, see www.ricksteves.com/update.

building (although not its bedrooms) has been painstakingly restored to its turn-of-the-20th-century glory. While this makes it a bit overpriced and it's far from friendly, the location and public areas help compensate (Db-12,800-19,200 Ft, price depends on type of room—more for air-con or more recently renovated rooms, elevator, pay Wi-Fi, Király utca 5, tel. 72/889-400, www.danubiushotels.com/palatinus, palatinus.reservation@danubiushotels.com).

$$$ Aranyhajó Fogadó ("Golden Ship Inn"), a lesser value, is ideally situated at the start of the Király utca pedestrian zone. In operation since the 18th century, the hotel's 18 rooms are old and a bit musty, with once-classy furniture. The front rooms are a bit bigger, noisier, and more expensive—I'd request a quieter back room (Sb-12,000 Ft, Db-16,000 Ft, extra bed-4,000 Ft; Internet access, Király utca 3, tel. 72/210-685, www.aranyhajo.hu, hotel@aranyhajo.hu).

$$ Diána Hotel has 20 rooms just up the street from the synagogue, between the town center and the Árkád shopping mall (Sb-11,000 Ft, Db-15,000 Ft, rates about 1,000 Ft cheaper if you pay cash, air-con-1,500 Ft, some street noise, Wi-Fi, Tímár utca 4a, tel. 72/328-594, www.hoteldiana.hu, rikopecs0275@t-online.hu).

$$ Hotel Főnix is a tidy and well-run little 13-room place just beyond the mosque/church at the top of the main square. There's no parking nearby, as it's in a quiet, traffic-free zone (Sb-7,500 Ft, Db-12,000 Ft, Tb-15,000 Ft, no air-con, free Wi-Fi, Hunyadi János út 2, tel. 72/311-680, fax 72/324-113, www.fonixhotel.com, sales@fonixhotel.com, Nándor Zagyi).

$$ Szinbád Panzió is on a busy street in a dull urban area just outside the city wall. But it feels more hotelesque than the other mid-range options in town: Its public areas are classy, the 27 rooms are nice, and it's a short walk from the cathedral area (Sb-11,200 Ft, Db-14,200 Ft, Tb-17,200 Ft, request quieter courtyard room, pay Internet access, free Wi-Fi in some rooms, free parking, Klimó György utca 9, tel. 72/221-110, www.szinbadpanzio.hu, szinbadpanzio@freemail.hu).

$ Náp Hostel ("Sun") is colorful and well-run by Tamás. Hiding upstairs in an apartment building on the main walking street, its four bedrooms share three WCs and two showers (D-13,000 Ft, bunk in 8-bed dorm-3,000 Ft, in 6-bed dorm-4,300 Ft, in 6-bed dorm with balcony-4,800 Ft, no breakfast, free Internet access and Wi-Fi, kitchen, laundry service, Király utca 23-25, tel. 72/950-684, www.naphostel.com).

Eating in Pécs

On the Pedestrian Drag, Király Utca

The walking streets branching off from the main square are lined with restaurants and cafés that feature outdoor tables with ideal people-watching. Király utca (described earlier, under "Sights in Pécs") is Pécs' "restaurant row," with a fine variety of eating options. Window-shop for your favorite, considering the following choices (generally open long hours daily):

Dóm Vendéglő serves traditional Hungarian cuisine along with pizzas and other international dishes. It has both indoor and outdoor seating (1,500-2,000-Ft main dishes, 1,000-1,500-Ft pizzas, 3,000-Ft steaks, Király utca 3, tel. 72/210-088).

Enoteca Corso, serving modern international cuisine, considers itself the finest dining establishment in town. Its upstairs restaurant defines Hungarian pretense (gourmet meals served with matching local wines, 8,000 Ft/three courses, 10,000 Ft/four courses, 12,000 Ft/five courses, more for wine, daily 8:00-24:00). Its street-level **Bistro Corso** is more accessible, with good 2,000-Ft plates and fine Hungarian wine by the glass (see blackboard inside for daily selections; Mon-Fri 12:00-14:30 & 18:30-22:30, Sat 18:30-22:30, closed Sun; both at Király utca 14, tel. 72/525-198).

Oázis is the place for a simple, cheap, fast, and good gyro or falafel. Grab one to go, or enjoy it at their outdoor tables on this main street (600-Ft sandwiches, Király utca 17).

Cool Tour Music & Café is a "ruin pub" with a bohemian vibe and rickety tables strewn around its hidden garden. It's a fine place for a toasted sandwich, pastry, coffee, or drink (Király utca 26). Consider dropping by after dinner for a cocktail or beer (nightly until wee hours).

Fregatt Arizona Pub is an enthusiastically American steakhouse considered by locals to be a fine value. Choose from three dining zones: a Buffalo Bill interior, a cool back courtyard, or streetside seating ideal for people-watching (2,000-4,000-Ft main dishes, daily 11:00-24:00, Király utca 21, tel. 72/511-068).

Elsewhere in Pécs

Elefántos Ház ("House at the Elephant") features good Italian fare in its ho-hum interior or at its inviting outdoor tables on a delightful shopping square in the town center (1,000-1,500-Ft pizzas and pastas, 2,000-3,000-Ft meat dishes, daily 11:30-23:30, Jókai tér 6, tel. 72/216-055).

Aranykacsa ("Golden Duck") is in all the guidebooks thanks to its well-respected, traditional Hungarian fare, specializing in duck. Choose between two distinct dining rooms: the smoky pub or a bright and elegant, smoke-free room with a Zsolnay porcelain theme (1,000-2,000-Ft main dishes, pricier duck specialties, Tue-Sat 11:30-22:00, Sun 11:30-15:30, closed Mon, Teréz utca 4, tel. 72/518-860).

Pécs Connections

From Pécs by Train: For destinations (including **Eger, Sopron,** and **Bratislava**), you'll generally change trains in Budapest. Direct trains connect Pécs and **Budapest** (8 fast IC trains/day, every 2 hours, 3 hours; a few additional connections are possible with a transfer at the suburban Budapest-Kelenföld station). One handy train each afternoon (departing at 15:30) follows a different route, near the Croatian border, connecting Pécs directly to **Sopron** (5 hours), then **Vienna** (6 hours).

SLOVENIA
Slovenija

SLOVENIA

Tiny, overlooked Slovenia is one of Europe's most unexpectedly charming destinations. At the intersection of the Slavic, German, and Italian worlds, Slovenia is an exciting mix of the best of each culture. Though it's just a quick trip away from the tourist throngs in Venice, Munich, Salzburg, and Vienna, Slovenia has stayed off the tourist track—making it a handy detour for in-the-know Back Door travelers. Be warned: I've never met anyone who visited Slovenia and didn't wish they'd allotted more time for this delightful, underrated land.

Today, it seems strange to think that Slovenia was ever part of Yugoslavia. Both in the personality of its people and in its landscape, Slovenia feels more like Austria. Slovenes are more industrious, organized, and punctual than their fellow former Yugoslavs...yet still friendly, relaxed, and Mediterranean. Locals like the balance. Visitors expecting minefields and rusting Yugo factories are pleasantly

surprised to find Slovenia's rolling countryside dotted instead with quaint alpine villages and the spires of miniature Baroque churches, with breathtaking, snowcapped peaks in the distance.

Only half as big as Switzerland, Slovenia is remarkably diverse for its size. Travelers can hike on alpine trails in the morning and explore some of the world's best caves in the afternoon, before relaxing with a seafood dinner on the Adriatic.

Slovenia enjoys a powerhouse economy—the healthiest of all of Europe's former communist countries. The Austro-Hungarian Empire left it with a strong industrial infrastructure, which the Yugoslav government expanded. By 1980, 60 percent of all Yugoslav industry was in little Slovenia (which had only 8 percent of Yugoslavia's population and 8 percent of its territory). With independence, Slovenia continued this trend, pushing their mighty little economy into the future. Of the 12 new nations that

have joined the European Union since 2004, Slovenia was the only one rich enough to be a net donor (with a higher per-capita income than the average), and the first one to join the euro currency zone (it adopted the euro in January 2007). Thanks to its long-standing ties to the West and can-do spirit, Slovenia already feels more "Western" than any other destination in this book.

The country has a funny way of making people fall in love with it. Slovenes are laid-back, easygoing, stylish, and fun. They won't win any world wars (they're too well-adjusted to even try)... but they're exactly the type of people you'd love to chat with over a cup of coffee.

The Slovenian language is as mellow as the people. While Slovenes use Serb, German, and English curses in abundance, the worst they can say in their native tongue is, "May you be kicked by a horse." For "Darn it!" they say, "Three hundred hairy bears!"

Coming from such a small country, locals are proud of the few

things that are distinctly Slovenian, such as the roofed hayrack. Foreigners think that Slovenes' fascination with these hayracks is strange...until they visit and see them absolutely everywhere (especially in the northwest). Because of the frequent rainfall, the hayracks are covered by a roof that allows the hay to dry thoroughly. The most

Slovenia Almanac

Official Name: Republika Slovenija, or simply Slovenija.

Snapshot History: After being dominated by Germans for centuries, Slovenian culture proudly emerged in the 19th century. In the aftermath of World War I, Slovenia merged with its neighbors to become Yugoslavia, then broke away and achieved independence for the first time in 1991.

Population: Slovenia's two million people (a count similar to Nevada's) are 83 percent ethnic Slovenes who speak Slovene, plus a smattering of Serbs, Croats, and Muslim Bosniaks. Almost 60 percent of the country is Catholic.

Latitude and Longitude: 46° N and 14° E (latitude similar to Lyon, France; Montreal, Canada; or Bismarck, North Dakota).

Area: At 7,800 square miles, it's about the size of New Jersey, but with one-fourth the population.

Geography: Tiny Slovenia has four extremely different terrains and climates: the warm Mediterranean coastline (just 29 miles long—about one inch per inhabitant); the snow-capped, forested alpine mountains in the northwest (including 9,400-foot Mount Triglav); the moderate-climate, central limestone plateau that includes Ljubljana and the cave-filled Karst region; and to the east, a corner of the Great Hungarian Plain (the Prekmurje region, near Maribor and Ptuj). If you look at a map of Slovenia and squint your eyes a bit, it looks like a chicken running toward the east.

Biggest Cities: Nearly one in five Slovenes lives in the two biggest cities: Ljubljana (the capital, pop. 270,000) and Maribor (in the east, pop. 158,000). Half of the population lives in rural villages.

Economy: With a Gross Domestic Product of $56 billion and a GDP per capita of $28,000, Slovenia's economy is extremely healthy (especially compared to most other post-communist states). Slovenia's wealth comes largely from manufactured metal products (trucks and machinery) traded with a diverse group of partners.

Currency: Slovenia uses the euro: €1 = about $1.40.

Government: The country is led by the prime minister (currently Janez Janša), who heads the leading vote-getting party in legislative elections. He governs along with the figurehead president (currently Danilo Türk). Slovenia's relatively peaceful secession is credited largely to former Prime Minister Milan Kučan, who remains a popular figure. The National Assembly consists of about 90 elected legislators; there's also a second house of parliament, which has much less power. Despite the country's small size, it is divided into some 200 municipalities.

Flag: Three horizontal bands of white (top), blue, and red. A shield in the upper left shows Mount Triglav, with a wavy-line sea below and three stars above.

The Average Slovene: The average Slovene skis, in this largely alpine country, and is an avid fan of team handball (yes, handball). He or she lives in a 250-square-foot apartment, earns $1,400 a month, watches 16 hours of TV a week (much of it in English with Slovene subtitles), and enjoys a drink-and-a-half of alcohol every day.

Notable Slovenes: A pair of prominent Ohio politicians—perennial presidential candidate Dennis Kucinich and Senator George Voinovich, both from the Cleveland area—are each half-Slovene. (In 1910, Cleveland had the biggest Slovenian population of any city in the world—just ahead of Trieste and Ljubljana.) Classical musicians might know composers Giuseppe Tartini and Hugo Wolf. Even if you haven't heard of architect Jože Plečnik yet, you'll hear his name a hundred times while you're in Slovenia—especially in Ljubljana (see page 742). Perhaps most famous of all is the illustrious Melania Knauss—a GQ cover girl who's also the current Mrs. Donald Trump.

Sporty Slovenes: If you follow alpine sports or team handball, you'll surely know some world-class athletes from Slovenia. NBA fans might recognize basketball players Primož Brezec and Bostjan Nachbar, as well as some lesser players. Slovenian hockey player Anže Kopitar plays in the NHL. The athletic Slovenes—perhaps trying to compensate for the miniscule size of their country—have accomplished astonishing feats: Davo Karničar has skied down from the summits of some of the world's tallest mountains (including Everest, Kilimanjaro, and McKinley). Benka Pulko became the first person ever to drive a motorcycle around the world (that is, all seven continents, including Antarctica; total trip: 118,000 miles in 2,000 days—also the longest solo motorcycle journey by a woman; www.benka pulko.com). Dušan Mravlje ran across all the continents (www .dusanmravlje.si). And ultra-marathon swimmer Martin Strel has swum the entire length of several major rivers, including the Danube (1,775 miles), the Mississippi (2,415 miles), the Yangtze (3,915 miles), and the Amazon (3,393 miles; for more, see www .martinstrel.com).

traditional kind is the *toplar*, consisting of two hayracks connected by one big roof. It looks like a skinny barn with open, fenced sides. Hay hangs on the sides to dry; firewood, carts, tractors, and other farm implements sit on the ground inside; and dried hay is stored in the loft above. But these wooden *toplarji* are firetraps, and a stray bolt of lighting can burn one down in a flash. So in recent years, more farmers are moving to single hayracks *(enojni);* these are still roofed, but have posts made of concrete, rather than wood. You'll find postcards and miniature wooden models of both kinds of hayracks (a fun souvenir).

Another good (and uniquely Slovenian) memento is a cre-

atively decorated front panel from a beehive *(panjske končnice)*. Slovenia has a strong beekeeping tradition, and beekeepers once believed that painting the fronts of the hives made it easier for bees to find their way home. Replicas of these panels are available at gift shops all over the country. (For more on the panels and Slovenia's beekeeping heritage, see page 787.)

Slovenia is also the land of polka. Slovenes claim that polka music was invented here, and singer/accordionist Slavko Avsenik—from the village of Begunje near Bled—cranks out popular oompah songs that make him bigger than the Beatles (and therefore, presumably, Jesus) in Germany. You'll see the Avsenik ensemble and other oompah bands on Slovenian TV, where hokey Lawrence Welk-style shows are a local institution.

To really stretch your euros, try one of Slovenia's more than 400 farmhouse B&Bs, called "tourist farms" *(turistične kmetije)*. These are actual, working farms (often organic) that sell meals and/or rent rooms to tourists to help make ends meet. You can use a tourist farm as a home base to explore the entire country—remember, the farthest reaches of Slovenia are only a day trip away. A comfortable, hotelesque double with a private bathroom—plus a traditional Slovenian dinner and a hearty breakfast—costs as little as €50. Request a listing from the Slovenian Tourist Board (see page 1228), or find information at www.slovenia.info.

Most visitors to Slovenia are, in my experience, completely charmed by the place. With all it has going for it, it's hard to believe that Slovenia is not already overrun with tourists. Somehow, this little country continues to glide beneath the radar. Exploring its mountain trails and meeting its friendly locals, you'll feel like you're in on a secret.

Helpful Hints

Sunday Closures: Slovenia can be extremely sleepy on Sundays, even in the larger towns and cities, where virtually all shops are closed. Plan ahead. Fortunately, many restaurants remain open, plus a select few grocery stores.

Smoking Ban: Smoking is prohibited in public places, unless it's a specially designated (and well-ventilated) smoking room. Larger hotels still have some "smoking" rooms, but smoking isn't allowed in public areas.

Telephones: Slovenian phone numbers beginning with 080 are toll-free; 090 and 089 denote expensive toll lines. Most mobile phone numbers begin with 030, 031, 040, 041, 051, 059, 070, or 071. For more details on how to dial to, from, and within Slovenia, see page 1231.

Toll Sticker: To drive on Slovenia's expressways *(avtocesta)*, you'll need to display a toll sticker *(vinjeta,* veen-YEH-tah; €15/week, €30/month). If renting your car in Slovenia, it probably comes with a toll sticker (but ask just to be sure); if you're driving in from elsewhere, such as Croatia, you can buy one at a gas station, post office, or some newsstands. **Be warned:** This rule is taken very seriously. If you're found driving on expressways without the sticker, you'll immediately be fined €150.

Cruise Port: The Slovenian coastal town of **Koper** is becoming a popular port of call for Mediterranean cruises. Koper is connected by frequent buses to the nearby and enjoyable coastal resort of Piran; a longer bus trip takes you to the Italian city of Trieste. However, as the country is so small, it's possible to see just about any of the Slovenia destinations covered in this book in a single day in port (provided you use your time efficiently and have a private driver—I recommend Tina Hiti and Sašo Golub, listed on page 767).

Slovenian History

Slovenia has a long and unexciting history as part of various larger empires. Charlemagne's Franks conquered the tiny land in the eighth century, and, ever since, Slovenia has been a backwater of the Germanic world—first as a holding of the Holy Roman Empire and later, the Habsburg Empire. Slovenia seems as much German as Slavic. But even as the capital, Ljubljana, was populated by Austrians (and called Laibach by its German-speaking residents), the Slovenian language and cultural traditions survived in the countryside.

Ljubljana rose to international prominence for half a decade (1809-1813) when Napoleon named it the capital of his "Illyrian Provinces," stretching from Austria's Tirol to Croatia's Dalmatian

SLOVENIA

Slo-what?-ia

The only thing I know about Slovakia is what I learned first-hand from your foreign minister, who came to Texas.

—George W. Bush, to a Slovak journalist (Bush had actually met with Dr. Janez Drnovšek, who was then Slovenia's prime minister)

Maybe it's understandable that many Americans confuse Slovenia with Slovakia. Both are small, mountainous countries that not too long ago were parts of bigger, better known, now defunct nations. But anyone who has visited Slovenia and Slovakia will set you straight—they feel worlds apart.

Slovenia, wedged between the Alps and the Adriatic, is a tidy, prosperous country with a strong economy. Until 1991, Slovenia was one of the six republics that made up Yugoslavia. Historically, Slovenia has had very strong ties with Germanic culture—so it feels like its neighbor to the north, Austria.

Slovakia—two countries away, to the northeast—is slightly bigger. Much of its territory is covered by the Carpathian Mountains, most notably the dramatic, jagged peaks of the High Tatras. In 1993, the Czechs and Slovaks peacefully chose to go their separate ways, so the nation of Czechoslovakia dissolved into the Czech Republic and the Slovak Republic (a.k.a. Slovakia).

To make things even more confusing, there's also **Slavonia.** This is the thick, inland "panhandle" that makes up the northeast half of Croatia, along Slovenia's southeast border. Much of the warfare in Croatia's 1991-1995 war took place in Slavonia (including Vukovar; see the Understanding Yugoslavia chapter).

I won't tell on you if you mix them up. But if you want to feel smarter than a former president, do a little homework and get it right.

Coast. During this time, the long-suppressed Slovene language was used for the first time in schools and the government. This kicked off a national revival movement (as in so many other Central and Eastern European countries at the time)—asserting the worthiness of the Slovenian language and culture compared to the dominant Germanic worldview of the time. Inspired by the patriotic poetry of France Prešeren, national pride surged.

The last century saw the most interesting chapter of Slovenian history. Some of World War I's fiercest fighting occurred at the Soča (Isonzo) Front in northwest Slovenia—witnessed by young Ernest Hemingway, who drove an ambulance (see sidebars on pages 800 and 808). After the war, from 1918 to 1991, Slovenia was Yugoslavia's smallest, northernmost, and most affluent republic.

Concerned about Serbian strongman Slobodan Milošević's nationalistic politics, Slovenia seceded in 1991. Because more than 90 percent of the people here were ethnic Slovenes, the break with Yugoslavia was simple and virtually uncontested. Its war for independence lasted just 10 days and claimed only a few dozen lives. (For more details, see the Understanding Yugoslavia chapter, page 1207.)

After centuries of looking to the West, in May of 2004 Slovenia became the first of the former Yugoslav republics to join the European Union. The Slovenes have been practical about this move, realizing it's essential for their survival as a tiny nation in a modern world. But there are trade-offs, and "Euroskeptics" are down on EU bureaucracy. As borders disappear, Slovenes are experiencing more crime. Traditional farms are grappling with strict EU standards. Slovenian businesses are having difficulty competing with big German and other Western European firms. Before EU membership, only Slovenes could own Slovenian land. But now wealthy foreigners are buying property, driving up the cost of real estate.

Yet EU membership seems to be agreeing with the Slovenes. For one thing, it allowed this generally low-key, conflict-averse little country a rare chance to flex its political muscles when, in 2009, they temporarily vetoed Croatia's bid for EU membership over a longstanding border rivalry along the Istrian coastline (for details, see page 831). Slovenia also became the first post-communist country to adopt the euro currency in January of 2007. Despite the worldwide economic crisis, business here is booming. As throughout their history, the Slovenes are adjusting to the 21st century with their characteristic sense of humor and easygoing attitude.

Slovenian Food

Slovenian cuisine offers more variety and better quality than Croatian fare. Slovenes brag that their cuisine melds the best of

Italian and German cooking—but they also embrace other international influences, especially French. Like Croatian food, Slovenian cuisine also features some pan-Balkan elements: The savory phyllo-dough pastry *burek* is the favorite fast food here, and when Slovenes host a backyard barbecue, they grill up *čevapčiči* and *ražnjiči*, topped off with the eggplant-and-red-bell-pepper condiment *ajvar* (see the "Balkan Flavors" sidebar on page 1090). Slovenia enjoys Italian-style

SLOVENIA

Pršut

In Slovenia and Croatia, *pršut* (purr-SHOOT) is one of the essential food groups. This air-cured ham (like Italian prosciutto) is soaked in salt and sometimes also smoked. Then it hangs in open-ended barns for up to a year and a half, to be dried and seasoned by the howling Bora wind. Each region produces a slightly different *pršut*. In Dalmatia, a layer of fat keeps the ham moist; in Istria, the fat is trimmed, and the *pršut* is dryer.

Since Slovenia joined the European Union, strict new standards have swept the land. Separate rooms must be used for the slaughter, preparation, and curing of the ham. While this seems fair enough for large producers, small family farms that want to produce just enough *pršut* for their own use—and maybe sell one or two ham hocks to neighbors—find they have to invest thousands of euros to be compliant.

fare, with a pizza or pasta restaurant on seemingly every corner. Hungarian food simmers in the northeast corner of the country (where many Magyars reside). And in most of the country, traditional Slovenian food has a distinctly Germanic vibe—including the "four S's": sausages, schnitzels, strudels, and sauerkraut.

Traditional Slovenian dishes are prepared with groats—a grainy mush made with buckwheat, barley, or corn. Buckwheat, which thrives in this climate, often appears on Slovenian menus. You'll also see plenty of *štruklji* (dumplings), which can be stuffed with cheese, meat, or vegetables. *Repa* is turnip prepared like sauerkraut. Among the hearty soups in Slovenia is *jota*—a staple for Karst peasants, made from *repa*, beans, and vegetables.

The cuisine of Slovenia's Karst region (the arid limestone plain south of Ljubljana) is notable. The small farms and wineries of this region have been inspired by Italy's Slow Food movement—their owners believe that cuisine is meant to be gradually appreciated, not rushed—making the Karst a destination for gourmet tours. Karstic cuisine is similar to France's nouvelle cuisine—several courses in small portions, with a focus on unusual combinations and preparations—but with a Tuscan flair. The Karst's tasty air-dried ham *(pršut)*, available throughout the country, is worth seeking out (see sidebar). Istria (the peninsula just to the south of the Karst, in southern Slovenia and Croatia) produces truffles that, locals boast, are as good as those from Italy's Piedmont (see page 1016).

Voda is water, and *kava* is coffee. Radenska, in the bottle with the three little hearts, is Slovenia's best-known brand of mineral water—good enough that the word *Radenska* is synonymous with bottled water all over Slovenia and throughout the former Yugoslavia. It's not common to ask for (or receive) tap water, but you can try requesting *voda iz pipe.*

Adventurous teetotalers should forego the Coke and sample

Cockta, a Slovenian cola with an unusual flavor (which supposedly comes from berry, lemon, orange, and 11 herbs). Originally called "Cockta-Cockta," the drink was introduced during the communist period, as an alternative to the difficult-to-get Coca-Cola. This local variation developed a loyal following...until the Iron Curtain fell, and the real Coke became readily available. Cockta sales plummeted. But in recent years—prodded by the slogan "The Taste of Your Youth"—nostalgic Slovenes are drinking Cockta once more.

To toast, say, *"Na ZDROW-yeh!"*—if you can't remember it, think of "Nice driving!" The premier Slovenian brand of *pivo* (beer) is Union (OO-nee-ohn), but you'll also see a lot of Laško (LASH-koh), whose mascot is the Zlatorog (or "Golden Horn," a mythical chamois-like animal).

Slovenia produces some fine *vino* (wine). The Celts first made wine in Slovenia; the Romans improved the process and spread it throughout the country. Slovenia has three primary wine regions. Podravje, in the northeast, is dominated by *laški* and *renski riesling.* Posavje, in the southeast, produces both white and red wines, but is known mostly for the light, russet-colored *cviček* wine. Primorska, in the southwest, has a Mediterranean climate and produces mostly reds. One of the most popular is *teran,* made from *refošk* grapes, which grow in iron-rich red soil *(terra rossa)*—infusing them with a high lactic acid content that supposedly gives the wine healing properties.

Slovenia's national dessert is *potica,* a rolled pastry with walnuts and sometimes also raisins. For more tasty treats, see the "Bled Desserts" sidebar on page 781. Locals claim that Ljubljana has the finest gelato outside of Italy—which, after all, is just an hour down the road.

Slovenian Language

Slovene is surprisingly different from languages spoken in the other former Yugoslav republics. While Serbian and Croatian are mutually intelligible, Slovene is gibberish to Serbs and Croats.

Most Slovenes, on the other hand, know Serbo-Croatian because, a generation ago, everybody in Yugoslavia had to learn it.

Linguists have identified some 46 official dialects of Slovene, and there are probably another 100 or so unofficial ones. Locals can tell which city—or sometimes even which remote mountain valley—someone comes from by their accent.

The tiny country of Slovenia borders Italy and Austria, with important historical and linguistic ties to both. For self-preservation, Slovenes have always been forced to function in many different languages. All of these factors make them excellent linguists. Most young Slovenes speak effortless, flawless English—then admit that they've never set foot in the United States or Britain, but love watching American movies and TV shows (which are always subtitled, never dubbed).

Slovene has a few letters that are pronounced differently than in English, and they add a few diacritics—little markings below and above some letters. Here are a few rules of thumb for sounding out unfamiliar words:

J / j sounds like "y" as in "yellow"

C / c sounds like "ts" as in "cats"

Č / č sounds like "ch" as in "chicken"

Š / š sounds like "sh" as in "shrimp"

Ž / ž sounds like "zh" as in "leisure"

V / v is pronounced as "u"—so the word *avto* sounds like "auto"

Slovene is notorious for its seemingly unpronounceable consonant combinations. Most difficult are **hv** (as in *hvala*, "thank you") and **nj** (as in Bohinj, a lake in Slovenia). Foreigners are notorious for over-pronouncing these combinations. In the combination hv, the h is nearly silent; if you struggle with it, simply leave off the h (for *hvala*, just say "VAH-lah"). When you see nj, the j is mostly silent, with a slight "y" sound that can be omitted: for Bohinj, just say BOH-heen. Listen to locals and imitate.

The only trick: As in English, which syllable gets the emphasis is unpredictable. Slovenes use many of the same words as Croatians, but put the stress on an entirely different place.

Learn some key Slovenian phrases (see the Slovenian survival phrases on page 1269). You'll make more friends and your trip will go more smoothly.

A few key words are helpful for navigation: *trg* (pronounced "turg," square), *ulica* (OO-leet-sah, road), *cesta* (TSEH-stah, avenue), *avtocesta* (OW-toh-tseh-stah, expressway), and *most* (mohst, bridge).

LJUBLJANA

Slovenia's capital, Ljubljana (lyoob-lyee-AH-nah), with a lazy Old Town clustered around a castle-topped mountain, is often likened to Salzburg. It's an apt comparison—but only if you inject a healthy dose of breezy Adriatic culture, add a Slavic accent, and replace favorite son Mozart with local architect Jože Plečnik.

Ljubljana feels smaller than its population of 270,000. While big-league museums are in short supply, the town itself is an idyllic place that sometimes feels too good to be true. Festivals fill the summer, and people enjoy a Sunday stroll any day of the week. Fashion boutiques and al fresco cafés jockey for control of the Old Town, while the leafy riverside promenade crawls with stylishly dressed students sipping *kava* and polishing their near-perfect English. Laid-back Ljubljana is the kind of place where graffiti and crumbling buildings seem elegantly atmospheric instead of shoddy. But more and more of those buildings have been getting a facelift recently, as a spunky mayor has been spiffing up the place and creating gleaming traffic-free zones left and right—making what was already an exceptionally livable city into a true pedestrians' paradise.

Batted around by history, Ljubljana has seen cultural influences from all sides—most notably Prague, Vienna, and Venice. This has left the city a happy hodgepodge of cultures. Being the midpoint between the Slavic, Germanic, and Italian worlds gives Ljubljana a special spice. People often ask me: What's the "next Prague"? And I have to answer Kraków. But Ljubljana is the *next* "next Prague."

The Story of Ljubljana

In ancient times, Ljubljana was on the trade route connecting the Mediterranean (just 60 miles away) to the Black Sea (toss a bottle off the bridge here, and it can float to the Danube and, eventually, all the way to Russia). Legend has it that Jason and his Argonauts founded Ljubljana when they stopped here for the winter on their way home with the Golden Fleece. The town was Romanized (and called Emona) before being overrun by Huns, only to be resettled later by Slavs.

In 1335, Ljubljana fell under the jurisdiction of the Habsburg emperors (who called it Laibach). After six centuries of Habsburg rule, Ljubljana still feels Austrian—especially thanks to its abundant Austrian Baroque and Viennese Art Nouveau architecture—but with a Mediterranean flair.

Napoleon put Ljubljana on the map when he made it the capital of his Illyrian Provinces, a realm that stretched from the Danube to Dubrovnik, and from Austria to Albania (for just four short years, 1809-1813). For the first time, the Slovene language was taught in schools, awakening a newfound pride in Slovenian cultural heritage. People still look back fondly on this very brief era, which was the first (and probably only) time when Ljubljana rose to prominence on the world stage. After more than 600 years of being part of the Habsburg Empire, Ljubljana has no "Habsburg Square"...but they do have a "French Revolution Square."

In the mid-19th century, the railway connecting Vienna to the Adriatic (Trieste) was built through town—and Ljubljana boomed. An earthquake hit the city in 1895, damaging many

Planning Your Time

Ljubljana deserves a full day. While there are few must-see sights, the city's biggest attraction is its ambience. You'll spend much of your time strolling the pleasant town center, exploring the many interesting squares and architectural gems, shopping at the boutiques, and sipping coffee at sidewalk cafés along the river.

Here's the best plan for a low-impact sightseeing day: Begin on Prešeren Square, the heart of the city. Cross the Triple Bridge and wander through the riverside produce market before joining the town walking tour at 10:00 (at 11:00 in Oct-March). After the tour, wander south along the Ljubljanica River and through the Krakovo gardens to my favorite Ljubljana museum, the Jože Plečnik House (as this sight may close for renovation, confirm it's open before making the trip). In the afternoon, commit some quality time to people-watching at a riverside café, window-shop at some colorful boutiques, or consider more sightseeing (good options include the Serbian Orthodox Church and Tivoli Park, with the Contemporary History Museum, west of downtown;

buildings. Locals cleverly exaggerated the impact (propping up buildings that were structurally sound, and even tearing down unwanted old houses that had been unharmed) in preparation for a visit of Emperor Franz Josef—who took pity on the city and invested generously in its reconstruction. Ljubljana was made over in the Art Nouveau style so popular in Vienna, its capital at the time. A generation later, architect Jože Plečnik bathed the city in his distinctive, artsy-but-sensible, classical-meets-modern style.

In World War II, Slovenia was occupied first by the Italians, then by the Nazis. Ljubljana had a thriving resistance movement that the Nazis couldn't suppress—so they simply fenced off the entire city and made it a giant prison for three years, allowing only shipments of basic food supplies to get in. But the Slovenes—who knew their land far better than their oppressors did—continued to slip in and out of town undetected, allowing them to agitate through the end of the war.

In 1991, Ljubljana became the capital of one of Europe's youngest nations. Today the city is filled with university students, making it a very youthful-feeling town. Ljubljana has always felt free to be creative, and recent years—with unprecedented freedoms—have been no exception. This city is on the cutting edge when it comes to architecture, public art, fashion, and trendy pubs—a tendency embodied by its recent mayor-turned-parliamentarian, Zoran Janković (see page 728). And yet, Ljubljana's scintillating avant-garde culture has soft edges—hip, but also nonthreatening and user-friendly.

or the Slovenian Ethnographic Museum and other sights in Metelkova, north of downtown).

Plenty of good day trips are a short distance from Ljubljana. With a second day, visit Lake Bled (see next chapter).

Ljubljana is dead and disappointing on Sundays (virtually all shops are closed and the produce market is quiet, but museums are generally open (except for the Jože Plečnik House), a modest flea market stretches along the riverfront, and the TI's walking tour still runs). The city is also relatively quiet in August, when the students are on break and many locals head to beach resorts. They say that in August, even homeless people go to the coast.

Orientation to Ljubljana

(area code: 01)

Ljubljana—with narrow lanes, architecture that mingles the Old World and contemporary Europe, and cobbles upon cobbles of wonderful distractions—can be disorienting for a first-timer.

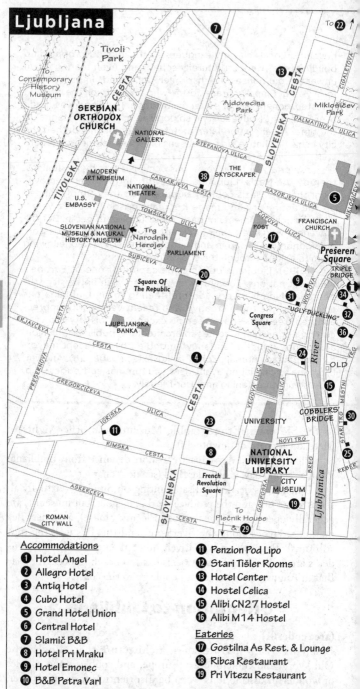

Ljubljana

LJUBLJANA

Accommodations

1 Hotel Angel
2 Allegro Hotel
3 Antiq Hotel
4 Cubo Hotel
5 Grand Hotel Union
6 Central Hotel
7 Slamič B&B
8 Hotel Pri Mraku
9 Hotel Emonec
10 B&B Petra Varl
11 Penzion Pod Lipo
12 Stari Tišler Rooms
13 Hotel Center
14 Hostel Celica
15 Alibi CN27 Hostel
16 Alibi M14 Hostel

Eateries

17 Gostilna As Rest. & Lounge
18 Ribca Restaurant
19 Pri Vitezu Restaurant

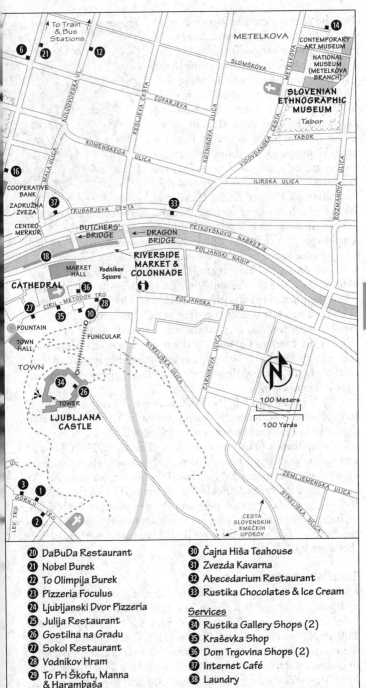

⑳ DaBuDa Restaurant	㉚ Čajna Hiša Teahouse
㉑ Nobel Burek	㉛ Zvezda Kavarna
㉒ To Olimpija Burek	㉜ Abecedarium Restaurant
㉓ Pizzeria Foculus	㉝ Rustika Chocolates & Ice Cream
㉔ Ljubljanski Dvor Pizzeria	
㉕ Julija Restaurant	<u>Services</u>
㉖ Gostilna na Gradu	㉞ Rustika Gallery Shops (2)
㉗ Sokol Restaurant	㉟ Kraševka Shop
㉘ Vodnikov Hram	㊱ Dom Trgovina Shops (2)
㉙ To Pri Škofu, Manna & Harambaša	㊲ Internet Café
	㊳ Laundry

But the charming central zone is compact, and with a little wandering, you'll quickly get the hang of it.

The Ljubljanica River—lined with cafés, restaurants, and a buzzing outdoor market—bisects the city, making a 90-degree turn around the base of a castle-topped mountain. Most sights are either along or just a short walk from the river. Visitors enjoy the distinctive bridges that span the Ljubljanica, including the landmark Triple Bridge (Tromostovje) and pillared Cobblers' Bridge (Čevljarski Most)—both designed by Jože Plečnik. Between these two is a very plain wooden bridge (with great views) dubbed the "Ugly Duckling." The center of Ljubljana is Prešeren Square, watched over by a big statue of Slovenia's national poet, France Prešeren.

I've organized the sights in this chapter based on which side of the river they're on: the east (castle) side of the river, where Ljubljana began, with more medieval charm; and the west (Prešeren Square) side of the river, which has a more Baroque/Art Nouveau feel and most of the urban sprawl. At the northern edge of the tourist's Ljubljana is the train station and Metelkova museum and nightlife zone; at the southern edge are the garden district of Krakovo and the Jože Plečnik House; and at the western edge is Tivoli Park.

Ljubljana's Two Big Ps: You'll hear the following two easy-to-confuse names constantly during your visit. Mind your Ps, and your visit to Ljubljana becomes more meaningful:

Jože Plečnik (YOH-zheh PLAYCH-neek, 1872-1957) is the architect who shaped Ljubljana, designing virtually all of the city's most important landmarks. For more information, see page 742.

France Prešeren (FRAHN-tseh preh-SHAY-rehn, 1800-1849) is Slovenia's greatest poet and the namesake of Ljubljana's main square. Some civic-minded candy shops—trying to imitate the success of Austria's "Mozart Ball" chocolates—sell chocolate "Prešeren Balls."

Tourist Information

Ljubljana's helpful, businesslike TI has a useful website (www.visitljubljana.si) and three branches: at the **Triple Bridge,** across from Prešeren Square (daily June-Sept 8:00-21:00, Oct-May 8:00-19:00, Stritarjeva 1, tel. 01/306-1215); at the upper corner of the **market** (with pay Internet access, bike rental, and information about the rest of Slovenia; June-Sept daily 8:00-21:00; Oct-May Mon-Fri 8:00-19:00, Sat-Sun 9:00-17:00; Krekov trg 10, tel. 01/306-4575); and at the **train station** (June-Sept daily 8:00-22:00; Oct-May Mon-Fri 10:00-19:00, Sat 8:00-15:00, closed Sun; Trg O.F. 6, tel. 01/433-9475).

At any TI, pick up a pile of free resources: the big city map, the *Tourist Guide*, the monthly *Where to?* events guide, and a wide range of informative brochures. The TI also offers a free room-finding service. The **Ljubljana Tourist Card,** which includes access to public transportation and covers entry to many city museums as well as the TI's walking tours and boat trips, could save busy sight-seers some money (€23/24 hours, €30/48 hours, €35/72 hours).

Arrival in Ljubljana

By Train: Ljubljana's modern, user-friendly train station (Železniška Postaja) is at the northern edge of the city center. Emerging from the passage up to track 1a, turn right and walk under the long canopy along the train tracks to find the yellow arrivals hall. Everything is well-signed in English, including a **TI,** the handy train-information office next door (with useful handouts outlining trips to several domestic and international destinations, daily 5:30-21:30), and—near the front of the station—a big **ticket office** with clearly marked ticket windows and an **ATM** (office open daily 5:00-22:00). Arrivals are *prihodi*, departures are *odhodi*, and track is *tir*.

The main square is an easy 10-minute **walk** from the station; you can walk to any of my recommended hotels within about 20 minutes (often less). To reach Prešeren Square at the city's center, leave the arrivals hall to the right and walk a long block along the busy Trg Osvobodilne Fronte (or "Trg O.F." for short, with the bus station in the middle). After passing all of the bus stalls, turn left across Trg O.F. and go down Miklošičeva, at the building with the round red-brick columns. This takes you past some of Ljubljana's most appealing architecture to Prešeren Square.

Unscrupulous **taxis** crouch in front of the station, waiting to spring on unsuspecting tourists. The fair metered rate to any of my recommended hotels is around €3 (maybe up to €4-5 in heavy traffic or after hours). But, because the city refuses to regulate taxi tariffs, train-station taxis uniformly charge exorbitant rates—generally around €3-5 per kilometer (plus an extra fee of around €2-3 for bags), which is exponentially more than the €1 per kilometer charged by legitimate outfits. Simply put, it's impossible to hail a taxi on the street in front of the station and get anything resembling a fair fare. But all hope is not lost—to avoid giving these crooks the satisfaction, you can simply call for a taxi that charges fair rates (dial 041-731-831 or 080-1190); if you're uncomfortable calling yourself, just ask the train station TI to call for you (since they're familiar with the situation, they're usually happy to do this if they're not too busy). Taking the time to call, then waiting just a few more minutes for your cab, could easily save you €10 or more. For more on taxis—and how to avoid rip-offs—see "Getting Around Ljubljana—By Taxi," later.

By Bus: Ljubljana's bus station (Autobusna Postaja) is a low-profile building (with ticket windows, Internet access, a bakery, and newsstands) in the middle of Trg O.F., right in front of the train station. To get into the city center, see "By Train," above.

By Car: As you approach Ljubljana on the expressway, the toll road ends. Once you're on the ring road, simply follow signs for *Center*. Once you get into the city center, you'll begin to see directional signs to individual hotels. Ask your hotel about parking—most have some available, usually for a price. If you need to gas up your rental car before returning it, you'll find a huge gas station on Tivolska Cesta (just west of the train station, near the big Union brewery). Otherwise, your options in the center are limited—it's better to look for a gas station on the expressway before you reach the city.

By Plane: See "Ljubljana Connections," at the end of this chapter.

Helpful Hints

Pedestrian Safety: Many Ljubljana residents commute by bike. As a pedestrian, I've had many close calls with bikes whizzing by. Keep your eyes open and stay out of the designated bike lanes on the sidewalks (often marked in red).

Closed Days: Most Ljubljana museums (except the castle and a few less-important museums) are closed on Mondays. The recommended Jože Plečnik House is closed Sundays, Mondays, and Fridays, and might be closed entirely for restoration during your visit.

Markets: In addition to the regular **market** that sprawls along the riverfront (described under "Sights in Ljubljana"), a colorful **flea market** hops along the Ljubljanica River's Breg embankment (across the river from the castle) every Sun 8:00-14:00. On summer Saturdays, there's also a lively and colorful **arts and handicrafts market** in the same place (Sat 8:00-14:00).

Money: Most banks are open Mon-Fri 8:00-12:00 & 15:00-17:00, a few also open Sat 9:00-12:00, closed Sun.

Internet Access: Most hotels offer free Internet access and/or Wi-Fi for their guests. The **TI** at the upper end of the market has several terminals (€1/30 minutes, see "Tourist Information," earlier). **Cyber Café Xplorer** is twice as expensive but has longer hours (Mon-Fri 10:00-22:00, Sat-Sun 12:00-22:00, Cankarjeva 9).

Post Office: The main post office *(pošta)* is in a beautiful yellow Art

Ljubljana Essentials

English	Slovene	Pronounced
Ljubljana Castle	Ljubljanski Grad	lyoob-lyee-AHN-skee grahd
Prešeren Square	Prešernov trg	preh-SHEHR-nohv turg
Congress Square	Kongresni trg	kohn-GREHS-nee turg
French Revolution Square	Trg Francoske Revolucije	turg frant-SOH-skeh reh-voh-LOOT-see-yeh
Square of the Republic	Trg Republike	turg-reh-POOB lee-keh
Triple Bridge	Tromostovje	troh-moh-STOHV-yeh
Cobblers' Bridge	Čevljarski Most	chehv-LAR-skee mohst
Dragon Bridge	Zmajski Most	ZMAY-skee mohst
Jože Plečnik, the architect	Jože Plečnik	YOH-zheh PLAYCH-neek
France Prešeren, the poet	France Prešeren	FRAHN-tseh preh-SHAY-rehn

Nouveau building a block up Čopova from Prešeren Square, at the intersection with the busy Slovenska cesta (Mon-Fri 8:00-19:00, Sat 8:00-13:00, closed Sun).

Architecture Guidebooks: Ljubljana is a turn-on for architecture buffs. If you want to learn more about this city's quirky buildings, consider the excellent €27 *Let's See the City: Ljubljana* architecture guidebook, or the €17 book about Jože Plečnik's work (sold at the Jože Plečnik House, some TIs, and many bookstores).

Laundry: Most hotels can do your laundry, but it's pricey. **Hostel Celica** serves as the town's self-serve launderette—but it has only one machine, and hostel guests have priority (€7/load, not very central at Metelkova 8). For full service, try **Tekstilexpress,** between the city center and Tivoli Park (€2.25/kilo, figure about €12-15 for a full load, takes 24 hours, Mon-Fri 7:00-19:00, Sat 9:00-13:00, closed Sun, Cankarjeva 10B, tel. 01/252-7354).

Car Rental: Figure about €60 per day (includes tax and insurance, no extra charge for drop-off elsewhere in Slovenia). Handy options include **Hertz** (Trdinova 9, tel. 01/434-0147, www.hertz.si), **Europcar** (in City Hotel at Dalmatinova 15, mobile 031-382-052, www.europcar.si), **Avis** (Čufarjeva 2, tel.

01/430-8010, www.avis.si), **Budget** (in Grand Hotel Union at Miklošičeva 3, tel. 01/421-7340, www.budget.si), and **Sixt** (at the train station, tel. 01/234-4650).

Best Views: The Skyscraper's observation deck offers the best views in town (see page 738). Views from the castle are nearly as good. At street level, my favorite views are from the wooden bridge called the "Ugly Duckling" (between the Triple and Cobblers' bridges), especially at night. On sunny, blue-sky days, the colorful architecture on and near Prešeren Square pops, and you'll take photos like crazy along the river promenade.

Getting Around Ljubljana

By Bus: Virtually all of Ljubljana's sights are easily accessible by foot, so public transportation probably isn't necessary. And it's a bit of a headache: To ride a bus, you first have to buy a plastic "Urbana" card for €2 (nonrefundable), which you then load with credit to pay for rides. A ride costs €0.80, and you can't pay the driver—you have to use the card (shareable by up to three people). You can buy the Urbana card at any TI, the bus station, and some newsstands. Transit info: www.lpp.si.

By Taxi: Always call for a cab, or you'll get ripped off. Because cabbies can legally charge whatever they want, even if they use the meter you'll still pay way too much. Legitimate taxis usually start at about €1.50, and then charge €1 per kilometer. But because city leaders refuse to regulate taxi tariffs, many unscrupulous cabbies (including all of those that wait at the train station) legally charge far more, and tack on bogus additional "surcharges." Crooked cabbies are a big problem in Ljubljana, but you can avoid this headache entirely by always calling a reputable taxi company instead of hailing one on the street. If you do this, Ljubljana is a fantastic taxi town with very affordable rates—a ride within the city center (such as from the station to a hotel) should run only a few euros, generally less than €5. Good companies include **Yellow Taxi** (mobile 041-731-831) and **Metro Taxi** (tel. 080-1190). Don't be intimidated—dispatchers speak English, and your hotel, restaurant, or maybe the TI (if they're not too busy) can call a cab for you.

By Bike: Ljubljana is a cyclist's delight, with lots of well-marked bike lanes. A few hotels have rental or loaner bikes, or you can rent bikes at the market square TI (€1/2 hours, €5/day; see "Tourist Information," earlier). Like many European cities, Ljubljana has a subsidized bike-rental program (called BicikeLJ) with 30 locations around the city center. While this program is cheap, it requires advance registration with a credit card, and you have to get the local public-transit Urbana card—probably not worth it for a short visit (for details, see http://en.bicikelj.si).

Tours in Ljubljana

Most of Ljubljana's museums are disappointing; the town's ambience, architecture, and public art are its best attraction. To help you appreciate it all, taking a walking tour—either through the TI or by hiring your own local guide—is worth ▲▲.

Walking Tour—The TI organizes excellent two-hour guided town walks of Ljubljana in English, led by knowledgeable guides. In summer, the walk also includes either a trip up to the castle (by funicular or tourist train) or a 30-minute boat ride on the river. From April through September, there are three tours daily: at 10:00, 14:00, and 17:00. From October through March, the walking tour goes daily at 11:00 (€10, or €9 if you pay at TI, meet at Town Hall around corner from Triple Bridge TI).

Local Guides—Having an expert show you around his or her hometown for two hours for €50 has to be the best value in town. Ljubljana's hardworking guides lead tours on a wide variety of topics and can tailor their tour to your interests (figure €60/2 hours, 50 percent more for same-day booking, contact TI for details, arrange at least 24 hours before). **Marijan Krišković,** who leads tours for me throughout Europe, is an outstanding guide (mobile 040-222-739, kriskovic@yahoo.com). **Barbara Jakopič,** soft-spoken and extremely knowledgeable, is also good (mobile 040-530-870, b_lucky2@yahoo.com). **Minka Kahrič,** who's traveled to the North Pole, also leads tours closer to home—including walks around Ljubljana and excursions into the countryside (€60/2-hour walking tour; driving: €100/up to 4 hours, €140/up to 8 hours; mobile 041-805-962, polarnimedo@yahoo.com).

Boat Cruise—Consider seeing the town from the Ljubljanica River. You have two options for your one-hour cruise: with English commentary from a live guide (€10, 2/day in summer), or unguided (€8, hourly in summer 10:00-20:00). For details, check with the TI (weather permitting, departs from near the Triple Bridge—about one block along the embankment away from the market). Because Ljubljana is a small town that's easily seen by foot, this trip is more romantic than informative.

Bike Tour—The TI offers a bike tour of the city by request (€15, 2 hours, 4-person minimum, arrange at least 24 hours ahead, get details at TI).

Excursions from Ljubljana—Slovenia is a tiny country with many well-worthwhile sights that are near Ljubljana but tricky to reach by public transportation. To hit several efficiently in one day, consider joining an excursion. Tour companies tend to come and go here—drop by any TI to ask about the latest options and which companies have the best reputations. You'll find fliers everywhere. Two relatively well-established outfits are **Roundabout** (their

Ljubljana at a Glance

▲▲▲People-Watching Ljubljana's single best activity is sitting at an outdoor café along the river and watching the vivacious, stylish, fun-loving Slovenes strut their stuff. **Hours:** 24/7.

▲▲Riverside Market Lively market area in the Old Town with produce, clothing, and souvenirs. **Hours:** Best in the morning, especially Sat; market hall open Mon-Fri 7:00-16:00, Sat 7:00-14:00, closed Sun.

▲▲Serbian Orthodox Church of Sts. Cyril and Methodius Beautifully decorated house of worship giving insight into the Orthodox faith. **Hours:** Sun 9:00-12:00 & 17:00-18:00, Mon 8:00-9:00 & 17:00-18:00, Tue-Sat 8:00-12:00 & 14:00-18:00.

▲▲National and University Library Jože Plečnik's pièce de résistance, with an intriguing facade, piles of books, and a bright reading room. **Hours:** Main staircase open Mon-Fri 9:00-20:00, Sat 9:00-14:00, closed Sun; student reading room open to the public only mid-July-mid-Aug Mon-Fri 14:00-20:00.

▲▲Jože Plečnik House Final digs of the famed hometown architect who shaped so much of Ljubljana, explained by an enthusiastic guide. **Hours:** English tours begin at the top of each hour Tue-Thu 10:00-18:00, Sat 9:00-15:00, last tour departs one hour before closing, closed Sun-Mon and Fri, and possibly closed at other times while undergoing renovation—call ahead.

one-day "Karst and Coast Mystery" tour takes you to Predjama Castle, Škocjan Caves, Lipica, and Piran for €45 plus admission to the caves; www.roundabout.si) and **Slovenia Explorer** (their ambitious "Slovenia in 1 Day" trip visits Lake Bled, Lake Bohinj, and Postojna Caves for €115; www.slovenia-explorer.com).

Self-Guided Spin-Tour

▲▲Prešeren Square

The heart of Ljubljana is lively Prešeren Square (Prešernov trg). It's always been bustling, but now it's more people-friendly than ever, since the mayor recently outlawed buses and taxis here.

The city's meeting point is the large **statue of France Prešeren,** Slovenia's greatest poet, whose works include the lyrics to the Slovenian national anthem (and whose silhouette adorns Slovenia's €2 coin). The statue shows Prešeren, an important catalyst of 19th-century Slovenian nationalism, being inspired from overhead by a Muse. This statue provoked a scandal and outraged

▲▲Slovenian Ethnographic Museum Engaging, well-presented collection celebrating Slovenian culture. **Hours:** Tue-Sun 10:00-18:00, closed Mon.

▲Cathedral Italian Baroque interior and highly symbolic, intricately carved doors. **Hours:** Open long hours daily but closed 12:00-15:00.

▲Dragon Bridge Distinctive Art Nouveau bridge adorned with the city's mascot. **Hours:** Always roaring.

▲Ljubljana Castle Tower with good views and so-so 3-D film. **Hours:** Grounds open daily April-Sept 9:00-23:00, Oct-March 10:00-21:00; castle open daily April-Sept 9:00-21:00, Oct-March 10:00-18:00, film plays all day on the half-hour.

▲Contemporary History Museum Baroque mansion in Tivoli Park, with exhibit highlighting Slovenia's last 100 years. **Hours:** Tue-Sun 10:00-18:00, closed Mon.

▲City Museum of Ljubljana Modern, high-tech exhibit on the city's history. **Hours:** Tue-Sun 10:00-18:00, Thu until 21:00, closed Mon.

▲Cobblers' Bridge Columned bridge that epitomizes Jože Plečnik's distinctive architectural style. **Hours:** Always open.

the bishop when it went up a century ago—a naked woman sharing the square with a church! To ensure that nobody could be confused about the woman's intentions, she's conspicuously depicted with typical Muse accessories: a laurel branch and a cloak. Even so, for the first few years they covered the scandalous statue with a tarp each night. And the model who posed for the Muse was so disgraced that no one in Slovenia would hire her—so she emigrated to South America and never returned.

Stand at the base of the statue to get oriented. The bridge crossing the Ljubljanica River is one of Ljubljana's most important landmarks, Jože Plečnik's **Triple Bridge** (Tromostovje). The middle (widest) part of this bridge already existed, but Plečnik added the two side spans to more efficiently funnel the six streets of traffic on this side of the bridge to the one street on the other side. The bridge's Venetian vibe is intentional: Plečnik recognized that Ljubljana, located midway between

Venice and then-capital Vienna, is itself a bridge between the Italian and Germanic worlds. Across the bridge are the TI, WCs, ATMs, market and cathedral (to the left), and the Town Hall (straight ahead).

Now turn 90 degrees to the right, and look down the first street after the riverbank. Find the pale woman in the picture frame on the second floor of the first yellow house. This is **Julija,** the unrequited love of Prešeren's life. Tour guides spin romantic tales about how the couple met. But the truth is far less exciting: He was a teacher in her father's house when he was in his 30s and she was four. Later in life, she inspired him from afar—as she does now, from across the square—but they never got together. She may have been his muse, but when it came to marriage, she opted for wealth and status.

When Ljubljana was hit by an earthquake in 1895, locals took the opportunity (and an ample rebuilding fund from the Austro-Hungarian Empire) to remake their city in style. Today Ljubljana—especially the streets around this square—is an architecture-lover's paradise. The **Hauptmann House,** to the right

of Julija, was the only building on the square to survive the quake. A few years later, the owner redecorated it in the then-trendy Viennese Art Nouveau style you see today, using bright colors (since his family sold dyes). All that remains of the original structure is the little Baroque balcony above the entrance.

Just to the right of the Hauptmann House is a car-sized **model** of the city center—helpful for orientation. The street next to it (with the McDonald's) is **Čopova,** once the route of Ljubljana's Sunday promenade. A century ago, locals would put on their Sunday best and stroll from here to Tivoli Park, listening to musicians and dropping into cafés along the way. Plečnik called it the "lifeline of the city," connecting the green lungs of the

LJUBLJANA

park to this urban center. Today, Slovenska avenue and railroad tracks cross the route, making the promenade less inviting. But in the last decade, Ljubljana has been trying to recapture its golden age, and some downtown streets are pedestrian-only on weekends once again. The new evening *paseo* thrives along the river from the Triple Bridge all the way up the river.

Continue looking to the right, past the big, pink landmark Franciscan Church of St. Mary. The characteristic glass awning marks **Centromerkur**—the first big post-quake department store, today government-protected. At the top of the building is Mercury, god of commerce, watching over the square that has been Ljubljana's commercial heart since the city began. (If you look carefully, you can see the

mustachioed face of the building's owner hiding in the folds of cloth by Mercury's left foot.) Since this area was across the river from medieval Ljubljana (beyond the town's limits...and the long arm of its tax collector), it was the best place to sell and buy goods. Today this recently restored, fine old building houses the top-end Galerija Emporium fashion mall, making it the heart of Ljubljana's boutique culture. Step inside for a glimpse at the sumptuous interior, with a grand staircase that gives way to a modern zone.

The street between Centromerkur and the pink church is **Miklošičeva cesta,** which connects Prešeren Square to the train station. When Ljubljana was rebuilding after the 1895 earthquake, town architects and designers envisioned this street as a showcase of its new, Vienna-inspired Art Nouveau image.

Up Miklošičeva street and on the left is the prominent **Grand Hotel Union,** with a stately domed spire on the corner. When these buildings were designed, Prague was the cultural capital of the Slavic world. The new look of Ljubljana paid homage to "the golden city of a hundred spires" (and copied Prague's romantic image). The city actually had a law for several years that new corner buildings had to have these spires. Even the trees you'll see around town were part of the vision. When the architect Plečnik designed the Ljubljanica River embankments a generation later, he planted tall, pointy poplar trees and squat, rounded willows—imitating the spires and domes of Prague.

Detour a block up Miklošičeva cesta to see two more architectural gems of that era (across from the Grand Hotel Union): First is a Secessionist building—marked **Zadružna Zveza**—with classic

red, blue, and white colors (for the Slovenian flag). Next is the noisy, pink, zigzagged **Cooperative Bank.** The bank was designed by Ivan Vurnik, an ambitious Slovenian architect who wanted to invent a distinctive national style after World War I, when the Habsburg Empire broke up and Eastern Europe's nations were proudly emerging for the first time.

Prešeren Square is the perfect springboard to explore the rest of Ljubljana. Now that you're oriented, visit some of the areas listed next.

Sights in Ljubljana

Ljubljana is bursting with new, well-presented, we-try-harder museums celebrating Slovenian history and culture. These include the Slovenian History Exhibition at the castle, the City Museum of Ljubljana, and the Contemporary History Museum in Tivoli Park. Those of us who've fallen in love with this city and country find each of these fascinating in its own right, but—since the museums are similar and largely overlapping—some visitors might find them redundant and dull. If you get museumed out easily, just visit the one that's handiest to your sightseeing plan.

East of the River, Under the Castle: The Market and Old Town

The castle side of the river is the city's most colorful and historic quarter, packed with Old World ambience.

▲▲**Riverside Market (Tržnice)**—In Ljubljana's thriving Old Town market, big-city Slovenes enjoy buying directly from the producer. Prices go down as the day gets late and as the week goes on. The market, worth an amble anytime, is best on Saturday mornings, when the townspeople take their time wandering the stalls. In this tiny capital of a tiny country, you may even see the president searching for the perfect melon.

Begin your walk through the market at the Triple Bridge (and TI). The riverside **colonnade,** which echoes the long-gone medieval city wall, was designed by (who else?) Jože Plečnik. This first stretch—nearest the

Triple Bridge—is good for souvenirs: woodcarvings, miniature painted frontboards from beehives, honey products (including honey brandy), and lots of colorful candles (bubbly Marta will gladly paint a special message on your candle for no extra charge).

Farther in, the market is almost all local, and the colonnade is populated by butchers, bakers, fishermen, and lazy cafés. Peek down at the actual river and see how the architect wanted the town and river to connect. The lower arcade (which you can access directly from the Triple Bridge, or by going down the spiral staircase by the beehive panels) is a people zone, with public WCs, inviting cafés, and a stinky fish market *(ribarnica)* offering a wide variety. The recommended restaurant just below, **Ribca,** serves fun fishy plates, beer, and coffee with great riverside seating.

Across from the stairs down into the fish market, about where the souvenir stands end, you reach the first small market square. On your right, notice the 10-foot-tall concrete **cone.** Plečnik wanted to make Ljubljana the "Athens of the North" and imagined a huge hilltop cone crowning the center of a national acropolis—a complex for government, museums, and culture. This ambitious plan didn't make it off the drawing board, but part of Plečnik's Greek idea came true: this marketplace, based on an ancient Greek *agora*. Plečnik's cone still captures the Slovenes' imaginations...and adorns Slovenia's €0.10 coin.

At the top of this square, you'll find the 18th-century **cathedral** standing on the site of a 13th-century Romanesque church (check out its finely decorated doors and consider going inside; for a complete description, see later).

The building at the end of the first market square is the seminary palace. In the basement is a **market hall,** with vendors selling cheeses, meats, baked goods, dried fruits, nuts, and other goodies (Mon-Fri 7:00-16:00, Sat 7:00-14:00, closed Sun). This place is worth a graze. Most merchants are happy to give you a free sample (point to what you want, and say *probat, prosim*—"a taste, please").

Leaving the market hall, notice where the colonnade ends at a modern bridge. Jože Plečnik designed a huge, roofed **Butchers' Bridge** to be built here, but—like so many of his designs—the plans were scuttled. Decades later, aware of Plečnik's newfound touristic currency, some town politicians dusted off the old plans and proposed building the bridge. The project stalled for years until the arrival of Mayor Zoran Janković, who swiftly constructed this modern version of the bridge. While it looks nothing like Plečnik's original plans, the bridge kept the old name and has been embraced by the community (there's a handy public WC down below on the lower level). The sculptures on the bridge, by local artist Jakov Brdar, were originally intended to be temporary—but people loved them, so they stayed. Notice the mournful pose of the

Zoran Janković

The latest chapter in Ljubljana's story has been written by a recent mayor, Zoran Janković. As chairman of the huge Mercator supermarket chain, Janković was famous for prowling around the front lines of his stores, micromanaging all the day-to-day business. After corporate political shuffling forced him out, Janković turned his attention to the municipal realm—and, in 2006, was elected mayor of Ljubljana in a landslide.

The people of this city, who had grown accustomed to well-intentioned but ineffectual leaders who proposed, then cancelled, ambitious projects, were stunned to see Janković's corporate-minded, no-nonsense follow-through. Project after project materialized, on time and under budget: the funicular to the castle, several new bridges (including the Butchers' Bridge at the market), the creation of quaintly cobbled traffic-free zones throughout almost the entire town center, and the pedestrianization of miles of riverfront embankment. The sweeping changes have had their critics—among them elderly people who can no longer easily drive to their homes in the now-traffic-free center—but ultimately most Ljubljanans are thrilled with the changes. It's a good example of how a progressive electorate can trust a capable leader to wisely invest public funds in urban-beautification projects that benefit the common good.

After winning re-election to the mayor's office in another landslide in 2010, Janković turned his sights to the national arena. In the parliamentary elections of December, 2011, the party he formed—Positive Slovenia—eked out a nationwide victory. Fittingly, it was the Ljubljana vote that put him over the top. However, some last-minute political wrangling among members of his coalition cost him the prime-ministership—he merely has a seat in the parliament. While some Slovenes were optimistic about what this bold innovator might do on a national scale, others were troubled by his virtually complete lack of foreign policy experience. Will Janković's mastery at managing the capital city ultimately translate to nationwide success in challenging economic times? Stay tuned.

Adam and Eve statues (being evicted from the Garden of Eden) at the market end of the bridge. And don't miss the bizarre smaller sculptures along the railing—such as the ones that look like mischievous lizards breaking out of their eggs. Almost as soon as it was built, the bridge's railings were covered with padlocks—part of the recent Europe-wide craze for young couples to commemorate their love by locking a padlock to a bridge railing. But all those locks are just too much for the railing to support—they are regularly cut off, soon to be replaced by new ones.

Sprawling up from the bridge is the **main market square,** packed with produce and clothing stands. (The colorful flower

market hides behind the market hall.) The row of vendors nearest the colonnade sell fruit from all over, but the ones located deeper in the market sell only locally grown produce. These producers go out of their way to be old-fashioned—a few of them still follow the tradition of pushing their veggies on wooden carts (called *cizas*) to the market from their garden patches in the suburbs. Once at the market, they simply display their goods on top of their cart, turning it into a sales kiosk. Tell the vendor what you want—it's considered rude for customers to touch the fruits and vegetables before they're bought. Over time, shoppers develop friendships with their favorite producers. On busy days, you'll see a long line at one stand, while the other merchants stand bored. Your choice is simple: Get in line, or eat subpar produce.

Near the market hall, look for the little **scales** in the wooden kiosks marked *Kontrolna Tehtnica*—allowing buyers to immediately check whether the producer cheated them (not a common problem, but just in case). The Habsburg days left locals with the old German saying, "Trust is good; control is better." Nearby, look for the innovative "Nonstop Mlekomat" stand, a vending machine that lets you buy a plastic bottle, then fill it with a liter of raw, unskimmed, farm-fresh milk for €1.

Two more sights are immersed in the market action (both described next); the cathedral sits at the top of the market area, near the Triple Bridge, while the Dragon Bridge spans the river just beyond the end of the market colonnade.

▲**Cathedral (Stolnica)**—Ljubljana's cathedral is dedicated to St. Nicholas, protector against floods and patron saint of the fish-

ermen and boatmen who have long come to sell their catch at the market. While the interior is worth a peek (free, open long hours daily but closed 12:00-15:00), the intricately decorated doors—created for Pope John Paul II's visit here in 1996—are even more interesting.

Go under the high arch, then take a close look at the remarkable side **door** on the left. Buried deeply in the fecund soil of their ancient and pagan history, the nation's linden tree of life sprouts with the story of the Slovenes. The ceramic pots represent the original Roman settlement here. Just to the left, above the tree, are the Byzantine missionaries Cyril and Methodius, who came here to convert the Slavs to Christianity in the ninth century. Just above, Crusaders and Ottomans do battle. Near the top, see the Slovenes going into the cave—entering the dark 20th century (World War I, World War II, and communism). At the top is Pope John Paul II (the first Slavic pontiff, who also oversaw the fall of communism). Below him are two men who are on track for becoming Slovenia's first saints; the one on the right is Frederic Baraga, a 19th-century bishop who became a missionary in Michigan and codified Chippewa grammar (notice the Native American relief on the book he's holding). In the upper right-hand corner is a sun, which has been shining since Slovenia gained its independence in 1991. Around back of the cathedral is a similar door, carved with images of the six 20th-century bishops of Ljubljana.

The cathedral's **interior** is stunning Italian Baroque. The transept is surrounded by sculptures of four bishops of Roman Ljubljana (when it was called Emona, or Aemon). Left of the main altar, notice the distinctive chair. This was designed by the very religious Jože Plečnik, whose brother was a priest here. Look up over the nave to enjoy the recently restored, gorgeous ceiling fresco.

▲Dragon Bridge (Zmajski Most)—The dragon has been the symbol of Ljubljana for centuries, ever since Jason (of Argonauts and Golden Fleece fame) supposedly slew one in a nearby swamp. This is one of the few notable bits of Ljubljana architecture not by Plečnik (but by Jurij Zaninović, a fellow student of Vienna architect Otto Wagner). While the dragon is the star of this very photogenic Art Nouveau bridge, the bridge itself was officially  dedicated to the 40th anniversary of Habsburg Emperor Franz Josef's reign (see the dates on the side: 1848-1888). Tapping into the emp's vanity got new projects funded—vital as the city rebuilt after the 1895 earthquake. But the Franz Josef name never stuck; those dragons are just too darn memorable.

From the Dragon Bridge, it's an easy funicular ride or steep hike up to Ljubljana Castle (described later). Or you can head back through the market to reach the Town Square and Old Town (see next).

▲Town Square (Mestni Trg) and the Old Town—Ljubljana's Town Square, just across the Triple Bridge and up the street from

Prešeren Square, is home to the **Town Hall** (Rotovž), highlighted by its clock tower and pillared loggia. Step inside the Renaissance courtyard to see paintings, artifacts, and a map of late 17th-century Ljubljana. Studying this map, notice how the river, hill, and wall worked together to fortify the town. Courtyards like this (but humbler) are hidden throughout the city. As rent in these old places is cheap, many such courtyards host funky and characteristic little businesses. Be sure to get off the main drag and poke into Ljubljana's nooks and crannies.

In the square is a recent replica of the **Fountain of Three Carniolian Rivers,** inspired in style and theme by Rome's many

fountains. (The original is in a museum.) The figures with vases represent this region's three main rivers: Ljubljanica, Sava, and Krka. This is one of many works in town by Francesco Robba, an Italian who came to Ljubljana for one job, fell in love with a Slovene, and stayed here the rest of his life—decorating the city's churches with beautiful Baroque altars. At the nearby corner, check out the wild interior of the Nova KBM Bank, which looks more like a cutting-edge nightclub.

In the early 19th century, Ljubljana consisted mainly of this single street, running along the base of Castle Hill (plus a small "New Town" across the river). Stretching south from here are two other "squares"—Stari trg (Old Square) and Gornji trg (Upper Square)—which have long since grown together into one big, atmospheric promenade lined with quaint boutiques, great restaurants, and cafés (perfect for a stroll). Virtually every house along this drag has a story to tell of a famous resident or infamous incident. As you walk, keep your eyes open for Ljubljana's mascot dragon—it's everywhere. Near the Town Hall, look for a pair of interesting spots on the left: At #4, Čupterija Bar has one of the most creative interiors in this very creative town. Next door at #5, Café Galerija is the city art gallery, with changing exhibits and a cool café in back. Continuing along this drag, stow your guidebook and enjoy some boutique window-shopping and people-watching; you'll also pass some recommended eateries (see "Eating in Ljubljana," later). At the end of the pedestrian zone (at Gornji trg), look uphill and notice the village charms of some of the oldest buildings in town (four medieval houses with rooflines slanted at the ends, different from the others on this street).

▲Ljubljana Castle (Ljubljanski Grad)—The castle above town offers enjoyable views of Ljubljana and the surrounding countryside. There has probably been a settlement on this site since prehistoric times, though the first fortress here was Roman. The 12th-century version was gradually added on to over the centuries, until it fell into disrepair in the 17th century. Today's castle was rebuilt in the 1940s, renovated in the 1970s, and is still technically unfinished (subject to ongoing additions). The castle houses a climbable tower, a good exhibit about Slovenian history, a fine restaurant, the good Rustika

gift shop, temporary exhibition halls, and a Gothic chapel with Baroque paintings of the coat of arms of St. George (Ljubljana's patron saint, the dragon-slayer). Above the restaurant are two wedding halls—Ljubljana's most popular places to get married (free for locals). The castle is also home to the Ljubljana Summer Festival, with concerts throughout the summer (tel. 01/306-4293, www.ljubljanafestival.si). While the castle and its attractions are ho-hum, the views are worth the trip.

Cost and Hours: You can hike up to the castle and wander the grounds for free (daily April-Sept 9:00-23:00, Oct-March 10:00-21:00). But if you want to enter the three sights at the castle (history exhibition, film, and castle tower), you'll pay €4 (€6 combo-ticket also includes funicular; €8 combo-ticket includes sights, funicular, and guided tour; sights open daily April-Sept 9:00-21:00, Oct-March 10:00-18:00, tel. 01/232-9994, www.ljubljanskigrad.si).

Tours: Guided tours of the castle in Slovene and English leave from the castle information center daily June through mid-September at 10:00, 11:00, 14:00, and 16:00 (€6, or included in €8 combo-ticket with castle sights and funicular; tour lasts 1-1.5 hours; winter tours possible to arrange upon request for at least 3 people—call a day ahead).

Getting to the Castle: A slick **funicular** whisks visitors to the top in a jiff (€1.50 one-way, €3 round-trip, also included in combo-tickets described above, runs every 10 minutes, 1-minute ride, daily April-Sept 9:00-23:00, Oct-March 10:00-21:00, catch it at Krekov trg—across the street from the market square TI). From the top, you'll find free WCs and a few easy flights of stairs up into the heart of the castle complex (or take the elevator). Another sweat-free route to the top is via the **tourist train** that leaves at the top of each hour (or more frequently with demand) from in front of the Town Hall (€3 round-trip, daily in summer 9:00-21:00, shorter hours off-season, doesn't run in snow or other bad weather). There are also two handy **trails** to the castle. The steeper-but-faster route begins near the Dragon Bridge: Find Študentovska lane, just past the statue of Vodnik in the market. This lane dead-ends at a gravel path, which you'll follow up to a fork. Turn left to zigzag up the steepest and fastest route, which deposits you just below the castle wall; from here, turn left again and curl around the wall to reach the main drawbridge. Slower but a bit less steep is Reber, just off Stari trg, a few blocks south of the Town Hall: Walk up to the top of Reber, and, at the dead end, turn right and start climbing up the stairs. From here on out, always bear left, then go right when you're just under the castle (follow *Grad* signs).

Sights at the Castle: Three sights cluster around the tallest tower: You can see a **film** about the history of Ljubljana (plays all day on the half-hour); climb the 92 steps up to the **castle tower,** with one of the best views in town; or tour the good exhibition about Slovenian history. From a sightseeing perspective, the castle's highlight is its **Slovenian History Exhibition,** which offers a concise but engaging overview of this little country's story. As you enter, ask to borrow the free audioguide, then head downstairs and work your way up. Dark display cases light up when you approach, revealing actual artifacts, video clips, and touchscreens with more information. A unique feature of the museum is that you're invited to touch replicas of important historic items (generally displayed next to the original items). Don't miss the top floor of the exhibit (go up the glassed-in staircase), which is the most interesting— covering the tumultuous 20th century. You'll learn about topics ranging from the battlefields of World War I, to the creation of the first Yugoslavia, to the fascist occupation and harrowing Italian-run concentration camps of World War II, to the cult of personality around Partisan war hero-turned-Yugoslav president Tito, to Slovenia's bid for independence.

Eating: Combine your visit to the castle with a meal at the recommended Gostilna na Gradu, with the best traditional Slovenian food in town (in the castle courtyard; described later, under "Eating in Ljubljana").

West of the River, Beyond Prešeren Square: The Museum Zone and Tivoli Park

The Prešeren Square (west) side of the river is the heart of modern Ljubljana, and home to several prominent squares and fine museums. These sights are listed roughly in order from Prešeren Square and can be linked to make an interesting walk.

• *Leave Prešeren Square in the direction the poet is looking, bear to your left (up Wolfova, by the picture of Julija), and walk a block to...*

Congress Square (Kongresni Trg)—This grassy, tree-lined square is ringed by some of Ljubljana's most important buildings: the University headquarters, the Baroque Ursuline Church of the Holy Trinity, a classical mansion called the Kazina, and the Philharmonic Hall. Once clogged with traffic, the area around the square was recently pedestrianized, including the broad strip along the far side. At the top end of the square, by the entry to a pedestrian underpass, a Roman sarcophagus sits under a gilded statue of a **Roman citizen**—a replica of an artifact from 1,700 years ago, when this town was called Emona. The busy street above you has been the main trading route through town since ancient Roman times. This square hosts the big town events.

• *Take the underpass beneath Slovenska avenue (the town's main traffic thoroughfare—which may be open only to buses in the coming years). As you go down into the underpass, you can turn left to find a surviving chunk of the old Roman wall. Continuing through the underpass and emerging at the far end, walk straight through the gap in the shopping mall into the...*

▲**Square of the Republic (Trg Republike)**—This unusual square is essentially a parking lot ringed by an odd collection of buildings. While hardly quaint, the Square of the Republic gives you a good taste of a modern corner of Ljubljana. And it's historic—this is where Slovenia declared its independence in 1991.

The **twin office towers** (with the world's biggest digital watch, flashing the date, time, and temperature) were designed by Plečnik's protégé, Edvard Ravnikar. As harrowing as these structures seem, imagine if the builders had followed the original plans—the towers would be twice as tall as they are now, and connected by a bridge, representing the gateway to Ljubljana. These buildings were originally designed as the Slovenian parliament, but they were scaled back when Tito didn't approve (since it would have made Slovenia's parliament bigger than the Yugoslav parliament in Belgrade). Instead, the **Slovenian Parliament** is across the square, in the strangely low-profile office building with the sculpted entryway. The carvings are in the Socialist Realist style, celebrating the noble Slovenian people conforming to communist ideals for the good of the entire society. Completing the square are a huge conference center (Cankarjev Dom, the white building behind the skyscrapers), a shopping mall, and some public art.

• *Just a block north, through the grassy park (Trg Narodni Herojev), you'll find the...*

Slovenian National Museum (Narodni Muzej Slovenije) and Slovenian Museum of Natural History (Prirodoslovni Muzej Slovenije)—These two museums share a single historic building facing a park behind the Parliament. While neither collection is particularly good, they're both worth considering if you have a special interest or if it's a rainy day.

The **National Museum** occupies the ground floor, featuring a lapidarium with carved-stone Roman monuments and exhibits on Egyptian mummies. (Temporary exhibits are also on this level.) Upstairs and to the right are more exhibits of the National Museum, with archaeological findings ranging from old armor and pottery to the museum's two prized possessions: a fragment of a 45,000-year-old Neanderthal flute fashioned from a cave bear's femur, supposedly the world's oldest musical instrument; and the "figural situla," a beautifully decorated bronze bucket from 500 B.C.

Upstairs and to the left is the **Natural History** exhibit, featuring the flora and fauna of Slovenia. You'll see partial skeletons of a mammoth and a cave bear, plenty of stuffed reptiles, fish, and birds, and an exhibit on "human fish" (*Proteus anguinus*—long, skinny, pale-pink, sightless salamanders unique to caves in this part of Europe).

Cost and Hours: €3 for each museum, or €5 for both, some English descriptions, free audioguide for Natural History Museum, both open daily 10:00-18:00, Thu until 20:00, Prešernova 20, tel. 01/241-4400, www.nms.si and www.pms-lj.si.

• At the far end of the building is a glassed-in annex displaying Roman stone monuments (free). Turning left around the museum building and walking one block, you'll see the...

US Embassy—This pretty yellow chalet (with brown trim and a red roof, at Prešernova cesta 31) wins my vote for quaintest embassy building in the world. Resist the urge to snap a photo... those guards are all business.

• Just up Prešernova street from the embassy are two decent but skippable art museums.

National Gallery (Narodna Galerija)—This museum has three parts: European artists (in the new building), Slovenian artists (in the old building), and temporary exhibits. Find the work of Ivana Kobilca, a late 19th-century Slovenian Impressionist. Art-lovers enjoy her self-portrait in *Summer*. If you're going to Bled, you can get a sneak preview with Marko Pernhart's huge panorama of the Julian Alps.

Cost and Hours: €7, more for special exhibits, permanent collection free first Sun of the month, open Tue-Sun 10:00-18:00, closed Mon, enter through old-fashioned facade at Cankarjeva 20, another entrance is at big glass box between two older buildings at Prešernova 24, tel. 01/241-5418, www.ng-slo.si.

Museum of Modern Art (Moderna Galerija Ljubljana)— Newly renovated, this museum has a permanent collection of modern and contemporary Slovenian artists, as well as temporary exhibits by both Slovenes and international artists. To explore the "Continuities and Ruptures" permanent collection (aptly named for a place with such a fractured, up-and-down recent history), borrow the English floor plan and take a chronological spin through the 20th century. Unusual for a "modern" art museum is the room with Partisan art, with stiff, improvised, communist-style posters from the days when Tito and his crew were just a ragtag militia movement.

Cost and Hours: €5, Tue-Sun 10:00-18:00, closed Mon, Tomšičeva 14, tel. 01/241-6800, www.mg-lj.si.

• *By the busy road near the art museums, look for the distinctive Neo-Byzantine design (tall domes with narrow slits) of the...*

▲▲Serbian Orthodox Church of Sts. Cyril and Methodius— Ljubljana's most striking church interior isn't Catholic, but

Orthodox. This church was built in 1936, soon after the Slovenes joined a political union with the Serbs. Wealthy Slovenia attracted its poorer neighbors from the south—so it built this church for that community. Since 1991, the Serb population continues to grow, as people from the struggling corners of the former Yugoslavia flock to prosperous Slovenia.

Step inside for the best glimpse of the Orthodox faith this side of Dubrovnik. The church is colorfully decorated without a hint of the 21st century, mirroring a very conservative religion. You'll see Cyrillic script in this building, which feels closer to Moscow than to Rome. Notice that there are no pews, because worshippers stand throughout the service. On the left, find the little room with tubs of water, where the faithful light tall, skinny beeswax candles (purchased at the little window in the back corner). The painted screen, or iconostasis, is believed to separate our material world from the spiritual realm behind it. Ponder the fact that several centuries ago, before the Catholic Church began to adapt to a changing world, all Christians worshipped this way. For more on the Orthodox faith, see the sidebar on page 876.

Cost and Hours: Free, Sun 9:00-12:00 & 17:00-18:00, Mon 8:00-9:00 & 17:00-18:00, Tue-Sat 8:00-12:00 & 14:00-18:00.

• *On the other side of the busy street is...*

Tivoli Park (Park Tivoli)—This huge park, just west of the center, is where Slovenes relax on summer weekends. The easiest access is through the graffiti-covered underpass from Cankarjeva cesta (between the Serbian Orthodox Church and the Museum of

Modern Art). As you emerge, the Neoclassical pillars leading down the promenade clue you in that this part of the park was designed by Jože Plečnik. Along this "main boulevard" of the park, various changing photographic exhibitions are displayed.

• *Aside from taking a leisurely stroll, the best thing to do in the park is visit the...*

▲**Contemporary History Museum (Muzej Novejše Zgodovine)**—In a Baroque mansion (Cekinov Grad) in Tivoli Park, a well-done exhibit called "Slovenians in the 20th Century" traces the last hundred years of Slovenia—essentially from the end of World War I to independence in 1991. Out front is a T-55 Yugoslav tank that was commandeered by the Slovenes during their war for independence. Inside, the ground floor displays temporary exhibits, and upstairs you'll find several rooms using models, dioramas, light-and-sound effects, and English explanations to creatively tell the story of one of Europe's youngest nations. While it's a little difficult to fully appreciate, the creativity and the spunky spirit of the place are truly enjoyable.

Cost and Hours: €3.50, permanent exhibit free first Sun of the month, guidebook-€15, open Tue-Sun 10:00-18:00, closed Mon, in Tivoli Park at Celovška cesta 23, tel. 01/300-9610, www.muzej-nz.si.

Getting There: The museum is a 20-minute walk from the center, best combined with a wander through Tivoli Park. The fastest approach: As you emerge from the Cankarjeva cesta underpass into the park, climb up the stairs, then turn right and go straight ahead for five minutes. You'll continue straight up the ramp, then turn left after the tennis courts and look for the big pink-and-white mansion on the hill.

Touring the Museum: The exhibit begins at the dawn of the 20th century, during Slovenia's waning days as part of the Austro-Hungarian Empire. You'll walk through a simulated trench from the Soča Front, then learn about the creation of the post-World War I Kingdom of Serbs, Croats, and Slovenes (or, as this exhibit pointedly puts it, "Kingdom of Slovenes, Croats, and Serbs").

Your footfalls echo loudly as you enter the room describing Slovenia's WWII experience (ask them to start the 12-minute "multivision" wrap-around slideshow with music and sound effects). You'll learn how during that war, Slovenia was divided between neighboring fascist powers Germany, Italy, and Hungary. Each one tried (but failed) to exert linguistic and cultural control over the people, hoping to eradicate Slovenian language, culture, and national identity. Video screens show subtitled interviews with people who lived through those war years.

Passing through the ballroom, you reach the "Slovenia 1945-1960" exhibit, outlining both the good (modernization) and the bad (prison camps and secret police) of the early Tito years. Despite his ruthless early rule, Tito remains popular here; under his stern bust, page through the photo album of Tito's visits to Slovenia. Find the display of the country's former currencies. Examining the Yugoslav dinar, notice that the figureheads on that communist currency were generic, idealized workers, farmers, and other members of the proletariat...except for a few notable individuals (including Tito). Meanwhile, Slovenia's short-lived post-Yugoslav currency, the *tolar* (1991-2006), featured artists and scientists rather than heads of state and generals.

The most evocative room has artifacts from the Slovenes' brave declaration of independence from a hostile Yugoslavia in 1991. The well-organized Slovenes had only to weather a 10-day skirmish to gain their freedom. It's chilling to think that at one point bombers were en route to level this gorgeous city. The planes were called back at the last minute, by a Yugoslav People's Army officer with allegiances to Slovenia.

• *Hungry? Straight ahead and down the stairs from the museum, look for the "Hot Horse" food kiosk, selling €4 horseburgers (no joke). A local institution, this is a popular place to get together with friends and neighbors. The giant, modern, blocky, light-blue building across the busy road is the Pivovarna Union—the brewery for Ljubljana's favorite brew.*

On your way back to the center, consider stopping by...

▲**The Skyscraper (Nebotičnik)**—This 1933 Art Deco building was the first skyscraper in Slovenia, for a time the tallest building in Central Europe, and one of the earliest European buildings that was clearly influenced by American architecture. The Skyscraper's top floor, which hosts a pricey restaurant, café, and observation deck, offers the best view of Ljubljana's skyline. Zip up in the elevator just to take a peek, or stay for a drink or meal. There are three levels: The best is the open-air, top-level terrace (floor #12—ride up to #11 and walk up the spiral stairs), where you can enjoy unobstructed views over the city and castle. While up on the terrace, you can enjoy a light meal (€4-9), cocktail (€5-8), or beer, wine, or coffee (€3). One floor below (#11) is the indoor club/lounge, with a similar menu. And on the next floor down is the restaurant (floor #10), with pricey food (€8-10 starters, €12-14 pastas, €20-24 main dishes) and less-impressive views. I'd skip the restaurant and the club, and just grab a drink or snack up on the terrace.

Cost and Hours: Free to ride the elevator up for a peek, but

LJUBLJANA

you should buy at least a drink if you want to stick around; terrace and club open Sun-Wed 9:00-1:00 in the morning, Thu-Sat 9:00-3:00 in the morning; restaurant open Mon-Sat 12:00-21:00, closed Sun; 2 blocks from Prešeren Square at Štefanova 1, tel. 040-601-787, www.neboticnik.si.

• *A few blocks south, near several Jože Plečnik sights (see next section) at the river end of French Revolution Square, you'll find the...*

▲**City Museum of Ljubljana (Mestni Muzej Ljubljana)**—This thoughtfully presented museum, located in the recently restored Auersperg Palace, offers a high-tech, in-depth look at the story of this city. You'll learn how Ljubljana has belonged to 10 different states over the last 200 years, ranging from the genteel Habsburg Empire to the oppressive Nazi regime to membership in the benevolent EU. You'll begin your visit in the cellar, with Roman ruins (including remains of the original Roman road and sewer system, found right here) and layers of medieval artifacts. You may see one of the museum's prize pieces, the world's oldest wooden wheel on an axle, dating from around 3200 B.C. and discovered in the Ljubljana marshlands (often not on display because it's incredibly fragile). Rounding out the collection is an evolving permanent collection and a range of temporary exhibits (generally on the second floor). Though everything is well-described in English (and touchscreens provide more information), a student on the museum's staff might be able to show you around if it's not too busy—ask.

Cost and Hours: €4, Tue-Sun 10:00-18:00, Thu until 21:00, closed Mon, kid-friendly, Gosposka 15, tel. 01/241-2500, www.mestnimuzej.si.

Nearby: Included in your ticket is an audio/videoguide that leads you on a walking tour to two nearby archaeological sites.

• *If visiting the museum, don't miss the nearby National and University Library and French Revolution Square—both described in the next section.*

South of Prešeren Square: Jože Plečnik's Architecture

Jože Plečnik is to Ljubljana what Antoni Gaudí is to Barcelona: a homegrown and amazingly prolific genius who shaped his town with a uniquely beautiful vision. And, as in Barcelona, Ljubljana has a way of turning people who couldn't care less about architecture into Plečnik fans. There's plenty to see. In addition to the Triple Bridge, the riverside market, and the sights listed here, Plečnik designed the embankments along the Ljubljanica and Gradaščica Rivers in the Trnovo neighborhood; the rebuilt Roman wall along Mirje street, south of the center; the Church of St. Francis, with its classicist bell tower; St. Michael's Church on the Marsh; Orel Stadium; Žale Cemetery; and many more buildings throughout Slovenia.

Some of the best Plečnik sights are near the river, just south of Congress and Prešeren squares. I've linked them up in the order of a short self-guided walk.

• *From Prešeren Square, stroll south along the river. After the plain wooden bridge called the "Ugly Duckling," you'll come to the...*

▲**Cobblers' Bridge (Čevljarski Most)**—Named for the actual cobblers (shoemakers) who set up shop along the river in olden

times, the bridge encapsulates Plečnik's style perhaps better than any other structure: simple, clean lines adorned with classical columns. Ideal for people-watching (with the castle hovering scenically overhead), this is one of Ljubljana's most appealing spots.

• *Continue past the Cobblers' Bridge on the right side of the river, past the fountain. After about a block, turn right up the parked-up street called Novi trg. At the top of this street, on the left, is a red-brick building embedded with gray granite blocks in an irregular checkerboard pattern. This is the...*

▲▲**National and University Library (Narodna in Univerzitetna Knjižnica, or NUK)**—Widely regarded as Plečnik's mas-

terpiece, this building is a bit underwhelming...until an understanding of its symbolism brings it to life. On the surface, the red-and-gray color scheme evokes the red soil and chunks of granite of the Karst region, south of Ljubljana. But on a

deeper level, the library's design conveys the message of overcoming obstacles to attain knowledge. The odd-sized and -shaped blocks in the facade represent a complex numerological pattern that suggests barriers on the path to enlightenment. The sculpture on the river side is Moses—known for leading his people through 40 years of hardship to the Promised Land. On the right side of the building, find the horse-head doorknobs—representing the winged horse Pegasus (grab hold, and he'll whisk you away to new levels of enlightenment). Step inside. The main staircase is dark

and gloomy—modeled after an Egyptian tomb. But at the top, through the door marked *Velika Čitalnica,* is the bright, airy main reading room: the ultimate goal, a place of learning. The top-floor windows are shaped roughly like open books.

Aside from being a great work of architecture, the building also houses the most important library in Slovenia, with more than two million books (about one per Slovene). The library is supposed to receive a copy of each new book printed in the country. In a freaky bit of bad luck, this was the only building in town damaged in World War II, when a plane crashed into it. But the people didn't want to see their books go up in flames—so hundreds of locals formed a human chain, risking life and limb to save the books from the burning building.

Cost and Hours: Free, staircase open Mon-Fri 9:00-20:00, Sat 9:00-14:00, closed Sun. The quiet main reading room is officially open for visitors only during very limited hours (mid-July-mid-Aug Mon-Fri 14:00-20:00). If you're not here during that one-month span, and you're really determined to see it, you can go up the stairs and try sticking close to a student going inside the reading room—but note that the guards frown on uninvited visitors. To get out, follow another student or push gently on the door (it'll likely open easily).

• *Directly behind the library is a mellow square with an obelisk in the middle. This is...*

French Revolution Square (Trg Francoske Revolucije)—Plečnik designed the **obelisk** in the middle of the square to commemorate Napoleon's short-lived decision to make Ljubljana the capital of his Illyrian Provinces. It's rare to find anything honoring Napoleon outside of Paris, but he was good to Ljubljana. Under his rule, Slovenian culture flourished, schools were established, and roads and infrastructure were improved. The monument contains ashes of the unknown French soldiers who died in 1813, when the region went from French to Austrian control.

The Teutonic Knights of the Cross established the nearby **monastery** (Križanke, ivy-capped wall and gate, free entry) in 1230. The adaptation of these monastery buildings into the Ljubljana Summer Theatre was Plečnik's last major work (1950-1956).

• *From here, it's a scenic 10-minute walk to the next sight. From the obelisk, walk down Emonska toward the twin-spired church. You'll pass (on the left) the delightful Krakovo district—a patch of green countryside in downtown Ljubljana. Many of the veggies you see in the riverside market come from these carefully tended gardens. When you reach the Gradaščica stream, head over the bridge (also designed by Plečnik) and go around the left side of the church to find the house.*

▲▲Jože Plečnik House (Plečnikova Zbirka)—Ljubljana's favorite son lived here from 1921 until his death in 1957. He added

Jože Plečnik
(1872-1957)

There is probably no other single architect who has shaped one city as Jože Plečnik (YOH-zheh PLAYCH-neek) shaped Ljubljana. From libraries, office buildings, cemeteries, and stadiums to landscaping, riverside embankments, and market halls, Plečnik left his mark everywhere. While he may not yet register very high on the international Richter scale of important architects, the Slovenes' pride in this man's work is understandable.

Plečnik was born in Ljubljana and trained as a furniture designer before his interest turned to architecture. He studied  in Vienna under the Secessionist architect Otto Wagner. His first commissions, done around the turn of the 20th century in Vienna, were pretty standard Art Nouveau stuff. Then Tomáš Masaryk, president of the new nation of Czechoslovakia, decided that the dull Habsburg design of Prague Castle could use a new look to go with its new independence. But he didn't want an Austrian architect; it had to be a Slav. In 1921, Masaryk chose Jože Plečnik, who sprinkled the castle grounds with his distinctive touches. By now, Plečnik had perfected his simple, eye-pleasing style, which mixes modern and classical influences, with lots of columns and pyramids—simultaneously austere and playful.

By the time Plečnik finished in Prague, he had made a name

on to an existing house, building a circular bedroom for himself and filling the place with bric-a-brac he designed, as well as artifacts, photos, and gifts from around the world that inspired him as he shaped Ljubljana. Living a simple, almost monastic life-style, Plečnik knew what he  liked, and these tastes are mirrored in his house.

Today the house is decorated exactly as it was the day Plečnik died, containing much of his equipment, models, and plans. The house can be toured only with a guide, whose enthusiasm brings the place to life. There are very few barriers, so you are in direct contact with the world of the architect. Still furnished with unique,

for himself. His prime years were spent creating for the Kingdom of Yugoslavia (before the ideology-driven era of Tito). Plečnik returned home to Ljubljana and set to work redesigning the city, both as an architect and as an urban planner. He lived in a humble house behind the Trnovo Church (now a tourable and recommended museum), and on his walk to work every day, he pondered ways to make the city even more livable. Wandering through town, notice how thoughtfully he incorporated people, nature, the Slovenian heritage, town vistas, and symbolism into his works—it's feng shui on a grand urban scale.

For all of Plečnik's ideas that became reality, even more did not. After World War II, the very religious Plečnik fell out of favor with the new communist government and found it more difficult to get his projects completed. (It's fun to imagine how this city might look if Plečnik had always gotten his way.) After his death in 1957, Plečnik was virtually forgotten by Slovenes and scholars alike. His many works in Ljubljana were taken for granted.

But in 1986, an exposition about Plečnik at Paris' Pompidou Center jump-started interest in the architect. Within a few years, Plečnik was back in vogue. Today, scholars laud him as a genius who was ahead of his time...while locals and tourists enjoy the elegant simplicity of his works.

Plečnik-designed furniture, one-of-a-kind inventions, and favorite souvenirs from his travels, the house paints an unusually intimate portrait of an artist.

While the house initially underwhelms some visitors, it's a ▲▲▲ pilgrimage for those who get caught up in Ljubljana's idiosyncratic sense of style. As you tour the place, be patient. Listen to its stories. Appreciate the subtle details. Notice how reverently your guide (and other Slovenes) speak of this man. Contrast the humbleness of Plečnik's home with the dynamic impact he had on the cityscape of Ljubljana and the cultural heritage of Slovenia. Wandering Plečnik's hallways, it's hard not to be tickled by this man's sheer creativity and the unique world he forged for himself to live in. As a visitor to his home, you're in good company. He invited only his closest friends here—except during World War II, when Ljubljana was occupied by Nazis and the university was closed, Plečnik allowed his students to work with him here.

Possible Closure: As the house is slated to be closed for restoration sometime soon, it's important to ask the TI, check the website, or call the museum to be sure it's open before making the trek out here.

Cost and Hours: €4, Tue-Thu 10:00-18:00, Sat 9:00-15:00, 45-minute English tours begin at the top of each hour, last tour departs one hour before closing, closed Sun-Mon and Fri, Karunova 4, tel. 01/280-1600, www.mgml.si, info@mgml.si. It's well-run by Ana and Natalija, who sometimes lead the tours.

Getting There: It's directly behind the twin steeples of the Trnovo Church. The 15-minute stroll from the center—the same one Plečnik took to work each day—is nearly as enjoyable as the house itself. You can either walk south along the river, then turn right onto Gradaška and stroll along the stream to the church; or, from French Revolution Square, head south on Emonska. Either way, you'll pass through the garden-patch district of Krakovo, where pea patches and characteristic Old World buildings gracefully cohabitate. On the way to or from the museum, consider getting a meal in Krakovo (three restaurants—Pri Škofu, Manna, and Harambaša—are described later, under "Eating in Ljubljana").

Museums in Metelkova, Northeast of Prešeren Square

These three museums, about a 10-minute walk northeast of Prešeren Square in the dull but up-and-coming district of Metelkova, face each other on a slick modern plaza next to the park called Tabor.

▲▲**Slovenian Ethnographic Museum (Slovenski Etnografski Muzej)**—Housed in a brand-new facility, this delightful museum is Ljubljana's most underrated attraction. With both permanent and temporary exhibits, the museum strives to explain what it is to be Slovene, with well-presented and well-described cultural artifacts from around the country. If you've caught the Slovenian folk culture itch, this is the place to scratch it.

Cost and Hours: €4.50, free last Sun of month, Tue-Sun 10:00-18:00, closed Mon, great café, Metelkova 2, tel. 01/300-8745, www.etno-muzej.si.

Touring the Museum: The ground and first floors have good temporary exhibits, while upstairs you'll find two permanent exhibits.

The best exhibit, filling the third floor, is called **"Between Nature and Culture."** As you exit the elevator, turn left and consider the surprisingly frank exhibit that acknowledges the shortsighted tendency for museum curators—including at this museum—to emphasize things that are foreign or different. Continue through collections of "Distant Worlds" (non-European cultures) to reach the core of the collection, which focuses on Slovenia. A good but slow-moving film visits the country's four major regions. Another exhibit ponders how people half a world away—in Slovenia and in North America—simultaneously invented a similar solution (snowshoes) for a common problem. One display deconstructs Slovenian clichés (including this country's odd fascination with its traditional hayracks). The arrangement of the collection emphasizes the evolution of an increasingly complicated civilization, from basic farming tools to ceramics to modern technology. The children's "Ethnoalphabet" area features an A-to-Ž array of engaging, hands-on activities.

The other permanent exhibit, on the second floor (from the elevator, turn left to find the entrance), is called "**I, We, and Others.**" A bit too conceptual for its own good, this heady exhibit ponders the notion of belonging. Designed for Slovenes more than foreigners (with very limited posted English information—borrow the free English audioguide from the ticket desk before heading up), it considers various aspects of how people define who they are, from individual and family to community and nation. Videos and sounds enhance the exhibits, and the curators neatly juxtapose well-known icons from different cultures (such as various national parliament buildings) in thought-provoking ways. While it's easy to get lost amid the navel-gazing, there is something particularly poignant about this topic here in the identity-obsessed Balkans.

Slovenian National Museum-Metelkova (Narodni Muzej Slovenije)—Next door to the Ethnographic Museum is this facility, where items from the Slovenian National Museum that were formerly tucked away in storage are now displayed on two floors. The very pretty historical bric-a-brac is neatly presented without much context—it's just an excuse to get a bunch of interesting stuff out into public view. Each room has a different collection: furniture, pottery and ceramics, church vestments, weapons and armor, and more. The painting gallery is nicely organized by century and style. Everything's labeled in English, and on weekday afternoons (after 15:00) and all day on weekends, a guide can show you around, if they're not too busy.

Cost and Hours: €3, Tue-Sun 10:00-18:00, closed Mon, Maistrova 1, tel. 01/230-7032.

Contemporary Art Museum—This brand-new collection, featuring changing exhibitions of present-day, mostly Slovenian artists, is scheduled to open next to the National Museum in 2012.

Shopping in Ljubljana

Ljubljana, with its easygoing ambience and countless boutiques, is made to order for whiling away an afternoon shopping. It's also a fun place to stock up on souvenirs and gifts for the folks back home. Popular items include wood carvings and models (especially of the characteristic hayracks that dot the countryside), different flavors of schnapps (the kind with a whole pear inside—cultivated to actually grow right into the bottle—is considered a particularly classy gift), honey mead brandy (*medica*—sweet and smooth), and those adorable painted panels from beehives (described on page 787). Rounding out the list of traditional Slovenian items are wrought-iron products from Kropa, crystal from Rogaska, lace from Idrija, salt from Piran, and Peko shoes (similar to high-fashion Italian models, but cheaper; the name is an abbreviation of its founder's name: Peter Kozina).

Souvenirs: The most atmospheric trinket-shopping is in the first stretch of the **market colonnade,** along the riverfront next to the Triple Bridge (described earlier, under "Sights in Ljubljana"). If you're looking for serious handicrafts rather than trinkets, drop by the **Rustika** gallery, just over the Triple Bridge (on the castle side). In addition to beehive panels, they also have lace, painted chests and boxes, and other tasteful local-style mementos (daily 9:00-20:00, Stritarjeva 9, mobile 031-459-509). There's another Rustika location up at the castle courtyard. **Kraševka** sells high-quality artisanal products (mostly foods) from the Karst region, and also acts as a sort of information office for that area (Mon-Fri 9:00-19:00, Sat 9:00-15:00, closed Sun, Ciril-Metodov trg 10, tel. 01/232-1445). A somewhat more downscale souvenir shop with a wide variety is **Dom Trgovina,** with two locations: One is a block across the Triple Bridge from Prešeren Square and facing the Town Hall (Mon-Fri 9:00-19:00, Sat 9:00-15:00, closed Sun, Mestni trg 24, tel. 01/241-8390), and the other is across from the TI on the main market square (Mon-Fri 8:00-19:00, Sat 8:00-15:00, closed Sun, Ciril-Metodov trg 5).

Boutiques and Galleries: Of the many fun and funky boutique streets in town, my two favorites are along the main drag through the **Old Town** (Mestni trg/Stari trg/Gornji trg), and along **Trubarjeva street,** a block up from the river (easy to find from Prešeren Square).

Sleeping in Ljubljana

Ljubljana has a good range of accommodations in all price ranges. I've focused my listings in or within easy walking distance of the city center. To get the best value, book ahead. The most expensive hotels raise their prices even more during conventions (Sept-Oct, and sometimes also June). The TI can give you a list of cheap private rooms *(sobe)*. To locate the following accommodations, see the map on page 714.

LJUBLJANA

Sleep Code

(€1 = about $1.40, country code: 386, area code: 01)
S = Single, **D** = Double/Twin, **T** = Triple, **Q** = Quad, **b** = bathroom. Unless otherwise noted, credit cards are accepted and breakfast is included, but the modest tourist tax (about €1 per person, per night) is not. Everyone listed here speaks English.

To help you easily sort through these listings, I've divided the accommodations into three categories based on the price for a double room with bath during high season:

$$$ **Higher Priced**—Most rooms €110 or more.
$$ **Moderately Priced**—Most rooms between €70-110.
$ **Lower Priced**—Most rooms €70 or less.

Prices can change without notice; verify the hotel's current rates online or by email. For other updates, see www.ricksteves.com/update.

$$$ *Boutique Hotels in the Old Town:* Three similar (but unrelated), expensive boutique hotels cluster idyllically on a cobbled square in Ljubljana's Old Town. While a bit overpriced (catering to deep-pocketed business travelers), they offer Old World charm with upscale touches (the rates listed are for May-mid-June and Sept-Oct, followed by mid-June-Aug, then Nov-April). **Hotel Angel,** part of the Lesar group, has 12 rooms with crisp white decor and hardwoods (Db-€165/€120/€110, pricier suites, air-con, free Wi-Fi, Gornji trg 7, tel. 01/425-5089, www.angelhotel.si, info@angelhotel.si). **Allegro Hotel** has a musical theme and 16 rooms around a checkerboard-tiled garden courtyard (classic Db-€140/€130/€100, superior Db-€170/€150/€120, air-con, free Internet access and Wi-Fi, Gornji trg 6, tel. 059/119-620, www.allegrohotel.si, info@allegrohotel.si). The family-run **Antiq Hotel** has 16 idiosyncratically decorated rooms sprawling through two buildings with lots of stairs and a mazelike floor plan (small S-€80, Sb-€125-145, small D-€120, Db-€157-180, price depends on size, air-con, free Internet access and Wi-Fi, some rooms have low beams and doors, Gornji trg 3, tel. 01/421-3560, fax 01/421-3565, www.antiqhotel.eu, info@antiqhotel.eu).

$$$ Cubo Hotel is a jolt of trendy minimalism on Ljubljana's hotel scene. Its 26 rooms are the best place in town for sleek, mod elegance. Choose between streetside rooms, which enjoy castle views but get some traffic noise, or quieter courtyard rooms (very flexible rates but generally Sb-€135, Db-€140-180, palatial suite-€200-250, cheaper off-season, non-smoking, air-con, elevator, free Wi-Fi, Slovenska cesta 15, tel. 01/425-6000, fax 01/425-6020, www.hotelcubo.com, reception@hotelcubo.com).

$$$ **Grand Hotel Union** is Ljubljana's top address, as much an Art Nouveau landmark as a hotel. You'll pay dearly for its Old World elegance, hundred years of history, professional staff, big pool, and perfect location (right on Prešeren Square). While their rack rates are outrageously high, you can often snare a great deal in the summer (July-Aug), winter, and on many weekends. The 194 plush "Executive" rooms are in the main building (official rates: Sb-€194, Db-€224; in slow times maybe as low as Sb-€110, Db-€120; non-smoking floors, air-con, elevator, free Wi-Fi, Miklošičeva cesta 1, tel. 01/308-1877, fax 01/308-1015, www .gh-union.si, hotel.union@gh-union.si). Its 133 "Business" rooms next door are less luxurious, almost as expensive, and a lesser value (official rates: Sb-€178, Db-€208; same potential deals as "Executive" rooms, non-smoking floors, air-con, elevator, free cable Internet, Miklošičeva cesta 3, tel. 01/308-1170, fax 01/308-1914, www.gh-union.si, hotel.business@gh-union.si). Both branches have access to parking (€17/day), as well as a pool and sauna on the top floor of the Business branch, and a free Internet terminal in the Executive branch. Because of a noisy nearby disco, request a quieter room at either building if you're here on a weekend.

$$$ **Central Hotel,** technically part of the Grand Hotel Union up the street, has 74 rooms similar to (but slightly smaller than) the "Business" rooms at the main hotel, but cheaper and in a friendlier, less-pretentious package. The hotel is conveniently situated between Prešeren Square and the train station (official rates: Sb-€139, Db-€167; much lower prices likely July-Aug, in winter, and on weekends—maybe as low as Sb-€75, Db-€90; extra bed-€27, non-smoking rooms, air-con, elevator, free Internet access and cable Internet, parking garage-€19/day, Miklošičeva cesta 9, tel. 01/308-4300, fax 01/230-1181, www.centralhotel.si, central .hotel@gh-union.si).

$$ **Slamič B&B** has 11 modern rooms with hardwood floors, tasteful decor, and absentee management. Over an upscale café in a nondescript neighborhood, this is a fine spot for affordable elegance (Sb-€65-75, Db-€95-99, price depends on size; suite: Sb-€135, Db-€165; air-con, lots of stairs with no elevator, free Wi-Fi, Kersnikova 1, tel. 01/433-8233, fax 01/433-8022, www .slamic.si, info@slamic.si). As the café hours are limited (Mon-Thu 7:30-22:00, Fri 7:30-21:00, Sat 9:00-16:00, closed Sun), clearly communicate your arrival time.

$$ **Hotel Pri Mraku** has 35 comfortable, slightly over-priced rooms in a pleasant neighborhood near French Revolution Square. While it's a bit rough around the edges and not without its quirks, this trusty old place is my sentimental favorite in Ljubljana

(Sb-€73, Db-€106, ground-floor and top-floor rooms have air-con and cost €4-5 extra, 8 percent discount for Rick Steves readers if you reserve ahead, extra bed-€23, cheaper mid-Oct-April, non-smoking floor, elevator, free Internet access and Wi-Fi, lunch restaurant with terrace under an old vine, Rimska 4, tel. 01/421-9650, fax 01/421-9655, www.daj-dam.si, hotelmrak@daj-dam.si).

$$ Hotel Emonec (eh-MOH-nets), with some of the most centrally located cheap beds in Ljubljana, hides just off Wolfova lane between Prešeren and Congress squares. Its 41 sleek rooms—in two buildings across a courtyard from each other—feel institutional and characterless, with tight bathrooms and a shoestring staff, but the price and location are hard to beat. As it's near a noisy disco, light sleepers should try requesting a quiet room (Sb-€64, small Db-€67, bigger "standard" Db-€77, Tb-€90-96, Qb-€105-111, price depends on demand, cheaper Nov-April, pay Internet access, free Wi-Fi in some areas, free cable Internet in rooms, free loaner bikes for guests, Wolfova 12, tel. 01/200-1520, fax 01/200-1521, www.hotel-emonec.com, hotelemonec@siol.net).

$ B&B Petra Varl offers comfortable, affordable, nicely appointed rooms on a courtyard across from the bustling riverside market. Petra, who's an artist and speaks good English, will help you feel at home. As this place is Ljubljana's top budget option, book early (Db-€60, extra bed-€10, includes kitchenette with basic do-it-yourself breakfast, cash only, air-con, free Wi-Fi, go into courtyard at Vodnikov trg 5 and look for *B&B* sign at 5A, mobile 041-389-470, petra@varl.si).

$ Penzion Pod Lipo has 10 rooms above a restaurant in a mostly residential area about a 12-minute walk from Prešeren Square. While the rooms are old and simple, it's thoughtfully run by Marjan (Db-€65, Tb-€75, Qb-€100, breakfast in restaurant-€3.50 extra, cash only, reception open 8:00-22:00, non-smoking, free Internet access, free cable Internet, guest kitchen, putting green on terrace, tel. 01/251-1683, mobile 031-809-893, www.penzion-podlipo.com, info@penzion-podlipo.com).

$ Stari Tišler ("Old Carpenter") is a good budget option in a characteristically old, time-warp house immersed in a commercial zone a 10-minute walk from Prešeren Square. Its four modern rooms—which are nicely appointed (with mod, colorful splashes) for this price range—share two toilets and one shower, keeping prices low. It's above a restaurant that's popular at lunchtime with local businesspeople (D-€50, T-€75, breakfast-€5, air-con, up 2 flights of stairs, free Wi-Fi, Kolodvorska 8, tel. 01/430-3370, www.stari-tisler.com, info@stari-tisler.com, Sandra).

$ Hotel Center (not to be confused with "Central Hotel," listed earlier) is a good value. Marko's eight small, modern rooms deliver on his promise of "three-star furnishings at two-star prices." While the location, just across Slovenska avenue from the main part of town, is convenient, this place suffers from noise—from the busy road on one side, and from the bar downstairs on the other...bring earplugs (Db-€60-66 depending on season, breakfast-€4.20, free Wi-Fi, down the passage at Slovenska cesta 51 and around back, mobile 041-263-347, www.hotelcenter.si, info@hotel center.si).

Hostels

Ljubljana has several good hostels. The ones listed here are particularly well-established.

$ Hostel Celica, a proud, innovative, and lively place, is funded by the city and run by a nonprofit student organization. This former military prison's 20 cells *(celica)* have been converted into hostel rooms—each one unique, decorated by a different designer (tours of the hostel daily at 14:00). The top floor features more typical hostel rooms (each with its own bathroom, for 3-12 people). The building also houses an art gallery, tourist information, Internet access and Wi-Fi, self-service laundry (€8/load), good restaurant, and shoes-off "Oriental café" (all prices listed are per person—cell rooms: S-€53-61, D-€28-32, T-€25-30; bed in top-floor rooms with bathrooms: 3- to 5-bed room-€25-30, 7-bed dorm-€23-27, 12-bed dorm-€21-25; price depends on demand—most expensive on June-Sept weekends, cheaper Nov-March; includes breakfast, sheets, towels, and tax; no curfew, non-smoking, bike and car rental, active excursions around Slovenia, Metelkova 8, a dull 15-minute walk to Prešeren Square, 8 minutes to the train station, tel. 01/230-9700, fax 01/230-9714, www.hostelcelica.com, recepcija@hostelcelica.com). Light sleepers take note: The hostel hosts live music events about two nights per week until around 24:00, but otherwise maintains "quiet time" after 23:00. However, the surrounding neighborhood—a bit rundown and remote, but safe—is a happening nightlife zone, which can make for noisy weekends.

$ Alibi Hostel, an official IYHF hostel creatively run by Gorazd, has two very different branches. For a grungy, funky backpacker-slumbermill scene, head for **Alibi CN27,** with 100 beds (including 20 private rooms). The rooms are colorful and scruffy, and it's ideally located right on Ljubljana's main riverfront-café drag. The imaginative graffiti murals—featuring a stripper with memorable piercings and a certain cowboy president—are guaranteed to offend just about anyone over 30 (dorm bed-€17, or €19 Fri-Sat; D-€50, or €60 Fri-Sat; includes sheets and tax, cheaper Oct-May, no breakfast, free Internet access and Wi-Fi, self-service laundry, lockers, Cankarjevo nabrežje 27, tel. 01/251-1244, www.alibi.si). When backpackers grow a bit older and more sedate, they're more interested in comfort than socializing—and it's time to head for **Alibi M14,** across the street from Grand Hotel Union, a few steps off Prešeren Square. With four small but well-appointed private rooms with private bathrooms, seven private rooms with shared baths, a 10-bed dorm (sharing one bathroom), and a pleasant kitchen—but not a lot of rowdy hangout areas—it's a good compromise (dorm bed-€15-19, €1 extra Fri-Sat; D-€40-50, €6 extra Fri-Sat; Db-€50-60, €6 extra Fri-Sat; cheaper Oct-May, includes sheets and towels, free Internet access and Wi-Fi, self-service laundry, lockers, Miklošičeva cesta 14, tel. 01/232-2770, www.alibi.si, m14@alibi.si).

Eating in Ljubljana

At this crossroads of cultures (and cuisines), Italian and French flavors are just as "local" as meat-and-starch Slovenian food. This cosmopolitan city also dabbles in other cuisines; you'll find Thai, Indian, Chinese, Mexican, and more. To locate these restaurants, see the map on page 714.

see the map on page 714.

In the City Center

Gostilna As ("Ace"), tucked into a courtyard just off Prešeren Square, offers fish-lovers the best blowout in town. It's dressy,

pricey, and pretentious (waiters ignore the menu and recommend what's fresh). Everything is specially prepared each day and beautifully presented. It's loosely based on the Slow Food model: Servings are small, and you're expected to take your time and order two or three courses (mostly fish and Italian, €6-15 starters, €18-30 main courses, daily 12:00-24:00, reservations smart, Čopova 5A, or enter courtyard with *As* sign near image of Julija on Wolfova, tel. 01/425-8822). For cheaper food from the same kitchen, eat at their attached **As Lounge.**

This much livelier, more casual spot features drinks, €8-11 salads and sandwiches, €7-10 pastas, and €11-19 main courses. You'll sit in the leafy courtyard or the glassed-in winter garden (food served daily 12:00-23:00, longer hours for drinks). The courtyard also has a couple of other fun eateries—and, in the summer only, live music and a much-loved gelato stand.

Ribca ("Fish") hides under the first stretch of market colonnade near the Triple Bridge. This is your best bet for a relatively quick and cheap riverside lunch. Choose between the two straightforward menus: grilled fillets or fried small fish. With the fragrant fish market right next door, you know it's fresh. If you just want to enjoy sitting along the river below the bustling market, this is also a fine spot for a coffee or beer (€6-7 salads, €4 seafood salads, €4-8 main courses, €7.50 lunches, Mon-Fri 8:00-16:00, Sat 8:00-14:00, closed Sun).

Pri Vitezu is well-respected for its seasonal menu of classic Mediterranean dishes. It sits along the newly spiffed-up Breg embankment, just beyond the Cobblers' Bridge; sit out on the pedestrian mall, or in the Old World-elegant interior. This place is especially worth considering for its excellent-value €9 lunch special, which includes soup, salad bar, a main dish, and a dessert (available Mon-Fri, on Sat they have a €14 traditional Slovenian lunch; otherwise €10-18 starters, €14-28 main dishes, €40 five-course meal, Mon-Fri 11:00-23:00, Sat 12:00-22:00, closed Sun, Breg 18-20, tel. 01/426-6058).

Asian Fusion: **DaBuDa** is the best spot in Ljubljana for Asian cuisine, featuring good Thai dishes (salads, curries, wok meals, and noodles) in a very mod, dark-wood, split-level setting frequented by hip young professionals (good-value €6-7 lunch specials, €8-14 main courses at dinner, Mon-Fri 11:00-23:00, Sat-Sun 12:00-23:00, also a few outdoor tables, between Congress Square and Square of the Republic at Šubičeva 1A, tel. 01/425-3060).

Fast and Cheap: Burek, the typical Balkan phyllo-dough snack (see the "Balkan Flavors" sidebar on page 1090), can be picked up at street stands around town. Most are open 24 hours and charge about €2 for a hearty portion. An easy choice is **Nobel Burek,** next to Miklošičeva cesta 30; but many locals prefer **Olimpija Burek,** around the corner at Pražakova 14 (across from the post office).

Pizzerias: Ljubljana has lots of great sit-down pizza places. Expect to pay €5-10 for an average-sized pie (wide variety of toppings). **Pizzeria Foculus,** tucked in a boring alleyway a few blocks up from the river, has a loyal local following, a happening atmosphere, an innovative leafy interior, a few outdoor tables, and Ljubljana's best pizza (over 50 types for €6-10, €6-8 salads, daily 11:00-24:00, just off French Revolution Square across the street from Plečnik's National and University Library at Gregorčičeva 3, tel. 01/251-5643). **Ljubljanski Dvor** enjoys the most convenient and scenic location of any pizzeria in town. On a sunny summer day, the outdoor riverside terrace is unbeatable. The interior has a simple pizza parlor downstairs (€5-11 pizzas and pastas), with a more refined dining room upstairs (selling the same pizzas and pastas, plus €12-20 Italian main courses; pizza parlor open daily 10:00-24:00, upstairs restaurant opens at 12:00, just 50 yards from Cobblers' Bridge at Dvorni trg 1, tel. 01/251-6555). Ljubljanski Dvor also has a handy, cheap pizza **take-out window** (go around back to the walk-up window on Congress Square, €2 slices to go, picnic in the park or down on the river—plenty of welcoming benches, Mon-Fri 7:00-24:00, Sat 9:00-24:00, Sun 12:00-24:00).

In the Old Town

The main drag through the Old Town (which starts at the Town Hall and changes names as it goes: Mestni trg, then Stari trg, then Gornji trg) is lined with inviting eateries. Tables spill into the cobbled pedestrian street, filled with happy diners. If you're at a loss for where to eat in town, stroll here to survey your options, then pick your favorite menu and ambience. As many restaurants along here are uniformly good, no one place really has the edge. One popular choice is **Julija,** with homey country-Slovenian decor inside, great outdoor seating, Mediterranean-Slovenian cuisine, and good €10 lunch deals (otherwise figure €8-12 starters, €12-19 main dishes, daily 12:00-22:00, Stari trg 9, tel. 01/425-6463). Romeo, across the street, is a lowbrow bar serving unexceptional Mexican food...but the name sure is clever (get it? "Romeo and Julija"). I've also enjoyed a great salad lunch at the **Čajna Hiša** teahouse (described later, under "Coffee, Tea, and Treats.")

Traditional Slovenian Food

Because Slovenes head into the countryside when they want traditional fare, Ljubljana isn't the best place to find authentic Slovenian grub. And, frankly, most visitors prefer the Mediterranean/international restaurants that are more common in the capital anyway. But you do have some good options in the city center.

Gostilna na Gradu, in the castle courtyard high above town, is your single best option for true Slovenian food in Ljubljana—if you don't mind going up to the castle to get it (the handy funicular costs €3 round-trip). Run by a well-respected chef, it serves up a seasonal menu of traditional flavors with modern flair. The portions are small, but the prices are surprisingly affordable. Choose between the dull vaulted interior, the glassed-in arcade, or the outdoor tables. Reservations are recommended before you make the trip up here (€8-12 pastas, €6-15 main dishes, €30 five-course meal lets you sample several flavors, Sun-Fri 10:00-24:00, Sat 10:00-16:00, Grajska Planota 1, mobile 031-301-777).

Touristy but Acceptable Options: Two places near the market are easy and popular options for Slovenian dishes. Both of these places cater mostly to tourists—so don't expect top quality or a great value. **Sokol,** with brisk, traditionally clad waiters, fills a fun, sprawling Slovenian-village interior with jaunty polkas on the soundtrack and a very central location. It's in all the guidebooks and deluged by tourists, so don't expect an authentic experience

(€9-21 main courses, a few veggie options, Mon-Sat 7:00-23:00, Sun 10:00-23:00, on castle side of Triple Bridge at Ciril-Metodov trg 18, tel. 01/439-6855). A few blocks away, across from the main market square, **Vodnikov Hram** has an Old World interior and outdoor tables overlooking a parking lot. While a variation on the same theme as Sokol, it's marginally less touristy, and has slightly lower prices (€7-8 pastas, €7-24 main courses, Mon-Sat 9:00-24:00, Sun 10:00-24:00, Vodnikov trg 2, tel. 01/234-5260).

In Krakovo

The Krakovo district—just south of the city center, where garden patches nearly outnumber simple homes—is a pleasant area to wander. It's also home to a trio of tasty restaurants. Consider combining a meal here with your trip to the Jože Plečnik House (which is just beyond Krakovo).

Pri Škofu ("By the Bishop") is a laid-back, informal place with mostly outdoor seating and a focus on freshness, serving international cuisine with a Slovenian flair. There's no menu—the waiter tells you what's good today...and it is. They'll ask what kind of pasta or meat you want, then help you narrow down your options (sauces, sides, etc.) to get to your ideal meal. This hidden gem is deliciously memorable and worth seeking out. Reservations are essential (creative €3 soups, €7-8 lunches, €7-23 main courses at dinner, homemade €3 desserts, Mon-Fri 10:00-24:00, Sat-Sun 12:00-24:00, Rečna 8, tel. 01/426-4508).

Manna, with artfully presented Slovenian-Mediterranean fusion cuisine, sits along the pleasant Gradaščica canal. The interior is pure Secession—the Gustav Klimt-era, early-20th-centry, gold-accented Viennese style that was so influential in Ljubljana. I prefer the more artistic, café-like downstairs to the stuffy upstairs dining room, but the seating out front is hard to beat on a nice day (€12 lunch special Mon-Fri, otherwise €7-12 starters, €9-25 main dishes, Mon-Sat 12:00-24:00, closed Sun, Eipprova 1A, tel. 01/283-5294).

Harambaša is the closest thing to a ticket to Sarajevo. Serving Balkan grilled meats, this popular-with-students eatery has Bosnian-flavored decor, old pictures, and cuisine reminiscent of the Bosnian capital. For a refresher on the meat dishes, see "Balkan Flavors" on page 1090. The menu is limited, which makes ordering easy. Their handy €7 *pola-pola* combo-plate—with lotsa meat combined with chopped onions, *kajmak* (a soft cheese spread), and *lepinja* (pita bread)—makes for a simple but filling lunch. Also consider the Bosnian coffee (a high-octane brew with "mud" at the bottom) and baklava. Vegetarians need not apply (€5-7 main courses, Mon-Fri 10:00-22:00, Sat 12:00-22:00, Sun 12:00-18:00, Vrtna 8, mobile 041-843-106).

Coffee, Tea, and Treats

Riverfront Cafés: Enjoying a coffee, beer, or ice-cream cone along the Ljubljanica River embankment (between the Triple and

Cobblers' bridges) is Ljubljana's single best experience—worth ▲▲▲. Tables spill into the street, and some of the best-dressed, best-looking students on the planet happily fill them day and night. (A common question from first-time visitors to Ljubljana: "Doesn't anybody here have a job?") This is some of the top people-watching in Europe. Rather than recommend a particular place (they're all about the same), I'll leave you to explore and find the spot with the breezy ambience you like best. When ordering, the easiest choice is a *bela kava*—"white coffee," basically a caffè latte.

Teahouse: If coffee's not your cup of tea, go a block inland to the teahouse **Čajna Hiša**. They have a shop (called "Cha") with over 100 varieties of tea, plus porcelain teapots and cups from all over (Mon-Fri 9:00-20:00, Sat 9:00-15:00, closed Sun). The café serves about 50 different types of tea, light food (including great salads), and desserts (€2-4 cakes and sandwiches, €7-9 salads, Mon-Fri 9:00-22:30, Sat 9:00-15:00 & 18:00-22:00, closed Sun, on the atmospheric main drag in the Old Town a few steps from Cobblers' Bridge at Stari trg 3, tel. 01/252-7010).

Cakes: **Zvezda Kavarna,** a trendy, central place at the bottom of Congress Square, is a local favorite for cakes, pastries, and ice cream (decadent €3-5 cakes, Mon-Sat 7:00-23:00, Sun 10:00-20:00, a block up from Prešeren Square at Wolfova 14, tel. 01/421-9090). **Abecedarium** (ah-beh-tseh-dah-ree-oom, like the alphabet) serves up delicious €4 Nutella-banana cake (and other food) with indoor or outdoor seating near the Triple Bridge. It's located in the oldest house in town, named for a work by one of Slovenia's greatest thinkers, who once lived in the house (daily 8:00-24:00, Ribji trg 2, tel. 01/426-9514).

Chocolates and Ice Cream: **Rustika** is a local chain that sells tasty homemade chocolates (€3.80/100 grams), cookies (including one kind with four different types of chocolate), and a wide variety of unusual and delicious artisan ice cream flavors. The menu changes from day to day, but highlights can include balsamic vinegar with vanilla or strawberry, very dark chocolate, Kanada (with maple syrup and walnuts), and Greek yogurt with honey and nuts. The handiest location is about an eight-minute walk from Prešeren Square, and comes with a delightful stroll along colorful Trubarjeva street (€1.20/scoop, ice cream available summer only, Mon-Fri 8:00-19:00, Sat 9:00-13:00, closed Sun, Trubarjeva 44, mobile 059-935-730). Don't confuse this sweet shop with the Rustika gift shop.

More Ice Cream: Ljubljana is known for its Italian gelato-style ice cream. You'll see fine options all along the Ljubljanica River embankment. Favorites include **Rustika**, the courtyard garden at **Gostilna As** (summer only) and **Zvezda Kavarna** (all described earlier).

Ljubljana Connections

As Slovenia's transportation hub, Ljubljana is well-connected to both domestic and international destinations. When checking schedules, be aware of name variations: In Slovene, Vienna is "Dunaj" and Budapest is "Budimpešta."

Getting to Croatia

To reach **Istria** by public transportation, you have two relatively straightforward options: In summer (June-late Sept), a direct bus departs Ljubljana for Rovinj once each day (around 13:45, 5.5 hours, €21, also stops en route in Piran and Poreč; off-season runs 2/week—generally Mon and Fri, departing 16:30). From mid-July through August, there's also a train connection to Pula (Thu-Sun only, 4.75 hours, transfer in Hrpelje-Kozina); once in Pula, you can connect by bus to other Istrian destinations. On off-season weekends, you might have to get creative (try connecting through Rijeka).

If connecting directly to Croatia's **Dalmatian Coast,** you have three options: Train to Zagreb (2.5 hours), where you can catch a cheap Croatia Air flight or a bus (see "Zagreb Connections" on page 1045); take the long, once-daily train connection from Ljubljana to Split (9 hours, requires a change in Zagreb); or, much slower, take the train to Rijeka, then cruise on a boat down the coast from there.

By Train

From Ljubljana by Train to: Lesce-Bled (roughly hourly, 40-60 minutes—but bus is better because it goes right to Bled town center), **Postojna** (nearly hourly, 1 hour), **Divača** (close to Škocjan Caves and Lipica, nearly hourly, 1.75 hours), **Sežana** (close to Lipica, nearly hourly, 2 hours), **Piran** (direct bus is better—see below; otherwise allow 4 hours, train to Koper, 4/day, 2.5 hours; then bus to Piran, 7/day, 30 minutes), **Maribor** (hourly, 2-3 hours, more with a transfer in Zidani Most), **Ptuj** (3/day, 2.5 hours, more with transfer in Pragersko), **Zagreb** (7/day, 2.5 hours), **Rijeka** (2/day direct, 2.75 hours), **Pula** (1/day mid-July-Aug Thu-Sun only,

4.75 hours, transfer in Hrpelje-Kozina), **Split** (1/day, 9 hours, transfer in Zagreb), **Vienna** (that's *Dunaj* in Slovene, 1/day direct, 6 hours; otherwise 4/day with transfer in Maribor, 6-7 hours), **Budapest** (that's *Budimpešta* in Slovene; 2/day direct, 8-9 hours, other connections possible with 1-2 changes but complicated, night train departs Ljubljana around 1:50 in the morning), **Venice** (1/day with a change to a bus in Villach, 6.75 hours; also possible by train to Sežana, then change to Nova Gorica, then transfer by bus to Gorizia, then train to Venice), **Salzburg** (2/day direct, 4-5 hours, more with transfer in Villach), **Munich** (3/day direct, 6 hours, including 1 night train; otherwise transfer in Salzburg). Train info: tel. 01/291-3332, www.slo-zeleznice.si.

By Bus

The bus station is a low-profile building in front of the train station. Buses depart from the numbered stalls in the middle of the street. For any bus, you have to buy tickets at the bus station ticket windows or at the automated e-kart kiosk (pay with credit card or cash), not from the driver. For bus information, pick up one of the blue phones inside the station to be connected to a helpful English-speaking operator. Bus info: www.ap-ljubljana.si, toll tel. 1991 (about €0.75/minute).

By Bus to: **Bled** (Mon-Sat hourly—usually at the top of each hour, fewer on Sun, 1.25 hours, €6.30), **Postojna** (at least hourly, 1 hour, €6), **Divača** (close to Škocjan Caves and Lipica, about every 2-3 hours, 1.5 hours, €7.90), **Piran** (5/day Mon-Fri, 2/day Sat, 4/day Sun, 2.5 hours, €12), over the **Vršič Pass** to **Bovec** (1/day June-Sept, departs Ljubljana 6:30, arrives Bovec 10:45, €14, none Oct-May), **Rovinj** (1/day June-late Sept, departs Ljubljana around 13:45, 5.5 hours, €21; off-season: 2/week, generally Mon and Fri, departs 16:30), **Rijeka** (2/day in summer, sporadic off-season, 2.5 hours, €23), **Zagreb** (1/day Mon-Fri only, €12).

By Plane

Slovenia's only **airport** (airport code: LJU) is 14 miles north of Ljubljana, about halfway to Bled. Confusingly, the airport goes by three names: Ljubljana Airport (the international version); Brnik (for the town that it's near); and Jože Pučnik Airport (a politician for whom it was controversially renamed in 2007). Most flights are operated by Slovenia's national airline, Adria Airways (www.adria-airways.com), but additional flights are run by easyJet (www.easyjet.com), Wizz Air (www.wizzair.com), Czech Airlines (www.csa.cz), and others. If you need to kill time here, follow signs (around to the left as you exit the terminal) to *Razgledna Terasa* and *Terasa Avionček* and ride the elevator up to the rooftop terrace with a café (daily 9:00-19:00). Here you can sip a coffee while you watch planes land and take off. Airport info: tel. 04/206-1000, www.lju-airport.si.

Getting Between Downtown Ljubljana and the Airport: Two kinds of buses connect the airport with Ljubljana's bus station: **public bus** #28 (to the right as you exit the airport; Mon-Fri hourly until 20:00, only 7/day Sat-Sun, 45 minutes, €4.10), and a **minibus** (to the left as you exit the airport, scheduled to depart after various arriving flights—look for schedule posted near bus stop). Two different companies run the minibus transfers, which take about 30 minutes: Markun (€5 to train station, €9 to your hotel, mobile 041-792-865) and Marko Nowotny (€9 regardless of your destination, mobile 040-771-771, www.mnj.si). I'd take whichever one is departing first. For a transfer *to* the airport, your hotel or any TI can make arrangements with one of these companies a day or so in advance (same price). Unfortunately, certain evening arrivals don't coordinate well with either the bus or the minibus, so you might have to wait a while or take a pricey **taxi** (figure €20-25 to the airport if you call a reputable company, but more like €42 *from* the airport—since you have to use the pricey taxi stand out front).

The Austrian Alternative: Since Ljubljana's airport is the only one in the country (and thus charges extremely high taxes and airport fees), many Slovenes prefer to fly out of Austria. The airport in **Klagenfurt** (airport code: KLU, also known as "Alpe-Adria Airport"), just over the Austrian border to the north, is subsidized by the local government to keep prices low and compete with Ljubljana's airport. Especially if you're connecting to Bled, it's somewhat handy to reach (from Ljubljana or Bled, take the train to Villach, then to Klagenfurt's Annabichl station, which is a 5-minute walk from the airport; total trip 3 hours from Ljubljana, or 2 hours from Bled; www.klagenfurt-airport.com). A taxi transfer to Bled runs a hefty €120 and takes about an hour (see "By Taxi" on page 720). Austrian Airlines (www.austrian.com) flies from Klagenfurt, as do low-cost carriers such as Ryanair (www.ryanair.com), TUIfly (www.tuifly.com), Germanwings (www.germanwings.com), and Air Berlin (www.airberlin.com).

LAKE BLED

Lake Bled—Slovenia's leading mountain resort—comes complete with a sweeping alpine panorama, a fairy-tale island, a cliff-hanging medieval castle, a lazy lakeside promenade, and the country's most sought-after desserts. There are few more enjoyable places to simply be on vacation.

Since the Habsburg days, Lake Bled (locals pronounce it "blayd") has been *the* place where Slovenes wow visiting diplomats. Tito had one of his vacation homes here (today's Hotel Vila Bled), and more recent visitors have included Prince Charles, Madeleine Albright, and Laura Bush. But above all, Lake Bled feels like a place that Slovenes enjoy alongside their visitors.

Lake Bled has plenty of ways to idle away an afternoon. While the lake's main town, also called Bled, is more functional than quaint, it offers postcard views of the lake and handy access to the region. Hike up to Bled Castle for intoxicating vistas. Make a wish and ring the bell at the island church. Wander the dreamy path around the lake. Sit on a dock, dip your feet in the water, and feed some of the lake's resident swans. Then dive into some of Bled's famous cakes while you take in the view of Triglav, Slovenia's favorite mountain (see "Mount Triglav" sidebar on page 798). Bled quiets down at night—no nightlife beyond a handful of pubs—giving hikers and other holiday-makers a chance to recharge. Bled is also a great jumping-off point for a car trip through the Julian Alps (see next chapter).

Planning Your Time

Bled and its neighboring mountains deserve two days. With one day, spend it in and around Bled (or, to rush things, spend the morning in Bled and the afternoon day-tripping). With a second day and a car, drive through the Julian Alps using the self-guided tour in the next chapter. The circular route takes you up and over the stunning Vršič Pass, then down the scenic and historic Soča River Valley. Without a car, skip the second day, or spend it doing nearby day trips: Bus or bike to Radovljica to see the bee museum, hike to Vintgar Gorge, or visit the more rustic Lake Bohinj (all described under "Near Lake Bled," later in this chapter).

Orientation to Lake Bled

(area code: 04)
The town of Bled is on the east end of 1.5-mile-long Lake Bled.

The lakefront is lined with cafés and resort hotels. A 3.5-mile path meanders around the lake. As no motorized boats are allowed, Lake Bled is particularly peaceful.

The tourists' center of Bled is a cluster of big resort hotels, dominated by the giant, red Hotel Park (dubbed the "red can"). The busy street called **Ljubljanska cesta** leads out of Bled town toward Ljubljana and most other destinations. Just up from the lakefront, across Ljubljanska cesta from Hotel Park, is the modern **commercial center** (Trgovski Center Bled), with a travel agency, grocery store, ATM, shops, and a smattering of lively cafés. Nicknamed "Gaddafi" by the people of Bled, the commercial center was designed for a Libyan city, but the deal fell through—so the frugal Slovenes built it here instead. Just up the road from the commercial center, you'll find the post office and library (with Internet access).

Bled's less-touristy Old Town is under the castle, surrounding the pointy spire of St. Martin's Church. There you'll find the bus station, some good restaurants, a few hostels, and more locals than tourists.

The mountains poking above the ridge at the far end of the lake are the Julian Alps, crowned by the three peaks of Mount Triglav. The big mountain behind the town of Bled is Stol ("Chair"), part of the Karavanke range that defines the Austrian border.

Tourist Information

Bled's helpful TI is in the long, lakefront casino building across the street from the big, red Hotel Park (as you face the lake, the TI is hiding around the front at the far left end, overlooking the lake). Pick up the good map (with the lake on one side and the whole region on the other) and the free Bled information booklet.

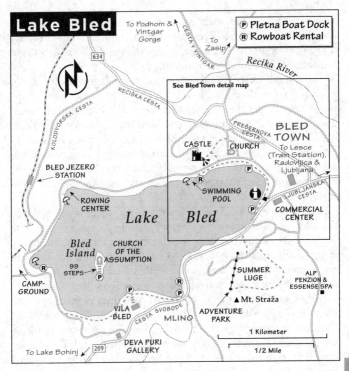

Get advice on hikes and day trips, confirm transit schedules, and if you're doing any serious hiking, spring for a good regional map (July-Aug Mon-Sat 8:00-21:00, Sun 9:00-18:00; May-June and Sept-Oct Mon-Sat 8:00-19:00, Sun 11:00-17:00; Nov-April Mon-Sat 8:00-18:00, Sun 8:00-13:00; Cesta Svobode 10, tel. 04/574-1122, www.bled.si). The TI can give you a list of accommodations, and if they're not too busy, they may be able to call around to check availability for you (Kompas Bled travel agency has a room-booking service—see "Helpful Hints," later).

For more details on hiking in Triglav National Park, visit the **Triglav National Park Information Center** on the main road out of town (free information, maps and guidebooks for sale; May-Sept daily 10:00-18:00; Oct-April Mon-Fri 12:00-16:00, Sat-Sun 10:00-18:00; Ljubljanska cesta 27, tel. 04/578-0205, www.tnp.si).

Arrival in Bled

By Train: Two train stations have the name "Bled." The **Bled Jezero** ("Bled Lake") station is across the lake from Bled town and is used only by infrequent, slow, tourist-oriented trains into the mountains. You're much more likely to use the **Lesce-Bled** station in the nearby village of Lesce. The Lesce-Bled station is on the main line and has far better connections to Ljubljana and international destinations. So if you're buying a train ticket or checking schedules, request "Lesce-Bled" rather than just "Bled." (This is so important, I'll remind you again later.)

The small **Lesce-Bled station** is in the village of Lesce, about 2.5 miles from Bled. The nearest ATM is upstairs in the shopping center across the street (at the Gorenjska Banka on the third floor, across the parking lot from Mercator supermarket). From the Lesce station, you can take the bus into Bled town (2/hour, 10 minutes, €1.30, catch it across the street from the train station); or pay about €10 for a taxi into town. If taking the train out of Lesce-Bled, you can buy tickets at this station or on the train—nobody in Bled town sells tickets.

By Bus: Bled's main bus station is just up from the lake in the Old Town. To reach the lake, walk straight downhill on Cesta Svobode. Note that many buses also stop on the way into town, along Ljubljanska cesta; this stop is handier for walking to many of my recommended accommodations—though some bus drivers may not want to stop here (for details, see "Sleeping in Bled," later).

By Car: Coming from Ljubljana, you'll wind your way into Bled on Ljubljanska cesta, which rumbles through the middle of town before swinging left at the lake. There's a short-term parking lot just above the commercial center, but it's often full; for a longer stay, turn right at the traffic light by Gostilna Union to reach a larger lot that's not far from the lake (near the sports hall). If you're sleeping in town, ask your hotel about parking. Also see "Route Tips for Drivers" on page 783.

By Plane: For details on getting from Ljubljana's airport to Bled, see "Lake Bled Connections," later.

Helpful Hints

Money: Bled town's handiest ATMs are at **SKB Banka** (upstairs in round building at commercial center) and **Gorenjska Banka** (at far end of Hotel Park; this ATM does not accept Visa cards).

Internet Access: Most hotels offer free Internet access and/or Wi-Fi for their guests. In a pinch, the public library has terminals with fast access (free up to one hour per day, Mon-Fri 10:00-19:00, Sat 8:00-12:00, closed Sun, next to the post office on Ljubljanska cesta).

Post Office: If you're coming up from the lake on Ljubljanska cesta, it's just past the commercial center and library (Mon-Fri 8:00-19:00, Sat 8:00-12:00, closed Sun, slightly longer hours July-Aug, tel. 04/575-0200).

Laundry: Most hotels can do laundry for you, but it's expensive (priced by the piece). You'll get a better deal from a can-do

Bled and the Julian Alps Essentials

English	Slovene	Pronounced
Slovenia's Biggest Mountain	Triglav	TREE-glau
Lake Bled	Blejsko Jezero	BLAY-skoh YAY-zay-roh
The Island	Otok	OH-tohk
Bled Castle	Blejski Grad	BLAY-skee grahd
Town near Bled with Train Station	Lesce	lest-SEH
Town with Bee Museum	Radovljica	rah-DOH-vleet-suh
Gorge near Bled	Vintgar	VEENT-gar
Rustic Lake near Bled	Bohinj	BOH-heen
Scenic High-Mountain Pass	Vršič	vur-SHEECH
Historic River Valley	Soča	SOH-chah

local, **Anže Štalc.** Call Anže to arrange drop-off (possibly at the Amigo travel agency, Cesta Svobode 15, next to the Casino), and pick it up cleaned and folded 24 hours later (€15/load, €5 more for same-day express service, mobile 041-575-522).

Car Rental: The Julian Alps are ideal by car. Several big chains rent cars in Bled—figure €60 per day, including tax, insurance, and unlimited mileage (generally no extra charge for drop-off elsewhere in Slovenia). Various major companies have branches in Bled, including **Europcar** (mobile 031-382-055), **Budget** (mobile 041-644-626), **Sixt** (mobile 030-645-350), **Hertz** (tel. 04/574-5588), and the local **Avantcar** (mobile 041-400-980); as the offices tend to move around, inquire in Bled about the current locations.

Travel Agency: Kompas Bled, in the commercial center, rents bikes, sells books and maps, offers a room-booking service (including many cheap rooms in private homes—though most are away from the lake), and sells various tours around the region (May-Sept Mon-Sat 8:00-19:00, Sun 8:00-12:00 & 16:00-19:00; Oct-April Mon-Sat 8:00-19:00, closed Sun; Ljubljanska cesta 4, tel. 04/572-7500, www.kompas-bled.si, kompas.bled@siol.net).

Massage: If you're here to relax, consider a massage at the **Essense** wellness center at the recommended Alp Penzion. This

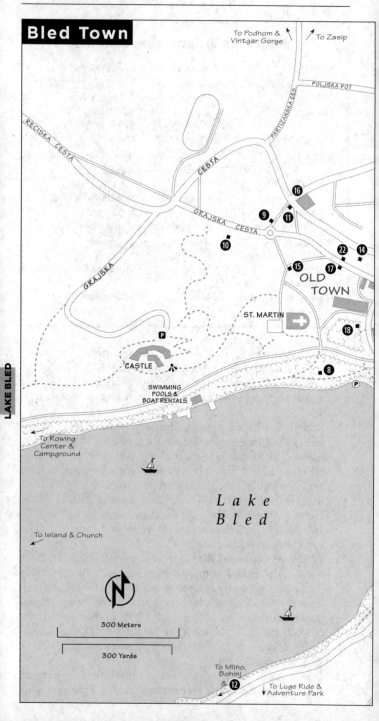

Bled Town

To Podhom &
Vintgar Gorge

To Zasip

POLJSKA POT

RECISKA CESTA

PARTIZANSKA CES.

CESTA

GRAJSKA CESTA

GRAJSKA

16

9 11

10

22 14

15 17

OLD
TOWN

ST. MARTIN

18

8

CASTLE

SWIMMING
POOLS &
BOAT RENTALS

To Rowing
Center &
Campground

LAKE BLED

Lake
Bled

To Island & Church

N

300 Meters

300 Yards

To Mlino,
Bohinj
&

12

To Luge Ride &
Adventure Park

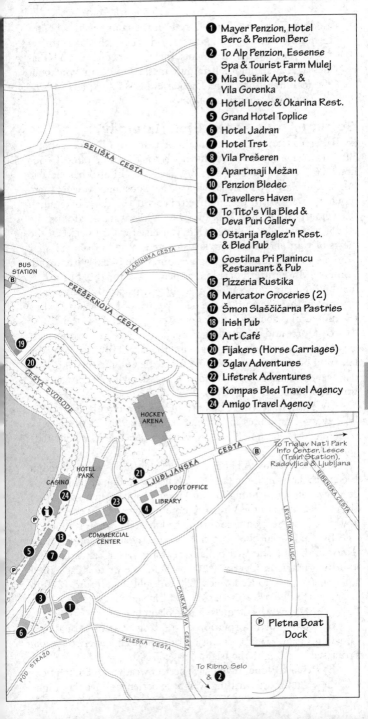

1. Mayer Penzion, Hotel Berc & Penzion Berc
2. To Alp Penzion, Essense Spa & Tourist Farm Mulej
3. Mia Sušnik Apts. & Vila Gorenka
4. Hotel Lovec & Okarina Rest.
5. Grand Hotel Toplice
6. Hotel Jadran
7. Hotel Trst
8. Vila Prešeren
9. Apartmaji Mežan
10. Penzion Bledec
11. Travellers Haven
12. To Tito's Vila Bled & Deva Puri Gallery
13. Oštarija Peglez'n Rest. & Bled Pub
14. Gostilna Pri Planincu Restaurant & Pub
15. Pizzeria Rustika
16. Mercator Groceries (2)
17. Šmon Slaščičarna Pastries
18. Irish Pub
19. Art Café
20. Fijakers (Horse Carriages)
21. 3glav Adventures
22. Lifetrek Adventures
23. Kompas Bled Travel Agency
24. Amigo Travel Agency

LAKE BLED

SELIŠKA CESTA

BUS STATION

MLADINSKA CESTA

PREŠERNOVA CESTA

CESTA SVOBODE

HOCKEY ARENA

To Triglav Nat'l Park Info Center, Lesce (Train Station), Radovljica & Ljubljana

LJUBLJANSKA CESTA

HOTEL PARK

CASINO

POST OFFICE

LIBRARY

COMMERCIAL CENTER

RIBENSKA CESTA

LEVSTIKOVA ULICA

CANKARJEVA CESTA

ŽELEŠKA CESTA

POD STRAŽO

To Ribno, Selo & 2

Ⓟ Pletna Boat Dock

modern, classy facility—hiding in the countryside about a 15-minute walk or 5-minute taxi ride above the lake—offers a wide range of spa treatments, including pedicures and Thai massage. A standard 50-minute massage will run you about €36 (call first to arrange, Cankarjeva cesta 20A, tel. 04/576-7450, www.alp-penzion.com).

Getting Around Lake Bled (Literally)

By Bike: You can rent a mountain bike at the TI or at Kompas Bled travel agency (both listed earlier) for the same rates (€3.50/hour, €6/3 hours, €8/half-day, €11/day). The TI also has electric bikes, which give you a much-appreciated boost once you get them moving—well worth the small extra cost if you don't bike much (€5/1 hour, €10/4 hours, €15/8 hours). While walking around the lake is slo-mo bliss, biking it lets you fast-forward between the views of your choice. Biking is also a great way to reach Vintgar Gorge—perfect for combining a countryside pedal with a walk immersed in nature. For a longer pedal, ask for the TI's excellent biking map, with various great bike trips clearly marked and described. The bike path to the nearby town of Radovljica (and its bee museum) is about four miles one-way (get details at the TI).

By Horse and Buggy: Buggies called *fijakers* are the romantic, expensive, and easy way to get around the lake. Hire one along the lakefront between Hotel Park and the castle (around the lake-€40, one-way up to castle-€40, round-trip to castle with 30-minute wait time-€50, mobile 041-710-970).

By Tourist Train: A little train makes a circuit around the lake every 40 minutes in summer (€3, daily 9:00-21:00 in peak season, shorter hours off-season, weather-dependent, mobile 051-337-478).

By Tourist Bus: A handy but pricey shuttle bus passes through Bled once daily in summer. It leaves the bus station at 10:00, stops at a few hotels (including Grand Hotel Toplice), then goes up to the castle and on to the Vintgar Gorge entrance (€3.50 one-way to any stop, June-Sept only, confirm schedule at TI or bus station).

By Taxi: Your hotel can call a taxi for you. Or contact **Bled Tours,** run by friendly, English-speaking driver Sandi Demšar and his girlfriend Cvetka (€10 to the castle or to Lesce-Bled train station, €14 to Radovljica, €50 to Ljubljana airport, €120 to Klagenfurt airport in Austria, office at Ljubljanska cesta 19, mobile 031-205-611, www.bledtours.si, info@bledtours.si).

By Boat: For information on renting your own boat, see "Boating," page 773. For details on riding the characteristic *pletna* boats, see "Getting to the Island," page 770.

By Private Plane: If you have perfect weather and deep pockets, there's no more thrilling way to experience Slovenia's high-mountain scenery than from a small propeller plane soaring over the peaks. Flights depart from a grass airstrip near the village of Lesce, a 10-minute drive or taxi ride from Bled. Expensive...but unforgettable (€75 for 15-minute hop over Lake Bled only, €135 for 30-minute flight that also buzzes Lake Bohinj, €195 for deluxe 45-minute version around the summit of Triglav, arrange at least a day in advance, tel. 04/532-0100, www.alc-lesce.si, info@alc-lesce.si).

Tours at Lake Bled

Local Guides—**Tina Hiti** and **Sašo Golub,** an energetic young couple, are both excellent guides who enjoy sharing the town and region they love with American visitors. Hiring one of them can add immeasurably to your enjoyment and understanding of Bled and the surrounding area (€45/2-hour tour of Bled, arrange several days in advance, info@pg-slovenia.com, Tina's mobile 040-166-554, Sašo's mobile 040-524-774, www.pg-slovenia.com). Tina and Sašo are especially handy for side-tripping into the countryside if you don't want to drive yourself. I've spent great days with both of them and was thankful they were behind the wheel. Their most popular trip is a day in the Julian Alps (€150 round-trip from Bled, €180 to pick up or drop off in Ljubljana—these prices are for two people; it's more expensive for three or more people, since they have to rent a van), but they also offer many other options, including all-day shore excursions from the cruise port in Koper (€230 for a day visiting Ljubljana and Bled) and trips in the Slovenian countryside to research your roots (price depends on distance). As Tina and Sašo both lead tours for me in Europe—and have two young kids—they may send you off with a well-trained substitute, such as Tina's father, Gorazd, a former Yugoslav Olympian (in ice hockey) who brings the older generation's perspective to the trip.

Excursions—To hit several far-flung day-trip destinations in one go, you could take a package tour from Bled. Destinations range from Ljubljana and the Karst region to the Austrian Lakes to Venice. For example, an all-day Julian Alps trip to the Vršič Pass and Soča Valley runs about €36 per person (sold by various agencies, including Kompas Bled). This tour is handy, but two people can rent a car for the day for about the same price and do it at their own pace using the self-guided driving tour in the next chapter.

Adventure Trips—Various Bled-based companies specialize in taking tourists on active, outdoorsy excursions into the surrounding countryside and mountains. One popular, all-day trip is white-water rafting on the Soča River (around €90/person). Other options include canyoning, river tubing, mountain biking, paragliding, rock climbing, and more. Various outfits cluster near the commercial center; these include **3glav Adventures** (just above commercial center at Ljubljanska cesta 1, mobile 041-683-184, www.3glav-adventures.com), **Lifetrek Adventures** (near the bus station at Grajska 4, mobile 040-508-853, www.lifetrek-slovenia .com), and **Amigo** (next to the Casino at Cesta Svobode 15, tel. 05/597-3250, www.amigo.si). Note that these companies tend to attract a young, sometimes rowdy crowd that enjoys lubricating their adventures with alcohol.

Sights at Lake Bled

Bled doesn't have many "sights," but there are plenty of rewarding and pleasant activities.

▲▲▲**Walk Around the Lake**—Strolling the 3.5 miles around the lake is enjoyable, peaceful, and scenic. At a leisurely pace, it takes about an hour and a half...not counting stops to snap photos of the ever-changing view. On the way, you'll pass some great villas, mostly from the beginning of the 19th century. The most significant one was a former residence of Marshal Tito— today the Hotel Vila Bled, a great place to stop for a coffee and pretend Tito invited you over for a visit (described next). For the more adventurous, hiking paths lead up into the hills surrounding the lake (ask TI for details and maps; or hike to Vintgar Gorge, described on page 783).

▲**Tito's Vila Bled**—Before World War II, this villa on Lake Bled was the summer residence for the Yugoslav royal family. When Tito ran Yugoslavia, the part-Slovene communist leader took over the place and had it renovated using plans from the architect Jože Plečnik. During his heyday, Tito entertained international guests here (big shots from the communist and non-aligned world, from Indira Gandhi to Nikita Khrushchev to Kim Il Sung to Raúl Castro). Since 1984, it's been a classy hotel and restaurant, offering guests grand Lake Bled views and James Bond ambience. The garden surrounding the villa is filled with exotic trees, brought here by Tito's guests from distant lands.

The terrace has a restaurant that welcomes visitors to drop in for a meal, a piece of cake, or just a cup of coffee. Tito fans might want to splurge for an overnight (standard Db-€230, tel. 04/575-3710, www.vila-bled.si). But even if you're not a guest here, the hotel's staff is generally tolerant of curious tourists poking around the public areas inside. From the marbled lobby, head upstairs. This is where Tito sympathizers have a nostalgic opportunity to

send an email from his desk, sip tea in his lounge, and gawk at his **Socialist Realist wall murals.** Those murals, decorating the upper walls of a vast ballroom on the second floor, are a fascinating peek at the propaganda of the time. Follow the rousing story of the origins of postwar Yugoslavia, starting on the upper left as you enter: First you see the Nazi destruction of Belgrade in 1941, a dark moment that inspired the South Slavs to band together to fight these foreign occupiers. See Tito raising his ragtag army, then leading them into pivotal battles in Bosnia-Herzegovina (notice the minaret and the destroyed bridge over the Neretva River), followed by a winter spent enduring hardship. At the end of this long wall, Tito's victorious Partisans crush the final vestiges of the Nazis; in the upper-right corner, the spring blossoms represent a promising future for the people of Yugoslavia. The large panel at the end of the room trumpets the idealized postwar world that Tito envisioned: proud workers from all walks of life coming together for the betterment of Yugoslavia. In the shadow of a mighty factory—a symbol of heavy industry, which communists embraced as the way of the future—notice that the ironworker and the farmer are holding hands in unity. The room's focal point is the mother hoisting a young child with one arm, and the flag of the nascent Socialist Federal Republic of Yugoslavia with the other.

Getting There: The villa is a 20-minute lakeside walk from the town of Bled at Cesta Svobode 26 (it's the big, white villa with the long staircase at the southern end of the lake, just beyond the village of Mlino). You can also ask your *pletna* gondolier to drop you off here after visiting the island. Those hiking around the lake will pass the gate leading up through Tito's garden to the restaurant and lobby.

▲▲**The Island (Otok)**—Bled's little island—capped by a supercute church—nudges the lake's quaintness level over the top. Locals call it simply "The Island" *(Otok).* While it's pretty to look at from afar, it's also fun to visit.

The island has long been a sacred site with a romantic twist. On summer Saturdays, a steady procession of brides and grooms, cheered on by their entourages, heads

LAKE BLED

for the island. Ninety-nine steps lead from the island's dock up to the Church of the Assumption on top. It's tradition for the groom to carry—or try to carry—his bride up these steps. About four out of five are successful (proving themselves "fit for marriage"). During the communist era, the church was closed, and weddings were outlawed here. But the tradition re-emerged—illegally—even before the regime ended, with a clandestine ceremony in 1989.

An eighth-century Slavic pagan temple dedicated to the goddess of love and fertility once stood here; the current Baroque version (with Venetian flair—the bell tower is separate from the main church) is the fifth to occupy this spot. Go inside (€3, daily May-Sept 9:00-19:00, April and Oct until 18:00, Nov-March until 16:00) and find the rope for the church bell, hanging in the middle of the aisle just before the altar. A local superstition claims that if you can get this bell to ring three times with one big pull of the rope, your dreams will come true. Worth a try.

If you're waiting for a herd of tourists to ring out their wishes, pass the time looking around the front of the church. When the church was being renovated in the 1970s, workers dug up several medieval graves (you can see one through the glass under the bell rope). They also discovered Gothic frescoes on either side of the altar, including, above the door on the right, an unusual ecclesiastical theme: the *bris* (Jewish circumcision ritual) of Christ.

A café (with a WC) and souvenir shop (with an exhibit of nativity scenes) are near the church at the top of the steps.

To descend by a different route, walk down the trail behind the church, then follow the path around the island's perimeter back to where your *pletna* boat awaits.

Getting to the Island: The most romantic route to the island is to cruise on one of the distinctive ***pletna*** boats (€12 per person round-trip, includes 30-minute stay on the island; catch one at several spots around the lake—most convenient from in front of Grand Hotel Toplice or just below Hotel Park, might have to wait for more passengers to fill the boat; generally run from dawn, last boat leaves one hour before church closes—see hours above; replaced by enclosed electric boats in winter—unless the lake freezes, in which case there are no boats; mobile 031-316-575). Other places to catch a *pletna* include the village of Mlino, partway around the lake; the bottom of the grand staircase leading up to Vila Bled (it's a shorter trip from here—though the same cost—as it's much closer to the island); and at the campground. For more on these characteristic

Pletna Boats

The *pletna* is an important symbol of Lake Bled. In addition to providing a pleasant way to reach the island, these boats also

carry on a tradition dating back for generations. In the 17th century, Habsburg Empress Maria Theresa granted the villagers from Mlino—the little town along the lakefront just beyond Bled—special permission to ferry visitors to the island. (Since Mlino had very limited access to farmland, the people needed another source of income.) Mlino residents built their *pletnas* by hand, using a special design passed down from father to son for centuries—like the equally iconic gondolas of Venice. Eventually, this imperial decree and family tradition evolved into a modern union of *pletna* oarsmen, which continues to this day.

Today *pletna* boats are still hand-built according to that same centuries-old design. There's no keel, so the skilled oarsmen work hard to steer the flat-bottomed boat with each stroke—boats piloted by an inexperienced oarsman can slide around on very windy days. There are 21 official *pletnas* on Lake Bled, all belonging to the same union. The gondoliers dump all of their earnings into one fund, give a cut to the tourist board, and divide the rest evenly among themselves. Occasionally a new family tries to break into the cartel, underselling his competitors with a "black market" boat that looks the same

as the official ones. While some see this as a violation of a centuries-old tradition, others view it as good old capitalism. Either way, competition is fierce.

little vessels, see the "*Pletna* Boats" sidebar. You can also **rent your own boat** to row to the island (see "Boating," later). It's even possible to **swim** to the island, especially from the end of the lake nearest the island (see "Swimming," later), but you're not allowed into the church in your swimsuit. Guess you'll just have to go in naked.

▲**Bled Castle (Blejski Grad)**—Bled's cliff-hanging castle, dating in one form or another from 1,000 years ago, was the seat of the Austrian Bishops of Brixen, who controlled Bled in the

Middle Ages. Today it's merely a fine tourist attraction with a little history and lots of big views. The various sights at the castle are more cute than interesting, but the real reason to come up here is to bask in the sweeping panoramas over Lake Bled and the surrounding mountainscapes.

Cost and Hours: €8, daily May-Oct 8:00-20:00, Nov-April 9:00-18:00, tel. 04/572-9782, www.blejski-grad.si.

Getting to the Castle: To really earn those views, you can **hike** up the steep hill (20-30 minutes). The handiest trails are behind big St. Martin's Church: Walk past the front door of the church with the lake at your back, and look left after the first set of houses for the *Grad* signs marking the steepest route (follow the wooden stakes all the way up the steep switchback steps); or, for a longer but less steep route, continue past the church on the same street about five minutes, bearing uphill (left) at the fork, and find the *Grad 1* sign just after the Pension Bledec hostel on the left. Once you're on this second trail, don't take the sharp-left uphill turn at the fork (instead, continue straight up, around the back of the hill). If you'd rather skip the hike, you can take the 10:00 **tourist bus** (see "Getting Around Lake Bled," earlier), your **rental car,** a **taxi** (around €10), or—if you're wealthy and romantic—a **horse and buggy** (€40, €10 extra for driver to wait 30 minutes and bring you back down). However, these options take you only to the parking lot, from which it's still a steep and slippery-when-wet five-minute hike up to the castle itself.

Touring the Castle: Your castle admission includes a newly spruced-up castle museum (described next); a small theater continuously showing a fun 20-minute movie about Bled (under the restaurant); a tiny chapel with 3-D frescoes that make it seem much bigger than it is (next to the museum entrance); and a rampart walk with an "herbal gallery" (gift shop of traditional-meets-modern herbal brandies, cosmetics, and perfumes—find the stairs up to the right as you enter the castle complex).

The **museum** strains to make the story of Bled, the castle, and the surrounding region of Carniola interesting. The ground floor has exhibits about old furniture, geology, and the seasonal life cycle of the region, while upstairs are a cool 3-D model of the surrounding mountains, smaller models illustrating the growth of the building, and exhibits on the development of tourism at Lake Bled (including its many fine vacation villas). While video screens and some English information are helpful, there's really not much to say.

In addition, the castle is home to a pair of interesting, old-fashioned shops: You can visit Mojster Janez's working replica of a **printing press** *(grajska tiskarna/manufaktura)* from Gutenberg's time and print your own custom-made souvenir certificate for €8-14 (next to the castle's oldest tower—from the 11th century). There's also an exhibition in English about early printing methods and the importance of movable type for advancing the Protestant Reformation, whose goal was to get the word of God more easily into the hands of everyday people. Near the "herbal gallery" (to the right as you enter the castle) is a **wine cellar** *(grajska klet de Adami)* where you can bottle and cork your own bottle of wine (€12-15). Slovenian wines are well-explained by one of two guys (both, coincidentally, named Andrej) who dress as monks, since winemaking was a monastic responsibility in the Middle Ages. Both the printing press and the wine cellar may close earlier than the castle grounds (possibly around 18:00).

Eating at the Castle: The **restaurant** at the castle is fairly expensive, but your restaurant reservation gets you into the castle grounds for free (international cuisine and some local specialties, €12-14 pastas, €18-25 main courses, daily in summer 10:00-22:00, less off-season, tel. 04/579-4424). Better yet, bring your own picnic to munch along the wall with million-dollar views over Lake Bled (buy sandwiches at the Mercator grocery store in the commercial center before you ascend—described later, under "Eating in Bled").

Boating—Bled is the rowing center of Slovenia. Town officials even lengthened the lake a bit so it would perfectly fit the standard two-kilometer laps, with 100 meters more for the turn (on maps, you can see the little divot taken out of the far end). Bled hosted its fourth world championship in August of 2011. The town has produced many Olympic medalists, winning gold in Sydney and silver in Athens. You'll notice that local crew team members are characters—with a tradition of wild and colorful haircuts. You'll likely see them running or rowing. This dedication to rowing adds to Bled's tranquility, since no motorized boats are allowed on the lake.

If you want to get into the action, you'll find **rental rowboats** at the swimming pool under the castle (small 3-person boat: first hour-€15, additional hours-€8 each; bigger 5-person boat: first hour-€17, additional hours-€9 each; daily in summer 10:00-18:00, last rental at 17:00). Two other places farther from Bled town also rent rowboats (4-person boat-€10/hour, closed in bad weather and off-season): Pension Pletna in Mlino (a 15-minute walk around the lake past Grand Hotel Toplice) and the campground on the far end of the lake.

Swimming—Lake Bled has several suitable spots for a swim. The swimming pools under the castle are filled with lake water and routinely earn the "blue flag," meaning the water is top-quality (swim all day–€7, less for afternoon only, June-Sept daily 8:00-19:00, closed Oct-May and in bad weather, tel. 04/578-0528). Lake Bled's main beach is at the campground, at the far end of the lake, though you can also swim near the

village of Mlino. If you swim to the island, remember that you can't get into the church in your swimsuit.

Luge Ride (Polento Sankanje)—Bled's "summer toboggan" luge ride, atop Mount Straža overlooking the lake, allows you to scream down a steep, curvy metal rail track on a little plastic sled. A chairlift takes you to the top of the track, where you'll sit on your sled, take a deep breath, and remind yourself: Pull back on the stick to slow down, push forward on the stick to go faster. You'll drop 480 feet in altitude on the 570-yard-long track, speeding up to about 25 miles per hour as you race toward the lake. You'll see the track on the hillside just south of town, beyond the Grand Hotel Toplice.

Cost and Hours: €8/ride, cheaper for multiple rides, chairlift only–€4, weather-dependent—if it rains, you can't go; mid-June-Aug daily 10:00-20:00; May-mid-June and Sept Sat-Sun only 11:00-18:00, closed Mon-Fri; Oct Sat-Sun only 11:00-16:30; most of April Sat-Sun only 11:00-17:00; closed Nov-early April.

Nearby: The affiliated **Adventure Park** (Pustolovski Park), next to the luge, has a series of five high-ropes courses designed for everyone from five-year-olds to adults (same hours as luge, €18 for adults, €13 for kids 7-14, €10 for kids under 7; various combotickets—for example, €23 covers the lift, adventure park, and one luge ride; mobile 031-761-661, www.pustolovski-park-bled.si).

Deva Puri Gallery—Just away from the lake (on the road to Lake Bohinj, behind Vila Bled), this gallery hosts good changing exhibits of mostly modern art. You'll see the latest exhibits advertised around town; recent installations have included Picasso's ceramics and Slovenian Impressionism. While the gallery is a bit out of town (a long walk or a quick bike, car, or taxi ride), it's worth the trek for art-lovers.

Cost and Hours: Price depends on exhibit but generally around €7, daily 10:00-19:00, open roughly mid-summer through Nov, Pristava, mobile 051-336-834, www.deva.si.

Day Trips—For details on some easy and enjoyable nearby sidetrips—including a scenic gorge hike, a quirky bee museum, an old blacksmithing town, and a more remote lake experience—see "Near Lake Bled" later in this chapter.

Nightlife in Bled

Bled Pub Crawl

Bled is quiet after hours. However, the town does have a few fun bars that are lively with a young crowd (all open nightly until late). Since many young people in Bled are students at the local tourism school, they're likely to speak English...and eager to practice with a native speaker. Try a "Smile," a Corona-type Slovenian lager. *Šnops* (schnapps) is a local specialty—popular flavors are plum *(slivovka)*, honey *(medica)*, blueberry *(borovničevec)*, and pear *(hruškovec)*.

Kick things off with the fun-loving local gang at **Gostilna Pri Planincu** near the bus station (described later, under "Eating in Bled"). Then head down Cesta Svobode toward the lake; just below Hotel Jelovica, you'll find the rollicking **Irish Pub** (a.k.a. "The Pub"), with Guinness and indoor or outdoor seating. For a more genteel atmosphere, duck across the street and wander a few more steps down toward the lake to find the **Art Café**, with a mellow ambience reminiscent of a Van Gogh painting. Around the lake near the commercial center, **Bled Pub** (a.k.a. "The Cocktail Bar" or "Troha"—for the family that owns it) is a trendy late-night spot where bartenders sling a dizzying array of mixed drinks to an appreciative crowd (between the commercial center and the lake, above the recommended Oštarija Peglez'n restaurant). If you're still standing, several other, more low-key bars and cafés percolate in the commercial center.

Sleeping in Bled

Bled is dominated by a few giant, gradually decaying, communist-era convention hotels. Some have been nicely renovated, but most are stale, outmoded, and overpriced. (It's a strange, incestuous little circle—the majority of the town's big hotels and restaurants are owned by the same company.) Instead, I prefer staying in smaller, countryside, pension-type accommodations—many of them just a short walk above the lake. These quaint little family-run pensions book up early with Germans and Brits; reserve as far ahead as possible. I've listed the high-season prices (May-Oct) unless noted. Off-season, prices are typically 10-20 percent lower. For even cheaper beds, consider one of the many *sobe* (rooms in private homes) scattered around the lake (about €21 per person in peak season, €16 per person if you stay three nights or longer, breakfast-€6 extra). Kompas Bled travel agency can book you a *soba* (see page 763), but be sure the location is convenient before you accept.

Sleep Code

(€1 = about $1.40, country code: 386, area code: 04)

S = Single, **D** = Double/Twin, **T** = Triple, **Q** = Quad, **b** = bathroom. Unless otherwise noted, credit cards are accepted and breakfast is included, but the modest tourist tax (about €1 per person, per night) is not. Everyone listed here speaks English.

To help you easily sort through these listings, I've divided the accommodations into three categories based on the price for a double room with bath during high season:

$$$ Higher Priced—Most rooms €100 or more.
 $$ Moderately Priced—Most rooms between €60-100.
  $ Lower Priced—Most rooms €60 or less.

Prices can change without notice; verify the hotel's current rates online or by email. For other updates, see www .ricksteves.com/update.

Above the Lake

These friendly, cozy, characteristic accommodations are Bled's best values. The only catch is that they're perched on a hilltop a steep five- to ten-minute climb up from the lake (easier than it sounds). There are two ways to find them from the town center: Walk around the lake to Grand Hotel Toplice, then go up the stairs around the right side of the Hotel Jadran (on the hill across the street from Grand Hotel Toplice). Or, from the main road into town (Ljubljanska cesta), take the small service road just above the commercial center (in front of Hotel Lovec), and loop up around the big Kompas and Golf hotels. Some buses (including those to/from Ljubljana) stop at a bus stop higher up on Ljubljanska cesta, just above the traffic light; this stop is handier to these hotels than the main bus station (though bus drivers don't always want to stop since it's a hassle to open the luggage compartment here—try asking nicely). From the bus stop, you can walk down Ljubljanska cesta and take the road just above the post office, which leads up to this area. If you're sleeping up here, Mayer Penzion's restaurant is the easiest choice for dinner (described later, under "Eating in Bled").

$$ Mayer Penzion, thoughtfully run by the Trseglav family, comes with 13 great-value rooms, a helpful staff, a tasty restaurant, an atmospheric wine-tasting cellar, and beautifully handcrafted

Slovenian woodwork inside and out. They book up fast in summer with return clients, so reserve early (Sb-€57, Db-€82, €5 less for 3 nights or more, extra bed-€20, family deals, elevator, free Internet access and Wi-Fi, Želeška cesta 7, tel. 04/576-5740, fax 04/576-5741, www.mayer-sp.si, penzion@mayer-sp.si). They also rent a cute, newly restored two-story Slovenian farm cottage next door (Db-€120, Tb/Qb-€150).

$$ Hotel Berc and **Penzion Berc** (pronounced "berts"), run by the Berc brothers, are next door to Mayer Penzion. Both have cozy public spaces, free Internet access and Wi-Fi, and free loaner bikes, and are worth reserving ahead (both cash only, www.berc -sp.si). The new hotel building has 15 rooms with pleasantly woody decor (Sb-€40-50, Db-€70-80; price depends on size, season, and length of stay; all rooms have balconies, Pod Stražo 13, tel. 04/576-5658, fax 04/576-5659, hotel@berc-sp.si, run by Luka). The older, adjacent *penzion* offers 11 cheaper, older, but nearly-as-nice rooms (Sb-€40, Db-€65, €5 more for 1-night stays, 10 percent cheaper off-season, most rooms have balconies, closed Nov-Christmas and sporadically off-season, Želeška cesta 15, tel. 04/574-1838, fax 04/576-7320, penzion@berc-sp.si, run by Miha).

$$ Alp Penzion is in a tranquil countryside setting amid hayfields. It's a long hike beyond the others listed here, but still within a 15-minute walk of the lake (better for drivers or for those who don't mind the walk). With 12 rooms (some with balconies), this place is enthusiastically run by the Sršen family, who offer lots of fun extras, including a tennis court and summer barbecue grill/outdoor pub (June-Sept: Sb-€60, Db-€75-80—higher price for rooms with balcony; Oct-May: Sb-€45, Db-€68; extra bed-€15, 3 percent cheaper if you pay cash, prices can be flexible—based on demand, family rooms, dinner possible—ask when you book, air-con, free Internet access and Wi-Fi, free loaner bikes, Cankarjeva cesta 20A, tel. 04/574-1614, fax 04/574-4590, www .alp-penzion.com, bled@alp-penzion.com). Just next door is the relaxing Essense spa (described earlier, under "Helpful Hints").

$ Friendly **Mia Sušnik** rents out two comfortable apartments. Modern, tidy, and equipped with kitchens, these are a good budget choice for families (Db-€57, Tb-€68, Qb-€79, 20 percent extra for fewer than 3 nights, includes tax, no breakfast, cash only, free Wi-Fi, laundry service-€10, free parking, Želeška cesta 3, tel. 04/574-1731, www.bled-holiday.com, susnik@bled-holiday.com). It's just toward the lake from the bigger pensions, with a big crucifix out front. Her sister Ivanka also rents apartments, but they're farther from the lake.

$ Tourist Farm Mulej, farther out of town than my other listings and better for drivers, is a new but traditional farmhouse in a tranquil valley about a half-mile from the lake (1.5 miles from

Bled town). Damjana and Jože, who run a working farm, rent out eight modern rooms and four apartments—all with balconies—and serve breakfasts and dinners made with food they produce (Db-€60, or €80 with dinner; €30 per extra person in apartments, or €40 with dinner; 20 percent extra for 1- or 2-night stays in June-Aug, cash only, family rooms, free cable Internet, free loaner bikes, horseback riding, Selo pri Bledu 42a, tel. & fax 04/574-4617, www.mulej-bled.com, info@mulej-bled.com). It's in the farm village of Selo—drive along the lakeside road south from Bled, then turn off in Mlino toward Selo, and look for the signs (to the right) once in the village.

$ Vila Gorenka is your non-hostel, low-budget option. The Žerovec family's old-fashioned house has 10 basic, faded, musty rooms sharing two bathrooms (S-€20, D-€36, cash only, no extra charge for 1-night stays, no breakfast, free Internet access and Wi-Fi, just below the bigger pensions at Želeška cesta 9, mobile 040-958-624, http://freeweb.siol.net/mz2, vila.gorenka@siol.net, Janez).

Near the Lake

You'll pay a premium to be closer to the lake—but it's hard to argue with the convenience.

$$$ Hotel Lovec (LOW-vets), a Best Western Premier, sits in a convenient (but non-lakefront) location just above the commercial center. Gorgeously renovated inside and out, and run by a helpful and friendly staff, it's a welcoming, cheery, well-run alternative to Bled's many old, dreary communist hotels. Its 60 plush rooms come with all the comforts (Sb-€128, Db-€151, €20 more for a lake-view balcony, very soft rates fluctuate with demand—email to ask for best price, cheaper Nov-Feb, family and "executive" suites available, delicious breakfast, elevator, free Internet access and Wi-Fi, indoor pool, free parking garage for guests, Ljubljanska cesta 6, tel. 04/620-4100, fax 04/576-8625, www.lovechotel.com, booking@kompas-lovec.eu).

$$$ Grand Hotel Toplice (TOHP-leet-seh) is the grande dame of Bled, with 87 high-ceilinged rooms, parquet floors, a genteel lakeview café/lounge, posh decor, all the amenities, and a long list of high-profile guests—from Madeleine Albright to Jordan's King Hussein to Slovene-by-marriage Donald Trump (ask to see their "wall of fame"). Once elegant, this place is a bit faded these days, but it's still a classic. Rooms in the back are cheaper, but have no lake views and overlook a noisy street—try to get one as high up as possible (I've listed the official rates followed by what you'll likely pay in slower times—non-view: Sb-€150/€110, Db-€170/€140; lake view: Sb-€180/€160, Db-€230/€200; suites with lake views-€280;

15-20 percent less Nov-April, very flexible rates—check online, air-con, elevator, free Internet access and cable Internet, free one-hour boat rental for guests, free parking, Cesta Svobode 12, tel. 04/579-1000, fax 04/574-1841, www.hotel-toplice.com, ghtoplice @hotelibled.com). The hotel's name—*toplice*—means "spa"; guests are free to use the hotel's swanky, natural-spring-fed indoor swimming pool (a chilly 72 degrees Fahrenheit). This hotel also runs two smaller, far less luxurious hotels nearby with very dated and faded rooms and lower rates (Hotel Trst and Hotel Jadran, details at Toplice's website).

$$$ Vila Prešeren has eight stylish, pricey rooms above a popular restaurant right on the lake. As the rooms are an afterthought to the busy restaurant, don't expect much personal attention from the staff (Sb-€112, Db-€150, apartment-€200-214 depending on size, cheaper mid-Oct-early May, no reception—check in at the restaurant, air-con, free Wi-Fi, Veslaška promenada 14, tel. 04/575-2510, www.vilapreseren.si, vilapreseren@sprtina resorts.si).

$ Apartmaji Mežan, run by young couple Janez and Saša, has three apartments in a modern home buried in the middle of town, just uphill from the church. As it's next to an old barn, it's technically a tourist farm (Db-€50, cash only, no breakfast, free Internet access and Wi-Fi, Riklijeva 6, mobile 041-210-290 or 041-516-688, www.apartmaji-mezan.si, sasa.mezan@gmail.com).

$ Penzion Bledec (BLED-ets), a family-run, official IYHF hostel, is just below the castle at the top of the Old Town. Each of the 12 rooms has its own bathroom. They have dorms (bed in 4- to 7-bed dorm-€22-24 depending on number of bunks) as well as rooms that can be rented as doubles (though "doubles" are actually underutilized triples and quads, with separate beds pushed together—so they might not be reservable July-Aug or at other busy times, Db-€54, Tb-€72; cheaper Nov-April, members pay 10 percent less, includes sheets and breakfast, great family rooms, free Internet access and Wi-Fi, full-service laundry for guests-€9/load, restaurant, Grajska 17, tel. 04/574-5250, fax 04/574-5251, www .youth-hostel-bledec.si, bledec@mlino.si).

$ Travellers Haven is a low-key hostel run by Mirjam and Karmen. The 27 beds fill six rooms in a nicely renovated hundred-year-old villa in the Old Town. The lodgings are well-maintained and the hangout areas are inviting, though the tight bathrooms offer little privacy (€19 for a bunk in a 4- to 6-bed room, D-€48, no breakfast but guest kitchen, reception open 8:00-13:00 & 16:00-23:00; free Internet access, Wi-Fi, laundry machines, and loaner bikes; Riklijeva cesta 1, mobile 031-704-455 or 041-396-545, www .travellers-haven.si, travellers-haven@t-2.net).

Eating in Bled

Bled has several good restaurants, but most everything is quite similar. For variety, wait for Ljubljana.

Okarina, run by charming, well-traveled Leo Ličof, serves a diverse array of cuisines, all of them well-executed: international fare, traditional Slovenian specialties, and Indian (Himalayan) dishes. Leo has a respect for salads and vegetables and a passion for fish. Creative cooking, fine presentation, friendly service, and an atmosphere as tastefully eclectic as the food make this place a great splurge (€9-14 pastas, €10-23 main courses, plus a few pricier splurges, daily 12:00-15:00 & 18:00-24:00, next to Hotel Lovec at Ljubljanska cesta 8, tel. 04/574-1458). In the back of the menu, look for the copy of the guest book page with Paul McCartney's visit from May 2005. Around the left side of the building, Leo runs a smaller pavilion restaurant out back, with different ambience and food (as the details are expected to change, ask when you arrive).

Oštarija Peglez'n ("The Old Iron"), conveniently located on the main road between the commercial center and the lake, cooks up tasty Slovenian and Mediterranean meals, with an emphasis on fish and fun family-style shareable plates. Choose between the delightful Slovenian cottage interior or the shady streetside terrace. Reservations are smart in summer (€7-9 salads and pastas, €11-19 main courses, daily 12:00-23:00, Cesta Svobode 19A, tel. 04/574-4218).

Vila Prešeren is the best choice for lakeside dining, with a giant terrace reaching all the way down to the lakefront path. Featuring tasteful, mod decor, international cuisine, and slow service, this is a great spot to linger over a meal, a drink, or a classic Lake Bled dessert (€10-12 salads, €8-14 pastas, €11-21 main courses, daily 7:00-23:00, Veslaška promenada 14, tel. 04/575-2510).

Mayer Penzion, just up the hill from the lakefront, has a dressy restaurant with good traditional cooking that's worth the short hike. This is where a Babel of international tourists come to swap hiking tips and day-trip tales. As this is the only real restaurant in the pension neighborhood, it can be very busy—reserve ahead (€8-21 main courses, Tue-Sun 18:00-24:00, closed Mon, indoor or outdoor seating, above Hotel Jadran at Železka cesta 7, tel. 04/576-5740).

Gostilna Pri Planincu ("By the Mountaineers") is a homey, informal bar coated with license plates and packed with fun-loving and sometimes rowdy natives. A larger dining area sprawls behind the small, local-feeling pub, and there's outdoor seating out front and on the side patio. The menu features huge portions of stick-to-your-ribs Slovenian pub grub, plus Balkan grilled-meat specialties (€9-19 main courses). Look for their €6-8 daily specials—huge,

Bled Desserts

While you're in Bled, be sure to enjoy the town's specialty, a cream cake called **kremna rezina** (KRAYM-nah ray-ZEE-nah; often referred to by its German-derived name, **kremšnita,** KRAYM-shnee-tah). It's a layer of cream and a thick layer of vanilla custard artfully sandwiched between sheets of delicate, crispy crust. Heavenly. Slovenes travel from all over the country to sample this famous dessert.

Slightly less renowned—but just as tasty—is **grmada** (gur-MAH-dah, "bonfire"). This dessert was developed by Hotel Jelovica as a way to get rid of their day-old leftovers. They take yesterday's cake, add rum, milk, custard, and raisins, and top it off with whipped cream and chocolate syrup.

Finally, there's *prekmurska gibanica*—or just **gibanica** (gee-bah-NEET-seh) for short. Originating in the Hungarian corner of the country, *gibanica* is an earthy pastry filled with poppy seeds, walnuts, apple, and cheese, and drizzled with rum.

These desserts are typically enjoyed with a lake-and-mountains view—the best spots are the terrace at Vila Prešeren, the Panorama restaurant by Grand Hotel Toplice, and the terrace across from the Hotel Park (figure around €5 for cake and coffee at any of these places). For a more local (but non-lake view) setting, consider Šmon Slaščičarna (only slightly cheaper; see next page).

home-style traditional dishes. Upstairs is a timbered pizzeria selling €5-9 wood-fired pies (daily 9:00-23:00, pizzeria open from 11:00, Grajska cesta 8, tel. 04/574-1613). The playful cartoon mural along the outside of the restaurant shows different types of mountaineers (from left to right): thief, normal, mooch ("gopher"), climber, and naked (...well, almost).

Pizzeria Rustika, in the Old Town, offers wood-fired pizzas and salads. Its upstairs terrace is relaxing on a balmy evening (€6-9 pizzas, daily 12:00-23:00, service can be slow when it's busy, Riklijeva cesta 13, tel. 04/576-8900).

The **Mercator** grocery store, in the commercial center, has the makings for a bang-up picnic. They sell pre-made sandwiches for about €3, or will make you one to order (point to what you want). This is a great option for hikers and budget travelers (Mon-Fri 7:00-19:00, Sat 7:00-15:00, Sun 8:00-12:00). There's another location closer to the Old Town and castle (Mon-Sat 7:00-20:00, Sun 8:00-16:00).

Dessert: While tourists generally gulp down their cream cakes on a hotel restaurant's lakefront terrace, local residents favor the desserts at **Šmon Slaščičarna** (a.k.a. the "Brown Bear," for the bear on the sign). It's nicely untouristy, but lacks the atmosphere of the lakeside spots (€2-3 cakes, daily 7:30-21:00, near bus station at Grajska cesta 3, tel. 04/574-1616).

Lake Bled Connections

The most convenient train connections to Bled leave from the Lesce-Bled station, about 2.5 miles away (see details under "Arrival in Bled," earlier). Remember, when buying a train ticket to Lake Bled, make it clear that you want to go to the Lesce-Bled station (not the Bled Jezero station, which is poorly connected to the main line). No one in the town of Bled sells train tickets; buy them at the station just before your train departs (open Mon-Fri 5:30-21:00, Sat 7:00-15:00, Sun 14:30-19:30). If the ticket window there is closed, buy your ticket on board from the conductor (who will likely waive the €2.50 additional fee).

Note that if you're going to **Ljubljana,** the bus (which leaves from Bled town itself) is better than the train (which leaves from the Lesce-Bled train station).

From Lesce-Bled by Train to: Ljubljana (roughly hourly, 40-60 minutes), **Salzburg** (5/day, 4 hours, some change in Villach, Austria), **Munich** (5/day, 6 hours, some change in Salzburg), **Vienna** (that's *Dunaj* in Slovene, 5/day, 6 hours, transfer in Villach or Salzburg), **Venice** (3/day with transfer in Villach—likely partway by bus, 6 hours), **Zagreb** (6/day direct, 3/day with a change in Ljubljana, 3.5 hours).

By Bus to: Ljubljana (Mon-Sat hourly—usually at :30 past the hour, fewer on Sun, 1.25 hours, €6.30), **Radovljica** (Mon-Fri at least 2/hour, Sat hourly, Sun almost hourly, 15 minutes, €1.80), **Lesce-Bled train station** (2/hour, 10 minutes, €1.30), **Lake Bohinj** (hourly, 40 minutes and €3.60 to Bohinj Jezero stop, 50 minutes and €4.10 to Bohinj Vogel or Bohinj Zlatorog stop, 3/day in summer continue all the way to Savica Waterfall trailhead), **Podhom** (15-minute hike away from Vintgar Gorge, Mon-Fri 5/day in the morning, 1/day Sat, none Sun, 15 minutes, €1.30), **Spodnje Gorje** (also 15-minute hike from Vintgar Gorge, take bus in direction of Krnica, hourly, 15 minute, €1.30). Confirm times at the TI or using the schedules posted at the unstaffed Bled bus station. Buy tickets on the bus.

By Plane: Ljubljana Airport is between Lake Bled and Ljubljana, about a 45-minute drive from Bled. Connecting by taxi costs around €40-50 (set price up front—since it's outside of town, they don't use the meter; be sure to use a Bled-based taxi, rather than a Ljubljana-based taxi, which will likely be more expensive). The Zup Prevozi shuttle bus is a more affordable option at €13, but it runs only three times each day (generally coordinated to meet easyJet flights). However, at other times you can arrange for a shuttle from Zup Prevozi for a bit less than a taxi (€34/1 person, €35/2 people, €37/3 people, €39/4 people, mobile 031-304-141, www.zup-prevozi.eu). The bus connection from Bled to the airport is cheap (total cost: about €5.40) but complicated and time-consuming: First, go to Kranj (Mon-Fri 12/day, Sat-Sun 8/day, 35 minutes), then transfer to a Brnik-bound bus (at least hourly, 20 minutes). Many Bled residents prefer to fly from Klagenfurt, Austria. For details on both the Ljubljana and Klagenfurt airports, see page 757.

Route Tips for Drivers: Bled is less than an hour north of Ljubljana on the slick A2 expressway. The exit is marked for *Lesce*, but you'll also see signs for *Bled*, which will lead you directly to the lake (where the road becomes Ljubljanska cesta).

To reach Radovljica (bee museum) or Lesce (train station), drive out of Bled on Ljubljanska cesta toward the expressway. Watch for the turnoff to those two towns on the right. They're on the same road: Lesce first (to reach train station, divert right when entering town), then Radovljica.

Near Lake Bled

The countryside around Bled offers several day trips that can be done easily without a car (bus connection information is described in each section). The four trips listed here are the best (two small-town/museum experiences, two hiking/back-to-nature options). They're more convenient than can't-miss, but each is worthwhile on a longer visit, and all give a good taste of the Julian Alps. For a self-guided driving tour through farther-flung (and even more striking) parts of the Julian Alps, see the next chapter.

Vintgar Gorge

Just north of Bled, the river Radovna has carved this mile-long, picturesque gorge into the mountainside. For hikers, Vintgar (VEENT-gar) Gorge is worth ▲▲. Boardwalks and bridges put you right in the middle of the action of this "poor man's Plitvice." You'll cross over several waterfalls and marvel at the clarity of the water. The easy hike is on a boardwalk trail with handrails (sometimes narrow and a bit slippery). At the end of the gorge, you'll find a snack stand, WCs, and a bridge with a fine view. Go back the way you came, or take a prettier return to Bled (see "Scenic Hike Back to Bled," later). The gorge is easily reachable from Bled by bus or foot and is the best option for those who are itching for a hike but don't have a car.

Cost and Hours: €4 to enter gorge, open daily May-late Oct 8:00-19:00 or until dusk, June-Aug maybe until 20:00, closed late Oct-April, tel. 04/572-5266.

Getting to Vintgar Gorge: The gorge is 2.5 miles north of Bled. To reach the gorge entrance, you can walk (takes at least one hour one-way), pedal a rental bike (about 30 minutes, easiest with an electric bike rented at the TI), take a bus (15-minute ride plus 15-minute walk, or 30-minute ride on summer tourist bus), or drive (less than 10 minutes).

Walkers and **cyclists** leave Bled on the road between the castle and St. Martin's Church and take the uphill (left) road at the fork. Just after the little yellow chapel, turn right on the road with the big tree, then immediately left at the Mercator grocery store. When the road swings left, continue straight onto Partizanska (marked for *Podhom* and a walking sign for *Vintgar;* ignore the bus sign for *Vintgar* pointing left). At the fork just after the little bridge, go left for Podhom, then simply follow signs for *Vintgar*.

In summer, the easy **tourist bus** takes you right to the gorge entrance in 30 minutes (see "Getting Around Lake Bled," page 766). Otherwise, you can take a **local bus** to one of two stops: Podhom (Mon-Fri 5/day in the morning, 1/day Sat, none Sun, 15 minutes, €1.30) or Spodnje Gorje (take bus in direction of Krnica, hourly, 15 minutes, €1.30). From either the Podhom or the Spodnje Gorje bus stop, it's a 15-minute walk to the gorge (follow signs for *Vintgar*).

Drivers follow signs to *Podhom*, then *Vintgar* (see walking/cycling instructions).

Scenic Hike Back to Bled: If you still have energy once you reach the end of the gorge, consider this longer hike back with panoramic views. Behind the snack stand deep in the gorge, find the trail marked *Katarina Bled*. You'll go uphill for 25 strenuous minutes (following the red-and-white circles and arrows) before cresting the hill and enjoying beautiful views over Bled town and the region. Continue straight down the road 15 minutes to the typical, narrow, old village of Zasip, then walk (about 30 minutes) or take the bus back to Bled.

Near Lake Bled

Radovljica

The town of Radovljica (rah-DOH-vleet-suh, "Radol'ca" for short), perched on a plateau above the Sava River, has the charming Old Town that Bled lacks. The traffic-free core of the town, once hemmed in by a stout wall (still faintly visible in some areas), is jammed with historic buildings that surround the long, skinny main square called Linhartov trg. While Radovljica's Old Town is a pleasant place to stroll or nurse a coffee, you can see it all in a few minutes. The main reason to visit here is to tour its offbeat but strangely fascinating beekeeping museum—which, with only a few rooms, still ranks as one of Europe's biggest on the topic. Skip the town on Mondays, when the museum is closed (and be aware that the museum closes for a three-hour lunch break off-season).

LAKE BLED

Getting to Radovljica

Buses to Radovljica generally leave Bled every half-hour (fewer on weekends, €1.80, buy ticket from driver, trip takes about 15 minutes). To reach the town center and the bee museum from the bus station, leave the station going straight ahead, cross the bus parking lot and the next street, then turn left down the far street (following brown sign for *Staro Mesto*). In five minutes, you'll reach the start of the pedestrianized Linhartov trg (with the TI—on the right—and the start of the Old Town, a few short blocks from the bee museum).

Drivers leave Bled on Ljubljanska cesta, then turn right at the sign for *Radovljica* and go through the village of Lesce; the road dead-ends at Radovljica's pedestrian zone, where you'll find a parking lot (by the rustic garage), the TI, and the start of the Old Town.

A handy **bike** path scenically and peacefully connects Bled with Radovljica (about 4 miles, get details at TI).

Orientation to Radovljica

Tourist Information

The enthusiastic TI loves to help visitors appreciate the town of "Radol'ca" (daily May-Sept 9:00-19:00, Oct-April 9:00-18:00, Linhartov trg 1, tel. 04/531-5112, www.radolca.si).

Sights in Radovljica

▲Apicultural Museum (Čebelarski Muzej)

This museum celebrates Slovenia's long and very proud beekeeping heritage. Since the days before Europeans had sugar, Slovenia has been a big honey producer. Slovenian farmer Anton Janša is considered the father of modern beekeeping and was Europe's first official teacher of this art (in Habsburg Vienna). And even today, beekeeping is considered a crucial part of Slovenian culture. The surrounding area (Carniola) has about 6,000 inhabitants, including 65 beekeepers who manage 5,000 hives—the most bees per capita of any place in Europe. Slovenes reserve an importance and affection for bees that's rare in our modern times. For example, the Slovene language has two different words for "to give birth" and "to die": One they use exclusively for humans and bees, and a different one for all other animals. If a beekeeper dies, it's believed (with some pretty incontrovertible evidence) that the new beekeeper must be formally "introduced" to the hive by going there and explaining to the bees what has happened; otherwise, they become confused and agitated, and often die themselves.

Cost and Hours: €3, good English descriptions, €1.60 English guidebook is a nice souvenir; May-Oct Tue-Sun 10:00-18:00, closed Mon; March-April and Nov-Dec Wed and Sat-Sun 10:00-12:00 & 15:00-17:00, Tue and Thu-Fri 8:00-15:00, closed Mon; Jan-Feb Tue-Fri 8:00-15:00, closed Sat-Mon; upstairs at Linhartov trg 1, tel. 04/532-0520, www.muzeji-radovljica.si.

◐ **Self-Guided Tour:** Everything is well-described in English, but this commentary will help you locate the highlights.

The first room of the museum traces the history of beekeeping, from the time when bees were kept in hollowed-out trees to the present day. The bust celebrates beekeeper extraordinaire Anton Janša.

In the second room are old-fashioned tools. When a new queen bee is born, the old queen takes half the hive's bees to a new location. Experienced beekeepers used the long, skinny instrument (a beehive stethoscope) to figure out when the swarm was ready to fly the coop. Then, once the bees had moved to a nearby tree, the beekeeper used the big spoons to retrieve the queen—surrounded by an angry ball of her subjects—from her new home before she could get settled in. The beekeeper transferred the furious gang into a manmade hive designed for easier, more sanitary collection of the honey. You can also see the tools beekeepers used to create smoke, which makes bees less aggressive. Even today, some of Slovenia's old-fashioned beekeepers simply light up a cigarette and blow smoke on any bees that get ornery.

The third room features the museum's highlight: whimsically painted beehive frontboards (called *panjske končnice*). Beekeepers,

believing these paintings would help the bees find their way home, developed a tradition of decorating their hives with religious, historical, and satirical folk themes. The oldest panel dates from 1758, but the practice really took off in the 19th century. Take your time perusing these delightful illustrations. The depiction of a hunter's funeral shows all the animals happy...except his dog. One popular panel shows two farmers fighting over a cow, while a lawyer milks the cow. There's everything from portraits of Habsburg emperors, to a "true crime" sequence of a man murdering his family as they sleep, to proto-"Lockhorns" cartoons of marital strife, to 18th-century erotica (one with a woman showing some leg and another with a flip-up, peek-a-boo panel). A few panels blur the line between humorous and misogynistic: Look for the devil sharpening a woman's tongue on a wheel, or the man carrying a cross—and his wife—on his back. The life-size wooden statues were used to "guard" the beehives—and designed to look like fearsome Ottoman and Napoleonic soldiers.

The fourth room examines the biology of bees. In the summer only, look for the actual, functioning beehive. Try to find the queen—she's usually marked with a dot on her back. The surround-sound hive nearby lets you step inside to hear the sound of a buzzing queen.

Finally, you'll have the opportunity to watch a good but dry, detailed 14-minute film about the Carniolan bee, and check out special exhibits. Back at the entrance, the ticket desk sells a few choice souvenirs, including hand-painted replicas of frontboards, honey brandy, candles, ornaments, and other bee products.

Nearby: Sharing a ticket desk with the bee museum, the **Linhart Museum** celebrates one of Slovenia's leading Enlightenment thinkers. Radovljica-born Anton Linhart was an 18th-century playwright, politician, pedagogue, and historian who wrote some of the first plays in the Slovenian language and set the stage for France Prešeren. While he's important to Slovenes, it's hard to drum up much excitement for this earnest but fairly obscure-to-outsiders two-room museum (€5 combo-ticket with Apicultural Museum, same hours).

Eating in Radovljica

Several Radovljica restaurants near the bee museum have view terraces overlooking the surrounding mountains and valleys.

Lectar offers pricey, hearty Slovenian fare in a rural-feeling setting with a user-friendly, super-traditional menu. Its several heavily decorated rooms are often filled with tour groups, but in good weather, don't miss the terrace out back. Come here if you want to linger over rustic Slovenian specialties—not if you're in a hurry. The restaurant is known for its heart-shaped gingerbread cookies (called *lect*), inscribed with messages of love. In the cellar is a €1 "living museum" where you can watch costumed bakers make and decorate these hearts according to the traditional recipe (€6-10 starters, €9-14 main courses, Wed-Mon 12:00-22:00, closed Tue, family-friendly, Linhartov trg 2, tel. 04/537-4800).

Gostilna Avguštin, across the street, is the simpler local alternative for unpretentious, stick-to-your-ribs Slovenian fare. Their terrace in back enjoys an even better view than Lectar's (€6-8 starters, €10-19 main dishes, daily 10:00-24:00, Linhartov trg 15, tel. 04/531-4163).

Grajska Gostilnica, outside of the Old Town and closer to the bus station, dishes up good, basic pub grub (salads, pizza, pastas, open long hours daily, across from the bus station and to the left, inside Hotel Grajski Dvor at Kranjska 2, tel. 04/531-5585).

Lake Bohinj

The pristine alpine Lake Bohinj (BOH-heen), 16 miles southwest of Bled, enjoys a quieter scene and (in clear weather) even better vistas of Triglav and the surrounding mountains. This is a real back-to-nature experience, with just a smattering of hotels and campgrounds, rather than the well-oiled resort machine of Bled. Some people adore Bohinj; others are bored by it. While spectacular in clear, sunny weather, it's disappointing in the clouds (and, because of its position deep in the mountains, it can be socked in here even when it's clear in Bled). But if the weather is great and you're finding Bled too touristy to allow you to really enjoy nature, go to Bohinj.

Getting to Lake Bohinj: From Bled, hourly **buses** head for Bohinj, stopping at three different destinations: Bohinj Jezero (the

village of Ribčev Laz, 40 minutes, €3.60), then Bohinj Vogel (a 10-minute walk from the base of the Vogel Mountain cable car, 50 minutes, €4.10), and finally a few hundred yards more to Bohinj Zlatorog (Hotel Zlatorog and the one-hour hike to the Savica waterfall trailhead, 50 minutes, €4.10). In summer, a few buses continue all the way to the Savica Waterfall trailhead (see details under "Savica Waterfall," later). Off-season, there are fewer buses—confirm times before you depart.

Drivers leave Bled going south along the lakefront road, Cesta Svobode; in the village of Mlino, you'll peel off from the lake and follow signs to *Boh Bistrica* (a midsize town near Lake Bohinj). Once in the town of Bohinjska Bistrica, turn right, following *Boh Jezero* signs. The road takes you to the village of Ribčev Laz and along the lakefront road with all the attractions—the drive from Bled to the lake takes about 30 minutes. You can follow this road all the way to the Vogel cable-car parking lot; at the Vogel turn-off, you can continue straight ahead to reach the Savica Waterfall trailhead, or turn right and cross the bridge to curl around the far end of the lake and see the pristine river that feeds the lake (which flows out of the pool at the base of the Savica Waterfall).

Sights at Lake Bohinj

A visit to Bohinj has three parts: a village (offering boat trips on the lake), a cable car (and nearby cemetery), and a waterfall hike. I've listed them as you'll reach them along the main road from

Bled, which runs along the south side of the lake. If you plan to do everything (boat trip, cable car, waterfall hike), ask at the TI in Ribčev Laz about a combo-ticket to save some money.

Ribčev Laz Village—Coming from Bled, your first views of Bohinj will be from the little village called Ribčev Laz (loosely translated as "Good Fishin' Hole") at the southeast corner of the lake. Here you'll find a TI, a handful of hotels and ice-cream stands, and the Bohinj Jezero bus stop. The town's main landmark is its picturesque lakefront church, **St. John the Baptist** (to your right as you face the lake, past the stone bridge; not open to visitors).

A five-minute stroll down the main lakefront road is a dock where you can catch an electric **tourist boat** to make a silent circuit around the lake (€10 round-trip, €7 one-way, daily 10:00-18:00, runs hourly, less off-season). The boat stops at the far end of the lake, at Camp Zlatorog—a 10-minute walk from the Vogel cable car (see below). Across from the Ribčev Laz dock is a fun concrete 3-D model of Triglav. Finally, a few more steps down the road, just beyond a boat rental dock, you'll see a statue of Zlatorog, the "Golden Horn"—a mythical chamois-like creature native to the Julian Alps.

▲Vogel Mountain Cable Car—For a mountain perch without the sweat, take the cable car up to the top of Vogel Mountain,

offering impressive panoramic views of Mount Triglav and the Julian Alps. On a clear day, this is the best mountain panorama you can get without wings (the light is best in the morning). The summit is a ski-in-winter, hike-in-summer area with a pasture filled with grazing cows (summer only) and smaller chairlifts to various recreation areas. The first, short chairlift you'll see is designed for skiers and doesn't run in summer, but if you hike down into the little valley, you can take the second chairlift up the adjacent summit (Orlove Glave) for views into another valley on the other side. Then, from Orlove Glave, you can hike or ride the chairlift back to where you started. With plenty of time and very strong knees, you could even hike from Orlove Glave all the way back down to Lake Bohinj. If you need a break near the cable-car station, the alpine hut Merjasec ("Wild Boar") offers tasty strudel and a wide variety of local brandies (including the notorious "Boar's Blood"—a concoction of several different flavors guaranteed to get you snorting).

Cost and Hours: €13 round-trip, Dec-Oct daily 8:00-18:00, runs every 30 minutes in summer and continuously in winter, closed Nov, www.vogel.si.

Getting There: To reach the cable-car station, drivers follow signs to *Vogel* (to the left off the main lakefront road); by bus, get off at the Bohinj Vogel stop (request this stop from driver) and hike about 10 minutes up the steep road on the left (away from the lake).

World War I Cemetery—Back down below the cable car, on the main road just beyond the cable-car station and Bohinj Vogel bus stop, look for the metal gate on the left marking a World War I cemetery—the final resting place for some Soča Front soldiers (see sidebar on page 808). While no fighting occurred here (it was mostly on the other side of these mountains), injured soldiers were brought to a nearby hospital, and those who didn't recover ended up here. Notice that many of the names are not Slovenian, but Hungarian, Polish, Czech, and so on—a reminder that the entire multiethnic Austro-Hungarian Empire was involved in the fighting. If you're walking down from the cable-car station, the cemetery makes for a poignant detour on your way to the main road (look for it through the trees).

Savica Waterfall (Slap Savica)—Up the valley beyond the end of the lake is Bohinj's final treat, a waterfall called Slap Savica

(sah-VEET-seh). Hardy hikers enjoy following the moderate-to-strenuous uphill trail (including 553 stairs) to see the cascade, which dumps into a remarkably pure pool of aquamarine snowmelt.

Cost and Hours: €2.50, daily in summer from 8:00 until dusk, allow up to 1.5 hours for the round-trip hike.

Getting There: Drivers follow the lakefront road to where it ends, right at the trailhead. Without a car, getting to the trailhead is a hassle. Boats on the lake, as well as most public buses from Bled, take you only as far as the Bohinj Zlatorog stop—the end of the line, and still a one-hour hike from the trailhead (from the bus stop, follow signs to *Slap Savica*). However, during the summer (Mon-Sat late June-Sept only, none Sun or off-season), three buses a day run from Bled all the way to the Savica trailhead (likely departing Bled at 10:00, 14:20, and 16:20, about an hour to the trailhead, returning at 15:20 and 18:20—but confirm times locally before making the trip). But frankly, if the connections don't work out for you, it's not worth worrying about.

Sleeping at Lake Bohinj

If you'd like to get away from it all and settle in at Bohinj, consider **$$ Stare Pension** (STAH-reh). Well-run by mild-mannered Jože, it has 10 older, rustic, but well-maintained rooms (five of them with balconies) in a pristine setting at the far end of the lake (Db-€80 July-Aug, €70 May-June and Sept, €60 Oct-April, €5 less without balcony, half-board-€10 per person, free Internet access and Wi-Fi, Ukanc 128, mobile 040-558-669, www.impel-bohinj.si, info@impel-bohinj.si).

THE JULIAN ALPS

Vršič Pass • Soča River Valley • Bovec • Kobarid

The countryside around Lake Bled is plenty spectacular. But to crescendo your Slovenian mountain experience, head for the hills. The northwestern corner of Slovenia—within yodeling distance of Austria and Italy—is crowned by the Julian Alps (named for Julius Caesar). Here, mountain culture has a Slavic flavor.

The Slovenian mountainsides are laced with hiking paths, blanketed in deep forests, and speckled with ski resorts and vacation chalets. Beyond every ridge is a peaceful alpine village nestled around a quaint Baroque steeple. And in the center of it all is Mount Triglav—ol' "Three Heads"—Slovenia's symbol and tallest mountain.

The single best day in the Julian Alps is spent driving up and over the 50 hairpin turns of breathtaking Vršič Pass (vur-SHEECH, open May-Oct) and back down via the Soča (SOH-chah) River Valley, lined with offbeat nooks and Hemingway-haunted crannies. As you curl on twisty roads between the cut-glass peaks, you'll enjoy stunning high-mountain scenery, whitewater rivers with superb fishing, rustic rest stops, thought-provoking World War I sights, and charming hamlets.

A pair of Soča Valley towns holds watch over the region. Bovec is all about good times (it's the whitewater adventure-sports hub), while Kobarid attends to more serious matters (WWI history). Though neither is a destination in itself, both Bovec and Kobarid are pleasant, functional, and convenient home bases for exploring this gloriously beautiful region.

Getting Around the Julian Alps

The Julian Alps are best by **car.** Even if you're doing the rest of your trip by train, consider renting a car here for maximum mountain day-trip flexibility. I've included a self-guided driving tour incorporating the best of the Julian Alps (Vršič Pass and Soča Valley).

If you're without your own wheels, hiring a **local guide with a car** can be a great value, maximizing not only what you see, but what you learn. Cheaper but less personalized, you could join a day-trip **excursion** from Bled. (Both options are explained under "Tours at Lake Bled," page 767.) A public **bus** follows more or less the driving-tour route described below, leaving Ljubljana each morning at 6:30, arriving in Bovec at 10:45 (daily July-Aug, Sat-Sun only June and Sept, none Oct-May). Or stay closer to Bled, and get a taste of the Julian Alps by taking advantage of easy and frequent bus connections to more convenient day-trip destinations (the Vintgar Gorge and Lake Bohinj—both described under "Near Lake Bled" in the previous chapter).

Self-Guided Driving Tour

This all-day, self-guided driving tour—rated ▲▲▲—takes you over the highest mountain pass in Slovenia, with stunning scenery and a few quirky sights along the way. From waterfalls to hiking trails, World War I history to queasy suspension bridges, this trip has it all.

Orientation to the Julian Alps

Most of the Julian Alps are encompassed by Triglav National Park (Triglavski Narodni Park). This drive is divided into two parts: the Vršič Pass and the Soča River Valley. While not for stick-shift novices, all but the most timid drivers will agree the scenery is worth the many hairpin turns. Frequent pull-outs offer plenty of opportunity to relax, stretch your legs, and enjoy the vistas.

Planning Your Time: This drive can be done in a day, but consider spending the night along the way for a more leisurely pace. You can start and end in Bled or Ljubljana. You can return to your starting point, or do this trip one-way as a very scenic detour between these two destinations.

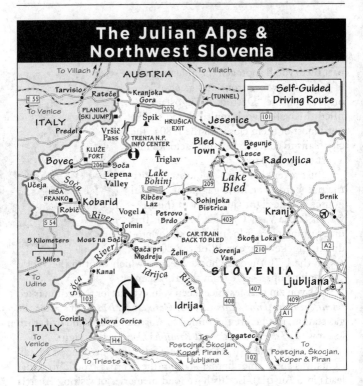

The Julian Alps & Northwest Slovenia

Length of This Tour: These rough estimates do not include stops: Bled to the top of Vršič Pass—1 hour; Vršič Pass to Trenta (start of Soča Valley)—30 minutes; Trenta to Bovec—30 minutes; Bovec to Kobarid—30 minutes; Kobarid to Ljubljana or Bled—2 hours (remember, it's an hour between Ljubljana and Bled). In other words, if you started and ended in Bled and drove the entire route without stopping, you'd make it home in less than five hours...but you'd miss so much. It takes at least a full day to really do the region justice.

Tourist Information: The best sources of information are the Bled TI (see page 760), the Triglav National Park Information Centers in Trenta (page 799) and Bled (page 761), and the TIs in Bovec and Kobarid (both listed in this chapter).

Maps: Pick up a good map before you begin (available at local TIs, travel agencies, and gas stations). The all-Slovenia *Autokarta Slovenija* or the TI's *Next Exit: Goldenhorn Route* map both include all the essential roads, but several more detailed options are also available. The 1:50,000 Kod & Kam *Posoče* map covers the entire Vršič Pass and Soča Valley (but doesn't include the parts of the drive near Bled and Ljubljana).

OK...let's ride.

THE JULIAN ALPS

Part 1: Vršič Pass

From Bled or Ljubljana, take the A2 expressway north, enjoying views of Mount Triglav on the left as you drive. About 10 minutes past Bled, you'll approach the industrial city of **Jesenice,** whose iron- and steelworks—once called the "Detroit of Yugoslavia"—filled this valley with multicolored smoke until most of them closed in the 1980s. The city plans to convert these old factories into a sort of theme park.

Just after the giant smokestack with the billboards, the little gaggle of colorful houses on the right (just next to the freeway) is **Kurja Vas** ("Chicken Village"). This unassuming place is locally famous for producing hockey players: 18 of the 20 players on the 1971 Yugoslav hockey team—which went to the World Championships—were from this tiny hamlet.

As you zip past Jesenice, keep your eye out for the exit marked *Jesenice-zahod, Trbiž/Tarvisio, Kr. Gora,* and *Hrušica* (it's after the gas station, just before the tunnel to Austria). When you exit, turn left toward *Trbiž/Tarvisio* and *Kranjska Gora* (yellow sign).

Just after the exit, the big, blue building surrounded by tall lights was the former border station (the overpass you'll go under leads into Austria). Locals have fond memories of visiting Austria during the Yugoslav days, when they smuggled home forbidden Western goods. Some items weren't available back home (VCRs, Coca-Cola, designer clothes), while other goods were simply better in Austria (chocolate, coffee, dishwasher soap).

Slovenes brag that their country—"with 56 percent of the land covered in forest"—is Europe's second-greenest. As you drive toward Kranjska Gora, take in all this greenery...and the characteristic Slovenian hayracks (recognized as part of the national heritage and now preserved; see page 701). The Vrata Valley (on the left) is a popular starting point for climbing Mount Triglav. Paralleling the road on the left is a "rails-to-trails" bike path converted from an old railway bed that loops from here through Italy and Austria, allowing bikers to connect three countries in one day. On the right, watch for the statue of Jakob Aljaž, who actually bought Triglav, back when such a thing was possible (he's pointing at his purchase). Ten minutes later, in Gozd Martuljek, you'll cross a bridge and enjoy a great head-on view of Špik Mountain.

Kranjska Gora was once Yugoslavia's leading winter resort, and remains popular with Croatian skiers. As every Slovene and Croatian wants a ski bungalow here, it has some of the highest property values in the country. Entering Kranjska Gora, you'll see a turnoff to the left marked for *Bovec* and *Vršič*. This leads up to the pass, but winter sports fanatics may first want to take a 15-minute detour to see the biggest ski jump in the world, a few miles ahead (stay straight through Kranjska Gora, then turn left at signs for **Planica,** the last stop before the Italian border). Every few years, tens of thousands of sports fans flock here to watch the ski-flying world championships. This is where a local boy was the first human to fly more than 100 meters (328 feet) on skis. Today's competitors routinely set new world records (currently 784 feet—that's 17 seconds in the air). From the ski jump, you're a few minutes' walk from Italy or Austria. This region—spanning three nations—lobbied unsuccessfully under the name Senza Confini (Italian for "without borders") to host the 2006 Winter Olympics. This philosophy is in tune with the European Union's vision for a Europe of regions, rather than nations.

Back in Kranjska Gora, follow the signs for *Vršič*. Before long, you'll officially enter **Triglav National Park** and come to the first of this road's 50 hairpin turns (24 up, then 26 down)—each one numbered and labeled with the altitude in meters. Notice that the turns are cobbled to provide better traction. If the drive seems daunting, remember that 50-seat tour buses routinely conquer this pass...if they can do it, so can you. Better yet, imagine the bicyclists who routinely pedal to the top. The best can do it in less than 30 minutes—faster than driving.

After switchback #8, with the cute waterfall, park your car on the right and hike up the stairs on the left to the little **Russian**

chapel. This road was built during World War I by at least 10,000 Russian POWs of the Austro-Hungarian Empire to supply the front lines of the Soča Front. The POWs lived and worked in terrible conditions, and several hundred died of illness and exposure. On March 8, 1916, an avalanche thundered down the mountains, killing hundreds more workers. This chapel was built where the final casualty was found. Take a minute to pay your respects to the men who built the road you're enjoying today. Because it's a Russian Orthodox chapel, notice that the crosses topping the steeples have three crossbars. (For more on the Orthodox faith, see page 876.)

Back on the road, after #17, look as high as you can on the cliff face to see sunlight streaming through a **"window"** in the rock. This natural formation, a popular destination for intrepid hikers, is big enough for the Statue of Liberty to crawl through.

After #22, at the pullout for Erjavčeva Koča restaurant, you

THE JULIAN ALPS

Mount Triglav

Mount Triglav ("Three Heads") stands watch over the Julian Alps and all of Slovenia. Slovenes say that its three peaks are the guardians of the water, air, and earth. This mountain defines Slovenes, even adorning the nation's flag: You'll often see the national seal, with three peaks (the two squiggly lines under it represent the Adriatic). Or take a look at one of Slovenia's €0.50 coins.

From the town of Bled, you'll see Triglav peeking up over the ridge on a clear day. (You'll get an even better view from nearby Lake Bohinj.)

It's said that you're not a true Slovene until you've climbed Triglav. One native took these words very seriously and climbed the mountain 853 times...in one year. Climbing to the summit—at 9,396 feet—is an attainable goal for any hiker in decent shape. If you're here for a while and want to become an honorary Slovene, befriend a local and ask if he or she will take you to the top.

If mountain climbing isn't your style, relax at an outdoor café with a piece of cream cake and a view of Triglav. It won't make you a Slovene...but it's close enough on a quick visit.

may see tour-bus groups making a fuss about the mountain vista. They're looking for a ghostly face in the cliff wall, supposedly belonging to the mythical figure **Ajda**. This village girl was cursed by the townspeople after correctly predicting the death of the Zlatorog (Golden Horn), a magical, beloved, chamois-like animal. Her tiny image (with a Picasso nose) is just above the tree line, a little to the right—try to get someone to point her out to you (you can see her best if you stand at the signpost near the road).

After #24, you reach the **summit** (5,285 feet). Consider getting out of the car to enjoy the views (in peak season, you'll pay

an attendant to park here). Hike up to the hut for a snack or drink on the grand view terrace. On the right, a long gravel chute gives hikers a thrilling glissade. (From the pullout just beyond #26, it's easy to view hikers "skiing" down.)

As you begin the descent, keep an eye out for old WWI debris. A lonely guard tunnel stands after #28, followed by a tunnel marked *1916* (on the left) that was part of the road's original path. Then you'll see abandoned checkpoints from when this was the border between Italy and the Austro-Hungarian Empire. At #48 is a statue of **Julius Kugy,** an Italian botanist who wrote books about alpine flora.

At #49, the road to the right (marked *Izvir Soče*) leads to the **source of the Soča River.** If you feel like stretching your legs after all that shifting, drive about five minutes down this road to a restaurant parking lot. From here, you can take a challenging 20-minute uphill hike to the Soča source. This is also the starting point for the well-explained, 12-mile Soča Trail (Soška Pot), which leads all the way to the town of Bovec, mostly following the road we're driving on today.

Nearing the end of the switchbacks, follow signs for *Bovec.* Crossing the Soča River, you begin the second half of this trip.

Part 2: Soča River Valley

During World War I, the terrain between here and the Adriatic made up the Soča (Isonzo) Front. As you follow the Soča River south, down what's nicknamed the "Valley of the Cemeteries," the scenic mountainsides around you tell the tale of this terrible warfare. Imagine a young Ernest Hemingway driving his ambulance through these same hills (see sidebar).

But it's not all so gloomy. There are plenty of other diversions—interesting villages and churches, waterfalls and suspension bridges, and lots more. Perhaps most impressive is the remarkable clarity and milky-blue color of the Soča itself, which Slovenes proudly call their "emerald river."

After switchback #49, you'll cross a bridge, then pass a church and a botanical garden of alpine plants (Alpinum Juliana). Across the street from the garden (on the right) is the parking lot for the Mlinarica Gorge. While the gorge is interesting, the bridge leading to it was damaged in a severe storm and hasn't yet been rebuilt—so it's best left to hardy hikers.

The last Vršič switchback (#50) sends you into the village of **Trenta.** As you get to the cluster of buildings in Trenta's "downtown," look on the left for the **Triglav National Park Information Center,** which also serves as a regional TI (daily July-Aug 8:00-20:00, May-June and Sept-Oct 10:00-18:00, Dec-April 10:00-14:00, closed Nov, tel. 05/388-9330, www.tnp.si). The €5 museum here provides a look (with English explanations) at the park's flora, fauna, traditional culture, and mountaineering history. An AV show celebrates the region's forests, and a poetic 15-minute slideshow explains the wonders and fragility of the park (included in

Hemingway in the Julian Alps

It was against the scenic backdrop of the Slovenian Alps that a young man from Oak Park, Illinois, first came to Europe—the continent with which he would forever be identified. After graduating from high school in 1917 and working briefly as a newspaper reporter, young Ernest Hemingway wanted to join the war effort in Europe. Bad vision kept him out of the army, but he craved combat experience—so he joined the Red Cross Ambulance Corps instead.

After a short detour through Paris, Hemingway was sent to the Italian Front. On his first day, he was given the job of retrieving human remains—gruesomely disfigured body parts—after the explosion of a munitions factory. Later he came to the Lower Piave Valley, not far from the Soča Front. In July 1918, his ambulance was hit by a mortar shell. Despite his injuries, he saved an Italian soldier who was also wounded. According to legend, he packed his own wound with cigarette butts to stop the flow of blood.

Sent to Milan to recuperate, Hemingway fell in love with a nurse, but she later left him for an Italian military officer. A decade later, Hemingway wrote about Kobarid (using its Italian name, Caporetto), the war, and his case of youthful heartbreak in the novel *A Farewell to Arms*.

museum entry, ask for English version as you enter).

THE JULIAN ALPS

After Trenta, you'll pass through a tunnel; then, on the left, look for a classic **suspension bridge.** Pull over to walk out for a bounce, enjoying the river's crystal-clear water and the spectacular mountain panorama.

About five miles beyond Trenta, in the town of Soča, is the **Church of St. Joseph** (with red onion dome, hiding behind the big tree on the right). The church was damaged in the earthquakes of 1998 and 2004, so the interior is likely covered with scaffolding. But if it's not covered, you'll see some fascinating art. During World War II, an artist hiding out in the mountains filled this church with patriotic symbolism. The interior is bathed in Yugoslav red, white, and blue—a brave statement made when such nationalistic sentiments were dangerous. On the ceiling is St. Michael (clad in Yugoslav colors) with Yugoslavia's three WWII enemies at his feet: the eagle (Germany), the wolf (Italy), and the serpent (Japan). The tops of the walls along the nave are lined with saints, but these are

Slavic, not Catholic. Finally, look carefully at the Stations of the Cross and find the faces of hated Yugoslav enemies: Hitler (fourth from altar on left) and Mussolini (first from altar on right). Behind the church, the stylized cross on the hill marks a **WWI cemetery**—the final resting place of some 600 Austro-Hungarian soldiers who were killed in action.

For another good example of how the Soča River cuts like God's band saw into the land, stop about two minutes past the church at the small gravel lot (on the left) marked *Velika Korita Soče* ("Grand Canyon of Soča"). Venture out onto the suspension bridge over the gorge...and bounce if you dare. Just beyond this bridge is the turnoff (on the left) to the Lepena Valley, home of the recommended Pristava Lepena ranch, with accommodations and Lipizzaner horses (described later, under "Sleeping in Bovec").

Roughly five miles after the town of Soča, you exit the national park, pass a WWI graveyard (on the left), and come to a fork in the road. The main route leads to the left, through Bovec. But first, take a two-mile detour to the right (marked *Trbiž/Tarvisio* and *Predel/Kluže*), where the WWI **Kluže Fort** keeps a close watch over the narrowest part of a valley leading to

Italy (€3; July-Aug daily 9:00-20:00; June and Sept Sun-Fri 9:00-17:00, Sat 9:00-18:00; May and Oct Sat-Sun 10:00-17:00, closed Mon-Fri; closed Nov-April; www.kluze.net). In the 15th century, the Italians had a fort here to defend against the Ottomans. Half a millennium later, during World War I, it was used by Austrians to keep Italians out of their territory. Notice the ladder rungs fixed to the cliff face across the road from the fort—allowing soldiers to quickly get up to the mountaintop.

Back on the main road, continue to **Bovec**. This town, which saw some of the most vicious fighting of the Soča Front, was hit hard by earthquakes in 1994 and 1998 (and by another tremor in 2004). Today, it's been rebuilt and remains the adventure-sports capital of the Soča River Valley—also known as the "Adrenaline Valley," famous for its whitewater activities. (Since the water comes from high-mountain runoff, the temperature of the Soča never goes above 68 degrees Fahrenheit.) For a good lunch stop in Bovec, take the turnoff as you first reach the town, and you'll pass an inviting restaurant terrace on the right (Martinov Hram; for details, see "Eating in Bovec," later). But if you're not eating or spending the night in Bovec, you could skip the town entirely and not miss much (continue along the main road to bypass the town center).

Heading south along the river—with water somehow both perfectly clear and spectacularly turquoise—watch for happy kayakers. When you pass the intersection at Žaga, you're just four miles from Italy. Along the way, you'll also pass a pair of **waterfalls**: the well-known Boka ("Slovenia's second-longest waterfall," on the right just before Žaga) and the hidden gem Veliki Kozjak (on the left just before Kobarid). It's possible—but challenging—to hike to either fall (Boka's trailhead is just after the bridge on the right, but it's an extremely strenuous hike; Veliki Kozjak is a bit more manageable, but still not level or easy—for details, see page 812).

Signs lead to the town of **Kobarid**, home to a sleepy main square and some fascinating WWI sights. Even if you don't think you're interested in the Soča Front, consider dropping in the Kobarid Museum. Driving up to the Italian mausoleum hovering over the town is a must. (These sights are described later, under "Sights in Kobarid.")

Leaving Kobarid, continue south along the Soča to **Tolmin.** Before you reach Tolmin, decide on your route back to civilization...

Finishing the Drive

While you could go back over the pass the way you came, there are various ways to make your trip a loop by circling through some more varied scenery. Which way you go depends on your final destination: Ljubljana or Bled.

To Ljubljana (or Southern Slovenia/Croatia)

From Tolmin, you have two possible driving routes to the capital. Either option brings you back to the A1 expressway south of Ljubljana, and will get you to the city in about two hours (though the second route has fewer miles).

Nova Gorica Route: The option you'll encounter first (turnoff to the right before Tolmin) is the smoother, longer route southwest to Nova Gorica. Along this road, you'll pass a hydroelectric dam and go under a 1906 rail viaduct that once connected this area to the port of Trieste (now in Italy). In the charming town of Kanal, you'll cross over the Soča on a picturesque bridge that's faintly reminiscent of Mostar's (as in that city, young people stage a competition for jumping off this bridge into the raging river below). Father along, the striking Solkan Bridge (another link in the Trieste rail line) is the longest single-span stone arch bridge in the world. Soon after, you arrive in Nova Gorica. This fairly dull city is divided in half by the Italian border (the Italian side is called "Gorizia"). Because Italians aren't allowed to gamble in their home towns, Nova Gorica is packed with casinos catering to Italian gamblers. In fact, it's home to Europe's biggest casino. Rocks spell out the name "TITO" on a hillside above town—a strange relic of an earlier age. From Nova Gorica, you can hop on the H4 expressway, which links easily to the main A1 expressway. **Idrija Route:** For a more off-the-beaten-path, ruggedly scenic approach, take this rural option: Continue through Tolmin, then head southeast through the hills back toward Ljubljana. Along the way, you could stop for a bite and some sightseeing at the town of Idrija (EE-dree-yah), known to all Slovenes for three things: its tourable mercury mine, fine delicate lace, and tasty *žlikrofi* (like ravioli). Back at the expressway (at Logatec), head north to Ljubljana.

To Bled

To reach Bled, you could follow either of the Ljubljana-bound routes outlined above, then carry on northward for another hour to Bled (allow about 3 hours total). But the following options are more direct.

Car Train: The fastest option is to load your car onto a "Car Train" (Autovlak) that cuts directly through the mountains. The train departs at 18:30 from Most na Soči (just south of Tolmin, along the Idrija route described above) and arrives at Bohinjska Bistrica, near Lake Bohinj, at 19:14 (€12 for the car; confirm schedule at the Bled TI before making the trip). From Bohinjska Bistrica, it's just a half-hour drive back to Bled. No reservations are necessary, but arrive at the train station about 30 minutes before the scheduled departure to allow time to load the car.

Through Italy via Predel Pass: Although this route requires some backtracking, it also includes a detour through Italy. From Kobarid, drive back the way you came (through Bovec), then turn off for the Kluže Fort (described on page 801), marked for *Predel* and Italy. In a few miles, after passing the fort, the road curves up through two small villages (first Log pod Mangartom, then Strmec na Predelu directly above it). Continue past the ruined fortress and cross the Italian border (there's no need to stop). Then curl down a few hairpin turns past the end of Lake Predel, and continue straight through the ghost city of Cave del Predil (a former lead-mining town) and along the valley road, following signs for Slovenia. Approaching Tarvisio, turn right (continuing to follow signs for Slovenia); from here, it's about a half-hour (10 miles) back across the Slovenian border to Kranjska Gora. This is where you first began your ascent of the Vršič Pass—just retrace your steps back to Bled.

Other Driving Routes: The fastest route (about 2 hours) is partially on a twisty, rough, very poor-quality road (go through Tolmin, turn off at Bača pri Modreju to Podbrdo, then from Petrovo Brdo take a very curvy road through the mountains into Bohinjska Bistrica and on to Bled). For timid drivers, it's more sane and not too much longer to start out on the Idrija route toward Ljubljana (described above), but turn off in Želin (before Idrija) toward Skofja Loka and Kranj, then on to Bled.

Bovec

The biggest town in the area, Bovec (BOH-vets) has a happening main square and all the tourist amenities. It's best known as a hub for whitewater adventure sports. While not exactly quaint, Bovec is charming enough to qualify as a good lunch stop or overnight home base. If nothing else, it's a nice jolt of civilization wedged between the alpine cliffs.

Orientation to Bovec

Tourist Information
The helpful TI on the main square offers fliers on mountain biking and water sports (flexible hours, generally June-Sept daily 9:00-19:00; off-season Mon-Fri 9:00-17:00, Sat-Sun 9:00-14:00 & 14:30-17:00; Trg Golobarskih Žrtev 8, tel. 05/384-1444, www.bovec.si).

Arrival in Bovec
The main road skirts Bovec, but you can turn off (watch for signs on the right) to take the road that goes through the heart of town, then rejoins the main road farther along. As you approach the city center, you can't miss the main square, Trg Golobarskih Žrtev, with the TI and a good restaurant (described later, under "Eating in Bovec").

Sleeping in Bovec

$$$ Hotel Mangart is a big chalet-style modern hotel with 36 rooms on the edge of Bovec (toward the Vršič Pass). All of the rooms have balconies, except the cheaper bunkbed hostel rooms (Db-€110 in July-Aug, €100 in May-June and Sept, €90 in Oct, cheaper Nov-April, bigger superior rooms have bathtubs and nicer decor—not worth the extra €20; hostel rooms are a great value-

Sleep Code

(€1 = about $1.40, country code: 386, area code: 05)
S = Single, **D** = Double/Twin, **T** = Triple, **Q** = Quad, **b** = bathroom. Unless otherwise noted, credit cards are accepted and breakfast is included, but the modest tourist tax (about €1 per person, per night) is not. Everyone listed here speaks English.

To help you easily sort through these listings, I've divided the accommodations into three categories based on the price for a double room with bath during high season:

$$$ **Higher Priced**—Most rooms €100 or more.
$$ **Moderately Priced**—Most rooms between €50-100.
$ **Lower Priced**—Most rooms €50 or less.

Prices can change without notice; verify the hotel's current rates online or by email. For other updates, see www .ricksteves.com/update.

€25/person in a small 2-, 4-, or 6-bed room with a tight bathroom; elevator, free Wi-Fi, Mala vas 107, tel. 05/388-4250, www.hotel -mangart.com, booking@hotel-mangart.com).

$$ Martinov Hram has 11 nice, modern rooms over a popular restaurant a few steps from Bovec's main square. While the rooms are an afterthought to the busy restaurant (reception at the bar), they're comfortable (very flexible rates, in peak season figure Sb-€40, Db-€70, a few euros less off-season, no extra charge for 1-night stays, rooms on sunny side have air-con, free Wi-Fi in restaurant and cable Internet in rooms, Trg Golobarskih Žrtev 27, tel. 05/388-6214, www.martinov-hram.si, sara.berginc@gmail.com).

Near Bovec

$$$ Pristava Lepena is a relaxing oasis hiding out in the Lepena Valley just north of Bovec. Well-run by Milan and Silvia Dolenc, this place is its own little village: a series of rustic-looking cabins, a restaurant, a sauna/whirlpool, and an outdoor swimming pool. Hiding behind the humble split-wood shingle exteriors is surprising comfort: 13 cozy apartments (with wood-burning stoves, TV, telephone, Wi-Fi, and all the amenities) that make you feel like relaxing. This place whispers "second honeymoon" (Db-€138 in July-Aug, €122 in May-June and Sept, €106 in early Oct and late April, closed in winter except mid-Dec-early Jan, multi-night stays preferred, 1-night stays may be possible for 20 percent extra, dinner-€19, lunch and dinner-€31, nonrefundable 30 percent advance payment when you reserve; just before Bovec, turn left off the main road toward Lepena, and follow the white horses to Lepena 2; tel. 05/388-9900, fax 05/388-9901, www.pristava-lepena.com, pristava .lepena@siol.net). The Dolences also have three Welsh ponies and five purebred Lipizzaner horses (two mares, three geldings) that guests can ride (in riding ring–€16/hour, on trail–€20/hour, riding lesson–€24; non-guests may be able to ride for a few euros more—call ahead and ask).

$$ Boka Pension fills a big modern-but-tasteful building squeezed between the road and the Soča near the big Boka waterfall. The 20 rooms are simple but have nice woody touches (Db–€66 in mid-July-Aug, €62 in May-mid-July and Sept, cheaper off-season, €10 more for a bigger suite, elevator, free cable Internet, some road noise, Žaga 156a, tel. 05/384-5512, www.boka-bovec.si, penzion@boka-bovec.si).

$ Tourist Farm Pri Plajerju is on a picturesque plateau at the edge of Trenta (the first town at the bottom of the Vršič Pass road). Run by the Pretner family (gregarious Marko is a park ranger, shy Stanka is "the boss"), this organic farm raises sheep and rents five apartments in three buildings separate from the main house. As the Soča Valley doesn't have many tourist farms, this is one of your best options if you want to stay at one. However, its location deeper in the mountains makes it a bit less convenient for side-tripping—it's 30 minutes to Bovec, and 45 minutes to Kobarid (July-Aug: Db–€45-55, Tb–€55-65, Qb–€68-78; Sept-June: Db–€40-50, Tb–€50-60, Qb–€63-70; price depends on size, breakfast–€7, dinner–€11—available some but not all nights, watch for signs to the left after coming over the pass and going through the village of Trenta, Trenta 16a, tel. & fax 05/388-9209, mobile 041-600-590, www.eko-plajer.com, info@eko-plajer.com).

Eating in Bovec

Martinov Hram, run by the Berginc family, has an inviting outdoor terrace under a grape trellis. Inside, the nicely traditional decor goes well with Slovenian specialties with a focus on sheep (good homemade bread, €7-12 pastas, €8-20 main courses, Tue-Sun 10:00-23:00, closed Mon, on the main road through Bovec, just before the main square on the right at Trg Golobarskih Žrtev 27, tel. 05/388-6214).

THE JULIAN ALPS

Kobarid

Kobarid (KOH-bah-reed) feels older, and therefore a bit more appealing, than its big brother Bovec. This humble settlement was

immortalized by a literary giant, Ernest Hemingway, who drove an ambulance in these mountains during World War I. He described Kobarid as "a little white town with a campanile in a valley. It was a clean little town and there was a fine fountain in the square." Sounds about right. Even though Kobarid loves to tout its Hemingway connection, historians believe that Papa did not actually visit Kobarid until he came back after the war to research his book.

Aside from its brush with literary greatness, Kobarid is known as a hub of Soča Front information (with an excellent WWI museum, a hilltop Italian mausoleum, and walks that connect the nearby sights). You won't find the fountain Hemingway wrote about—it's since been covered up by houses (though the town government hopes to excavate it as a tourist attraction). You will find a modern statue of Simon Gregorčič (overlooking the main intersection), the beloved Slovenian priest-slash-poet who came from and wrote about the Soča Valley.

Orientation to Kobarid

(area code: 05)
The main road cuts right through the heart of little Kobarid, bisecting its main square (Trg Svobode). The Kobarid Museum is along this road, on the left before the square. To reach the museum from the main square, simply walk five minutes back toward Bovec.

Tourist Information
The TI has good information on the area, and Internet access (May-June Mon-Fri 9:00-13:00 & 14:00-18:00, Sat-Sun 10:00-14:00; July-Sept daily 9:00-19:00; Oct-April Mon-Fri 9:00-13:00 & 14:00-16:00, Sat-Sun 10:00-14:00; on the main square at Trg Svobode 16—follow the white footprints behind the statue of Gregorčič, tel. 05/380-0490, www.dolina-soce.com and www.kobarid.si).

The Soča (Isonzo) Front

The valley in Slovenia's northwest corner—called Soča in Slovene and Isonzo in Italian—saw some of World War I's fiercest fighting. While the Western Front gets more press, this eastern border between the Central Powers and the Allies was just as significant. In a series of 12 battles involving 22 different nationalities along a 60-mile-long front, 300,000 soldiers died, 700,000 were wounded, and 100,000 were declared MIA. In addition, tens of thousands of civilians died. A young Ernest Hemingway, who drove an ambulance for the Italian army in nearby fighting, would later write the novel *A Farewell to Arms* about the battles here (see "Hemingway in the Julian Alps" sidebar on page 800).

On April 26, 1915, Italy joined the Allies. A month later, it declared war on the Austro-Hungarian Empire (which included Slovenia). Italy unexpectedly invaded the Soča Valley, quickly taking the tiny town of Kobarid, which it planned to use as a home base for attacks deeper into Austro-Hungarian territory. For the next 29 months, Italy launched 10 more offensives against the Austro-Hungarian army, which was encamped on higher ground on the mountaintops. All of these Italian offensives were unsuccessful, even though the Italians outnumbered their opponents three to one. This was unimaginably difficult warfare—Italy had to attack uphill, waging war high in the mountains, in the harshest of conditions. Trenches had to be carved into rock instead of mud, and many unprepared conscripts—brought here from faraway lands and unaccustomed to the harsh winter conditions atop the Alps—froze to death. During one brutal winter alone, some 60,000 soldiers were killed by avalanches.

Visitors take a look at this tight valley, hemmed in by seemingly impassible mountains, and wonder: Why would people fight so fiercely over such inhospitable terrain? At the time, Slovenia was the natural route from Italy to the Austro-Hungarian capital at Vienna. The Italians believed that if they could hold this val-

Sights in Kobarid

▲▲▲**Kobarid Museum (Kobariški Muzej)**—This modest but world-class museum, offering a haunting look at the tragedy of the Soča Front, was voted Europe's best museum in 1993. The tasteful exhibits, with fine English descriptions and a pacifist tone, take an even-handed approach to the fighting—without getting hung up on identifying the "good guys" and the "bad guys." The museum's

ley and push over the mountains, Vienna—and victory—would be theirs. Once committed, they couldn't turn back, and the war devolved into one of exhaustion—who would fall first?

In the fall of 1917, Austro-Hungarian Emperor Karl appealed to his ally Germany, and the Germans agreed to assemble an army for a new attack to retake Kobarid and the Soča Valley. In an incredible logistical accomplishment, they spent just six weeks building and supplying this new army by transporting troops and equipment high across the mountaintops under cover of darkness...above the heads of their oblivious Italian foes dozing in the valley.

On October 24, Austria-Hungary and Germany launched an attack that sent 600,000 soldiers down into the town of Kobarid. This crucial 12th battle of the Soča Front, better known as the Battle of Kobarid, was the turning point—and saw the introduction of battlefield innovations that are commonplace in the military today. German field commanders were empowered to act independently on the battlefield, reacting immediately to developments rather than waiting for approval. Also, for the first time ever, the Austrian-German army used elements of a new surprise-attack technique called *Blitzkrieg*. (One German officer, Erwin Rommel, made great strides in the fighting here, and later climbed the ranks to become famous as Hitler's "Desert Fox" in North Africa.)

The attack caught the Italian forces off-guard, quickly breaking through three lines of defense. Within three days, the Italians were forced to retreat. (Because the Italian military worked from the top down, the soldiers were sitting ducks once they were cut off from their commanders.) The Austrians called their victory the "Miracle at Kobarid." But Italy felt differently. The Italians see the battle of Caporetto (the Italian name for Kobarid) as their Alamo. To this day, when an Italian finds himself in a mess, he might say, "At least it's not a *Caporetto*."

A year later, Italy came back—this time with the aid of British, French, and US forces—and easily retook this area. On November 4, 1918, Austria-Hungary conceded defeat. After more than a million casualties, the fighting at Soča was finally over.

THE JULIAN ALPS

focus is not on the guns and heroes, but on the big picture of the front and on the stories of the common people who fought and died here.

Cost and Hours: €5, good selection of books; April-Sept Mon-Fri 9:00-18:00, Sat-Sun 9:00-19:00; Oct-March Mon-Fri 10:00-17:00, Sat-Sun 9:00-18:00; Gregorčičeva 10, tel. 05/389-0000, www.kobariski-muzej.si.

Tours: History buffs can call ahead to arrange a private guide to lead them through the collection (€20/hour), or tour the sights outside (€25/hour). You can also arrange a guide through the Walk of Peace Visitors Center, listed later.

🢒 **Self-Guided Tour:** The entry is lined with hastily made cement and barbed-wire gravestones, flags representing all the nationalities involved in the fighting, and pictures of soldiers and nurses from diverse backgrounds who were brought together here (for example, the men wearing fezzes were from Bosnia-Herzegovina, annexed by the Austro-Hungarian Empire shortly before the war).

Buy your ticket and ask to watch the English version of the 19-minute film on the history of the Soča Front (informative but dry, plays on top floor).

The first floor up is divided into several rooms. The White Room, filled with rusty crampons, wire-cutters, pickaxes, and shovels, explains wintertime conditions at the front. What looks like a bear trap was actually used to trap enemy soldiers. The Room of the Rear shows the day-to-day activities away from the front line, from supplying troops to more mundane activities (milking cows, washing clothes, getting a shave, lifting weights, playing with a dog). The Black Room is the museum's most somber, commemorating the more than one million casualties of the Soča Front. These heartbreaking exhibits honor the common people whose bodies fertilized the battlefields of Europe. Horrific images of war injuries are juxtaposed with a display of medals earned—prompting the question, was it worth it? The little altar was purchased by schoolchildren, who sent it to the front to offer the troops some solace.

Through the door marked *Room of the Krn Range* (also on the first floor up), find your way to the Kobarid Rooms, which trace the history of this region from antiquity to today. High on the wall, look for the timelines explaining the area's turbulent history. The one in the second room shows wave after wave of invaders (including Ottomans, Habsburgs, and Napoleon). In the next room, above a display case with military uniforms, another timeline shows the many flags that flew over Kobarid's main square during the 20th century.

On the top floor, across from the room where the film plays (described above), you'll see a giant model of the surrounding mountains, painstakingly tracing the successful Austrian-German *Blitzkrieg* attack during the Battle of Kobarid.

▲▲**Italian Mausoleum (Kostnica)**—The 55 miles between here and the Adriatic are dotted with more than 75 cemeteries,

reminders of the countless casualties of the Soča Front. One of the most dramatic is this mausoleum, overlooking Kobarid. The access road, across Kobarid's main square from the side of the church, is marked by stone gate towers (with the word *Kostnica*—one tower is topped with a cross and the other with a star for the Italian army).

Take the road up Gradič Hill—passing Stations of the Cross—to the mausoleum. Built in 1938 (when this was still part of Italy) around the existing Church of St. Anthony, this octagonal pyramid holds the remains of 7,014 Italian soldiers. The stark, cold, Neoclassical architecture is pure Mussolini. Names are listed alphabetically, along with mass graves for more than 1,700 unknown soldiers *(militi ignoti)*.

Walk behind the church and enjoy the **view.** Find the WWI battlements high on the mountain's rock face (with your back to church, they're at 10 o'clock). Incredibly, the fighting was done on these treacherous ridges; civilians in the valleys only heard the distant battles. Looking up and down the valley, notice the "signal churches" evenly spaced on hilltops, each barely within view of the next—an ancient method for quickly spreading messages or warnings across long distances.

If the **church** is open, go inside and look above the door to see a brave soldier standing over the body of a fallen comrade and fending off enemies with nothing but rocks.

When Mussolini came to dedicate the mausoleum, local revolutionaries plotted an assassination attempt that couldn't fail. A young man planned to suicide-bomb Mussolini as the leader came back into town from this hilltop. But as Mussolini's car drove past, the would-be assassin looked at his fellow townspeople around him, realized the innocent blood he would also spill, and had a last-minute change of heart. Mussolini's trip was uneventful, and fascism continued to thrive in Italy.

▲**Walk of Peace (Pot Miru)**—This relatively new walking route—which, as of a 2012 expansion, extends more than 140 miles from these mountains all the way to the Adriatic—is designed to link museums, cemeteries, churches, and other sites related to the warfare of the Soča Front. In addition to the excellent museum here in Kobarid, several other "outdoor museums" in the area let you get close to the places where the fighting actually occurred. Some are reachable by car, while others require a challenging mountain hike. To learn more about all of these options, visit the **Walk of Peace Foundation Information Center,** across the street from the Kobarid Museum. They hand out good, free maps and booklets about these places, and sell a fine €10 guidebook to WWI sights in the area. They also plan a new exhibition featuring a touchscreen map of the route, a film offering a bird's-eye view over the territory of the front, and photographs of the area (free; July-Aug Mon-Fri 9:00-13:00 & 14:00-19:00, Sat-Sun 10:00-13:00 & 14:00-19:00; April-June and Sept-Oct slightly shorter hours; Nov-March Sat-Sun only 10:00-15:00, closed Mon-Fri; Gregorčičeva 8, tel. 05/389-0167, www.potmiru.si). They also arrange guides that can join you for part of the walk (€25/hour for up to 4 hours, €20/hour for longer tours), and in the summer, they offer excursions to related sights nearby (for example, to the open-air museum in Kolovrat, 2/week, €15).

Kobarid Historical Walk—This shorter walk to WWI sights around Kobarid is well-explained by the free brochure available at the TI, museum, and information center (3 miles, mostly uphill, allow 3-5 hours; or you can just do a shorter, easier stretch along the river, 1-2 hours).

Alpine Cheese Museum—This humble exhibit, at the big Planika ("Edelweiss") dairy at the edge of town, examines the history of cheesemaking in this area since ancient times.

Cost and Hours: €2, May-mid-Sept Mon-Sat 10:00-18:00; March-April and mid-Sept-Oct Mon-Sat 10:00-16:00, closed Sun and off-season; Gregorčičeva 32, www.mlekarna-planika.si /muzej.

Great Kozjak Waterfall (Veliki Kozjak) Hike—If you have time to kill in Kobarid and want to go for a sturdy hike, consider trekking to the Great Kozjak Waterfall—a dramatic cascade that flows through an extremely narrow gorge and plunges 50 feet into a beautiful pool. While local signs clock the hike at 30 minutes from the town center, plan on closer to 45 minutes each way. The trailhead is at the Bovec end of Kobarid: As you approach town from Bovec, turn right into the town, then take an immediate and sharp left to go back under the main road, following signs for Kamp Koren. Wind down to cross the bridge over the Soča, then turn left and head up the hill (you'll pass Kamp Koren). You can park in the big gravel lot across the street from the camp, or, to get closer to the trailhead, turn left just after Kamp Koren at the Slap Kozjak sign and follow the gravel road (park your car at the pullout after the multicolored beehives). Continue walking along the gravel path down into the ravine, passing views of a smaller waterfall. Go right at the fork, continue into the gorge, and take the high, narrow bridge over the stream (no railing—a little nerve-racking for those afraid of heights). Finally, follow the boardwalk as it curls around a cliff for great views of the falls.

Sleeping in Kobarid

(€1 = about $1.40, country code: 386, area code: 05)
My first listing is right on the main square. The other two hide
on side streets about a block off the main road through town,
between the museum and the main square (about a 3-minute walk
to either).

$$$ Hotel Hvala is the only real hotel in town. Run by the
Hvala family, its 32 contemporary rooms are comfortable, and the
location can't be beat. The mural on the wall in the elevator shaft
tells the story of the Soča Valley as you go up toward the top floor
(mid-July-Aug: Sb-€76, Db-€112, cheaper third-floor "mansard"
Sb-€62, Db-€98; Sept-mid-July: Sb-€72, Db-€104, cheaper third-
floor "mansard" Sb-€58, Db-€90; pricier superior Db with air-con
and sleek new decor-€160-200; cheaper off-season, hotel closed
parts of Feb and Nov, elevator, free Internet access and Wi-Fi, Trg
Svobode 1, tel. 05/389-9300, fax 05/388-5322, www.hotelhvala.si,
topli.val@siol.net).

$ Apartmaji Lia, run by sweet Alenka Likar, has six tidy
apartments in two buildings in the town center (Db-€40, extra
adult-€20, kids under 15-€10, cash only, no breakfast, some rooms
have air-con, free Wi-Fi, main house at Volaričeva 9, mobile 051-
415-058, www.apartmaji-lia.si, apartmajilia@gmail.com).

$ Picerija Fedrig is a pizzeria that rents five simple but fine
rooms upstairs (Db-€40, less for more than 1 night, 10 percent
more in Aug, between the main square and the Kobarid Museum
at Volaričeva 11, tel. 05/389-0115, fedrig@t-2.net).

Eating in Kobarid

Topli Val ("Heat Wave"), Hotel Hvala's restaurant, is pricey but
good, with a menu that emphasizes fish (€8-16 pastas, €9-23 main
courses, lengthy list of Slovenian wines, daily 12:00-15:00 & 18:00-
23:00, Trg Svobode 1, tel. 05/389-9300).

Kotlar Restaurant, across the square from Hotel Hvala, is
similarly priced and well-regarded (Thu-Mon 12:00-15:00 &
18:00-22:00, closed Tue-Wed, Trg Svobode 11, tel. 05/389-1110).
Kotlar also rents rooms if you're in a pinch.

Picerija Fedrig (also listed under "Sleeping in Kobarid,"
above) serves up good €5-7 pizzas (Tue-Thu 17:00-22:00, Fri-Sun
12:00-22:00, closed Mon, also closed Tue in Nov-April, Volaričeva
11, tel. 05/389-0115).

Sleeping and Eating near Kobarid

$$$ Hiša Franko is a gourmet restaurant that also rents 10 rooms less than a five-minute drive outside of Kobarid. The modern-style rooms in the main building are upscale and comfortable, while the rooms in the adjacent yellow house are much simpler, dated, and affordable (main-building Db-€110-135 depending on size and amenities, yellow-house Db-€80, includes breakfast, free Wi-Fi, bike rental-€7, Staro Selo 1, tel. 05/389-4120, www.hisafranko .com, info@hisafranko.com).

What brings most people here is the upscale **restaurant,** which combines Slovenian cuisine and ingredients with modern international influences to create a memorable, if pricey, meal. The dining room is spiffy but casual and unpretentious, and the service is attentive and welcoming (€12-15 starters, €22-24 main dishes, €50-75 fixed-price meals, Wed-Sun 12:00-15:00 & 17:00-23:00, closed Mon-Tue).

Getting There: To reach Hiša Franko, leave Kobarid heading toward Robič on the pleasant tree-lined road, and look for the sign on the right.

THE JULIAN ALPS

CROATIA
Hrvatska

CROATIA

Sunny beaches, succulent seafood, and a taste of *la dolce vita*...in Eastern Europe?

With thousands of miles of seafront and more than a thousand islands, Croatia's coastline is Eastern Europe's Riviera. Holiday-makers love its pebbly beaches, predictably balmy summer weather, and dramatic mountains. Croatia is also historic. From ruined Roman arenas and Byzantine mosaics to Venetian bell towers, Habsburg villas, and even communist concrete, past rulers have left their mark.

Croatia feels more Mediterranean than "Eastern European." Historically, Croatia has more in common with Venice and Rome than Vienna or Budapest. Especially on the coast, it's sometimes difficult to distinguish this lively place from Italy. If you've become accustomed to the Germanic-style efficiency of Slovenia or Hungary, Croatia's relaxed and unpredictable style can come as a shock.

Aside from its fun-in-the-sun status, Croatia is also known as one of the sites, just over a decade and a half ago, of the most violent European war in generations. Locals call it "The Homeland War" or, more casually, "The Last War" (though it's ambiguous whether they mean "final" or "most recent"). Thankfully, the bloodshed is in the past. While a trip to Croatia offers thoughtful travelers the opportunity to understand a complicated chapter of recent history, most visitors focus instead on its substantial natural wonders: mountains, waterfalls, sun, sand, and sea.

Croatia's 3,600 miles of coastline—its main draw for tourists—is loosely divided into three regions. Most people flock to the Dalmatian Coast, in the south—where dramatic limestone cliffs rise from the deep and islands are scattered just offshore (Korčula is the most appealing). Here you'll find Croatia's top tourist town, Dubrovnik, and the big city of Split, with its impressive Roman

Croatia

AUSTRIA

HUNGARY

Drava

Maribor •
Ptuj •

Varaždin •

Pécs •

SERBIA

Bled •

Ljubljana ✿

SLOVENIA

Samobor ✿

Zagreb ✿

CROATIA

SLAVONIA

Osijek •
Vukovar •

ITALY

Trieste •
Piran •

Motovun •
Poreč •

Opatija • Rijeka

Slunj •

Karlovac •

Sava

ISTRIA

Krk

Senj •

Plitvice Lakes
National Park

BOSNIA-
HERZEGOVINA

Rovinj •

Pula •

Cres

Rab

Otočac •

Brijuni
Islands

KVARNER

GULF

Pag

Knin •

Sarajevo •

Zadar •

Dugi
Otok

Šibenik •

Adriatic

Trogir •

Split

Mostar •

Sea

DALMATIAN

Makarska •

Hvar

Hvar

Korčula

Korčula

Medugorje ■

Ploče •

Neum

MONTE-
NEGRO

Trebinje •

Kotor •

Ston •
Mljet •

Dubrovnik

ITALY

COAST

Cavtat •

Cetinje •
Budva •

Bay of
Kotor

Sveti
Stefan

100 Kilometers

100 Miles

N

Danube

ruins. Way up at the northern corner of the country is the
wedge-shaped peninsula called
Istria, which has less dramatic
scenery but arguably even more
romantic towns—including my
favorite, the Venetian-flavored
Rovinj—along with the city of
Pula (more great Roman ruins)
and a hilly interior blanketed with vineyards and topped with hill
towns (Motovun is the best).

Enjoy the coast, but don't ignore the interior. The bustling
capital of Zagreb is urban, engaging, and full of great museums.
And Croatia's single best natural wonder (in this country that's so
full of them) are the stunning waterfalls at Plitvice Lakes National
Park.

It's possible to blow a lot of money here. Croatian hotels, especially on the coast, are a terrible value, and there are plenty of touristy restaurants happy to overcharge you. But if you know where to

CROATIA

look, you can find some wonderful budget alternatives—foremost among them *sobe* (rooms in private homes). *Sobe* are a comfortable compromise: fresh, hotelesque doubles with a private bathroom, air-conditioning, and TV, for a fraction of the cost of an anonymous room in an overpriced resort hotel just down the beach (for details, see "Croatian Accommodation," later).

Europeans are reverent sun-worshippers, and on clear days, virtually every square inch of coastal Croatia is occupied by a sunbather on a beach towel. Nude beaches are a big deal, especially for vacationing Germans and Austrians. If you want to work on an all-around tan, seek out a beach marked *FKK* (from the German *Freikörper Kultur*, or "free body culture"). First-timers get comfortable in a hurry, finding they're not the only pink novices on the rocks. But don't get too excited—these beaches are most beloved by people you'd rather see with their clothes on.

Perhaps because sunshine is so important to the economy, Croatians are particularly affected by weather. They complain that the once-predictable climate has become erratic, with surprise rainy spells or heat waves in the once perfectly consistent, balmy summer months. Historically, the Dubrovnik senate was legally forbidden from making any major decision if the hot, humid Jugo wind was blowing, as that wind tended to make people cranky and ill-tempered. And today, the weather report includes a *biometeorološka prognoza* that indicates how the day's weather will affect your mood. Weather maps come with smiley or frowny faces, and forecasts predict, "People will be tired in the afternoon and not feel like working." Hmm...good excuse.

Every Croatian coastal town has two parts: The time-warp old town, and the obnoxious resort sprawl. Main drags are clogged

with gift shops selling shell sculptures and tasteless T-shirts. While European visitors enjoy this tacky-trinket tourism, Americans are generally more interested in Old World charm. Fortunately, it's relatively easy to ignore the touristy scene and instead poke your way into twisty old medieval lanes, draped with drying laundry and populated by gossiping neighbors, humble fishermen's taverns, and soccer-playing kids.

Croatian popular music, the mariachi music of Europe, is the ever-present soundtrack of a Dalmatian vacation. Oliver Dragojević—singing soulful Mediterranean ballads with his gravelly, passionate voice—is the Croatian Tom Jones. Known simply as "Oliver," this beloved crooner gets airplay across Europe and has spawned many imitators (such as the almost-as-popular Gibonni).

More traditional is the hauntingly beautiful *klapa* music—men's voices harmonizing a cappella, like barbershop with a sooth-ing Adriatic flavor. Typically the leader begins the song, and the rest of the group (usually 3 to 12 singers) follow behind him with a slight delay. You'll see mariachi-style *klapa* groups performing in touristy areas; a CD of one of these performances (or of a professional group—Cambi is great) is a fun souvenir.

Croatia may be Europe's second most ardently Catholic country (after Poland). Under communism, religion was downplayed and many people gave up the habit of attending Mass regularly. But as the wars raged in the early 1990s, many Croatians rediscovered religion. You may be surprised by how many people you see worshipping in Croatia's churches today.

In the Yugoslav era, Croatia was flooded with tourists—both European and American—who fell in love with its achingly beautiful beaches and coves. In its heyday, Croatia hosted about 10 million visitors a year, who provided the country with about a third of its income. But then, for several years after the war, Croatia floundered. Just a decade ago, the streets of Dubrovnik were empty, lined with souvenir shops tended by desperate-looking vendors. But in the last few years, locals are breathing a sigh of relief as the number of visitors returns to pre-war highs. With astonishing speed, Croatia is becoming one of Europe's top destinations.

Even so, the standards for service (at restaurants, hotels, and so on) can be lower than you might expect. While you'll meet plenty of wonderfully big-hearted Croatians, many of my readers characterize the Croatian waiters or hotel receptionists they've encountered as "gruff" or even "rude." Be prepared for two universal gestures: the classic eye-roll, directed at anyone asking someone to do something that's not precisely in their job description; and the "Croatian Shrug"—a simple gesture meaning, "Don't know, don't care." It helps me to make an attitude adjustment when I cross into Croatia. We're used to thinking, "I should be waited upon." But Croatians think, "This is our world, and you're visiting it...so you can just wait."

Maybe this mindset is understandable, even forgivable. After all, how would you like it if a tidal wave of sweaty, ill-behaved, clueless tourists took over your entire town for the nicest months of each year? (No, I'm not talking about you...but just look around

Croatia Almanac

Official Name: Republika Hrvatska, or just Hrvatska for short.

Snapshot History: After losing their independence to Hungary in 1102, the Croats watched as most of their coastline became Venetian and their interior was conquered by Ottomans. Croatia was "rescued" by the Habsburgs, but after World War I it became part of Yugoslavia—a decision many Croats regretted until they finally gained independence in 1991 through a bitter war with their Serb neighbors.

Population: Of the country's 4.5 million people, 90 percent are ethnic Croats (Catholic) and 4.5 percent are Serbs (Orthodox). (The Serb population was more than double that before the ethnic cleansing of the 1991-1995 war.) About 1.3 percent of Croatians are Bosniak (Muslim). "Croatians" are citizens of Croatia; "Croats" are a distinct ethnic group made up of Catholic South Slavs. So Orthodox Serbs living in Croatia are Croatians (specifically "Croatian Serbs"), but they aren't Croats.

Latitude and Longitude: 45°N and 15°E (similar latitude to Venice, Italy; Ottawa, Canada; or Portland, Oregon).

Area: 22,000 square miles, similar to West Virginia.

Geography: This boomerang-shaped country has two terrains: Stretching north to south is the long, rugged Mediterranean coastline (3,600 miles of beach, including more than 1,100 offshore islands), which is warm and dry. Rising up from the sea are the Dinaric Mountains. To the northeast, beginning at about Zagreb, Croatia's flat, inland "panhandle" (called Slavonia) is an extension of the Great Hungarian Plain, with hot summers and cold winters.

Biggest Cities: The capital, Zagreb (in the northern interior), has 780,000 people; Split (along the Dalmatian Coast) has 178,000; and Rijeka (on the northern coast) has 129,000.

Economy: Much of the country's wealth ($78 billion GDP, $17,400 GDP per capita) comes from tourism, banking, and trade with Italy. Unemployment is a stiff 17 percent.

Currency: 1 kuna (kn, or HRK) = about 20 cents, and 5 kunas = about $1. One kuna is broken down into 100 lipa. Kuna is Croatian for "marten" (a foxlike animal), recalling a time when fur pelts were used as currency. A lipa is a linden tree.

CROATIA

you.) The one-two punch of several decades of communism, followed by a devastating war, wasn't exactly the best preparation for being the perfect host. On the other hand, it can be a bit jarring in a place so dependent upon tourism to find such a stubborn disregard for the fundamentals of hospitality. The good news is that I've noticed some improvement over the last few years. My advice: Expect the worst, then be pleasantly surprised by the posi-

Government: The single-house assembly (Sabor) of 153 legislators is elected by popular vote. The country's prime minister (the head of the majority party in parliament, the center-left Social Democrats) is currently Zoran Milanović; the directly elected (but more figurehead) president is Ivo Josipović (whose first term expires in 2015).

Flag: The flag has three horizontal bands (red on top, white, and blue) with a traditional red-and-white checkerboard shield in the center.

The Average Croatian: The average Croatian will live to age 76 and have 1.4 children. One in four uses the Internet. The average Croatian absolutely adores the soccer team Dinamo Zagreb and absolutely despises Hajduk Split...or vice versa.

Notable Croatians: A pair of big-league historical figures were born in Croatia: Roman Emperor Diocletian (A.D. 245-313) and explorer Marco Polo (1254?-1324). More recently, many Americans whose names end in "-ich" have Croatian roots, including actor John Malkovich and Ohio politicians Dennis Kucinich and John Kasich, not to mention baseball legend Roger Marich...I mean, Maris. More Croatian athletes abound: NBA fans might recognize Toni Kukoč or Gordan Giricek, and at the 2002 and 2006 Winter Olympic Games, the women's downhill skiing events were dominated by Janica Kostelić; her brother Ivica Kostelić medaled in 2006 and 2010. Actor Goran Višnjić (from TV's ER) was born and raised in Croatia, and served in the army as a paratrooper. You've likely never heard of the beloved Croatian sculptor Ivan Meštrović, but you'll see his expressive works all over the country (see page 926). Inventor Nikola Tesla (1856-1943)—who, as a rival of Thomas Edison's, invented alternating current (AC)—was a Croatian-born Serb. And a band of well-dressed 17th-century Croatian soldiers stationed in France gave the Western world a new fashion accessory—the *cravate*, or necktie (for the full story, see page 924).

CROATIA

tive interactions you have, rather than getting hung up on the frustrating ones.

Today's Croatia is crawling with a Babel of international guests speaking German, French, Italian, every accent of English...and a smattering of Croatian. And yet, despite the tourists, this place remains distinctly and stubbornly Croatian. You'd have to search pretty hard to find a McDonald's.

Helpful Hints

Hotel Prices: In this book's Croatian destinations, I've listed rates in euros for ease of comparison—though most hotels expect payment in the local currency, kunas. If you need to convert prices between kunas and euros (7 kunas = about €1), it's simple: just divide the kuna price by 7 to get euros, or multiply the euro price by 7 to get kunas.

Seasonality: Croatia is the most seasonal destination in this book. In a little coastal resort village, a few weeks can mean the difference between being a ghost town or being deluged with crowds. Peak season is July and August, though late June and most of September are becoming nearly as popular. During these busy times, accommodations, boats, and beaches are jam-packed. Shoulder season—the most appealing time to travel here—is late May through mid-June, and late September through early October. During the off-season (mid-October–mid-May), many small towns close down entirely, with only one hotel and one restaurant remaining open during the lean winter months.

Telephones: Mobile phone numbers begin with 091, 098, or 099. Numbers beginning with 060 are pricey toll lines. For more details on how to dial to, from, and within Croatia, see page 1231.

Free Tourist Help by Phone: The "Croatian Angels" service gives free information in English over a toll-free line (tel. 062-999-999, daily June-Aug 8:00–24:00, April-May and Sept-mid-Oct 9:00–17:00, closed mid-Oct–March).

Addresses: Addresses listed with a street name and followed by "b.b." have no street number. In most small towns, locals ignore not only street numbers but also street names—navigate with a map or by asking for directions.

Slick Pavement: Old towns, with their well-polished pavement stones and many slick stairs, can be quite treacherous, especially after a rainstorm. (On a recent trip, one of your co-authors almost broke his arm slipping down a flight of stairs.) Tread with care.

Beaches: Croatia is known for its glimmering beaches. However, most are pebbly or rocky rather than sandy—and spiny sea urchins are not uncommon. In addition to your swimsuit, you may want to pack (or buy in Europe) a pair of water shoes for wading. Bring good sunscreen, and—if you'll be hiking on Croatia's many scenic coastal trails, which can be rugged and often lack shade—also take a sun hat and sturdy shoes.

Siesta: Croatians eat their big meal at lunch, then take a traditional Mediterranean siesta. This means that many stores, museums, and churches are closed in the mid-afternoon.

CROATIA

Business Closures on Sundays: During the busier tourist months, from June through December, stores are allowed to be open on Sundays. Off-season, from January through May, most shops are legally required to close.

Land Mine Warning: Certain parts of the Croatian interior were once full of land mines. Most of these mines have been removed, and fields that may still be dangerous are usually clearly marked. As a precaution, if you're in a former war zone, stay on roads and paths, and don't go wandering through overgrown fields and deserted villages.

Croatian Accommodation

For most travelers, Croatian hotels are a bad value. You basically have two options: over-the-top, fancy, overpriced splurge hotels catering to the international jet-set crowd; or run-down, communist-era, overpriced resort hotels desperate for a renovation. Whether old or new, Croatian hotels all seem to carry on the old Yugoslav aesthetic of mass tourism. That means crowded "beach" access (often on a concrete pad), typically surly staff, a travel-agency desk selling excursions in the lobby, corny live music in the lounge a few nights each week, and a seaview apéritif bar. More money buys you a friendlier, more polished staff and newer decor.

Fortunately, the void of mid-range sleeps is filled perfectly by what locals call "private accommodations": a rented apartment (*apartman*, plural *apartmani*) or a room in a private home (*soba*, pronounced SOH-bah; plural *sobe*, SOH-bay). Private accommodations offer travelers a characteristic and money-saving alternative for a fraction of the price of a hotel.

Often run by empty-nesters, private accommodations are similar to British bed-and-breakfasts...minus the breakfast (ask your host about the best nearby breakfast spot). Generally the more you pay, the more privacy and amenities you get: private bathroom, TV, air-conditioning, kitchenette, and so on. The fanciest *sobe* are downright swanky and offer near-hotel anonymity. Apartments are bigger and cost more than *sobe*, but they're still far cheaper than hotels.

Registered *sobe* are rated by the government using a system that assigns stars based on amenities. Three or more stars means that you'll have your own bathroom, two stars puts the bathroom down the hall, and one star is rock-bottom basic. (Apartments always have private bathrooms, plus modest kitchen facilities.) Many, but not all, three-star *sobe* also have TV and air-conditioning (but usually no telephone). The prices for private accommodations generally fluctuate with the seasons; stays of fewer than three nights usually come with a 20-50 percent surcharge (though this is often waived outside peak season).

CROATIA

Getting Around the Dalmatian Coast

Although it's a long haul from the other destinations in this book, the Dalmatian Coast is well worth it: It's the cherry on top of your grand Eastern European adventure. To reach the Dalmatian Coast, you can drive or take the bus (about five hours on the A1 expressway from Zagreb to Split); take a train (about 6 hours from Zagreb to Split); or catch a flight (Croatia Airlines often has reasonable deals—see www.croatiaairlines.com—but also check low-cost carriers, using the search engine at www.skyscanner.net). Once on the coast, you'll rely on boats, buses, or a rental car. The following tips are useful for connecting Dubrovnik, Split, and Korčula (covered in the next three chapters); for specifics, I've listed the most useful boat and bus departures in the "Connections" section for each destination.

By Boat: Plodding car ferries and speedy catamarans inexpensively shuttle tourists between major coastal cities and quiet island towns. Boat rides are cheap for deck passengers. A short hop, such as from Split to the island of Korčula, costs around $5-10; for a longer trip, such as from Split to Dubrovnik, figure $20. Most of the ferries are run by Jadrolinija, which conveniently connects the three destinations in this book plus a

lot more (www.jadrolinija.hr). Advance reservations are not necessary for deck passengers; you can almost always find a seat on the deck or in the on-board café. You can't reserve a space for a car, so in peak season, drivers will want to arrive at the boat early (ask the local TI what time you should arrive). The faster, passenger-only catamarans are run by smaller companies. These include the *Krilo* between Split, Hvar, and Korčula (www.krilo.hr); and the *Nona Ana* between Dubrovnik and Korčula (www.gv-line.hr). Because space is limited on the catamarans, it's essential to buy your tickets as early as possible (I've suggested strate-

Since the best-value *sobe* deservedly book up early, reservations are highly recommended. For the *sobe* listed in this book, **always book direct.** Many of my recommended *sobe* are listed on room-booking websites (Booking.com is especially popular), but going through a middleman costs your host an extra 15 percent commission and gains you absolutely nothing. Do your hosts a favor and email or phone *sobe* directly to request reservations; it's also an opportunity to ask any questions you have about the accommodations, and to start to get to know your host.

Once you've reserved, keep in mind that your host loses money if you don't show up. For this reason, some hosts may request your

gies for each destination). Then, to get a good seat on board, it's wise to show up 30-60 minutes before departure time. The boat schedule information in this book changes every year, without fail. It's essential to confirm before you make your plans. Jadrolinija's website (www.jadrolinija.hr) is useful, but they don't post future schedules very far in advance. Once again, local TIs are the single best source of information for how their town is connected to the rest of the coast.

By Bus: Buses can be a good way to connect destinations when there are gaps in the boat schedule, even for islands. Confusingly, a single bus route can be operated by a variety of different companies, making it difficult to find comprehensive schedules (though Split has a handy online timetable: www.ak-split.hr). Confirm schedules with a local TI or bus station. Prices vary among companies, even for identical journeys. For popular routes during peak season, drop by the station to buy your ticket a few hours—or even days—in advance to ensure getting a seat (ask the bus station ticket office or the local TI how far ahead you should arrive). You'll pay about $2 per bag to stow your luggage under the bus. If you're headed south along the coast, sitting on the right side comes with substantially better scenery (sit on the left for northbound buses). When choosing a seat, also take the direction of the sun into consideration.

By Car: Considering the long distances, cheap and frequent buses, long ferry lines for cars (as opposed to quick and fun connections for walk-ons), and worthlessness of a car in Dubrovnik or Split, those simply lacing together the major sights are better off without a car. Drivers should be prepared for twisty seaside roads, wonderful views, and plenty of tempting stopovers. As you approach any town, follow the signs to *Centar* (usually also signed with a bull's-eye symbol). Note that Croatia's expressway extends only as far south as the town of Ploce, about 80 miles south of Split; from there, you'll take the slower coastal road. For detailed route tips on driving in Dalmatia, see page 947; for driving to Mostar, see page 1093.

credit-card number to secure the reservation. (They'll generally ask for payment in cash when you're there; your credit card won't

be charged.) Other hosts might ask you to wire or mail money as a deposit. Because wiring money can come with substantial fees—which you (rather than the *sobe* host) will incur—it usually works better to mail them a check or travelers check. Ask your *sobe* host which options they accept. If the request seems too complicated for you, reserve elsewhere.

If you like to travel spontaneously, during most of the year you'll have no problem finding *sobe* as you go (late July and August are the exceptions). Locals hawking rooms meet each arriving boat, bus, and train. Many of these *sobe* have not been vetted by the government, but they can sometimes turn out to be a good deal. In fact, I've found some of my favorite *sobe* in this book this way. The person generally shows photos of her place, you haggle for a price, then she escorts you to your new home. Be sure you understand exactly where it's located (i.e., within easy walking distance of the attractions) before you accept—ask to see the location on a map, and find out how long it takes to walk into town.

You can also keep an eye out for rooms as you walk or drive through town—you'll see blue *sobe* and *apartmani* signs everywhere. It's actually fun to visit a few homes and make a deal. While it takes nerve to just show up without a room, this is standard operating procedure for backpackers.

As a last resort, you can enlist the help of a travel agency to find you a room—but you'll pay 10-30 percent extra (various agencies are listed in this book; to search from home, try www.dubrovnik apartmentsource.com for Dubrovnik, or www.adriatica.net for all of Croatia).

Discos and nightclubs are proliferating in the old town centers of many cities in this book—including Dubrovnik, Split, and Ljubljana. I've noted the specific hotels that suffer the worst noise. If you're a light sleeper, make a point of requesting a quiet room. And bring earplugs.

If there seems to be no hot water, try flipping the switch with a picture of a water tank, usually next to the light switch. In many *sobe,* the hot-water tank is tiny—barely big enough for one American-length shower. So two people traveling together may want to practice the "navy shower" method (douse yourself, turn off water, soap up, then turn water back on for a quick rinse)...or the second one may be in for a chilly surprise. The incredibly high water pressure in most Croatian showers just makes the hot water go that much faster (turn the faucet on only partway to help stretch the precious hot water).

I'm accustomed to staying in hotels. But a few years ago, I found all the hotels in Dubrovnik booked up. With some trepidation, I stayed in a *soba*...and I'll never go back to a Croatian resort hotel again. I've made it my mission to convince you to sleep in *sobe,* too.

CROATIA

Croatian History

For nearly a millennium, bits and pieces of what we today call "Croatia" were batted back and forth between foreign powers: Hungarians, Venetians, Ottomans, Habsburgs, and Yugoslavs. Only in 1991 did Croatia (violently) regain its independence.

Early History

Croatia's first inhabitants were the Illyrians (ancestors of today's Albanians). During antiquity, the Greeks and Romans both sailed ships up and down the strategic Dalmatian Coast, founding many towns that still exist today, and littering the Adriatic seabed with shipwrecks. Romans built larger settlements on the Dalmatian Coast as early as 229 B.C., and in the fourth century A.D., Emperor Diocletian built his retirement palace in the coastal town of Split. As Rome fell in the fifth century, Slavs (the ancestors of today's Croatians) and other barbarians flooded Europe. The northern part of Croatia's coast fell briefly under the Byzantines, who slathered churches with shimmering mosaics (the best are in the Euphrasian Basilica in Poreč, Istria).

Beginning in the seventh century, Slavic Croats began to control most of the land that is today's Croatia. In A.D. 925, the Dalmatian Duke Tomislav united the disparate Croat tribes into a single kingdom. By consolidating and extending Croat-held territory and centralizing power, Tomislav created the first "Croatia."

Loss of Independence

By the early 12th century, the Croatian kings had died out, and neighboring powers (Hungary, Venice, and Byzantium) threatened the Croats. For the sake of self-preservation, Croatia entered an alliance with the Hungarians in 1102, and for the next 900 years, the Croats were ruled by foreign states. The Hungarians gradually took more and more power from the Croats, exerting control over the majority of inland Croatia. Meanwhile, the Venetian Republic conquered most of the coast and peppered the Croatian Adriatic with bell towers and statues of St. Mark. Through it all, the tiny Republic of Dubrovnik flourished—paying off whomever necessary to maintain its independence and becoming one of Europe's most important shipbuilding and maritime powers...a plucky rival to powerful Venice.

The Ottomans conquered most of inland Croatia in the 15th century and challenged the Venetians—unsuccessfully—for control of the coastline. Most of the stout walls, fortresses, and other fortifications you'll see all along the Croatian coast date from this time, built by the Venetians to defend against Ottoman attack. In the 17th century, the Habsburgs forced the Ottomans out of inland Croatia. Then, after Venice and Dubrovnik fell to Napoleon in the early 19th century, the coast also went to the Habsburgs—beginning a long tradition of Austrians basking on Croatian beaches.

The Yugoslav Era, World War II, and the Ustaše

When the Austro-Hungarian Empire broke up at the end of World War I, the Croats banded together with the Serbs, Slovenes, and Bosnians in the union that would become Yugoslavia. But virtually as soon as Yugoslavia was formed, many Croats began to fear that the Serbs would steer Yugoslavia to their own purposes. So when the Nazis invaded and installed a puppet government—run by the homegrown, fascist Ustaše party—many Croats supported them, believing that fascism could provide them with greater independence. Under the watchful eye of the Nazis, the Ustaše operated one of the most brutal Nazi puppet states during World War II, the misnamed "Independent State of Croatia" (which also controlled most of today's Slovenia and Bosnia). Ustaše concentration camps were used to murder not only Jews and Roma (Gypsies), but also Serbs. Hot-tempered debate rages even today about how many Serbs died at the hands of the Ustaše—estimates vary wildly, from 25,000 to over a million, but most legitimate historians put the number in the hundreds of thousands.

Cardinal Alojzije Stepinac was one Croat who made the mistake of backing the Ustaše. By most accounts, Stepinac was a mild-mannered, extremely devout man who didn't agree with the extremism of the Ustaše...but also did little to fight it. Following the war, Stepinac was arrested, tried, and imprisoned, dying under house arrest in 1960. In the years since, Stepinac has become a martyr for Catholics and Croat nationalists. Even though he's the single most revered figure of Croatian Catholicism, Stepinac remains highly unpopular among Serbs.

At the end of World War II, the Ustaše and the Nazis were forced out by Yugoslavia's homegrown Partisan Army, led by a charismatic war hero named Josip Broz, who went by his nickname, "Tito." Tito became "president for life," and Croatia once again became part of a united Yugoslavia. The union would hold together for more than 40 years, until it broke apart under Serbian President Slobodan Milošević and Croatian President Franjo Tudman.

For more details on Yugoslavia and its breakup, see the Understanding Yugoslavia chapter.

Independence Regained

Croatia's declaration of independence from Yugoslavia in 1991 was met with fear and anger on the part of its more than half-million Serb residents. Even before independence, the first volleys of a bloody war had been fired. The war had two phases: First, in 1991, Croatian Serbs declared independence from the new nation of Croatia, forming their own state and forcing out or murdering any Croats in "their" territory (with the thinly disguised support of Slobodan Milošević). Then a tense cease-fire fell over the region until 1995, when the second phase of the war ignited: Croatia pushed back through the Serb-dominated territory, reclaiming it for Croatia and forcing out or murdering Serbs living there.

Imagine becoming an independent nation after nine centuries of foreign domination. Croatians seized their hard-earned freedom with a nationalist fervor that bordered on fascism. It was a heady and absurd time, which today's Croatians recall with disbelief, sadness...and maybe a tinge of nostalgia.

In the Croatia of the early 1990s, even the most bizarre notions seemed possible. Croatia's first post-Yugoslav president, the extreme nationalist Franjo Tuđman (see sidebar on page 830), proposed implausible directives for the new nation—such as privatizing all of the nation's resources and handing them over to 200 super-elite families (which, thankfully for everyone else, never happened). The government began calling the language "Croatian" rather than "Serbo-Croatian" and created new words from specifically Croat roots. The Croats even briefly considered replacing the Roman alphabet with the ninth-century Glagolitic script to invoke Croat culture and further differentiate Croatian from Serbia's Cyrillic alphabet. Fortunately for tourists, this plan didn't take off.

After Tuđman's death in 1999, Croatia began the new millennium with a more truly democratic leader, Stipe Mesić. The popular Mesić, who was once aligned with Tuđman, had split off and formed his own political party when Tuđman's politics grew too extreme. Tuđman spent years tampering with the constitution to give himself more and more power, but when Mesić took over, he reversed those changes and handed more authority back to the parliament.

Croatia Today

In 2003, Croatia applied for membership in the European Union. It cleared the final hurdles in the summer of 2011, and—assuming all goes as scheduled—is slated to officially join the EU on July 1, 2013.

Croatia's road to EU membership has been rocky. Initially, Croatia's biggest barrier was its human-rights record during the recent war. Several Croatian officers were indicted for war crimes by the International Criminal Tribunal for the Former Yugoslavia (ICTY) in The Hague, Netherlands. But many Croatians feel that the soldiers branded as "war criminals" by The Hague are instead

Franjo Tuđman
(1922-1999)

Independent Croatia's first president was the controversial Franjo Tuđman (FRAHN-yoh TOOJ-mahn). Tuđman began his career fighting for Tito on the left, but later had a dramatic ideological swing to the far right. His anticommunist, highly nationalistic HDZ party was the driving force for Croatian statehood, making him the young nation's first hero. But even as he fought for independence from Yugoslavia, his own ruling style grew more and more authoritarian. Today Tuđman remains a polemical figure.

Before entering politics, Tuđman was a military officer (he fought for the Partisans in World War II, and later became the youngest general in the Yugoslav People's Army) and a historian. Tuđman revered the Ustaše, Croatia's Nazi-affiliated government during World War II, who murdered hundreds of thousands of Serbs and Jews in concentration camps. (Because the Ustaše governed the first "independent" Croatian state since the 12th century, Tuđman figured that these quasi-Nazis were the original Croatian "freedom fighters.") When Croatia voted for independence and Tuđman was elected president in 1990, he immediately reintroduced many Ustaše symbols, including their currency (the kuna, still used today). His actions raised eyebrows worldwide, and raised alarms in Croatia's Serb communities.

Tuđman espoused many of the same single-minded attitudes about ethnic divisions as the ruthless Serbian leader Slobodan Milošević. Croat forces—which may or may not have been acting under Tuđman's orders—carried out wide-scale ethnic cleansing, targeting Serb and Muslim minorities. Tuđman and Milošević had secret, Hitler-and-Stalin-esque negotiations even as they were ripping into each other rhetorically. According to some reports, at one meeting they drew a map of Bosnia-Herzegovina on a cocktail napkin, then drew lines divvying up

heroes of their war of independence. The highest-profile Croatian figure to be arrested was Ante Gotovina, a lieutenant general accused of atrocities against Serb civilians. After four years in hiding, Gotovina was found and arrested in Spain in December 2005 and sent to stand trial in The Hague; he was convicted and sentenced to a prison term in April 2011. As a sign of support, photos of Gotovina have appeared in towns throughout Croatia. Gotovina's name means "cash." Many Croatians grouse, "To get into the EU, we have to pay cash *(gotovina)*!"

GENERAL
ANTE GOTOVINA

Later in the process, when it was time for current EU mem-

the country between themselves. Their so-called "Karađorđevo Agreement" completely left out the Bosniaks, who constituted the largest ethnic group within the nation whose fate was being decided. When Tuđman's successor moved into the president's office, he discovered a top-secret hotline to Milošević's desk.

To ensure that he stayed in power, Tuđman played fast and loose with his new nation's laws. He was notorious for changing the constitution as it suited him. By the late 1990s, when his popularity was slipping, Tuđman extended Croatian citizenship to anyone in the world who had Croatian heritage—a ploy aimed at getting votes from Croats living in Bosnia-Herzegovina, who were sure to line up with him on the far right.

Through it all, Tuđman kept a tight grip on the media, making it illegal to report anything that would disturb the public—even if true. When Croatians turned on their TV sets and saw the flag flapping in the breeze to the strains of the national anthem, they knew something was up...and switched to CNN to get the real story. In this oppressive environment, many bright, young Croatians fled the country, causing a "brain drain" that hampered the postwar recovery.

Tuđman died of cancer at the end of 1999. While history will probably judge him harshly, the opinion in today's Croatia is qualified. Most agree that Tuđman was an important and even admirable figure in the struggle for Croatian statehood, but he ultimately went too far and got too greedy. Tuđman's political party is still active, frequently naming streets, squares, and bridges for this "hero" of Croatian nationalism. The most elaborate tomb in Zagreb's national cemetery (Mirogoj) honors this "Croatian founding father." And yet, if he were alive, Tuđman would be standing trial before the International Criminal Tribunal in The Hague.

bers to approve Croatia's accession, spunky Slovenia (one of the smallest EU members) flexed its mighty little muscles. For years, Croatia and Slovenia have wrangled over some disputed borders (most notably, the border through the middle of the Bay of Piran). In 2009, when Croatia needed Slovenia's support to join the EU, the Slovenes said, "Not so fast..." and vetoed Croatia's EU bid for 10 months. (Eventually US Secretary of State Hilary Clinton intervened, and cooler heads prevailed.) The EU dust-up has contributed to a palpable friction between the Croatians and Slovenes. On my last trip, when I'd show people the cover of my *Croatia & Slovenia* book, people in both countries expressed displeasure that they were grouped together. Ironically, even Croatians who are vehemently opposed to EU membership are bugged that Slovenia tried to prevent it.

Some Croatians remain skeptical about joining the EU for other reasons. One Croatian said to me, "We were just badly divorced. We're not ready to be married again." For the other countries that recently joined the EU, a concern with EU membership was that the new members' citizens would flood to the West. Some Croatians are worried about the opposite: Westerners buying up Adriatic beachfront property.

Perhaps not surprisingly for a post-communist country, Croatia's government can be excessively bureaucratic. Expats who want to work here find it a tough place to do business. Laws tend to be implemented, then quickly overturned. In the last few years, a ban on shops being open on Sundays, a smoking ban, and a zero blood-alcohol limit for drivers have all come and gone. (The last one was contested by priests, who pointed out that if the blood-alcohol limit is zero, parishioners can't take the wine at communion.) The country also has a penchant for corruption—perhaps best embodied by Croatia's previous prime minister, Ivo Sanader, who served from 2003 to 2009. After abruptly resigning, he was eventually arrested in Austria and extradited to Croatia in 2010 to stand trial for corruption charges.

After a successful decade as president, the term-limited Stipe Mesić stepped down in 2010. Ivo Josipović, running on a strong anti-corruption platform, won by a landslide, and within months had exceeded his predecessor's already high popularity rating. With EU membership on the horizon and some of the growing pains of new nationhood behind it, Croatia seems poised for an ever-brighter future.

Croatian Food

Croatian food is good, but tends to be fairly expensive and unimaginative—and all too often comes with less than cheerful service.

The country's tourist board has gone to great lengths to promote its cuisine and wines as major components of any trip— inflating the culinary dreams of some visitors, only to leave them disappointed by the reality of Croatian restaurants. Adjust your expectations and you'll eat well here—it ain't Tuscany, but it ain't bad, either.

Like its people, the food in Croatia's different regions has been shaped by various influences—predominantly Italian, Turkish, and Hungarian. And yet, the cuisine here is surprisingly uniform: 90 percent of coastal restaurants have a similar menu of seafood, pasta, and pizza. Because it's so easy to get into a culinary rut here, I've also tried to recommend a few more exotic alternatives.

Two staples of Croatian food, as in most Mediterranean lands, are wine and olive oil. You'll see vineyards and olive groves blanketing the Croatian countryside and islandscapes. Croatians joke that grapes are like a new bride—they demand a lot of attention, while olives are like a mother—low-maintenance. Another major part of the local diet is the air-dried ham called *pršut* (a.k.a. prosciutto—see sidebar on page 708).

While you'll find places called *restaurant*, you'll more often see the name *konoba*—which means an unpretentious traditional restaurant, like an inn. To request a menu, say, *"Meni, molim"* (MEH-nee, MOH-leem; "Menu, please"). To get the attention of your waiter, say *"Konobar"* (KOH-noh-bahr; "Waiter"). When he brings your food, he'll likely say, *"Dobar tek!"* ("Enjoy your meal!"). When you're ready for the bill, ask for the *račun* (RAH-choon).

Main Dishes

On the coast, seafood is a specialty, and the Italian influence is obvious. According to Dalmatians, "Eating meat is food; eating fish is pleasure." They also say that a fish should swim three times: first in the sea, then in olive oil, and finally in wine—when you eat it. If you see something described as "Dalmatian-style," it usually means with lots of olive oil, parsley, and garlic.

You can get all kinds of seafood: fish, scampi, mussels, squid, octopus, you name it. At fish restaurants, seafood is often priced by weight—either by kilogram or by hectogram (100 grams, or one-tenth of a kilogram). A one-kilogram portion feeds two hungry people or three light eaters. While this is a land of fisherfolk, frozen fish is not unheard of—if you want something fresh from the market, ask. When ordering, be prepared for surprises. For example, *škampi* (shrimp) often come still in their shells (sometimes with crayfish-like claws), which can be messy and time-consuming to eat. Before you order shrimp, ask if it's shelled. The menu item called "small fried fish" is generally a plate of deep-fried minnows. If you're not clear on exactly what something is, feel free to ask for clarification (though some waiters are more forthcoming than others).

Sometimes it's a pleasant surprise. Many menu items that

don't sound appetizing can be delicious. Jump at the chance to sample a good, fresh anchovy—which, when done right, has a pleasant flavor and a melt-in-your-mouth texture that's a world away from the salty, withered little fish you might find topping a pizza back home. Those not accustomed to

Croatian Wine

The quality of Croatia's wine was devastated by the phylloxera epidemic in the late 19th century, and further declined under the communists, when much of the indus-try was state-run and focused on mass production. Today vintner families are returning to their roots—literally—and bringing quality back to Croatian wine. Thanks partly to the interest and invest-ment of American vintners, Croatian wine are gaining respect worldwide. Because very few Croatian wines are exported, this is a good chance for wine-lovers to sample some new tastes.

The northern part of the country primarily produces whites *(bijelo vino)*, usually dry *(suho)* but sometimes semi-dry *(polusuho)* or sweet *(slatko)*. The sunny mountains just north of Zagreb are cov-ered with vineyards producing whites. From Slavonia (Croatia's inland panhandle), you'll find *graševina*—crisp, dry, and acidic (like Welsh Riesling); Krauthaker and Enjingi are well-respected brands. The Istrian Peninsula corks up some good whites, includ-ing *malvazija*, a very popular, light, mid-range wine (Muscat is also popular).

As you move south, along the Dalmatian Coast, the wines turn red—which Croatians call "black wine" *(crno vino,* TSUR-noh VEE-noh). The most common grape here is *plavac mali* ("lit-tle blue")—a distant relative of Californian Zinfandel and Italian *primitivo* grapes. Generally speaking, the best coastal reds are produced on the long Pelješac Peninsula, across from Korčula (the most well-respected regions are Dingač and Postup). But each island also produces its own good wines. Korčula makes excellent white wine from *pošip* grapes (especially near the vil-

eating octopus might want to try octopus salad—a flavorful mix of octopus, tomatoes, onions, and spices (pictured on previous page). In the interior, trout is popular.

If you're not a seafood-eater, there are plenty of meat options. A delicious Dalmatian specialty is *pašticada*—braised beef in a slightly sweet wine-and-herb sauce, usually served with gnocchi. Dalmatia is also known for its mutton. Since the lambs graze on salty seaside herbs, the meat—often served on a spit—has a dis-tinctive flavor. The most widely available meat dish is the "mixed grill"—a combination of various Balkan grilled meats, best accom-panied by the eggplant-and-red-pepper condiment *ajvar* (see the "Balkan Flavors" sidebar on page 1090).

lages of Čara and Smokvica), as well as *grk* and *korčulanka*. Hvar has *bogdanuša*.

When looking at wine labels, watch for these three official classifications: *stolno* ("table," the lowest grade), *kvalitento* ("quality"—actually mid-range), and *vrhunsko* (top-quality). In general, if only the grape is listed (e.g., *mali plavac*), the quality isn't as good as when the region is prominently noted (e.g., Dingač or Postup)—though there are some exceptions (Miljenko Grgić, described next, produces a top-tier red, with mostly Dingač grapes, that he markets as simply *plavac mali*). You may also see the words *vinogorje* (vineyard) and *položaj* (location).

The big name in Croatian wines is Miljenko Grgić. Born in Croatia in 1923, Grgić emigrated from communist Yugoslavia to the US and—as "Mike Grgich"—worked at the Chateau Montelena in Napa Valley. In the famous so-called "Judgment of Paris" in 1976, Grgić's 1973 Chardonnay beat out several well-respected French wines in a blind taste test. Considered a turning point in the winemaking world, this event brought new respect to American winemakers and put Napa on the *mapa*.

Having revolutionized American winemaking, Grgić turned his sights on his Croatian homeland. He imported know-how (not to mention equipment) from California to the slopes of the Pelješac Peninsula, where he set about to making some of Croatia's first truly well-respected wines. Grgić grows his red *plavac mali* on the Pelješac Peninsula (at Dingač and nearby, at Trstanik), and his white *pošip* wine on Korčula Island. The prices for Grgić's wines match his reputation; for producers that are comparable but a bit more affordable, look for these red-wine alternatives: Madirazza (they make a great Postup), Frano Miloš (try the full-bodied Stagnum), and Matuško and Skaramuća (good Dingač). Philipp, by a famously meticulous Swiss-Croatian vintner, produces a good Postup, as well as fine summer white that blends Rukatac and Chardonnay.

The best meat dish in Croatia is veal or lamb prepared under a *peka*—a metal baking lid that's covered with red-hot coals, to allow the meat to gradually cook to tender perfection. (*Ispod peka*

means "under the bell.") Available only in traditional restaurants, this dish typically must be ordered in advance and for multiple people. You'll also find a break from seafood in the north (Zagreb) and east (Slavonia), where the food has more of a Hungarian flavor—heavy on meat served with cabbage, noodles, or potatoes.

Budget-conscious tourists reserve meat and fish for splurge dinners and mostly dine on cheaper and faster pastas and pizzas. You'll see familiar dishes, such as spaghetti Bolognese (with meat sauce) and spaghetti carbonara (with a sauce of egg, parmesan, and bacon), gnocchi (*njoki,* potato dumplings), and lasagna. Risotto (*rižoto,* a rice dish) is popular here; most common is "black risotto," mixed with squid ink and various kinds of seafood.

Side Dishes

There are many good local varieties of cheese made with sheep's or goat's milk. Pag, an island in the Kvarner Gulf, produces a famous, very salty, fairly dry sheep's-milk cheese *(paški sir),* which is said to be flavored by the herbs the sheep eat.

A common side dish is boiled potatoes and mangold *(blitva),* similar to Swiss chard. When ordering salad, choose between mixed (typically shredded cabbage, tomatoes, and maybe some beets and a little lettuce) or green (mostly lettuce). Throughout Croatia, salad is typically served with the main dish unless you request that it be brought beforehand.

Dessert and Beverages

For dessert, look no further than the mountains of delicious, homemade ice cream *(sladoled)* that line every street in Dalmatia.

I've worked hard to sample and recommend the best ice-cream parlors in each town. (Poor me.) Dalmatia's typical dessert is a flan-like, crème caramel custard, called *rozata. Prošek* is a sweet dessert wine.

Water is *voda,* and mineral water is *mineralna voda.* Jamnica is the main Croatian brand of bottled water, but you'll also see Bistra and Studenac. Many restaurants—especially fancier ones—might not want to bring you a glass of tap water, but you can try asking for *voda iz slavine.* For coffee *(kava),* the easiest choice is *bijela kava* (BEE-yeh-lah KAH-vah)—"white coffee," or espresso with lots of milk (similar to a *caffè latte*). To get it black, ask for *crna kava* (TSUR-nah KAH-vah).

The most popular Croatian beers *(pivo)* are Ožujsko and Karlovačko, but you'll also see the Slovenian brand Laško (which is also brewed here in Croatia). Fans of dark beer *(crno pivo)* enjoy Tomislav. Most places also serve non-alcoholic beers *(bezalkoholno pivo);* most common are Ožujsko Cool and Stella Artois NA.

Even more beloved in Croatia is wine (*vino;* see "Croatian

Wine" sidebar, page 834). Along the coast, locals find it refreshing to drink wine mixed with mineral water (called, as in English, *špricer*). When toasting with some new Croatian friends, raise your glass with a hearty *"Živjeli!"* (ZHEE-vyeh-lee).

Croatian Language

Croatian was once known as "Serbo-Croatian," the official language of Yugoslavia. Most Yugoslav republics—including Croatia, Serbia, and Bosnia-Herzegovina—spoke this same language (though Slovene is quite different). And while each of these countries has tried to distance its language from that of its neighbors since the war, the languages spoken in all of these places are still very similar. The biggest difference is in the writing: Croatians and Bosniaks use our Roman alphabet, while Serbs use Cyrillic letters.

In recent years, Croatia has attempted to artificially make its vocabulary different from Serbian. A decade ago, you'd catch a plane at the *aerodrom*. Today, you'll catch that same flight at the *zračna luka*—a new coinage that combines the old Croatian words for "air" and "port." These new words, once created, are actively injected into the lexicon. Croatians watching their favorite TV show will suddenly hear a character use a word they've never heard before...and think, "Oh, we have another new word." In this way, Croatian really is becoming quite different from Serbian (in much the same way Norwegian evolved apart from Swedish a century ago).

Here are some tips for Croatian pronunciation:

J / j sounds like "y" as in "yellow"

C / c sounds like "ts" as in "cats"

Č / č and **Ć / ć** sound like "ch" as in "chicken"

Š / š sounds like "sh" as in "shrimp"

Ž / ž sounds like "zh" as in "leisure"

Đ / đ is like the "dj" sound in "jeans" (often replaced with **dj** in English)

Croatian has the same tricky consonant combinations as in Slovene, most notably hv (as in *hvala*, "thank you") and nj (as in Rovinj). Don't over-pronounce these. For **hv,** the h is nearly silent—it's easiest just to omit the h (for *hvala*, just say "VAH-lah," not "huh-VAH-lah"). In the combination **nj,** the j is mostly silent, with a slight "y" sound that can be omitted: Rovinj sounds like roh-VEEN.

When attempting to pronounce an unfamiliar word, remember that the accent is usually on the first syllable (and never on the last). Confusingly, Croatian pronunciation—even of the same word—can vary in different parts of the country. This is because modern Croatian has three distinct dialects, called Kajkavian,

Shtokavian, and Chakavian—based on how you say "what?" (*kaj?*, *što?*, and *ča?*, respectively). That's a lot of variety for a language with only five million speakers.

For a smoother trip, take some time to learn a few Croatian survival phrases (listed on page 1271).

As you navigate through Croatia, these words might help: *trg* (pronounced "turg," square), *ulica* (OO-leet-sah, road), *cesta* (TSEH-stah, avenue), *autocesta* (OW-toh-tseh-stah, expressway), *most* (mohst, bridge), *otok* (OH-tohk, island), *trajekt* (TRAH-yehkt, ferry), and *Jadran* (YAH-drahn, Adriatic).

DUBROVNIK

Dubrovnik is a living fairy tale that shouldn't be missed. It feels like a small town today, but 500 years ago, Dubrovnik was a major maritime power, with the third-biggest navy in the Mediterranean. Still jutting confidently into the sea and ringed by thick medieval walls, Dubrovnik deserves its nickname: the Pearl of the Adriatic. Within the ramparts, the traffic-free Old Town is a fun jumble of quiet, cobbled back lanes; low-impact museums; narrow, steep alleys; and kid-friendly squares. After all these centuries, the buildings still hint at old-time wealth, and the central promenade (Stradun) remains the place to see and be seen. If I had to pick just one place to visit in Croatia, this would be it.

The city's charm is the sleepy result of its no-nonsense past. Busy merchants, the salt trade, and shipbuilding made Dubrovnik rich. But the city's most valued commodity was always its freedom—even today, you'll see the proud motto *Libertas* displayed all over town (see *"Libertas"* sidebar).

Dubrovnik flourished in the 15th and 16th centuries, but an earthquake destroyed nearly everything in 1667. Most of today's buildings in the Old Town are post-quake Baroque, although a few palaces, monasteries, and convents displaying a rich Gothic-Renaissance mix survive from Dubrovnik's earlier Golden Age. Dubrovnik remained a big tourist draw through the Tito years, bringing in much-needed hard currency from Western visitors. Consequently, the city was never given the hard socialist patina of other Yugoslav cities (such as the nearby Montenegrin capital Podgorica, then known as "Titograd").

As Croatia violently separated from Yugoslavia in 1991, Dubrovnik became the only coastal city to be pulled into the

Libertas

Libertas—liberty—has always been close to the heart of every Dubrovnik citizen. Dubrovnik was a proudly independent republic for centuries, even as most of Croatia became Venetian and Hungarian. Dubrovnik believed so strongly in *libertas* that it was the first foreign state in 1776 to officially recognize an upstart, experimental republic called the United States of America.

In the Middle Ages, the city-state of Dubrovnik (then called Ragusa) bought its independence from whoever was strongest— Byzantium, Venice, Hungary, the Ottomans—sometimes paying off more than one at a time. Dubrovnik's ships flew whichever flags were necessary to stay free, earning the nickname "Town of Seven Flags." It was sort of a Hong Kong of the Middle Ages—a spunky, trading-oriented statelet that maintained its sovereignty while being completely surrounded by an often-hostile mega-state (in Dubrovnik's case, the Ottoman Empire). As time went on, Europe's big-league nations were glad to have a second major seafaring power in the Adriatic to balance the Venetian threat; Dubrovnik emerged as an attractive alternative at times when Venetian ports were blockaded by the Ottomans. A free Dubrovnik was more valuable than a pillaged, plundered Dubrovnik.

In 1808, Napoleon conquered the Adriatic and abolished the Republic of Dubrovnik. After Napoleon was defeated, the fate of the continent was decided at the Congress of Vienna. But Dubrovnik's delegate was denied a seat at the table. The more powerful nations, no longer concerned about Venice and fed up after years of being sweet-talked by Dubrovnik, were afraid that the delegate would play old alliances off each other to re-establish an independent Republic of Dubrovnik. Instead, the city became a part of the Habsburg Empire and entered a long period of decline.

Libertas still hasn't died in Dubrovnik. In the surreal days of the early 1990s, when Yugoslavia was reshuffling itself, a movement for the creation of a new Republic of Dubrovnik gained some momentum (led by a judge who, in earlier times, had convicted others for the same ideas). Another movement pushed for Dalmatia to secede as its own nation. But now that the dust has settled, today's locals are content and proud to be part of an independent Republic of Croatia.

DUBROVNIK

fighting (see "The Siege of Dubrovnik" sidebar). Imagine having your youthful memories of good times spent romping in the surrounding hills replaced by visions of tanks and warships shelling your hometown. The city was devastated, but Dubrovnik has been repaired with amazing speed. The only physical reminders of the war are lots of new, bright-orange roof tiles. Locals, relieved the fighting is over but forever hardened, are often willing to talk openly about the experience with visitors—offering a rare opportunity to grasp the harsh realities of war from an eyewitness perspective.

Though the war killed tourism in the 1990s, today the crowds are most decidedly back—even exceeding prewar levels. In fact, Dubrovnik's biggest downside is the overwhelming midday crush of multinational tourists who converge on the Old Town when their cruise ships dock. These days the city's economy is based almost entirely on tourism, and most locals have moved to the suburbs so they can rent their Old Town apartments to travelers. All of this can make the Old Town feel, at times, like a very pretty but soulless theme park. Dubrovnik lacks the gritty real-world vibe of Split or the charming local vitality of Ljubljana. But, like Venice, Dubrovnik rewards those who get off the beaten path and stick around beyond the normal midday cruise-ship window. Europeans set up here for a full week or two to explore the entire region, and even busy Americans might want to build some slack into their Dubrovnik time for a wide array of worthwhile side-trips.

Planning Your Time

While Dubrovnik's museums are nothing special, the town is one of those places that you never want to leave. The real attraction here is the Old Town and its relaxing, breezy ambience. While Dubrovnik could easily be "seen" in a day, a second or third day to unwind (or even more time, for side-trips) makes the long trip here more worthwhile.

To hit all the key sights in a single day, start at the Pile Gate, just outside the Old Town. Walk around the city's walls to get your bearings (before it gets too hot and crowded), then work your way down the main drag (following my "Strolling the Stradun" self-guided walk). As you explore, drop in at any museums or churches that appeal to you. To squeeze the most into a single day (or with a second day), hit the beach or consider a boat excursion from the Old Port (Lokrum Island, just offshore, requires the least brainpower, while the seafront town of Cavtat has some great art treasures).

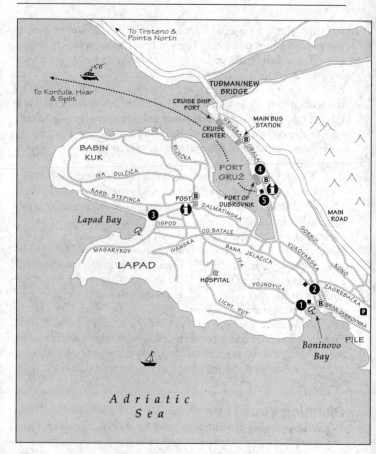

Orientation to Dubrovnik

(area code: 020)

Nearly all of the sights worth seeing are in Dubrovnik's traffic-free, walled **Old Town** (Stari Grad) peninsula. The main pedestrian promenade through the middle of town is called the **Stradun;** from this artery, the Old Town climbs steeply uphill in both directions to the walls. The Old Town connects to the mainland through three gates: the **Pile Gate,** to the west; the **Ploče Gate,** to the east; and the smaller **Buža Gate,** at the top of the stepped lane called Boškovićeva. The **Old Port** (Gradska Luka), with leisure boats to nearby destinations, is at the east end of town. While greater Dubrovnik has about 50,000 people, the local population within the Old Town is just a few thousand in the winter—and even smaller in summer, when many residents move out to rent their apartments to tourists.

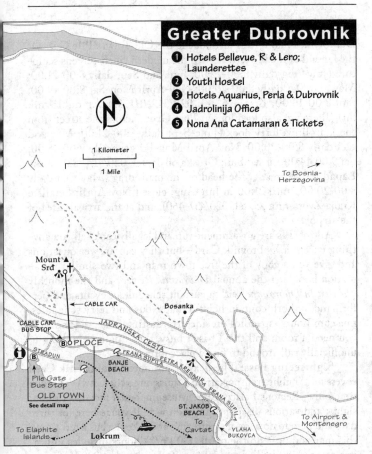

Greater Dubrovnik

1. Hotels Bellevue, R & Lero; Launderettes
2. Youth Hostel
3. Hotels Aquarius, Perla & Dubrovnik
4. Jadrolinija Office
5. Nona Ana Catamaran & Tickets

1 Kilometer

1 Mile

To Bosnia-Herzegovina

Mount Srđ

CABLE CAR

Bosanka

"CABLE CAR" BUS STOP

JADRANSKA CESTA

PLOČE

STRADUN

FRANA SUPILA

PETRA KREŠIMIRA

Pile Gate Bus Stop

BANJE BEACH

FRANA SUPILA

OLD TOWN

See detail map

ST. JAKOB BEACH

To Cavtat

To Airport & Montenegro

VLAHA BUKOVCA

To Elaphite Islands

Lokrum

The **Pile** (PEE-leh) neighborhood, a pincushion of tourist services, is just outside the western end of the Old Town (through the Pile Gate). In front of the gate, you'll find the main TI, ATMs, a post office, taxis, buses (fanning out to all the outlying neighborhoods), a cheap Konzum grocery store, and the Atlas Travel Agency (described later, under "Helpful Hints"). Just off this strip are some good *sobe* (rooms in private homes—described under "Sleeping in Dubrovnik"). This is also the starting point for my "Strolling the Stradun" self-guided walk.

A mile or two away from the Old Town are beaches peppered with expensive resort hotels. The closest area is **Boninovo Bay** (a 20-minute walk or 5-minute bus trip from the Old Town), but most cluster on the lush **Lapad Peninsula** to the west (a 15-minute bus trip from the Old Town); I've recommended accommodations in each of these areas. Across the bay from the Lapad Peninsula is **Port Gruž**, with the main bus station, ferry terminal, and cruise-ship port.

Tourist Information

Dubrovnik's main TI is just outside the Old Town's **Pile Gate**, at the far end of the big terrace with the modern video-screens sculpture (July-Aug daily 8:00-22:00; June and Sept daily 8:00-21:00; May and Oct daily 8:00-20:00; Nov-April Mon-Sat 8:00-19:00, Sun 8:00-16:00; Brsalje 5, tel. 020/312-011, www.tzdubrovnik .hr). There are also locations at **Port Gruž,** across the street from the Jadrolinija ferry dock (June-Sept daily 8:00-21:00; May and Oct daily 8:00-20:00; Nov-April Mon-Fri generally 9:00-15:00, Sat 9:00-14:00, closed Sun; Gruška obala, tel. 020/417-983); in the **Lapad** resort area, at the head of the main drag (May-Oct daily 8:00-20:00, until 21:00 in July-Aug; closed Nov-April; Šetalište Kralja Zvonimira 25, tel. 020/437-460); and at the arrivals area of the **airport**.

All the TIs are government-run and legally can't sell you anything except a Dubrovnik Card—but they can answer questions and give you a copy of the free town map and two similar information booklets: the annual *Dubrovnik Riviera* and the monthly *The Best in Dubrovnik* (with a current schedule of events and performances); both contain helpful maps, bus and ferry schedules, museum hours, specifics on side-trip destinations, and more. If you need a room and the TI isn't busy, they might be willing to unofficially call around to find a place for you.

Sightseeing Pass: The heavily promoted **Dubrovnik Card** covers local public transportation; admission to the City Walls (one time only), Rector's Palace, Rupe Museum, and a few other minor sights; and various discounts around town. If you're here for three days and plan to do a lot of sightseeing and take the bus a few times, this may add up—do the math (130 kn/24 hours includes unlimited transit, 180 kn/3 days includes 10 transit rides, 220 kn/7 days includes 20 transit rides, sold at TIs and many sights and hotels).

Arrival in Dubrovnik

As is the case throughout Croatia, you'll be met at the boat dock or bus station by locals trying to get you to rent a room *(soba)* at their house. If you've already reserved elsewhere, honor your reservation; if not, consider the offer (but be very clear on the location before you accept—many are nowhere near the Old Town).

By Bus: Dubrovnik's **main bus station** (Autobusni Kolodvor) is just beyond the ferry terminal along the Port Gruž embankment (about 2.5 miles northwest of the Old Town). It's straightforward and user-friendly, with pay toilets, baggage storage, and a helpful bus information window. To reach the Old Town's Pile Gate, walk straight ahead through the bus stalls, then bear right at the main road to the city bus stop, where you can hop on a bus (#1, #1a, #1b, or #1c) to the Pile stop. A taxi from the main bus station to the Old

Dubrovnik Essentials

English	Croatian	Pronounced
Old Town	Stari Grad	STAH-ree grahd
Old Port	Stara Luka	STAH-rah LOO-kah
Pile Gate	Gradska Vrata Pile	GRAHD-skah VRAH-tah PEE-leh
Ploče Gate	Gradska Vrata Ploče	GRAHD-skah VRAH-tah PLOH-cheh
Main Promenade	Stradun	STRAH-doon
Adriatic Sea	Jadran	YAH-drahn

Town and most accommodations runs about 75 kn.

Some buses (especially southbound regional buses, such as those to Cavtat) originate at the main bus station, but also use another stop, much handier to the Old Town. The **"cable car" bus stop** (a.k.a. "fire station" bus stop) is just uphill from the Buža Gate, overlooking the old wall, right next to the bottom station of the cable car up to Mount Srđ. From this bus stop, simply walk downhill (and through the pedestrian underpass)—you'll be inside the Old Town walls within a few minutes.

By Car Ferry or Catamaran: The big car ferries currently arrive at Port Gruž, two miles northwest of the Old Town. On the road in front of the ferry terminal, you'll find a bus stop (#1, #1a, #1b, and #1c go to the Old Town's Pile Gate; wait on the embankment side of the street) and a taxi stand (figure 70 kn to the Old Town and most accommodations). Across the street is the Jadrolinija office (with an ATM out front) and a TI. You can book a private room *(soba)* at Atlas Travel Agency (room-booking desk in boat terminal building, May-Sept only) or at Gulliver Travel Agency (behind TI). The fast *Nona Ana* catamaran from Mljet and Korčula also arrives near this big ferry dock.

By Cruise Ship: Some ships anchor just offshore from the Old Port, then send their passengers into the Old Town on tenders. Others put in at Port Gruž, just beyond the bus station. To reach the Old Town, take a public bus or pay 80 kn for a taxi (described earlier, under "By Bus").

By Plane: Dubrovnik's small airport (Zračna Luka) is near a village called Čilipi, 13 miles south of the city. A Croatia Airlines bus meets arriving flights for most major airlines at the airport, and brings you to the main bus station (35 kn, 40 minutes; may also stop near the Old Town—ask driver or airport TI). Legitimate cabbies charge around 220 kn for the ride between the airport and the center (though some cabbies charge as much as 300 kn;

Dubrovnik at a Glance

▲▲▲**Stradun Stroll** Charming walk through Dubrovnik's vibrant Old Town, ideal for coffee, ice cream, and people-watching. **Hours:** Always open. See page 853.

▲▲▲**Town Walls** Scenic mile-long walk along top of 15th-century fortifications encircling the city. **Hours:** July-Aug daily 8:00-19:30, progressively shorter hours off-season until 10:00-15:00 in mid-Nov-mid-March. See page 863.

▲▲▲**Mount Srđ** Napoleonic fortress above Dubrovnik with spectacular views and a modest museum to the recent war. **Hours:** Mountaintop—always open; cable car—daily June-Aug 9:00-24:00, April-May and Sept-Oct 9:00-20:00, Feb-March and Nov 9:00-17:00, Dec-Jan 9:00-16:00; museum—same hours as cable car except closes at 22:00 in summer. See page 878.

▲**Franciscan Monastery Museum** Tranquil cloister, medieval pharmacy-turned-museum, and a century-old pharmacy still serving residents today. **Hours:** Daily April-Oct 9:00-18:00, Nov-March 9:00-17:00. See page 868.

▲**Rector's Palace** Sparse antiques collection in the former home of rectors who ruled Dubrovnik in the Middle Ages. **Hours:** Daily May-Oct 9:00-18:00, Nov-April 9:00-16:00. See page 868.

▲**Cathedral** Eighteenth-century Roman Baroque cathedral and treasury filled with unusual relics such as a swatch of Jesus' swaddling clothes. **Hours:** Church—daily 8:00-20:00, treasury—generally open same hours as church, both have shorter hours off-season. See page 870.

▲**Dominican Monastery Museum** Another relaxing cloister with precious paintings, altarpieces, and manuscripts. **Hours:** Daily May-Sept 9:00-18:00, Oct-April 9:00-17:00. See page 871.

▲**Synagogue Museum** Europe's second-oldest synagogue and Croatia's only Jewish museum, with 13th-century Torahs and

consider arranging your transfer in advance with one of the drivers listed on page 852, or through your *sobe* host). Airport info: tel. 020/773-333, www.airport-dubrovnik.hr.

To get *to* the airport, you can take the same Croatia Airlines bus, which typically leaves from Dubrovnik's main bus station 1.5 hours before each Croatia Airlines or Austrian Airlines flight, or two hours before other airlines' international flights (the schedule is posted the day before—ask at the TI). It's possible that the bus

Holocaust-era artifacts. **Hours:** May-mid-Nov daily 10:00-20:00; mid-Nov-April Mon-Fri 10:00-13:00, closed Sat-Sun. See page 874.

▲**War Photo Limited** Thought-provoking photographic look at contemporary warfare. **Hours:** June-Sept daily 10:00-22:00; May and Oct Tue-Sun 10:00-16:00, closed Mon; closed Nov-April. See page 875.

▲**Serbian Orthodox Church and Icon Museum** Active church serving Dubrovnik's Serbian Orthodox community and museum with traditional religious icons. **Hours:** Church—daily May-Sept 8:00-14:00 & 16:00-21:00, until 19:00 in shoulder season, until 17:00 in winter; museum—May-Oct Mon-Sat 9:00-13:00, closed Sun; Nov-April Mon-Fri 9:00-13:00, closed Sat-Sun. See page 875.

▲**Rupe Granary and Ethnographic Museum** Good folk museum with tools, jewelry, clothing, and painted eggs above immense underground grain stores. **Hours:** Wed-Mon 9:00-16:00, closed Tue. See page 877.

Maritime Museum Contracts, maps, paintings, and models from Dubrovnik's days as a maritime power and shipbuilding center. **Hours:** Flex with demand, usually March-Oct Tue-Sun 9:00-18:00, until 16:00 in Nov-Feb, closed Mon year-round. See page 874.

Aquarium Tanks of local sea life housed in huge, shady old fort. **Hours:** Daily July-Aug 9:00-21:00, progressively shorter hours off-season until 9:00-13:00 Nov-March. See page 874.

Institute for the Restoration of Dubrovnik Photos and videos of the recent war and an exhibit on restoration work. **Hours:** Completely unpredictable—just drop by and see if it's open. See page 875.

may also stop at a point closer to the Old Town (maybe at the Pile Gate, or possibly at the Buža Gate above the Old Town). As of this writing, this has not been decided—ask at the TI to see if it can save you some time.

Bad-Weather Warning: If you're considering flying into or out of Dubrovnik, be aware that the airport is located right in the blast zone of the fierce Bora winds that periodically howl along the Dalmatian Coast (especially in the late fall). It's not uncommon for flights coming into Dubrovnik to be diverted to Split instead, with passengers forced to take a dull five-hour bus journey to their intended destination. Departing flights are usually less affected (though disruptions to incoming planes could, obviously, cause delays for departures as well). Personally, I've flown out of Dubrovnik a dozen times without incident, but it's not unheard of for travelers to be inconvenienced by this.

Nearby: If you have time to kill at the airport, you can go spelunking in the karstic **Đurović Cave**, which was recently discovered beneath the runway and opened to the public. It's filled with a "skycellar," allowing you to sample local wines in an underground cavern while waiting for your flight...no joking (40 kn to enter, 75 kn to taste up to 10 wines, sporadic hours; as you face the terminal, go to the right end and buzz the bell, or enter through the cafeteria).

By Car: Coming from the north, you'll drive over the super-modern Tuđman Bridge (which most locals, mindful of their former president's tarnished legacy, call simply "the New Bridge"). Immediately after crossing the bridge, you have two options: To get to the main bus station, ferry terminal (with some car-rental drop-off offices nearby), and Lapad Peninsula, take the left turn just after the bridge, wind down to the waterfront, then turn left and follow this road along the Port Gruž embankment. Or, to head for the Old Town, continue straight after the bridge. You'll pass above the Port Gruž area, then take the right turn-off marked *Dubrovnik* (with the little bull's-eye). You'll go through a tunnel, then turn left for *Centar,* and begin following the brown signs for *Grad* (Old Town); individual big hotels are also signed from here. Turn right to get to the Buža Gate at the top of the Old Town; first you'll pass the Old Town parking garage (described next), then wind up just above the walls (with more parking options—also described next). From this point, the direction you choose determines which one-way loop you'll be stuck on. Turning right takes you to the Pile Gate, then back up out of town toward Boninovo Bay and Lapad; turning left takes you the pretty Viktorija area, then (after looping down again) to the Ploče Gate.

If you're sleeping in or near the Old Town, **parking** is tricky. The handiest place to park long-term is the Old Town garage, which you'll pass on the right as you head toward the Old Town (15 kn/hour, 180 kn/day, half-price Oct-May). From here, it's about a 10-minute downhill walk to the Old Town, or you can take a shuttle bus (2/hour, free if you're paying to park here). If you'd like to be closer to the Old Town, you can take your chances on finding a spot—either on the street directly behind and above the town walls (pay at meter), or in the convenient but often-crammed pay lot nicknamed "the tennis court," just behind the wall (10 kn/hour). Another option is to drive to this area near the Old Town to unload your bags, then leave your car at the Old Town garage (or a cheaper, more distant one) for the duration of your visit. When in doubt, ask your *sobe* host or hotel for parking tips.

If you're sleeping at Lapad or Boninovo Bay, you'll have an easier time finding parking at or near your hotel—ask.

Helpful Hints

Festivals: Dubrovnik is most crowded during its Summer Festival, a month and a half of theater and musical performances held annually from July 10 to August 25 (www.dubrovnik-festival.hr). This is quickly followed by the "Rachlin & Friends" classical music festival in September (www.julianrachlin.com). For other options, see "Entertainment in Dubrovnik," later.

Crowd-Beating Tips: Dubrovnik has been discovered—especially by cruise ships (nearly 800 of which visit each year, bringing a total of around 900,000 passengers). Cruise-ship crowds descend on the Old Town on most summer days, roughly between 8:30 and 14:00 (the streets are most crowded 9:00-13:00). In summer, try to avoid the big sights—especially walking around the wall—during these peak times, and hit the beach or take a siesta midday, when the town is hottest and most crowded. On very busy days, as many as 9,000 cruise-ship day-trippers deluge Dubrovnik (three big ships' worth). If you're caught off-guard, it can be miserable. For others, it's entertaining to count the dozens of tour guides toting numbered paddles through the Old Town, and to watch the blocky orange tenders going back and forth to the ships moored offshore.

No Euros: Dubrovnik's merchants can be stubborn about accepting only kunas—no euros. (While it's technically illegal for vendors to accept any payment other than kunas, this is rarely enforced.) Even some of the top sights—including the City Walls and the cable car to Mount Srd—accept only kunas (or, sometimes, credit cards). Even if you're in town for just a few hours, visit an ATM to avoid hassles when it comes time to pay.

Wine Shop: For the best wine-tasting selection in a cool bar atmosphere, don't miss **D'Vino Wine Bar** (described on page 884). If you want to shop rather than taste, **Vinoteka Miličić** offers a nice variety of local wines; wry Dolores can explain your options, though she does tend to push Miličić wines (daily June-Aug 9:00-23:00, April-May and Sept-Oct 9:00-20:00, Nov-March 9:00-16:00, near the Pile end of the Stradun, tel. 020/321-777).

Internet Access: Most accommodations in Dubrovnik offer free Wi-Fi, and several cafés and bars around town provide Wi-Fi for customers. In the Old Town, the modern **Netcafé** has several speedy terminals and pay Wi-Fi right on Prijeko street, the "restaurant row" (daily 9:00-24:00, Prijeko 21, tel. 020/321-025).

English Bookstore: The **Algoritam** shop, right on the Stradun, has a wide variety of guidebooks, nonfiction books about Croatia and the former Yugoslavia, novels, and magazines—all in English (July-Aug Mon-Sat 9:00-23:00, Sun 10:00-13:00 & 18:00-22:00; June and Sept Mon-Sat 9:00-21:00, Sun 10:00-14:00; shorter hours off-season; Placa 8, tel. 020/322-044).

Laundry: Hotels charge a mint to wash your clothes; *sobe* hosts are cheaper, but often don't have the time (ask). The handy, fun, retro, self-service **Sanja and Rosie's Launderette** is just outside the Ploče Gate (cross the bridge and look left; 50-kn wash, 30-40-kn dry, clear English instructions, machines take bills, daily 8:00-22:00, 100-kn drop-off service available Mon-Sat before 14:00, put od Bosanke 2, mobile 099-254-6959, www.dubrovniklaundry.com). Two full-service launderettes are near the hotels at **Boninovo Bay**, a 20-minute uphill walk or five-minute bus trip from the Pile Gate: one at Pera Čingrije 8 (145-kn wash and dry in about 3 hours, no self-service, Mon-Fri 9:00-13:00 & 15:00-18:00, Sat 9:00-15:00, closed Sun, shorter hours off-season, across from the big seafront Hotel Bellevue, tel. 020/333-347), and another a few steps toward the main road at bana Jelačića 1 (120 kn to wash and dry up to an 11-pound load, same-day service possible if you bring it in by 10:00, open Mon-Fri 8:00-20:00, Sat 9:00-14:00, closed Sun, mobile 091-190-0888).

Car Rental: The big international chains, such as **Avis** (tel. 020/313-633), have offices both at the airport and near the Port Gruž embankment where the big boats come in. In addition, the many travel agencies closer to the Old Town also have a line on rental cars. Figure €50-60 per day, including taxes, insurance, and unlimited mileage (at the bigger chains, there's usually no extra charge for drop-off elsewhere in Croatia). Be sure the agency knows if you're crossing a border (such as Bosnia-Herzegovina or Montenegro) to ensure you have the proper paperwork.

Travel Agency: You'll see travel agencies all over town. At any of them, you can buy seats on an excursion, rent a car, book a room, buy Jadrolinija ferry tickets, and pick up a pile of brochures. The most established company is **Atlas,** with an office just outside the Pile Gate from the Old Town—though the location might change (June-Sept Mon-Sat 8:00-21:00, Sun 8:00-13:00; Oct-May Mon-Sat 8:00-20:00, closed Sun; down the little alley at Sv. Đurđa 4, otherwise look for signs to new location around the bus-stop area, tel. 020/442-574, fax 020/323-609, www.atlas-croatia.com, atlas.pile@atlas.hr).

Best Views: Walking the **Old Town walls** late in the day, when the city is bathed in rich light, is a treat. The cable car up to **Mount Srđ** provides bird's-eye panoramas over the entire region, from the highest vantage point without wings. The **Fort of St. Lawrence,** perched above the Pile neighborhood cove, has great views over the Old Town. A stroll up the road east of the city walls offers nice views back on the Old Town (best light early in the day). Better yet, if you have a car, head south of the city in the morning for gorgeously lit Old Town views over your right shoulder; various turn-offs along this road are ideal photo stops. The best one, known locally as the **"panorama point,"** is where the road leading up and out of Dubrovnik meets the main road that passes above the town (look for the pull-out on the right, with tour buses). Even if you're heading north, in good weather it's worth a quick detour south for this view.

Getting Around Dubrovnik

If you're staying in or near the Old Town, everything is easily walk-able. But those sleeping on Boninovo Bay or the Lapad Peninsula will want to get comfortable using the buses. Once you understand the system, commuting to the Old Town is a breeze.

By Bus: Libertas runs Dubrovnik's public buses. Tickets, which are good for an hour, are cheaper if you buy them in advance from a newsstand or your hotel (10 kn, ask for *autobusna karta,* ow-toh-BOOS-nah KAR-tah) than if you buy them from the bus driver (12 kn). A 24-hour ticket costs 30 kn (only sold at special bus-ticket kiosks, such as the one near the Pile Gate bus stop).

When you board the bus, validate your ticket in the machine next to the driver (insert it with the orange arrow facing out). Because most tourists can't figure out how to validate their tickets, it can take a long time to load the bus (which means drivers are understandably grumpy, and locals aren't shy about cutting in line).

All buses stop near the Old Town, just in front of the Pile Gate (buy tickets at the newsstand or bus-ticket kiosk right by the stop). From here, they fan out to just about anywhere you'd want to go (hotels on Boninovo Bay, Lapad Peninsula, and the ferry terminal and main bus station). You'll find bus schedules and a map in the TI booklet (for more information, visit www.libertas dubrovnik.hr).

By Taxi: Taxis start at 25 kn, then charge 8 kn per kilometer. The handiest taxi stand for the Old Town is just outside the Pile Gate. The biggest operation is Radio Taxi (tel. 0800-0970).

Tours in Dubrovnik

Walking Tours—Two companies—**Dubrovnik Walking Tours** and **Dubrovnik Walks**—offer similar one-hour walking tours of the Old Town daily at 10:00 and usually also at 18:00 (90 kn, also other departures and topics—look for fliers at TI). I'd skip these tours—they're pricey and brief, touching lightly on the same information explained in this chapter.

Local Guide—For an in-depth look at the city, consider hiring your own local guide. **Štefica Curić** is a sharp professional guide who offers a great by-the-book tour and an insider's look at the city (500 kn/2 hours, mobile 091-345-0133, www.dubrovnikprivate guide.com, dugacarapa@yahoo.com). If Štefica is busy, she can refer you to another good guide for the same price. **Roberto de Lorenzo** and his mother **Marija Tiberi** are both warm people enthusiastic about telling evocative stories from medieval Dubrovnik, including some off-the-beaten-path stops tailored to your interests (480 kn/2 hours, mobile 091-541-6637, bobdel70@yahoo.com). The TI can also suggest guides.

Bus-plus-Walking Tours—Two big companies (**Atlas** and **Elite**) offer expensive tours of Dubrovnik (about 250 kn, 2 hours).

From Dubrovnik

Package Excursions—Various travel agencies in Dubrovnik offers guided excursions (by bus and/or boat) to nearby destinations, including Mostar, Korčula, Montenegro, islands and villages near Dubrovnik, Albania, and others (figure €30-100/person, depending on the itinerary; one of the biggest operations is Dubrovnik—listed earlier, under "Helpful Hints"). While these excursions can be a convenient way to see otherwise difficult-to-reach destinations, the experience is generally disappointing: The buses are packed, the guides are uninspired (reading from a dull script—often in multiple languages), and quality time at the destinations is short. If you have no other way to reach a place you're dying to visit, guided excursions can still be worth considering. But I'd exhaust my other options first—consider renting a car for the day, or hiring your own driver (described next).

For pointers on excursions by boat from Dubrovnik's Old Port, see page 873.

Hire Your Own Driver—I enjoy renting my own car to see the sights around Dubrovnik (see "Helpful Hints," earlier). But if you're more comfortable having someone else do the driving, consider hiring a driver. While the drivers listed here are not official tour guides, they speak great English and offer ample commentary as you roll, and can help you craft a good day-long itinerary to Mostar, Montenegro, or anywhere else near Dubrovnik (typically departing around 8:00 and returning in the early evening). They're flexible about tailoring the tour to your interests: Because there are lots of options en route to either Mostar or Montenegro, do your homework so you can tell them what you'd like to see (and not see). Or you can just leave it up to them and go along for the ride.

Friendly **Pepo Klaić,** a veteran of the recent war, is enjoyable to get to know and has a knack for making the experience both informative and meaningful (€250/day, €125 for half-day trip to nearer destinations, airport transfer for about €30—cheaper than a taxi, these prices for up to 4 people—more expensive for bigger group, mobile 098-427-301, www.dubrovnikshoretrip.com, pepo klaic@yahoo.com). For €70, Pepo can drive you to the fortress at Mount Srđ up above the Old Town, with sweeping views of the entire area (about 1-1.5 hours round-trip). **Petar Vlašić** does similar tours for similar prices, and specializes in wine tours to the Pelješac Peninsula, with stops at various wineries along the way (€30 airport transfers, €190-200 for 2-person trip to Pelješac wineries, €230 to Mostar including guide, €250 to Montenegro including local guide and boat to Our Lady of the Rock, these prices for 1-3 people—more for larger groups, mobile 091-580-8721, www.dubrovnikrivieratours.com, meritum@du.t-com.hr). **Pero Carević,** who runs the recommended Villa Ragusa guest house, also drives travelers on excursions (similar prices, mobile 098-765-634, villa.ragusa@du.t-com.hr). If your destination is Mostar, likeable Bosnian driver **Ermin Elezović** will happily come pick you up for less than the Dubrovnik-based drivers (for up to 3 people: €100 for one-way transfer from Dubrovnik to Mostar, €150 for an all-day excursion with stops en route, €200 for round-trip to Mostar with same-day return to Dubrovnik; for contact information and details, see page 1067).

Self-Guided Walk

▲▲▲Strolling the Stradun

Running through the heart of Dubrovnik's Old Town is the 300-yard-long Stradun promenade—packed with people and lined with sights. This walk offers an ideal introduction to Dubrovnik's charms. It takes about a half-hour, not counting sightseeing stops.

• *Begin at the busy square in front of the west entrance to the Old Town, the Pile (PEE-leh) Gate.*

Pile Neighborhood

This bustling area is the nerve center of Dubrovnik's tourist industry—it's where the real world meets the fantasy of Dubrovnik (for

details on services offered here, see "Orientation to Dubrovnik," earlier). Near the modern, mirrors-and-TV-screens monument (which honors the "Dubrovnik Defenders" who protected the city during the 1991-1992 siege) is a leafy café terrace. Wander over to the edge of the terrace and take in the imposing walls of the Pearl of the Adriatic. The huge, fortified peninsula just outside the city walls is the **Fort of St. Lawrence** (Tvrđava Lovrijenac), Dubrovnik's oldest fortress and one of the top venues for the Dubrovnik Summer Festival. Shakespearean plays are often performed here, occasionally starring Goran Višnjić, the Croatian actor who became an American star on the TV show *ER*. You can climb this fortress for great views over the Old Town (30 kn, or covered by same ticket as Old Town walls on the same day).

• *Cross over the moat (now a shady park) to the round entrance tower in the Old Town Wall. This is the...*

Pile Gate (Gradska Vrata Pile)

Just before you enter the gate, notice the image above the entrance of **St. Blaise** (Sveti Vlaho in Croatian) cradling Dubrovnik in

his arm. You'll see a lot more of Blaise during your time here—we'll find out why later on this walk.

Inside the outer wall of the Pile Gate and to the left, a white **map** shows where each bomb dropped on the Old Town during the siege. Once inside town, you'll see virtually no signs of the war—demonstrating the townspeople's impressive resilience in rebuilding so well and so quickly.

Passing the rest of the way through the gate, you'll find a lively little square surrounded by landmarks. To the left, a steep stairway leads up to the imposing **Minčeta Tower**. It's possible to enter here to begin Dubrovnik's best activity, walking around the top of the wall (described later, under "Sights in Dubrovnik")—but this walk ends near a better entry point.

Next to the stairway is the small **Church of St. Savior** (Crkva

Svetog Spasa). Appreciative locals built this votive church to thank God after Dubrovnik made it through a 1520 earthquake. When the massive 1667 quake destroyed the city, this church was one of the only buildings left intact. And during the recent war, the church survived another close call when a shell exploded on the ground right in front of it (you can still see faint pockmarks from the shrapnel).

The big building on the left just beyond the small Church of St. Savior is the **Franciscan Monastery Museum.** This building, with a delightful cloister and one of Europe's oldest pharmacies, is worth touring (described later).

The giant, round structure in the middle of the square is **Onofrio's Big Fountain** (Velika Onofrijea Fontana). In the

Middle Ages, Dubrovnik had a complicated aqueduct system that brought water from the mountains seven miles away. The water ended up here, at the town's biggest fountain, before continuing through the city. This plentiful supply of water, large reserves of salt (a key source of Dubrovnik's wealth, from the town of Ston), and a massive granary (now the Rupe Ethnographic Museum, described later) made little, independent Dubrovnik very siege-resistant.

Tucked across the square from the church is the **Visia Dubrovnik Multimedia Museum,** showing a badly produced 3-D film about the city's history that isn't worth your 35 minutes or 75 kn (schedule posted at entry). In the evening, the theater shows first-run 3-D movies.

• *When you're finished taking in the sights on this square, continue along...*

The Stradun

Dubrovnik's main promenade—officially called the Placa, but bet-

ter known as the Stradun—is alive with locals and tourists alike. This is the heartbeat of the city: an Old World shopping mall by day and sprawling cocktail party after dark, when everybody seems to be doing the traditional evening stroll—flirting, ice-cream-licking, flaunting, and gawking. A coffee and some of Europe's best

Dubrovnik's Old Town

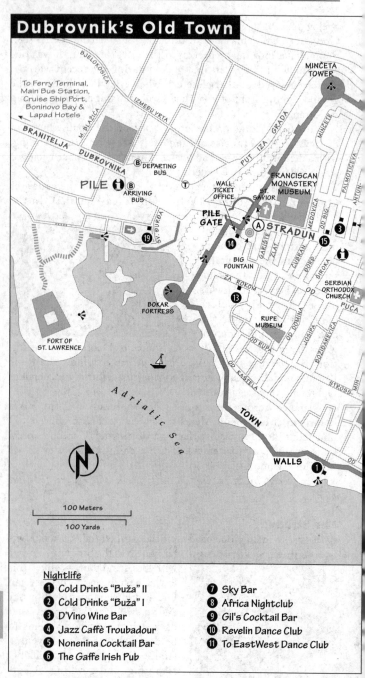

To Ferry Terminal,
Main Bus Station,
Cruise Ship Port,
Boninovo Bay &
Lapad Hotels

BJELOKOSIĆA

IZMEĐU VRTA

BRANITELJA DUBROVNIKA

M. BLAŽIĆA

MINČETA TOWER

PUT IZA GRADA

MINČETE

PALMOTIĆEVA

ANTUN

PILE

B DEPARTING BUS

T

WALL TICKET OFFICE

FRANCISCAN MONASTERY MUSEUM

OD SIG.

MEDOVIĆA

3

B ARRIVING BUS

ST. SAVIOR

A STRADUN

15

PILE GATE

14

GARIŠTE

ZLAT.

ĆUBRAN.

POBJ.

ORD

ŠIROKA

19

SV. ĐURĐA

BIG FOUNTAIN

SERBIAN ORTHODOX CHURCH

PUČA

BOKAR FORTRESS

ZA ROKOM

13

OD

RUPE MUSEUM

JOSIPA

BOŽIDAREVIĆA

FORT OF ST. LAWRENCE

OD DOMINA

OD RUPA

STROSS-

MIH.

Adriatic Sea

OD KAŠTELA

TOWN

WALLS

1

OD

N

100 Meters

100 Yards

Nightlife

1. Cold Drinks "Buža" II
2. Cold Drinks "Buža" I
3. D'Vino Wine Bar
4. Jazz Caffè Troubadour
5. Nonenina Cocktail Bar
6. The Gaffe Irish Pub
7. Sky Bar
8. Africa Nightclub
9. Gil's Cocktail Bar
10. Revelin Dance Club
11. To EastWest Dance Club

DUBROVNIK

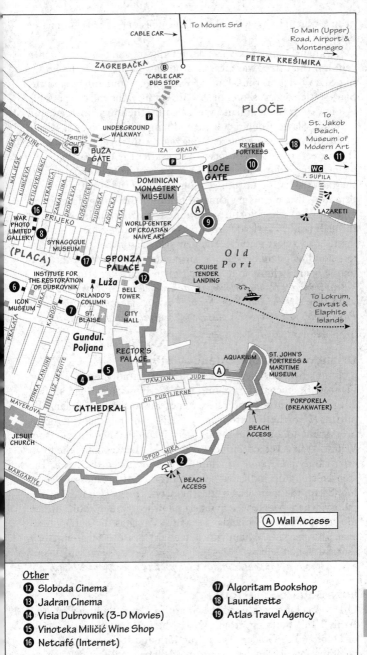

Other

⑫ Sloboda Cinema
⑬ Jadran Cinema
⑭ Visia Dubrovnik (3-D Movies)
⑮ Vinoteka Miličić Wine Shop
⑯ Netcafé (Internet)

⑰ Algoritam Bookshop
⑱ Launderette
⑲ Atlas Travel Agency

people-watching in a prime Stradun café is one of travel's great $3 bargains.

When Dubrovnik was just getting its start in the seventh century, this street was a canal. Romans fleeing from the invading Slavs lived on the island of Ragusa (on your right), and the Slavs settled on the shore. In the 11th century, the canal separating Ragusa from the mainland was filled in, the towns merged, and a unique Slavic-Roman culture and language blossomed. While originally much more higgledy-piggledy, this street was rebuilt in the current, more straightforward style after the 1667 earthquake.

During your time in Dubrovnik, you'll periodically hear the rat-a-tat-tat of a drum echoing through the streets from the Stradun. This means it's time to head for this main drag to get a glimpse of the colorfully costumed **"town guards"** parading through (and a cavalcade of tourists running alongside them, trying to snap a clear picture). You may also see some of these characters standing guard outside the town gates. It's all part of the local tourist board's efforts to make their town even more atmospheric.

• *Branching off from this promenade are several museums and other attractions. At the end of the Stradun is a passageway leading to the Ploče Gate. Just before this passage is the lively Luža Square. Its centerpiece is...*

Orlando's Column (Orlandov Stup)

Columns like this were typical of towns in northern Germany. Dubrovnik erected the column in 1417, soon after it had shifted allegiances from the oppressive Venetians to the Hungarians. By putting a northern European symbol in the middle of its most prominent square, Dubrovnik decisively distanced itself from Venice. Whenever a decision was made by the Republic, the town crier came to Orlando's Column and announced the news. The step he stood on indicated the importance of his message—the higher up, the more important the news. It was also used as the pillory, where people were publicly punished. The thin line on the top step in front of Orlando is exactly as long as the statue's forearm. This mark was Dubrovnik's standard measurement—not for a foot, but for an "elbow."

• *Now stand in front of Orlando's Column and orient yourself with a...*

Luža Square Spin-Tour

Orlando is looking toward the **Sponza Palace** (Sponza-Povijesni Arhiv). This building, from 1522, is the finest surviving example of Dubrovnik's Golden Age in the 15th and 16th centuries. It's a combination of Renaissance (ground-floor arches) and Venetian Gothic (upstairs windows). Houses up and down the main promenade used to look like this, but after the 1667 earthquake, they were replaced with boring uniformity. This used to be the customs office *(dogana),* but now it's an exhaustive archive of the city's history, with temporary art exhibits and a war memorial. The poignant **Memorial Room of Dubrovnik Defenders** (on the left as you enter) has photos of dozens of people from Dubrovnik who were killed fighting Yugoslav forces in 1991. A TV screen and images near the ceiling show the devastation of the city. Though the English

descriptions are pointedly—if unavoidably—slanted to the Croat perspective, it's compelling to look in the eyes of the brave young men who didn't start this war...but were willing to finish it (free, long hours daily in peak season, shorter hours off-season). Beyond the memorial room, the impressive **courtyard,** which generally displays temporary exhibits, is worth a peek (25 kn, generally free after-hours).

To the right of Sponza Palace is the town's **Bell Tower** (Gradski Zvonik). The original dated from 1444, but it was rebuilt when it started to lean in the 1920s. The big clock may be an octopus, but only one of its hands tells time. Below that, the golden circle shows the phase of the moon. At the bottom, the old-fashioned digital readout tells the hour (in Roman numerals) and the minutes (in five-minute increments). At the top of each hour (and again three minutes later), the time is clanged out on the bell up top by two bronze bell-ringers, Maro and Baro. (If this all seems like a copy of the very similar clock on St. Mark's Square in Venice, locals are quick to point out that this clock predates that one by several decades.) The clock still has to be wound every two days. Notice the little window between the moon phase and the "digital" readout: The clock-winder opens this window to get some light. The Krasovac family was in charge of winding the clock for generations (1877-2005). During the 1991-1992 siege, their house was destroyed—with the winding keys inside. For days, the clock bell didn't run. But then, miraculously, the keys were discovered lying in the street. The excited Dubrovnik citizens came together in this square and cheered as the clock was wound and the bell chimed, signaling to the soldiers surrounding the city that they hadn't won yet.

It's possible to climb up to the **gallery** next to the tower for a fine view of the Stradun, but only in the evening (July-Aug nightly 20:00-23:00, spring and fall nightly 19:00-21:00 or 22:00, closed in winter) and—as of this writing—only if you have a Dubrovnik

The Siege of Dubrovnik

In June 1991, Croatia declared independence from Yugoslavia. Within weeks, the nations were at war (for more on the war, see the Understanding Yugoslavia chapter). Though warfare raged in the Croatian interior, nobody expected that the bloodshed would reach Dubrovnik.

As refugees from Vukovar (in northeastern Croatia) arrived in Dubrovnik that fall, telling horrific stories of the warfare there, local residents began fearing the worst. Warplanes from the Serb-dominated Yugoslav People's Army buzzed threateningly low over the town, as if to signal an impending attack.

Then, at 6:00 in the morning on October 1, 1991, Dubrovnik residents awoke to explosions on nearby hillsides. The first attacks were focused on Mount Srđ, high above the Old Town. First the giant cross was destroyed, then a communications tower (both have been rebuilt and are visible today). This first wave of attacks cleared the way for Yugoslav land troops—mostly Serbs and Montenegrins—who surrounded the city. The ragtag, newly formed Croatian army quickly dug in at the old Napoleonic-era fortress at the top of Mount Srđ, where just 25 or 30 soldiers fended off a Yugoslav takeover of this highly strategic position.

At first, shelling targeted military positions on the outskirts of town. But soon, Yugoslav forces began bombing residential neighborhoods, then the Pearl of the Adriatic itself: Dubrovnik's Old Town. Defenseless townspeople took shelter in their cellars, and sometimes even huddled together in the city wall's 15th-century forts. It was the first time in Dubrovnik's long history that the walls were actually used to defend against an attack.

Dubrovnik resisted the siege better than anyone expected. The Yugoslav forces were hoping that residents would flee the town, but the people of Dubrovnik stayed. Though severely outgunned and outnumbered, Dubrovnik's defenders managed to hold the fort atop Mount Srđ, while Yugoslav forces controlled the nearby mountaintops. All supplies had to be carried up to the fort by foot or by donkey. Dubrovnik wasn't prepared for war, so its citizens had to improvise their defense. Many brave young locals lost their lives when they slung old hunting rifles over their shoulders and, under cover of darkness, climbed the hills above Dubrovnik to meet Yugoslav soldiers face-to-face.

After eight months of bombing, Dubrovnik was liberated by

the Croatian army, which attacked Yugoslav positions from the north. By the end of the siege, 100 civilians were dead, as well as more than 200 Dubrovnik citizens who lost their lives actively fighting for their hometown (much revered today as "Dubrovnik Defenders"); in the greater Dubrovnik area, 420 "Defenders" were killed, and another 900 wounded. More than two-thirds of Dubrovnik's buildings had been damaged, and more than 30,000 people had to flee their homes—but the failed siege was finally over.

Why was Dubrovnik—so far from the rest of the fighting—dragged into the conflict? Yugoslavia wanted to catch the city and surrounding region off-guard, gaining a toehold on the southern Dalmatian Coast so they could push north to Split. They also hoped to ignite pro-Serb passions in the nearby Serb-dominated areas of Bosnia-Herzegovina and Montenegro. But perhaps most of all, Yugoslavia wanted to hit Croatia where it hurt—its proudest, most historic, and most beautiful city, the tourist capital of a nation dependent on tourism. (It seems their plan backfired. Locals now say, "When Yugoslavia attacked Dubrovnik, they lost the war"—because images of the historic city under siege swayed international public opinion *against* Yugoslavia.)

The war initially devastated the tourist industry. Now, to the casual observer, Dubrovnik seems virtually back to normal. Aside from a few pockmarks and bright, new roof tiles, there are scant reminders of what happened here two decades ago. But even though the city itself has been repaired, the people of Dubrovnik are forever changed. Imagine living in an idyllic paradise, a place that attracted and awed visitors from around the world...and then watching it gradually blown to bits. It's understandable if Dubrovnik citizens are a little less in love with life than they once were.

It's clear that in the case of this siege, the Croats of Dubrovnik were the largely innocent victims of a brutal surprise attack. But keep in mind the larger context of the war: The cousins of these Croats, who were defending the glorious monument that is Dubrovnik, bombarded another glorious monument—the Old Bridge of Mostar (see page 1071). It's just another reminder that the "good guys" and "bad guys" in these wars are far from clear-cut.

Dubrovnik has several low-key attractions related to its recent war, including the museum in the ruined fortress atop Mount Srđ, the Memorial Room of Dubrovnik Defenders in the Sponza Palace on Luža Square, and the Institute for the Restoration of Dubrovnik. Another sight, War Photo Limited, expands the scope to war photography from around the world.

Card. Even if you don't have the card, you can try asking nicely (the entrance is in the passageway just to the left of the tower).

The big building to the right of the Bell Tower is the **City Hall** (Vijećnica). Next to that is **Onofrio's Little Fountain** (Mala Onofrijea Fontana), the little brother of the one at the other end of the Stradun. Beyond that is the **Gradska Kavana,** or "Town Café." This hangout—historically Dubrovnik's favorite spot for gossiping and people-watching—has pricey drinks and seating all the way through the wall to the Old Port. Just down the street from the Town Café is the Rector's Palace, and then the cathedral (for more on each, see "Sights in Dubrovnik").

Behind Orlando is **St. Blaise's Church** (Crkva Sv. Vlaha), dedicated to the patron saint of Dubrovnik. You'll see statues and paintings of St. Blaise all over town, always holding a model of the city in his left hand. According to legend, a millennium ago St. Blaise came to a local priest in a dream and warned him that the up-and-coming Venetians would soon attack the city. The priest alerted the authorities, who

prepared for war. Of course, the prediction came true. St. Blaise has been a Dubrovnik symbol—and locals have resented Venice—ever since.

• *Your tour is finished. From here, you've got plenty of sightseeing options. As you face the Bell Tower, you can go up the street to the right to reach the Rector's Palace and cathedral; you can walk through the gate straight ahead to reach the Old Port; or you can head through the gate and jog left to find the Dominican Monastery Museum. Even more sights—including an old synagogue, an Orthodox church, two different exhibits of war photography, and the medieval granary—are in the steep streets between the Stradun and the walls.*

Sights in Dubrovnik

Nearly all of Dubrovnik's sights are inside the Old Town's walls.

Combo-Tickets: The Rector's Palace, Maritime Museum, and Rupe Granary and Ethnographic Museum—which normally cost 40 kn apiece—are covered by a combo-ticket (55 kn to visit any two, 70 kn to visit all three, tickets sold at all three sights, valid for three days). The TI's Dubrovnik Card—which covers the same three sights, plus the City Walls and a few lesser attractions—can also be a good deal for busy sightseers (see "Tourist Information," earlier).

▲▲▲Town Walls (Gradske Zidine)

Dubrovnik's single best attraction is strolling the scenic mile-and-a-quarter around the city walls. As you meander along this lofty perch—with a sea of orange roofs on one side, and the actual sea on the other—you'll get your bearings and snap pictures like mad of the ever-changing views. Bring your map, which you can use to pick out landmarks and get the lay of the land.

Cost: 70 kn to enter walls, also includes the St. Lawrence Fort outside the Pile Gate (kunas or credit cards only—no euros).

Hours: July-Aug daily 8:00-19:30, progressively shorter hours off-season until mid-Nov-mid-March 10:00-15:00. Since the hours change with the season, confirm them by checking signs posted at the entrance (essential if you want to time your wall walk to avoid the worst crowds—explained below). The posted closing time indicates when the walls shut down, *not* the last entry—ascend well before this time if you want to make it all the way around. (If you want to linger, begin at least an hour ahead; if you're speedy, you can ascend 30 minutes before closing time.) Attendants begin circling the walls about 30 minutes after the posted closing time to lock the gates. There's talk of someday illuminating the walls at night, in which case the hours would be extended until after dark.

Entrances and Strategies: There are three entry points for the wall (see map on page 856), and wall-walkers are required to proceed counterclockwise. The best plan is to begin at the far side of the Old Town, using the entrance **near the Ploče Gate** and Dominican Monastery. This entrance is the least crowded, and you'll tackle the steepest part (and enjoy the best views) first, as you climb up to the landward side of the wall with magnificent views across the entire Old Town and the Adriatic. If you're wiped out, overheated, or fed up with crowds after that, you can bail out halfway (at the Pile Gate), having seen the best—or you can continue around the seaward side. The other two entrances are **just inside the Pile Gate** (by far the most crowded; for this location only, you must buy your tickets at the desk across the square; if you begin here, you'll reach the Minčeta Tower—with the steepest ascent and best views—last) and **near St. John's Fort** overlooking the Old Port (next to the Maritime Museum).

Crowd Control: Because this is Dubrovnik's top attraction, it's extremely crowded. Your best strategy is to avoid the walls during the times when the cruise ships are in town. On days when the walls open at 8:00, try to get started around that time. The walls are the most crowded from about 8:30 until 11:00, when the cruise ships are docked. There's generally an afternoon lull in the crowds (11:00-15:00), but that's also the hottest time to be atop the walls. Crowds pick up again in the late afternoon (starting around 15:00), peaking about an hour before closing time (18:30 in high season). So your peak-season options are either early, crowded, or hot; the ticket-takers told me that, all things considered, they'd ascend either at 8:00 or 30-60 minutes before closing.

Tips: Speed demons with no cameras can walk the walls in about an hour; strollers and shutterbugs should plan on longer. Because your ticket is electronically scanned as you enter, you can't leave and re-enter the wall later; you have to do it all in one go. If you have a Dubrovnik Card—even a multiple-day one—you can only use it to ascend the walls once.

Warning: The walls can get deliriously hot—all that white stone and seawater reflect blazing sunshine something fierce, and there's virtually no shade. It's essential to bring sunscreen, a hat, and water. Take your time: There are several steep stretches, and you'll be climbing up and down the whole way around. A few scant shops and cafés along the top of the wall (mostly on the sea side) sell water and other drinks, but it's safest to bring what you'll need with you.

Audioguide: You can rent a 40-kn audioguide, separate from the admission fee, for a dryly narrated circular tour of the walls (look for vendors near the Pile Gate entrance—not available at other entrances). But I'd rather just enjoy the views and lazily pick out the landmarks with my map.

Background: There have been walls here almost as long as there's been a Dubrovnik. As with virtually all fortifications on the Croatian Coast, these walls were beefed up in the 15th century, when the Ottoman navy became a threat. Around the perimeter are several substantial forts, with walls rounded so that cannonballs would glance off harmlessly. These stout forts intimidated would-be invaders during the Republic of Dubrovnik's Golden Age, and protected residents during the 1991-1992 siege.

➋ Self-Guided Tour: It's possible to just wander the walls and snap photos like crazy as you go. And trying to hew to closely to guided commentary kind of misses the point of being high above the Dubrovnik rooftops. But this brief tour will help give you bearings to what you're seeing, as you read Dubrovnik's unique and illustrious history into its street plan.

Part 1—Ploče Gate to Pile Gate: Begin by ascending near the **Ploče Gate** (go through the gate under the Bell Tower, walk along the stoutly walled passageway between the port and the Dominican Monastery, and look for the wall entrance on your right). Buy your ticket, head up, turn left, and start walking counterclockwise, with Mount Srd and the cable car on your right. Passing the Dominican Monastery's fine courtyard on the left, you're walking above what was the poorest part of medieval Dubrovnik, the domain of the craftsmen—with narrow, stepped lanes that had shops on the ground floor and humble dwellings up above.

As you walk, keep an eye on the different-colored **rooftops** for

an illustration of the damage Dubrovnik sustained during the 1991-1992 siege. It's easy to see that nearly two-thirds of Dubrovnik's roofs were replaced after the bombings (notice the new, bright-orange tiles—and how some buildings salvaged the old tiles, but have 20th-century ones underneath). The pristine-seeming Old Town was rebuilt using exactly the same materials and methods with which it was originally constructed.

As the level path you're on becomes stepped, you are rewarded with higher and higher views. Nearing the summit, you pass a juice bar (you can use the WCs if you buy a drink). At the very top, you enjoy the best possible view of the Old Town—you can see the rooftops,

churches, and the sea. For an even better view, if you have the energy, huff up the steep stairs to the (empty) **Minčeta Tower.** From either viewpoint, observe the valley-like shape of Dubrovnik. It's easy to imagine how it began as two towns—one where you are now, and the other on the hilly island with the church spires across the way—originally separated by a seawater canal. Notice the relatively regular, grid-like pattern of houses on this side, but the more higgledy-piggledy arrangement on the far side (a visual clue that the far side is older).

The sports court at your feet is a reminder that Dubrovnik is a living city—though it's not as vibrant as it once was. While officially 2,000 people live within these walls, most locals estimate the real number at about half that; the rest rent out their homes to tourists. And with good reason: Imagine the challenges that come with living in such a steep medieval townscape well into the 21st century. Delivery trucks rumble up and down the Stradun early each morning, and you'll see hardworking young men delivering goods on hand carts throughout the day. Looking up at the fortress atop Mount Srđ—seemingly custom-made for keeping an eye on a large swathe of coastline—the strategic position of Dubrovnik is clear. Independent Dubrovnik was not just this walled city, but an entire region.

Now continue downhill (you've earned it) until you get to the flat stretch. If you're bushed and ready to head back to town, you can turn left and head downstairs to the exit—but be aware that once you leave, you can't re-enter on the same ticket. Better yet, carry on straight for part 2.

Part 2—Pile Gate to Old Port: Pause to enjoy the full frontal view of the **Stradun**, barreling right at you. In the Middle

Ages, lining this drag were the merchants, and before that, this was a canal. At your feet is Onfrio's Big Fountain, which supplied water to a thirsty town. From here, you can see a wide range of church steeples representing the cosmopolitan makeup of a thriving medieval trade town (from left to right): Dominican, Franciscan (near you), the town Bell Tower, St. Blaise's (the round dome—hard to see from here), Serbian Orthodox, Cathedral, and (high on the hill) Jesuit. Sit and watch the river of humanity, flowing constantly up and down one of Europe's finest main streets.

Carry on through the guard tower and along the wall, climbing uphill again. On the right across the little cove is the **Fort of St. Lawrence,** which worked in concert with these stout walls to make Dubrovnik virtually impenetrable. Climbing higher and looking to your left, into town, you'll see that this area is still damaged—not from the 1991-1992 siege, but from the 1667 earthquake. Notice that, unlike the extremely dense construction on the poorer far side of town, this area has more breathing space—and even some gardens. Originally this was also densely populated, but after the quake, rather than rebuild, the wealthy folks who lived here decided to turn some former homes into green space. Grates cover the openings to old wells and grain stores that once supplied homes here—essential for surviving a siege.

As the walkway levels out, you pass a bar with drinks; more (with WCs) are coming up. Farther along, at the picturesque little turret, are gift shops and WCs. Looking down to your right (outside the wall), you'll begin to see tables and umbrellas clinging to the rocks at the base of the wall. This is the recommended "Cold Drinks" Buža II, the best spot in town for a scenic drink). On the horizon is the isle of Lokrum and—often—cruise ships at

anchor, sending their passengers to and fro on tenders. After passing Buža, look down on the left to see the local kids' makeshift soccer pitch, wedged between the walls—the best they can do in this vertical town. Soon you'll see the "other" Buža (technically Buža I) ahead; nearby, notice the little statue of St. Blaise, Dubrovnik's patron, enjoy some shade under the turret.

Rounding the bend, you see the facade of the Jesuit church. Notice that the homes in this area are much larger. These are aristocratic palaces—VIPs wanted to live as close as possible to the Cathedral and Rector's Palace, which are just below—and this also happens to be the oldest part of town, where "Ragusa" was born on a steep offshore island.

Continue around the wall, passing another snack bar (with WCs) and more ruined houses. From the high plateau, you have another opportunity to head down into town. (In the little plant-filled square at the bottom of these stairs is a cute little cat hospice, with a donation box for feeding some homeless feline residents.) But the final stretch of our wall walk is shorter than the other two, and mostly level.

Part 3—Old Port to Ploče Gate: Continuing along the wall, you'll pass near the entrance to the skippable Maritime Museum, then walk along the top of the wall overlooking the Old Port. Imagine how this heavily fortified little harbor (facing away from Dubrovnik's historic foes, the Venetians) was busy with trade in the Middle Ages. Today it's still the economic lifeline for town—watch the steady stream of cruise-ship tenders injecting dose after dose of tourist cash into town. As you curl around the far side of the port, you'll see the inviting outdoor tables of Gil's, a cocktail bar/restaurant catering to high-rolling yachters. While it looks appealing, it's a very exclusive place that frowns on would-be visitors who dress like normal people. Gussied-up jet-set diners enjoy coming here for good but extremely expensive designer fare. (One local told me, "The food is great—just eat a hamburger before you go.")

Just past Gil's, you come to the stairs back down to where you started this wall walk. Nice work. Now head on down and reward yourself with an ice-cream cone...and some shade.

The "Other" Wall Climb: Your ticket for the Old Town Walls also includes the Fort of St. Lawrence just outside the Old Town (valid same day only; fort described on page 854). If you've already bought a 30-kn ticket there, show it when buying your main wall ticket and you'll pay only the difference.

Near the Pile Gate

This museum is just inside the Pile Gate.

▲Franciscan Monastery Museum (Franjevački Samostan-Muzej)—In the Middle Ages, Dubrovnik's monasteries flourished. While all you'll see here are a fine cloister and a one-room museum in the old pharmacy, it's a delightful space. Enter through the gap between the small church and the big monastery. Just inside the door (before the ticket-seller), a century-old pharmacy still serves residents.

Explore the peaceful, sun-dappled **cloister.** Examine the capitals at the tops of the 60 Romanesque-Gothic double pillars.

Each one is different. Notice that some parts of the portals inside the courtyard are made with a lighter-colored stone—these had to be repaired after being hit during the 1991-1992 siege. The damaged 19th-century frescoes along the tops of the walls depict the life of St. Francis, who supposedly visited Dubrovnik in the early 13th century.

In the far corner stands the monastery's original medieval **pharmacy.** Part of the Franciscans' mission was to contribute to the good health of the citizens, so they opened this pharmacy in 1317. The monastery has had a pharmacy in continual operation ever since. On display are jars, pots, and other medieval pharmacists' tools. The sick would come to get their medicine at the little window (on left side), which limited contact with the pharmacist and reduced the risk of passing on disease. Around the room, you'll also find some relics, old manuscripts, and a detailed painting of early 17th-century Dubrovnik.

The adjoining **church** (enter next door) has a fine Baroque interior.

Cost and Hours: 30 kn, daily April-Oct 9:00-18:00, Nov-March 9:00-17:00, Placa 2, tel. 020/321-410, www.malabraca.hr.

Near Luža Square

These sights are at the far end of the Stradun (nearest the Old Port). As you stand on Luža Square facing the Bell Tower, the Rector's Palace and cathedral are up the wide street called Pred Dvorom to the right, and the Dominican Monastery Museum is through the gate by the Bell Tower and to the left.

▲Rector's Palace (Knežev Dvor)—In the Middle Ages, the Republic of Dubrovnik was ruled by a rector (similar to a Venetian doge), who was elected by the nobility. To prevent any one person from becoming too powerful, the rector's term was limited to one

month. Most rectors were in their 50s—near the end of the average life span and when they were less likely to shake things up. During his term, a rector lived upstairs in this palace. Because it's been plundered twice (most recently by Napoleon's forces, who stole all the furniture), this empty-feeling museum isn't as interesting as most other European palaces. What little you'll see was donated by local aristocrats to flesh out the pathetically empty complex. The palace collection, which requires a ticket and has good English explanations, is skippable, but it does offer a glimpse of Dubrovnik in its glory days. Even if you pass on the interior, the palace's exterior and courtyard are viewable at no charge.

Cost and Hours: 40 kn, covered by 55-kn or 70-kn combo-ticket, daily May-Oct 9:00-18:00, Nov-April 9:00-16:00, some posted English information, 6-kn English booklet is helpful, Pred Dvorom 3, tel. 020/322-096.

Visiting the Palace: The **exterior** is decorated in the Gothic-Renaissance mix (with particularly finely carved capitals) that was so common in Dubrovnik before the 1667 earthquake. Above the entrance is the message *Obliti privatorum publica curate*—loosely translated, "Forget your personal affairs and concern yourself with the affairs of state." This was a bold statement in a feudal era before democracy, when aristocrats were preoccupied exclusively with their self-interests.

Standing at the main door, you can generally get a free look at the palace's impressive **courtyard**—a venue for the Summer Festival, hosting music groups ranging from the local symphony to the Vienna Boys' Choir. In the courtyard (and also visible from the door) is the only secular statue created during the centuries-long Republic. Dubrovnik republicans, mindful of the dangers of hero-worship, didn't believe that any one citizen should be singled out. They made only one exception—for Miho Pracat (a.k.a. Michaeli Prazatto), a rich citizen who donated vast sums to charity and willed a fleet of ships to the city. But notice that Pracat's statue is displayed in here, behind closed doors, not out in public.

If you pay to go **inside,** you'll start on the ground floor, where you'll see dull paintings, the green-stucco courtroom (with explanations of the Republic's unique governmental system), and one of the palace's highlights, the original bronze bell-ringers from the town Bell Tower (named Maro and Baro). Like antique robots (from the Renaissance, c. 1470), these eerily lifelike sculptures could pivot at the waist to ring the bell. Then you'll see some iron chests (including a few with elaborate locking mechanisms) before entering some old prison cells, which supposedly were placed within earshot of the rector's quarters, so he would hear the moans of the prisoners...and stay honest. Leaving the prison, you'll enter the courtyard described earlier, where you can get a better look at the Pracat statue.

On the mezzanine level (stairs near the main entrance, above the prison), you'll find a decent display of furniture, a wimpy gun exhibit, votive offerings (mostly silver), a ho-hum coin collection, and an interesting painting of "Ragusa" in the early 17th century—back when it was still bisected by a canal.

Head back down to the courtyard and go to the upper floor (using the staircase across from mezzanine stairs, near the Pracat statue—notice the "hand" rails). Upstairs, you'll explore old apartments that serve as a painting gallery. The only vaguely authentic room is the red room in the corner, decorated more or less as it was in 1500, when it was the rector's office. Mihajlo Hamzić's exquisite *Baptism of Christ* painting, inspired by Italian painter Andrea Mantegna, is an early Renaissance work from the "Dubrovnik School" (see "Dominican Monastery Museum" listing, later).

▲**Cathedral (Katedrala)**—Dubrovnik's original 12th-century cathedral was funded largely by the English King Richard the Lionhearted. On his way back

from the Third Crusade, Richard was shipwrecked nearby. He promised God that if he survived, he'd build a church on the spot where he landed—which happened to be on Lokrum Island, just offshore. At Dubrovnik's request, Richard agreed to build his token of thanks inside the city instead. It was the finest Romanesque church on the Adriatic...before it was destroyed by the 1667 earthquake. This version is 18th-century Roman Baroque.

Cost and Hours: Church—free, daily 8:00-20:00; treasury—15 kn, generally open same hours as church; both have shorter hours off-season.

Touring the Cathedral: Inside, you'll find a painting from the school of Titian *(Assumption of the Virgin)* over the stark contemporary altar, and a quirky treasury *(riznica)* packed with 187 relics. Examining the treasury collection, notice that there are three locks on the treasury door—the stuff in here was so valuable, three different VIPs (the rector, the bishop, and a local aristocrat) had to agree before it could be opened. On the table near the door are several of St. Blaise's body parts (pieces of his arm, skull, and leg—

all encased in gold and silver). In the middle of the wall directly opposite the door, look for the crucifix with a piece of the True Cross. On a dig in Jerusalem, St. Helen (Emperor Constantine's mother) discovered what she believed to be the cross that Jesus was crucified on. It was brought to Constantinople, and the Byzantine czars doled out pieces of it to Balkan kings. Note the folding three-paneled altar painting (underneath the cross). Dubrovnik ambassadors packed this on road trips (such as their annual trip to pay off the Ottomans) so they could worship wherever they traveled.

On the right side of the room, the silver casket supposedly holds the actual swaddling clothes of the Baby Jesus (or, as some locals call it somewhat less reverently, "Jesus' nappy"). Dubrovnik bishops secretly passed these clothes down from generation to generation...until a nun got wind of it and told the whole town. Pieces of the cloth were cut off to miraculously heal the sick, especially new mothers recovering from a difficult birth. No matter how often it was cut, the cloth always went back to its original form. Then someone tried to use it on the wife of a Bosnian king. Since she was Muslim, it couldn't help her, and it never worked again. True or not, this legend hints at the prickly relationships between faiths (not to mention the male chauvinism) here in the Balkans.

▲Dominican Monastery Museum (Dominikanski Samostan-Muzej)—You'll find many of Dubrovnik's art treasures—paintings,

altarpieces, and manuscripts—gathered around the peaceful Dominican Monastery cloister inside the Ploče Gate. Historically, this was the church for wealthy people, while the Franciscan Church (down at the far end of the Stradun) was for poor people. Services were staggered by 15 minutes to allow servants to drop off their masters here, then rush down the Stradun for their own service.

Cost and Hours: 20 kn, art buffs enjoy the 50-kn English book, daily May-Sept 9:00-18:00, Oct-April 9:00-17:00.

Touring the Museum: Turn left from the entry and work your way clockwise around the cloister. The room in the far corner contains paintings from the **"Dubrovnik School,"** the Republic's circa-1500 answer to the art boom in Florence and Venice. Though the 1667 earthquake destroyed most of these paintings, about a dozen survive, and five of those are in this room. Don't miss the triptych by Nikola Božidarović with St. Blaise holding a detailed model of 16th-century Dubrovnik (left panel)—the most famous depiction of Dubrovnik's favorite saint. You'll also see reliquaries shaped like the hands and feet that they hold.

Continuing around the courtyard, duck into the next room. Here you'll see a painting by **Titian** depicting St. Blaise, Mary Magdalene, and the donor who financed this work.

At the next corner of the courtyard is the entrance to the striking **church** at the heart of this still-active monastery. Step

inside. The interior is decorated with modern stained glass, a fine 13th-century stone pulpit that survived the earthquake (reminding visitors of the intellectual approach to scripture that characterized the Dominicans), and a precious 14th-century Paolo Veneziano crucifix hanging above the high altar. The most memorable piece of art in the church is the *Miracle of St. Dominic*, showing the founder of the order bringing a child back to life (over the altar to the right, as you enter). It was painted in the Realist style (late 19th century) by Vlaho Bukovac.

World Center of Croatian Naive Art—Just inside the entrance to the Dominican Monastery complex, look left to find this Croatian naive art center. The gallery displays and sells works of this little-known art movement (described in detail on page 1031). In addition to some less-impressive starving artists, the gallery has some pieces by movement founder Ivan Generalić (priced at €15,000), Ivan Večenaj, and Mijo Kovačić. If you're not going to the excellent Naive Art Museum in Zagreb, this is a good chance to get a peek at this unique art form.

Cost and Hours: Free, Mon-Sat 10:00-18:00, closed Sun, 4 Sv. Dominika, tel. 020/321-565.

Museum of Modern Art (Umjetnička Galerija)—While salty old Dubrovnik and modern art don't quite seem to go together, the city has a fine modern art gallery a 10-minute walk outside the Ploče Gate. You'll see a permanent collection with 20th-century Croatian art (including some paintings by local artist Vlaho Bukovac—whose home in Cavtat offers a more intimate look at his life and works), as well as changing exhibits.

Cost and Hours: 30 kn, Tue-Sun 10:00-20:00, closed Mon, put Frana Supila 23, tel. 020/426-590, www.ugdubrovnik.hr.

Near the Old Port (Stara Luka)

The picturesque Old Port, carefully nestled behind St. John's Fort, faces away from what was Dubrovnik's biggest threat, the Venetians. The long seaside building across the bay on the left is the Lazareti, once the medieval quarantine house. In those days, all visitors were locked in here for 40 days before entering town.

(Today it hosts folk-dancing shows—described later,
under "Entertainment in
Dubrovnik.") A bench-
lined harborside walk leads
around the fort to a breakwater, providing a peaceful
perch. From the breakwater,
rocky beaches curl around
the outside of the wall.

Excursions—At the port, you can haggle with captains selling
excursions. The basic option is a 50-minute **"panorama cruise"**
out into the water and back again (75 kn, departures every hour).
Other popular trips are to **Lokrum Island,** just offshore (40 kn
round-trip, 10 kn for a map, runs April-Sept, 2/hr, 9:00-17:00,
mid-June-Aug until 19:00, none Oct-March); and to the archipelago called the **Elaphite Islands,** with visits to three different islands about 250 kn with lunch, 180 kn without, several boats
depart daily around 10:30-11:00, return around 15:45-19:30; so they
can buy enough food, companies prefer you to reserve and pay a
50-kn deposit the day before). You generally spend about three
hours on Lopud and about an hour each on Koločep and Šipan,
with about 2.5 hours on the boat.

    Cavtat: For sightseeing rather than sunning and lazing, con-
sider a cruise to the nearby resort town of Cavtat (TSAV-taht).
Cavtat is set within an idyllic, horseshoe-shaped harbor hemmed
in by a pair of peninsulas. Even those suffering from beach-resort
fatigue will enjoy a side-trip to Cavtat, if they appreciate local art.
Capping the hill just above town is a breathtaking mausoleum
by the great Croatian sculptor **Ivan Meštrović** (Račić Family
Mausoleum, 10 kn, Mon-Sat 10:00-17:00, closed Sun and mid-
Oct-mid-April; for more on Meštrović, see page 926). Right along
the main drag, a half-block up a side-street, is the former home-
turned-museum of the Cavtat-born, early-20th-century painter
Vlaho Bukovac (Kuća Bukovac, 20 kn, good 40-kn guidebook;
May-Oct Tue-Sat 9:00-13:00 & 16:00-20:00, Sun 16:00-20:00,
closed Mon; Nov-April Tue-Sat 9:00-13:00 & 14:00-17:00, Sun
14:00-17:00, closed Mon; Bukovčeva 5, tel. 020/478-646, www
.kuca-bukovac.hr). Boats to Cavtat leave about hourly from
Dubrovnik's Old Port (80 kn round-trip, 50 kn one-way, about
45 minutes each way, hourly return boats from Cavtat). Note that
a round-trip ticket is cheaper, but you'll have to return with the
same company (rather than on whichever boat is leaving next). You
can also reach Cavtat by public bus #10 (departs from Dubrovnik's
main bus station and also stops at the "cable car" bus stop above
the Old Town, 1-2/hour, 30-40 minutes, 17 kn).

Maritime Museum (Pomorski Muzej)—By the 15th century, when Venice's nautical dominance was on the wane, Dubrovnik emerged as a maritime power and the Mediterranean's leading shipbuilding center. The Dubrovnik-built "argosy" boat (from "Ragusa," an early name for the city) was the Cadillac of ships, mentioned by Shakespeare. This small museum traces the history of Dubrovnik's most important industry with contracts, maps, paintings, and models—all well-described in English. The main floor takes you through the 18th century, and the easy-to-miss upstairs covers the 19th and 20th centuries. Boaters will find the museum particularly interesting.

Cost and Hours: 40 kn, covered by 55-kn or 70-kn combo-ticket, 5-kn English booklet, hours flex on demand—usually March-Oct Tue-Sun 9:00-18:00, until 16:00 in Nov-Feb, closed Mon year-round, upstairs in St. John's Fort, at far/south end of Old Port, tel. 020/323-904.

Aquarium (Akvarij)—Dubrovnik's aquarium, housed in the cavernous St. John's Fort, is an old-school place, with 31 tanks on one floor. A visit here allows you a close look at the local marine life and provides a cool refuge from the midday heat.

Cost and Hours: 40 kn, kids-15 kn, English descriptions, daily July-Aug 9:00-21:00, progressively shorter hours off-season until 9:00-13:00 Nov-March, ground floor of St. John's Fort, enter from Old Port, tel. 020/323-484.

Between the Stradun and the Mainland

These two museums are a few steps off the main promenade toward the mainland.

▲**Synagogue Museum (Sinagoga-Muzej)**—When the Jews were forced out of Spain in 1492, a steady stream of them passed through here en route to today's Turkey. Finding Dubrovnik to be a flourishing and relatively tolerant city, many stayed. Žudioska ulica ("Jewish Street"), just inside Ploče Gate, became the ghetto in 1546. It was walled at one end and had a gate (which would be locked at night) at the other end. Today, the same street is home to the second-oldest continuously functioning synagogue in Europe (after Prague's), which contains Croatia's only Jewish museum. The top floor houses the synagogue itself. Notice the lattice windows that separated the women from the men (in accordance with Orthodox Jewish tradition). Below that, a small museum with good English descriptions gives meaning to the various Torahs (including a 14th-century one from Spain) and other items—such as the written orders *(naredba)* from Nazi-era Yugoslavia, stating that Jews were to identify their shops as Jewish-owned and wear armbands. (The Ustaše—the Nazi puppet government in Croatia—interned and executed not only Jews and Roma/Gypsies, but also Serbs and other people they considered undesirable; see page 828.) Of Croatia's 24,000 Jews, only 4,000 survived the Holocaust. Today Croatia has about 2,000 Jews, including a dozen Jewish families who call Dubrovnik home.

Cost and Hours: 20 kn, 10-kn English booklet; May-mid-Nov daily 10:00-20:00; mid-Nov-April Mon-Fri 10:00-13:00, closed Sat-Sun; Žudioska ulica 5, tel. 020/321-028.

▲**War Photo Limited**—If the tragic story of wartime Dubrovnik has you in a pensive mood, drop by this gallery with images of warfare from around the world. The brainchild of Kiwi-turned-Croatian photojournalist Wade Goddard, this thought-provoking museum attempts to show the ugly reality of war through raw, often disturbing photographs taken in the field. You'll find well-displayed exhibits on two floors; a small permanent exhibit depicts the wars in the former Yugoslavia through photography and video footage. Each summer, the gallery also houses various temporary exhibits. Note that the focus is not solely on Dubrovnik, but on war anywhere and everywhere.

Cost and Hours: 30 kn; June-Sept daily 10:00-22:00; May and Oct Tue-Sun 10:00-16:00, closed Mon; closed Nov-April; Antuninska 6, tel. 020/322-166, www.warphotoltd.com.

Between the Stradun and the Sea
Institute for the Restoration of Dubrovnik (Zavod za Obnovu Dubrovnika)—This small photo gallery considers the eight-month siege of Dubrovnik from late 1991 to mid-1992 (see "The Siege of Dubrovnik" sidebar, earlier). You'll see images of bombed-out Dubrovnik, each one juxtaposed with an image of the same building after being rebuilt, as well as rotating exhibits about efforts to restore Dubrovnik to its pre-siege glory. The photos are too few, but still illuminating. The highlight of the exhibit is a video showing a series of breathless news reports from a British journalist stationed here during the siege. As you watch shells devastating this glorious city, and look in the eyes of its desperate citizens at their darkest hour, you might just begin to grasp what went on here not so long ago.

Cost and Hours: Free, completely unpredictable hours—just drop by and see if it's open, a half-block off the Stradun at Miha Pracata, tel. 020/324-060.

▲**Serbian Orthodox Church and Icon Museum (Srpska Pravoslavna Crkva i Muzej Ikona)**—Round out your look at Dubrovnik's major faiths (Catholic, Jewish, and Orthodox) with a visit to this house of worship—one of the most convenient places in Croatia to learn about Orthodox Christianity. Remember that people from the former Yugoslavia who follow the Orthodox faith are, by definition, ethnic Serbs. With all the (perhaps

The Serbian Orthodox Church

While the former Yugoslav destinations covered in this book are either Catholic (Slovenia and Croatia) or Muslim (Mostar), don't overlook the rich diversity of faiths in this region. Dubrovnik's Serbian Orthodox church—as well as the Orthodox church in Ljubljana, Slovenia (page 736)—offer an invaluable opportunity to learn about a faith that's often unfamiliar to visitors.

As you explore an Orthodox church, keep in mind that these churches carry on the earliest traditions of the Christian faith. Orthodox and Catholic Christianity came from the same roots, so the oldest surviving early-Christian churches (such as the stave churches of Norway) have many of the same features as today's Orthodox churches.

Notice that there are no pews. Worshippers stand through the service, as a sign of respect (though some older parishioners sit on the seats along the walls). Women stand on the left side, men on the right (equal distance from the altar—to represent that all are equal before God). The Orthodox Church uses essentially the same Bible as Catholics, but it's written in the Cyrillic alphabet, which you'll see displayed around any Orthodox church. Following Old Testament Judeo-Christian tradition, the Bible is kept on the altar behind the iconostasis, the big screen in the middle of the room covered with curtains and icons (golden paintings of saints), which separates the material world from the spiritual one. At certain times during the service, the curtains or doors are opened so the congregation can see the Holy Book.

Unlike the decorations in many Catholic churches, Orthodox icons are not intended to be lifelike. Packed with intricate symbolism, and cast against a shimmering golden background, they're meant to remind viewers of the metaphysical nature of Jesus and the saints rather than their physical form, which is considered irrelevant. You'll almost never see a statue, which is thought to overemphasize the physical world...and, to Orthodox people, feels a little too close to violating the commandment, "Thou shalt not worship graven images." Orthodox services generally involve chanting (a dialogue that goes back and forth between the priest and the congregation), and the church is filled with the evocative aroma of incense.

The incense, chanting, icons, and standing up are all intended to heighten the experience of worship. While many Catholic and Protestant services tend to be more of a theoretical and rote consideration of religious issues (come on—don't tell me you've never dozed through the sermon), Orthodox services are about creating a religious experience. Each of these elements does its part to help the worshipper transcend the physical world and enter communion with the spiritual one.

understandably) hard feelings about the recent war, this church serves as an important reminder that all Serbs aren't bloodthirsty killers.

Dubrovnik never had a very large Serb population (an Orthodox church wasn't even allowed inside the town walls until the mid-19th century). During the recent war, most Serbs fled, created new lives for themselves elsewhere, and saw little reason to return. But some old-timers remain, and Dubrovnik's dwindling, aging Orthodox population is still served by this **church.** The candles stuck in the sand (to prevent fire outbreaks) represent prayers: The ones at knee level are for the deceased, while the ones higher up are for the living. The gentleman selling candles encourages you to buy and light one, regardless of your faith, so long as you do so with the proper intentions and reverence.

A few doors down, you'll find the **Icon Museum.** This small collection features 78 different icons (stylized paintings of saints, generally on a golden background—a common feature of Orthodox churches) from the 15th through the 19th centuries, all identified in English. In the library—crammed with old shelves holding some 12,000 books—look for the astonishingly detailed calendar, with portraits of hundreds of saints. The gallery on the ground floor, run by Michael, sells original icons and reproductions (open longer hours than museum).

Cost and Hours: Church—free but donations accepted, good 20-kn English book explains church and museum; daily May-Sept 8:00-14:00 & 16:00-21:00, until 19:00 in shoulder season, until 17:00 in winter; short services daily at 8:30 and 19:00, longer liturgy Sun 9:30-11:00; museum—10 kn; May-Oct Mon-Sat 9:00-13:00, closed Sun; Nov-April Mon-Fri 9:00-13:00, closed Sat-Sun, Od Puča 8, tel. 020/323-283.

▲Rupe Granary and Ethnographic Museum (Etnografski Muzej Rupe)—This huge, 16th-century building was Dubrovnik's biggest granary, and today houses the best folk museum I've seen in Croatia. *Rupe* means "holes"—and it's worth the price of entry just to peer down into these 15 cavernous underground grain stores, designed to maintain the perfect temperature to preserve the seeds (63 degrees Fahrenheit). When the grain had to be dried, it was moved upstairs—where today you'll find a surprisingly well-presented ethnographic museum, with tools, jewelry, clothing, instruments, painted eggs, and other folk artifacts from Dubrovnik's colorful history. Borrow the free English information guide at the entry. The museum hides several blocks uphill from the main promenade, toward the sea (climb up Široka—the widest side street from the Stradun—which becomes Od Domina on the way to the museum).

Cost and Hours: 40 kn, covered by 55-kn or 70-kn combo-ticket, Wed-Mon 9:00-16:00, closed Tue, od Rupa 3, tel. 020/323-013.

Above Dubrovnik

▲▲▲**Mount Srđ**—After adding Dubrovnik to his holdings, Napoleon built a fortress atop the hill behind the Old Town to keep an eye on his new subjects (in 1810). During the city's 20th-century tourism heyday, a cable car was built to effortlessly whisk visitors to the top so they could enjoy the fine views from the fortress and the giant cross nearby. Then, when war broke out in the 1990s, Mount Srđ (pronounced

like "surge") became a crucial link in the defense of Dubrovnik—the only high land that locals were able to hold. The fortress was shelled and damaged, and the cross and cable car were destroyed. Minefields and unexploded ordnance left the hilltop a dangerous no-man's land. But more recently, the mountain's fortunes have reversed. The land mines have been removed, and in 2010, the cable car was rebuilt to once again connect Dubrovnik's Old Town to its mountaintop. Visitors head to the top both for the spectacular sweeping views and for a ragtag museum about the war.

Warning: While this area has officially been cleared of land mines, nervous locals remind visitors that this was a war zone. Be sure to stay on clearly defined paths and roads.

Getting There: The **cable car** is easily the best option for summiting Mount Srđ (80 kn round-trip, 50 kn one-way, kunas or credit cards only—no euros; 2/hour—generally departing at :00 and :30 past each hour, maybe more frequent with demand, 3-minute ride; daily June-Aug 9:00-24:00, April-May and Sept-Oct 9:00-20:00, Feb-March and Nov 9:00-17:00, Dec-Jan 9:00-16:00; doesn't run in Bora wind or heavy rain, last ascent 30 minutes before closing, tel. 020/325-393, www.dubrovnikcablecar.com). The lower station is just above the Buža Gate at the top of the Old Town (from the main drag, huff all the way to the top of Boškovićera, exit through gate, and climb uphill one block, then look right). You may see travel agencies selling tickets elsewhere in town, but there's no advantage to buying them anywhere but here.

If you have a **car,** you can drive up. From the high road above the Old Town, watch for the turnoff to Bosanka, which leads you to that village, then up to the fortress and cross—follow signs for *Srđ* (it's twisty but not far—figure a 20-minute drive from the Old Town area). If you're coming south from the Old Town, once you reach the main road above, you'll have to turn left and backtrack a bit to reach the Bosanka turnoff. A **taxi** to the top is needlessly expensive (figure €50-70 round-trip, including some waiting time at the top); this is worthwhile only if you hire recommended driver Pepo Klaić to take you to the summit while sharing his firsthand experiences defending the fortress (€70, listed on page 853). For **hikers,** a switchback trail (used to supply the fortress during the siege) connects the Old Town to the mountaintop—but it's very steep and provides minimal shade. (If you're in great shape and it's not too hot, you could ride the cable car up, then hike down.)

Mountaintop: From the top cable-car station, head up the stairs to the panoramic terrace. The bird's-eye **view** is truly spec-

tacular, looking straight down to the street plan of Dubrovnik's Old Town. From this lofty perch, you can see north to the Dalmatian islands (the Elaphite archipelago, Mljet, Korčula, and beyond); south to Montenegro; and east into Bosnia-Herzegovina. Gazing upon those looming mountains that define the border with Bosnia-Herzegovina—which, centuries ago, was also the frontier of the huge and powerful Ottoman Empire—you can appreciate how impressive it was that stubborn little Dubrovnik managed to remain independent for so much of its history.

The **cross** was always an important symbol in this very Catholic town. After it was destroyed, a temporary wooden one was erected to encourage the townspeople who were waiting out the siege below. During a visit in 2003, Pope John Paul II blessed the rubble from the old cross; those fragments are now being used in the foundations of the city's newest churches.

To reach the museum in the old fortress, walk behind the cable-car station along the rocky red soil.

Fort and Museum: The Napoleonic-era Fort Imperial (Tvrđava Imperijal) houses the **Dubrovnik During the Homeland War (1991-1995) Museum** (20 kn, 40-kn booklet, same hours as cable car except closes at 22:00 in summer). Photos, video clips, documents, and artifacts tell the story (with English descriptions) of the overarching war with Yugoslavia and how the people defended this fortress. The descriptions are too dense and detailed for casual visitors, but you'll see lots of photos and some actual items used in the fighting: primitive, rusty rifles (some dating from World War II) that the Croatians used for their improvised defense, and mortar shells and other projectiles that Yugoslav forces hurled at the fortress and the city. Look for the wire-guided Russian rockets. After being launched at their target, the rockets would burrow into a wall, waiting to be detonated once their operators saw the opportunity for maximum destruction. You'll also learn how a squadron of armed supply ships became besieged Dubrovnik's only tether to the outside world.

While the devastation of Dubrovnik was disturbing, this museum could do a far better job of fostering at least an illusion of impartiality. Instead, descriptions rant one-sidedly against "Serbian and Montenegrin aggression" and the "Serbian imperialist war," and the exhibits self-righteously depict Croats exclusively as victims (which was basically true here in Dubrovnik, but ignores Croat atrocities elsewhere). All of this serves only to trivialize and distract from the human tragedy of this war.

After seeing the exhibit, climb up a few flights of stairs to the **rooftop** for the view. The giant communications tower overhead flew the Croatian flag during the war, to inspire the besieged residents below. You might see some charred trees around here—these were claimed not by the war but more recently, by forest fires. (Fear of land mines and other explosives prevented locals from fighting the wildfires as aggressively as they might otherwise, making these fires more dangerous than ever.)

Eating: Boasting undoubtedly the best view in Dubrovnik, **Restaurant/Snack Bar Panorama** has reasonable prices and drop-dead, astonishing views over the rooftops of the Old Town and to the most beautiful parts of three different countries (25-35-kn drinks, 55-70-kn cocktails, 10-kn ice cream, 27-kn cakes, 65-90-kn pastas, 85-145-kn main dishes, open same hours as cable car).

Activities in Dubrovnik

Swimming and Sunbathing—If the weather's good and you've had enough of museums, spend a sunny afternoon at the beach. There are no sandy beaches on the mainland near Dubrovnik, but there are lots of suitable pebbly options, plus several concrete perches. The easiest and most atmospheric place to take a dip is right off the Old Town. From the Old Port and its breakwater, uneven steps clinging to the outside of the wall lead to a series of great sunbathing and swimming coves (and even a showerhead sticking out of the town wall). Another delightful rocky beach hangs onto the outside of the Old Town's wall (at the bar called Cold Drinks "Buža" I; for more on this bar, and how to find it, see page 883). Locals prefer to swim on Lokrum Island, because there are (relatively) fewer tourists there; for details on taking a boat to Lokrum, see page 873. Other convenient public beaches are Banje (just outside Ploče Gate, east of Old Town) and the beach in the middle of Lapad Bay (near Hotel Kompas).

My favorite hidden beach—**St. Jakob**—takes a lot longer to reach, but if you're up for the hike, it's worth it to escape the crowds. Figure about a 25-minute walk (each way) from the Old Town. Go through the Ploče Gate at the east end of the Old Town, and walk along the street called Frana Supila as it climbs uphill above the waterfront. At Hotel Argentina, take the right (downhill) fork and keep going on Vlaha Bukovca. Eventually you'll reach the small church of St. Jakob. You'll see the beach—in a cozy protected cove—far below. Curl around behind the church and keep an eye out for stairs going down on the right. Unfortunately, these stairs are effectively unmarked, so it might take some trial and error to find the right ones. (If you reach the rusted-white gateway of the old communist-era open-air theater, you've gone too far.) Hike down the very steep stairs to the gentle cove, which has rentable chairs and a small restaurant for drinks (and a WC). Enjoy the pebbly beach and faraway views of Dubrovnik's Old Town.

Sea Kayaking—Paddling a sleek kayak around the outside of Dubrovnik's imposing walls is a memorable experience. Several outfits in town offer half-day tours (most options 250-350 kn); popular itineraries include loops along the City Walls, to secluded beaches, and around Lokrum island. As this scene is continually evolving, look for fliers locally.

Shopping in Dubrovnik

Most souvenirs sold in Dubrovnik—from lavender sachets to plaster models of the Old Town—are pretty tacky. Whatever you buy, prices are much higher along the Stradun than on the side streets.

A classy alternative to the knickknacks is a type of local jewelry called *Konavoske puce* ("Konavle buttons"). Sold as earrings,
pendants, and rings, these distinctive
and fashionable filigree-style pieces
consist of a sphere with several small
posts. Though they're sold around town,
it's least expensive to buy them on Od
Puča street, which runs parallel to the
Stradun two blocks toward the sea
(near the Serbian Orthodox Church).
The high concentration of jewelers

along this lane keeps prices reasonable. You'll find the "buttons" in
various sizes, in both silver (affordable) and gold (pricey).

You'll also see lots of jewelry made from red coral, which
can only be legally gathered in small amounts from two small
islands in northern Dalmatia. If you see a particularly large
chunk of coral, it's likely imported. To know what you're getting, shop at an actual jeweler instead of a souvenir shop.

Gift-Shop Chains: Several pleasant gift shops in Dubrovnik
(with additional branches throughout Dalmatia) hawk fun, if
sometimes made-in-China, items. Look for these chains, which
are a bit classier than the many no-name shops around town: **Aqua**
sells pleasant nautical-themed gifts, blue-and-white-striped sailor
shirts, and other gear. **Bonbonnière Kraš** is Croatia's leading
chocolatier, selling a wide array of tasty candies.

Entertainment in Dubrovnik

Musical Events

Dubrovnik annually hosts a full schedule of events for its Summer
Festival (July 10-Aug 25, www.dubrovnik-festival.hr). Lovers of
classical music enjoy the "Rachlin & Friends" festival in September
(www.julianrachlin.com). But the town also works hard to offer
traditional music outside of festival time. Spirited folk-music concerts are performed for tourists twice weekly in the Lazareti (old
quarantine building) just outside the Old Town's Ploče Gate (100
kn, usually at 21:30). About one night per week through the winter,
you can watch the Dubrovnik Symphony Orchestra (usually at the
Rector's Palace in good weather, or Dominican Monastery in bad
weather). And since Dubrovnik is trying to become a year-round
destination, the city also offers tourist-oriented musical events
most nights throughout the winter (often at a hotel). For the latest
on any of these festivals and concerts, check the events listings in
the *Best in Dubrovnik* brochure, or ask the TI.

Also consider the folk dancing and market each Sunday
morning at Čilipi, a small town near the airport (see page 845).

Dubrovnik-based companies offer excursions that include transportation there and back (230 kn).

Nightlife

Dubrovnik's Old Town is one big, romantic parade of relaxed and happy people out strolling.
The main drag is brightly lit and packed with shops, cafés, and bars, all open late. This is a fun scene. And if you walk away from the crowds or out on the port, you'll be alone with the magic of the Pearl of

the Adriatic. Everything feels—and is—very safe after dark.

If you're looking for a memorable bar after dark, consider these:

▲▲▲**Drinks with a View**—**Cold Drinks "Buža"** offers, without a doubt, the most scenic spot for a drink. Perched on a cliff above the sea, clinging like a barnacle to the outside of the city walls, this

is a peaceful, shaded getaway from the bustle of the Old Town...the perfect place to watch cruise ships disappear into the horizon. *Buža* means "hole in the wall"—and that's exactly what you'll have to go through to get to this place. There are actually two different Bužas, with separate owners. My favorite is Buža II (which is actually the older and bigger of the pair). Filled with mellow tourists and bartenders pouring wine from tiny screw-top bottles into plastic cups, Buža II comes with castaway views and Frank Sinatra ambience. This is

supposedly where Bill Gates hangs out when he visits Dubrovnik (25-40-kn drinks, summer daily 9:00-into the wee hours, closed mid-Nov-Jan). Buža I, with a different owner, is more casual, plays hip rather than romantic music, and has concrete stairs leading down to a beach on the rocks below (18-45-kn drinks). If one Buža is full, check the other one.

Getting There: Both Bužas are high above the bustle of the main drag, along the seaward wall. To reach them from the cathedral area, hike up the grand staircase to St. Ignatius' Church, then go left to find the lane that runs along the inside of the wall. To find the classic Buža II, head right along the lane and look for the *Cold Drinks* sign pointing to a literal hole in the wall. For the hipper Buža I, go left along the same lane, and locate the hole in the wall with the *No Toples No Nudist* graffiti.

Wine-Tasting—D'Vino Wine Bar, just a few steps off the main drag, has a relaxed atmosphere and a knowledgeable but unpretentious approach—making it the handiest place in Dalmatia to taste and learn about Croatian wines. Run by gregarious Aussie/Croat Sasha, this cozy bar (with a few outdoor tables) sells more than 60 wines by the glass and lots more by the bottle. The emphasis is on Croatian wines by small-production wineries, but they also have a few international vintages. Each wine is well-described on the menu, and the staff is happy to guide you through your options— just tell them what you like (18-80-kn glasses—most around 25-35 kn, 50-kn wine flights; light food—70-kn 2-person cheese plate, 90-kn antipasti plate; daily 10:30-2:00 in the morning, possibly less in winter, Palmotićeva 4a, tel. 020/321-130, www.dvino .net). Sasha takes wine-lovers on all-day wine tours to the Pelješac Peninsula (for details and prices, email him at sasha@dvino.net); also ask about his wine dinners.

Cocktails and People-Watching—Jazz Caffè Troubadour is a cool place, originally owned by a former member of the Dubrovnik Troubadours—Croatia's answer to the Beatles (or, perhaps more accurately, the Turtles). On balmy evenings, 50 chairs with tiny tables are set up theater-style in the dreamy alley facing the musicians. Step inside to see old 1970s photos of the band (50-60-kn cocktails, daily 9:00-24:00, happy hour 14:00-19:00 with 20-kn drinks, live jazz nightly from about 20:30, often live piano at other times, next to cathedral at Bunićeva Poljana 2).

The square just around the corner from Troubadour, alongside the cathedral, is another happening nightspot. Several cafés that ring the square have outdoor seating, filling the entire space with a convivial hubbub of people out enjoying the al fresco ambience.

Nonenina, a few steps from the cathedral on Pred Dvorom, is an outdoor lounge with big, overstuffed chairs at a fine vantage point for people-watching. They brag that they serve 180 different types of cocktails (55-80 kn, also 35-45-kn beers, daily 9:00-2:00 in the morning, shorter hours off-season, across from Rector's Palace).

The Gaffe Irish Pub, with a nicely pubby interior and a small courtyard, is a rollicking spot to drain a pint and watch some rugby (Miha Pracata 4, mobile 098-196-2149, see full listing under "Eating in Dubrovnik," later).

Nightclubs—Dubrovnik has a variety of nightclubs. The streets branching off from the Stradun are lined with several options with drinks and pumping music, including **Sky Bar** (toward the water on Marojice Kaboge) and **Africa** (toward the mountain at Vetranićeva 3). Just follow the beat.

More places are near or just beyond the Ploče Gate at the east end of town. Head under the bell tower, then up the street past the Dominican Monastery. You'll pass the hole-in-the-wall entrance (right) for the snobby, upscale **Gil's** cocktail bar and "pop lounge" (www.gilsdubrovnik.com). Then, after crossing the bridge, look (on the left) for the entrance to **Revelin**—a dance club that fills one of the city wall's fortress towers (nightly 22:00-6:00, www.revelinclub-dubrovnik.com). Then head out and up the street until you reach Banje Beach, half of which is occupied by the **EastWest** dance club (www.ew-dubrovnik.com). Note that some of these are more exclusive and may charge admission on weekends.

Movies

The Old Town has a trio of movie theaters showing American blockbusters (usually in English with Croatian subtitles, unless the film's animated or for kids). The **Sloboda** cinema, right under the Bell Tower on Luža Square, is nothing special. But in good weather, head for the fun outdoor **Jadran** cinema, where you can lick ice cream (B.Y.O.) while you watch a movie with a Dubrovnik-mountaintop backdrop. This is a cheap, casual, and very Croatian scene, where people smoke and chat, and the neighbors sit in their windowsills to watch the movie (most nights in summer only, shows begin shortly after sundown; in the Old Town near the Pile Gate). For first-run 3-D movies, head to the **Visia Dubrovnik Multimedia Museum** just inside the Pile Gate (tel. 020/324-714, www.visiadubrovnik.com).

Sleeping in Dubrovnik

You basically have two options in Dubrovnik: a centrally located room in a private home *(soba)*; or a resort hotel on a distant beach, a bus ride away from the Old Town. Since Dubrovnik hotels are generally a poor value, I highly recommend giving the *sobe* a careful look. For locations, see the map on page 888.

Be warned that the Old Town is home to many popular discos. My listings are quieter than the norm, but if you're finding a place on your own, you may discover you have a late-night soundtrack—particularly if you're staying near the Stradun.

No matter where you stay, prices are much higher mid-June through mid-September, and highest in July and August. Reserve ahead for these peak times, especially during the Summer Festival (July 10-Aug 25 every year).

Sobe (Private Rooms): A Dubrovnik Specialty

In Dubrovnik, you'll almost always do better with a *soba* than with a hotel. Before you choose, carefully read the information on page 823. All of my favorite *sobe* are run by friendly

Sleep Code

(5 kn = about $1, €1 = about $1.40, country code: 385, area code: 020)

S = Single, **D** = Double/Twin, **T** = Triple, **Q** = Quad, **b** = bathroom. The modest tourist tax (about 7 kn per person, per night) is not included in these rates. Hotels generally accept credit cards and include breakfast in their rates, while most sobe accept only cash and don't offer breakfast. While rates are listed in euros, you'll pay in kunas. Everyone listed here speaks English.

Rates: If I've listed two sets of rates for an accommodation, I've noted when the second rate applies (generally off-season, Oct-May); if I've listed three sets of rates, separated by slashes, the first is for peak season (July-Aug), the second is for shoulder season (May-June and Sept-Oct), and the third is for off-season (Nov-April). The dates for seasonal rates vary by hotel, and prices can change without notice; verify the hotel's current rates online or by email. For other updates, see www.ricksteves.com/update.

Price Ranges: To help you easily sort through these listings, I've divided the accommodations into three categories based on the price for a double room with bath during high season:

$$$ Higher Priced—Most rooms €95 or more.
$$ Moderately Priced—Most rooms between €55-95.
$ Lower Priced—Most rooms €55 or less.

English-speaking Croatians and are inside or within easy walking distance of the Old Town. There's a range of places, from simple and cheap rooms where you'll share a bathroom, to downright fancy places with private facilities, air-conditioning, kitchenettes, and satellite TV, where you can be as anonymous as you like. Most *sobe* don't include breakfast, so I've listed some suggestions later, under "Eating in Dubrovnik."

Book direct, using the email addresses I've listed for each place—middleman agencies (including booking websites) tack on fees, making it more expensive for both you and your host. Note that many Dubrovnik *sobe* hosts might ask you to send them a deposit to secure your reservation. Sometimes they'll accept your credit-card number; others might want you to mail them a check or traveler's check (the better option) or wire them the money (which can be expensive). While it's a bit of a hassle, this request is reasonable and part of the experience of sleeping at a *soba*. Remember that you'll usually need to pay your bill in cash (kunas), not with a credit card.

In the Old Town, Above the Stradun Promenade

These are some of my favorite accommodations in Dubrovnik. All are located at the top of town, high above the Stradun, and all are excellent values. The first three are within a few steps of each other, along a little block dubbed by some "Rickova ulica." If you don't mind the very steep hike up, you'll find this to be a wonderful enclave of hospitality. When one of these places is full, they work together to find space for you. The last two listings are a few blocks over, and nearly as nice (and equally steep). Because all of these hosts live off-site, be sure to let them know when you'll arrive so they can let you in.

$$ Villa Ragusa, offers my favorite rooms for the price in the Old Town. Pero and Valerija Carević have renovated a 600-year-

old house at the top of town that was damaged during the war. The five comfortable, modern rooms come with atmospheric old wooden beams, antique furniture, and thoughtful touches. There are three doubles with bathrooms (including a top-floor room with breathtaking Old Town views for no extra charge—request when you reserve) and two singles that share a bathroom (S-€40/€35/€25, Db-€80/€70/€50, €8 breakfast can be eaten here or at nearby Stradun café, cash only, air-con, lots of stairs with no elevator, free Wi-Fi, Žudioska ulica 15, tel. 020/453-834, mobile 098-765-634, www .villaragusa-dubrovnik.com, villa.ragusa@du.t-com.hr). Pero offers his guests airport transfers for a reasonable €30, and can drive you on an all-day excursion (such as to Montenegro or Mostar) for €250—if you can split this cost with other guests, it's a good value (same price for up to 6 people).

$$ Apartments Paviša, next door to Villa Ragusa and run by Pero and Davorka Paviša, has three good, older-feeling rooms at the top of the Old Town (Db-€100/€70/€50, 10 percent discount if you book direct with this book, no breakfast, cash only, air-con, lots of stairs, free Wi-Fi, Žudioska ulica 19, mobile 098-427-399 or 098-175-2342, www.apartmentspavisa.com, davorka.pavisa@du .t-com.hr). They have two more rooms in the **Viktorija** neighborhood, about a 20-minute mostly uphill walk east of the Old Town. While it's a long-but-scenic walk into town, the views from these apartments are spectacular (same prices as in-town rooms, Frana Supila 59, bus stop nearby). Pero and Davorka also manage **Apartments Martecchini,** three units a bit closer to the main drag in the Old Town (small apartment-€100/€70/€50, bigger

Old Town Hotels & Restaurants

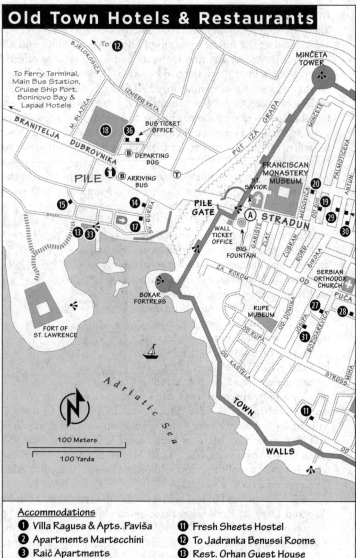

Accommodations

1. Villa Ragusa & Apts. Paviša
2. Apartments Martecchini
3. Raič Apartments
4. Plaza Apartments
5. Minerva Apartments
6. Karmen Apartments
7. Apartments Amoret (3)
8. Apartments Placa
9. Garden Cottage
10. Renata Zijadić Rooms
11. Fresh Sheets Hostel
12. To Jadranka Benussi Rooms
13. Rest. Orhan Guest House
14. Nedjeljka Benussi Rooms
15. Paulina Čumbelić Rooms
16. Villa Adriatica
17. Atlas Travel Agency
18. Hilton Imperial Dubrovnik
19. Hotel Stari Grad

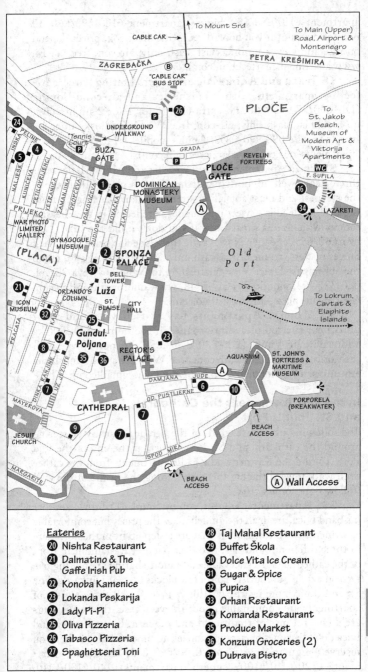

Eateries

20 Nishta Restaurant
21 Dalmatino & The Gaffe Irish Pub
22 Konoba Kamenice
23 Lokanda Peskarija
24 Lady Pi-Pi
25 Oliva Pizzeria
26 Tabasco Pizzeria
27 Spaghetteria Toni
28 Taj Mahal Restaurant
29 Buffet Škola
30 Dolce Vita Ice Cream
31 Sugar & Spice
32 Pupica
33 Orhan Restaurant
34 Komarda Restaurant
35 Produce Market
36 Konzum Groceries (2)
37 Dubrava Bistro

apartment-€110/€80/€50, biggest apartment-€120/€90/€60; 10 percent discount if you book direct with this book, prices depend on size and views, no breakfast, cash only, air-con, free Wi-Fi, www.apartmentsmartecchini.com).

$$ Ivana and Anita Raič are sisters renting three new-feeling apartments with kitchenettes and air-conditioning (Db-€90/€70/€50-60, no extra charge for 1- or 2-night stays, no breakfast, cash only, air-con, free Wi-Fi, Žudioska ulica 16, Ivana's mobile 098-996-0858, Anita's mobile 091-537-6035, www .apartments-raic.com, ivanaraic@gmail.com).

$$ Plaza Apartments, run by Lidija and Maro Matić, rents three clean, well-appointed apartments on a plant-filled lane—the steepest and most appealing stretch of stairs leading up from the Stradun. Lidija's sweet personality is reflected in the cheerful rooms, which are a great value if you don't mind the hike (Db-€75/€60/€55, cheaper Nov-April, these special prices for Rick Steves readers, no breakfast, cash only, air-con, free Wi-Fi, climb the stairs past Dolce Vita gelato shop to Nalješkovićeva 22, tel. 020/321-493, mobile 091-517-7048, www.dubrovnik-online.com /apartment_plaza, lidydu@yahoo.com).

$$ Minerva Apartments has two cozy ground-floor units near the top of a similar lane, in the home of Dubravka Vidosavljević-Vučić (Db-€80/€75/€65, cheaper Nov-April, cash only, no breakfast, air-con, free Wi-Fi, washing machine, Antuninska 14, mobile 091-252-9677, duvivu@gmail.com).

In the Old Town, near the Cathedral and St. John's Fort

The following places are south of the Stradun, mostly clustering around the cathedral and St. John's Fort, at the end of the Old Port. To find the Karmen and Zijadić apartments from the cathedral, walk toward the big fort tower along the inside of the wall (follow signs for *akvarji*).

$$$ Apartments Amoret, run by Branka Dabrović and her husband Ivica, are in all the guidebooks. The pricey but comfortable apartments, with furnishings that are a step up from the norm, are in three different buildings: two over Amoret Restaurant in front of the cathedral (at Restićeva 2); eight more sharing an inviting terrace on a quiet, untouristy lane a few blocks east (at Dinka Ranjine 5); and three more nearby (at Ilije Sarake 4). All three classes of apartments are comparably good; in every case, the furnishings are a tasteful mix of traditional and modern. Since Branka and Ivica don't live on-site, arrange a meeting time and place when you reserve ("regular" apartments-€100/€90/€80; "standard" apartments-€120/€110/€100; "superb" apartments-€140/€130/€110, cheaper Nov-April, 30 percent more for 1-night stays, 20 percent more for 2-night stays, 10 percent more for 3-night stays, no breakfast, cash only, air-con, free Wi-Fi, mobile 091-530-4910, tel. & fax 020/324-005, www.dubrovnik-amoret.com, dubrovnik@post.t-com.hr).

$$ Karmen Apartments are well-run by a Brit named Marc and his Croatian wife Silva, who offer four apartments just inside the big fort. The prices are very high, and they're in all the guidebooks, but the apartments are big, well-equipped, and homey-feeling, each with a bathroom and kitchen. The decor is eclectic but tasteful, and Marc and Silva are good hosts, with a virtual mini-museum of historic Dubrovnik maps and documents in the stairwell (smaller apartment-€90/€70, mid-sized apartment-€135/€108, bigger apartment-€155/€110; higher price is for May-Sept, less Dec-March, usually 3-night minimum, no breakfast, cash only, air-con, free Wi-Fi, near the aquarium at Bandureva 1, tel. 020/323-433, mobile 098-619-282, www.karmendu.com, marc.van-bloemen@du.t-com.hr).

$$ Apartments Placa (PLAH-tsah; not to be confused with Plaza Apartments, described earlier) is run by Tonči (TOHN-chee). He rents three apartments with some antique furnishings and some modern, overlooking the market square in the heart of the Old Town. You might get some early-morning noise from the market set-up, but the double-paned windows help, and the location is wonderfully central. Since Tonči lives elsewhere, clearly communicate your arrival time (Db-€90/€80/€70, cheaper Nov-April, no breakfast, cash only, no extra charge for 1- or 2-night stays, several flights of stairs, air-con, free Wi-Fi, Gundulićeva poljana 5, mobile 091-721-9202, www.dubrovnik-online.com/apartments_placa, tonci.korculanin@du.t-com.hr).

$$ Garden Cottage is exactly that: a small freestanding house nestled in a very rare patch of green. It's a peaceful oasis smack-dab in the heart of the bustling city (just off the plaza in front of the Jesuit church). Roberto and his mother Marija (also recommended tour guides—see page 852) live in an old Dubrovnik mansion with a fine little garden, and they've converted the old laundry building into a simple rental apartment that sleeps up to four people. When you book this place, you're also renting the entire garden for your own use...very cool, particularly in a city with virtually no green space (€80/€70/€60 per night for 4 or more nights, €90/€80/€70 per night for 2-3 nights, €100/€90/€80 for 1 night, extra bed-€15, cash only, air-con, washing machine, kitchenette, mobile 091-541-6637, bobdel70@yahoo.com).

$$ Renata Zijadić, a friendly mom who speaks good English, offers four well-located rooms with slanting floors, funky colors, and over-the-top antique furniture. A single and a double (both with great views) share one bathroom; another double features an ornate old cabinet and its own bathroom; and the top-floor apartment comes with low ceilings and fine vistas (S-€30/€28, D-€50/€45, Db-€60/€50, apartment-€85/€75, second price is for June and Sept, cheaper Oct-May, no extra charge for 1- or 2-night stays, no breakfast, cash only, all rooms have air-con except the single, free Wi-Fi; follow signs for wall access and walk up the steps marked *ulica Stajeva* going over the street to find Stajeva 1; tel. 020/323-623, www.dubrovnik-online.com/house_renata, renatadubrovnik@yahoo.com).

$ Fresh Sheets, a bright, stylish, and appealingly funky hostel run by a fun-loving Canadian-Croatian couple, is your best youth hostel option in the Old Town. The 22 bunks (two 8-bed dorms, one 4-bed dorm, and a double room) sit above a tight but enjoyable common area. Located at the very top of town just inside the town walls, it's a steep hike up from the main drag, but worth it if you enjoy youthful backpacker bonding (€22-33/bunk in a dorm, €25-38/person in a private room, likely closed Nov-March, free breakfast, free Internet access and Wi-Fi, lockers, kitchen, Svetog Šimuna/Smokvina 15, mobile 091-799-2086, www.freshsheets hostel.com, beds@igotfresh.com).

In the Pile Neighborhood, Just Outside the Old Town

There's a concentration of good *sobe* just outside the Old Town's Pile Gate. The Pile (PEE-leh) neighborhood offers all the conveniences of the modern world (grocery store, bus stop, post office, travel agency, etc.), just steps from Dubrovnik's magical Old Town. The first place is up the hill (away from the water) from the Pile Gate's bus stop; the rest cluster around a quiet, no-name cove near

Restaurant Orhan. From the bus stop area in front of Pile Gate, various lanes lead down toward this cove.

$$ Jadranka and Milan Benussi, a middle-aged professional couple, rent four rooms in a quiet, traffic-free neighborhood. Their delightful stony-chic home, complete with a leafy terrace, is a steep 10-minute hike above the Old Town—close enough to be convenient, but far enough to take you away from the bustle and into a calm residential zone. Jadranka speaks good English, enjoys visiting with her guests, and gives her place a modern Croatian class unusual for *sobe.* This is one of your best values and most comfortable home bases in Dubrovnik, if you don't mind the walk (small Db-€60/€55, big Db-€70/€65, small apartment-€90/€85, big apartment with balcony-€100/€95, cheaper Oct-May, 20 percent more for stays less than 4 nights, no breakfast, cash only, air-con, kitchenettes, free Wi-Fi, Miha Klaića 10, tel. 020/429-339, mobile 098-928-1300, www.dubrovnik-benussi.com, jadranka @dubrovnik-benussi.com). To find the Benussis, go to the big Hilton Hotel just outside the Pile Gate (across from the TI). Walk up the little stepped lane called Marijana Blažića at the upper-left corner of the Hilton cul-de-sac. When that lane dead-ends, go left up ulica Don Iva Bjelokosića (more steps) until you see a little church on the left. The Benussis' house is just before this church.

$$ Restaurant Orhan Guest House allows hotel anonymity at *sobe* prices. Its 11 basic, old-fashioned, ramshackle rooms—in a couple of different buildings around the corner from the restaurant—are well-located and quiet, with modern bathrooms. As the rooms are an afterthought to the restaurant, don't expect a warm welcome (Sb or Db-€60-75/€40, includes breakfast, cash only, air-con, free Wi-Fi, Od Tabakarije 1, tel. & fax 020/414-183, www .restaurant-orhan.com, restoran.orhan@yahoo.com). Their restaurant is also a good spot for a scenic meal (described later, under "Eating in Dubrovnik").

$$ Nedjeljka Benussi, the sister-in-law of Jadranka Benussi (listed earlier), rents three modern, spacious, straightforward rooms sharing two bathrooms and a pretty view (D-€70/€55, T-€80/€75, cheaper Dec-March, same price for 1-night stays, no breakfast, cash only, fans but no air-con, Sv. Đurđa 4, tel. 020/423-062, mobile 098-170-5699).

$ Paulina Čumbelić is a kind, gentle woman renting four old-fashioned rooms in her homey, clean, and peaceful house (S-€30/€27, D-€50/€40, T-€60/€55, 20 percent more for 1- or 2-night stays, no breakfast, cash only, closed in winter, can be noisy outside, Od Tabakarije 2, tel. 020/421-327, mobile 091-530-7985).

Beyond the Ploče Gate, East of the Old Town

To reach these options, you'll go through the Ploče Gate and walk along the road stretching east from the Old Town (with fine views back on the Old Port). This area is shared by giant waterfront luxury hotels and residential areas, so it has a bit less character than the Pile and Old Town listings (which I prefer).

$$ Apartments Paviša, described on page 887, has two fine apartments in the Viktorija neighborhood about a 20-minute walk or short bus ride from town.

$$ Villa Adriatica has four old-fashioned rooms above a travel agency and a family home just outside the Ploče Gate, a few steps from the Old Town. The rooms are antique-furnished, but have modern bathrooms, TVs, and air-conditioning. While impersonal and a lesser value than my other listings, it's worth considering just for the huge, shared terrace with priceless Old Port views, plus a common living room and kitchen furnished with museum-piece antiques. Teo manages the rooms; ask for him at the Perla Adriatic travel agency, just outside the Ploče Gate (Db-€85-95/€80-90/€75-85, cheaper Nov-April, price depends on size and view, 20 percent more for 1- or 2-night stays, no breakfast, cash only, air-con, free Wi-Fi in some areas, Frana Supila 4, mobile 098-334-500, tel. 020/411-962, fax 020/422-766, www.villa-adriatica.net, booking @villa-adriatica.net, Tomšić family).

Sobe-Booking Websites and Agencies

Several websites put you in touch with Dubrovnik's *sobe* and apartments. Of course, you'll save yourself and your host money if you book direct, but these sites are convenient. For example, www .dubrovnikapartmentsource.com, run by an American couple, offers a range of carefully selected, well-described accommodations. You can browse a variety of options, then reserve your choice and pay a nonrefundable deposit by credit card. Another, bigger operation—with a wider selection but less personal attention—is www.adriatica.net; international sites such as www.booking.com are another good option.

If you arrive without a reservation and the TI isn't too busy, they might be able to call around and find you a *soba* for no charge. Otherwise, just about any travel agency in town can help you, on the spot or in advance...for a fee. **Atlas** is the biggest company (figure Db-€55-60 and apartment-€75-100 in June-Sept, €15-20 less in shoulder season; for more on Atlas, see page 850).

Hotels

If you must stay in a hotel, you have only a few good options. There are just two hotels inside the Old Town walls—and one of them charges $500 a night (Pucić Palace, www.thepucicpalace.com). Any big, resort-style hotel within walking distance of the Old Town will run you at least €200. These inflated prices drive most visitors to Boninovo Bay or the Lapad Peninsula, a bus ride west of the Old Town. In the mass-tourism tradition, many European visitors choose to take the half-board option at their hotel (i.e., dinner in the hotel restaurant). This can be convenient and a good value—especially considering the relatively low quality of Dubrovnik's restaurants (explained later, under "Eating in Dubrovnik")—but the Old Town is a much more atmospheric place to dine.

In and near the Old Town

$$$ Hilton Imperial Dubrovnik, sitting regally just outside the Pile Gate, is the closest big hotel to the Old Town. This grand 19th-century building was recently overhauled to create 147 plush rooms. If you want predictable Hilton comfort at outlandish prices a short walk from the Old Town, this is the place (Db-€300, less off-season, €55 extra for sea view, €65 extra for balcony but no view, €120 extra for balcony and view, most rates include breakfast but not the 10 percent tax, elevator, air-con, pay Wi-Fi in lobby and pay cable Internet in rooms, parking-€27/night, $7 bottles of water at the reception desk, Marijana Blažića 2, tel. 020/320-320, fax 020/320-220, www.hilton.com, sales.dubrovnik@hilton.com).

$$$ Hotel Stari Grad knows it's the only real hotel option inside the Old Town—and charges accordingly. It has eight modern yet nicely old-fashioned rooms a half-block off the Old Town's main drag. The rooftop terrace enjoys an amazing view over orange tiles. This place books up fast, so reserve early (Sb-€180/€134/€99, Db-€240/€192/€140, no extra charge for 1- or 2-night stays, includes breakfast, air-con, lots of stairs with no elevator, free Wi-Fi, Od Sigurate 4, tel. 020/322-244, fax 020/321-256, www .hotelstarigrad.com, info@hotelstarigrad.com).

Near Boninovo Bay

Boninovo Bay (boh-NEE-noh-voh) is your best bet for an affordable and well-located hotel. Above this bay are Dubrovnik's only three-star hotels within walking distance of the Old Town (not to mention the city's only official youth hostel). These places offer slightly better prices and closer proximity to the Old Town than the farther-out Lapad Bay resorts. They're on or near the water, but don't have views of the Old Town (which is around the bend). Boninovo Bay is an uphill 20-minute walk or five-minute bus ride from the Old Town (straight up Branitelja Dubrovnika). Once you're comfortable with the buses, the location is great: Any bus that leaves the Pile Gate stops first at Boninovo Bay. You'll see the bay on your left as you climb the hill, then get off at the stop after the traffic light (or stay on bus #4, which stops even closer to the hotels). To reach the hotels from the Boninovo bus stop, go up Pera Čingrije (the busy road running along the top of the cliff overlooking the sea). There's a super little bakery, Pekarnica Klas, on the right (across the street from Hotel Bellevue).

$$$ Hotel Bellevue has a striking location, with its back against the cliff rising up from Boninovo Bay and an elevator plunging directly to its own pebbly beach. Completely gutted and rebuilt just a few years ago, its 91 top-notch rooms—all but two with sea views, many with balconies—offer upscale wood-grain elegance (standard Db-generally €250/€220, less Nov-April, very flexible rates, €50 more for balcony, air-con, elevator, free Internet access and Wi-Fi, Pera Čingrije 7, tel. 020/330-000, fax 020/330-100, www.hotel-bellevue.hr, welcome@hotel-bellevue.hr).

$$$ Hotel R, a homey enclave with just 10 rooms, feels friendlier and less greedy than all the big resort hotels. Well-run by

DUBROVNIK

the Rešetar family, it's a good small-hotel value (Sb-€72/€56/€50, Db-€110/€86/€77, closed Nov-Easter, 10 percent more for balcony, half-board-€13, air-con, free Wi-Fi, just beyond the big Hotel Lero at Iva Vojnovića 16, tel. 020/333-200, fax 020/333-208, www .hotel-r.hr, helpdesk@hotel-r.hr).

$$$ Hotel Lero, 250 yards up the street from the bus stop, has 140 recently renovated rooms and a fine outdoor pool. Choose between so-so sea views with some road noise, or quieter back rooms (soft rates, but generally Sb-€110/€85, Db-€140/€106, cheaper mid-Oct-April; in busy times, you may be quoted more than these rates—try asking for a better deal; "superior" rooms with balcony not worth the extra €30/person, air-con, elevator, pay Internet access, free Wi-Fi, half-board-€6, Iva Vojnovića 14, tel. 020/341-333, fax 020/332-123, www.hotel-lero.hr, sales@hotel -lero.hr).

$ Dubrovnik's official **Youth Hostel** is quiet, modern, and well-run by proud manager Laura. It's institutional, with 82 beds in 19 fresh, woody dorms and few extra hostel amenities (bunk in 4- to 6-bed dorm-€18/€17/€16, cheaper Nov-March, €1.50 more for nonmembers, includes sheets, includes breakfast, no air-con in rooms, free Internet access, no Wi-Fi; reception open daily June-Oct 7:00-3:00 in the morning, Nov-May 8:00-14:00 & 18:00-20:00; 2:00 a.m. curfew in summer, none in winter; up the steps at ulica bana Jelačića 15-17 to ulica Vinka Sagrestana 3, tel. 020/423-241, fax 020/412-592, www.hfhs.hr, dubrovnik@hfhs.hr). From the Boninovo bus stop, go down Pera Čingrije toward Hotel Bellevue, but take the first right uphill onto ulica bana Jelačića and look for signs up to the hostel on your left, on ulica Vinka Sagrestana. Several houses nearby rent rooms to those who prefer a double...and pick off would-be hostelers as they approach.

In Lapad

For a real resort-style vacation (at premium prices), many travelers call the touristy area around Lapad (LAH-pahd) Bay home. The main drag running through the middle of this scene, called Šetalište Kralja Zvonimira, is a nicely pedestrianized people zone buzzing with tourists, restaurants, cafés, and mild diversions. From the bus stop, the main drag leads to a pleasant pebble beach good for swimming and a romantic bayside path. While I much prefer sleeping near the Old Town, this is an appealing place to be on vacation (even if the Old Town weren't just a short bus ride away). To get here from the Old Town's Pile Gate, pile onto bus #6 with all the other tourists and get off at the Pošta Lapad stop (poorly marked—after bus turns left away from the big harbor, watch for low-profile yellow *pošta* sign on left; 4-6 buses/hour until 24:30, 15 minutes). A taxi costs about 60 kn.

$$$ *Small Hotels in Lapad:* In this area, I like three new-ish, interchangeable small hotels. While not affiliated with each other, each one has similar amenities—air-con, elevator (except Hotel Dubrovnik), Internet access either in lobby or in room—and similar prices (roughly Db-€160/€140/€110, but prices are very soft and can flex with demand, season, and length of stay; check online for the latest, and ask for a deal when you reserve). **Hotel Aquarius,** hiding a block off the main drag, has 24 comfortable, plush-feeling rooms and an inviting terrace out front (Mata Vodopića 8, tel. 020/456-111, fax 020/456-100, www.hotel-aquarius.net, stjepanka@hotel-aquarius.net). **Hotel Perla,** right on the main drag, has 25 modern rooms (tel. 020/438-244, fax 020/438-245, www.perla-dubrovnik.com, info@perla-dubrovnik.com). **Hotel Dubrovnik,** two doors up from the Perla, has 25 simpler rooms (tel. 020/435-030, fax 020/435-999, www.hoteldubrovnik.hr, info@hoteldubrovnik.com).

Eating in Dubrovnik

Dubrovnik disappoints diners with high prices, surly service, and mediocre quality. With the constant influx of deep-pocketed tour-

ists corrupting greedy restaurateurs, places here tend to go downhill faster than a game of marbles on the *Titanic.* Promising new restaurants open all the time, but most quickly fade, and what's great one year can be miserable the next. Therefore, lower your expectations, take my suggestions

with a grain of salt, and ask around locally for what's good this month. Don't bother looking for a "local" favorite anywhere near the Old Town—people who live here eat out at restaurants in the 'burbs. The good news is that it's atmospheric. Anywhere you dine, breezy outdoor seating is a no-brainer, and scrawny, adorable kittens beg for table scraps. In general, seafood restaurants are good only at seafood; if you want pasta, go to a pasta place.

In the Old Town

Nishta ("Nothing"), featuring a short menu of delicious vegetarian fusion cuisine with Asian flair, offers a welcome change of pace from the Dalmatian seafood-pasta-pizza rut. Busy Swiss owner/chef Gildas cooks, while his wife Ruža cheerfully serves a steady stream of return diners. This tiny place—which, in my experience, is just about the only reliably good eatery in town—has just a few indoor and outdoor tables. Even if you're not a vegetarian, it's worth a visit; reserve a day ahead in peak season (60-85-kn main courses, May-Oct Mon-Sat 11:30-22:00, Nov-April generally open Mon-Sat for lunch only, closed Sun year-round, on the restaurant-clogged Prijeko street—near the Pile Gate end of the street, tel. 020/322-088).

Dalmatino has some of the best traditional Dalmatian cooking in the city—without having to pay a premium. South African-Croatian owner Robert prides himself on cooking each dish to order; while this may take a few minutes longer, you can taste the results. While there's no seating on a street or square, you'll find cozy tables tucked along the alley leading to the spacious, classy-but-not-stuffy dining room (45-110-kn pastas, 65-125-kn main dishes, daily 11:00-23:00, Miha Pracata 6, tel. 020/323-070).

Konoba Kamenice, a no-frills fish restaurant, is a local institution offering inexpensive, fresh, and good meals on a charming market square, as central as can be in the Old Town. On the limited menu, the seafood dishes are excellent (try their octopus salad, even if you don't think you like octopus), while the few non-seafood dishes are uninspired. Some of the waitstaff are notorious for their playfully brusque service, but loyal patrons happily put up with it. Arrive early, or you'll have to wait (35-70-kn main courses, daily 8:00-23:00, until 22:00 off-season, Gundulićeva poljana 8, tel. 020/323-682).

Lokanda Peskarija enjoys an enticing setting, with a sea of tables facing the Old Port. Servings are hearty and come in a pot, "home-style." The 70-kn seafood risotto easily feeds two, and sharing is no problem. The menu's tiny—with only seafood options, and not much in the way of vegetables. Locals complain that the quality has taken a nosedive (crank-'em-out food and disinterested service) ever since the restaurant's following has grown and its idyllic dining area has been expanded to the hilt. But for reasonably priced seafood dishes on the water, this remains an acceptable option (60-85-kn main courses, daily 12:00-24:00, very limited indoor seating fills up fast, plenty of outdoor tables—which can also fill up, tel. 020/324-750, no reservations taken in summer).

Lady Pi-Pi, named for a comical, anatomically correct, and slightly off-putting statue out front, sits high above town just inside the wall. The food, prepared on an open grill, is just an excuse to sit out on their terrace, with several tables overlooking the rooftops of Dubrovnik (65-70-kn pastas, 65-110-kn main dishes, daily May-Sept 9:00-24:00, closed Oct-April, Peline b.b., tel. 020/321-288).

Pizza: Dubrovnik seems to have a pizzeria on every corner. Little separates the various options—just look for a menu and outdoor seating option that appeals to you. I've eaten well at **Oliva Pizzeria,** just behind St. Blaise's Church (40-65-kn pizzas, Lučarica 5, daily 10:00-24:00, tel. 020/324-594). Around the side is a handy take-out window for a bite on the go (though **Tutto Bene,** a few blocks down on od Puča, has better take-away slices). Close to the Old Town, but just far enough away to cater mostly to locals, **Tabasco Pizzeria** is tucked at the corner of the parking lot beneath the cable-car station. Unpretentious and affordable, this is the place to come if the pizza is more important than the setting—though the outdoor terrace does have views of the Old Town walls...over a sea of parked cars (40-50-kn pizzas, 70-80-kn "jumbo" pizzas, daily 9:00-23:00, Hvarska 48A, tel. 020/429-595).

Pasta: **Spaghetteria Toni** is popular with natives and tourists. While it's nothing fancy, it offers good pastas at reasonable prices. Choose between the cozy 10-table interior or the long alley filled with outdoor tables (45-80-kn pastas, 45-65-kn salads, daily in summer 11:00-23:00, closed Sun in winter, closed Jan, Nikole Božidarevića 14, tel. 020/323-134).

Bosnian Cuisine: For a break from Croatian fare, consider the grilled meats and other tasty Bosnian dishes at the misnamed **Taj Mahal.** Though the service can be lacking, the menu offers an enticing taste of the Turkish-flavored land to the east. Choose between the tight interior, which feels like a Bosnian tea house, or tables out on the alley (40-55-kn salads, 50-120-kn main courses, daily 10:00-24:00, Nikole Gučetića 2, tel. 020/323-221). For a primer on Bosnian food, see the "Balkan Flavors" sidebar on page 1090.

Sandwiches: **Buffet Škola** is a rare bit of pre-glitz Dubrovnik just a few steps off the Stradun, serving take-away or sit-down sandwiches on homemade bread. Squeeze into the hole-in-the-wall interior, or sit at one of the outdoor tables (25-30 kn, 60-80-kn plates, daily 8:00-22:00 or 23:00, Antuninska 1, tel. 020/321-096).

Pub Grub: **The Gaffe Irish Pub** offers a break from traditional Dalmatian food, with a simple menu of British Isles-style pub food, including burgers and some international flavors (Thai curry, tandoori, and so on). It isn't exactly high cuisine...but at least it's a break from seafood risotto (40-52-kn light meals, 50-90-kn big meals, open long hours daily, Miha Pracata 4, mobile 098-196-2149).

Ice Cream: Dubrovnik has lots of great *sladoled,* but locals swear by the stuff at **Dolce Vita** (daily 9:00-24:00, a half-block off the Stradun at Nalješkovićeva 1A, tel. 020/321-666).

Other Desserts: Two good dessert shops in Dubrovnik have been getting raves from locals and visitors. If you have a sweet tooth, drop by one or both to survey their display cases (12-20-kn cakes). They're within a few short blocks of each other: **Sugar and Spice** (pink-and-stone hole-in-the-wall, "global desserts with a Dalmatian twist," Mon-Sat 9:00-22:00, Sun 11:00-19:00, Sv. Josipa 5, mobile 091-361-9550) and **Pupica** (also has good coffee drinks, long hours daily, Cvijete Zuzorić b.b., mobile 099-216-545).

The Old Town's "Restaurant Row," Prijeko Street: The street called Prijeko, a block toward the mainland from the Stradun promenade, is lined with outdoor, tourist-oriented eateries—each one with a huckster out front trying to lure in diners. (Many of them aggressively try to snare passersby down on the Stradun, as well.) Don't be sucked into this vortex of bad food at outlandish prices. The only place worth seeking out here is Nishta (described earlier); the rest are virtually guaranteed to disappoint. Still, it can be fun to take a stroll along here—the atmosphere is lively, and the sales pitches are entertainingly desperate.

Just Outside the Old Town, with a View

Orhan Restaurant, overlooking the tranquil cove at the Pile neighborhood outside the Old Town, feels just beyond the tourist crush. It features disinterested service and unremarkable food, but great views on a large terrace (reserve a seat here in advance). Watch the people walk the Old Town walls across the cove. This is a handy spot for a scenic breakfast (75-100-kn pastas, 80-180-kn main courses, daily 8:00-23:00, cash only, Od Tabakarije 1, tel. 020/414-183).

Komarda serves up forgettable food on a memorably romantic terrace, with views of Dubrovnik's walls and Old Port. Tables are scattered around a tranquil garden just above the sea and a concrete beach. As there's no point eating here unless you have a good view, consider dropping by early in the day to pick out and reserve the table of your choice for dinner (50-80-kn pastas, 75-135-kn main courses, 60-kn lunch special, daily 7:00-2:00 in the morning, reservations essential in summer, mobile 098-428-239). To find it, exit the Old Town through the Ploče Gate (east). After walking through the final fortification, you'll reach a block of travel agencies. Once you pass these, look for the stairs down to Komarda, on the right.

Picnic Tips

Dubrovnik's lack of great restaurant options makes it a perfect place to picnic. You can shop for fresh fruits and veggies at the open-air produce market (each morning near the cathedral, on the square called Gundulićeva Poljana). Supplement your picnic with grub from the cheap **Konzum grocery store** (one location on the market square near the produce-vendors: Mon-Sat 7:00-21:00, Sun 7:00-13:00; another near the bus stop just outside Pile Gate: Mon-Sat 7:00-21:00, Sun 8:00-13:00). Good picnic spots include the shaded benches overlooking the Old Port; the Porporela breakwater (beyond the Old Port and fort—comes with a swimming area, sunny no-shade benches, and views of Lokrum Island); and the green, welcoming park in what was the moat just under the Pile Gate entry to the Old Town.

Breakfast

If you're sleeping in a *soba*, you'll likely be on your own for breakfast. Fortunately, you have plenty of cafés and pastry shops to choose from, and your host probably has a favorite she can recommend. In the Old Town, **Dubrava Bistro**—which locals call "Snack Bar"— has great views and fine outdoor seating at the most colorful end of the Stradun. While the ham resembles Spam and the continental breakfast is paltry, you can't beat the real estate. Locals who hang out here—catching up with their friends as they stroll by—call this their low-tech version of "Facebook" (basic 38-46-kn egg dishes, 24-kn caffè lattes; you'll pay 25 percent less if you sit inside—but then there's no point eating here; daily 8:00-24:00, Placa 6, tel. 020/321-229). For better food in a less atmospheric setting, **The Gaffe Irish Pub** has a good menu of breakfast options (30-42 kn, served daily 9:00-11:30, Miha Pracata 4, mobile 098-196-2149). In the Pile neighborhood, I like **Orhan Restaurant,** right on the cove (described earlier; 50 kn for omelet or continental breakfast, served daily 8:00-11:00). Some of the other restaurants listed in this section (including **Konoba Kamenice**) also serve breakfast. Not many places serve before 9:00 or 10:00; if you'll be departing early, stock up on groceries the night before.

On Lapad Bay

If you want a break from the Old Town, consider venturing to Lapad Bay. The ambience is pleasant and Lapad is worth an evening stroll (for details on getting here, see page 896 under "Sleeping in Dubrovnik"). This area's main drag, **Šetalište Kralja Zvonimira,** is an amazingly laid-back pedestrian lane where bars have hammocks, Internet terminals are scattered through a forested park, and a folksy Croatian family ambience holds its own against the better-funded force of international tourism. Stroll from near Hotel Zagreb to the bay, marked by Hotel Kompas. From Hotel Kompas, a romantic walk—softly lit at night—leads past some splurge restaurants along the bay through the woods, with plenty of private little stone coves for lingering.

Dubrovnik Connections

For general tips on getting around the Dalmatian Coast, see page 824. Note that the boats listed here leave from Dubrovnik's Port Gruž, a bus ride away from the Old Town (described earlier, under "Arrival in Dubrovnik—By Car Ferry or Catamaran"). Be aware that eventual redevelopment of the port area will likely move the

Jadrolinija ferries and *Nona Ana* catamaran departure point out to the far end of the port, under the big bridge. If I've listed a range of prices, the specific fare depends on the season.

From Dubrovnik by Big Jadrolinija Car Ferry: From June to September only, the big boats leave Dubrovnik twice weekly in the morning and go to **Sobra** on Mljet Island (1.25 hours, plus a 1.25-hour bus ride to the national park, 75-90 kn), **Korčula** (4.5 hours, 90-110 kn), **Stari Grad** on Hvar Island (8.75 hours, 110-130 kn), **Split** (11 hours, 110-130 kn), and **Rijeka** (21 hours including overnight from Split to Rijeka, 215-255 kn). These ferries do not run October through May, and the price range depends on the season. However, boat schedules are subject to change—confirm your plans at a local TI, or see www.jadrolinija.hr.

From Dubrovnik by Speedy *Nona Ana* Catamaran: This handy service connects Dubrovnik to popular islands to the north (Mljet, Korčula, and Lastovo). This schedule is subject to change from year to year, so carefully confirm the details before planning your trip. In the summer (June-Sept), the boat departs Dubrovnik each morning and heads for **Sobra** (1.5 hours, 40 kn) and **Polače** (1.75 hours, 54 kn) on Mljet Island. In the peak months of July and August, it sometimes continues on to **Korčula** (4/week, 2.75 hours, 58 kn) and **Lastovo Island** (2/week, 4 hours, 68 kn). In the winter (Oct-May), the boat goes each afternoon at 14:30 to Sobra and Polače on Mljet, but does not go all the way to Korčula or Lastovo. The catamaran leaves from Dubrovnik's Port Gruž (buy tickets at the kiosk next to the boat, ticket window opens 1 hour before departure; in peak season, it's smart to show up about an hour ahead to be sure you get on the boat). Confirm schedules at the Dubrovnik TI, or check www.gv-line.hr.

By Bus to: Split (almost hourly, generally at the top of each hour, less off-season, 3.5-5 hours, 100 kn), **Korčula** (summer: 2/day at 9:00 and 15:00; off-season: Mon-Sat 1/day at 15:00, Sun 2/day at 15:00 and 18:00; 3.5 hours, 90 kn; also consider the shuttle-bus service described below), **Rijeka** (5/day, 12.5-13 hours, 410-510 kn), **Zagreb** (7/day including some overnight options, 10 hours, 200-220 kn), **Kotor** in Montenegro (2/day, 2.5 hours, 90-110 kn), **Mostar** (5/day in summer, 3/day in winter, 4-5 hours, 80-115 kn), **Sarajevo** (2/day at 8:00 and 15:15, 5-6.5 hours, 245-255 kn; also a night bus at 21:00; only 1/day in winter), **Pula** and **Rovinj** (nightly, 15 hours to Pula, 16 hours to Rovinj). As usual, schedules are subject to change—confirm locally before making the trip to the bus station. For bus information, call 060-305-070 (a pricey toll line, but worth it).

By Shuttle Bus to Korčula: Korčula-based Korkyra Info Travel Agency runs a handy door-to-door shuttle service from your Dubrovnik accommodations to Korčula (departs at various times—call to ask and to reserve, may stop briefly in Ston if you want, by request only Nov-Feb, 2 hours, 150 kn one-way, mobile 091-571-4355, www.korkyra.info, info@korkyra.info).

By Plane: To quickly connect remote Dubrovnik with the rest of your trip, consider a cheap flight. For information on Dubrovnik's airport, see "Arrival in Dubrovnik—By Plane," earlier.

By Car: For tips on driving along the Dalmatian Coast between Dubrovnik and Split, see page 947 in the Split chapter.

Can I Get to Greece from Dubrovnik? Not easily. Your best bet is to fly (though there are no direct flights, aside from the occasional charter flight from Dubrovnik to Athens—you'll generally have to transfer elsewhere in Europe). Even though Croatia and Greece are nearly neighbors, no direct boats connect them, and the overland connection is extremely long and rugged.

What About Italy? Flying is the easiest option, though there are only a few direct flights (on Croatia Airlines to Rome, Venice, or Milan; or on easyJet to Rome or Milan). You can take a direct night boat from Dubrovnik to Bari, or head to Split for more boat connections (for more on all of these boats, see page 942). The overland connection is overly long (figure 5 hours to Split, then 5 hours to Zagreb, then 7 hours to Venice).

SPLIT

Dubrovnik is the darling of the Dalmatian Coast, but Split (pronounced as it's spelled) is Croatia's "second city" (after Zagreb), bustling with 178,000 people. If you've been hopping along the coast, landing in urban Split feels like a return to civilization. While most Dalmatian coastal towns seem made for tourists, Split is real and vibrant—a shipbuilding city with ugly sprawl surrounding an atmospheric Old Town, which teems with Croatians living life to the fullest.

Though today's Split throbs to a modern, young beat, its history goes way back—all the way to the Roman Empire. Along with all the trappings of a modern city, Split has some of the best Roman ruins this side of Italy. In the fourth century A.D., the Roman Emperor Diocletian (245-313) wanted to retire in his native Dalmatia, so he built a huge palace here. Eventually, the palace was abandoned. Then locals, fleeing seventh-century Slavic invaders, moved in and made themselves at home, and a medieval town sprouted from the rubble of the old palace. In the 15th century, the Venetians took over the Dalmatian Coast. They developed and fortified Split, slathering the city with a new layer of Gothic-Renaissance architecture.

But even as Split grew, the nucleus remained the ruins of Diocletian's Palace. To this day, 2,000 people live or work inside the former palace walls. A maze of narrow alleys is home to fashionable boutiques and galleries, wonderfully atmospheric cafés, and Roman artifacts around every corner.

Today's Split has a split personality, as it struggles to decide how it fits into Croatia's tourist-mecca image: Is it a big, drab

metropolis; a no-nonsense transit point; an impressive destination in its own right, with sights to rival Dubrovnik's...or all
three? While largely lacking Dubrovnik's over-the-top romance,
Split settles for being nobody's "second-best." It's its own city—an
antidote to all that's quaint and cutesy in Dalmatia.

Planning Your Time

Split is southern Croatia's hub for bus, boat, train, and flight connections to other destinations in the country and abroad. This
means that many visitors stop in Split only long enough to change
boats. But the city is the perfect real-life contrast to the lazy, prettified Dalmatian beach resorts—it deserves a full day. Begin by
strolling the remains of Diocletian's Palace, then take a coffee
break along the Riva promenade or lunch in the Old Town. After
lunch, browse the shops or visit a couple of Split's museums (the
Meštrović Gallery, which is a long walk or short bus or taxi ride
from the Old Town, is tops). Promenading along the Riva with the
natives is *the* evening activity, while nursing a drink at an atmospheric open-air café is a close second.

Orientation to Split

(area code: 021)

Split sprawls, but almost everything of interest to travelers is
around the City Harbor (Gradska Luka). At the top of this harbor is the Old Town (Stari
Grad). Between the Old
Town and the sea is the
Riva, a waterfront pedes-
trian promenade lined with
cafés and shaded by palm
trees. The main ferry terminal (Trajektni Terminal,
a.k.a. Trajektna Luka) juts
into the harbor from the east
side. Along the harborfront embankment between the ferry terminal and the Old Town are the long-distance bus station (Autobusni
Kolodvor) and the forlorn little train station (Željeznička Stanica).
West of the Old Town, poking into the Adriatic, is the lush and
hilly Marjan peninsula.

Split's domino-shaped Old Town is made up of two square
sections. The east half was once Diocletian's Palace, and the west
half is the medieval town that sprang up next door. The shell of
Diocletian's ruined palace provides a checkerboard street plan,
with a gate at each end. But the streets built since are anything

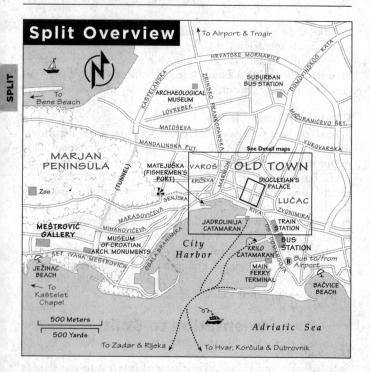

but straight, making the Old Town a delightfully convoluted maze (double-decker in some places). At the center of the former palace is a square called the Peristyle (Peristil), where you'll find the TI, cathedral, and highest concentration of Roman ruins.

Tourist Information

Split's TI is in the little chapel on the square called the Peristyle, in the very center of Diocletian's Palace (Easter-mid-Oct Mon-Sat 8:00-20:30, Sun 8:00-13:00; mid-Oct-Easter Mon-Fri 8:00-20:00, Sat 8:00-13:00, closed Sun; tel. 021/345-606, www.visitsplit.com). Pick up the free town map, monthly *Visit Split* booklet (with information on museums, events, restaurants, and more), and other brochures.

Sightseeing Pass: The TI sells the **Splitcard,** which includes free admission to several sights (including the City Museum, Ethnographic Museum, and cathedral), a 50 percent discount at other sights (including the Meštrović Gallery, Archaeological Museum, and Museum of Fine Arts), and minor discounts at other attractions, shops, and restaurants around town (35 kn/72 hours). This card might save busy sightseers some money—do the arithmetic. The Splitcard is free if you're staying at least three nights in town; to claim yours, bring a note from your hotel to the TI.

Split Essentials

English	Croatian	Pronounced
Old Town	Stari Grad	STAH-ree grahd
City Harbor	Gradska Luka	GRAHD-skah LOO-kah
Harborfront promenade	Riva	REE-vah
Peristyle (old Roman square)	Peristil	PEH-ree-steel
Soccer team	Hajduk	HIGH-dook
Local sculptor	Ivan Meštrović	EE-vahn MESH-troh-veech
Adriatic Sea	Jadran	YAH-drahn

Arrival in Split

By Boat, Bus, or Train: Split's ferry terminal (Trajektni Terminal), main bus station (Autobusni Kolodvor), and train sta-

tion (Željeznička Stanica) all share a busy and practical strip of land called Obala Kneza Domagoja, on the east side of the City Harbor. From any of them, you can see the Old Town and Riva; just **walk** around the harbor toward the big bell tower (about a 10-minute walk). Along the way, you'll pass travel agencies, baggage-storage offices, people trying to rent rooms, a post office, Internet cafés, shops, and cafés. Arriving or leaving from this central location, you never need to deal with the concrete, exhaust-stained sprawl of outer Split.

Boats arrive at various piers. The **Jadrolinija passenger catamaran** to and from Hvar and Korčula docks at the Obala Lazareta embankment, right in front of the Old Town. The *Krilo* **passenger catamaran** to those destinations uses pier #11, the shorter pier partway along the harbor. Bigger **car ferries** use various docks along the harbor. The main terminal, at the far end, has ATMs, WCs, a grocery store, and offices for all of the main ferry companies. The large Jadrolinija ticket and information office, which is open long hours daily, generally has a helpful English-speaking staff.

By Cruise Ship: In recent years—as packed-to-the-gills Dubrovnik has had to turn away cruise ships—Split has become

SPLIT

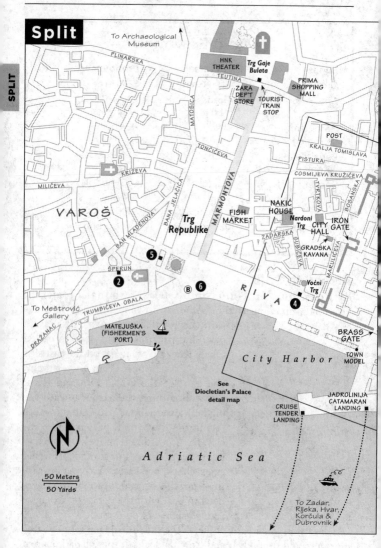

a popular port of call for Mediterranean cruises. Dubrovnik's loss is Split's gain—and passengers' gain, as the city is particularly easy to see in a quick visit. Cruise ships either dock along the main harbor in front of the Old Town, or anchor in the harbor and send tenders to shore (for directions on the short walk to the Old Town, see previous page).

By Plane: Split's airport (Zračna Luka Split-Kaštela) is across the big bay, 15 miles northwest of the center, near the town of Trogir (tel. 021/203-506, www.split-airport.hr). A handy Croatia Airlines bus connects the airport with downtown Split (30 kn, 40

1. Backpacker Internet C@fé
2. Modrulj Launderette
3. Travel49 Travel Agency
4. Turistički Biro Travel Agency
5. Vinoteka Bouquet Wine Shop
6. Bus #12 to Meštrović Gallery & Marjan Peninsula

minutes). This bus meets most arriving flights at the airport—just exit the airport, turn right, and look for the bus stop. To take this *to* the airport, catch it at the stop just beyond the bus station, across the street from the main ferry terminal (departs 1.5 hours before each Croatia Airlines flight and some other companies' flights). Cheaper long-distance buses also run regularly between the airport and Split's main bus station on their way to other destinations (15 kn, 7/day Mon-Fri, none Sat-Sun, 40 minutes). Yet another option is to take public bus #37, which stops along the main road in front of the airport (20 kn, 3/hour Mon-Fri, 2/hour Sat-Sun, 45 minutes); the catch is that bus #37 uses Split's suburban bus station, which is a dreary 10-minute walk north of downtown. The most expensive option is a taxi, which costs a hefty 300 kn between the airport and downtown Split.

By Car: For details on arriving in Split by car, driving between northern Croatia and Split, and driving south to the rest of the Dalmatian Coast, see "Route Tips for Drivers," on page 947.

Helpful Hints

Festivals: For one week in late August, Split celebrates Diocletian Days, when 50 actors from Rome walk the streets in ancient garb. A boat brings "Diocletian" to the Riva, people wearing togas attend dinner in the palace cellars, and the Diocletian Games are staged along the Riva.

Internet Access: Internet cafés are plentiful in the Old Town; look for signs, especially around the Peristyle, or try **Modrulj Launderette** or **Travel49** (both described later). Closer to the stations and ferry terminal, **Backpacker C@fé** has Internet access, coffee and drinks with outdoor seating, luggage storage, and used paperbacks for sale (30 kn/hour, Wi-Fi-15 kn/hour, daily July-Aug 6:00-23:00, shoulder season 6:30-22:00, even shorter hours off-season, near the beginning of Obala Kneza Domagoja, tel. 021/338-548). For locations, see map on page 908.

Post Office: A modern little post office is next to the bus station (Mon-Fri 7:30-19:00, Sat 7:30-14:30, closed Sun, on Obala Kneza Domagoja).

Luggage Storage: Seemingly custom-made for a quick stopover between Dalmatian destinations, this transit hub has no shortage of luggage-storage options. The train station has lockers (15 kn), and the adjacent bus station has a left-luggage desk *(garderoba)*. A small luggage-storage kiosk is along the sidewalk between the stations and the Old Town. Other options in and near the Old Town include Backpacker C@fé (listed earlier) and Modrulj Launderette and Travel49 (both listed later).

Laundry: Modrulj Launderette, a rare coin-operated launderette, is well-run by an Australian couple, Shane and Julie. It's conveniently located in the Varoš neighborhood at the west end of the Old Town, near several recommended restaurants—handy if multitasking is your style (self-service-50 kn/load, full-service-75 kn/load, air-con, Internet access, left-luggage service; April-Oct daily 8:00-20:00; Nov-March Mon-Sat 9:00-17:00, closed Sun; Šperun 1—see map on page 908, tel. 021/315-888).

Bike Rental: The staff at **Travel49** can rent you some wheels and enjoys suggesting biking routes. One good—if strenuous— option is a loop around the nearby Marjan peninsula, with a stop at a beach (15 kn/hour, 60 kn/4 hours, 100 kn/day, 20 percent discount with this book; for contact information, see below). They also offer three-hour **bike tours** (180 kn, 20 percent discount with this book).

Travel Agencies: Travel49, run by gregarious Josip, is a jack-of-all-trades agency buried deep in the Old Town. Josip offers walking tours (see "Tours in Split," later), bike tours, excursions, a room-booking service, car and bike rental, Internet access, luggage storage, and other services (daily May-Nov 8:00-22:00, Dec-April 9:00-17:00, Dioklecijanova 5, mobile 098-858-141, www.travel49.com). **Turistički Biro,** between the two halves of the Old Town on the Riva, books *sobe* and hotels; they also sell guidebooks, maps, and tickets for excursions (May-Sept daily 8:00-20:00; Oct-April Mon-Fri 8:00-20:00, Sat 8:00-13:00, closed Sun; Riva 12, tel. & fax 021/347-100, turist.biro.split@st.t-com.hr). For locations, see map on page 908.

Wine Shop: At **Vinoteka Bouquet,** at the west end of the Riva (near the restaurants and launderette on Šperun street), knowledgeable Denis can help you pick out a bottle of Croatian wine to suit your tastes (Mon-Fri 8:30-12:30 & 17:00-20:30, Sat 9:00-13:30, closed Sun, Obala Hrvatskog Narodnog Preporoda 3, tel. 021/348-031). For a wine primer before you visit, see page 834.

Who's Hajduk?: You'll see the word *Hajduk* (HIGH-dook), and a distinctive red-and-white checkerboard circle design (or red-and-blue stripes), all over town and throughout northern Dalmatia. Hajduk Split is the fervently supported soccer team, named for a band of highwaymen bandits who rebelled against Ottoman rule in the 17th-19th centuries. Most locals adore Hajduk as much as they loathe their bitter rivals, Dinamo Zagreb.

G'day, *Gospod:* You may notice a surprising concentration of Australians in Split. Many of them are actually Australian-born Croats, returning to the cosmopolitan capital city of their parents' Dalmatian homeland.

Getting Around Split

Most of what you'll want to see is within walking distance, but some sights (such as the Meštrović Gallery) are more easily reached by bus or taxi.

By Bus: Local buses, run by Promet, cost 10 kn per ride (or 9 kn if you buy a ticket at a newsstand or Promet kiosk, ask for a *putna karta;* zone I is fine for any ride within Split). For a round-trip within the city, buy a 16-kn transfer ticket, which works like two individual tickets (must buy at kiosk). Validate your ticket in the machine or with the driver as you board the bus. Suburban buses to towns near Split generally use the suburban bus station (Prigradski Autobusni Kolodvor), a 10-minute walk due north of the Old Town on Domovinskog rata. Bus information: www .promet-split.hr.

By Taxi: Taxis start at 20 kn, then cost around 7 kn per kilometer. Figure 50 kn for most rides within the city (for example, from the ferry terminal to most hotels)—but if going from one end of the Old Town to the other, it can be faster to walk. To call for a taxi, try Radio Taxi (tel. 021/970).

By Tourist Train: An hourly tourist train leaves from the square at the top of Marmontova and does a loop around the Marjan peninsula with a stop at Bene Beach (20 kn one-way, departs on the hour 9:00-20:00, mobile 095-530-6962).

Tours in Split

Walking Tours—Various companies offer walking tours of Split's Old Town. The most established is **Unique Walking Tours,** part of Travel49, whose 1.5-hour tours depart from the Peristyle (80 kn, 20 percent discount if you buy tickets at Travel49 office and show this book; May-Oct daily at 10:30, 12:00, and 19:00; April and Nov daily at 11:00 only; Dec-March no scheduled tours but possible upon request; mobile 098-858-141, www.diodetianpalace tour.com).

Local Guides—Consider hiring an insider to show you around. **Maja Benzon** is a smart and savvy local guide; she leads good walking tours through the Old Town (500 kn/up to 2 hours, 600 kn/3 hours, mobile 098-852-869, maja.benzon@gmail.com). You can also hire a guide through the **guide association,** which has an office at the Peristyle (525 kn/1.5-2 hours; June-Aug Mon-Fri 9:00-17:00, closed Sat-Sun; Sept-May generally open weekday mornings only; tel. 021/360-058, tel. & fax 021/346-267, mobile 098-361-936, www.guides.hr, info@guides.hr).

From Split

Bus Tours—Various companies run excursions to outlying sights. Options include the town of Trogir; the Roman ruins of Solin (ancient Salona); whitewater rafting on the Cetina River; the islands of Brač, Hvar, and Šolta (either separately or together); the pilgrimage site at Međugorje; Dubrovnik; and the waterfalls at Krka National Park or Plitvice Lakes National Park. This can be an efficient way to get to places that take a while to reach by public transportation. **Travel49** runs youthful, fun-loving excursions, and offers a 20 percent discount to Rick Steves readers if you book at their office (listed earlier, under "Helpful Hints"). **Atlas Travel** is a much larger operation and offers a wider variety of excursions, but their guiding can be hit-or-miss (about 300-700 kn, most are full-day tours). For details on excursions, look for fliers around town. Buy tickets at any travel agency, such as the Turistički Biro on the Riva (listed earlier, under "Helpful Hints").

Self-Guided Walk

▲▲▲Diocletian's Palace (Dioklecijanova Palača)

Split's top activity is visiting the remains of Roman Emperor Diocletian's enormous retirement palace, sitting on the harbor in the heart of the city. This monstrous complex was two impressive structures in one: luxurious villa and fortified Roman town. My walk takes you through Diocletian's back door; down into the labyrinth of cellars that supported the palace; up to the Peristyle (the center of the palace); into Diocletian's mausoleum—now the town's cathedral, with a crypt, treasury/museum, and climbable tower; over to Jupiter's Temple (later converted into a baptistery); down the main artery of the palace; and ends at what was once the front entrance to the palace. The ruins themselves are now integrated with the city's street plan, so exploring them is free—except for the cellars and the cathedral sights/temple, which you'll pay to enter. In peak season, the cellars are open late (on most days until 20:00 or 21:00), and the cathedral sights generally close at 19:00. If visiting off-season, do this walk as early as possible, as the cathedral sights close at noon. For exact hours, see the individual sight listings.

Fragments of the palace are poorly marked, and there are no good guidebooks or audioguides for tracking down the remains. For most visitors, this walk provides enough details; for more in-depth information, consider joining a walking tour or hiring a guide (see "Tours in Split," earlier).

Background

Diocletian grew up just inland from Split, in the town of Salona (Solin in Croatian), which was then the capital of the Roman province of Dalmatia. He worked his way up the Roman hierarchy and ruled as emperor for the unusually long tenure of 20 years (A.D. 284-305). Despite all of his achievements, Diocletian is best remembered for

DIOCLETIANVS

two questionable legacies: dividing the huge empire among four emperors (which helped administer it more efficiently, but began a splintering effect that arguably led to the empire's decline); and torturing and executing Christians, including thousands right here on the Dalmatian Coast.

As Diocletian grew older, he decided to return to his homeland for retirement. Since he was in poor health, the medicinal sulfur spring here was another plus. His massive palace took only 11 years to build—and this fast pace required a big push (more than 2,000 slaves died during construction). Huge sections of his palace still exist, modified by medieval and modern developers alike.

• *Start in front of the palace, at the east end of the Riva. To get a sense of the original palace, check out the big illustration posted across from the palace entry. Across the street at the end of the Riva, notice the big car-size model of today's Old Town, which is helpful for orientation. (Both the sign and the model are usually crowded with tour groups.) Now study the...*

Palace Facade

The "front" of today's Split—facing the harbor—was actually the back door of Diocletian's Palace. There was no embankment in front of the palace back then, so the water came right up to this door—sort of an emergency exit by boat. Looking out to the water, appreciate the palace's strategic location, easy to fortify and to watch for enemies approaching either by land or by sea.

Visually trace the outline of the gigantic palace, which was more than 600 feet long on each side. On the corner to the right stands a big, rectangular guard tower (one of the original 16). To the left, the tower is gone and the corner is harder to pick out (look for the beginning of the newer-looking buildings). Mentally erase the ramshackle two-story buildings added 200 years ago, which obscure the grandness of the palace wall.

Halfway up the facade, notice the row of 42 arched window frames (mostly filled in today). Diocletian and his family lived in the seaside half of the palace. Imagine him strolling back and forth along this fine arcade, enjoying the views of his Adriatic homeland. The inland, non-view half of the palace was home to 700 servants, bodyguards, and soldiers.

• *Go through the door in the middle of the palace (known as the "Brass Gate," located under the* Substructure of Diocletian's Palace *banner). Just inside the door and to the left is the entrance to...*

Diocletian's Cellars (Podromi)

Since the palace was constructed on land that sloped down to the sea, these chambers were built to level out a foundation for

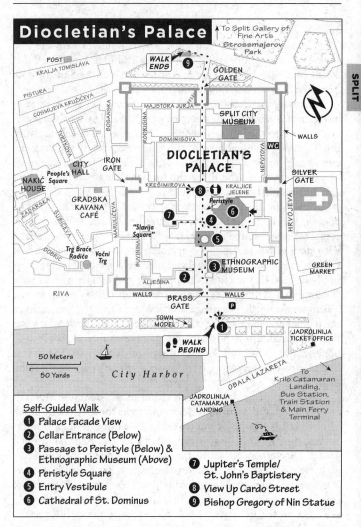

Diocletian's Palace

To Split Gallery of Fine Arts
Strossmajerov Park

POST
KRALJA TOMISLAVA

PISTURA

COSMIJEVA KRUŽIČEVA

BOSANSKA

WALK ENDS

GOLDEN GATE

MAJSTORA JURJA

RODRIGINA

DOMINISOVA

SPLIT CITY MUSEUM

WALLS

TYCHOVA

CITY HALL

IRON GATE

DIOCLETIAN'S PALACE

NEPOTOVA

WC

SILVER GATE

NAKIĆ HOUSE

People's Square

KREŠIMIROVA

KRALJICE JELENE

ZADARSKA

SUBIĆEVA

GRADSKA KAVANA CAFÉ

MARULIĆEVA

BUVININA

"Slavija Square"

Peristyle

HRVOJEVA

Trg Braće Radića

DOBRIC

Voćni Trg

ALJEŠINA

ETHNOGRAPHIC MUSEUM

GREEN MARKET

RIVA

WALLS

BRASS GATE

WALLS

P

TOWN MODEL

JADROLINIJA TICKET OFFICE

WALK BEGINS

50 Meters
50 Yards

City Harbor

OBALA LAZARETA

To Krilo Catamaran Landing, Bus Station, Train Station & Main Ferry Terminal

JADROLINIJA CATAMARAN LANDING

Self-Guided Walk

1. Palace Facade View
2. Cellar Entrance (Below)
3. Passage to Peristyle (Below) & Ethnographic Museum (Above)
4. Peristyle Square
5. Entry Vestibule
6. Cathedral of St. Dominus
7. Jupiter's Temple/ St. John's Baptistery
8. View Up Cardo Street
9. Bishop Gregory of Nin Statue

the massive structure above (like a modern "daylight basement"). These cellars were filled with water from three different sources:

a freshwater spring, a sulfur spring, and the sea. Later, medieval residents used them as a dump. Rediscovered only in the last century, the cellars enabled archaeologists to derive the floor plan of some of the palace's long-gone upper sections. These underground chambers also house art exhibits and a little strip of souvenir stands.

Cost and Hours: 35 kn, some posters inside explain the site; June-Sept daily 9:00-21:00; April-May and Oct Mon-Sat 9:00-20:00, Sun 9:00-18:00 except in April, when it closes Sun at 14:00; Nov-March Mon-Sat 9:00-18:00, Sun 9:00-14:00.

Touring the Cellars: Use the free map you get at the entry to navigate this labyrinthine complex of cellars. First visit the **western cellars** (to the left as you enter). Near the ticket-seller, notice the big **topographical map** of the Split area, clearly showing the city's easily defensible location—with a natural harbor sheltered by tall mountains. You'll see the former Roman city of Salona, Diocletian's birthplace, just inland.

Head into the main part of the cellars by going through the door on the right, just past the ticket-seller. This takes you into the complex's vast, vaulted **main hall**—the biggest space in the cellars, with stout pillars to support everything upstairs. When those first villagers took refuge in the abandoned palace from the rampaging Slavs in 641, the elite lived upstairs, grabbing what was once the emperor's wing. They carved the rough holes you see in the ceiling to dump their garbage and sewage. Over the generations, the basement (where you're standing) filled up with layers of waste that solidified, ultimately becoming a once-stinky, then-precious bonanza for 19th- and 20th-century archaeologists. Today this hall is used for everything from flower and book shows to fashion catwalks.

Exit the main hall through either of the doors on the left, cross through the narrow corridor, and enter the long room. Look just overhead—the holes you see once held beams to support floorboards, making this a two-story cellar. Face the giant replica of a golden Diocletian coin at the far end, and turn left, then immediately right into a small circular room, which has a headless, pawless black granite sphinx—one of 13 that Diocletian brought home from Egypt (only four survive, including a mostly intact one we'll see soon on the Peristyle). Look up to admire the circular brickwork. Then continue straight. In the small room just beyond is a stone olive-oil press.

Backtrack past the round room and into a room that displays two petrified beams, like the ones that once filled the double-decker holes we saw earlier. At the far end of this room is an unexcavated wing—a compost pile of ancient lifestyles, awaiting the tiny shovels and toothbrushes of future archaeologists.

Facing the mound of ancient garbage, turn left into another round room, featuring a bust of Diocletian (or is it Sean Connery?). From here, loop through a few more rooms back into the long room you were in earlier, then turn right and exit out the bottom of this hall. On your right, look for original Roman sewer pipes—square outside and round inside—designed to fit into each other to create long pipes.

From here, head back out to the exit. If you'd like to see more cellars—mostly with their ceilings missing, so they're open to the air—cross over into the **eastern cellars** (same ticket). This section is less interesting than the western part, but worth a quick visit.

• *When you're finished, head back to the main gallery. Ignore the tacky made-in-Malaysia trinket shops as you head down the passage and up the stairs into the...*

Peristyle (Peristil)

This square was the centerpiece of Diocletian's Palace. As you walk up the stairs, the entry vestibule into the residence is above

your head, Diocletian's mausoleum (today's Cathedral of St. Dominus) is to your right, and the street to Jupiter's Temple is on your left. The TI is in the small chapel. Straight ahead, beyond the TI/chapel, is the narrow street that leads to the palace's former main entrance, the Golden Gate.

Go to the middle of the square and take it all in. The red granite pillars—which you'll see all over Diocletian's Palace—are from Egypt, where Diocletian spent many of his pre-retirement years. Imagine the pillars defining fine arcades—now obscured by medieval houses. The black sphinx is the only one of Diocletian's collection of 13 that's still (mostly) intact.

In summer (mid-June-mid-Sept), costumed pageantry brings the square to life. "Roman soldiers" pose for tips (daily 9:00-17:00), and every day at noon an actor playing Diocletian appears at the top of the stairs to address the crowd in Latin.

• *Climb the stairs (above where you came in) into the domed, open-ceilinged...*

Entry Vestibule

Impressed? That's the idea. This was the grand entry to Diocletian's living quarters, meant to wow visitors. Emperors were believed to be gods. Diocletian called himself "Jovius"— the son of Jupiter, the most powerful of all gods. Four times a year (at the changing of the seasons), Diocletian would stand here and overlook the Peristyle. His subjects would lie on the ground in worship, praising his name and kissing his scarlet robe. Notice the four big niches at floor level, which once held statues of the four tetrarchs who ruled the unwieldy empire after Diocletian retired. The empty hole in the ceiling was once capped by a dome (long since collapsed), and the ceiling itself was covered with frescoes and mosaics.

In this grand space, you'll likely run into an all-male band of *klapa* singers, performing traditional a cappella harmonies. Just stand and enjoy a few glorious tunes—you'll rarely find a better group or acoustics. A 100-kn *klapa* CD is the perfect souvenir.

Wander out back to the harbor side through medieval buildings (some with seventh-century foundations), which evoke the way local villagers came in and took over the once-spacious and elegant palace. Back in this area, you'll find the beautifully restored home of the **Ethnographic Museum** (described later, under "Sights in Split").

• *Now go back into the Peristyle and turn right, climbing the steps to the...*

Cathedral of St. Dominus (Katedrala Sv. Duje)

The original octagonal structure was Diocletian's elaborate mausoleum, built in the fourth century. But after the fall of Rome, it was converted into the town's cathedral. Construction of the bell tower began in the 13th century and took 300 years to complete. Before you go inside, notice the sarcophagi ringing the cathedral. In the late Middle Ages, this was prime post-mortem real estate, since being buried closer to a cathedral improved your chances of getting to heaven.

Cost and Hours: You'll need a ticket for the cathedral interior, the crypt, the unimpressive treasury/museum, the tower climb, and—a block away—Jupiter's Temple (described later). Various combo-ticket options are available (but note that these are constantly changing and may be different during your visit). A basic 15-kn ticket covers the cathedral, crypt, and Jupiter's Temple (probably your best option on a brief visit). The 35-kn combo-ticket adds the tower and the treasury/museum. You can also buy individual tickets for the tower climb (10 kn, buy ticket at tower door) and the treasury/museum (15 kn). All of the sights are open similar hours, but the cathedral can close unexpectedly for services. In general, hours are summer Mon-Sat 8:00-19:00, Sun 12:30-18:30, cathedral often closed Sat afternoons for weddings; winter daily 7:00-12:00, maybe later on request; Kraj Sv. Duje 5, tel. 021/344-121.

Touring the Cathedral: To get inside in peak season (April-Oct), you must loop around the outside of the cathedral. Facing the main door at the bottom of the stairs, circle around the left side to find the door in the building behind. Buy your ticket here and climb up the stairs to the **treasury/museum.** This single room contains dusty display cases of vestments, giant books, icon-like paintings, reliquaries, chalices, monstrances, and other church art, with very sparse English descriptions. Go up one more floor to get into the cathedral. In winter (Nov-March), you can simply enter the cathedral through the main door.

Step into the church interior. This is the oldest—and likely smallest—building used as a cathedral anywhere in Christendom.

Imagine the place in pre-Christian times, with Diocletian's tomb in the center. The only surviving decor from those days are the granite columns and the relief circling the base of the dome (about 50 feet up)—a ring of carvings heralding the greatness of the emperor. The small red-marble pillars around the top of the pulpit (near the entry) were scavenged from Diocletian's sarcophagus. These pillars are all that remain of Diocletian's remains.

Diocletian brutally persecuted his Christian subjects. Just before he moved to the Dalmatian Coast, he had Bishop Dominus of Salona killed, along with several thousand Christians. When Diocletian died, there were riots of happiness. In the seventh century, his mausoleum became a cathedral dedicated to the martyred bishop. The extension behind the altar was added in the ninth century. The sarcophagus of St. Dominus (to the right of the altar, with early-Christian carvings)

was once the cathedral's high altar. To the left of today's main altar is the impressively detailed, Renaissance-era altar of St. Anastasius, who is lying on a millstone that is tied to his neck. On Diocletian's orders, this Christian martyr was drowned in A.D. 302. To the left of St. Anastasius' altar is the "new" altar of St. Dominus; his relics lie in the 18th-century Baroque silver reliquary, above a stone relief showing him being beheaded. Posthumous poetic justice: Now Christian saints are entombed in Diocletian's mausoleum...and Diocletian is nowhere to be found. As you exit through the 13th-century main doors, notice the 14 panels on each of the two wings—showing 28 scenes from the life of Christ.

Climbing the 183 steep steps to the top of the 200-foot-tall **bell tower** rewards you with sweeping views of Split, but it's not for claustrophobes or those scared of heights.

If you circle down and around the right side of the cathedral as you face the main stairs, you'll find the entrance to the **crypt** *(kripta)*. This musty, domed cellar (with eerie acoustics) was originally used to level the foundation of Diocletian's mausoleum. Later, Christians turned it into another chapel. The legend you'll likely hear about Diocletian torturing and murdering Christians in this very crypt, which began about the same time this became a church, is probably false.

• *Remember that Diocletian believed himself to be Jovius (Jupiter, Jr.). As worshippers exited the mausoleum of Jovius, they would look straight ahead to the temple of Jupiter. (Back then, there were none of these medieval buildings cluttering up the view.) Make your way through the narrow alley (directly across from the cathedral entry), past another headless, pawless sphinx, to explore the small...*

Jupiter's Temple/St. John's Baptistery

About the time the mausoleum became a cathedral, this temple was converted into a baptistery (same ticket and hours as cathedral; off-season, if it's locked, go ask the person at the cathedral to let you in). Inside, the big 12th-century baptismal font—large enough to immerse someone (as was the tradition in those days)—is decorated with the intricate, traditional *pleter* design also used around the border of Croatia's current passport stamp. On the font, notice the engraving: a bishop (on the left) and the king on his throne (on the right).

At their feet (literally under the feet of the bishop) is a submissive commoner—neatly summing up the social structure of the Middle Ages. Standing above the font is a statue of St. John the Baptist counting to four, done by the great Croatian sculptor Ivan Meštrović (see page 926). The half-barrel vaulted ceiling, completed later, is considered the best-preserved of its kind anywhere. Every face and each patterned box is different.

• *Back at the Peristyle, stand in front of the little chapel with your back to the entry vestibule. The small street just beyond the chapel (going left to right) connects the east and west gates. If you've had enough Roman*

SPLIT

history, head right (east) to go through the Silver Gate and find Split's busy, open-air Green Market. Or, head to the left (west), which takes you to the Iron Gate and People's Square (see "Sights in Split," later) and, beyond that, the fresh-and-smelly fish market. But if you want to see one last bit of Roman history, continue straight ahead up the...

Cardo

A traditional Roman street plan has two roads: Cardo (the north-south axis) and Decumanus (the east-west axis). Split's Cardo street was the most important in Diocletian's Palace, connecting the main entry with the heart of the complex. As you walk, you'll pass several noteworthy sights: in the first building on the right, a bank with modern computer gear all around its exposed Roman ruins (look through window); at the first gate on the left, the courtyard of a Venetian merchant's palace (a reminder that Split was dominated by Venice from the 15th century on); on the right, an alley to the **City Museum** (described later, under "Sights in Split"); and, on the right, **Nadalina,** an artisan chocolatier selling mostly dark chocolate creations with some innovative Dalmatian flavors (30 kn/100 grams, 13-kn chocolate bars, Mon-Fri 9:00-21:00, Sat 9:00-12:00, closed Sun).

Just before the Golden Gate, detour a few steps to the left along skinny **Majstora Jurja** street—lined with some of the most appealing outdoor cafés in town, lively both day and night (described later, under "Nightlife in Split"). Near the start of this street, just after its initial jog, stairs climb to the miniscule **St. Martin's Chapel,** burrowed into the city wall. Dating from the fifth century, this is one of the earliest Christian chapels anywhere. St. Martin is the patron saint of soldiers, and the chapel was built for the troops who guarded this gate (free, sporadic hours—just climb the stairs to see if it's open).

• *Backtrack to the main drag and go inside the huge...*

Golden Gate (Zlatna Vrata)

This great gate was the main entry of Diocletian's Palace. Its name wasn't literal—rather, the "gold" suggests the importance of this gateway to Salona, the Roman provincial capital at the time. Standing inside the gate itself, you can appreciate the double-door design that kept the palace safe. Also notice how this ancient building is now being used in very different ways from its original purpose. Above, on the outer wall, you can see the bricked-in windows that contain part of a Dominican convent. At the top of the inner wall is somebody's garden terrace.

Go outside the gate and look back at the recently restored fortification—with all its structural elements gleaming. This mostly uncluttered facade gives you the best opportunity in town to

SPLIT

visualize how the palace looked before so many other buildings were grafted on. Straight ahead as you exit this gate is Salona (Solin), which was a major city of 60,000 (and Diocletian's hometown) before there was a Split. The big statue by Ivan Meštrović is **Bishop Gregory of Nin,** a 10th-century Croatian priest who tried to convince the Vatican to allow sermons during Mass to be said in Croatian, rather than Latin. People rub his toe for good luck (though only non-material wishes are given serious consideration). The big building beyond the statue houses Split's **Gallery of Fine Arts** (described later, under "Sights in Split").

• *Your tour is finished. Now enjoy the rest of Split.*

Sights in Split

In or near the Old Town

In addition to the palace, cellars, and cathedral described on my self-guided walk, you can also enjoy these attractions.

▲**People's Square (Narodni Trg)**—Locals call this lively square at the center of the Old Town *Pjaca*, pronounced the same as the Italian *piazza* (PYAH-tsah). Stand in the center and enjoy the bustle. Look around for a quick lesson in Dalmatian history. When Diocletian lived in his palace, a Roman village popped up here, just outside the wall. Face the former wall of Diocletian's Palace (behind and to the right of the 24-hour

clock tower). This was the western entrance, or so-called "Iron Gate." By the 14th century, a medieval town had developed, making this the main square of Split.

On the wall just to the right of the lane leading to the Peristyle, look for the life-size relief of **St. Anthony.** Notice the creepy "mini-me" clutching the saint's left leg—depicting the sculptor's donor, who didn't want his gift to be forgotten. Above this strange statue, notice the smaller, faded relief of a man and a woman arguing.

Turn around and face the square. On your left is the city's grand old café, **Gradska Kavana,** which has been the Old Town's venerable meeting point for generations. Today it's both a café and a restaurant with disappointing food but the best outdoor ambience in town (35-kn breakfasts, 60-80-kn pastas, 85-145-kn main courses, daily 7:00-24:00, Narodni trg 1, tel. 021/317-835).

Across the square, the white building jutting into the square was once the **City Hall,** and now houses temporary exhibitions. The loggia is all that remains of the original Gothic building.

At the far end of the square is the out-of-place **Nakić House,** built in the early 20th-century Viennese Secession style—a reminder that Dalmatia was part of the Habsburg Empire, ruled by Vienna, from Napoleon's downfall through World War I.

The lane on the right side of the Nakić House leads to Split's **fish market** (Ribarnica), where you can see piles of the still-wriggling catch of the day. No flies? It's thanks to the sulfur spring in the nearby spa building (with the gray statues, on the corner). Just beyond the fish market is the pedestrian boulevard Marmontova (described on page 929).

Ethnographic Museum (Etnografski Muzej)—This museum uses well-presented temporary exhibits to show off the culture, costumes, furniture, tools, jewelry, weapons, and paintings of Dalmatia. It's all displayed in a gorgeously renovated early-medieval palace with a confusing treehouse floor plan. You'll find it in the upper level of the Old Town, behind Diocletian's entry vestibule. Check out the artsy "golden fleece" entry door. The ground floor sports the remains of a seventh-century church, and the exhibits usually include a good look at traditional folk dress. Your ticket also includes access to the roof of the vestibule (find the stairs at the far end of the museum); while it's not high enough to be thrilling, and you can't actually see down into the vestibule, it provides a nice view over the rooftops of Split.

Cost and Hours: 10 kn, some English explanations; July-mid-Sept Mon-Fri 9:00-21:00, Sat 9:00-13:00, closed Sun; June Mon-Fri 9:00-18:00, Sat 9:00-13:00, closed Sun; mid-Sept-May Mon-Fri 9:00-15:00, Sat 9:00-13:00, closed Sun; Severova 7, tel. 021/344-164, www.etnografski-muzej-split.hr.

Split City Museum (Muzej Grada Splita)—This museum traces how the city grew over the centuries. It's a bit dull, but it can help you appreciate a little better the layers of history you're seeing in the streets. The ground floor displays Roman fragments (including coins from the days of Diocletian), temporary exhibits, and the museum's highlight: a semicircular marble table used by the Romans. As depicted in Hollywood movies, the Romans ate lying down (three people would lounge and feast, while servants dished things up from the straight side). This table has been painstakingly reconstructed from shreds and splinters discovered in the cellars. The upstairs focuses on the Middle Ages (find the terrace displaying carved stone monuments), and the top floor covers the 16th century to the present.

The 15th-century Papalić Palace, which houses the City Museum, is a sight all its own. At the end of the palace, near Cardo street, look up to see several typical Venetian-style Gothic-Renaissance windows. The stone posts sticking out of the wall next to them were used to hang curtains.

Cost and Hours: 10 kn, some English descriptions, 40-kn guidebook is overkill; May-Oct Tue-Fri 9:00-21:00, Sat-Mon 9:00-16:00; Nov-April generally Tue-Fri 10:00-17:00, Sat-Sun 10:00-13:00, closed Mon, possibly even shorter hours off-season, Papalićeva 1, tel. 021/360-171, www.mgst.net.

Radić Brothers Square (Trg Braće Radića)—Also known as Voćni Trg ("Fruit Square") for the produce that was once sold here, this little piazza is just off the Riva between the two halves of the Old Town. Overhead is a **Venetian citadel.** After Split became part of the Venetian Republic, there was a serious danger of attack by the Ottomans, so octagonal towers like this were built all along the coast. But this imposing tower had a second purpose: to encourage citizens of Split to forget about any plans of rebellion.

In the middle of the square is a studious sculpture by Ivan Meštrović of the 16th-century poet **Marko Marulić,** who is considered the father of the Croatian language. Marulić was the first to write literature in the Croatian vernacular, which before then had generally been considered a backward peasants' tongue.

On the downhill (harbor) side of the square is **Croata,** a necktie boutique that loves to explain how Croatian soldiers who fought with the French in the Thirty Years' War (1618-1648) had a distinctive way of tying their scarves. The French found it stylish, adopted it, and called it *à la Croate*—or eventually, *cravate*—thus creating the modern necktie that many people wear to work every day throughout the world. Croata's selection includes ties with traditional Croatian motifs, such as the checkerboard pattern from the flag or writing in the ninth-century Glagolitic alphabet. Though pricey, these ties make nice souvenirs (250-700 kn, Mon-Fri 8:00-20:30, Sat 8:00-13:00, closed Sun, shorter hours off-season). Croata has a bigger, second location on the Peristyle.

Green Market—This lively open-air market bustles at the east end of Diocletian's Palace. Residents shop for produce and clothes here, and there are plenty of tourist souvenirs as well. Browse the wide selection of T-shirts, and ignore the creepy black-market tobacco salesmen who mutter at you: *"Cigaretta?"*

Split Gallery of Fine Arts (Galerija Umjetnina Split)—This collection, beautifully displayed in a finely restored old hospital just behind Diocletian's Palace, features mostly Croatian artwork from the 14th to the 21st centuries. It's basically a hodgepodge with few highlights—best reserved for art-lovers. Cross through the courtyard, climb up the stairs, and follow the one-way route through the chronologically displayed collection, which is heavy on the 20th century.

Cost and Hours: 20 kn; May-Sept Mon 11:00-16:00, Tue-Fri 11:00-19:00, Sat 11:00-15:00, closed Sun; Oct-April Mon 9:00-14:00, Tue-Fri 9:00-17:00, Sat 9:00-13:00, closed Sun; mod café, go straight out the Golden Gate and a bit to the left—behind the statue of Gregory of Nin—to Kralja Tomislava 15, tel. 021/350-110, www.galum.hr.

Archaeological Museum (Arheološki Muzej)—If you're intrigued by all the "big stuff" from Split's past (buildings and ruins), consider paying a visit to this collection of its "little stuff." A good exhibit of artifacts (mostly everyday domestic items) traces this region's history from its Illyrian beginnings chronologically through its notable Roman period (items from Split and Salona) to the Middle Ages. About a 10-minute walk north of the Old Town, it's worth the trip for archaeology fans. Don't confuse this with the less-interesting Museum of Croatian Archaeological Monuments, on the way to the Ivan Meštrović Gallery.

Cost and Hours: 20 kn; June-Sept Mon-Sat 9:00-14:00 & 16:00-20:00, closed Sun; Oct-May Mon-Fri 9:00-14:00 & 16:00-20:00, Sat 9:00-14:00, closed Sun; Zrinsko Frankopanska 25, tel. 021/329-340, www.mdc.hr/split-arheoloski.

Ivan Meštrović Sights, West of the Old Town

The excellent Meštrović Gallery and nearby Kaštelet Chapel are just outside the Old Town. Both sights are covered by the same ticket and have the same hours.

Cost and Hours: 30 kn, covers both the gallery and the chapel; May-Sept Tue-Sun 9:00-19:00, closed Mon; Oct-April Tue-Sat 9:00-16:00, Sun 10:00-15:00, closed Mon; gallery tel. 021/340-800, chapel tel. 021/358-185, www.mdc.hr/mestrovic.

Getting There: Both sights are located along Šetalište Ivana Meštrovića. You can take **bus** #12 from the little cul-de-sac at the west end of the Riva (departs hourly, get off at the stop in front of the gallery—just after your bus passes a museum prominently marked *Muzej Hrvatskih Arheoloških Spomenika*). You can also **walk** (about 25 minutes): Follow the harbor west of town toward the big marina, swing right with the road, and follow the park until you see the gallery on your right (at #46). A **taxi** from the west end of the Old Town to the gallery costs about 50 kn (much more from the east end of the Old Town). To reach the chapel, it's a five-minute walk past the gallery down Šetalište Ivana Meštrovića to #39 (on the left, in an olive grove).

▲▲Meštrović Gallery (Galerija Meštrović)—Split's best art museum is dedicated to the sculptor Ivan Meštrović, the most

Ivan Meštrović
(1883-1962)

Ivan Meštrović (EE-vahn MESH-troh-veech), who achieved international fame for his talents as a sculptor, was Croatia's answer to Rodin. You'll see Meštrović's works everywhere in the streets, squares, and museums of Croatia.

Meštrović came from humble beginnings. He grew up in a family of poor, nomadic farm workers just inland from Split. At an early age, his drawings and wooden carvings showed promise, and a rich family took him in and made sure he was properly trained. He eventually went off to school in Vienna, where he fell in with the Secession movement and found fame and fortune. He lived in Prague, Paris, and Switzerland, fully engaged in the flourishing European artistic culture at the turn of the 20th century (he counted Rodin among his friends). After World War I, Meštrović moved back to Croatia and established an atelier, or workshop, in Zagreb (now a museum—see page 1035).

Later in life—like Diocletian before him—Meštrović returned to Split and built a huge seaside mansion (today's Meštrović Gallery). The years between the World Wars were Meštrović's happiest and most productive. It was during this time that he sculpted his most internationally famous works, a pair of giant Native American warriors on horseback in Chicago's Grant Park. But when World War II broke out, Meštrović—an outspoken supporter of the ideals of a united Yugoslavia—was briefly imprisoned by the anti-Yugoslav Ustaše (Croatia's Nazi puppet government). After his release, Meštrović fled to Italy, then the US, where he lectured at prominent universities such as Notre Dame and Syracuse. After the war, the Yugoslav dictator Tito invited Meštrović to return, but the very religious artist refused to cooperate with an atheist regime. (Meštrović was friends with the Archbishop Alojzije Stepinac, who was imprisoned by Tito.) Meštrović died in South Bend, Indiana.

Meštrović worked in wood, plaster, marble, and bronze, and dabbled in painting. His sculptures depict biblical, mythological, political, and everyday themes. Meštrović's figures typically have long, angular fingers, arms, and legs. Whether whimsical or emotional, Meštrović's expressive, elongated faces—often with a strong-profile nose—powerfully connect with the viewer.

important of all Croatian artists. Many of Meštrović's finest works are housed in this palace, designed by the sculptor himself to serve as his residence, studio, and exhibition space. If you have time, it's worth the trek. The gallery offers a free guide-booklet and pricey, downloadable smartphone audio tours. The 80-kn guidebook is overkill for most visitors.

◆ Self-Guided Tour: After buying your ticket (and asking about the time for your return bus to the Old Town), climb the stairs toward Meštrović's house, pausing in the **garden** to admire a smattering of sculptures (including several female nudes, Cyclops hurling a giant shot put, and an eagle).

Go up another set of stairs to reach the **Entrance Hall,** displaying sculptures mostly of Carrara marble, Michelangelo's favorite medium. Notice the black sculptures by the two staircases: on the left, representing birth, and on the right, representing death—Meštrović strove to capture the full range of human experience in his work.

Go to the left, and enter the **Dining Room** at the end of the main floor. It's decorated with portraits of Meštrović's wife, mother, and children. Meštrović often used his mother as a model for older women and his second wife Olga as a model for younger women. Also look for the self-portrait and two painted portraits of Meštrović (one as a young man, another shortly before his death). A painting of the *Last Supper* hangs in virtually every Dalmatian dining room. Meštrović's is no exception—he painted this version himself. At the end of the room are two giant caryatids carved from Dalmatian stone (embedded with fragments of seashells).

Now climb the stairs and go to the right, into the **Secession Room.** Some of these works—including the girl singing and the intimate portrait of a family—show the influence of Meštrović's contemporary, Rodin.

Pass through the room of drawings into the **Long Hall,** lined with life-size figures and a view terrace. The woman sitting with her knees apart and feet together is demonstrating a favorite pose of Meštrović's.

At the end of the hall is the **Study Room,** filled with miniature sculptures Meštrović created to prepare for larger-scale works. Notice the small study of *Job*, then go into the small side-room to see the much larger final version. One of Meštrović's most powerful works, *Job*—howling with an agony verging on insanity—was carved by the artist in exile, as his country was turned upside-down by World War II. Meštrović sketched his inspiration for this piece (displayed on the wall) while he was imprisoned by the Ustaše.

Head down the stairs and turn left into the **Sacral Room.**
Meštrović was very religious, and here you can
see some of his many works depicting biblical
figures. The giant, wood-carved *Adam* and
Eve dominate the room, but don't miss the
smaller side-room, with another of the gallery's highlights: the quietly poignant *Roman
Pietà*. Meštrović follows the classical pyramid
form, with Joseph of Arimathea (top), Mary
(left), and Mary Magdalene (right) surrounding the limp body of Christ. But the harmony
is broken by the painful angles of the mourning faces. While this sculpture is plaster,
Meštrović also completed a marble version for
the campus of Notre Dame in the US.

▲**Kaštelet Chapel**—If you enjoy the gallery, don't miss the
nearby Kaštelet Chapel ("Chapel of the Holy Cross"). Meštrović
bought this 16th-century fortified palace to display his 28 wood
reliefs of Jesus' life. You can see how Meštrović's style changed
over time, as he carved these over a nearly 30-year span, completing the last 12 when he was in the US. (However, note that he
didn't carve the reliefs in chronological order—ask for a booklet
identifying the topic and year for each one.) While the earlier
pieces are well-composed and powerful, the later ones seem more
hastily done, as Meštrović rushed to complete his opus. Work
clockwise around the room, tracing the life of Christ. Notice
that some of the Passion scenes are out of order (a side-effect of
Meštrović's nonlinear schedule). The beautiful *pietà* near the end
still shows some of the original surface of the wood, demonstrating the skill required to create depth and emotion in just a few
inches of medium. Dominating the chapel is an extremely powerful wooden crucifix, with Christ's arms, legs, fingers, and toes bent
at unnatural angles—a typically expressionistic flair Meštrović
used to exaggerate suffering.

Activities in Split

▲▲**Strolling the Riva**—The official name for this seaside pedestrian drag is the "Croatian National Revival Embankment" (Obala
Hrvatskog Narodnog Preporoda) but locals just call it "Riva"
(Italian for "harbor"). This is the town's promenade, an integral
part of Mediterranean culture. After dinner, Split residents collect
their families and friends for a stroll on the Riva. It offers some
of the best people-watching in Croatia; make it a point to be here
for an hour or two after dinner. The stinky smell that sometimes

accompanies the stroll (especially at the west end) isn't from a sewer. It's sulfur—a reminder that the town's medicinal sulfur spas have attracted people here since the days of Diocletian.

The Riva recently underwent an extensive, costly, and controversial renovation. The old potholed pavement and scrubby gardens were torn up and replaced with a broad, sleek, carefully landscaped people zone. A clean, synchronized line of modern white lampposts and sun screens sashays down the promenade. But many residents miss the colorful quirks of the old version. For example, when the promenade was first renovated, cafés were forced to buy identical tables and chairs to make everything match. In protest, some cafés offered no outdoor seating at all...until the city relented, and now any chairs are allowed. Some think that the starkly modern strip is at odds with the rest of the higgledy-piggledy Old Town, while others see this as simply the early-21st century's contribution to the architectural hodgepodge that is Split.

At the west end of the Riva, the people-parade of Croatian culture turns right and heads away from the water, up **Marmontova.** Although it lacks the seafront cachet, this drag is equally enjoyable and feels more local. As you walk up Marmontova, on the left is the plain-Jane outer facade of the arcade that defines Trg Republike, a grand and genteel Napoleonic-era square. Duck through the passage across from the fish market to bask in its "poor man's St. Mark's Square" ambience, and maybe to linger over a drink at the recommended Bajamonti café. A bit farther up Marmontova, on the right, look for the whimsical fountain nicknamed "The Teacup," with a hand squirting water across the sidewalk into a funnel. At the top of Marmontova are some department stores, a lively café square, and the Croatian National Theater (Hrvatsko Narodno Kazalište, HNK).

Exploring Matejuška Fishermen's Port—While Split's harborfront Riva is where the beautiful people stroll, the city's fishermen roots still thrive just to the west. The neighborhood called Matejuška—at the little harbor where the Varoš district hits the water (a five-minute walk beyond the end of the Riva, with the water on your left)—has long been Split's working

fishermen's harbor. While the area has received a facelift to match the one along the Riva, it still retains its striped-collar character. The enclosed harbor area is filled with working fishing boats and colorful dinghies that bob in unison. Along the breakwater, notice the new fishermen's lockers, where people who earn their living from the Adriatic still keep their supplies. You'll see the most fisherman action here in the mornings.

The far side of the breakwater—all glitzy white marble—is another world, with a pebbly beach, inviting plaza, and some of the best views looking back on the Riva. After its recent facelift, this jetty has become a popular open-air, after-hours hangout spot for young people. Like Split itself, these two worlds—that of grizzled fishermen mending nets, and that of teenagers living it up—coexist more smoothly than anyone might have guessed.

Hiking the Marjan Peninsula—This huge, hilly, and relatively undeveloped spit of parkland—improbably located right next to Split's Old Town—feels like a chunk of Dalmatian island wilderness, a stone's throw from the big city. With out-of-the-way beaches and miles of hiking trails, the Marjan (MAR-yahn) Peninsula is where residents go to relax. Most people here seem to have their favorite hidden paths and beach coves on Marjan, so ask around for tips.

From the Šperun neighborhood at the west end of the Old Town, you can hike to various lookout points. The best views are from the lowest point. If you're in shape, figure about an hour to hike to the top viewpoint, then another 45 minutes back down.

Start by climbing the stairs past the recommended Šperun Restaurant, and continue straight up Senjska ulica. Follow the stairs all the way up for 10-15 steep minutes to reach a spectacular view terrace (with sweeping vistas over Split's Old Town), next to a little café.

If you like, you can keep ascending for more good views (though you can't really see the Old Town beyond here). To continue on, curl around past the restaurant (following signs for *Crkva sv. Nikole* and *Sedlo*) and follow the steep pathway up, passing the fenced-in park on your right. Soon you'll reach the small chapel of St. Nicholas. Just behind it, find the steps up and to the right (look for *Marjanske Skale* signs). At the top of these stairs is Split's very humble zoo (adults-10 kn, kids-5 kn, daily 8:00-18:00). From here, a broad path cuts through the woods, with smaller paths branching off downhill. For the highest viewpoint, follow signs for *Sedlo* and hike up the steps to the terrace. This top-of-the-world perch offers a 360-degree panorama of Split's urban sprawl, receding layers of jagged and majestic mountains, offshore islands, and the bay behind the Marjan peninsula (but little in the way of Old Town views).

It's easiest to go back down the way you came. But for a longer hike, continue down the stairs at the far end of the view terrace, and follow signs for *Crkva sv. Jere*. This path takes you along the length of the peninsula, mostly through trees (read: no views). A series of switchbacks leads back down to the main road running along the perimeter of Marjan; from here, you can turn left to get back to town or right for an even longer walk around the far end of Marjan.

The peninsula also has a pair of good beaches (Ježinac and Bene, described next).

Hitting the Beach—Since it's more of a big city than a resort, Split's beaches aren't as scenic (and the water not as clear) as small towns elsewhere along the coast. The beach that's most popular—and crowded—is **Bačvice,** in a sandy cove just a short walk east of the main ferry terminal. As it's very shallow, it's especially popular with kids. After dark, it becomes a hopping meat-market nightlife zone for older "kids." You'll find less crowded beaches just to the east of Bačvice.

Or head in the other direction to Marjan, the peninsular city park, which is ringed with several sunbathing beaches. Along the southern edge of Marjan, just below the Meštrović Gallery, is a rocky but more local-feeling and less crowded beach called **Ježinac** (Croatian for "sea urchin"...be sure to wear water shoes). **Bene Beach** is along the northern edge of Marjan—reachable by bus #12 (the same one that goes to the Meštrović Gallery), tourist train (described earlier, under "Getting Around Split"), bike, or foot (about a 45-minute walk from the Old Town).

Nightlife in Split

The Riva—Every night, the sea of Croatian humanity laps at the walls of Diocletian's Palace along the town's pedestrian promenade. Choose a bench and watch life go by, or enjoy a drink at one of the many outdoor cafés. Live music (funded  by the tourist board) enlivens the Riva nightly through the summer (June-mid-Sept).

Old Town Bars—The labyrinthine lanes of the Old Town are packed with mostly interchangeable bars and cafés featuring inviting tables crammed between ancient stone buildings under a starry Croatian sky. If you're staying in the Old Town, you'll hear bar-goers late into the night. If you can't beat 'em, join 'em. One way is to simply lose yourself in the twisty lanes by following the music and the sound of socializing Croatians to the spot you like best. Or, if you prefer a little direction to your ramblings, explore the following neighborhoods. Note that, while each of the bars listed here has an interior, there's little reason to sit anywhere but under the open sky. Prices and menus are similar at most places (beer, wine, cocktails, coffee drinks); ordering something simply gives you an excuse to sit in a gorgeous outdoor space, nurse a drink, and focus on your travel partner. The action at these places really gets rolling around 22:00 and peaks around 23:00 (when bars are supposed to close their outdoor seating areas—but rarely do).

On the Peristyle: The obvious choice is right on the main square of the Old Town, Diocletian's former entry hall. All day long, the Peristyle steps serve as makeshift café tables for the bar called **Luxor,** with red cushions and small tables scattered along the steps. If you sit on a cushion, you're expected to order a drink (but you can sit or stand elsewhere for free). In the evening—as twilight encroaches and floodlights transform the square into one of the most atmospheric public spaces in Europe—live music breaks out (generally starting between 20:00 and 21:00 and continuing until around midnight). The smooth marble tiles of the Peristyle—worn to a slippery sheen by two millennia of visitors—becomes a dance floor, as people salsa, foxtrot, or pop-and-lock their way around the majestic space. Where else can you cut a rug in the grand entry hall of a Roman palace?

Majstora Jurja: This street, which runs along the north edge of Diocletian's Palace (just inside the wall), is lined with a mellow gaggle of low-key hangouts. Some mood music plays, but the soundtrack here is mostly chatting, laughing, and flirting. West of the Golden Gate, the lineup of café/bars includes **Teak** (with a namesake woody interior that feels almost distinguished) and the nondescript **Kala** and **Mosquito.** Up the side street at Dominisova 9, **Galerija** has the classiest atmosphere, with an upscale-feeling (but not stuffy), gallery-like ambience and a display case of cakes. East of the Golden Gate is the requisite **Irish Pub** (the best place in town to watch a rugby match) and **Red Room,** filling a large square with tables.

"Slavija Square": This is my own nickname for the tight, stepped area that's squeezed in front of Hotel Slavija, near Radić Brothers Square (Trg Braće Radića; from the square's statue of Marulić, enter the Old Town and bear right, following the beat).

This area is more youthful and rowdy, with throbbing techno music and cocktails that flow freely. Clambering up the steps are several bars, including the hip and roughly interchangeable **Puls** and **Fluid,** with predictable thumpa-thumpa atmosphere. Near the top of the stairs, the engagingly scruffy **Rakijarnica** boasts magic-marker walls, free stick-on moustaches, the motto "User Friendly," and *rakija*, the ubiquitous Balkan firewater, in several different flavors (mostly fruit). A few steps beyond, through the enclosed court-yard on the right, **Ghetto** has a mellower sailors' bordello-theme interior, with heart-shaped tables, red velvet, and randy graffiti. In the opposite direction, around the corner toward Jupiter's Temple, is a pair of bars facing each other (**Jupiter** and **San Giovanni**), with outdoor café tables and corny American music.

Behind the Loggia: For the youngest, trendiest scene in the Old Town, head for the zone locals call *Iza Loda* ("Behind the Loggia"). From the grand People's Square, follow the beat behind the former City Hall loggia to discover a well-dressed meat mar-ket populated by sleazy young men and tipsy American girls determined to make bad decisions. The main magnet here is the standing-room-only **Gaga,** with a pounding dance beat, indoor and outdoor bar areas, and a laser-light show on the ancient stones above. At the far end of the little square, like a mellow grandpar-ent observing the rowdy younger generation, is **La Linea** (which locals call simply "taverna")—an old sailors' pub decorated with nautical flags.

Other Areas: The large square at the top of Marmontova, just before the **Zara** store, is crammed with tables belonging to a half-dozen, identical-feeling cafés. And with the arrival of the rec-ommended Bajamonti café, **Trg Republike** (the grand Napoleonic square just west of the Riva) could also become a happening and inviting nightlife option.

Clubbing at Bačvice Beach—This family-friendly beach by day becomes a throbbing party area for young locals late at night. Since all Old Town bars have to close by 1:00 in the morning, night owls hike on over to the Bačvice crescent of clubs. The three-floor club complex is a cacophony of music, with the beat of each club melt-ing into the next—all with breezy terraces overlooking the harbor.

Sleeping in Split

Split has very expensive sleeps. Since there aren't enough beds in peak season, many hoteliers are shameless about gouging their cus-tomers. Lower your expectations. Split also suffers from perhaps the worst nighttime noise of any destination in this book—bring earplugs, and always ask for a quiet room (if possible). If you're on your own for breakfast, see my suggestions on page 940.

Sleep Code

(5 kn = about $1, €1 = about $1.40, country code: 385, area code: 021)

S = Single, **D** = Double/Twin, **T** = Triple, **Q** = Quad, **b** = bathroom. The modest tourist tax (about 7 kn per person, per night) is not included in these rates. Hotels generally accept credit cards and include breakfast in their rates, while most *sobe* accept only cash and don't offer breakfast. While rates are listed in euros, you'll pay in kunas.

Rates: If I've listed two sets of rates for an accommodation, I've noted when the second rate applies (generally off-season, Oct-May); if I've listed three sets of rates, separated by slashes, the first is for peak season (July-Sept), the second is shoulder season (May-June and Oct), and the third is off-season (Nov-April). The dates for seasonal rates vary by hotel, and prices can change without notice; verify the hotel's current rates online or by email. For other updates, see www.ricksteves.com/update.

Price Ranges: To help you easily sort through these listings, I've divided the accommodations into three categories based on the price for a double room with bath during high season:

  $$$ Higher Priced—Most rooms €125 or more.
   $$ Moderately Priced—Most rooms between €70-125.
    $ Lower Priced—Most rooms €70 or less.

Outside of the Old Town

These good values are within a five-minute walk of the Old Town. They're nearly as convenient as the Old Town options, but cheaper. Note that none of these places has a full-time reception desk; call ahead to arrange your arrival time.

In the Lučac Neighborhood, East of the Old Town

The Lučac neighborhood—which lines up along the busy street called Kralja Zvonimira—feels urban and a bit gritty, but it's handy to the Old Town. You'll find more Old World atmosphere on Petrova street, a block below the main road.

$$$ Hotel Luxe, a mod, minimalist hotel with 30 elegant-feeling rooms, is your best bet near the Old Town for sea views. While it fronts a dreary, busy urban street, all of its rooms face the quieter back side, and most have views over the harbor (non-view Sb-€140/€115/€105, sea-view Sb-€160/€130/€115, non-view Db-€155/€130/€120, sea-view Db-€200/€165/€140, bigger "superior" room with balcony for about €50 more, cheaper Nov-Feb, one-time €25 cleaning fee, air-con, elevator, free Wi-Fi, spa with small gym and Jacuzzi, Kralja Zvonimira 6, tel. 021/314-444, www.hotelluxesplit.com, hotelluxe@hotelluxesplit.com).

$$$ Villa Diana has six overpriced, mostly small rooms in a stone house over a restaurant (Sb-€104/€90/€80, Db-€129/€115/€100, Tb-€159/€145/€130, pricier apartment also available, cheaper Nov-March, air-con, free Wi-Fi, free parking, next door to Villa Ana at Kuzmanića 3—see directions in next listing, tel. & fax 021/482-460, www.villadiana.hr, info@villadiana.hr).

$$ Villa Ana, my favorite small hotel in Split, has five modern, comfortable rooms in a smart little freestanding stone house (Sb-€80, Db-€100, Tb-€115, roughly €20 less Nov-March, includes breakfast, air-con, free Wi-Fi, reception open sporadically 7:00-22:00, may be closed mid-Dec-mid-Jan, a few tight free parking spots out front; 2 long blocks east of Old Town up busy Kralja Zvonimira, follow the driveway-like lane opposite the lonely skyscraper to Vrh Lučac 16; tel. 021/482-715, fax 021/482-721, www.villaana-split.hr, info@villaana-split.hr, Danijel Bilobrk and helpful Branka).

$ Villa Art, run by sweet Tatijana, has five color-coded rooms that are unusually thoughtfully appointed. Decorated by a local artist, they have an almost French flair. Although it's on a drab alley, it's handy to the center (Db-€70/€55, apartment-€100/€85, lower prices are for Sept-June, no extra charge for 1- or 2-night stays, air-con, free Wi-Fi, Vickotina 7, tel. 021/482-288, mobile 098-170-4769, www.splitartapartments.com, booking@splitart apartments.com).

$ Dioclecijan Apartments, run by Tomislav Skalić and his wife Ivana, has two small rooms and one apartment in a pleasant local neighborhood. The decor is a tasteful mix of new and traditional (Db-€55/€40, apartment-€80/€65, lower price is for Oct-March, 1-night stays cost €5 more in rooms or €10 more in apartment, prices soft, cash only, no breakfast, air-con, free Wi-Fi, Petrova 19, Tomislav's mobile 091-537-1826, Ivana's mobile 091-536-7486, tskalic@globalnet.hr). From near the Green Market, head up Kralja Zvonimira, and turn right down Petrova. The apartments are on your left as the road bends.

In the Varoš Neighborhood, West of the Old Town

In addition to hosting the following accommodations, the atmospheric Varoš neighborhood—with twisty lanes climbing up towards the forested peak of the Marjan peninsula—is also home to several recommended eateries and the self-service Modrulj Launderette.

$$ Villa Matejuška has six apartments with old-fashioned beams and stone walls on a tight lane (small apartment-€109/€79, bigger apartment-€117/€79, biggest apartment-€136/€89, lower

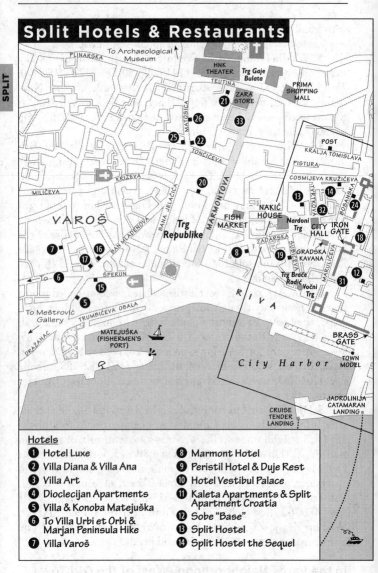

Split Hotels & Restaurants

Hotels

1. Hotel Luxe
2. Villa Diana & Villa Ana
3. Villa Art
4. Dioclecijan Apartments
5. Villa & Konoba Matejuška
6. To Villa Urbi et Orbi & Marjan Peninsula Hike
7. Villa Varoš
8. Marmont Hotel
9. Peristil Hotel & Duje Rest
10. Hotel Vestibul Palace
11. Kaleta Apartments & Split Apartment Croatia
12. Sobe "Base"
13. Split Hostel
14. Split Hostel the Sequel

prices are for Oct-mid-April, cash only, no extra charge for 1-night stays, no breakfast, air-con, free Wi-Fi, Tomića Stine 3, mobile 098-222-822, www.villamatejuska.hr, info@villamatejuska.hr or villamatejuska93@gmail.com). A second branch, **$$ Villa Urbi et Orbi,** has six cheaper units a steep five-minute hike up the street (Sb-€79/€59, Db-€89/€59, small apartment-€119/€89, big apartment-€169/€129, lower prices are for Oct-mid-April; from Villa Matejuška, continue up Senjska, head straight up the stairs,

Restaurants & Nightlife

15 Šperun Restaurant & Bistrot Šperun Deva
16 Konoba Varoš Restaurant
17 Tonik Juice Bar
18 Trattoria Bajamont
19 Apetit Restaurant
20 Bajamonti Restaurant
21 Maslina Restaurant
22 Ristorante Pizzeria Galija
23 Zlatna Vrata Pizza & Pasta
24 Fast Food None
25 Kantun Paulina
26 Hajduk Ice Cream
27 Ivona Ice Cream
28 Nadalina Chocolate Shop
29 Luxor Bar
30 Majstora Jurja Nightlife
31 "Slavija Square" Nightlife
32 "Behind the Loggia" Nightlife
33 Marmontova Nightlife
34 To Bačvice Beach

then turn right on Šenoina to #2; mobile 099-734-2777, www.villa urbietorbi.hr, info@villaurbietorbi.hr).

\$\$ Villa Varoš, run with class by Croatian-American Joanne Đonlić and her son Jure, has eight rooms and an apartment (with its own terrace) on a residential lane just beyond the appealing, restaurant-lined Šperun street. Thin walls and echoey halls can make for a noisy night (Db-€80/€65, Tb-€85/€70, apartment-€120/€90, lower prices are for Oct-March, rates include tax, optional 30-kn breakfast at nearby restaurant, air-con, stairs with no elevator, free Wi-Fi, Miljenka Smoje 1, tel. 021/483-469, Joanne's mobile 098-469-681, Jure's mobile 098-229-408, www.villavaros.hr, joanne.d.o.o@st.t-com.hr).

Inside the Old Town

While the Old Town is convenient, it's also a happening nightlife zone, so you're likely to encounter some noise (especially on weekends). Old Town bars are required to close by 23:00, though this is loosely enforced (especially in summer). Earplugs are essential.

$$$ Marmont Hotel is a very inviting oasis offering four-star comfort, with 21 mod-feeling rooms in a quiet corner of the Old Town. The slight aroma you may notice is from the fish market, just around the corner (standard Sb-€145/€95/€85, superior Sb-€185/€120/€118, Db-€188/€136/€105, superior Db-€260/€189/€145, "deluxe" rooms also available, air-con, elevator, free Wi-Fi, sun terrace, Zadarska 13, tel. 021/308-060, fax 021/308-070, www.marmonthotel.com, booking@marmonthotel.com).

$$$ Hotel Peristil has 12 classy rooms over a restaurant just steps from the couldn't-be-more-central square of the same name. Run by the Caktaš family, it's homey and convenient, if pricey (Sb-€135/€110/€95, Db-€160/€135/€120, extra bed-€15, air-con, stairs with no elevator, free Wi-Fi, some noise from nearby bars, just behind TI and inside the Silver Gate at Poljana Kraljice Jelene 5, tel. 021/329-070, fax 021/329-088, www.hotelperistil.com, booking@hotelperistil.com).

$$$ Hotel Vestibul Palace is the swankiest splurge in Split's Old Town, with modern decor in an old shell. Tucked in a corner just behind the entry vestibule on the upper level of Diocletian's Palace, this plush place offers seven rooms with maximum comfort and style for maximum prices. Throughout the day, you'll hear the harmonious voices of the *klapa* singers echoing up from the vestibule below (Sb-€190/€158/€126, small Db-€230/€189/€147, standard Db-€315/€275/€217, pricier suites also available, air-con, no elevator, free Internet access and Wi-Fi, valet parking-100 kn, Iza Vestibula 4, tel. 021/329-329, fax 021/329-333, www.vestibul palace.com, info@vestibulpalace.com). They also have four more rooms in a nearby annex, called Villa Dobrić.

$$ Kaleta Apartments, run by the Raić family, consists of several tastefully decorated apartments spread across two buildings. Two stylish, modern apartments are squeezed between cafés along a tight alley in a lively area at the back of the Old Town (the good windows do a heroic job of keeping noise to a minimum). Their other three units, including a larger one with a couch and eat-in space, share a common lounge in a quieter building a few blocks away, near the People's Square (Db-€75-90, €60-80 in Oct-May, price depends on size of room, cash only, air-con, free Internet access and Wi-Fi, Majstora Jurja 4, mobile 099-509-4299, www.kaletaapartments.hr, kaletaapartments@email.t-com.hr).

$$ Split Apartment Croatia, run by go-getter Nikša, is an agency with a line on apartments around Split. Nikša rents two of his own rooms, near the People's Square (Db-€75/€55/€40, air-con, free Wi-Fi). He can also arrange a room for you elsewhere for similar prices (you pay him 20 percent, then the rest to the owner, cash only; his office at Majstora Jurja 4 serves as a sort of reception desk, offering free coffee and Internet access; mobile 091-390-9411, www.split-apartment.com, info@split-apartment.com).

$ Sobe "Base" has three of the nicest rooms in the Old Town. Tina and her dad, retired ship's captain Ivo, offer many amenities unusual for this price range, including free Wi-Fi and Internet terminals in each room. You can't be more central: All of the colorful rooms—located over a gift shop—overlook the front steps of the cute little Jupiter's Temple. Although it's in the midst of some bustling bar action, the double-paned windows do their darnedest to provide reasonable peace; earplugs help, too (Db-€70, €60 in Sept-June, cash only, no extra charge for 1- or 2-night stays, no breakfast, air-con, Kraj Svetog Ivana 3, tel. 021/317-375, mobile 098-361-387, www.base-rooms.com, mail@base-rooms.com).

$ *Other* Sobe: Several *sobe* are inside Split's Old Town, and many more are within a 10-minute walk. As in any coastal town, you can simply show up at the boat dock or bus station, be met by locals trying to persuade you into their rooms, and check out the best offer (Db-about 250 kn). Or you can try booking through a travel agency, such as **Travel49** or **Turistički Biro** (both listed earlier, under "Helpful Hints"), or **Split Apartment Croatia** (listed above).

$ Split Hostel is centrally located just off the People's Square in the heart of town. This small, youthful hostel has 23 beds in four cramped rooms and a shared outdoor terrace to give everyone some much-needed breathing room. Run by a pair of Croat-Aussie women with the simple slogan "booze & snooze," it's Split's most central hostel option (bunk in 6-bed room-€25/€20/€17/€15, cash only, no breakfast, free Internet access and Wi-Fi, laundry service, excursions, 8 Narodni Trg, tel. 021/342-787, www.splithostel.com, info@splithostel.com). Their second location—**Split Hostel the Sequel**—is also in the Old Town, a short walk away, and has 25 dorm beds in five rooms at similar prices, plus a wider range of rooms, including 8-, 5-, 4-, and 2-bed rooms (D-€70 in summer, downstairs bar, Kružićeva 5).

SPLIT

Eating in Split

Split's Old Town has oodles of atmosphere, but the Varoš district, just a couple of blocks west of the Old Town, has several characteristic *konoba*s (traditional restaurants). I've listed options in both areas. Service in Split's restaurants tends to be a bit grouchy, and you may be unceremoniously turned away if they're very busy (reservations are wise, especially for dinner).

In Varoš, West of the Old Town

Šperun Restaurant has a classy, cozy Old World ambience and a passion for good Dalmatian food. Owner Damir Banović (with the help of his animated dad, Zdravko) serves a mix of Croatian and "eclectic Mediterranean," specializing in seafood. A "buffet" table of *antipasti* (starters) in the lower dining room shows you what you're getting, so you can select your ideal meal (not self-service—order from the waiter). This place distinguishes itself by offering a warm welcome and good food for reasonable prices (35-70-kn pastas, 50-120-kn meat and seafood dishes, daily 9:00-23:00, air-con, a few sidewalk tables, reservations wise in summer, Šperun 3, tel. 021/346-999). Their annex across the street, **Bistrot Šperun Deva,** has a simpler and cheaper menu, lots of outdoor seating, and a handy à la carte breakfast for *sobe*-dwellers (20-50-kn salads, 50-60-kn main courses, daily 8:00-23:00, closed off-season, Šperun 2).

Konoba Matejuška offers charm, good food, and fair prices in a cozy, inviting, mellow, five-table cellar (30-55-kn starters, 50-150-kn main courses, daily 13:00-16:00 & 19:00-23:00, below Villa Matejuška hotel at Tomića Stine 3, tel. 021/355-152).

Konoba Varoš, though bigger and more impersonal than others listed here, is beloved by natives and tourists alike for its great food. Serious waiters serve a wide range of Croatian cooking (including pastas, seafood, and meat dishes) under droopy fishnets in a slightly gloomy throwback interior (50-80-kn pastas, 60-110-kn main courses, daily 9:00-24:00, lots of groups, reservations smart—busiest 20:00-22:00, Ban Mladenova 7, tel. 021/396-138).

Smoothies and Fruit Juices: For a healthier energy boost, head for **Tonik Juice Bar,** run by Croat-Aussie Stefanie. Select from the diverse menu of smoothies and juice combos (16-40 kn). In summer, they also serve light meals (30-kn wraps, 25-kn muesli for breakfast, June-Sept daily 7:00-22:00, shoulder season daily 8:00-21:00, closed Nov-March, near the launderette and Šperun street restaurants at Ban Mladenova 5, mobile 098-641-376).

In and near the Old Town

Trattoria Bajamont, not to be confused with Bajamonti (listed below), is buried on a narrow lane deep in the Old Town. This is a great choice for unpretentious, affordable Dalmatian home cooking with an emphasis on fish. The handwritten menu pinned to a bulletin board informs you of the day's options—all fresh from the market. In this tight, casual, and cozy eatery, the busy kitchen and seven tables are all crammed into a single room. Because the place can get crowded, you may have to share your table—and be prepared for the service to be chaotic and a bit quirky (60-80-kn pastas, 70-150-kn fish dishes, Mon-Sat 8:00-24:00, closed Sun, Bajamontijeva 3, mobile 091-253-7441).

Apetit serves up traditional Dalmatian cuisine in an appealingly modern, second-floor dining room (the restaurant on the ground floor of the same building, which enjoys hijacking Apetit's customers, is a different operation). As there's no outdoor seating, this is a good bad-weather option (50-70-kn pastas, 60-115-kn main courses; 90-kn daily special in summer includes soup, salad, and main dish; lots of groups, daily 10:00-24:00, Šubićeva 5, tel. 021/332-549).

Bajamonti sits regally at the top of Split's beautiful, arcaded square, Trg Republike, just off the west end of the Riva. This place brings a certain grand-café elegance to Split's otherwise rustic *konoba*-heavy dining scene. The interior is classy, with checkerboard-tiled, split-level elegance, but the best seating is on the grand square out front (55-80-kn pastas, 80-160-kn main courses, daily 7:30-24:00, Trg Republike 1, tel. 021/341-033).

Maslina ("Olive"), an unpretentious family-run spot filled with locals, hides behind a shopping mall on the busy Marmontova pedestrian street. They serve a wide range of 45-70-kn pizzas and pastas, plus 65-110-kn meat and fish dishes (Tue-Sat 10:00-24:00, Sun-Mon 12:00-24:00, Teutina 1A, tel. 021/314-988, Pezo family). It's virtually impossible to find on your own, so follow these directions carefully: Approaching the top of Marmontova from the harbor, look for the low-profile archway on the left beyond the café tables (just before the big Zara store). Walk along the skinny path behind the building to reach the restaurant.

Pizzerias: **Ristorante Pizzeria Galija,** at the west end of the Old Town, has a boisterous local following and good wood-fired pizza, pasta, and salads (40-70 kn, Mon-Sat 9:00-24:00, Sun 12:00-24:00, air-con, just a block off of Marmontova at Tončićeva 12, tel. 021/347-932; the recommended Hajduk ice-cream shop is nearby). **Zlatna Vrata** ("Golden Gate"), right in the Old Town, offers wood-fired pizzas and pasta dishes. The food and interior are nothing special, but there's wonderful outdoor seating in a tingle-worthy Gothic courtyard with pointy arches and lots of pillars (40-60 kn, Mon-Sat 7:00-24:00, closed Sun, just inside the Golden Gate and—as you face outside—up the skinny alley to the left, on Majstora Jurja, tel. 021/345-015).

Take-Away: **Fast Food None** ("Grandma's") is a stand-up or take-away pizza joint handy for a quick bite in the Old Town. In addition to pizzas and bruschettas with various toppings, they serve up a pair of traditional pizza-like specialties (with crust on bottom and top, like a filled pizza): *viška pogača,* with tomatoes, onion, and anchovy; and *soparnik,* with a thin layer of spinach, onion, and olive oil. They can also make you a grilled sandwich—just point to what you want (10-30 kn, Mon-Sat 7:00-23:00, closed Sun, just outside Diocletian's Palace on the skinny street that runs along the wall at Bosanska 4, tel. 021/347-252). **Kantun Paulina** ("Paulina's Corner") is a local favorite for take-away *čevapčići*—Balkan grilled meats (17-20 kn, Mon-Sat 8:00-23:00, Sun 17:00-23:00, Matošića 1). For descriptions of your options, see the "Balkan Flavors" sidebar on page 1090.

Breakfast: **Hotel Peristil** serves breakfast to non-guests for 50 kn (all-you-can-eat, including eggs; daily 7:00-12:00); the adjacent **Duje Restaurant**, just behind the cathedral, has a similar deal. The only place serving breakfast along the Riva is **Adriana**, which charges a hefty 80 kn for eggs, rolls, coffee, and juice; alternatively, you could just buy some pastries at a bakery and eat them on a harborfront bench. For a cheap alternative, head over to the Matejuška fishermen's port, where **Leut** restaurant serves a 30-kn breakfast on their terrace (from 10:00). Several of my recommended restaurants also serve breakfast.

Gelato: Split has several spots for delicious ice cream *(sladoled).* Most ice-cream parlors *(kuća sladoleda)* are open daily 8:00-24:00. Natives recommend two in particular: **Hajduk,** named for Split's soccer team, is a block off the main Marmontova pedestrian drag; ask them to dip your cone in milk chocolate for no extra charge (around the corner from Pizzeria Galija at Matošićeva 4). More central, at the east end of the Riva, look for **Ivona** (near entrance to Diocletian's cellars at Kaštelanska cesta 65).

Split Connections

For general tips on getting around the Dalmatian Coast, see page 824.

By Boat

As the transport hub for the Dalmatian Coast, Split has good boat connections to nearly anywhere you want to go. The fast passenger catamarans dock close to the Old Town: the *Krilo* catamaran uses dock #11, which is along the pier halfway between the main ferry terminal and the Old Town; and the Jadrolinija catamaran arrives and departs at the handy Obala Lazareta embankment just in front of the Old Town. Big car ferries can arrive or depart from all along the harbor (electronic boards display which dock each boat leaves

from). Note that these locations sometimes change according to boat traffic.

Note: The following boat information is subject to change—always confirm before you make your plans. To check Jadrolinija schedules, see www.jadrolinija.hr; for *Krilo* catamaran schedules, see www.krilo.hr. Or drop by Split's helpful Jadrolinija boat ticket office, in the main ferry terminal (open 24/7 in summer, daily 5:30-24:00 off-season, tel. 021/338-333).

Buying Tickets

Tickets for the fast passenger **catamarans** (either *Krilo* or Jadrolinija) are not sold until 6:00 in the morning on the day of departure. As these boats can sell out quickly in peak season, buy your tickets in the morning. For the 11:30 Jadrolinija catamaran, try to get your tickets by 9:00 (or, on busy days in July-Aug, even earlier—by about 8:30). For afternoon boats, purchase tickets by noon (or earlier on summer weekends). *Krilo* tickets are only sold at the kiosk at its departure dock (#11). For Jadrolinija catamarans, you can buy tickets at three locations: the kiosk on the parking island right in front of the Old Town; next to the *Krilo* kiosk alongside the harbor; and in the main terminal (if the kiosk near the Old Town has a long line, consider walking five minutes to the next one, where the wait is probably shorter).

If you're a passenger walking onto a Jadrolinija **car ferry**, there's no need to buy tickets in advance. However, if you're driving onto a car ferry, it's smart to buy your tickets from one of the Jadrolinija kiosks mentioned above and line up early—ask locally for advice on your particular boat. For the connections below, I've listed the passenger fare.

If I've listed a price range for a specific journey, it depends on the season.

Weather Disruptions: Catamarans are the quickest way to the islands, but they're also the most susceptible to bad weather. In very rough or windy weather, cancellations are possible (decisions are made a couple of hours before departure—ask at the ticket booth what time you should come back to check). In poor

Sailing Between Croatia and Italy

Many travelers are tempted to splice a little bit of Croatia into their Italian itinerary, or vice versa. But zipping across the Adriatic isn't as effortless as it seems. Most sea crossings involve an overnight on the boat, and the Italian towns best connected to Croatia—Ancona, Pescara, and Bari—are far from Italy's top sights. Plan thoughtfully. For example, if you're in northern Italy and want to sample Croatia, it's much easier to dip into Istria than it is to get all the way down to Croatia's Dalmatian Coast.

If you decide to set sail, you have several options, run by various companies. Split is the primary hub, but you can also go from other cities (usually Dubrovnik or Zadar; some international ferries also call at the small Dalmatian islands). Almost all boats go to Ancona, Italy, which is about two-thirds of the way up the Italian coast (on the calf of Italy's "boot"). Others go to Pescara, about 100 miles south of Ancona; and to Bari, near the southern tip of Italy (the "heel"). Most trips are overnight and last 8-10 hours, but there are faster daytime catamarans. Note that these connections are highly subject to change from year to year; do an Internet search to be confident you know all of your options.

Slow Night Boats: Figure about €55 per person for one-way deck passage (about 10-20 percent more in peak season, roughly July-Aug; sometimes even more on weekends). Onboard accommodation costs extra (about €20 per person for a couchette in a 4-berth compartment, €60-75 per person in 2-bed compartment with private shower and WC). These companies operate night boats to Italy:

Jadrolinija goes from Split to Ancona, from Zadar to Ancona, and from Dubrovnik to Bari (tel. 051/211-444 or 021/338-333, www.jadrolinija.hr).

Blue Line sails from Split to Ancona; on weekends in Aug, it stops en route at Stari Grad on Hvar Island (can book at Split

weather, the *Krilo* is more stable (and provides a more comfortable ride) than Jadrolinija's *Adriana* catamaran; if you have an option, go with *Krilo*. If the catamarans aren't running, look into taking the slower car ferries instead (which typically go in any weather).

Getting from Split to Other Destinations in Croatia

Big Jadrolinija Car Ferries: Twice weekly in summer, these hulking boats make the long trip down the Dalmatian Coast, connecting key destinations. They leave Split early in the morning (at 7:30) and head south, stopping at **Stari Grad on Hvar Island** (20-minute bus ride from Hvar town; 1.75 hours, 39-47 kn; the catamarans described next are faster and take you right to Hvar town), **Korčula town** (6 hours, 90-110 kn; again, catamarans to Korčula Island

Tours travel agency in Split, tel. 021/352-533, www.blueline -ferries.com).

Azzurra Line/Jadrolinija goes between Bari and Dubrovnik, and between Bari and Kotor, Montenegro (Croatian tel. 020/313-178, Montenegrin tel. 085/313-617, Italian tel. 080-592-8400, www.azzurraline.com).

Other companies serving these routes come and go each year—ask the Split TI or poke around Split's main terminal building to discover the latest.

Fast Daytime Boats: Some speedier crossings are available. But because these boats are faster and smaller, they're also weather-dependent—so they don't run off-season. In recent years, due to decreased demand, these boats have run only in July and August—check online for a current schedule. **SNAV** connects Split and Ancona in just 4.5 hours; they also zip from Split to Stari Grad (on Hvar Island), then on to the Italian town of Pescara (6 hours total; either trip €60-100 one-way, depending on season; Croatian tel. 021/322-252, Italian tel. 081-428-5555, www.snav.it).

Trains Within Italy: From **Ancona,** you can catch a train to Venice (almost hourly, 4.25-5.25 hours, most transfer in Bologna), Florence (almost hourly, 3-4.25 hours, most transfer in Bologna), or Rome (8/day direct, 3-4.5 hours). From **Pescara,** trains head to Rome (6/day direct, 3.75-4.25 hours) and Florence (almost hourly, 4.5-5.25 hours, transfer in Bologna). From **Bari,** you can hop a train to Naples (6/day, 3.75-6 hours, most transfer in Caserta), Rome (3/day direct, 4.75 hours), or Florence (8/day, 6.75-8.5 hours, transfer in Rome or Bologna). For timetables, check www.ferroviedellostato.it or www.bahn.com (Germany's excellent all-Europe website).

Note that in Italian, Split is called "Spalato" (which is also the sound you hear if seasickness gets the best of you).

are faster), **Sobra on Mljet Island** (1.25-hour bus ride from the national park; 8.75 hours, 110-130 kn), and **Dubrovnik** (11 hours, 110-130 kn). You can also take a boat to **Rijeka**, on the northern Croatian coast, 4 hours by train from Zagreb and 2.75 hours by train from Ljubljana (2/week, June-Sept only, 11 hours overnight, 160- to 190-kn deck passage, more if you want a bed).

Other Boats to Hvar Island: To reach Hvar, ideally catch a boat heading to Hvar town, the most interesting part of the island. Two companies run speedy catamarans (50-60 minutes) from Split to Hvar town: **Jadrolinija** (June-Sept: 2/day, departing Split at 11:30 and 15:00, 45-47 kn; Oct-May: 1/day, departing Split at 14:00, 45 kn; occasionally stops at Milna on Brač Island; a different catamaran, bound for Vis, stops at Hvar only on Tuesdays) and

Krilo (June-Sept: departs Split daily at 17:00; Oct-May: departs Split daily at 16:00; 35-45 kn). You can also reach Hvar Island on the **local car ferries** from Split; these are frequent but take longer and are less convenient, since they take you to the town of Stari Grad, across the island and a 20-minute bus trip from Hvar town. On the other hand, these are the only way to get to Hvar in the morning—and a good backup plan if the 11:30 catamaran sells out, or if the catamaran stops running due to bad weather (7/day in summer, 3/day in winter, 1.75 hours, 39-47 kn).

Other Boats to Korčula Island: Many of the same boats that go to Hvar town continue on to Korčula Island. The most convenient is the *Krilo* **catamaran,** which takes you right to Korčula town (June-Sept: departs Split daily at 17:00; Oct-May: departs Split daily at 16:00; 2.5-2.75 hours; 60-65 kn; in summer, it also stops en route at Prigradica on Korčula Island). The other boats leave you at Vela Luka, at the far end of the island from Korčula town (buses meet arriving boats to take passengers on the one-hour trip into Korčula town). One **Jadrolinija catamaran** goes from Split to Hvar town, then to Vela Luka (June-Sept: departs Split at 15:00, Oct-May: departs at 14:00, 2 hours, 40-50 kn). You can also take Jadrolinija's slower **local car ferries** from Split to Vela Luka (1-2/day, 3 hours, 50-60 kn).

By Bus

Each of the following routes is served by multiple companies, which charge slightly different rates, so the prices listed here are rough estimates. Always ask about the fastest option—which can save hours of bus time. It's smart to arrive about 30 minutes before your bus departs to buy tickets (better yet, during peak season, come to the station to buy them earlier in the day). The generally English-speaking staff at Split's bus station gives out handy little schedules for popular journeys. Bus info: www.ak-split.hr, toll tel. 060-327-777.

By Bus to: Zagreb (at least hourly, 5-8 hours, depending on route, about 175-200 kn), **Dubrovnik** (almost hourly, less off-season, 3.5-5 hours, 100 kn), **Korčula** (1 night bus leaves at 1:00 in the morning and arrives at 6:00, 125 kn), **Trogir** (1-2/hour, 30 minutes, about 20 kn), **Zadar** (at least hourly, 3 hours, about 80-120 kn), **Mostar** (6/day, 4-4.5 hours, about 115 kn), **Međugorje** (3/day, 3.5 hours, about 100 kn), **Sarajevo** (5/day in summer, 3/day in winter, 5.5-6 hours, 7.5 hours, about 200 kn), **Rijeka** (7-10/day including some night buses, 7.75-8.5 hours, 260-350 kn). Zagreb-bound buses sometimes also stop at **Plitvice** (confirm with driver and ask him to stop at the national park entrance; about 4/day, 4-6 hours, 155 kn).

By Train

From Split, trains go to **Zagreb** (3/day, 6 hours, 190 kn; 1 direct night train, 9 hours, 172 kn); in Zagreb, you can transfer to **Ljubljana** (1/day, 9 hours total). Train info: tel. 021/338-525 or toll tel. 060-333-444, www.hznet.hr.

Route Tips for Drivers

Driving around the city center can be tricky—Split is split by its Old Town, which is welded to the harbor by the pedestrian-only Riva promenade. This means drivers needing to get 300 yards from one side of the Old Town to the other must drive about 15 minutes entirely around the center, which can be miserably clogged with traffic. A semicircular ring road and a tunnel under the Marjan peninsula help relieve the situation a bit.

Arriving in Split: Drivers are treated to the ugly side of Split as they approach town (don't worry—it gets better). From the expressway, you'll pass through an industrial zone, then curl through a few tunnels as you twist your way down into Split's striking, bowl-like setting. While you're still quite a distance from downtown, you'll come to a fork where you'll have to make a decision about which side of town you want to drive to (east or west); ask your hotel in advance for directions, and be ready for your turn. (While many hotels are individually signposted at the fork, it's a long list and hard to read quickly as you zip past.)

At the main fork, turning to the right (marked with *Centar* signs) takes you to the **west end** of the Old Town, including the Varoš neighborhood. Or, if you continue straight (marked *Trajekt*—"ferry"), you'll eventually reach other *Centar* signs and the **east end** of the Old Town, with the ferry terminal, the bus and train stations, and the Lučac neighborhood. You'll pop out right at the southeast corner of Diocletian's Palace (by the Green Market). For handy (but expensive) parking, when the road swings left to the ferry terminal, continue straight, right into a parking lot just outside the palace walls (10 kn/hour).

Connecting Split with Destinations to the North: Thanks to Croatia's A1 super-expressway, the road trip from Zagreb to Split takes less than five hours. You can leave Zagreb after an early dinner and arrive in Split before bedtime. If you're heading north from Split, simply drive up out of the city's bowl-like setting and follow signs to the A1 expressway north (toward Zagreb; if you're going to Plitvice, turn off at Otočac and drive east from there).

Connecting Split with Destinations to the South: If you're heading to Dubrovnik, other Dalmatian Coast destinations, or Mostar—it's a bit more complicated, as the expressway southbound from Split is only partially completed (to check the latest progress,

A Bridge Too Far?

If you're driving along the coast between Split and Dubrovnik, you may be surprised when you have to stop and show your passport to enter another country—Bosnia-Herzegovina, around the resort town of Neum. How is it that Bosnia wound up with its very own five-and-a-half-mile stretch of the Dalmatian Coast? During the heyday of the Republic of Dubrovnik, the city's leaders granted this land to the Ottoman Empire to provide a buffer between Dubrovnik's holdings and the Republic of Venice, to the north. (They knew the Venetians would never enter the territory of the Ottomans—their fearsome enemy—in order to invade Dubrovnik.) Later, as the borders of Europe were being redrawn in modern times, Bosnia retained possession of this strip of land as a sort of inheritance from their former rulers.

For years, coastal Bosnians and their Croatian neighbors have coexisted, albeit tensely at times. Prices for hotel rooms, groceries, and other staples are slightly cheaper in Neum, whose rest stops lure tourist buses with low prices and generous kickbacks for bus drivers. Visitors are inconvenienced by having to go through a passport checkpoint as they enter Bosnia and again, just a few minutes later, as they exit Bosnia. From a practical standpoint, this is rarely an issue. But on busy days, there can be lines, and it's always smart to have your passport and rental car's "green card" (proof of insurance) ready.

Croatians are irritated with the red tape, and—even more—by the way Neum merchants undersell the Croatian alternatives nearby. As Croatia extends its expressway southward, the most logical approach would be a route through Bosnia to Dubrovnik. But some Croatian politicians have been looking for a way to avoid Neum altogether. One solution is to build a 1.5-mile-long bridge from just north of Neum to the Pelješac Peninsula, then re-join the coastal road back in Croatia, just south of Neum—effectively bypassing Bosnian territory. Environmentalists worry about the impact the bridge will have on the ecosystem around Mali Ston. But, because of the proposed bridge's popularity with a certain segment of the voting population, work actually began on this project prior to a recent election (notice that one mountaintop on Pelješac has already been cleared). After the election—and with the global economic crisis—plans were put on hold. It remains to be seen whether this very expensive project will ever come to fruition...and if so, whether the bridge will be completed before Croatia and Bosnia both join the EU and open their borders anyway.

see www.hac.hr or www.hak.hr). You have two options. The main **coastal road** twists slowly but scenically along some fantastic scenery, in an area dubbed the "Makarska Riviera." (Along this road is the town of Drvenik, where you can take a ferry to Sućuraj on Hvar Island; from Sućuraj, a surprisingly long and twisty road traverses the length of the island to Hvar town. If you're going to Hvar Island, taking a car ferry directly from Split to Stari Grad is far faster and less stressful.) Continuing south, you'll wind up in the town of Ploče (described later).

To save some time, most travelers prefer to take the **expressway** part of the way. To do this, as you leave Split, follow blue expressway signs to *Dubrovnik*. You can take A1 south as far as it goes; it cuts inland from the sea, running behind the tall coastal mountain range, near the Bosnian border. As of early 2012, A1 was complete to the remote town of Vrgorac, about 100 km (60 miles) south of Split; a small section around the coastal town of Ploče, about 25 km (15 miles) south of Vrgorac, was also complete. Until A1 is finished (possibly in late 2012 or early 2013), you'll have to transfer to rough and rugged surface roads between Vrgorac and Ploče. (Note that if you're headed to Mostar, the fastest way from here is to pass into Bosnia-Herzegovina just south of Vrgorac, at Veliki Prolog, then follow signs to *Mostar* from there.)

Ploče has a ferry that runs to the town of Trpanj, on the landward side of the Pelješac Peninsula—not far from Orebić, where another boat plods across to Korčula town. If you're headed to Korčula and plan your timing to catch this ferry, it could save you some driving.

Just south of Ploče is the dramatic Neretva River Delta, a scenic and lush zone of farmland (described on page 1094). This also marks the end of the A1 expressway. Here you'll hop on the main Dalmatian coastal road. Halfway along the delta, you'll see the turnoff to Metković, the gateway town on the main, heavily touristed road between Croatia and Mostar.

South of the Neretva River Delta—after twisting up to a high perch overlooking the delta—is a border crossing. Here begins an odd little stretch of coastline that's technically in Bosnia, around the town of Neum (for details on Neum—and the bridge Croatia is building to bypass it—see sidebar). Have your passport ready, but don't panic—the border is generally a quick wave-through. After a few more miles, you'll cross back into Croatia, and shortly come to a crossroads where, if you like, you can turn right and detour a few minutes to the impressively walled little villages of Ston and Mali Ston, at the base of the Pelješac Peninsula. If you're headed to Korčula, continue beyond Ston to the far end of the Pelješac Peninsula, where the ferry plods from Orebić to Dominče, near Korčula town.

After Ston, you're less than an hour from Dubrovnik. Along the way, you'll have fine views of Mljet and the Elaphite Islands. As you near Dubrovnik, you'll pass through the town of Trsteno, which has a good arboretum. When you cross the giant, modern bridge, you'll know Dubrovnik is just around the bend; for arrival tips, see page 848.

KORČULA

The island town of Korčula (KOHR-choo-lah) boasts an atmospheric Old Town, a smattering of surprisingly engaging museums, and a dramatic, fjord-like mountain backdrop. While certainly on the tourist trail, Korčula is sleepy and has an appealing (and occasionally frustrating) backwater charm. All things considered, Korčula is the most enjoyable Back Door stopover between Split and Dubrovnik.

Like so many other small Croatian coastal towns, Korčula was founded by the ancient Greeks. It became part of the Roman Empire and was eventually a key southern outpost of the Venetian Republic. Four centuries of Venetian rule left Korčula with a quirky Gothic-Renaissance mix and a strong siesta tradition. Korčulans take great pride in the fact that Marco Polo was born here in 1254—the explorer remains the town's poster boy. Korčula is also known for its traditional *Moreška* sword dance.

You'll discover that there are two Korčulas: the tacky seaside resort and the historic Old Town. Savvy visitors ignore the tourist sprawl and focus on Korčula's medieval quarter, a mini-Dubrovnik poking into the sea on a picture-perfect peninsula. Tiny lanes branch off the humble main drag like ribs on a fish's backbone. This street plan is designed to catch both the breeze and the shade. All in all, this laid-back island village is an ideal place to take a vacation from your busy vacation.

Planning Your Time

Korčula deserves the better part of a day, but you'll quickly exhaust the town's sightseeing options. Spend the morning wandering the medieval Old Town and exploring the handful of tiny museums (many close for siesta in the early afternoon, especially outside of peak season). In the afternoon, kick back at a café or restaurant and bask on the beach. If you're here on a Thursday, be sure to catch the performance of the *Moreška* dance (also Mon July-Aug). With a second day, really be on vacation.

Off-Season Challenges: While Korčula is reasonably well-connected to the rest of Dalmatia in the summertime, things change off-season. The handy *Nona Ana* express boat to Dubrovnik runs only in July and August. From October to May, things get even more sparse: The Dubrovnik car-ferry is discontinued entirely, bus connections to Dubrovnik are cut in half (leaving only one early-morning option), and express boat service from Split and Hvar is also halved. You may find that you'll have to spend two nights in Korčula just to have any daylight time here.

Orientation to Korčula

(area code: 020)
The long, skinny island of Korčula runs alongside the even longer, skinnier Pelješac Peninsula. The main town and best destination on the island—just across a narrow strait from Pelješac—is also called Korčula.

Korčula town is centered on its compact **Old Town** (Stari Grad) peninsula, which is connected to the mainland at a big staircase leading to the Great Land Gate. In the area in front of this staircase, you'll find ATMs, travel agencies, the Jadrolinija ferry office, Internet cafés, the Konzum supermarket, a colorful outdoor produce market, and other handy tourist services.

Stretching to the south and east of the Old Town is **"Shell Bay,"** surrounded by a strip of tacky tourist shops and resort hotels. This seamier side of Korčula—best avoided—caters mostly to Brits and Germans here to worship the sun for a week or two.

To the west of Old Town is the serene waterfront street **Put Svetog Nikole,** where you'll find a few *sobe* (including some recommended under "Sleeping in Korčula," later), inviting swimming areas, great views back on the Old Town, and more locals than tourists.

Tourist Information
Korčula's TI, run by Stanka Kraljević and slyly smiling Smilija, is next to Hotel Korčula on the west side of the Old Town waterfront (mid-June-Sept Mon-Sat 8:00-15:00 & 16:00-22:00, Sun

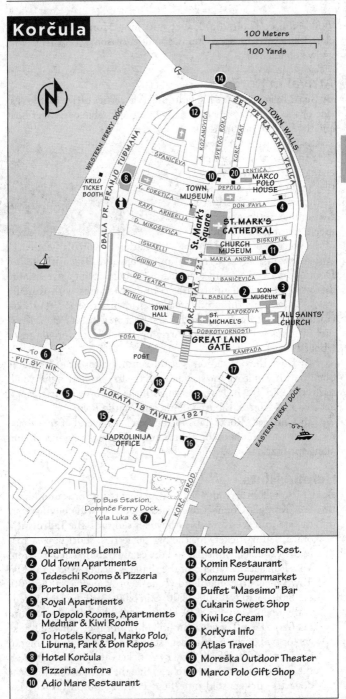

Korčula

100 Meters
100 Yards

ŠET. PETRA KANAVELICA

OLD TOWN WALLS

WESTERN FERRY DOCK

A. ROZANOVIĆA

SVETOG ROKA

KORC. BRAT

ŠPANIĆEVA

LENTICA

KRILO TICKET BOOTH

OBALA DR. FRANJO TUĐMANA

V. FORETIĆA

TOWN MUSEUM

DEPOLO

MARCO POLO HOUSE

RAFA ARNERIJA

DON PAVLA

D. MIROŠEVIĆA

ST. MARK'S CATHEDRAL

ISMAELLI

CHURCH MUSEUM

BISKUPIJE

GIUNIO

MARKA ANDRIJIĆA

OD TEATRA

J. BANIČEVIĆA

ŽITNICA

L. BABLIĆA

ICON MUSEUM

TOWN HALL

ST. MICHAEL'S

KAPOROVA

ALL SAINTS' CHURCH

FOSA

DOBROTVORNOSTI

GREAT LAND GATE

RAMPADA

POST

KORC. STAT. 1214

St. Mark's Square

PUT SV. NIK.

PLOKATA 19 TRAVNJA 1921

JADROLINIJA OFFICE

EASTERN FERRY DOCK

KORC. BROD

To Bus Station,
Dominče Ferry Dock,
Vela Luka & ⑦

1 Apartments Lenni
2 Old Town Apartments
3 Tedeschi Rooms & Pizzeria
4 Portolan Rooms
5 Royal Apartments
6 To Depolo Rooms, Apartments Medmar & Kiwi Rooms
7 To Hotels Korsal, Marko Polo, Liburna, Park & Bon Repos
8 Hotel Korčula
9 Pizzeria Amfora
10 Adio Mare Restaurant
11 Konoba Marinero Rest.
12 Komin Restaurant
13 Konzum Supermarket
14 Buffet "Massimo" Bar
15 Cukarin Sweet Shop
16 Kiwi Ice Cream
17 Korkyra Info
18 Atlas Travel
19 Moreška Outdoor Theater
20 Marco Polo Gift Shop

9:00-13:00 & 17:00-20:00; Oct-mid-June Mon-Sat 8:00-14:00, closed Sun, may be open Sun in shoulder season; tel. 020/715-701, www.korcula.net).

Arrival in Korčula

By Boat: In general, the big Jadrolinija car ferries arrive on the east side of the Old Town peninsula, while the Orebić passenger boat and the fast catamarans dock at the west side of town. (But inclement weather can change the arrival or departure point.) From either side of the peninsula, it's just a two-minute walk to where it meets the mainland and all

of the services described under "Orientation to Korčula," earlier.

A few boats (car ferries from Orebić and Drvenik) use the Dominče dock two peninsulas east of Korčula, about a five-minute drive from town. Regular buses connect this dock with Korčula town. Some boats from Split and Hvar town arrive at Vela Luka, at the far end of Korčula Island. Each boat arriving at Vela Luka is met by a bus waiting to bring arriving travelers to Korčula town (about 1 hour).

By Bus: The bus station is at the southeast corner of Korčula's Shell Bay. If you leave the station with the bay on your right, you'll reach the Old Town. If you leave with the bay on your left, you'll get to hotels Korsal, Liburna, Park, and Marko Polo.

By Car: See "Route Tips for Drivers" at the end of this chapter. Once in Korčula town, there's free parking at the bus station along the marina.

Helpful Hints

Boat Tickets: On arrival, plan for your departure (for your options, see "Korčula Connections," later). Don't dawdle buying your tickets to leave Korčula—they can sell out. The **Jadrolinija** office, selling tickets for the big car ferries, short hops across to the Pelješac Peninsula, and the catamaran that departs from Vela Luka at the far end of the island is located where the Old Town meets the mainland (June-Sept Mon-Fri 8:00-20:00, Sat 8:00-13:30 & 18:00-22:00, Sun 6:00-13:30; Oct-May generally open Mon-Fri 8:00-14:00, Sat 8:00-13:00, closed Sun; tel. 020/715-410, www.jadrolinija.hr). But they don't sell tickets for two of the handy, fast catamarans: the *Krilo* catamaran to Hvar town and Split (buy *Krilo* tickets at the small kiosk on the embankment near Hotel Korčula the night before the boat departs—tickets sold June-Sept 19:00-20:00 only, Oct-May

18:00-19:00 only), and the *Nona Ana* catamaran to Mljet and Dubrovnik (buy *Nona Ana* tickets at the Korkyra Info travel agency, listed next).

Travel Agencies: Korčula has several travel agencies where you can book an excursion, browse shelves of books and souvenirs, and get information about car rental and other activities. **Korkyra Info,** well-run by Vlado, provides all the usual services (car rental, room booking, excursions) and runs a handy shuttle bus to Dubrovnik (May-Sept daily 9:00-22:00, until 20:00 and sometimes closed for mid-afternoon break in shoulder season, just outside the Great Land Gate, mobile 091-571-4355, www.korkyra.info, info@korkyra.info). **Atlas Travel** is well-established but more institutional (long hours daily in summer, closed for mid-afternoon break and sometimes closed Sun in shoulder season, open Mon-Sat mornings and closed Sun in winter; a few steps down from the Great Land Gate at Trg 19 Travnja, tel. 020/711-231).

Sights in Korčula

Korčula's few sights cluster within a few yards of each other in the Old Town. I've listed them roughly in order from the Great Land Gate (the Old Town's main entry) to the tip of the Old Town peninsula. All museums are officially "closed" November through April, but most will usually open by request (ask the TI to call for you...or just try knocking on the door).

▲▲*Moreška* **Dance**—Lazy Korčula snaps to life when locals perform a medieval folk dance called the *Moreška* (moh-REHSH-kah). The plot helps Korčulans remember their hard-fought past: A bad king takes the good king's bride, the dancing forces of good and evil battle, and there's always a happy ending.

Cost and Hours: 100 kn, June-mid-Oct every Thu at 21:00, July-Aug also Mon at 21:00, in outdoor theater next to the Great Land Gate—to the left as you face the gate, or in a nearby congress center if bad weather; buy tickets from travel agency, at your hotel, or at the door.

▲**Great Land Gate (Veliki Revelin)**—A noble staircase leads up to the main entrance to the Old Town. Like all of the town's towers, it's adorned with the Venetian winged lion and the coats of arms of the doge of Venice (left) and the rector of Korčula (right; the offset coat of

arms below was the rector who later renovated the gate). Climb the tower to visit a small exhibit with costumes and photos from the *Moreška* dance, then head up to the top level to enjoy panoramic town views.

Cost and Hours: 15 kn, daily 10:00-16:00, until 19:00 or 21:00 in summer, generally closed Nov-May, English descriptions.

Nearby: On the left inside the gate is the 16th-century **Town Hall and Rector's Palace.** The seal of Korčula (over the center arch) symbolizes the town's importance as the southernmost bastion of the Venetian Republic: St. Mark standing below three defensive towers. The little church on the other side of the square is dedicated to **St. Michael** (Crkva Sv. Mihovila). Throughout Croatia, many towns have churches dedicated to St. Michael just inside the town gates, as he is believed to offer saintly protection from enemies. Notice that a passageway connects the church to the building across the street—home to the Brotherhood of St. Michael, one of Korčula's many religious fraternal organizations (see "Icon Museum," later).

• *Now begin walking up the...*

Street of the Korčulan Statute of 1214 (Ulica Korčulanskog Statuta 1214)—This street is Korčula's backbone, in more ways than one: While most medieval towns slowly evolved with twisty, mazelike lanes, Korčula was carefully planned to resemble a fish skeleton. The streets to the west (left) of this one are straight, to allow the refreshing northwesterly Maestral winds into town. To the east (right), they're curved (notice you can't see the sea) to keep out the bad-vibe southeasterly Jugo winds.

The street's complicated name honors a 1214 statute—the oldest known written law in Central Europe—with regulations about everyday life and instructions on maintaining the city walls, protecting nature, keeping animals, building a house, and so on. As you head up the street, look up to notice some interesting decorations on the houses' upper floors.

• *If you continue up the street, you'll reach St. Mark's Square (Trg Sv. Marka). From here, you're a few steps from the next four sights.*

▲St. Mark's Cathedral (Katedrala Sv. Marka)—Korčula became a bishopric in the 14th century. In the 19th century—36

bishops later—the Habsburgs decided to centralize ecclesiastical power in their empire, and they removed Korčula's bishop. The town still has this beautiful "cathedral"—but no bishop. On the ornately decorated tympanum above the main door, you'll see another Venetian statue of St.

Mark (flanked by Adam and Eve). Inside, above the main altar, is an original Tintoretto painting. At the altar to the left, find the statue of St. Rok (better known by his Italian name, San Rocco) pointing to a wound on his leg. This popular-in-Croatia French saint is believed to help cure disease. As you leave, notice the weapons on the back wall, used in some of the pivotal battles that have taken place near strategically situated Korčula.

Cost and Hours: Free except in Aug, when you'll pay 4 kn; open May-Oct daily 9:00-14:00 & 17:00-19:00, may be open all day long in peak season, closed during church services, generally closed Nov-April but may be open Mon-Fri 9:00-12:00 after Easter.

▲**Church Museum (Opatska Riznica)**—This small museum has an eclectic and fascinating collection. Go on a scavenger hunt for the following items: a ceremonial necklace from Mother Teresa (who came from Macedonia, not far from here—she gave this necklace to a friend from Korčula), some 12th-century hymnals, copies of two tiny drawings by Leonardo da Vinci, a coin collection (including a 2,400-year-old Greek coin minted here in Korčula), some Croatian modern paintings, three amphora jugs, and two framed reliquaries with dozens of miniscule relics.

Cost and Hours: 20 kn, 25-kn guidebook covers both museum and cathedral; May-Oct Mon-Sat 9:00-14:00 & 17:00-19:00, closed Sun except sometimes open in the morning; generally closed Nov-April but may be open Mon-Fri 9:00-12:00 after Easter.

▲**Town Museum (Gradski Muzej)**—Housed in an old mansion, this museum does a fine job of bringing together Korčula's various claims to fame. It's arranged like a traditional Dalmatian home: shop on the ground floor, living quarters in the middle floors, kitchen on top. Notice that some of the walls near the entry have holes in them. Archaeologists are continually doing "digs" into these walls to learn how medieval houses here were built.

On the ground floor is a lapidarium, featuring fragments of Korčula's stone past (see the first-century Roman amphora jugs). Upstairs is a display on Korčula's long-standing shipbuilding industry, including models of two modern steel ships built here (the town still builds ship parts today). There's also a furnished living room and, in the attic, a kitchen. This was a smart place for the kitchen—if it caught fire, it was less likely to destroy the whole building. Notice the little WC in the corner. A network of pipes took kitchen and other waste through town and out to sea.

Cost and Hours: 15 kn, limited posted English information but free smartphone audiotour available for download on their Wi-Fi network; June-Sept Mon-Sat 10:00-21:00, closed Sun; Oct and April-May Mon-Sat 8:00-14:00, closed Sun;

Nov-March Mon-Fri 8:00-14:00, closed Sat-Sun; tel. 020/711-420. If it's locked, try knocking.

Marco Polo's House (Kuća Marka Pola)—Korčula's favorite son is the great 13th-century explorer Marco Polo. Though Polo sailed under the auspices of the Venetian Republic, and technically was a Venetian (since the Republic controlled this region), Korčulans proudly claim him as their own. Marco Polo was the first Westerner to sail to China, bringing back amazing stories and exotic goods (like silk) that Europeans had never seen before. After his trip, Marco Polo fought in an important naval battle against the Genoese near Korčula. He was captured, taken to Genoa, and imprisoned. He told his story to a cellmate, who wrote it down, published it, and made the explorer a world-class and much-in-demand celebrity. To this day, kids in swimming pools around the world try to find him with their eyes closed.

Today, Korčula is the proud home to "Marco Polo's House"—actually a more recent building on the site of what may or may not have been his family's property, with a stubby tower you can climb for an uninspiring view...and nothing else. In the future, the town hopes to turn the complex into a world-class museum about the explorer, with exhibits about Polo himself, Korčula in the 13th century, the big 1298 naval battle during which Polo was taken prisoner, and the Silk Road trading route.

Cost and Hours: 15 kn, daily July-Aug 9:00-21:00, Easter-June and Sept-Oct 10:00-13:00 & 15:00-18:00, closed Nov-Easter, just north of cathedral on—where else?—ulica Depolo.

Nearby: Across the street from the house's entrance, you'll find a clever **Marco Polo gift shop** selling various items relating to the explorer—herbs, brandies, honey, ice cream, and so on. Each one comes with a little tag telling a legend about M.P.—for example, how the word "million" was based on his middle name, Emilio (because no existing word was superlative enough for his discoveries). There's even a life-size Marco Polo and Kublai Khan keeping an eye on the cash register (daily in summer 9:00-24:00, progressively shorter hours and closed for mid-afternoon break off-season, closed in winter, ulica Depolo 1A, mobile 091-189-8048).

▲Icon Museum (Zbirka Ikona)—Korčula is known for its many brotherhoods—centuries-old fraternal organizations that have sprung up around churches. The Brotherhood of All Saints has been meeting every Sunday after Mass since the 14th century, and they run a small but interesting museum of icons. Maja, who lives upstairs, speaks no English but will point out what's worth seeing. These golden religious images were brought back from Greece in the 17th century by Korčulans who had been fighting the Ottomans on a Venetian warship.

Brotherhoods' meeting halls are often connected to their church by a second-story walkway. Use this one to step in to the Venetian-style **All Saints' Church** (Crkva Svih Svetih). Under the loft in the back of the church, notice the models of boats and tools—donated by Korčula's shipbuilders. Look closely at the painting to the right of the altar. See the guys in the white robes kneeling under Jesus? That's the Brotherhood, who commissioned this painting.

Cost and Hours: 15 kn, hours depend on demand—generally May-Oct daily 10:00-14:00 & 17:00-20:00, may be open all day long in peak season, closed Nov-April—but try ringing the bell, on Kaprova ulica at the Old Town's southeast tip.

▲**Old Town Walls**—For several centuries, Korčula held a crucial strategic position as one of the most important southern outposts of the Venetian Republic (the Republic of Dubrovnik started at the Pelješac Peninsula, just across the channel). The original town walls around Korčula date from at least the 13th century, but the fortifications were extended (and new towers built) over several centuries to defend against various foes of Venice—mostly Ottomans and pirates.

The most recent tower dates from the 16th century, when the Ottomans attacked Korčula. The rector and other VIPs fled to the mainland, but a brave priest remained on the island and came up with a plan. All of the women of Korčula dressed up as men, and then everybody in town peeked over the wall—making the Ottomans think they were up against a huge army. The priest prayed for help, and the strong northerly Bora wind blew. Not wanting to take their chances with the many defenders and the weather, the Ottomans sailed away, and Korčula was saved.

By the late 19th century, Korčula was an unimportant Habsburg beach town, and the walls had no strategic value. The town decided to quarry the top half of its old walls to build new homes (and to improve air circulation inside the city). Though today's walls are half as high as they used to be, the town has restored many of the towers, giving Korčula its fortified feel. Each one has a winged lion—a symbol of Venice—and the seal of the rector of Korčula when the tower was built.

Activities in Korčula

Swimming—The water around Korčula is clean and suitable for swimming. You'll find pebbly beaches strewn with holiday-goers all along Put Svetog Nikole, the street that runs west from the Old Town. While this shoreline doesn't have much flat land for sunning yourself, you can generally find a relatively comfy rock to recline on. Another good swimming spot is at the very end of the Old Town peninsula. Or trek to the beaches near Lumbarda (described next).

Lumbarda—For a break from Korčula town, venture about three miles southeast to Lumbarda, a tranquil end-of-the-road village. Lumbarda is known for its wine (the sweet *grk* dessert wine) and for its beaches: the pebbly Bilin Žal, just east of town; and the sandy Vela Pržina, about a 20-minute walk through vineyards to the south. While not worth going out of your way for, Lumbarda and its beaches are fun to explore on a lazy vacation day. From Korčula town, you can get to Lumbarda by water taxi (50 kn) or by bus (hourly Mon-Sat, fewer buses Sun, 15 minutes, 15 kn).

Excursions—Various companies offer day-long excursions to nearby destinations (generally available June-Oct, each itinerary offered 2-4 times per week). The most popular options are Dubrovnik and the national park on Mljet Island. Korkyra Info runs their own tours, with smaller groups, or you can go with the bigger, most established, and more impersonal Atlas (see "Helpful Hints," earlier). Several new, more active tour companies have popped up recently, offering canoe trips, snorkeling, kayaking, and other "adventures"—look for flyers around town.

Other Activities—You'll see travel agencies all over where you can rent a car, bike, scooter, boat, sea kayak, or anything else you want for some vacation fun. Local captains take tourists on cruises to nearby bays and islands to get out on the water, swim, and enjoy a local-style "fish picnic." Inquire at any travel agency, or simply talk to a captain at the

harbor (near the eastern ferry dock, at Shell Bay; figure about 200 kn per hour regardless of number of people). If you're a wine-lover, consider hiring a driver to take you on a tour of Korčula Island, including stops at some wineries (ask at TI or travel agency).

Nightlife in Korčula

This town is much sleepier than some, but you'll still find a fair share of late-night discos in the summertime, including one near the eastern base of the Old Town peninsula, and others along the waterfront between the Old Town and the resort hotels (east of town). Just below the Great Land Gate, Caffe Bar Step often has live music outside.

The best setting for drinks is at **Buffet "Massimo,"** a youthful-feeling cocktail bar in a city-wall tower at the very tip of the Old Town peninsula. You can have a drink on one of three levels:

the downstairs bar, the main-floor lounge, or climb the ladder (at your own risk) to the tower-top terrace (terrace is only for cocktail-sippers—no beer or wine). If you're up top, notice the simple dumbwaiter for hauling up drinks (50-55-kn cocktails, 20-kn beer, daily in summer 18:00-2:00 in the morning, shoulder season 17:00-1:00 in the morning, closed Nov-April, tel. 020/715-073).

Sleeping in Korčula

Korčula has six hotels—five of which are owned by the same company (which is, in turn, government-run). The lack of competition keeps quality low and prices ridiculously high—which makes *sobe* a particularly good alternative.

Sobe

My favorite *sobe* in Korčula offer similar comfort to the hotels at far lower prices—most of them with TVs and air-conditioning, to boot. If you arrive without a room and all of my recommendations are full, you still have several options: Entertain the offers

---

Sleep Code

(5 kn = about $1, €1 = about $1.40, country code: 385, area code: 020)

S = Single, **D** = Double/Twin, **T** = Triple, **Q** = Quad, **b** = bathroom. The modest tourist tax (about 7 kn per person, per night) is not included in these rates. Hotels generally accept credit cards and include breakfast in their rates, while most *sobe* accept only cash and don't offer breakfast. While rates are listed in euros, you'll pay in kunas. Everyone listed here speaks English (or has a relative or neighbor who can help translate).

Rates: If I've listed two sets of rates for an accommodation, prices for peak season (generally July and August) precede those for shoulder season (May-June and Sept-Oct). The few places that remain open through the winter charge even less during those months. The dates for seasonal rates vary by hotel, and prices can change without notice; verify the hotel's current rates online or by email. For other updates, see www.ricksteves.com/update.

Price Ranges: To help you easily sort through these listings, I've divided the accommodations into three categories based on the price for a double room with bath during high season:

$$$ **Higher Priced**—Most rooms €100 or more.
  $$ **Moderately Priced**—Most rooms between €55-100.
    $ **Lower Priced**—Most rooms €55 or less.

that greet you as you step off your boat or bus; walk through an area with lots of *sobe* and *apartman* signs (such as the Put Svetog Nikole waterfront and the streets just above it) and ring some doorbells; or enlist the help of a local travel agency, such as Korkyra Info or Atlas (see "Helpful Hints," earlier). If you book a place sight-unseen, be very clear on the location, and expect locals to underestimate walking times (a place they swear is a "10-minute walk" from town may take you more like 15 or 20 minutes). The options I've listed below are safe bets and worth reserving ahead.

Apartments come equipped with kitchens, and *sobe* often have refrigerators and kettles. For something more substantial, several cafés in town offer breakfast for 30-40 kn; ask your *sobe* host for suggestions.

In the Old Town

Sleeping in the Old Town nestles you squarely in the historic heart of Korčula, in immediate proximity to all of the sights. The likely trade-offs: steep and tight staircases, small rooms in centuries-old houses, and no sea views.

$$ Apartments Lenni is run by Lenni and Periša (Peter) Modrinić, both of whom are outgoing and speak good English.

They rent three tight, modern, comfortable rooms (one with a private bathroom across the hall) and three apartments in a nicely renovated house right in the heart of the Old Town. Since they live off-site, confirm your reservation the day before and let them know your arrival time (Db-€65/€55,

apartment-€90/€70, book direct for these rates, air-con, free Wi-Fi, near Konoba Marko Polo restaurant at Jakova Baničevića 13, tel. 020/721-444, fax 020/711-400, mobile 091-551-6592, www .ikorcula.net/lenni, perisa.modrinic@du.t-com.hr). Peter offers minibus transfers to Dubrovnik with a few fun stops en route (1,100 kn for groups of 1-8 people—team up with other guests to cut costs), and can drive you on a day trip to Mostar (1,500 kn) or on a four-hour tour around the island (750 kn).

$$ Old Town Apartments, well-run by Branko and Ulrike Ristić (who have lived in Germany for many years), has three modern apartments wedged into an old shell right in the heart of town (studio-€75/€65, bigger "comfort" studio-€85/€75, one-bedroom apartment-€95/€85, air-con, free Wi-Fi, Don Iva Matijace 14, tel. 020/711-320, mobile 098-180-2553, www.juristic.de/korcula, branko.r@onlinehome.de).

$ Ivo and Katja Tedeschi, who also run a recommended pizzeria, rent four small, simple rooms and a big, low-ceilinged, top-floor apartment up lots of steep stairs just inside the seawall. The apartment and two of the rooms have sea views and air-conditioning, while two other rooms have neither (Db-€50/€40-45, apartment-€90/€60, Don Iva Matijace, tel. 020/711-354, Ivo's mobile 091-762-7803, tedeschi@hi.t-com.hr).

$ Anka Portolan, with her helpful English-speaking granddaughter Vesna, rents two fine, older-feeling rooms perfectly located near the wall in the Old Town (Db-€35/€30, bigger apartment-€50/€40, 30 percent more for 1- or 2-night stays, cash only, air-con, Don Pavla Poše 7, tel. 020/711-711, ankaportolan.apartmani @gmail.com).

West of the Old Town

The pleasant residential neighborhood west of the Old Town, along the waterfront drag called Put Svetog Nikole, comes with an easy, level walk into town and gorgeous views of the Old Town peninsula. The main advantages to sleeping here are a bit more space and (in many cases) sea views. I've listed these in the order you'll reach them as you walk along the water—from one minute (the first listing) to 10 minutes (last listing) away from the Old Town.

$$ Royal Apartments are run by Zvonko and Marija Jelavić, who have lived in Toronto and have built some of the most hotelesque (and most expensive) rooms in town—using comfortingly familiar North American fixtures imported from Home Depot. Their five classy apartments feel more like a small hotel with no real reception desk (small apartment-€80, big apartment-€95, same prices all season, closed mid-Oct-mid-April, no extra charge for 1- or 2-night stays, air-con, free Wi-Fi, well-marked with green awning just west of Old Town at Trg Petra Šegedina 4, mobile 098-184-0444, royalapt@ica.net, Jelavić family).

$ Rezi and Andro Depolo, probably distant relatives of Marco, rent four comfy, good-value rooms on the bay west of the Old Town. Three of the rooms offer beautiful views to the Old Town, and the five-minute stroll into town is pleasant and scenic. Friendly, English-speaking Rezi works to make her guests feel welcome (Db-€40/€35, room with kitchen-€5 more, about €3 cheaper without sea view, 30 percent more for 1-night stays, continental breakfast-25 kn, big breakfast-35 kn, air-con, free Wi-Fi; walk along waterfront from Old Town with bay on your right to the yellow house at Put Svetog Nikole 28—it's set back from the street, just before the two monasteries; tel. 020/711-621, mobile 098-964-3687, rezi.depolo@gmail.com).

$ Apartments Medmar, run by colorful Mađa Marović, has three well-appointed, well-stocked apartments and two rooms in a modern yellow house with great sea views at the tip of land just beyond the monastery. Ursa-Međa (as in "Ursa Major") speaks limited English, but her son Pero translates reservation emails (Db-€45 year-round but discounted for longer stays off-season, apartment-€80/€50, air-con, Put Svetog Nikole 38—just as the road bends left, above the family's natural-products shop, tel. 020/711-640, mobile 098-244-974, marovicp@yahoo.com).

$ Kiwi Rooms, run by gregarious English-speaking Nado Andrijić and his artist wife Marica, has two bright, modern, nicely decorated rooms with gorgeous seaview balconies. While there's no air-conditioning, they often get a good breeze and there's only a bit of road noise (Db-€50/€40, 25 percent more for 1-night stays, Put Svetog Nikole 42, tel. 020/711-608, mobile 091-543-8265).

Hotels

$$$ Hotel Korsal is Korčula's best hotel option—and the only one in town not owned by the sinking ship called HTP Korčula (see next listing). The Korsal's 10 rooms fill two buildings just above the promenade connecting the Old Town to the resort area, less than a 10-minute walk from downtown. While the standard rooms are smallish, all rooms come with sea views and stylish, colorful decor (standard Db-€156/€136, bigger "comfort" Db-€196/€176, family room for up to four-€296/€260, 20 percent more for 1-night stays, includes breakfast, free Wi-Fi, air-con, closed Nov-April, Šetalište Frana Kršinića 80, tel. 020/715-722, mobile 091-533-8302, www.hotel-korsal.com, info@hotel-korsal.com). Their restaurant has a good menu that mixes traditional Dalmatian cooking with international dishes; you can sit inside, or out on the seaview terrace—ask about the proposal-perfect tables (60-95-kn pastas and starters, 80-170-kn main dishes, daily 12:00-24:00).

HTP Korčula Hotels

This company owns Korčula's five big hotels, all in need of renovation. But if you don't want to stay in a *soba,* and the Korsal is full, these are the only game in town. You can reserve rooms at any of them through the main office (tel. 020/726-336, fax 020/711-746, www.korcula-hotels.com, marketing@htp-korcula.hr). I've listed peak-season prices with breakfast only; rates are progressively lower the farther you get into off-season. You can pay €10 more per person for half-board (dinner at the hotel). It's much cheaper to stay a week or longer. There's a long-term plan to renovate all of these hotels, but so far the Marko Polo is the only one that's seen any progress (and the only one that has air-conditioning).

$$$ Hotel Korčula has by far the best location, right on the waterfront alongside the Old Town. It has a fine seaside terrace restaurant and friendly staff, even if the 20 rooms are outmoded and waaay overpriced. The rooms are on two floors: The more expensive "first-floor" rooms (actually on the third floor) have big windows and sea views; the cheaper "second-floor" rooms (actually on the fourth floor) have tiny windows and no views (Sb-€105-120/€85, Db-€140-160/€120, less off-season, reception tel. 020/711-078).

$$$ Hotel Marko Polo, the only one of the chain that has been renovated, has 94 rooms, air-conditioning, an elevator, and a big pool. All of this makes it the town's only real "splurge"... and it's priced accordingly (Db-€120-165/€85-132 depending on size and amenities, cheaper off-season, pay Wi-Fi, reception tel. 020/726-100).

$$$ Other Hotels: Three more HTP hotels cluster a 15-minute walk away, around the far side of Shell Bay. All are rough around the edges, overpriced, and relatively inconvenient to the Old Town, but they share a nice beach. **Hotel Liburna,** with a clever split-level design that reflects the skyline of the Old Town, has 109 rooms, most of them accessible by elevator; half the rooms face the sea and cost an additional 10 percent (Db-€130/€100-110, pay Wi-Fi, reception tel. 020/726-006). Dreary **Hotel Park** has 153 cheaper rooms (some the same price as Liburna, others cheaper, reception tel. 020/726-100). The fifth hotel, **Hotel Bon Repos**—another 15 minutes by foot from the Old Town—is, in every sense, the last resort.

Eating in Korčula

Korčula lacks the culinary scene of bigger destinations; things are pretty static here, and the place is awash in interchangeable *konobas*—simple restaurants serving pastas and seafood dishes. These are all decent options, but everything in town is pretty similar—make your decision based on atmosphere and what looks best to you. Note that almost all of these eateries close from mid-October to Easter.

Pizzeria Amfora, on a side lane off the people-parade up Korčula's main drag in the Old Town, features delicious and well-priced pastas and pizzas—nothing fancy, just good ol' comfort food. Squeeze into the small dining room or enjoy the sidewalk tables (50-70-kn pizzas and pastas, 60-100-kn main courses, daily 11:00-24:00, closed 15:00-18:00 and Sun dinner for a few weeks at start and end of season, closed mid-Oct-mid-April, ulica od Teatra 4, tel. 020/711-739).

Adio Mare, with fine seafood, may have the best decor in town: a cavernous stone dining room with long shared tables and a thick vine scaling one wall. Or climb the stairs and cross the little bridge to the delightful rooftop garden terrace (60-70-kn pastas,

50-120-kn main courses, descriptive menu, Mon-Sat 12:00-24:00, Sun 17:30-24:00, on the main drag just past Marco Polo's House, tel. 020/711-253).

Konoba Marinero has pleasantly nautical decor, outdoor tables on an atmospherically tight lane, and a simple menu of Dalmatian specialties (70-120-kn main courses, Easter-mid-Oct daily 17:00-24:00, Marka Andrijića 13, tel. 020/711-170).

Along the Seawall: Various restaurants line up scenically along the Old Town's seawall, providing al fresco dining with salty views. Their tables, spilling out along the seafront, are ideal for romantic harborside meals. On the eastern side of the peninsula, several interchangeable places serve uninspired, overpriced crank-'em-out food with jaded service; for something more affordable, try **Pizzeria Tedeschi,** which serves up good pizzas closer to the base of the peninsula (40-50-kn pizzas and pastas, daily 9:00-24:00, closed mid-Oct-April, tel. 020/711-586). On the western side, near the tip and perfectly situated for viewing the sunset, **Komin** offers traditional Dalmatian meals cooked on a grill inside (45-70-kn pastas, 65-150-kn main dishes, daily 9:00-24:00, Šetalište Petra Kanavelica 26, mobile 098-847-057).

Around Shell Bay: Prices inside the Old Town are generally the highest in Korčula. But several cheaper eateries lie just outside the Old Town. Window-shop menus along the harbor, then hang a left at the bus station and continue up the road toward the big resort hotels. You'll find plenty of cafés, pizzerias, and *konoba*s (traditional restaurants), most with outdoor seating. For something a bit more upscale, consider the restaurant at **Hotel Korsal,** which strives to bring a bit more class to Korčula's cuisine scene (see "Sleeping in Korčula," earlier).

Picnics: Just outside the main gate, you'll find a lively produce market and a big, modern, air-conditioned **Konzum** supermarket (Mon-Sat 7:00-20:00, Sun 8:00-13:00). A short stroll from there down Put Svetog Nikole takes you to rocky seafront perches with the best Korčula views. Otherwise, there are many inviting picnic spots along the Old Town embankment.

Sweet Shop: For good (if pricey) local sweets, stop by **Cukarin,** which sells tasty traditional cookies such as the delicious flourless (and gluten-free) *amareta* almond cake; the Marko Polo cake (flourless chocolate cake with buttercream); and the walnut-cream-filled *klašun*. They also sell homemade wine, liqueur, honey, and jam (Mon-Sat 8:30-12:00 & 17:30-20:00, closed Sun and Jan-Feb, a block behind the Jadrolinija office on Hrvatske Bratske Zajednice, tel. 020/711-055).

Ice Cream: My favorite *sladoled* in Korčula is at **Kiwi** (just up the lane across from Konzum supermarket, open long hours daily).

Korčula Connections

For general tips on getting around the Dalmatian Coast, see page 824. Korčula is reasonably well-connected to the rest of the Dalmatian Coast by boat, but service becomes sparse in the off-season. If you're here during a lull in the sailing schedule, buses are your ticket out of town (making the short crossing to the Pelješac Peninsula on the Dominče-Orebić ferry). No matter when you travel, it's smart to carefully study current boat schedules, as they are always subject to change.

By Boat

Boats big and small depart from the embankment surrounding Korčula's Old Town peninsula. Which side of the peninsula a boat uses can depend on the weather—be flexible and inquire locally about where to meet your boat. Some boats leave from other parts of the island, most notably the town of Vela Luka (at the opposite tip of the island, a 1-hour bus ride from Korčula town—described later). Other boats, including the car ferries to Orebić and Drvenik (described later, under "Route Tips for Drivers"), leave from the Dominče dock, about a five-minute drive east of Korčula town. If I've listed two prices for a journey, the specific fare depends on the season.

Big Jadrolinija Car Ferries: Running twice weekly in summer (June-Sept only), these huge, handy vessels go north from Korčula town to **Stari Grad** on Hvar Island (20-minute bus ride from Hvar town; 3.75 hours, 90-110 kn; the catamaran described next is faster and takes you right to Hvar town) and **Split** (6 hours, 90-110 kn—catamaran described next is faster and cheaper); or south, to **Sobra** on Mljet Island (1.25-hour bus ride from the national park, 2.25 hours, 75-90 kn) and **Dubrovnik** (4.5 hours, 90-110 kn). These ferries do not run off-season (Oct-May).

Speedy *Krilo* Catamaran from Korčula Town to Hvar Town and Split: The speedy *Krilo* catamaran leaves Korčula town at 6:00 in the morning every day year-round (except Sun in Oct-May, when it departs at 13:00 instead), and zips to Hvar town and Split (to Hvar: 1.5 hours, 40-50 kn; to Split: 2.5-2.75 hours, 60-65 kn; in summer, it also stops en route at Prigradica on Korčula Island). In Korčula, tickets for the *Krilo* are sold at a small waterfront kiosk near Hotel Korčula—not at the Jadrolinija office. While you can, in theory, buy *Krilo* tickets starting a half-hour before the boat departs (at 5:30), they often sell out—so it's essential to buy them the night before (they're sold at the kiosk only during a one-hour time period, which is posted at the kiosk—generally June-Sept 19:00-20:00, Oct-May 18:00-19:00, mobile 099-194-6903). Since it returns from Split and Hvar the same afternoon, this extremely

KORČULA

handy catamaran allows you to effortlessly day-trip to either place (see "Split Connections" on page 942). For the latest schedule, see www.krilo.hr.

Speedy *Nona Ana* Catamaran to Mljet and Dubrovnik: In July and August, this convenient boat zips travelers from Korčula to Polače (on Mljet Island, handy to the national park there), then to Sobra (a less-appealing spot on Mljet) and on to Dubrovnik (4/week, generally departs Korčula at 16:00; to Polače: 1 hour, 39 kn; to Sobra: 1.25 hours, 45 kn; to Dubrovnik: 2.75 hours, 58 kn). Unfortunately, the boat doesn't serve Korčula at other times (Sept-June). Confirm schedules at www.gv-line.hr, and buy tickets at the Korkyra Info travel agency (see "Helpful Hints," earlier).

From Vela Luka to Hvar Town and Split: Additional boats connect to points north, but they depart from the port at Vela Luka, an hour away from Korčula town, at the other end of the island. A Jadrolinija **fast catamaran** goes daily from Vela Luka to both Hvar town and Split; unfortunately, on most days it leaves extremely early, with no bus connection from Korčula to get you there in time—if you're desperate, you could pay about 400 kn for an early-morning taxi, or sleep overnight in Vela Luka (Mon-Sat departs at 5:30, Sun at 8:00; to Hvar: 45 minutes, 27-32 kn; to Split: 2 hours, 40-50 kn). A **car ferry** also travels daily from Vela Luka to Split—it's slower, but generally departs at a more convenient time that's coordinated with a bus from Korčula (1-2/day, 3 hours, 50-60 kn, no stop at Hvar town). Since reaching Vela Luka from Korčula town is a hassle, carefully confirm these boat schedules at the Korčula TI or Jadrolinija office, and understand all your options before you get up early to make the trip.

Bus Connections

All buses from Korčula town (except those to Vela Luka) first drive to Dominče, where they meet the car ferry to cross over to Orebić, on the Pelješac Peninsula. Don't be surprised if you have to get off the bus, walk onto the ferry, and meet a different bus across the channel. It takes just over an hour to drive the length of the Pelješac Peninsula and meet the main coastal road.

From Korčula Town by Bus to: Dubrovnik (peak season: 2/day, 3.5 hours, likely departs at 6:45 and 15:45; off-season: 1/day, Mon-Sat generally at 6:45, Sun at 14:45; trip costs 90 kn), **Zagreb** (1/day, 9-13.5 hours depending on route), **Split** (1/day, 5 hours, inconveniently timed—departs Korčula at 19:45 and arrives in Split after midnight, same bus goes to Zagreb), **Vela Luka** (at far end of island, Mon-Fri 7/day, Sat 6/day, Sun 4/day, 1 hour).

Shuttle Bus to Dubrovnik: Korkyra Info Travel Agency runs a handy minibus that costs only slightly more than the bus and takes you right to your accommodations in Dubrovnik (150 kn one-way, runs daily March-Oct generally at 9:00, Nov-Feb by request only, 2 hours, includes croissant and juice and room-finding help through their Dubrovnik agency if needed, reserve ahead, mobile 091-571-4355, www.korkyra.info, info@korkyra.info).

Route Tips for Drivers: Between Korčula and the Mainland

The island of Korčula is connected to the mainland by a small car ferry that runs between Dominče—about a mile east of Korčula town—and Orebić, across the channel on the Pelješac Peninsula (76 kn/car, 16 kn/passenger, 15-minute crossing, departs Dominče at the top of most but not all hours—check carefully in Korčula, departs Orebić at :30 past most hours).

If you're driving via the mainland, you'll first cross on this car ferry to Orebić on the vineyard-strewn Pelješac Peninsula. The Pelješac Peninsula is extremely long and narrow, and the roads are very rough, so it can take longer than you'd expect to reach the main coastal road (figure 1-1.5 hours from Orebić). Where the peninsula meets the mainland, you'll see the cute little "Great Wall of Croatia" town of Ston.

If you're heading south to **Dubrovnik,** the coastal road zips you right there (about an hour from Ston). If you're heading north to **Split,** soon after joining the coastal road you'll actually pass through Bosnia-Herzegovina for a few miles (around the town of Neum; for details, see page 948).

Because of the ferry crossing and the long drive along the Pelješac Peninsula, driving **between Split and Korčula** is time-consuming and tiring. Instead, I prefer to take the longer car ferry the whole way between Split and Vela Luka, at the far end of Korčula Island (described earlier; allow 1 hour for the drive from Korčula town to Vela Luka, costs about 300 kn per car for ferry ride). The scenic and relaxing 2.75-hour boat ride from Vela Luka to Split saves you more than that much driving time.

If you're headed north, note that there's also a car ferry from Dominče north, to **Drvenik** on the mainland (about halfway to Split).

ROVINJ and ISTRIA

Pula • Motovun

Rising dramatically from the Adriatic as though being pulled up to heaven by its grand bell tower, Rovinj (roh-VEEN; in Italian: Rovigno/roh-VEEN-yoh) is a welcoming Old World oasis in a sea of tourist kitsch. Among the villages of Croatia's coast, there's something particularly romantic about Rovinj—the most Italian town in Croatia's most Italian region. Rovinj's streets are delightfully twisty, its ancient houses are characteristically crumbling, and its harbor—lively with real-life fishermen—is as salty as they come. Like a little Venice on a hill, Rovinj is the stage set for your Croatian seaside dreams.

Rovinj was prosperous and well-fortified in the Middle Ages. It boomed in the 16th and 17th centuries, when it was flooded with refugees fleeing both the Ottoman invasions and the plague. Because the town was part of the Republic of Venice for five centuries (13th to 18th centuries), its architecture, culture, and even language are strongly Venetian. The local folk groups sing in a dialect actually  considered more Venetian than what the Venetians themselves speak these days. (You can even see Venice from Rovinj's church bell tower on a very clear day.)

After Napoleon seized the region, then was defeated, Rovinj became part of Austria. The Venetians had neglected the town, but the Austrians invested in it, bringing the railroad, gas lights, and a huge Ronhill tobacco factory. (This factory—recently replaced by an enormous, state-of-the-art facility you'll pass on the highway farther inland—is one of the town's most elegant structures, and is slated for extensive renovation in the coming years.) The Habsburgs tapped Pula and Trieste to be the empire's major ports—cursing those cities with pollution and sprawl, while allowing Rovinj to linger in its trapped-in-the-past quaintness.

Before long, Austrians discovered Rovinj as a handy escape for a beach holiday. Tourism arrived in the late 1890s, when a powerful Austrian baron bought one of the remote, barren islands offshore and brought it back to life with gardens and a grand villa. Before long, another baron bought another island...and a tourist boom was underway. In more recent times, Rovinj has become a top destination for nudists. The resort of Valalta, just to the north, is a popular spot for those seeking "southern exposure"... as a very revealing brochure at the TI illustrates (www.valalta.hr). Whether you want to find PNBs (pudgy nude bodies), or avoid them, remember that the German phrase *FKK* (*Freikörper Kultur*, or "free body culture") is international shorthand for nudism.

Rovinj is the star attraction of Croatia's wedge-shaped Istrian Peninsula. With more time in Istria (EE-stree-ah; "Istra" in Croatian), visit the striking Roman ruins in urban Pula and the laid-back hill town of Motovun (both described later in this chapter; for more on Istria, see page 996).

Rovinj is the most atmospheric of all of Croatia's small coastal towns. Maybe that's because it's always been a real town, where poor people lived. You'll find no fancy old palaces here—just narrow streets lined with skinny houses that have given shelter to humble families for generations. While it's becoming known on the tourist circuit, Rovinj retains the soul of a fishermen's village; notice that the harbor is still filled not with glitzy yachts, but with a busy fishing fleet.

Planning Your Time

While you can reach Rovinj by bus (see "Rovinj Connections," later), it's most worthwhile by car (which allows you to easily visit nearby destinations, such as Pula and Motovun). For drivers, Rovinj fits neatly between Slovenia and Croatia (for example, on a Ljubljana-Lake Bled-Julian Alps-Rovinj-Plitvice-Split itinerary).

Rovinj is hardly packed with diversions. You can get the gist of the town in a one-hour wander. The rest of your time is for enjoying the ambience or pedaling a rental bike to a nearby beach.

With a second day, side-trip to Pula and Motovun; to fill a lazy afternoon on a single day, choose just one of these attractions. Be aware that much of Rovinj closes down from mid-October through Easter.

Orientation to Rovinj

(area code: 052)
Rovinj, once an island, is now a peninsula. The Old Town is divided in two parts: a particularly charismatic chunk on the oval-shaped peninsula, and the rest on the mainland (with similarly time-worn buildings, but without the commercial cuteness that comes with lots of tourist money). Where the mainland meets the peninsula is a broad, bustling public space called Tito Square (Trg Maršala Tita). The Old Town peninsula—traffic-free except for the occasional moped—is topped by the massive bell tower of the Church of St. Euphemia. At the very tip of the peninsula is a small park.

Tourist Information
Rovinj's TI, facing the harbor, has several handy, free materials, including a town map and an info booklet (June-Sept daily 7:00-22:00; Oct and May daily 8:00-21:00; Nov-April Mon-Fri 8:00-15:00, Sat 8:00-13:00, closed Sun; along the embankment at Obala Pina Budičina 12, tel. 052/811-566, www.tzgrovinj.hr). In summer, the TI may offer a free Old Town walking tour (possibly Tue at 10:00) and a free bike tour (possibly Tue at 16:00); ask for details and reserve a spot at the TI.

Arrival in Rovinj
By Car: Only local cars are allowed to enter the Old Town area. To get as close as possible—whether you're staying in the Old Town, or just visiting for the day—use the big waterfront parking lots just north of the Old Town Peninsula: Approaching Rovinj, follow *Centar* signs, eventually taking you through the little round-about and directly into the parking lot (July-Aug: 6.5 kn/hour, April-June and Sept: 5 kn/hour, Oct-March: 1-2 kn/hour). There are two big parking lots, side-by-side, called "Valdibora 1" (a.k.a. "Big Valdibora," farther from the Old Town), and "Valdibora 2" (a.k.a. "Little Valdibora," closer to the Old Town). The slightly closer Valdibora 2 is sometimes reserved for residents, in which case you won't be able to take a ticket to enter.

While these Valdibora lots are the most convenient—and come with the classic Rovinj view—the cost adds up fast if you're parking overnight. If it's full, you'll be pushed to another pay lot farther out, along the bay northwest of the Old Town (a scenic

15-minute walk from town; summer: 5-6 kn/hour, free 23:00-6:00; winter: 2 kn/hour, free 20:00-6:00 and on Sun). If you're sleeping at a hotel away from the Old Town, carefully track individual blue hotel signs as you approach town.

By Bus: The bus station is on the south side of the Old Town, close to the harbor. Leave the station to the left, then walk on busy Carera street directly into the center of town. Note that there are plans to move the bus station to the other side of the Old Town, just above the long waterfront parking lots. If your bus stops here instead, simply head down to the main road and walk along the parking lots into town.

By Boat: The few boats connecting Rovinj to Venice, Piran, Trieste, and other Istrian towns dock at the long pier protruding from the Old Town peninsula. Just walk up the pier, and you're in the heart of town.

Helpful Hints

Internet Access: A-Mar Internet Club has several terminals and long hours (40 kn/hour, Mon-Fri 8:00-22:00, Sat-Sun 9:00-23:00, less off-season, on the main drag in the mainland part of the Old Town, Carera 26, tel. 052/841-211).

Laundry: The full-service **Galax** launderette hides up the street beyond the bus station. You can usually pick up your laundry after 24 hours, though same-day service might be possible if you drop it off early enough in the morning (70 kn/load wash and dry; Easter-Sept daily 6:00-20:00, until later in summer; Oct-Easter Mon-Fri 7:00-19:00, Sat 9:00-15:00, closed Sun; up Benussia street past the bus station, on the left after the post office, tel. 052/816-130).

Local Guides: Vukica Palčić is a very capable guide who knows her town intimately and loves to share it with visitors (€50 for a 2-hour tour, mobile 098-794-003, vukica.palcic@pu.t-com.hr). **Renato Orbanić** is a laid-back musician (sax) who also enjoys wandering through town with visitors. While light on heavy-hitting facts, his casual tour somehow suits this easy-going little town (€60 for a 2-hour tour, mobile 091-521-6206, rorbanic@inet.hr).

Best Views: The town is full of breathtaking views. Photography buffs will be busy in the "magic hours" of early morning and evening, and even by moonlight. The postcard view of Rovinj is from the parking lot embankment at the north end of the Old Town (at the start of the "Self-Guided Walk," next). For a different perspective on the Old Town, head for the far side of the harbor on the opposite (south) end of town. The church bell tower provides a virtual aerial view of the town and a grand vista of the outlying islands.

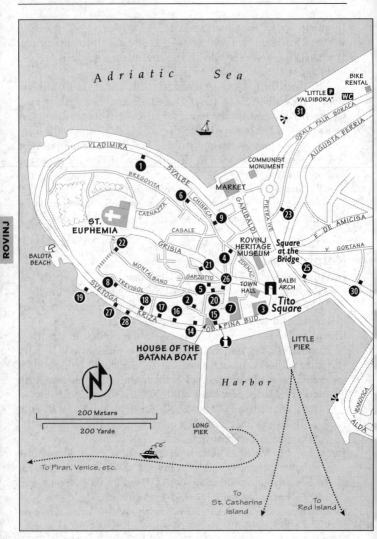

Self-Guided Walk

▲▲▲Rovinj Ramble

This orientation walk introduces you to Rovinj in about an hour. Begin at the parking lot just north of the Old Town.

Old Town View

Many places offer fine views of Rovinj's Old Town, but this is the most striking. Boats bob in the harbor, and behind them Venetian-looking homes seem to rise from the deep. (For an aerial per-

Rovinj

1. Hotel Villa Angelo d'Oro
2. Villa Markiz
3. Hotel Adriatic
4. Villa Cissa
5. Casa Garzotto (Reception & Apts.)
6. Casa Garzotto (Rooms)
7. Porta Antica Apartments
8. Trevisol Apartments
9. Miranda Fabris Rooms
10. To Hotels Vila Kristina, Vila Lili, Villa Baron Gautsch, Monte Mulini, Lone & Eden
11. To Hotel Park, Elda Markulin Apts., Apartmani Tomo & Restaurant Maestral
12. Futura Travel Agency
13. Natale Travel Agency
14. Planet Travel Agency
15. Scuba Restaurant
16. Veli Jože Restaurant
17. Santa Croce Restaurant
18. Lampo Restaurant
19. La Puntuleina Restaurant
20. Barba Zuane Restaurant
21. Krčma Ulika Restaurant
22. Monte Restaurant
23. Gostionica/Trattoria Toni
24. Sidro Restaurant
25. Bacchus Wine Bar
26. Piassa Granda Wine Bar
27. Valentino Champagne & Cocktail Bar
28. Monte Carlo Bar
29. Launderette
30. Internet Café
31. Start of Self-Guided Walk

ROVINJ

spective, notice the big billboard overhead and to the left.)

The Old Town is topped by the church, whose bell tower is capped by a weathervane in the shape of Rovinj's patron saint, Euphemia. Local fishermen look to this saintly weathervane for direction: When Euphemia is looking out to sea, it means the stiff, fresh Bora wind is blowing, bringing dry air from the interior...a sailor's delight. But if she's facing the land, the humid Jugo wind will soon bring bad weather from the sea. After a day or so, even a tourist learns to look to St. Euphemia for the weather report.

As you soak in this scene, ponder how the town's history created its current shape. In the Middle Ages, Rovinj was an island, rather than a peninsula, and it was surrounded by a double wall—a protective inner wall and an outer seawall. Because it was so well-defended against pirates and other marauders (and carefully quarantined from the plague), it was extremely desirable real estate. And yet, it was easy to reach from the mainland, allowing it to thrive as a trading town. With more than 10,000 residents at its peak, Rovinj became immensely crowded, explaining today's pleasantly claustrophobic Old Town.

Over the centuries—as demand for living space trumped security concerns—the town walls were converted into houses, with windows grafted on to their imposing frame. Gaps in the wall, with steps that seem to end at the water, are where fishermen would pull in to unload their catch directly into the warehouses on the bottom level of the houses. (Later you can explore some of these lanes from inside the town.) Today, if you live in one of these houses, the Adriatic is your backyard.

• *Now head into town. In the little park near the sea, just beyond the end of the parking lot, look for the big, blocky...*

Communist-Era Monument

Dating from the time of Tito, this celebrates the Partisan Army's victory over the Nazis in World War II and commemorates the victims of fascism. The minimalist reliefs on the ceremonial tomb show a slow prisoners' parade of victims prodded by a gun in the back from a figure with a Nazi-style helmet. Notice that one side of the monument is in Croatian, and the other is in Italian. With typical Yugoslav grace and subtlety, this jarring block shatters the otherwise harmonious time-warp vibe of Rovinj.

Fortunately, it's the only modern structure anywhere near the Old Town.

• *Now walk a few more steps toward town, stopping to explore the covered...*

Market

The front part of the market, near the water, is for souvenirs. But natives delve deeper in, to the local produce stands. Separating the gifty stuff from the nitty-gritty produce is a line of merchants aggressively pushing free samples. Everything is local and mostly homemade. Consider this snack-time tactic: Loiter around, joking with the farmers while sampling their various tasty walnuts, figs, cherries, grapes, olive oils, honey, *rakija* (the powerful schnapps popular throughout the Balkans), and more. If the sample is good, buy some more for a picnic. In the center of the market, a delightful and practical fountain from 1908 reminds locals of the infrastructure brought in by their Habsburg rulers a century ago. The hall labeled *Ribarnica/Pescheria* at the back of the market is where you'll find fresh, practically wriggling fish. This is where locals gather ingredients for their favorite dish, *brodet*—a stew of various kinds of seafood mixed with olive oil and wine...all of Istria's best bits rolled into one dish. It's slowly simmered and generally served with polenta (unfortunately, it's rare in restaurants).

• *Continue up the broad street, named for* **Giuseppe Garibaldi**—*one of the major players in late-19th-century Italian unification. Imagine: Even though you're in Croatia, Italian patriots are celebrated in this very Italian-feeling town (see the "Italo-Croatia" sidebar). After one long block, on your left, you'll come to the wide cross-street called...*

Square at the Bridge (Trg na Mostu)

This marks the site of the medieval bridge that once connected the fortified island of Rovinj to the mainland (as illustrated in the small painting above the door of the Kavana al Ponto—"Bridge Café"). Back then, the island was populated mostly by Italians, while the mainland was the territory of Slavic farmers. But as Rovinj's strategic importance waned, and its trading status rose, the need for easy access became more important than the canal's protective purpose—so in 1763, it was filled in. The two populations integrated, creating the bicultural mix that survives today.

Notice the breeze? Via Garibaldi is nicknamed Val di Bora ("Valley of the Bora Wind") for the constant cooling wind that blows here. On the island side of Trg na Mostu is the Rovinj Heritage Museum (described later, under "Sights in Rovinj"). Next door, the town's cultural center posts lovingly hand-lettered signs in Croatian and Italian announcing upcoming musical events (generally free, designed for locals, and worth noting and enjoying).

Nearby (just past Kavana al Ponto, on the left), the Viecia Batana Café—named for Rovinj's unique, flat-bottomed little fishing boats—has a retro interior with a circa-1960 fishermen mural that evokes an earlier age. The café is popular for its chocolate cake and "Batana" ice cream.

• *Now proceed to the little fountain in the middle of the square (near Hotel Adriatic).*

ROVINJ

Italo-Croatia

Apart from its tangible attractions, one of Istria's hallmarks is its biculturalism: It's an engaging hybrid of Croatia and Italy.

Like most of the Croatian Coast, Istria has variously been controlled by Illyrians, Romans, Byzantines, Slavs, Venetians, and Austrians. After the Habsburgs lost World War I, most of today's Croatia joined Yugoslavia—but Istria became part of Italy. During this time, the Croatian vernacular was suppressed, while the Italian language and culture flourished. But this extra chapter of Italian rule  was short-lived. After World War II, Istria joined Yugoslavia, and Croatian culture and language returned. What followed was a so-called "Italian exodus," during which many Istrian Italians chose to relocate to Italy—leaving behind hill towns, valley villages, and farm estates that are abandoned even to this day.

The Istrians who stayed behind were saddled with an identity crisis. Many people here found it difficult to abandon their ties to Italy, and continued to speak the language and embrace the culture. Today, depending on who you ask, Istria is the most Italian part of Croatia...or the most Croatian part of Italy. Istria pops up on Italian weather reports. A few years ago, Italy's then-Prime Minister Silvio Berlusconi declared that he still considered Istria part of Italy—and he wanted it back. When I wrote an article about Istria for a newspaper, some Italian readers complained that I made it sound "too Croatian," while some Croatians claimed my depiction was "too Italian."

People who actually live here typically don't worry about the distinction. Locals insist that they're not Croatians and not Italians—they're Istrians. They don't mind straddling two cultures. Both languages are official (and often taught side-by-side in schools), street signs are bilingual, and most Istrians dabble in each tongue—often seeming to foreign ears as though they're mixing the two at once.

As a result of their tangled history, Istrians have learned how to be mellow and take things as they come. They're gregarious, open-minded, and sometimes seem to thrive on chaos. A twentysomething local told me, "My ancestors lived in Venice. My great-grandfather lived in Austria. My grandfather lived in Italy. My father lived in Yugoslavia. I live in Croatia. My son will live in the European Union. And we've all lived in the same town."

ROVINJ

Tito Square (Trg Maršala Tita)

This wide-open square at the entrance to the Old Town is the crossroads of Rovinj. The **fountain,** with a little boy holding a water-spouting fish, celebrates the government-funded water system that finally brought running water to the Old Town in 1959. Walk around the fountain, with your eyes on the relief, to see a successful socialist society at the inauguration of this new water system. Despite the happy occasion, the figures are pretty stiff—conformity trumped most other virtues in Tito's world.

Now walk out to the end of the concrete pier, called the **Mali Molo ("Little Pier").** From here, you're surrounded by Rovinj's

crowded harbor, with fishing vessels and excursion boats that shuttle tourists out to the offshore islands. If the weather's good, a **boat trip** can be a memorable way to get out on the water for a different angle on Rovinj (see "Activities in Rovinj," later, for details).

ROVINJ

Scan the **harbor.** On the left is the MMC, the local meeting and concert hall (described later, under "Nightlife in Rovinj"). Above and behind the MMC, the highest bell tower inland marks the Franciscan monastery, which was the only building on the mainland before the island town was connected to shore. Along the waterfront to the right of the MMC is Hotel Park, a typical monstrosity from the communist era, now tastefully renovated inside. A recommended bike path starts just past this hotel, leading into a nature preserve and the best nearby beaches (which you can see in the distance; for more on bike rental, see "Activities in Rovinj," later).

Now head back to the base of the pier. If you were to walk down the **embankment** between the harbor and the Old Town

(past Hotel Adriatic), you'd find the TI, the recommended House of the Batana Boat museum, and a delightful "restaurant row" with several tempting places for a drink or a meal. Many fishermen pull their boats into this harbor, then simply carry their catch across the street to a waiting restaurateur. (This self-guided walk finishes with a stroll down this lane.)

Backtrack 10 paces past the fountain and face the Old Town entrance gate, called the **Balbi Arch.**

The winged lion on top is a reminder that this was Venetian territory for centuries.

• *Head through the gate into the Old Town. Inside and on the left is the red...*

Town Hall

On the old Town Hall, notice another Venetian lion, as well as other historic crests embedded in the wall. The Town Hall actually sports an Italian flag (along with ones for Croatia and Rovinj) and faces a square named for Giacomo Matteotti, a much-revered Italian patriot.

Continue a few more steps into town. Gostionica/Trattoria Cisterna faces another little square, which once functioned as a cistern (collecting rainwater, which was pulled from a subterranean reservoir through the well you see today). The building on your left (which often has a *batana* boat out front) is the Italian Union—yet another reminder of how Istria has an important bond with Italy.

• *Now begin walking up the street to the left of Gostionica/Trattoria Cisterna.*

Grisia Street

The main "street" (actually a tight lane) leading through the middle of the island is choked with tourists during the midday rush and lined with art galleries. This inspiring

town has attracted many artists, some of whom display their works along this colorful stretch. Notice the rusty little nails speckling the walls—each year in August, an art festival invites locals to hang their best art on this street. With paintings lining the lane, the entire community comes out to enjoy each other's creations.

As you walk, keep your camera cocked and ready, as you can find delightful scenes down every side lane. Remember that, as crowded as it is today, little Rovinj was even more packed in the Middle Ages. Keep an eye out for arches that span narrow lanes (such as on the right, at Arsenale street)—the only way a walled city could grow was up. Many of these additions created hidden little courtyards, nooks, and crannies that make it easy to get away from the crowds and claim a corner of the town for yourself. Another sign of Rovinj's overcrowding are the distinctive chimneys poking up above the rooftops. These chimneys, added long after the buildings were first constructed, made it possible to heat previously underutilized rooms...and squeeze in even more people.

• *Continue up to the top of Grisia. Capping the town is the can't-miss-it...*

▲Church of St. Euphemia (Sv. Eufemija)

Rovinj's landmark Baroque church dates from 1754. It's watched over by an enormous 190-foot-tall campanile, a replica of the

famous bell tower on St. Mark's Square in Venice. The tower is topped by a copper weather-vane with the weather-predicting St. Euphemia, the church's namesake.

Cost and Hours: Free, generally open May-Sept daily 10:00-18:00, Easter-April and Oct-Nov open only for Mass and with demand, generally closed Dec-Easter.

Touring the Church: The vast, somewhat gloomy interior boasts some fine altars of Carrara marble (a favorite medium of Michelangelo's). Services here are celebrated using a combination of Croatian and Italian, suiting the town's mixed population.

To the right of the main altar is the church's highlight: the chapel containing the relics of St. Euphemia. Before stepping into the chapel, notice the altar featuring Euphemia—depicted, as she usually is, with her wheel (a reminder of her torture) and a palm frond (symbolic of her martyrdom), and holding the fortified town of Rovinj, of which she is the protector.

St. Euphemia was the virtuous daughter of a prosperous early fourth-century family in Chalcedon (near today's Istanbul). Euphemia used her family's considerable wealth to help the poor. Unfortunately, her pious philanthropy happened to coincide with anti-Christian purges by the Roman Emperor Diocletian. When she was 15 years old, Euphemia was arrested for refusing to worship the local pagan idol. She was brutally tortured, her bones broken on a wheel. Finally she was thrown to the lions as a public spectacle. But, the story goes, the lions miraculously refused to attack her—only nipping her gently on one arm. The Romans murdered Euphemia anyway, and her remains were later rescued by Christians. In the year 800, a gigantic marble sarcophagus containing St. Euphemia's relics somehow found its way into the Adriatic and floated all the way up to Istria, where Rovinj fishermen discovered it bobbing in the sea. They towed it back to town, where a crowd gathered. The townspeople realized what it was and wanted to take it up to the hilltop church (an earlier version of the one we're in now). But nobody could move it...until a young boy with two young calves showed up. He said he'd had a dream of St. Euphemia—and, sure enough, he succeeded in dragging her relics to where they still lie.

The small chapel behind the altar is dominated by Euphemia's famous sarcophagus. The front panel (with the painting of Euphemia) is opened with much fanfare every September 16, St. Euphemia's feast day, to display the small, withered, waxen face of Rovinj's favorite saint. The sarcophagus is flanked by frescoes depicting her most memorable moment (protected by angels, as a bored-looking lion tenderly nibbles at her right bicep) and her arrival here in Rovinj (with burly fishermen looking astonished as the young boy succeeds in moving the giant sarcophagus). Note the depiction of Rovinj fortified by a double crenellated wall—looking more like a castle than like the creaky fishing village of today. At the top of the hill is an earlier version of today's church.

• *If you have time and energy, consider climbing the...*

Bell Tower

Scaling the church bell tower's creaky wooden stairway requires an enduring faith in the reliability of wood. It rewards those who brave the climb with a commanding view of the town and surrounding islands. The climb doubles your altitude, and from this perch you can also look down—taking advantage of the quirky little round hole in the floor to photograph the memorable staircase you just climbed.

Cost and Hours: 10 kn, same hours as church, enter from inside church—to the left of the main altar.

• *Leave the church through the main door. A peaceful café on a park terrace (once a cemetery) is a bit to your right. Farther to the right, a winding lane leads down toward the water, then forks. A left turn zigzags you past a WWII pillbox and leads along the "restaurant row," where you can survey your options for a drink or a meal (see "Eating in Rovinj," later). A right turn curls you down along the quieter northern side of the Old Town peninsula. Either way, Rovinj is yours to enjoy.*

Sights in Rovinj

▲**House of the Batana Boat (Kuća o Batani)**—Rovinj has a long, noble shipbuilding tradition, and this tiny but interesting museum gives you the story of the town's distinctive *batana* boats.

Locals say this museum puts you in touch with the soul of this town.

The flat-bottomed vessels are favored by local fishermen for their ability to reach rocky areas close to shore that are rich with certain shellfish. The museum explains how the boats are built, with the help of an entertaining elapsed-time video showing a boat built from scratch in five minutes. You'll also meet some of the salty old sailors who use these vessels (find the placemat with wine stains, and put the glass in different red circles to hear various seamen talk in the Rovinj dialect). Another movie shows the boats at work. Upstairs is a wall of photos of *batana* boats still in active use, a tiny library (peruse photos of the town from a century ago), and a video screen displaying *bitinada* music—local music with harmonizing voices that imitate instruments. Sit down and listen to several (there's a button for skipping ahead). The museum has no posted English information, so pick up the comprehensive English flyer as you enter.

Cost and Hours: 10 kn; June-Sept daily 10:00-14:00 & 19:00-23:00; Oct-Dec and March-May Tue-Sun 10:00-13:00 & generally also 16:00-18:00, closed Mon; closed Jan-Feb; Obala Pina Budicina 2, tel. 052/812-593, mobile 091-154-6598, www.batana.org.

Activities: The museum, which serves as a sort of cultural heritage center for the town, also presents a variety of engaging

batana-related activities. On some summer evenings, you can take a boat trip on a *batana* from the pier near the museum. The trip, which is accompanied by traditional music, circles around the end of the Old Town peninsula and docks on the far side, where a traditional wine cellar has a fresh fish dinner ready, with local wine and more live music (June-mid-Sept, generally 2 days per week—likely Tue and Thu at 20:30, boat trip-50 kn, dinner-120 kn extra, visit or call the museum the day before to reserve). Also on some summer evenings, you can enjoy an outdoor food market with traditional Rovinj foods and live *bitinada* music. The centerpiece is a *batana* boat being refurbished before your eyes (in front of museum, 20-30-kn light food, mid-June-early Sept generally Tue and Sat 20:00-23:00—but confirm details at museum). Even if you're here off-season, ask at the museum if anything special is planned.

Rovinj Heritage Museum (Zavičajni Muzej Grada Rovinja)— This ho-hum museum combines art old (obscure classic painters) and new (obscure contemporary painters from Rovinj) in an old mansion. Rounding out the collection are some model ships, a small archaeological exhibit, and temporary exhibits.

Cost and Hours: 15 kn; mid-June-mid-Sept Tue-Sun 10:00-14:00 & 18:00-22:00, closed Mon; off-season Tue-Sat 10:00-13:00, closed Sun-Mon; Trg Maršala Tita 11, tel. 052/816-720, www.muzej-rovinj.com.

Aquarium (Akvarij)—This century-old collection of local sea life is one of Europe's oldest aquariums. Unfortunately, it's also tiny (with three sparse rooms holding a few tanks of what you'd see if you snorkeled here), disappointing, and overpriced.

Cost and Hours: 20 kn, daily June-Aug 9:00-21:00, Sept 9:00-20:00, Oct-May 10:00-16:00 or longer depending on demand, across the street from the end of the waterfront parking lot at Obala G. Paliage 5, tel. 052/804-712.

Activities in Rovinj

Boat Trips—Excursion boats leave from the end of the concrete pier in the Old Town known as the Mali Molo ("Little Pier"). In Rovinj's own little archipelago, the two most popular islands to visit by boat are **St. Catherine** (Sv. Katarina—the lush, green island just across the harbor, about a 5-minute trip, boats run about hourly in summer, 30 kn) and **Red Island** (Crveni Otok—farther out, about a 15-minute trip, boats run hourly in summer, 40 kn). Each island has a hotel and its own share of beaches.

If you're more interested in the boat trip than the destination, it's also fun to simply go for a **cruise** to the various coves and islands around Rovinj. Your two basic options are a straightforward 1.5-hour loop trip around the offshore islands for around 100 kn (often available—and especially atmospheric—at sunset); or a four-hour, 150-kn sail north along the coast and into the disappointing **"Limski Canal"** (a.k.a. "Limski Fjord"), where you'll have one to two hours of free time. Dolphin sightings are not unusual, and some outfits throw in a "fish picnic" en route for extra. To sort through your options, chat with the captains hawking excursions at the pier.

▲Swimming and Sunbathing—Rovinj doesn't have any sandy beaches—just rocky ones. (The nearest thing to a sandy beach is the small, finely pebbled beach on Red Island/Crveni Otok.) The most central spot to swim or sunbathe is at **Balota Beach,** on the rocks along the embankment on the south side of the Old Town penin-

sula (no showers, but scenic and central). For bigger beaches, go to the wooded **Golden Cape** (Zlatni Rt) south of the harbor (past the big, waterfront Hotel Park). This cape is lined with walking paths and beaches, and shaded by a wide variety of trees and plants. For a scenic and memorable sunbathing spot, choose a perch facing Rovinj on the north side of the Golden Cape. Another beach, called **Kuvi**, is beyond the Golden Cape. To get away from it all, take a boat to an island on Rovinj's little archipelago (see previous listing).

▲**Bike Ride**—The TI's free, handy biking map suggests a variety of short and long bike rides. The easiest and most scenic is a

quick loop around the Golden Cape (Zlatni Rt, described above). You can do this circuit and return to the Old Town in about an hour (without stops). Start by biking south around the harbor and past the waterfront Hotel Park, where you leave the cars and enter the wooded Golden Cape. Peaceful miniature beaches abound. The lane climbs to a quarry (much of Venice was paved with Istrian stone), where you're likely to see beginning rock climbers inching their way up and down. Cycling downhill from the quarry and circling the peninsula, you hit the Lovor Grill (open daily in summer 10:00-16:00 for drinks and light meals)—a cute little restaurant housed in the former stables of the Austrian countess who planted what today is called "Wood Park." From there, you can continue farther along the coast or return to town (backtrack two minutes and take the right fork through the woods back to the waterfront path).

Bike Rental: Bikes are rented at subsidized prices from the city parking lot kiosk (5 kn/hour, open 24 hours daily except no rentals in winter, fast and easy process; choose a bike with enough air in its tires or have them pumped up, as the path is rocky and gravelly). Various travel agencies around town rent bikes for much more (10-20 kn/hour); look for signs or ask around.

Nightlife in Rovinj

Rovinj After Dark

Rovinj is a delight after dark. Views that are great by day become magical in the moonlight and floodlight. The streets of the Old Town are particularly inviting when empty and under stars.

Concerts—Lots of low-key, small-time music events take place right in town (ask at the TI, check the events calendar at www .tzgrovinj.hr, and look for handwritten signs on Garibaldi street near the Square at the Bridge). Groups perform at various venues around town: right along the harborfront (you'll see the bandstand set up); in the town's churches (especially St. Euphemia and the Franciscan church); in the old cinema/theater by the market; at the pier in front of the House of the Batana Boat (described earlier, under "Sights in Rovinj"); and at the Multi-Media Center (a.k.a. the "MMC," which locals call "Cinema Belgrade"—its former name), in a cute little hall above a bank across the harbor from the Old Town.

Wine Bars—Rovinj has two good places to sample Istrian and Croatian wines, along with light, basic food—such as prosciutto-like *pršut*, truffles, and olive oil. Remember, two popular local wines worth trying are *malvazija* (mahl-VAH-zee-yah, sometimes spelled Malvasia in English—a light white wine that can be either sweet/*slatko* or dry/*suho*) and *teran* (a heavy red). At **Bacchus Wine Bar,** owner Paolo is happy to explain how the local wine has improved since communist times, when wine production stagnated. About 80 percent of his wines are Istrian, with the rest from elsewhere in Croatia and international vintners (15-60 kn/deciliter, most around 20-30 kn, 65-250-kn bottles, daily 7:00-1:00 in the morning, shorter hours off-season, Carera 5, tel. 052/812-154). **Piassa Granda,** on a charming little square right in the heart of the Old Town, has a classy, cozy interior and 140 types of wine (18-25-kn glasses, 30-70-kn Istrian small plates, more food than Bacchus, daily 10:00-24:00, Veli trg 1, mobile 098-824-322, Helena).

Lounging—**Valentino Champagne and Cocktail Bar** is a memorable, romantic, justifiably pretentious place for an expensive late-night waterfront drink with jazz.
Fish, attracted by its underwater lights, swim by from all over the bay...to the enjoyment of those nursing a cocktail on the rocks (literally—you'll be given a small seat cushion and welcomed to find your own seaside niche). Or you can choose to sit on one of
the terraces. Classy candelabras twinkle in the twilight, as couples cozy up to each other and the view. Patricia opens her bar nightly from 19:00 until as late as there's any action. While the drinks are extremely pricey, this place is unforgettably cool (50-65-kn cocktails, 50-kn non-alcoholic drinks, Via Santa Croce 28, tel. 052/830-683). Valentino sometimes plays thumping techno music; if you're in the mood to chill out instead, check out the **Monte Carlo** bar, along the same drag but a bit closer to the harbor, with generally mellower Rat Pack-type music and cheaper cocktails; it has fine

waterfront seating, but lacks the atmospheric "on the rocks" setting of Valentino. Or consider **La Puntuleina,** beyond Valentino, with a similarly rocky ambience but lower prices (30-40-kn drinks) and a bit less panache (listed later, under "Eating in Rovinj").

Batana **Boat Activities**—In summer, the House of the Batana Boat often hosts special events such as a boat trip and traditional dinner, and an outdoor food court. For details, see the listing earlier, under "Sights in Rovinj."

Sleeping in Rovinj

Most Rovinj accommodations (both hotels and *sobe*) prefer longer stays of at least four or five nights, so in peak season (mid-July–mid-Sept), you may run into strict minimum-stay requirements or high surcharges for shorter stays (though I've noted the ones that waive this fee). Hoteliers and *sobe* hosts are somewhat more flexible in the shoulder season. Don't show up here without a room in August: Popular Rovinj is packed during that peak month.

Sleep Code

(5 kn = about $1, €1 = about $1.40, country code: 385, area code: 052)

S = Single, **D** = Double/Twin, **T** = Triple, **Q** = Quad, **b** = bathroom. The modest tourist tax (about 7 kn per person, per night) is not included in these rates. Hotels generally accept credit cards and include breakfast in their rates, while most *sobe* accept only cash and don't offer breakfast. While rates are listed in euros, you'll pay in kunas. Everyone listed here speaks English (or has a relative or neighbor who can help translate).

    Rates: If I've listed three sets of rates, separated by slashes, the first is for peak season (typically mid-July through late Aug), the second is for shoulder season (roughly June–mid-July and late Aug-Sept), and the third is for off-season (Oct-May). If I've listed only two rates, the first is for peak season and the second for shoulder/ off-season. The dates for seasonal rates vary by hotel, and prices can change without notice; verify the hotel's current rates online or by email. For other updates, see www.ricksteves.com/update.

    Price Ranges: To help you easily sort through these listings, I've divided the accommodations into three categories based on the price for a double room with bath during high season:

$$$ **Higher Priced**—Most rooms €110 or more.
  $$ **Moderately Priced**—Most rooms between €70-110 kn.
   $ **Lower Priced**—Most rooms €70 or less.

In the Old Town

All of these accommodations are on the Old Town peninsula, rather than the mainland section of the Old Town. Rovinj has no real hostel, but *sobe* are a good budget option.

$$$ Hotel Villa Angelo d'Oro is your Old Town splurge. The location—on a peaceful street just a few steps off the water—is ideal, and the public spaces (including a serene garden bar and sauna/whirlpool area) are rich and inviting. The 23 rooms don't quite live up to the fuss, but if you want your money to talk your way into the Old Town, this is the place (Sb-€137/€121/€103, Db-€222/€204/€170, sea view-€20 more, family room for up to 4 people-€332/€298/€238, no extra charge for 1-night stays, closed Jan-Feb, no elevator, air-con, free Wi-Fi in lobby, free loaner bikes for guests, Vladimira Švalbe 38-42, tel. 052/840-502, fax 052/840-111, www.rovinj.at, hotelangelo@rovinj.at).

$$$ Villa Markiz, run by Danijela, has four extremely mod, stylish apartments in an old shell in the heart of the Old Town. You'll climb a steep and narrow staircase to reach the apartments, each of which has a small terrace (Db-€120/€80-100/€60; gorgeous top-floor apartment with seaview terrace-€250/€150-180/€140; no breakfast, air-con, free Wi-Fi, Pod Lukovima 1, tel. 052/841-380, mobile 095-804-0375, dani7cro@msn.com).

$$$ Hotel Adriatic, a lightly renovated holdover from the communist days, features 27 rooms overlooking the main square, where the Old Town peninsula meets the mainland. The quality of the drab, worn rooms doesn't justify the outrageously high prices... but the location might. Of the big chain of Maistra hotels, this is the only one in the Old Town (rates flex with demand, in top season figure Sb-€150, Db-€225; these prices are per night for 1- or 2-night stays—cheaper for 3 nights or more, all Sb are non-view, most Db have views—otherwise €20 less, closed mid-Oct-March, no elevator, air-con, pay Wi-Fi, some nighttime noise—especially on weekends, Trg Maršala Tita, tel. 052/803-520, fax 052/813-573, www.maistra.hr, adriatic@maistra.hr).

$$ Villa Cissa, run by Zagreb transplant Veljko Despot, has three apartments with tastefully modern, artistic decor above an art gallery in the Old Town. Kind, welcoming Veljko—who looks a bit like Robin Williams—is a fascinating guy who had an illustrious career as a rock-and-roll journalist (he was the only Eastern Bloc reporter to interview the Beatles) and record-company executive. Now his sophisticated, artistic style is reflected in these comfortable apartments. Because the place is designed for longer stays, you'll pay a premium for a short visit (50 percent extra for 2-night stays, prices double for 1-night stays), and it comes with some one-time fees, such as for cleaning. Veljko lives off-site, so be sure to clearly communicate your arrival time (smaller apartment-€98/€88/€78 plus €30 one-time cleaning fee, bigger apart-ment-€100 more plus €50 one-time cleaning fee, extra person-20 percent more, cash only, air-con, free Wi-Fi, lively café across the street, Zdenac 14, tel. 052/813-080, www.villacissa.com, info @villacissa.com).

$$ Casa Garzotto is an appealing mid-range option, with four apartments, four rooms, and one large family apart-ment in three different Old Town buildings. These classy and classic lodgings have modern facilities but old-fashioned charm, with antique furniture and historic family portraits on the walls. Thoughtfully run by a friendly staff, it's a winner (rooms—Sb-€80/€80/€70, Db-€110/€105/€90; apartments—Sb-€105/€95/€90, Db-€140/€125/€115; 2-bedroom family apart-ment—Sb-€105/€95/€90, Db-€145/€125/€115, Tb-€180/€160/€150; includes breakfast, off-site parking, loaner bikes, and other thoughtful extras; 25 percent extra for 1-night stays, air-con, lots of stairs, free Wi-Fi in main building, reception and most apart-ments are at Garzotto 8, others are a short walk away, tel. 052/811-884, mobile 099-247-9887, www.casa-garzotto.com, casagarzotto @gmail.com).

$$ Porta Antica rents 16 comfortable, nicely decorated apart-ments in five different buildings around the Old Town (all except La Carera are on the peninsula). Review your options on their website and be specific in your request—though in busy times (July-Aug), you may be asked to pay a surcharge to guarantee a particular apartment (Db-€100/€90/€80, cheaper for longer stays, sea views-€10-20 extra, extra person-€25, no breakfast, air-con, tries to be non-smoking, free Wi-Fi, open year-round, recep-tion and main building next door to TI on Obala Pina Budičina, mobile 099-680-1101, www.portaantica.com, portaantica@yahoo .it, Marino).

$$ Trevisol Apartments has four new, modern units on a sleepy Old Town street, plus a few others around town. Check your options on their website, reserve your apartment, and arrange a time to meet (Db-€90/€75/€50; bigger seaview Db-€110/€80/€60; extra charge for 1-night stays: 50 percent in peak season, 30 percent off-season; no breakfast, air-con, free Wi-Fi, Trevisol 40, main office at Sv. Križa 33, mobile 098-177-7404, www.lvi.hr, Adriano).

$ Miranda Fabris is an outgoing local teacher who rents four basic, tight apartments with kitchenettes. While rough around the edges, the rooms are the cheapest I could find in the Old Town (Db-€50/€40, no extra charge for 1- or 2-night stays, cash only, no breakfast, lots of steep stairs, across from Villa Valdibora at Chiurca 5, mobile 091-881-8881, miranda_fabris@yahoo.com).

$ Other Sobe: Try looking for your own room online (www .inforovinj.com is helpful). Several agencies have a line on private

ROVINJ

rooms in the Old Town—but in peak season, you'll pay about 70 percent extra for a one-night stay, and 30 percent extra for a two- or three-night stay. These agencies are English-friendly and handy to the bus station (open sporadic hours, based on demand): **Futura Travel** (across from bus station at Benussi 2, tel. 052/817-281, fax 052/817-282, www.futura-travel.hr) and **Natale** (Carducci 4, tel. & fax 052/813-365, www.rovinj.com). In the Old Town, try **Planet,** near the TI (Sv. Križa 1, tel. 052/840-494, www.planetrovinj .com).

On the Mainland, Southeast of the Old Town

To escape the high prices of Rovinj's Old Town, consider the resort neighborhood just south of the harbor. These are a 10- to 20-minute walk from the Old Town (in most cases, at least partly uphill), but most of that walk is along the very scenic harborfront—hardly an unpleasant commute. While the big Maistra hotels are an option, I prefer cheaper alternatives in the same area. The big hotels are signposted as you approach town (follow signs for *hoteli,* then your specific hotel). Once you're on the road to Hotels Eden and Park, the smaller ones are easy to reach: Villa Baron Gautsch is right on the road to Hotel Park; Hotel Vila Lili and Vila Kristina are a little farther on the main road toward Eden (to the left just after turnoff for Hotel Park, look for signs).

Guest Houses and Small Hotels

These are a bit closer to the Old Town than the Maistra hotels, and offer much lower rates and more personality. The first three are hotelesque and sit up on the hill behind the big resort hotels, while the last two choices lack personality but are a great budget option relatively close to the Old Town (an easy and scenic 10-minute walk).

\$\$ Vila Kristina, run by friendly Kristina Kiš and her family, has 10 rooms and five apartments along a busy road. All but one of the units has a balcony (Db-€75/€70, extra bed-€40/€35, includes breakfast, air-con, no elevator, free Wi-Fi, Luje Adamovića 16, tel. 052/815-537, www.kis-rovinj.com, kristinakis@mail.inet.hr).

\$\$ Hotel Vila Lili is a family-run hotel with 20 rooms above a restaurant on a quiet, leafy lane. While the rooms are a bit overpriced, the extra cost buys you more hotel amenities than the cheaper guest houses listed here (Sb-€60/€50, Db-€105/€75, pricier suites also available, no extra charge for 1-night stays, elevator, air-con, free Wi-Fi, parking-30 kn/day, Mohorovičića 16, tel. 052/840-940, fax 052/840-944, www.hotel-vilalili.hr, info@hotel -vilalili.hr, Petričević family).

\$\$ Villa Baron Gautsch, named for a shipwreck, is a German-owned pension with 17 comfortable rooms and an inviting, shared view terrace (Db-€72/€62/€52, €10 more for balcony, they also have two Sb for half the Db price, 20 percent more for 1- or 2-night stays, only non-balcony rooms have air-con, closed late Oct-Easter, cash only, no elevator, free Wi-Fi, Ronjgova 7, tel. 052/840-538, fax 052/840-537, www.baron-gautsch.com, baron .gautsch@gmx.net).

$ Elda Markulin, whose son runs the Baccus Wine Bar, rents three rooms and four apartments in a new, modern house a short walk up from the main harborfront road (Db-€50/€45/€40, apart-ment-€75/€60/€50, small surcharge possible for short stays, cash only, air-con, free Wi-Fi, Mate Balote 12, tel. 052/811-018, mobile 091-170-7453, markulin@hi.t-com.hr). To reach it from the Old Town, walk along the waterfront; after you pass the recommended Maestral restaurant and the ragtag boatyard on your right, turn left onto the uphill Mate Balote.

$ Apartmani Tomo, next door to Elda (see directions above), is run with Albanian pride by Tomo Lleshdedaj, who rents seven rooms and nine studio apartments. While the lodgings are basic and communication can be a bit challenging, it's a handy loca-tion and the price is right (Db-€40/€35, Db with kitchen-€45/€40, smaller studio Db-€70/€60, bigger studio Db-€60/€50, extra person-€10, cash only, air-con, free Wi-Fi, Mate Balote 10, tel. 052/813-457, mobile 091-578-1518, no email—reserve by phone).

Maistra Hotels

The local hotel conglomerate, Maistra, has several hotels in the lush parklands just south of the Old Town. As all of the hotels were recently either completely renovated or built from scratch, these are a very expensive option; most of my readers—looking for proximity to the Old Town rather than hanging out at a fancy hotel—will prefer to save money and stay at one of my other list-ings. These hotels have extremely slippery pricing, based on the type of room, the season, and how far ahead you book. (I've listed the starting rate for a 1- or 2-night stay in July-Aug; you'll pay less if you stay longer or visit off-season. Complete rates are explained on the website, www.maistra.hr.) I've listed the hotels in the order you'll reach them as you approach from the Old Town. All hotels have air-conditioning, elevators, free parking, Internet access, and Wi-Fi, and include breakfast in their rates. The Maistra chain also has several other properties (including the Old Town's Hotel Adriatic, described earlier, and other more distant, cheaper options). Most Maistra hotels close during the winter.

$$$ Hotel Park is the humblest of the pack, with just three stars. It has 202 renovated but dull rooms in a colorized commu-nist-era hull, and a seaside swimming pool with sweeping views to the Old Town. This is the handiest for walking into the Old

Town—it's a 10-minute stroll, entirely along the stunning harborfront promenade (non-view Sb-€125, non-view Db-€225, view Db-€250, tel. 052/808-000, park@maistra.hr).

$$$ Hotel Monte Mulini is the fanciest of the bunch, with five stars, 99 rooms and 14 suites (all with seaview balconies), a beautiful atrium with a huge glass wall overlooking the cove, an infinity pool, and over-the-top prices (Db-€540, tel. 052/636-000, www.montemulinihotel.com, montemulini@maistra.hr).

$$$ Hotel Lone (LOH-neh), named for the cove it overlooks, is the newest and by far the most striking in the collection—the soaring atrium of this "design hotel" feels like a modern art museum. Also extremely expensive, its 248 rooms come wrapped in a memorable package (Db-€540, tel. 052/632-000, www.lone hotel.com, lone@maistra.hr).

$$$ Hotel Eden offers four stars and 325 upscale, imaginatively updated rooms with oodles of contemporary style behind a brooding communist facade (rates about €30 more than Hotel Park, tel. 052/800-400, eden@maistra.hr).

Eating in Rovinj

It's expensive to dine in Rovinj, but the food is generally very good-quality. Interchangeable restaurants cluster where Rovinj's Old Town peninsula meets the mainland, and all around the harbor. Be warned that most eateries—like much of Rovinj—close for the winter (roughly mid-Oct to Easter). If you're day-tripping into the Istrian interior, consider dining at one of the excellent restaurants in or near Motovun (see page 1014), then returning to Rovinj after dark.

Along Rovinj's "Restaurant Row"

The easiest dining option is to stroll the Old Town embankment overlooking the harbor (Obala Pina Budičina), which changes its name to Svetoga Križa and cuts behind the buildings after a few blocks. Window-shop the pricey but scenic eateries along here, each of which has its own personality (all open long hours daily). Some have sea views, others are set back on charming squares, and still others have atmospheric interiors. I've listed these in the order you'll reach them. You'll pay top dollar, but the ambience is memorable.

Scuba, at the start of the row, is closest to the harbor—so, they claim, they get first pick of the daily catch from arriving fishing boats. They serve both seafood and tasty Italian dishes, in a contemporary interior or at a few outdoor tables with harbor views (50-80-kn pastas, 60-150-kn main dishes, daily 11:00-24:00, Obala Pina Budičina 6, mobile 098-219-446).

Veli Jože, with a smattering of outdoor tables (no real views) and a rollicking, folksy interior decorated to the hilt, is in all the guidebooks but still delivers on its tasty, traditional Istrian cuisine (35-80-kn pastas, 45-160-kn main courses, daily 12:00-24:00, Sv. Križa 1, tel. 052/816-337).

Santa Croce, with tables scenically scattered along a terraced incline that looks like a stage set, is well-respected for its pricey seafood and pastas (50-70-kn pastas, 70-160-kn main courses, no sea views, daily 18:00-24:00, Sv. Križa 11, tel. 052/842-240).

Lampo is simpler, with a basic menu of salads, pizzas, and pastas. The only reason to come here is for the fine waterfront seating at a reasonable price (30-45-kn pastas, 60-100-kn main courses, Sv. Križa 22, tel. 052/811-186).

La Puntuleina, at the end of the row, is the most scenic (and most expensive) option. This upscale restaurant/cocktail bar/wine bar features Italo-Mediterranean cuisine served in the contemporary dining room, or outside—either on one of the many terraces, or at tables scattered along the rocks overlooking a swimming hole. The menu is short, and the selection each day is even less, since Miriam and Giovanni insist on serving only what's fresh in the market. I wouldn't pay these prices unless I got a nice table out on a terrace. Reservations are recommended (80-100-kn pastas, 120-160-kn main courses, Thu-Tue 12:00-15:00 & 18:00-22:00, closed Wed except in peak season, closed Nov-Easter, on the Old Town embankment past the harbor at Sv. Križa 38, tel. 052/813-186). You can also order just a drink to sip while sitting down on the rocks.

Just before La Puntuleina, don't miss the inviting **Valentino Champagne and Cocktail Bar**—with no food but similar "drinks on the rocks" ambience (described earlier, under "Nightlife in Rovinj"). If you're on a tight budget, dine cheaply elsewhere, then come here for an after-dinner finale.

Barba Zuane, while not on "Restaurant Row," is just a couple of blocks behind it, buried deep in the Old Town. As it has some of the best indoor atmosphere in Rovinj—with rustic old Venetian coziness, and a well that looks down into a cistern now filled with the kitchen's stock room—it's a good rainy-day option. Chef Boris spent 20 years cooking in Italy before returning to his native Croatia (60-80-kn pastas, 90-130-kn main dishes, daily 12:00-23:00, Via Montalbano 1, tel. 052/811-884).

International Fare on the Old Town Peninsula

Offering upscale, international (rather than strictly Croatian) food and presentation, these options are expensive but memorable.

Krčma Ulika, a classy hole-in-the-wall run by Inja Tucman, has a mellow, cozy, art-strewn interior. Inja enjoys surprising diners with unexpected flavor combinations. The food is a bit overpriced and can be hit-or-miss, but the experience feels like an innovative break from traditional Croatian fare. Explore your options with Inja's help before ordering (12-kn cover, 100-130-kn main courses, daily 19:00-1:00 in the morning, Sun-Thu also 13:00-15:00, until 23:00 in shoulder season, closed Nov-Easter, cash only, Porečka 6, tel. 052/818-089, mobile 098-929-7541).

Monte Restaurant is your upscale, white-tablecloth splurge—made to order for a memorable dinner out. With tables strewn around a covered terrace just under the town bell tower, this atmospheric place features inventive cuisine that melds Istrian products with international techniques. Come here only if you value a fine dining experience, polished service, and the chance to learn about local food and wines more than you value the price tag (plan to spend 350-600 kn per person for dinner, daily 12:00-14:30 & 18:30-23:00, reserve ahead in peak season, Montalbano 75, tel. 052/830-203, Đekić family).

Affordable Alternatives on the Mainland

These options are a bit less expensive than most of those described above. I've listed them in the order you'll reach them as you walk around Rovinj's harbor.

Gostionica/Trattoria Toni is a hole-in-the-wall serving up small portions of good Istrian and Venetian fare. Choose between the cozy interior (tucked down a tight lane), or the terrace on a bustling, mostly pedestrian street (40-95-kn pastas, 40-130-kn main courses, Thu-Tue 12:00-15:00 & 18:00-22:30, closed Wed, just up ulica/via Driovier on the right, tel. 052/815-303).

Sidro offers a break from pasta, pizza, and fish; it's well-respected for its Balkan meat dishes such as *ćevapčići* (see the "Balkan Flavors" sidebar on page 1090) and a spicy pork-and-onion stew called *mućkalica*. With unusually polite service and a long tradition (run by three generations of the Paoletti family since 1966), it's a popular local hangout (45-70-kn pastas, 55-90-kn grilled meat dishes, 75-135-kn steaks and fish, daily 11:00-23:00, closed Nov-Feb, harborfront at Rismondo 14, tel. 052/813-471).

Maestral combines affordable, straightforward pizzas and seafood with Rovinj's best view. If you want an outdoor table overlooking bobbing boats and the Old Town's skyline—without breaking the bank—this is the place. It fills a big building surrounded by workaday shipyards about a 10-minute walk from the

Old Town, around the harbor toward Hotel Park (30-kn sandwiches, 45-60-kn pizzas and pastas, 45-100-kn fish and meat dishes, May-Sept open long hours daily, closed Oct-April, obala N. Nazora b.b., look for *Bavaria* beer sign).

Breakfast

Most rental apartments come with a kitchenette handy for breakfasts (stock up at a neighborhood grocery shop). Cafés and bars along the waterfront serve little more than an expensive croissant with coffee. The best budget breakfast (and a fun experience) is a picnic. Within a block of the market, you have all the necessary stops: the Brionka bakery (fresh-baked cheese or apple strudel); mini-grocery stores (juice, milk, drinkable yogurt, and so on); market stalls (cherries, strawberries, walnuts, and more, as well as an elegant fountain for washing); an Albanian-run bread kiosk/café between the market and the water...plus benches with birds chirping, children playing, and fine Old Town views along the water. For a no-fuss alternative, you can shell out 50 kn for the buffet breakfast at Hotel Adriatic (daily 7:00-10:00, until 11:00 July-Aug; described earlier, under "Sleeping in Rovinj").

Rovinj Connections

By Bus

Rovinj's bus station is open limited hours (Mon-Fri 6:30-9:15 & 9:45-16:30 & 17:00-20:00, Sat 7:30-13:30, Sun 8:30-13:30). As always, confirm the following times before planning your trip. Fares listed below are approximate and vary based on the company and route. Bus schedules are dramatically reduced on Saturdays and especially on Sundays, as well as (in some cases) off-season. Bus information: tel. 060-333-111.

From Rovinj by Bus to: Pula (about hourly, 45 minutes, 30-40 kn), **Poreč** (6-9/day, 1 hour, 30-45 kn), **Rijeka** (4-7/day, 2-3.25 hours, 90-125 kn), **Zagreb** (6-9/day, 3-6 hours, 150-200 kn), **Venice** (1/day Mon-Sat departing very early in the morning—likely at 5:40, arriving Venice at 10:00, none Sun, 185 kn). In the summer, you can reach Slovenia—including **Piran** (2.5 hours) and **Ljubljana** (5.5 hours)—by hopping on the 8:00 bus from Rovinj (June-late Sept only; off-season, a similar bus may run 2/week at 6:00, stopping at Portorož near Piran en route to Ljubljana). A second bus to Ljubljana may run sporadically on summer afternoons (around 17:00). You can also reach Piran (and other Slovenian destinations) with a transfer in Umag and Portorož. A bus departs Rovinj every evening at 19:00 for the Dalmatian Coast, arriving in **Split** at 6:00 (445 kn) and **Dubrovnik** at 11:00 (630 kn). (If this

Istria

Rovinj is just one of many worthwhile attractions on the peninsula called Istria. In Istria, pungent truffles, Roman ruins, striking hill towns, quaint coastal villages, carefully cultivated food and wine, and breezy Italian culture all compete for your attention.

While you could spend days exploring Istria, two destinations outside Rovinj are especially worthwhile (each one deserves a half-day side-trip). Down at the tip of Istria is big, industrial Pula, offering a bustling urban contrast to the rest of the time-passed coastline, plus some remarkable Roman ruins (including an amphitheater so intact, you'll marvel that you haven't heard of it before). The charming hill town of Motovun—with sweeping views over the surrounding terrain, including a truffle-packed forest—is one of the country's most appealing reasons to head inland.

Getting Around Istria

Istria is a cinch for **drivers,** who find distances short and roads and attractions well-marked (though summer traffic can be miserable, especially on weekends). Istria is neatly connected by a speedy highway nicknamed the *ipsilon* (the Croatian word for the letter Y, which is what the highway is shaped like). One branch of the "Y" (A9) runs roughly parallel to the coast from Slovenia to Pula, about six miles inland; the other branch (A8) cuts diagonally northeast to the Učka Tunnel (leading to Rijeka). You'll periodically come to toll booths, where you'll pay a modest fee for using the *ipsilon.* Following road signs here is easy (navigate by town names), but if you'll be driving a lot, pick up a good map to more easily navigate the back roads. My favorite is the Kod & Kam 1:100,000 *Istra* map (available in local bookstores and some TIs).

If you're relying on **public transportation,** Istria can be frustrating: The towns that are easiest to reach (Poreč and Pula) are less appealing than Istria's highlights (Rovinj and Motovun). Linking up the coastal towns by bus is doable if you're patient and check schedules carefully, but the hill towns probably aren't worth the hassle. Even if you're doing the rest of your trip by public trans-

portation, consider renting a car for a day or two in Istria.

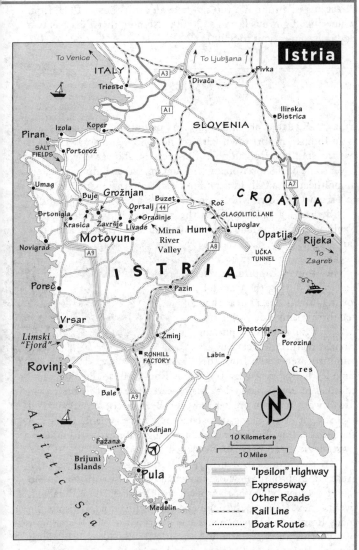

By Boat to Venice, Piran, or Trieste: Venezia Lines (www .venezialines.com) and **Commodore Cruises** (www.commodore -cruises.hr) connect Venice daily in summer with Rovinj, Poreč, and Pula. **Trieste Lines** (www.triestelines.it) connects Rovinj and Poreč to Piran (Slovenia), then Trieste (Italy). While designed for day-trippers from Istria to Venice or Trieste, these services can also be used one-way. Since schedules tends to change from year to year, check their websites for details.

direct bus isn't running, you can take an earlier bus to Pula, from where this night bus leaves at 20:00; also note that Pula has two daytime connections to Split.)

Pula

Pula (POO-lah, Pola in Italian) isn't quaint. Istria's biggest city is an industrial port town with traffic, smog, and sprawl...but it has the soul of a Roman poet. Between the shipyards, you'll discover some of the top Roman ruins in Croatia, including its stately amphitheater—a fully intact mini-Colosseum that marks the entry to a seedy Old Town with ancient temples, arches, and columns.

Strategically situated at the southern tip of the Istrian Peninsula, Pula has long been a center of industry, trade, and military might. In 177 B.C., the city became an important outpost of the Roman Empire. It was destroyed during the wars following Julius Caesar's death and rebuilt by Emperor Augustus. Many of Pula's most important Roman features—including its amphitheater—date from this  time (early first century A.D.). But as Rome fell, so did Pula's fortunes. The town changed hands repeatedly, caught in the crossfire of wars between greater powers—Byzantines, Venetians, and Habsburgs. After being devastated by Venice's enemy Genoa in the 14th century, Pula gathered dust as a ghost town...still militarily strategic, but otherwise abandoned.

In the mid-19th century, Italian unification forced the Austrian Habsburgs—whose navy had been based in Venice—to look for a new home for their fleet. In 1856, they chose Pula, and over the next 60 years, the population grew thirtyfold. (Despite the many Roman and Venetian artifacts littering the Old Town, most of modern Pula is essentially Austrian.) By the dawn of the 20th century, Pula's harbor bristled with Austro-Hungarian warships, and it had become the crucial link in a formidable line of imperial defense that stretched from here to Montenegro. As one of the most important port cities of the Austro-Hungarian Empire, Pula attracted naval officers, royalty...and a young Irishman named James Joyce on the verge of revolutionizing the literary world.

Today's Pula, while no longer quite so important, remains a vibrant port town and the de facto capital of Istria. It offers an enjoyably urban antidote to the rest of this stuck-in-the-past peninsula.

PULA

Planning Your Time

Pula's sights, while top-notch, are quickly exhausted. Two or three hours should do it: Visit the amphitheater, stroll the circular Old Town, and maybe see a museum or two. As it's less than an hour from Rovinj, there's no reason to spend the night.

Orientation to Pula

(area code: 052)
Although it's a big city, the tourist's Pula is compact: the amphitheater and, beside it, the ring-shaped Old Town circling the base of an old hilltop fortress. The Old Town's main square, the Forum, dates back to Roman times.

Tourist Information

Pula's TI overlooks the Old Town's main square, the Forum. It offers a free map and information on the town and all of Istria (daily May-Oct 8:00-22:00, Nov-April 9:00-16:00, Forum 3, tel. 052/219-197, www.pulainfo.hr).

Arrival in Pula

By Car: Pula is about a 45-minute drive south of Rovinj. Approaching town, follow *Centar* signs, then look for the amphitheater. You'll find a large pay lot just below the amphitheater, toward the waterfront (4 kn/hour, 20 kn/all day).

By Bus: As you exit the bus station, walk toward the yellow mansion, then turn left onto the major street (ulica 43 Istarske Divizije); at the roundabout, bear left again, and you'll be headed for the amphitheater (about a 10-minute walk total).

By Train: The train station is a 15-minute walk from the amphitheater, near the waterfront (in the opposite direction from the Old Town). Walk with the coast on your right until you see the amphitheater.

By Plane: Pula's small airport, which is served by various low-cost airlines, is about 3.5 miles northeast of the center. Since there's no convenient public bus option, count on paying 100 kn for the taxi ride into town. Airport info: tel. 052/530-105, www.airport-pula.com.

Helpful Hints

Car Rental: To rent a car in Pula, **Avis** is the most central (Riva 14, tel. 052/224-350). Several other companies have offices at the airport, which is a 100-kn taxi ride outside of town (see "Arrival in Pula," above).

Local Guide: If you'd like a local guide to help you uncover the story of Pula, **Mariam Abdelghani** leads great tours of the

PULA

major sites (€80 for a 2-hour city tour, €160 for an all-day tour of Istria, mobile 098-419-560, mariam.abdelghani@gmail.com).

Self-Guided Walk

Welcome to Pula

This walk is divided between Pula's two most interesting attractions: the Roman amphitheater and the circular Old Town. About an hour for each is plenty. More time can be spent sipping coffee al fresco or dipping into museums.

· *Begin at Pula's main landmark, its...*

Amphitheater (Amfiteatar)

Of the dozens of amphitheaters left around Europe and North Africa by Roman engineers, Pula's is the sixth-largest (435 feet long and 345 feet wide) and one of the best-preserved anywhere. This is the top place in Croatia to resurrect the age of the gladiators.

Cost and Hours: 40 kn, daily May-Sept 8:00-21:00—sometimes later for special events, April 8:00-20:00, Oct 9:00-19:00, Nov-March 9:00-17:00. The 30-kn audioguide narrates 20 stops with 30 minutes of flat, basic data on the structure.

➲ Self-Guided Tour: Go inside and explore the interior, climbing up the seats as you like. An "amphi-theater" is literally a "double theater"—imagine two theaters, without the back wall behind the stage, stuck together to maximize seating. Pula's amphitheater was built over several decades (first century A.D.) under the reign of three of Rome's top-tier emperors: Augustus,

Claudius, and Vespasian. It was completed around A.D. 80, about the same time as the Colosseum in Rome. It remained in active use until the beginning of the fifth century, when gladiator battles were outlawed. The location is unusual but sensible: It was built just outside town (too big for tiny Pula, with just 5,000 people) and near the sea (so its giant limestone blocks could more easily be transported here from the quarry six miles away).

Notice that the amphitheater is built

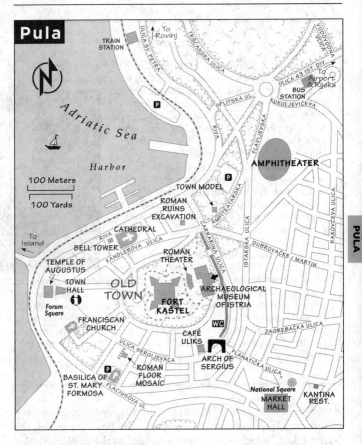

into the gentle incline of a hill. This economical plan, unusual for Roman amphitheaters, saved on the amount of stone needed, and provided a natural foundation for some of the seats (notice how the upper seats incorporate the slope). It may seem like the architects were cutting corners, but they actually had to raise the ground level at the lower end of the amphitheater to give it a level foundation. The four rectangular towers anchoring the amphitheater's facade are also unique (two of them are mostly gone). These once held wooden staircases for loading and unloading the amphitheater more quickly. At the top of each tower was a water reservoir, used for powering fountains that sprayed refreshing scents over the crowd to mask the stench of blood.

And there was plenty of blood. Imagine this scene in the days of the gladiators. More than 25,000 cheering fans from all social classes filled the seats. The Romans made these spectacles cheap or even free—distracting commoners with a steady diet of mindless entertainment prevented discontent and rebellion. (Hmm...

PULA

Amphorae

In museums, hotels, and restaurants all along the Croatian coast, you'll see amphorae. An amphora is a jug that was used to transport goods when the ancient Greeks ruled the seas, through about the second century B.C. Later, the Romans also used their own amphorae. These tall and skinny ceramic jugs—many of them lost in ancient shipwrecks—litter the Adriatic coastline.

Amphorae were used to carry oil, wine, and fish on long sea journeys. They're tapered at the bottom because they were stuck into sand (or placed on a stand) to keep them upright in transit. They also have a narrow neck at the top, often with two large handles. In fact, the name comes from the Greek *amphi pherein,* "to carry from both sides." The taller, skinnier amphorae were generally used for wine, while the fat, short ones were for olive oil. Because amphorae differ according to their purpose and nationality, archaeologists find them to be a particularly useful clue for dating shipwrecks and determining the country of origin of lost ships. This is made easier by later Roman amphorae, which are actually stamped with the place they came from and what they held.

American Idol, anyone?) Canvas awnings rigged around the top of the amphitheater shaded many seats. The fans surrounded the "slaying field," which was covered with sand to absorb blood spilled by man and beast, making it easier to clean up after the fight. This sand *(harena)* gave the amphitheater its nickname...arena.

The amphitheater's "entertainers" were gladiators (named for the *gladius,* a short sword that was tucked into a fighter's boot). Some gladiators were criminals, but most were prisoners of war from lands conquered by Rome, who dressed and used weapons according to their country of origin. A colorful parade kicked off the spectacle, followed by simulated fights with fake weapons. Then the real battles began. Often the fights represented stories from mythology or Greek or Roman history. Most ended in death for the loser. Sometimes gladiators fought exotic animals—gathered at great expense from far corners of the empire—which would enter the arena from the two far ends (through the biggest arches). There were female gladiators, as well, but they always fought other women.

While the life of a gladiator seems difficult, consider that it wasn't such a bad gig—compared to, say, being a soldier. Gladiators were often better paid than soldiers, enjoyed terrific celebrity (both in life and in death), and only had to fight a few times each year.

Ignore the modern seating, and imagine when the arena (sandy oval area in the center) was ringed with two levels of stone seating and a top level of wooden bleachers. Notice that the outline of the arena is marked by a small moat—just wide enough to keep the animals off the laps of those with the best seats, but close enough so that blood still sprayed their togas.

After the fall of Rome, builders looking for ready-cut stone picked apart structures like this one—scraping it as clean as a neat slice of cantaloupe. Sometimes the scavengers were seeking the iron hooks that were used to connect the stone; in those oh-so "Dark Ages," the method for smelting iron from ore was lost. Most of this amphitheater's interior structures—such as steps and seats—are now in the foundations and walls of Pula's buildings...not to mention palaces in Venice, across the Adriatic. In fact, in the late 16th century, the Venetians planned to take this entire amphitheater apart, stone by stone, and reassemble it on the island of Lido on the Venetian lagoon. A heroic Venetian senator—still much revered in Pula—convinced them to leave it where it is.

Despite these and other threats, the amphitheater's exterior has been left gloriously intact. The 1999 film *Titus* (with Anthony Hopkins and Jessica Lange) was filmed here, and today the amphitheater is still used to stage spectacles—from Placido Domingo to Elton John—with seating for about 5,000 fans. Recently, the loudest concerts were banned, because the vibrations were damaging the old structure.

Before leaving, don't miss the museum exhibit (in the "subterranean hall," down the chute marked #17). This takes you to the lower level of the amphitheater, where gladiators and animals were kept between fights. When the fight began, gladiators would charge up a chute and burst into the arena, like football players being introduced at the Super Bowl. As you go down the passage, you'll walk on a grate over an even lower tunnel. Pula is honeycombed with tunnels like these, originally used for sewers and as a last-ditch place of refuge in case of attack. Inside, the exhibit—strangely dedicated to "viniculture and olive-oil production in Istria in the period of antiquity" instead of, you know, gladiators—is surprisingly interesting. Browse the impressive collection of amphorae (see sidebar), find your location on the replica of a fourth-century A.D. Roman map (oriented with east on top), and ogle the gigantic grape press and two olive-oil mills.

• *From the amphitheater, it's a few minutes' walk to Pula's Old Town, where more Roman sights await. Exit the amphitheater to the left and walk one long block up the busy road (Amfiteatarska ulica) along the small wall, bearing right at the fork. When you reach the big park on your right, look for the little, car-sized...*

Town Model

Use this handy model of Pula to get oriented. Next to the amphitheater, the little water cannon spouting into the air marks the blue house nearby, the site of a freshwater spring (which makes this location even more strategic). The big star-shaped fortress on the hill is Fort Kaštel, designed by a French architect but dating from the Venetian era (1630). Read the street plan of the Roman town into this model: At the center (on the hill) was the *castrum,* or military base. At the base of the hill (the far side from the amphitheater) was the forum, or town square. During Pula's Roman glory days, the hillsides around the *castrum* were blanketed with the villas of rich merchants. The Old Town, which clusters around the base of the fortress-topped hill, still features many fragments of the Roman period, as well as Pula's later occupiers. We'll take a counterclockwise stroll around the fortified old hill through this ancient zone.

The huge anchor across the street from the model celebrates Pula's number-one employer—its shipyards.

• *Continue along the street. At the fork, again bear right (on Kandlerova ulica—level, not uphill). Notice the* **Roman ruins** *on your right. Just about any time someone wants to put up a new building, they find ruins like these. Work screeches to a halt while the valuable remains are excavated. In this case, they've discovered three Roman houses, two churches, and 2,117 amphorae—the largest stash found anywhere in the world. (Notice the harbor just behind, which suggests this might have been a storehouse for off-loaded amphorae.) I guess the new parking garage has to wait.*

After about three more blocks strolling through gritty, slice-of-life Pula, on your right-hand side, you'll see Pula's...

Cathedral (Katedrala)

This church combines elements of the two big Italian influences on Pula: Roman and Venetian. Dating from the fifth century A.D., the Romanesque core of the church (notice the skinny, slitlike windows) marks the site of an early-Christian seafront settlement in Pula. The Venetian Baroque facade and bell tower are much more recent (early 18th century). Typical of the Venetian style, notice how far away the austere bell tower is from the body of the church. The bell tower's foundation is made of stones that were scavenged from the amphitheater. On the square is an instructive poster illustrating the physical development of the town through the ages. The church's interior features a classic Roman-style basilica floor plan, with a single grand hall—the side naves were added in the 15th century, after a fire.

Cost and Hours: Free, generally open daily 7:00-12:00 & 16:00-18:00, but often closed.

· *Keep walking through the main pedestrian zone, past all the tacky souvenir shops and Albanian-run fast-food and ice-cream joints. After a few more blocks, you emerge into the...*

Forum

Every Roman town had a forum, or main square. Twenty centuries later, Pula's Forum not only serves the same function but has kept the old Roman name.

Two important buildings front the north end of the square, where you enter. The smaller building (on the left, with the col-

umns) is the first-century A.D. Roman **Temple of Augustus** (Augustov Hram). Built during the reign of, and dedicated to, Augustus Caesar, this temple took a direct hit from an Allied bomb in World War II. After the war, the Allied occupiers rebuilt it as a sort of mea culpa—notice the patchwork repair job. It's the only one remaining of three such temples that once lined this side of the square. Inside the temple is a single room with fragments of ancient sculptures (10 kn, May-Sept Mon-Sat 9:00-20:00, Sun 10:00-15:00, often closed Oct-April—but you can try asking at the Archaeological Museum if you want to go in, sparse English labels). The statue of Augustus, which likely stood on or near this spot, dates from the time of Christ. Other evocative chips and bits of Roman Pula include the feet of a powerful commander with a pathetic little vanquished barbarian obediently at his knee (perhaps one of the Histri—the indigenous Istrians that the Romans conquered in 177 B.C.).

Head back out on to the square. As Rome fell, its long-subjugated subjects in Pula had little respect for the former empire's symbols, and many temples didn't survive. Others were put to new use: Part of an adjacent temple (likely dedicated to Diana) was incorporated into the bigger building on the right, Pula's medieval **Town Hall** (Gradska Palača). If you circle around behind this building, you can still see Roman fragments embedded in the back. The Town Hall encapsulates many centuries of Pula architecture: Romanesque core, Gothic reliefs, Renaissance porch, Baroque windows...and a few Roman bits and pieces. Notice the interesting combination of flags above the door: Pula, Croatia, Istria (with its mascot goat), Italy (for the large ethnic minority here), and the European Union (since Croatia is a candidate country).

• *Consider dropping by the TI on this square before continuing our circular stroll down the main drag, Sergijevaca. You'll pass by a small park on your right, then a block of modern shops. Immediately after the Kenvelo shop on the right (with a red-and-black K sign), turn right into the white, unmarked doorway. Emerging on the other side, turn left, walk to the metal grill, and look down to see the...*

Roman Floor Mosaic (Rimski Mozaik)

This hidden mosaic is a great example of the Roman treasures that lie below the old center of Pula. Uncovered by locals who were cleaning up from World War II bombs, this third-century floor was carefully excavated and cleaned up for display right where it was laid nearly two millennia ago. (Notice that the Roman floor level was about six feet below today's.) The centerpiece of the mosaic depicts the punishment of Dirce. According to the ancient Greek legend, King Lykos of Thebes was bewitched by Dirce and abandoned his pregnant queen. The queen gave birth to twin boys (depicted in this mosaic), who grew up to kill their deadbeat dad and tie Dirce to the horns of a bull to be bashed against a mountain. This same story is famously depicted in the twisty *Toro Farnese* sculpture partly carved by Michelangelo (on display in Naples' Archaeological Museum).

• *For an optional detour to Byzantine times, walk into the parking lot just beyond the mosaic. Near the end of the lot, on the left-hand side, is a fenced-off grassy field. At the far end of the field is the small...*

Basilica of St. Mary Formosa
(Kapela Marije Formoze)

We've seen plenty of Roman and Venetian bric-a-brac, but this chapel survives from the time of another Istrian occupier: Byzantium. For about 170 years after Rome fell (the sixth and seventh centuries A.D.), this region came under the control of the Byzantine Empire and was ruled from Ravenna (now in Italy, across the Adriatic, south of Venice). Much of this field was once occupied by a vast, richly decorated basilica. This lonely chapel is all that's left, but it still gives a feel for the architecture of that era—including the Greek cross floor plan (with four equal arms) and heavy brick vaulting. An informational sign posted nearby outlines the original basilica and floor plan.

• *Back on the main drag (Sergijevaca), continue a few more blocks through Pula's most colorful and most touristy neighborhood, until you arrive at the...*

Arch of Sergius (Slavoluk Sergijevaca)

This triumphal arch, from the first century B.C., was Michelangelo's

favorite Roman artifact in Pula. Marking the edge of the original Roman town, it was built to honor Lucius Sergius Lepidus. He fought on the side of Augustus in the civil wars that swept the empire after Julius Caesar's assassination. The proto-feminist inscription proudly explains, "Silvia of the Sergius family paid for this with her own money." Statues of Silvia's husband, Lucius, plus her son and her brother-in-law, once stood on the three blocks at the top of the arch. (Squint to see the *Sergivs* name on each block.) On the underside of

the arch is a relief of an eagle (Rome) clutching an evil snake in its talons.

• *Before going under the arch, look to your left to see a famous Irishman appreciating the view from the terrace of...*

Café Uliks

In October 1904, a young writer named James Joyce moved from Dublin to Pula with his girlfriend, Nora Barnacle. By day, he

taught English to Austro-Hungarian naval officers at the Berlitz language school (in the yellow building just behind). By night, he imagined strolling through his hometown as he penned short stories that would eventually become the collection *Dubliners*. But James and Nora quickly grew bored with little Pula and moved to Trieste in March 1905. Even so, Pula remains proud of its literary connections.

• *Now pass through the arch, into a square next to remains of the town wall. Continue straight ahead (up two bustling blocks, along the in-love-with-life Flanatička street) to...*

PULA

National Square (Nardoni Trg) and Market Hall

Pula's market hall was an iron-and-glass marvel when inaugurated in the 19th century. This structure is yet another reminder of the way the Austro-Hungarian Empire modernized Pula with grace and gentility. You'll find smelly fish on the ground floor (Mon-Sat 7:00-13:30, Sun 7:00-12:00) and an inviting food circus upstairs (Mon-Fri 7:00-15:00, Sat 7:00-14:00, Sun 7:00-12:00). All around is a busy and colorful

farmers' market that bustles until about 13:00, when things quiet down.

• *Our tour is finished. If you're ready for lunch, consider one of the cheap options inside the market hall, or walk one block to Kantina (see "Eating in Pula," later).*

When you're done here, backtrack to the town wall. As you face the Arch of Sergius, take a right and walk under the leafy canopy next to the wall. Keep an eye out (mostly on your left, along the wall) for more Roman remains. Among these are the **Twin Gates** *(Porta Gemina), marking the entrance to a garden that's home to the* **Archaeological Museum of Istria** *(described next, under "Sights in Pula"). With more time, you can also consider a trip to the hilltop fortress,* **Fort Kaštel.** *Otherwise, we've completed our circular tour—the amphitheater is just around the corner.*

Sights in Pula

Archaeological Museum of Istria (Arheološki Muzej Istre)—If Pula's many ruins intrigue you, here's the place to scratch your Roman itch. This museum, over a century old, shows off some of what you've seen in the streets, plus lots more—stone monuments, classical statues, ancient pottery...you name it.

Cost and Hours: 20 kn; May-Sept Mon-Fri 9:00-20:00, Sat-Sun 10:00-15:00; Oct-April Mon-Fri 9:00-14:00, closed Sat-Sun; Carrarina 3, tel. 052/351-301, www.ami-pula.hr.

Nearby: On the hill behind the museum (and free to visit even if you don't buy a museum ticket) is its highlight, the remains of a **Roman Theater** (Rimsko Kazalište). Part of the stage is still intact, along with the semicircle of stone seats (some of which are still engraved with the names of the wealthy theatergoers who once sat there). To find it, go up the hill around the right side of the museum. This was the smaller of the two theaters in Roman Pula; the second was south of the center (and is no longer intact).

Fort Kaštel—For a bird's-eye view over the town, head up to its centerpiece fortress. This deserted-feeling place, hosting the Historical Museum of Istria, is worth visiting only for the chance to wander the ramparts. While neither the museum nor the fortress is worth the hike up here, it's a good way to kill some extra time in Pula and sample the views over the town and amphitheater (various trails lead up from the streets below).

Eating in Pula

The best lunch options are in and near the town's **market hall** (which is also where my self-guided walk ends). The top floor of the market is a food circus with a number of cheap and tempting eateries with both indoor and terrace seating. Upstairs in the back, look for **Laterna,** with unusually classy decor and fish specialties. Back outside, **Pekarna Corona**—a bakery across from the right side of the market (as you face the main entrance)—serves up good, fresh, cheap *burek,* the phyllo-dough pastry (Mon-Fri 6:30-18:00, Sat 6:30-15:00, closed Sun).

Kantina Restaurant, a block away, serves good lunches (including veggie options) and hearty, creative 35-kn salads both in an elegant vaulted cellar and on a lazy shady terrace. The service can be slow—if you're in a rush, eat at the market hall instead (50-75-kn pastas, 90-130-kn meat dishes, daily 12:00-23:00, at the end of the pedestrian zone at Flanatička 16, tel. 052/214-054). They also have a smaller café (drinks only, no food) directly across from the market hall.

Pula Connections

By Bus from Pula to: Rovinj (about hourly, 45 minutes, 30-40 kn), **Poreč** (12/day, 1.5 hours, 75 kn), **Opatija** (12-14 day, 2 hours), **Rijeka** (nearly hourly, 2-2.5 hours, 100 kn), **Zagreb** (almost hourly, 3.75-6 hours, 190 kn), **Split** (2/day, 10 hours, plus 1 night bus—described below, 400 kn), **Venice** (1/day departing at 5:30, arrives Venice 10:45). A night bus departs Pula at 20:00, going to **Split** (arrives 6:00), where you can connect to **Dubrovnik** (arrives 11:00). To reach destinations in **Slovenia** (including Piran and Ljubljana), you'll first transfer in Umag; or, in the summer, you can take the 8:00 bus from Rovinj (described on page 995); these buses, which tend to be in flux, may originate in Pula—ask at the bus station. Be aware that bus connections are more frequent on weekdays (fewer departures Sat-Sun). Bus info: toll tel. 060-304-090.

By Train to: Zagreb (3/day, 6 hours, transfer in Rijeka), **Ljubljana** (1/day Thu-Sun mid-July-Aug only, 4.75 hours, transfer in Hrpelje-Kozina).

Motovun

Most tourists in Croatia focus on the coast. For a dash of variety, head inland. Some of the best bits of the Croatian interior lie just a short drive from Rovinj. Dotted with picturesque hill towns, speckled with wineries and olive-oil farms, embedded with precious truffles, and grooved by meandering rural roads, the Istrian interior is worth a visit.

Dramatically situated high above vineyards and a truffle-filled forest, Motovun (moh-toh-VOON, Montona in Italian, pop. 531) is the best-known and most-touristed of the Istrian hill towns. And for good reason: Its hilltop Old Town is particularly evocative, with a colorful old church and a rampart walk with the best spine-tingling vistas in the Istrian interior. It's hard to believe that race-car driver Mario Andretti was born in such a tranquil little traffic-free hamlet. Today Motovun's quiet lanes are shared by locals, tourists, and artists—who began settling here a generation ago, when it was nearly deserted.

Orientation to Motovun

(area code: 052)

Motovun is steep. Most everything of interest to tourists is huddled around its tippy-top. The main, upper entrance gate into town deposits you at the main square, with the church on your left and Hotel Kaštel on the right. From there, you're just about two blocks in every direction from a sheer drop-off. This hilltop zone is circled by an old rampart that today offers Motovun's most scenic stroll.

Tourist Information

Motovun's main square has a small TI (Mon and Wed-Sat 11:00-15:00, closed Tue and Sun, Trg Andrea Antico 1, tel. 052/681-726); if it's closed, the gang at Hotel Kaštel dispenses tourist information.

Arrival in Motovun

Motovun's striking hilltop setting comes with a catch: Visitors usually have to hike up part of the way. A steep, twisty road connects the base of the hill with the Old Town up top. If it's not too crowded, drive as far up this road as possible until you're directed to park in the lot partway up (near the lower church, a steep 10-minute uphill walk to the main square, 20 kn/day). On extremely busy days, this lot might be full, so you may have to wait a few minutes for a car to leave; or you can park in the big lot at the foot of the hill and walk all the way up (during special events, such as the film festival, a shuttle bus may take visitors up the hill). If you're staying at Hotel Kaštel, follow the procedure explained under "Sleeping in Motovun," later. If staying elsewhere, ask your *sobe* host for advice.

Self-Guided Walk

Welcome to Motovun

The following commentary will bring some meaning to your Motovun hilltop stroll. The walk begins at the traffic barrier half-way up the hill (the highest you can drive unless you're sleeping at Hotel Kaštel).

The main drag leading up into town is lined with wine-and-truffle shops. My favorite is the Lanča family's **Etnobutiga ČA** (just above the parking lot on the right, at Gradiziol 33). This restored 17th-century house has a beautiful view terrace and a wide selection of local wines, brandies, and truffle products (most of them from the Zigante company, just across the valley). Like many people around here, Livio Lanča makes his own mistletoe brandy laced with honey (daily in season 10:00-22:00, closed Mon in Nov and entirely in Feb-mid-March, tel. 052/681-767). On the enclosed terrace downstairs, they also have a small restaurant, **Pod Napun** (45-150-kn pastas, 55-250-kn main dishes, same hours as shop).

Hike several more steep minutes up the hill. Soon you'll pass yet another traffic barrier and reach the base of the town's wall (and the recommended Mondo Konoba restaurant). Continuing up, you'll go through the first of two **defensive gateways.** Inside this passage (under the fortified gate), notice the various insignias from Motovun's history lining the walls—look for the Venetian lion, the Latin family tombstone, and the seal of Motovun (with five towers being watched over by an angel). The area above the gate was a storehouse for weapons in the 15th century, when Motovun first flourished.

Emerging from the gateway, you're greeted by sweeping views of the valley below on your right-hand side. (A coffee or light meal with this view is unforgettable; the town's lone ATM is to your left.) Just up and to the left, you'll find another defensive gateway, which is the main entrance into the heart of the **Old Town.** (Inside this gateway, notice the recommended Konoba pod Voltom restaurant.)

To your left as you come through the main gate is the yellow

town church, **St. Stephen's.** The crenellated tower is a reminder of a time when this hilltop town needed to be defended. While unassuming from the outside, this austere house of worship has an impressive pedigree: It's based on designs by the famous Venetian architect Andrea Palladio (1508-1580), who greatly influenced the Neoclassical architecture of Washington, DC. The interior is a little gloomy but refreshingly lived-in—used more by locals than by tourists. On the left, notice a painting of the heart of Jesus, its eyes following you around the church (free, generally open daily 10:00-18:00 and during frequent services).

As you stand on the square in front of the church, imagine Motovun during its annual **film festival,** when it's filled with 20,000 movie-lovers from throughout the region and around the world—often including a minor celebrity or two. This square fills to capacity, and films are projected on a giant screen at the far end (generally late July or early Aug, www.motovunfilmfestival.com).

Facing the church is the **Italian Cultural Center,** which plays an important role in this very Italian corner of Croatia. While the building is not open to the public, if your timing is right you'll enjoy beautiful music spilling out from its windows and filling the square. The local *klapa* music troupe—with men's voices harmonizing a cappella—practices here twice weekly (usually Mon and Fri evenings, at 21:00 in summer and 20:00 in winter, www.klapa motovun.com). If you hear them, find a bench and enjoy the show.

At the other end of the square is a leafy little piazza dominated by the big **Hotel Kaštel**—the main industry in town. This is also where bigwigs in town for the local film festival call home—ask the staff about recent sightings of B-, C-, and D-list celebrities. (For example, if you're staying here, you may be showering in the same bathroom once graced by Jason Biggs, star of *American Pie.* Lucky you.) In the fall, they can also arrange truffle-finding excursions for tourists (about 400 kn/person).

Between the church and Hotel Kaštel, follow the lane to the **ramparts.** Take the five-minute stroll around the Old Town on these fortifications. While most of Croatia is overrun by stray cats, Motovun seems populated by dog lovers. If you see or hear dogs in

people's backyards, it's a safe bet that they are trained to hunt for truffles in the surrounding forest.

As you breathe in the stunning panorama, notice that well-defended Motovun has been fortified three times—two layers of wall up top, and a third down below.

Sleeping in Motovun

(5kn = about $1, €1 = about $1.40, country code: 385, area code: 052)

Because it's not on the coast, Motovun's accommodations don't charge extra for one- or two-night stays. In fact, if you're staying for three or more nights, try to score a discount. Except for the big hotel, all of the places here keep the same rates all year long. Most Motovun accommodations lack air-conditioning; thick old walls and a nice breeze generally keep things cool without it.

$$ Hotel Kaštel, dominating Motovun's hilltop (and its tourist industry), is can-do, ideally located, and the only real hotel in this little burg. Most of the 33 colorful rooms have views. True to its name, the building used to be a castle, so the floor plan can be confusing (Sb-€60/€56/€53, standard Db-€102/€94/€87, Db suite or "superior" Db with air-con-€123/€116/€108, "exclusive" Db with air-con and balcony-€154/€146/€135; 10 percent discount with this book if you book direct, elevator, air-con only in some rooms, laundry service, pay Internet access and Wi-Fi, Trg Andrea Antico 7, tel. 052/681-607, fax 052/681-652, www.hotel-kastel-motovun.hr, info@hotel-kastel-motovun.hr). Guests have free access to part of the spa facilities, with a beautiful indoor pool and a spa offering a wide range of massages (starting at 150 kn/30 min, 10 percent discount with this book). Guests with cars should tell the attendant at the traffic barrier that you're staying here (he'll likely charge you a one-time 20-kn parking fee). If there's room on top, he'll let you drive up. Otherwise he'll tell you where to park and call the hotel, which will send down a free car to shuttle you up (runs until about 18:00); either way, call ahead to the hotel to figure out your options.

$ House of Gold is an injection of creativity in creaky old Motovun, filling a historic house on the road up into town with modern, minimalist, artsy decor. Youthful but still respectable—and just the right kind of funky—the three rooms share a common room with a big-screen TV, wood stove, and kitchen (non-view Db-€50, bigger view Db-€64, huge attic Db-€74, includes breakfast, cash only, free Wi-Fi, Gradziol 46—across from Etnobutiga ČA gift shop at the bottom of town, mobile 098-353-968, www.motovunaccommodation.com, brankarusnov@gmail.com, Branka). It's on the main road just above the parking lot halfway up into town—a steep 10- to 15-minute walk to the main square.

MOTOVUN

MOTOVUN

$ At Bella Vista, just below the lower defensive gateway (a five-minute uphill walk to the main square), the Kotiga family rents five apartments with cute decor and balconies that offer sweeping views across the countryside (Db-€50, no breakfast, cash only, air-con, Gradiziol 1, check in at gift shop, clearly communicate arrival time if coming after 21:00 in summer or 20:00 off-season, tel. & fax 052/681-724, mobile 091-523-0321, www.apartmani-motovun .com, info@apartmani-motovun.com, Mirjana).

$ Sobe Nena, run by sweet Nevija and Ricardo, is a good budget option at the very bottom of Motovun's hill. The two rooms are old-fashioned and basic, sharing a bathroom, but there's a fine garden to relax in. Ricardo speaks only a little English (Nevija speaks none), but they can call their daughter Doris to translate if necessary. It's a steep hike up into town, but you can try catching the shuttle bus from the lower parking lot, or—if you have a car— drive up to the parking lot partway up the hill (S-€20, D-€40, cash only, across from the gas station at Kanal 32, tel. 052/681-719, mobile 099-609-0883, sobe.nena@gmail.com).

$ Villa Maria has two fine rooms with view terraces in the Sviličić family home (Db-€50, no breakfast, cash only, air-con, free Wi-Fi, facing the defensive gate turn right and go down and around to Borgo 32, tel. 052/681-559, lorenasvilicic@gmail.com).

$ Antico Rooms is five simple rooms above the lively Café/ Bar Antico, a few steps around the corner from the main square. As the rooms are not affiliated with the bar, arrange a meeting time when you reserve (Db-€30, apartment with air-con-€40, no breakfast, cash only, closed Oct-March, some rooms get late-night noise from the café—try requesting a quieter one, Pietra Kandlera 2, mobile 098-173-0019, antico_motovun@hi.t-com.hr, Tomislav and Sandra).

Eating in Motovun

Considering this is a small hill town with just a few real restaurants, all of them are impressively good; the first two listings are particularly notable. Every menu is topped by pricey (but tasty) truffle dishes—but keep in mind that these are a better investment when truffles are in season and the flavors are pungent (see sidebar, page 1016); otherwise you'll get older, blander truffles.

Mondo Konoba, run by a typical Croatian-Italian hybrid family and located just below the lower town gate (on the left, at the base of the wall), serves up Sicilian-Istrian fusion cuisine. Most diners skip the forgettable dining room in favor of the inviting little outdoor terrace. The Mondo family's pack of five truffle-hunting dogs occasionally pay a visit (55-95-kn pastas, 60-170-kn main courses, June-Sept daily 12:00-15:30 & 18:00-22:00, closed

Tue Oct-May and all of Jan, Barbakan 1, tel. 052/681-791).

Konoba pod Voltom is actually inside the town's upper, main gate (on the right, with the *Taberna* sign above the door). Motovun's most traditional eatery serves excellent, well-presented Istrian food in a cozy dining room. In good weather (June-Sept only), it's hard to beat their view loggia, just below and outside the gate (40-60-kn pastas, 60-110-kn main courses, 80-260-kn truffle splurges, Thu-Tue 12:00-22:00, closed Wed and Jan, tel. 052/681-923).

Hotel Kaštel's **Palladio Restaurant** has good food and delightful seating right on the leafy main square—but I'd skip the dull interior (40-50-kn pastas, 55-185-kn main dishes, 10 percent discount with this book, daily 7:00-22:00; also listed under "Sleeping in Motovun," earlier).

The simple **Montona Gallery** café, with tables along the rampart between the two gates, serves drinks and ice cream with mammoth views (open long hours daily).

Near Motovun

While Motovun's eateries, listed above, are excellent, several other places are nearby. If good food is your priority, consider driving about 10 minutes down to Livade (in the valley below Motovun), or about 30 minutes to Brtonigla (between Motovun and the coast).

In Livade

The flat little crossroads village of Livade, sitting in the valley facing the back of Motovun's hill, is home to the first and last name in Istrian truffles. In 1999, Giancarlo Zigante unearthed the biggest white truffle the world had ever seen—2.9 pounds, as verified by *The Guinness Book of World Records.* (In 2007, the record was broken by a 3.3-pound Tuscan truffle.) Zigante's hunk of fungus—now revered as if a religious relic—kicked off a truffle craze that continues in Istria today (see sidebar on page 1016). Today Zigante has a virtual monopoly on Istria's truffle industry, producing a wide range of truffle goodies. If you're a connoisseur, or just curious, make a pilgrimage to this truffle mecca.

Zigante's large facility here is divided into two parts: The **Zigante Tartufi shop** offers shelves upon shelves of both fresh and packaged truffle products (plus local wines, olive oils, brandies, and more). There's also a little tasting table where you can sample the earthy goods, and a brain-sized replica of that famously massive chunk of white truffle. A small jar of preserved truffles will run you 80-150 kn, depending on the size, type of truffle, and preparation. You can even pick up a recipe sheet telling you what to do with the precious stuff once you get it home (daily 9:00-21:00, off-season 10:00-20:00, Livade 7, tel. 052/664-030,

Truffle Mania

A mysterious fungus with a pungent, unmistakable flavor has been all the rage in Istria for the last decade or so. Called *tartufi* in both Croatian and Italian, these precious tubers have been gathered here since Roman times and were favored by the region's Venetian and Austrian rulers. More recently, local peasants ate them as a substitute for meat (often mixed with polenta) during the lean days after World War II.

In 1999, local entrepreneur Giancarlo Zigante discovered a nearly three-pound white truffle. In addition to making Giancarlo Zigante a very wealthy man (see "Zigante Tartufi" listing, previous page), this giant truffle legitimized Istria on the world truffle scene. Today, Istria is giving France's Provence and Italy's Piedmont a run for their money in truffle production. Most of Istria's truffles are concentrated in the Motovun Forest, the damp, oak-tree-filled terrain surrounding Motovun, Livade, and Buzet.

A truffle is a tuber that grows entirely underground, usually at a depth of eight inches near the roots of oak trees. Since no part of the plant grows aboveground, they're particularly difficult to find...and, therefore, valuable. Traditionally, Istrian truffle-gatherers use specially trained dogs to find truffles. This

www.zigantetartufi.com). The adjacent **Restaurant Zigante,** one of Istria's fanciest (and most expensive), dishes up all manner of truffle specialties. The decor—inside or out on the terrace—is white-tablecloth classy, the service is deliberate but friendly, and the truffles, as if on a cooking game show, are prepared in a dizzying variety of ways. If you want the full dose of this local delicacy from a place that knows its truffles, this is a worthwhile splurge (250-350-kn main dishes, 500-kn-plus fixed-price meals—even more during white truffle season, daily 12:00-23:00, until 22:00 in winter, Livade 7, tel. 052/664-302).

Livade's more affordable dining option, **Konoba Dorjana,** is across the roundabout and just down the street from Zigante. This family-run eatery has a cozy old-fashioned dining room around a giant fireplace, an inviting terrace covered by a canopy of ivy, and plenty of truffle options (45-150-kn pastas, 50-200-kn main dishes, Thu-Tue 11:00-22:00, closed Wed, Livade 4a, tel. 052/664-093).

Eating near Livade, in Gradinje: A five-minute drive east of Livade, in the hamlet of Gradinje, is a rustic, unpretentious eat-is most productive at night, when the darkness forces the dog to rely more on its sense of smell rather than sight.

There are two general types of truffles: white (more valuable and with a milder flavor—*Tuber magnatum,* known as the "Queen of the Truffles") and black. Each type of truffle has a "season"—a specific time of year when its scent is released, making it easier to find (May-Nov for black, Oct-Jan for white). Once dug up, they look pretty unassuming—like a tough, dirty pinecone.

Truffles can be eaten in a variety of ways. Thanks to their powerful and distinctive kick, they're often used sparingly for flavor—grated like parmesan cheese, or as truffle oil sprinkled over a dish. But you'll also find them in cheese, salami, olive oil, pâté, and even ice cream. Some people find that the pungent, musty aftertaste follows them around all day...and all night, when its supposed aphrodisiac qualities kick in. Because they're so rare and difficult to find, truffles are incredibly expensive—but many people are more than happy to pay royally for that inimitable flavor. Long overshadowed by other famous truffle regions, Istria is becoming more well-known for this precious local product. In 2011, American chef and TV personality Anthony Bourdain filmed a show here highlighting Istrian truffle meals (airing in 2012).

If you're a truffle nut, you'll find yourself in heaven here; if not, you may still appreciate the chance to sample a little taste of truffle. While you do that, ponder how one giant tuber changed the economy of an entire region.

---

ery serving up the most affordable truffle dishes around. **Konoba Dolina** ("Valley Inn") has a nondescript interior and a pleasant terrace out front. Because it's just beyond the tourist trail, the prices are reasonable and the ambience is more authentic (45-95-kn meals, truffle splurges up to 120 kn, Wed-Mon 12:00-22:00, closed Tue, tel. 052/664-091). First make your way to Gradinje (go into Livade and turn right at the main roundabout, then drive through the countryside for a few minutes). Once in Gradinje, go all the way through town, then look for signs on the left.

In Brtonigla, between Motovun and Rovinj

Brtonigla (bur-toh-NEEG-lah, Verteneglio in Italian, literally "black soil") is a tiny wine village surrounded by vineyards. It's a bit closer to the sea than the other hill towns in this chapter, and sits above gentle slopes rather than a dramatic hilltop. Once in town, you'll find just a handful of haphazard streets, and this fine restaurant.

Konoba Astarea, a restaurant down the street and around the

corner (on the main road toward
Buje), is a local favorite for traditional, take-your-time Istrian
cuisine with a focus on fish and
lamb. While this isn't gourmet
cooking and truffles are an afterthought, it's rustic food done well.
Anton and Alma Kernjus don't
print an English menu, but Anton

will pull up a chair to explain your options. Choose between the
warmly cluttered, borderline-kitschy dining room huddled around
the blazing open fire, where Alma does a lot of the cooking, or
the cool and welcoming terrace with faraway sea views. It's smart
to reserve ahead (figure 210 kn per person for a full-blown multi-
course meal, or 70-120 kn for individual dishes, daily 11:00-23:00,
closed Nov, tel. 052/774-384).

MOTOVUN

ZAGREB

In this land of time-passed coastal villages, Zagreb (ZAH-grehb) offers a welcome jolt of big-city sophistication. You can't get a complete picture of modern Croatia without a visit here—away from the touristy resorts, in the lively and livable city that is home to one out of every six Croatians (pop. 780,000). In Zagreb, you'll find historic neighborhoods, a thriving café culture, my favorite urban people-watching in Croatia, and virtually no tourists. The city is also Croatia's best destination for museum-going, with wonderful collections highlighting distinctively Croatian artists (the Naive Art movement and sculptor Ivan Meštrović), a quirky exhibit telling the tales of fractured relationships, and a smattering of other fine options (modern art, city history, arts and crafts, and much more). Get your fill here before heading to smaller cities and towns, where worthwhile museums are in short supply.

Zagreb began as two walled medieval towns, Gradec and Kaptol, separated by a river. As Croatia fell under the control of various foreign powers—Budapest, Vienna, Berlin, and Belgrade—the two hill towns that would become Zagreb gradually took on more religious and civic importance. Kaptol became a bishopric in 1094, and it's still home to Croatia's most important church. In the 16th century, the Ban (Croatia's governor) and the Sabor (parliament) called Gradec home. The two towns officially merged in 1850, and soon after, the railroad connecting Budapest with the Adriatic port city of Rijeka was built through the city. Zagreb prospered. After centuries of being the de facto religious, cultural, and political center of Croatia, Zagreb officially became a European capital when the country declared its independence in 1991. Today, while many Croatian destinations are becoming more popular, Zagreb is an underrated, unsung exception that still feels relatively undiscovered. The city rewards those who choose to visit.

Planning Your Time

Most visitors just pass through Zagreb, but the city is worth a look. Throw your bag in a locker at the station and zip into the center for a quick visit—or, better yet, spend the night.

If you're very tight on time, you can get a decent sense of Zagreb in just a few hours. Make a beeline for Jelačić Square to visit the TI and get oriented. Take the funicular up to Gradec, visit the excellent Croatian Museum of Naive Art and/or the Museum of Broken Relationships, and stroll St. Mark's Square. Then wander down through the Stone Gate to the lively Tkalčićeva scene (good for a drink or meal), through the market (closes at 14:00), and on to Kaptol and the cathedral. Depending on how much you linger, this loop can take anywhere from three hours to a full day.

With additional time, visit more of Zagreb's museums (the Meštrović Atelier and City Museum, both in the compact Gradec zone, are both good), wander the series of parks called the "Green Horseshoe" (with even more museums), or pay a visit to the beautiful Mirogoj Cemetery (one of Europe's finest final resting places).

If you're moving on from Zagreb to Plitvice Lakes National Park (described in the next chapter), be warned that the last bus leaves in the mid-afternoon (usually 16:00); confirm your bus departure carefully to ensure that you don't get stranded in Zagreb.

Orientation to Zagreb

(area code: 01)

Zagreb, just 30 minutes from the Slovenian border, stretches from the foothills of Medvednica ("Bear Mountain") to the Sava River. In the middle of the sprawl, you'll find the modern **Lower Town** (Donji Grad, centered on **Jelačić Square**) and the historic **Upper**

Town (Gornji Grad, comprising the original hill towns of **Gradec** and **Kaptol**). To the south is a U-shaped belt of parks, squares, and museums that make up the **"Green Horseshoe."** The east side of the U is a series of three parks, with the train station at the bottom (south) and Jelačić

ZAGREB

Zagreb Essentials

English	Croatian	Pronounced
Jelačić Square	Trg bana Jelačića	turg BAH-nah YEH-lah-chee-chah
Gradec (original civic hill town)	Gradec	GRAH-dehts
Kaptol (original religious hill town)	Kaptol	KAHP-tohl
Café street between Gradec and Kaptol	Tkalčićeva (or "Tkalči" for short)	tuh-KAHL-chee-chay-vah (tuh-KAHL-chee)
Main train station	Glavni Kolodvor	GLAHV-nee KOH-loh-dvor
Bus station	Autobusni Kolodvor	OW-toh-boos-nee KOH-loh-dvor

Square at the top (north).

Zagrebians have devised a brilliant scheme for confusing tourists: Street names can be given several different ways. For example, the street that is signed as ulica Kralja Držislava ("King Držislav Street") is often called simply Držislavova ("Držislav's") by locals. So if you're looking for a street, don't search for an exact match—be willing to settle for something that just has a lot of the same letters.

Tourist Information

Zagreb has Croatia's best-organized TI, right on Jelačić Square (Mon-Fri 8:30-20:00, until 21:00 in June-Sept; Sat 9:00-18:00, Sun 10:00-17:00; Trg bana Jelačića 11, tel. 01/481-4051, www .zagreb-touristinfo.hr). They also have an office in the train station (Mon-Fri 8:30-20:00, Sat-Sun 12:30-18:30). Both TIs offer piles of free, well-produced tourist brochures; highlights include the one-page city map (with handy transit map and regional map on back), the monthly events guide, and the great *Step By Step* brochure (with a couple of good self-guided walking tours). I'd skip the TI's Zagreb Card (free transportation and discounts at most Zagreb museums, 60 kn/24 hours, 90 kn/72 hours).

Arrival in Zagreb

By Train: Zagreb's main train station (Glavni Kolodvor) is a few long blocks south of Jelačić Square, at the base of the Green Horseshoe. The straightforward arrivals hall has a train information desk, ticket windows, luggage lockers (lining the hallway to the left as you exit the platform, 15 kn/day), ATMs, WCs, Konzum

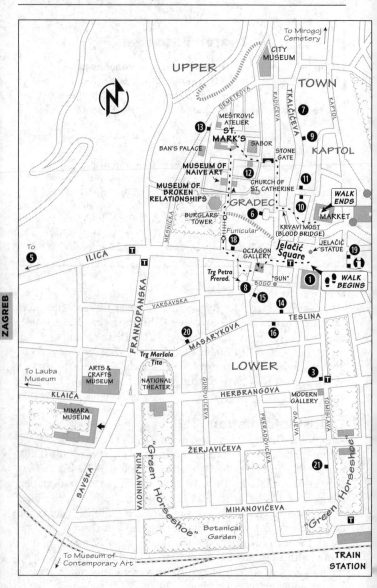

grocery store, and newsstands. To reach the city center, go straight out the front door. You'll run into a taxi stand, and then the tracks for **tram #6** (direction: Črnomerec zips you to Jelačić Square; direction: Sopot takes you to the bus station—the third stop, just after you turn right and go under the big overpass). You can also take tram #13 to Jelačić Square (direction: Žitnjak). For either tram, buy an 8-kn ticket from the kiosk, and validate it when you board

Zagreb

1. Hotel Dubrovnik
2. Hotel Astoria
3. Palace Hotel
4. Hotel Central
5. To Hotel Ilica
6. Apartments Lessi & Fulir Backpackers Inn
7. Tkalčićeva St. Eateries
8. Trg Petra Preradovića Eateries
9. Pivnica Medvedgrad Pub
10. Nokturno Restaurant
11. The Cookie Factory
12. Trilogija Wine Bar & Old Pharmacy
13. Konoba Didov San
14. Vinodol Restaurant
15. Ribice i Tri Točkice
16. Sandwich Bar Pingvin
17. Mimice Restaurant
18. Slastičarnica Vincek Ice Cream
19. Gradska Kavana Café
20. Marko Polo Travel Agency
21. Plitvice Lakes Office

the tram. If you **walk** straight ahead through the long, lush park, you'll wind up at the bottom of Jelačić Square in 10 minutes.

By Bus: The user-friendly but inconveniently located bus station (Autobusni Kolodvor) is a few long blocks southeast of the main train station. The station has all the essentials—ATMs, post office, mini-grocery store, left-luggage counter...everything from a smut store to a chapel. Upstairs, you'll find ticket windows and access to the buses (follow signs to *perone;* wave ticket in front of turnstile to open gate). Tram #6 (direction: Črnomerec) takes you to the main train station, then on to Jelačić Square. Walking from the bus station to Jelačić Square takes about 25 minutes.

By Plane: Zagreb's small airport is 10 miles south of the center (tel. 01/626-5222, www.zagreb-airport.hr). If you have time to kill, head up the stairs (near the main security checkpoint) to the rooftop café view terrace, where you can enjoy a drink while watching planes take off and land, with the Zagreb skyline on the distant horizon. Once you get through security, your only food and drink option is one very expensive bar. While a shuttle bus connects the airport to the bus station (2/hour, 30 minutes, 30 kn), it can be worth the convenience to pay for a taxi right to your hotel (30 minutes; the fair metered rate is around 180-200 kn, but some crooked cabbies might try to charge you more).

Getting Around Zagreb

The main mode of public transportation is the **tram,** operated by ZET (Zagreb Electrical Transport). For longer rides, a single ticket (good for 1.5 hours in one direction, including transfers) costs 10 kn if you buy it from the driver (8 kn at kiosk, ask for *ZET karta*—zeht KAR-tah). A day ticket *(dnevna karta)* costs 25 kn. The most useful tram for tourists is #6, connecting Jelačić Square with the train and bus stations.

Taxis start at 15-19 kn, then run 5-7 kn per kilometer (exact rate depends on company, 20 percent more Sun and 22:00-5:00, 3 kn extra for each piece of baggage). Beware of corrupt cabbies— ask for an estimate up front, or call one of the main companies: Radio Taxi (tel. 01/661-0200 or 060-800-800), Cammeo (tel. 060-700-700), or Oryx (tel. 1888). A typical ride within the city center shouldn't run more than about 30 kn, and the trip to the airport should cost no more than 200 kn (agree on a price first).

Helpful Hints

Schedule Quirks: Virtually all of Zagreb's museums are closed on Sunday afternoon and all day Monday. Some museums stay open late one night a week in summer (usually Thu). On Sunday morning, the city is thriving—but by afternoon, it's extremely quiet.

Changing of the Guard: Zagreb's "Changing of the Guard" ceremony (a very recent innovation) enlivens the city center on summer weekends. The 17th-century-costumed guards wear jaunty red scarves (an homage to the tale of how Croat soldiers "invented" the necktie) as they proceed through the center of town—passing landmarks such as Tkalčićeva street, St. Mark's Square, Jelačić Square, and the statue of Mary in front of the cathedral (mid-April-mid-Oct only, Sat-Sun 11:40-14:20, ask for complete schedule at TI). While little more than a photo op, this ceremony is one of the many ways Zagreb is working hard to please visitors.

Ferry Tickets: If you're heading for the coast, you can get time-table information and buy Jadrolinija ferry tickets at the **Marko Polo** travel agency (Mon-Fri 9:00-17:00, closed Sat-Sun, Masarykova 24, tel. 01/481-5216).

Plitvice Lakes Office: If you're going to Plitvice Lakes National Park, visit their information office in Zagreb to get your questions answered—I've found this office far better-informed and more helpful than anyplace at Plitvice itself (Mon-Fri 8:00-16:00, closed Sat-Sun, a block in front of main train station at Trg Kralja Tomislava 19, tel. 01/461-3586).

Tours in Zagreb

Local Guide—**Dijana Bebek Miletić** is an energetic, knowledge-able guide who helps visitors appreciate Zagreb's charms (3-hour walking tour-630 kn, mobile 091-303-3979, dijana.bebek@vip.hr).

Hop-On, Hop-Off Bus Tour—The local transit company runs two hop-on, hop-off routes through the city, a handy way to get to Zagreb's many outlying sights. Unfortunately, the frequency is sparse—only four per day on one route, and three per day on the other (70 kn, May-Sept only, daily 12:00-16:30, details at TI).

Bike Tours—**Blue Bike** runs three different bike-tour routes through the city, starting in front of the Mimara Museum on the west end of the Green Horseshoe (170 kn, daily at 10:00 and 15:00, for details ask at TI or see www.zagrebbybike.com).

Bus-plus-Walking Tours—This option, which combines a two-hour town walk with a one-hour bus tour, can help you get your bearings (165 kn, April-Oct daily at 10:00, www.ibus.hr).

Self-Guided Walk

▲▲Welcome to Zagreb

The following one-way circular orientation walk begins at Jelačić Square. The entire route takes about an hour at a leisurely pace (not counting museum stops).

▲▲Jelačić Square (Trg bana Jelačića)

The "Times Square" of Zagreb bustles with life. Watching the crowds pile in and out of trams and seeing the city buzz with activity, you feel the energy of an on-the-rise capital of a vibrant new nation. The city's busy pedestrian scene, sense of style, and utter lack of tourists make it arguably Croatia's best people-watching destination.

It's hard to believe that this frenetic Donji Grad ("lower town") once held the townspeople's farm fields. Today, it features a prominent equestrian statue of national hero **Josip Jelačić** (YOH-seep YEH-lah-cheech, 1801-

1859), a 19th-century governor who extended citizens' rights and did much to unite the Croats within the Habsburg Empire. In Jelačić's time, the Hungarians were exerting extensive control over Croatia, even trying to make Hungarian the official language. Meanwhile, Budapesters revolted against Habsburg rule in 1848. Jelačić, ever mindful of the need to protect Croatian cultural autonomy, knew that he'd have a better shot at getting his way from

Austria than from Hungary. Jelačić chose the lesser of two evils and fought alongside the Habsburgs to put down the Hungarian uprising. A century later, in the Yugoslav era, Jelačić was considered a dangerously nationalistic symbol, and this statue was dismantled and stored away. But when Croatia broke away in 1991, Croatian patriotism was in the air, and Jelačić returned. Though Jelačić originally faced his Hungarian foes to the north, today he's staring down the Serbs to the south.

Get oriented. As you face Jelačić's statue, down a long block to your left is a funicular that takes you up to one of Zagreb's original villages, Gradec. To the right, look for the TI. At the top-right corner of the square is the **Gradska Kavana,** Zagreb's top café (with an elegant white-and-purple Art Deco interior that was recently renovated with gleaming style). If you were to leave the square ahead and to the right, you'll reach the city's other original village, Kaptol, and the cathedral (you can't miss its huge, pointy, Neo-Gothic spires—visible from virtually everywhere in Zagreb).

Taking the small street behind Jelačić and then going a little to the left would lead you to the market (Dolac) and the lively café street, Tkalčićeva (where this walk ends). On the left side of this small street (still on the square), stop at the modern building with an arcade of blocky pillars to take in a creative bit of public art. Look closely at the first pillar and find the small silver plaque with a little ball labeled *Venus* (about eight feet up, facing the building). This is one piece of the 10-part work called "**Zagreb's Solar System.**" Its center lies a short walk away, two blocks in front of Jelačić (on Bogovićeva street): a large spherical sculpture called *The Grounded Sun*, made in 1971. Decades later, a different artist decided to piggyback on that idea, and created nine new sculptures, together titled *Nine Views*. Scattered around the city are each of the nine planets—completely to scale (both the size of each planet—from the size of a marble to the size of a basketball—and each one's distance from the "sun"). The artist, Davor Preis, did the project in secret, so Zagrebians had to seek out each of the nine planets on their own, in a kind of citywide scavenger hunt. If you've got of the time and interest, see if you can track them down (ask locals or search online)—if nothing else, it's a good excuse to see some parts of Zagreb most tourists miss.

But for now, head up to the hill called Gradec. Go a long block down busy Ilica street (to the left as you face Jelačić), then enter the big **"Octagon" shopping gallery** on the left (at #5, enter under *Privedna Banka Zagreb* sign). This was the ultimate in iron-and-glass shopping elegance a century ago, and still features a few of the city's top shops (including Croata, the tie store that loves to explain how Croatians invented the necktie; for the whole story, see page 924).

Walk all the way through the gallery, exiting into the inviting café-lined square called **Trg Petra Preradovića.** It hosts a flower market all day, and inviting al fresco cafés throughout the day and into the night. Survey your options for a coffee break, then turn right and head back out to Ilica street, then turn left and continue the way you were headed before (noticing, at #18, the popular and recommended ice cream and cake shop Slastičarnica Vincek).

After another block, cross the tram tracks and turn right up Tomičeva, where you'll see a small **funicular** (ZET Uspinjača) crawling up the hill. Dating from the late 19th century, this funicular is looked upon fondly by Zagrebians—both as a bit of nostalgia and as a way to avoid some steps. You can walk up if you want, but the ride is more fun and takes only 55 seconds (4 kn, validate ticket in orange machine before you board, leaves every 10 minutes daily 6:30-22:00).

Gradec

From the top of the funicular, you'll enjoy a fine panorama over

Zagreb. The tall tower you face as you exit is one of Gradec's original watchtowers, the **Burglars' Tower** (Kula Lotrščak). After the Tatars ransacked Central Europe in the early 13th century, King Béla IV decreed that towns be fortified— so Gradec built a wall and guard towers (just like Kraków and

Budapest did). Look for the little cannon in the top-floor window. Every day at noon, this cannon fires a shot, supposedly to commemorate a 15th-century victory over the besieging Ottomans. Zagrebians hold on to other traditions, too—the lamps on this hill are still gas-powered, lit by a city employee every evening.

Head up the street next to the tower. Little remains of medieval Gradec. When the Ottomans overran Europe, they never managed to take Zagreb, but the threat was enough to scare the nobility into the countryside. When the Ottomans left, the nobles came back, and they replaced the medieval buildings here with Baroque mansions. At the first square, to the right, you'll see the Jesuit **Church of St. Catherine.** It's not much to look at from the outside, but the interior is intricately decorated. The same applies to several mansions on Gradec. This simple-outside, ornate-inside style is known as "Zagreb Baroque."

As you continue up the street, notice the old-timey **street signs,** holdovers from the Austro-Hungarian era: in both Croatian (Gospodska ulicza) and German (Herren Gasse).

From here, you're a few steps from Zagreb's two most interesting museums: On the right is the **Museum of Broken Relationships,** and a few steps down on the left is the **Croatian Museum of Naive Art** (both listed later, under "Sights in Zagreb").

In the next block, on the left, look for the monument to **Nikola Tesla** (1856-1943), a prominent Croatian-born scientist who moved to America and championed alternating current as a better electrical system than Thomas Edison's direct current.

While born in Croatia, Tesla was of Serb ancestry—so both ethnicities claim him.

At the end of the block, you'll come to **St. Mark's Square** (Markov trg), centered on the **Church of St. Mark.** The original church here was from the 13th century, but only a few fragments remain. The present church's colorful tile roof, from 1880, depicts two coats of arms. On the left, the red-and-white checkerboard symbolizes north-central Croatia, the three lions' heads stand for the Dalmatian Coast, and the marten (*kuna*, like the money) running between the two rivers (Sava and Drava) represents Slavonia—Croatia's northern, inland panhandle. On the right is the seal of Zagreb, featuring a walled city. (The seal typically shows wide-open doors—to demonstrate that Zagreb is strong, but still welcoming to visitors—but on this seal, the doors are closed.) The church interior (open sporadically) features frescoes with Bible scenes, and was redecorated in the early 20th century by local artists. Sculptures by the talented artist Ivan Meštrović flank the main altar: a *pietà* on the left, and Madonna and Child on the right (sitting cross-legged, in a typical Meštrović pose). He also sculpted the crucifix over the main altar. If you like these works, consider visiting **Meštrović's former home,** nearby, which is now a museum of his works (it's about a block away: go down the street behind the church on the left-hand side, and you'll see the museum on the right; see the Ivan Meštrović Atelier listing under "Sights in Zagreb").

As you face the church, to the right is the **Sabor,** or parliament. From the 12th century, Croatian noblemen would gather here to make important decisions regarding their territories. This gradually evolved into today's modern parliament. (If you walk along the front of the Sabor and continue straight ahead two blocks, you'll run into the excellent **Zagreb City Museum,** described later, under "Sights in Zagreb.")

Across the square from the Sabor (to your left as you face the church) is **Ban's Palace** (Banski Dvori), today the offices for the prime minister. This was one of the few buildings in central Zagreb damaged in the war following Croatia's independence. In October of 1991, Yugoslav forces shelled it from afar, knowing that Croatian President Franjo Tuđman was inside...but Tuđman survived. (Notice the different-colored tiles where the roof had to be patched.)

Walk from Gradec to Kaptol

For an interesting stroll from St. Mark's Square to the cathedral, head down the street (Kamenita ulica) to the right of the parliament building. Near the end of the street, on the right, you'll see the oldest **pharmacy** in town—recently restored and gleaming (c. 1355, marked *gradska ljekarna*).

Just beyond, you'll reach Gradec's only surviving town gate, the **Stone Gate** (Kamenita Vrata). Inside is an evocative chapel. The focal point is a painting of Mary that miraculously survived a major fire in the adjoining house in 1731. When this medieval gate was reconstructed in the Baroque style, they decided to turn it into

a makeshift chapel. The candles (purchased in the little shop and lit in the big metal bin) represent Zagrebians' prayers. Notice the soot-blackened ceiling over the forest fire of blazing candles in the bin. The stone plaques on the wall give thanks *(hvala)* for prayers that were answered. You may notice people making
the sign of the cross as they walk through here, and often a crowd of worshippers gather, gazing intently at the painting. Mary was made the official patron saint of Zagreb in 1990.

As you leave the Stone Gate and come to Radićeva, turn right and walk downhill. Take the next left, onto the street called **Krvavi Most**—"Blood Bridge." At the end of Krvavi Most, you'll come to Tkalčićeva. This lively café-and-restaurant street used to be a river—the natural boundary between Gradec and Kaptol. The two towns did not always get along, and sometimes fought against each other. Blood was spilled, and the bridge that once stood here between them became known as Blood Bridge. By the late 19th century, the towns had united, and the polluted river began to stink—so they covered it over with this street.

As you cross the pedestrian drag called **Tkalčićeva,** you enter the old town of Kaptol. Consider taking a detour up delightful, in-love-with-life Tkalčićeva to scout your options for a coffee, beer, or meal (I've listed a few recommendations under "Eating in Zagreb," later).

Just beyond Tkalčićeva is the **market** *(dolac)*, packed with colorful stalls selling produce of all kinds (Mon-Sat 7:00-14:00, Sun 7:00-13:00). At the back-left corner is the fragrant fish market *(ribarnica)*, and under your feet is an indoor part of the market *(tržnica)*, where farmers sell farm-fresh eggs and dairy products (same hours as outdoor market, entrance below in the direction of Jelačić Square).

Your walk is over. On the other side of the market, you can visit the **cathedral** (described later, under "Sights in Zagreb").

Sights in Zagreb

Zagreb has more than its share of museums, and many of them are excellent—making up for the lack of great Croatian museums outside of the capital. It would take you days to see all of the city's museums; I've selected the most worthwhile (still enough to fill a couple of days—choose the ones that interest you the most).

▲▲▲Croatian Museum of Naive Art (Hrvatski Muzej Naivne Umjetnosti)

This remarkable spot, founded in 1952 as the "Peasant Art Gallery," is one of the most enjoyable little museums in Croatia. It features expressionistic paintings by untrained peasant artists. On one easy floor, the museum displays 80 paintings made mostly by Croatians from the 1930s to the 1980s.

Cost and Hours: 20 kn, pick up the English explanations as you enter, Tue-Fri 10:00-18:00, Sat-Sun 10:00-13:00, closed Mon, ulica Sv. Ćirila i Metoda 3, tel. 01/485-1911, www.hmnu.org.

Background: Starting in the late 19th century, the art world began to broaden its definition of great art, seeking out worthy art originating outside the esteemed academies and salons of the day. Their goal: to demonstrate that art was not simply a trained skill, but an inborn talent. Intellectuals began to embrace an "anti-intellectual" approach to art. Interest grew in the indigenous art of Africa, Mesoamerica, and Polynesia (Picasso went through an African mask phase, and Gauguin went to live in Tahiti); composer Béla Bartok collected traditional folk melodies from the Hungarian countryside; the "art brut" movement preserved artwork by people deemed "insane" by mainstream society; the autodidactic (self-taught) painter Grandma Moses became well-known in the US and Europe; and art by children gained acclaim.

Here in Croatia in the 1930s, the focus was on art by untrained peasants. At that time, as in much of rural Europe, 85 percent of Croatians lived virtually medieval lifestyles—with no electricity or other modern conveniences—and about 60 percent were illiterate and uneducated. These artists captured this humble reality, creating figurative works in an increasingly abstract age. By the 1950s and 1960s, Croatian "naive art" had emerged at the forefront of a Europe-wide phenomenon.

This museum presents an easily digestible sampling of the top names from this movement. Viewing these evocative works, it's important to remember that this isn't considered "folk art" or "amateur art"—but top-quality works by great artists who were, by fluke of fate, never formally trained.

❍ **Self-Guided Tour:** Buy your ticket and follow the one-way route through the six numbered rooms, which you'll circle counter-clockwise.

Room 1: Immediately to the right as you enter is the first of many paintings by **Ivan Generalić** (1914-1992), the founder and star of Croatian naive art (his self-portrait, with a blue background, dominates the room). Generalić was discovered in the 1930s by a Paris-trained Croatian artist. The first few paintings show his evolution as an artist (and the evolution of Croatian naive art in general): While his early works came with a social or political agenda (such as *The Requisition*, where two policemen repo a cow from

an impoverished couple), he eventually mellowed his focus to simply show typical village scenes. These start out as purely representational of peasant life *(Village Dance)*, gradually become more and more fantastical *(Harvesters)*, and eventually strip away people entirely to focus on the land (1939's *Landscape*). In 1953, Generalić—still relatively unknown outside his homeland—did a show in Paris, sold everything, and came home rich. This put Croatian naive art on the international map and kick-started a new

vigor in the movement. *Woodcutters*, from 1959, shows the next phase, as Generalić's works became even more rich with fantasy—the peacock, the men clinging to tree tops, and the trademark "coral trees." Instead of showing, Generalić is evoking; naive art strove to capture the spirit and emotion of peasant life. Paintings such as this one inspired Generalić's followers (called the "Hlebine School," for the village where Generalić lived).

Flanking the door to the next room are works by the next generation of naive art—two big-name followers who were inspired (if not trained) by Generalić: on the left, the gruesome *Evangelists at Cavalry* crucifix, by **Ivan Večenaj,** who focused on religious scenes; and on the right, *Winter Landscape with Woman*, by **Mijo Kovačić,** who specialized in peasant landscapes.

Room 2: The next room features more works by Večenaj and Kovačić. Studying Kovačić's many landscapes, notice how he took a style of painting pioneered by Generalić and brought it to the next level. Winter scenes were most common, because the peasant artists were busy working the fields the rest of the year. (Early on, such artists were sometimes

called "Sunday painters," because they had to work their "real" jobs from Monday to Saturday.) Kovačić also enjoyed winter scenes for the evocative black-and-white contrast they allowed. Like Dalí, Magritte, and other surrealists, Kovačić juxtaposed super-realism (look at each individual hair on the swine in his painting *Swineherd*, pictured below) with fantastical, almost otherworldly settings. Also in this room are some landscapes and portraits by **Dragan Gaži,** a friend and neighbor of Generalić's.

You may notice that these supposedly "untrained" artists seem to borrow from other painters—most notably, the countryside

peasant scenes often feel ripped from a Pieter Bruegel canvas. While not formally schooled, there's no doubt that these artists were aware of, and often inspired by, their artistic forebears.

Also notice that naive artists frequently painted on glass. It was cheaper and more readily available in rural areas than art canvases, and—because it required no special technique—was an easier medium for the untrained naive artists to work on.

Room 3: On the right, find the portraits of Roma (Gypsy) people by **Martin Mehkek.** For the one depicting his cross-eyed neighbor Steve, Mehkek mostly painted with his fingers, using brushes only for fine details (such as the Hitler-style moustache). On the other side of the door is *Guiana '78*—by **Josip Generalić,** the founder's less-talented son—showing the gruesome aftermath of the Jim Jones mass suicide, with a pair of monkeys surveying the smiling corpses. (While vivid, this painting doesn't reflect the Croatian peasant experience, and the curator admits it's not the best representative of naive art.) Filling out the room are more of those distinctive coral-style trees that pervade naive works, these by **Ivan Lacković Croata.**

Room 4: This room shows off two big names from the latter part of the movement. On the left are lyrical landscapes by **Ivan Rabuzin,** arguably the movement's second most important artist, after Ivan Generalić. Like a visual haiku, Rabuzin's dreamlike world of hills, trees, and clouds is reminiscent of Marc Chagall. Rabuzin's works are especially popular among

the museum's many Japanese visitors. On the right are **Emerik Feješ**'s colorful scenes of famous monuments from around Europe—Paris, Venice, Vienna, and Milan. Feješ never traveled to any of these places—his paintings are based on romantic black-and-white postcards of the era, which Feješ "colorized" in his unique style.

Rooms 5 and 6: Room 5 displays works mostly by naive artists from other countries. And Room 6 features pencil sketches used by naive artists to create their works. After the sketch was complete, the artist would put it against a pane of glass to paint the scene—small details first, gradually filling in more and more of the background. Then the glass painting would literally be flipped over to be viewed. All of the works on glass you've seen in this collection were actually painted backward.

Other Museums in Gradec

▲▲Museum of Broken Relationships—Newly opened in 2010, this extremely clever museum lives up to all the attention it's received in the international press.

The museum's mission is simple: collect true stories of failed couples from around the world, tell their story in their own words, and display the tale alongside an actual item that embodies the relationship. The items and stories provide insights into a shared human experience—we can all relate to the anger, sadness, and relief expressed in these poignant, at times hilarious, displays. In addition to the predictable "he cheated on me so I broke his favorite fill-in-the-blank" items, the ever-changing collection delves into other types of fractured connections: an unrequited childhood crush, the slow fade of lovers who gradually grew apart, disappointment in a politician who failed to live up to lofty expectations, the premature end of a love cut short by death, and so on. You'll see discarded wedding albums, sex toys with stories about unreasonable requests for kinky acts, films that attempt to capture the essence of a relationship, children's playthings representing the innocence of young love, and plenty of items broken with vengeful wrath. The museum is small—just a few rooms—but rewards those who take the time to read each story. The collection has been such a hit, they've taken it on the road, garnering fans in cities worldwide.

Cost and Hours: 20 kn, daily June-Sept 9:00-22:30, Oct-May 9:00-21:00, café, 230-kn catalog tells all the stories with photos, Sv. Čirila i Metoda 2, tel. 01/485-1021, www.brokenships.com.

▲**Ivan Meštrović Atelier**—Ivan Meštrović—Croatia's most famous artist—lived here from 1922 until 1942 (before he fled to the US after World War II). The house, carefully decorated by Meštrović himself, has been converted into a delightful gallery of the artist's works, displayed in two parts: residence and studio. Split's Meštrović Gallery (described on page 925) is the definitive museum of this 20th-century Croatian sculptor, but if you're not going there, Zagreb's gallery is a convenient place to gain an appreciation for this prolific, thoughtful artist. For more on Meštrović, see page 926.

Cost and Hours: 30 kn, 20-kn English catalog, Tue-Fri 10:00-18:00, Sat-Sun 10:00-14:00, closed Mon, behind St. Mark's Square at Mletačka 8, tel. 01/485-1123, www.mestrovic.hr.

Touring the Museum: When you buy your ticket, be sure to pick up the large floor plan—it's the only way to identify the pieces on display here (they're marked only by number). Then enter the high-ceilinged dining room of Meštrović's **home**. He designed the wood-carved chandeliers and the furniture, right down to the carvings on the backs of the chairs. Overlooking the table is a portrait of his mother, legs crossed, hands clasped in intent prayer—a favorite pose of Meštrović's. Head upstairs to see sketches and plaster casts Meštrović did in preparation for some of his larger works. The rooms on this floor are filled with busts and small, characteristically elongated statues, all of them expressive. In the far room, appreciate his fine ceiling frescoes. Continue up to the top floor, where you'll find several evocative pieces: Meštrović's wife breastfeeding their son; a portrait of Michelangelo, Meštrović's artistic ancestor, holding a chisel and hammer, and portrayed with his trademark high forehead and smashed nose; and a copy of the powerful *pietà* from St. Mark's Church. The next room holds a cowering Job, the head of an archangel, a tender portrait of a mother teaching her child to pray, and a small model of one of Meštrović's biggest and best-known works, *Bishop Gregory of Nin* (in Split, described on page 922).

Head back downstairs and through the courtyard (with the large *Woman in Agony* in the center, and less-agonized women all around) and into Meštrović's **studio**. Immediately to the left as you enter is a skinny, Modigliani-esque sculpture of Meštrović's first wife, Ruža. Farther in the room are two sculptures modeled after his second wife, Olga: the unfinished, walnut-carved *Mother*

ZAGREB

and Child, and the exquisite, white-marble *Woman Beside the Sea* (one of the collection's highlights). Nearby is a sculpture of the Evangelist Luke. Upstairs around the gallery are smaller pieces, including a study for the spiny-fingered hand of Split's *Bishop Gregory of Nin*.

Now head (or look) out into the **garden,** with several more fine pieces, including another one of the museum's top works: *The History of the Croats,* with a woman sitting cross-legged (remember this pose?) with a book resting on her lap. The top of the book has a unique Croatian spiral design, and along the front of it are the letters of Croatia's Glagolitic alphabet.

▲**Zagreb City Museum (Muzej Grada Zagreba)**—This collection, with a modern, well-presented exhibit that sprawls over two floors of an old convent, traces the history of the city through town models, paintings, furniture, clothing, and lots of fascinating artifacts. After buying your ticket, head through the door and turn left, then work your way up through the ages. Each display has a fine English description. The colorfully painted shooting targets in the 19th-century wing help give it a folk-museum feel. Find the giant map on the floor, punctuated with models of key buildings. The coverage of the tumultuous 20th century is perhaps most engaging, evincing an understandably bad attitude about the Serb-dominated first Yugoslav period. It features stirring videos, a hall of propaganda posters, and artifacts from World War II and the Tito period (when Croatia was a player in Belgrade). The historical heaviness is balanced by a lighthearted exhibit about Zagreb's popular cartoon industry. The finale is a room dedicated to the creation of independent Croatia, including an exhibit on damage sustained during the war, and a film showing the return of the statue of Jelačić to his namesake square.

Cost and Hours: 30 kn, 20-kn audioguide nicely supplements the posted descriptions, Tue-Fri 10:00-18:00, Sat 11:00-19:00, Sun 10:00-14:00, closed Mon, at north end of Gradec at Opatička 20, tel. 01/485-1361, www.mgz.hr.

▲▲Cathedral (Katedrala)

By definition, Croats are Catholics. Before the recent war, relatively few people practiced their faith. But as the Croats fought against their Orthodox and Muslim neighbors, Catholicism took on a greater importance. Today, more and more Croats are attending Mass. This is Croatia's single most important church.

In 1094, when a diocese was established at Kaptol, this church

quickly became a major center of high-ranking church officials. In the mid-13th century, the original cathedral was destroyed by invading Tatars, who actually used it as a stable. It was rebuilt, only to be destroyed again by an earthquake in 1880. The current version—undergoing yet another renovation for the last several years—is Neo-Gothic (about a hundred years old inside and out). Surrounding the church are walls with pointy-topped towers (part of a larger archbishop's palace) that were built for protection against the Ottomans. The full name is the Cathedral of the Assumption of the Blessed Virgin Mary and the Saintly Kings Stephen and Ladislav (whew!)—but most locals just call it "the cathedral."

Cost and Hours: Free, Mon-Sat 10:00-17:00, Sun 13:00-17:00.

Touring the Cathedral: As you stand out front, appreciate the stately facade and modern tympanum (carved semicircular section over the door). Then step inside and wander down the nave.

First, look closely at the silver relief on the main **altar:** a whimsical scene of the Holy Family doing chores around the house (Mary sewing, Joseph and Jesus building a fence...and angels helping out).

In the front-left corner (on the wall, between the confessionals), find the modern tombstone of **Alojzije Stepinac.** He was the Archbishop of Zagreb during World War II, when he shortsightedly supported the Ustaše (Nazi puppet government in Croatia)—thinking, like many Croatians, that this was the ticket to greater independence from Serbia. When Tito came to power, he put Stepinac on trial and sent him to jail for five years. But Stepinac never lost his faith, and he remains to many the most important inspirational figure of Croatian Catholicism. (He's also respected in the US, where some Catholic schools bear his name.

But many Serbs today consider Stepinac a villain who cooperated with the brutal Ustaše.)

Facing the nearby altar, on the right look for the grave of **Josip Jelačić,** the statesman whose statue adorns Zagreb's main square.

As you leave the church, look high on the wall to the left of the door. This strange script is the **Glagolitic alphabet** *(glagoljca)*, invented by Byzantine missionaries Cyril and Methodius in the ninth century to translate the Bible into Slavic languages. Though these missionaries worked mostly in Moravia (today's eastern Czech Republic), their alphabet caught on only here, in Croatia.

(Glagolitic was later adapted in Bulgaria to become the Cyrillic alphabet—still used in Serbia, Russia, and other parts east.) In 1991, when Croatia became its own country and nationalism surged, the country flirted with the idea of making this the official alphabet.

The Green Horseshoe

With extra time, stroll around the Green Horseshoe (the U-shaped belt of parks and museums in the city center). The museums here aren't nearly as interesting as those on Gradec, but may be worth a peek on a rainy day.

Mimara Museum (Muzej Mimara)—This grand, empty-feeling building displays the eclectic art collection of a wealthy Dalmatian, ranging from ancient artifacts to paintings by European masters. After buying your ticket, head up to the top floor (2) and tour the fine painting gallery. While the names are major—Rubens, Rembrandt, Velázquez, Renoir, Manet—the paintings themselves are minors (I wouldn't prioritize these over the works of Croatian artists on display elsewhere in Zagreb, especially those at the Naive Art Museum or the Meštrović Atelier). The first floor displays sculpture and applied arts, while the ground floor has vases, carpets, and objects from the Far East.

Cost and Hours: 40 kn, 90-kn English guidebook, free and excellent smartphone audio tour available for download on their Wi-Fi network, Tue-Sat 10:00-17:00, Thu until 19:00, Sun 10:00-14:00, closed Mon, Rooseveltov trg 5, tel. 01/482-8100.

Arts and Crafts Museum (Muzej za Umjetnost i Obrt)—This decorative arts collection of furniture, ceramics, and clothes is well-displayed. From the entry, go upstairs, then work your way clockwise and up to the top floor—passing through each artistic style, from Gothic to the present. It's mostly furniture, with a few paintings and other items thrown in. The ground floor features temporary exhibits.

Cost and Hours: 30 kn, some rooms have laminated English descriptions to borrow, otherwise very limited English, Tue-Sat

10:00-19:00, Thu until 22:00, Sun 10:00-14:00—sometimes later depending on special exhibits, closed Mon, Trg Maršala Tita 10, tel. 01/488-2125, www.muo.hr.

Botanical Garden (Botanički Vrt)—For a back-to-nature change of pace from the urban cityscape, wander through this relaxing garden, run by the University of Zagreb.

Cost and Hours: Free, Mon-Tue 9:00-14:30, Wed-Sun 9:00-18:00—until 19:00 in summer, at southwest corner of the Green 'Shoe.

Elsewhere in Zagreb

▲**Mirogoj Cemetery (Groblje Mirogoj)**—Of Europe's many evocative cemeteries, Mirogoj (MEE-roh-goy) is one of the finest,

studded with great architecture and beautifully designed tombs. This peaceful spot, a short bus ride from the city center, memorializes many of the greats who built the Croatian nation. Anyone can enjoy a quiet walk here, but to provide context to your stroll, stop by the TI first for their free, thorough booklet of maps and descriptions identifying the most significant graves.

The cemetery was designed by Herman Bollé, an Austrian architect who lived and worked for most of his career in Zagreb, leaving his mark all over the city before becoming a permanent resident in this cemetery. From the stately domed main mausoleum, a long arcade (with VIP tombs) stretches along the road in both directions, punctuated by smaller domes. Entering through the main gate, circle behind the mausoleum to find the biggest tomb here: of Franjo Tuđman, the (now-controversial) leader who spearheaded the creation of independent Croatia. Continuing straight past Tuđman's grave, you'll reach the Central Cross, which usually has a field of flowers around it, and beyond that, a monument to the dead of World War I. In every direction, as far as the eye can see, are the final resting places of great Croatians.

Cost and Hours: Free, daily April-Sept 6:00-20:00, Oct-March 7:30-18:00.

Getting There: Catch bus #106 from in front of the Cathedral (3/hour) and ride six stops, or about 10 minutes, to the stop called simply "Mirogoj" (the one *after* the stop called "Mirogoj Arkada"). The return bus leaves from across the street.

Art Museums—In addition to the art gallery at the Mimara Museum (described earlier), art-lovers may want to visit a trio of other Zagreb art museums. Three different collections cover works from the 20th century through today: The **Modern Gallery** features art from the early 20th century (a few blocks south of Jelačić Square at Andrije Hebranga 1, www.moderna-galerija.hr); the new **Museum of Contemporary Art** focuses on mid-century art (south of the river and not as convenient to visit, avenija Dubrovnik 17, www.msu.hr); and the innovative **Lauba,** with more cutting-edge works from the last few years (Baruna Filipovića 23A, www.lauba.hr). For details on any of these, check their websites or ask at the TI.

Sleeping in Zagreb

Hotels in central Zagreb are expensive. As this is a convention and business town, rates at business-oriented hotels are highest on weekdays mid-February through mid-July, then again from September through November. At other times of year, and weekends year-round, you'll generally enjoy lower rates. I've listed the average rates—they may be slightly higher or lower with demand. If I've listed two sets of rates separated by slashes, the first is for high season and the second is for low season.

$$$ Hotel Dubrovnik is a professional-feeling, business-class hotel with 245 rooms, ideally located at the bottom of Jelačić Square (small Sb-€95, bigger Sb-€110, Db-€135, bigger and nicer "deluxe" Db-€175, suite-€200-220, extra bed-€35, rooms overlooking the square don't cost extra but come with some tram noise, often cheaper on weekends, prices can flex up or down with demand, air-con, non-smoking floors, elevator, free Internet access and Wi-Fi, Gajeva 1, tel. 01/486-3555, fax 01/486-3506, www.hotel-dubrovnik.hr, reservations@hotel-dubrovnik.hr).

$$$ Hotel Astoria, a Best Western, offers 100 smallish but plush, recently renovated rooms and a high-class lobby. It's conveniently located between the train station and Jelačić Square, albeit on a somewhat grimy street. If you can get a good price, it's worth considering (Sb-€89/€79, Db-€103/€93, rates flex up and down with demand, various discounts offered—including military, fancier suites also available, air-con, elevator, non-smoking rooms, free Internet access and Wi-Fi, Petrinjska 71, tel. 01/480-8900, fax 01/480-8908, www.hotelastoria.hr, recepcija@hotelastoria.hr).

$$$ Palace Hotel, conveniently located on the big park halfway between the train station and Jelačić Square, comforts business travelers and low-level visiting dignitaries with its Old World elegance. Its 120 rooms are divided between smaller, older, perfectly fine standard rooms (Db-€105/€94), and larger, recently renovated "comfort" rooms (Db-€120/€100; rates can flex with demand, air-con, elevator, non-smoking rooms, free Wi-Fi, Strossmayerov Trg 10, tel. 01/4899600, www.palace.hr, palace@palace.hr).

Sleep Code

(5 kn = about $1, €1 = about $1.40, country code: 385, area code: 01)
S = Single, **D** = Double/Twin, **T** = Triple, **Q** = Quad, **b** = bathroom. Unless otherwise noted, credit cards are accepted and breakfast is included, but the modest tourist tax (about 7 kn per person, per night) is not. While rates are listed in euros, you'll pay in kunas. Everyone listed here speaks English.

To help you easily sort through these listings, I've divided the accommodations into three categories based on the price for a double room with bath during high season:

$$$ Higher Priced—Most rooms €100 or more.
$$ Moderately Priced—Most rooms between €60-100.
$ Lower Priced—Most rooms €60 or less.

Prices can change without notice; verify the hotel's current rates online or by email. For other updates, see www.ricksteves.com/update.

$$ InZagreb, run by Ivana and Ksandro Kovačić, rents nine mostly one-bedroom apartments in various buildings around the city. While locations vary, most are in untouristy urban zones within a 15- to 20-minute walk of the main square. The units are nicely equipped and come with several welcoming, creative touches. Visit their website, find the apartment that appeals to you, and make a reservation. Clearly communicate your arrival time, and they'll pick you up at the train or bus station (no extra charge) or at the airport (150 kn extra) and take you to your home-away-from-home in Zagreb (Db-€65-89 depending on apartment and location, no 1-night stays, no breakfast, kitchenettes, air-con, free Wi-Fi, laundry machine, mobile 091-652-3201, fax 01/652-3201, www.inzagreb.com, info@inzagreb.com).

$$ Hotel Central's 76 overly perfumed rooms are comfortable and modern, and the price is right. Despite the disinterested staff, the location—right across from the main train station—makes it a good option for rail travelers (Sb-€70, larger Sb-€75, Db with one big bed-€90, twin Db-€95, Tb-€150, rates can flex with demand, air-con, elevator, free Internet access and Wi-Fi, Branimirova 3, tel. 01/484-1122, fax 01/484-1304, www.hotel-central.hr, info @hotel-central.hr).

$ Hotel Ilica is a 15-minute walk or short tram ride from Jelačić Square. The hotel's idiosyncratic sense of style—with faux chandeliers and Roman busts that Liberace would find gaudy—helps compensate for its dull urban neighborhood. It's set back on its own courtyard with a garden behind it, making it an oasis of quiet in the heart of the city. With 24 rooms, four apartments, and a staff that prides itself on its personal service, this quirky place is an excellent value if you don't mind commuting to your sightseeing by tram (Sb-€40, Db-€56, twin Db-€60—or €56 for a bunkbed, Tb-€76, big apartment-€96, air-con, free Internet access and Wi-Fi, off-street courtyard parking-29 kn/€4, Ilica 102, two tram stops from Jelačić Square at Britanski trg stop, tel. 1/377-7522, www.hotel-ilica.hr, info@hotel-ilica.hr).

$ Apartments Lessi, run by youthful and English-speaking Tin, are three rooms that share a centrally located courtyard with a bar and the Fulir Backpackers Inn (see next listing). The rooms (one of which is up a tight spiral staircase) have pleasantly rustic decor with modern comforts (smaller room: Sb-€27, Db-€50; apartments: Sb-€47, Db-€60, Tb-€80, Qb-€95; cheaper Jan-April, cash only, no breakfast, air-con, free Wi-Fi, tucked down the courtyard at Radićeva 3a, mobile 091-288-8858, www.lessi.com.hr, info@lessi.com.hr).

$ Fulir Backpackers Inn, a funky slumbermill named for a legendary Zagrebian bon vivant, is loosely run by Davor and Leo, a pair of can-do Croats who lived in Ohio. It's colorful, friendly, and youthful, with a big 10-bunk dorm, one seven-bed dorm, three six-bed rooms, and a quad. Just a few steps from Jelačić Square, this hostel puts you in the heart of Zagreb (€18-20/bunk depending on season—cheaper Oct-April, includes sheets, no breakfast, free lockers, free Internet access and Wi-Fi, self-service laundry, upstairs at the end of the courtyard at Radićeva 3a, tel. 01/483-0882, mobile 098-193-0552, www.fulir-hostel.com, fulir@fulir-hostel.com).

Eating in Zagreb

As a cosmopolitan European capital, Zagreb enjoys a refreshingly varied restaurant scene. If you're heading for (or have just returned from) the coast, consider skipping traditional Croatian food here in Zagreb—your non-Croatian options are limited almost everywhere else in the country. Look beyond restaurants, too: Several enticing boutique sandwich shops and gourmet coffee bars are scattered around the center, catering to businesspeople on their lunch breaks.

People-Watching and Coffee-Sipping

One of my favorite Zagreb pastimes is nursing a drink along its thriving people zones, watching an endless parade of fashionable locals saunter past, and wondering why they don't create such an inviting space in my hometown. The best place is on **Tkalčićeva**

street, Zagreb's main café street and urban promenade rolled into one. It's a parade of fashionable locals and *the* place to see and be seen (starts a block behind Jelačić Square, next to the market). I've listed my favorite Tkalčićeva eateries next. Honorable mention goes to **Trg Petra Preradovića,** an inviting square just a short walk from Jelačić Square (up Ilica street) that bustles with appealing outdoor cafés and bars.

Eating on or near Tkalčićeva Street

Most places along Tkalčićeva serve only drinks. For a meal, consider these options.

Pivnica Medvedgrad is a rollicking brewpub serving five different in-house beers and heavy, stick-to-your-ribs pub grub that feels closer to Prague than to Dubrovnik. The food offers a welcome break from the pizzas-pastas-and-seafood rut you'll encounter on the coast, and the outdoor seating right on Tkalčićeva's most colorful stretch will seduce you into staying for another beer—if you can score a table. The pubby interior is convivial, but less enticing (20-60-kn meals, daily 10:00-24:00, food served until 22:00, Tkalčićeva 36, tel. 01/492-9613).

Nokturno, just off of Tkalčićeva, serves up good pizza and pasta in a lively interior and has ample outdoor seating on a terrace that cascades down the street (cheap 20-35-kn pizzas, pastas, and salads; 35-100-kn meat and fish dishes; daily 9:00-1:00 in the morning, Skalinska 4, tel. 01/481-3394).

At the Market **(Dolac):** Zagreb's busy market offers plenty of options (Mon-Sat 7:00-14:00, Sun 7:00-13:00). Assemble a fresh picnic direct from the producers. Or, for something already prepared, duck into one of the many cheap restaurants and cafés on the streets around the market. The middle level of the market, facing Jelačić Square, is home to a line of places with cheap food and indoor or outdoor seating.

Dessert: **The Cookie Factory** has a wide array of American-style cookies, brownies, smoothies, and other goodies. Pull up a table for a brownie à la mode, or get an ice-cream cookie sandwich to go (10-20-kn treats, Mon-Sat 9:00-23:00, Sun 14:00-21:00, next to Nokturno at Skalinska 3, tel. 01/481-3901).

In the Upper Town (Gradec)

Trilogija, just above the Stone Gate, is a casual wine bar serving up delicious, well-presented, and affordable international dishes made with local ingredients. There's no printed menu because they cook what they find at the market—your server will translate and explain the chalkboard menu. Reservations are smart (30-70-kn small dishes, 65-90-kn large dishes, Mon-Sat 11:00-24:00, closed Sun, Kamenita 5, tel. 01/485-1394).

Konoba Didov San ("Grandfather's Dream") serves up traditional food from the Dalmatian hinterland (specifically the Neretva River Delta, near Metković). You'll find the normal Dalmatian specialties, plus eel, frogs, and snails. Choose between the homey, traditional interior and the outdoor tables (25-60-kn starters, 60-120-kn main courses, daily 10:00-24:00, a few steps up from the Ivan Meštrović Atelier at Mletačka 11, tel. 01/485-1154).

In the Lower Town, near Jelačić Square

These places are all within a level five-minute walk of Jelačić Square.

Vinodol is your white-tablecloth-classy dinner spot, with a peaceful covered terrace and a smartly appointed dining room under an impressive vaulted ceiling. The good, reasonably priced cuisine includes veal prepared *peka*-style, in a pot covered with hot coals (*peka* portion costs 90 kn, served only at certain times—generally at 12:30 and 18:30; 50-120-kn main courses, open daily 10:00-24:00, Teslina 10, tel. 01/481-1427).

Ribice i Tri Točkice ("Fish and...") serves up fish, seafood, and...whatever else they feel like. Enjoy the casual, colorful upstairs dining room and the affordably priced fish, bought daily at the market. Restaurants on the coast offer ample opportunity to sample Croatian fish, but this is a good opportunity to have some in the big city (30-80-kn dishes, order sides separately, daily 9:00-24:00, Petra Preradovića 7/1, tel. 01/563-5479).

Fast and Cheap: **Sandwich Bar Pingvin,** busy with locals dropping by for take-away, is a favorite for quick, cheap, tasty sandwiches with chicken, turkey, steak, or fish (plus some pasta dishes). They'll wrap it all in a piece of grilled bread and top it with your choice of veggies and sauces to go—or, to eat here, sit at one of the few tiny tables or stools (17-30 kn, Mon-Sat 8:00-late, Sun 18:00-late, about a block below Jelačić Square at Teslina 7).

Fried and Fishy: **Mimice** is a local institution and an old-habits-die-hard favorite of the older generation. While a bit tired and dreary, I like it as a cheap and memorable time-warp serving up simple fish dishes (15-35 kn, order starches and sauces separately). Choose what you want from the limited menu (if confused, survey the room for a plate that looks good and ask what it is), pay, and take your receipt to the next counter to claim your food. Order the smelt to get a plate of tiny deep-fried fish (Mon-Sat 7:00-21:00, closed Sun, Jurišićeva 21). As Zagreb is a Catholic town, you'll have to wait in line if you're here on a Friday.

Dessert: As the long line out front suggests, Zagreb's favorite *sladoled* (Italian gelato-style ice cream) is at **Slastičarnica Vincek,** two blocks west of Jelačić Square. Choose from a wide variety of flavors (6 kn/scoop), giving special consideration to the Vincek flavor—chocolate and walnuts. They also have other desserts, including *Zagrebačka kremšnita*—a variation on the famous cream-and-custard cake from Lake Bled (see page 781), but with chocolate (Mon-Sat 8:30-23:00, closed Sun, on the busy tram-lined Ilica street at #18).

Zagreb Connections

From Zagreb by Train to: Rijeka (2/day, 4 hours), **Pula** (3/day, 6 hours, transfer in Rijeka), **Split** (3/day, 2/day off-season, 6 hours, plus 1 direct night train, 9 hours), **Sarajevo** (2/day, 9 hours, including a night train), **Mostar** (1/day, 13.5 hours, bus is faster), **Ljubljana** (7/day, 2.5 hours), **Vienna** (2 direct/day, 6-6.5 hours, others with 1-2 changes take 7.5-8.5 hours), **Budapest** (3 direct/day, 6 hours, others with 1-2 changes), **Lake Bled** (via Lesce-Bled, 6/day, 3.5 hours), **Venice** (1 night train/day, 7.5 hours), **Munich** (3/day, 9 hours). Train info: tel. 060-333-444.

By Bus to: Samobor (about 2-3/hour, 30-50 minutes), **Plitvice Lakes National Park** (about hourly until around 16:00, 2-2.5 hours), **Rijeka** (hourly, 2.5 hours), **Rovinj** (6-9/day, 3-6 hours), **Pula** (almost hourly, 3.75-6 hours), **Split** (at least hourly, 5-8 hours), **Mostar** (5/day, 8-9.5 hours, includes a night bus), **Dubrovnik** (7/day including some overnight options, 10 hours), **Korčula** (1/day, 9-13.5 hours depending on route), **Kotor** (1/night, 14.5 hours).

Bus schedules can be sporadic (e.g., several departures clustered around the same time, then nothing for hours)—confirm your plans carefully (inquire locally, or use the good online schedules at www.akz.hr). The TI is very helpful with providing bus information. Popular buses, such as the afternoon express to Split, can fill up quickly in peak season. Unfortunately, it's impossible to buy bus tickets anywhere in the center, so to guarantee a seat, you'll have to get to the station early (locals suggest even two hours in advance). Better yet, call the central number for the bus station to check schedules and reserve the bus you want, ideally at least 24 hours ahead: tel. 060-313-333 (from abroad, dial +385-1-611-2789). If you can't get an English-speaker on the line, and the TI isn't too busy, they might be willing to call for you.

ZAGREB

PLITVICE LAKES NATIONAL PARK

Nacionalni Park Plitvička Jezera

Plitvice (PLEET-veet-seh) is one of Europe's most spectacular natural wonders. Imagine Niagara Falls diced and sprinkled over a heavily forested Grand Canyon. There's nothing like this lush valley of 16 terraced lakes, laced together by waterfalls and miles of pleasant plank walks. Countless cascades and water that's both strangely clear and full of vibrant colors make this park a misty natural wonderland. Years ago, after eight or nine visits, I thought I really knew Europe. Then I discovered Plitvice and realized you can never exhaust Europe's surprises.

Planning Your Time

Plitvice deserves at least a few good hours. Since it takes some time to get here (two hours by car or bus from Zagreb), the most sensible plan is to spend the night in one of the park's hotels (no character, but comfortable and convenient) or a nearby private home (cheaper, but practical only if you're driving). If you're coming from the north (e.g., Ljubljana), you can take the train to Zagreb in the morning, spend a few hours seeing the Croatian capital, then take the bus (generally no buses after about 16:00) or drive to Plitvice in the late afternoon to spend the night at the park. Get up early and hit the trails (ideally by 8:30); by early afternoon, you'll be ready to move on (by bus to the coast, or back to Zagreb). The most interesting and accessible part of the park can be seen very efficiently, in

a three- to four-hour hike; while there are other hiking opportunities, they pale in comparison to this "greatest hits" section. Therefore, two nights and a full day at Plitvice is probably overkill for all but the most avid hikers.

Crowd-Beating Tips: Plitvice is swamped with international tour groups, many of whom aren't shy about elbowing into position for the best photos. The park's trails are most crowded between 10:00 and 15:00. I try to hit the trails by 8:30; that way, the crowds are moving in just as I'm finishing up. If arriving in the afternoon, starting your hike after 15:00 also works well.

Getting to Plitvice

Plitvice Lakes National Park, a few miles from the Bosnian border, is two hours by car south of Zagreb on the old highway #1 (a.k.a. D1).

By **car** from Zagreb, take the A1 expressway south for about an hour, exiting at Karlovac (marked for *1* and *Plitvice*). From here, D1 takes you directly south about another hour to the park. If you're staying at the park hotels, you can park for free at the hotel lot; to park at the lots at Entrance 1 or Entrance 2, you'll have to pay (7 kn/hour). For information about driving onward from Plitvice, see "Route Tips for Drivers" at the end of this chapter.

Buses leave from Zagreb's main bus station in the direction of Plitvice. Various bus companies handle the route; just go to the ticket window and ask for the next departure (81-95 kn depending on company, trip takes 2-2.5 hours). Buses run from Zagreb about hourly until about 16:00; avoid the sporadic late-night buses, which don't get you to the park until after midnight. Confirm that your bus will actually stop at Plitvice. (The official Plitvice bus stop is along the main road, about a 5- to 10-minute walk beyond the hotels.) Confirm the schedule online (www.akz.hr) or at the Plitvice office in Zagreb (Mon-Fri 8:00-16:00, closed Sat-Sun, Trg Kralja Tomislava 19, tel. 01/461-3586).

By car or bus, you'll see some thought-provoking terrain between Zagreb and Plitvice. As you leave Karlovac, you'll pass through the village of **Turanj,** part of the war zone from two decades ago. The destroyed, derelict houses belonged to Serbs who have not come back to reclaim and repair them. Farther along, about 25 miles before Plitvice, you'll pass through the striking village of **Slunj,** picturesquely perched on travertine formations (like Plitvice's) and surrounded by sparkling streams and waterfalls. If you're in a car, this is worth a photo stop. This town, too, looks very different from how it did before the war—when it was 30 percent Serb. As in countless other villages in the Croatian interior, the Orthodox church has been destroyed...and locals still seethe when they describe how the Serbs "defiled" the town's delicate beauty.

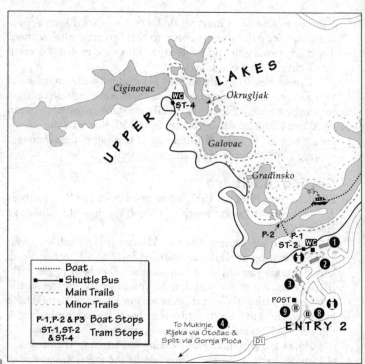

Legend:
- .... Boat
- ━■━ Shuttle Bus
- ----- Main Trails
- -·-·- Minor Trails
- P-1, P-2 & P3 Boat Stops
- ST-1, ST-2 & ST-4 Tram Stops

To Mukinje, Rijeka via Otočac & Split via Gornja Ploča

ENTRY 2

PLITVICE LAKES

Orientation to Plitvice

(area code: 053)

Plitvice's 16 lakes are divided into the Upper Lakes (Gornja Jezera) and the Lower Lakes (Donja Jezera). The park officially has two entrances *(ulaz),* each with ticket windows and snack and gift shops. Entrance 1 is at the bottom of the Lower Lakes, across the busy D1 road from the park's best restaurant, Lička Kuća (described later, under "Eating in Plitvice"). Entrance 2 is about 1.5 miles south, below the cluster of Plitvice's three hotels (Jezero, Plitvice, and Bellevue; see "Sleeping in Plitvice," later). There is no town at Plitvice. The nearest village, Mukinje, is a residential community mostly for park workers (boring for tourists, but has some good private room options).

Cost: The price to enter the park during peak season (April-Oct) is 110 kn (80 kn Nov-March; covers park entry, boat, and shuttle bus). Park hotel guests pay the entry fee only once for their entire stay; if you're staying off-site and want to visit the park on several days, you'll have to buy separate tickets each day.

Hours: The park is open every day, but the hours vary by season. In summer, it's generally open 7:00-20:00; in spring and fall,

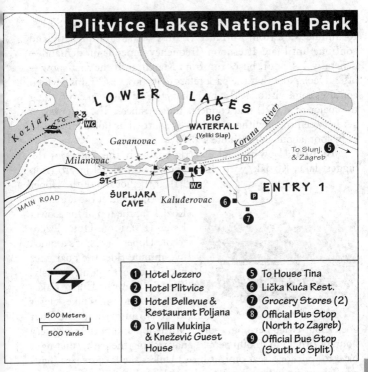

Plitvice Lakes National Park

LOWER LAKES

Kozjak

P-3 WC

BIG WATERFALL (Veliki Slap)

Gavanovac

Korana River

Milanovac

To Slunj 5
& Zagreb

ST-1

7 WC

ŠUPLJARA CAVE

Kaluđerovac

Kaluderovac 6

D1

ENTRY 1

P

7

MAIN ROAD

500 Meters
500 Yards

1 Hotel Jezero
2 Hotel Plitvice
3 Hotel Bellevue & Restaurant Poljana
4 To Villa Mukinja & Knežević Guest House

5 To House Tina
6 Lička Kuća Rest.
7 Grocery Stores (2)
8 Official Bus Stop (North to Zagreb)
9 Official Bus Stop (South to Split)

8:00-18:00; and in winter, 8:00-15:00. The last boats and shuttle buses depart one hour before the park closes. Night owls should note that the park never really "closes"; these hours are for the ticket booths and the boat and shuttle bus system. You can just stroll right into the park at any time, provided that you aren't using the boat or bus. Again, for fewer tour-group crowds, visit early or late in the day.

Tourist Information

A handy map of the trails is on the back of your ticket, and big maps are posted all over the park. The big map is a good investment; the various English-language guidebooks are generally poorly translated and not very helpful (both sold at entrances, hotels, and shops throughout the park). The park has a good website: www.np-plitvicka-jezera.hr.

Getting Around Plitvice

Plitvice is designed for hikers. But the park has a few ways (included in entry cost) to help you connect the best parts.

By Shuttle Bus: Buses connect the hotels at Entrance 2 (stop ST2, below Hotel Jezero) with the top of the Upper Lakes (stop

ST4) and roughly the bottom of the Lower Lakes (stop ST1, a 10-minute walk from Entrance 1). Buses start running early and continue until late afternoon (frequency depends on demand—generally 3-4/hour; buses run from March until the first snow—often Dec). Note that the park refers to its buses as "trains," which confuses some visitors. Also note that no local buses take you along the major road (D1) that connects the entrances. The only way to get between them without a car is by shuttle bus (inside the park) or by foot (about a 40-minute walk).

By Boat: Low-impact electric boats ply the waters of the biggest lake, Kozjak, with three stops: below Hotel Jezero (stop

P1), at the bottom of the Upper Lakes (P2), and at the far end of Kozjak, at the top of the Lower Lakes (P3). From Hotel Jezero to the Upper Lakes, it's a quick five-minute ride; the boat goes back and forth continuously. The trip from the Upper Lakes to the Lower Lakes takes closer to 20 minutes, and the boat goes about twice per hour—often at the top and bottom of every hour. (With up to 10,000 people a day visiting the park, you might have to wait for a seat on this boat.) Unless the lake freezes (happens about every five years), the boat also runs in the off-season—though frequency drops to hourly, and it stops running earlier.

Sights in Plitvice

Plitvice is a refreshing playground of 16 terraced lakes, separated by natural travertine dams and connected by countless waterfalls. Over time, the water has simultaneously carved out, and, with the help of mineral deposits, built up this fluid landscape.

Plitvice became Croatia's first national park in 1949, and was a popular destination during the Yugoslav period. On Easter Sunday in 1991, the first shots of Croatia's war with Yugoslavia

were fired right here—in fact, the war's first casualty was a park policeman, Josip Jović. The Serbs held Plitvice until 1995, and most of the Croatians you'll meet here were evacuated and lived near the coast as refugees. During those five years, the park saw virtually no tourists, and was allowed to grow wild—allowing the ecosystem to recover from the impact of so many visitors. Today, the war is a fading memory, and the park is again a popular tourist destination, with nearly a million visitors each year (though relatively few are from the US).

▲▲▲Hiking the Lakes

Plitvice's system of trails and boardwalks makes it possible for visitors to get immersed in the park's beauty. (In some places, the path

leads literally right up the middle of a waterfall.) The official park map and signage recommend a variety of hikes, but there's no need to adhere strictly to these suggestions; invest in the big map and create your own route.

Most visitors stick to the main paths and choose between two basic plans: uphill or downhill. Each one has pros and cons. Park officials generally recommend hiking uphill, from the Lower Lakes to the Upper Lakes, which offers slightly better head-on views of the best scenery (this is the route described below). It also saves the most scenic stretch of lakes and falls—the Upper Lakes—for last. Hiking downhill, from Upper to Lower, is easier (though you'll have to hike steeply up out of the canyon at the end), and since most groups go the opposite way, you'll be passing—but not stuck behind—the crowds. Either way you go, walking briskly and with a few photo stops, figure on an hour for the Lower Lakes, an hour for the Upper Lakes, and a half-hour to connect them by boat.

Lower Lakes (Donja Jezera)—The lower half of Plitvice's lakes are accessible from Entrance 1. If you start here, the route marked *B* leads you along the boardwalks to Kozjak, the big lake that connects the Lower and the Upper Lakes (described later).

From the entrance, you'll descend a steep path with lots of **switchbacks,** as well as thrilling views over the canyon of the Lower Lakes. As you reach the lakes and begin to follow the boardwalks, you'll have great up-close views of the travertine formations that make up Plitvice's many waterfalls. Count the trout. If you're tempted to throw in a line, don't. Fishing is strictly forbidden. (Besides, they're happy.)

After you cross the path over the first lake, an optional 10-minute detour (to the right) takes you down to the **Big Waterfall** (Veliki Slap). It's the biggest

The Science of Plitvice

Virtually every visitor to Plitvice eventually asks the same question: How did it happen? A geologist once explained to me that Plitvice is a "perfect storm" of unique geological, climatic, and biological features found in very few places on Earth.

Plitvice's magic ingredient is calcium carbonate ($CaCO_3$), a mineral deposit from the limestone. Calcium is the same thing that makes "hard water" hard. If you have hard water, you may get calcium deposits on your cold-water faucet. But these deposits build up only at the faucet, not inside the pipes. That's because when hard water is motionless (as it usually is in the pipes), it holds on to the calcium. But at the point where the water is subjected to pressure and movement—as it pours out of the faucet— it releases the calcium.

Plitvice works the same way. As water flows over the park's limestone formations, it dissolves the rock, and the water becomes supersaturated with calcium carbonate. When the water is still, it holds on to the mineral—which helps create the beautiful deep-blue color of the pools. But when the water speeds up and spills over the edge of the lakes, it releases carbon dioxide gas. Without the support of the carbon dioxide, the water can't hold on to the calcium carbonate, so it gets deposited on the lake bed and at the edges of the lakes. Eventually, these deposits build up to form a rock called travertine (the same composition as the original limestone, but formed in a different way). The travertine coating becomes thicker, and barriers—and eventually

of Plitvice's waterfalls, where the Plitvica River plunges 250 feet over a cliff into the valley below. Depending on recent rainfall, the force of the Big Waterfall varies from a light mist to a thundering deluge.

If you're a hardy hiker, consider climbing the steep steps from the Big Waterfall up to a **viewpoint** at the top of the canyon (marked *Sightseeing Point/Vidikovac*; it's a strenuous 10-minute hike to the top). Take the stairs up, bearing to the right at the top (near the shelter) to find a nice viewpoint overlooking the Big Waterfall. From here, you can carry on along the road that actually goes up over the top of the Big Waterfall, offering more views over the park. (Go as far as you like, then return the way you came.) The giant mill perched at the top of the Big Waterfall was used to grind grains; this very poor part of Croatia was traditionally inhabited by farmers.

After seeing the Big Waterfall, backtrack up to the main trail and continue on the boardwalks. After you pass another bank of waterfalls, a smaller trail branches off (on the left) toward **Šupljara** ("Bottomless") **Cave**. You can actually climb through this slip-

dams and new waterfalls—are formed. The moss and grass serve as a natural foundation for the calcification. In other words, the stone hangs down like the foliage because the foliage guides the growth of the stone. Because of this ongoing process, Plitvice's landscape is always changing.

And why is the water so clear? For one thing, it comes directly from high-mountain runoff, giving it little opportunity to become polluted or muddy. And because the water calcifies everything it touches, it prevents the creation of mud—so the bottoms of the lakes are entirely stone. Also, a different mineral in the water, magnesium carbonate, both gives the water its special color (which, park rangers brag, changes with the direction of the sunshine) and makes it highly basic, preventing the growth of plant life (such as certain algae) that could cloud the water.

The park contains nearly 1,300 different species of plants. Wildlife found in the park include deer, wolves, wildcats, lynx, wild boar, voles, otters, 350 species of butterflies, 42 types of dragonflies, 21 species of bats, and more than 160 species of birds (including eagles, herons, owls, grouse, and storks). The lakes (and local menus) are full of trout, and you'll also see smaller, red-finned fish called *klen* ("chub" in English). Perhaps most importantly, Plitvice is home to about 40 or 50 brown bears—a species now extremely endangered in Europe. You'll see bears, the park's mascot, plastered all over the tourist literature (and one scary representative in the lobby of Hotel Jezero).

PLITVICE LAKES

pery cave all the way up to the trail overlooking the Lower Lakes (though it's not recommended). This unassuming cavern is a surprisingly big draw. In the 1960s, several German and Italian "Spaghetti Westerns" were filmed at Plitvice and in other parts of Croatia (which, to European eyes, has terrain similar to the American West). The most famous, *Der Schatz im Silbersee (The Treasure in Silver Lake)*, was filmed here at Plitvice, and the treasure was hidden in this cave. The movie—complete with *Deutsch*-speaking "Native Americans"—is still a favorite in Germany, and popular theme tours bring German tourists to movie locations here in Croatia. (If you drive the roads near Plitvice, keep an eye out for strange, Native American-sounding names such as Winnetou—fictional characters from these beloved stories of the Old West, by the German writer Karl May.)

After Šupljara Cave, you'll stick to the east side of the lakes, then cross over one more time to the west, where you'll cut through a comparatively dull forest. You'll emerge at a pit-stop-perfect clearing with WCs, picnic tables, a souvenir shop, and a self-service restaurant. Here you can catch the shuttle boat across Lake Kozjak to the bottom of the Upper Lakes (usually every 30 minutes).

Lake Kozjak (Jezero Kozjak)—The park's biggest lake, Kozjak, connects the Lower and Upper Lakes. The 20-minute boat ride between Plitvice's two halves offers a great chance for a breather. You can hike between the lakes along the west side of Kozjak, but the scenery's not nearly as good as in the rest of the park.

Upper Lakes (Gornja Jezera)—Focus on the lower half of the Upper Lakes, where nearly all the exotic beauty is. From the boat dock, signs for *B* direct you up to Gradinsko Lake through the most striking scenery in the whole park. Enjoy the stroll, taking your time...and lots of photos.

After Gradinsko Lake, you'll have two options:

1. Make your hike a loop by continuing around the far side of Gradinsko Lake and back to the P2 boat dock, where you can take the boat back over to the hotels (P1 stop).

2. Continue hiking up to the top of the Upper Lakes (following the icon for the shuttle bus); you'll get away from the crowds and feel like you've covered the park thoroughly. From here on up, the scenery is less stunning, and the waterfalls are fewer and farther between. At the top, you'll finish at shuttle bus stop ST4 (with food stalls and a WC), where the bus zips you back to the entrances and hotels.

Nice work!

Sleeping in Plitvice

At the Park

The most convenient way to sleep at Plitvice is to stay at the park's lodges, which are run by the same office (reservation tel. 053/751-015, fax 053/751-013, www.np-plitvicka-jezera.hr, info@np-plitvicka-jezera.hr; reception numbers for each hotel listed below). Warning: Because of high volume in peak season, the booking office often doesn't respond to emails. Instead, to make a reservation, use the park's website to book your room (look for the "Online booking" box). In a pinch, try calling the booking office or the hotel directly (they speak English), or emailing the park information office in Zagreb (np.zg.info@np-plitvicka-jezera.hr), which is more likely to respond in the busy summer months.

$$$ Hotel Jezero is big and modern, with all the comfort—and charm—of a Holiday Inn. It's well-located right at the park entrance and offers 200 rooms that feel newish, but generally have at least one thing that's broken. Rooms facing the park have big glass doors and balconies (July-Aug: Sb-€83/€76/€61, Db-€118/€108/€86; elevator, reception tel. 053/751-400).

$$ Hotel Plitvice, a better value than Jezero, offers 50 rooms and mod, wide-open public spaces on two floors with no

---

Sleep Code

(5 kn = about $1, €1 = about $1.40, country code: 385, area code: 053)

Unless otherwise noted, credit cards are accepted and breakfast is included, but the tourist tax (about 7 kn per person, per night) is not. While rates are listed in euros, you'll pay in kunas. Everyone listed here speaks English (or has a relative or neighbor who can help translate).

Rates: If I've listed three sets of rates, separated by slashes, the first is for peak season (July-Aug), the second is for shoulder season (May-June and Sept-Oct), and the third is for off-season (Nov-April). The dates for seasonal rates vary by hotel, and prices can change without notice; verify the hotel's current rates online or by email. For other updates, see www.ricksteves.com/update.

Price Ranges: To help you easily sort through these listings, I've divided the accommodations into three categories based on the price for a double room with bath during high season:

$$$ Higher Priced—Most rooms €100 or more.
$$ Moderately Priced—Most rooms between €50-100.
$ Lower Priced—Most rooms €50 or less.

---

elevators. For rooms, choose from economy (fine, older-feeling; Sb-€72/€65/€50, Db-€96/€82/€70), standard (just a teeny bit bigger; Sb-€77/€70/€55, Db-€106/€96/€74), or superior (bigger still, with a sitting area; Sb-€82/€75/€60, Db-€116/€106/€84, reception tel. 053/751-100).

$$ Hotel Bellevue is simple and bare-bones (no TVs or elevator). It has an older feel to it, but the price is right and the 80 rooms are perfectly acceptable (Sb-€55/€50/€40, Db-€74/€68/€54, reception tel. 053/751-700).

Sobe near the Park

While the park's lodges are the easiest choice for non-drivers, those with a car should consider sleeping at one of the **$-$$** *sobe* (rooms in private homes) near the park. You'll see *sobe* signs for miles on either side of the park. A few that have good reputations include **Villa Mukinja** (in the village of Mukinje just south of the park, tel. 01/652-1857, www.plitvice-lakes.com, info@plitvice-lakes.com), **House Tina** (just north of the park in the village of Grabovac, tel. 04/778-4197), and **Knežević Guest House** (also in the village of Mukinje, tel. 053/774-081, mobile 098-168-7576, www.knezevic.hr, guest_house@vodatel.net, daughter Kristina speaks English).

Eating in Plitvice

The park runs all of the restaurants at Plitvice. These places are handy, and the food is affordable and decent. If you're staying at the hotels, you have the option of paying for half-board with your room (lunch or dinner, €12/90 kn each). This option is designed for the restaurants inside hotels Jezero and Plitvice, but you can also use the voucher at other park eateries (you'll pay the difference if the bill is more). The half-board option is worth doing if you're here for dinner, but don't lock yourself in for lunch—you'll want more flexibility as you explore Plitvice (excellent picnic spots and decent food stands abound inside the park).

Hotel Jezero and **Hotel Plitvice** both have big restaurants with adequate food and friendly, professional service (half-board for dinner, described above, is a good deal; or order à la carte; both open daily until 23:00).

Lička Kuća, across the pedestrian overpass from Entrance 1, has a wonderfully dark and smoky atmosphere around a huge open-air wood-fired grill (pricey, daily 11:00-24:00, tel. 053/751-024).

Restaurant Poljana, behind Hotel Bellevue, has the same boring, park-lodge atmosphere in both of its sections: cheap, self-service cafeteria and sit-down restaurant with open wood-fired grill (same choices and prices as the better-atmosphere Lička Kuća, above; both parts open daily but closed in winter, tel. 053/751-092).

For **picnic** fixings, there's a small grocery store at Entrance 1 and another one with a larger selection across road D1 (use the pedestrian overpass). At the P3 boat dock, you can buy grilled meat and drinks. Friendly old ladies sell homemade goodies (such as strudel and hunks of cheese) throughout the park, including at Entrance 1.

Plitvice Connections

To reach the park, see "Getting to Plitvice," earlier in this chapter. Moving on from Plitvice is trickier. **Buses** pass by the park in each direction—northbound (to **Zagreb,** 2-2.5 hours) and southbound (to coastal destinations such as **Split,** 4-6 hours). The reception desk should have a printout of the schedule, or you can check at www.akz.hr.

There is no bus station at the park—just a low-profile *Plitvice*

Centar bus stop shelter. To reach it from the park, go out to the main road from either Hotel Jezero or Hotel Plitvice, then turn right; the bus stops are just after the pedestrian overpass. The one on the hotel side of the road is for buses headed for the coast (southbound); the stop on the opposite side is for Zagreb (northbound). Try to carefully confirm the bus schedule with the park or hotel staff, then head out to the bus stop and wave down the bus. (It's easy to confuse public buses with private tour buses, so don't panic if a bus doesn't stop for you—look for a bus with your final destination marked in the windshield.)

But here's the catch: If the bus is full, they won't stop at Plitvice to pick you up. This is most common on days when the buses are jammed with people headed to or from the coast. For example, on Fridays—when everyone is going from Zagreb to Split—you're unlikely to have any luck catching a southbound bus at Plitvice after 12:00, as they tend to be full. Similarly, on Sunday afternoons, northbound buses are often full. In general, don't plan on taking the last bus of the day.

While there's a chance you'll miss a bus and have to wait for the next one, in practice bus travel from Plitvice usually works fine...if you're patient.

Route Tips for Drivers

Plitvice's biggest disadvantage is that it's an hour away from the handy A1 expressway that connects northern Croatia to the Dalmatian Coast. You have three ways to access this expressway from Plitvice, depending on which direction you're heading.

Going North: If you're heading north (to Zagreb or Slovenia), get on the expressway at **Karlovac:** From Plitvice, drive about one hour north on D1 to the town of Karlovac, where you can access A1 northbound. Alternatively, you can take A1 southbound to A6, which leads west to Rijeka, Opatija, and Istria (though this route is more boring and only slightly faster than the route via Otočac, next).

Going to Central Croatia: If you're going to central destinations on the coast, such as Istria (Rovinj or Pula), get on the expressway at **Otočac.** From Plitvice, go south on D1, then go west on road #52 to the town of Otočac (about an hour through the mountains from Plitvice to Otočac). After Otočac, you can get on A1 (north to Zagreb, south to the Dalmatian Coast); or continue west and twist down the mountain road to the seaside town of Senj, on the main coastal road of the Kvarner Gulf. From Senj, it's about an hour north along the coast to Rijeka, then on to Istria.

During the recent war, the front line between the Croats and Serbs ran just east of **Otočac** (OH-toh-chawts), and bullet holes still mar the town's facades. (Watch for minefield warning signs

just east of Otočac, but don't let them make you too nervous: It's safe to drive here, but not necessarily safe to get out of your car and wander through the fields.) Today Otočac is putting itself back together, and it's a fine place to drop into a café for a coffee, or pick up some produce at the outdoor market. The Catholic church in the center of town, destroyed in the war but now rebuilt, displays its damaged church bells in a memorial out back. The crucifix nearby is made of old artillery shells. Just up the main street, beyond the big, grassy park, is the Orthodox church. Otočac used to be about one-third Serbian, but the Serbs were forced out during the war, and this church fell into disrepair. But, as Otočac and Croatia show signs of healing, about two dozen Serbs have returned to town and reopened their church (for more on the Serbian Orthodox Church, see page 876).

Going South: If you're heading south (to Split and the rest of Dalmatia) from Plitvice, catch the expressway at **Gornja Ploča.** Drive south from Plitvice on D1, through Korenica, Pećane, and Udbina, then follow signs for the A1 expressway (and *Lovinac*) via Kurjak to the Gornja Ploča on-ramp. Once on A1, you'll twist south through the giant Sveti Rok tunnel to Dalmatia.

BOSNIA-HERZEGOVINA
Bosna i Hercegovina

MOSTAR

The mid-1990s weren't kind to Bosnia-Herzegovina: War. Destruction. Genocide. But apart from the tragic way it separated from Yugoslavia, the country has long been—and remains—a remarkable place, with ruggedly beautiful terrain, a unique mix of cultures and faiths, kind and welcoming people who pride themselves on their hospitality, and some of the most captivating sightseeing in southeastern Europe. After all, little Bosnia-Herzegovina is still a country with three faiths, three languages, and two alphabets.

There's so much to see in this country. But for the scope of this book, I've selected just one destination: Mostar (MOH-star). Safe, stable, and within easy reach of the Dalmatian Coast, Mostar is worth considering as a detour—both geographical and cultural—from the Croatian mainstream. In Mostar's cobbled Old Town, you can poke into several mosques, tour old-fashioned Turkish-style houses, shop your way through a bazaar of souvenir stands, and hear the call to prayer echoing across the rooftops. For me, it's the single best side-trip from Dubrovnik.

Mostar encapsulates the best and the worst of Yugoslavia. During the Tito years, its residents enjoyed an idyllic mingling of cultures—Catholic Croats, Orthodox Serbs, and Muslim Bosniaks living together in harmony, their differences spanned by an Old Bridge that epitomized an optimistic vision of a Yugoslavia where ethnicity didn't matter. But then, as the country unraveled in the early 1990s, Mostar was gripped by a gory three-way war among those same peoples...and that famous bridge crumbled into the Neretva River.

Mostar is still rebuilding, and the bullet holes and destroyed

buildings are ugly reminders that the last time you saw this place, it was probably on the nightly news. Western visitors may also be struck by the immediacy of the Muslim culture that permeates Mostar. Here at a crossroads of civilizations, minarets share the horizon with church steeples. During the Ottomans' 400-year control of this region, many Slavic subjects converted to Islam (see sidebar on page 1074). And, although they retreated in the late 19th century, the Ottomans left behind a rich architectural, cultural, and religious legacy that has forever shaped Mostar. Five times each day, loudspeakers on minarets crackle to life, and the call to prayer warbles through the streets. In many parts of the city, you'd swear you were in Turkey.

If these images intrigue you, read on—Mostar has so much more to offer. Despite the scars of war, its setting is stunning: straddling the banks of the gorgeous Neretva River, with tributaries and waterfalls carving their way through the rocky landscape. The sightseeing—mosques, old Turkish-style houses, and that spine-tingling Old Bridge—is more engaging than much of what you'll find in Croatia or Slovenia. And it's cheap—hotels, food, and museums are less than half the prices you'll pay in Croatia.

While a visit to Mostar was depressing just a few years ago, the city gets more uplifting all the time: Mostarians are rebuilding at an impressive pace and working hard to make Mostar tourist-friendly. Before long, Mostar will reclaim its status as one of the premier destinations in the former Yugoslavia. Visit now, while it still has its rough-around-the-edges charm—you'll have seen it before it really took off.

Planning Your Time

Because of its cultural hairiness, a detour into Bosnia-Herzegovina feels like a real departure from a Dalmatian vacation. And yet, Mostar is easier to reach from Dubrovnik or Split than many popular Dalmatian islands (it's within a three-hour drive or bus ride from either city).

The vast majority of tourists in Mostar are day-trippers from the coast, which means the Old Town is packed at midday, but empty in the morning and evening. You can get a good feel for Mostar in just a few hours, but a full day gives you time to linger and ponder. My self-guided walk provides a framework for a visit of any duration.

You have three basic options for getting here: take a package

MOSTAR

Bosnia-Herzegovina Almanac

Official Name: Bosna i Hercegovina (abbreviated "BiH"); the i means "and"—Bosnia *and* Herzegovina (the country's two regions). For simplicity, I generally call it "Bosnia" in this book. "Bosna" (literally "running water") is the name of a major river here, while the tongue-twisting name "Herzegovina" (hert-seh-GOH-vee-nah) comes from the German word for "dukedom" (*Herzog* means "duke").

Snapshot History: Bosnia-Herzegovina's early history is similar to the rest of the region: Illyrians, Romans, and Slavs (oh, my!). In the late 15th century, Turkish rulers from the Ottoman Empire began a 400-year domination of the country. Many of the Ottomans' subjects converted to Islam, and their descendants remain Muslims today. Bosnia-Herzegovina became part of the Austro-Hungarian Empire in 1878, then Yugoslavia after World War I, until it declared independence in the spring of 1992. The bloody war that ensued came to an end in 1995. (For details, see the Understanding Yugoslavia chapter.)

Population: About 4.6 million. (There were about 100,000 identified casualties of the recent war, but many estimates of total casualties are double that number.) Someone who lives in Bosnia-Herzegovina, regardless of ethnicity, is called a "Bosnian." A southern Slav who practices Islam is called a "Bosniak." Today, about half of all Bosnians are Bosniaks (Muslims), a little more than a third are Orthodox Serbs, and about 15 percent are Catholic Croats.

Political Divisions: As a part of the Dayton Peace Accords that ended the conflict here in 1995, the nation is divided into three separate regions: the Federation of Bosnia and Herzegovina (FBiH, shared by Bosniaks and Croats, very roughly in the western and central parts of the country), the Republika Srpska (RS, dominated by Serbs, generally to the north and east), and the Brčko District (BD, a tiny corner of the country, with a mix of the ethnicities). For the most part, each of the three native ethnic groups stay in "their" part of this divided country, but tourists can move freely between them.

Language: Technically, Bosnia-Herzegovina has three languages—Bosnian, Serbian, and Croatian. But all three are mutually intelligible dialects of what was until recently considered a single language: Serbo-Croatian. Bosniaks and Croats use basically the same Roman alphabet we do, while Serbs generally use the Cyrillic alphabet. You'll see both alphabets on currency and other official documents. Many people also speak English.

Area: 19,741 square miles (about the size of West Virginia). In both size and population, Bosnia is comparable to Croatia.

Geography: Bosnia and Herzegovina are two distinct regions that share the same mountainous country. Bosnia constitutes the majority of the country (in the north, with a continental climate), while Herzegovina is the southern tip (about a fifth of the total area, with a hotter Mediterranean climate). The nation's capital, Sarajevo, has an estimated 310,000 people; Mostar is Herzegovina's biggest city (with approximately 130,000 people) and unofficial capital.

Red Tape: To enter Bosnia-Herzegovina, Americans and Canadians need only a passport (no visa required).

Economy: The country's economy has struggled since the war—the per capita GDP is just $6,600, and the official unemployment rate is around 43 percent.

Currency: The official currency is the Convertible Mark (Konvertibilna Marka, abbreviated KM locally, BAM internationally). The official exchange rate is $1 = about 1.40 KM. But merchants are usually willing to take euros, and often also Croatian kunas, roughly converting prices with a simple formula:

2 KM = €1 = 8 kn (= about $1.40)

Telephones: Bosnia-Herzegovina's country code is 387. If calling from another country, first dial the international access code (00 in Europe, 011 in the US), then 387, then the area code (minus the initial zero), then the number.

Flag: The flag of Bosnia-Herzegovina is a blue field with a yellow triangle along the top edge. The three points of the triangle represent Bosnia-Herzegovina's three peoples (Bosniaks, Croats, Serbs), and the triangle itself resembles the physical shape of the country. A row of white stars underscores the longest side of the triangle. These stars—and the yellow-and-blue color scheme—echo the flag of the European Union (a nod to the EU's efforts to bring peace to the region). While this compromise flag sounds like a nice idea, almost no Bosnian embraces it as his or her own; each group has its own unofficial but highly prized symbols and flags (such as the fleur-de-lis for the Bosniaks, the red-and-white checkerboard shield for the Croats, and the cross with the four C's for the Serbs)—many of which offend the other groups.

tour from Dalmatia; rent a car for a one-day side-trip into Mostar; or (my favorite) spend the night here en route between Croatian destinations. To work a Mostar overnight into your itinerary, consider a round-trip plan that takes you south along the coast, then back north via Bosnia-Herzegovina (for example, Split-Korčula-Dubrovnik-Mostar-back to Split).

Getting to Mostar

By Car: Coming with your own car gives you maximum flexibility, and a variety of interesting routes connect Mostar to the coast (for detailed route information, see "Route Tips for Drivers" on page 1093). If you do plan to drive here, let your car-rental company know in advance, to ensure you have the appropriate paperwork for crossing the border. If you're not up for driving yourself, consider splurging on a **driver** to bring you here (for drivers based in Dubrovnik, see page 852; for a Mostar-based driver, see page 1067). Drivers may suggest several detours en route—do your homework to know which ones interest you (for example, Međugorje isn't worth the extra time for most visitors), and don't hesitate to say you want to just max out on time in Mostar itself.

By Bus: Especially if you're spending the night in Mostar, bus connections with destinations on the Dalmatian Coast (especially Split and Dubrovnik) are workable—though getting clear and consistent schedule information can be a headache. For details, see "Mostar Connections," later.

By Package Tour: Taking a package excursion from a Dalmatian resort town seems like an efficient way to visit Mostar. Unfortunately, in reality it can be less rewarding than doing it on your own—count on lots and lots of hours on a crowded bus, listening to a lackluster, multilingual tour guide reading from a script, and relatively little time in the destinations themselves. But if you just want a quick one-day look at these places, an excursion could be a necessary evil. These all-day tours are sold from Split, Korčula, Dubrovnik, and other Croatian coastal destinations for about €50-60. The best tours focus almost entirely on Mostar (it still won't be enough time); avoid tours that include a pointless boat trip on the Neretva River or time in Međugorje. Those that add a quick visit to the worthwhile town of Počitelj are a better deal. Ask for details at any travel agency in Dalmatia.

Orientation to Mostar

(country code: 387; area code: 036)
Mostar—a mid-sized city with just over 100,000 people—is situated in a basin surrounded by mountains and split down the middle by the emerald-green Neretva River. Bosniaks live mostly on

the east side of the river (plus a strip on the west bank) and Croats in the modern sprawl to the west. The populations are beginning to mix again, albeit with tentative baby steps. Virtually all of the sights are in the Bosniak zone, but visitors move freely throughout the city, and most don't even notice the division. The cobbled, Turkish-feeling Old Town (called the "Stari Grad" or—borrowing a Turkish term—the "Stara Čaršija") surrounds the town's centerpiece, the Old Bridge.

The skyline is pierced by the minarets of various mosques, but none is as big as the two major Catholic (Croat) symbols in town, both erected since the recent war: the giant white cross on the hilltop (placed where Croat forces shelled the Bosniak side of the river, including the Old Bridge); and the enormous (almost 100-foot-tall) bell tower of the Franciscan Church of Sts. Peter and Paul. A monumental Orthodox cathedral once stood on the hillside across the river, but it was destroyed in the war when the Serbs were forced out. Funds are now being collected to rebuild it.

A note about safety: Mostar is as safe as any city its size, but it doesn't always *feel* safe. You'll see bombed-out buildings everywhere, even in the core of the city. Some are marked with *Warning! Dangerous Ruin* signs, but for safety's sake, never wander into any building that appears damaged or deserted. In terms of petty theft, the Old Town has as many pickpockets as any tourist zone in Europe: Watch your valuables, especially on the Old Bridge.

Tourist Information

The virtually worthless TI shares a building with a tour office, but it does give out a free town map and a few other brochures on Mostar and Herzegovina (sporadic hours, generally open June-Sept daily 9:00-17:00, maybe later in busy times, likely closed Oct-May, just a block from the Old Bridge on Rade Bitange street, tel. 036/580-275, www.bhtourism.ba).

Arrival in Mostar

By Bus or Train: The **main bus station** (where most buses arrive in town) sits next to the giant but mostly deserted **train station,** north of the Old Town on the east side of the river. At the bus station, you'll find ticket windows and a left-luggage counter (2 KM/bag) in the Autoprevoz lobby facing the bus stalls. You can check schedules and buy tickets in this office for most buses *except* the many connections operated by Globtour, whose office is nearby (exit Autoprevoz, turn left, and walk to the end of the bus-station area). Because these two companies don't cooperate, you have to check with both to get the complete schedule. To find your way to the town center, walk through the bus stalls and parking lot and turn left at the big road, which leads you to the Old Town area in

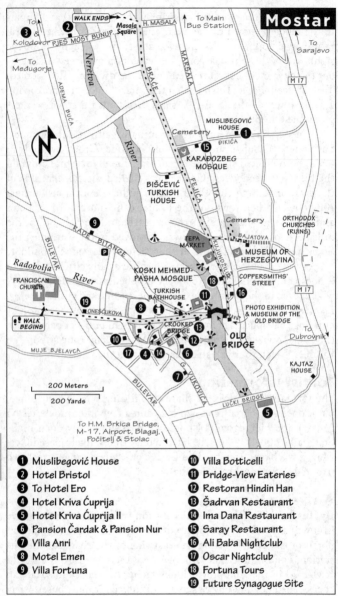

Mostar

WALK ENDS

Masala Square

To Main Bus Station

To Sarajevo

PJEŠ MOST BUNUP

Kolodvora

To Medugorje

MUSLIBEGOVIĆ HOUSE ❶

Cemetery

ĐIKIĆA ❶⑮

KARADOZBEG MOSQUE

BIŠĆEVIĆ TURKISH HOUSE

Cemetery

ORTHODOX CHURCHES (RUINS)

BAJATOVA

TEPA MARKET

MUSEUM OF HERZEGOVINA

RADE BITANGE ❾

P

Radobolja River

FRANCISCAN CHURCH

KOSKI MEHMED-PASHA MOSQUE

COPPERSMITHS' STREET

❶⑱

TURKISH BATHHOUSE

ONEŠĆUKOVA

❽⑲

PHOTO EXHIBITION & MUSEUM OF THE OLD BRIDGE

WALK BEGINS

CROOKED BRIDGE

OLD BRIDGE

To Dubrovnik

MUJE BJELAVCA

⑩⑰④⑭⑥⑬⑫

❼

KAJTAZ HOUSE

200 Meters
200 Yards

LUČKI BRIDGE ❺

To H.M. Brkica Bridge, M-17, Airport, Blagaj, Počitelj & Stolac

MOSTAR

❶ Muslibegović House
❷ Hotel Bristol
❸ To Hotel Ero
❹ Hotel Kriva Ćuprija
❺ Hotel Kriva Ćuprija II
❻ Pansion Čardak & Pansion Nur
❼ Villa Anri
❽ Motel Emen
❾ Villa Fortuna

⑩ Villa Botticelli
⑪ Bridge-View Eateries
⑫ Restoran Hindin Han
⑬ Šadrvan Restaurant
⑭ Ima Dana Restaurant
⑮ Saray Restaurant
⑯ Ali Baba Nightclub
⑰ Oscar Nightclub
⑱ Fortuna Tours
⑲ Future Synagogue Site

about 15 minutes. A taxi into town costs about 10 KM.

If you're arriving by bus it's possible (though unlikely) that you'll arrive at Mostar's makeshift secondary bus station, called "**Kolodvor,**" on the west/Croat side of town. From here, it's a dreary 15-minute walk into town: Turn right out of the bus station area, turn left down the busy Dubrovačka street, and head straight to the river to reach the main bus station. From the station, head south along the river into the Old Town.

For details on both stations—and how to get reliable schedule information—see "Mostar Connections," later.

By Car: For tips on driving to Mostar from the Dalmatian Coast, see page 947.

Helpful Hints

Local Cash: Need Convertible Marks? The most convenient ATM in town is to the left of Fortuna Tours' door, right at the top of Coppersmiths' Street (but on a short visit, you can generally skip a trip to the ATM, as most vendors here also accept Croatian kunas and euros).

Travel Agency: The handy **Fortuna Tours** travel agency, right in the heart of the Old Town (at the top of Coppersmiths' Street), sells all the tourist stuff, can book you a local guide, and answers basic questions (open long hours daily, Kujundžiluk 2, tel. 036/551-887, main office tel. 036/552-197, fax 036/551-888, www.fortuna.ba, fortuna_mostar1@bih.net.ba).

Local Guides: Hiring a guide is an excellent investment to help you understand Mostar. I've enjoyed working with **Alma Elezović,** a warm-hearted Bosniak who loves sharing her city and her wartime stories with visitors (€20/person, up to €70/group for 2-3-hour tour, includes entrance to a Turkish house and a mosque, tel. 036/550-514, mobile 061-467-699, aelezovic@gmail.com). If Alma is busy, various companies around town can arrange for a local guide at extremely reasonable prices (2-hour tour—€30/2 people, €40/4 people, includes entrance to mosque and/or Turkish house); try **Fortuna Tours,** listed previously.

If someone approaches you offering to be your guide, ask the price in advance (many charge ridiculously high rates). If they seem cagey or overpriced, decline politely. The official guides are better anyway.

Local Driver: **Ermin Elezović,** husband of local guide Alma (see above), is a gregarious, English-speaking driver who enjoys taking visitors on day trips from Mostar. You can also hire him for a transfer between Mostar and destinations anywhere in Croatia (prices for a van for up to 6 people: €100 for one-way transfer to Sarajevo, Split, or Dubrovnik, or €150 to add some extra time for sightseeing en route; €200 round-trip from Mostar to Sarajevo, Split, or Dubrovnik; tel. 036/550-514, mobile 061-908-597, elezovicermin@gmail.com).

Sights in Mostar

Mostar's major sights line up along a handy L-shaped axis. I've laced them together as an enjoyable orientation walk: From the Franciscan Church, you'll walk straight until you cross the Old Bridge. Then you'll turn left and walk basically straight (with a couple of detours) to the big square at the far end of town.

• *Begin at the...*

▲Franciscan Church of Sts. Peter and Paul

In a town of competing religious architectural exclamation points, this spire is the tallest. The church, which adjoins a working Franciscan monastery, was built in 1997, after the fighting subsided (the same year as the big cross on the hill). The tower, which looks at first glance like a minaret on steroids, is actually modeled after typical Croatian/Venetian campanile bell towers. Step inside to see how the vast and coarse concrete shell awaits completion. In the meantime, the cavernous interior is already hosting services. (Sunday Mass here is an inspiration.)

• *The church fronts the busy boulevard called...*

▲Bulevar

"The Boulevard" was once the modern main drag of Mostar. In the early 1990s, this city of Bosniaks, Croats, and Serbs began to fracture under the pressure of politicians' propaganda. In October 1991, Bosnia-Herzegovina—following Croatia's and Slovenia's example, but without the blessing of its large Serb minority—declared independence from Yugoslavia. Soon after, the Serb-dominated Yugoslav People's Army invaded. Mostar's Bosniaks and Croats joined forces to battle the Serbs and succeeded in claiming the city as their own and forcing out the Serb residents.

But even as they fended off the final, distant bombardments of

Serb forces, Mostar's Bosniaks (Muslims) and Croats (Catholics) began to squabble. Neighbors, friends, and even relatives took up arms against each other. As fighting raged between the Croat and Bosniak forces, this street became the front line—and virtually all of its buildings were destroyed. Then as now, the area to the east of here (toward the river) was held by Bosniaks, while the western part of town was Croat territory.

While many of the buildings along here have been rebuilt, some damage is still evident. Stroll a bit, imagining the hell of a split community at war. Mortar craters in the asphalt leave poignant scars. During those dark war years, the Croats on the hill above laid siege to the Bosniaks on the other side, cutting off electricity, blocking roads, and blaring Croatian rabble-rousing pop music and Tokyo Rose-type propaganda speeches from loudspeakers. Through '93 and '94, when the Bosniaks dared to go out, they sprinted past exposed places, for fear of being picked off by a sniper. Local Bosniaks explain, "Night was time to live" (in black clothes). When people were killed along this street, their corpses were sometimes left here for months, because it wasn't safe to retrieve the bodies. Tens of thousands fled. Scandinavian countries were the first to open their doors, but many Bosnians ended up elsewhere in Europe, the US, and Canada.

The stories are shocking, and it's difficult to see the war impartially. But looking back on this complicated war, I try not to broadly cast one side as the "aggressors" and another as the "victims." Bosniaks were victimized in Mostar, just as Croats were victimized during the siege of Dubrovnik (explained on page 860). And, as the remains of a destroyed Orthodox cathedral on the hillside above Mostar (not quite visible from here) attest, Serbs also took their turn as victims. Every conflict has many sides, and it's the civilians who often pay the highest toll—no matter their affiliation.

Cross the boulevard and head down Onešćukova street. A few steps down on the left, the vacant lot with the menorah-ornamented metal fence will someday be the **Mostar Synagogue**. While the town's Jewish population has dwindled to a handful of families since World War II, many Jews courageously served as aid workers and intermediaries when Croats and Bosniaks were killing each other. In recognition of their loving help, the community of Mostar gave them this land for a new synagogue.

• *Continue past the synagogue site, entering the Old Town and following the canyon of the...*

Radobolja River Valley

Cross the creek called Radobolja, which winds over waterfalls and several mills on its way to join the Neretva, and enter the city's

cobbled historic core (keeping the small river on your right). As you step upon the smooth, ankle-twisting river stones, you suddenly become immersed in the Turkish heritage of Mostar. Around you are several fine examples of Mostar's traditional heavy limestone-shingled roofs. From the arrival of the Ottomans all the way through the end of World War II, Mostar had fewer than 15,000 residents—this compact central zone was pretty much all there was to the city. It wasn't until the Tito years that it became industrialized and grew like crazy. As you explore, survey the atmospheric eateries clinging to the walls of the canyon—and choose one for a meal or drink later in the day (I've noted a couple under "Eating in Mostar," later).

Walk straight ahead until you reach a square viewpoint platform on your right. It's across from a charming little mosque and above the stream (you may have to squeeze between souvenir stands to get there). The mosque is one of 10 in town. Before the recent war, there were 36, and before World War II, there were even more (many of those damaged or destroyed in World War II were never repaired or replaced, since Tito's communist Yugoslavia discouraged religion). But the recent war inspired Muslims to finally rebuild. Each of the town's newly reconstructed mosques was financed by a Muslim nation or organization (this one was a gift from an international association for the protection of Islamic heritage). Some critics (read: Croats) allege that these foreign Muslim influences—which generally interpret their faith more strictly than the extremely progressive and laid-back Bosniaks—are threatening to flood the country with a rising tide of Islamic fundamentalism.

• *Spanning the river below the mosque is the...*

▲Crooked Bridge (Kriva Ćuprija)

This miniature Old Bridge was built nearly a decade before its more famous sibling, supposedly to practice for the real deal. Damaged—but not destroyed—during the war, the bridge was swept away several years later by floods. The bridge you see today is a recent reconstruction.

• *Continue deeper on the same street into the city center. After a few steps, a street to the left (worth a short detour) leads to the **TI**, then a copper-domed hammam (Turkish bathhouse), which was destroyed in World War II and only recently rebuilt. A happening nightlife and restaurant scene tumbles downhill toward the river from here, offering spectacular views of the Old Bridge.*

Back on the main drag, continue along the main shopping zone, past several market stalls, to the focal point of town, the...

▲▲▲Old Bridge (Stari Most)

One of the most evocative sights in the former Yugoslavia, this iconic bridge confidently spanned the Neretva River for more than

four centuries. Mostarians of all faiths love the bridge and speak of "him" as an old friend. Traditionally considered the point where East meets West, the Old Bridge is as symbolic as it is beautiful. Dramatically arched and flanked by two boxy towers, the bridge is stirring—even if you don't know its history.

Before the Old Bridge, the Neretva was spanned only by a rickety suspension bridge, guarded by *mostari* ("watchers of the bridge"), who gave the city its name. Commissioned in 1557 by the Ottoman Sultan Süleyman the Magnificent, and completed just nine years later, the Old Bridge was a technological marvel for its time..."the longest single-span stone arch on the planet." (In other words, it's the granddaddy of the Rialto Bridge in Venice.) Because of its graceful keystone design—and the fact that there are empty spaces inside the structure—it's much lighter than it appears. And yet, nearly 400 years after it was built, the bridge was still sturdy enough to support the weight of Nazi tanks that rolled in to occupy Mostar. Over the centuries, it became the symbol for the town and region—a metaphor in stone for the way the diverse faiths and cultures here were able to bridge the gaps that divided them.

All of that drastically changed in the early 1990s. Beginning in May of 1993, as the city became engulfed in war, the Old Bridge frequently got caught in the crossfire. Old tires were slung over its sides to absorb some of the impact from nearby artillery and shrapnel. In November of 1993, Croats began shelling the bridge from the top of the mountain (where the cross is now—you can just see its tip peeking over the hill from the top of the bridge). The bridge took several direct hits on November 8; then, on November 9, another shell caused the venerable Old Bridge to lurch, then tumble in pieces into the river. The mortar inside, which contained pink bauxite, turned the water red as it fell in. Locals said that their old friend was bleeding.

The decision to destroy the bridge was partly strategic—to cut off a Bosniak-controlled strip on the west bank from Bosniak forces on the east. (News footage from the time shows Bosniak soldiers scurrying back and forth over the bridge.) But there can be no doubt that, like the Yugoslav Army's siege of Dubrovnik, the attack was also partly symbolic: the destruction of a bridge representing the city's Muslim legacy.

After the war, city leaders decided to rebuild the Old Bridge. Chunks of the original bridge were dredged up from the river. But the limestone had been compromised by soaking in the water for so long, so it couldn't be used (you can still see these pieces of the old Old Bridge on the riverbank below). Having pledged to rebuild the bridge authentically, restorers cut new stone from the original quarry, and each block was hand-carved. Then they assembled the  stones with the same technology used by the Ottomans 450 years ago: Workers erected wooden scaffolding and fastened the blocks together with iron hooks cast in lead. The project cost over $13 million, funded largely by international donors and overseen by UNESCO.

It took longer to rebuild the bridge in the 21st century than it did to build it in the 16th century. But on July 23, 2004, the new Old Bridge was inaugurated with much fanfare and was immediately embraced by both the city and the world as a sign of reconciliation.

Since its restoration, another piece of bridge history has fully returned, as young men once again jump from the bridge 75 feet down into the Neretva (which remains icy cold even in summer). Done both for the sake of tradition and to impress girls, this custom was carried on even during the time when the destroyed bridge was temporarily replaced by a wooden one. Now the tower on the west side of the bridge houses the office of the local "Divers Club," a loosely run organization that carries on this long-standing ritual. On hot summer days, you'll see divers making a ruckus and collecting donations at the top of the bridge. They tease and tease, standing up on the railing and pretending they're about to jump... then getting down and asking for more money. (If he's wearing trunks rather than Speedos, he's not a diver—just a teaser.) Once they collect about €30, one of them will take the plunge.

Before moving on, see how many of the town's 10 mosques you can spot from the top of the bridge (I counted seven minarets).

• If you'd like to see one of the best **views** in town—looking up at the Old Bridge from the riverbank below—backtrack the way you came into the shopping zone, take your first left (at Šadran restaurant—a good place to try the powerful "Bosnian coffee"), then find the steps down to the river on the left.

When you're ready to continue, hike back up to the Old Bridge and cross to the other side. After the bridge on the right are two different exhibits worth a quick visit.

Bookstore near the Old Bridge

This excellent bookstore has a good, free photo exhibition of powerful images of war-torn Mostar, displayed inside a former mosque for soldiers who guarded the bridge. They play a montage of videos and photos of the bridge—before, during, and after the war—that's nearly as good as the similar film shown at the Museum of Herzegovina (described later). The shop also sells an impressively wide range of books about the former Yugoslavia and its troubled breakup.

Cost and Hours: Free, daily 7:00-24:00.

• *Just beyond the bookstore, tucked into the corner on the right, look for the stairs leading up to the...*

Museum of the Old Bridge (Muzej Stari Most)

Located within one of the Old Bridge's towers, this museum features a film and photos about the reconstruction of the bridge, archaeological findings, and a few other paltry exhibits about the history of the town and bridge, all in English. First climb up the stairs just after the bridge and buy your ticket, before hiking the rest of the way up to the top of the tower, where you can enjoy fine views through grubby windows. Then go around below to the archaeological exhibit. The museum offers more detail than most casual visitors need; consider just dropping into the smaller, free photo exhibition described previously, then moving along.

Cost and Hours: 5 KM, Tue-Sun 10:00-18:00, closed Mon, lots of stairs, Bajatova 4, mobile 061-707-307.

• *After the Old Bridge, the street swings left and leads you along...*

▲▲Coppersmiths' Street (Kujundžiluk)

This lively strip, with the flavor of a Turkish bazaar, offers some of the most colorful shopping this side of Istanbul. You'll see Mostar's characteristic bridge depicted in every possible way, along with blue-and-white "evil eyes" (believed in the Turkish culture to keep bad spirits at bay), old Yugoslav Army kitsch, and hammered-copper decorations (continuing the long tradition that gave the street its name). Partway up, the homes with the colorfully painted facades double as galleries for local artists. The artists live

The Muslims of Mostar

While Muslim immigrants have only recently become a fixture in many European cities, Bosnia-Herzegovina is one place where Muslims have continuously been an integral part of the cultural tapestry for centuries.

During the more than 400 years that Mostar was part of the Ottoman Empire, the Muslim Turks (unlike some Catholic despots at the time) did not forcibly convert their subjects. However, it was advantageous for non-Turks to adopt Islam (for lower taxes and better business opportunities), so many Slavs living here became Muslims. In fact, within 150 years of the start of Ottoman rule, half of the population of Bosnia-Herzegovina was Muslim.

The Ottomans became increasingly intolerant of other faiths as time went on, and uprisings by Catholics and Orthodox Christians eventually led to the end of Ottoman domination in the late 19th century. But even after the Ottomans left, many people in this region continued practicing Islam, as their families had been doing for centuries. These people constitute an ethnic group called "Bosniaks," and many of them are still practicing Muslims today (following the Sunni branch of the Muslim faith). Most Bosniaks are Slavs—of the same ethnic stock as Croats and Serbs—and look pretty much the same as their neighbors; however, some Bosniaks have ancestors who married into Turkish families, and they may have some Turkish features.

The actions of a small but attention-grabbing faction of Muslim extremists have burdened Islam with a bad reputation in the Western world. But judging Islam based on Osama bin Laden and al-Qaeda is a bit like judging Christianity based on the Oslo gunman and the Ku Klux Klan. Visiting Mostar is a unique opportunity to get a taste of a fully Muslim society, made a bit less intimidating because it wears a more-familiar European face.

Here's an admittedly basic and simplistic outline (written

and work upstairs, then sell their work right on this street. Pop into the *atelier d'art* ("Đul Emina") on the right to meet Sead Vladović and enjoy his impressive iconographic work (daily 9:00-20:00). This is the most touristy street in all of Bosnia-Herzegovina, so don't expect any bargains. Still, it's fun. As you stroll, check out the fine views of the Old Bridge.

• *Continue uphill. After the street levels out, about halfway along the street on the left-hand side, look for the entrance to the...*

▲Koski Mehmed-Pasha Mosque (Koski Mehmed-Paša Džamija)

Mostar's Bosniak community includes many practicing Muslims. Step into this courtyard for a look at one of Mostar's many mosques. This mosque, dating from the early 17th century, is

by a non-Muslim) designed to help travelers from the Christian West understand a very rich but often misunderstood culture worthy of respect:

Muslims, like Christians and Jews, are monotheistic. They call God "Allah." The most important person in the Islamic faith is Muhammad, Allah's most important prophet, who lived in the sixth and seventh centuries A.D.

The "five pillars" of Islam are the same among Muslims in Bosnia-Herzegovina, Turkey, Iraq, Indonesia, the US, and everywhere else. Followers of Islam should:

1. Say and believe, "There is only one God, and Muhammad is his prophet."

2. Pray five times a day, facing Mecca. Modern Muslims explain that it's important for this ritual to include several elements: washing, exercising, stretching, and thinking of God.

3. Give to the poor (one-fortieth of your wealth, if you are not in debt).

4. Fast during daylight hours through the month of Ramadan. Fasting is a great social equalizer and helps everyone to feel the hunger of the poor.

5. Visit Mecca. This is interpreted by some Muslims as a command to travel. Muhammad said, "Don't tell me how educated you are, tell me how much you've traveled."

Good advice for anyone, no matter what—or if—you call a higher power.

notable for its cliff-hanging riverside location, and because it's particularly accessible for tourists. But Mostar's other mosques share many of its characteristics—much of the following information applies to them as well.

Cost and Hours: 4 KM to enter mosque, 4 KM more to climb minaret, daily April-Oct 9:00-18:00, until 19:00 at busy times, Nov-March 9:00-15:00; if it seems crowded with tour groups, you can enter a very similar mosque later on this walk instead.

Touring the Mosque: The **fountain** *(šadrvan)* in the courtyard allows worshippers to wash before entering the mosque, as directed by Islamic law. This practice, called ablution, is both a literal and a spiritual cleansing in preparation for being in the presence of Allah. It's also refreshing in this hot climate, and the sound of running water helps worshippers concentrate.

The **minaret**—the slender needle jutting up next to the dome—is the Islamic equivalent of the Christian bell tower, used to call people to prayer. In the old days, the *muezzin* (prayer leader) would climb the tower five times a day and chant, "There is only one God, and Muhammad is his prophet." In modern times, loudspeakers are used instead. Climbing the minaret's 89 claustrophobic, spiral stairs is a memorable experience, rewarding you at the top with the best views over Mostar—and the Old Bridge—that you can get without wings (entrance to the right of mosque entry).

Because this mosque is accustomed to tourists, you don't need to take off your shoes to enter (but stay on the green carpet), women don't need to wear scarves, and it's fine to take photos inside. Near the front of the mosque, you may see some of the small, overlapping rugs that are below this covering (reserved for shoes-off worshippers).

Once **inside,** notice the traditional elements of the mosque. The niche *(mihrab)* across from the entry is oriented toward Mecca

(the holy city in today's Saudi Arabia)—the direction all Muslims face to pray. The small stairway *(mimber)* that seems to go nowhere is symbolic of the growth of Islam—Muhammad had to stand higher and higher to talk to his growing following. This serves as a kind of pulpit, where the cleric gives a speech, similar to a sermon or homily in Christian church services. No priest ever stands on the top stair, which is symbolically reserved for Muhammad.

The balcony just inside the door is traditionally where women worship. For the same reason I find it hard to concentrate on God at yoga classes, Muslim men decided prayer would go better without the enjoyable but problematic distraction of bent-over women between them and Mecca. These days, women can also pray on the main floor with the men, but they must avoid physical contact.

Muslims believe that capturing a living creature in a painting or a sculpture is inappropriate. (In fact, depictions of Allah and the prophet Muhammad are strictly forbidden.) Instead, mosques are filled with ornate patterns and Arabic calligraphy (of the name "Muhammad" and important prayers and sayings from the Quran). You'll also see some floral and plant designs, which you'd never see in a more conservative, Middle Eastern mosque.

Before leaving, ponder how progressive the majority of Mostar's Muslims are. Most of them drink alcohol, wear modern European clothing (you'll see virtually no women wearing head scarves or men with beards), and almost never visit a mosque to pray. In so many ways, these people don't fit our preconceived notions of Islam...and yet, they consider themselves Muslims all the same.

The mosque's **courtyard** is shared by several merchants. When you're done haggling, head to the terrace behind the mosque for the best view in town of the Old Bridge.

• *Just beyond this mosque, the traffic-free cobbles of the Old Town end. Take a right and leave the cutesy tourists' world. Walk up one block to the big...*

▲▲New Muslim Cemetery

In this cemetery, which was a park before the war, every tomb is dated 1993, 1994, or 1995. As the war raged, more exposed

cemeteries were unusable. But this tree-covered piece of land was relatively safe from Croat snipers. As the casualties mounted, locals buried their loved ones here under cover of darkness. Many of these people were soldiers, but some were civilians. Strict Muslim graves don't display images of

people, but here you'll see photos of war dead who were young, less-traditional members of the Muslim community. The fleur-de-lis shape of many of the tombstones is a patriotic symbol for the nation of Bosnia. The Arabic squiggles are the equivalent of an American having Latin on his or her tombstone—old-fashioned and formal.

• *Go up the wide stairs to the right of the cemetery (near the mosque). At #4 on the right, just before and across from the bombed-out tower, you'll find the...*

Museum of Herzegovina (Muzej Hercegovine)

This humble little museum is made worthwhile by a deeply moving **film**, rated ▲▲, that traces the history of the town through its Old Bridge: fun circa-1957 footage of the diving contests; harrowing scenes of the bridge being pummeled, and finally toppled, by artillery; and a stirring sequence showing the bridge's reconstruction and grand reopening on that day in 2004—with high-fives, Beethoven's *Ode to Joy*, fireworks, and more divers.

The museum itself displays fragments of this region's rich history, including historic photos and several items from its Ottoman period. There are sparse English descriptions, but without a tour guide the exhibits are a bit difficult to appreciate. Topics include the Turkish period, Herzegovina under the Austro-Hungarian

MOSTAR

Empire, village life, and local archaeology. One small room commemorates the house's former owner, Dzemal Bijedić, who was Tito's second-in-command during the Yugoslav period until he was killed in a mysterious plane crash in 1977. (If Bijedić had lived, many wonder whether he might have succeeded Tito...and succeeded in keeping Yugoslavia together.)

Cost and Hours: 5-KM museum entry includes 12-minute film, no narration—works in any language, ask about "film?" as you enter; Mon-Fri 9:00-14:00, Sat 10:00-12:00, closed Sun; Bajatova 4—walking up these stairs, it's the second door that's marked for the museum, under the overhanging balcony, www.muzejherce govine.com.

• *Backtrack to where you left the Old Town. Notice the* **Tepa Market***, with locals buying produce, in the area just beyond the pedestrian zone. Now walk (with the produce market on your left) along the lively street called* **Braće Fejića.** *(There's no sign, but the street is level and busy with cafés.) You're in the "new town," where locals sit out in front of boisterous cafés sipping coffee while listening to the thumping beat of distinctly Eastern-sounding music.*

Stroll down this street for a few blocks. At the palm trees (about 50 yards before the minaret—look for sign to Ottoman House*), you can side-trip a block to the left to reach...*

▲Bišćević Turkish House (Bišćevića Ćošak)

Mostar has three traditional Turkish-style homes that are open for tourists to visit. The Bišćević House is the oldest, most interesting, and most convenient for a quick visit, but two others are described at the end of this listing. Dating from 1635, the Bišćević House is typical of old houses in Mostar, which mix Oriental style with Mediterranean features.

Cost and Hours: 4 KM, daily March-Oct 8:00-19:00 or 20:00, Nov-Feb 9:00-15:00—but can close unexpectedly, Bišćevića 13.

Touring the House: First you'll step through the outer (or animals') garden, then into the inner (or family's) garden. This inner zone is surrounded by a high wall—protection from the sun's rays, from thieves...and from prying eyes, allowing women to take off the veil they were required to wear in public. Enjoy the geometrical patters of the smooth river stones in the floor (for example, the five-sided star), and keep an eye out for the house's pet turtles. It's no coincidence that the traditional fountain *(šadrvan)* resembles those at the entrance to a mosque—a reminder of the importance of running water in Muslim culture. The little white building is a kitchen—cleverly located apart from the house so that the heat and smells of cooking didn't permeate the upstairs living area.

Buy your ticket and take off your shoes before you climb up the wooden staircase. Imagine how a stairway like this one could be pulled up for extra protection in case of danger (notice that this one has a "trap door" to cover it). The cool, shady, and airy living room is open to the east—from where the wind rarely blows. The overhanging roof also prevented the hot sun from reaching this area. The loom in the corner was the women's workplace—the carpets you're standing on would have been woven there. The big chests against the wall were used to bring the dowry when the homeowner took a new wife. Study the fine wood carving and the heavy stonework of the roof.

Continue back into the main gathering room *(divanhan)*. This space—whose name comes from the word "talk"—is designed in a circle so people could face each other, cross-legged, for a good conversation while they enjoyed a dramatic view overlooking the Neretva. The room comes with a box of traditional costumes—great for photo fun. Put on a pair of baggy pants and a fez and really lounge.

Other Turkish Houses: If you're intrigued by this house, consider dropping by Mostar's two other Turkish houses. The **Muslibegović House** (Muslibegovića Kuća) feels newer because it dates from 1871, just a few years before the Ottomans left town. This homey house—which also rents out rooms to visitors (see "Sleeping in Mostar," later)—has many of the same features as the Bišćević House. If they're not too busy, Sanela or Gabriela can give you an English tour (4 KM, mid-April-mid-Oct daily 10:00-18:00, closed to visitors off-season, just two blocks uphill from the Karađozbeg Mosque at Osman Đikića 41, tel. 036/551-379, www.muslibegovichouse.com). To find it, go up the street between the Karađozbeg Mosque and the cemetery, cross the busy street, and continue a long block uphill on the alley. The wall with the slate roof on the left marks the house.

The **Kajtaz House** (Kajtazova Kuća), hiding up a very residential-feeling alley a few blocks from the Old Bridge, feels lived-in because it still is (in the opposite direction from most of the other sights, at Gaše Ilića 21).

• *Go back to the main café street and continue to the...*

▲Karađozbeg Mosque (Karađozbegova Džamija)

The city's main mosque was completed in 1557, the same year work began on the Old Bridge. This mosque, which welcomes visitors,

feels less touristy than the one back in the Old Town. Before entering the gate into the complex, look for the picture showing the recent war damage sustained by this mosque. You'll see that this mosque has most of the same elements as the Koski Mehmed-Pasha Mosque (described earlier). But here, some of the decorations are original. Across the street is another cemetery with tombstones from that terrible year, 1993.

Cost and Hours: 4 KM to enter mosque, 4 KM more to climb minaret, daily May-Sept 9:00-19:30, Oct-April 10:00-15:00. Inside the mosque, either stay on the green carpet or remove your shoes.

• *Now continue into modern, urban Mostar along the street in front of the Karađozbeg Mosque. This grimy, mostly traffic-free street is called...*

▲Braće Fejića

Walking along the modern town's main café strip, enjoy the opportunity to observe this workaday Bosniak town. You'll see the humble offices of the ragtag B&H Airlines; a state-run gambling office taxing its less-educated people with a state lottery; and lots of cafés that serve drinks but no food. People generally eat at home before going out to nurse an affordable drink. (Café ABC has good cakes and ice cream; the upstairs is a popular pizza hangout for students and families.)

At the small mosque on the left, obituary announcements are tacked to the outer wall, listing the bios and funeral times for locals who have recently died. A fig tree grows out of the mosque's minaret, just an accident of nature illustrating how that plant can thrive with almost no soil (somehow, the Bosniaks can relate). Walking farther, look up to see a few ruins—still ugly nearly two decades after the war. There's a messy confusion about who owns what in Mostar. Surviving companies have no money. Yugo Bank, which held the mortgages, is defunct. No one will invest until clear ownership is established. Until then, the people of Mostar sip their coffee and rip up their dance clubs in the shadow of these jagged reminders of the warfare that wracked this town not so long ago.

Near the end of the pedestrian zone, through the parking lot on the right, look for the building with communist-era reliefs of 12th-century Bogomil tomb decor—remembering the indigenous culture before the arrival of the Ottomans.

When you finally hit the big street (with car traffic), head left one block to the big **Masala Square** (literally, "Place for Prayer").

The Dawn of War in Mostar

Mostar was always one of the most stubbornly independent parts of the former Yugoslavia. It had one of the highest rates of mixed-ethnicity marriages in all of Bosnia-Herzegovina. In the early 1990s, Mostar's demographics were proportioned more-or-less evenly—about 35 percent of its residents were Bosniaks, 34 percent Croats, and 19 percent Serbs. But this delicate balance was shattered in a few brutal months of warfare.

On April 1, 1992, Bosnia-Herzegovina—led by Muslim president Alija Izetbegović—declared independence from Yugoslavia. Very quickly, the Serb-dominated Yugoslav People's Army moved to stake their claim on territory throughout the country, including the important city of Mostar. That spring, Serb forces occupied the east end of town (including the Ottoman Old Town), forcing many residents—predominantly Croats and Bosniaks—to hole up in the western part of the city. Meanwhile, Serbian and Croatian leaders were secretly meeting to divvy up Bosnian territory, and that summer, they agreed that Croatia would claim Mostar. Several weeks later, when the joint Croat-Bosniak forces crossed back over the river, the Serb forces mysteriously withdrew from the city (having been directed to capitulate), and retreated to the mountaintops above town, where they watched...and waited. The Croats and Bosniaks, believing they'd achieved peace, began putting their city back together. During this time, some factions also rounded up, tortured, and killed Serbs still living in Mostar. Many Bosniaks moved back to their homes on the east side of town, but, rather oddly, many of the Croats who had previously resided there instead stayed in the west—in many cases, moving into apartments vacated by Serbs.

On May 9, 1993—the Yugoslav holiday of "Victory over Fascism Day"—Mostarians were rocked awake by the terrifying sounds of artillery shells. Croat military forces swept through the city, forcibly moving remaining Bosniaks from the west part of town into the east. Throughout that summer, Bosniak men were captured and sent to concentration camps, while the Croats virtually sealed off the east side of town—creating a giant ghetto with no way in or out. The long and ugly siege of Mostar had begun.

Historically this was where pilgrims gathered before setting off for Mecca on their hajj. This is a great scene on balmy evenings, when it's a rendezvous point for the community. The two busts near the fountain provide perfect goal posts for budding soccer stars.

• For a finale, you can continue one block more out onto the bridge to survey the town you just explored. From here, you can backtrack to linger in the places you found most inviting. Or you can venture into...

Western (Croat) Mostar

Most tourists stay on the Bosniak side of town. For a complete look at this divided city, consider a stroll to the west. While there are few attractions here, and it's not particularly pretty—it fees like any dreary mid-size Balkan city—it provides an interesting contrast to the Muslim side of town.

Crossing the river and Bulevar, the scarred husks of destroyed buildings begin to fade away, and within a block you're immersed in concrete apartment buildings—making it clear that, when the city became divided, the Muslims holed up in the original Ottoman Old Town, while the Croats claimed the modern Tito-era sprawl. The relative lack of war damage (aside from a few stray bullet holes) emphasizes that it was the Croats laying siege to the Muslims of Mostar. Looking at a map, you'll notice that many streets on this side of town are named for Croatian cities (Dubrovačka, Splitska, Vukovarska) or historical figures (Kralja Tomislava, for the duke who first united the Croats in the 10th century). This side of town also has several remnants of Habsburg rule (including genteel buildings that look like they'd be at home in Vienna, and fine boulevards lined with plane trees). A few of these streets converge at the big roundabout called the Rondo, where *Centar* signs pointedly direct traffic *away* from the (Bosniak) Old Town. Also notice the many road signs pointing toward Široki Brijeg—a Bosnian Croat stronghold. A block toward the Old Town from the Rondo, notice the big cemetery with Muslim tombstones from the early 1990s. These are the graves of those killed during the first round of fighting, when the Croats and Bosniaks teamed up to fight the Serbs. You'll also notice some glitzy new shopping centers and more pizza and pasta restaurants than *ćevapčići* joints (in other words, even the food over here is more Croatian than Bosnian).

Near Mostar

While Mostar has its share of attractions, there's also plenty to see within a short drive. Ideally try to splice one or two of these stops into your trip between Mostar and the coast (see my "Route Tips for Drivers," later, for tips on linking them up).

Blagaj—Blagaj (BLAH-gai, rhymes with "pie") was the historical capital of this region until the arrival of the Ottomans. Deep in Blagaj is an impressive cliff face with a scenic house marking the source of the Buna River. The building, called the Tekija, is actually a former monastery for Turkish dervishes (an order that emphasizes poverty and humility, famous for the way they whirl in a worshipful trance); inside is a modest museum with the graves of two important dervishes. Blagaj is easiest to see on the way to or from Mostar—just turn off from the main road and follow the Buna River to the big parking lot.

▲**Počitelj**—Počitelj (POTCH-ee-tell) is an artists' colony filled with a compelling mix of Christian and Muslim architecture. Ideally situated right along the main Mostar-to-Croatia road, it's one of the most popular rest stops for passing tour buses, so it's hardly undiscovered. But it's still worth a stop for its dramatically vertical townscape and beautifully restored Ottoman architecture. Hike up steeply through town to the mosque (free entry—women must cover their heads), then continue up to the fortress for panoramic views over the countryside to appreciate Počitelj's strategic position.

Stolac—Unless you're fascinated by archaeology, Stolac (STOH-lats) isn't worth a long detour—but since it's on the way between

Mostar and Dubrovnik (on the back-roads route), consider stopping off. On the outskirts of Stolac (on the road toward Mostar), you'll find a necropolis with a bonanza of giant tombstones called *stećak*s, engraved with evocative reliefs. These date from the 13th through the 15th centuries, when the Bogomils ruled here. Soon after these were erected, the Ottomans arrived, and conversions to Islam commenced. Archaeological treasures aside, today's Stolac is a workaday village that was particularly hard-hit during the recent war, when it was taken over by Croat forces and its majority Muslim residents forced to flee to Mostar. The mosque and surrounding area were completely leveled; it's now rebuilt, and the town's population is divided evenly—albeit tensely—between Croats and Bosniaks.

Međugorje—Međugorje is an unassuming little village "between the hills" (as its name implies) that ranks with Lourdes, Fátima, and Santiago de Compostela as one of the most important pilgrimage sites in all of Christendom. To the cynical non-Catholic, it's just a strip of crassly commercial hotels, restaurants, and rosary shops leading up to a dull church, all tied together by a silly legend about a hilltop apparition. But if you look into the tear-filled eyes

MOSTAR

Međugorje Mary

What compels millions to flock to this little village in the middle of nowhere? The official story goes like this: On the evening of June 24, 1981, two young women were gathering their sheep on the hillside above Mostar. They came across a woman carrying a baby who told them to come near. Terrified, they fled, only to realize later that this might have been a vision of the Virgin Mary. They returned the next night with some friends and saw the apparition again.

In the nearly three decades since, six different locals  (including the two original seers) claim to have seen the vision, and some of them even say they see it regularly to this day. They also say that Mary has given them 10 secrets—predictions of future events that will portend Judgment Day. Written on a piece of parchment, these are kept safely at the home of one of the seers. They have said they will reveal each of these secrets, 10 days before the event occurs, to the local parish priest, who will then alert the world.

But official representatives of the Vatican are not among the believers. According to Catholic law, such visions must be "certified" by the local bishop—and the one around here didn't buy it. One cause for suspicion is that the six seers, before witnessing the visions, were sometimes known to be troublemakers. (In fact, they later admitted that they went up the hill that fateful night not to chase wayward sheep, but to sneak a smoke.) One investigator even suggested that they invented the story as a prank, only to watch it snowball out of control once they told it to the local priest. After decades of reluctance, in mid-2010 the Vatican formed a commission to determine whether to officially endorse this "miracle." (For now, priests are allowed to accompany pilgrimages to Međugorje, but not to *lead* them.)

Whether or not the story is true is, to a certain extent, beside the point—that people *believe* it's true is why they come here.

of the pilgrims who've journeyed here, it's clear that to some, this place offers much more than what you see on the surface. For true believers, Međugorje represents a once-in-a-lifetime opportunity to tread on sacred soil: a place where, over the last three decades, the Virgin Mary has appeared to six local people. More than 30 million pilgrims have visited Međugorje since the sightings began—summer and winter, war (which didn't touch Međugorje) and peace, rain and shine.

The center of pilgrim activity is **St. James' Church** (Crkva Sv. Jakova), which was built before the apparitions. As you face the church, you'll see two trails leading up to the hills. Behind and to the left of the church is **Apparition Hill** (at Podbrdo), where the sightings occurred (a 1-mile hike, topped by a statue of Mary). Directly behind the church is the **Great Hill** (Križevac, or "Cross Mountain"), where a giant hilltop cross, which predates the visions,

has become a secondary site of pilgrimage (1.5-mile hike). Pilgrims often do one or both of these hikes barefoot, as a sign of penitence. Beyond the church is a path lined with scenes from the life of Jesus. Farther along, on the right, is a giant statue of the **Resurrected Savior** (Uskrsli Spasitelj), also known as the "Weeping Knee." While the elongated, expressionistic sculpture—exemplifying Christ's suffering—is striking in itself, the eternal dampness of its right knee attracts the most attention from pilgrims. Miraculously (or not), it's always wet—go ahead and touch the spot that's been highly polished by worshippers and skeptics alike.

Nightlife in Mostar

Be sure to enjoy the local scene after dark in Mostar. Though the town is touristy, it's also a real urban center with a young popula-

tion riding a wave of raging hormones. The meat market in the courtyard next to the old Turkish bathhouse near the TI is fun to observe. The Old Bridge is a popular meeting place for locals as well as tourists (and pickpockets).

A stroll from the Old Bridge down the café-lined Braće Fejića boulevard, to the modern Masala Square at the far end of town (described earlier), gives a great peek at Mostarians socializing away from the tourists.

Ali Baba is an actual cave featuring a fun, atmospheric, and youthful party

MOSTAR

scene. Order a cocktail or try a Turkish-style hubbly-bubbly (*šiša*, SHEE-shah). Ask to have one of these big water pipes fired up for you and choose your flavored tobacco: apple, cappuccino, banana, or lemon (20 KM per pipe per group, 8-KM cocktails, open late daily; look for low-profile, cave-like entrance along Coppersmiths' Street, just down from the Old Bridge—watch for "Open Sesame" sign tucked down a rocky alley).

Oscar Nightclub is a caravanserai for lounge lizards—an exotic world mixing babbling streams, terraces, lounge chairs, and big sofas where young and old enjoy 5-10-KM cocktails and *šiša* (10 KM will last you about 40 minutes; June-Aug open "non-stop," closed Sept-May, up from the Old Bridge on Onešćukova street, near the Crooked Bridge at the end of the pedestrian zone).

Sleeping in Mostar

The Ero and Bristol are big, full-service hotels, but a bit farther from the charming Old Town. The rest are small, friendly, accessible, affordable guest houses in or very near the Old Town. Many hotels and pensions in town promise "parking," but it's often street parking out front—private lots are rare. Mostar's Old Town can be very noisy on weekends, with nightclubs and outdoor restaurants rollicking into the wee hours. If you're a light sleeper, consider Villa Fortuna and the Muslibegović House, which are quieter than the norm.

$$$ The Muslibegović House, a Bosnian national monument that also invites tourists in to visit during the day, is in an actual

Turkish home dating from 1871. The complex houses 10 homey rooms and two suites, all of which combine classic Turkish style (elegant and comfortable old beds, creaky wooden floors with colorful carpets, lounging sofas; guest remove shoes at the outer door) with modern comforts (air-con, free Wi-Fi, flatscreen TVs). Situated on a quiet residential lane just above the bustle of Mostar's main pedestrian drag and Old Town zone, this is a memorable experience (Sb-€55, Db-€90/€75, "pasha suite"-€105, includes a tour of the house, closed Nov-Feb, 2 blocks uphill from the Karađozbeg Mosque at Osman Đikića 41, tel. 036/551-379, www.muslibegovichouse.com, muslibegovichouse@gmail .com; Taž, Sanela, and Gabriela).

$$$ Hotel Bristol is the only business-class place near central Mostar. Its 47 rooms don't quite live up to their four stars, but

Sleep Code

($1 = about 1.40 KM, €1 = about $1.40, country code: 387, area code: 036)

S = Single, **D** = Double/Twin, **T** = Triple, **Q** = Quad, **b** = bathroom. Unless otherwise noted, credit cards are accepted, and breakfast is included. Everyone listed here speaks English.

Rates: If I list two rates separated by a slash, the first is for peak season (June-Sept), and the second is for off-season (Oct-May).

Price Ranges: To help you easily sort through these listings, I've divided the accommodations into three categories based on the price for a double room with bath during peak season:

$$$ Higher Priced—Most rooms €70 or more.
 $$ Moderately Priced—Most rooms between €40-70.
  $ Lower Priced—Most rooms €40 or less.

Prices can change without notice; verify the hotel's current rates online or by email. For other updates, see www.ricksteves.com/update.

the location is handy, overlooking the river a 10-minute walk from the heart of the Old Town (Sb-€42, Db-€76, apartment-€90, extra bed-€16, air-con, elevator, free Internet access and Wi-Fi, some street noise, limited parking, Mostarskog Bataljona, tel. 036/500-100, fax 036/500-502, www.bristol.ba, info@bristol.ba).

$$$ Hotel Ero, a 20-minute walk north of the Old Town, is a good big-hotel option, with 91 fine rooms and a professional staff. This was one of the only big buildings in the center not damaged during the war, since it hosted journalists and members of the international community and was therefore off-limits (Sb-€51, Db-€86, suite-€110, air-con, elevator, free Wi-Fi, some traffic noise, ulica Dr. Ante Starčevića, tel. 036/386-777, fax 036/386-700, www.ero.ba, hotel.ero@tel.net.ba).

$$ Hotel Kriva Ćuprija ("Crooked Bridge"), by the bridge of the same name, is tucked between waterfalls in a picturesque valley a few steps from the Old Bridge. It's an appealing oasis with five rooms, four apartments, and a restaurant with atmospheric outdoor seating (Sb-€39, Db-€65, apartment-€75, extra bed-€18, 10 percent discount on rooms and food with this book, can be noisy, air-con, free Wi-Fi, free parking, call to reconfirm if arriving after 19:00, enter at Onešćukova 23 or Kriva Ćuprija 2, tel. 036/550-953, mobile 061-135-286, www.motel-mostar.ba, info@motel-mostar.ba, Sami). Their second location—creatively named **Hotel Kriva Ćuprija II**—offers 10 modern rooms with a business-class vibe in a Habsburg-style building overlooking the river from a drab urban street, about 200 yards to the south (same prices, discount, amenities, and contact information as main hotel; some traffic noise, Maršala Tita 186, next to the Lučki Bridge, reception tel. 036/554-125).

$$ Pansion Čardak, run by sweet Suzana and Nedžad Kasumović, has four rooms sharing a kitchen and Internet nook in a stone house set just back from the bustling Crooked Bridge area (Db-€50/€45, Tb-€75/€60, Qb-€90/€75, cash only, no breakfast, air-con, free Wi-Fi, free parking, Jusovina 3, tel. 036/578-249, mobile 061-385-988, www.pansion-cardak.com, info@pansion-cardak.com).

$$ Pansion Nur, run by Feđa, a relative of Suzana and Nedžad (above), also has four rooms and a shared kitchen (twin Db-€40/€35, Db-€50/€40, Tb-€70/€60, suite-€80/€70, cash only, no breakfast, air-con, free Wi-Fi, free parking, Jusovina 8b, tel. 036/580-296, mobile 062-160-872, www.pansion-nur.com, info@pansion-nur.com).

$$ Villa Anri, a bit more hotelesque than other pensions in Mostar, sits a block farther from the bustle near the Bulevar. The stony facade hides seven rooms (five with balconies) combining old Herzegovinian style and bright colors. The big draw is the rooftop terrace, shared by two rooms, which enjoys grand views over the Old Bridge area (Db-€60/€50, Db with grand terrace-€70/€60, Tb-€85/€70, Tb with grand terrace-€100/€80, Qb-€110/€90, cash only, air-con, free Wi-Fi, free parking, Braće Đukića 4, tel. 036/578-477, www.villa-anri-mostar.ba, villa.anri@gmail.com).

$$ Motel Emen has six modern, sleek rooms overlooking a busy café street a few cobbled blocks from the Old Bridge (Sb-€50, Db-€70, bigger Db with balcony-€80, all rooms €10 less Oct-May, air-con, free Internet access and Wi-Fi, free parking, Onešćukova 32, tel. 036/581-120, www.motel-emen.com, info@motel-emen.com).

$ Villa Fortuna is an exceptional value, located in a nondescript urban neighborhood a few minutes' walk farther away from the Old Bridge. Owners Nela and Mili Bijavica rent eight tasteful, modern rooms above the main office of Fortuna Tours. The courtyard in front offers free, secure parking, and in back there's a pleasant garden with a traditional Herzegovinian garden cottage (Sb-€30, Db-€40, apartment-€80, these prices if you book direct, breakfast-€5, non-smoking, air-con, free Wi-Fi, Rade Bitange 34, tel. & fax 036/580-625, mobile 063-315-017, www.villafortuna.ba, villa_fortuna@bih.net.ba). Fortuna Tours can also put you in touch with locals renting rooms and apartments.

$ Villa Botticelli, overlooking a charming waterfall garden just up the valley from the Crooked Bridge, has five colorful rooms (Sb-€30, Db-€40, Tb-€60, breakfast-€3, air-con, free Wi-Fi,

Muje Bjelavca 6, enter around back along the alley, mobile 063-809-658, www.villabotticelli.com, botticelli@bih.net.ba, Snježana and Zoran).

Eating in Mostar

Most of Mostar's tourist-friendly restaurants are conveniently concentrated in the Old Town. If you walk anywhere that's cobbled, you'll stumble onto dozens of tempting restaurants charging the same reasonable prices and serving rustic, traditional Bosnian food. In my experience, the menus at most places are virtually identical—though quality and ambience can vary greatly. As eateries tend to come and go quickly here, and little distinguishes these places anyway, don't be too focused on a particular spot. Grilled meats are especially popular—read the "Balkan Flavors" sidebar before you dine. Another specialty is *dolma*—a pepper stuffed with minced meat, vegetables, and rice. On menus, look for the word *domaća*—"homemade." Sarajevska beer is on tap at most places.

On the Embankment, with Old Bridge Views

For the best atmosphere, find your way into the several levels of restaurants that clamber up the riverbank and offer perfect views of the Old Bridge. In terms of the setting, this is the most memorable place to dine in Mostar—but be warned that the quality of the food along here is uniformly low, and prices are relatively high (figure 8-15 KM for a meal). If you want a good perch, it's fun and smart to drop by earlier in the day and personally reserve the table of your choice.

To reach two of the most scenic eateries, go over the Old Bridge to the west side of the river, and bear right on the cobbles until you get to the old Turkish bathhouse (with the copper domes on the roof). To the right of the bathhouse is the entrance to a lively courtyard surrounded with cafés. Continuing toward the river from the courtyard, stairs lead down to several riverfront terraces belonging to two different restaurants: **Teatar,** a bit closer to the bridge, has unobstructed views and lower-quality food, while **Babilon** has slightly better (but still not great) food and nearly as good views. Poke around to find your favorite bridge panorama before settling in for a drink or a meal.

Two other places (including a pizzeria) are a bit closer to the bridge—to reach these, look for the alley on the left just before the bridge tower.

Near the Old Bridge

While they lack the Old Bridge views, these places are just as central as those listed above, and serve food that's generally a step up.

MOSTAR

Balkan Flavors

All of the countries of the Balkan Peninsula—basically from Slovenia to Greece—have several foods in common: The Ottomans from today's Turkey, who controlled much of this territory for centuries, imported some goodies that remained standard fare here long after they left town. Whether you're in Mostar, Croatia, or Slovenia, it's worth seeking out some of these local tastes.

A popular, cheap fast food you'll see everywhere is **burek** (BOO-rehk)—phyllo dough filled with meat, cheese, spinach, or apples. The more familiar **baklava** is phyllo dough layered with honey and nuts.

Grilled meats are a staple of Balkan cuisine. You'll most often see **čevapčići** (cheh-VAHP-chee-chee), or simply **čevap** (cheh-VAHP)—minced meat formed into a sausage-link shape, then grilled. **Ražnjići** (RAZH-nyee-chee) is small pieces of steak on a skewer, like a shish kebab. **Pljeskavica** (plehs-kah-VEET-suh) is similar to *čevapčići,* except the meat is in the form of a hamburger-like patty.

While Balkan cuisine favors meat, a nice veggie complement is **đuveđ** (JOO-vedge)—a spicy mix of stewed vegetables, flavored with tomatoes and peppers.

And you just can't eat any of this stuff without the ever-present condiment **ajvar** (EYE-var). Made from red bell pepper and eggplant, *ajvar* is like ketchup with a kick. Many Americans pack a jar of this distinctive sauce to remember the flavors of the Balkans when they get back home. (You may even be able to find it at specialty grocery stores in the US—look for "eggplant/red pepper spread".) Particularly in Bosnia, another side-dish you'll see is the soft, spreadable—and tasty—cheese called **kajmak.** **Lepinje** is a pita-like grilled bread, which is often wrapped around *čevapčići* or *pljeskavica* to make a sandwich.

Ajvar, kajmak, lepinje, and diced raw onions are the perfect complement to a **"mixed grill"** of various meats on a big platter—the quintessence of Balkan cuisine on one plate.

The first three places are in the atmospheric Old Town, while the last one is in the modern part of town.

Restoran Hindin Han is pleasantly situated on a woody terrace over a rushing stream. It's respected locally for its good cooking and fair prices (big 12-16-KM salads, 7-13-KM grilled dishes, 12-20-KM fish and other main dishes, Sarajevsko beer on tap, daily 11:00-24:00, Jusovina 10, tel. 036/581-054). To find it,

MOSTAR

walk west from the Old Bridge, bear left at the Šadrvan restaurant, cross the bridge, and you'll see it on the left.

Šadrvan ("Fountain"), situated smack-dab in the center of the tourist zone, where cobbled paths converge near the Old Bridge, is undoubtedly touristy. But it also has fine service, good food, and pleasant outdoor seating under a tree around its namesake fountain. This is also a good place to nurse a "Bosnian coffee"—like Turkish coffee, unfiltered, with "mud" in the bottom of the cup (7-10-KM vegetarian options, 10-15-KM pastas, 7-20-KM main dishes, daily 7:00-23:00, Jusovina 11, tel. 036/579-057).

Ima Dana ("Someday") is woven into a tangle of terraces over a rushing little stream facing the Crooked Bridge, with good food and a pleasant riverside setting (7-10-KM pizzas and pastas, 7-18-KM meat and fish meals, daily 11:00-24:00, on Jusovina street at the end of the Crooked Bridge, head waiter Miro's mobile is 061-529-408).

Local Alternative in the New Town: **Saray** is an untouristy, nondescript little eatery just uphill from the Karađozbeg Mosque in the modern part of town. They have a basic menu of cheap and very tasty grilled meats—specializing in the classic *ćevapčići* (little sausage-shaped meat patties)—and outdoor seating overlooking a playground that offers good people- and kid-watching while you eat (4-10-KM grilled meat dishes, big 6-7-KM salads, daily 9:00-17:00, Karađozbegova 3, mobile 062-062-301).

Mostar Connections

By Bus

Not surprisingly for a divided city, Mostar has two different, autonomous bus terminals, each served by different companies. Mostar's **main bus station** (called "Autobusna Stanica") is on the east/Bosniak side of the river, about a 15-minute walk north of the Old Town (for details, see "Arrival in Mostar," earlier). Most buses you're likely to take use this station; for information on the other station (on the west/Croat side of town), see the end of this section.

Schedules and Tickets: At the main station, two primary companies (one Bosniak, one Croat) operate independent offices, providing schedule information and tickets only for their own buses. Because the companies refuse to cooperate, there's no single information or ticket office for all Mostar buses—so it's essential to visit both companies to know your options before buying tickets. (You may be lucky and encounter a helpful person in one office who'll clue you in on options at the other, but don't count on it—they're just as likely to pretend the other company doesn't exist.) As you face the bus station, near the left end is the Bosniak company

Autoprevoz (tel. 036/551-900, www.autoprevoz-bus.ba); they also sell tickets for a few other companies (including Eurolines and Bogdan Bus). Near the right end is the Croat-owned **Globtour** (tel. 036/318-333, www.globtour.com), which sells tickets only for its own buses. Local and regional connections (not listed below) are operated by Mostar Bus, whose buses depart from across the street from the main bus station (www.mostarbus.ba).

Tracking down reliable **schedule** information in Mostar is tricky, but you can start by checking the websites listed above, then calling or visiting both companies at the station to confirm your options and buy tickets. While this may sound intimidating, it's workable—just be sure to double-check your plans. Note that buses to seasonal destinations (such as along the Dalmatian Coast) run more frequently in peak season, roughly June through mid-September. The prices I've listed are estimates; it can depend on the company.

From Mostar's Main Bus Station to: Međugorje (6-7/day, 40 minutes, all operated by Globtour, 4-5 KM), **Sarajevo** (at least hourly, 2.5 hours, several different companies—check with both offices to know all your options, 20 KM), **Zagreb** (4/day on Globtour, 1/day on Autoprevoz, 8-9.5 hours, includes a night bus, 45 KM), **Split** (2/day with Globtour, 2-3/day with Autoprevoz, 4-4.5 hours, plus 1 night bus with Eurolines/Autoprevoz, 20-30 KM), **Dubrovnik** (2/day with Globtour, 1/day with Eurolines/Autoprevoz—or 3/day in summer, 4-5 hours, 25-30 KM). The important Dubrovnik connection is tricky: Most days, all Dubrovnik buses depart early in the day, making an afternoon return from Mostar to Dubrovnik impossible. In summer, however, Eurolines adds two more departures each day—including a handy 17:30 departure, which makes day-tripping from Dubrovnik workable (tickets sold at Autoprevoz office). Globtour also runs a handy bus to Montenegro's **Bay of Kotor** (departs Mostar at 7:00, arrives at Kotor at 12:30 and Budva at 13:30, then returns the same day).

From Mostar's West/Croat Bus Station: A few additional buses, mostly to Croatian destinations and to Croat areas of Bosnia-Herzegovina, depart from the west side of town. These use a makeshift "station" (actually a gravel lot behind a gas station) on Vukovarska street, called "Kolodvor." It's about a 15-minute walk due west of the main bus station. Most buses using the Kolodvor station are operated by the Euroherc company. In addition to one daily bus apiece to **Zagreb, Split,** and **Sarajevo,** this station has several departures to **Metković** (at the Croatian border, with additional connections to Croatian destinations; 8/day) and to **Međugorje** (7/day Mon-Fri, 3/day Sat, none Sun, 5 KM). Additionally, some Croat buses leave from a bus stop near the

Franciscan Church. But since the connections from this side are sparse, the location is inconvenient, and the "station" is dreary, I'd stick with the main bus station and ignore this option unless you're desperate.

By Train

Mostar is on the train line that runs from Ploče (on the Croatian coast between Split and Dubrovnik) to Zagreb, via Mostar and Sarajevo. This train—which leaves from next to the main bus station—generally runs once daily, leaving **Ploče** soon after 6:00 in the morning, with stops at **Mostar** (1.75 hours), **Sarajevo** (4.25 hours), and **Zagreb** (13.5 hours; bus is faster). Going the opposite direction, the train leaves Zagreb at about 9:00 in the morning. There's also a night train connection running in both directions along the same track (leaving Ploče northbound at 16:25, arriving in Mostar at 18:35, Sarajevo at 20:59, and Zagreb at 6:44; and southbound leaving Zagreb at 21:24, arriving in Sarajevo at 6:39 and Mostar at 9:31). Train info: tel. 036/550-608.

Route Tips for Drivers
From Dubrovnik to Mostar

You have two ways to drive between Dubrovnik and Mostar: easy and straightforward along the coast, or adventurous and off the beaten path through the Herzegovinian mountains. I've narrated each route as you'd encounter it driving from Dubrovnik to Mostar, but you can do either one in reverse—just hold this book upside-down.

The Main Coastal Road

The vast majority of traffic from Dubrovnik to Mostar follows the coastal road north, then cuts east into Bosnia. Because this is one of the most direct routes, it can be crowded (allow about 2.5 hours). It's also a bit inconvenient, as you have to cross the border three times (into and out of Bosnia at Neum, and into Bosnia again at Metković).

Begin by driving north of Dubrovnik, passing some of the places mentioned in the Near Dubrovnik chapter: **Trsteno** (with its arboretum), and **Ston** and **Mali Ston** (with a mighty wall and waterfront restaurants, respectively). After passing the Ston turn-off, you'll see the long, mountainous, vineyard-draped **Pelješac Peninsula** across the bay on your left.

Soon you'll come to a surprise border crossing, at **Neum**. Here you'll cross into Bosnia-Herzegovina—then, six miles later, cross back out again (for details on this odd little stretch of Bosnian coast, see page 948).

You won't be back in Croatia for long. Just north of Neum, the main coastal road jogs away from the coast and around the striking **Neretva River Delta**—the extremely fertile "garden patch of Croatia," which produces a significant portion of Croatia's fruits and vegetables. The Neretva is the same river that flows under Mostar's Old Bridge upstream—but in Metković, it spreads out into 12 branches as it enters the Adriatic, flooding a vast plain and creating a bursting cornucopia in the middle of an otherwise rocky and arid region. Enjoying some of the most plentiful sunshine on the Croatian coast, as well as a steady supply of water for irrigation, the Neretva Delta is as productive as it is beautiful.

At the Neretva Delta, turn off for the town of **Metković**; at the far end of that town, you'll cross the border into **Bosnia-Herzegovina,** then continue straight on the main road (M17) directly into Mostar. As you drive, you'll see destroyed buildings and occasional roadside memorials bearing the likenesses of fresh-faced soldiers who died in the recent war.

Along the way are a few interesting detours: In Čapljina, you can turn off to the left to reach **Međugorje** (see page 1083). If you stay on the main road, keep your eyes peeled soon after the Čapljina turnoff for a mountaintop castle tower (on the right side of the road), which marks the medieval town of **Počitelj** (see page 1083). With extra time, just before Mostar (in Buna), you can detour a few miles along the Buna River into **Blagaj** (see page 1082).

Approaching **Mostar** on M17, you'll pass the airport, then turn left at your first opportunity to cross the river. After crossing the bridge, bear right onto Bulevar street, and continue on that main artery for several blocks (passing several destroyed buildings). At the street called Rade Bitange (just after the giant church bell tower), turn right to find the public parking lot (2 KM/hour, 10 KM/8 hours)—less than a 10-minute walk from the Old Bridge. Be warned that signage is poor; if you get lost, try asking for directions to "Stari Most" (STAH-ree most)—the Old Bridge.

Rugged-but-Scenic Backcountry Journey through Serb Herzegovina

While the coastal route outlined above is the most common way to connect Dubrovnik to Mostar, I enjoy getting out of the tourist rut by twisting up the mountains behind Dubrovnik and cutting across the scenic middle of Herzegovina. (If you're traveling by road between Dubrovnik and Split at another point in your trip, you'll see the coastal road anyway—so this alternative helps you avoid the rerun.) This route feels much more remote, but the roads are good and the occasional gas station and restaurant break up the journey. I find this route particularly interesting because it offers an easily digestible taste of the **Republika Srpska** part of

Herzegovina—controlled by the country's Serb minority, rather than its Bosniak and Croat majority. You'll see Orthodox churches and monasteries, the Cyrillic alphabet, and various symbols of the defiantly proud Serb culture (such as the red, white, and blue flag with the four golden C's). You can't get a complete picture of the former Yugoslavia without sampling at least a sliver of Serb culture. (Because this road goes through the Serbian part of Herzegovina, it's not popular among Bosniaks or Croats—in fact, locals might tell you this road "does not exist." It does.) If you want a little taste of Republika Srpska, consider just day-tripping into Trebinje—especially on Saturday, when the produce market is at its liveliest.

The first step is to climb up into the mountains and the charming market town of Trebinje. From there, two different roads lead to Mostar: via Stolac or via Nevesinje. If you take the Stolac route, the whole journey from Dubrovnik to Mostar takes about as long as the coastal road (and potentially even faster, thanks to the light traffic and lack of an extra border). The Nevesinje route takes a good hour longer than the Stolac route, and immerses you in an even more remote landscape.

Dubrovnik to Trebinje: From Dubrovnik, head south toward Cavtat, the airport, and Montenegro. Shortly after leav-

ing Dubrovnik, watch for—and follow—signs on the left directing you to *Brgat Gornji*. (Signage completely ignores the large Serb town of Trebinje, just past this obscure border village.) As you drive through the border into Bosnia-Herzegovina, notice the faint remains of a long-abandoned old rail line cutting sharp switch-

backs up the hill. This once connected Dubrovnik to Mostar and Sarajevo. The charred trees you may see are not from the war, but from more recent forest fires.

Carry on across the plateau, where you may begin to notice Cyrillic lettering on signs: You've crossed into the Republika Srpska. About 20 minutes after the border, you'll come upon **Trebinje** (Требиње)—a pleasant and relatively affluent town with a leafy main square that hosts a fine Saturday market. Trebinje is a good place to stretch your legs, get some Bosnian Convertible Marks (ATMs are scattered around the town center), and maybe nurse a coffee while people-watching on the main square. Overlooking the town from its hilltop perch is the striking Orthodox Church of Nova Gračanica, built to resemble the historically important Gračanica Monastery in Kosovo. If you have time, drive up to the church's viewpoint terrace for great views over Trebinje and the valley, and step inside the church to immerse yourself in a gorgeously vibrant world of Orthodox icons.

From Trebinje, you have two options for getting to Mostar: The faster route via Stolac, or the very rugged slower route via Nevesinje.

Stolac Route: As you enter Trebinje, after crossing the river, follow signs for *Mostar* and *Ljubinje*. Follow the Trebišnjica River into a high-altitude karstic basin, where waterwheels power a primitive irrigation system. From here, the river flows down to the coast—providing hydroelectric power for Dubrovnik—before detouring south and emptying into the sea near Herceg Novi, Montenegro...one river, three countries, in just a few miles. This area is blanketed with vineyards and dotted with old monasteries. Passing the village of Mesari ("Butchers"), you'll also see flocks of sheep. In this part of the Balkans, Croats were traditionally the city-dwellers, while Serbs were farmers. There used to be sheep like these in the pastures near Dubrovnik, but when the Serbs left during the war, so did the sheep.

The large field you're driving along is called **Popovo Polje** ("Priests' Field"). Because it floods easily, the canal was built to remove floodwater. Pull over at one of the humble, slate-roofed Orthodox chapels by the road. In the cemeteries, many of the gravestones are from 1991—when soldiers from this area joined the war effort against Dubrovnik.

At the fork, carry on straight to Ljubinje. Climbing up into the mountains, you'll see garbage along the side of the road—an improvised dump in this very poor land, where a fractured government struggles to provide even basic services. Twisting up through even higher mountains, you'll wind up in the town of **Ljubinje** (Љубиње). In this humble burg, roadside stands with *med* signs advertise homegrown honey. The partially built houses are not signs of war damage (the war didn't reach here); it's a form of "savings" in the Balkans, where people don't trust banks: Rather than deposit money in an account, they spend many years gradually adding on to a new house.

Continuing toward Mostar, you'll pass through more desolate countryside to the town of **Stolac** (Столац); the town's defiant mosque minaret tells you that you've crossed from Serb territory into Bosnia's Muslim-Croat Federation. Stolac is home to some fascinating history, and worth a stroll if you have the time (see page 1083). Leaving Stolac, keep an eye out (on the left) for its fascinating **necropolis**—a cluster of centuries-old traditional Bosnian tombstones (worth a quick photo-op stop).

Past Stolac, you'll soon pop out at an intersection with the main road between Mostar and the coast. From here, turn right to head into **Počitelj** (see page 1083), then the turnoff for **Blagaj** (page 1082) and on to **Mostar**. (If you want to go to **Međugorje**—see page 1083—turn left here, then turn right once you get to Čapljina.) For arrival tips in Mostar, see the end of the driving directions above.

Nevesinje Route: This longer, more remote, middle-of-nowhere adventure takes about an hour longer than the Stolac route. But if you're adventurous, it's a fun ride. From Trebinje, drive north toward **Bilećko Lake**—a vast, aquamarine lake you'll see on your right (the Vikiovac Restaurant offers a great viewpoint). Then you'll go through the town of **Bileća** (Билећа), turning west at the gloomy industrial town of **Gacko** (Гацко, with a giant coal mine), and onward to the humble but proud little town of **Nevesinje** (Невесиње). From Nevesinje, it's a quick drive up over the mountains, then down into Mostar—passing spectacular views of Herzog Stjepan's imposing castle over the town of Buna. Follow signs on into Mostar.

AUSTRIA
Österreich

VIENNA

Wien

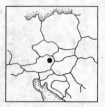

Vienna is the capital of Austria, the cradle of classical music, the home of the rich Habsburg heritage, and one of Europe's most livable cities. The city center is skyscraper-free, pedestrian-friendly, dotted with quiet parks, and traversed by quaint electric trams. Many buildings still reflect 18th- and 19th-century elegance, when the city was at the forefront of the arts and sciences. Compared with most modern European urban centers, the pace of life is slow.

Vienna (*Wien* in German—pronounced "veen") has always been considered the easternmost city of the West. For 640 years, Vienna was the capital of the enormous Austrian Empire (a.k.a. the Austro-Hungarian Empire, a.k.a. the Habsburg Empire). Stretching from the Alps of northern Italy to the rugged Carpathians of Romania, and from the banks of the Danube to sunny Dubrovnik, this multiethnic empire was arguably the most powerful European entity since Rome. And yet, of its 60 million people, only eight million were Austrian; Vienna was a kind of Eastern European melting pot. Today, the truly Viennese person is not Austrian, but a second-generation Habsburg cocktail, with grandparents from the distant corners of the old empire—Hungary, the Czech Republic, Slovakia, Poland, Slovenia, Croatia, Bosnia-Herzegovina, Serbia, Romania, and Italy.

Vienna reached its peak in the 19th century. Politically, it hosted European diplomats at the 1814 Congress of Vienna,

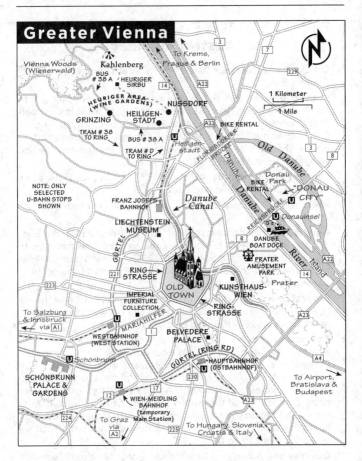

Greater Vienna

Vienna Woods (Wienerwald)

Kahlenberg

BUS # 38 A

HEURIGER SIRBU

HEURIGER AREA (WINE GARDENS)

GRINZING

HEILIGEN-STADT

TRAM # 38 TO RING

BUS # 38 A

TRAM # D TO RING

NOTE: ONLY SELECTED U-BAHN STOPS SHOWN

To Krems, Prague & Berlin

NUSSDORF

BIKE RENTAL

Heiligen-stadt

Danube

Old Danube

Donau Park

BIKE RENTAL

"DONAU CITY"

Donauinsel

FRANZ JOSEFS BAHNHOF

Danube Canal

LIECHTENSTEIN MUSEUM

1 Kilometer

1 Mile

River

Island

DANUBE BOAT DOCK

RING-STRASSE

OLD TOWN

PRATER AMUSEMENT PARK

Prater

IMPERIAL FURNITURE COLLECTION

KUNSTHAUS-WIEN

RING-STRASSE

To Salzburg & Innsbruck via A1

MARIAHILFER

WESTBAHNHOF (WEST STATION)

BELVEDERE PALACE

GÜRTEL (RING RD)

HAUPTBAHNHOF (OSTBAHNHOF)

SCHÖNBRUNN PALACE & GARDENS

Schönbrunn

WIEN-MEIDLING BAHNHOF (temporary Main Station)

To Airport, Bratislava & Budapest

To Graz via A2

To Hungary, Slovenia, Croatia & Italy

which reaffirmed Europe's conservative monarchy after the French Revolution and Napoleon. Vienna became one of Europe's cultural capitals, home to groundbreaking composers (Beethoven, Mozart, Brahms, Strauss), scientists (Doppler, Boltzmann), philosophers (Freud, Husserl, Schlick, Gödel, Steiner), architects (Wagner, Loos), and painters (Klimt, Schiele, Kokoschka). In 1900, Vienna's 2.2 million inhabitants made it the world's fifth-largest city—after New York, London, Paris, and Berlin. By the turn of the 20th century, Vienna sat on the cusp between stuffy Old World monarchy and subversive modern trends.

However, after starting and losing World War I, the Habsburgs lost their far-flung holdings. Then came World War II: While Vienna's old walls had long held out would-be invaders—Germanic barbarians (in Roman times), marauding Magyars (today's Hungarians, 10th century), Mongol hordes (13th century), Ottoman Turks (the sieges of 1529 and 1683)—they were no match

Austria Almanac

Official Name: Republik Österreich ("Eastern Empire"), or simply Österreich.

Population: Austria's 8.3 million people (similar population to the state of Georgia) are 91 percent ethnic Austrian, plus 4 percent from the former Yugoslavia. Three out of four Austrians are Catholic; about 1 in 20 is Muslim. German is the dominant language (though there are a few Slovene- and Hungarian-speaking villages in border areas).

Latitude and Longitude: 47°N and 13°E. The latitude is the same as Minnesota or Washington state.

Area: With 32,400 square miles, Austria is similar in size to South Carolina or Maine.

Geography: The northeast is flat and well-populated; the less-populated southwest is mountainous, with the Alps rising up to the 12,450-foot Grossglockner. The 1,770-mile-long Danube River meanders west-to-east through the upper part of the country, passing through Vienna.

Biggest Cities: One in five Austrians lives in the capital of Vienna (1.7 million in the city; 2.2 million in the greater metropolitan area). Graz has 262,000, and Linz has 189,000.

Economy: Austria borders eight other European countries and is well-integrated into the EU economy. The Gross Domestic Product is $332 billion (similar to Massachusetts'). It has a GDP per capita of $40,000—among Europe's highest. One of its biggest moneymakers is tourism. Austria produces wood, paper products (nearly half the land is forested)...and Red Bull Energy Drink. The country faces an aging population that increasingly collects social security—a situation that will strain the national budget in years to come.

Government: Austria has been officially neutral since 1955 and its citizens take a dim view of European unity. Although right-leaning

for WWII bombs, which destroyed nearly a quarter of the city's buildings. In the Cold War, neutral Austria took a big bite out of the USSR's Warsaw Pact buffer zone—and Vienna became, for a time, a den of spies.

Today Vienna has settled down into a somewhat sleepy, pleasant place where culture is still king. Classical music is everywhere. People nurse a pastry and coffee over the daily paper at small cafés. It's a city of world-class museums, big and small. Anyone with an interest in painting, music, architecture, beautiful objects, or Sacher-Torte with whipped cream will feel right at home.

From a practical standpoint, Vienna serves as a prime "gateway" city. The location is central and convenient to most major Eastern European destinations. Actually farther east than Prague,

parties made substantial gains in recent elections, the government continues to be a center-left coalition, currently headed by Federal President Heinz Fischer and Chancellor Werner Faymann (both Social Democrats). The resurgent right—buoyed by anti-immigrant and anti-EU sentiment—was dealt a blow in October 2008 when its "yuppie fascist" leader Jörg Haider died in a car accident. Austria is the only EU nation that lets 16- and 17-year-olds vote.

Flag: Three horizontal bands of red, white, and red.

Cuisine: Austrian treats include Wiener schnitzel (breaded veal cutlet), *Knödel* (dumplings), *Apfelstrudel* (apple strudel), *Kaiserschmarr'n* (fluffy, caramelized pancake strips), and fancy desserts like the Sacher-Torte, Vienna's famous chocolate cake.

Language: Austria's official language is German. It's important to greet people in the breakfast room and those you pass on the streets or meet in shops. The Austrian version of "Hi" is a cheerful *"Grüss Gott."* You'll get the correct pronunciation after the first volley—listen and copy. For German Survival Phrases, see page 1273.

Gemütlichkeit: Austrians are not Germans—they cherish their distinct cultural and historical traditions. Austria is mellow and relaxed compared to Deutschland. *Gemütlichkeit* is the word most often used to describe this special Austrian cozy-and-easy approach to life. On the other hand, Austria feels relatively stiff and formal compared to most of Eastern Europe (except, possibly, Hungary).

The Average Austrian: A typical Austrian is 43 years old, has 1.4 children, and will live to be 80. He or she inhabits a 900-square-foot home, and spends leisure time with a circle of a few close friends. Chances are high that someone in that closely knit circle is a smoker—Austrians smoke more cigarettes per day than any other Europeans.

Ljubljana, and Zagreb, and just upstream on the Danube from Budapest and Bratislava, Vienna is an ideal launchpad for a journey into the East.

Planning Your Time

For a big city, Vienna is pleasant and laid-back. Packed with sights, it's worth two days and two nights on even the speediest trip. If you have more time, Vienna can easily fill it; art- and music-lovers in particular won't regret adding a third or fourth day. If you're visiting Vienna as part of a longer European trip, you could sleep on the train on your way in and out—Prague, Kraków, Warsaw, Berlin, Venice, Rome, the Swiss Alps (via Zürich), Paris, and the Rhine Valley are each handy night trains away, and easy daytime trains connect Vienna to Budapest, Zagreb, Ljubljana, and Prague.

Palace Choices: The Hofburg and Schönbrunn are both world-class palaces, but seeing both is redundant—with limited time or money, I'd choose just one. The Hofburg comes with the popular Sisi Museum and is right in the town center, making for an easy visit. With more time, a visit to Schönbrunn—set outside town amid a grand and regal garden—is also a great experience.

Vienna in One to Four Days

Below is a suggested itinerary for how to spend your time. I've left the **evenings** open for your choice of activities. The best options are taking in a concert, opera, or other musical event; enjoying a leisurely dinner (and people-watching) in the stately old town or atmospheric Spittelberg Quarter; heading out to the *Heuriger* wine pubs in the foothills of the Vienna Woods; or touring the Haus der Musik interactive music museum (open nightly until 22:00). Plan your evenings based on the schedule of musical events while you're in town.

Day 1

9:00	Take the 1.5-hour Red Bus City Tour, or circle the Ringstrasse by tram, to get your bearings.
10:30	Drop by the TI for planning and ticket needs.
11:00	Enjoy the Albertina Museum.
13:00	Take the Opera tour (buy tickets at 12:40).
14:00	Follow my Vienna City Walk, including Kaisergruft visit and St. Stephen's Cathedral Tour (nave closes at 16:30, or 17:30 June-Aug).

Day 2

9:00	Browse the colorful Naschmarkt, or shop along Mariahilfer Strasse.
11:00	Tour the Kunsthistorisches Museum.
14:00	After a short break (and maybe a picnic) in the Burggarten, tour the Hofburg Palace Imperial Apartments and Treasury; if time, interest, and energy hold out, dip into the New Palace museums.

Day 3

Choose from among the following sights: Belvedere Palace, with its fine collection of Viennese art and great city views; the engaging Karlsplatz sights (Karlskirche, Wien Museum, Academy of Fine Arts, and The Secession); or a wide range of honorable mentions (Natural History Museum, Liechtenstein Museum, KunstHausWien and Hundertwasserhaus, Museum of Applied

Art, Imperial Furniture Collection, Sigmund Freud Museum, Jewish sights, and so on).

If you need a break, linger in a classic Viennese café.

Or, to get out of town, tromp through the Vienna Woods, ending at the *Heuriger* wine pubs for dinner.

Day 4

9:00	Head out to Schönbrunn Palace to enjoy the royal apartments and grounds.
12:00	If the weather's good, picnic at Schönbrunn (on the lawn in front of the Gloriette), then return to downtown.
13:00	Rent a bike and head out to the modern Danube City "downtown" sector, Danube Island (for fun people-watching), and the Prater amusement park.

Orientation to Vienna

(area code: 01)

Vienna sits between the Vienna Woods (Wienerwald) and the Danube (Donau). To the southeast is industrial sprawl. The Alps,

which arc across Europe from Marseille, end at Vienna's wooded hills, providing a popular playground for walking and sipping new wine. This greenery's momentum carries on into the city. More than half of Vienna is parkland, filled with ponds, gardens, trees, and statue-maker memories of Austria's glory days.

Think of the city map as a target with concentric sections: The bull's-eye is St. Stephen's Cathedral, the towering cathedral south of the Danube. Surrounding that is the old town, bound tightly by the circular road known as the Ringstrasse, marking what used to be the city wall. The Gürtel, a broader ring road, contains the rest of downtown. Outside the Gürtel lies the uninteresting sprawl of modern Vienna.

Addresses start with the district, or *Bezirk,* followed by the street and building number. The Ringstrasse (a.k.a. the Ring) circles the first *Bezirk*. Any address higher than the ninth *Bezirk* is beyond the Gürtel, far from the center.

Much of Vienna's sightseeing—and most of my recommended restaurants—are located in the old town (inside the Ringstrasse). Walking across this circular district takes about 30 minutes. St. Stephen's Cathedral sits in the center, at the intersection of the two main (pedestrian-only) streets: Kärntner Strasse runs north-south

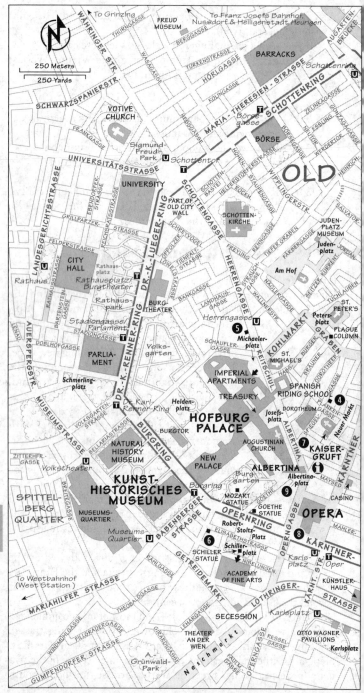

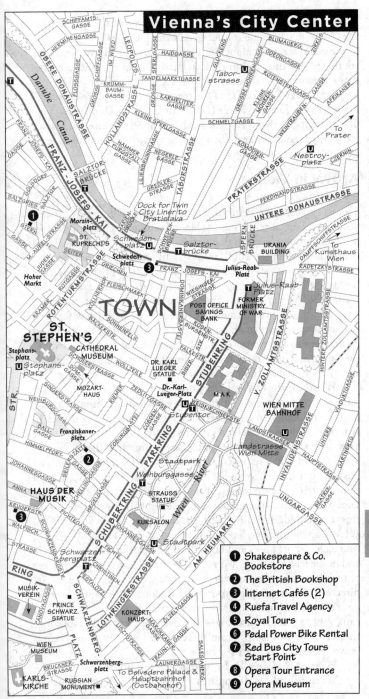

Vienna's City Center

1. Shakespeare & Co. Bookstore
2. The British Bookshop
3. Internet Cafés (2)
4. Ruefa Travel Agency
5. Royal Tours
6. Pedal Power Bike Rental
7. Red Bus City Tours Start Point
8. Opera Tour Entrance
9. Opera Museum

and Graben runs east-west. To the northwest of the cathedral is the "Bermuda Triangle" of pubs and cafés for nightlife.

Several sights sit along, or just beyond, the Ringstrasse: to the southwest are the Hofburg and related Habsburg sights, and the Kunsthistorisches Museum; to the south is a cluster of intriguing sights near Karlsplatz; to the southeast is Belvedere Palace. A branch of the Danube River (*Donau* in German, DOH-now) borders the Ring to the north. As a tourist, concern yourself only with this compact old center. When you do, sprawling Vienna suddenly becomes manageable.

Arrival in Vienna
By Train
Vienna's many train stations will be in disarray for the next few years, as a central train station (Hauptbahnhof) is built in the former Südbahnhof location that will handle most of the traffic. Until this is done (likely in 2013), trains to different destinations depart from various stations scattered around the city. As these departure points are prone to change, confirm carefully which station your train uses. As the stations themselves are also in flux (the main ones are all being renovated), the details I've listed below for each one are also subject to change. From most stations, the handiest connection to the center is usually the U-Bahn (subway) system; line numbers and stop names are noted below. For some stations, there's also a handy tram connection.

Westbahnhof (West Station): In the midst of a massive renovation, this station (at the west end of Mariahilfer Strasse, on the U-3 and U-6 lines) serves trains to/from many points in **Austria** (including Melk, Hallstatt, Salzburg, and Innsbruck), as well as **Germany, Switzerland,** and **Hungary.** The Reisebüro am Bahnhof office sells maps, books hotels (for a pricey fee), and answers questions (Mon-Fri 8:00-19:00, Sat 8:00-13:00, closed Sun). During the ongoing construction, this station's many services are scattered throughout a provisional hall—including a train ticket office (daily 5:30-22:45), grocery store (daily 5:30-23:00), ATMs, change offices, a post office, and luggage lockers (€2-3.50). To reach airport buses and taxis, from the platforms, head outside and to the left. For the city center, ride the U-3 line (buy your ticket or transit pass from a machine, then follow *U-3* signs to the tracks; direction: Simmering). If your hotel is along Mariahilfer Strasse, your stop is on this line. If you're sleeping in the center—or just can't wait to start sightseeing—ride five stops to Stephansplatz, at the very center of town. From there, the TI is a five-minute stroll down pedestrian Kärntner Strasse.

Wien-Meidling Bahnhof: This temporary "main station" (a mile and a half southeast of Schönbrunn Palace, at the

Philadelphiabrücke stop on the U-6 subway line and tram #62) serves most international trains, including southbound trains to/from **Italy, Slovenia,** and **Croatia,** as well as northbound trains to/from the **Czech Republic** and **Poland.** The once-small sub-urban station has been souped up to accommodate the traffic that formerly passed through the Südbahnhof. It has train info desks (near track 1 and underground, near track 4), ATMs (near tracks 1 and 6), luggage lockers (underground, near track 7), and airport bus services. To reach the hotels on Mariahilfer Strasse, or to head to Stephansplatz, take the U-Bahn on the U-6 line (direction: Floridsdorf) to the Westbahnhof, then change to the U-3 line (see "Westbahnhof," above). If you're staying near the Opera, catch the direct tram #62 (direction: Karlsplatz). For Schwedenplatz, take the U-6 (direction: Floridsdorf) two stops to Längenfeldgasse, then change to the U-4 (direction: Heiligenstadt).

Ostbahnhof (East Station), a.k.a. Südbahnhof (South Station): The temporary Ostbahnhof (just south of Belvedere Palace) is near the former Südbahnhof, and is in the midst of the massive construction zone for the brand-new Hauptbahnhof (Main Station)—so, confusingly, it goes by any of these three names. For now, this station serves trains to/from **Bratislava,** Slovakia. To reach the city center, take tram #D to the Ring; to reach Mariahilfer Strasse, hop on bus #13A (U-1: Südtiroler Platz is also nearby).

Franz Josefs Bahnhof: This small station in the northern part of the city serves **Krems** and other points on the **north bank of the Danube** (as well as **Český Krumlov,** Czech Republic). Although the station doesn't have a U-Bahn stop, convenient tram #D con-nects it to the city center. Also note that trains coming into town from this direction stop at the Spittelau station (on the U-4 and U-6 lines), one stop before they end at the Franz Josefs station; consider hopping off your train at Spittelau for a handy connec-tion to other points in Vienna. (Similarly, if you're headed out of town and you're not near the tram #D route, take the U-Bahn to Spittelau and catch your train there.)

By Plane

Vienna International Airport, 12 miles from the center, has easy connections to Vienna's various train stations (airport tel. 01/700-722-233, www.viennaairport.com).

Two different trains transport airport passengers into Vienna. Both go to the same point in the city center: the Wien-Mitte Bahnhof, on the east side of the Ring (adjacent to the Landstrasse U-Bahn stop, with a handy connection to Mariahilfer Strasse hotels and other accommodations neighborhoods). The main dif-ferences between them are time and cost. The **S-Bahn** commuter

VIENNA

train (S-7 yellow line) works just fine and is plenty fast (€3.60, 2/hour, 24 minutes, buy 2-zone ticket from machines on the platform, price includes any bus or S- or U-Bahn transfers). The fast **CAT** (City Airport Train) takes a third less time but costs nearly triple (€10, €11.50 includes a ride to your final destination on Vienna's transit system, 2/hour, usually departs at :05 and :35, 16 minutes, www.cityairporttrain.com). I'd take the S-Bahn, unless the CAT is departing first and you're in a hurry. You can see when the next trains are leaving by looking on the overhead screens in the arrivals hall (with a red strip along the top—note that the green screens show only the premium CAT train, not the cheaper S-Bahn alternative).

Both trains leave from underground tracks just outside the arrivals hall: Exit straight ahead, go through the green entrance (marked *CAT*), and go down the stairs. The CAT train is to the left. The S-Bahn is to the right, then left down the dull hallway (poorly marked—look for train logo).

Convenient express airport **buses** go to various points in Vienna: the Schwedenplatz U-Bahn station (for city-center hotels), Westbahnhof (for Mariahilfer Strasse hotels), and Wien-Meidling Bahnhof (while this train station is acting as Vienna's main station during construction). To reach these buses from the arrivals hall, go outside and to your left (note destination and times on curbside TV monitors; €6, 2-3/hour, generally 20-30 minutes, buy ticket from driver, tel. 0810-222-333 for timetable info, www.postbus.at).

The 30-minute ride into town by **taxi** costs about €35-40 (including the €11 airport surcharge). From the arrivals hall, the taxi stand is out the door to the right; taxis also wait at the downtown terminus of each airport transit service (save money by riding the cheap train/bus downtown, then take a taxi to your destination). Hotels arrange for a €30 fixed-rate car service to the airport; you'll also see several desks for this in the arrivals hall.

For details on arriving at the airport in nearby Bratislava, Slovakia—a hub for some low-cost flights and just an hour away from Vienna—see page 241.

Tourist Information

Vienna's one real TI is a block behind the Opera at Albertinaplatz (daily 9:00-19:00, tel. 01/211-140, www.vienna.info). At the TI, confirm your sightseeing plans, and pick up the free and essential city map with a list of museums and hours (also available at most hotels), the monthly program of concerts (called *Wien-Programm*) and the *Vienna from A to Z* booklet (both described below), and the annual city guide (called *Vienna Journal*). Ask about their program of guided walks (€14 each). The TI also books rooms for a €3 fee.

While hotel and ticket-booking agencies at the train station and airport can answer questions and give out maps and brochures, I'd rely on the official TI if possible.

Wien-Programm: This monthly entertainment guide is particularly important, listing all of the events, including music, walks, expositions, and evening museum hours. Note the key for abbreviations on the inside cover, which helps make this dense booklet useful even for non-German speakers.

Vienna from A to Z: Consider this handy booklet, sold by TIs for €3.60. Every major building in Vienna sports a numbered flag banner that keys into this booklet and into the TI's city map—handy for finding your way if you get turned around.

Vienna Card: The much-promoted €18.50 Vienna Card is not worth the mental overhead for most travelers. It gives you a 72-hour transit pass (worth €13.60) and discounts of 10-40 percent at the city's museums. It might save the busy sightseer a few euros (though seniors and students will do better with their own discounts).

Helpful Hints

Sisi Ticket: This €23.50 ticket covers the Royal Imperial Apartments at the Hofburg (including the Sisi Museum and Imperial Porcelain and Silver Collection—but *not* the Hofburg Treasury), Schönbrunn Palace's Grand Tour, and the Imperial Furniture Collection; the ticket saves €0.50 off the combined cost of the Hofburg apartments and Schönbrunn, making the good Furniture Collection effectively free (sold at any participating sight).

Teens Sightsee Free: Those under 19 get in free to state-run museums and sights.

Music Sightseeing Priorities: Be wary of Vienna's various music sights. Many "homes of composers" are pretty disappointing. My advice to music-lovers is to concentrate on these activities: Take in a concert, tour the Opera house, snare cheap standing-room tickets to see an opera there (even just part of a performance), enjoy the Haus der Musik, and scour the wonderful Collection of Ancient Musical Instruments in the Hofburg's New Palace. If in town on a Sunday, don't miss the glorious music at the Augustinian Church Mass (see page 1147).

Internet Access: The TI has a list of Internet cafés. **Surfland Internet Café** is near the Opera (€6/hour, daily 10:00-23:00, Krugerstrasse 10, tel. 01/512-7701).

Post Offices: The main post office is near Schwedenplatz at Fleischmarkt 19 (Mon-Fri 7:00-22:00, Sat-Sun 9:00-22:00). Branch offices are at the Westbahnhof (Mon-Fri 7:00-22:00,

Sat-Sun 9:00-20:00), near the Opera (Mon-Fri 7:00-19:00, closed Sat-Sun, Krugerstrasse 13), and scattered throughout town.

English Bookstore: Stop by the woody and cool Shakespeare & Co. (Mon-Sat 9:00-19:00 and sometimes later, generally closed Sun, north of Hoher Markt at Sterngasse 2, tel. 01/535-5053). Also inside the Ring is The British Bookshop (Mon-Fri 9:30-18:30, Sat 9:30-18:00, closed Sun, between Franziskaner Platz and the Ring at Weihburggasse 24, tel. 01/512-194-522).

Keeping Up with the News: Don't buy newspapers. Read them for free in Vienna's marvelous coffeehouses. It's much classier.

Travel Agency: Conveniently located just off the Graben, **Ruefa** sells tickets for flights, trains, and boats to Bratislava. They'll waive the service charge for train tickets for my readers (Mon-Fri 9:00-18:00, Sat 10:00-13:00, closed Sun, Spiegelgasse 15, tel. 01/513-4000).

Getting Around Vienna

By Public Transportation: Take full advantage of Vienna's simple, cheap, and super-efficient transit system, which includes trams (a.k.a. streetcars), buses, U-Bahn (subway), and S-Bahn (faster suburban trains). The smooth, modern trams are Porsche-designed, with "backpack technology" that locates the engines and mechanical hardware on the roofs for a lower ride and easier entry. I generally stick to the tram to zip

around the Ring and take the U-Bahn to outlying sights or hotels. Trams #1, #2, and #D all travel partway around the Ring.

The free Vienna map, available at TIs and hotels, includes a smaller schematic map of the major public transit lines, making the too-big €2.50 transit map unnecessary. (Transit maps are also posted conveniently on U-Bahn station walls.) As you study the map, note that tram lines are marked with numbers or letters (such as #38 or #D). Buses have numbers followed by an *A* or *B* (such as #38A); three-digit numbers are for buses into the outskirts. Night buses, which start with *N* (such as #N38), run after other public transit stops running. U-Bahn lines begin with U (e.g., U-1), and the directions are designated by the end-of-the-line stops. Blue lines are the speedier S-Bahns. Transit info: tel. 01/790-9100, www.wienerlinien.at.

Trams, buses, the U-Bahn, and the S-Bahn all use the same tickets. Buy tickets from *Tabak-Trafik* shops, station machines, marked *Vorverkauf* offices in the station, or—for trams or buses only—on board (tickets only, more expensive). You have lots of choices:

- Single tickets (€2, €2.20 if bought on tram or bus, good for one journey with necessary transfers)
- 24-hour transit pass (€6.70)
- 48-hour transit pass (€11.70)
- 72-hour transit pass (€14.50)
- 7-day transit pass (*Wochenkarte*, €15—but the catch is that it starts on Monday, even if you buy it on a Saturday)
- 8-day "Climate Ticket" (*Acht-Tage-Klimakarte*, €33.80, can be shared—for example, 4 people for 2 days each). With a per-person cost of about €4.25/day (compared to €6.70/day for a 24-hour pass), this can be a real saver for groups.

Kids under 15 travel free on Sundays and holidays; kids under 6 always travel free.

Stamp a time on your ticket as you enter the Metro system, tram, or bus (stamp it only the first time for a multiple-use pass). Cheaters pay a stiff €100 fine, plus the cost of the ticket. Rookies miss stops because they fail to open the door. Push buttons, pull latches—do whatever it takes. Before you exit a U-Bahn station, study the wall-mounted street map. Choosing the right exit—signposted from the moment you step off the train—saves lots of walking.

Cute little electric buses wind through the tangled old center. Bus #1A is best for a joyride—hop on and see where it takes you.

By Car: Vienna's comfortable, civilized, and easy-to-flag-down **taxis** start at €2.50. You'll pay about €10 to go from the Opera to the Westbahnhof. Pay only what's on the meter—any surcharges (other than the €2 fee for calling a cab or €10 fee for the airport) are just crude cabbie rip-offs. Rates are legitimately higher at night.

Consider the luxury of having your own **car and driver.** Johann (a.k.a. John) Lichtl is a kind, honest, English-speaking cabbie who can take up to four passengers in his car (€27/1 hour, €25/hour for 2 hours or more, €27 to or from airport, mobile 0676-670-6750). Consider hiring gentle Johann for a day trip to the Danube Valley (€160, up to 8 hours) or to drive you to Salzburg with Danube sightseeing en route (€350, up to 14 hours; other trips can be arranged). These special prices are valid with this book in 2013 and 2014.

By Bike: Vienna is a great city for biking. The bike path along the Ring is wonderfully entertaining. Your best sightseeing by bike is around the Ring, through the City Park, across the Danube Island, and out to the modern "Donau City" business district and nearby beach.

Borrowing a Free/Cheap Bike: Citybike Wien lets you borrow bikes from public racks all over town (toll tel. 0810-500-500, www.citybikewien.at). The bikes are heavy, clunky, and difficult to maneuver—with a solid wheel, single gear, basket, built-in lock, and ads on the side—but they're perfect for a short, practical joy-ride in the center (such as around the Ringstrasse).

While bike programs in other European cities are difficult for tourists to take advantage of, Vienna's system is easy to use. Bikes are locked into more than 50 stalls scattered through the city center. To borrow a bike, use the computer terminal at any rack to register: Press the credit card button, insert and pull out your card, register your name and address, and select a username and password for future rentals (you can also register online at www.citybikewien.at). Then punch in the number of the bike that you want to use to unlock it. Registration costs €1 (first time only), and they'll place a refundable €20 hold on your card while you're using the bike (only one bike per credit card—couples must use two different cards). Since the bikes are designed for short-term use, it costs more per hour the longer you keep it (first hour free, second hour €1, third hour €2, €4/hour after that). To avoid registering at a machine, you can also get a Citybike Tourist Card (sold for €2/day at Royal Tours, near the Hofburg at Herrengasse 1-3)—but this extra step isn't worth the trouble. When you're done, drop off your bike at any stall, and make sure it's fully locked into the rack to avoid getting charged for more time.

Renting a Higher-Quality Bike: If you want to ride beyond the town center—or you simply want a better set of wheels—check out **Pedal Power,** with a handy central location near the Opera house. The local authority on bike touring both in town and from here to points along the Danube, Pedal Power rents bikes and provides good biking info (€5/hour, €17/4 hours, €27/24 hours, daily 8:30-18:00, Elisabethstrasse 13 at the corner of Eschenbachgasse). They can also deliver a bike to your hotel and pick it up when you're done (€32/day including delivery, tel. 01/729-7234, www.pedalpower.at), and they organize bike tours (described later). **Crazy Chicken** bike rental, a short tram ride from the Westbahnhof, is less convenient but a lot cheaper (€3/hour, €12/day, daily 8:30-19:00, near recommended Pension Fünfhaus at Sperrgasse 12—see page 1193 for directions, tel. 01/892-2134, mobile 0664-421-4789, www.crazychicken.at).

Rick Steves Free Audio Tours

I've produced free, self-guided audio tours of some of the main attractions in this chapter (download them via the Rick Steves Audio Europe smartphone app, www.ricksteves .com/audioeurope, or iTunes). These user-friendly, easy-to-follow, fun, and informative audio tours are available for my Vienna City Walk, Ringstrasse Tram Tour, and St. Stephen's Cathedral. Compared to live tours, my audio tours are hard to beat: Nobody will stand you up, the quality is reliable, you can take the tour exactly when you like, and they're free.

Tours in Vienna

Walking Tours—The TI's *Walks in Vienna* brochure describes the city's many guided walks. The basic 1.5-hour "Vienna at First Glance" introductory walk is offered daily throughout the summer (€14, leaves at 14:00 from near the Opera, in both English and German, just show up, tel. 01/876-7111, mobile 0664-260-4388, www.wienguide.at). Various specialized tours go once a week and are listed on their website.

Bike Tours—Several companies offer city tours. **Pedal Power** runs two different three-hour tours daily from May to September (€26/tour includes bike, €44 for both tours, €14 extra to keep the bike for the day, departs at 9:45 and 14:15 in front of Opera at corner of Operngasse and the Kärntner Ring, also rents bikes, tel. 01/729-7234, www.pedalpower.at). **Wolfgang Höfler** leads bike tours as well as walking tours (€140/2 hours, mobile 0676-304-4940, www.vienna-aktivtours.com, office@vienna-aktivtours.com; also listed later, under "Local Guides").

Bus Tours—**Red Bus City Tours'** convertible buses do a 1.5-hour loop, hitting the highlights of the city with a 20-minute shopping break in the middle. It covers the main first-district attractions as well as a big bus can, along with the entire Ringstrasse. But the most interesting part of the tour is outside the center—zipping through Prater Park, over the Danube for a glimpse of the city's Danube Island playground, and into the "Donau City" skyscraper zone. If the weather's good, the bus goes topless and offers great opportunities for photos (€14, departs hourly April-Oct 10:00-18:00, less frequently off-season, tours start one block behind the Opera at Lobkowitzplatz 1, pretty good recorded narration in any language, your own earbuds are better than the beat-up headphones they provide, tel. 01/512-4030, www.redbuscitytours .at). The boss, Gabriel, gives those with this book a free cold drink from the shop where you buy your tickets.

Vienna at a Glance

▲▲▲**Opera** Dazzling, world-famous opera house. **Hours:** By guided tour only, July-Aug generally daily at the top of each hour 10:00-16:00; Sept-June fewer tours, afternoon only, and none on Sun. See page 1130.

▲▲▲**St. Stephen's Cathedral** Enormous, historic Gothic cathedral in the center of Vienna. **Hours:** Church—daily 7:00-22:00; main nave—Mon-Sat 9:00-11:30 & 13:00-16:30, Sun 13:00-16:30, until 17:30 June-Aug. See page 1133.

▲▲▲**Hofburg Imperial Apartments** Lavish main residence of the Habsburgs. **Hours:** Daily July-Aug 9:00-18:00, Sept-June 9:00-17:30. See page 1138.

▲▲▲**Hofburg Treasury** The Habsburgs' collection of jewels, crowns, and other valuables—the best on the Continent. **Hours:** Wed-Mon 10:00-18:00, closed Tue. See page 1143.

▲▲▲**Kunsthistorisches Museum** World-class exhibit of the Habsburgs' art collection, including works by Raphael, Titian, Caravaggio, Bosch, and Bruegel. **Hours:** Tue-Sun 10:00-18:00, Thu until 21:00, closed Mon. See page 1151.

▲▲▲**Schönbrunn Palace** Spectacular summer residence of the Habsburgs, rivaling the grandeur of Versailles. **Hours:** Daily July-Aug 8:30-18:00, April-June and Sept-Oct 8:30-17:00, Nov-March 8:30-16:30. See page 1168.

▲▲**Haus der Musik** Modern museum with interactive exhibits on Vienna's favorite pastime. **Hours:** Daily 10:00-22:00. See page 1131.

▲▲**Hofburg New Palace Museums** Uncrowded collection of armor, musical instruments, and ancient Greek statues, in the elegant halls of a Habsburg palace. **Hours:** Wed-Sun 10:00-18:00, closed Mon-Tue. See page 1146.

▲▲**Albertina Museum** Habsburg residence with decent apartments and world-class temporary exhibits. **Hours:** Daily 10:00-18:00, Wed until 21:00. See page 1148.

▲▲**Kaisergruft** Crypt for the Habsburg royalty. **Hours:** Daily 10:00-18:00. See page 1149.

▲▲**Belvedere Palace** Elegant palace of Prince Eugene of Savoy, with a collection of 19th- and 20th-century Austrian art (including Klimt). **Hours:** Daily 10:00-18:00, Lower Palace only open Wed until 21:00. See page 1160.

▲**St. Peter's Church** Beautiful Baroque church in the old center. **Hours:** Mon-Fri 7:00-19:00, Sat-Sun 9:00-19:00. See page 1132.

▲**Spanish Riding School** Prancing white Lipizzaner stallions. **Hours:** Late Aug-late June performances Sun at 11:00 and either Sat at 11:00 or Fri at 19:00, plus less-impressive training sessions generally early Aug-late June Tue-Fri 10:00-12:00. See page 1146.

▲**St. Michael's Church Crypt** Final resting place of about 100 wealthy 18th-century Viennese. **Hours:** By tour Mon-Sat at 11:00 and 13:30. See page 1151.

▲**Natural History Museum** Big building facing the Kunsthistorisches, featuring the ancient *Venus of Willendorf*. **Hours:** Wed-Mon 9:00-18:30, Wed until 21:00, closed Tue. See page 1154.

▲**Karlskirche** Baroque church offering the unique (and temporary) chance to ride an elevator up into the dome. **Hours:** Mon-Sat 9:00-18:00, Sun 13:00-18:00. See page 1156.

▲**Academy of Fine Arts** Small but exciting collection by 15th- to 18th-century masters. **Hours:** Tue-Sun 10:00-18:00, closed Mon. See page 1157.

▲**The Secession** Art Nouveau exterior and Klimt paintings *in situ*. **Hours:** Tue-Sun 10:00-18:00, closed Mon. See page 1158.

▲**Naschmarkt** Sprawling, lively outdoor market. **Hours:** Mon-Fri 6:00-18:30, Sat 6:00-17:00, closed Sun, closes earlier in winter. See page 1160.

▲**KunstHausWien** Modern art museum dedicated to zany local artist/environmentalist Hundertwasser. **Hours:** Daily 10:00-19:00. See page 1165.

▲**Liechtenstein Museum** Impressive Baroque collection. **Hours:** Fri-Tue 10:00-17:00, closed Wed-Thu. See page 1167.

▲**Imperial Furniture Collection** Eclectic collection of Habsburg furniture. **Hours:** Tue-Sun 10:00-18:00, closed Mon. See page 1168.

Vienna Sightseeing offers a longer, three-hour city tour, including a tour of Schönbrunn Palace (€39, 3/day April-Oct, 2/day Nov-March). They also run hop-on, hop-off bus tours with recorded commentary. The schedule is posted curbside (three different routes, €13/1 hour, €16/2 hours, €20/all day, departs from the Opera 4/hour July-Aug 10:00-20:00, runs less frequently and stops earlier off-season, tel. 01/7124-6830, www.viennasightseeing .at). Given the city's excellent public transportation and this outfit's meager frequency, I'd skip this tour; if you just want a quick, guided city tour, take the Red Bus tours recommended above.

Ring Tram Tour—One of Europe's great streets, the Ringstrasse is lined with many of the city's top sights. Take a tram ride around the Ring with my free audio tour (see sidebar), which gives you a fun orientation and a ridiculously quick glimpse of some major sights as you glide by. Neither tram #1 nor #2 makes the entire loop around the Ring, but you can see it all by making one transfer between them (at the Schwedenplatz stop). A single transit ticket can be used to cover the whole route, including the transfer (though you're not allowed to interrupt your trip, except to transfer). For more on riding Vienna's trams, see page 1112.

The **Vienna Ring Tram,** a made-for-tourists streetcar, is a slightly easier but much pricier option, running clockwise along the entire Ringstrasse (€6 for one 30-minute loop, €9 for 24-hour hop-on, hop-off privileges, 2/hour 10:00-18:00, July-Aug until 19:00, recorded narration). The tour starts at the top and bottom of each hour on the Opera side of the Ring at Kärntner Ring. At each stop, you'll see an ad for this tram tour (look for *VRT Ring-Rund Sightseeing*). The schedule clearly notes the next departure time.

Horse-and-Buggy Tour—These traditional horse-and-buggies, called *Fiakers,* take rich romantics on clip-clop tours lasting 20 minutes (€40-old town), 40 minutes (€65-old town and the Ring), or one hour (€95-all of the above, but more thorough). You can share the ride and cost with up to five people. Because it's a kind of guided tour, talk to a few drivers before choosing a carriage, and pick someone who's fun and speaks English (tel. 01/401-060).

Local Guides—You'll pay about €140 for two hours. Get a group of six or more together and call it a party. The tourist board's website (www.vienna.info) has a long list of local guides with their specialties and contact information. **Lisa Zeiler** is an excellent guide (tel. 01/402-3688, lisa.zeiler@gmx .at). **Wolfgang Höfler,** a generalist with a knack for having psychoanalytical fun with history, enjoys the big changes of the 19th and 20th centuries (€135/2 hours, mobile 0676-304-4940, www.vienna-aktivtours.com, office@vienna-aktivtours.com, also leads bike tours—described earlier). If Lisa and Wolfgang are booked, they work with other good guides and can set you up.

Self-Guided Walk

Vienna City Walk

This walk connects the top three sights in Vienna's old center: the Opera, St. Stephen's Cathedral, and the Hofburg Palace. Along the way, you'll see sights covered elsewhere in this chapter (to find the full descriptions, flip to "Sights in Vienna," later), and get an overview of Vienna's past and present. Allow one hour, and more time if you plan to stop into any of the major sights along the way. You can download a free Rick Steves audio tour of this walk (see page 1115).

• *Begin at the square outside Vienna's landmark Opera house. (The Opera's entrance faces the Ringstrasse; we're starting at the busy pedestrian square that's to the right of the entrance as you're facing it.)*

Opera

If Vienna is the world capital of classical music, this building is its throne room, one of the planet's premier houses of music. It's

typical of Vienna's 19th-century buildings in that it features a revival style—Neo-Renaissance—with arched windows, half-columns, and the sloping, copper mansard roof typical of French Renaissance châteaux. Since the structure was built in 1869, almost all of the opera world's luminaries have passed

through here. Its former musical directors include Gustav Mahler, Herbert von Karajan, and Richard Strauss. Luciano Pavarotti, Maria Callas, Placido Domingo, and many other greats have sung from its stage.

In the pavement along the side of the Opera (and all along Kärntner Strasse, the bustling shopping street we'll visit shortly), you'll find star plaques forming a Hollywood-style walk of fame. These represent the stars of classical music—famous composers, singers, musicians, and conductors.

Looking up at the Opera, notice the giant outdoor screen onto which some live performances are projected (as noted in the posted schedules).

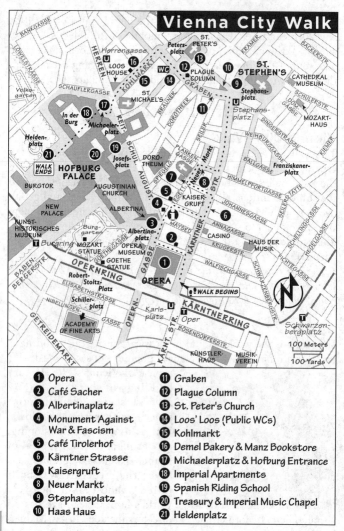

Vienna City Walk

1. Opera
2. Café Sacher
3. Albertinaplatz
4. Monument Against War & Fascism
5. Café Tirolerhof
6. Kärntner Strasse
7. Kaisergruft
8. Neuer Markt
9. Stephansplatz
10. Haas Haus
11. Graben
12. Plague Column
13. St. Peter's Church
14. Loos' Loos (Public WCs)
15. Kohlmarkt
16. Demel Bakery & Manz Bookstore
17. Michaelerplatz & Hofburg Entrance
18. Imperial Apartments
19. Spanish Riding School
20. Treasury & Imperial Music Chapel
21. Heldenplatz

VIENNA

If you're a fan, take a guided tour of the Opera. If you're not, you still might consider springing for an evening performance (standing-room tickets are surprisingly cheap; see page 1180). Regular opera tickets are sold at various points near here: The closest one is the small ticket office just below the screen, while the main one is across from the opposite side of the Opera, on Operngasse. For information about other entertainment options during your visit, check in at the Wien Ticket kiosk in the booth on this square.

The Opera marks a busy intersection in Vienna, where

Kärntner Strasse meets the Ring. The Karlsplatz U-Bahn station in front of the Opera is an underground shopping mall with fast food, newsstands, lots of pickpockets, and even a Vienna Opera Toilet experience (€0.60, *mit Musik*).

• *Walk behind the Opera and across the street toward the dark-red awning to find the famous...*

Café Sacher

This is the home of the world's classiest chocolate cake, the Sacher-Torte: two layers of cake separated by apricot jam and covered in

dark-chocolate icing, usually served with whipped cream. It was invented in a fit of improvisation in 1832 by Franz Sacher, dessert chef to Prince Metternich (the mastermind diplomat who redrew the map of post-Napoleon Europe). The cake became world-famous when the inventor's son served it next door at his hotel (you may have noticed the fancy doormen). Many locals complain that the cakes here have gone downhill, and many tourists are surprised by how dry they are—you really need that dollop of *Schlagobers*. Still, coffee and a slice of cake here can be €8 well invested for the historic ambience alone. While the café itself is grotesquely touristy, the adjacent Sacher Stube has ambience and natives to spare (same prices). For maximum elegance, sit inside.

• *Continue past Hotel Sacher. At the end of the street is a small, triangular, cobbled square adorned with modern sculptures.*

Albertinaplatz

As you enter the square, to the right you'll find the **TI**. On your left, the tan-and-white Neoclassical building with the statue

alcoves marks the tip of the Hofburg Palace—the sprawling complex of buildings that was long the seat of Habsburg power (we'll end this walk at the palace's center). The balustraded terrace up top was originally part of Vienna's defensive rampart. Later, it was the balcony

of Empress Maria Theresa's daughter Maria Christina, who lived at this end of the palace. Today, her home houses the **Albertina Museum,** topped by a sleek, controversial titanium canopy (called the "diving board" by critics). The museum's plush, 19th-century rooms are hung with facsimiles of its graphic collection, and an entire floor is dedicated to the Batliner collection, covering each artistic stage from Impressionism to the present day.

Albertinaplatz itself is filled with statues that make up the powerful, thought-provoking **Monument Against War and Fascism,** which commemorates the dark years when Austria came under Nazi rule (1938-1945).

The statue group has four parts. The split white monument, *The Gates of Violence,* remembers victims of all wars and violence. Standing directly in front of it, you're at the gates of a concentration camp. Then, as you explore the statues, you step into a montage of wartime images: clubs and WWI gas masks, a dying woman birthing a future soldier, and chained slave laborers sitting on a pedestal of granite cut from the infamous quarry at Mauthausen concentration camp. The hunched-over figure on the ground behind is a Jew forced to scrub anti-Nazi graffiti off a street with a toothbrush. Of Vienna's 200,000 Jews, more than 65,000 died in Nazi concentration camps. The statue with its head buried in the stone is Orpheus entering the underworld, meant to remind Austrians (and the rest of us) of the victims of Nazism...and the consequences of not keeping our governments on track. Behind that, the 1945 declaration that established Austria's second republic—and enshrined human rights—is cut into the stone.

Viewing this monument gains even more emotional impact when you realize what happened on this spot: During a WWII bombing attack, several hundred people were buried alive when the cellar they were using as shelter was demolished.

Austria was led into World War II by Germany, which annexed the country in 1938, saying Austrians were wannabe Germans anyway. But Austrians are not Germans—never were, never will be. They're quick to proudly tell you that Austria was founded in the 10th century, whereas Germany wasn't born until 1870. For seven years, just before and during World War II (1938-1945), there was no Austria. In 1955, after 10 years of joint occupation by the victorious Allies, Austria regained total independence on the condition that it would be forever neutral (and never join NATO or the Warsaw Pact). To this day, Austria is outside of NATO (and Germany).

Behind the monument is **Café Tirolerhof,** a classic Viennese café full of things that time has passed by: chandeliers, marble tables, upholstered booths, waiters in tuxes, and newspapers. For more on Vienna's cafés, see page 1173.

Often parked on the same square are the Red Bus City Tour buses, offering a handy way to get a quick overview of the city (see "Tours in Vienna," earlier).

• *From the café, turn right on Führichsgasse, passing the recommended cafeteria-style Rosenberger Markt Restaurant. Walk one block until you hit...*

Kärntner Strasse

This grand, mall-like street (traffic-free since 1974) is the people-watching delight of this in-love-with-life city. Today's Kärntner

Strasse (KAYRNT-ner SHTRAH-seh) is mostly a crass commercial pedestrian mall—its famed elegant shops are long gone. But locals know it's the same road Crusaders marched down as they headed off from St. Stephen's Cathedral for the Holy Land in the 12th century. Its name indicates that it leads south, toward the region of Kärnten (Carinthia, a province divided between Austria and Slovenia). Today it's full of shoppers and street musicians.

Where Führichsgasse meets Kärntner Strasse, note the city **Casino** (across the street and a half-block to your right, at #41)—once venerable, now tacky, it exemplifies the worst of the street's evolution. Turn left to head up Kärntner Strasse, going away from the Opera. As you walk along, be sure to look up, above the modern storefronts, for glimpses of the street's former glory. Near the end of the block, on the left at #26, **J & L Lobmeyr Crystal** ("Founded in 1823") still has its impressive brown storefront with gold trim, statues, and the Habsburg double-eagle. In the market for some $400 napkin rings? Lobmeyr's your place. Inside, breathe in the classic Old World ambience as you climb up to the glass museum (free entry, Mon-Fri 10:00-19:00, Sat 10:00-18:00, closed Sun).

• *At the end of the block, turn left on Marco d'Aviano Gasse (passing the fragrant flower stall) to make a short detour to the square called Neuer Markt. Straight ahead is an orange-ish church with a triangular roof and cross, the Capuchin Church. In its basement is the...*

Kaisergruft

Under the church sits the Imperial Crypt, filled with what's left of Austria's emperors, empresses, and other Habsburg royalty. For centuries, Vienna was the heart of a vast empire ruled by the Habsburg family, and here is where they lie buried in their fancy pewter coffins. You'll find all the Habsburg greats, including Maria Theresa, her son Josef II (Mozart's patron), Franz Josef, and Empress Sisi. Before moving on, consider paying your respects here.

• *Stretching north from the Kaisergruft is the square called...*

Neuer Markt

A block farther down, in the center of Neuer Markt, is the **four rivers fountain** showing Lady Providence surrounded by figures

symbolizing the rivers that flow into the Danube. The sexy statues offended Empress Maria Theresa, who actually organized "Chastity Commissions" to defend her capital city's moral standards. The modern buildings around you were rebuilt after World War II. Half of the city's inner center was intentionally destroyed by Churchill to demoralize the Viennese, who were disconcertingly enthusiastic about the Nazis.

• *Lady Providence's one bare breast points back to Kärntner Strasse (50 yards away). Before you head back to the busy shopping street, you could stop for a sweet treat at the heavenly, recommended Kurkonditorei Oberlaa (to get there, disobey the McDonald's arrows—it's at the far-left corner of the square).*

Leave the square and return to Kärntner Strasse. Turn left and continue down Kärntner Strasse. As you approach the cathedral, you're likely to first see it as a reflection in the round-glass windows of the modern Haas Haus. Pass the U-Bahn station (which has WCs) where the street spills into Vienna's main square...

Stephansplatz

The cathedral's frilly spire looms overhead, worshippers and tourists pour inside the church, and shoppers and top-notch street entertainers buzz around the outside. You're at the center of Vienna.

The Gothic **St. Stephen's Cathedral** (c. 1300-1450) is known for its 450-foot south tower, its colorful roof, and its place in Viennese history. When it was built, it was a huge church for what was then a tiny town, and it helped put the fledgling city on the map. At this point, you may want to take a break from the walk to tour

the church (see my self-guided tour on page 1134).

Where Kärntner Strasse hits Stephansplatz, the grand, soot-covered building with red columns is the **Equitable Building** (filled with lawyers, bankers, and insurance brokers). It's a fine example of Neoclassicism from the turn of the 20th century—look up and imagine how slick Vienna must have felt in 1900.

Facing St. Stephen's is the sleek concrete-and-glass **Haas Haus,** a postmodern building by noted Austrian architect Hans Hollein (finished in 1990). The curved facade is supposed to echo the Roman fortress of Vindobona (its ruins were found near here). Although the Viennese initially protested having this stark modern tower right next to their beloved cathedral, since then, it's become a fixture of Vienna's main square. Notice how the smooth, rounded glass reflects St. Stephen's pointy architecture, providing a great photo opportunity—especially at twilight.

• *Exit the square with your back to the cathedral. Walk past the Haas Haus, and bear right down the street called...*

Graben

This was once a *Graben,* or ditch—originally the moat for the Roman military camp. Back during Vienna's 19th-century heyday, there were nearly 200,000 people packed into the city's inner center (inside the Ringstrasse), walking through dirt streets. Today this area houses 20,000. Graben was a busy street with three lanes of traffic until the 1970s, when it was turned into one of Europe's first pedestrian-only zones. Take a moment to absorb the scene—you're standing in an area surrounded by history, postwar rebuilding, grand architecture, fine cafés, and people enjoying life...for me, quintessential Europe.

Two blocks after leaving Stephansplatz, you reach Dorotheergasse, on your left, which leads (after two more long blocks) to the **Dorotheum** auction house. Consider poking your nose in here later for some fancy window-shopping. Also along this street are

two recommended eateries: the sandwich shop Buffet Trześniewski—one of my favorite places for lunch—and the classic Café Hawelka (both described later).

In the middle of this pedestrian zone is the extravagantly blobby **Holy Trinity plague column** *(Pestsäule).* The 60-foot pillar of clouds sprouts angels and cherubs, with the wonderfully gilded Father, Son, and Holy Ghost at the top (all protected by an anti-pigeon net).

In 1679, Vienna was hit by a massive epidemic of bubonic plague. Around 75,000

Viennese died—about a third of the city. Emperor Leopold I dropped to his knees (something emperors never did in public) and begged God to save the city. (Find Leopold about a quarter of the way up the monument, just above the brown banner. Hint: The inbreeding typical of royal families left him with a gaping underbite.) His prayer was heard by Lady Faith (the statue below Leopold, carrying a cross). With the help of a heartless little cupid, she tosses an old naked woman—symbolizing the plague—into the abyss and saves the city. In gratitude, Leopold vowed to erect this monument, which became a model for other cities ravaged by the same plague.

• *Thirty yards past the plague monument, look down the short street to the right, which frames a Baroque church with a stately green dome.*

St. Peter's Church

Leopold I ordered this church to be built as a thank-you for surviving the 1679 plague. The church stands on the site of a much older church that may have been Vienna's first (or second) Christian church. Inside, St. Peter's shows Vienna at its Baroque best. Note that the church offers free organ concerts (Mon-Fri at 15:00, Sat-Sun at 20:00).

• *Continue west on Graben, where you'll immediately find some stairs leading underground to...*

Loos' Loos

In about 1900, a local chemical-maker needed a publicity stunt to prove that his chemicals really got things clean. He purchased two wine cellars under Graben and had them turned into classy WCs in the Modernist style (designed by Adolf Loos—see sidebar), complete with chandeliers and finely crafted mahogany. While the chandeliers are gone, the restrooms remain a relatively appealing place to do your business—in fact, they're so inviting that they're used for poetry readings. Locals and tourists happily pay €0.50 for a quick visit.

• *Graben dead-ends at the aristocratic supermarket Julius Meinl am Graben. From here, turn left. In the distance is the big green and gold dome of the Hofburg, where we'll end this walk. The street leading up to the Hofburg is...*

Kohlmarkt

This is Vienna's most elegant and unaffordable shopping street, lined with Cartier, Armani, Gucci, Tiffany, and the emperor's palace at the end. Strolling Kohlmarkt, daydream about the edible

Adolf Loos
(1870-1933)

"Decoration is a crime," wrote Adolf Loos, the turn-of-the-20th-century architect who was Vienna's answer to Frank Lloyd Wright. Foreshadowing the Modernist style of "less is more" and "form follows function," Loos stripped buildings down to their structural skeletons. In his day, most buildings were plastered with fake Greek columns, frosted with Baroque balustrades, and studded with statues. Even the newer buildings featured flowery Art Nouveau additions. Loos' sparse, geometrical style stood out at the time—and it still does more than a century later. Loos was convinced that unnecessary ornamentation was a waste of workers' valuable time and energy, and was a symbol of an unevolved society. He even went so far as to compare decoration on a facade with a lavatory wall smeared with excrement. You'll still find many of Loos' once-revolutionary, now tame-seeming buildings scattered around Vienna.

window displays at **Demel,** the ultimate Viennese chocolate shop (#14, daily 10:00-19:00). The room is filled with Art Nouveau boxes of Empress Sisi's choco-dreams come true: *Kandierte Veilchen* (candied violet petals), *Katzenzungen*

(cats' tongues), and so on. The cakes here are moist (compared to the dry Sacher-Tortes). The enticing window displays change monthly, reflecting current happenings in Vienna. Inside, there's an impressive cancan of Vienna's most beloved cakes—displayed to tempt visitors into springing for the €10 cake-and-coffee deal (point to the cake you want). You can sit inside, with a view of the cake-making, or outside, with the street action (upstairs is less crowded). Shops like this boast "K.u.K."—signifying that during the Habsburgs' heyday, it was patronized by the *König und Kaiser* (king and emperor—same guy). If you happen to be looking through Demel's window at exactly 19:01, just after closing, you can witness one of the great tragedies of modern Europe: the daily dumping of its unsold cakes.

Next to Demel, the **Manz Bookstore** has a Loos-designed facade (see "Adolf Loos" sidebar, earlier).

• *Kohlmarkt ends at the square called...*

Michaelerplatz

This square is dominated by the **Hofburg Palace.** Study the grand Neo-Baroque facade, dating from about 1900. The four heroic giants illustrate Hercules wrestling with his great challenges (Emperor Franz Josef, who commissioned the gate, felt he could relate).

In the center of this square, a scant bit of **Roman Vienna** lies exposed just beneath street level.

Do a slow, clockwise pan to get your bearings, starting (over your left shoulder as you face the Hofburg) with **St. Michael's Church,** which offers fascinating tours of its crypt. To the right of that is the fancy **Loden-Plankl shop,** with traditional Austrian formalwear, including dirndls. Farther to the right, across Augustinerstrasse, is the wing of the palace that houses the **Spanish Riding School** and its famous white Lipizzaner stallions. Farther down this street lies **Josefsplatz,** with the Augustinian Church, and the Dorotheum auction house. At the end of the street are Albertinaplatz and the Opera (where we started this walk).

Continue your spin: Two buildings over from the Hofburg (to the right), the modern **Loos House** (now a bank) has a facade featuring a perfectly geometrical grid of square columns and windows. Although the Loos House might seem boring today, in its time, it was considered to be Vienna's first "modern" building—with a trapezoidal footprint that makes no attempt to hide the awkwardly shaped street corner it stands on. Windows lack the customary cornice framing the top—a "house without eyebrows." Compared to the Neo-Rococo facade of the Hofburg, the stern Modernism of the Loos House appears to be from an entirely different age. And yet, both of these—as well as the Eiffel Tower and Mad Ludwig's fairy-tale Neuschwanstein Castle—were built in the same generation, roughly around 1900. In many ways, this jarring juxtaposition exemplifies the architectural turmoil of the turn of the 20th century, and represents the passing of the torch from Europe's age of divine monarchs to the modern era.

• *We'll finish up our tour where Austria's glorious history began—at the...*

Hofburg

This is the complex of palaces where the Habsburg emperors lived (except in summer, when they lived out at Schönbrunn Palace). Enter the Hofburg through the gate, where you immediately find

yourself beneath a big rotunda (the netting is there to keep birds from perching). The doorway on the right is the entrance to the **Imperial Apartments,** where the Habsburg emperors once lived in chandeliered elegance. Today you can tour its lavish rooms, as well as a museum on Empress Sisi, and a porcelain and silver collection. To the left is the ticket office for the **Spanish Riding School.**

Continuing on, you emerge from the rotunda into the main courtyard of the Hofburg, called **In der Burg.** The Caesar-like statue is of Habsburg Emperor Franz II (1768-1835), grandson of Maria Theresa, grandfather of Franz Josef, and father-in-law of Napoleon. Behind him is a tower with three kinds of clocks (the yellow disc shows the phase of the moon tonight). To the right of Franz are the Imperial Apartments, and to the left are the offices of Austria's mostly ceremonial president (the more powerful chancellor lives in a building just behind this courtyard).

Franz Josef faces the oldest part of the palace. The colorful red, black, and gold gateway (behind you), which used to have a drawbridge, leads over the moat and into the 13th-century Swiss Court (Schweizerhof), named for the Swiss mercenary guards once stationed there. As you enter, you're passing into the historic core of the palace, the site of the first fortress, and, historically, the place of last refuge. Here you'll find the **Treasury** (Schatzkammer) and the **Imperial Music Chapel** (Hofmusikkapelle), where the Boys' Choir sings the Mass.

Back at In der Burg, face Franz and turn left, passing through the **tunnel,** with a few tourist shops and restaurants.

The tunnel spills out into spacious **Heldenplatz** (Heroes' Square). On the left is the impressive curved facade of the **New Palace** (Neue Burg). This vast wing was built in the early 1900s to be the new Habsburg living quarters (and was meant to have a matching building facing it). But in 1914, the heir-to-the-throne, Archduke Franz Ferdinand—while waiting politely for his long-lived uncle, Emperor Franz Josef, to die—was assassinated in Sarajevo. The archduke's death sparked World War I and the eventual end of eight centuries of Habsburg rule.

This impressive building saw even sadder days a few decades later, when Adolf Hitler addressed adoring throngs from the New Palace balcony in 1938, after Austria had been annexed.

Today the building houses the **New Palace museums,** an eclectic collection of weaponry, suits of armor, musical instruments, and ancient Greek statues. The two equestrian statues depict Prince Eugene of Savoy (1663-1736), who battled the Ottoman Turks, and Archduke Charles (1771-1847), who battled Napoleon. Eugene gazes toward the far distance at the prickly spires of Vienna's City Hall.

The Hofburg's **Burggarten** (with its much-photographed Mozart statue) is not visible from here, but it's just behind the New Palace. If you continued on through the Greek-columned passageway (the Äussere Burgtor), you'd reach the Ringstrasse, the Kunsthistorisches Museum, and the MuseumsQuartier.

• *Our walk is finished. You're in the heart of Viennese sightseeing. The Hofburg contains some of Vienna's best sights and museums. From the Opera to the Hofburg, from chocolate to churches, from St. Stephen's to Sacher-Tortes—Vienna waits for you.*

Sights in Vienna

In the Old Town, Within the Ring

These sights are listed roughly from south to north. For a self-guided walk connecting many of central Vienna's top sights—including some of the ones below—see my "Vienna City Walk," earlier.

▲▲▲**Opera (Staatsoper)**—The Opera, facing the Ring and near the TI, is a central point for any visitor. Vienna remains one of the world's great cities for classical music, and this building still belts out some of the finest opera, both classic and cutting-edge. While the critical reception of the building 130 years ago led the architect to commit suicide, and though it's been rebuilt since its destruction by WWII bombs, it's still a sumptuous place. The interior has a chandeliered lobby and carpeted staircases perfect for making the scene. The theater itself features five wrap-around balconies, gold and red decor, and a bracelet-like chandelier.

Depending on your level of tolerance for opera, you can simply admire the Neo-Renaissance building from the outside, take a guided tour of the lavish interior, visit the Opera Museum, or attend a performance.

Performances: For information on buying tickets and attending a performance, see page 1180.

Tours: You can only enter the Opera if you're attending a performance or if you join a guided 45-minute tour in English (€6.50, ticket covers modest Opera Museum, described below; tours run July-Aug generally daily at the top of each hour 10:00-16:00; Sept-June fewer tours, afternoons only, and none on Sun; buy tickets 20 minutes before tour departs—ticket office is around the left side, as you face the main entrance; tel. 01/514-442-606). Note that tour times are often changed or cancelled due to rehearsals and performances. Schedules with daily listings for each month (including tour times) are posted all around the building; you can also pick up the monthly *Prolog* program, which includes the schedule for tours.

Opera Museum: Included in your opera tour ticket (whether you like it or not), this museum is a let-down. The permanent exhibit chronologically traces the illustrious history of the Vienna State Opera, highlighting the most famous singers, directors (including Gustav Mahler and Herbert von Karajan), and performances. It also features old posters, costumes, and lots of photographs (main topics in English, but most descriptions in German only). There are also rotating three-month-long special exhibits (€3, or included in the Opera tour ticket; Tue-Sun 10:00-18:00, closed Mon; across the street and a block away from the Opera toward the Hofburg, tucked down a courtyard at Hanuschgasse 3, near Albertina Museum, tel. 01/514-442-100).

▲▲**Haus der Musik**—Vienna's "House of Music" is a high-tech experience that celebrates this hometown specialty. The museum is unique for its effective use of interactive touchscreen computers and headphones to explore the physics of sound. Really experiencing the place takes time. It's open late and makes a good evening activity. The first floor features a small exhibit on the Vienna Philharmonic Orchestra, including the batons of prominent conductors and Leonard Bernstein's tux. On the second floor, wander through the "sonosphere" and marvel at the amazing acoustics. Spend some time at the well-presented, interactive headphone stations to learn about the nature of sound and music; I could actually hear what I thought only a piano tuner could discern. The third floor features fine audiovisual exhibits on each of the famous hometown boys (Haydn, Mozart, Beethoven, Schubert, Strauss, and Mahler). Before leaving, pick up a virtual baton to conduct the Vienna Philharmonic. Each time you screw up, the musicians put their instruments down and ridicule you; make it through the piece, and you'll get a rousing round of applause.

Cost and Hours: €11, includes audioguide for third floor only, half-price Tue after 17:30, €17 combo-ticket with Mozarthaus, daily 10:00-22:00, last entry one hour before closing, 2 blocks from the Opera at Seilerstätte 30, tel. 01/513-4850, www.hdm.at.

▲**The Dorotheum: Vienna's Auction House**—For an aristocrat's flea market, drop by Austria's answer to Sotheby's. The ground floor has shops, an info desk with a schedule of upcoming auctions, and a few auction items. Some items are available for immediate sale (marked *VKP*, for *Verkaufpreis*—"sales price"), while others are up for auction (marked *DIFF. RUF*). Labels on each item predict the auction value.

The three upstairs floors have antique furniture and fancy

knickknacks (some for immediate sale, others for auction), many brought in by people who've inherited old things and don't have room. Wandering through here, you feel like you're touring a museum with exhibits you can buy (Mon-Fri 10:00-18:00, Sat 9:00-17:00, closed Sun, classy little café on second floor, between the Graben pedestrian street and Hofburg at Dorotheergasse 17, tel. 01/51560, www.dorotheum.com).

Afterwards, you can continue your hunt for the perfect curio on the streets around the Dorotheum, lined with many fine antique shops.

▲**St. Peter's Church (Peterskirche)**—Baroque Vienna is at its best in this gem, tucked away a few steps from the Graben. Admire the rose-and-gold, oval-shaped Baroque interior, topped with a ceiling fresco of Mary kneeling to be crowned by Jesus and the Father, while the dove of the Holy Spirit floats way up in the lantern. Taken together, the church's elements—especially the organ, altar painting, pulpit, and coat of arms (in the base of the dome) of church founder Leopold I—make St. Peter's one of the city's most beautiful and ornate churches.

To the right of the altar, a dramatic golden statue shows the martyrdom of St. John Nepomuk (c. 1340-1393). The Czech saint defied the heretical King Wenceslas, so he was tossed to his death off the Charles Bridge in Prague (for the story, see page 88). In true Baroque style, we see the dramatic peak of his fall, when John has just passed the point of no return. The Virgin Mary floats overhead in a silver cloud.

The present church (from 1733) stands atop earlier churches dating back 1,600 years. On either side of the nave are glass cases containing skeletons of Christian martyrs from Roman times. Above the relic on the left is a painting of the modern saint Josemaría Escrivá, founder of the conservative Catholic organization Opus Dei, of *Da Vinci Code* notoriety.

Cost and Hours: Free, Mon-Fri 7:00-19:00, Sat-Sun 9:00-19:00; free organ concerts Mon-Fri at 15:00, Sat-Sun at 20:00; just off the Graben between the Plague Monument and Kohlmarkt, tel. 01/533-6433.

Mozarthaus Vienna—Opened in 2006 to commemorate Wolfgang's 250th birthday, this museum is easy to get excited about, but it disappoints. Exhibits fill the only surviving Mozart residence in Vienna, where he lived from 1784 to 1787, when he had lots of money (and produced some of his most famous works, including *The Marriage of Figaro* and *Don Giovanni*). While the museum might be worth the time and money for enthusiasts, I much prefer the Haus der Musik (described earlier).

Cost and Hours: €10, includes audioguide, €17 combo-ticket with Haus der Musik, daily 10:00-19:00, last entry 30 minutes before closing, a block behind the cathedral, go through arcade at #5a and walk 50 yards to Domgasse 5, tel. 01/512-1791, www .mozarthausvienna.at.

Judenplatz Memorial and Museum—The classy square called Judenplatz marks the location of Vienna's 15th-century Jewish community, one of Europe's largest at the time. The square, once filled with a long-gone synagogue, is now dominated by a blocky **memorial** to the 65,000 Viennese Jews killed by the Nazis. The memorial—a library turned inside out—symbolizes Jews as "people of the book" and causes viewers to ponder the huge loss of culture, knowledge, and humanity that took place between 1938 and 1945.

The **Judenplatz Museum,** while sparse and overpriced, has displays on medieval Jewish life and a well-done video re-creating the ghetto as it looked five centuries ago. Wander the scant remains of the medieval synagogue below street level—discovered during the construction of the Holocaust memorial. This was the scene of a medieval massacre. Since Christians weren't allowed to lend money, Jews were Europe's moneylenders. As so often happened in Europe, when Viennese Christians fell too deeply into debt, they found a convenient excuse to wipe out the local ghetto—and their debts at the same time. In 1421, 200 of Vienna's Jews were burned at the stake. Others who refused a forced conversion committed mass suicide in the synagogue (€10 ticket also covers a different Jewish Museum on Dorotheergasse; alternatively, consider €15 "Vienna Museum Melange" combo-ticket with either Haus der Musik, Hundertwasser's KunstHausWien, or Mozarthaus; Sun-Thu 10:00-18:00, Fri 10:00-14:00, closed Sat, Judenplatz 8, tel. 01/535-0431, www.jmw.at).

▲▲▲St. Stephen's Cathedral (Stephansdom)

This massive church is the Gothic needle around which Vienna spins. According to the medieval vision of its creators, it stands like a giant jeweled reliquary, offering praise to God from the center of the city. The church and its towers, especially the 450-foot south tower, give the city its most iconic image. (Check your pockets for €0.10 coins; ones minted in Austria feature the south tower on the back.) The cathedral has survived Vienna's many wars and today symbolizes the city's spirit and love of freedom.

Cost: It's free to enter the back part and north aisle of the church, but it costs €3.50 to get into the main nave, where most of the interesting items are located (more for special exhibits). Going up the towers costs €3.50 (by stairs, south tower) or €4.50 (by elevator, north tower). The €14.50 combo-ticket—covering entry, audioguide, both towers, and the catacombs tour—is overkill for most visitors.

Hours: The church doors are open daily 7:00-22:00, but the main nave is open for tourists Mon-Sat 9:00-11:30 & 13:00-16:30, Sun 13:00-16:30, until 17:30 June-Aug. During services, you can't enter the main nave (unless you're attending Mass) or access the north tower elevator or catacombs, but you can go into the back of the church.

Information: Tel. 01/515-523-526, www.stephanskirche.at.

Tours: The €4.50 tours in English are entertaining (daily at 15:45, check information board inside entry to confirm schedule, price includes main nave entry). The €1 audioguide is helpful. You can download a free Rick Steves audio tour of the cathedral (see page 1115).

◆ **Self-Guided Tour:** This tour will give you a good look at the cathedral, inside and out.

Cathedral Exterior: Before we go inside, let's circle around the cathedral for a look at its impressive exterior.

• *As you face the church's main entry, go to the right across the little square, and find the old-time photos next to the door marked* 3a Stephansplatz. *From here, you can take in the sheer magnitude of this massive church, with its skyscraping spire.*

The church we see today is the third one on this spot. It dates mainly from 1300-1450, when builders expanded on an earlier structure and added two huge **towers** at the end of each transept. The impressive 450-foot south tower—capped with a golden orb and cross—took two generations to build (65 years) and was finished in 1433. The tower is a rarity among medieval churches in that it was completed before the Gothic style—and the age of faith—petered out. The half-size north tower (223 feet), around the other side of the church, was meant to be a matching steeple. But around 1500, it was abandoned in mid-construction, when the money was used to defend the country against the Ottomans rather than to build church towers. You can ascend both towers (stairs to the south tower, an elevator to the north tower); for details, see the end of this tour.

The cathedral was heavily damaged at the end of World War II. Near where you are standing are **old photos** showing the destruction. In 1945, Vienna was caught in the chaos between the occupying Nazis and the approaching Soviets. Allied bombs sparked fires in nearby buildings. The embers leapt to the cathedral rooftop. The original timbered Gothic roof burned, the cathedral's huge bell crashed to the ground, and the fire raged for two days. Civic pride prompted a financial outpouring, and the roof was rebuilt to its original splendor by 1952—doubly impressive considering the bombed-out state of the country at that time.

• *Circle the church exterior counterclockwise, passing the entrance to the south tower. If you're up for climbing the 343 stairs to the top, you could do it now, but it's better to wait until the end of this tour (tower climb described at the end of this tour).*

As you hook around behind the church, look for the cathedral bookshop (Dombuchhandlung) at the end of the block. Pause in front of that shop and look toward the cathedral.

Just above street level, notice the marble **pulpit** under the golden starburst. The priest would stand here, stoking public opinion against the Ottomans to crowds far bigger than could fit into the church. Above the pulpit (in a scene from around 1700), a saint stands victoriously atop a vanquished Turk.

To your right, notice the entrance to the forlorn **Cathedral Museum.** This pricey, skippable sight provides a close-up look at piles of religious paintings, statues, stained-glass windows, illuminated manuscripts, and a treasury (€7, Tue-Sat 10:00-17:00, closed Sun-Mon, Stephansplatz 6, tel. 01/515-523-689).

• *Continue circling the church, passing a line of horse carriages waiting to take tourists for a ride. Go all the way around to the west facade.*

The Romanesque-style **main entrance** is the oldest part of the church (c. 1240—part of a church that stood here before). Right behind you is the site of Vindobona, a Roman garrison town. Before the Romans converted to Christianity, there was a pagan temple here, and this entrance pays homage to that ancient heritage. Roman-era statues are embedded in the facade, and the two **octagonal towers** flanking the main doorway are dubbed the "heathen towers" because they're built with a few recycled Roman stones (flipped over to hide the pagan inscriptions and expose the smooth sides).

• *Step inside.*

Cathedral Interior: Find a spot to peer through the gate down the immense **nave**—more than a football field long and nine stories tall. Stylistically, the nave is Gothic with a Baroque overlay. The nave's columns are richly populated with 77 life-size stone statues, making a saintly parade to the high altar.

To the right as you enter, in a gold-and-silver sunburst frame, is a crude Byzantine-style **Maria Pócs Icon** (Pötscher Madonna), brought here from a humble Hungarian village church. The picture of Mary and Child is said to have wept real tears in 1697, as Central Europe was once again being threatened by the Turks.

Along the left side of the nave is the **gift shop.** Step in to marvel at the 14th-century statuary decorating its wall—some of the finest carvings in the church.

To the left of the gift shop is the gated entrance to the **Chapel of Prince Eugene of Savoy.** Prince Eugene (1663-1736), a teenage seminary student from France, arrived in Vienna in 1683 as the city was about to be overrun by the Ottoman Turks. He volunteered for the army and helped save the city, launching a brilliant career as a military man for the Habsburgs. His specialty was conquering the Ottomans. When he died, the grateful Austrians buried him here, under this chapel, marked by a tomb hatch in the floor.

• *To access the main nave of the church, you'll have to pay admission. Once through the ticket line, start down the nave toward the altar.*

At the second pillar on the left is the Gothic sandstone **pulpit** (c. 1500), a masterpiece carved from three separate blocks (see if you can find the seams). A spiral stairway winds up to the lectern, surrounded and supported by the four church "fathers," whose writings influenced early Catholic dogma. The pulpit is as crammed with religious meaning as it is with beautifully realistic carvings. The top of the stairway's railing swarms with lizards (animals of light), and toads (animals of darkness). The "Dog of the Lord" stands at the top, making sure none of those toads pollutes the sermon. Below the toads, wheels with three parts (the Trinity) roll up, while wheels with four spokes (the four seasons and the four cardinal directions, symbolizing mortal life) roll down.

Find the guy peeking out from under the stairs. This may be a **self-portrait** of the sculptor. In medieval times, art was done for the glory of God, and artists worked anonymously. But this pulpit was carved as humanist Renaissance ideals were creeping in from Italy—and individual artists were becoming famous. So the artist included what may be a rare self-portrait bust in his work.

• *Continue up to the main altar.*

During World War II, many of the city's top art treasures were stowed safely in cellars and salt mines—hidden by both the Nazi occupiers (to protect against war damage) and by citizens (to protect against Nazi looters). The **stained-glass windows** behind the high altar were meticulously dismantled and packed away. The pulpit was encased in a shell of brick. As the war was drawing to a close, it appeared St. Stephen's would escape major damage. But as the Nazis were fleeing, the bitter Nazi commander in charge of the

VIENNA

city ordered that the church be destroyed. Fortunately, his under-lings disobeyed. Unfortunately, the church accidentally caught fire during Allied bombing shortly thereafter, and the wooden roof collapsed onto the stone vaults of the ceiling. The Tupperware-colored glass on either side of the nave dates from the 1950s. Before the fire, the church was lit mostly with clear Baroque-era windows.

To the right of the main altar is the **tomb of Frederick III.** This imposing, red-marble tomb is like a big king-size-bed coffin with an effigy of Frederick lying on top (not visible—but there's a photo of the effigy on the left). The top of the tomb is decorated with his coats of arms, representing the many territories he ruled over. Frederick III (1415-1493) is considered the "father" of Vienna for turning the small village into a royal town with a cosmopolitan feel.

· *After exploring the nave, consider three more church-related sights: touring the catacombs, and ascending either one of the two towers.*

Catacombs (Katakomben): The catacombs (viewable by guided tour only) hold the bodies—or at least the innards—of 72 Habsburgs, including that of Rudolf IV, the man who began build-ing the south tower. This is where Austria's rulers were buried before the Kaisergruft was built (see page 1149), and where later Habsburgs' entrails were entombed. The copper urns preserve the imperial organs in alcohol. I touched Maria Theresa's urn...and it wobbled (€4.50, daily 10:00-11:30 & 13:30-16:30, until 17:30 June-Aug, tours depart about every 30 minutes and are in German and English). Just be at the stairs in the left/north transept to meet the guide.

Ascending the North Tower: This tower, reached from inside the church (look for the *Aufzug zur Pummerin* sign), holds the famous "Pummerin" bell—cast from captured Ottoman cannons, this bell rings in the New Year. This tower is easier to ascend than the south tower (described next), but it's much shorter and not as exciting, with lesser views (€4.50, daily 9:00-11:30 & 13:00-16:30, until 17:30 in June-Aug, entrance inside the church on the left/north side of the nave; you can access this elevator without buying a ticket for the main nave).

Climbing the South Tower: The iconic south tower offers a far better view than the north one, but you'll earn it by climb-ing 343 tightly wound steps up the spiral staircase (€3.50, daily 9:00-17:30; this hike burns about one Sacher-Torte of calories). To reach the entrance, exit the church and make a U-turn to the left. This tower, once key to the city's defense as a lookout point, is still dear to Viennese hearts. (It's long been affectionately nicknamed "Steffl," Viennese for "Stevie.") No church spire in (what was) the Austro-Hungarian Empire is taller—by Habsburg decree. From the top, use your city map to locate the famous sights.

The Hofburg Palace

The complex, confusing, and imposing Imperial Palace, with 640 years of architecture, demands your attention. This first Habsburg residence grew with the family empire from the 13th century until 1913, when the last "new wing" opened. The winter residence of the Habsburg rulers until 1918, it's still the home of the Austrian president's office, 5,000 government workers, and several important museums. For an overview of the palace layout, see map on next page.

Planning Your Time: Don't get confused by the Hofburg's myriad courtyards and many museums. Focus on three sights: the Imperial Apartments, Treasury, and the museums at the New Palace (Neue Burg). With more time, consider the Hofburg's many other sights, covering virtually all facets of the imperial lifestyle.

Eating at the Hofburg: Down the tunnel to Heroes' Square is a tiny but handy sandwich bar called **Hofburg Stüberl.** It's ideal for a cool, quiet sit and a drink or snack (same €3 sandwich price whether you sit or go, Mon-Fri 7:00-18:00, Sat-Sun 10:00-16:00). For a cheap, quick meal, duck into the mod and efficient, cafeteria-style **Restaurant zum Alten Hofkeller** in a cellar under the palace (€5 plates, Mon-Fri 7:30-13:30, closed Sat-Sun and in Aug, on the street that runs along the right side of the Hofburg as you face the main entry, on the left-hand side at Schauflergasse 7). The **Soho Kantine,** in the basement of the National Library, is a cheap-but-not-cheery option (described on page 1202).

▲▲▲Hofburg Imperial Apartments (Kaiserappartements)

These lavish, Versailles-type, "wish-I-were-God" royal rooms are the downtown version of the grander Schönbrunn Palace. If you're rushed and have time for only one palace, make it this one. Palace visits are a one-way romp through three separate exhibits: a porcelain and silver collection, a museum dedicated to the enigmatic and troubled Empress Sisi, and the luxurious apartments themselves.

The Imperial Apartments are a mix of Old World luxury and modern 19th-century conveniences. Here, Emperor Franz Josef I lived and worked along with his wife Elisabeth, known as Sisi. The Sisi Museum traces the development of her legend, analyzing how her fabulous but tragic life created a 19th-century Princess Diana. You'll read bits of her poetic writing, see exact copies of her now-lost jewelry, and learn about her escapes, dieting mania, and chocolate bills.

Cost and Hours: €10.50, includes well-done audioguide, also covered by €23.50 Sisi Ticket (see page 1111), daily July-Aug 9:00-18:00, Sept-June 9:00-17:30, last entry one hour before closing, enter from courtyard through St. Michael's Gate—just off

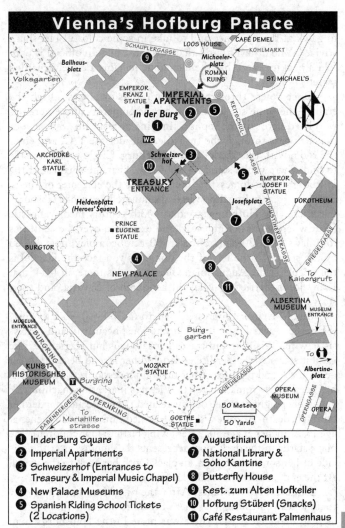

Vienna's Hofburg Palace

1. In der Burg Square
2. Imperial Apartments
3. Schweizerhof (Entrances to Treasury & Imperial Music Chapel)
4. New Palace Museums
5. Spanish Riding School Tickets (2 Locations)
6. Augustinian Church
7. National Library & Soho Kantine
8. Butterfly House
9. Rest. zum Alten Hofkeller
10. Hofburg Stüberl (Snacks)
11. Café Restaurant Palmenhaus

Michaelerplatz, tel. 01/533-7570, www.hofburg-wien.at.

Information: With the included audioguide and the self-guided tour below, you won't need the €8 *Imperial Apartments/Sisi Museum/Silver Collection* guidebook. If you listen to the entire audioguide, allow 40 minutes for the silver collection, 30 minutes for the Sisi Museum, and 40 minutes for the apartments.

⊙ **Self-Guided Tour:** Your visit (and the excellent audioguide) starts on the ground floor.

Imperial Porcelain and Silver Collection: Here you'll see the Habsburg court's vast tableware collection, which the audioguide actually manages to make fairly interesting. Browse the collection to gawk at the opulence and to take in some colorful Habsburg trivia. (Who'd have thunk that the court had an official way to fold a napkin—and that the technique remains a closely guarded secret?)

Once you're through all those rooms of dishes, climb the stairs—the same staircase used by the emperors and empresses who lived here. At the top is a timeline of Sisi's life. Swipe your ticket to pass through the turnstile, consider the WC, and enter the room with the **Model of the Hofburg.** Circle to the far side to find where you're standing right now, near the smallest of the Hofburg's three domes. The Hofburg was the epicenter of one of Europe's great political powers—six hundred years of Habsburgs lived here. The Hofburg started as a 13th-century medieval castle (near where you are right now) and expanded over the centuries to today's 240,000-square-meter (60-acre) complex, now owned by the state. To the left of the dome (as you face the facade) is the steeple of the Augustinian Church. It was there, in 1854, that Franz Josef married 16-year-old Elisabeth of Bavaria, and their story began.

Sisi Museum: Empress Elisabeth (1837-1898)—a.k.a. "Sisi" (SEE-see)—was Franz Josef's mysterious, beautiful, and narcissistic wife. This museum traces her fabulous but tragic life. The exhibit starts where her life ended and her legend began (see her death mask and pictures of her funeral procession). Although Sisi has been overly romanticized by Vienna's marketing machine, it's genuinely poignant to see objects related to her life and ponder her untimely death. Admire Sisi's hard-earned thin waist (20 inches at age 16, 21 inches at age 50...after giving birth to four children). The black statue in the dark room represents the empress after the suicide of her son—aloof, thin, in black, with her back to the world. At the end, ponder the crude, knife-like file that killed Sisi.

Imperial Apartments: After the Sisi Museum, a one-way route takes you through a series of royal rooms. The first room—as if to make clear that there was more to the Habsburgs than Sisi—shows a family tree tracing the Habsburgs from 1273 to their messy WWI demise. From here, enter the private apartments of the royal family (Franz Josef's first, then Sisi's).

Franz Josef's apartments illustrate the lifestyle of the last great Habsburg ruler. In these rooms, he presided over defeats and liberal inroads as the world was changing and the monarchy becoming obsolete. Here he met with advisors and welcomed foreign dignitaries, hosted lavish, white-gloved balls and stuffy formal dinners, and raised three children. He slept (alone) on his austere bed while his beloved wife Sisi retreated to her own rooms. He suffered through the assassination of his brother, the suicide

Sisi
(1837-1898)

Empress Elisabeth—Franz Josef's beautiful wife—was the 19th-century equivalent of Princess Diana. Known as "Sisi" since childhood, she became an instant celebrity when she married Franz Josef at the age of 16.

Sisi's main goals in life seem to have been preserving her reputation as a beautiful empress, maintaining her Barbie-doll figure, and tending to her fairy-tale, ankle-length hair. In the 1860s, she was considered one of the most beautiful women in the world. But, in spite of severe dieting and fanatic exercise, age took its toll. After turning 30, she refused to allow photographs or portraits, and was generally seen in public with a delicate fan covering her face (and bad teeth).

Complex and influential, Sisi was adored by Franz Josef, whom she respected. Although Franz Josef was supposed to have married her sister Helene (in an arranged diplomatic marriage), he fell in love with Sisi instead. It was one of the Habsburgs' few marriages for love.

Sisi's personal mission and political cause was promoting Hungary's bid for autonomy within the empire. Her personal tragedy was the death of her son Rudolf, the crown prince, in an apparent suicide (an incident often dramatized as the "Mayerling Affair," named after the royal hunting lodge where it happened). Disliking Vienna and the confines of the court, Sisi traveled more and more frequently. (She spent so much time in Budapest, and with Hungarian statesman Count Andrássy, that many believe her third daughter to be the count's.) As the years passed, the restless Sisi and her hardworking husband became estranged. In 1898, while visiting Geneva, Switzerland, she was murdered by an Italian anarchist.

Sisi's beauty, bittersweet life, and tragic death helped create her larger-than-life legacy. However, her importance is often inflated by melodramatic accounts of her life. The Sisi Museum seeks to tell a more accurate story.

of his son and heir, the murder of his wife, and the assassination of his nephew, Archduke Ferdinand, which sparked World War I and spelled the end of the Habsburg monarchy.

Among the Franz Josef rooms you'll see is the **audience room,** where Franz Josef received commoners from around the empire. They came from far and wide to show gratitude or to make a request. Imagine you've traveled for days to have your say before the

Emperor Franz Josef
(1830-1916)

Franz Josef I—who ruled for 68 years (1848-1916)—was the embodiment of the Habsburg Empire as it finished its six-century-long ride. Born in 1830, Franz Josef had a stern upbringing that instilled in him a powerful sense of duty and—like so many men of power—a love of all things military.

His uncle, Ferdinand I, suffered from profound epilepsy, which prevented him from being an effective ruler. As the revolutions of 1848 rattled royal families throughout Europe, the Habsburgs forced Ferdinand to abdicate and put 18-year-old Franz Josef on the throne. Ironically, as one of his first acts as emperor, Franz Josef—whose wife would later become closely identified with Hungarian independence—put down the 1848 revolt in Hungary with bloody harshness. He spent the first part of his long reign understandably paranoid, as social discontent continued to simmer.

Franz Josef was very conservative. But worse, he wrongly believed that he was a talented military tactician, leading Austria into catastrophic battles against Italy (which was fighting for its unification and independence) in the 1860s. As his army endured severe, avoidable casualties, it became clear: Franz Josef was a disaster as a general.

Wearing his uniform to the end, Franz Josef never saw what a dinosaur his monarchy was becoming, and never thought it strange that the majority of his subjects didn't even speak German. Franz Josef had no interest in democracy and pointedly never set foot in Austria's parliament building. But, like his contemporary, Queen Victoria, he was a microcosm of his empire—old-fashioned but sacrosanct. His passion for low-grade paperwork earned him the nickname "Joe Bureaucrat." Mired in these petty details, he missed the big picture. In 1914, he helped start a Great War that ultimately ended the age of monarchs. The year 1918 marked the end of Europe's big royal families: Hohenzollerns (Prussia), Romanovs (Russia), and Habsburgs (Austria).

emperor. You're wearing your new fancy suit—Franz Josef required that men coming before him wear a tailcoat, women a black gown with a train. You've rehearsed what you want to say. You hope your hair looks good. Suddenly, you're face-to-face with the emp himself. (The portrait on the easel shows Franz Josef in 1915, when he was more than 80 years old.) Despite your efforts, you probably weren't in this room long. He'd stand at the high table (far left) as the visiting commoners had their say. (Standing kept things moving.) You'd hear a brief response from him (quite likely the same he'd given all day), and then you'd back out of the room while bowing (also required). On the table is a partial list of 56 appointments he had on January 3, 1910 (three columns: family name, meeting topic, and *Anmerkung*—the emperor's "action log").

Franz Josef's **bedroom** shows off his spartan lifestyle. Notice his no-frills iron bed. He typically rose at 3:30 and started his day in prayer, kneeling at the prayer stool against the far wall. While he had a typical emperor's share of mistresses, his dresser was always well-stocked with photos of Sisi.

Sisi's Rooms include her exercise/dressing room, where servants worked three hours a day on the empress' famous hair. She'd exercise on the wooden structure and on the rings suspended from the doorway to the left. Afterward, she'd get a massage on the red-covered bed. In Sisi's main bathroom, you'll see her huge copper tub (with the original wall coverings behind it), where servants washed her hair—an all-day affair. Sisi was the first Habsburg to have running water in her bathroom (notice the hot and cold faucets). In the small salon, the portrait is of Crown Prince Rudolf, Franz Josef and Sisi's only son. On the morning of January 30, 1889, the 30-year-old Rudolf and a beautiful baroness were found shot dead in an apparent murder-suicide in his hunting lodge in Mayerling. The scandal shocked the empire and tainted the Habsburgs; Sisi retreated further into her fantasy world, and Franz Josef carried on stoically with a broken heart.

The tour ends in the **dining room.** It's dinnertime, and Franz Josef has called his extended family together. The settings are modest...just silver. Gold was saved for formal state dinners. Next to each name card was a menu listing the chef responsible for each dish. (Talk about pressure.) While the Hofburg had tableware for 4,000, feeding 3,000 was a typical day. The cellar was stocked with 60,000 bottles of wine. The kitchen was huge—50 birds could be roasted at once on the hand-driven spits. Franz Josef enforced strict protocol at mealtime: No one could speak without being spoken to by the emperor, and no one could eat after he was done. While the rest of Europe was growing democracy and expanding personal freedoms, the Habsburgs preserved their ossified worldview to the bitter end.

In 1918, World War I ended, Austria was created as a modern nation-state, the Habsburgs were tossed out...and Hofburg Palace was destined to become a museum.

▲▲▲Hofburg Treasury (Weltliche und Geistliche Schatzkammer)

One of the world's most stunning collections of royal regalia, the Hofburg Treasury shows off sparkling crowns, jewels, gowns, and assorted Habsburg bling in 21 darkened rooms. The treasures, well-explained by an audioguide, include the crown of the Holy Roman Emperor, Charlemagne's saber, a "unicorn horn," and more precious gems than you can shake a scepter at.

Cost and Hours: €12, €18 combo-ticket with Kunsthistorisches Museum and New Palace museums, Wed-Mon 10:00-18:00, closed Tue; from the Hofburg's central courtyard pass through the black, red, and gold gate, then follow *Schatzkammer* signs to the Schweizerhof; tel. 01/525-240, www.khm.at.

Audioguide Tours: A basic audioguide covering the top 11 jewels is included with your ticket. Or, for €2, you can rent an audioguide programmed to describe the top 100 stops—well worth it to get the most out of this dazzling collection.

❍ Self-Guided Tour: Here's a rundown of the highlights (the audioguide is much more complete).

Room 2: The personal crown of Rudolf II has survived since 1602—it was considered too well-crafted to cannibalize for other crowns. It's a big deal because it's the adopted crown of the Austrian Empire, established in 1806 after Napoleon dissolved the Holy Roman Empire (an alliance of Germanic kingdoms so named because it wanted to be considered the continuation of the Roman Empire). Pressured by Napoleon, the Austrian Francis II—who had been Holy Roman Emperor—became Francis I, Emperor of Austria (the stern guy on the wall, near where you entered). Look at the crown. Its design symbolically merges a bishop's miter ("Holy"), the arch across the top of a Roman emperor's helmet ("Roman"), and the typical medieval king's crown ("Emperor").

Rooms 3 and 4: These rooms contain some of the **coronation vestments and regalia** needed for the new Austrian (not Holy Roman) Emperor. There was a different one for each of the emperor's subsidiary titles, e.g., King of Hungary or King of Lombardy. So many crowns and kingdoms in the Habsburgs' vast empire!

Room 5: Ponder the **Cradle of the King of Rome,** once occupied by Napoleon's son, who was born in 1811 and made King of Rome. While pledging allegiance to democracy, Napoleon in fact crowned himself Emperor of France and hobnobbed with Europe's royalty. When his wife, Josephine, could not bear him a male heir, Napoleon divorced her and married into the Habsburg family. With the birth of the baby King of Rome, Napoleon and his new wife, Marie Louise, were poised to start a new dynasty of European rulers...but then Napoleon met his Waterloo, and the Habsburgs remained in power.

Room 6: For Divine Right kings, even child-rearing was a sacred ritual that needed elaborate regalia for public ceremonies. The 23-pound **gold basin and pitcher** were used to baptize noble children, who were dressed in the **hooded baptismal dresses** displayed nearby.

Room 7: These jewels are the true "treasures," a cabinet of wonders used by Habsburgs to impress their relatives (or to hock when funds got low).

Room 8: The eight-foot-tall, 500-year-old **"unicorn horn"** (a narwhal tusk), was considered to have magical healing powers bestowed from on high. This one was owned by the Holy Roman Emperor—clearly a divine monarch.

Religious Rooms: The next several rooms contain **religious objects**—crucifixes, chalices, mini-altarpieces, reliquaries, and bishops' vestments. Habsburg rulers mixed the institutions of church and state, so these precious religious accoutrements were also part of their display of secular power.

Room 10: The big red-silk and gold-thread **mantle,** nearly 900 years old, was worn by Holy Roman Emperors at their coronation.

Room 11: The collection's highlight is the 10th-century

crown of the Holy Roman Emperor. It was probably made for Otto I (c. 960), the first king to call himself Holy Roman Emperor. The Imperial Crown swirls with symbolism "proving" that the emperor was both holy and Roman: The cross on top says the HRE ruled as Christ's representative on earth, and the jeweled arch over the top is reminiscent of the parade helmet of ancient Romans. The jewels themselves allude to the wearer's kinghood in the here and now. Imagine the impression this priceless, glittering crown must have made on the emperor's medieval subjects.

Nearby is the 11th-century **Imperial Cross** that preceded the emperor in ceremonies. Encrusted with jewels, it had a hollow compartment (its core is wood) that carried substantial chunks thought to be from *the* **cross** on which Jesus was crucified and *the* **Holy Lance** used to pierce his side (both pieces are displayed in the same glass case). Holy Roman Emperors actually carried the lance into battle in the 10th century. Look behind the cross to see how it was a box that could be clipped open and shut, used for holding holy relics. You can see bits of the "true cross" anywhere, but this is a prime piece—with the actual nail hole.

Room 12: Now picture all this regalia used together. The **painting** shows the coronation of Maria Theresa's son Josef II as Holy Roman Emperor in 1764. Set in a church in Frankfurt (filled with the bigwigs—literally—of the day), Josef is wearing the same crown and royal garb that you've just seen.

Room 12 also displays the **leather cases** used to store and transport the crowns, crosses, and other objects. Another glass case contains **relics**—such as a fragment of Jesus' manger, a piece of Christ's loincloth, and a shred of the Last Supper tablecloth.

The Rest of the Treasury: Rooms 13-15 have (among other things) **portraits of important Habsburgs,** such as Maximilian I and Mary of Burgundy. Room 16 contains the **royal vestments** (15th century), which display perhaps the most exquisite workmanship in the entire Treasury. Look closely—they're "painted" with gold and silver threads. But after seeing so much bling, by the time you view these vestments, they can seem downright understated—just another example of the pomp and circumstance of the majestic Habsburgs.

More Hofburg Sights

▲▲**Hofburg New Palace Museums**—The New Palace (Neue Burg) houses three separate collections (covered by a single ticket): The **Arms and Armor Collection** displays weaponry and body armor from all over the vast Habsburg Empire, including exotic Turkish suits of armor. The **Ancient Musical Instruments Collection** shows instruments through the ages, especially the rapid evolution from harpsichord to piano. Admire Beethoven's (supposed) clarinet, Leopold Mozart's violin, a keyboard perhaps played by Wolfgang Mozart, and Brahms' piano. The **Ephesus Museum** has artifacts from the bustling ancient Roman city of 300,000 people (located in modern-day Turkey, near Kuşadası on the southwestern coast). The *Bronze Statue of an Athlete* is a jigsaw of 234 shattered pieces meticulously put back together. The *Statue of Artemis,* representing a pagan fertility goddess, is draped with sexy round objects—which may have symbolized breasts, eggs, or bulls' testicles. The included audioguide brings the exhibits to life and lets you hear the collection's fascinating old instruments being played. An added bonus is the chance to wander alone among the royal Habsburg halls, stairways, and painted ceilings.

Cost and Hours: €12, ticket covers all three collections and the Kunsthistorisches Museum across the Ring, €18 combo-ticket also includes the Hofburg Treasury, Wed-Sun 10:00-18:00, closed Mon-Tue, last entry 30 minutes before closing, almost no tourists, tel. 01/525-240, www.khm.at.

▲**Spanish Riding School**—This stately 300-year-old Baroque Hall at the Hofburg Palace is the home of the renowned Lipizzaner stallions. The magnificent building was an impressive expanse in its day. Built without pillars, it offers clear views of the prancing horses under lavish chandeliers, with a grand statue of Emperor Charles VI on horseback at the head of the hall.

Lipizzaner stallions were a creation of horse-loving Habsburg Archduke Charles, who wanted to breed the perfect animal. He imported Andalusian horses from his homeland of Spain, then mated them with a local line to produce an extremely intelligent and easily trainable breed. Italian and Arabian bloodlines were later added to tweak various characteristics. Lipizzaner stallions are known for their noble gait and Baroque profile. These regal horses have changed shape with the tenor of the times: They were bred strong and stout during wars, and frilly and slender in more cultured eras. But they're always born black, fade to gray, and turn a distinctive white in adulthood.

The school offers three options for seeing the horses:

Performances: The Lipizzaner stallions put on great 80-minute shows in spring and fall (late Aug-late June Sun at 11:00 and either Sat at 11:00 or Fri at 19:00, fewer shows in Jan-Feb, none late June-late Aug, tel. 01/533-9031, www.srs.at). The formal emcee thoughtfully introduces each number in German and English as horses do their choreographed moves to jaunty recorded Viennese classical music (in 4:4 meter rather than 3:4—I guess the horses don't waltz). The pricey seats book up months in advance, but standing room is usually available the same day, and there's not a bad view in the house (seats: €47-173, standing room: €23-31; box office opens at 9:00 and is located inside the Hofburg—go through the main Hofburg entryway from Michaelerplatz, then turn left into the first passage).

Training Sessions: Luckily for the masses, training sessions with music take place in the same hall and are open to the public. Don't have high expectations, as the horses often do little more than trot and warm up (€14 at the door, roughly early Aug-late June Tue-Fri 10:00-12:00—but only when the horses are in town). Tourists line up early at Josefsplatz (the large courtyard between Michaelerplatz and Albertinaplatz), at the door marked *Spanische Hofreitschule*. But there's no need to show up when the doors open at 10:00, since tickets never really "sell out." Only the horses stay for the full two hours. As people leave, new tickets are printed, so you can just prance in with no wait at all. You can also buy tickets for the training sessions at the box office.

Stables: Any time of day, you can see the horses in their stalls and view videos of them prancing in the Reitschulgasse corridor. Guided one-hour tours of stalls are given daily (€16; tours at 14:00, 15:00, and 16:00; in English and German, reserve by calling 01/533-9031).

▲**Augustinian Church (Augustinerkirche)**—This is the Gothic and Neo-Gothic church where the Habsburgs got latched (weddings took place here), then dispatched (the royal hearts are in the vault—not open to the public). Don't miss the exquisite, tomb-like Canova memorial (Neoclassical, 1805) to Maria Theresa's favorite daughter, Maria Christina, with its incredibly sad white-marble procession. The church's 11:00 Sunday Mass is a hit with music-lovers—both a Mass and a concert, often with an orchestra accompanying the choir (acoustics are best in front). Pay by contributing to the offering plate and buying a CD afterwards. Programs are posted by the entry (church open long hours daily, Augustinerstrasse 3—facing Josefsplatz, with its statue of the great reform emperor Josef II and the imperial library next door).

Austrian National Library—Next to the Augustinian Church, this was once the library of the Habsburgs. Wandering through this impressive temple of learning—with a statue of Charles VI in the center— you find yourself whispering. The setting takes you back to 1730 and gives you the sense that, in imperial times, knowledge of the world was for the elite—and with that knowledge, the elite had power (€7, Tue-Sun 10:00-

18:00, Thu until 21:00, closed Mon, recommended Soho Kantine in the basement good for a cheap lunch).

Burggarten (Palace Garden) and Butterfly House—This greenbelt, once the backyard of the Hofburg and now a people's park, welcomes visitors to loiter on the grass. On nice days, it's lively with office workers enjoying a break. The statue of Mozart facing the Ringstrasse is popular. The iron-and-glass pavilion now houses the recommended Café Restaurant Palmenhaus and a small but fluttery butterfly exhibit (€5.50; April-Oct Mon-Fri 10:00-16:45, Sat-Sun 10:00-18:15; Nov-March daily 10:00-15:45).

▲▲Albertina Museum—This building, at the southern tip of the Hofburg complex (near the Opera), was the residence of Maria Theresa's favorite daughter, Maria Christina, who was the only one allowed to marry for love rather than political strategy. Her many sisters were jealous. (Marie-Antoinette had to marry the French king...and lost her head over it.)

Maria Christina's husband, Albert of Saxony, was a great collector of original drawings and amassed an enormous assortment of works by Dürer, Rembrandt, Rubens, Schiele, and others. Today, reproductions of some of these works hang in the Albertina's elegant French-Classicist-style **state rooms** *(Prunkräume)*. Head to these rooms first for a great opportunity to wander freely under the chandeliers of a Habsburg palace, with its pure 19th-century imperial splendor unconstrained by velvet ropes.

Then follow signs for *Meisterwerke der Moderne* (*Die Sammlung Batliner,* on the top floor). These modern galleries hold a wonderful rotating exhibit from the museum's **Batliner collection** of modern art (from Impressionism to Abstract Expressionism, with minor works by major artists—Monet, Picasso, Chagall, Matisse), along with temporary exhibits.

To understand both the imperial apartments and the wonderful Batliner works, invest in the €4 **audioguide,** which makes this collection a luxurious lesson in modern art appreciation—from Monet to today.

Cost and Hours: €11, generally meaningless without €4 audioguide, daily 10:00-18:00, Wed until 21:00, overlooking Albertinaplatz across from the TI and Opera, tel. 01/534-830, www.albertina.at.

Church Crypts near the Hofburg

Two churches near the Hofburg offer starkly different looks at dearly departed Viennese: the Habsburg coffins in the Kaisergruft, and the commoners' graves in St. Michael's Church.

▲▲**Kaisergruft: The Remains of the Habsburgs**—Visiting the imperial remains is not as easy as you might imagine. These original organ donors left their bodies—about 150 in all—in the unassuming Kaisergruft (the Imperial Crypt at the Capuchin Church), their hearts in the Augustinian Church (vaults closed to public), and their entrails in the crypt below St. Stephen's Cathedral (described on page 1133). Don't tripe.

Cost and Hours: €5, daily 10:00-18:00, last entry at 17:40, behind the Opera on Neuer Markt, tel. 01/512-6853.

Highlights: As you enter, be sure to buy the €0.50 map with a Habsburg family tree and a chart locating each coffin.

Find the pewter double-coffin under the dome. This tomb of **Maria Theresa** (1717-1780) and her husband, **Franz I** (1708-1765), is worth a close look for its artwork. Maria Theresa outlived her husband by 15 years—which she spent in mourning. Old and fat, she installed a special lift enabling her to get down into the crypt to be with her dear, departed Franz (even though he had been far from faithful). The couple reclines—Etruscan-style—atop a fancy lead coffin. At each corner are the crowns of the Habsburgs—the Holy Roman Empire, Hungary, Bohemia, and Jerusalem. Notice the contrast between the Rococo splendor of Maria Theresa's tomb and the simple box holding her more modest son, **Josef II** (at his parents' feet). This understated tomb is in keeping with his enlightened politics.

Nearby, find the appropriately austere military tomb of **Franz Josef** (1830-1916; see sidebar on page 1142) in the more brightly lit modern section. Flanking Franz Josef are the tombs of his son, the archduke **Rudolf,** and Empress Elisabeth. Rudolf and his teenage mistress supposedly committed suicide together in 1889 at Mayerling hunting lodge and—since the Church figured he forced her to take her own life and was therefore a murderer—it took considerable legal hair-splitting to win Rudolf this spot (after examining his brain, it was determined that he was mentally disabled and therefore incapable of knowingly killing himself and his girl).

Empress Maria Theresa (1717-1780) and Her Son, Emperor Josef II (1741-1790)

Maria Theresa was the only woman to officially rule the Habsburg Empire in that family's 640-year reign. She was a strong and effective empress (r. 1740-1780). People are quick to remember Maria Theresa as the mother of 16 children (10 survived into adulthood). Imagine that the most powerful woman in Europe either was pregnant or had a newborn for most of her reign. Maria Theresa ruled after the Austrian defeat of the Ottomans, when Europe recognized Austria as a great power. (Her rival, the Prussian emperor, said, "When at last the Habsburgs get a great man, it's a woman.") The last of the Baroque imperial rulers, and the first of the modern rulers of the Age of Enlightenment, Maria Theresa marked the end of the feudal system and the beginning of the era of the grand state. She was a great social reformer. During her reign, she avoided wars and expanded her empire by skillfully marrying her children into the right families. For instance, after daughter Marie-Antoinette's marriage into the French Bourbon family (to Louis XVI), a country that had been an enemy became an ally. (Unfortunately for Marie-Antoinette, Maria Theresa's timing was off.)

To stay in power during the era of revolution, Maria Theresa had to be in tune with her age. She taxed the Church and the nobility, provided six years of obligatory education to all children, and granted free health care to all in her realm. Maria Theresa also welcomed the boy genius Mozart into her court.

The empress' legacy lived on in her son, Josef II, who ruled as emperor himself for a decade (1780-1790). He was an even more avid reformer, building on his mother's accomplishments. An enlightened monarch, Josef mothballed the too-extravagant Schönbrunn Palace, secularized the monasteries, established religious tolerance within his realm, freed the serfs, made possible the founding of Austria's first general hospital, and promoted relatively enlightened treatment of the mentally ill. Josef was a model of practicality (for example, reusable coffins à la *Amadeus,* and no more than six candles at funerals)—and very unpopular with other royals. But his policies succeeded in preempting the revolutionary anger of the age, enabling Austria to largely avoid the turmoil that shook so much of the rest of Europe.

Kaiserin Elisabeth (1837-1898), a.k.a. **Sisi,** always gets the "Most Flowers" award (see sidebar on page 1141).

In front of those three are the two most recent Habsburg tombs. **Empress Zita** was laid to rest here in 1989, followed by her son, **Karl Ludwig,** in 2007. The funeral procession for Karl, the fourth son of the last Austrian emperor, was probably the last such Old Regime event in European history. The monarchy died hard in Austria. Today there are about 700 living Habsburg royals, mostly living in exile. When they die, they get buried in their countries of exile.

Body parts and ornate tombs aside, the real legacy of the Habsburgs is the magnificence of this city. Step outside. Pan up. Watch the clouds glide by the ornate gables of Vienna.

▲**St. Michael's Church Crypt**—St. Michael's Church, which faces the Hofburg on Michaelerplatz, offers a striking contrast to the imperial crypt. Regular tours take visitors underground to see a typical church crypt—filled with the rotting wooden coffins of well-to-do commoners.

Climbing below the church, you'll see about a hundred 18th-century coffins and stand on three feet of debris, surrounded by niches filled with stacked lumber from decayed coffins and countless bones. You'll meet a 1769 mummy in lederhosen and a wig, along with a woman clutching a cross with flowers painted on her high heels. You'll learn about death in those times—from how the wealthy didn't want to end up in standard shallow graves, instead paying to be laid to rest below the church, to how, in 1780, the enlightened emperor Josef II ended the practice of cemetery burials in cities but allowed the rich to become the stinking rich in crypts under churches. You'll also discover why many were buried with their chins strapped shut (because when the muscles rot, your jaw falls open and you get that ghostly skeleton look that nobody wants).

Cost and Hours: €5 for 45-minute tour, Mon-Sat at 11:00 and 13:30, mostly in German but with enough English, wait at the sign that advertises the tour at the church entrance and pay the guide directly.

Kunsthistorisches Museum and Nearby

▲▲▲**Kunsthistorisches Museum**—This exciting museum, across the Ring from the Hofburg Palace, showcases the grandeur and opulence of the Habsburgs' collected artwork in a grand building (purpose-built in 1888 to display these works). While there's

Kunsthistorisches Museum

To Opera

VAN DER WEYDEN & VAN EYCK

COREGGIO & PARMIGIANINO

DÜRER   BOSCH   EARLY NORTHERN ART   MANTEGNA

RAPHAEL

17   16   14   1   2   3   4

HOLBEIN   Saal XI   SNYDERS   Saal X   Saal IX   WC   WC   TITIAN Saal I   VERONESE Saal II   TINTO-RETTO

THESEUS STATUE   Saal III

RINGSTRASSE

MORE   NORTHERN ART   BRUEGEL   TOUR BEGINS   MORE   ITALIAN ART

NORTHERN EUROPEAN ART   **ITALIAN, SPANISH & FRENCH ART**

MAIN STAIRCASE   CAFÉ

RUBENS   CANALETTO   BAROQUE   CARA-VAGGIO

Saal XIII   Saal XIV   Saal XV   Saal VII   Saal VI   Saal V   7

ARCIMBOLDO

21   22   VERMEER   23   VELÁZQUEZ   10

TOUR ENDS

REMBRANDT

ENTRANCE
(on ground level)

Not to Scale

MARIA-THERESIEN-PLATZ

little Viennese art here, you will find world-class European masterpieces galore (including canvases by Raphael, Caravaggio, Velázquez, Dürer, Rubens, Vermeer, Rembrandt, and a particularly exquisite roomful of Bruegels), all well-hung on one glorious floor, plus a fine display of Egyptian, classical, and applied arts.

Cost and Hours: €12, also includes New Palace museums across the Ring; free for kids under 18, €18 combo-ticket also includes the Hofburg Treasury, Tue-Sun 10:00-18:00, Thu until 21:00, closed Mon, on the Ringstrasse at Maria-Theresien-Platz, U-2 or U-3: Volkstheater/Museumsplatz (exit toward *Burgring*), tel. 01/525-240, www.khm.at.

Audioguide Tours: You can rent an audioguide at the desk in the atrium. The free "Highlights" audioguide covers a selection of 20 pieces (including just 13 paintings). The €3 "Total" audioguide is far more comprehensive, covering 560 items (worth it if you want an in-depth tour).

❍ **Self-Guided Tour:** The Kunsthistorwhateveritis Museum—let's just say "Koonst"—houses some of the most beautiful, sexy, and fun art from two centuries (c. 1450-1650). The collection reflects the joie de vivre of Austria's luxury-loving Habsburg rulers. At their peak of power in the 1500s, the Habsburgs ruled Austria, Germany, northern Italy, the Netherlands, and Spain—and you'll see a wide variety of art from all these places and beyond.

If you're short on time, focus on the Painting Gallery *(Gemäldegalerie)* on the first floor. Climb the main staircase, featuring Antonio Canova's statue of *Theseus Clubbing the Centaur.* Italian, Spanish, and French art is in the right half of the building (as you face Theseus), and Northern European art to the left. Notice that the museum labels the largest rooms with Roman numerals (Saal I, II, III), and the smaller rooms around the perimeter with Arabic (Rooms 1, 2, 3).

Italian, Spanish, and French Art: Saals I-III cover the Venetian renaissance. The first spans the long career of **Titian,** who painted portraits, Christian Madonnas, and sexy Venuses with equal ease. Next comes Paolo **Veronese,** whose colorful works reflect the wealth of Venice, the funnel through which luxury goods from the exotic East flowed into northern

Europe. And **Tintoretto**'s many portraits give us a peek at the movers and shakers of the Venetian Empire.

Rooms 1-4 hold some of the museum's most important works: **Mantegna**'s *St. Sebastian,* **Correggio**'s *Jupiter and Io,* and **Raphael**'s *Madonna of the Meadow (Die Madonna im Grünen),* a geometrically perfect masterpiece of the High Renaissance, painted when Raphael was just 22.

Farther along, through the small rooms along the far end of this wing (likely Room 7, or possibly out on loan), find the cleverly deceptive portraits by Giuseppe **Arcimboldo.** With a pickle nose, pear chin, and corn-husk ears, Arcimboldo's subject literally is what he eats.

Caravaggio (in Saal V) shocked the art world with bru-

tally honest reality. Compared with Raphael's super-sweet *Madonna of the Meadow,* Caravaggio's *Madonna of the Rosary (Die Rosenkranzmadonna,* the biggest canvas in the room) looks perfectly ordinary, and the saints kneeling around her have dirty feet. In *David with the Head of Goliath (David mit dem Haupt des Goliath)* Caravaggio turns a third-degree-interrogation light on a familiar Bible story. David shoves the dripping head of the slain giant—the artist's self portrait—right in our noses.

When the Habsburgs ruled both Austria and Spain, cousins kept in touch through portraits of themselves and their kids. Diego **Velázquez** (in Room 10) was the greatest of Spain's "photojournalist" painters: heavily influenced by Caravaggio's realism, capturing his subjects without passing judgment, flattering, or glorifying them.

Northern European Art: The other half of this floor features works of the "Northern Renaissance," which was more secular and Protestant than Catholic-funded Italian art (that means fewer Madonnas, saints, and Greek gods and more peasants, landscapes, and food). Paintings are smaller and darker, full of down-to-earth objects. Northern artists sweated the details, encouraging the patient viewer to appreciate the beauty in everyday things.

The undisputed master of the slice-of-life village scene was Pieter **Bruegel** the Elder—the Norman Rockwell of the 16th century. Saal X contains the largest collection of Bruegels in captivity. Despite his many rural paintings, Bruegel was actually a cultivated urbanite who liked to wear peasants' clothing to observe country folk at play (a trans-fest-ite?). He celebrated their simple life, but he also skewered their weaknesses—not to single them out as hicks, but as universal examples of human folly. *The Peasant Wedding (Bauernhochzeit)*, Bruegel's most famous work, is less about the wedding than the food. It's a farmers' feeding frenzy, as the barnful of wedding guests scrambles to get their share of free eats. Bruegel's *Peasant Dance (Bauerntanz)* shows a celebration at the consecration of a village church. The three Bruegel landscape paintings are part of an original series of six "calendar" paintings, depicting the seasons of the year.

Also in this section, don't miss **Rubens**' large, lush canvases (including *The Little Fur/Das Pelzchen*, depicting his much younger, dimpled bride); **Vermeer**'s *The Art of Painting (Die Malkunst)*, showing the painter at work in his studio, with a painstaking attention to detail; and **Rembrandt**'s frank self-portraits—one as a defiant young artist, the other as a broken old man.

▲Natural History Museum—In the twin building facing the Kunsthistorisches Museum, you'll find moon rocks, dinosaur stuff, and the fist-sized *Venus of Willendorf*—at 25,000 years old, the world's oldest sex symbol. This four-inch-tall, chubby stone statuette, found in the Danube Valley, is a generic female (no face or feet) resting her hands on her ample breasts. The statue's purpose is unknown, but she may have been a symbol of fertility for our mammoth-hunting ancestors. Even though the museum is not glitzy or high-tech, it's a hit with children and scientifically curious grown-ups. Of the museum's 20 million objects, you're sure to find something interesting.

Cost and Hours: €10, Wed-Mon 9:00-18:30, Wed until 21:00, closed Tue, on the Ringstrasse at Maria-Theresien-Platz, U-2 or U-3: Volkstheater/Museumsplatz, tel. 01/521-770, www.nhm-wien.ac.at.

MuseumsQuartier—The vast grounds of the former imperial stables now corral a cutting-edge cultural center for contemporary

arts and design, including several impressive museums; the best are the Leopold Museum and the Museum of Modern Art.

Walk into the complex from the Hofburg side, where the main entrance (with visitors center, shop, and ticket office) leads to a big courtyard with cafés, fountains, and ever-changing "installation lounge furniture," all surrounded by the quarter's various museums. At the visitors center, various **combo-tickets** are available for those interested in more than just the Leopold and Modern Art museums. You can also rent a €4 **audioguide** that explains the complex (behind Kunsthistorisches Museum, U-2 or U-3: Volkstheater/Museumsplatz, tel. 01/525-5881, www.mqw.at).

The **Leopold Museum** features several temporary exhibits of modern Austrian art. The top floor holds the largest collection of works by Egon Schiele (1890-1918; these works make some people uncomfortable—Schiele's nudes are *really* nude) and a few paintings by Gustav Klimt, Kolo Moser, and Oskar Kokoschka. While this is a great collection, you can see even better works from these artists in the Belvedere Palace, described later (€11, €3 audioguide—worth it only for enthusiasts; June-Aug daily 10:00-18:00, Thu until 21:00; Sept-May Wed-Mon 10:00-18:00, Thu until 21:00, closed Tue; tel. 01/525-700, www.leopoldmuseum.org).

The **Museum of Modern Art** (Museum Moderner Kunst Stiftung Ludwig, a.k.a. "MUMOK") is Austria's leading gallery for international modern and contemporary art. It's the striking lava-paneled building—three stories tall and four stories deep, offering seven floors of far-out art that's hard for most visitors to appreciate. This huge, state-of-the-art museum owns works by "classical" modernists (Paul Klee, Pablo Picasso, Pop artists) and shows off up-to-the-minute contemporary art in revolving exhibits (€9, €3 audioguide has more than you probably want to hear, daily 10:00-18:00, Thu until 21:00, tel. 01/52500, www.mumok.at).

Rounding out the sprawling MuseumsQuartier are an architecture center, Electronic Avenue, design forum, children's museum, "Quartier 21" (with gallery space and shops), and the **Kunsthalle Wien**—an exhibition center for contemporary art (two halls with different exhibitions, €8.50 for one, €7 for the other, €11.50 for both; daily 10:00-19:00, Thu until 22:00, tel. 01/521-8933, www.kunsthallewien.at).

Karlsplatz and Nearby

These sights cluster around Karlsplatz, just southeast of the Ringstrasse (U-1, U-2, or U-4: Karlsplatz). From the U-Bahn station's passageway, it's a 30-minute walk around the sights on Karlsplatz: the Karlskirche, Secession, and Naschmarkt (allow more time to actually visit these sights).

Karlsplatz—This picnic-friendly square, with its Henry Moore sculpture in the pond, is ringed with sights. The massive, domed Karlskirche and its twin spiral columns dominate the square. The small green, white, and gold pavilions that line the street across the square from the church are from the late-19th-century municipal train system *(Stadtbahn)*. One of Europe's first subway systems, this precursor to today's U-Bahn was built with a military purpose in mind: to move troops quickly in time of civil unrest—specifically, out to Schönbrunn Palace. With curvy iron frames, decorative marble slabs, and painted gold trim, these are pioneering works in the *Jugendstil* style (see sidebar, page 1159), designed by Otto Wagner, who influenced Klimt and the Secessionists. One of the pavilions has an exhibit on **Otto Wagner** (€2, April-Oct Tue-Sun 10:00-18:00, closed Mon and Nov-March, near the Ringstrasse, tel. 01/5058-7478-5173).

▲Karlskirche (St. Charles' Church)—Charles Borromeo, a 16th-century bishop from Milan, was an inspiration during plague times. This "votive church" was dedicated to him in 1713, when an epidemic spared Vienna. The church offers the best Baroque in Vienna, with a unique combination of columns (showing scenes from the life of Charles Borromeo, à la Trajan's Column in Rome), a classic pediment, and an elliptical dome. The dome's colorful 13,500-square-foot fresco—painted in the 1730s by Johann Michael Rottmayr—shows Signor Borromeo (in red-and-white bishops' robes) gazing up into heaven, spreading his arms wide, and pleading with Christ to spare Vienna from the plague.

The church is especially worthwhile for the chance to ride an **elevator**

(installed for renovation work) up into the cupola. While the restoration of the interior is complete, work on the exterior will likely continue into 2013; when it's finished, the scaffolding and elevator will likely be taken down. Until that happens, the industrial lift takes you to a platform at the base of the 235-foot dome (if you're even slightly afraid of heights, skip this trip). Consider that the church was built and decorated with a scaffolding system essentially the same as this one. Once up top, you'll climb stairs to the steamy lantern at the extreme top of the church. At that dizzying height, you're in the clouds with cupids and angels. Many details that appear smooth and beautiful from ground level—such as gold leaf, paintings, and fake marble—look rough and sloppy up close. It's surreal to observe the 3-D figures from an unintended angle—check out Christ's leg, which looks dwarf-sized up close. Give yourself a minute to take it in: Faith, Hope, and Charity triumph and inspire. Borromeo lobbies heaven for plague relief. Meanwhile, a Protestant's Lutheran Bible is put to the torch by angels. At the very top, you'll see the tiny dove representing the Holy Ghost, surrounded by a cheering squad of nipple-lipped cupids.

Cost and Hours: €6, ticket covers church interior, elevator ride, and skippable one-room museum; audioguide-€2; Mon-Sat 9:00-18:00, Sun 13:00-18:00, last entry 30 minutes before closing; elevator runs until 17:30, last ascent at 17:00. The entry fee may seem steep, but remember that it funds the restoration.

Wien Museum Karlsplatz—This underappreciated city history museum, worth ▲ for those intrigued by Vienna's illustrious past, walks you through the story of Vienna with well-presented artifacts. Work your way up chronologically. The ground floor exhibits prehistoric and Roman fragments, along with some original statues from St. Stephen's Cathedral (c. 1350). The first floor focuses on the Renaissance and Baroque eras, including suits of armor, old city maps, booty from an Ottoman siege, and an 1850 city model showing the town just before the wall was replaced by the Ring. Finally, the second floor displays a city model from 1898 (with the new Ringstrasse), sentimental Biedermeier paintings and objets d'art, and early 20th-century paintings (including four by Klimt, as well as works by Schiele, Kokoschka, and other Secessionists).

Cost and Hours: €6, free first Sun of the month, open Tue-Sun 10:00-18:00, closed Mon, tel. 01/505-8747, www.wienmuseum.at.

▲Academy of Fine Arts (Akademie der Bildenden Künste)—Recently refurbished, this museum features a small but impressive collection of works by big-name artists, including quick, sketchy cartoons Rubens used to create his giant canvases; a Venice series by Guardi; a self-portrait by a 15-year-old Van Dyck; and a round Botticelli canvas, recently cleaned to show off its vivid colors, depicting the Madonna tenderly embracing the Baby Jesus. The collection's highlight is the captivating, harrowing *Last Judgment* triptych by Hieronymus Bosch (c. 1482, with some details added by Lucas Cranach). Read the altarpiece from left to right, following the pessimistically medieval narrative about humankind's fall from God's graces: In the left panel, at the bottom, God pulls Eve from Adam's rib in the Garden of Eden. Just above that, we see a female representing the serpent hold out the forbidden fruit to tempt Eve. Above that, Adam and Eve are being shooed away by an angel. At the top of this panel, God sits on his cloud, evicting the fallen angels (who turn into insect-like monsters). In the middle panel, Christ holds court over the living and the dead. Notice the jarring contrast between Christ's serene expression and the grotesque scene playing out beneath him. These disturbing images crescendo in the final (right) panel, showing an unspeakably horrific vision of hell that few artists have managed to top in the more than half-millennium since Bosch.

The collection is magnificently lit and well-described by the €2 audioguide, and comes with comfy chairs. The fact that it's housed upstairs in a working art academy gives it a certain authenticity. As you wander the halls of the academy, ponder how history might have been different if Hitler—who applied to study architecture here but was rejected—had been accepted as a student. Before leaving, peek into the ground floor's central hall—textbook Historicism, the Ringstrasse style of the late 1800s.

Cost and Hours: €8, audioguide-€2; Tue-Sun 10:00-18:00, closed Mon, 3 blocks from the Opera at Schillerplatz 3; once inside, go up two floors, following signs for *Gemäldegalerie;* tel. 01/588-162-201, www.akademiegalerie.at.

▲**The Secession**—This little building, strategically located behind the Academy of Fine Arts, was created by the Vienna Secession movement, a group of nonconformist artists led by Gustav Klimt, Otto Wagner, and friends. (For more on the art movement, see the sidebar on the opposite page.)

The young trees carved into the walls and the building's bushy "golden cabbage" rooftop are symbolic of a renewal cycle. Today, the Secession continues to showcase cutting-edge art, as well as one of Gustav Klimt's most famous works.

While the staff hopes you take a look at the temporary exhibits (and they're included in the ticket price whether you like it or not), most tourists head directly for the basement, home to the museum's highlight: Klimt's classic *Beethoven Frieze* (a.k.a. the

Art Nouveau (a.k.a. *Jugendstil* or the Vienna Secession), c. 1896-1914

As Europe approached the dawn of a new *(nouveau)* century, it embraced a new art: Art Nouveau. Though the movement began in Paris and Belgium, each country gave it its own spin. In German-speaking lands (including Austria), Art Nouveau was called *Jugendstil* (meaning "youth style").

Art Nouveau was forward-looking and modern, embracing the new technology of iron and glass. But it was also a reaction against the sheer ugliness of the mass-produced, boxy, rigidly geometrical art of the Industrial Age. Art Nouveau artists returned to nature (which abhors a straight line) and were inspired by the curves of plants. Art Nouveau street lamps twist and bend like flower stems. Ironwork fountains sprout buds that squirt water. Dining rooms are paneled with leafy garlands of carved wood. Advertising posters feature flowery typefaces and beautiful young women rendered in pure, curving lines. Art Nouveau was a total "look" that could be applied to furniture, jewelry, paintings, and the building itself.

Imagine being a cutting-edge artist in late-19th-century Vienna, surrounded not by creativity, but by conformity. Take, for example, the Ringstrasse, with its Neo-Greek, Neo-Gothic, Neo-Baroque architecture. There was nothing daring or new—it was simply redoing what had already been done (Historicism). This drove Vienna's impatient young generation of artists (Gustav Klimt, Otto Wagner, Egon Schiele, Oskar Kokoschka, and company) to escape, or "secede," from all this conventionalism. They established "The Secession" (Vienna's own *Jugendstil* movement) and transcended into a world of pure beauty, hedonism, eroticism, and aesthetics.

The Secession preferred buildings that were simple and geometrically pure, decorated with a few unadulterated Art Nouveau touches. Architects, painters, and poets had no single unifying style, except a commitment to what was new. The Secessionist motto was: "To each age its art, and to art its liberty."

"Searching Souls"). One of the masterpieces of Viennese Art Nouveau, this 105-foot-long fresco was the multimedia centerpiece of a 1902 exhibition honoring Ludwig van Beethoven. Read the free flier, which explains Klimt's still-powerful work, inspired by Beethoven's Ninth Symphony. Klimt embellished the work with painted-on gold (his brother, and colleague, was a goldsmith), and by gluing on reflecting glass and mother-of-pearl for the ladies' dresses and jewelry. For more on Klimt, see the "Gustav Klimt" sidebar, on page 1164.

Cost and Hours: €5, as high as €8.50 during special exhibits,

Tue-Sun 10:00-18:00, closed Mon, Friedrichstrasse 12, tel. 01/587-5307, www.secession.at.

▲**Naschmarkt**—In 1898, the city decided to cover up its Vienna River. The long, wide square they created was filled with a lively produce market that still bustles most days (closed Sun). It's long been known as *the* place to get exotic faraway foods. In fact, locals say, "From here start the Balkans."

From near the Opera, the Naschmarkt (roughly, "Munchies Market") stretches along Wienzeile street. This "Belly of Vienna" comes with two parallel lanes—one lined with fun and reasonable eateries, and the other featuring the town's top-end produce and gourmet goodies. This is where top chefs like to get their ingredients. At the gourmet vinegar stall, you sample the vinegar like perfume—with a drop on your wrist (see photo). Farther from the center, the Naschmarkt becomes  likeably seedy and surrounded by sausage stands, Turkish *Döner Kebab* stalls, cafés, and theaters. At the market's far end is a line of buildings with fine Art Nouveau facades. Each Saturday, the Naschmarkt is infested by a huge flea market where, in olden days, locals would come to hire a monkey to pick little critters out of their hair.

Hours and Location: Mon-Fri 6:00-18:30, Sat 6:00-17:00, closed Sun, closes earlier in winter; U-1, U-2, or U-4: Karlsplatz. For a picnic in the park, pick up your grub here and walk over to Karlsplatz (described earlier).

More Sights Beyond the Ring
South of the Ring

▲▲**Belvedere Palace (Schloss Belvedere)**—This is the elegant palace of Prince Eugene of Savoy (1663-1736), the still-much-appreciated conqueror of the Ottomans. Today you can tour Eugene's lavish palace, see sweeping views of the gardens and the Vienna skyline, and enjoy world-class art starring Gustav Klimt, French Impressionism, and a grab-bag of other 19th- and early-20th-century artists. While Vienna's other art collections show off works by masters from around Europe, this has the city's

best collection of homegrown artists.

Cost and Hours: €11 for Upper Belvedere Palace only, €16 for Upper and Lower palaces—generally not worth it, gardens are free except for privy garden—included in big ticket, audioguide-€4 or €6/2 people, daily 10:00-18:00, Lower Palace only open Wed until 21:00, grounds open until dusk, no photos allowed inside, entrance at Prinz-Eugen-Strasse 27, tel. 01/7955-7134, www.belvedere.at.

Getting There: The palace is a 15-minute walk south of the Ring. To get there from the center, catch tram #D at the Opera (direction: Südbahnhof). Get off at the Schloss Belvedere stop (just below the Upper Palace gate), cross the street, walk uphill one block, and look for the gate on your right.

➲ Self-Guided Tour: The Belvedere Palace is actually two grand buildings—the Upper Palace and Lower Palace—separated by a fine garden. For our purposes, the Upper Palace is what matters. Buy your ticket at the office behind the palace, then go around to the front to enter. Once inside, the palace's eclectic collection is tailor-made for browsing. It's organized roughly chronologically as you go up.

Ground Floor: The main floor displays a collection of Austrian Baroque (on the left) and medieval art (on the right). The Baroque section includes a fascinating room of grotesquely grimacing heads by **Franz Xaver Messerschmidt** (1736-1783), a quirky 18th-century Habsburg court sculptor who left the imperial life to follow his own, somewhat deranged muse. After his promising career was cut short by mental illness, Messerschmidt relocated to Bratislava and spent the rest of his days sculpting a series of eerily lifelike "character heads" *(Kopfstücke)*. Their most unusual faces are contorted by extreme emotions.

• *From the entrance, climb the staircase to the first floor and enter the grand red-and-gold, chandeliered...*

Marble Hall (First Floor): This was Prince Eugene's party room. *Belvedere* means "beautiful view," and the view from the Marble Hall is especially spectacular.

• *To the right is the...*

East Wing (First Floor): Alongside Renoir's ladies, Monet's landscapes, and Van Gogh's rough brushstrokes are similar works by their lesser-known Austrian counterparts. Around 1900, Austrian artists come to the fore, soaking up Symbolism, Expressionism, and other Modernist trends.

In the two rooms full of sumptuous paintings by **Gustav Klimt,** you can get caught up in his fascination with the beauty and danger he saw in women. To Klimt, all art was erotic art. He painted during the turn of the century, when Vienna was a splendid laboratory of hedonism. The famous painting of *Judith I* (1901) shows no biblical heroine—Klimt paints her as a high-society

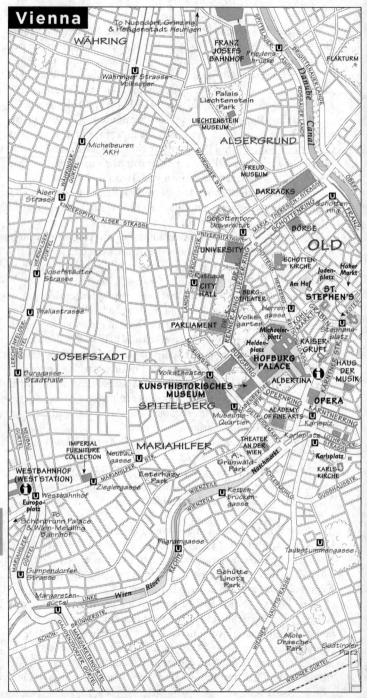

VIENNA

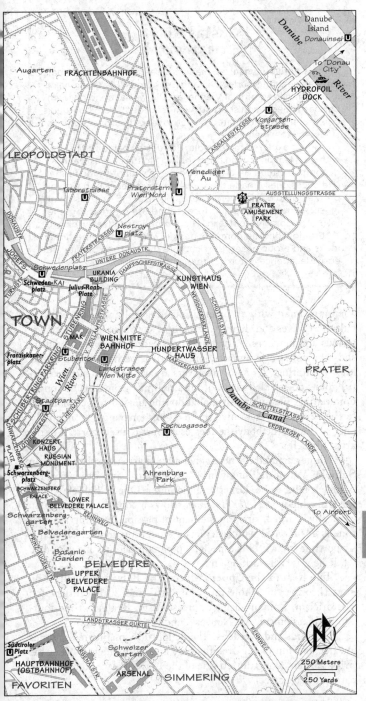

Gustav Klimt
(1862-1918)

Klimt, a noted womanizer, made a career painting the female form as beautiful, seductive, and dangerous. His erotic paintings scandalized official Vienna, and he was a founding member of the Secessionist artists who "seceded" from bourgeois constraints. He dedicated his later years to works commissioned by the liberal elite.

Klimt explored multimedia. Besides oil paints, he painted with gold leaf or applied bright objects to the canvas/panel for decorative effect. He often worked in a square-frame format. (He occasionally made the frames themselves, along with his brother, a gold engraver.) There's no strong 3-D in his paintings; the background and foreground are merged together into a decorative pattern. His women are clearly drawn, emerging from the complex design. With their come-hither looks and erotic poses, they capture the overripe beauty and edgy decadence of turn-of-the-century Vienna.

Vienna woman with an ostentatious dog-collar necklace. With half-closed eyes and slightly parted lips, she's dismissive...yet mysterious and bewitching. Holding the head of her biblical victim, she's the modern femme fatale. In what is perhaps Klimt's best-known painting, *The Kiss,* two lovers are wrapped up in the colorful gold-and-jeweled cloak of bliss. Klimt's woman is no longer dominating, but submissive, abandoning herself to her man in a fertile field and a vast universe. In a glow emanating from a radiance of desire, the body she presses against is a self-portrait of the artist himself.

Klimt nurtured the next generation of artists, especially **Egon Schiele.** While Klimt's works are mystical and otherworldly, Schiele's tend to be darker and gloomier. One of Schiele's most recognizable works, *The Embrace,* shows a couple engaged in an erotically charged, rippling moment of passion. Striking a darker tone is *The Family,* which depicts a crouching couple. This family portrait from 1918 is especially poignant because his wife died while he was still working on it.

The Rest of the Upper Palace: The Belvedere's collection goes through the whole range of 19th- and 20th-century art: Historicism, Romanticism, Impressionism, Realism, tired tourism, Expressionism, Art Nouveau, and early Modernism.

Grounds and Gardens: The delightfully manicured grounds are free and fun to explore. The only area with an entry fee is the **privy garden,** along the left side of the Lower Palace (and accessed through that palace).

Lower Palace: Covered by a separate ticket, this is the home where Prince Eugene actually hung his helmet. Today it contains a small stretch of three of his private apartments (relatively uninteresting compared to the sumptuous Habsburg apartments elsewhere in town). The Lower Palace also houses some generally good special exhibits, as well as the entrance to the privy garden, orangerie, and stables (until 12:00). If the special exhibits intrigue you, it's worth buying the combo-ticket to get in here; otherwise, I wouldn't bother to visit.

East of the Ring

Museum of Applied Art (Österreichisches Museum für Angewandte Kunst)—Facing the old town from across the Ring, the MAK, as it's called, is Vienna's answer to London's Victoria and Albert Museum. The MAK is more than just another grand building on the Ringstrasse. It was built to provide models of historic design for Ringstrasse architects and is a delightful space in itself (many locals stop in to enjoy a coffee on the plush couches in the main lobby). The relatively sparse collection shows off the fancies of local aristocratic society, including fine *Jugendstil* pieces (among them Klimt designs for a palace in Brussels). Each wing is dedicated to a different era. Exhibits, well-described in English (borrow the captions in each room), come with a playful modern flair—notable modern designers were assigned various spaces. The unique gift shop also makes for a fun diversion.

Cost and Hours: €8, €10 includes a hefty English guidebook, free on Sat, open Tue-Sun 10:00-18:00, Tue until 24:00, closed Mon, Stubenring 5, tel. 01/711-360, www.mak.at.

Eating at the MAK: The beautiful lobby hosts an inviting **café.** The **Restaurant Österreicher im MAK,** in the same building, is named for Chef Helmut Österreicher, who's renowned for his classic and modern Viennese cuisine. Classy and mod, it's trendy for locals (€9-23 plates, daily 8:30-1:00 in the morning, reserve for evening, tel. 01/714-0121).

▲KunstHausWien: Hundertwasser Museum—This "make yourself at home" museum and nearby apartment complex are a hit with lovers of modern art, mixing the work and philosophy of local painter/environmentalist Friedensreich Hundertwasser (1928-2000). Stand in front of the colorful checkerboard building and consider Hundertwasser's style. He was against "window racism": Neighboring houses allow only one kind of window, but 100H$_2$O's windows are each different—and he encouraged residents in the Hundertwasserhaus (a 5-10 minute walk away, described below) to personalize them. He recognized "tree tenants" as well as human tenants. His buildings are spritzed with a forest and topped with dirt and grassy little parks—close to nature and good for the soul.

Floors and sidewalks are irregular—to "stimulate the brain" (although current residents complain it just causes wobbly furniture

and sprained ankles). Thus 100H$_2$O waged a one-man fight—during the 1950s and 1960s, when concrete and glass ruled—to save the human soul from the city. (Hundertwasser claimed that "straight lines are godless.")

Inside the museum, start with his interesting biography. His fun paintings are half psychedelic *Jugendstil* and half just kids' stuff. Notice the photographs from his 1950s days as part of Vienna's bohemian scene. Throughout the museum, keep an eye out for the fun philosophical quotes from an artist who believed, "If man is creative, he comes nearer to his creator."

Cost and Hours: €9 for Hundertwasser Museum, €12 combo-ticket includes special exhibitions, half-price on Mon, open daily 10:00-19:00, extremely fragrant and colorful garden café, tel. 01/712-0491, www.kunsthauswien.com.

Getting There: It's located at Untere Weissgerberstrasse 13 (tram #1: Radetzkyplatz or U-3: Landstrasse). Note that the tram stop is much closer than the U-Bahn stop. From the Landstrasse U-Bahn stop, walk 10 minutes downhill (north) along Untere Viaduktgasse (a block east of the station), or ride tram #0 three stops to Radetzkyplatz; from there signs point to the museum.

Hundertwasserhaus: The KunstHausWien provides by far the best look at Hundertwasser, but for an actual lived-in apartment complex by the green master, walk five minutes to the one-with-nature Hundertwasserhaus (at Löwengasse and Kegelgasse). This complex of 50 apartments, subsidized by the government to

provide affordable housing, was built in the 1980s as a breath of architectural fresh air in a city of boring, blocky apartment complexes. While not open to visitors, it's worth visiting for its fun and colorful patchwork exterior and the Hundertwasser festival of shops across the street. Don't miss the view from Kegelgasse to see the "tree tenants" and the internal winter garden that residents enjoy.

Hundertwasser detractors—of which there are many—remind visitors that 100H$_2$O was a painter, not an architect.

They describe the Hundertwasserhaus as a "1950s house built in the 1980s" that was colorfully painted with no real concern for the environment, communal living, or even practical comfort. Almost all of the original inhabitants got fed up with the novelty and moved out.

North of the Ring

▲**Liechtenstein Museum**—The noble Liechtenstein family (who own only a tiny country, but whose friendship with the Habsburgs goes back generations) amassed an incredible private art collection. Their palace was long a treasure for Vienna art-lovers. Then, in 1938—knowing Hitler was intent on plundering artwork to create an immense "Führer Museum"—the family fled to their pint-size homeland with their best art. Since the museum reopened in 2004, attendance has been disappointing, but the problem is its location (and perhaps its steep price)...not its worthiness. The Liechtensteins' "world of Baroque pleasures" includes the family's rare "Golden Carriage," which was used for their grand entry into Paris in 1738. It was carted to the edge of town and assembled there. It's a rare example of the French Rococo style, as nearly all such carriages were destroyed in the French Revolution. The museum also has a plush Baroque library, an inviting English Garden, and an impressive collection of paintings, including a complete cycle of early Rubens.

Cost and Hours: €10 on Fri-Sat and Mon-Tue, more for temporary exhibits; €30 on Sun—when ticket includes permanent and temporary exhibits, lunch, and concerts at 11:00 and 15:00; gardens are free but aren't worth the trip on their own; audioguide-€1; Fri-Tue 10:00-17:00, last entry 30 minutes before closing, closed Wed-Thu, gardens open until 20:30; Fürstengasse 1—take tram #D to Bauernfeldplatz/Porzellangasse, tel. 01/319-5767-252, www.liechtensteinmuseum.at.

Sigmund Freud Museum—Freud enthusiasts enjoy seeing the humble apartment and workplace of the man who fundamentally changed our understanding of the human psyche. Dr. Sigmund Freud (1856-1939), a graduate of Vienna University, established his practice here in 1891. For the next 47 years, he received troubled patients who hoped to find peace by telling him their dreams, life traumas, and secret urges. It was here that he wrote his influential works, including the landmark *Interpretation of Dreams* (1899). Today, you can walk through his three-room office (but not the apartments next door, where Freud lived with his large family). The rooms are tiny and disappointingly bare. Freud, who was Jewish, fled Vienna when the Nazis came to power. He took most of his furniture with him, including the famous couch that patients reclined on (now in a London museum). All in all, the museum is quite old-fashioned—tediously described in a three-ring binder loaned to visitors, which complements the more general audioguide.

Cost and Hours: €7, audioguide-€2, daily July-Sept 9:00-18:00, Oct-June 9:00-17:00, cool shop, half a block downhill from the Schlickgasse tram #D stop, Berggasse 19, tel. 01/319-1596, www.freud-museum.at.

West of the Ring, on Mariahilfer Strasse
▲Imperial Furniture Collection (Hofmobiliendepot)—
Bizarre, sensuous, eccentric, or precious, this collection is your peek at the Habsburgs' furniture—from grandma's wheelchair to the emperor's spittoon—all thoughtfully described in English. The Habsburgs had many palaces, but only the Hofburg was permanently furnished. The rest were done on the fly—set up and taken down by a gang of royal roadies called the "Depot of Court Movables" (Hofmobiliendepot). When the monarchy was dissolved in 1918, the state of Austria took possession of the Hofmobiliendepot's inventory—165,000 items. Now this royal storehouse is open to the public in a fine and sprawling museum. Don't go here for the *Jugendstil* furnishings. The older Baroque, Rococo, and Biedermeier pieces are the most impressive and tied most intimately to the royals. Combine a visit to this museum with a stroll down the lively shopping boulevard, Mariahilfer Strasse.

Cost and Hours: €7.90, covered by €23.50 Sisi Ticket (see page 1111), Tue-Sun 10:00-18:00, closed Mon, Mariahilfer Strasse 88, main entrance around the corner at Andreasgasse 7, U-3: Zieglergasse, tel. 01/5243-3570, www.hofmobiliendepot.at.

▲▲▲Schönbrunn Palace (Schloss Schönbrunn)
Among Europe's palaces, only Schönbrunn rivals Versailles. This former summer residence of the Habsburgs is big, with 1,441 rooms. But don't worry—only 40 rooms are shown to the public. Of the plethora of sights at the palace, the highlight is a tour of the Royal Apartments—the chandeliered rooms where the Habsburg nobles lived. You can also stroll the gardens, tour the coach museum, and visit a handful of lesser sights nearby.

Getting There: While on the outskirts of Vienna, Schönbrunn is an easy 10-minute subway ride from downtown. Take U-4 to Schönbrunn and follow signs for *Schloss Schönbrunn*. Exit bearing right, then cross the busy road and continue to the right along the yellow building to the main

VIENNA

entry courtyard, which will be on your left.

▲▲▲**Royal Apartments**—While the palace's exterior is Baroque, the interior was finished under Maria Theresa in let-them-eat-cake Rococo. As with the similar apartments at the Hofburg (the Habsburgs' winter home), these apartments give you a sense of the quirky, larger-than-life personalities who lived here—especially Franz Josef (r. 1848-1916) and Sisi. Your tour of the apartments, accompanied by an audioguide, covers one small section of the palace's grand interior on a clearly signed route. You have two tour options: Imperial (shorter and cheaper) or Grand (longer and more expensive). Both follow the same route at first, but after a certain point the Imperial group is politely excused while the Grand gang continues on to see a few more rooms.

Moving from room to room, you're immersed in imperial splendor. The chandeliers are made either of Bohemian crystal or hand-carved wood with gold-leaf gilding. Highlights include Franz Josef's study and bedroom (and the bed he actually died in). The Mirrored Room was where six-year-old Wolfie Mozart performed his first concert. The opulent, chandeliered Great Gallery—with its mirrored walls and dramatically frescoed ceilings—was the site of a famous 1961 summit between John F. Kennedy and Nikita Khrushchev.

Fortunately, the palace managed to escape destruction when WWII bombs rained on the city and the palace grounds. The palace itself took only one direct hit. Thankfully, that bomb, which crashed through three floors—including the sumptuous central ballroom—was a dud. Most of the public rooms are decorated in Neo-Baroque, as they were under Franz Josef and Sisi. The rest of the palace was converted to simple apartments and rented to the families of 260 civil servants, who enjoy rent control and governmental protections so they can't be evicted.

Cost: The 22-room **Imperial Tour** (€10.50, 35 minutes, Grand Palace rooms plus apartments of Franz Josef and Sisi—mostly 19th-century and therefore least interesting) or the 40-room **Grand Tour** (€13.50, one hour, includes Imperial Tour plus Maria Theresa's apartments—18th-century Rococo). If venturing beyond the apartments, consider one of two combo-tickets: The **Schönbrunn Classic Pass Light** includes the Grand Tour, as well as other sights on the grounds—the Gloriette viewing terrace, maze, and privy garden (€16.50, available April-Oct only). The **Schönbrunn Classic Pass** includes all of the above, plus the court bakery (complete with *Apfelstrudel* demo and tasting; €19.50). However, none of these extra sights is really worth the cost of entry, so I'd skip them and just do the Grand Tour, followed by a mosey through the impressive grounds (which are free).

Hours: Daily July-Aug 8:30-18:00, April-June and Sept-Oct

8:30-17:00, Nov-March 8:30-16:30.

Crowd-Beating Tips: Schönbrunn suffers from crowds. It can be a jam-packed sauna in the summer. It's busiest from 9:30 to 11:30, especially on weekends and in July and August; it's least crowded after 14:00, when there are no groups. To avoid the long delays in summer, make a reservation by telephone for no extra charge a few days in advance (tel. 01/8111-3239, answered daily 8:00-17:00, wait through the long message for the operator). You can also book online with a credit card at www.schoenbrunn .at. You'll get an appointment time and a ticket number. Check in at least 30 minutes early. Upon arrival, go to the "Group and Reservations" desk, give your number, pick up your ticket, and jump in ahead of the masses (for most of 2012, the reservations desk is located immediately inside the gate on the left at the gate house—long before the actual palace; in fall of 2012, it may move to a new visitors center). If you have any time to kill, spend it exploring the gardens or Coach Museum.

▲▲Palace Gardens—Unlike the gardens of Versailles, meant to shut out the real world, Schönbrunn's park was opened to the pub-

lic in 1779 while the monarchy was in full swing. It was part of Maria Theresa's reform policy, making the garden a celebration of the evolution of civilization from autocracy into real democracy. Today it's a delightful, sprawling place to wander—especially on a sunny day. You can spend hours here, enjoying the views and the people-watching. And most of the park is free, as it has been for more than two centuries (open daily sunrise to dusk, entrance on either side of the palace).

The large, manicured grounds are laid out on angled, tree-lined axes that gradually incline, offering dramatic views back to the palace. The small side gardens flanking the palace are the most elaborate. As you face the back of the palace, to the right is the **privy garden** (*Kronprinzengarten*, €2); to the left are the free **Sisi Gardens.** Better yet, just explore, using a map (pick one up at the palace) to locate several whimsical **fountains;** a kid-friendly **maze** (*Irrgarten*) and playground area (€2.90); and the **Gloriette,** a purely decorative monument celebrating an obscure Austrian military victory and offering a fine city view (pay for a pricey drink in the café or shell out €2 to hike up to the viewing terrace—or skip the whole thing, as views are about as good from the lawn in front; included in Schönbrunn Passes described earlier, daily April-Sept 9:00-18:00, July-Aug until 19:00, Oct 9:00-17:00, closed Nov-March).

At the west end of the grounds is Europe's oldest **zoo**

(Tiergarten), built by Maria Theresa's husband for the entertainment and education of the court in 1752 (€14, €20 combo-ticket with desert and palm house, daily April-Sept 9:00-18:30, closes earlier off-season, tel. 01/877-9294). Nearby are two skippable sights: The **palm house** *(Palmenhaus;* €4, €6 combo-ticket with desert house, €20 combo-ticket also includes zoo, daily May-Sept 9:30-18:00, Oct-April 9:30-17:00, last entry 30 minutes before closing) and the **Desert Experience House** *(Wüstenhaus;* €4, same combo-tickets and hours as palm house).

A **tourist train** makes the rounds all day, connecting Schönbrunn's many attractions (€6, 2/hour in peak season, none Nov-mid-March, one-hour circuit). Unfortunately, there's no bike rental nearby.

▲**Coach Museum Wagenburg**—The Schönbrunn coach museum is a 19th-century traffic jam of 50 impressive royal carriages and sleighs. Highlights include silly sedan chairs, the death-black hearse carriage (used for Franz Josef in 1916, and most recently for Empress Zita in 1989), and an extravagantly gilded imperial carriage pulled by eight Cinderella horses. This was rarely used other than for the coronation of Holy Roman Emperors, when it was disassembled and taken to Frankfurt for the big event. You'll also get a look at one of Sisi's impossibly narrow-waisted gowns, and (upstairs) Sisi's "Riding Chapel," with portraits of her 25 favorite horses.

Cost and Hours: €6, audioguide-€2, daily April-Oct 9:00-18:00, Nov-March 10:00-16:00, last entry 15 minutes before closing, 200 yards from palace, walk through right arch as you face palace, tel. 01/525-24-3470.

East of the Danube Canal

▲**Prater**—Since the 1780s, when the reformist Emperor Josef II gave his hunting grounds to the people of Vienna as a public park, this place has been Vienna's playground. While tired and a bit run-down these days, Vienna's sprawling amusement park still tempts visitors with its huge 220-foot-tall, famous, and lazy Ferris wheel *(Riesenrad),* roller coaster, bumper cars, Lilliputian railroad, and endless eateries. Especially if you're traveling with kids, this is a fun, goofy place to share the evening with thousands of Viennese (rides run May-Sept 9:00-24:00—but quiet after 22:00, March-April and Oct 10:00-22:00, Nov-Dec 10:00-20:00, grounds always open, U-1: Praterstern, www.prater.at). For a local-style family dinner, eat at Schweizerhaus (good food, great Czech Budvar—the original "Budweiser"—beer, classic conviviality).

Donauinsel (Danube Island)—In the 1970s, the city dug a canal parallel to the mighty Danube River, creating both a flood barrier and a much-loved island escape from the city (easy U-Bahn access on U-1 to Donauinsel). This skinny, 12-mile-long island provides a natural wonderland. All along the traffic-free, grassy park, you'll find locals—both Viennese, and especially immigrants and those who can't afford their own cabin or fancy vacation—at play. The swimming comes tough, though, with rocky entries rather than sand. The best activity here is a bike ride. If you venture far from the crowds, you're likely to encounter nudists on inline skates.

"Donau City"—This modern part of town, just beyond the Donauinsel, is the skyscraping "Manhattan" of Austria. A business, residential, and shopping zone surrounded by inviting parkland, this corner of the city is likely to grow as Vienna expands. Its centerpiece is the futuristic UNO City, a major outpost of offices for the United Nations. While it lacks the Old World character, charm, and elegance of the rest of Vienna, Donau City may interest travelers who are into contemporary glass-and-steel architecture (U-1: Kaisermühlen VIC).

Shopping in Vienna

Traditional Austrian Clothing—If you're interested in picking up a classy felt suit or dirndl, you'll find shops all over town. Most central is the fancy Loden-Plankl shop, with a vast world of traditional Austrian formalwear upstairs (across from the Hofburg, at Michaelerplatz 6). The Tostmann Trachten shop is the ultimate for serious shopping. Frau Tostmann powered the resurgence of this style. Her place is like a shrine to traditional Austrian and folk clothing (called Tracht)—handmade and very expensive (Schottengasse 3A, 3-minute walk from Am Hof, tel. 01/533-5331).

Artsy Gifts—Vienna's museum shops are some of Europe's best. The design store in the Museum of Applied Art (MAK) is a delight; the shops of the Albertina Museum, Kunsthistorisches Museum, Belvedere Palace, KunstHausWien, Sigmund Freud Museum, and the MuseumsQuartier museums are also particularly good.

Mariahilfer Strasse—Ride the underground to Neubaugasse and just stroll along this thriving shopping street. Near the U-Bahn stop, the Bushplanet Headshop and Growshop offers a convivial opportunity to see how Austrians are dealing with their marijuana culture (Mon-Fri 10:00-19:00, Sat 10:00-18:00, closed Sun, Esterhazygasse 32, www.bushplanet.at).

Window-Shopping—The narrow streets north and west of the cathedral are sprinkled with old-fashioned shops that seem to belong to another era, carrying a curiously narrow range of items for sale (old clocks, men's ties, gloves, and so on). Dedicated window-shoppers will enjoy the Dorotheum auction house (see page 1131).

Experiences in Vienna

Vienna's Café Culture

In Vienna, the living room is down the street at the neighborhood coffeehouse. This tradition is just another example of Viennese expertise in good living. Each of Vienna's many long-established (and sometimes even legendary) coffeehouses has its individual character (and characters). Today these classic cafés can be a bit tired, with a shabby patina and famously grumpy waiters who treat you like an uninvited guest invading their living room. Yet these spaces somehow also feel welcoming, offering newspapers, pastries, sofas, quick and light workers' lunches, elegant ambience, and "take all the time you want" charm for the price of a cup of coffee. Rather than buy the *International Herald Tribune* ahead of time, spend the money on a cup of coffee and read the paper for free, Vienna-style, in a café.

Viennese Coffee Terms

As in Italy and France, Viennese coffee drinks are espresso-based. Obviously, *Kaffee* means coffee and *Milch* is milk; *Obers* is cream, while *Schlagobers* is whipped cream. Beyond those basics, here are some uniquely Viennese coffee terms (use them elsewhere, and you'll probably get a funny look):

Schwarzer, Mokka	straight, black espresso; order it *kleiner* (small) or *grosser* (big)
Verlängeter ("lengthened")	espresso with water, like an Americano
Brauner	with a little milk
Schale Gold ("golden cup")	with a little cream
Melange	like a cappuccino
Franziskaner	a *Melange* with whipped cream rather than foamed milk, often topped with chocolate flakes
Kapuziner	strong coffee with a dollop of sweetened cream (oddly, not a cappuccino, which derives its name from the same word)
Verkehrt ("incorrect"), *Milchkaffee*	with lots and lots of milk—similar to a *caffè latte*
Einspänner ("buggy")	with lots and lots of whipped cream, served in a glass with a handle (as it was the drink of horse-and-buggy drivers, who only had one hand free)
Fiaker ("horse-and-buggy driver")	black, with kirsch liqueur or rum, served with a cherry

(Wiener) Eiskaffee   coffee with ice cream
Maria Theresia   coffee with orange liqueur

Americans who ask for a "latte" are mistaken for Italians and given a cup of hot milk.

Cafés

These are some of my favorite Viennese cafés. All of them, except for Café Sperl, are located inside the Ring (see map on page 1196).

Café Hawelka has a dark, "brooding Trotsky" atmosphere, paintings by struggling artists who couldn't pay for coffee, a saloon-wood flavor, chalkboard menu, smoked velvet couches, an international selection of newspapers, and a phone that rings for regulars. Frau Hawelka died just a couple weeks after Pope John Paul II. Locals suspect the pontiff wanted her much-loved *Buchteln* (marmalade-filled doughnuts) in heaven. Herr Hawelka, now alone and understandably a bit forlorn, still oversees the action (Wed-Mon 8:00-2:00 in the morning, Sun from 10:00, closed Tue, just off the Graben, Dorotheergasse 6, U-1 or U-3: Stephansplatz, tel. 01/512-8230).

Café Central, while a bit touristy, remains a classic place, lavish under Neo-Gothic columns. They serve fancy coffees (€4-6) and two-course lunches (€10), as well as entertain guests with live piano each evening from 17:00-22:00 (daily 7:30-22:00, corner of Herrengasse and Strauchgasse, U-3: Herrengasse, tel. 01/533-3764).

Café Sperl dates from 1880 and is still furnished identically to the day it opened—from the coat tree to the chairs (Mon-Sat 7:00-23:00, Sun 11:00-20:00 except closed Sun July-Aug, just off Naschmarkt near Mariahilfer Strasse, Gumpendorfer 11, U-2: Museumsquartier, tel. 01/586-4158; see map on page 1190).

Café Bräunerhof, between the Hofburg and the Graben, offers classic ambience with no tourists and live music on weekends (light classics, no cover, Sat-Sun 15:00-18:00), along with a practical menu with daily specials (open long hours daily, Stallburgasse 2, U-1 or U-3: Stephansplatz, tel. 01/512-3893).

Other Classics in the Old Center: All of these places are open long hours daily: **Café Pruckel** (at Dr.-Karl-Lueger-Platz, across from Stadtpark at Stubenring 24); **Café Tirolerhof** (2 blocks from the Opera, behind the TI on Tegetthoffstrasse, at Führichgasse 8); and **Café Landtmann** (directly across from the City Hall on the Ringstrasse at Dr.-Karl-Lueger-Ring 4). The Landtmann is unique, as it's the only grand café built along the Ring with all the other grand buildings. **Café Sacher** (see page 1196) and **Demel** (see page 1126) are famous for their cakes, but they also serve good coffee drinks.

Wein in Wien: Vienna's Wine Gardens

The *Heuriger* (HOY-rih-gur) is a uniquely Viennese institution. When the Habsburgs let Vienna's vintners sell their own new wine (called *Sturm*) tax-free, several hundred families opened *Heurigen* (HOY-rih-gehn)—wine-garden restaurants clustered around the edge of town. A tradition was born. Today, they do their best to maintain the old-village atmosphere, serving their homemade wine (the most recent vintage, until November 11, when a new vintage year begins) with small meals and strolling musicians. Most *Heurigen* are decorated with enormous antique presses from their vineyards. Wine gardens might be closed on any given day; call ahead to confirm if you have your heart set on a particular place. (For a near-*Heuriger* experience in downtown Vienna, drop by Gigerl Stadtheuriger—see page 1195.)

I've listed three good *Heuriger* neighborhoods—all on the outskirts of Vienna (see the map on page 1101). I've listed them in order from east to west, and from least to most touristy. To reach the neighborhoods from downtown Vienna, it's best to use public transportation (cheap, 30 minutes, runs late in the evening, directions given per listing below), or you can take a 15-minute taxi ride from the Ring (about €15-20).

Planning Your Time: While there are some "destination" *Heurigen*, it can be disappointing to seek out a particular place, as the ambience can change depending with that evening's clientele (i.e., locals vs. tour groups). I've described a few neighborhoods that are worth exploring; wander around one or two of them, then choose the *Heuriger* with the best atmosphere. It's easiest to stick to one *Heuriger* neighborhood, though it's potentially more fun to hop from area to area; the handy bus #38A (described below) connects Heiligenstadt, Grinzing, and (with a transfer to tram #D) Nussdorf.

Getting Around the *Heurigen*: The three neighborhoods I list are relatively close to each other—within a few minutes' bus ride or about a half-hour walk. The handiest public-transit connections are these:

Tram #D runs from the Ring to Nussdorf, the least touristy *Heuriger* neighborhood. On the way, it passes the Grinzinger Strasse stop, where you can catch bus #38A (toward the other two neighborhoods). Tram #D runs every 5-10 minutes (fewer trams after 23:00, last tram around 24:30).

Bus #38A connects the Heiligenstadt U-Bahn station (U-4 line) with the *Heurigen* in Heiligenstadt (Fernsprechamt/Heiligenstadt stop), and then Grinzing (Grinzing or Himmelstrasse stops). Bus #38A runs frequently into the evening (8/hour until 19:00, then 6/hour until 22:00, then 4/hour until 24:00; last bus around midnight).

The *Heuriger* Experience

There are more than 1,700 acres of vineyards within Vienna's city limits and countless *Heuriger* taverns. Here's what you can expect when you visit a *Heuriger*:

First go to the buffet to get your food—simply tell them what you want, and they'll fill your plate. Many *Heuriger* staff members speak English, but pointing also works. Food is generally sold by the weight, often in *"10 dag"* units (that's 100 grams, or about a quarter-pound). The buffet has several sections: The core of your meal is a warm dish, generally meat (such as ham, roast beef, roast chicken, roulade, or meat loaf) carved off a big hunk. There are also warm sides *(Beilagen),* such as casseroles and sauerkraut. And there's a wide variety of cold sides—various salads and spreads. Rounding out the menu are bread and cheese (they'll slice it off for you).

Dishes to look for...or look out for: *Leberkäse* (meat loaf), *Stelze* (grilled knuckle of pork), *Fleischlaberln* (fried ground-meat patties), *Schinkenfleckerln* (pasta with cheese and ham), *Spanferkel* (suckling pig), *Schmalz* (a spread made with pig fat), *Blunzen* (black pudding...sausage made from blood), *Presskopf* (jellied brains and innards), *Bratlfett* (gelatinous goo made from fat drippings), *Liptauer* (spicy cheese spread), *Kornspitz* (whole-meal bread roll), and *Kummelbraten* (crispy roast pork with caraway).

Pay for your food at the buffet, then find a table. Once seated, order your wine (or other drinks) from a server. A quarter-liter *(Viertel,* FEER-tehl, 8 oz) glass of new wine costs about €2-3. *Most* (mohst) is lightly alcoholic grape juice—wine in its earliest stages. Once it gets a little more oomph, it's called *Sturm* (shtoorm). Teetotalers can order *Traubenmost* (TROW-behn-mohst), grape juice.

Tram #38 starts on the Ring at the Schottentor stop and goes to Grinzing (roughly the same hours as Tram #D).

Taxis stand by in touristy Grinzing; from the other places, you might need to ask the *Heuriger* to call one for you (figure about €15-20 between the *Heurigen* and the Ring or any hotel I list).

Nussdorf—An untouristy district, characteristic and popular with the Viennese, Nussdorf has plenty of *Heuriger* ambience. This area feels more real than the other two—with a working-class vibe, streets lined with local shops, and characteristic *Heurigen* that feel a little bit rougher around the edges. Right at the last stop on tram #D's route (Beethovengang), you'll find three long and skinny places side by side. Of these, **Schübel-Auer Heuriger** is my favorite—bigger, classier, and with the most user-friendly buffet (many dishes are labeled—see the menu decoder in the sidebar—and the patient staff speaks English). Its rustic ambience can be enjoyed indoors or out (Tue-Sat 16:00-24:00, closed Sun-Mon, Kahlenberger Strasse 22, tel. 01/370-2222). The other two are also worth considering: **Heuriger Kierlinger** has a particularly rollicking, woody room around its buffet (daily 15:30-24:00, Kahlenberger Strasse 20, tel. 01/370-2264). **Steinschaden** feels a bit more like a traditional restaurant. Though it has a typical *Heuriger* buffet, it also has menus and table service (daily 15:00-24:00, Kahlenberger Strasse 18, tel. 01/370-1375).

Getting to the Nussdorf *Heurigen*: Take tram #D from the Ringstrasse (stops include the Opera, Hofburg/Kunsthistorisches Museum, and City Hall) to its endpoint (the stop labeled *Nussdorf* isn't the end—stay on for one more stop to Beethovengang). Exit the tram, cross the tracks, bear right down the street, and look for the *Heurigen* on your left.

Heiligenstadt (Pfarrplatz)—Between Nussdorf and Grinzing, hiding just above the unappealing main road, is Pfarrplatz, which feels like a charming village square watched over by a church. Beethoven lived—and began work on his Ninth Symphony—here in 1817; he'd previously written his Sixth Symphony *(Pastorale)* while staying in this then-rural district. He hoped the local spa would cure his worsening deafness. (Confusingly, the name "Heiligenstadt" is used for two different locations: this little neighborhood, and the big train and U-Bahn station near the river.) Right next to the church, **Mayer am Pfarrplatz** (a.k.a. Beethovenhaus) is famous, touristy, and feels more polished—almost trendy—compared to the other *Heurigen* I list. This place has a charming inner courtyard under cozy vines with an accordion player, along with a sprawling backyard with a big children's play zone (Mon-Fri 16:00-24:00, Sat-Sun 11:00-24:00, Pfarrplatz 2, tel. 01/370-1287). **Weingut and Heuriger Werner Welser** is a block uphill (go up Probusgasse). It's big (serving large tour groups) and traditional, with dirndled waitresses and lederhosened waiters. It feels a bit crank-'em-out, but it's still lots of fun, with music nightly from 19:00 (open daily 15:30-24:00, Probusgasse 12, tel. 01/318-9797).

Getting to the Heiligenstadt *Heurigen*: Take the U-4 line to its last station, Heiligenstadt, then transfer to bus #38A. Get off at Fernsprechamt/Heiligenstadt, walk uphill, and take the first right onto Nestelbachgasse, which leads to Pfarrplatz and the Beethovenhaus. Bus #38A also runs uphill from here, past the Grinzing *Heurigen*, to the Kahlenberg viewpoint (described later).

Grinzing—Of the many *Heuriger* suburbs, Grinzing is the most famous, lively...and touristy. If you're looking to avoid tour groups, head elsewhere. But it's the easiest, most accessible zone that I list. You can't walk down the street without stumbling over great, interchangeably touristy options—so much so, in fact, that I won't bother pointing you to a specific place. Just find your favorite ambience. (Since this isn't exactly fine wine anyway, the difference in quality is negligible.) The district is also simply pretty. Like the other two, it feels like a charming town all its own, with an onion-domed church and carefully manicured streetscape.

Getting to the Grinzing *Heurigen*: Take tram #38 from the Schottentor stop on the Ring to its endpoint. If you are coming from the other *Heurigen* neighborhoods, bus #38A makes two stops in this district: The Grinzing stop is at the bottom of town (and just across the street from the stop for tram #38); the next stop is Himmelstrasse, a bit uphill (and easier for strolling down past your options). If you get off at the Grinzing stop, follow Himmelgasse uphill toward the green onion-top dome. You'll pass plenty of wine gardens—and tour buses—on your way up. Just past the dome, you'll find the heart of the Heurigen.

Entertainment in Vienna

Vienna—the birthplace of what we call classical music—still thrives as Europe's music capital. On any given evening, you'll have your choice of opera, Strauss waltzes, Mozart chamber concerts, and lighthearted musicals. The Vienna Boys' Choir lives up to its worldwide reputation. If techno or rock are more your scene, you'll find plenty in the pubs and clubs of the "Bermuda Triangle" neighborhood near St. Stephen's Cathedral and along the Gürtel.

Besides music, you can spend an evening enjoying art, watching a classic film, or sipping Viennese wine in a village wine garden. Save some energy for Vienna after dark.

Music

As far back as the 12th century, Vienna was a mecca for musicians—both sacred and secular (troubadours). The Habsburg emperors of the 17th and 18th centuries were not only generous supporters of music, but fine musicians and composers themselves. (Maria Theresa played a mean double bass.) Composers such as Haydn, Mozart, Beethoven, Schubert, Brahms, and Mahler gravitated to this music-friendly environment. They taught each other, jammed together, and spent a lot of time in Habsburg palaces. Beethoven was a famous figure, walking—lost in musical thought—through the Vienna Woods. In the city's 19th-century belle époque, "Waltz King" Johann Strauss and his brothers kept

Vienna's 300 ballrooms spinning.

This musical tradition continues into modern times, leaving some prestigious Viennese institutions for today's tourists to enjoy: the Opera, the Boys' Choir, and the great Baroque halls and churches, all busy with classical and waltz concerts. As you poke into churches and palaces, you may hear groups practicing. You're welcome to sit and listen.

The best-known entertainment venues are the Staatsoper (a.k.a., "the Opera"), the Volksoper (for musicals and operettas), the Theater an der Wien (newly reopened, opera and other performances), the Wiener Musikverein (home of the Vienna Philharmonic Orchestra), and the Wiener Konzerthaus (various events). These events are listed in the monthly *Wien-Programm* (available at TI).

In Vienna, it's music *con brio* from October through June, reaching a symphonic climax during the Vienna Festival each May and June. Sadly, in summer (generally July and August), the Boys' Choir, Opera, and many other serious music companies are—like you—on vacation. But Vienna hums year-round with live classical music; touristy, crowd-pleasing shows are always available.

Buying Tickets: Most tickets run from €40 to €55 (plus a stiff booking fee when booked in advance or through a box office like the one at the TI). A few venues charge as little as €25; look around if you're not set on any particular concert. While it's easy to book tickets online long in advance, spontaneity is also workable, as there are invariably people selling their extra tickets at face value or less outside the door before concert time. If you call a concert hall directly, they can advise you on the availability of (cheaper) tickets at the door. Vienna takes care of its starving artists (and tourists) by offering cheap standing-room tickets to top-notch music and opera (generally an hour before each performance).

Vienna Boys' Choir (Wiener Sängerknaben)—The boys sing (from a high balcony, heard but not seen) at the 9:15 Sunday Mass from September through June in the Hofburg's Imperial Music Chapel (Hofmusikkapelle). The entrance is at Schweizerhof; you can get there from In der Burg square or go through the tunnel from Josefsplatz.

Reserved seats must be booked two months in advance (€5-29; reserve by fax, email, or mail: fax from the US 011-431-533-992-775, whmk@chello.at, or write Hofmusikkapelle, Hofburg-Schweizerhof, 1010 Wien; call 01/533-9927 for information only—they can't book tickets at this number).

Much easier, standing room inside is free and open to the first 60 who line up. Even better, rather than line up early, you can simply swing by and stand in the narthex just outside, where you can hear the boys and see the Mass on a TV monitor.

Boys' Choir concerts are also given Fridays at 16:00 in late April, May, June, September, and October on stage at the Musikverein, near the Opera and Karlsplatz (€36-56, around 30 standing-room tickets go on sale at 15:30 for €15, Karlsplatz 6; U-1, U-2, or U-4: Karlsplatz; tel. 01/5880-4173).

They're talented kids, but, for my taste, not worth all the commotion. Remember, many churches have great music during Sunday Mass. Just 200 yards from the Boys' Choir chapel, the Augustinian Church has a glorious 11:00 service each Sunday (see page 1147).

The Opera—The Vienna State Opera (Staatsoper), featuring Vienna Philharmonic Orchestra musicians in the pit, is one of the world's top opera houses. They put on 300 performances a year, but in July and August the singers rest their voices (or go on tour). Since there are different operas nearly nightly, you'll see big trucks out back and constant action backstage—all the sets need to be switched each day. Even though the expensive seats normally sell out long in advance, the opera is perpetually in the red and subsidized by the state. The excellent "electronic libretto" translation screens help make the experience worthwhile for opera newbies. (Press the button to turn yours on; press again for English.)

Opera Tickets: Seats range from €8 to €168. You can book tickets in advance by phone (tel. 01/513-1513, phone answered daily 10:00-21:00) or online (www.wiener-staatsoper.at); you'll give them your credit-card number, then pick up your tickets at the box office just before show time. If you want to inquire about tickets in person, head to the theater's box office, which is open from 9:00 until one hour before each performance. The Opera has two ticket offices. The main one is on the west side of the building, across Operngasse and facing the Opera. A smaller one is just under the big screen on the east side of the Opera (facing Kärntner Strasse).

Unless Placido Domingo is in town, it's easy to get one of 567 **standing-room tickets** (*Stehplätze*, €3 up top or €4 downstairs). While the front doors open one hour before the show starts, a side door (middle of building, on the Operngasse side) opens 80 minutes before curtain time, giving those in the know an early grab at standing-room tickets (tickets sold until 20 minutes after curtain time). Just walk straight in, then head right until you see the ticket booth marked *Stehplätze*. If fewer than 567 people are in line, there's no need to line up early. If you're one of the first 160 in line, try for the "Parterre" section and you'll end up dead-center at stage level, directly under the Emperor's Box (otherwise, you can choose between the third floor—*Balkon*, or the fourth floor—*Galerie*). Dress is casual (but do your best) at the standing-room bar. Locals save their spot along the rail by tying a scarf to it.

Rick's Crude Tips: For me, three hours is a lot of opera.

But just to see and hear the Opera in action for half an hour is a treat. You can buy a standing-room spot and drop in for part of the show. Ending time is posted in the lobby—you could stop by for just the finale. If you go at the start or finish, you'll get the added entertainment of seeing Vienna all dressed up. Of the 567 people with cheap standing-room tickets, invariably many will not stand through the entire performance. If you drop by after showtime, you can wait for people to leave and bum their tickets off them—be sure to ask them for clear directions to your spot. (While it's perfectly legal to swap standing-room spots, be discreet if finding your spot mid-performance—try to look like you know where you're going.) Even those with standing-room tickets are considered "ticket-holders," and are welcome to explore the building. As you leave, wander around the first floor (fun if skipping out early, when halls are empty) to enjoy the sumptuous halls (with prints of famous stage sets and performers) and the grand entry staircase. The last resort (and worst option) is to drop into the Café Oper Vienna and watch the performance live on TV screens (inside the Opera, reasonable menu and drinks).

"Live Opera on the Square": Demonstrating its commitment to bringing opera to the masses, each summer the Vienna Opera projects several performances live on a huge screen on its building, and even puts out chairs for the public to enjoy...and it's all free (these projected performances are noted as *Oper live am Platz* in the official Opera schedule—posted all around the Opera building; they are also listed in the *Wien-Programm* brochure).

Vienna Volksoper—For less-serious operettas and musicals, try Vienna's other opera house, located along the Gürtel, west of the city center (see *Wien-Programm* brochure or ask at TI for schedule, Währinger Strasse 78, tel. 01/5144-4360, www.volksoper.at).

Theater an der Wien—Considered the oldest theater in Vienna, this venue was designed in 1801 for Mozart operas—intimate, with just a thousand seats. Reopened in 2006 for Mozart's 250th birthday, it treats Vienna's music-lovers to a different opera every month—generally Mozart with a contemporary setting and modern interpretation—with the excellent Vienna Radio Orchestra in the pit. With the reopening of Theater an der Wien, Vienna now supports three opera companies; this one is the only company playing through the summer. They also feature occasional ballet, operetta, and other performances (facing the Naschmarkt at Linke Wienzeile 6, tel. 01/5883-0660 for information, tickets available at www.theater-wien.at).

Touristy Mozart and Strauss Concerts—If the music comes to you, it's touristy—designed for flash-in-the-pan Mozart fans. Powdered-wig orchestra performances are given almost nightly in grand traditional settings (€25-50). Pesky wigged-and-powdered

Mozarts peddle tickets in the streets. They rave about the quality of the musicians, but you'll get second-rate chamber orchestras, clad in historic costumes, performing the greatest hits of Mozart and Strauss. These are casual, easygoing concerts with lots of tour groups. While there's not a Viennese person in the audience, the tourists generally enjoy the evening.

To sort through your options, check with the ticket office in the TI (same price as on the street, but with all venues to choose from). Savvy locals suggest getting the cheapest tickets, as no one seems to care if cheapskates move up to fill unsold pricier seats. Critics explain that the musicians are actually very good (often Hungarians, Poles, and Russians working a season here to fund an entire year of music studies back home), but that they haven't performed much together so aren't "tight."

Of the many fine venues, the **Mozarthaus** might be my favorite. Intimate chamber-music concerts take place in a small room richly decorated in Venetian Renaissance style (€35-42, Thu-Fri at 19:30, Sat at 18:00, near St. Stephen's Cathedral at Singerstrasse 7, tel. 01/911-9077).

Strauss Concerts in the Kursalon—For years, Strauss concerts have been held in the Kursalon, where the "Waltz King" himself

directed wildly popular concerts 100 years ago (€39-56, concerts nightly generally at 20:15, tel. 01/512-5790 to reserve). Shows last two hours and are a mix of ballet, waltzes, and a 15-piece orchestra. It's touristy—tour guides holding up banners with group numbers wait out front after the show. Even so, the performance is playful, visually fun, fine quality for most, and with a tried-and-tested, crowd-pleasing format. The conductor welcomes the crowd in German (with a wink) and English; after that...it's English only.

Musicals—The Wien Ticket pavilion next to the Opera (near Kärntner Strasse) sells tickets to contemporary American and British musicals performed in German (€10-109). Same-day tickets are available at a 24 percent discount from 14:00 until 18:00 (ticket pavilion open daily 10:00-19:00). Or you can reserve (full-price) tickets for the musicals by phone (call Wien Ticket at tel. 01/58885).

Films of Concerts—To see free films of great concerts in a lively, outdoor setting near City Hall, see "Nightlife in Vienna," next.

Ballroom Dancing—If you like to dance (waltz and ballroom), or watch people who are really good at it, consider the Dance Evening at the Tanz Café in the Volksgarten (€5-6, May-Aug Sun from 18:00, www.volksgarten.at).

Organ Concerts—St. Peter's Church puts on free organ concerts weekdays at 15:00 and weekends at 20:00 (see page 1132).

Classical Music to Go—To bring home Beethoven, Strauss, or the Wiener Philharmonic on a top-quality CD, shop at Gramola on the Graben or EMI on Kärntner Strasse.

Nightlife in Vienna

If powdered wigs and opera singers in Viking helmets aren't your thing, Vienna has plenty of alternatives. For an up-to-date run-down on fun after dark, check www.viennahype.at.

City Hall Open-Air Classical-Music Cinema and Food Circus—A thriving people scene erupts each evening in summer (mid-July-mid-Sept) at the park in front of City Hall (Rathaus, on the Ringstrasse). Thousands of people keep a food circus of 24 simple stalls busy. There's not a plastic cup anywhere, just real plates and glasses—Vienna wants the quality of food to be as high as the music that's about to begin. About 3,000 folding chairs face a 60-foot-  wide screen up against the City Hall's Neo-Gothic facade. When darkness falls, an announcer explains the program, and then the music starts. The program is different every night—mostly movies of opera and classical concerts, with some films. The TI has the schedule (programs generally last about 2 hours, starting when it's dark—between 21:30 in July and 20:30 in Aug and early Sept).

Since 1991, the city has paid for 60 of these summer event nights each year. Why? To promote culture. Officials know that the City Hall Music Festival is mostly a "meat market" where young people come to hook up. But they believe many of these people will develop a little appreciation of classical music and high culture on the side.

Bermuda Triangle (Bermuda Dreieck)—The area known as the "Bermuda Triangle"—north of St. Stephen's Cathedral, between Rotenturmstrasse and Judengasse—is the hot nightspot in the old town. You'll find lots of music clubs and classy pubs, or *Beisl* (such as Krah Krah, Salzamt, Bermuda Bräu, and First Floor—for cocktails with a view of live fish). The serious-looking guards have nothing to do with the bar scene—they're guarding the synagogue nearby.

Gürtel—The Gürtel is Vienna's outer ring road. The arches of a lumbering viaduct (which carries a train track) are now filled with trendy bars, sports bars, dance clubs, strip clubs, antique shops, and restaurants. To experience—or simply see—the latest scene in town, head out here. The people-watching—the trendiest kids on the block—makes the trip fun even if you're looking for exercise rather than a drink. Ride U-6 to Nussdorfer Strasse or Thaliastrasse and hike along the viaduct.

English Cinema—Several great theaters offer three or four screens of English movies nightly (€6-9): **Burg Kino,** a block from the Opera, facing the Ring (see below); **English Cinema Haydn,** near my recommended hotels on Mariahilfer Strasse (Mariahilfer Strasse 57, tel. 01/587-2262, www.haydnkino.at); and **Artis International Cinema,** right in the town center a few minutes from the cathedral (Schultergasse 5, tel. 01/535-6570).

***The Third Man* at Burg Kino**—This movie, voted the best British film ever by the British Film Institute, takes place in 1949 Vienna—when it was divided, like Berlin, between the four victorious Allies. With a dramatic Vienna cemetery scene, coffee-house culture surviving amid the rubble, and Orson Welles being chased through the sewers, the tale of a divided city about to fall under Soviet rule and rife with smuggling is an enjoyable two-hour experience while in Vienna (€8, in English; 3-4 showings weekly—usually Friday evening, Sunday afternoon, and Tuesday early evening; Opernring 19, tel. 01/587-8406, www.burgkino.at).

Sleeping in Vienna

As you move out from the center, hotel prices drop. My listings are in the old center (figure at least €100 for a decent double), along the likeable Mariahilfer Strasse (about €90), and near the Westbahnhof (about €70).

Book ahead for Vienna if you can, particularly for holidays (see sidebar on page 1255; for tips on making reservations, see page 30). Business hotels have their highest rates in September and October, when it's peak convention time. Prices are also high right around New Year's Eve. Steer clear of Internet booking sites—hotels lose big and you pay more. Book direct by phone, fax, or email.

While few accommodations in Vienna are air-conditioned, you can generally get fans on request. Places with elevators often have a few stairs to climb, too. Viennese elevators can be confusing: In most of Europe, 0 is the ground floor, and 1 is the first

Sleep Code

(€1 = about $1.40, country code: 43, area code: 01)
S = Single, **D** = Double/Twin, **T** = Triple, **Q** = Quad, **b** = bathroom,
s = shower only. Unless otherwise noted, credit cards are
accepted, and breakfast is included. Everyone listed here
speaks English.

To help you easily sort through these listings, I've divided
the accommodations into three categories, based on the price
for a double room with bath during high season:

$$$ Higher Priced—Most rooms €120 or more.
$$ Moderately Priced—Most rooms between €75-120.
$ Lower Priced—Most rooms €75 or less.

Prices can change without notice; verify the hotel's
current rates online or by email. For other updates, see www
.ricksteves.com/update.

floor up (our "second floor"). But in Vienna, elevators can also have
floors P, U, M, and A before getting to 1—so floor 1 can actually
be what we'd call the fifth floor.

For tips on reaching your hotel upon arrival in Vienna, see
"Vienna Connections" at the end of this chapter.

Within the Ring, in the Old City Center

You'll pay extra to sleep in the atmospheric old center, but if you can
afford it, staying here gives you the best classy Vienna experience.

$$$ Hotel am Stephansplatz is a four-star business hotel
with 56 rooms. It's plush but not over-the-top, and reasonably
priced for its sleek comfort and incredible location facing the
cathedral. Every detail is modern and quality; breakfast is superb,
with a view of the city waking up around the cathedral; and
the staff is always ready with a friendly welcome (Sb-€160-180,
Db-€210-250, prices vary with season and room size, prices shoot
up during conventions—most often in Sept-Oct; generally less
Fri-Sun, July-Aug, and in winter; extra bed-€50, children stay for
free or very cheap, air-con, free Internet access and Wi-Fi, gym
and sauna, elevator, Stephansplatz 9, U-1 or U-3: Stephansplatz,
tel. 01/534-050, fax 01/5340-5710, www.hotelamstephansplatz.at,
office@hotelamstephansplatz.at).

$$$ Hotel Pertschy, circling an old courtyard, is big and
hotelesque. Its 56 huge rooms are elegantly creaky, with chande-
liers and Baroque touches. Those on the courtyard are quietest (Sb-
€95-114, Db-€139-169 depending on room size, €20-30 cheaper
off-season, extra bed-€36, non-smoking rooms, free Internet access

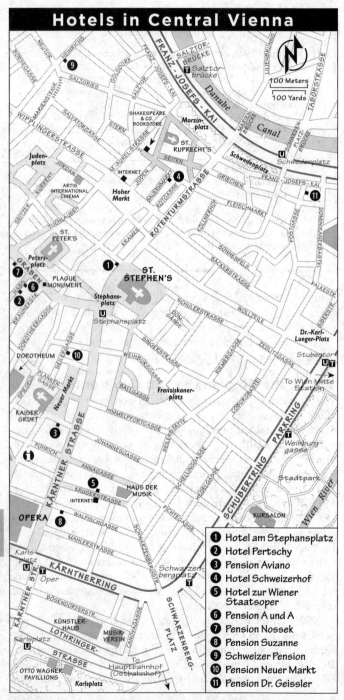

Hotels in Central Vienna

1. Hotel am Stephansplatz
2. Hotel Pertschy
3. Pension Aviano
4. Hotel Schweizerhof
5. Hotel zur Wiener Staatsoper
6. Pension A und A
7. Pension Nossek
8. Pension Suzanne
9. Schweizer Pension
10. Pension Neuer Markt
11. Pension Dr. Geissler

and Wi-Fi, elevator, Habsburgergasse 5, U-1 or U-3: Stephansplatz, tel. 01/534-490, fax 01/534-4949, www.pertschy.com, pertschy @pertschy.com).

$$$ Pension Aviano is another peaceful, family-run place. It has 17 comfortable rooms with flowery carpet and other Baroque frills, all on the fourth floor above lots of old-center action (Sb-€104, Db-€148-169 depending on size, roughly €20-30 cheaper per room in July-Aug and Nov-March, 5 percent discount if you book direct and mention Rick Steves, extra bed-€25-33, non-smoking, fans, free Internet access and Wi-Fi, elevator, between Neuer Markt and Kärntner Strasse at Marco d'Avianogasse 1, tel. 01/512-8330, fax 01/5128-3306, www.secrethomes.at, aviano @secrethomes.at).

$$$ Hotel Schweizerhof is classy, with 55 big rooms, all the comforts, shiny public spaces, and a formal ambience. It's centrally located midway between St. Stephen's Cathedral and the Danube Canal (Sb-€85-95, Db-€120-140, low prices are for July-Aug and slow times, with cash and this book get your best price and then claim a 10 percent discount, extra bed-€35, grand breakfast, free Wi-Fi, elevator, Bauernmarkt 22, U-1 or U-3: Stephansplatz, tel. 01/533-1931, fax 01/533-0214, www.schweizerhof.at, office @schweizerhof.at). Since this is in the "Bermuda Triangle" night-club area, it can be noisy on weekends (Thu-Sat). If you'll be here then, ask for a quiet room when you reserve.

$$$ Hotel zur Wiener Staatsoper, the Schweizerhof's sister hotel, is quiet, with a more traditional elegance. Its 22 tidy rooms come with high ceilings, chandeliers, and fancy carpets on parquet floors (tiny Sb-€80-100, Db-€115-150, Tb-€135-175, rates depend on demand, cheaper prices are for July-Aug and Dec-March, extra bed-€22, fans on request, elevator, free Wi-Fi, a block from the Opera at Krugerstrasse 11; U-1, U-2, or U-4: Karlsplatz; tel. 01/513-1274, fax 01/513-127-415, www.zurwienerstaatsoper.at, office@zurwienerstaatsoper.at, manager Claudia).

$$$ Pension A und A, a friendly eight-room B&B run by Andreas and Andrea, offers a sleek, mod break from crusty old Vienna. This pricey place, wonderfully located just off the Graben, replaces Baroque doilies with contemporary style and blinding-white minimalist public spaces (Sb-€98-128 depending on sea-son; Db-€149 in May-Aug, €179 in Sept-Oct, €129 in Nov-Feb; includes breakfast, air-con, free Wi-Fi, Habsburgergasse 3, floor M, tel. 01/890-5128, www.aunda.at, office@aunda.at).

$$ At Pension Nossek, an elevator takes you above any street noise into Frau Bernad and Frau Gundolf's world, where the chil-dren seem to be placed among the lace and flowers by an interior designer. With 32 rooms right on the wonderful Graben, this is a particularly good value (S-€52-60, Ss-€62, Sb-€76-80, Db-€120,

€30 extra for sprawling suites, extra bed-€35, cash only, air-con, elevator, pay Internet access and Wi-Fi, Graben 17, U-1 or U-3: Stephansplatz, tel. 01/5337-0410, fax 01/535-3646, www.pension -nossek.at, reservation@pension-nossek.at).

$$ Pension Suzanne, as Baroque and doily as you'll find in this price range, is wonderfully located a few yards from the Opera. It's small, but run with the class of a bigger hotel. The 25 rooms are packed with properly Viennese antique furnishings and paintings (Sb-€82, Db-€106-127 depending on size, 4 percent discount with this book and cash, extra bed-€25, spacious apartment for up to 6 also available, discounts in winter, fans on request, elevator, free Internet access and Wi-Fi, Walfischgasse 4; U-1, U-2, or U-4: Karlsplatz and follow signs for Opera exit; tel. 01/513-2507, fax 01/513-2500, www.pension-suzanne.at, info@pension-suzanne.at, manager Michael).

$$ Schweizer Pension has been family-owned for four generations. Anita and her son Gerald offer lots of tourist info and 11 homey rooms for a great price, with parquet floors. True to its name, it feels very Swiss—tidy and well-run (S-€46-55, big Sb-€68-81, D-€68-79, Db-€89-98, Tb-€109-125, prices depend on season and room size, cash only, entirely non-smoking, elevator, free Wi-Fi, laundry-€18/load, Heinrichsgasse 2, U-2 or U-4: Schottenring, tel. 01/533-8156, fax 01/535-6469, www.schweizer pension.com, schweizer.pension@chello.at). They also rent a quad with bath (€129-139—too small for 4 adults but great for a family of 2 adults/2 kids under age 15).

$$ Pension Neuer Markt is family-run, with 37 comfy but faded rooms in a perfectly central locale. Its hallways have the ambience of a cheap cruise ship (Ss-€70-80, Sb-€90-110, smaller Ds-€80-90, Db-€90-135, prices vary with season and room size, extra bed-€20, request a quiet room when you reserve, fans, elevator, free Internet access and Wi-Fi, Seilergasse 9, tel. 01/512-2316, fax 01/513-9105, www.hotelpension.at/neuermarkt, neuermarkt @hotelpension.at).

$$ Pension Dr. Geissler has 23 plain-but-comfortable rooms in a modern, nondescript apartment building about 10 blocks northeast of St. Stephen's, near the canal (S-€48, Ss-€68, Sb-€76, D-€65, Ds-€77, Db-€95, 20 percent less in winter, elevator, Postgasse 14, U-1 or U-4: Schwedenplatz—Postgasse is to the left as you face Hotel Capricorno, tel. 01/533-2803, fax 01/533-2635, www.hotelpension.at/dr-geissler, dr.geissler@hotelpension.at).

On or near Mariahilfer Strasse

Lively Mariahilfer Strasse connects the Westbahnhof (West Station) and the city center. The U-3 line, starting at the Westbahnhof, goes down Mariahilfer Strasse to the cathedral.

This tourist-friendly, vibrant area is filled with shopping malls, simpler storefronts, and cafés. Its smaller hotels and private rooms are generally run by people from the non-German-speaking part of the former Habsburg Empire (i.e., Eastern Europe). Most hotels are within a few steps of an U-Bahn stop, just one or two stops from the Westbahnhof (direction from the station: Simmering). The nearest place to do laundry is **Schnell & Sauber Waschcenter** (wash-€4.50 for small load or €9 for large load, plus a few euros to dry, daily 6:00-23:00, a few blocks north of Westbahnhof on the east side of Urban-Loritz-Platz).

$$$ NH Hotels, a Spanish chain, runs two stern, stylish-but-passionless business hotels a few blocks apart on Mariahilfer Strasse. Both rent ideal-for-families suites, each with a living room, two TVs, bathroom, desk, and kitchenette (rack rate: Db suite-€99-200, going rate usually closer to €110-125, €17/person for optional breakfast, apartments for 2-3 adults, 1 kid under 12 free, non-smoking rooms, elevator, pay Wi-Fi). The 73-room **NH Atterseehaus** is at Mariahilfer Strasse 78 (U-3: Zieglergasse, tel. 01/524-5600, fax 01/524-560-015, nhatterseehaus@nh-hotels.com), and **NH Wien** has 105 rooms at Mariahilfer Strasse 32 (U-3: Neubaugasse—follow *Stiftgasse* signs to exit and turn left from top of escalator; from Mariahilfer Strasse, enter through shop passageway between Nordsee and Tchibo—or from Lindengasse 9, tel. 01/521-720, fax 01/521-7215, nhwien@nh-hotels.com). The website for both is www.nh-hotels.com.

$$ Hotel Pension Corvinus is bright, modern, and proudly and warmly run by a Hungarian family: Miklós, Judit, Anthony, and Zoltan. Its 12 comfortable rooms are spacious, and some are downright sumptuous (Sb-€69-79, Db-€99-109, Tb-€119-129, get these special Rick Steves prices with this book, extra bed-€26, also has apartments with kitchens, most rooms non-smoking, air-con, elevator, free Internet access and Wi-Fi, parking garage-€17/day, on the third floor at Mariahilfer Strasse 57-59, U-3: Neubaugasse, tel. 01/587-7239, fax 01/587-723-920, www.corvinus.at, hotel@corvinus.at).

$$ Hotel Pension Mariahilf's 12 rooms are clean, well-priced, and good-sized (if outmoded), with a slight Art Deco flair (Sb-€60-75, twin Db-€78-98, Db-€88-109, Tb-€99-139, 5-6-person apartment with kitchen-€129-169, lower prices are for Nov-Feb or longer stays, book direct and ask about a Rick Steves discount, elevator, free Wi-Fi, parking-€18, Mariahilfer Strasse 49, U-3: Neubaugasse, tel. 01/586-1781, fax 01/586-178-122, www.mariahilf-hotel.at, office@mariahilf-hotel.at).

$$ K&T Boardinghouse rents spacious, comfortable, good-value rooms in two locations. The first has three bright and airy rooms three flights above lively Mariahilfer Strasse (no elevator).

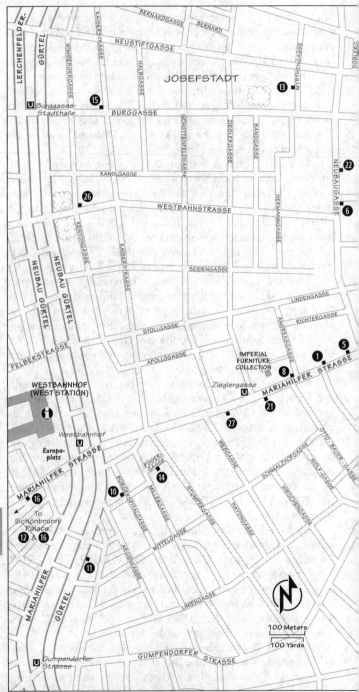

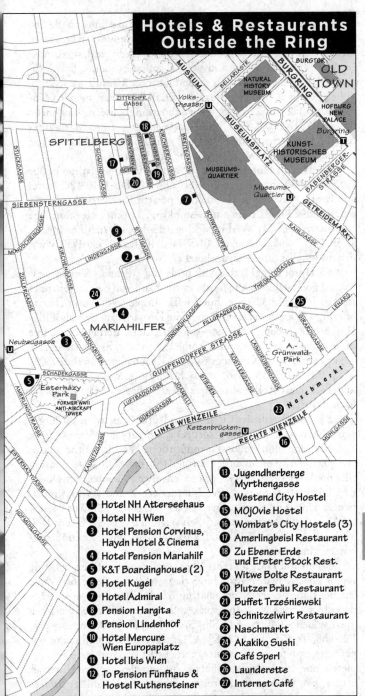

Hotels & Restaurants Outside the Ring

1. Hotel NH Atterseehaus
2. Hotel NH Wien
3. Hotel Pension Corvinus, Haydn Hotel & Cinema
4. Hotel Pension Mariahilf
5. K&T Boardinghouse (2)
6. Hotel Kugel
7. Hotel Admiral
8. Pension Hargita
9. Pension Lindenhof
10. Hotel Mercure Wien Europaplatz
11. Hotel Ibis Wien
12. To Pension Fünfhaus & Hostel Ruthensteiner
13. Jugendherberge Myrthengasse
14. Westend City Hostel
15. MOjOvie Hostel
16. Wombat's City Hostels (3)
17. Amerlingbeisl Restaurant
18. Zu Ebener Erde und Erster Stock Rest.
19. Witwe Bolte Restaurant
20. Plutzer Bräu Restaurant
21. Buffet Trześniewski
22. Schnitzelwirt Restaurant
23. Naschmarkt
24. Akakiko Sushi
25. Café Sperl
26. Launderette
27. Internet Café

The second location, just across the street, has five units on the first floor (Db-€79, Tb-€99, Qb-€119, 2-night minimum, no breakfast, air-con-€10/day, cash only but reserve with credit card, non-smoking, free Internet access and Wi-Fi, coffee in rooms; first location: Mariahilfer Strasse 72, second location: Chwallagasse 2; for either, get off at U-3: Neubaugasse; tel. 01/523-2989, mobile 0676-553-6063, fax 01/522-0345, www.ktboardinghouse.at, k.t@chello .at, Tina). To reach the Chwallagasse location from Mariahilfer Strasse, turn left at Café Ritter and walk down Schadekgasse one short block; tiny Chwallagasse is the first right.

$$ Haydn Hotel is big and formal, with masculine public spaces and 50 spacious rooms (Sb-€80-90, Db-€110-120, suites and family apartments, ask about 10 percent Rick Steves discount, extra bed-€30, all rooms non-smoking, air-con, elevator, free Internet access, pay Wi-Fi, parking-€15/day, Mariahilfer Strasse 57-59, U-3: Neubaugasse, tel. 01/5874-4140, fax 01/586-1950, www .haydn-hotel.at, info@haydn-hotel.at, Nouri).

$$ Hotel Kugel is run with pride and attitude. "Simple quality and good value" is the motto of the hands-on owner, Johannes Roller. It's a big 32-room hotel with simple Old World charm, offering a fine value (Db-€85, supreme Db with canopy beds-€105-115, cash only, completely non-smoking, free Internet access, free cable Internet in some rooms, some tram noise, Siebensterngasse 43, at corner with Neubaugasse, U-3: Neubaugasse, tel. 01/523-3355, fax 01/5233-3555, www.hotelkugel.at, office@hotel kugel.at). Herr Roller also offers several cheaper basic rooms for backpackers.

$$ Hotel Admiral is huge and practical, with 80 large, workable rooms. This last resort is on a dreary street across from a rowdy nightclub (request a quiet room), and lacks the charm and personality of my other listings (Sb-€70, Db-€94, mention this book for these special prices, cheaper in winter, extra bed-€25, breakfast-€6/person, free Internet access and Wi-Fi; limited free parking is first-come, first-served—otherwise €10/day; a block off Mariahilfer Strasse at Karl-Schweighofer-Gasse 7, U-2 or U-3: Volkstheater, tel. 01/521-410, fax 01/521-4116, www.admiral.co.at, hotel@admiral.co.at).

$ Pension Hargita rents 19 generally small, bright, and tidy rooms (mostly twins) with Hungarian woody-village decor. While the pension is directly on bustling Mariahilfer Strasse, its windows block noise well. This spick-and-span, well-located place is a great value (S-€40, Ss-€47, Sb-€57, D-€54, Ds-€60, tiny Db-€65, Db-€68, Ts-€75, Tb-€82, Qb-€112, reserve with credit card but pay with cash to get these rates, extra bed-€12, breakfast-€5, completely non-smoking, lots of stairs and no elevator, free Internet access, pay Wi-Fi in some rooms, corner of Mariahilfer Strasse and Andreasgasse, Andreasgasse 1, U-3: Zieglergasse, tel. 01/526-1928, fax 01/526-0492, www.hargita.at, pension@hargita.at, Erika and Tibor).

$ Pension Lindenhof rents 19 very basic, very worn but clean rooms. It's a dark and mysteriously dated time warp filled with plants (and a fun guest-generated postcard wall); the stark rooms have outrageously high ceilings and teeny bathrooms (S-€32, Sb-€40, D-€54, Db-€72, T-€81, Tb-€108, Q-€108, Qb-€144, cheaper during slow times, hall shower-€2, cash only, elevator, next door to a harmless strip bar at Lindengasse 4, U-3: Neubaugasse, tel. 01/523-0498, fax 01/523-7362, www.pensionlindenhof.at, pensionlindenhof@yahoo.com, run by Gebrael family; Zara, Keram, and his father George speak English).

Near the Westbahnhof (West Station)

$$$ Hotel Mercure Wien Europaplatz offers high-rise modern efficiency and comfort in 211 air-conditioned rooms, directly across from the Westbahnhof (Db-€130-170 depending on season, online deals as cheap as Db-€69 if you book well in advance, breakfast-€15, free Internet access and Wi-Fi in lobby, pay Wi-Fi in rooms, elevator, parking-€15/day, Matrosengasse 6, U-3: Westbahnhof, tel. 01/5990-1181, fax 01/597-6900, www.mercure.com, h1707@accor.com).

$$ Hotel Ibis Wien, a modern high-rise hotel with American charm, is ideal for anyone tired of quaint old Europe. Its 340 cookie-cutter rooms are bright, comfortable, and modern, with all the conveniences (Sb-€69-75, Db-€87-93, Tb-€106, breakfast-€10, air-con, elevator, free Internet access and Wi-Fi in lobby, parking garage-€12/day; exit Westbahnhof to the right and walk 400 yards, Mariahilfer Gürtel 22-24, U-3: Westbahnhof; tel. 01/59998, fax 01/597-9090, www.ibishotel.com, h0796@accor.com).

$ Pension Fünfhaus is big, plain, clean, and bare-bones—almost institutional—with tile floors. The neighborhood is run-down (with a few ladies loitering late at night), but this 47-room pension offers the best doubles you'll find for under €60 (S-€34, Sb-€43, D-€49, Db-€58, Tb-€84-92, 4-person apartment-€98-104, cash only, closed mid-Nov-Feb, includes basic breakfast, Sperrgasse 12, U-3: Westbahnhof, tel. 01/892-3545 or 01/892-0286, fax 01/892-0460, www.pension5haus.at, vienna@pension5haus.at, Frau Susi Tersch). Half the rooms are in the main building and half are in the annex, which has good rooms but is near the train tracks and a bit scary on the street at night. From the station, ride tram #52 or #58 two stops down Mariahilfer Strasse away from center, and ask for Sperrgasse. Crazy Chicken bike rental, listed on page 1114, is just a block farther down Sperrgasse.

VIENNA

Cheap Dorms and Hostels
near Mariahilfer Strasse

$ Jugendherberge Myrthengasse is your classic huge and well-run HI youth hostel, with 280 beds (€17-21/person in 2- to 6-bed rooms, price depends on season, includes sheets and breakfast, non-members pay €3.50 extra, pay Internet access, free Wi-Fi in lobby, always open, no curfew, lockers and lots of facilities, coin-op laundry, Myrthengasse 7, tel. 01/523-6316, fax 01/523-5849, hostel@chello.at).

$ Westend City Hostel, just a block from the Westbahnhof and Mariahilfer Strasse, is well-run and well-located, with 180 beds in 4- to 12-bed dorms (€22-29/person depending on how many in the room, Db-€66-92, rates vary by season, cheaper Nov-mid-March—except around New Year's; includes sheets, breakfast, and locker; cash only, pay Internet access, free Wi-Fi, laundry-€7, Fügergasse 3, tel. 01/597-6729, fax 01/597-672-927, www.westend hostel.at, info@westendhostel.at).

$ MOjOvie is a creative "little neighbourette," combining a residential apartment feel with a hostel vibe. This network of apartments offers dorm beds as well as private units sleeping two to four (dorm bed-€20, €23-26/person in a private room with shared bathroom, €35-45/person for apartment with private bathroom, includes sheets and towels, cash only for charges under €100, free Wi-Fi, laundry service, shared kitchen, reception open 8:00-23:00, Kaiserstrasse 77, tram #5 or a 10-minute walk from Westbahnhof, mobile 0699-1155-5505, www.mymojovie.at, accommodation @mymojovie.at).

$ *More Hostels:* Other hostels with €17-20 beds and €50 doubles near Mariahilfer Strasse are **Wombat's City Hostel** (3 locations: one near tracks behind the station at Grangasse 6, another even closer to station at Mariahilfer Strasse 137, and a new one near the Naschmarkt at Rechte Wienzeile 35; tel. 01/897-2336, www.wombats-hostels.com, office@wombats-vienna.at) and **Hostel Ruthensteiner** (smoke-free; leave the Westbahnhof to the right and follow Mariahilfer Strasse behind the station, then left on Haidmannsgasse for a block, then turn right and find Robert-Hamerling-Gasse 24; tel. 01/893-4202, www.hostelruthensteiner .com, info@hostelruthensteiner.com).

Eating in Vienna

The Viennese appreciate the fine points of life, and right up there with waltzing is eating. The city has many atmospheric restaurants. As you ponder the Eastern European specialties on menus, remember that Vienna's diverse empire may be no more, but its flavors linger.

While cuisines are routinely named for countries, Vienna claims to be the only *city* with a cuisine of its own: Vienna soups come with fillings (semolina dumpling, liver dumpling, or pancake slices). *Gulasch* is a beef ragout based on a traditional Hungarian shepherd's soup (spiced with onion and paprika). Of course, Wiener schnitzel is traditionally a breaded and fried veal cutlet (though pork is more common these days). Another meat specialty is boiled beef *(Tafelspitz)*. While you're sure to have *Apfelstrudel*, try *Topfenstrudel*, too (wafer-thin strudel pastry filled with sweet cheese and raisins). The *dag* you see in some prices stands for "dekagram" (10 grams). Therefore, *10 dag* is 100 grams, or about a quarter-pound.

On nearly every corner, you can find a colorful *Beisl* (BYE-zul). These uniquely Viennese taverns are a characteristic cross between an English pub and a French brasserie—filled with poetry teachers and their students, couples loving without touching, housewives on their way home from cello lessons, and waiters who enjoy serving hearty food and drinks at an affordable price. Ask at your hotel for a good *Beisl*. (Beware: Despite non-smoking laws, *Beisls* may still be quite smoky; fortunately, most have outdoor seating.)

Two other don't-miss Viennese institutions, its cafés and wine gardens, are covered under "Experiences in Vienna" on page 1173.

Many restaurants offer a *"menu,"* a fixed-price bargain meal, at lunchtime.

Near St. Stephen's Cathedral
Each of these eateries is within about a five-minute walk of the cathedral (U-1 or U-3: Stephansplatz).

Gigerl Stadtheuriger offers a fun, near-*Heuriger* wine cellar experience (described on page 1175), without leaving the city center. Just point to what looks good. Food is sold by the piece or weight; 100 grams *(10 dag)* is about a quarter-pound (cheese and cold meats cost about €3 per 100 grams, salads are about €2 per 100 grams; price sheet posted on wall to right of buffet line). The *Karree* pork with herbs is particularly tasty and tender. They also have menu entrées, spinach strudel, quiche, *Apfelstrudel*, and, of course, casks of new and local wines (sold by the *Achtel*, about 4 oz). Meals run €7-12, and there's often accordion or live music on weekends (daily 15:00-24:00, indoor/outdoor seating, behind cathedral, a block off Kärntner Strasse, a few cobbles off Rauhensteingasse on Blumenstock, tel. 01/513-4431).

Zu den Drei Hacken, another fun and typical *Weinstube,* is famous for its local specialties (€10 plates, Mon-Sat 11:00-23:00, closed Sun, indoor/outdoor seating, Singerstrasse 28, tel. 01/512-5895).

Buffet Trześniewski is an institution—justly famous for its

VIENNA

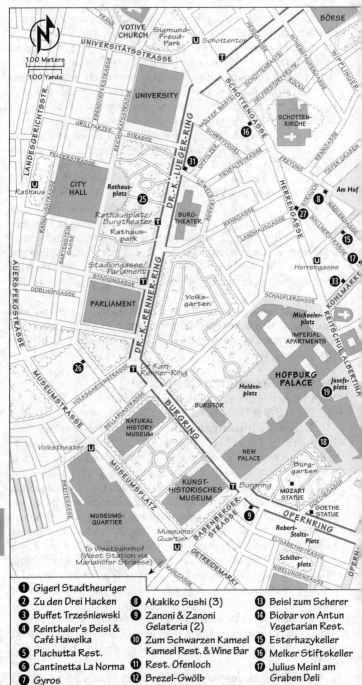

VIENNA

1. Gigerl Stadtheuriger
2. Zu den Drei Hacken
3. Buffet Trześniewski
4. Reinthaler's Beisl & Café Hawelka
5. Plachutta Rest.
6. Cantinetta La Norma
7. Gyros
8. Akakiko Sushi (3)
9. Zanoni & Zanoni Gelateria (2)
10. Zum Schwarzen Kameel Kameel Rest. & Wine Bar
11. Rest. Ofenloch
12. Brezel-Gwölb
13. Beisl zum Scherer
14. Biobar von Antun Vegetarian Rest.
15. Esterhazykeller
16. Melker Stiftskeller
17. Julius Meinl am Graben Deli

Restaurants in Central Vienna

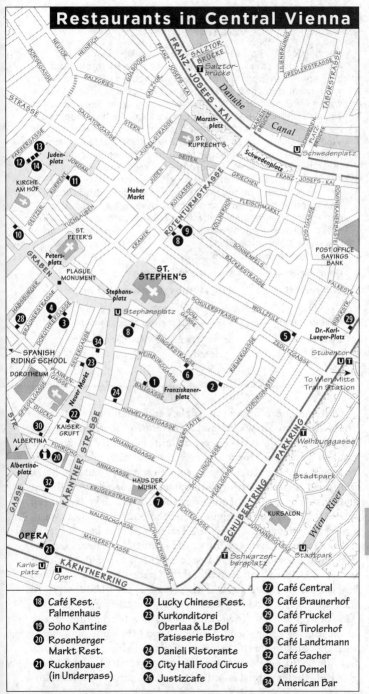

18 Café Rest. Palmenhaus
19 Soho Kantine
20 Rosenberger Markt Rest.
21 Ruckenbauer (in Underpass)

22 Lucky Chinese Rest.
23 Kurkonditorei Oberlaa & Le Bol Patisserie Bistro
24 Danieli Ristorante
25 City Hall Food Circus
26 Justizcafe

27 Café Central
28 Café Braunerhof
29 Café Pruckel
30 Café Tirolerhof
31 Café Landtmann
32 Café Sacher
33 Café Demel
34 American Bar

Wieners in Wien

For hardcore Viennese cuisine, drop by a *Würstelstand*. The local hot-dog stand is a fixture on city squares throughout the old center, serving a variety of hot dogs and pickled side dishes with a warm corner-meeting-place atmosphere. The *Wiener* we know is named for Vienna, but the guy who invented the weenie studied in Frankfurt. Out of nostalgia for his school years, he named his fun fast food for that city...a Frankfurter. Only in Vienna are *Wieners* called *Frankfurters*. (Got that?) Convenient sausage stands are on Hoher Markt, the Graben, and in front of the Albertina Museum. Explore the fun menus. Be adventurous. The many varieties of hot dogs cost €3-4 each.

Your *Wurst* options go far beyond the hometown hot dog. The generic term *Bratwurst* simply means "grilled sausage," and regional variations of it abound. Some sausages are boiled *(gekocht)*, and some are grilled *(gegrillt)*. Generally, the darker the weenie, the spicier it is.

Here are some key words:

Frankfurter	our hot dog
Burenwurst	pork sausage similar to what we'd call "kielbasa"
Käsekrainer	boiled, with melted cheese inside
Debreziner	boiled, thin, spicy Hungarian, with paprika

elegant and cheap finger sandwiches and small beers (€1 each). Three different sandwiches and a *kleines Bier (Pfiff)* make a fun, light lunch. Point to whichever delights look tasty (or grab the English translation sheet and take time to study your 22 sandwich options). The classic favorites are *Geflügelleber* (chicken liver), *Matjes mit Zwiebel* (herring with onions), and *Speck mit Ei* (bacon and eggs). Pay for your sandwiches and a drink. Take your drink tokens to the lady on the right. Sit on the bench and scoot over to a tiny table when a spot opens up. Trześniewski has been a Vienna favorite for more than a century...and many of its regulars seem to have been here for the grand opening (Mon-Fri 8:30-19:30, Sat 9:00-17:00, closed Sun; 50 yards off the Graben, nearly across from brooding Café Hawelka, Dorotheergasse 2; tel. 01/512-3291). In the fall, this is a good opportunity to try the fancy grape juices—*Most* or *Traubenmost*. Their other location, at Mariahilfer Strasse 95 (near many recommended hotels), serves the same sandwiches with the same menu in the same ambience (Mon-Fri 8:30-19:00, Sat 9:00-18:00, closed Sun, U-3: Zieglergasse, tel. 01/596-4291).

Reinthaler's Beisl is a time warp that serves simple, tradi-

Bosna	with onions and sometimes curry
Waldviertler	smoked sausage
Beinwurst	made of smoked pork, herbs, and wine
Bockwurst	thick pork sausage (white)
Weisswurst	boiled white sausage (typically Bavarian; peel off the casing before you eat it)
Nürnberger	short and spicy pork sausage
Blutwurst, Blunzn	made from congealed blood
frische	fresh ("eat before the noon bells")

Sauces and sides include *Senf* (mustard; ask for *süss*—sweet; or *scharf*—sharp), *Ketchup, Curry-Ketchup* (a tasty curry-infused ketchup), and sometimes *Kren* (horseradish) or *Kraut* (sauerkraut). You also have a choice between a slice of bread *(Brot)* or a roll *(Semmel)*. They might ask you: *Brot oder Semmel?* (Bread or roll?). Neither one of these resembles an American hot-dog bun.

They'll give the sausage and bread or roll to you on a paper plate, with a squirt of mustard or ketchup. Only a tourist puts the sausage in a bun like a hot dog. Munch alternately between the meat and the bread ("that's why you have two hands"), and you'll look like a native.

tional *Beisl* fare all day. It's handy for its location (a block off the Graben, across the street from Buffet Trześniewski) and because it's a rare restaurant in the center that's open on Sunday. Its fun, classic interior winds way back (use the handwritten daily menu rather than the printed English one, €6-12 plates, daily 11:00-22:30, at Dorotheergasse 4, tel. 01/513-1249).

Plachutta Restaurant, with a stylish green-and-cream, elegant-but-comfy interior and breezy covered terrace, is famous for the best beef in town. You'll find an enticing menu with all the classic Viennese beef dishes, fine desserts, attentive service, and an enthusiastic and sophisticated local clientele. They've developed the art of beef to the point of producing popular cookbooks. Their specialty is a page-long list of *Tafelspitz*—a traditional copper pot of boiled beef with broth and vegetables. Treat the broth as your soup course. A chart on the menu lets you choose your favorite cut. Make a reservation for this high-energy Vienna favorite (€16-21/pot, daily 12:00-22:30, 10-minute walk from St. Stephen's Cathedral to Wollzeile 38, U-3: Stubentor, tel. 01/512-1577).

Cantinetta La Norma, a short walk from the cathedral,

serves fresh, excellent Italian dishes amid a cozy, yet energetic ambience. Even on weeknights the small dining area is abuzz with chatter among its multinational, loyal regulars (€8 pizzas and pastas, €7-18 entrées, lunch specials, daily 11:00-24:00, outdoor seating, Franziskaner Platz 3, tel. 01/512-8665, run by friendly Paco).

Gyros is a humble little Greek/Turkish joint run by Yilmaz, a fun-loving Turk from Izmir. He simply loves to feed people—the food is great, the prices are decent, and you almost feel like you took a quick trip to Istanbul (€8-12 plates, Mon-Sat 10:00-24:00, Sun 10:00-18:00, a long block off Kärntner Strasse at corner of Fichtegasse and Seilerstätte, mobile 0699-1016-3726).

Akakiko Sushi is a small chain of Japanese restaurants with an easy, pan-Asian menu that's worth considering if you're just schnitzeled out. They serve sushi, of course, but also noodles, stir-fry, and other meals. The €11 bento box meals are a decent value. There are several convenient locations: Singerstrasse 4 (a block off Kärntner Strasse near the cathedral), Rotenturmgasse 6 (also near the cathedral), Heidenschuss 3 (near other recommended eateries just off Am Hof, U-3: Herrengasse), and Mariahilfer Strasse 42-48 (fifth floor of Kaufhaus Gerngross, near many recommended hotels, U-3: Neubaugasse). Though they lack charm, these are fast and reasonable (€8-11 meals, all open daily 10:30-23:30).

Ice Cream!: **Zanoni & Zanoni** is a very Italian *gelateria* run by an Italian family. They're mobbed by happy Viennese hungry for their huge €2 cones to go. Or, to relax and watch the thriving people scene, lick your gelato in their fun outdoor area (daily 7:00-24:00, 2 blocks up Rotenturmstrasse from cathedral at Lugeck 7, tel. 01/512-7979). There's another location behind the Kunsthistorisches Museum, facing the Ring (at Burgring 1, U-2 or U-3: Volkstheater/Museumsplatz).

Near Am Hof Square

The square called Am Hof (U-3: Herrengasse) is surrounded by a maze of atmospheric medieval lanes; the following eateries are all within a block of the square.

Zum Schwarzen Kameel Wine Bar ("The Black Camel") is filled with a professional local crowd enjoying small plates from the same kitchen as their fancy restaurant, but at a better price. This is *the* place for horseradish and thin-sliced ham (*Beinschinken mit Kren*, €8.50 a plate, *Achtung*—the horseradish is *hot*). I'd order their *Vorspeisenteller* (a great antipasti dish that comes with ham and horseradish) or *Tafelspitz* (€16). Stand, grab a stool, find a table on the street, or sit anywhere you can—it's customary to share tables in the wine-bar section. Fine Austrian wines are sold by the *Achtel* (eighth-liter glass) and listed on the board; Aussie bartender Karl can help you choose. They also have a buffet of tiny €1-2 sandwiches. For a splurge, the **Zum Schwarzen Kameel Restaurant** is a tiny, elegant alternative. The dark-wood, 12-table, Art Nouveau restaurant serves fine gourmet Viennese cuisine (three-course lunch-€40, three-course dinner-€65 plus pricey wine, both open Mon-Sat 8:30-24:00, closed Sun, Bognergasse 5, tel. 01/533-8125).

Restaurant Ofenloch serves good, old-fashioned Viennese cuisine with formal service, both indoors and out. This 300-year-old eatery, with great traditional ambience, is dressy (with white tablecloths) but intimate and woodsy (€10 lunch specials, €13-19 main courses, Mon-Sat 11:00-22:30, closed Sun, Kurrentgasse 8, tel. 01/533-8844).

Brezel-Gwölb, a Tolkienesque wine cellar with outdoor dining on a quiet square, serves forgettable food in an unforgettable atmosphere. It's ideal for a romantic late-night glass of wine (daily 11:30-23:30; leave Am Hof on Drahtgasse, then take first left to Ledererhof 9; tel. 01/533-8811).

Beisl zum Scherer, around the corner, is untouristy and serves traditional plates for €8-15. Sitting outside, you'll face a stern Holocaust memorial. Inside comes with a soothing woody atmosphere and intriguing decor. Let friendly Sakis explain the daily specials—which don't show up on the English menu (Mon-Sat 11:30-22:00, closed Sun, Judenplatz 7, tel. 01/533-5164).

Biobar von Antun Vegetarian Restaurant is a cheery and earthy little place with a €7 lunch special and hearty €10 salads, plenty of vegan options, and the fancy juices you'd expect (daily 12:00-23:00, on Judenplatz at Drahtgasse 3, tel. 01/968-9351).

Esterhazykeller, both ancient and popular, has traditional fare deep underground. For a cheap and sloppy buffet, climb down to the lowest cellar. For table service on a pleasant square, sit outside (Mon-Sat 11:00-23:00, Sun 16:00-23:00, may close for lunch in Aug-Sept and/or in bad weather, just below Am Hof at Haarhof 1, tel. 01/533-3482).

Melker Stiftskeller is an untouristy *Stadtheuriger* in a deep and rustic circa-1626 cellar with hearty, inexpensive meals and new wine. Avoid this place when it's hot out, as there's no outdoor seating (Tue-Sat 17:00-24:00, closed Sun-Mon and mid-July-mid-Aug, between Am Hof Square and Schottentor U-Bahn stop at Schottengasse 3, tel. 01/533-5530).

Julius Meinl am Graben, a posh supermarket with two floors of temptations right on the Graben, has been famous since 1862 as a top-end delicatessen with all the gourmet fancies. Assemble a meal from the picnic fixings on the shelves. There's also a café, with light meals and great outdoor seating; a stuffy and pricey restaurant upstairs; and a take-away counter with good benches for people-watching while you munch (shop open Mon-Fri

8:00-19:30, Sat 9:00-18:00, closed Sun; restaurant open Mon-Sat until 24:00, closed Sun; Am Graben 19, tel. 01/532-3334).

Near the Opera

These eateries are within easy walking distance of the Opera (U-1, U-2, or U-4: Karlsplatz).

Café Restaurant Palmenhaus overlooks the Palace Garden (Burggarten—see page 1148). Tucked away in a green and peaceful corner two blocks behind the Opera in the Hofburg's backyard, this is a world apart. If you want to eat modern Austrian cuisine surrounded by palm trees rather than tourists, this is the place. And, since it's at the edge of a huge park, it's great for families. Their fresh fish with generous vegetables specials are on the board (€8.50 lunch plates available Mon-Fri, €15-18 entrées, open daily 10:00-24:00, serious vegetarian dishes, fish, extensive wine list, indoors in greenhouse or outdoors, Burggarten 1, tel. 01/533-1033).

Soho Kantine is a grim, government-subsidized cantina serving the National Library and offering the best cheap sit-down lunches in the Hofburg. Pay for your meal—your choice of bland meat or bland vegetarian—and a drink at the bar, take your token to the kitchen, and then sit down and eat with the locals (€6 two-course lunch, Mon-Fri 11:30-15:00, closed Sat-Sun and Aug, hard to find on ground floor of library—opposite the butterflies in a forlorn little square with no sign, Burggarten, Josefsplatz 1, tel. 01/532-8566, mobile 0676-309-5161).

Rosenberger Markt Restaurant is mobbed with tour groups. Still, if you don't mind a freeway-cafeteria ambience in the center of the German-speaking world's classiest city, this self-service eatery is fast and easy. It's just a block toward the cathedral from the Opera. The best cheap meal here is a small salad or veggie plate stacked high (daily 10:30-23:00, lots of fruits, veggies, fresh-squeezed juices, addictive banana milk, ride the glass elevator downstairs, Maysedergasse 2, tel. 01/512-3458).

Ruckenbauer, a favorite for a quick bite, is a fast-food kiosk in a transit underpass under the street in front of the Opera, between the entryways marked *U2/U4* and *U1*. Their €1.60 *Tramezzini* sandwiches and fine pastries make a classy, quick picnic lunch or dinner before the Opera, just 100 yards away (Mon-Fri 6:00-20:00, Sat-Sun 9:00-20:00).

Lucky Chinese Restaurant is simply a good, modern, and well-located option for Chinese food. The inside is fresh and air-conditioned, the outside seating is on a great square, and the service is friendly (€10-15 plates, daily 11:30-23:00, Neuer Markt 8, tel. 01/512-3428).

Kurkonditorei Oberlaa may not have the royal and plush

fame of Demel (see page 1127), but this is where Viennese connoisseurs serious about the quality of their pastries go to get fat.
With outdoor seating on Neuer Markt, it's particularly nice on a
hot summer day. Upstairs has more temptations and good seating (€10 daily three-course lunches, great selection of cakes, daily
8:00-20:00, Neuer Markt 16, other locations about town, including the Naschmarkt, tel. 01/5132-9360).

Le Bol Patisserie Bistro (next to Oberlaa) satisfies your need
for something French. The staff speaks to you in French, serving
fine €8 salads, baguette sandwiches, and fresh croissants (Mon-Sat
8:00-22:00, Sun 10:00-20:00, Neuer Markt 14).

Danieli Ristorante is your best classy Italian bet in the old
town. White-tablecloth dressy, but not stuffy, it has reasonable
prices. Dine in their elegant back room or on the street (€13-18
pizzas and pastas, €18-25 main courses, fresh fish specialties, daily
10:00-24:00, 30 yards off Kärntner Strasse opposite Neuer Markt
at Himmelpfortgasse 3, tel. 01/513-7913).

City Hall Food Circus

During the summer, scores of outdoor food stands and hundreds
of picnic tables are set up in the park in front of the City Hall
(Rathausplatz). Local mobs enjoy mostly ethnic meals for decent-
but-not-cheap prices and classical entertainment on a big screen.
The fun thing here is the energy of the crowd and a feeling that
you're truly eating as the Viennese do...not schnitzel and quaint
traditions, but trendy "world food" with young people out having
fun in a fine Vienna park setting (mid-July-mid-Sept daily from
11:00 until late, in front of City Hall on the Ringstrasse, U-2:
Rathaus).

Just West of the Ring

Justizcafe, the cafeteria serving Austria's Supreme Court of
Justice, offers a fine view, great prices, and a memorable lunchtime
experience—even if the food is somewhat bland. Enter the Palace
of Justice through its grand front door, pass through tight security, say "wow" to the Historicist architecture in the courtyard, and
ride the elevator to the rooftop. You can sit behind the windows
inside or dine outside on the roof, enjoying one of the best views
of Vienna while surrounded by legal beagles (€8-12 main dishes,
Mon-Fri 11:00-14:30, closed Sat-Sun, Schmerlingplatz 10, U-2 or
U-3: Volkstheater/Museumsplatz, mobile 0676-755-6100).

Spittelberg Quarter

A charming cobbled grid of traffic-free lanes and Biedermeier
apartments has become a favorite neighborhood for Viennese
wanting a little dining charm between the MuseumsQuartier

and Mariahilfer Strasse (handy to many recommended hotels; take Stiftgasse from Mariahilfer Strasse, or wander over here after you close down the Kunsthistorisches Museum; U-2 or U-3: Volkstheater/Museumsplatz). Tables tumble down sidewalks and into breezy courtyards filled with appreciative natives enjoying dinner or a relaxing drink. It's only worth the trip on a balmy summer evening, as it's dead in bad weather. Stroll Spittelberggasse, Schrankgasse, and Gutenberggasse, then pick your favorite. Don't miss the vine-strewn wine garden at Schrankgasse 1. To locate these restaurants, see the map on page 1190.

Amerlingbeisl, with a charming, casual atmosphere both on the cobbled street and in its vine-covered courtyard, is a great value, serving a mix of traditional Austrian and international dishes (always a €5 vegetarian daily special, other specials for €6-10, €9-14 dinners, daily 9:00-2:00 in the morning, Stiftgasse 8, tel. 01/526-1660).

Zu Ebener Erde und Erster Stock ("Downstairs, Upstairs") is a charming little restaurant with a near-gourmet menu. True to its name, it has two distinct eating zones (with the same menu): a casual, woody bistro downstairs (traditionally the quarters of the poor); and a fancy Biedermeier-style dining room with red-velvet chairs and violet tablecloths upstairs (where the wealthy convened). There are also a few al fresco tables out front. Reservations are smart (€10-19 main dishes, €25 traditional three-course fixed-price meal, seasonal specials, Mon-Fri 7:30-21:30, last seating at 20:00, closed Sat-Sun, Burggasse 13, tel. 01/523-6254).

Witwe Bolte is classy and a good choice for uninspired Viennese cuisine with tablecloths. The interior is tight, but its tiny square has wonderful leafy ambience (€11-17 main dishes, daily 11:30-23:30 except closed 15:00-17:30 mid-Jan-mid-March, Gutenberggasse 13, tel. 01/523-1450).

Plutzer Bräu, next door to Amerlingbeisl, feels a bit more touristy. It's a big, sprawling, impersonal brewpub serving stick-to-your-ribs pub grub (€7-9 vegetarian dishes, €9-20 meals, ribs, burgers, traditional dishes, Tirolean beer from the keg, also brew their own, daily 11:00-2:00 in the morning, food until 24:00, Schrankgasse 4, tel. 01/526-1215).

Near Mariahilfer Strasse

Mariahilfer Strasse (see map on page 1190) is filled with reasonable cafés serving all types of cuisine. For a quick yet traditional bite, consider the venerable **Buffet Trześniewski** sandwich bar at Mariahilfer Strasse 95.

Schnitzelwirt is an old classic with a 1950s patina and a clientele to match. In this smoky, working-class place, no one finishes their schnitzel ("to-go" for the dog is wrapped in newspaper,

VIENNA

"to-go" for you is wrapped in foil). You'll find no tourists, just cheap €6-11 schnitzel meals (Mon-Sat 10:00-23:00, closed Sun, Neubaugasse 52, U-3: Neubaugasse, tel. 01/523-3771).

The **Naschmarkt** (described on page 1160) is Vienna's best Old World market, with plenty of fresh produce, cheap local-style eateries, cafés, *Döner Kebab* and sausage stands, and the best-value sushi in town (Mon-Fri 6:00-18:30, Sat 6:00-17:00, closed Sun, closes earlier in winter; U-1, U-2, or U-4: Karlsplatz, follow *Karlsplatz* signs out of the station). Survey the lane of eateries at the end of the market nearest the Opera. The circa-1900 pub is inviting. Picnickers can buy supplies at the market and eat on nearby Karlsplatz (plenty of chairs facing the Karlskirche).

Vienna Connections

By Train

Remember, Vienna has several train stations, the biggest of which are undergoing an extensive renovation. Be sure you know which station your train departs from; see page 1108 for the basic rundown, but always confirm locally.

From Vienna by Train to: Bratislava (2/hour, 1 hour, alternating between Bratislava's main station and less-convenient Petržalka station; or try going by bus or boat, described on page 240), **Budapest** (every 2 hours direct, 3 hours; more with transfers), **Prague** (5/day direct, 4.75 hours; more with 1 change, 5-6 hours; 1 night train, 8 hours), **Český Krumlov** (6/day with at least one change, 5-6 hours), **Kraków** (3 decent daytime options, 6.25 hours direct or 7-8.5 hours with 1-3 changes, plus a night train), **Warsaw** (2/day direct including 1 night train, 7.75-8.5 hours), **Ljubljana** (1 convenient early-morning direct train, 6 hours; otherwise 6/day with change in Villach, Maribor, or Graz, 6-7 hours), **Zagreb** (2/day direct, 6-6.5 hours, others with 1-2 changes take 7.5-8.5 hours), **Melk** (2/hour, 1.25 hours, some with change in St. Pölten), **Krems** (at least hourly, 1 hour), **Mauthausen** (about hourly until 17:30, 2 hours, change in St. Valentin), **Salzburg** (almost hourly, 2.5-3 hours), **Hallstatt** (hourly, 4 hours, change in Attnang-Puchheim), **Innsbruck** (almost hourly, 5 hours), **Munich** (6/day direct, 4.25 hours; otherwise about hourly, 5-5.75 hours, transfer in Salzburg), **Berlin** (8/day, most with 1 change, 9.5 hours, some via Czech Republic; longer on night train), **Dresden** (2/day direct, 7 hours; plus 1 night train/day, 7.75 hours), **Zürich** (nearly hourly, 9-10 hours, 1 with changes in Innsbruck and Feldkirch, night train), **Rome** (3/day, 12-13 hours, plus several overnight options), **Venice** (3/day, 8-9.5 hours with changes—some may involve bus connection; plus 1 direct night train, 12 hours), **Frankfurt** (6/day direct, 7 hours; plus 1 direct night train, 10 hours), **Paris** (7/day, 12-17

VIENNA

hours, 1-3 changes, night train), **Strasbourg** (9/day, 9-11 hours, 2-3 changes), **Amsterdam** (3/day, 11.5-12.5 hours, 1-2 changes, longer night-train options involve change in Germany).

For **schedules,** the first place to check is Germany's excellent all-Europe timetable at www.bahn.com. You can also check Austria's own timetable website at www.oebb.at, which may have prices for more Austrian trains, but is not as easy to navigate as the German site. For general train information in Austria, call 051-717 (to get an operator, dial 2, then 2).

UNDERSTANDING YUGOSLAVIA

Americans struggle to understand the complicated breakup of Yugoslavia—especially when visiting countries that rose from its ashes, such as Croatia, Slovenia, and Bosnia-Herzegovina. Talking to the locals can make it even more confusing: Everyone in the former Yugoslavia seems to have a slightly different version of events. A very wise Bosniak once told me, "Listen to all three sides—Muslim, Serb, and Croat. Then decide for yourself what you think." That's the best advice I can offer. But since you likely won't have time for that on your brief visit, here's an admittedly oversimplified, as-impartial-as-possible history to get you started.

Balkan Peninsula 101

For starters, it helps to have a handle on the different groups who've lived in the Balkans—the southeastern European peninsula between the Adriatic and the Black Sea, stretching from Hungary to Greece. The Balkan Peninsula has always been a crossroads of cultures. The Illyrians, Greeks, and Romans had settlements here before the Slavs moved into the region from the north around the seventh century. During the next millennium and a half, the western part of the peninsula—which would become Yugoslavia—was divided by a series of cultural, ethnic, and religious fault lines.

The most important religious influences were **Western Christianity** (i.e., Roman Catholicism, first brought to the western part of the region by Charlemagne and later reinforced by the Austrian Habsburgs), **Eastern Orthodox Christianity** (brought to the east from the Byzantine Empire), and **Islam** (in the south, from the Ottomans).

Two major historical factors made the Balkans what they are today: The first was the **split of the Roman Empire** in the fourth century A.D., dividing the Balkans down the middle into Roman

Yugoslav Succession

Former Yugoslavia Border

Current Border

Province within Serbia

Slovene — Language

"Serbian Krajina" (Serb-Controlled Croatia 1991-1995)

Republika Srpska (Serb territory in Bosnia-Herz.)

100 Kilometers

100 Miles

Catholic (west) and Byzantine Orthodox (east)—roughly along today's Bosnian-Serbian border. The second was the **invasion of the Islamic Ottomans** in the 14th century. The Ottoman victory at the Battle of Kosovo Polje (1389) began five centuries of Islamic influence in Bosnia-Herzegovina and Serbia, further dividing the Balkans into Christian (north) and Muslim (south).

Because of these and other events, several distinct ethnic identities emerged. The major ethnicities of Yugoslavia—Croat, Slovene, Serb, and Bosniak—are all considered South Slavs. The huge Slav ethnic and linguistic family—some 400 million strong—is divided into three groups: South (the peoples of Yugoslavia, explained below, plus Bulgarians), West (Poles, Czechs, and Slovaks), and East (Russians, Ukrainians, and Belarusians).

The South Slavs, who are all descended from the same ancestors and speak closely related languages, are distinguished by their religious practices. Roman Catholic **Croats** or **Slovenes** are found mostly west of the Dinaric Mountains (Croats along the Adriatic coast and Slovenes farther north, in the Alps); Orthodox Christian

Who's Who in Yugoslavia

Yugoslavia was made up of six republics, which were inhabited by eight different ethnicities (not counting small minorities such as Jews, Germans, and Roma). This chart shows each ethnicity and the republic(s) in which they were most concentrated. Not coincidentally, the more ethnically diverse a region was, the more conflict it experienced.

	Serbia*	Croatia	Bosnia-Herz.	Slovenia	Montenegro	Macedonia
Serbs (Orthodox)	X	X	X		X	
Croats (Catholic)		X	X			
Bosniaks (Muslims)			X			
Slovenes (Catholic)				X		
Macedonians (like Bulgarians)						X
Montenegrins (like Serbs)					X	
Albanians	X		X			X
Hungarians	X	X		X		

*Within Serbia were two "autonomous provinces," each of which was dominated by a non-Slavic ethnic group: Hungarians in Vojvodina and Albanians in Kosovo.

Serbs live mostly east of the Dinaric range; and Muslim **Bosniaks** (whose ancestors converted to Islam under the Ottomans) live mostly in the Dinaric Mountains. Two other, smaller Orthodox ethnicities have been influenced by other larger groups: the **Montenegrins** (shaped by centuries of Croatian and Venetian Catholicism) and the **Macedonians** (with ties to Bulgarians and Greeks). To complicate matters, the region is also home to several non-Slavic minority groups, including **Hungarians** (in the northern province of Vojvodina) and **Albanians,** concentrated in Kosovo (descended from the Illyrians, who lived here long before the Greeks and Romans).

Of course, these geographic divisions are extremely general. The groups overlapped a lot—which is exactly why the breakup of Yugoslavia was so contentious. One of the biggest causes of this ethnic mixing came in the 16th century. The Ottomans were threatening to overrun Europe, and the Austrian Habsburgs wanted a buffer zone—a "human shield." The Habsburgs encouraged Serbs who were fleeing from Ottoman invasions to settle along today's Croatian-Bosnian border (known as *Vojna Krajina*, or "Military Frontier"). The Serbs stayed after the Ottomans left, establishing homes in predominantly Croat communities.

After the Ottoman threat subsided in the late 17th century, some of the Balkan states (basically today's Slovenia and Croatia) became part of the Austrian Habsburg Empire. The Ottomans stayed longer in the south and east (today's Bosnia-Herzegovina and Serbia)—making the cultures in these regions even more different. By the mid-19th century, the Ottoman Empire had become the dysfunctional "Sick Man of Europe," making it easy for Serbia to gain its independence; meanwhile, Bosnia-Herzegovina was taken into the Habsburg fold. But before long, World War I erupted, after a disgruntled Bosnian Serb nationalist killed the Austrian archduke and heir to the Habsburg throne during a visit to Sarajevo (see page 184).

South Slavs Unite

When the Austro-Hungarian Empire fell at the end of World War I, the map of Europe was redrawn for the 20th century. After centuries of being governed by foreign powers, the South Slavs began to see their shared history as more important than their differences. A tiny country of a few million Croats or Slovenes couldn't have survived on its own. Rather than be absorbed by a non-Slavic power, the South Slavs decided that there was safety in numbers, and banded together as a single state—first called the Kingdom of the Serbs, Croats, and Slovenes (1918), later known as the Kingdom of Yugoslavia (Land of the South Slavs—*yugo* means "south"). "Yugoslav unity" was in the air, but this new union was fragile and ultimately bound to fail (not unlike the partnership between the Czechs and Slovaks, formed at the same time and for similar reasons).

From the very beginning, the various ethnicities struggled for power within the new Yugoslavia. The largest group was the Serbs (about 45 percent), followed by the Croats (about 25 percent). Croats often felt they were treated as lesser partners under the Serbs. For example, many Croats objected to naming the country's official language "Serbo-Croatian"—why not "Croato-Serbian?" Serbia already had a very strong king, Alexander Karađorđević, who immediately attempted to give his nation a leading role in the federation. A nationalistic Croat politician named Stjepan Radić, pushing for a more equitable division of powers, was shot by a Serb during a parliamentary session in 1928. Karađorđević abolished the parliament and became dictator. Six years later, infuriated Croat separatists killed him. By the time World War II came to Yugoslavia, the kingdom was already on the verge of collapse. The conflicts between the various Yugoslav groups set the stage for a particularly complex and gruesome wartime experience.

World War II

Observers struggle to comprehend how it was possible for inter-ethnic conflict to escalate so quickly here in the early 1990s. Most of the answers can be found in the war that shook Europe 50 years earlier. In the minds of the participants, the wars of the 1990s were a continuation of unresolved conflicts from World War II.

The Nazis invaded Yugoslavia in April 1941; within 11 days, the country had surrendered. The core of the nation (much of today's Croatia and Bosnia-Herzegovina) became the misnamed Independent State of Croatia, which was actually run by a Nazi puppet government called the Ustaše. (Meanwhile, much of today's Serbia was occupied by Nazi Germany, and Montenegro by Mussolini's Italy.) Many Croat nationalists supported the Ustaše in the hopes that it would be their ticket to long-term independence from Serbia.

Emboldened by their genocide-minded Nazi overlords, Ustaše leaders used death camps to exterminate their enemies—specifically, the Serbs who, they felt, had wronged them in the days of the Kingdom of Yugoslavia. Not only were Jews, Roma, and other Nazi-decreed "undesirables" murdered in Ustaše concentration camps, but also hundreds of thousands of Serbs living in Croatia and Bosnia. Other Serbs were forced to flee the country or convert to Catholicism. Most historians consider the Ustaše camps to be the first instance of ethnic cleansing in the Balkans. (Half a century later, the Serbs justified their ruthless treatment of Croats and Bosniaks as retribution for these WWII atrocities.)

Meanwhile, in the eastern mountains of Yugoslavia rose the Četniks—a fearsome paramilitary band of mostly Serbian men fighting to re-establish a Serb-dominated monarchy. Wearing long beards and traditional mountain garb, and embracing a skull-and-crossbones logo adorned with the motto "Freedom or Death" in Cyrillic, the Četniks were every bit as brutal as their Ustaše enemies. In pursuit of their goal to create a purely Serb state, the Četniks expelled or massacred Croats and Muslims living in the territory they held. (To this day, if a Croat wants to really insult a Serb, he'll call him a "Četnik," and a Serb might use "Ustaše" to really hit a Croat where it hurts.)

Fighting against both the Četniks and the Ustaše was the ragtag Partisan Army, led by Josip Broz—better known by his code name, Tito. The clever and determined Partisans had dual aims: to liberate Yugoslavia as a free nation on its own terms, and to make that new state a communist one. Even while the war was still underway, the Partisan leadership laid the foundations for what would become a postwar, communist Yugoslavia.

After years of largely guerrilla fighting among these three groups, the Partisans emerged victorious. And so, as the rest of Eastern Europe was being "liberated" by the Soviets, the Yugoslavs regained their independence on their own. After the short but rocky Yugoslav union between the World Wars, it seemed that no one could hold the southern Slavs together in a single nation. But one man could, and did: Tito.

Tito's Yugoslavia

Communist Party president and war hero Tito emerged as a political leader after World War II. With a Slovene for a mother, a Croat for a father, a Serb for a wife, and a home in Belgrade, Tito was a true Yugoslav. Tito had a compelling vision that this fractured union of the South Slavs could function.

Tito's new incarnation of Yugoslavia aimed for a more equitable division of powers. It was made up of six republics, each with its own parliament and president: **Croatia** (mostly Catholic), **Slovenia** (mostly Catholic), **Serbia** (mostly Orthodox), **Bosnia-Herzegovina** (the most diverse—mostly Muslim Bosniaks, but with very large Croat and Serb populations), **Montenegro** (mostly Orthodox—a sort of a Serb/Croat hybrid), and **Macedonia** (with about 25 percent Muslim Albanians and 75 percent Orthodox Macedonians). Within Serbia, Tito set up two autonomous provinces, each dominated by an ethnicity that was a minority in greater Yugoslavia: Albanians in **Kosovo** (to the south) and Hungarians in **Vojvodina** (to the north). By allowing these two provinces some degree of independence—including voting rights—Tito hoped they would balance the political clout of Serbia, preventing a single republic from dominating the union.

Each republic managed its own affairs, but always under the watchful eye of president-for-life Tito, who said that the borders between the republics should be "like white lines in a marble column." Nationalism was strongly discouraged, and Tito's tight—often oppressive—control kept the country from unraveling. For more on Tito, see the sidebar.

Tito's Yugoslavia was communist, but it wasn't Soviet communism; you'll find no statues of Lenin or Stalin here. Despite strong pressure from Moscow, Tito refused to ally himself with the Soviets—and therefore received good will (and $2 billion) from the United States. He ingeniously played the East and the West against each other. He'd say to both Washington and Moscow, "If you don't pay me off, I'll let the other guy build a base here."

Everyone paid up.

Economically, Tito's vision was for a "third way," in which Yugoslavia could work with both East and West without being dominated by either. Yugoslavia was the most free of the communist states. While large industry was nationalized, Tito's system allowed for small businesses. This experience with a market economy benefited Yugoslavs when Eastern Europe's communist regimes eventually fell. And even during the communist era, Yugoslavia remained a popular tourist destination for visitors from both East and West, keeping its standards more in line with Western Europe than the Soviet states. Meanwhile, Yugoslavs, uniquely among communist citizens, were allowed to travel to the West. In fact, because Yugoslavs could travel relatively hassle-free in both East and West, their "red passports" were worth even more on the black market than American ones.

Things Fall Apart

With Tito's death in 1980, Yugoslavia's six constituent republics gained more autonomy, with a rotating presidency. But before long, the fragile union Tito had held together started to unravel.

The breakup began, in the late 1980s, with squabbles in the autonomous province of Kosovo between the Serb minority and the ethnic-Albanian majority. But, even though 9 of every 10 Kosovans were Albanian, the region remained important to the Serbs, who consider Kosovo the cradle of their civilization—the medieval homeland of their most important monasteries and historic sites. Most significantly, it was the location of the Battle of Kosovo Polje ("Field of Blackbirds"), an epic 14th-century battle at the foundation of Serbian cultural identity...even though the Serbs lost to the Ottoman invaders (sort of the Serbian Alamo). One Serb told me, "Kosovo is the Mecca and Medina of the Serb people."

Serbian politician Slobodan Milošević saw how the conflict could be used to Serbia's (and his own) advantage. In April of 1987, Milošević delivered a rabble-rousing speech in Kosovo, pledging that Serbia would come to the aid of its Kosovar-Serb brothers (famously asserting, "No one has the right to beat you"). He returned two years later for the 600th anniversary of the Battle of Kosovo Polje and delivered another inflammatory speech ("Six centuries later, now, we are being again engaged in battles....They are not armed battles, although such things cannot be excluded yet"). With these visits, Milošević upset the delicate balance that Tito had so carefully sought, while setting the stage for his own rise to the Serbian presidency.

When Milošević-led Serbia annexed Kosovo soon after, other republics (especially Slovenia and Croatia) feared that he would

Tito
(1892-1980)

The Republic of Yugoslavia was the vision of a single man, who made it reality. Josip Broz—better known as Marshal Tito—presided over the most peaceful and prosperous era in this region's long and troubled history. Three decades after his death, Tito is beloved by many of his former subjects...and yet, he was a communist dictator known for torturing and executing his political enemies. This love-him-and-hate-him autocrat is one of the most complex figures in the history of this very complicated land.

Josip Broz was born in 1892 to a Slovenian mother and a Croatian father in the northern part of today's Croatia, which then belonged to the Austro-Hungarian Empire. After growing up in the rural countryside, Tito was trained as a metalworker. He was drafted into the Austro-Hungarian army, went to fight on the Eastern Front during World War I, and was captured and sent to Russia as a prisoner of war. Freed by Bolsheviks, Broz fell in with the Communist Revolution...and never looked back.

At war's end, Broz returned home to the newly independent Yugoslavia, where he worked alongside the Soviets to build a national Communist Party. As a clandestine communist operative, he adopted the code name he kept for the rest of his life: Tito. (Some people half-joke that the name came from Tito's authoritarian style: *"Ti, to!"* means "You, do this!")

When the Nazis occupied Yugoslavia, Tito raised and commanded a homegrown, communist Partisan Army. Through guerilla tactics, Tito's clever maneuvering, and sheer determination, the Partisans liberated their country. And because they did so mostly without support from the USSR, Yugoslavia could set its own postwar course.

The war hero Tito quickly became the "president for life" of postwar Yugoslavia. But even as he introduced communism to his country, he retained some elements of a free-market economy—firmly declining to become a satellite of Moscow. He also led the creation of the worldwide Non-Aligned Movement, joining with nations in Africa, the Middle East, Asia, and Latin America in refusing to ally with the US or USSR (see page 1212). Stubborn but suitably cautious, Tito expertly walked a tightrope between East and West.

There was a dark side to Tito. In the early years of his regime, Tito resorted to brutal, Stalin-esque tactics to assert his control. Immediately following World War II, the Partisan Army massacred tens of thousands of soldiers who had supported the Nazis. Then Tito systematically routed out other Nazi supporters—arresting, trying, torturing, or executing those who did not accept his new regime (including the Croatian archbishop Alojzije Stepinac, whom Tito imprisoned for five years—see page 1037). Those whose lives were ruined during this reign of terror will never forgive Tito for what he did.

But once he gained full control, Tito moved away from strong-arm tactics and into a warm-and-fuzzy era of Yugoslav brotherhood. Tito believed that the disparate peoples of Yugoslavia could live in harmony. For example, every Yugoslav male had to serve in the People's Army, and Tito made sure that each unit was a microcosm of the complete Yugoslavia— with equal representation from each ethnic group. This meant that Yugoslavs from diverse backgrounds were forced to work together and socialize, and as a result, they became friends.

Tito's reign is a case study in the power of the cult of person-ality. Rocks on hillsides throughout Yugoslavia were rearranged to spell "TITO," and his portrait hung over every family's dinner table. Each of the six republics renamed one of its cities for their dictator. The main street and square in virtually every town was renamed for Tito (and many still are). Tito also had vacation villas in all of Yugoslavia's most beautiful areas, including Lake Bled, the Brijuni Islands, and the Montenegrin coast. People sang patri-otic anthems to their Druža (Comrade) Tito: "Comrade Tito, we bow to you."

Tito died in 1980 in a Slovenian hospital. His body was loaded onto his Blue Train and went on a grand tour of the Yugoslav capitals: Ljubljana, Zagreb, Sarajevo, and Belgrade, where he was buried before hundreds of thousands of mourners, including more heads of state than any other funeral in history.

The genuine outpouring of support at Tito's death might seem unusual for a man who was, on paper, an authoritarian communist dictator. But even today, many former Yugoslavs— especially Slovenes and Bosniaks—believe that his iron-fisted government was a necessary evil that kept the country strong and united. The eventual balance Tito struck between commu-nism and capitalism, and between the competing interests of his ethnically diverse nation, led to this region's most stable and prosperous era. Pictures of Tito still hang in many Croatians' homes. In a recent poll in Slovenia, Tito had a higher approval rat-ing than any present-day politician, and 80 percent of Slovenes said they had a positive impression of him.

And yet, the Yugoslavs' respect for their former leader was not enough to keep them together. Tito's death began a long, slow chain reaction that led to the end of Yugoslavia. As the decades pass, the old joke seems more and more appropriate: Yugoslavia had eight distinct peoples in six republics, with five languages, three religions (Orthodox Christian, Catholic, and Muslim), and two alphabets (Roman and Cyrillic), but only one Yugoslav—Tito.

gut their nation to create a "Greater Serbia," thereby destabilizing the friendly coalition of diverse Yugoslav republics. Some of the leaders—most notably Milan Kučan of Slovenia—tried to avoid warfare by suggesting a plan for a loosely united Yugoslavia, based on the Swiss model of independent yet confederated cantons. But other parties, who wanted complete autonomy, refused. Over the next decade, Yugoslavia broke apart, with much bloodshed.

The Slovene Secession

Slovenia was the first Yugoslav republic to hold free elections, in the spring of 1990. Voters wanted the communists out, and they wanted their own independent nation. The most ethnically homogeneous of the Yugoslav nations, Slovenia was also the most Western-oriented, prosperous, and geographically isolated—so secession just made sense. But that didn't mean it would be achieved without violence.

After months of stockpiling weapons, Slovenia closed its borders and declared independence from Yugoslavia on June 25, 1991. Belgrade sent in the Yugoslav People's Army to take control of Slovenia's borders with Italy and Austria, figuring that whoever controlled the borders had a legitimate claim on sovereignty. Fighting broke out around these borders. Because the Yugoslav People's Army was made up of soldiers from all republics, many Slovenian troops found themselves fighting their own countrymen. (The army had cut off communication between these conscripts and the home front, so they didn't know what was going on—and often didn't realize they were fighting their friends and neighbors until they were close enough to see them.)

Slovenian civilians bravely entered the fray, blockading the Yugoslav barracks with their own cars and trucks. Most of the Yugoslav soldiers—now trapped—were young and inexperienced, and were terrified of the improvised (but relentless) Slovenian militia, even though their own resources were far superior.

After 10 days of fighting and fewer than a hundred deaths, Belgrade relented. The Slovenes stepped aside and allowed the Yugoslav People's Army to leave with their weapons and to destroy all remaining military installations as they went. When the Yugoslav People's Army cleared out, they left the Slovenes with their freedom.

The Croatian Conflict

In April of 1990, a retired general and historian named Franjo Tuđman—and his highly nationalistic, right-wing party, the HDZ (Croatian Democratic Union)—won Croatia's first free elections (for more on Tuđman, see page 830). Like the Slovenian reformers, Tuđman and the HDZ wanted more autonomy from

Yugoslavia. But Tuđman's methods were more extreme than those of the gently progressive Slovenes. Tuđman invoked the spirit of the Ustaše, who had ruthlessly run Croatia's puppet government under the Nazis. He reintroduced symbols that had been embraced by the Ustaše, including the red-and-white checkerboard flag and the kuna currency. (While many of these symbols predated the Ustaše by centuries, they had become irrevocably tainted by their association with the Ustaše.) The 600,000 Serbs living in Croatia, mindful that their grandparents had been massacred by the Ustaše, saw the writing on the wall and began to rise up.

The first conflicts were in the Serb-dominated Croatian city of Knin. Tuđman had decreed that Croatia's policemen must wear a new uniform, which was strikingly similar to Nazi-era Ustaše garb. Infuriated by this slap in the face, and prodded by Slobodan Milošević's rhetoric, Serb police officers in Knin refused. Over the next few months, tense negotiations ensued. Serbs from Knin and elsewhere began the so-called "tree trunk revolution"—blocking important Croatian tourist roads to the coast with logs and other barriers. Meanwhile, the Croatian government—after being denied support from the United States—illegally purchased truckloads of guns from Hungary. (A UN weapons embargo—designed to prevent the outbreak of violence—had little effect on the Serb-dominated Yugoslav People's Army, which already had its own arsenal, but was devastating to separatist Croatian and—later—Bosnian forces, which were just beginning to build their armies.) Croatian policemen and Serb irregulars from Knin fired the first shots of the conflict on Easter Sunday 1991 at Plitvice Lakes National Park.

By the time Croatia declared its independence (on June 25, 1991—the same day as Slovenia), it was already embroiled in the beginnings of a bloody war. Croatia's more than a half-million Serb residents immediately declared their own independence from Croatia. The Serb-dominated Yugoslav People's Army swept in, supposedly to keep the peace between Serbs and Croats—but it soon became obvious that they were there to support the Serbs. The ill-prepared Croatian resistance, made up mostly of policemen and a few soldiers who defected from the People's Army, were quickly overwhelmed. The Serbs gained control over the parts of inland Croatia where they were in the majority: a large swath around the Bosnian border (including Plitvice) and part of Croatia's inland panhandle (the region of Slavonia). They called this territory—about a quarter of Croatia—the **Republic of Serbian Krajina** (*krajina* means "border"). This new "country" (hardly recognized by any other nations) minted its own money and raised its own army, much to the consternation of Croatia—which was now worried about the safety of Croats living in Krajina.

As the Serbs advanced, hundreds of thousands of Croats fled to the coast and lived as refugees in resort hotels. The Serbs began a campaign of ethnic cleansing, systematically removing Croats from contested territory—often by murdering them. The bloodiest siege was at the town of **Vukovar,** which the Yugoslav People's Army surrounded and shelled relentlessly for three months. By the end of the siege, thousands of Croat soldiers and civilians had disappeared. Many were later discovered in mass graves; hundreds are still missing, and bodies are still being found. In a surprise move, Serbs also attacked the tourist resort of **Dubrovnik**—which resisted and eventually repelled the invaders (see page 860). By early 1992, both Croatia and the Republic of Serbian Krajina had established their borders, and a tense ceasefire fell over the region.

The standoff lasted until 1995, when the now well-equipped Croatian army retook the Serb-occupied areas in a series of two offensives—**"Lightning"** *(Blijesak),* in the northern part of the country, and **"Storm"** *(Oluja),* farther south. Some Croats retaliated for earlier ethnic cleansing by doing much of the same to Serbs—torturing and murdering them, and dynamiting their homes. Croatia quickly established the borders that exist today, and the Erdut Agreement brought peace to the region. But most of the 600,000 Serbs who had once lived in Croatia/Krajina were forced into Serbia or were killed. While Serbs have long since been legally invited back to their ancestral Croatian homes, relatively few have returned—afraid of the "welcome" they might receive from the Croat neighbors who killed their relatives or blew up their houses just two decades ago.

The War in Bosnia-Herzegovina

As violence erupted in Croatia and Slovenia, Bosnia-Herzegovina was suspiciously quiet. Even optimists knew it couldn't last. At the crossroads of Balkan culture, Bosnia-Herzegovina was even more diverse than Croatia; it was populated predominantly by Muslim Bosniaks (43 percent of the population), but also by large numbers of Serbs (31 percent) and Croats (17 percent). Bosniaks tended to live in the cities, while Serbs and Croats were more often farmers.

In the fall of 1991, Bosnia-Herzegovina's president, Alija Izetbegović, began to pursue independence. While most Bosnian Croats and virtually all Bosniaks supported this move, Bosnia's substantial Serb minority resisted it. Bosnian Serbs preferred to remain part of an increasingly dominant ethnic group in a big country (Yugoslavia) rather than become second fiddle in a new, small country (Bosnia-Herzegovina). And so the Serbs within Bosnia-Herzegovina created their own "state," called the Republic of the Serb People of Bosnia-Herzegovina. Its president, Radovan Karadžić, enjoyed the semisecret military support of Slobodan Milošević and the Yugoslav People's Army. The stage was set for a bloody secession.

In the spring of 1992, as a referendum on Bosnian independence loomed, the Serbs made their move. To legitimize their claim to "their" land, the Serbs began a campaign of ethnic cleansing against Bosniaks and Croats residing in Bosnia. Initially Karadžić's forces moved to take control of a strip of Muslim-majority towns (including Foča, Srebrenica, Goražde, Višegrad, and Zvornik) along the Drina River, between Serbia proper and Serb-controlled areas closer to Sarajevo. They reasoned that their claim on this territory was legitimate, because the Ustaše had decimated the Serb population there during World War II. The well-orchestrated Karadžić forces secretly notified Serb residents to evacuate before they invaded each mixed-ethnicity town, then encircled the remaining Bosniaks and Croats with heavy artillery and sniper fire in an almost medieval-style siege. Many people were executed on the spot, while others were arrested and taken to concentration camps. Survivors were forced to leave the towns their families had lived in for centuries.

It was during this initial wave of Bosnian Serb ethnic cleansing—orchestrated by Radovan Karadžić and his generals—that the world began to hear tales as horrifying as anything you can imagine. Militia units would enter a town and indiscriminately kill anyone they saw—civilian men, women, and children. Pregnant women mortally wounded by gunfire were left to die in the street. Fleeing residents crawled on their stomachs for hours to reach cover, even as their family and friends were shot and blown up right next to them. Soldiers rounded up families, then forced parents to watch as they slit the throats of their children—and then the parents were killed, too. Dozens of people would be lined up along a bridge to have their throats slit, one at a time, so that their lifeless bodies would plunge into the river below. (Villagers downstream would see corpses float past, and know their time was coming soon.) While in past conflicts, houses of worships were considered off-limits, now Serbs actively targeted mosques and Catholic churches. Perhaps most despicable was the establishment of so-called "rape camps"—concentration camps where mostly Bosniak women were imprisoned and systematically raped by Serb soldiers. Many were intentionally impregnated and held captive until they had come to term (too late for an abortion), when they were released to bear and raise a child forced upon them by their hated enemy. These are the stories that turned "Balkans" into a dirty word.

The Bosnian Serb aggressors were intentionally gruesome and violent. Leaders roused their foot soldiers with hate-filled propaganda (claiming, for example, that the Bosniaks were intent on creating a fundamentalist Islamic state that would do even worse to its Serb residents), then instructed them to carry out unthinkable atrocities. For the people who carried out these attacks, the war represented a cathartic opportunity to exact vengeance for decades-old perceived injustices. But their superiors had even more dastardly motives. They sought not only to remove people from "their" land, but to ensure that the various groups could never again tolerate living together.

Bosnia-Herzegovina was torn apart. Even the many mixed families were forced to choose sides. If you had a Serb mother and a Croat father, you were expected to pick one ethnicity or the other—and your brother might choose the opposite. The majority of people, who did not want this war and couldn't comprehend why it was happening, now faced the excruciating realization that their very neighbors and friends were looting and burning their houses, and shooting at their loved ones. As families and former neighbors trained their guns on each other, proud and beautiful cities such as Mostar were turned to rubble, and people throughout Bosnia-Herzegovina lived in a state of constant terror.

Even as the Serbs and Croats fought brutally in the streets, their leaders—Slobodan Milošević and Franjo Tuđman, respectively—were secretly meeting to carve up Bosnia into Serb and Croat sectors, at the Bosniaks' expense (the so-called Karađorđevo Agreement). Bosniak President Alija Izetbegović was completely left out of the discussion. For his part, Izetbegović desperately pleaded with the international community to support the peaceful secession of a free Bosnian state. Motivated more by fear than by nationalism, Izetbegović insisted that the creation of an independent Bosnia-Herzegovina was the only way to protect the lives of the Bosniak people. He said, "I would sacrifice peace for a sovereign Bosnia-Herzegovina, but for that peace in Bosnia-Herzegovina I would not sacrifice sovereignty."

At first, the Bosniaks and Croats teamed up to fend off the Serbs. But even before the first wave of fighting had subsided, Croats and Bosniaks turned their guns on each other. The Croats split off their own mini-state, the Croatian Republic of Herzeg-Bosnia. A bloody war raged for years among the three groups: the Serbs (with support from Serbia proper), the Croats (with support from Croatia proper), and—squeezed between them—the internationally recognized Bosniak government, with little support from anybody.

The United Nations Protection Force (UNPROFOR)—dubbed "Smurfs" both for their light-blue helmets and for their ineffectiveness—exercised their very limited authority to provide humanitarian aid. Their charge allowed them only to feed civilians caught in the crossfire—an absurd notion in places like Sarajevo, where civilians were forced to live like soldiers. (A political cartoon from the time shows a Bosnian Serb preparing to murder a Bosniak with a knife. A UN solider appears and says, "Not so fast!" He proceeds to feed the Bosniak...then walks away, mission accomplished, while the Serb murders his victim.) Later, the UN tried to designate "safe areas" where civilians were protected, but because the UNPROFOR troops were not allowed to use force, even in self-defense, they became impotent witnesses to atrocities. This ugly situation was brilliantly parodied in the film *No Man's Land* (which won the Oscar for Best Foreign Film in 2002), a very dark comedy about the absurdity of the Bosnian war.

For three and a half years, the capital of Sarajevo—still inhabited by a united community of Sarajevans (who largely eschewed their individual ethnicities as Bosniaks, Croats, and Serbs)—was surrounded by Karadžić's Bosnian Serb army. Other Bosniak cities were also besieged, most notoriously Srebrenica in July 1995. After surviving as a UN-designated safe area, this mid-sized, predominantly Bosniak town near the Serbian border was left unprotected early that summer when UNPROFOR troops vacated. Bosnian Serb forces, led by General Ratko Mladić, swept in and rounded up all the men and boys in Srebrenica—about 8,000 civilians—and took them into the woods under cover of darkness. They were never again seen alive, and mass graves are still being found in the Srebrenica woods. Additionally, 35,000 to 40,000 Bosniak women and children were forcibly removed from the city; many of them (including babies) died en route.

After four long years, the mounting mass of atrocities—including the siege of Srebrenica and the bombing of innocent civilians at a market in Sarajevo—finally persuaded the international community to act. In the late summer of 1995, NATO began bombing Bosnian Serb positions, forcing them to relax their siege and come to the negotiating table. The Dayton Peace Accords—brokered by US diplomats at Wright-Patterson Air Force Base near Dayton, Ohio—finally brought an end to the wars of Yugoslav succession.

The Dayton Peace Accords carefully divided Bosnia-Herzegovina into three different units: the Federation of Bosnia and Herzegovina (Bosniaks and Croats), the Serb-dominated Republika Srpska, and the mixed-ethnicity Brčko District. This compromise, while successfully ending the war, also created a nation with four independent and redundant governments—further crippling this war-torn and impoverished nation.

The Fall of Milošević

After years of bloody conflicts, public opinion among Serbians had decisively swung against their president. The transition began gradually in early 2000, spearheaded by Otpor, a nonviolent, grassroots, student-based opposition movement, and aided by similar groups. Using clever PR strategies, these organizations convinced Serbians that real change was possible. As anti-Milošević sentiments gained momentum, opposing political parties banded together behind one candidate, Vojislav Koštunica. Public support for Koštunica mounted, and when the arrogant Milošević called an early election in September 2000, he was soundly defeated. Though Milošević tried to claim that the election results were invalid, determined Serbs streamed into their capital, marched on their parliament, and—like the Czechs and Slovaks a decade before—peacefully took back their nation.

In 2001, Milošević was arrested and sent to The Hague, in the Netherlands, to stand trial before the International Criminal Tribunal for the Former Yugoslavia (ICTY). Milošević served as his own attorney as his trial wore on for five years, frequently delayed due to his health problems. Then, on March 11, 2006—as his trial was coming to a close—Milošević was found dead in his cell. Ruled a heart attack, Milošević's death, like his life, was controversial. His supporters alleged that Milošević had been denied suitable medical care, some speculated that he'd been poisoned, and others suspected that he'd intentionally worsened his heart condition to avoid the completion of his trial. Whatever the cause, in the end Milošević escaped justice—he was never found guilty of a single war crime.

More War Leaders on Trial

On July 18, 2008, Serbian police announced that they had captured Radovan Karadžić, the former leader of the Bosnian Serb state who is considered one of the worst culprits in the brutal ethnic cleansing during the war.

Karadžić, who went into hiding shortly after the war (in 1996), had been living for part of that time in a residential neighborhood of Belgrade, posing as an alternative-medicine healer named Dr. Dragan David Dabić. (Karadžić had previously received training as a psychiatrist.) This expert on what he called "Human Quantum Energy" had his own website and even presented at conferences.

How did one of the world's most wanted men effectively disappear in plain sight for 12 years? He had grown a very full beard and wore thick glasses as a disguise, and frequented a neighborhood bar where a photo of him, in his earlier life, hung proudly on the wall...and yet, he was undetected even by those who saw him every day. It's alleged that at least some Serb authorities knew of his whereabouts, but, considering him a hero, refused to identify or arrest him.

After his arrest, Karadžić was indicted at The Hague for war crimes, including genocide. In May 2011, the last "most wanted" criminal of the conflict—Karadžić's military leader, General Ratko Mladić—was found and arrested. As of this writing, Karadžić and Mladić are both standing trial in The Hague.

Montenegro and Kosovo: Europe's Newest Nations

After the departures of Croatia, Slovenia, Bosnia-Herzegovina, and Macedonia (which peacefully seceded in 1991), by the late 1990s only two of the original six republics of Yugoslavia remained united: Serbia (which still included the provinces of Kosovo and Vojvodina) and Montenegro. But in 2003, Montenegro began a gradual, tiptoe secession process that ended when it peacefully gained its independence in 2006.

The Yugoslav crisis concluded in the place where it began: the Serbian province of Kosovo. Kosovo's majority Albanians rebelled against Serbian rule in 1998, only to become victims of Milošević's ethnic cleansing (until US General Wesley Clark's NATO warplanes forced the Serbian army out). For nearly a decade, Kosovo remained a UN protectorate within Serbia—still nominally part of Serbia, but for all practical purposes separate and self-governing (under the watchful eye of the UN).

But on Sunday, February 17, 2008, Kosovo's provisional government unilaterally declared its independence as the "Republic of Kosovo." The US, UK, France, Germany, and several other countries quickly recognized the new republic, but the UN didn't officially endorse it. Serbia opposed the move, and was backed by several countries involved in their own internal disputes with would-be breakaway regions: Russia (areas of Georgia), China (Taiwan), and Spain (Catalunya, the Basque Country, and others).

The new Kosovo government carefully stated that it would protect the rights of its minorities, including Serbs. But the Serbs deeply believed that losing Kosovo would also mean losing their grip on their own history and culture. They also feared for the safety of the Serb minority there (and potential retribution from Albanians who had for so long been oppressed themselves). For a few tense months, international observers watched nervously, worrying that war might erupt in the region once more. There have been a few scuffles, especially in some of the large Serb settlements. But as of this writing, Kosovo independence appears to be holding—representing, perhaps, the final chapter of a long and ugly Yugoslav succession. Kosovo is the seventh country to emerge from the breakup of Yugoslavia.

Finding Their Way:
The Former Yugoslav Republics

Today, Slovenia and Croatia are as stable as Western Europe, Bosnia-Herzegovina has made great strides in putting itself back together, Macedonia feels closer to Bulgaria than to Belgrade, and the sixth and seventh countries to emerge from "Yugoslavia"— Montenegro and Kosovo—are fledgling democracies.

And yet, nagging questions remain. Making the wars even more difficult to grasp is the uncomfortable reality that there were no clear-cut "good guys" and "bad guys"—just a lot of ugliness on all sides. When considering specifically the war between the Croats and the Serbs, it's tempting for Americans to take Croatia's "side" because we saw them in the role of victims first; because they're Catholic, so they seem more "like us" than the Orthodox Serbs; and because we admire their striving for independence. But in the streets and the trenches, it was never that straightforward. The Serbs believe that *they* were the victims first—back in World War II, when their grandparents were executed in Croat-run Ustaše concentration camps. And when Croats retook the Serb-occupied areas in 1995, they were every bit as brutal as the Serbs had been a few years before. Both sides resorted to genocide, both sides had victims, and both sides had victimizers.

Even so, many can't help but look for victims and villains. During the conflict in Bosnia-Herzegovina, several prominent and respected reporters began to show things from one "side" more than the others—specifically, depicting the Bosniaks (Muslims) as victims. This reawakened an old debate in the journalism community: Should reporters above all remain impartial, even if "showing all sides" might make them feel complicit in ongoing atrocities?

As for villains, it's easy to point a finger at Slobodan Milošević, Radovan Karadžić, Ratko Mladić, and other military leaders who have been arrested and tried at The Hague. Others condemn the late Croatian President Franjo Tuđman, who, it's now known, secretly conspired with Milošević to redraw the maps of their respective territories. And of course, the foot soldiers of those monstrous men—who followed their immoral orders—cannot be excused.

And yet, you can't paint an entire group with one brush. While some Bosnian Serbs did horrifying things, only a small fraction of all Bosnian Serbs participated in the atrocities. Travelers to this region quickly realize that the vast majority of people they meet here never wanted these wars. And so finally comes the inevitable question: Why did any of it happen in the first place?

Explanations tend to gravitate to two extremes. Some observers consider this part of the world to be inherently warlike—a place where deep-seated hatreds and age-old ethnic passions unavoidably flare up. This point of view sees an air of inevitability about the recent wars and the potential for future conflict. And it's hard to deny that the residents of the region tend to obsess about exacting vengeance for wrongdoings (real or imagined) that happened many decades or even centuries in the past.

For others, however, this theory is an insulting oversimplification. Sure, animosity has long simmered in the Balkans, but for centuries before World War II, the various groups had lived more or less in harmony. The critical component of these wars—what made them escalate so quickly and so appallingly—was the single-minded, self-serving actions of a few selfish leaders who exploited existing resentments to advance their own interests. It wasn't until Milošević, Karadžić, Tuđman, and others expertly manipulated the people's grudges that the region fell into war. By vigorously fanning the embers of ethnic discord, polluting the airwaves with hate-filled propaganda, and carefully controlling media coverage of the escalating violence, these leaders turned what could have been a healthy political debate into a holocaust.

Tension still exists throughout the former Yugoslavia—especially in the areas that were most war-torn. Croatians and Slovenes continue to split hairs over silly border disputes, Bosnia-Herzegovina groans under the crippling inefficiency of four autonomous governments, and Serbs ominously warn that they'll take up arms to reclaim Kosovo. Observers can't escape the uncomfortable truth that, just as grudges held over from World War II were quickly ignited in the 1990s, holdover tensions from the recent wars could someday ignite a new wave of conflict. When the people of this region encounter other Yugoslavs in their travels, they instantly evaluate each other's accent to determine: Are they one of us, or one of them?

For the visitor, it's tricky to get an impartial take on the current situation, or even on historical "facts." People you meet will tell you their stories, and sometimes it's just as important to listen to their tone and subtext as it is to judge the veracity of their tale. Are they preaching a message of reconciliation or one of provocation?

With time, hard feelings are fading. The appealing prospect of European Union membership is a powerful motivator for groups to set aside their differences and cooperate. The younger generations don't look back—teenaged Slovenes no longer learn Serbo-Croatian, have only known life in an independent little country, and get bored (and a little irritated) when their old-fashioned parents wax nostalgic about the days of a united Yugoslavia. A middle-aged Slovene friend of mine thinks fondly of his months of compulsory service in the Yugoslav People's Army, when his unit was made up of Slovenes, Croats, Serbs, Bosniaks, Albanians, Macedonians, and Montenegrins—all of them countrymen, and all good friends. To the young Yugoslavs, ethnic differences didn't matter. My friend still often visits with an army buddy from Dubrovnik—600 miles away, not long ago part of the same nation—and wishes there had been a way to keep the country all together. But he says, optimistically, "I look forward to the day when the other former Yugoslav republics also join the European Union. Then, in a way, we will all be united once again."

APPENDIX

Contents

Tourist Information

Before Your Trip

National tourist offices are a wealth of information. Before your trip, get the free general information packet and request any specifics you may want (such as regional and city maps and festival schedules).

Czech Tourist Office: Basic information and a map are free; additional materials are $4 (prepaid by Czech...er, check). Call 212/288-0830 or visit www.czechtourism.com (info-usa@czech tourism.com).

Slovakian Tourist Office: Call 212/679-7045 or visit www.slovakia.travel (slovakoffice@nyc.rr.com).

Polish Tourist Office: Ask for Warsaw and Kraków information, regional brochures, maps, and more. Call 212/338-9412 or visit www.poland.travel (info.na@poland.travel).

Hungarian Tourist Office: Request the free *Budapest Guide*. They also have regional and topical brochures. Call 212/695-1221 or visit www.gotohungary.com (info@gotohungary.com).

Slovenian Tourist Office: They have a *Slovenia Invigorates* brochure, map, and information on various regions, hiking, biking, winter travel, and tourist farms. From the US, call Slovenian tel. 01/306-4575 or visit www.slovenia.info (info@slovenia.info).

Croatian National Tourist Office: Ask for their free brochures and maps. In the US, call 212/279-8672 or visit http://us.croatia.hr (cntony@earthlink.net).

Bosnia-Herzegovina Tourist Office: From the US, call Bosnian tel. 33/233-886 or visit www.bhtourism.ba (tourinfo@bih.net.ba).

Austrian Tourist Office: They have maps and information on festivals, hiking, wine country, and more. Call 212/944-6880 or visit www.austria.info (travel@austria.info).

In Eastern Europe

Your best first stop in every town is generally the tourist information office—abbreviated **TI** in this book. You'll find local TIs are usually well-organized and always have an English-speaking staff.

TIs are great places to get a city map and information on public transit (including bus and train schedules), walking tours, special events, and nightlife. Many TIs have information on the entire country or at least the region, so try to pick up maps for destinations you'll be visiting later in your trip. If you're arriving in town after the TI closes, call ahead or pick up a map in a neighboring town.

The TIs in Eastern Europe are run by the government, which means their information isn't colored by a drive for profit. They're not allowed to make money by running a room-booking service—though they can almost always give you a list of local hotels and private rooms. If they're not too busy, they can call around for you to check on availability. While every major town has at least one travel agency with a room-booking service, even if there's no "fee," you'll save yourself and your host money by going direct with the listings in this book.

Communicating

Hurdling the Language Barrier

The language barrier in Eastern Europe is no bigger than in Western Europe. I find it much easier to communicate in Hungary or Croatia than in Italy or Spain.

Since the Eastern European countries are small and not politically powerful, their residents realize that it's unreasonable to expect visitors to learn Hungarian (with only 12 million speakers worldwide), Croatian (5 million), or Slovene (2 million). It's essential to find a common language with the rest of the world—so they learn English early and well. In Croatia, for example, all schoolchildren start learning English in the third grade. (I've had surprisingly eloquent conversations with Croatian grade-schoolers.)

Of course, not everyone speaks English. You'll run into the most substantial language barriers in situations when you need to deal with a clerk or service person aged 40 or above (train-station and post-office counters, maids, museum guards, bakers, and so on). Be reasonable in your expectations. Czech post-office clerks and Polish museum ticket-sellers are every bit as friendly, cheery, and multilingual as their American counterparts.

In these situations, it's relatively easy to get your point across. I've often bought a train ticket simply by writing out the name of my destination (preferably with the local spelling—for example, "Praha" instead of "Prague"); the time I want to travel (using the 24-hour clock); and, if I'm not traveling on the same day I'm buying the ticket, I include the date I want to leave (day first, then the month as a Roman numeral, then the year). Here's an example of what I'd show a ticket-seller at a train station: "Warszawa, 17:30, 15.VII.13."

Eastern Europeans, realizing that their language intimidates Americans, often invent easier nicknames for themselves—so Šárka goes by "Sara," András becomes "Andrew," and Jaroslav tells you, "Call me Jerry."

The people in most of this book's destinations—the Czech Republic, Slovakia, Poland, Slovenia, Croatia, and Bosnia-Herzegovina—speak Slavic languages. These languages are closely related to each other and to Russian, and are, to varying degrees, mutually intelligible (though many spellings change—for example, Czech *hrad*, or "castle," becomes Croatian *grad*). Slavic languages have simple vocabularies but are highly inflected—that is, the meaning of a sentence depends on complicated endings that are tacked onto the ends of the words (as in Latin).

Slavic words are notorious for their seemingly unpronounceable, long strings of consonants. Slavic pronunciation can be tricky. In fact, when the first Christian missionaries, Cyril and Methodius, came to Eastern Europe a millennium ago, they invented a whole new alphabet to represent these strange Slavic sounds. A modified version of that alphabet—called Cyrillic—is still used today in the eastern Slavic countries (such as Serbia and Russia).

Fortunately, the destinations covered in this book all use the same Roman alphabet we do, but they add lots of different diacritics—little markings below and above some letters—to represent a wide range of sounds (for example, č, ą, ó, đ, ł). I explain each of these diacritics in this book's various country introductions.

Hungarian is another story altogether—it's completely unrelated to Slavic languages, German, or English. For more on the challenging Magyar tongue, see page 521.

German is spoken in Vienna. As part of the same language family as English, German sounds more familiar to American ears than the Slavic languages. Throughout Eastern Europe, speaking German can come in handy, especially if you're interacting with somebody over age 40 (while few people under communism learned English, German ranked right up there with Russian as a popular second language). A few words of Italian can come in handy in Slovenia and Croatia.

There are certain universal English words all Eastern Europeans know: hello, please, thank you, super, pardon, stop, menu, problem, and no problem. Another handy word that people throughout the region will understand is *Servus* (SEHR-voos)—the old-fashioned greeting from the days of the Austro-Hungarian Empire. If you draw a blank on how to say hello in the local language, just offer a cheery, *"Servus!"*

Get an ear for the local language (see the language section in each of this book's country introductions), learn the key phrases (find survival phrases for each language starting on page 1263), and travel with a phrase book. Consider Lonely Planet's good *Eastern Europe Phrasebook*, which covers all of the destinations in this book (except Vienna).

Don't be afraid to interact with locals. Eastern Europeans can initially seem shy or even brusque—a holdover from the closed communist society—but often a simple smile is the only icebreaker you need to make a new friend. You'll find that doors open a little more quickly when you know a few words of the language. Give it your best shot, and the natives will appreciate your efforts.

Telephones

Smart travelers use the telephone to reserve or reconfirm rooms, get tourist information, reserve restaurants, confirm tour times, or phone home. This section covers dialing instructions, phone cards, and types of phones (for more in-depth information, see www .ricksteves.com/phoning).

How to Dial

Calling from the US to Europe, or vice versa, is simple—once you break the code. The European calling chart in this chapter will walk you through it.

Dialing Domestically in Eastern Europe

About half of all European countries use area codes; the other half use a direct-dial system without area codes.

In countries that use area codes (such as Slovakia, Slovenia, Croatia, Bosnia, and Austria), you dial the local number when calling within a city, and add the area code (which starts with a zero) if calling long distance within the same country. For example, Dubrovnik's area code is 020, and the number of one of my recommended Dubrovnik B&Bs is 453-834. To call the B&B within Dubrovnik, just dial 453-834. To call it from Split, dial 020/453-834.

Hungary, which also uses area codes, is a special case: To call within the same city, just dial the local number. But for long distance within Hungary, add the prefix 06, followed by the area code and number. For example, to call a hotel in Eger, I'd dial 411-711 if I'm calling from within Eger; but from Budapest, I'd have to dial 06, then 36 (Eger's area code), then 411-711. For more on the confusing Hungarian phone system, see page 506.

To make calls within a country that uses a direct-dial system (such as the Czech Republic or Poland), you dial the same number whether you're calling across the country or across the street.

Don't be surprised that in some countries, local phone numbers have different numbers of digits within the same city, or even the same hotel (e.g., a hotel can have a 6-digit phone number, a 7-digit mobile phone number, and an 8-digit fax number).

Dialing Internationally to or from Eastern Europe

If you want to make an international call, follow these steps:

• Dial the international access code (00 if you're calling from Europe, 011 from the US or Canada).

• Dial the country code of the country you're calling (see the European calling chart in this chapter).

• Dial the area code (if applicable) and the local number, keeping in mind that calling many countries requires dropping the initial zero of the phone number (the calling chart lists specifics per country).

Calling from the US to Europe: To call, for example, the Dubrovnik B&B from the US, dial 011 (the US international access code), 385 (Croatia's country code), 20 (Dubrovnik's area code without the initial zero), and 453-834.

Calling from any European country to the US: To call my

European Calling Chart

Just smile and dial, using this key:
AC = Area Code, LN = Local Number.

European Country	Calling long distance within ...	Calling from the US or Canada to ...	Calling from a European country to ...
Austria	AC + LN	011 + 43 + AC (without the initial zero) + LN	00 + 43 + AC (without the initial zero) + LN
Belgium	LN	011 + 32 + LN (without initial zero)	00 + 32 + LN (without initial zero)
Bosnia-Herzegovina	AC + LN	011 + 387 + AC (without initial zero) + LN	00 + 387 + AC (without initial zero) + LN
Britain	AC + LN	011 + 44 + AC (without initial zero) + LN	00 + 44 + AC (without initial zero) + LN
Croatia	AC + LN	011 + 385 + AC (without initial zero) + LN	00 + 385 + AC (without initial zero) + LN
Czech Republic	LN	011 + 420 + LN	00 + 420 + LN
Denmark	LN	011 + 45 + LN	00 + 45 + LN
Estonia	LN	011 + 372 + LN	00 + 372 + LN
Finland	AC + LN	011 + 358 + AC (without initial zero) + LN	999 (or other 900 number) + 358 + AC (without initial zero) + LN
France	LN	011 + 33 + LN (without initial zero)	00 + 33 + LN (without initial zero)
Germany	AC + LN	011 + 49 + AC (without initial zero) + LN	00 + 49 + AC (without initial zero) + LN
Gibraltar	LN	011 + 350 + LN	00 + 350 + LN
Greece	LN	011 + 30 + LN	00 + 30 + LN
Hungary	06 + AC + LN	011 + 36 + AC + LN	00 + 36 + AC + LN
Ireland	AC + LN	011 + 353 + AC (without initial zero) + LN	00 + 353 + AC (without initial zero) + LN

European Country	Calling long distance within ...	Calling from the US or Canada to ...	Calling from a European country to ...
Italy	LN	011 + 39 + LN	00 + 39 + LN
Montenegro	AC + LN	011 + 382 + AC (without initial zero) + LN	00 + 382 + AC (without initial zero) + LN
Morocco	LN	011 + 212 + LN (without initial zero)	00 + 212 + LN (without initial zero)
Netherlands	AC + LN	011 + 31 + AC (without initial zero) + LN	00 + 31 + AC (without initial zero) + LN
Norway	LN	011 + 47 + LN	00 + 47 + LN
Poland	LN	011 + 48 + LN	00 + 48 + LN
Portugal	LN	011 + 351 + LN	00 + 351 + LN
Slovakia	AC + LN	011 + 421 + AC (without initial zero) + LN	00 + 421 + AC (without initial zero) + LN
Slovenia	AC + LN	011 + 386 + AC (without initial zero) + LN	00 + 386 + AC (without initial zero) + LN
Spain	LN	011 + 34 + LN	00 + 34 + LN
Sweden	AC + LN	011 + 46 + AC (without initial zero) + LN	00 + 46 + AC (without initial zero) + LN
Switzerland	LN	011 + 41 + LN (without initial zero)	00 + 41 + LN (without initial zero)
Turkey	AC (if there's no initial zero, add one) + LN	011 + 90 + AC (without initial zero) + LN	00 + 90 + AC (without initial zero) + LN

- The instructions above apply whether you're calling a land line or mobile phone.

- The international access code (the first numbers you dial when making an international call) is 011 if you're calling from the US or Canada. It's 00 if you're calling from virtually anywhere in Europe (except Finland, where it's 999 or another 900 number, depending on the phone service you're using).

- To call the US or Canada from Europe, dial 00, then 1 (the country code for the US and Canada), then the area code and number. In short, 00 + 1 + AC + LN = Hi, Mom!

office in Edmonds, Washington, from anywhere in Europe, I dial 00 (Europe's international access code), 1 (the US country code), 425 (Edmonds' area code), and 771-8303.

Note: You might see a + in front of a European number. When dialing the number, replace the + with the international access code of the country you're calling from (00 from Europe, 011 from the US or Canada).

Prepaid Phone Cards

To make calls from public phones, you'll need a prepaid phone card. There are two kinds of phone cards: insertable (usable only in pay phones) and international (usable from any phone, but hard to find in Eastern Europe).

Insertable Phone Cards: This type of card is a convenient way to pay for calls from public pay phones and can be purchased at post offices, newsstands, and tobacco shops. Simply take the phone off the hook, insert the prepaid card, wait for a dial tone, and dial away. The price of the call (local or international) is automatically deducted while you talk. These cards only work in the country where you buy them (so your Czech phone card is worthless in Poland). Insertable phone cards are a good deal for calling within Europe, but calling the US can be pricey (at least 50 cents/minute). Be aware that with the prevalence of mobile phones, public phones are getting harder to find.

International Phone Cards: Although common throughout much of Western Europe, international phone cards are still relatively rare (and more expensive) in the East. You're more likely to find them in the Czech Republic than in other countries in this book (in Prague, look for the Smartcall brand—with a black-and-orange ad). Try looking for fliers advertising long-distance rates, or ask about the cards at Internet cafés, newsstands, exchange bureaus, souvenir shops, and youth hostels. Buy a low denomination in case the card is a dud. These cards generally work only in the country where you buy them.

If you can snare one of these cards, your calls to the US will generally cost around 25-50 cents per minute (and you can also use them for domestic calls). They work from any type of phone, including the one in your hotel room (but ask at the front desk about whether they'd charge you for calling the access number). To use the card, dial a toll-free access number, then enter your scratch-to-reveal PIN code. A few of the cards I've tried have an access number that's not toll-free—which means that you pay both for the call, and for the time being deducted from your card.

US Calling Cards: These cards, such as the ones offered by AT&T, Verizon, or Sprint, are the worst option. You'll save a lot of money by using a pay phone and a locally purchased, insertable phone card instead.

Types of Phones
Public Pay Phones
Coin-op phones are virtually extinct—you'll usually need an insertable phone card (described earlier) to make a call.

Hotel Room Phones
Calling from your hotel room can be cheap for local calls (ask for the rates at the front desk first), but is often a rip-off for long-distance calls, unless you use an international phone card (explained earlier). Some hotels charge a fee for dialing supposedly "toll-free" numbers, such as the one for your international phone card—ask before you dial. Incoming calls are free, making this a cheap way for friends and family to stay in touch (provided they have a good long-distance plan for calls to Europe—and a list of your hotels' phone numbers).

If you're staying at a private room—such as Croatia's *sobe*—be aware that you're unlikely to have a telephone in your room.

Metered Phones
These are available in phone offices and sometimes in bigger post offices. You can talk all you want, then pay the bill when you leave—but be sure you know the rates before you have a lengthy conversation.

Mobile Phones
Many travelers enjoy the convenience of traveling with a mobile phone.

Using Your Mobile Phone: Your US mobile phone works in Europe if it's GSM-enabled, tri-band or quad-band, and on a calling plan that includes international calls. Phones from AT&T and T-Mobile, which use the same GSM technology that Europe does, are more likely to work overseas than Verizon or Sprint phones (if you're not sure, ask your service provider). Most US providers charge $1.29-1.99 per minute while roaming internationally to make or receive calls, and 20-50 cents to send or receive text messages.

You'll pay cheaper rates if your phone is electronically "unlocked" (ask your provider about this); then in Europe, you can simply buy a **SIM card,** which gives you a European phone number. SIM cards are sold at mobile-phone stores and some newsstand kiosks for about $5-15, and generally include several minutes' worth of prepaid domestic calling time. When you buy a

SIM card, you may need to show ID, such as your passport. Insert the SIM card in your phone (usually in a slot on the side or behind the battery), and it'll work like a European mobile phone. Before purchasing a SIM card, always ask about fees for domestic and international calls, roaming charges, and how to check your credit balance and buy more time. When you're in the SIM card's home country, domestic calls are reasonable, and incoming calls are free. You'll pay more if you're roaming in another country.

Buying a European Mobile Phone: Mobile-phone shops all over Europe sell basic phones. The mobile-phone desk in a big department store is another good place to check. Phones that are "locked" to work with a single provider start around $40; "unlocked" phones (which allow you to switch out SIM cards to use your choice of provider) start around $60. You'll also need to buy a SIM card and prepaid credit for making calls.

Renting a European Mobile Phone: Car-rental companies and mobile-phone companies offer the option to rent a mobile phone with a European number. While this seems convenient, hidden fees (such as high per-minute charges or expensive shipping costs) can really add up—which usually makes it a bad value. One exception is Verizon's Global Travel Program, available only to Verizon customers.

Data Downloading on a Smartphone: Many smartphones, such as the iPhone, Android, and BlackBerry, work in Europe (note that some older Verizon iPhones don't work abroad). For voice calls and text messaging, smartphones work the same as other US mobile phones (explained earlier). But beware of sky-high fees for data downloading (checking email, browsing the Internet, streaming videos, and so on). The best solution: Disable data roaming entirely, and only use your device when you find free Wi-Fi. You can ask your mobile-phone service provider to cut off your account's data-roaming capability, or you can manually turn it off on your phone (look under the "Network" menu).

If you want Internet access without being limited to Wi-Fi, you'll need to keep data roaming on—but you can take steps to reduce your charges. Consider paying extra for a limited inter-national data-roaming plan through your carrier, then use data roaming selectively (if a particular task gobbles bandwidth, wait until you're on Wi-Fi). In general, ask your provider in advance how to avoid unwittingly roaming your way to a huge bill. If your smartphone is on Wi-Fi, you can use certain apps to make cheap or free voice calls (described next).

Calling over the Internet

Some things that seem too good to be true...actually are true. If you're traveling with a wireless device (such as a laptop or smartphone), you can use **VoIP** (Voice over Internet Protocol) to make free calls over the Internet to another wireless device (or you can pay a few cents to call from your computer to a telephone). If both devices have cameras, you can even see each other while you chat. The major providers are Skype (www.skype.com, also available as a smartphone app), Google Talk (www.google .com/talk), and FaceTime (this app comes standard on newer Apple devices). If you have a smartphone, you can get online at a hotspot and use these apps to make calls without ringing up expensive roaming charges (though call quality can be spotty on slow connections).

Useful Phone Numbers
Emergency Needs
In all of the countries in this book, dial 112 for medical or other emergencies. For police, dial 112 in Slovakia, Hungary, Poland, or Austria; dial 158 in the Czech Republic; dial 113 in Slovenia; dial 92 in Croatia; and dial 122 in Bosnia-Herzegovina.

US Embassies
In Austria: Parkring 12a, Vienna, passport services available Mon-Fri 8:00-11:30, tel. 01/313-397-535, http://austria.usembassy.gov.

In Bosnia-Herzegovina: Robert C. Frasure Street 1, Sarajevo, passport services available Mon-Fri 14:00-15:30 plus Fri 8:00-10:30, tel. 033/704-000, on weekends and after hours call the same number and press 0 after the recording, http://sarajevo.usembassy .gov. There's also a branch office in Mostar (Husnije Repca 3, tel. 036/580-580).

In Croatia: Ulica Thomasa Jeffersona 2, Zagreb, passport services available Mon-Thu 13:00-15:00 plus Wed 9:00-11:00, tel. 01/661-2200, after business-hours tel. 01/661-2400, consular services tel. 01/661-2300, http://croatia.usembassy.gov.

In the Czech Republic: Tržiště 15, Prague, passport services available Mon-Fri 9:00-11:30, tel. 257-022-000, http://prague .usembassy.gov.

In Hungary: Szabadság tér 12, Budapest, passport services available Mon-Thu 9:00-12:00 & 13:00-16:00, Fri 13:00-16:00, tel. 1/475-4164, after-hours emergency tel. 1/475-4703 or 1/475-4924, http://hungary.usembassy.gov.

In Poland: Ulica Piękna 12, Warsaw, passport services available Mon-Fri 9:00-12:00, tel. 022-625-1401, http://poland.usembassy .gov; also a US Consulate in Kraków at ulica Stolarska 9, passport services available Mon-Fri 8:30-15:00, tel. 012-424-5183.

In Slovakia: Hviezdoslavovo námestie 4, Bratislava, passport services available Mon-Fri 8:00-11:45 & 14:00-15:15, tel. 02/5443-0861, http://slovakia.usembassy.gov.

In Slovenia: Prešernova 31, Ljubljana, passport services available Mon-Fri 9:00-11:30 & 13:00-15:00, tel. 01/200-5595, after business hours tel. 01/200-5500, http://slovenia.usembassy.gov.

Canadian Embassies

For after-hours emergencies, Canadian citizens can call collect to the Foreign Services Office in Ottawa, Canada at 613/996-8885.

In Austria: Laurenzerberg 2, Vienna, passport services available Mon-Fri 8:30-12:30 & 13:30-15:30, tel. 01/313-83000, toll-free emergency tel. 800-2326-6831, www.austria.gc.ca.

In Bosnia-Herzegovina: Services provided by Canadian Embassy in Budapest, Hungary (listed below).

In Croatia: Prilaz Djure Deželića 4, Zagreb, passport services available Mon-Thu 10:00-12:00 & 13:00-15:00, Fri 10:00-13:00, tel. 01/488-1200, www.croatia.gc.ca.

In the Czech Republic: Muchova 6, Prague, consular services available Mon-Fri 8:30-12:30, tel. 272-101-800, www.czechrepublic.gc.ca; also provides services for Slovakia.

In Hungary: Ganz utca 12-14, Budapest, passport services available Mon-Thu 8:30-12:30 & 13:00-16:30, Fri 8:00-12:30, tel. 1/392-3342, www.hungary.gc.ca; also provides services for Bosnia-Herzegovina and Slovenia. For after-hours emergencies, call collect to Canadian tel. 613/996-8885.

In Poland: ulica Jana Matejki 1-5, Warsaw, passport services available Mon-Fri 8:30-16:30, tel. 022-584-3100, toll-free emergency tel. 800-111-4319, www.poland.gc.ca.

In Slovakia: Mostova 2, Bratislava, passport services available Mon-Fri 8:30-12:00 & 13:30-16:30, tel. 02/5920-4031; some services provided through Canadian Embassy in Prague, Czech Republic (listed above).

Canadian Consulate in Slovenia: Trg Republike 3, 12th floor, Ljubljana, passport services available Mon-Fri 9:00-13:00, tel. 01/252-4444; some services provided through Canadian Embassy in Budapest, Hungary (listed above).

Travel Advisories

US Department of State: tel. 202/647-5225, www.travel.state.gov
Canadian Department of Foreign Affairs: Canadian tel. 800-267-8376, www.international.gc.ca
US Centers for Disease Control and Prevention: tel. 800-CDC-INFO (800-232-4636), www.cdc.gov/travel

Directory Assistance

Dial 1188 in the Czech Republic, 913 in Poland, 198 in Hungary, 988 in Croatia or Slovenia, 1181 in Slovakia, and 118 in Austria.

Internet Access

It's useful to get online periodically as you travel—to confirm trip plans, check train or bus schedules, get weather forecasts, catch up on email, blog or post photos from your trip, or call folks back home (explained earlier, under "Calling over the Internet").

Internet Terminals: Some hotels offer a computer in the lobby with Internet access for guests. If you ask politely, smaller places may let you sit at their desk for a few minutes just to check your email. If your lodgings don't have access, ask your host to direct you to the nearest place to get online.

Traveling with a Laptop or Other Wireless Device: You can get online if your accommodations have Wi-Fi or a port in your room for plugging in a cable. Some places offer Wi-Fi for free; others charge by the minute or hour. A cellular modem—which lets your laptop access the Internet over a mobile phone network—provides more extensive coverage, but is much more expensive than Wi-Fi. On my last trip to Eastern Europe, staying in accommodations listed in this book, I was able to get online almost everywhere.

Warning: Anytime you access the Internet—especially over a public connection (such as a Wi-Fi signal or at an Internet café)—you're running the risk that someone could be looking over your shoulder, literally or virtually. Be careful about storing personal information (such as passport and credit-card numbers) online. If you're not convinced it's secure, avoid accessing any sites (such as online banking) that could be sensitive to fraud.

Mail

While you can arrange for mail delivery to your hotel (allow 10 days for a letter to arrive), phoning and emailing are so easy that I've dispensed with mail stops altogether.

You can mail one package per day to yourself worth up to $200 duty-free from Europe to the US (mark it "personal purchases"). If you're sending a gift to someone, mark it "unsolicited gift." For details, visit www.cbp.gov and search for "Know Before You Go."

Transportation

By Car or Public Transportation?

In Eastern Europe, I travel mostly by public transportation. For long distances between big cities (such as Prague to Kraków, Warsaw to Budapest, or Vienna to Dubrovnik), I prefer to take a cheap flight or a night train. For shorter distances (like Gdańsk to Warsaw or Ljubljana to Zagreb), I take a daytime train or bus. In areas with lots of exciting day-trip possibilities, such as the Czech countryside or Slovenia's Julian Alps, I rent a car for a day or two—

or hire a local with a car to drive me around (which can be cheaper than you might think; in this book, I recommend several drivers and tour guides with cars).

If you're debating between public transportation and car rental, consider these factors: Cars are best for three or more traveling together (especially families with small kids), those packing heavy, and those scouring the countryside. Trains, buses, and boats are best for solo travelers, blitz tourists, and city-to-city travelers; those with an ambitious, multi-country itinerary; and those who don't want to drive in Europe. While a car gives you more freedom—enabling you to search for hotels more easily and carrying your bags for you—trains, buses, and boats zip you effortlessly and scenically from city to city, usually dropping you in the center, often near a tourist office. Cars are great in the countryside, but a worthless headache in places like Prague, Budapest, and Dubrovnik.

Public Transportation

Throughout this book, I suggest whether trains, buses, or boats are better for a particular destination (in the "Connections" section at the end of each chapter).

Trains

Trains are punctual and cover cities well, but frustrating schedules make a few out-of-the-way recommendations difficult—or impossible—to reach (usually the bus will get you there instead; see "Buses," later).

Schedules: Pick up train schedules from stations as you go, or print them out from an online source. To study ahead on the Web, check www.bahn.com, Germany's excellent all-Europe timetable (use http://bahn.hafas.de/bin/query.exe/en to go directly to an English-language search page). Individual countries also have their own train timetable websites:

- **Czech Republic:** www.idos.cz
- **Slovakia:** www.cp.sk
- **Poland:** www.rozklad-pkp.pl
- **Hungary:** www.elvira.hu
- **Slovenia:** www.slo-zeleznice.si
- **Croatia:** www.hznet.hr
- **Austria:** www.oebb.at

Tickets: Buy tickets at the train station (or on board, if the station is unstaffed). In many big-city train stations, it can be tricky to find the correct line (you'll see separate ticket windows for domestic trips, international journeys, immediate departures, and other concerns—all of them poorly marked). Before getting in line, confirm with fellow travelers that you've chosen the right one.

Public Transportation in Eastern Europe

----- Bus Route ·············· Ferry Route

— · — Railway —o— Border Station

Not to Scale

Many ticket-sellers speak limited (or no) English—be prepared to write out your destination and time. Bigger cities have train-ticket offices, either downtown (such as in Prague and Budapest) or in the station (such as in Warsaw and Ljubljana) where you can take a number to wait for an English-speaking clerk to sort through your options; I've listed these in this book. Especially if you have a complicated request (such as reserving a night-train berth a few days ahead), these offices can save you some frustration, and—in some cases—a needless trip to the station. While most short-haul journeys do not require a reservation, you are required to reserve on some high-speed trains (such as the Warsaw-Kraków express). It's also smart to reserve a sleeping berth if you're taking a night train.

Night Trains: To cover the long distances between the major destinations in this book, consider using night trains. Each night on the train saves a day for sightseeing. Fortunately, most of Eastern Europe's big cities are connected by night trains. I appreciate the convenience of night trains and take them routinely. Still, some of my readers have complained that Eastern European night trains aren't as new, plush, and comfy as those they've used in the West. Expect a bumpy, noisy ride and gross WCs. In general, if a higher degree of comfort is important to you, look for an affordable flight (see "Cheap Flights," later) or take a day train. As in Western Europe, thefts on night trains do occur, so lock the door and secure your belongings (to make it difficult—or at least noisy—for thieves to rip you off). When sleeping on a night train, I wear my money belt.

Railpasses: While railpasses can be a good deal in Western Europe, they aren't necessarily the best option in the East for two reasons: Point-to-point tickets are cheap and simple here, and most railpasses don't conveniently combine Eastern European countries. For example, with the Eurail Selectpass, you can buy unlimited travel for up to 15 travel days (within a two-month period) in three, four, or five adjacent countries; but of the countries in this book, only Hungary, Austria, the Czech Republic, and Slovenia/Croatia are eligible. A more popular option is the European East Pass, covering the Czech Republic, Hungary, Poland, Slovakia, and Austria—but not Slovenia or Croatia. Each country except Slovakia and Bosnia-Herzegovina has its own individual railpass, valid for trips only within that country. Various pre-selected two- and three-country options are also available. Again, none of these passes is likely to save you much money, but if a pass matches your itinerary, give it a look and crunch the numbers. For options, including approximate point-to-point train fares, see www.rick steves.com/rail.

Buses

While the train can get you most places faster than a bus can, this book covers a few areas where buses are worth considering. For example, Ljubljana and Lake Bled are connected by both train and bus—but the bus station is right in the town center of Bled, while the train station is a few miles away. And a few destinations, including Croatia's Plitvice Lakes National Park and Rovinj, are accessible only by bus. In general, trains are best in Poland and Hungary; buses are often better in Slovakia and Croatia; and it's a toss-up in the Czech Republic and Slovenia. When in doubt, ask at the local TI for advice.

Boats

Boats can be your best option along the Croatian coast. For details, see "Getting Around the Dalmatian Coast" on page 824.

Renting a Car

If you're renting a car, bring your US driver's license. It's recommended, but not required, that you also have an International Driving Permit (sold at your local AAA office for $15 plus the cost of two passport-type photos; see www.aaa.com); however, I've frequently rented cars in Eastern Europe and traveled problem-free with just my US license.

Rental companies require you to be at least 18 years old and to have held your license for one year. Drivers under the age of 25 may incur a young-driver surcharge, and some rental companies do not rent to anyone 75 and over.

Research car rentals before you go. It's cheaper to arrange most car rentals from the US. Call several companies and look online to compare rates, or arrange a rental through your home-town travel agent.

Most of the major US rental agencies (such as Alamo/National, Avis, Budget, Dollar, Hertz, and Thrifty) have offices throughout Eastern Europe. It can be cheaper to use a consolidator, such as Auto Europe (www.autoeurope.com) or Europe by Car (www.ebctravel.com), which compares rates at several companies to get you the best deal. However, my readers have reported problems with consolidators, ranging from misinformation to unexpected fees; because you're going through a middleman, it can be more challenging to resolve disputes that arise with the rental agency.

Regardless of the car-rental company you choose, always read the contract carefully. The fine print can conceal a host of common add-on charges—such as one-way drop-off fees, airport surcharges, or mandatory insurance policies—that aren't included in the "total price," but can be tacked on when you pick up your

Driving: Distance & Time

N — Not to Scale

GERMANY

Berlin

120m 2.25h

Dresden

65m 1.5h

POLAND

To Gdańsk

Toruń — 110m 2.5h

215m 5h

180m • 3.75h

Poznań

190m • 4h

Warsaw

135m • 3.5h

265m • 6.5h

210m • 4h

140m • 3.5h

390m • 9.5h

185m • 4.5h

Częstochowa — 90m • 2h

65m 1.75h

40m 1.25h

Kraków

Terezín — 40m 1h

Prague

25k • .75h

Karlštejn Castle

40m 1.25h

Kutná Hora

290m • 5.5h

Auschwitz

CZECH REPUBLIC

100m • 2.75h

80m • 2h

175m • 3.5h

Zakopane

45m 1.5h

Poprad

115m 3.5h

100m • 2.25h

210m • 3.5h

130m • 2h

Brno — 80m 2h

200m

200m • 4h

SLOVAKIA

Český Krumlov

135m • 3.25h

80m 1.5h

240m 5.5h

Eger

Munich

240m • 4h

140m • 2.5h

200m • 3.5h

Vienna — 40m 1h

Bratislava

125m • 2.5h

80m • 2h

90m 1.5h

Salzburg

235m • 4h

240m 4h →

150m • 2.5h

Budapest

150m • 2.5h

AUSTRIA

150m • 2.5h

290m • 4.5h

145m • 2.5h

HUNGARY

Bled — 30m 1h

60m 1.5h

Ljubljana

Pécs

SLOVENIA

90m • 2h

150m • 3.5h

SERBIA

ITALY

75m 2h

140m • 2h

Zagreb

CROATIA

100m • 1.75h

Trieste

50m • 1.5h

100m 4h

85m • 2h

260m • 6h

Venice

Rovinj — 30m • .75h

Rijeka

90m • 2.5h

Plitvice

BOSNIA-HERZEGOVINA

Pula

55m 1.5h

140m • 3.5h

85m 1.75h

Sarajevo

90m 2.5h

Zadar

100m • 2h

Mostar

110m 2.5h

Adriatic Sea

105m • 2.5h

Split

65m 2h

Ston — 35m 1h

5.5h

35m • 1h

Korčula

3.4h

MONT.

Dubrovnik

Note: Your times may vary based on traffic, construction, and road conditions.

m = miles
h = hours
--- = car ferry

car. You may need to query rental agents pointedly to find out your actual cost.

For the best deal, rent by the week with unlimited mileage. To save money on fuel, ask for a diesel car. I normally rent a small, inexpensive model like a Ford Fiesta or Škoda Fabia. Expect to pay about $300-450 to rent a small economy car for two weeks with unlimited mileage, basic insurance, gas, and tolls. Note that short rentals cost significantly more per day.

An automatic transmission adds about 50 percent to the car-rental cost over a manual transmission. Almost all rentals are manual by default, so if you need an automatic, you must request one in advance; be aware that these cars are usually larger models (not as maneuverable on narrow, winding roads).

Be warned that dropping a car off in a different country—say, picking up in Prague and dropping in Dubrovnik—can be prohibitively expensive (depends on distance, but the extra fee averages a few hundred dollars and can exceed $1,000). If you're doing a multi-country trip by car, find out what the international drop-off fee will be. If it's exorbitant, consider instead doing a round-trip itinerary, renting a car per country...or using public transportation. Again, I prefer to connect long distances by train, bus, or plane, then rent cars for a day or two where they're most useful. But be aware that some companies have a minimum rental period (generally three days); you can keep the car for fewer days, but you'll pay for the minimum period anyway. If you want the car for just a day or two, try to find a company that allows short rentals.

As a rule, always tell your car-rental company up front exactly which countries you'll be entering. Some companies levy extra insurance fees for trips taken with certain types of cars (such as BMWs, Mercedes, and convertibles) in certain countries. Or the company may prohibit driving the car in off-the-beaten-track destinations, such as Bosnia-Herzegovina. As you cross borders, you may need to show the proper paperwork, such as proof of insurance (called a "green card"). Double-check with your rental agent that you have all the documentation you need before you drive off.

You can sometimes get a GPS unit with your rental car or leased vehicle for an additional fee (around $15/day; be sure it's set to English and has all the maps you need before you drive off). Or, if you have a portable GPS device at home, consider taking it with you to Europe (some devices come pre-loaded with Western European maps, but you may have to purchase and download separate maps for Eastern Europe). GPS apps are also available for smartphones, but downloading maps using one of these apps in Europe could lead to an exorbitant data-roaming bill.

Big companies have offices in most cities; ask whether they can pick you up at your hotel. Small local rental companies can be cheaper but aren't as flexible. Compare pickup costs (downtown can be less expensive than the airport), and explore drop-off options. Returning a car at a big-city train station can be tricky; get precise details on the car drop-off location and hours. Note that rental offices usually close from midday Saturday until Monday.

When you pick up the rental car, check it thoroughly and make sure any damage is noted on your rental agreement. Find out how your car's lights, turn signals, wipers, and gas cap function, and know what kind of fuel the vehicle takes. When you return the car, make sure the agent verifies its condition with you.

Car Insurance Options

When you rent a car, you are liable for a very high deductible, sometimes equal to the entire value of the car. Limit your financial risk by choosing one of these three options: Buy Collision Damage Waiver (CDW) coverage from the car-rental company, get coverage through your credit card (free if your card automatically includes zero-deductible coverage), or buy coverage through Travel Guard.

CDW includes a very high deductible (typically $1,000-1,500). Though each rental company has its own variation, basic **CDW** costs $15-25 a day (figure roughly 25 percent extra) and reduces your liability, but does not eliminate it. When you pick up the car, you'll be offered the chance to "buy down" the basic deductible to zero (for an additional $15-30/day; this is sometimes called "super CDW").

If you opt for **credit-card coverage,** there's a catch. You'll technically have to decline all coverage offered by the car-rental company, which means they can place a hold on your card (which can be up to the full value of the car). In case of damage, it can be time-consuming to resolve the charges with your credit-card company. Before you decide on this option, quiz your credit-card company about how it works.

Finally, you can buy collision insurance from **Travel Guard** ($9/day plus a one-time $3 service fee covers you for up to $35,000, $250 deductible, tel. 800-826-4919, www.travelguard.com). It's valid everywhere in Europe except the Republic of Ireland, and some Italian car-rental companies refuse to honor it. Note that various states differ on which products and policies are available to their residents.

For more information on car-rental insurance, see www.ricksteves.com/cdw.

Leasing

For trips of two and a half weeks or more, consider leasing (which automatically includes zero-deductible collision and theft insurance). By technically buying and then selling back the car, you save lots of money on tax and insurance, and get a brand-new car with unlimited mileage and a 24-hour emergency assistance program. However, leases aren't generally available in Eastern Europe—you'll have to pick up and drop off the car elsewhere in Europe (such as Germany or Italy). You can lease for as little as 17 days to as long as 6 months. Car leases must be arranged from the US. One of many companies offering affordable lease packages is Europe by Car (US tel. 800-223-1516, www.ebctravel.com).

Driving

Road Rules: Learn the universal road signs. Bring your driver's license. Seat belts are required, and two beers under those belts are enough to land you in jail. Be aware of typical European road rules; for example, many countries—including the Czech Republic, Poland, Hungary, Slovenia, Croatia, and Bosnia-Herzegovina—require headlights to be turned on at all times (even in broad daylight) and forbid drivers from talking on mobile phones without a hands-free headset. Ask your car-rental company about these rules, or check the US State Department website (www.travel.state.gov, click on "International Travel," then specify your country of choice and click "Traffic Safety and Road Conditions").

STOP AND LEARN THESE ROAD SIGNS

Speed Limit (km/hr) — Yield — No Passing — End of No Passing Zone

One Way — Intersection — Main Road — Freeway

Danger — No Entry — No Entry for cars — All Vehicles Prohibited

Parking — No Parking — Customs — Peace

Fuel: Gas is expensive—often about $6 per gallon. Diesel cars are more common in Europe than back home, so be sure you know what type of fuel your car takes before you fill up. Fuel pumps are color-coded for unleaded or diesel.

Road Conditions: Eastern Europe is nearing the end of an impressive binge of superhighway construction. It's not unusual to discover that a much faster road has been built between

major destinations since your five-year-old map was published. (This is another good reason to travel with the most up-to-date maps available and study them before each drive.) Over the last several years, superhighways have opened between Dresden and Prague (A17), and from Budapest all the way to Ploče, Croatia (via Zagreb and Split). As soon as a long-enough section is completed, the roads are opened to the public.

Occasionally backcountry roads are the only option (especially in Poland and Slovakia). These can be bumpy and slow, but they're almost always paved (or, at least, they once were). In Poland, where the network of new expressways is still far from complete, locals travel long distances on two-lane country roads. Since each lane is about a lane and a half wide, passing is commonplace. Slower drivers should keep to the far-right of their lane, and not be surprised when faster cars zip past them. Especially in Croatia and Slovenia, keep a close eye out for bikers—you'll see scads of them on mountain roads, struggling to earn a thrilling downhill run.

Tolls: In many countries, driving on highways requires a toll sticker (generally available at the border, post offices, gas stations, and sometimes car-rental agencies). You'll need a sticker in the **Czech Republic** (*dálniční známka*, 200 Kč/15 days, 300 Kč/2 months); **Slovakia** (*úhrada*, €10/10 days, €14/month, www.ndsas .sk); **Hungary** (*autópálya matrica*, 1,650 Ft/4 days, 2,750 Ft/week, 4,500 Ft/month, www.motorway.hu); **Slovenia** (*vinjeta*, €15/week, €30/month); and **Austria** (*Vignette*, €8/10 days, €23/2 months). Fines for not having a toll sticker can be stiff. Note that you don't need a toll sticker if you'll be dipping into the country on minor roads—only for major highways. Your rental car may already come with the necessary sticker—ask. In **Croatia**, you'll take a toll-ticket as you enter the expressway, then pay when you get off, based on how far you've traveled (figure about $8/hour). In **Poland**, drivers also pay tolls to use completed expressway segments.

Parking: Parking is a costly headache in big cities. You'll pay about $10-25 a day to park safely. Rental-car theft can be a problem in cities (especially Prague), so ask at your hotel for advice.

Cheap Flights

If you're considering a train ride that's more than five hours long, a flight may save you both time and money. When comparing your options, factor in the time it takes to get to the airport and how early you'll need to arrive to check in.

Low-cost airlines allow you to cheaply connect many of

the destinations in this book. Two well-established budget airlines are based in Eastern Europe: **Wizz Air** (www.wizzair.com, with hubs in Budapest, Prague, Warsaw, Gdańsk, and Katowice, near Kraków) and **Smart Wings** (www.smartwings.net, based in Prague). Well-known cheapo carriers that fly to Eastern European destinations include **easyJet** (www.easyjet.com), **Ryanair** (www.ryanair.com), **Air Berlin** (www.airberlin.com), and **Norwegian Air** (www.norwegian.no).

Now that the established airlines in Eastern Europe face more competition, they've been forced to adapt. Many national carriers charge reasonable fares for short-distance trips. For example, check out Croatia Airlines (www.croatiaairlines.com) and Poland's LOT Airlines (www.lot.com). On recent trips, I've flown affordably on LOT between Kraków and Ljubljana, and between Kraków and Budapest, avoiding lengthy overland journeys.

Good comparison search engines for international flights include www.kayak.com and www.hipmunk.com. For comparing inexpensive flights within Europe, try www.skyscanner.com. If you're not sure who flies to your destination, check its airport's website for a list of carriers.

Be aware of the potential drawbacks of flying on the cheap: nonrefundable and nonchangeable tickets, minimal or nonexistent customer service, and stingy baggage allowances with steep overage fees. If you're traveling with lots of luggage, a cheap flight can quickly become a bad deal. To avoid unpleasant surprises, read the small print before you book. Also be aware that you may fly out of less convenient, secondary airports. For example, some of Wizz Air's flights from "Kraków" actually depart from Katowice, 50 miles away.

Europe by Air offers a Flight Pass, starting at $99 per leg (plus taxes and airport fees) for flights within Europe. They partner with various well-established airlines, providing good coverage for low prices (most useful for Croatia Airlines flights to and from the Dalmatian Coast; tickets can be purchased only in US, www.europebyair.com, US tel. 888-321-4737).

Resources

Resources from Rick Steves

Books: *Rick Steves' Eastern Europe* is one of many books in my series on European travel, which includes country guidebooks (such as Croatia & Slovenia), city and regional guidebooks (including Budapest; Prague & the Czech Republic; and Vienna, Salzburg & Tirol), Snapshot guides (excerpted chapters from my country guides), Pocket Guides (full-color little books on big cities), and my budget-travel skills handbook, *Rick Steves' Europe Through the*

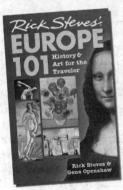

Back Door. Most of my titles are available as ebooks. My phrase books—for German, French, Italian, Spanish, and Portuguese—are practical and budget-oriented. My other books include *Europe 101* (a crash course on art and history), *Mediterranean Cruise Ports* (how to make the most of your time in port), and *Travel as a Political Act* (a travelogue sprinkled with tips for bringing home a global perspective). A more complete list of my titles appears near the end of this book.

Video: My public television series, *Rick Steves' Europe*, covers European destinations in 100 shows, including several episodes that explore Eastern Europe. To watch episodes, visit www.hulu .com/rick-steves-europe; for scripts and other details, see www .ricksteves.com/tv.

Audio: My weekly public radio show, *Travel with Rick Steves*, features interviews with travel experts from around the world. This audio content is available for free at Rick Steves' Audio Europe, an extensive online library organized by destination. Choose whatever interests you, and download it for free to your computer or mobile device via www.ricksteves.com/audio europe, iTunes, or the Rick Steves Audio Europe smartphone app.

Maps

The black-and-white maps in this book are concise and simple, designed to help you locate recommended places and get to local TIs, where you can pick up more in-depth maps of towns or regions (usually free).

Better maps are sold at newsstands and bookstores in Europe. Before you buy a map, look at it to be sure the map has the level of detail you want. Train travelers can usually manage fine with the freebies they get at the local tourist offices. Hikers will find no shortage of excellent, very detailed maps locally. For drivers, I'd recommend a 1:200,000- or 1:300,000-scale map for each country. Since new expressways are constantly being built in these countries, an up-to-date map is essential—it can mean the difference between choosing an old, slow road or saving an hour by finding the brand-new highway. In Croatia and Slovenia, my favorite maps of the region are by the Slovenian cartographer Kod & Kam (sold all over).

Begin Your Trip at www.ricksteves.com

At ricksteves.com, you'll discover a wealth of free information on European destinations, including fresh monthly news and helpful tips from thousands of fellow travelers. You'll find my latest guidebook updates (www.ricksteves.com/update), a monthly travel e-newsletter (easy and free to sign up), my personal travel blog, and my free Rick Steves Audio Europe smartphone app (if you don't have a smartphone, you can access the same content via podcasts). You can also follow me on Facebook and Twitter.

Our **online Travel Store** offers travel bags and accessories that I've specifically designed to help you travel smarter and lighter. These include my popular carry-on bags (roll-aboard and backpack versions), money belts, totes, toiletries kits, adapters, other accessories, and a wide selection of guidebooks, planning maps, and DVDs.

Choosing the right **railpass** for your trip—amidst hundreds of options—can drive you nutty. We'll help you choose the best pass for your needs and ship it to you for free, plus give you a bunch of free extras.

Rick Steves' Europe Through the Back Door travel company offers **tours** with more than three dozen itineraries and more than 450 departures reaching the best destinations in this book...and beyond. Our 16-day Eastern Europe tour visits the Czech Republic, Poland, Hungary, Croatia, and Slovenia, while our 14-day Adriatic tour focuses on Slovenia, Croatia, and a bit of Bosnia-Herzegovina. We also offer an 8-day tour that covers Prague and Budapest, and a 12-day tour of Berlin, Prague, and Vienna. You'll enjoy great guides, a fun bunch of travel partners (with small groups of generally around 24-28), and plenty of room to spread out in a big, comfy bus. You'll find European adventures to fit every vacation length. For all the details, and to get our Tour Catalog and a free Rick Steves Tour Experience DVD (filmed on location during an actual tour), visit www.ricksteves.com or call the Tour Department at 425/608-4217.

Other Guidebooks

If you're like most travelers, this book is all you need. But if you're heading beyond my recommended destinations, $40 for extra maps and books is money well spent. For more extensive coverage of this region and neighboring countries, consider *Rick Steves' Prague & the Czech Republic*, *Rick Steves' Budapest*, *Rick Steves' Croatia & Slovenia*, and *Rick Steves' Vienna, Salzburg & Tirol*.

The following books are worthwhile, though most are not updated annually; check the publication date before you buy. The Rough Guides, which individually cover the countries in this book, are packed with historical and cultural insight. The Lonely Planet guides are similar, but are designed more for travelers than for intellectuals. If choosing between these two titles, I'd buy the one that was published most recently. Lonely Planet's fat, far-ranging *Eastern Europe* overview book gives you little to go on for each destination, though their country- and city-specific guides are more thorough.

Dorling Kindersley publishes snazzy Eyewitness Guides, covering Prague, the Czech Republic, Slovakia, Budapest, Hungary, Kraków, Warsaw, Poland, Dubrovnik and the Dalmatian Coast, Croatia, and Vienna. While pretty to look at, these books weigh a ton and are skimpy on written content.

In Your Pocket publishes regularly updated magazines on major Eastern European cities (especially useful in Poland, including editions for Kraków, Warsaw, and Gdańsk). These handy guides are particularly good for their up-to-date hotel, restaurant, and nightlife recommendations (available locally, usually for a few dollars, but often free; condensed versions available free online at www.inyourpocket.com). The British entertainment publication *Time Out* sells a similarly well-researched annual magazine with up-to-date coverage on Croatia (look for it at newsstands for about $10, www.timeout.com).

Recommended Books and Movies

To learn about Eastern Europe past and present, check out a few of these books and films.

Nonfiction

Lonnie Johnson's *Central Europe: Enemies, Neighbors, Friends* is the best historical overview of the countries in this book. Timothy Garton Ash has written several good "eyewitness account" books analyzing the fall of communism in Eastern Europe, including *History of the Present* and *The Magic Lantern*. Michael Meyer's *The Year that Changed the World* intimately chronicles the exciting events of 1989, culminating in the fall of the Berlin Wall. Tina

Rosenberg's dense but thought-provoking *The Haunted Land* asks how those who actively supported communism in Eastern Europe should be treated in the post-communist age.

Patrick Leigh Fermor's *Between the Woods and the Water* is the vivid memoir of a young man who traveled by foot and on horseback across the Balkan Peninsula (including Hungary) in 1933. Rebecca West's classic, bricklike *Black Lamb and Grey Falcon* is the definitive travelogue of the Yugoslav lands (written during a journey between the two World Wars). For a more recent take, Croatian journalist Slavenka Drakulić has written a quartet of insightful essay collections from a woman's perspective: *Café Europa: Life After Communism; The Balkan Express; How We Survived Communism and Even Laughed;* and *A Guided Tour Through the Museum of Communism.* Drakulić's *They Would Never Hurt a Fly* profiles Yugoslav war criminals.

For a thorough explanation of how and why Yugoslavia broke apart, read *Yugoslavia: Death of a Nation* (by Laura Silber and Allan Little). Joe Sacco's powerful graphic novel *Safe Area Goražde* describes the author's experience living in a mostly Muslim town in Bosnia-Herzegovina while it was surrounded by Serb forces during the wars of the 1990s.

For information on Eastern European Roma (Gypsies), consider the textbook-style *We Are the Romani People* by Ian Hancock, and the more literary *Bury Me Standing* by Isabel Fonseca.

Fiction

The most prominent works of Eastern European fiction have come from the Czechs. These include *I Served the King of England* (Bohumil Hrabal), *The Unbearable Lightness of Being* (Milan Kundera), and *The Good Soldier Švejk* (Jaroslav Hašek). The Czech existentialist writer Franz Kafka wrote many well-known novels, including *The Trial* and *The Metamorphosis.* Bruce Chatwin's *Utz* is set in communist Prague.

James Michener's *Poland* is a hefty look into the history of the Poles. *Zlateh the Goat* (Isaac Bashevis Singer) includes seven folktales of Jewish Eastern Europe. Joseph Roth's *The Radetzky March* details the decline of an aristocratic family in the Austro-Hungarian Empire.

Imre Kertész, a Hungarian-Jewish Auschwitz survivor who won the Nobel Prize for Literature in 2002, is best known for his semi-autobiographical novel *Fatelessness (Sorstalanság),* which chronicles the experience of a young concentration-camp prisoner. Márai Sándor's reflective *Embers* paints a rich picture of cobblestoned, gaslit Vienna just before the empire's glory began to fade.

Arthur Phillips' confusingly titled 2002 novel *Prague* tells the story of American expats negotiating young-adult life in post-communist Budapest, where they often feel one-upped by their compatriots doing the same in the Czech capital (hence the title).

Films

Each of these countries has produced fine films. Here are a few highlights:

Czech Republic: *I Served the King of England* (2006); *Czech Dream* (2004); *Divided We Fall* (2000); *Kolya* (1996); *The Trial* (1993); *Kouř* (*Smoke*, 1991); *The Unbearable Lightness of Being* (1988); *The Firemen's Ball* (1967); *Closely Watched Trains* (1966); *The Loves of a Blonde* (1965).

Poland: *Katyń* (2007); *Karol: A Man Who Became Pope* (2005); *The Decalogue* (1989); *The Wedding* (1972).

Hungary: *Children of Glory* (*Szabadság, Szerelem*, 2006); *Fateless* (2005); *Kontroll* (2003); *Csinibaba* (1997); *Time Stands Still* (1981); *The Witness* (1969).

Croatia: *How the War Started on My Island* (1996); *Underground* (1995); *Tito and Me* (1992); *When Father Was Away on Business* (1985).

Slovenia: *No Man's Land* (2002, Slovenian-produced, but deals with Bosnian war; Oscar winner for Best Foreign Film).

Other Movies: Two recent German movies are excellent for their insight into the surreal and paranoid days of the Soviet Bloc. The Oscar-winning *The Lives of Others* (2006) chronicles the constant surveillance that the communist regime employed to keep potential dissidents in line. For a darkly funny and nostalgic look at post-communist Europe's fitful transition to capitalism, *Good Bye Lenin!* (2003) can't be beat.

Schindler's List (1993) and *The Pianist* (2002)—both of which won multiple Oscars—chronicle the plight of Jewish Holocaust victims in Kraków and Warsaw, respectively.

Sunshine (1999, starring Ralph Fiennes, directed by István Szabó; not to be confused with Danny Boyle's 2007 film of the same name) somewhat melodramatically traces three generations of an aristocratic Jewish family in Budapest, from the Golden Age, through the Holocaust, to the Cold War.

Documentaries about this region are also worth looking for. The BBC produced a remarkable six-hour documentary series called *The Death of Yugoslavia*, featuring interviews with all of the key players (it's difficult to find on DVD, but try searching for "Death of Yugoslavia" on YouTube; the book *Yugoslavia: Death of a Nation*, noted earlier, was a companion piece to this film). The 1998 Oscar-winning documentary *The Last Days* recounts the fate of Jews when the Nazis took over Hungary in 1944.

Holidays and Festivals

This list includes many—but not all—big festivals in this region, plus national holidays. Many sights and banks close down on national holidays—keep this in mind when planning your itinerary. Catholic holidays are celebrated in Poland, Slovakia, Croatia, and Slovenia (and to a lesser extent in Hungary and the Czech Republic). Muslims (most predominant in Bosnia) observe the month of Ramadan. Before planning a trip around a festival, make sure to verify the dates by checking the festival's website or contacting the various national TIs (listed at the beginning of this chapter).

For sports events, see www.sportsevents365.com for schedules and ticket information.

Jan 1	New Year's Day, all countries
Jan 6	Epiphany, Catholic countries
Jan 19	Anniversary of Jan Palach's Death, Prague (flowers in Wenceslas Square)
Feb 8	National Day of Culture, Slovenia (celebrates Slovenian culture and national poet France Prešeren)
Early March	One World International Human Rights Film Festival, Prague (1 week, www.oneworld.cz)
March 15	National Day, Hungary (celebrates 1848 Revolution)
Late March	Budapest Spring Festival (2 weeks, www.festivalcity.hu); last weekend is also Budapest Fringe Festival
Late March	Ski Flying World Championships, Planica, Slovenia (3 days, www.planica.info)
Easter	(April 8 in 2012, March 31 in 2013) all countries
April 27	National Resistance Day, Slovenia
April 30	Witches' Night, Czech Republic (similar to Halloween, with bonfires)
May 1	Labor Day, all countries
May 3	Constitution Day, Poland (celebrates Europe's first constitution)
May 8	Liberation Day, Czech Republic and Slovakia
Ascension	(May 17 in 2012, May 9 in 2013) Catholic countries
Whitsunday (Pentecost) and Whitmonday	(May 27-28 in 2012, May 19-20 in 2013) Catholic countries

Mid-May	Prague International Marathon (www .pim.cz)
Mid- to Late May	"Prague Spring" Music Festival (3 weeks, www.festival.cz)
Corpus Christi	(June 7 in 2012, May 30 in 2013) Catholic countries
Mid-May to Early June	Vienna Festival of Arts and Music (www.festwochen.or.at)
June-July	Prague Proms, Prague (music festival, www.pragueproms.cz)
Early June	Dance Week Festival, Zagreb, Croatia (www.danceweekfestival.com)
Mid-June	Celebration of the Rose, Český Krumlov, Czech Republic (3 days, medieval festival, music, theater, dance, knights' tournament)
June 22	Antifascist Struggle Day, Croatia
June 25	National Day, Slovenia; Statehood Day, Croatia
Late June	Floating of the Wreaths Midsummer Festival, Kraków, Poland (1 weekend, wreaths on rafts in Vistula River, fireworks, music)
Late June	Jewish Culture Festival, Kraków, Poland (1 week, www.jewishfestival.pl)
Late June	Midsummer Eve Celebrations, Austria
July 5	Sts. Cyril and Methodius Day, Czech Republic and Slovakia
July 6	Jan Hus Day, Czech Republic
July 10-Aug 25	(every year) Dubrovnik Summer Festival, Croatia (www.dubrovnik-festival.hr)
Early July-late Aug	Ljubljana Summer Festival, Slovenia (www.ljubljanafestival.si)
Mid-July-mid-Aug	International Music Festival, Český Krumlov, Czech Republic (www .festivalkrumlov.cz)
Ramadan	(Muslim holy month; July 20-Aug 18 in 2012, July 9-Aug 7 in 2013)
Late July	International Folklore Festival, Zagreb, Croatia (5 days, costumes, songs, dances from all over Croatia, www .msf.hr)
Late July	Formula 1 races, Budapest (1 day, www .hungaroinfo.com/formel1)
Aug 5	National Thanksgiving Day, Croatia

Early Aug	Sziget Festival, Budapest (1 week, rock and pop music, www.sziget.hu)
Aug 15	Assumption of Mary, Catholic countries
Aug 20	Constitution Day and St. Stephen's Day, Hungary (fireworks, celebrations)
Aug 29	National Uprising Day, Slovakia (commemorates uprising against Nazis)
Late Aug	Diocletian Days, Split, Croatia (1 week, toga-clad celebrations)
Late Aug-early Sept	Jewish Summer Festival, Budapest (2 weeks, www.jewishfestival.hu)
Aug-Sept	Dvořák's Prague Music Festival, Prague (www.dvorakovapraha.cz)
Sept	Radio Autumn, Prague (international music festival of radio orchestras)
Sept 1	Constitution Day, Slovakia
Sept 28	St. Wenceslas Day, Czech Republic (celebrates national patron saint and Czech statehood)
Oct	International Jazz Festival, Prague (www.jazzfestivalpraha.cz)
Oct 8	Independence Day, Croatia
Mid-Oct	Budapest Autumn Festival (1 week, music, www.festivalcity.hu)
Oct 23	Republic Day, Hungary (remembrances of 1956 Uprising)
Oct 26	National Day, Austria
Oct 28	Independence Day, Czech Republic
Oct 31	Reformation Day, Slovenia
Nov 1	All Saints' Day/Remembrance Day, Catholic countries (religious festival, some closures)
Nov 11	Independence Day, Poland; St. Martin's Day (official first day of wine season), Slovenia and Croatia
Nov 17	Velvet Revolution Anniversary, Czech Republic and Slovakia
Dec 5	St. Nicholas Eve, Prague (St. Nick gives gifts to children in town square)
Dec 24-25	Christmas Eve and Christmas Day, all countries
Dec 26	Boxing Day/St. Stephen's Day; Independence and Unity Day, Slovenia
Dec 31	St. Sylvester's Day, Prague and Vienna (fireworks)

Conversions and Climate

Numbers and Stumblers

- Europeans write a few of their numbers differently than we do. 1 = 1, 4 = 4, 7 = 7.
- In Europe, dates appear as day/month/year, so Christmas is 25/12/13.
- Commas are decimal points and decimals commas. A dollar and a half is 1,50, one thousand is 1.000, and there are 5.280 feet in a mile.
- When counting with fingers, start with your thumb. If you hold up your first finger to request one item, you'll probably get two.
- What Americans call the second floor of a building is the first floor in Europe.
- On escalators and moving sidewalks, Europeans keep the left "lane" open for passing. Keep to the right.

Metric Conversions (Approximate)

A kilogram is 2.2 pounds, and 1 liter is about a quart, or almost four to a gallon. A kilometer is six-tenths of a mile. I figure kilometers to miles by cutting them in half and adding back 10 percent of the original (120 km: 60 + 12 = 72 miles, 300 km: 150 + 30 = 180 miles).

1 foot = 0.3 meter	1 square yard = 0.8 square meter
1 yard = 0.9 meter	1 square mile = 2.6 square kilometers
1 mile = 1.6 kilometers	1 ounce = 28 grams
1 centimeter = 0.4 inch	1 quart = 0.95 liter
1 meter = 39.4 inches	1 kilogram = 2.2 pounds
1 kilometer = 0.62 mile	32°F = 0°C

Clothing Sizes

When shopping for clothing, use these US-to-European comparisons as general guidelines (but note that no conversion is perfect).

- Women's dresses and blouses: Add 30
  (US size 10 = European size 40)
- Men's suits and jackets: Add 10
  (US size 40 regular = European size 50)
- Men's shirts: Multiply by 2 and add about 8
  (US size 15 collar = European size 38)
- Women's shoes: Add about 30
  (US size 8 = European size 38-39)
- Men's shoes: Add 32-34
  (US size 9 = European size 41; US size 11 = European size 45)

Climate

First line is the average daily high; second line, average daily low; third line, average number of rainy days. For more detailed weather statistics for destinations in this book (as well as the rest of the world), check www.worldclimate.com.

	J	F	M	A	M	J	J	A	S	O	N	D
AUSTRIA • Vienna												
	34°	38°	47°	58°	67°	73°	76°	75°	68°	56°	45°	37°
	25°	28°	30°	42°	50°	56°	60°	59°	53°	44°	37°	30°
	15	14	13	13	13	14	13	13	10	13	14	15
CROATIA • Dubrovnik												
	53°	55°	58°	63°	70°	78°	83°	82°	77°	69°	62°	56°
	42°	43°	57°	52°	58°	65°	69°	69°	64°	57°	51°	46°
	13	13	11	10	10	6	4	3	7	11	16	15
CZECH REPUBLIC • Prague												
	31°	34°	44°	54°	64°	70°	73°	72°	65°	53°	42°	34°
	23°	24°	30°	38°	46°	52°	55°	55°	49°	41°	33°	27°
	13	11	10	11	13	12	13	12	10	13	12	13
HUNGARY • Budapest												
	34°	39°	50°	62°	71°	78°	82°	81°	74°	61°	47°	39°
	25°	28°	35°	44°	52°	58°	62°	60°	53°	44°	38°	30°
	13	12	11	11	13	13	10	9	7	10	14	13
POLAND • Kraków												
	32°	34°	45°	55°	67°	72°	76°	73°	66°	56°	44°	37°
	22°	22°	30°	38°	48°	54°	58°	56°	49°	42°	33°	28°
	16	15	12	15	12	15	16	15	12	14	15	16
SLOVENIA • Ljubljana												
	36°	41°	50°	60°	68°	75°	80°	78°	71°	59°	47°	39°
	25°	25°	32°	40°	48°	54°	57°	57°	51°	43°	36°	30°
	13	11	11	13	16	16	12	12	10	14	15	15

Temperature Conversion: Fahrenheit and Celsius

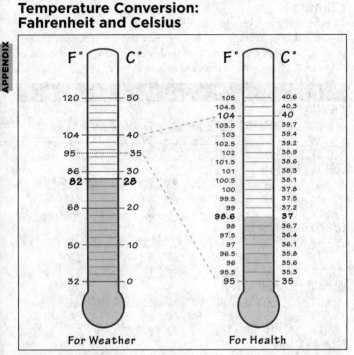

For Weather

For Health

Europe takes its temperature using the Celsius scale, while we opt for Fahrenheit. For a rough conversion from Celsius to Fahrenheit, double the number and add 30. For weather, remember that 28°C is 82°F—perfect. For health, 37°C is just right.

Packing Checklist

Whether you're traveling for five days or five weeks, here's what you'll need to bring. Pack light to enjoy the sweet freedom of true mobility. Happy travels!

- ❑ 5 shirts: long- and short-sleeve
- ❑ 1 sweater or lightweight fleece
- ❑ 2 pairs pants
- ❑ 1 pair shorts
- ❑ 1 swimsuit
- ❑ 5 pairs underwear and socks
- ❑ 1 pair shoes
- ❑ 1 rainproof jacket with hood
- ❑ Tie or scarf
- ❑ Money belt
- ❑ Money—your mix of:
  - ❑ Debit card (for ATM withdrawals)
  - ❑ Credit card
  - ❑ Hard cash (in easy-to-exchange $20 bills)
- ❑ Documents plus photocopies:
  - ❑ Passport
  - ❑ Printout of airline eticket
  - ❑ Driver's license
  - ❑ Student ID and hostel card
  - ❑ Railpass/car rental voucher
  - ❑ Insurance details
- ❑ Daypack
- ❑ Electronics—your choice of:
  - ❑ Camera (and related gear)
  - ❑ Computer/mobile devices (phone, MP3 player, ereader, etc.)
  - ❑ Chargers for each of the above
  - ❑ Plug adapter
- ❑ Empty water bottle

- ❑ Wristwatch and alarm clock
- ❑ Earplugs
- ❑ Toiletries kit
  - ❑ Toiletries
  - ❑ Medicines and vitamins
  - ❑ First-aid kit
  - ❑ Glasses/contacts/sunglasses (with prescriptions)
- ❑ Sealable plastic baggies
- ❑ Laundry soap
- ❑ Clothesline
- ❑ Small towel
- ❑ Sewing kit
- ❑ Travel information (guidebooks and maps)
- ❑ Address list (for sending postcards)
- ❑ Postcards and photos from home
- ❑ Notepad and pen
- ❑ Journal

If you plan to carry on your luggage, note that all liquids must be in 3.4-ounce or smaller containers and fit within a single quart-size sealable baggie. For details, see www.tsa.gov/travelers.

Hotel Reservation

To: _____ _____
           hotel   *email or fax*

From: _____ _____
            name   *email or fax*

Today's date: _____ / _____ / _____
                     day   *month*   *year*

Dear Hotel _____ ,
Please make this reservation for me:

Name: _____

Total # of people: _____ # of rooms: _____ # of nights: _____

Arriving: _____ / _____ / _____ My time of arrival (24-hr clock): _____
                day *month* *year*   (I will telephone if I will be late)

Departing: ____ / ____ / ____
                  day *month* *year*

Room(s): Single____ Double ____ Twin ____ Triple ____ Quad ____

With: Toilet ____ Shower ____ Bath ____ Sink only ____

Special needs: View____ Quiet____ Cheapest ____ Ground Floor ____

Please email or fax confirmation of my reservation, along with the type of room reserved and the price. Please also inform me of your cancellation policy. After I hear from you, I will quickly send my credit-card information as a deposit to hold the room. Thank you.

_____
Name

_____
Address

_____
City   *State*   *Zip Code*   *Country*

Before hoteliers can make your reservation, they want to know the information listed above. You can use this form as the basis for your email, or you can photocopy this page, fill in the information, and send it as a fax (also available online at www.ricksteves.com/reservation).

Czech Survival Phrases

The emphasis in Czech words usually falls on the first syllable—though don't overdo it, as this stress is subtle and can vary slightly. A vowel with an accent (á, é, í, ú, ý) is held longer, but the emphasis is not necessarily on that syllable. The combination *ch* sounds like the guttural "kh" sound in the Scottish word "loch." The uniquely Czech letter *ř* (as in Dvořák) sounds like a cross between a rolled "r" and "zh"; in the phonetics, I've simplified it to "zh." Here are a few English words that all Czechs know: super, OK, pardon, stop, menu, problem, and no problem.

Hello. (formal)	Dobrý den.	DOH-bree dehn
Hi. / Bye. (informal)	Ahoj.	AH-hoy
Do you speak English?	Mluvíte anglicky?	MLOO-vee-teh ANG-lits-kee
Yes. / No.	Ano. / Ne.	AH-noh / neh
I (don't) understand.	Nerozumím.	NEH-roh-zoo-meem
Please. / You're welcome. / Can I help you?	Prosím.	PROH-seem
Thank you (very much).	Děkuji.	DYACK-khuyi
Excuse me. / I'm sorry.	Promiňte.	PROH-meen-teh
(No) problem.	(To není) problém.	(toh NEH-nee) proh-BLEHM
Good.	Dobře.	DOHB-zhay
Goodbye.	Nashledanou.	NAH-skleh-dah-noh
one / two	jeden / dva	YAY-dehn / dvah
three / four	tři / čtyři	tzhee / CHTEE-zhee
five / six	pět / šest	pyeht / shehst
seven / eight	sedm / osm	SEH-dum / OH-sum
nine / ten	devět / deset	DEHV-yeht / DEH-seht
hundred / thousand	sto / tisíc	stoh / TEE-seets
How much?	Kolik?	KOH-leek
local currency	koruna (Kč)	koh-ROO-nah
Write it.	Napište to.	NAH-pish-teh toh
Is it free?	Je to zadarmo?	yeh toh ZAH-dar-moh
Is it included?	Je to v ceně?	yeh tohf TSAY-nyeh
Where can I find / buy...?	Kde mohu najít / koupit...?	gday MOH-hoo NAH-yeet / KOH-pit
I'd like...(said by a man)	Rád bych...	rahd bikh
I'd like...(said by a woman)	Ráda bych...	RAH-dah bikh
We'd like...	Rádi bychom...	RAH-dyee BEE-khohm
...a room.	...pokoj.	POH-koy
...a ticket to ___. (destination)	...jízdenka do ___.	YEEZ-dehn-kah doh ___
Is it possible?	Je to možné?	yeh toh MOHZH-neh
Where is...?	Kde je...?	gday yeh
...the train station	...nádraží	NAH-drah-zhee
...the bus station	...autobusové nádraží	OW-toh-boo-soh-veh NAH-drah-zhee
...the tourist information office	...turistická informační kancelář	TOO-rih-stit-skah EEN-for-mahch-nee KAHN-tseh-lahzh
...the toilet	...vécé	VEHT-seh
men / women	muži / ženy	MOO-zhee / ZHAY-nee
left / right	vlevo / vpravo	VLEH-voh / FPRAH-voh
straight	rovně	ROHV-nyeh
At what time...	V kolik...	FKOH-leek
...does this open / close?	...otevírají / zavírají?	OH-teh-vee-rah-yee / ZAH-vee-rah-yee
Just a moment.	Moment prosím.	MOH-mehnt PROH-seem
now / soon / later	teď / brzy / později	tedge / BIR-zih / POHZH-dyeh-yee
today / tomorrow	dnes / zítra	duh-NEHS / ZEE-trah

In a Czech Restaurant

I'd like to reserve... (said by a man)	Rád bych zarezervoval....	rahd bikh ZAH-reh-zehr-voh-vahl
I'd like to reserve... (said by a woman)	Ráda bych zarezervovala....	RAH-dah bikh ZAH-reh-zehr-voh-vah-lah
...a table for one person / two people.	...stůl pro jednoho / dva.	stool proh YEHD-noh-hoh / dvah
Non-smoking.	Nekuřácký.	NEH-kuhzh-aht-skee
Is this table free?	Je tento stůl volný?	yeh TEHN-toh stool VOHL-nee
Can I help you?	Mohu Vám pomoci?	MOH-hoo vahm poh-MOHT-see
The menu (in English), please.	Jídelní lístek (v angličtině) prosím.	YEE-dehl-nee LEE-stehk (FAHN-gleech-tee-nyeh) PROH-seem
Service is / is not included.	Spropitné je / není zahrnuto.	SPROH-pit-neh yeh / NEH-nee ZAH-har-noo-toh
"to go"	s sebou	SEH-boh
with / without	s / bez	suh / behz
and / or	a / nebo	ah / NEH-boh
ready-to-eat meal (available now)	hotová jídla	HOH-toh-vah YEED-lah
meal on request (takes longer)	minutky	MIH-noot-kee
appetizers	předkrm.	PZHEHD-krim
bread	chléb	khlehb
cheese	sýr	seer
sandwich	sendvič	SEHND-vich
soup	polévka	poh-LEHV-kah
salad	salát	SAH-laht
meat	maso	MAH-soh
poultry	drůbež	DROO-behzh
fish	ryby	RIH-bih
fruit	ovoce	OH-voht-seh
vegetables	zelenina	ZEH-leh-nyee-nah
dessert	dezert	DEH-zehrt
(tap) water	voda (z kohoutku)	VOH-dah (SKOH-hoht-koo)
mineral water	minerální voda	MIH-neh-rahl-nyee VOH-dah
carbonated / not carbonated (spoken)	s bublinkami / bez bublinek	SBOOB-leen-kah-mee / behz BOO-blee-nehk
carbonated / not carbonated (printed)	perlivá / neperlivá	PEHR-lee-vah / NEH-pehr-lee-vah
milk	mléko	MLEH-koh
(orange) juice	(pomerančový) džus	(POH-mehr-ahn-choh-vee) "juice"
coffee	káva	KAH-vah
tea	čaj	chai
wine	víno	VEE-noh
red / white	červené / bílé	CHEHR-veh-neh / BEE-leh
sweet / dry	sladké / suché	SLAHD-keh / SOO-kheh
glass / bottle	sklenka / lahev	SKLEHN-kah / LAH-hehv
beer	pivo	PEE-voh
light / dark	světlé / tmavé	SVYEHT-leh / TMAH-veh
Cheers!	Na zdraví!	nah zdrah-VEE
Enjoy your meal.	Dobrou chuť.	DOH-broh khoot
More. / Another.	Více. / Další.	VEET-seh / DAHL-shee
The same.	To samé.	toh SAH-meh
the bill	účet	OO-cheht
I'll pay.	Zaplatím.	ZAH-plah-teem
tip	spropitné	SPROH-pit-neh
Delicious!	Výborné!	VEE-bohr-neh

Polish Survival Phrases

Keep in mind a few Polish pronunciation tips: **w** sounds like "v," **ł** sounds like "w," **ch** is a back-of-your-throat "kh" sound (as in the Scottish "loch"), and **rz** sounds like the "zh" sound in "pleasure." The "shch" sound (indicated by various combinations, including *ść* and *szcz*) is easier than it seems—just say the two sounds in rapid succession (think of the phrase "fresh cheese"). The "khch" sound (denoted by *chci*) is similar: the guttural "kh" sound quickly followed by ch. The vowels with a tail (**ą** and **ę**) have a slight nasal "n" sound at the end, similar to French; depending on the word, this can have a strong n sound, or be nearly silent—just follow the phonetics below.

Hello. (formal)	Dzień dobry.	jehn DOH-brih
Hi. / Bye. (informal)	Cześć.	cheshch
Do you speak English? (asked of a man)	Czy Pan mówi po angielsku?	chih pahn MOO-vee poh ahn-GYEHL-skoo
Do you speak English? (asked of a woman)	Czy Pani mówi po angielsku?	chih PAH-nee MOO-vee poh ahn-GYEHL-skoo
Yes. / No.	Tak. / Nie.	tahk / nyeh
I (don't) understand.	(Nie) rozumiem.	(nyeh) roh-ZOO-myehm
Please. / You're welcome. / Can I help you?	Proszę.	PROH-sheh
Thank you (very much).	Dziękuję (bardzo).	jehn-KOO-yeh (BARD-zoh)
Excuse me. / I'm sorry.	Przepraszam.	psheh-PRAH-shahm
(No) problem.	(Żaden) problem.	(ZHAH-dehn) PROH-blehm
Good.	Dobrze.	DOHB-zheh
Goodbye.	Do widzenia.	doh veed-ZAY-nyah
one / two	jeden / dwa	YEH-dehn / dvah
three / four	trzy / cztery	tzhih / CHTEH-rih
five / six	pięć / sześć	pyench / sheshch
seven / eight	siedem / osiem	SHYEH-dehm / OH-shehm
nine / ten	dziewięć / dziesięć	JEH-vyench / JEH-shench
hundred / thousand	sto / tysiąc	stoh / TIH-shants
How much?	Ile?	EE-leh
local currency	złoty (zł)	ZWOH-tih
Write it.	Napisz to.	NAH-peesh toh
Is it free?	Czy to jest za darmo?	chih toh yehst zah DAR-moh
Is it included?	Czy jest to wliczone?	chih yehst toh vlee-CHOH-neh
Where can I find / buy...?	Gdzie mogę dostać / kupić...?	guh-DYEH MOH-geh DOH-statch / KOO-peech
I'd like...(said by a man)	Chciałbym...	KHCHAW-beem
I'd like...(said by a woman)	Chciałabym...	KHCHAH-wah-beem
We'd like...	Chcielibyśmy...	KHCHEHL-ee-bish-mih
...a room.	...pokój.	POH-kooey
...a ticket to ___.	...bilet do ___.	BEE-leht doh ___
Is it possible?	Czy jest to możliwe?	chih yehst toh mohzh-LEE-veh
Where is...?	Gdzie jest...?	guh-DYEH yehst
...the train station	...dworzec kolejowy	DVOH-zhehts koh-leh-YOH-vih
...the bus station	...dworzec autobusowy	DVOH-zhehts ow-toh-boos-OH-vih
...the tourist information office	...informacja turystyczna	een-for-MAHT-syah too-ris-TITCH-nah
...the toilet	...toaleta	toh-ah-LEH-tah
men / women	męska / damska	MEHN-skah / DAHM-skah
left / right	lewo / prawo	LEH-voh / PRAH-voh
straight	prosto	PROH-stoh
At what time...	O której godzinie...	oh kuh-TOO-ray gohd-ZHEE-nyeh
...does this open / close?	...będzie otwarte / zamknięte?	BEND-zheh oht-VAHR-teh / zahm-KNYEHN-teh
Just a moment.	Chwileczkę.	khvee-LETCH-keh
now / soon / later	teraz / niedługo / później	TEH-rahz / nyed-WOO-goh / POOZH-nyey
today / tomorrow	dzisiaj / jutro	JEE-shigh / YOO-troh

In the Restaurant

English	Polish	Pronunciation
I'd like to reserve... (said by a man)	Chciałbym zarezerwować...	KHCHAW-beem zah-reh-zehr-VOH-vahch
I'd like to reserve... (said by a woman)	Chciałabym zarezerwować...	KHCHAH-wah-beem zah-reh-zehr-VOH-vahch
We'd like to reserve...	Chcielibyśmy zarezerwować...	KHCHEHL-ee-bish-mih zah-reh-zehr-VOH-vahch
...a table for one person / two people.	...stolik na jedną osobę / dwie osoby.	STOH-leek nah YEHD-now oh-SOH-beh / dvyeh oh-SOH-bih
Non-smoking.	Niepalący.	nyeh-pah-LOHNT-sih
Is this table free?	Czy ten stolik jest wolny?	chih tehn STOH-leek yehst VOHL-nih
Can I help you?	W czym mogę pomóc?	vchim MOH-geh POH-moots
The menu (in English), please.	Menu (po angielsku), proszę.	MEH-noo (poh ahn-GYEHL-skoo) PROH-sheh
service (not) included	usługa (nie) wliczona	oos-WOO-gah (nyeh) VLEE-choh-nah
cover charge	wstęp	vstenp
"to go"	na wynos	nah VIH-nohs
with / without	z / bez	z / behz
and / or	i / lub	ee / loob
milk bar (cheap cafeteria)	bar mleczny	bar MLETCH-nih
fixed-price meal (of the day)	zestaw (dnia)	ZEHS-tahv (dih-NYAH)
specialty of the house	specjalność zakładu	speht-SYAHL-nohshch zah-KWAH-doo
half portion	pół porcji	poow PORTS-yee
daily special	danie dnia	DAH-nyeh dih-NYAH
appetizers	przystawki	pshih-STAHV-kee
bread	chleb	khlehb
cheese	ser	sehr
sandwich	kanapka	kah-NAHP-kah
soup	zupa	ZOO-pah
salad	sałatka	sah-WAHT-kah
meat	mięso	MYEHN-soh
poultry	drób	droob
fish	ryba	RIH-bah
seafood	owoce morza	oh-VOHT-seh MOH-zhah
fruit	owoce	oh-VOHT-seh
vegetables	warzywa	vah-ZHIH-vah
dessert	deser	DEH-sehr
(tap) water	woda (z kranu)	VOH-dah (SKRAH-noo)
mineral water	woda mineralna	VOH-dah mee-neh-RAHL-nah
carbonated / not carbonated	gazowana / niegazowana	gah-zoh-VAH-nah / NYEH-gah-zoh-vah-nah
milk	mleko	MLEH-koh
(orange) juice	sok (pomarańczowy)	sohk (poh-mah-rayn-CHOH-vih)
coffee	kawa	KAH-vah
tea	herbata	hehr-BAH-tah
wine	wino	VEE-noh
red / white	czerwone / białe	chehr-VOH-neh / bee-AH-weh
sweet / dry / semi-dry	słodkie / wytrawne / półwytrawne	SWOHT-kyeh / vih-TRAHV-neh / poow-vih-TRAHV-neh
glass / bottle	szklanka / butelka	SHKLAHN-kah / boo-TEHL-kah
beer	piwo	PEE-voh
vodka	wódka	VOOD-kah
Cheers!	Na zdrowie!	nah ZDROH-vyeh
Enjoy your meal.	Smacznego.	smatch-NEH-goh
More. / Another.	Więcej. / Inny.	VYEHNT-say / EE-nih-nih
The same.	Taki sam.	TAH-kee sahm
the bill	rachunek	rah-KHOO-nehk
I'll pay.	Ja płacę.	yah PWAHT-seh
tip	napiwek	nah-PEE-vehk
Delicious!	Pyszne!	PISH-neh

Hungarian Survival Phrases

Remember, the letter *a* is pronounced "aw," while *á* is a brighter "ah."
In the phonetics, *dj* is pronounced like the j in "jeans."

Hello. (formal)	Jó napot kívánok.	yoh NAH-pot KEE-vah-nohk
Hi. / Bye. (informal)	Szia. or Hello.	SEE-yaw, "Hello"
Do you speak English?	Beszél angolul?	BEH-sayl AWN-goh-lool
Yes. / No.	Igen. / Nem.	EE-gehn / nehm
I (don't) understand.	(Nem) értem.	(nehm) AYR-tehm
Please.	Kérem.	KAY-rehm
You're welcome.	Szívesen.	SEE-veh-shehn
Thank you (very much).	Köszönöm (szépen).	KUR-sur-nurm (SAY-pehn)
Excuse me. / I'm sorry.	Bocsánat.	BOH-chah-nawt
No problem.	Semmi gond.	SHEH-mee gohnd
Good.	Jól.	yohl
Goodbye.	Viszontlátásra.	VEE-sohnt-lah-tahsh-raw
one / two	egy / kettő	edj / KEH-tur
three / four	három / négy	HAH-rohm / naydj
five / six	öt / hat	urt / hawt
seven / eight	hét / nyolc	hayt / nyolts
nine / ten	kilenc / tíz	KEE-lehnts / teez
hundred / thousand	száz / ezer	sahz / EH-zehr
How much?	Mennyi?	MEHN-yee
local currency	forint (Ft)	FOH-reent
Where is it?	Hol van?	hohl vawn
Is it free (no charge)?	Ingyen van?	een-JEHN vawn
Is it included?	Benne van az árban?	BEH-neh vawn oz AHR-bawn
Where can I find / buy...?	Hol találok / vehetek...?	hohl TAW-lah-lohk / VEH-heh-tehk
I'd like...	Kérnék...	KAYR-nayk
We'd like...	Kérnénk...	KAYR-naynk
...a room	...egy szobát	edj SOH-baht
...a ticket (to ___)	...egy jegyet (___-ig)	edj YEHDJ-eht (___-ig)
Is it possible?	Lehet?	leh-HEHT
Where is the...?	Hol van a...?	hohl vawn aw
big train station (in Budapest)	pályaudvar	PAH-yood-vawr
small train station (elsewhere)	vasútállomás	VAW-shoot-ah-loh-mahsh
bus station	buszpályaudvar	BOOS-pah-yood-vawr
tourist information office	turista információ	TOO-reesh-taw EEN-for-maht-see-yoh
toilet	toalet or WC	TOH-aw-leht, VAYT-say
men	férfi	FAYR-fee
women	női	NUR-ee
left / right	bal / jobb	bawl / yohb
straight	egyenesen or előre	EDJ-eh-neh-shehn, EH-lew-reh
At what time...	Mikor...	MEE-kohr
...does this open / close?	...nyit / zár?	nyit / zahr
Just a moment.	Egy pillanat.	edj PEE-law-nawt
now / soon / later	most / hamarosan / később	mohsht / HAW-maw-roh-shawn / KAY-shurb
today / tomorrow	ma / holnap	maw / HOHL-nawp

In the Restaurant

English	Hungarian	Pronunciation
I'd like to reserve a table for one / two people.	Szeretnék foglalni egy asztalt egy / két fő részére.	SEH-reht-nayk FOG-lawl-nee edj AWS-tawlt edj / kayt few RAY-say-reh
Non-smoking.	Nem dohányzó.	nehm DOH-hayn-zoh
Is this table free?	Ez az asztal szabad?	ehz oz AWS-tawl saw-BAWD
Can I help you?	Tessék.	TEHSH-shayk
The menu (in English), please.	Kérem az (angol) étlapot.	KAY-rehm oz (AWN-gohl) AYT-law-poht
service (not) included	a számla a felszolgálási dijat (nem) tartalmazza	aw SAHM-law aw FEHL-sohl-gah-lah-shee DEE-yawt (nehm) TAWR-tawl-maw-zaw
cover charge	belépő	BEH-lay-pur
"to go"	elvitelre	EHL-vee-tehl-reh
with / without	___-val / nélkül	___-vawl / NAYL-kewl
and / or	és / vagy	aysh / vawdj
fixed-price meal (of the day)	(napi) menü	(NAW-pee) MEH-new
specialty of the house	a ház specialitása	aw hahz SHPEHT-see-aw-lee-tah-shaw
half portion	fél adag	fayl AW-dawg
daily special	napi ajánlat	NAW-pee AW-yahn-lawt
fixed-price meal (for tourists)	(turista) menü	(TOO-reesh-taw) MEH-new
main courses	főételek	FUR-ay-teh-lehk
appetizers	előételek	EH-lur-ay-teh-lehk
bread / cheese	kenyér / sajt	KEHN-yayr / shayt
sandwich	szendvics	SEND-veech
soup / salad	leves / saláta	LEH-vehsh / SHAW-lah-taw
meat / poultry	hús / szárnyasok	hoosh / SAHR-nyaw-shohk
fish	halak	HAW-lawk
seafood	tengeri halak	TEHN-geh-ree HAW-lawk
fruit	gyümölcs	JEWM-urlch
vegetables	zöldség	ZULRD-shayg
dessert	desszert	DEH-sehrt
vegetarian	vegetáriánus	VEH-geh-tah-ree-ah-noosh
(tap) water	(csap) víz	(chawp) veez
mineral water	ásványvíz	ASH-vawn-veez
milk	tej	TAYee
(orange) juice	(narancs) lé	(NAW-rawnch) lay
coffee / tea	kávé / tea	KAH-vay / TEH-aw
beer / wine	sör / bor	shohr / bohr
red / white	vörös / fehér	VUR-rursh / FEH-hayr
sweet / dry / semi-dry	édes / száraz / félszáraz	AY-dehsh / SAH-rawz / FAYL-sah-rawz
glass / bottle	pohár / üveg	POH-hahr / EW-vehg
Cheers!	Egészségedre!	EH-gehs-shay-geh-dreh
More. / Another.	Még. / Másikat.	mayg / MAH-shee-kawt
The same.	Ugyanazt.	OODJ-aw-nawst
Bill, please. (literally, "I'll pay.")	Fizetek.	FEE-zeh-tehk
tip	borravaló	BOH-raw-vaw-loh
Bon appétit!	Jó étvágyat!	yoh AYT-vah-yawt
Delicious!	Finom!	FEE-nohm

Slovenian Survival Phrases

When using the phonetics, pronounce ī / Ī as the long I sound in "light." The vowel "eh" sometimes sounds closer to "ay" (depending on the speaker).

English	Slovenian	Phonetics
Hello. (formal)	Dober dan.	DOH-behr dahn
Hi. / Bye. (informal)	Živjo.	ZHEEV-yoh
Do you speak English?	Ali govorite angleško?	AH-lee goh-voh-REE-teh ahn-GLEHSH-koh
Yes. / No.	Ja. / Ne.	yah / neh
I (don't) understand.	(Ne) razumem.	(neh) rah-ZOO-mehm
Please. / You're welcome.	Prosim.	PROH-seem
Thank you (very much).	Hvala (lepa).	HVAH-lah (LEH-pah)
Excuse me. / I'm sorry.	Oprostite.	oh-proh-STEE-teh
problem	problem	proh-BLEHM
No problem.	Ni problema.	nee proh-BLEH-mah
Good.	Dobro.	DOH-broh
Goodbye.	Na svidenje.	nah SVEE-dehn-yeh
one / two	ena / dve	EH-nah / dveh
three / four	tri / štiri	tree / SHTEE-ree
five / six	pet / šest	peht / shehst
seven / eight	sedem / osem	SEH-dehm / OH-sehm
nine / ten	devet / deset	deh-VEHT / deh-SEHT
hundred / thousand	sto / tisoč	stoh / TEE-sohch
How much?	Koliko?	KOH-lee-koh
local currency	euro	EE-oo-roh
Write it?	Napišite?	nah-PEESH-ee-teh
Is it free?	Ali je brezplačno?	AH-lee yeh brehz-PLAHCH-noh
Is it included?	Ali je vključeno?	AH-lee yeh vuk-LYOO-cheh-noh
Where can I find / buy...?	Kje lahko najdem / kupim...?	kyeh LAH-koh NĪ-dehm / KOO-peem
I'd / We'd like...	Želel / Želeli bi...	zheh-LEEoo / zheh-LEH-lee bee
...a room.	...sobo.	SOH-boh
...a ticket to ___.	...vozovnico do ___.	voh-ZOHV-neet-soh doh
Is it possible?	Ali je možno?	AH-lee yeh MOHZH-noh
Where is...?	Kje je...?	kyeh yeh
...the train station	...železniška postaja	zheh-LEHZ-neesh-kah pohs-TĪ-yah
...the bus station	...avtobusna postaja	OW-toh-boos-nah pohs-TĪ-yah
...the tourist information office	...turistično informacijski center	too-REES-teech-noh een-for-maht-SEE-skee TSEHN-tehr
...the toilet	...vece (WC)	VEHT-SEH
men	moški	MOHSH-kee
women	ženski	ZHEHN-skee
left / right	levo / desno	LEH-voh / DEHS-noh
straight	naravnost	nah-RAHV-nohst
At what time...	Ob kateri uri...	ohb kah-TEH-ree OO-ree
...does this open / close?	...se odpre / zapre?	seh ohd-PREH / zah-PREH
(Just) a moment.	(Samo) trenutek.	(sah-MOH) treh-NOO-tehk
now / soon / later	zdaj / kmalu / pozneje	zuh-DĪ / kuh-MAH-loo / pohz-NEH-yeh
today / tomorrow	danes / jutri	DAH-nehs / YOO-tree

In the Restaurant

I'd like to reserve...	Rezerviral bi...	reh-zehr-VEE-rahl bee
We'd like to reserve...	Rezervirali bi...	reh-zehr-VEE-rah-lee bee
...a table for one / two.	...mizo za enega / dva.	MEE-zoh zah EH-neh-gah / dvah
Non-smoking.	Za nekadilce.	zah NEH-kah-deelt-seh
Is this table free?	Ali je ta miza prosta?	AH-lee yeh tah MEE-zah PROH-stah
Can I help you?	Izvolite?	eez-VOH-lee-teh
The menu (in English), please.	Jedilni list (v angleščini), prosim.	yeh-DEEL-nee leest (vuh ahn-GLEHSH-chee-nee) PROH-seem
service (not) included	postrežba (ni) vključena	post-REHZH-bah (nee) vuk-LYOO-cheh-nah
cover charge	pogrinjek	poh-GREEN-yehk
"to go"	za s sabo	zah SAH-boh
with / without	z / brez	zuh / brehz
and / or	in / ali	een / AH-lee
fixed-price meal (of the day)	(dnevni) meni	(duh-NEW-nee) meh-NEE
specialty of the house	specialiteta hiše	speht-see-ah-lee-TEH-tah HEE-sheh
half portion	polovična porcija	poh-loh-VEECH-nah PORT-see-yah
daily special	dnevna ponudba	duh-NEW-nah poh-NOOD-bah
fixed-price meal for tourists	turistični meni	too-REES-teech-nee meh-NEE
appetizers	predjedi	prehd-yeh-DEE
bread	kruh	krooh
cheese	sir	seer
sandwich	sendvič	SEND-veech
soup	juha	YOO-hah
salad	solata	soh-LAH-tah
meat	meso	meh-SOH
poultry	perutnina	peh-root-NEE-nah
fish	riba	REE-bah
seafood	morska hrana	MOHR-skah HRAH-nah
fruit	sadje	SAHD-yeh
vegetables	zelenjava	zeh-lehn-YAH-vah
dessert	sladica	slah-DEET-sah
(tap) water	voda (iz pipe)	VOH-dah (eez PEE-peh)
mineral water	mineralna voda	mee-neh-RAHL-nah VOH-dah
milk	mleko	MLEH-koh
(orange) juice	(pomarančni) sok	(poh-mah-RAHNCH-nee) sohk
coffee	kava	KAH-vah
tea	čaj	chī
wine	vino	VEE-noh
red / white	rdeče / belo	ahr-DEH-cheh / BEH-loh
sweet / dry / semi-dry	sladko / suho / polsuho	SLAHD-koh / SOO-hoh / POHL-soo-hoh
glass / bottle	kozarec / steklenica	koh-ZAH-rehts / stehk-leh-NEET-sah
beer	pivo	PEE-voh
Cheers!	Na zdravje!	nah ZDROW-yeh
More. / Another.	Še. / Še eno.	sheh / sheh EH-noh
The same.	Isto.	EES-toh
Bill, please.	Račun, prosim.	rah-CHOON PROH-seem
tip	napitnina	nah-peet-NEE-nah
Delicious!	Odlično!	ohd-LEECH-noh

Croatian Survival Phrases

When using the phonetics, pronounce ī / Ī as the long I sound in "light."

Hello. (formal)	Dobar dan.	DOH-bahr dahn
Hi. / Bye. (informal)	Bog.	bohg
Do you speak English?	Govorite li engleski?	GOH-voh-ree-teh lee EHN-glehs-kee
Yes. / No.	Da. / Ne.	dah / neh
I (don't) understand.	(Ne) razumijem.	(neh) rah-ZOO-mee-yehm
Please. / You're welcome.	Molim.	MOH-leem
Thank you (very much).	Hvala (lijepa).	HVAH-lah (LYEH-pah)
Excuse me. / I'm sorry.	Oprostite.	oh-PROH-stee-teh
problem	problem	proh-BLEHM
No problem.	Nema problema.	NEH-mah proh-BLEH-mah
Good.	Dobro.	DOH-broh
Goodbye.	Do viđenija.	doh veed-JAY-neeah
one / two	jedan / dva	YEH-dahn / dvah
three / four	tri / četiri	tree / CHEH-teh-ree
five / six	pet / šest	peht / shehst
seven / eight	sedam / osam	SEH-dahm / OH-sahm
nine / ten	devet / deset	DEH-veht / DEH-seht
hundred / thousand	sto / tisuća	stoh / TEE-soo-chah
How much?	Koliko?	KOH-lee-koh
local currency	kuna	KOO-nah
Write it?	Napišite?	nah-PEESH-ee-teh
Is it free?	Da li je besplatno?	dah lee yeh BEH-splaht-noh
Is it included?	Da li je uključeno?	dah lee yeh OOK-lyoo-cheh-noh
Where can I find / buy...?	Gdje mogu pronaći / kupiti...?	guh-DYEH MOH-goo PROH-nah-chee / KOO-pee-tee
I'd like / We'd like...	Želio bih / Željeli bismo...	ZHEH-lee-oh beeh / ZHEH-lyeh-lee BEES-moh
...a room.	...sobu.	SOH-boo
...a ticket to ___.	...kartu do ___.	KAR-too doh
Is it possible?	Da li je moguće?	dah lee yeh MOH-goo-cheh
Where is...?	Gdje je...?	guh-DYEH yeh
...the train station	...željeznička stanica	ZHEH-lyehz-neech-kah STAH-neet-sah
...the bus station	...autobusna stanica	OW-toh-boos-nah STAH-neet-sah
...the tourist information office	...turističko informativni centar	TOO-ree-steech-koh EEN-for-mah-teev-nee TSEHN-tahr
...the toilet	...vece (WC)	VEHT-SEH
men	muški	MOOSH-kee
women	ženski	ZHEHN-skee
left / right	lijevo / desno	LEE-yeh-voh / DEHS-noh
straight	ravno	RAHV-noh
At what time...	U koliko sati...	oo KOH-lee-koh SAH-tee
...does this open / close?	...otvara / zatvara?	OHT-vah-rah / ZAHT-vah-rah
(Just) a moment.	(Samo) trenutak.	(SAH-moh) treh-NOO-tahk
now / soon / later	sada / uskoro / kasnije	SAH-dah / OOS-koh-roh / KAHS-nee-yeh
today / tomorrow	danas / sutra	DAH-nahs / SOO-trah

In a Croatian Restaurant

I'd like to reserve...	**Rezervirao bih...**	reh-zehr-VEER-ow beeh
We'd like to reserve...	**Rezervirali bismo...**	reh-zehr-VEE-rah-lee BEES-moh
...a table for one / two.	**...stol za jednog / dva.**	stohl zah YEHD-nog / dvah
Non-smoking.	**Za nepušače.**	zah NEH-poo-shah-cheh
Is this table free?	**Da li je ovaj stol slobodan?**	dah lee yeh OH-vī stohl SLOH-boh-dahn
Can I help you?	**Izvolite?**	EEZ-voh-lee-teh
The menu (in English), please.	**Jelovnik (na engleskom), molim.**	yeh-LOHV-neek (nah EHN-glehs-kohm) MOH-leem
service (not) included	**posluga (nije) uključena**	POH-sloo-gah (NEE-yeh) OOK-lyoo-cheh-nah
cover charge	**couvert**	KOO-vehr
"to go"	**za ponjeti**	zah POHN-yeh-tee
with / without	**sa / bez**	sah / behz
and / or	**i / ili**	ee / EE-lee
fixed-price meal (of the day)	**(dnevni) meni**	(duh-NEHV-nee) MEH-nee
specialty of the house	**specijalitet kuće**	speht-see-yah-LEE-teht KOO-cheh
half portion	**pola porcije**	POH-lah PORT-see-yeh
daily special	**jelo dana**	YEH-loh DAH-nah
fixed-price meal for tourists	**turistički meni**	TOO-ree-steech-kee MEH-nee
appetizers	**predjela**	PREHD-yeh-lah
bread	**kruh**	krooh
cheese	**sir**	seer
sandwich	**sendvič**	SEND-veech
soup	**juha**	YOO-hah
salad	**salata**	sah-LAH-tah
meat	**meso**	MAY-soh
poultry	**perad**	PEH-rahd
fish	**riba**	REE-bah
seafood	**morska hrana**	MOHR-skah HRAH-nah
fruit	**voće**	VOH-cheh
vegetables	**povrće**	POH-vur-cheh
dessert	**desert**	deh-SAYRT
(tap) water	**voda (od slavine)**	VOH-dah (ohd SLAH-vee-neh)
mineral water	**mineralna voda**	MEE-neh-rahl-nah VOH-dah
milk	**mlijeko**	mlee-YEH-koh
(orange) juice	**sok (od naranče)**	sohk (ohd NAH-rahn-cheh)
coffee	**kava**	KAH-vah
tea	**čaj**	chī
wine	**vino**	VEE-noh
red / white	**crno / bijelo**	TSEHR-noh / bee-YEH-loh
sweet / dry / semi-dry	**slatko / suho / polusuho**	SLAHT-koh / SOO-hoh / POH-loo-soo-hoh
glass / bottle	**čaša / boca**	CHAH-shah / BOHT-sah
beer	**pivo**	PEE-voh
Cheers!	**Živjeli!**	ZHEE-vyeh-lee
More. / Another.	**Još. / Još jedno.**	yohsh / yohsh YEHD-noh
The same.	**Isto.**	EES-toh
Bill, please.	**Račun, molim.**	RAH-choon MOH-leem
tip	**napojnica**	NAH-poy-neet-sah
Delicious!	**Izvrsno!**	EEZ-vur-snoh

German Survival Phrases

When using the phonetics, pronounce ī as the long I sound in "light."

English	German	Phonetics
Good day.	Guten Tag.	**goo**-tehn tahg
Do you speak English?	Sprechen Sie Englisch?	shprehkh-ehn zee **ehng**-lish
Yes. / No.	Ja. / Nein.	yah / nīn
I (don't) understand.	Ich verstehe (nicht).	ikh fehr-**shtay**-heh (nikht)
Please.	Bitte.	**bit**-teh
Thank you.	Danke.	**dahng**-keh
I'm sorry.	Es tut mir leid.	ehs toot meer līt
Excuse me.	Entschuldigung.	ehnt-**shool**-dig-oong
(No) problem.	(Kein) Problem.	(kīn) proh-**blaym**
(Very) good.	(Sehr) gut.	(zehr) goot
Goodbye.	Auf Wiedersehen.	owf **vee**-der-zayn
one / two	eins / zwei	īns / tsvī
three / four	drei / vier	drī / feer
five / six	fünf / sechs	fewnf / zehkhs
seven / eight	sieben / acht	**zee**-behn / ahkht
nine / ten	neun / zehn	noyn / tsayn
How much is it?	Wieviel kostet das?	**vee**-feel **kohs**-teht dahs
Write it?	Schreiben?	**shrī**-behn
Is it free?	Ist es umsonst?	ist ehs oom-**zohnst**
Included?	Inklusive?	in-kloo-**zee**-veh
Where can I buy / find...?	Wo kann ich kaufen / finden...?	voh kahn ikh **kow**-fehn / **fin**-dehn
I'd like / We'd like...	Ich hätte gern / Wir hätten gern...	ikh **heh**-teh gehrn / veer **heh**-tehn gehrn
...a room.	...ein Zimmer.	īn **tsim**-mer
...a ticket to ___.	...eine Fahrkarte nach ___.	ī-neh **far**-kar-teh nahkh
Is it possible?	Ist es möglich?	ist ehs **mur**-glikh
Where is...?	Wo ist...?	voh ist
...the train station	...der Bahnhof	dehr **bahn**-hohf
...the bus station	...der Busbahnhof	dehr **boos**-bahn-hohf
...tourist information	...das Touristen-informationsbüro	dahs too-**ris**-tehn-in-for-maht-see-**ohns-bew**-roh
...toilet	...die Toilette	dee toh-**leh**-teh
men	Herren	**hehr**-rehn
women	Damen	**dah**-mehn
left / right	links / rechts	links / **rehkhts**
straight	geradeaus	geh-**rah**-deh-**ows**
When is this open / closed?	Um wieviel Uhr ist hier geöffnet / geschlossen?	oom **vee**-feel oor ist heer geh-**urf**-neht / geh-**shloh**-sehn
At what time?	Um wieviel Uhr?	oom **vee**-feel oor
Just a moment.	Moment.	moh-**mehnt**
now / soon / later	jetzt / bald / später	yehtst / bahld / **shpay**-ter
today / tomorrow	heute / morgen	**hoy**-teh / **mor**-gehn

In the Restaurant

I'd like / We'd like...	Ich hätte gern / Wir hätten gern...	ikh **heh**-teh gehrn / veer **heh**-tehn gehrn
...a reservation for...	...eine Reservierung für...	ī-neh reh-zer-**feer**-oong fewr
...a table for one / two.	...einen Tisch für ein / zwei.	ī-nehn tish fewr īn / tsvī
Non-smoking.	Nichtraucher.	**nikht**-rowkh-er
Is this seat free?	Ist hier frei?	ist heer frī
Menu (in English), please.	Speisekarte (auf Englisch), bitte.	**shpī**-zeh-kar-teh (owf **ehng**-lish) **bit**-teh
service (not) included	Trinkgeld (nicht) inklusive	**trink**-gehlt (nikht) in-kloo-**zee**-veh
cover charge	Eintritt	**īn**-trit
to go	zum Mitnehmen	tsoom **mit**-nay-mehn
with / without	mit / ohne	mit / **oh**-neh
and / or	und / oder	oont / **oh**-der
menu (of the day)	(Tages-) Karte	(**tah**-gehs-) **kar**-teh
set meal for tourists	Touristenmenü	too-**ris**-tehn-meh-**new**
specialty of the house	Spezialität des Hauses	shpayt-see-ah-lee-**tayt** dehs **how**-zehs
appetizers	Vorspeise	**for**-shpī-zeh
bread	Brot	broht
cheese	Käse	**kay**-zeh
sandwich	Sandwich	**zahnd**-vich
soup	Suppe	**zup**-peh
salad	Salat	zah-**laht**
meat	Fleisch	flīsh
poultry	Geflügel	geh-**flew**-gehl
fish	Fisch	fish
seafood	Meeresfrüchte	**meh**-rehs-**frewkh**-teh
fruit	Obst	ohpst
vegetables	Gemüse	geh-**mew**-zeh
dessert	Nachspeise	**nahkh**-shpī-zeh
mineral water	Mineralwasser	min-eh-**rahl**-vah-ser
tap water	Leitungswasser	**lī**-toongs-vah-ser
milk	Milch	milkh
(orange) juice	(Orangen-) Saft	(oh-**rahn**-zhehn-) zahft
coffee	Kaffee	kah-**fay**
tea	Tee	tay
wine	Wein	vīn
red / white	rot / weiß	roht / vīs
glass / bottle	Glas / Flasche	glahs / **flah**-sheh
beer	Bier	beer
Cheers!	Prost!	prohst
More. / Another.	Mehr. / Noch ein.	mehr / nohkh īn
The same.	Das gleiche.	dahs **glīkh**-eh
Bill, please.	Rechnung, bitte.	**rehkh**-noong **bit**-teh
tip	Trinkgeld	**trink**-gehlt
Delicious!	Lecker!	**lehk**-er

For more user-friendly German phrases, check out *Rick Steves'
German Phrase Book and Dictionary* or *Rick Steves' French, Italian
& German Phrase Book*.

Pronouncing Eastern European Place Names

Remember that in all of these languages, j is pronounced as "y," and c is pronounced "ts." Diacritical markings over most consonants (such as č, š, ś, or ž) have the same effect as putting an h after it in English; for example, č is "ch," š or ś is "sh," ž is "zh."

Name	Pronounced
Auschwitz (Concentration Camp, Poland)	OWSH-vits
Birkenau (Concentration Camp, Poland)	BEER-keh-now
Bled (Slovenia)	bled (as it's spelled); locals say "blayd"
Bohinj (Slovenia)	BOH-heen
Bovec (Slovenia)	BOH-vets
Bratislava (Slovakia)	brah-tee-SLAH-vah
Brtonigla (Croatia)	bur-toh-NEEG-lah
Budapest (Hungary)	BOO-dah-pest in English, BOO-daw-pesht in Hungarian
Český Krumlov (Czech Republic)	CHESS-key KROOM-loff
Dubrovnik (Croatia)	doo-BROHV-nik
Dunajec (River Canyon, Slovakia)	DOO-nah-yets
Eger (Hungary)	EH-gehr
Egerszalók (Hungary)	EH-gehr-sah-lohk
Esztergom (Hungary)	EHS-tehr-gohm
Füzesabony (Hungary)	FOO-zesh-ah-boyn
Gdańsk (Poland)	guh-DAYNSK
Gdynia (Poland)	guh-DIN-yah
Gödöllő (Palace, Hungary)	GER-der-ler
Herzegovina (Bosnia-Herzegovina)	hert-seh-GOH-vee-nah
Istria (Croatia)	EE-stree-ah
Jadrolinija (Croatian Ferry Company)	yah-droh-LEE-nee-yah
Karlštejn (Castle, Czech Republic)	KARL-shtayn
Kazimierz (Poland)	kah-ZHEE-mezh
Kobarid (Slovenia)	KOH-bah-reed
Konopiště (Castle, Czech Republic)	KOH-noh-peesh-tyeh
Korčula (Croatia)	KOHR-choo-lah

Name	**Pronounced**
Kraków (Poland)	KRACK-cow in English, KROCK-oof in Polish
Křivoklát (Castle, Czech Republic)	KREE-vohk-laht
Kutná Hora (Czech Republic)	KOOT-nah HO-rah
Levoča (Slovakia)	LEH-voh-chah
Ljubljana (Slovenia)	lyoob-lyee-AH-nah
Malbork (Castle, Poland)	MAHL-bork
Mostar (Bosnia-Herzegovina)	MOH-star
Motovun (Croatia)	moh-toh-VOON
Nowa Huta (Poland)	NOH-vah HOO-tah
Oświęcim (Poland)	ohsh-VEENCH-im
Pécs (Hungary)	paych
Plitvice (National Park, Croatia)	PLEET-veet-seh
Praha (Czech name for Prague, Czech Republic)	PRAH-hah
Pula (Croatia)	POO-lah
Radovljica (Slovenia)	rah-DOH-vleet-suh
Rijeka (Croatia)	ree-YAY-kah
Rovinj (Croatia)	roh-VEEN
Soča (River Valley, Slovenia)	SOH-chah
Sopot (Poland)	SOH-poht
Sopron (Hungary)	SHOH-prohn
Spiš (Region, Slovakia)	speesh
Split (Croatia)	split (as it's spelled)
Szentendre (Hungary)	SEHN-tehn-dreh
Terezín (Concentration Camp, Czech Republic)	TEH-reh-zeen
Toruń (Poland)	TOH-roon
Vintgar (Gorge, Slovenia)	VEENT-gar
Visegrád (Hungary)	VEE-sheh-grahd
Vršič (Pass, Slovenia)	vur-SHEECH
Warszawa (Polish name for Warsaw, Poland)	vah-SHAH-vah
Wieliczka (Salt Mine, Poland)	veel-EECH-kah
Wien (German name for Vienna, Austria)	veen
Zagreb (Croatia)	ZAH-grehb

INDEX

INDEX

INDEX

MAP INDEX

Audio Europe

Rick's free app and podcasts

The FREE Rick Steves Audio Europe™ app for iPhone, iPad, iPod Touch and Android gives you self-guided audio tours of Europe's top museums, sights and historic walks—plus hundreds of tracks filled with cultural insights and sightseeing tips from Rick's radio interviews—all organized into geographic-specific playlists.

Let Rick Steves Audio Europe™ amplify your guidebook. This free app includes self-guided audio tours for all the most important museums and historical walks in London, Paris Rome, Venice, Florence, Athens, and more.

With Rick whispering in your ear, Europe gets even better.

Thanks Facebook fans for submitting photos while on location! From top: John Kuijper in Florence, Brenda Mamer with her mother in Rome, and Alyssa Passey with her friend in Paris.

Find out more at ricksteves.com

Join a Rick Steves tour

Enjoy Europe's warmest welcome... with the flexibility and friendship of a small group getting to know Rick's favorite places and people. It all starts with our free tour catalog and DVD.

Great guides, small groups, no grumps.

Free information and great gear

▶ Plan Your Trip

Browse thousands of articles and a wealth of money-saving tips for planning your dream trip. You'll find up-to-date information on Europe's best destinations, packing smart, getting around, finding rooms, staying healthy, avoiding scams and more.

▶ Eurail Passes

Find out, step-by-step, if a railp makes sense for your trip—and how to avoid buying more than need. Get free shipping on onlin orders

▶ Graffiti Wall & Travelers Helpline

Learn, ask, share—our online community of savvy travelers is a great resource for first-time travelers to Europe, as well as seasoned pros.

Rick Steves' Europe Through the Back Door, I.

Rick Steves

www.ricksteves.com

EUROPE GUIDES

Best of Europe
Eastern Europe
Europe Through the Back Door
Mediterranean Cruise Ports

COUNTRY GUIDES

Croatia & Slovenia
England
France
Germany
Great Britain
Ireland
Italy
Portugal
Scandinavia
Spain
Switzerland

CITY & REGIONAL GUIDES

Amsterdam, Bruges & Brussels
Budapest
Florence & Tuscany
Greece: Athens & the Peloponnese
Istanbul
London
Paris
Prague & the Czech Republic
Provence & the French Riviera
Rome
Venice
Vienna, Salzburg & Tirol

SNAPSHOT GUIDES

Barcelona
Berlin
Bruges & Brussels
Copenhagen & the Best of
  Denmark
Dublin
Dubrovnik
Hill Towns of Central Italy
Italy's Cinque Terre
Krakow, Warsaw & Gdansk
Lisbon
Madrid & Toledo
Munich, Bavaria & Salzburg
Naples & the Amalfi Coast
Northern Ireland
Norway
Scotland
Sevilla, Granada & Southern Spain
Stockholm

POCKET GUIDES

Athens
London
Paris
Rome

TRAVEL CULTURE

Europe 101
European Christmas
Postcards from Europe
Travel as a Political Act

Rick Steves guidebooks are published by Avalon Travel,
a member of the Perseus Books Group.

NOW AVAILABLE:
eBOOKS, APPS & BLU-RAY

eBOOKS

Most guides are available as eBooks from Amazon, Barnes & Noble, Borders, Apple, and Sony. Free apps for eBook reading are available in the Apple App Store and Android Market, and eBook readers such as Kindle, Nook, and Kobo all have free apps that work on smartphones.

RICK STEVES' EUROPE DVDs

10 New Shows 2011–2012
Austria & the Alps
Eastern Europe
England & Wales
European Christmas
European Travel Skills & Specials
France
Germany, BeNeLux & More
Greece & Turkey
Iran
Ireland & Scotland
Italy's Cities
Italy's Countryside
Scandinavia
Spain
Travel Extras

BLU-RAY

Celtic Charms
Eastern Europe Favorites
European Christmas
Italy Through the Back Door
Mediterranean Mosaic
Surprising Cities of Europe

PHRASE BOOKS & DICTIONARIES

French
French, Italian & German
German
Italian
Portuguese
Spanish

JOURNALS

Rick Steves' Pocket Travel Journal
Rick Steves' Travel Journal

APPS

Select Rick Steves guides are available as apps in the Apple App Store.

PLANNING MAPS

Britain, Ireland & London
Europe
France & Paris
Germany, Austria & Switzerland
Ireland
Italy
Spain & Portugal

Rick Steves books and DVDs are available at bookstores and through online booksellers.

Credits

Contributors
Honza Vihan

Honza, who co-authors *Rick Steves' Prague & the Czech Republic,* grew up roaming the Czech countryside in search of the Wild West. Once the borders opened, he set off for South Dakota. His journey took him to China, Honduras, India, and Iran, where he contributed to several travel guides. Honza lives in Prague with his family, teaches Chinese, and leads Rick Steves' tours through Eastern Europe.

Gene Openshaw

Gene is the co-author of ten Rick Steves books. For this book, he wrote material on Europe's art, history, and contemporary culture (including this book's tour of the Kunsthistorisches Museum in Vienna). When not traveling, Gene enjoys composing music, recovering from his 1973 trip to Europe with Rick, and living everyday life with his daughter.

Special Thanks

The authors would like to acknowledge our friends and colleagues for their invaluable insights. Thanks to Ian Watson, Dave Hoerlein, Rick Garman, and Trevor Holmes; *Děkuji* to Honza Vihan (Czech Republic); *Dziękuję* to Katarzyna Derlicka and Agnieszka Syroka (Poland); *Köszönjük szépen* to Péter Pölczman, Andrea Makkay, and Elemér Boreczky (Hungary); *Hvala lepa* to Marijan Krišković, Tina Hiti, Sašo Golub, Bojan Kočar, and Gorazd Hiti (Slovenia and Croatia); and *D'akujeme* to Susana Minich (Slovakia).

Chapter Images

Location	Photographer
Title Page: Széchenyi Baths, Budapest, Hungary	Cameron Hewitt
Full-Page Color: Ulica Długa, Gdańsk, Poland	Cameron Hewitt
Introduction: Wawel Cathedral, Kraków, Poland	Cameron Hewitt
Czech Republic (full-page image): Charles Bridge, Prague	Cameron Hewitt
Prague: Vltava River, Charles Bridge, and Prague Castle	Cameron Hewitt
Near Prague: Konopiště Castle	Rick Steves
Český Krumlov: Skyline	Rick Steves
Slovakia (full-page image): St. Michael's Gate, Bratislava	Cameron Hewitt
Bratislava: Bratislava Castle	Cameron Hewitt
The Spiš Region: Spiš Castle	Cameron Hewitt
Poland (full-page image): Old Town Square, Warsaw	Cameron Hewitt
Kraków: Main Market Square	Cameron Hewitt
Auschwitz-Birkenau: Birkenau Guard Tower	Rick Steves
Warsaw: Castle Square and the Old Town	Cameron Hewitt
Gdańsk: Artus Court on Ulica Długa	Cameron Hewitt
Pomerania: Malbork Castle	Cameron Hewitt
Hungary (full-page image): Parliament, Budapest	Cameron Hewitt
Budapest: Chain Bridge Panorama	Cameron Hewitt
Eger: View from the Castle	Cameron Hewitt
Pécs: Main Square	Cameron Hewitt
Slovenia (full-page image): Julian Alps	Cameron Hewitt
Ljubljana: Ljubljana Castle overlooking Prešeren Square	Cameron Hewitt
Lake Bled: Pletna Boat on Lake Bled	Cameron Hewitt
The Julian Alps: Mountain Hut	Cameron Hewitt
Croatia (full-page image): Rovinj	Cameron Hewitt
Dubrovnik: View of Old Town	Cameron Hewitt
Split: Riva Promenade and Old Town	Cameron Hewitt
Korčula: Old Town	Cameron Hewitt
Rovinj and Istria: Rovinj Harbor	Cameron Hewitt
Zagreb: Zagreb Skyline	Cameron Hewitt
Plitvice Lakes National Park: Plitvice	Rick Steves
Bosnia-Herzegovina (full-page image): Old Bridge, Mostar	Cameron Hewitt
Mostar: Old Bridge	Cameron Hewitt
Austria (full-page image): St. Peter's Church, Vienna	Rick Steves
Vienna: Schönbrunn Palace	Cameron Hewitt

Rick Steves' Guidebook Series

City, Regional, and Country Guides

Rick Steves' Amsterdam,
   Bruges & Brussels
Rick Steves' Best of Europe
Rick Steves' Budapest
Rick Steves' Croatia
   & Slovenia
Rick Steves' Eastern Europe
Rick Steves' England
Rick Steves' Florence
   & Tuscany
Rick Steves' France
Rick Steves' Germany
Rick Steves' Great Britain
Rick Steves' Greece: Athens
   & the Peloponnese
Rick Steves' Ireland

Rick Steves' Istanbul
Rick Steves' Italy
Rick Steves' London
Rick Steves' Paris
Rick Steves' Portugal
Rick Steves' Prague
   & the Czech Republic
Rick Steves' Provence
   & the French Riviera
Rick Steves' Rome
Rick Steves' Scandinavia
Rick Steves' Spain
Rick Steves' Switzerland
Rick Steves' Venice
Rick Steves' Vienna,
   Salzburg & Tirol

Snapshot Guides

Excerpted from country guidebooks, the Snapshots Guides
cover many of my favorite destinations, such as *Rick Steves'
Snapshot Barcelona*, *Rick Steves' Snapshot Scotland*, and
Rick Steves' Snapshot Hill Towns of Central Italy.

Pocket Guides

My new Pocket Guides are condensed, colorful guides to
Europe's top cities, including Paris, London, Rome, and Athens,
with more to come. These combine the top self-guided walks
and tours from my city guides with vibrant full-color photos,
and are sized to slip easily into your pocket.

Rick Steves' Phrase Books

French
French/Italian/German
German
Italian
Portuguese
Spanish

More Books

Rick Steves' Europe 101: History and Art for the Traveler
Rick Steves' Europe Through the Back Door
Rick Steves' European Christmas
Rick Steves' Mediterranean Cruise Ports
Rick Steves' Postcards from Europe
Rick Steves' Travel as a Political Act